A PRACTICAL MASTERCLASS AND MANUAL OF

DRAWING & PASTELS

PENCIL SKILLS, PENMANSHIP AND CALLIGRAPHY

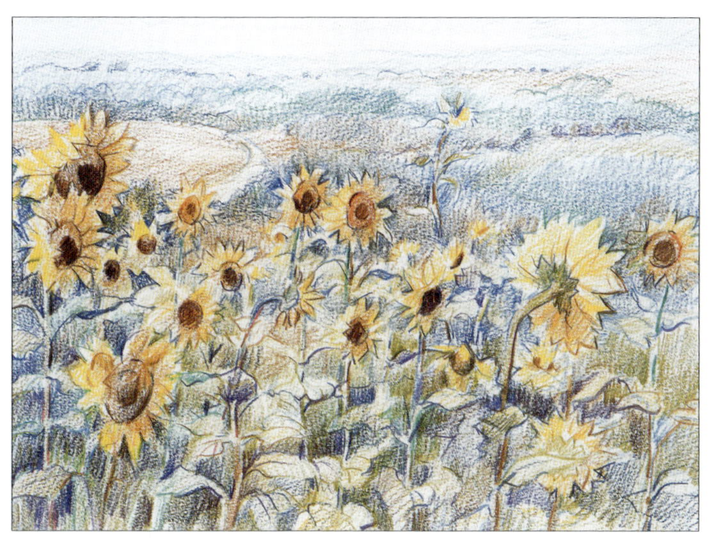

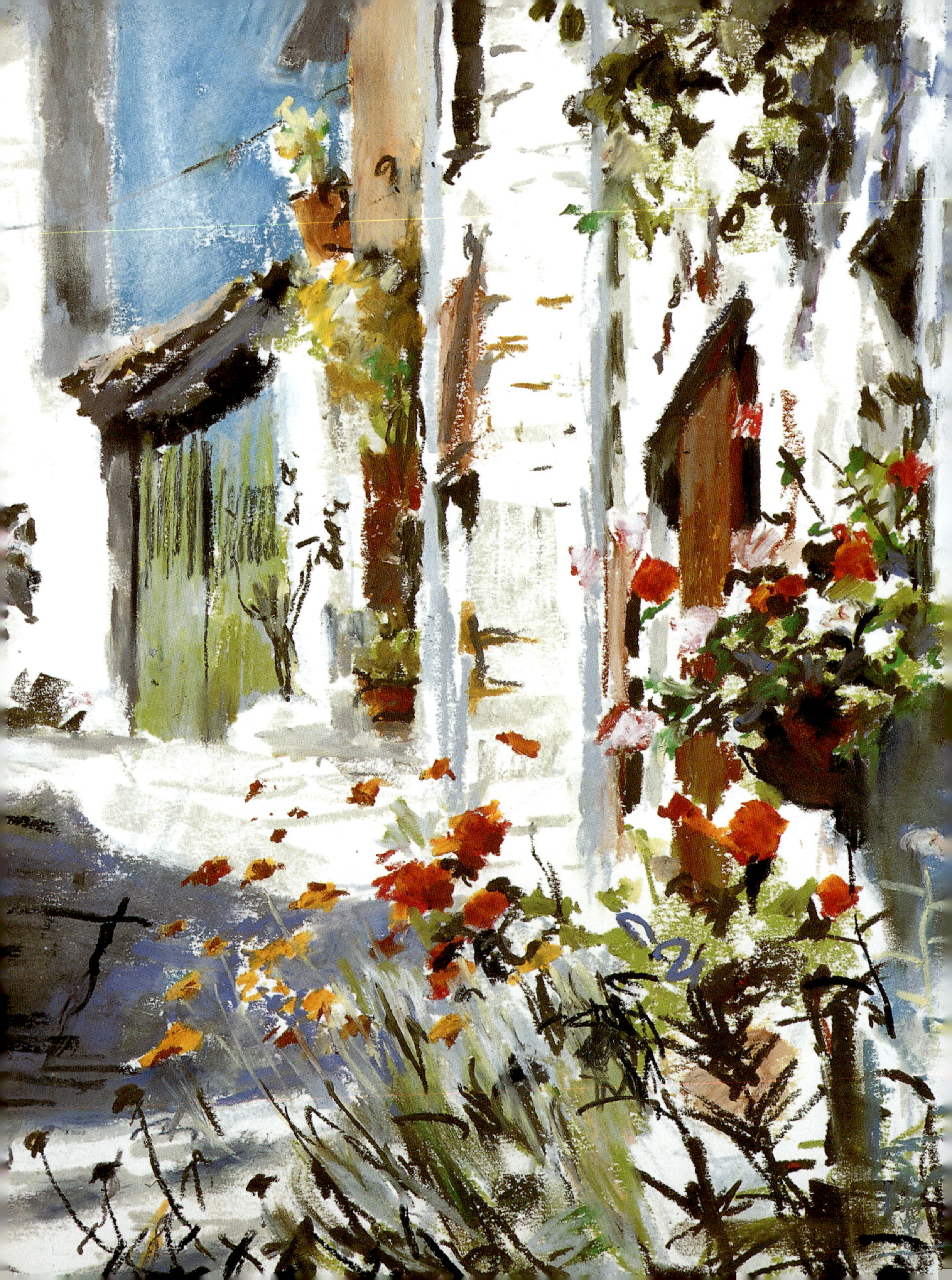

A PRACTICAL MASTERCLASS AND MANUAL OF

DRAWING & PASTELS

PENCIL SKILLS, PENMANSHIP AND CALLIGRAPHY

EXPERT TUITION ON HOW TO USE PENCILS, PENS, CHARCOAL AND PASTELS – FROM LIVELY SKETCHES TO IMPRESSIVE FULL-SCALE DRAWINGS AND BEAUTIFUL CALLIGRAPHIC LETTERING

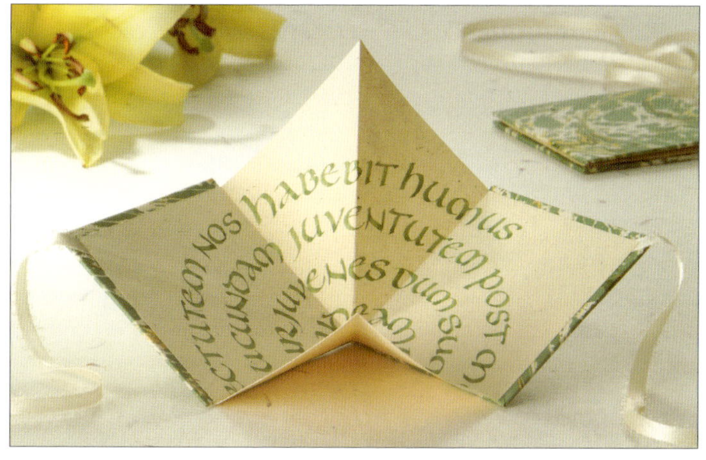

IAN SIDAWAY • SARAH HOGGETT • JANET MEHIGAN • HAZEL HARRISON

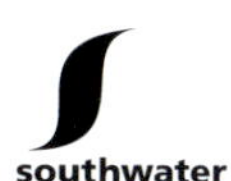

southwater

Contents

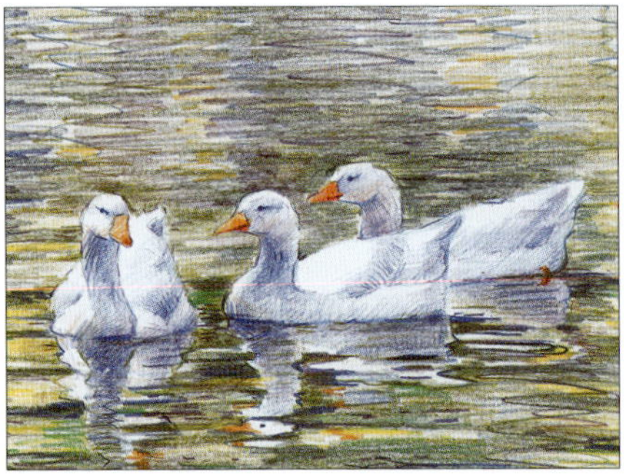

Introduction

Long predating the development of written language, drawing is a basic human skill, a universal means of interpreting the world, and one that has evolved with us: from an early age we are capable of recognizing a solid object from a sketch of a few lines, as our brains fill in the missing details, and in fact we have become so adept at this that we commonly see pictures in clouds and other natural formations. Pictorial art is a fundamental means of communication, conveying not just physical appearance but character, mood and atmosphere, and developing an aptitude for drawing opens a satisfying channel through which to express our emotions and creativity.

Many children love drawing and do it with enviable freedom and confidence, but as adults many of us become diffident about our artistic abilities. But all it really takes to regain that childlike enjoyment is practice and a little help getting started. So if you thought you had no talent for drawing, let this book change your mind. In a series of inspiring step-by-step demonstrations, it will show you how to look at the world with an artist's eye, and how to break down seemingly complex subjects into simple shapes, drawing what you are really seeing instead of what you think you already know about an object.

You don't need a lot of equipment to get started, but it's a good idea to experiment by making marks with different media to see what suits you, whether you naturally prefer the smudgy line and soft tone of charcoal, the delicacy of pencils or the precision of pen and ink. You may also want to explore more challenging media and techniques, such as brush drawing and working with masks, or introduce colour into your work using water-soluble pencils and washes.

Practice exercises show how to analyse complex objects as a series of basic shapes, seeing the 'bones' or underlying structure of your subject, whether it is a tree, a building or a person, and there are informative sections on technical skills such as reproducing tone and understanding perspective, which will help you to give your work solidity and depth. Numerous examples of artists' work show differing ways of treating subjects such as still life, architecture, animals and the human body, and each section of the book opens with a gallery of contemporary works in a wide range of styles and media to inspire you.

To build up your confidence and technical skill, each of the drawing projects includes a photographic reference for the subject and guides you through the development of the work in stages, with detailed explanations of the artist's intentions and methods. You can draw along with some of these to help you get the feel of subjects and styles that appeal to you, or use the techniques they demonstrate to refine your original work.

In addition to step-by-step projects, a series of quick sketches show what can be achieved in a limited time, starting with brief impressions drawn in a few minutes and working up to more finished, tonal studies. As well as giving an insight into the way that different approaches to a subject by the same artist can produce widely varying results, these are designed to inspire you to get out with a sketchbook and keep drawing; at home, in the garden, in the countryside or sitting in a park. The more you draw the better you will learn to see and understand your subjects with an artist's eye.

As your drawing skills progress you may find that you want to adopt a more painterly approach. Pastel is a unique medium, in that although it has all the directness and spontaneity of drawing,

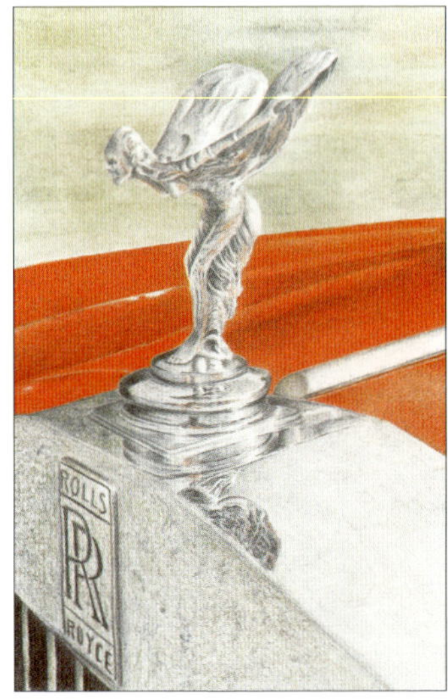

▲ Meticulous rendering of reflections conveys the texture of polished chrome in this coloured pencil study.

▼ This pencil drawing uses tone and texture to capture the atmosphere of a winter landscape drained of colour.

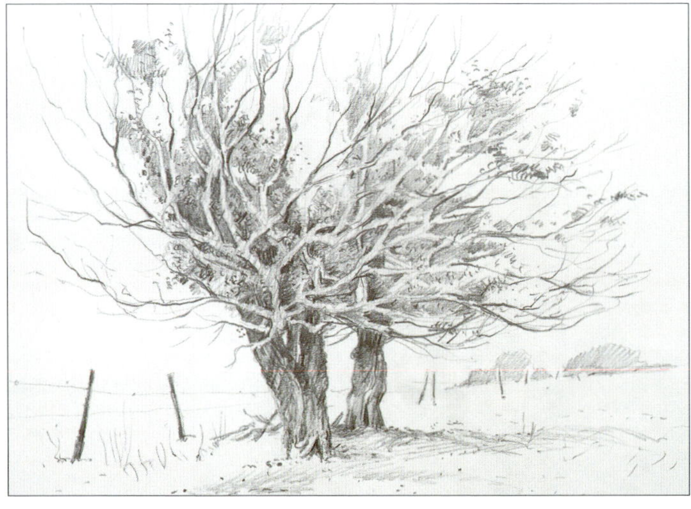

the blending and layering of colours are more closely related to painting. Pastel colours can be delicately blended to create misty, atmospheric effects, or jabbed into coarsely textured paper in thick layers of blunt strokes, resulting in pictures of great drama and depth. The pastel artists' works reproduced in this book show what a highly adaptable medium it is, and practice exercises explore the potential of the various kinds – powdery soft pastels, oil pastels and pastel pencils – showing how they can be mixed with other media, such as charcoal and watercolour, and how the use of coloured and textured papers can dramatically affect the final work. Again, a series of detailed projects guide you through the stages of building up pastel compositions, with a host of helpful hints and tips.

Skill in drawing depends on a delicate balance between freedom and control of the pencil or pen. The final section of this book takes that skilled penmanship in a new direction by introducing calligraphy, the art of beautiful handwriting. While not a pictorial form, it demands the same combination of aesthetic sensitivity and

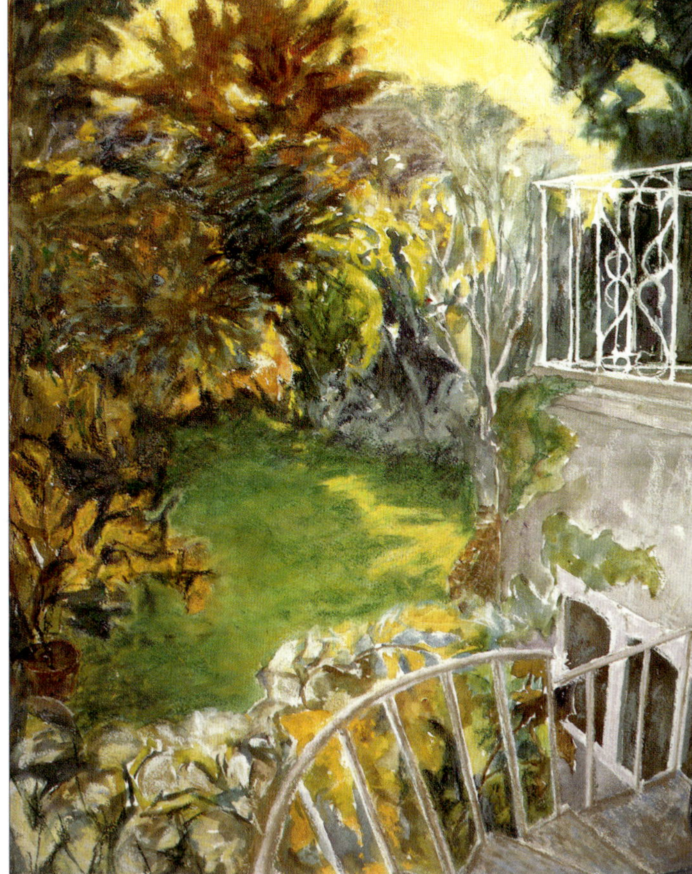

▶ Novel effects can be achieved in mixed media works, like this garden scene using pastel and watercolour.

▼ There are many beautiful and practical ways in which you can use your developing skills in penmanship.

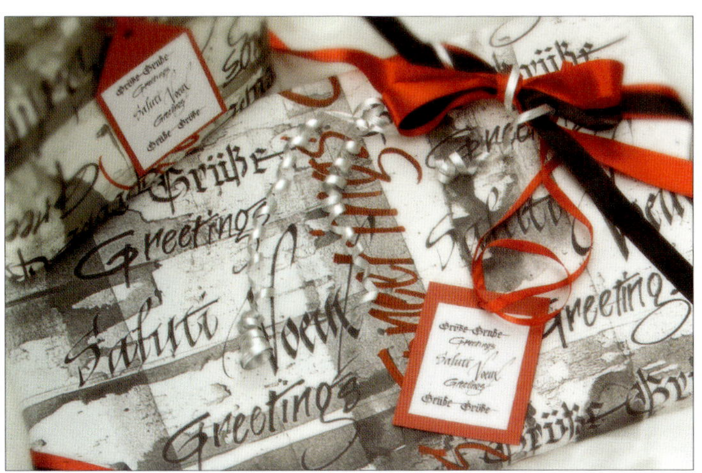

the confidence to handle a pen in a relaxed yet controlled way, producing lines of elegance and beauty.

The basic writing forms and techniques are explained, with information on materials and equipment, and there are sections on related skills such as gilding, bookbinding and making your own pens. Twelve complete alphabets are shown, with detailed instructions to help you achieve perfect letterforms. Finally, the calligraphy projects present ideas for using this lovely traditional art form in some very modern and unusual ways. Striking examples of the work of contemporary calligraphers are featured, to inspire you to practice and perfect your penmanship, producing unique and original artworks of your own.

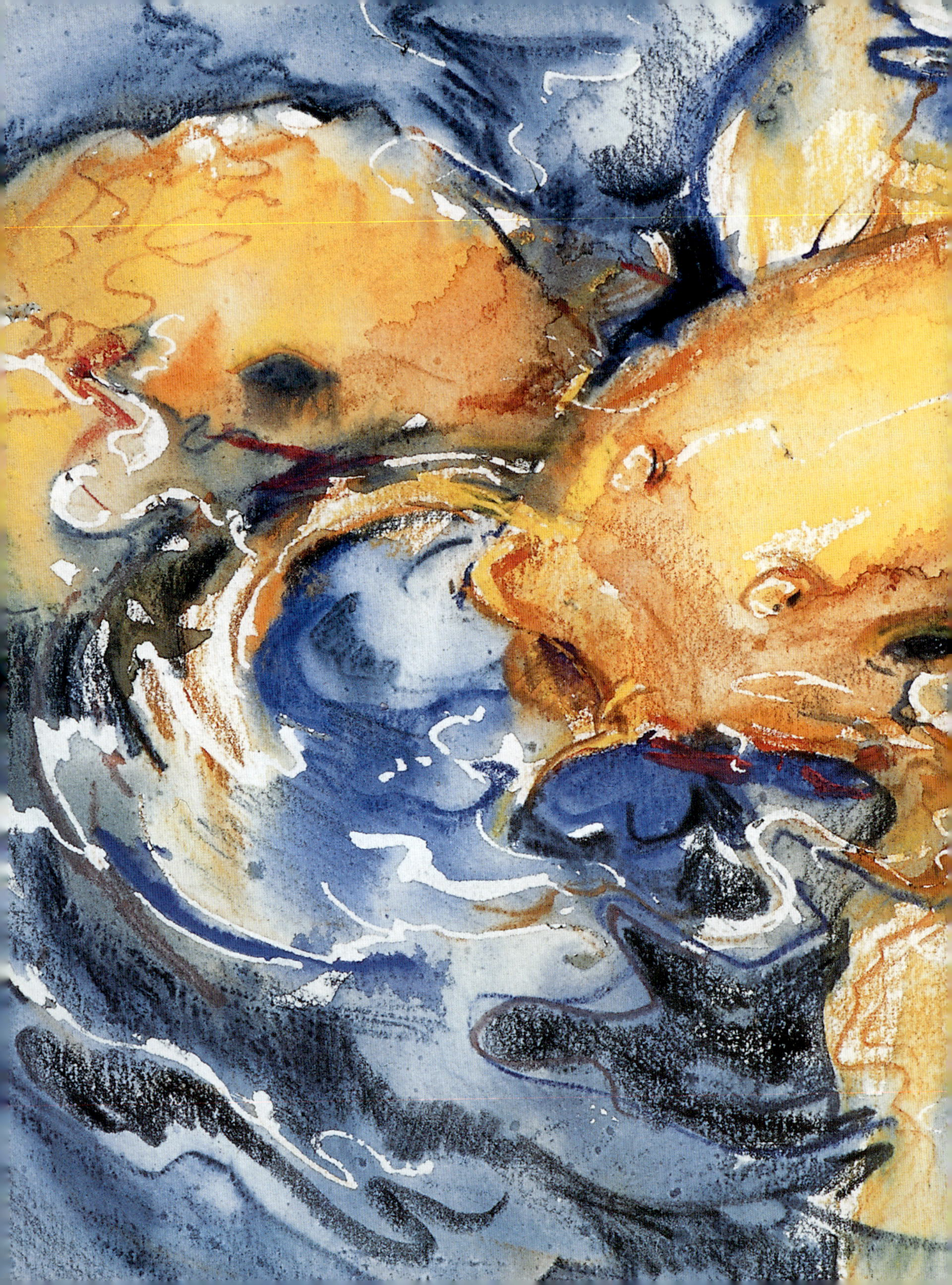

DRAWING

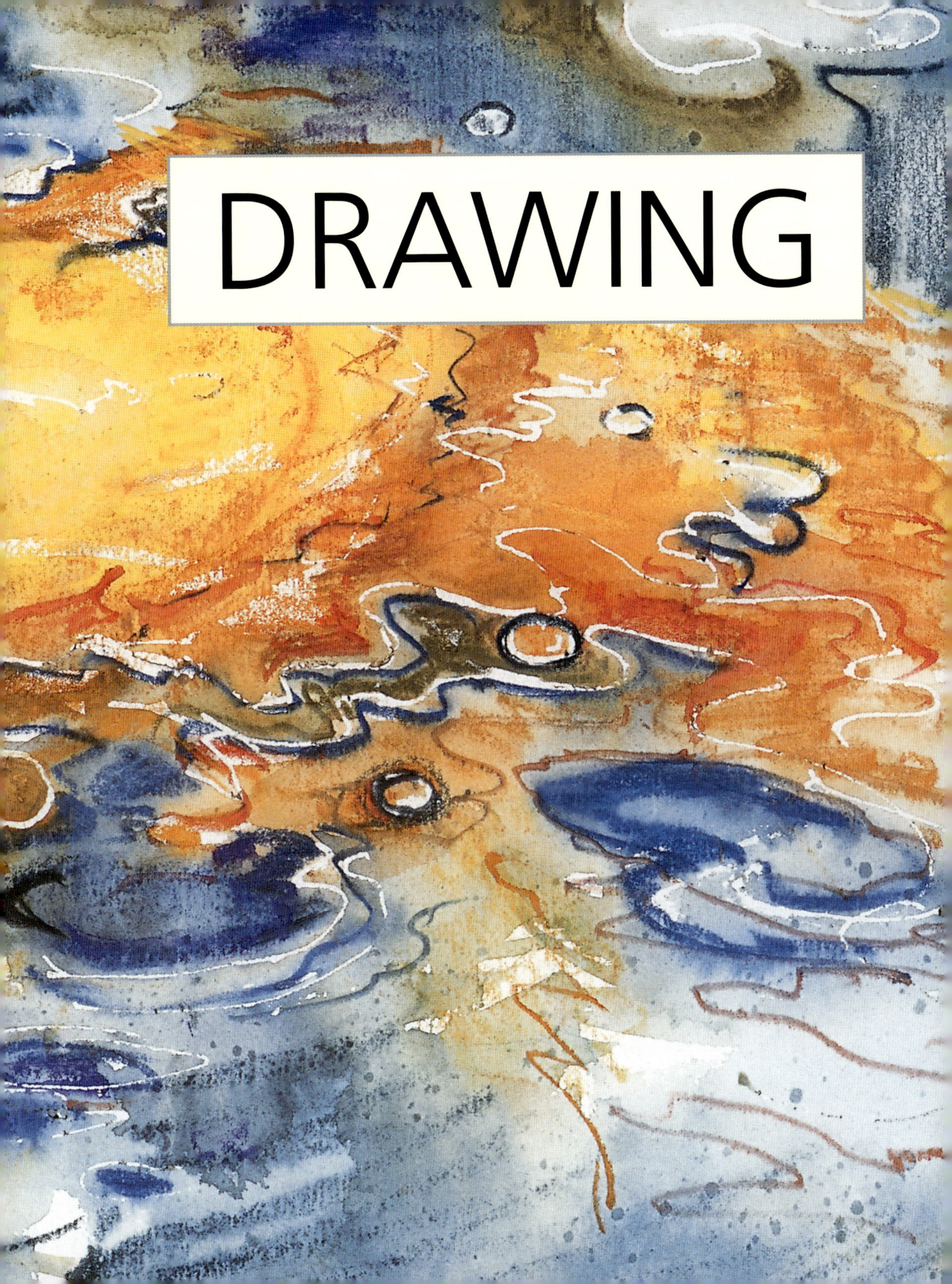

Introducing drawing

It is not easy to define the word 'drawing' because it embraces a wide range of related but different activities. At its simplest it can be described as marks made on a sheet of paper, and in this sense it is one of the most basic of all human activities. Young children enjoy scribbling with a pencil or crayon as soon as they have developed sufficient manual dexterity to grip the implement, and long before they consider relating what they are doing to the world they see around them.

This enjoyment of the lines and marks made by various drawing implements is an important factor in all drawing, and paramount in the work of some artists – the modern Swiss painter and draughtsman, Paul Klee, described his drawing as 'taking a line for a walk'. For most artists, however, drawing also performs a descriptive function: it is a direct response to the visual stimuli of our surroundings.

Learning to draw

The ability to draw is often regarded as a special gift, and it is true that there are people who seem to be able to draw quite effortlessly. Yet drawing, like writing, is a skill that can be acquired; if the motivation is there, most people can learn to draw accurately. In the past, students were taught to draw in a certain way, with the emphasis on mastering a specific set of techniques, but this ignored the essential fact that drawing is first and foremost about seeing, and each of us sees the world in a unique way.

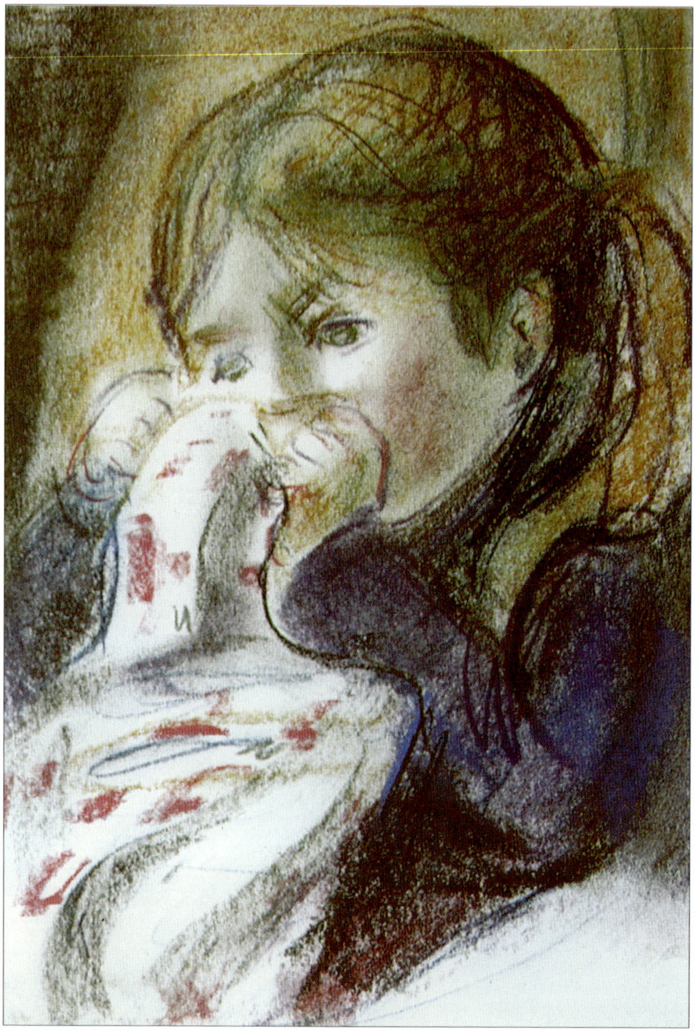

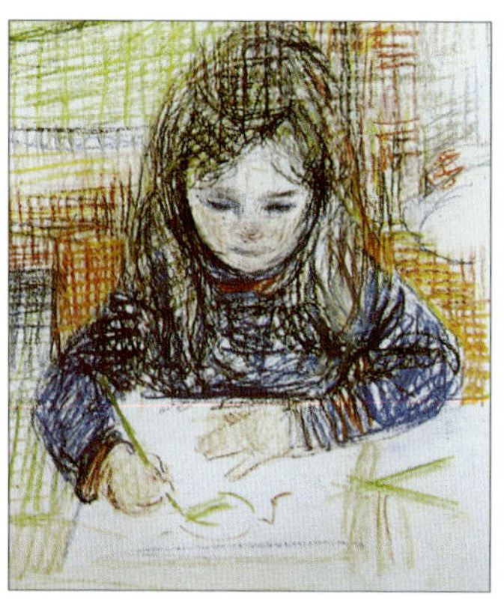

◀ **'Girl Sketching'**
Wax crayon is a less subtle drawing medium than pastel, but it has the advantage of not smudging and is thus useful for sketchbook drawings and quick impressions. In this lively drawing, the artist has built up the forms and colours with a network of loose hatching and cross-hatching lines.
Ted Gould

▲ **'Claire'**
Pastel is a lovely medium for portraiture and is particularly well-suited to studies of children, as it creates gentle effects in keeping with the subject. On the face and clothing the artist has applied the colours lightly, rubbing them slightly into the paper to create soft blends, reinforced with crisp linear drawing.
Ted Gould

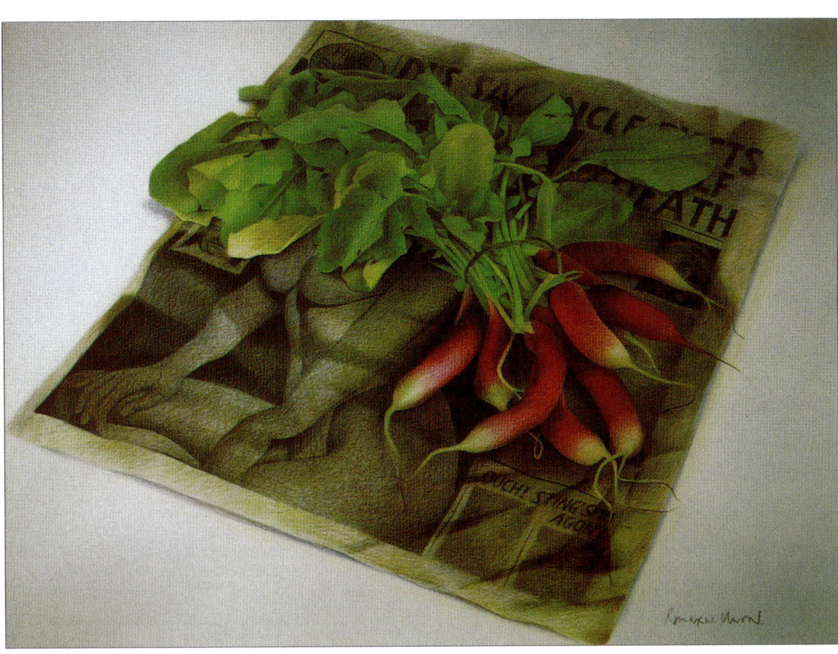

◀ **'Yesterday's Nudes, Radishes'**
In his picture, this artist uses coloured pencil in a very refined and highly wrought way. He achieves meticulous detail and considerable depth of colour with successive layers of coloured pencil, using a delicate shading technique so that almost no lines are visible.
Robert Maxwell Wood

▶ **'Summer View Beyond the Pool'**
This artist works out of doors directly from his subject, and uses coloured pencil in a free and instinctive manner, with bold hatching lines following form.
John Townend

▼ **'Swans on the Thames'**
Pastel need not be a soft and delicate medium; it is extremely versatile and responsive to the artist's visual interests and ways of working. Here the artist has created energetic and exciting effects in the picture by laying down heavy strokes of unblended colour, using the tip of the pastel stick.
Pip Carpenter

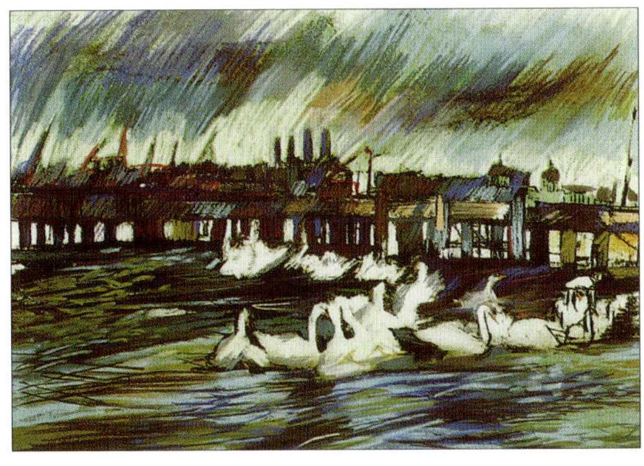

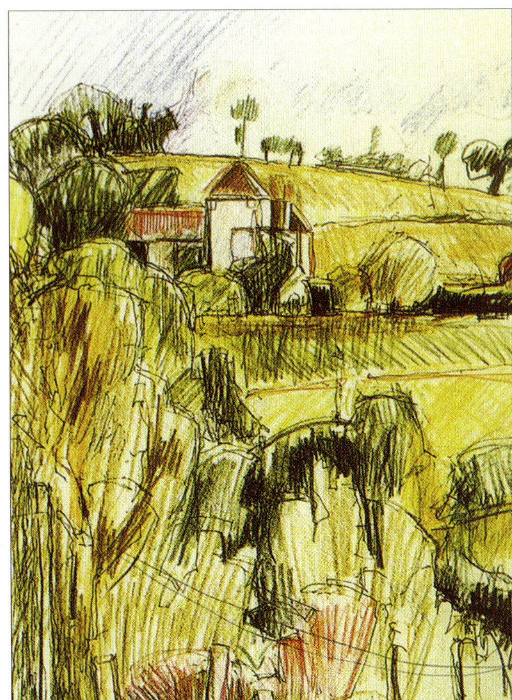

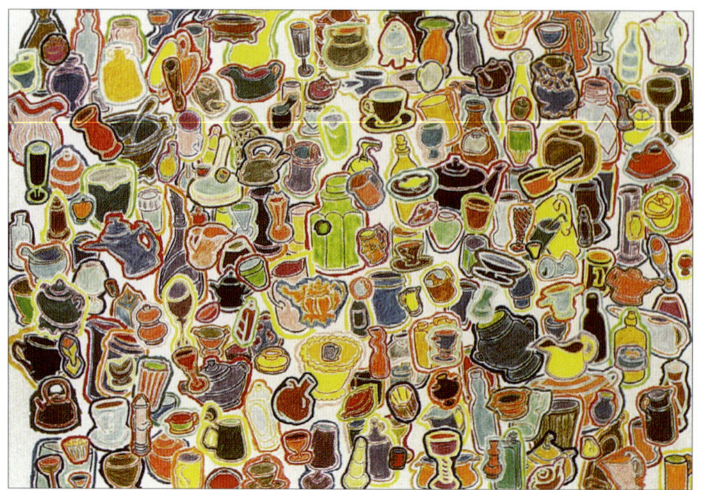

Although technical skill is important, it is not the first stage in learning how to draw, as it is pointless to develop techniques in a void. You may be capable of producing beautifully even lines of hatching and cross-hatching but still find that you have failed in the primary task of drawing, which is to describe the subject to your own satisfaction. Such failures are nearly always the direct result of poor observation of the subject, not of inadequate technique.

It sounds easy enough to say that if you want to learn how to draw all you need to do is to look at things, but it is not that simple, because you have to learn to look at them in a certain way – analytically and objectively. This skill can be surprisingly difficult to master, as it involves looking at a subject with a fresh eye every time,

▲ **'Polly Wants a Pot'**
In this delightful and inventive drawing, coloured pencil has been pressed heavily into the paper to achieve areas of heavy, almost flat colour. The two-dimensional pattern element is stressed by the use of coloured outlines.
David Cuthbert

▼ **'Still Life with Man-Made and Natural Objects'**
A combination of pastel and pastel pencil has been used for this exploration of forms. The brown paper has allowed the artist to build up both highlights and shadows and has given a touch of colour to an essentially monochrome drawing.
Paul Bartlett

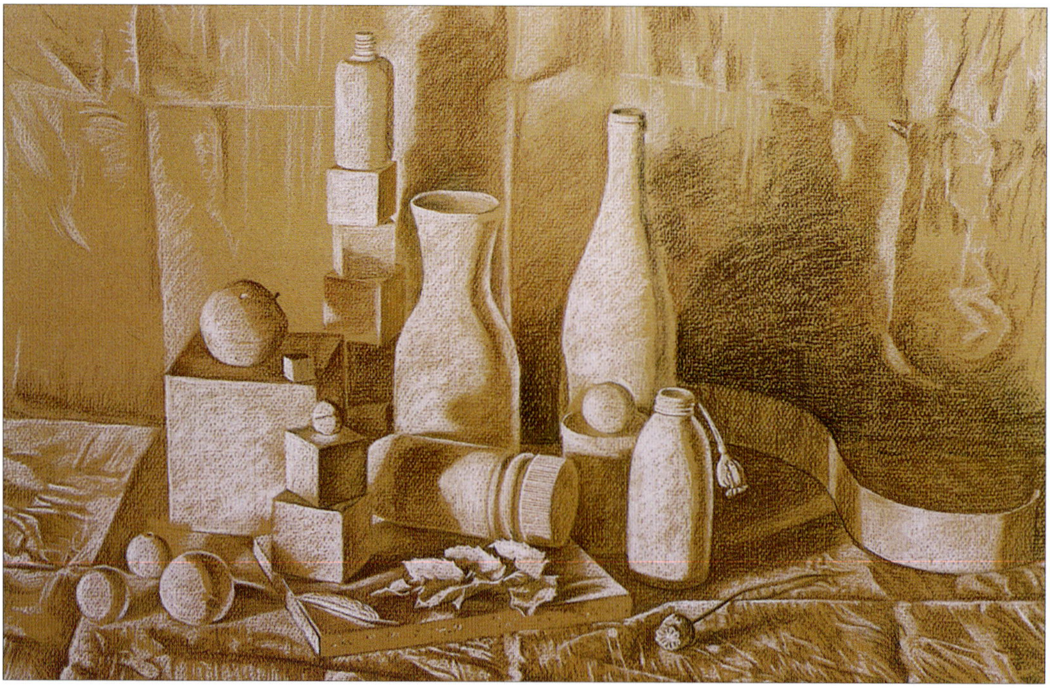

abandoning preconceptions. Our brains are cluttered with information that can be actively unhelpful in the context of drawing, leading us to quite the wrong conclusions – we tend to draw what we know from experience rather than what we see with our own eyes.

A classic example is relative size, which can be hard to get right, particularly when you are drawing familiar objects. If you place a large object on a table with a much smaller one in front of it, the chances are that in your drawing you will make the larger one too large because of your prior knowledge of it. But in fact the effects of perspective will have caused it to 'shrink', so that it may appear to be smaller than the nearer object. The only way to approach drawing a familiar subject, whether it be a portrait, an apple on a plate or a tree, is to force yourself to

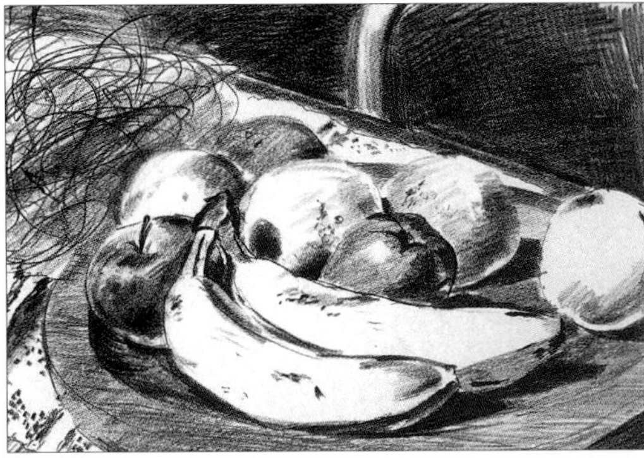

◀ **'Bananas and Other Fruit'**
This lovely drawing is also a study of form, done in very soft pencil, which blunts easily and thus provides broader, bolder effects than hard or medium pencil. Both this and Bartlett's still life are carefully composed, showing that a drawing in monochrome can make as complete a statement as a coloured drawing or painting.
Gerry Baptist

▼ **'Self portrait'**
A comparison between this drawing and Gerry Baptist's demonstrates the versatility of the pencil. Here the effect is almost photographic in its minute attention to detail and texture and its subtle gradations of tone.
Paul Bartlett

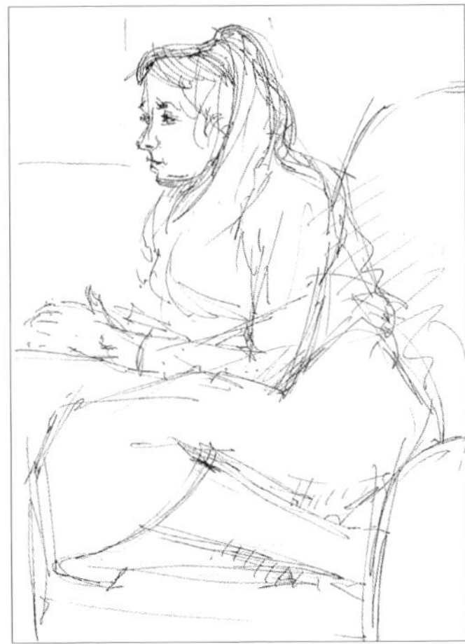

▲ **'Girl in an Armchair'**
Pen and ink can achieve intricate and elaborate effects, but it is also a lovely medium for rapid line drawings. In this figure study the artist has caught the essentials of the pose in a few pen strokes, sometimes superimposing lines where the first drawing was incorrect or needed clarifying.
Ted Gould

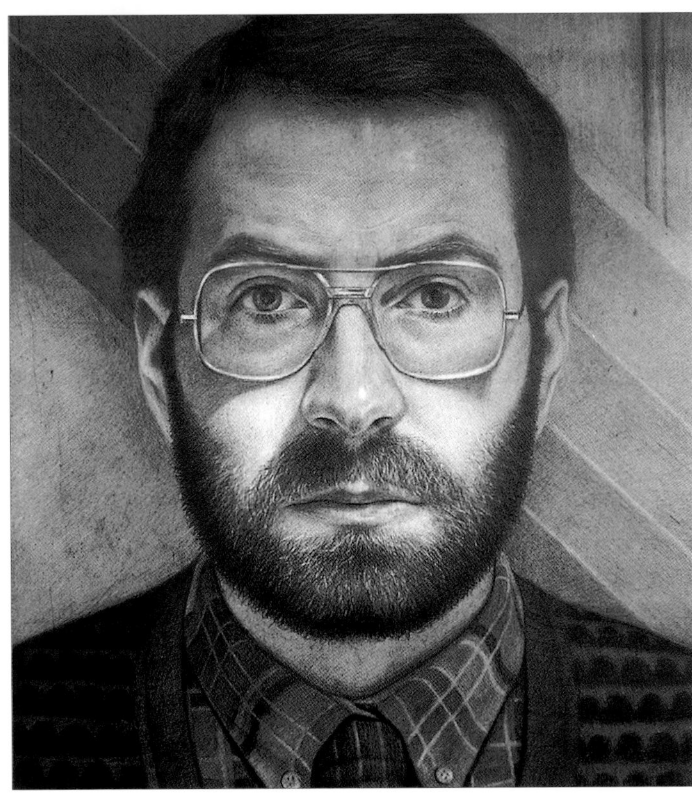

abandon your preconceptions by pretending to yourself that you have never seen this thing before. Only in this way will you be able to assess it thoroughly and draw it accurately.

Different kinds of drawing

A drawing can be many things: it can be a few lines of 'visual shorthand' in a sketchbook, made to remind the artist of some salient point in a subject; it can be a preliminary step in a painting, which will subsequently be hidden by layers of paint and thus have no independent existence; or it can be a finished work of art in its

▶ 'Shunting Locomotive at Bow'
For this robust sketch, made on location, the artist has used oil pastel. This is an ideal medium for bold effects and quick impressions, as the colours can be built up rapidly. Also, unlike soft pastel, oil pastel does not smudge and does not require fixing (setting). The sgraffito technique has been used to add touches of linear detail to the side of the locomotive.
John Townend

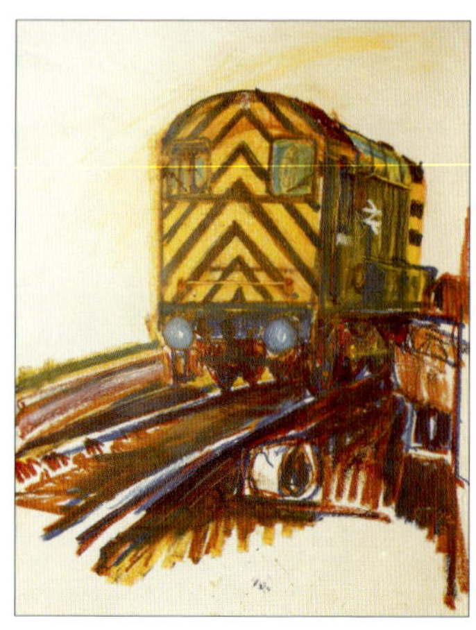

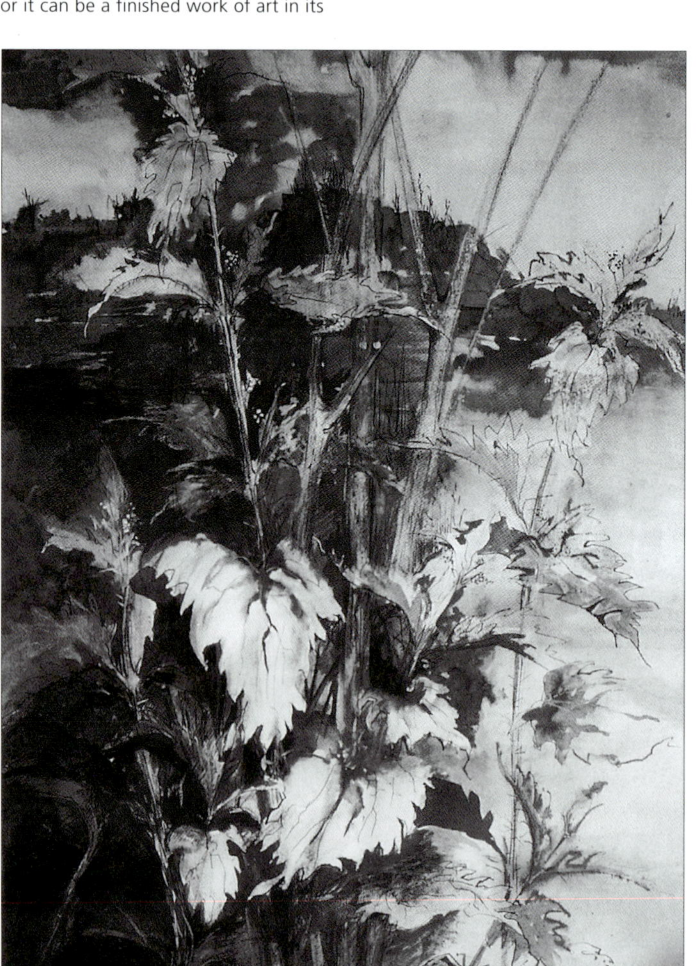

◀ 'Nettles'
The attractive combination of pen lines and washes of diluted ink allows tones to be built up faster than is possible with line alone. Pen and wash is ideal both for broad treatments and the kind of delicate effect seen in this drawing.
Elisabeth Harden

▼ 'East End Family House'
In this pen-and-ink drawing, tones have been built up by hatching and cross-hatching: this method can create a somewhat mechanical impression, but has been used loosely here, with the lines almost scribbled over one another in varying directions. Pen and ink is a good medium for rapid location sketches like this, as the impossibility of erasing encourages a decisive approach.
John Townend

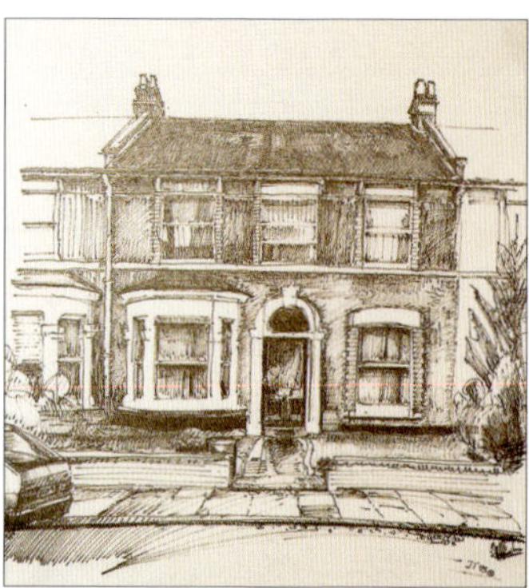

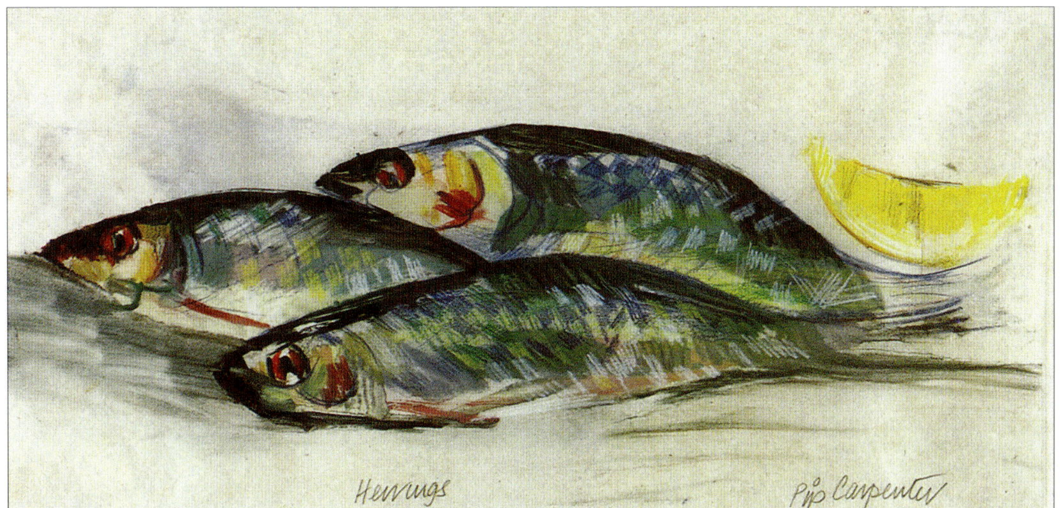

own right, planned, composed and executed with as much thought as the artist would give to a painting.

The kind of drawing you make depends on how you view the purpose of the activity – why are you drawing? You may draw simply because you love to do so, in which case, once you have mastered the 'alphabet' of drawing you will find it a satisfying means of self-expression. You may have aspirations to become an illustrator, or you may simply want to improve your observational skills because you enjoy painting.

If you view drawing as a necessary foundation for painting, accuracy will be your main aim, but for those who enjoy drawing for its own sake, it is rewarding to experiment with different media. The word 'drawing' should not conjure up an image of timid grey pencil marks on white paper – much more exciting effects are achievable. There is now a wider choice of drawing materials than ever before, from the traditional graphite pencil to a whole range of coloured pencils, inks and felt-tipped pens. The second part of this book explores the versatility of pastel, a drawing medium that can accommodate a more painterly approach. This first section explores the skills of observation and draughtsmanship that will enable you to create images of solid objects with integrity, using line and tone.

▲ **'Three Fishes'**
This mixed-media work uses an unusual combination: oil paint, used thinly on paper, and coloured pencils. There are no set rules about mixed-media drawing; only by experimenting with a variety of different materials will you discover which work well together and which do not.
Pip Carpenter

▼ **'White Village, South Spain'**
In this delightful drawing – which could be described equally well as a painting – the artist has used pen and ink with light washes of watercolour. These have spread the ink in places so that there is no obvious boundary between line and colour. When using a mixture of media it is important that the two work together, or the drawing will lack unity.
Joan Elliott Bates

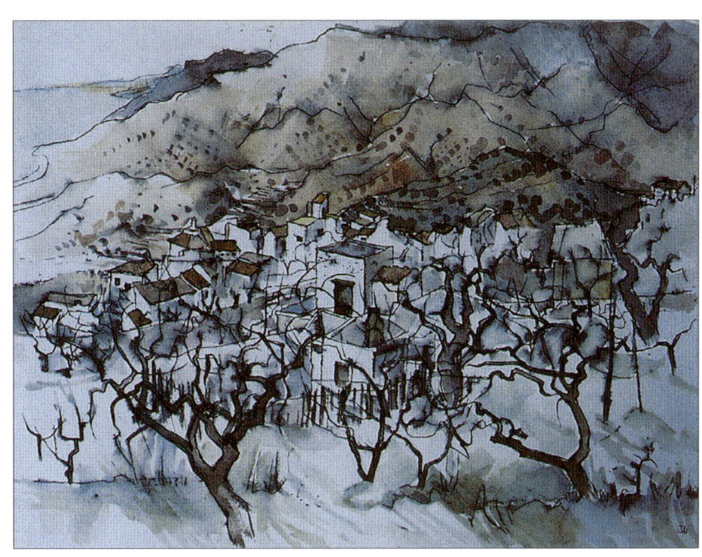

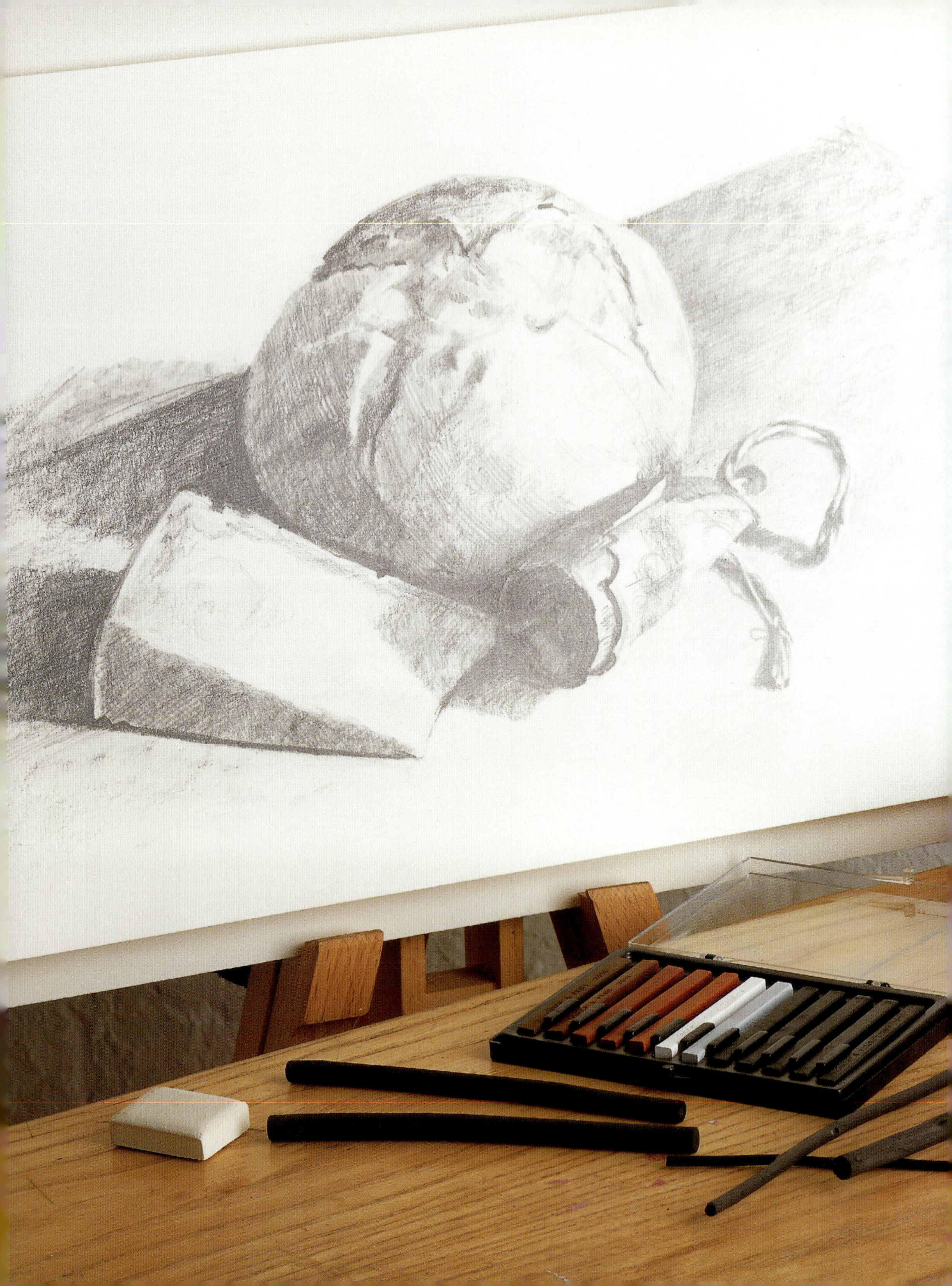

Getting Started in Drawing

There's something incredibly satisfying, not to say almost magical, about being able to recreate a three-dimensional subject on paper with just a few swift lines. This section sets out all the drawing techniques you need to know, using simple step-by-step exercises that you can follow in your own home. In the process, you will be introduced to the full range of drawing media, from graphite pencil and charcoal to coloured pencils, crayons, and pen and ink. Work through it systematically and you will acquire a comprehensive grasp of the fundamentals, which you can then apply to any subject you choose.

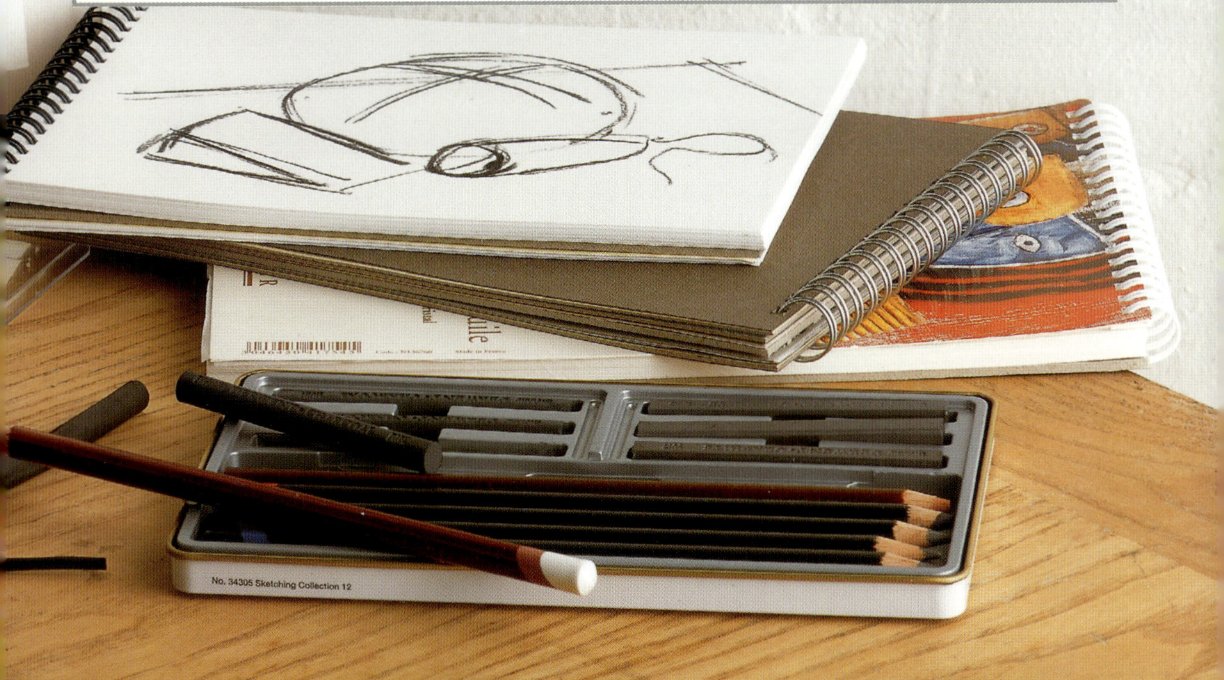

Monochrome media

The most commonly used drawing implement is the so-called 'lead' pencil, which is actually made not from lead but from a form of soft carbon known as graphite. The purest seams of graphite were discovered by chance in Borrowdale in Cumberland (northern England) in around 1500: after a heavy storm, local shepherds discovered that trees had been blown down, exposing large masses of an unknown black material. At first they thought it was coal, but it didn't burn; they then realized how good it was for making marks, and used it to mark their sheep. It was not long before people realized the potential of graphite as a drawing tool and it quickly spread across Europe, replacing the traditional silverpoint. To make a graphite pencil, graphite is reduced to a powder, which is then mixed with clay to make a paste; the paste is then extruded as a thin strip and encased in a wooden barrel made from a smooth-grain cedar.

The barrel of a graphite pencil may be round, hexagonal or triangular in shape. The choice of barrel shape is a personal one but, as a general rule, round barrels are easy to turn between the fingers while hexagonal and triangular ones are more stable to hold.

Pencils vary in hardness. Each grade is given a code that runs from 9H (the hardest) down to HB and F (for fine) and then up to 9B, which is the softest. The degree of hardness is determined by the relative proportions of graphite and clay: the more clay in the mix, the harder the grade. A selection of five different grades – say, a 2H, HB, 2B, 4B and 6B – should be adequate for most purposes.

Each grade of pencil is capable of making a mark of a certain density. Soft pencils give a very dense, black mark, while hard pencils give a grey, rather than a black, mark. If you require a darker mark, do not try to apply more pressure to the pencil, but switch to a softer grade.

Grades of pencil ▼
To make these marks, the same amount of pressure was applied to each pencil. You can clearly see how different grades of pencil produce marks of different density.

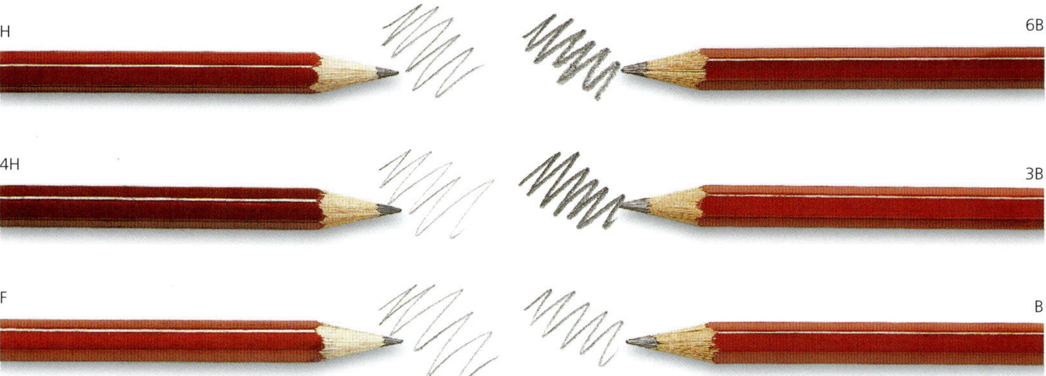

Water-soluble graphite pencils

There are also water-soluble graphite pencils, which are made with a binder that dissolves in water. Available in a range of grades, they can be used dry or worked into with a brush and water to create a range of watercolour-like effects.

Water-soluble graphite pencils are an ideal tool for sketching on location, as they offer you the versatility of combining linear marks with tonal washes. Use the tip to create fine details and the side of the pencil to cover large areas quickly.

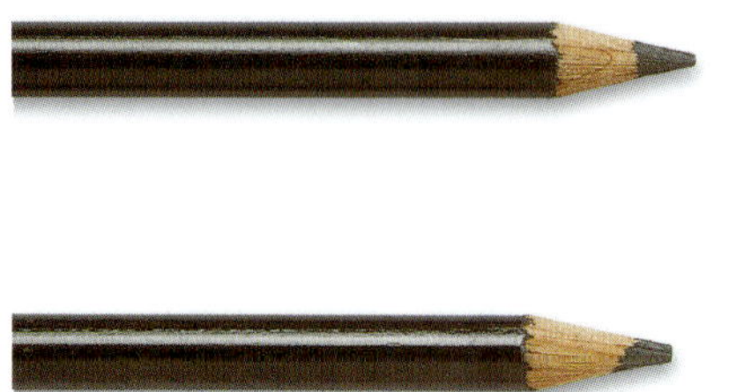

Tips: When you are sharpening a pencil in a pencil sharpener, the shaving should come out as a long, continuous strip. If it does not, then the sharpener is blunt and should be thrown away.

You can also sharpen pencils using a craft (utility) knife. Hold the knife at a very shallow angle and stroke the blade lightly along the wood of the pencil tip. (If you dig in too deeply, the graphite strip will almost certainly break.) Replace the knife blade regularly so that the blade is always sharp.

Graphite sticks

Solid sticks of graphite are available in various sizes and grades. Some resemble conventional pencils with a round profile, while others are shorter, thicker, and hexagonal in shape. Thick, short round sticks can also be found, as can sticks with a square or rectangular profile. You can also buy irregular-shaped chunks and fine graphite powder.

Thinner strips of graphite in varying degrees of hardness are also manufactured to fit in a barrel that has a clutch mechanism. These often have a sharpener hidden in the device that is pressed to operate the clutch.

Because of their shape, graphite sticks are capable of making a wider range of marks than conventional graphite pencils. For example, you can use the point or the side of a square- or rectangular-profile stick to make a thin mark, or stroke the whole side of the stick over the paper to make a broader mark.

Square-profile graphite stick ▼
Like graphite pencils, graphite sticks come in a range of grades, with a softer grade making a denser, blacker mark than a hard grade.

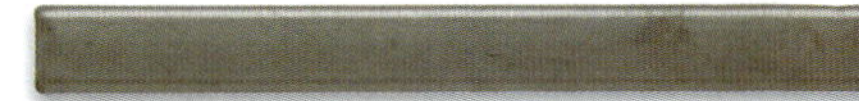

Charcoal

The other monochromatic drawing material popular with artists is charcoal. Charcoal is usually made from willow, although both vine and beech charcoal can also be found. It is made by charring the twigs at a very high temperature in airtight kilns.

Charcoal comes in different lengths and in thin, medium, thick and extra-thick sticks. You can also buy large, irregular-shaped chunks that are ideal for very large, expressive drawings. Stick charcoal is very brittle and breaks easily if you press hard. It is very powdery and is wonderful for creating broad areas of tone.

Compressed charcoal is made from charcoal dust mixed with a binder and fine clay and pressed into shape. It is harder than conventional charcoal and does not break so easily. It is also less messy to use. Rectangular or round compressed charcoal sticks are made in varying degrees of hardness.

Compressed charcoal is also made into pencils that either have a wooden barrel that is sharpened in the same way as a traditional graphite pencil or are set in a paper barrel that is torn away as the charcoal strip wears down. Because the charcoal is covered, charcoal pencils are much cleaner to handle than stick charcoal. They also have a slightly harder texture. Unlike stick charcoal, charcoal pencils are ideal for detailed, linear work. However, only the point can be used, so if you want to block in large areas of the paper quickly, it is perhaps preferable to use the side of a charcoal stick.

Charcoal smudges extremely easily, so you should wipe your fingers regularly when drawing with it so that you don't leave fingerprints on the paper. As with other powdery mediums, such as chalk and soft pastels, drawings made in charcoal should be sprayed with fixative to hold the pigment in place and prevent smudging. Fixative is readily available from art and craft stores, but hairspray makes a good and inexpensive alternative.

Various forms of charcoal ▼
From top to bottom: thick charcoal stick; thin charcoal stick; compressed charcoal stick; compressed charcoal pencil.

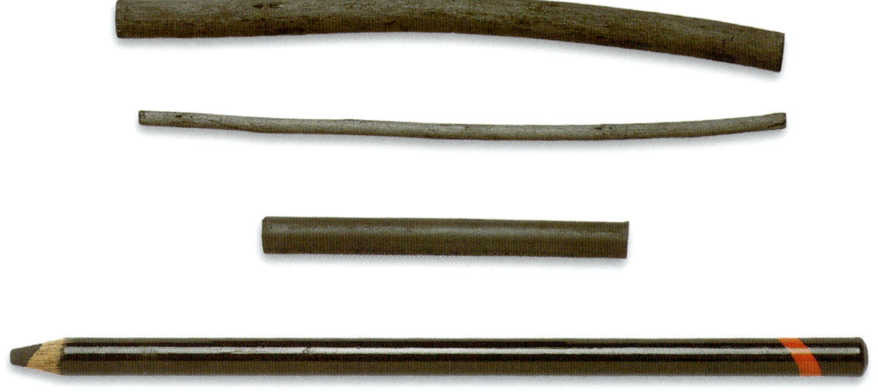

Coloured drawing media

Coloured pencils are as familiar as graphite pencils and are used in the same way. They contain a coloured pigment and clay, together with a binder. They are impregnated with wax to help the pigment hold on to the surface of the support with no need for a fixative. The coloured strip is held in a wooden barrel which, like graphite pencils, can be round, triangular or hexagonal in shape. The coloured strip can vary in diameter from one manufacturer to another, as can the wax content and hardness. Hard pencils will keep their point longer and so tend to be better for linear work or work that entails a lot of crosshatching, while a softer pencil might be better if you are working with large, loosely applied areas of colour. There are also coloured pencils that resemble graphite sticks and consist of a solid strip of pigment.

The range of colours available is extensive. Mixing takes place optically on the surface of the support rather than by physical blending. All brands are inter-mixable, although certain brands can be more easily erased than others; so always try out one or two individual pencils from a range before you buy a large set.

Coloured pencils are especially useful for making coloured drawings on location, as they are a very stable medium and not prone to smudging, so they do not need to be fixed (set).

Huge colour range
Artists who work in coloured pencil tend to accumulate a vast range in different shades – the variance between one tone and its neighbour often being very slight. This is chiefly because you cannot physically mix coloured pencil marks to create a new shade (unlike pastel or paint). So, if you want lots of different greens in a landscape, you will need a different pencil for each one.

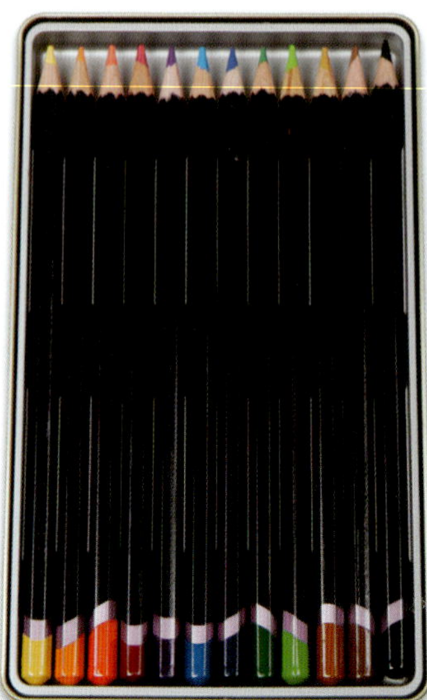

Water-soluble pencils

Most coloured-pencil manufacturers also produce a range of water-soluble pencils, which can be used to make conventional pencil drawings and blended with water to create watercolour-like effects. In recent years, solid pigment sticks that resemble pastels have been introduced that are also water-soluble and can be used in conjunction with conventional coloured pencils or on their own.

Water-soluble pencils ►
Like conventional coloured pencils, water-soluble pencils are available in many colours.

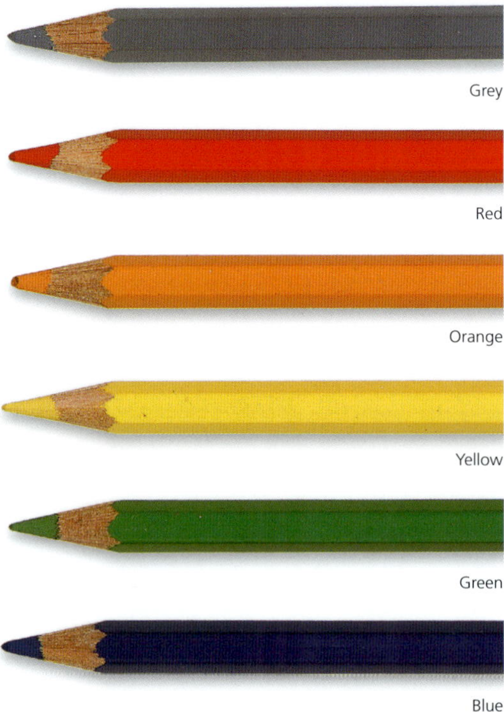

Wet and dry
Watercolour pencils can be used dry, in the same way as conventional pencils, to create linear marks (below left) or blended with water to make watercolour-like effects (right).

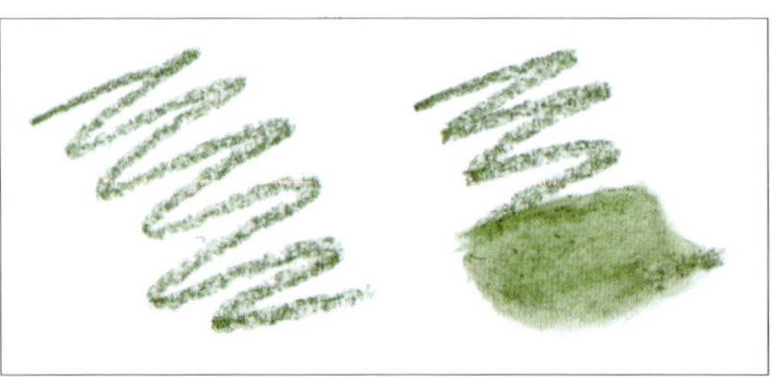

Conté crayons and pencils

Named after Nicolas-Jacques Conté, who invented them in the 18th century, Conté crayons are made in a range of traditional colours: white (made from chalk), sanguine (from iron oxide), sepia (from the ink of the cuttlefish) and bistre (from the soot of burnt beech wood). Terracotta, umber and black are also available, as are sets that provide a range of greys and browns. The crayons are also known as carré sticks – *carré* being the French word for 'square', referring to the square profile of the sticks.

The best way to use Conté crayons is to snap off a small section about 2–3cm (1in) long and use the side of the crayon to block in large areas, and a sharp edge or the tip to make more linear marks.

The pigment in Conté crayons is relatively powdery, which means that, like soft pastels and charcoal, it can be blended by rubbing with a finger, rag or torchon (tortillon, or blending stump). Conté crayon drawings benefit from being given a coat of fixative to prevent smudging. However, Conté crayons are slightly harder and more oily than soft pastels, so you can lay one colour over another, allowing the underlying colour to show through.

Conté is also available in pencil form in a similar range of colours. The pencils contain wax and need no fixing (setting); the other benefit is that the tip can be sharpened to a relatively fine point.

Pencils and sticks are particularly effective when used together, the pencil being used for precision and detail and the sticks to block in wide areas of tone. Drawings made using both pencils and sticks can be seen to best advantage when made on a light-coloured paper.

Most of the colours available in pencil and stick form can also be found in short 'lead' form intended for use in a holder. Different manufacturers make 'leads' in different diameters, not all interchangeable. Many of the holders have a sharpening mechanism in the end. Similar square holders are made to hold small pieces of the broken sticks.

Conté crayons ▼
These small, square-profile sticks are available in boxed sets of traditional colours. Drawings made using these traditional colours are reminiscent of the wonderful chalk drawings of such old masters as Michelangelo or Leonardo da Vinci.

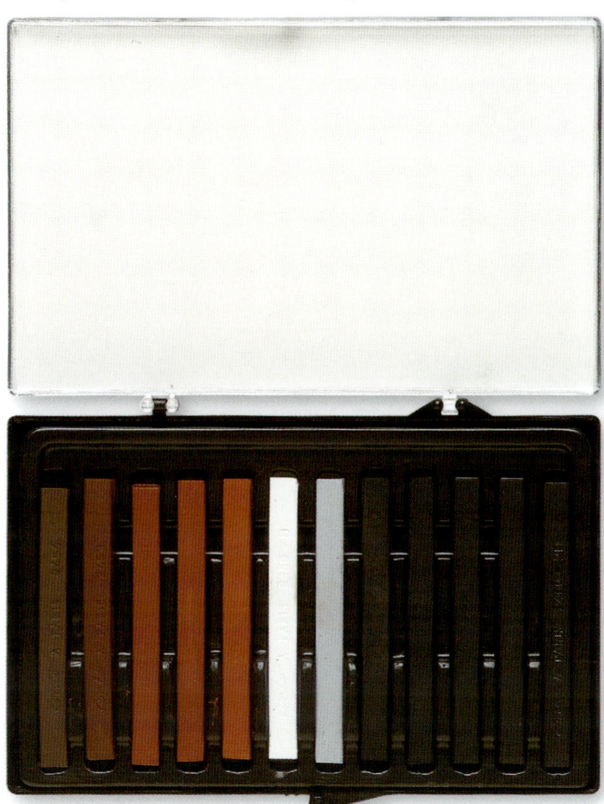

Conté pencils ▼
As they can be sharpened to a point, Conté pencils are ideal for drawings that require precision and detail.

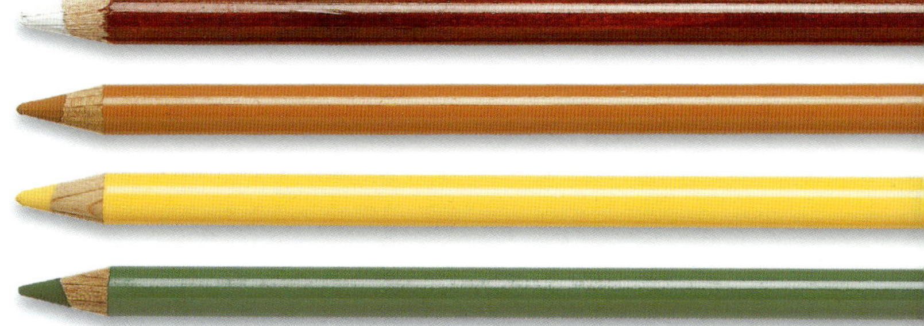

Pen and ink

Working in pen and ink can be a rather frightening prospect for beginners as, if you make a mistake, it's difficult to erase. However, with so many types of pens and colours of ink available, not to mention the possibility of combining linear work with washes of colour, it is an extremely versatile medium and one that is well worth exploring.

Begin by making a light pencil under-drawing of your subject – but beware of simply inking over your pencil lines, as this can look rather flat and dead. When you feel you've gained enough confidence, your aim should be to put in the minimum of lines in pencil, simply to ensure you've got the proportions and angles right, and do the majority of work in pen.

Inks

There are two types of inks used by artists – waterproof and non-waterproof. Waterproof inks can be diluted with water, but they are permanent once dry, which means that line work made using waterproof ink can be worked over with washes without any fear of it being removed. They often contain shellac, and thick applications dry to leave a slight sheen, which can be slightly distracting. Perhaps the most well-known waterproof ink is so-called Indian ink, which is not from India at all, but from China. Indian ink makes beautiful line drawings. Although it is a deep black when it is used straight from the bottle, Indian ink can be diluted to give a beautiful range of warm greys. Waterproof inks are also available in a limited range of basic colours that can be mixed prior to application.

Non-waterproof inks are more difficult to find, but they are worth the effort as they can be worked into once dry. Work can be lightened and corrections made. As with waterproof inks, the colour range is limited.

Finally, do not overlook the potential of liquid acrylics and watercolours. Both are found in bottles and can be used with pen and brush, just like ink. The colour range is slightly more extensive.

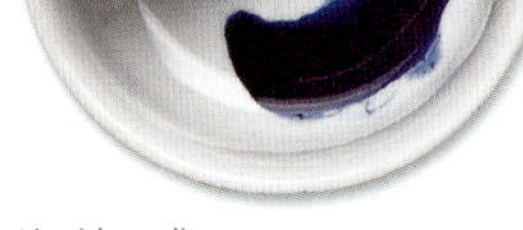

Liquid acrylic

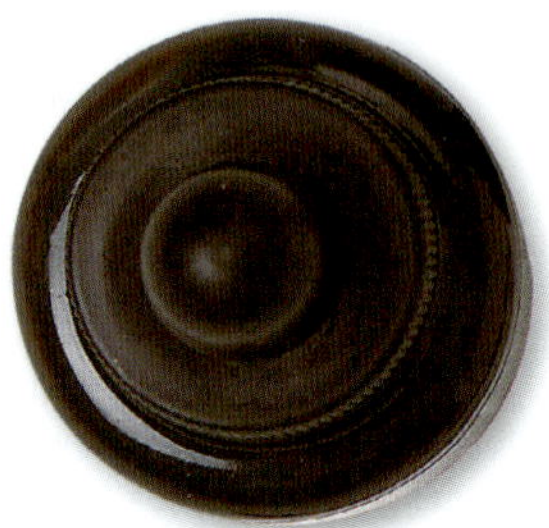

Water-soluble ink

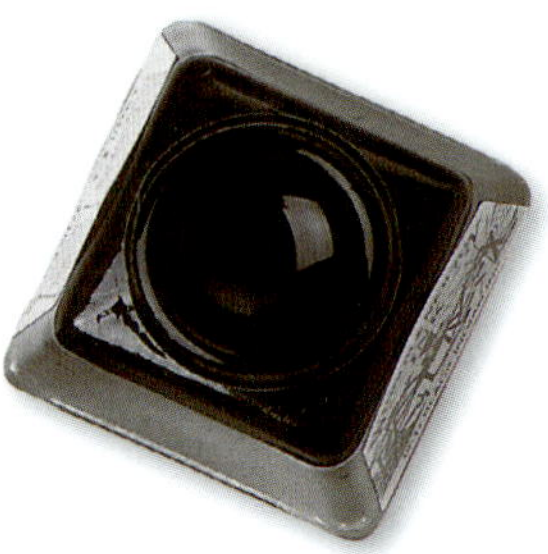

Waterproof ink

Dip pens and nibs

A dip pen does not have a reservoir of ink; as the name suggests, it is simply dipped into the ink to make marks. Drawings made with a dip pen have a unique quality, as the nib can make a line of varying width depending on how much pressure you apply. You can also turn the pen over and use the back of the nib to make broader marks. As you have to keep reloading the pen with ink, it is difficult to make a long, continuous line – but for many subjects the rather scratchy, broken lines that are produced are very attractive.

When you first use a new nib it can be reluctant to accept ink. To solve this, wet it with a little saliva.

Range of nibs

Dip pen barrels take a range of different shapes and sizes of nib. Each nib makes a different range of marks – and the more flexible the nib, the more variety you can achieve in the thickness of line. To put in a new nib, simply push the end into the slot in the barrel, taking care not to bend it. Not all nibs fit every pen, so make sure you buy nibs that are compatible with your pen barrel. The barrels are made from wood or plastic and are inexpensive to buy.

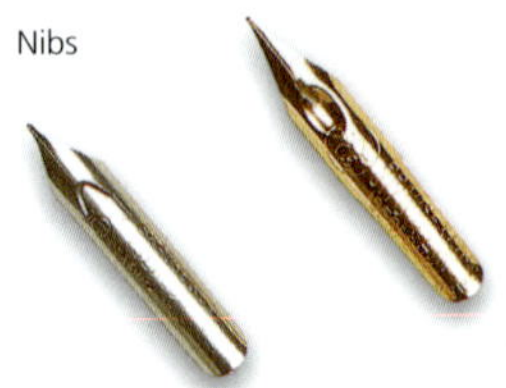

Nibs

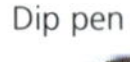

Dip pen

Bamboo, reed and quill pens

Cut from a short length of bamboo, bamboo pens vary in thickness. Some pens are cut so that they have a different sized nib at each end. The nib of a bamboo pen is inflexible and delivers a slightly 'dry', rather coarse line that is completely different to one made using a dip pen.

Reed pens are flexible and deliver a subtle line that does vary in thickness. The nib end breaks easily, although it can be reshaped using a sharp knife.

Quill pens can be made from any reasonably large feather – turkey, swan or goose, for example. The line quality is full of character, making a quill pen a joy to use. The cut nib can break easily but, like reed pens, can be re-cut.

Sketching pens, fountain pens and technical pens

Sketching pens and fountain pens make ideal sketching tools and enable you to use ink on location without having to carry bottles of ink. Use only water-soluble ink in fountain pens, or they will quickly become blocked.

Technical pens deliver ink through a tube rather than a shaped nib, so the line is of a uniform width. If you want to make a drawing that has a range of line widths, you will need several pens with different-sized tubular nibs.

Ink cartridges for sketching pens ▼
Sketching pens hold a cartridge that contains a specially formulated drawing ink that will not clog the nib.

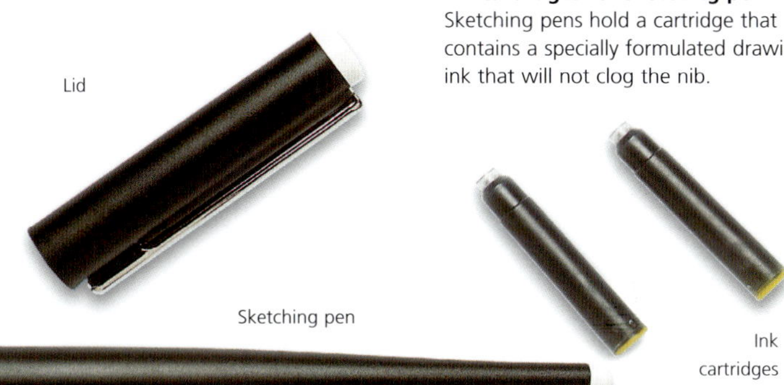

Lid

Sketching pen

Ink cartridges

Rollerball, fibre-tip and marker pens

All these types of pen are readily available from both art supply stores and normal stationery stores. Drawings made using a rollerball pen can have a rather mechanical feel to them, as the line does not vary in width, but, by working quickly, you can make a light line by delivering less ink.

Fibre-tip and marker pens nowadays come in an extensive range of tip widths from super-fine to calligraphic style tips and also in a wide range of colours.

While these types of pen may not be suitable for finished artworks, they are certainly very useful tools for working out ideas in sketchbooks and for making preparatory studies. One of the main benefits is that they are so easily portable, as you do not need to carry separate bottles of ink.

Fibre-tip pen ▼
The advantage of fibre-tip pens is that they come in a range of tip widths, so you can use broad tips to block in large areas of tone and fine tips for delicate details. The colour range is also extensive, so they are great for making quick colour notes on reference sketches. Like rollerball and technical pens, they tend to give a drawing a rather mechanical feel.

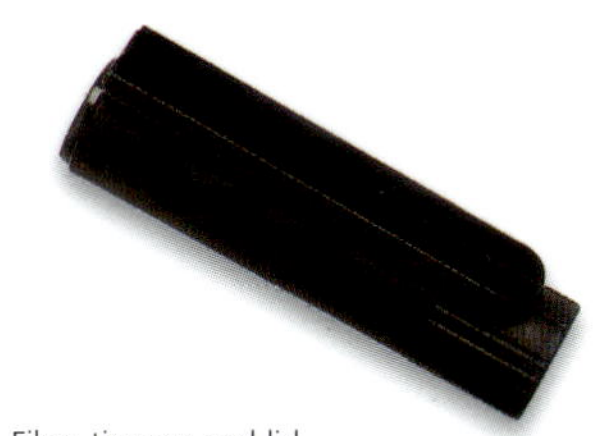

Fibre-tip pen and lid

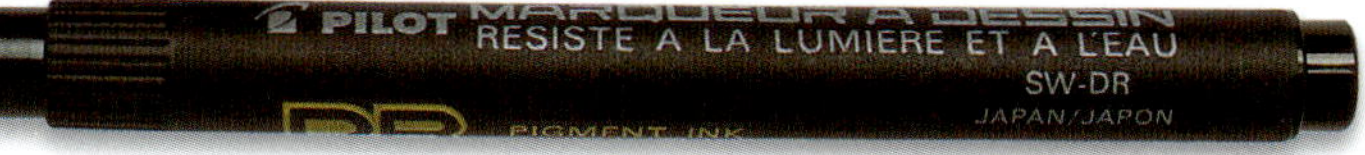

Rollerball pen ▼
For making quick reference sketches or thumbnail compositional sketches on location, rollerball pens are a good option as they are easy to transport and clean to handle.

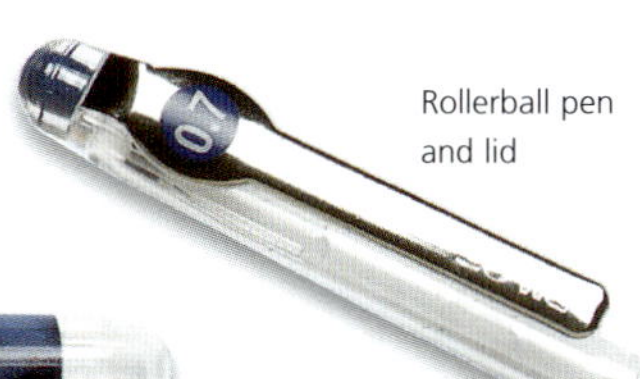

Rollerball pen and lid

Supports

The general name for the surface on which you draw is the 'support' – usually, but not always, some kind of paper. There are a number of types and qualities of paper available and the one you choose will depend on both your own personal taste and the subject you are drawing, as well as the medium in which you are working.

White paper

Drawing papers vary enormously in quality and cost, depending on whether the paper is handmade, machine-made, or mould-made.

The thickness of a paper is described in one of two ways. The first is in pounds (lb) and describes the weight of a ream (500 sheets). The second is in grams (gsm), and describes the weight of one square metre of a single sheet. Sheets vary in size.

Many papers can also be bought in roll form and cut to the size required. You can also buy pads, which are lightly glued at one end, from which you tear off individual sheets as required. One of the benefits of buying a pad of paper is that it usually has a stiff cardboard back, which gives you a solid surface to lean on when working on location and means that you don't have to carry a heavy drawing board around with you. Sketchbooks have the same advantage.

The most common drawing paper has a smooth surface that is suitable for graphite, coloured pencil and ink work. Papers intended for use with watercolour also make ideal drawing supports. These papers come in three distinctly different surfaces – HP (hot-pressed) papers, which are smooth; CP (cold-pressed) papers, also known as NOT, or 'not hot-pressed' papers, which have some surface texture; and rough papers which, not surprisingly, have a rougher texture.

Art and illustration boards are made from cardboard with paper laminated to the surface. They offer a stable, hard surface on which to work and are especially useful for pen line and wash, but can also be used with graphite and coloured pencil. They have the added advantage of not buckling when wet, as lightweight papers are prone to do, and are available in a range of sizes and surface textures, from very smooth to rough.

Drawing paper ▼
A medium-weight paper is suitable for most purposes, but if you are planning to use water-soluble pencils in combination with water, a heavier paper is best. For fine, detailed work, choose a smooth paper. For charcoal and pastel work, a paper with some 'tooth' to pick up the pigment is generally best.

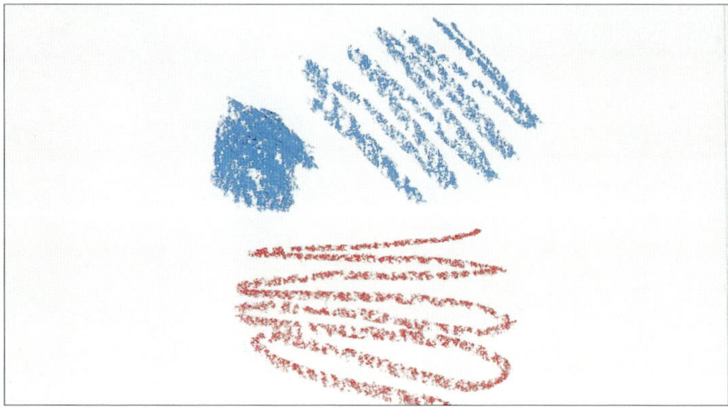

Sketchbooks ▼
Available in a wide range of formats and containing all the above-mentioned papers, sketchbooks are invaluable for working out ideas and for drawing on location. Spiral-bound, stitched or glued, the sketchbook is perhaps the most important piece of equipment for anyone who draws.

Coloured paper

The main advantage of making a drawing on coloured paper is that you can choose a colour that complements the subject and enhances the mood of the drawing. Coloured papers can be used with all drawing media. Some of these papers are laid rather than woven. Laid papers can be identified by the network of parallel lines that runs through the paper, which you can see by holding it up to the light.

Some papers are manufactured specifically for use with dusty, pigmented drawing materials such as pastel, chalk and charcoal. They are normally tinted in a range of pleasing natural colours that complement the pastel colours and give an overall colour harmony. Several brands are also available as boards, which makes them relatively easy to use on location.

Coloured papers ▼
Available in a wide range of colours with a good, even surface texture, coloured papers can be used with all drawing media.

Pastel and charcoal papers ▼
Papers for use with pastels and charcoals are coated with pumice powder or tiny cork particles that hold the pigment and allow for a build-up of colour.

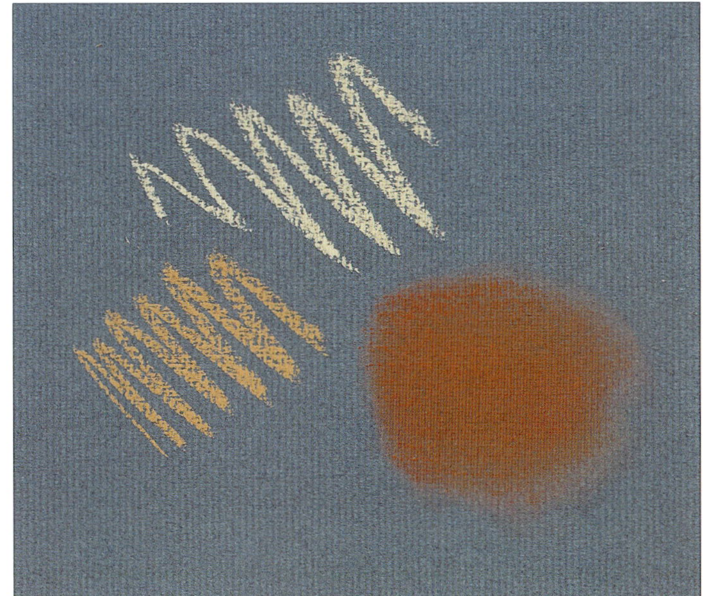

Preparing your own surfaces

It is both satisfying and surprisingly easy to prepare your own drawing surfaces. Acrylic gesso, a kind of primer that is used to prepare a surface such as canvas or board when painting in oils or acrylics, can also be painted on to paper to give a brilliant white, hard surface that receives graphite and coloured pencil beautifully.

To make a surface that is suitable for pastels, you can mix the gesso with pumice powder.

To create a toned or coloured ground, simply tint the gesso by adding a small amount of acrylic paint in the appropriate colour.

Additional equipment

In addition to drawing tools and paper, there are a number of other pieces of equipment that you will need – erasers, tools to sharpen your pencils, blending tools and easels. If you work in very soft media, such as charcoal, you will also need fixative. With the exception of easels, most are inexpensive and readily available from both art supply stores and general stationers.

Erasing tools

After tools that make marks, perhaps the next most used pieces of drawing equipment are tools that erase them. Erasing marks is not only a way of making corrections, but also a mark-making technique in its own right.

Kneaded erasers are good for cleaning up areas of a drawing. You can knead them to a point and even pull off small sections for delicate areas of a drawing. They do, however, get dirty very quickly, especially when used with charcoal or pastel.

India rubber, vinyl and plastic erasers are harder and able to erase precise, fine marks. Large soap-gum erasers are used for cleaning up areas of white paper, as are cleaning pads, consisting of a bag of rubber granules that is rubbed over the paper surface. Erasing knives can be used to scrape mistakes away gently, but they need to be used with care.

Types of eraser ▶
A plastic eraser (top) is hard and unyielding and can be used very precisely to erase small marks and areas. A kneaded eraser (bottom) is pliable and can be pulled to a point.

Sharpening tools

In order to sharpen your drawing tools and to repair and re-cut pen nibs, you will need a sharp craft (utility) knife. There are several types on the market, from those that require replaceable blades to models with retractable blades that break off to expose a new sharp section. Whichever type you use, keep plenty of spare, sharp blades to hand. Using a blunt knife will not only not sharpen your drawing implement well, but it is also dangerous.

Pencil sharpeners are also useful, provided the blade is sharp. Abrasive-paper blocks are another good way of keeping the points of pencils and chalks shaped and sharp.

Hand-held pencil sharpener ▼
Small, hand-held pencil sharpeners are useful but make sure they are large enough to hold the barrel of the pencil.

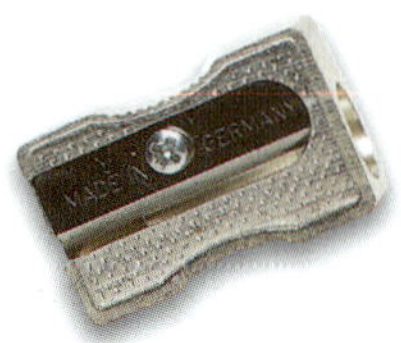

Craft/utility knife ▼
This knife has a retractable blade. When one section of the blade is blunt, simply snap it off and push the lever on the knife handle to expose the next section.

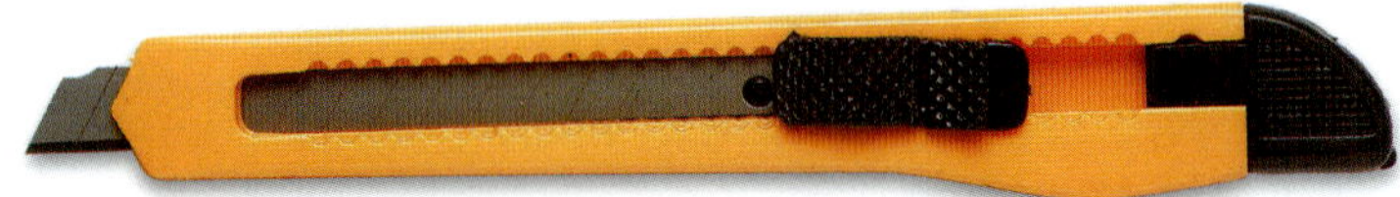

Battery-powered sharpener ▼
This battery-powered pencil sharpener is ideal if you do a lot of graphite or coloured-pencil work, as it sharpens quickly and evenly.

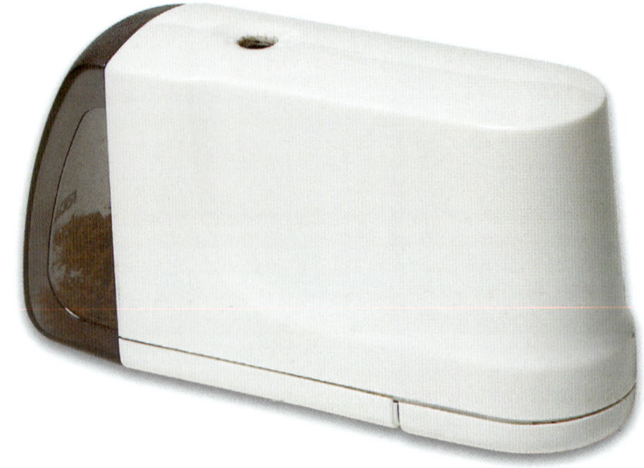

Fixative

Made from resin dissolved in a colourless spirit solvent, fixative is applied to drawings made with dusty, pigmented materials such as charcoal and soft pastels, to prevent smudging. Fixative is used not only on finished drawings, but also on work in progress to make it possible to build up layers of marks and to preserve areas of a drawing that you are happy with. Fixative is available in aerosol cans (like hairspray, which can be used as a cheap alternative), bottles with a mechanical spray mechanism or a mouth spray diffuser.

Blending tools

In order to blend marks and manipulate pigment or move it around on the support, you will need to acquire some torchons – also known as paper stumps, or tortillons. These are made from rolled or pulped paper fashioned into a point at one or both ends. They get dirty quickly, but can be cleaned by being rubbed on a sheet of glass paper.

Of course, you can also blend marks with a clean rag or piece of kitchen paper (although this method is best for large areas such as skies), or with your fingertips.

Torchons ▼
Invaluable for blending dusty, pigmented materials such as charcoal and soft pastels, torchons (also known as tortillons or paper stumps) come in a range of sizes. They are made of tightly rolled paper and have a tapered end (for working on large areas) or a pointed end (for small details).

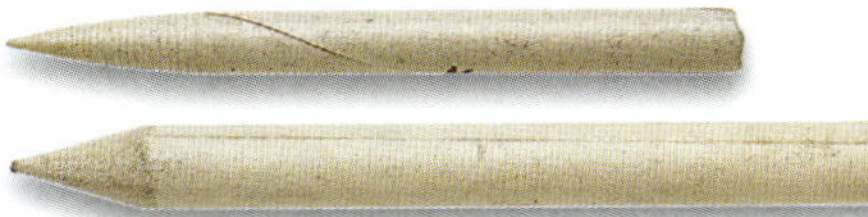

Drawing boards and easels

If you are working on loose sheets of paper, you will need a drawing board. You may find it worthwhile buying two in different sizes. Boards are made from plywood, which makes them relatively light and easy to use on location. Paper is fixed to the board by means of clips, drawing pins (thumb tacks) or masking tape; clips (see below) are easy to use and do not tear or puncture the paper.

The type of easel that you choose depends on your budget, the space in which you work, the type of work that you intend to do, and whether or not you plan to work on location. Table easels hold a medium-size drawing board and can be positioned so that the drawing surface is anything up to about 45 degrees above the horizontal. They do, however, need to be placed on a flat surface, so are not suitable for location work.

There are two main types of free-standing easel – those that are portable and those that are not. Portable easels are good for location work. Make sure you buy one that is stable when erected and can easily hold the size of support on which you intend to work, at a comfortable angle. Studio easels are a major investment; only buy one if you have room for it. There are two main shapes: an A frame and an H frame. The larger H-frame easels are on castors to make them easier to move and may have a ratchet or winding system to raise or lower the support.

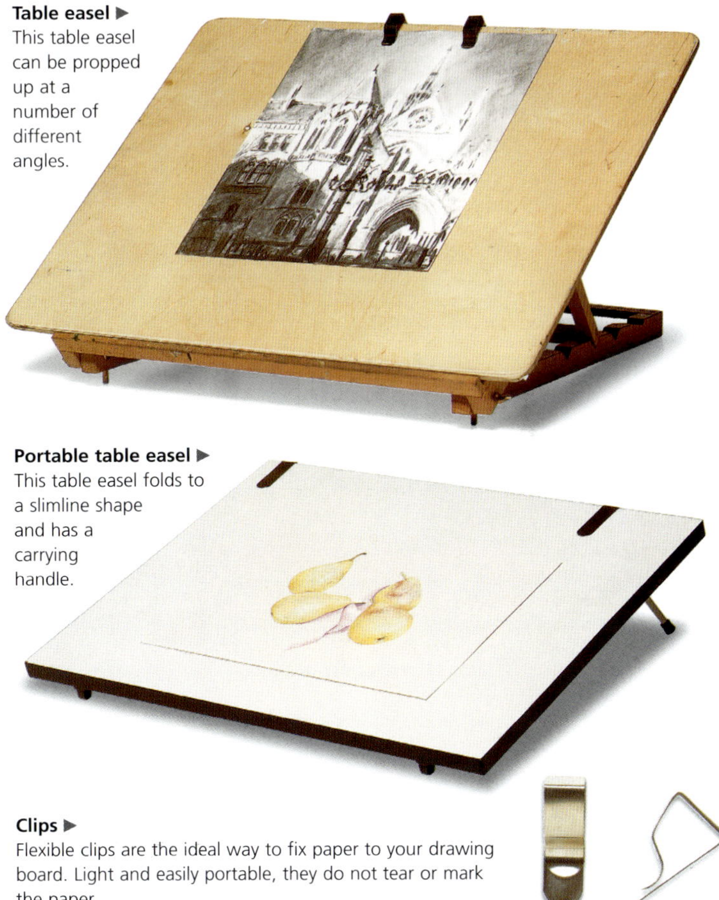

Table easel ▶
This table easel can be propped up at a number of different angles.

Portable table easel ▶
This table easel folds to a slimline shape and has a carrying handle.

Clips ▶
Flexible clips are the ideal way to fix paper to your drawing board. Light and easily portable, they do not tear or mark the paper.

Making marks

The success of your drawings depends on your ability to make as wide and as varied a range of marks as possible. This allows you to exploit the potential of your chosen material to the full. With practice, every drawing tool – even the simple graphite pencil – can be made to produce a surprisingly wide range of marks. Mark-making is something that you can practise whenever you have a few minutes spare; time that you spend doodling on a scrap piece of paper is never wasted.

Several things affect the quality of a mark, including pressure, direction, speed, and the angle at which the drawing tool is presented to the support. Marks made when drawing are used to represent three distinct things: line, tone and texture. Line is mainly used to describe the shape of a thing. In reality, these lines don't exist, but in the hands of an artist they are a graphic device that indicates where one thing ends and another begins. By varying the quality of a line, however, you can show much more than just the shape of something. You can also convey light, shade, and even the texture of the object.

Tone indicates how light or dark something is, the direction and strength of the light, and the form of the subject. Tone can be applied in several ways. Suffice to say here that being able to indicate tone in a controlled way is very important if you want to portray your subject in a way that looks convincing. Textures indicate the surface quality of an object and are directly affected by the quality and direction of the light. When a subject is lit from overhead, the texture of its surface can look flat and uninteresting; when lit from the side, that same surface will look dramatic and full of interest. In order to make these different types of mark, you will need to learn how to hold the drawing tool in a variety of different ways. These may feel slightly awkward at first, but with practice they will become second nature.

The shape of the drawing tool dictates the type and range of marks you make. Remember that, with all drawing tools, by turning them in your fingers you can use not only the point but also the side and the edge, allowing it to come into contact with the support in many different ways.

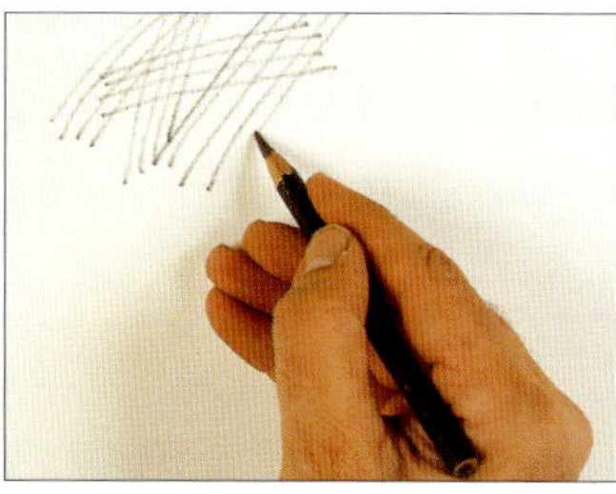

Controlling the point of a pencil
By gently cradling a pencil between your fingers, you can manipulate the point of the tool very precisely by using just your fingers and wrist.

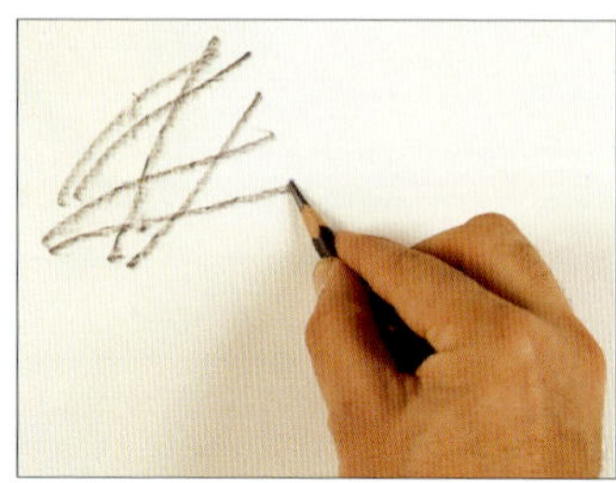

Making heavy marks with a pencil
By holding a pencil between the tips of your fingers and your thumb, you can bring the side of the lead into contact with the support and make thicker, heavier marks.

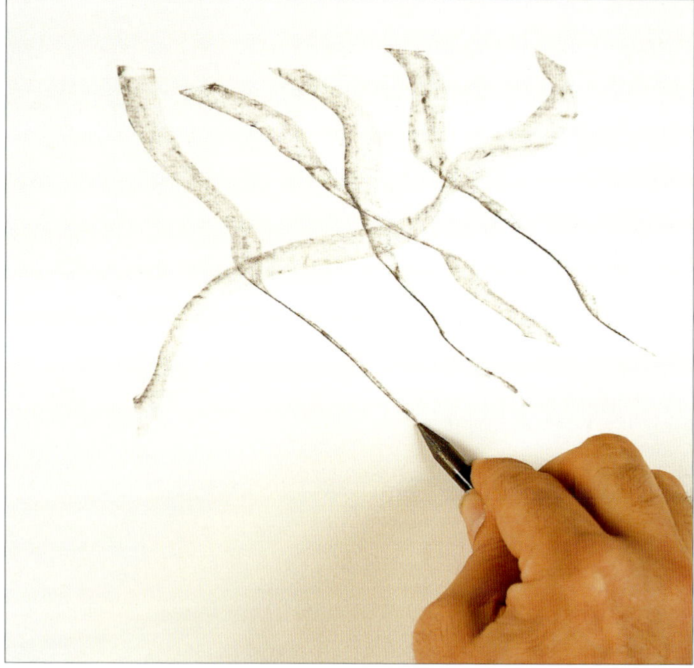

Altering the angle at which you hold a graphite stick
By holding a stick of graphite in the same way and altering the angle of the stick in relation to the support as you work, you can create a fluid line that varies in thickness from being as wide as the tapered section of the stick (shown at the top of the image above, and created by pressing the tapered section flat on to the support) to a crisp, thin line made using just the tip of the stick.

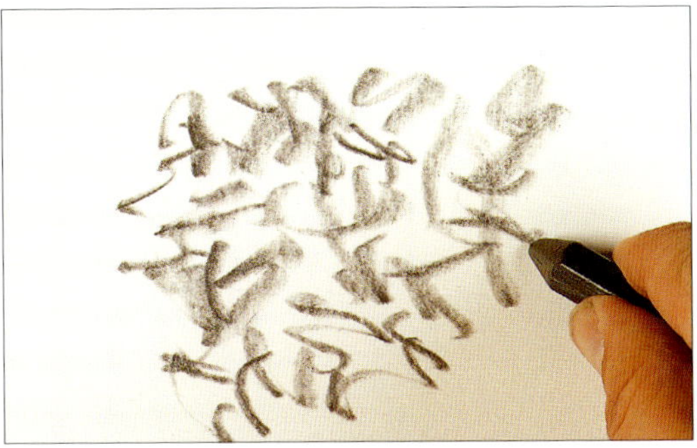

Textural marks
By jabbing the dull, blunted end of a thick stick of graphite on to the support, you can make textural marks that vary in tone, depending on how much pressure you apply.

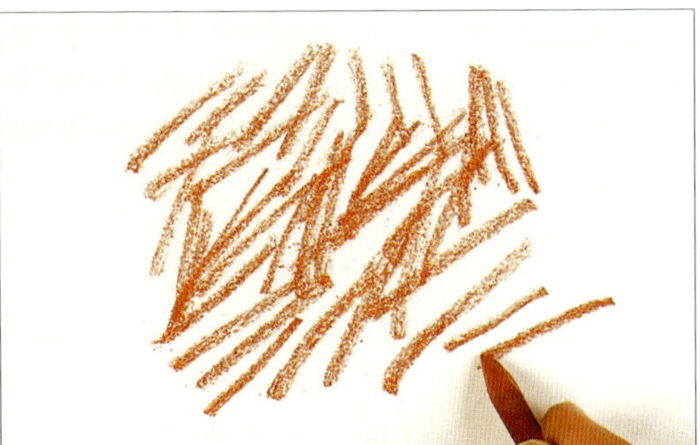

Using the point of a Conté or carré stick
Conté and carré sticks and chalks can be sharpened to various degrees in order to make lines of varying thickness similar to those made with a pencil.

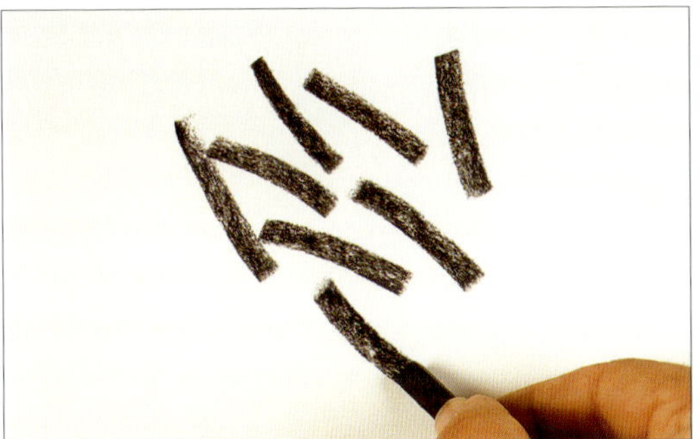

Using the full width of a Conté or carré stick
Here the width of a Conté stick is pressed on to the support to create a broad, dense mark.

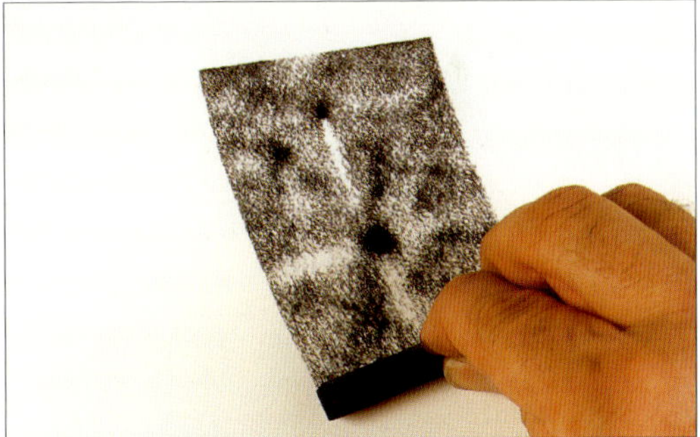

Using the flat side of a Conté or carré stick
By pulling the side of a Conté or carré stick across the support, you can lay down a broad area of dense pigment.

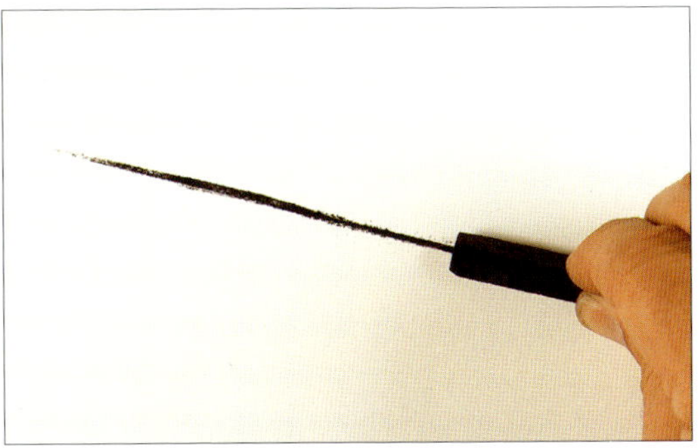

Using the sharp edge of a Conté or carré stick
By holding the stick between the tips of your fingers and your thumb and pulling it lengthways along the sharp edge of one side, you can make a straight line that gradually becomes thicker as the stick wears down.

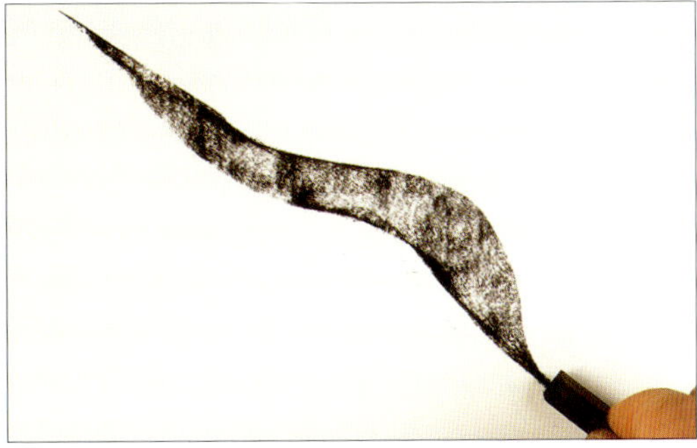

Twisting a Conté or carré stick
By holding the stick between the tips of your fingers and your thumb, pulling it lengthways along the sharp edge of one side, and turning it back and forth, you can create a wave-like line that varies in width from thin to thick and back again.

Line drawing

Lines around an object are merely a graphic device that artists use to describe the shape of things. A good line drawing will guide the eye over and around the subject, inviting you to 'feel' its shape. In order to use line in this way, you need to be able to alter its density and its width. When using dry pigmented materials like graphite, you can make a line darker by increasing the amount of pressure that you apply. To increase the width of a line, angle the drawing tool so that more of it comes into contact with the support. The quality of a line is also influenced by the speed with which it is made; a line applied with speed and confidence will look strong and fluid, whereas a line applied in a hesitant way looks laboured. If it is used well, the line can be made to describe light, shade and the texture of your subject. It can also be used to describe internal contours. If an object is drawn in outline only, all you will see is a silhouette-like shape – but if you use line to indicate internal contours, you will have a much better idea of the form of the object that you are drawing.

Practice exercise: **Simple line drawing**

You can adapt the approach used here to any subject you choose, and it is well worth setting aside ten or fifteen minutes every day to make a sketch like this as there is nothing better for improving your powers of observation and eye–hand co-ordination.

Whatever subject you choose, think of your eye as a laser, moving along the contours of the object and cutting it out. Try to move your eye and your pencil at the same speed, as this will make it easier for you to get the size of different parts of the subject right without having to measure anything. Work slowly to begin with, increasing your speed as you get more confident.

As a variation on this exercise, draw something without looking down at the paper. Don't worry if your lines don't join up: the point is to train yourself to really look at your subject and put down on paper the shapes you can see.

Materials

- *Smooth drawing paper*
- *4B pencil*

The subject

Here, the artist selected a trainer (sneaker) as her subject. The laces and the decorative lines within it help to convey the shape of the shoe.

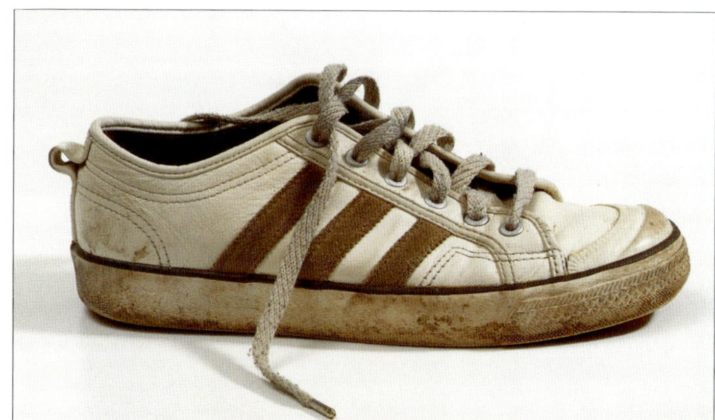

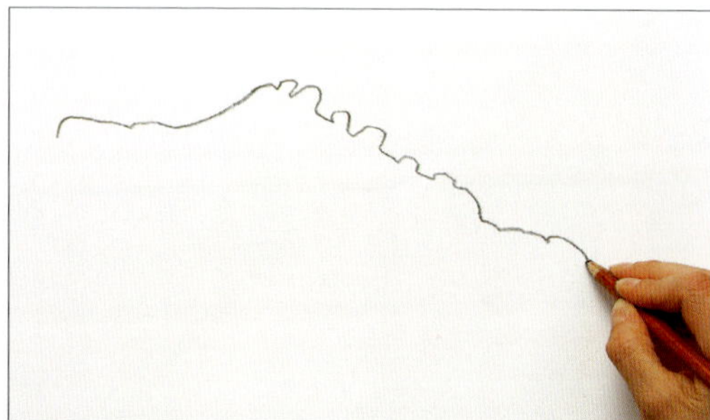

1 Working slowly and carefully, begin drawing the top of the trainer, looking at where the laces form the outer line of the silhouette. Try to think of the laces as being part of the overall shape of the shoe, rather than just things that are attached to it.

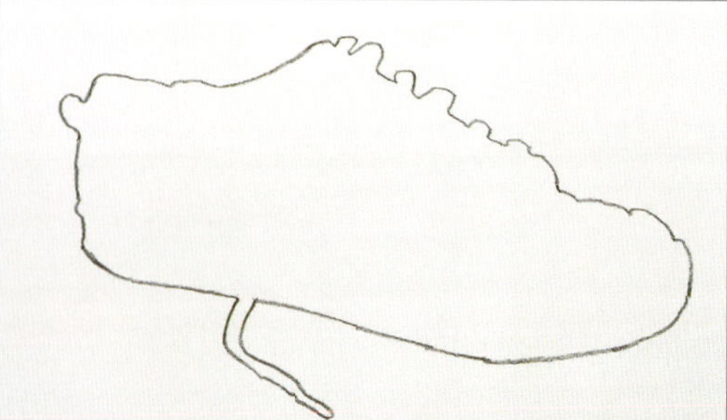

2 Continue around the base of the shoe, concentrating hard. It's very easy to draw something the way you think it ought to look, rather than putting down the shapes that are actually there. Note how the lace breaks the outline. Try to complete Steps 1 and 2 without lifting the pencil from the paper.

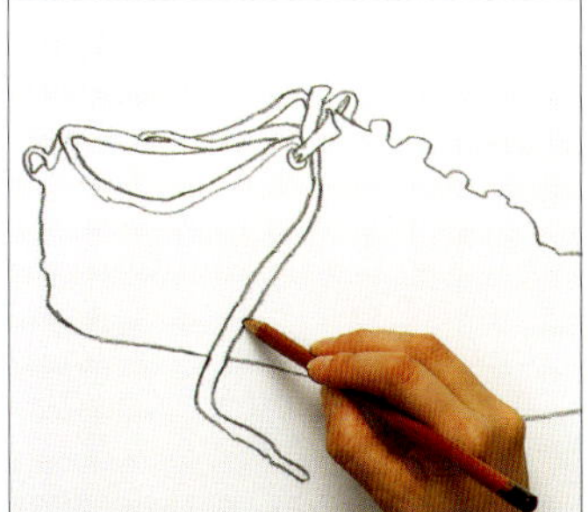

3 Once the outline is complete, you can begin to put in some of the internal lines such as the lace holes and the long lace that trails over the side of the shoe.

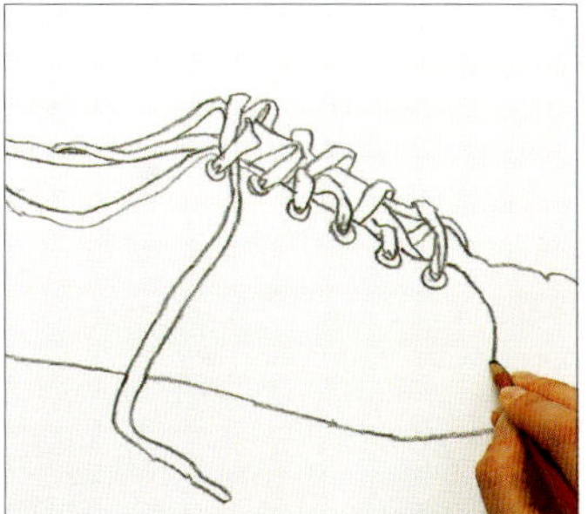

4 Now draw the laces, observing carefully how they twist and turn over one another. Also draw the decorative band on the side of the lace-hole panel.

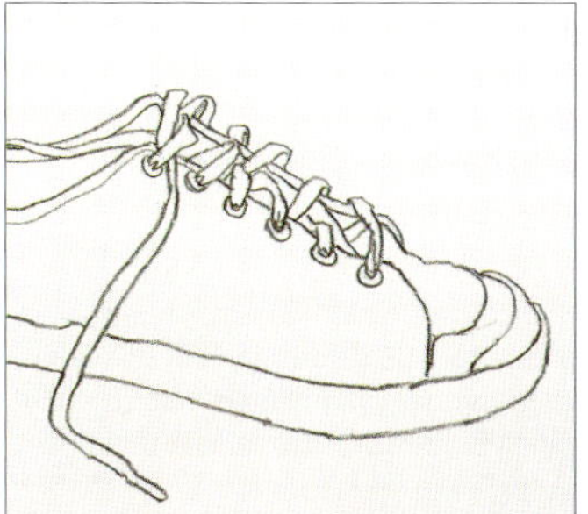

5 Next you will need to put in the broad lines across the toe of the shoe as well as along the raised tread around the base. This helps to give some sense of form.

The finished drawing

The decorative detailing completes the drawing. This is a simple sketch of an ordinary household object, but with just a few lines the artist has managed to convey both the shape and something of the form of her subject.

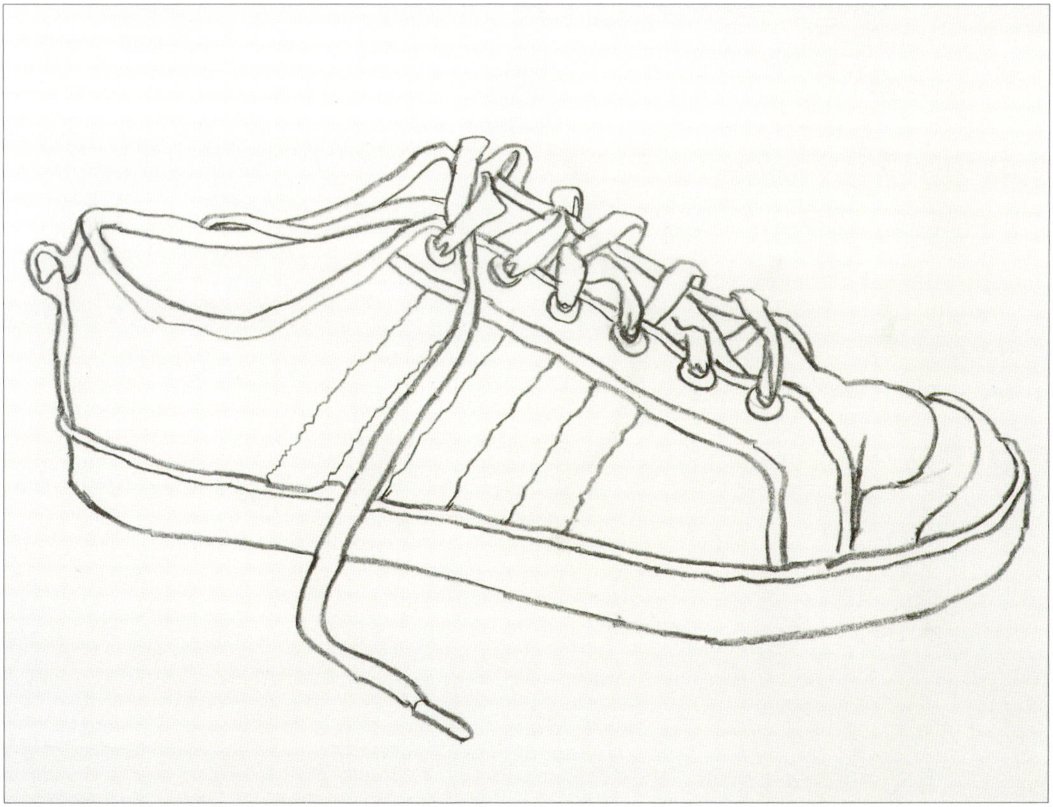

Seeing things as simple shapes

When you first look at your subject, the amount of information that you need to take in and assimilate can seem quite daunting. The answer is to simplify what you see into a series of simple geometric shapes. The shapes most commonly used are the cone, the cylinder, the cube and the sphere – all three-dimensional objects. They may be elongated or compacted, but essentially the shapes remain the same.

Make your initial sketch using these four shapes, or combinations of them, as appropriate. All these shapes are relatively easy to draw in perspective, which will help you to orientate and position the elements within the drawing quickly and correctly. Then you can elaborate, redefine the shape and gradually add tone and detail.

The illustrations on these two pages show how simple geometric shapes (the red lines in the illustrations) can be used as a starting point for drawing a number of ordinary household objects. Adopt the same approach when drawing other subjects; you will find it surprisingly beneficial.

Straight-sided bottle ▼
The shape of this bottle was established by first drawing a simple elongated box in perspective. The top of the bottle was then indicated by drawing a tall cylinder.

Bottle with round base ▼
The round-based bottle shown below was drawn by first creating an egg shape (an elongated sphere). The long neck of the bottle was then added, using a simple cylinder.

Wine glass ▼
The shape of this glass is contained within a cylinder. The bowl of the glass was made using a sphere. Make sure you draw the ellipses for the top rim and the base at the correct angle.

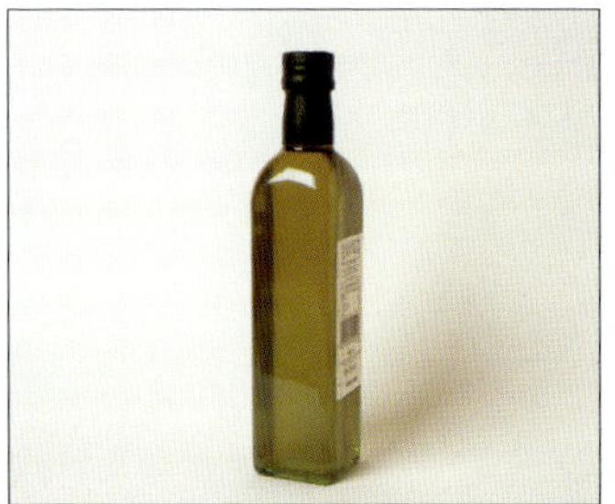

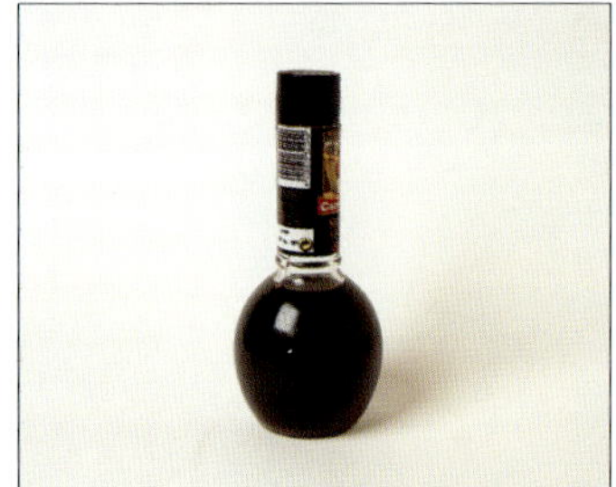

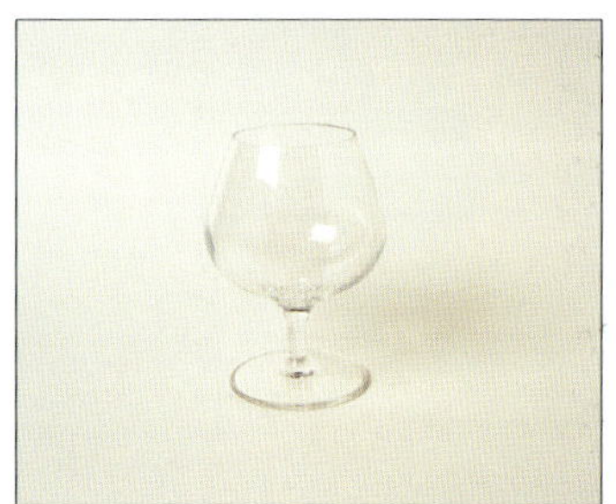

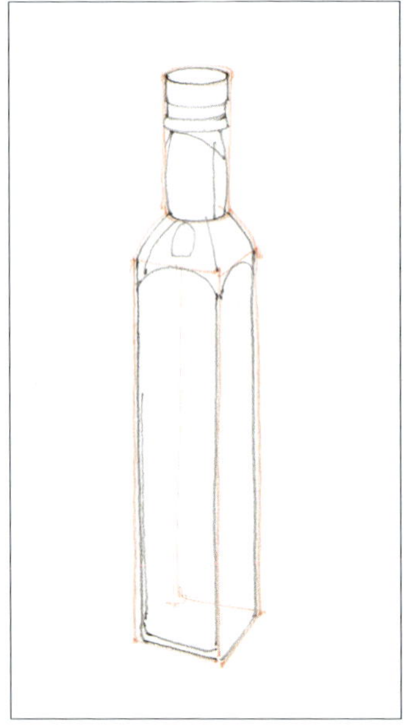

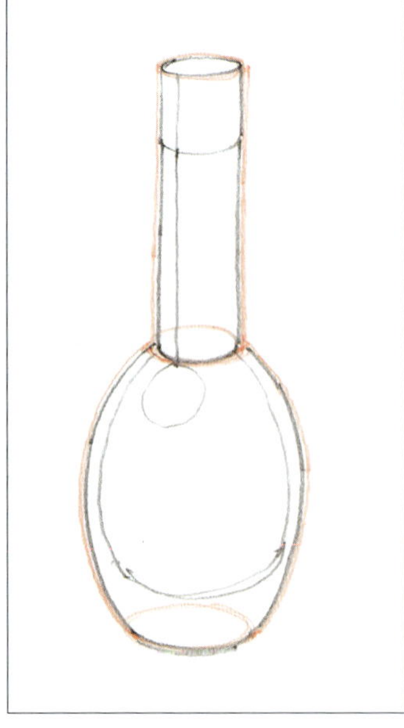

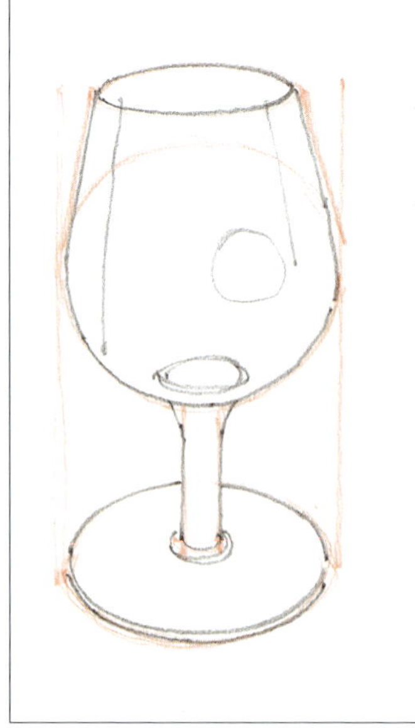

Olive oil pourer 1 ▼
This olive oil pourer was drawn by first sketching a tall cone surmounted by a short cylinder. The spout and handle were added last.

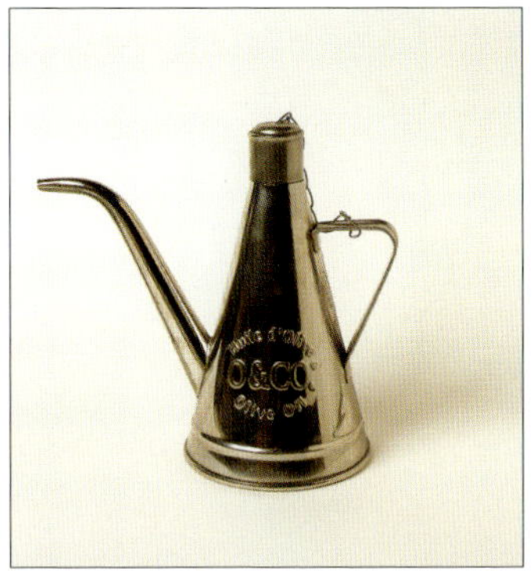

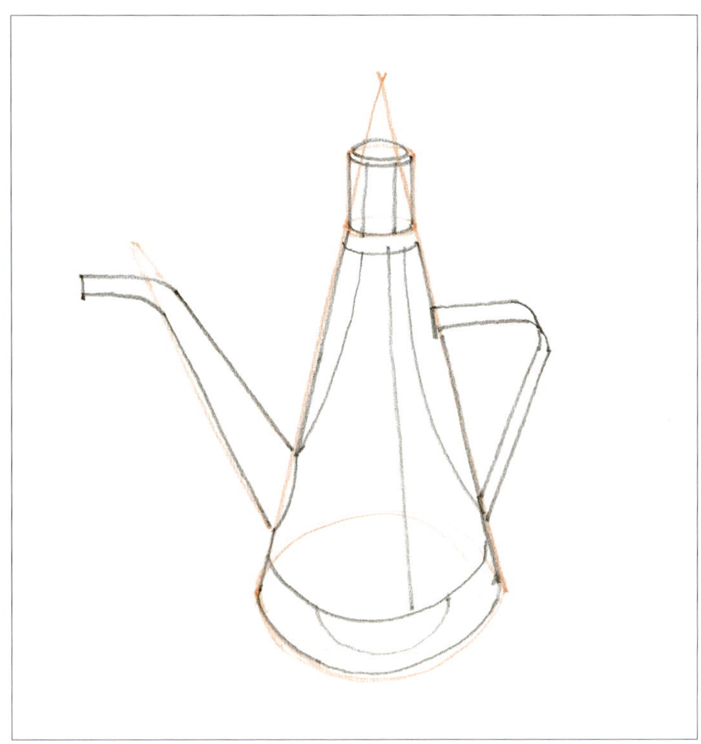

Tip: Even with apparently quite complex-looking objects such as teapots, coffee percolators and oil pourers, keep in mind the four most common geometric shapes: the cone, the cylinder, the cube and the sphere.

Olive oil pourer 2 ▼
For this pourer two cylinders were drawn, one on top of the other.

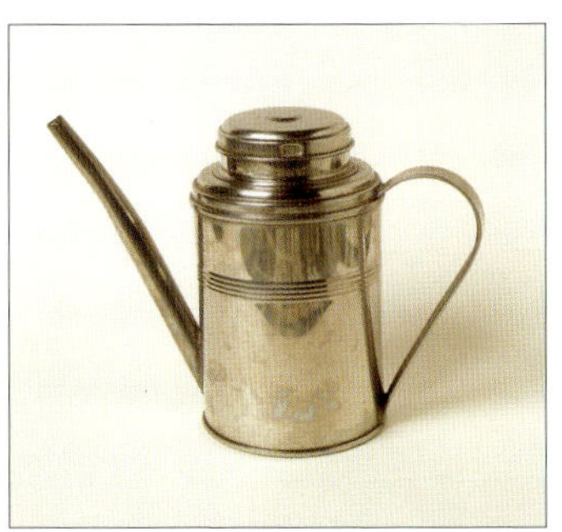

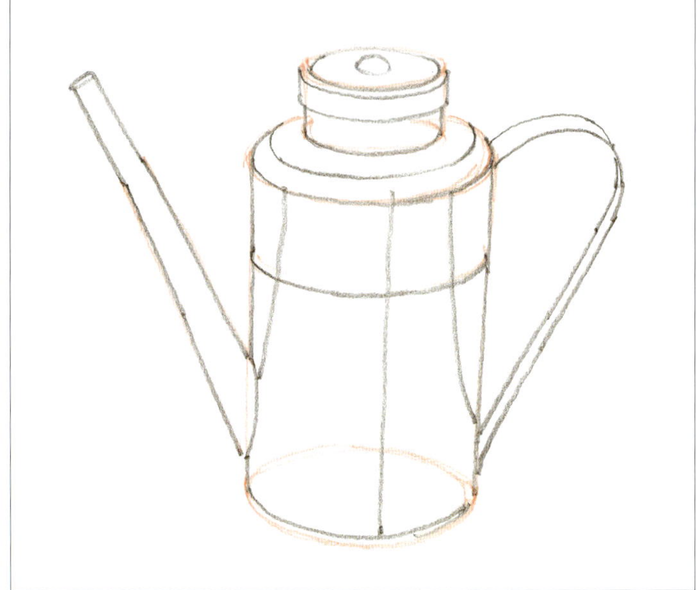

Practice exercise: **Reducing a simple still life to basic shapes**

Set up a still life with both rounded and straight-sided shapes. Thinking of your subject as a variation on a basic geometric shape will make it easier for you to draw it correctly. It is relatively easy to construct the basic shape of man-made objects using geometric shapes, as these things invariably started life on a drawing board as the same simple shapes that you are using to draw them now.

Materials

- *Smooth drawing paper*
- *HB pencil*

The set-up

For this exercise, the artist selected a range of objects from his kitchen that exemplify three of the main geometric shapes – the sphere (an apple), the cone (a coffee pot and a pear) and the cylinder (a coffee cup).

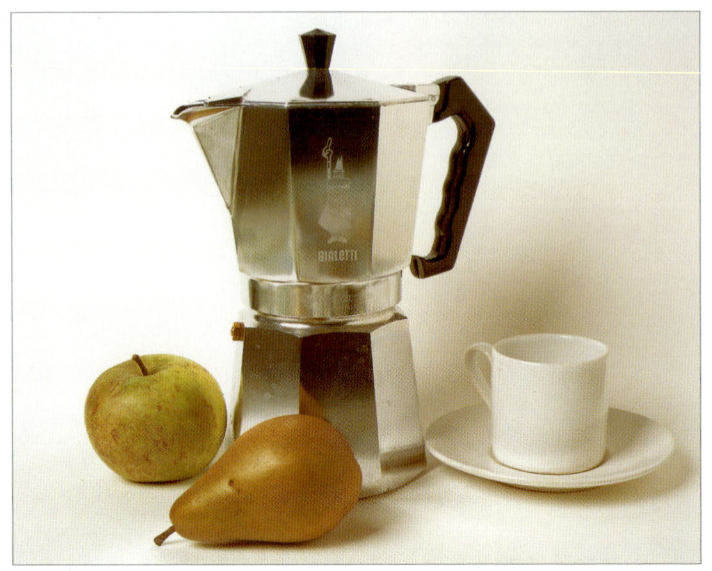

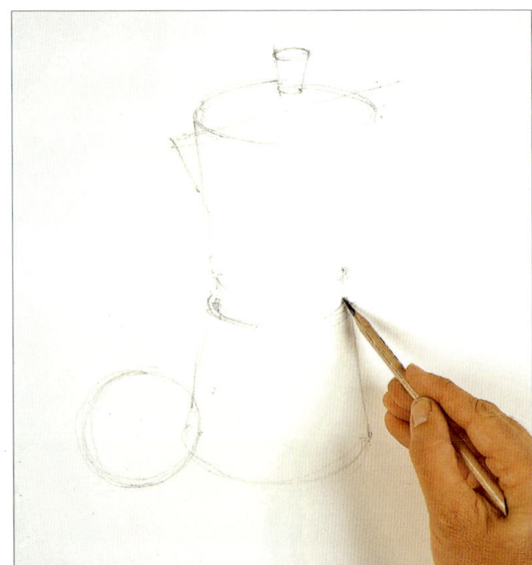

1 Lightly sketch the objects, thinking of them as simple geometric shapes. Indicate the position of the apple with a circle. The coffee pot consists in essence of two cones, one inverted on top of the other, with a short cylinder at the 'waist' and a small cone for the knob (on the lid). Put in a line across the top of the coffee pot to suggest the axis along which the spout and handle are positioned.

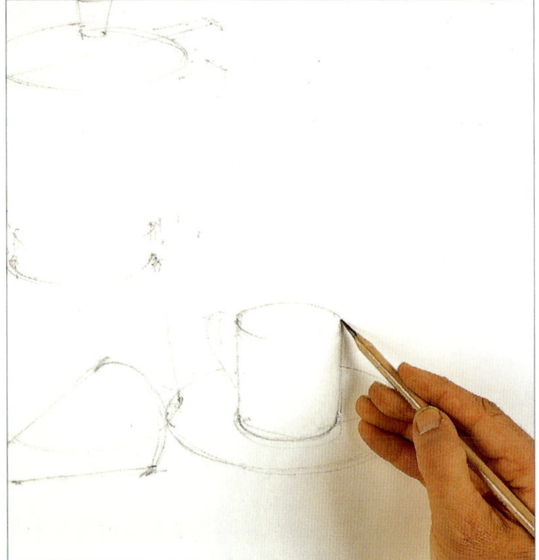

2 You need to indicate the position and shape of the pear by starting to draw a cone. Position the cup and saucer, drawing a cylinder to represent the cup. Note that the lines should be tentative at this stage. All you are doing is trying to search out the essential forms while still thinking of them as basic geometric shapes – the details can be revisited and refined later.

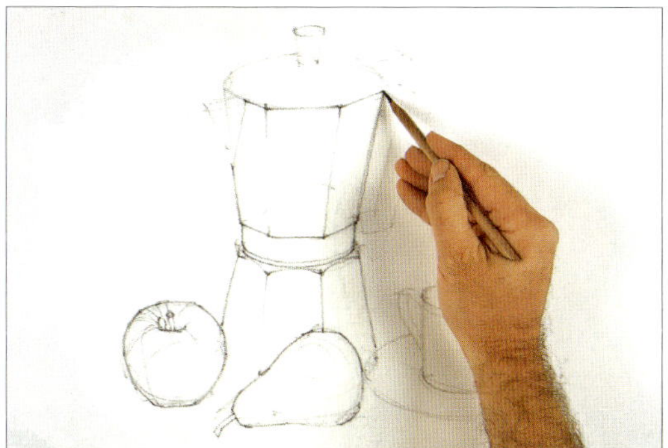

3 Once you have established the approximate shape and position of the elements, you can begin to refine the objects by drawing over the basic geometric shapes. Make a series of short, straight lines, for example, to establish the different facets of the coffee pot, which has straight sides. Position the stem at the top of the apple. Immediately the objects begin to look three-dimensional.

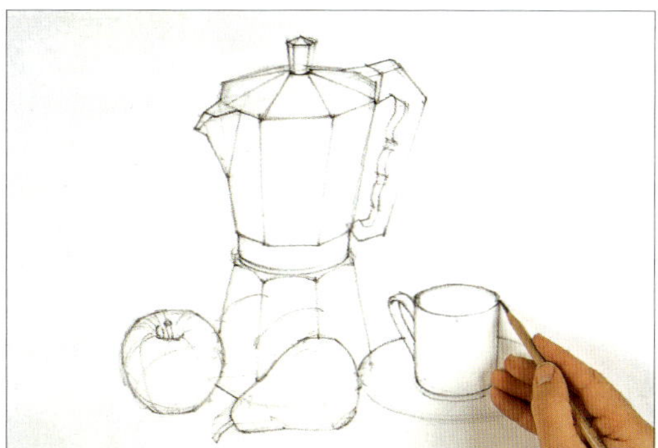

4 Complete the facets of the coffee pot and put in the ellipses that form the saucer and the top and bottom of the coffee cup.

The finished drawing

Add a few internal contour lines, which indicate the direction and angle of some of the surfaces, to complete the drawing.

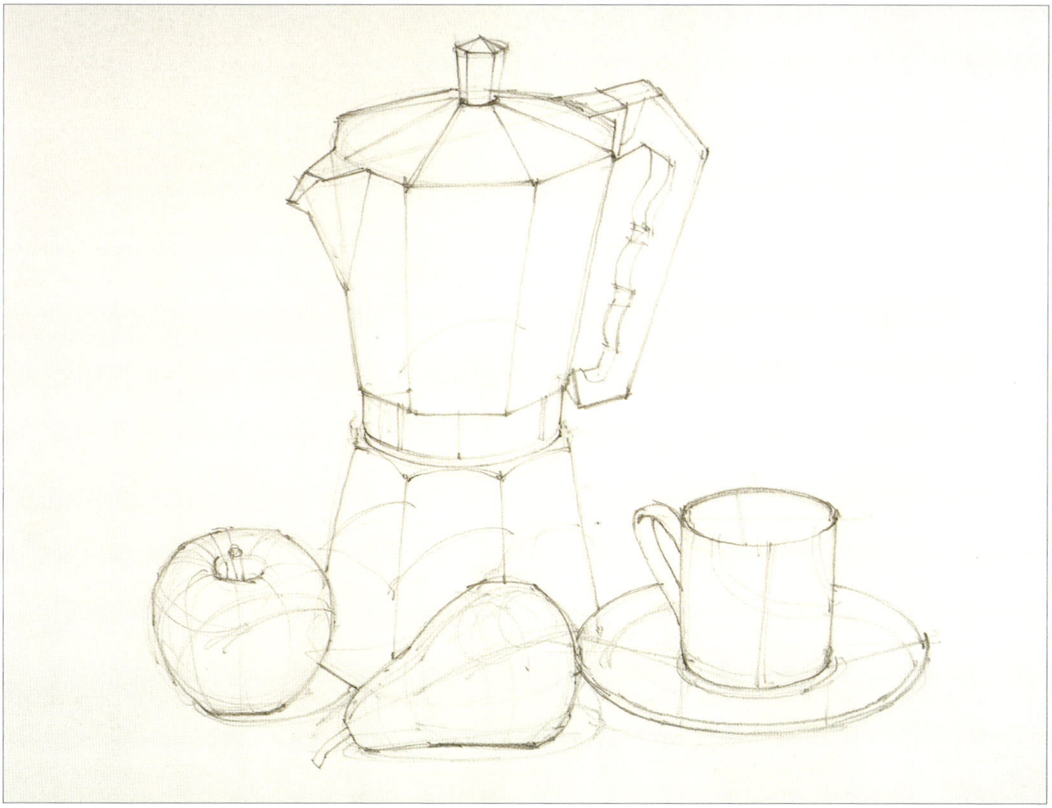

Practice exercise: **Simple landscape viewed as geometric shapes**

With natural subjects, such as elements of a landscape, it can be slightly more difficult to assign simple geometric shapes to objects. The answer, of course, is not to be too literal. See trees as spheres or cones: the cypress trees in this scene are basically conical in shape, for example, whereas the overall shapes of other trees such as oaks are more rounded. Try to think of any landscape that you are drawing as a series of interconnecting shapes. To practise this, make a series of quick sketches setting down your subjects as rough overall shapes, so that you can fine-tune your eye to this method of working.

Buildings are somewhat easier to deal with, as they are usually designed as geometric shapes in the first place. Most buildings are simply a series of interconnecting rectangles or cubes arranged around one another.

Your aim in the exercise below is not to produce a perfectly finished landscape, but simply to get used to analysing the shape of the things you are drawing.

Materials

- *Smooth drawing paper*
- *2B pencil*

The scene

This is a simple landscape scene of a church in rural Italy surrounded by tall cypresses and shorter, more rounded trees.

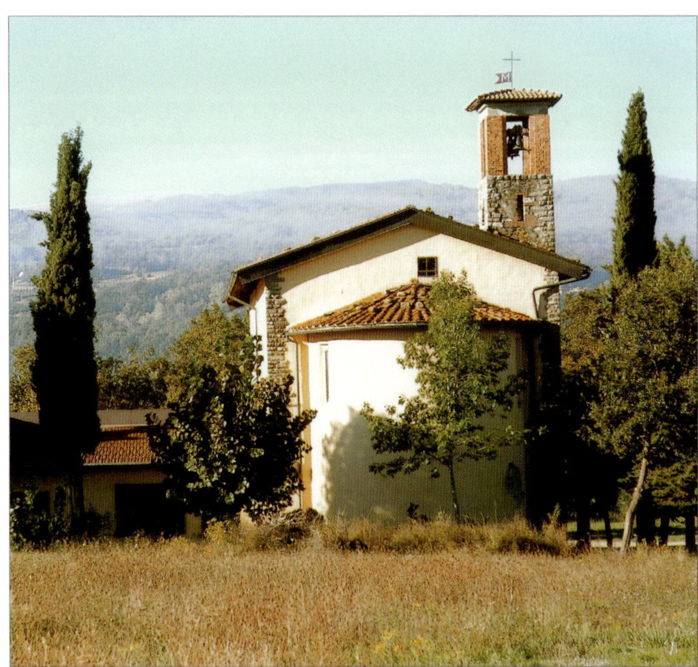

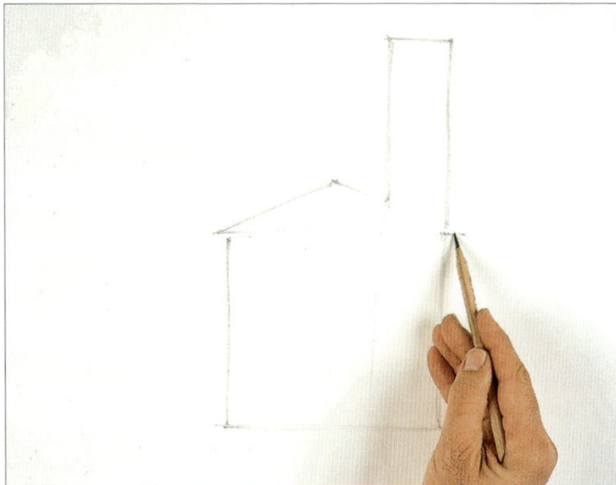

1 First, draw the position and shape of the church. It consists of a rectangle surmounted by a triangular shape that is, in turn, surmounted on one side by the long, thin rectangle of the bell tower. Make sure that the relative proportions of these three shapes are correct.

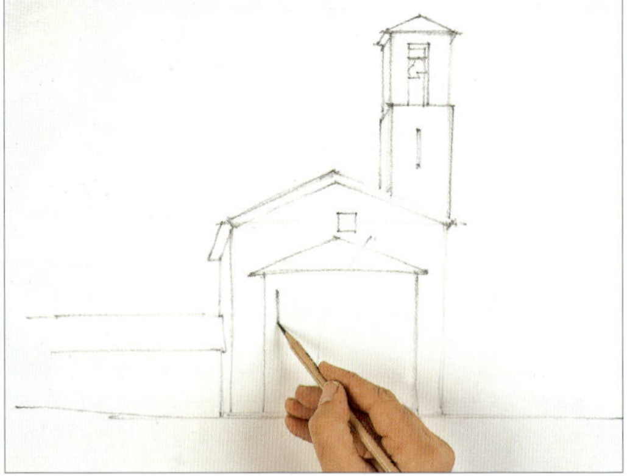

2 Draw the long building that lies to the left of the church as an elongated cube and put in the roof of the tall bell tower. Indicate the apse of the church by lightly drawing another rectangle, surmounting it with a triangle with a slightly curved base.

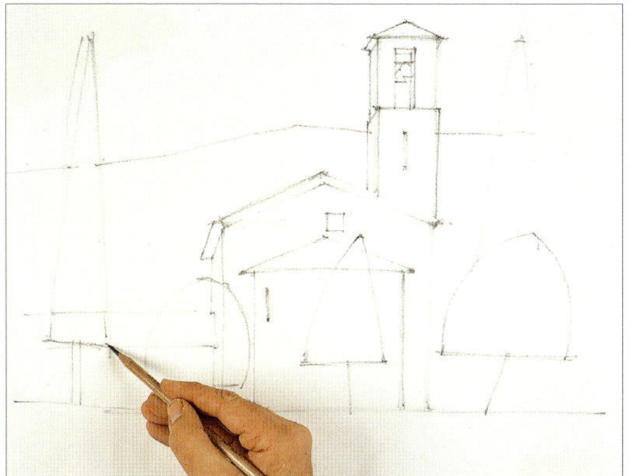

3 Next, indicate the position and shape of the trees. Although they do not conform strictly to any geometric shape, with a little imagination they can be simplified.

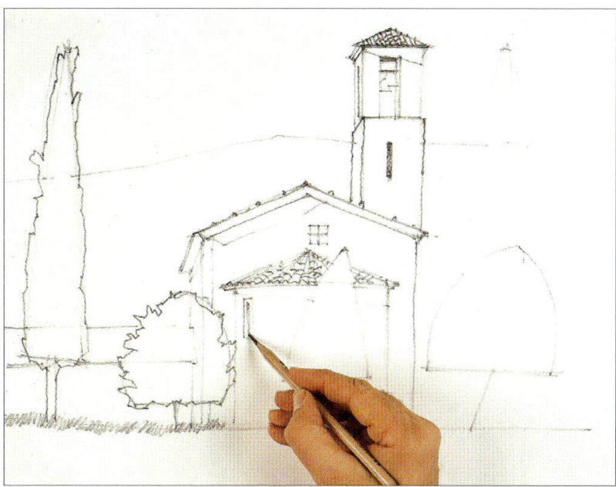

4 Once you have sketched the position and proportions of all the different elements in the scene, use the simple geometric shapes as a guide to refine your drawing.

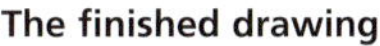

The finished drawing

With the addition of a little tone, the image comes to life. The tone not only begins to suggest the forms, but also covers up many of the construction lines that you used to search out the basic geometric forms.

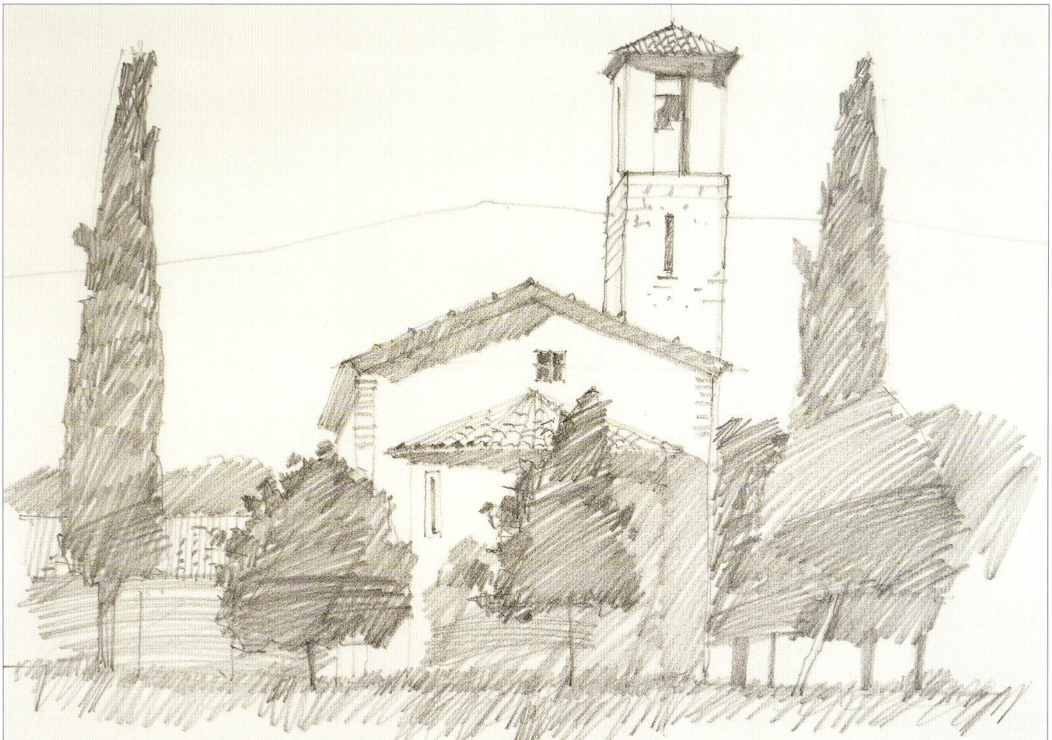

Understanding tone

The term 'tone' describes the degree of dark or light values that the artist uses to create the illusion of form and space in a picture. While it is possible to draw representational images with line alone, this is a more difficult process. Linear drawing encloses plain shapes that may appear to be flat if they are not observed very accurately. The most serviceable method of conveying form, or the three-dimensional nature of the subject, is tone. It is the fall of light across the surface of the objects, figure or landscape being drawn that reveals promontories, contours and the negative shapes of space. Even abstraction requires artists to create illusory picture space by using tone.

There are as many methods of creating tone as there are artists, and each beginner must devise a personal method of shading the paper to his or her satisfaction. Examine the works of the great masters for outstanding examples of the use of various media to create tonal values. Try studying the hatched pen drawings of Rembrandt, the wash drawings of Tiepolo, the chalk work of Seurat or pencil studies by Matisse. Whether you study them in books or in galleries, note how tonal density was achieved and choose a preferred method to enable you to find a starting point for toning work.

Once you have devised a way of creating tone, the quality and direction of lighting will also determine the character of the picture. For example, a sunlit rendition reveals the sparkling mass of a rocky outcrop, while storm light enlivens the boiling sea in coastal works. A dramatically lit stage will have more contrast than the calm, steady quality of a day-lit domestic interior.

The illustrations here show a plaster-cast head of the French writer and philosopher Voltaire, lit from different directions. Where light falls directly on the subject, very little detail is discernible. But on the sides that are turned away from the light, strong shadows are formed – and it is these shadows that show up the muscle formation and bone structure, making the cast look three-dimensional.

Light from the left, almost full profile

Here, the light was positioned to the left of the plaster cast and slightly above it. As a result, the forehead is brightly illuminated: the artist left the paper untouched in this part of the drawing. A few faint lines under the left eye hint at the bone structure, but the face is so brightly lit that few shadows are formed here.

On the left side of the head, however (the right side as we look at it), a mid-tone is used to draw deep shadows that reveal the sunken cheekbones and indentations in the skull. The slab of the neck is drawn using a tone that is even darker, as virtually no direct light hits this part of the cast.

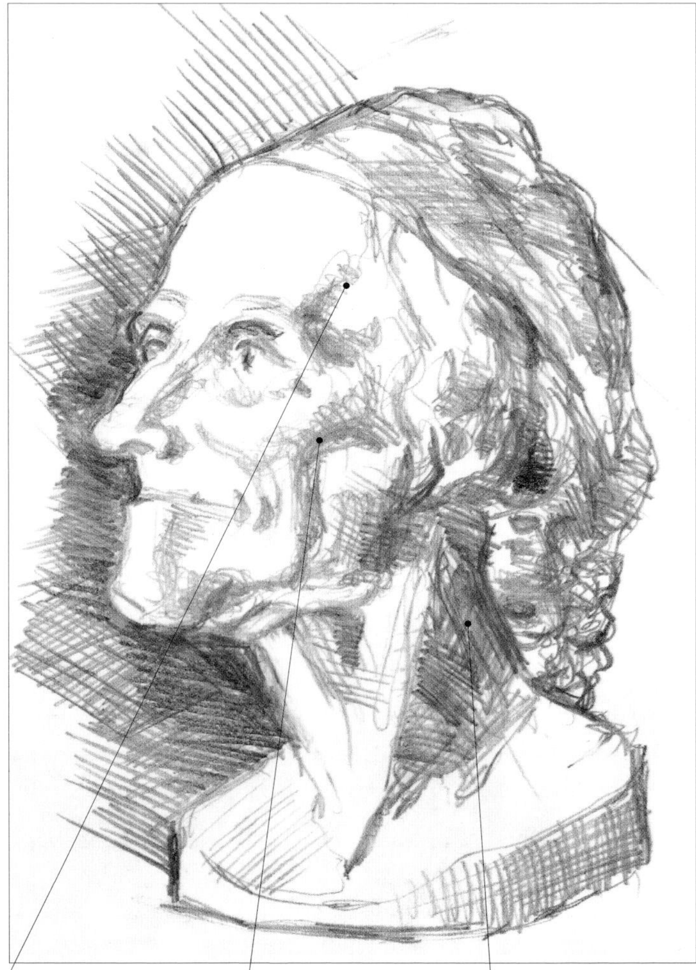

Light pencil marks indicate the change of plane from the brightly lit front of the skull to the side.

A mid-tone reveals the structure of the cheekbones, which are in moderate shadow.

Very little direct light reaches the side of the neck and so a very dark tone is used here.

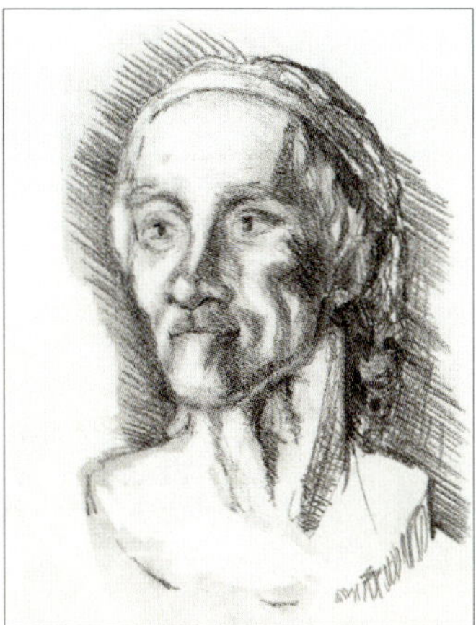

Light from the left, almost full face
Here, the head was turned to show more of the face.The light is from the left, so everything on the other side of the rather prominent nose is in shadow.

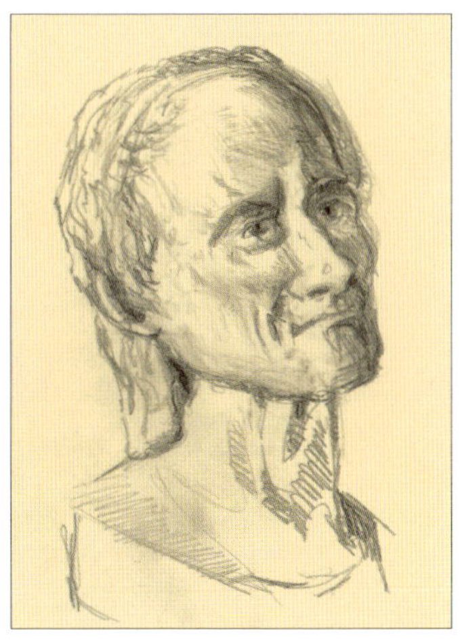

Light from the left, three-quarter view
Here, the light was again positioned to the left of the cast – but slightly lower down than in the previous two images, almost level with the cast, and the cast was turned further to the right. Again, every feature to the right of the nose as we look at the image is cast into deep shadow – but changing the angle of the cast emphasizes different features.

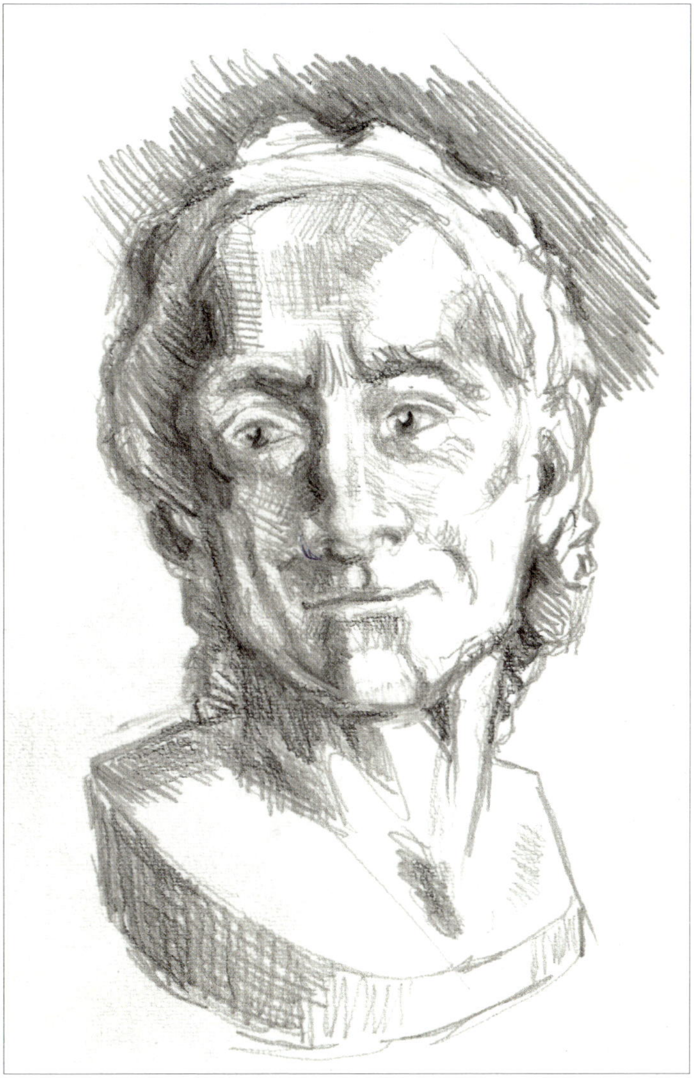

Light from the front, full face
Here the light was positioned in front of the cast – although, to make the drawing more interesting, the artist arranged it slightly to the right instead of placing it centrally, in line with the nose. As a result, the right side of the face (the left as we look at the image) is slightly shaded. The artist used mid-tones to convey this. (Compare this image with the other two on this page, where the light is from the side and the shadows are darker and more intense.)

Note, too, how the frontal lighting has the effect of flattening out some of the features: the cheekbones, in particular, look more rounded and less angular, although this is partly due to the fact that we are viewing the face full on, rather than from the side.

Adding tone

In drawing, the application of tone is sometimes referred to as 'shading', as in 'light and shade'. It is this tone or shading that describes the form of a thing and makes it appear three-dimensional.

The range of tones visible in an object depends entirely on the amount and quality of the light illuminating the subject. A very bright, directional light-source results in a range of tones that run from very dark to very light, with emphasis placed less on the mid-tones and more on the darker and lighter tones. An even but subdued light results in an equally wide tonal range, but with the mid-tones far more evident than strong darks or bright lights. In order to give your two-dimensional drawing the illusion of having the added dimension of depth, you will need to render light and shade convincingly. Fortunately, there are several ways of doing this.

Charcoal: dots and dashes
With soft materials such as charcoal or soft pastels, you can use dots and dashes to create tone. To make the tone darker or lighter, apply more or less pressure.

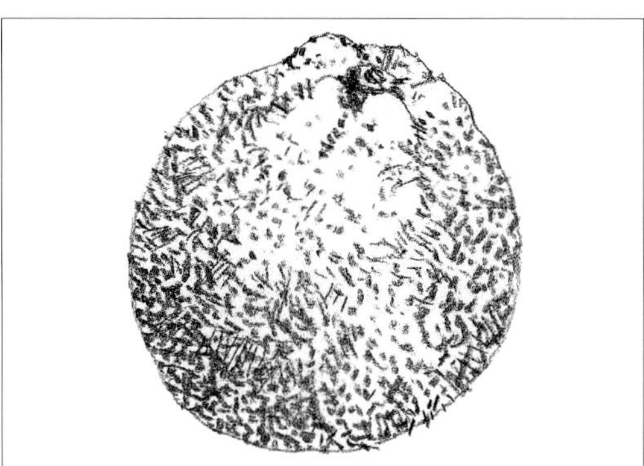

Charcoal: blending
With very soft, highly pigmented drawing materials, the drawn tones can be blended together using your finger, a torchon or a rag. Drawings like these are quite delicate and need to be fixed to prevent them from being smudged.

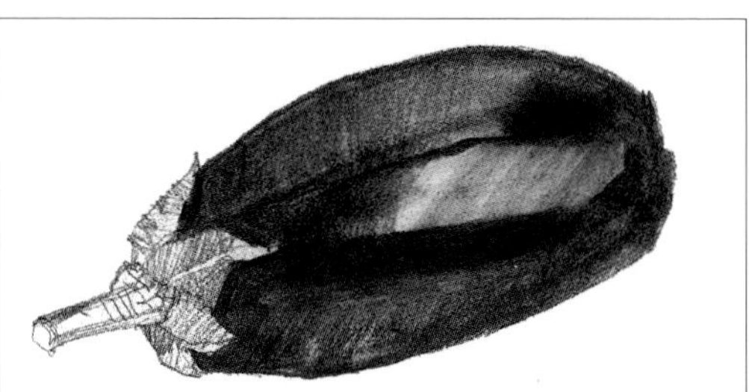

Graphite: scribbled tone
With a graphite pencil, you can scribble on tone. For a darker tone, vary the direction of the marks and the amount of pressure.

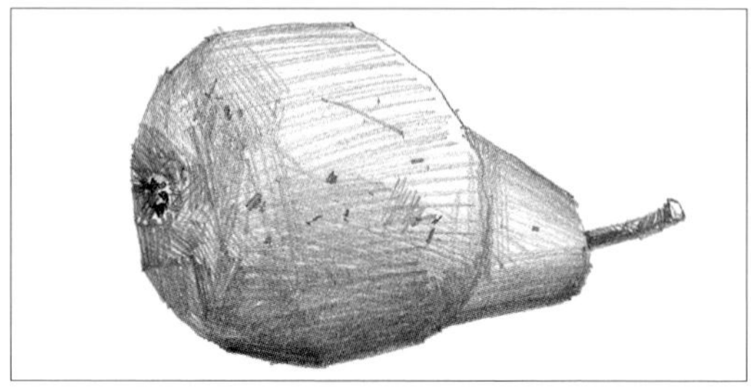

Graphite: contour shading
In contour shading, simple linear marks are made to follow the form of the object. This is sometimes called bracelet shading and can be seen on many old master drawings.

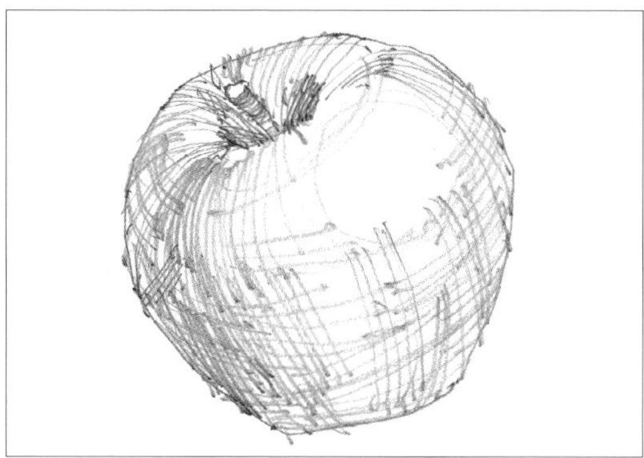

Graphite: crosshatching
With pens and pencils, you can create tone by drawing a series of parallel lines. Crosshatching consists of another series of lines drawn across the first set at an angle. To darken the tone, draw lines closer together and apply more pressure.

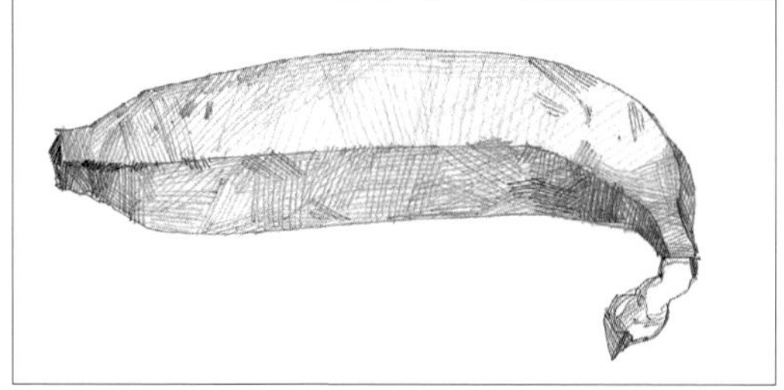

Chalks on a mid-toned ground

With chalks or charcoal, a particularly efficient way of achieving a tonal drawing is to work on a mid-grey ground (a ready-toned paper). Establish the mid- and dark tones first before bringing the whole thing to life by adding the lighter tones and the highlights.

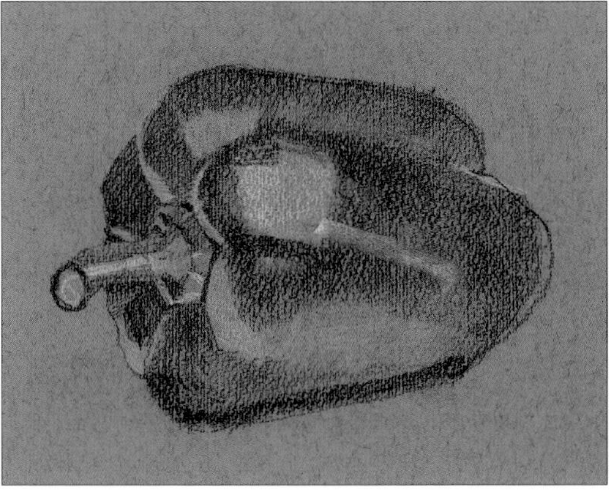

Ink: controlled hatching

When using a pen with a fixed-width nib, you can create tone by using hatched and crosshatched lines. To build up the depth of the tone, simply draw the lines closer together. For light areas and highlights, leave the paper untouched so that the white of the support stands for the brightest areas.

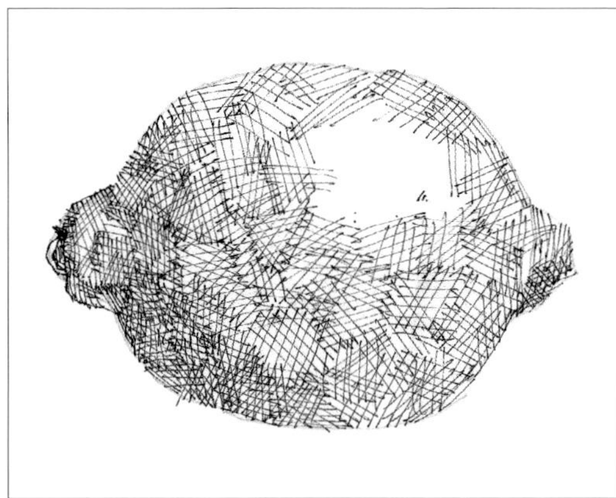

Ink: pen and wash

You can create tonal washes by diluting ink with clean water to differing degrees. These ink washes can be used on their own to build up the drawing or contained by linear work made using a dip pen.

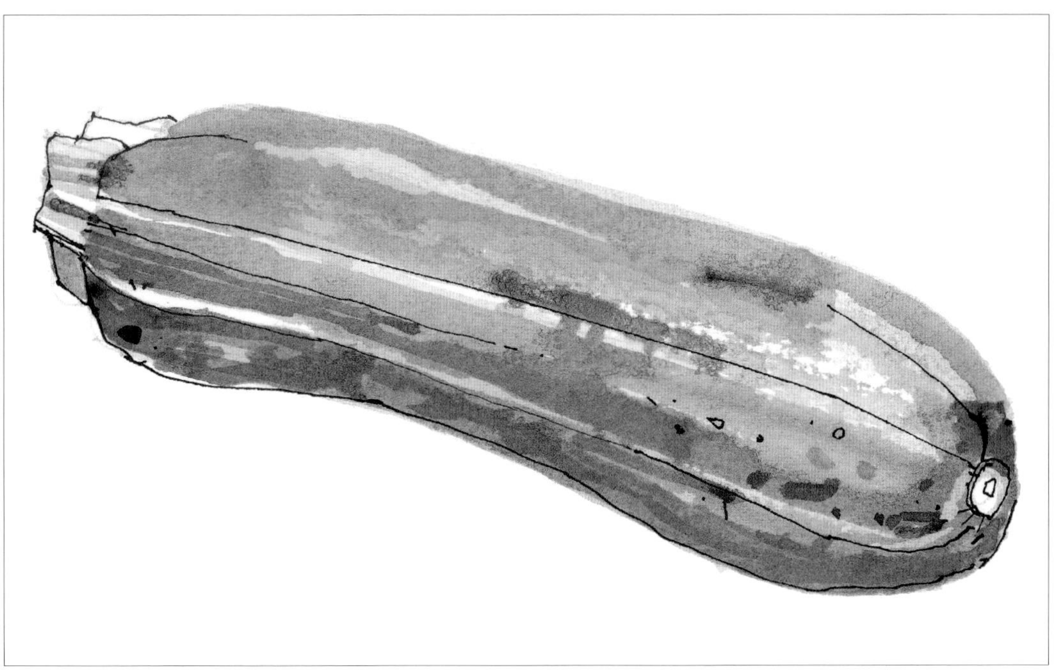

Practice exercise: **Shading straight-sided objects**

For your first practice exercises in shading, select straight-sided subjects and light them strongly from one side, as this makes it easier to see where changes in tone occur. You can find lots of suitable subjects around the home; books, stacked boxes in varying sizes, a pile of CD cases arranged so that they cast shadows on the table top and background, or children's play bricks would all make good subjects.

Start with a monochromatic object. As soon as you introduce different colours things become more complicated, as you are distracted by the colour and will probably find it harder to work out how light or dark the tones need to be.

Materials

- *White pastel paper*
- *Thin charcoal*

The set-up

The subject chosen for this exercise is a brown paper bag, which has a number of creases and folds within it. The lighting from the side creates interesting cast shadows on both the table top and the wall behind.

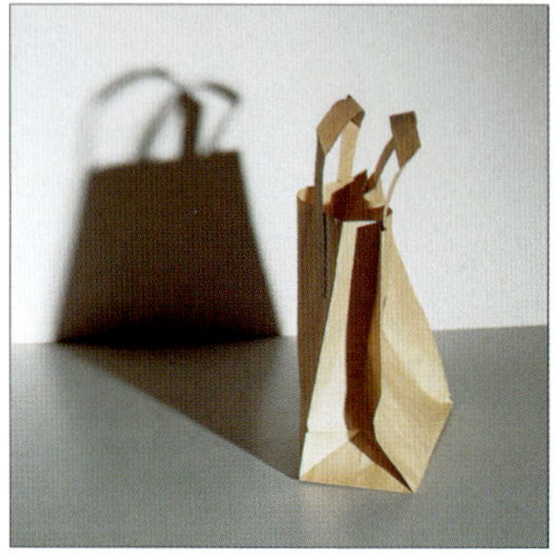

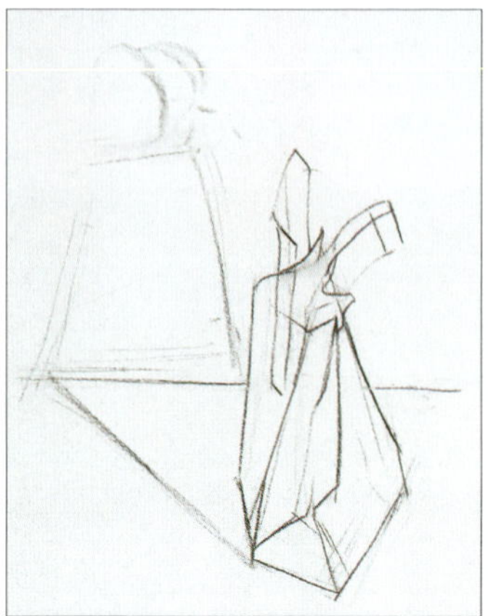

1 Using a thin charcoal stick, map out the composition, making strong lines for the bag and lighter ones for the cast shadows.

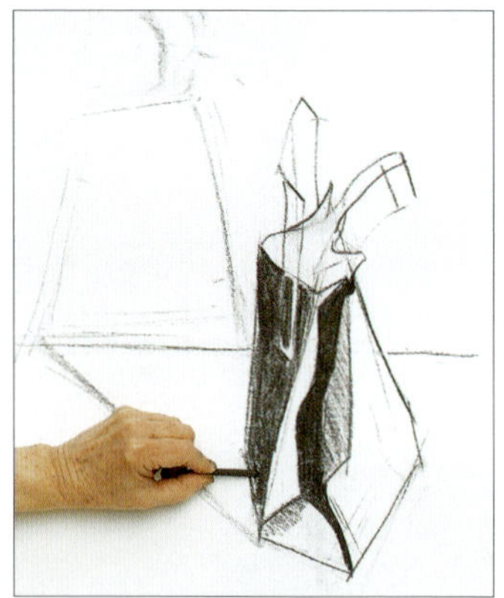

2 Half close your eyes to assess the tones and work out which areas of the bag are the darkest. (In the set-up shown here, you can see that the back of the bag and the cast shadow in the folded side of the bag are the darkest.) Roughly block them in, using the side of the charcoal stick. Don't make them too dark, however: if necessary, you can always darken the drawing later once the mid- and light tones are in place, but if you make it too dark to begin with, you will find that it's much more difficult to lighten it.

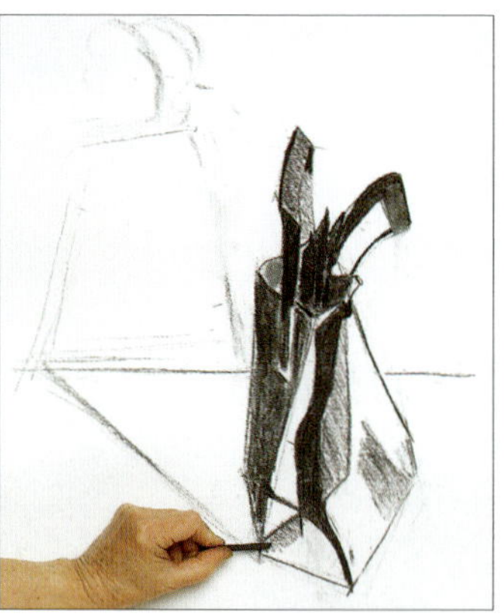

3 Put in the darkest tones and the mid-tones on the handles. The handles are twisted, so different facets catch the light in different ways, hence the differences in tone. Again using the side of the charcoal stick, put in the dark and mid-tones on the front and side of the bag. You can see how shading provides us with information about the form of the bag: without these subtle differences in tone, we would have no way of knowing how the handles are twisted or where the creases in the bag occur.

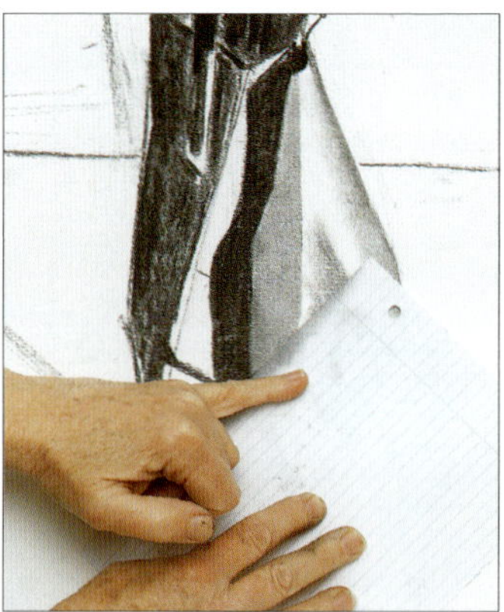

4 Line up a piece of scrap paper along the bottom edge of the bag and hold it firmly in place. Gently smooth out the mid-tones. (Use your little finger, as it is the coolest and driest part of your hand.) The scrap paper helps you to maintain a crisp edge to the bag; if your finger goes beyond the edge of the bag when you're blending, the charcoal will dirty only the scrap paper and not the background to the drawing. Blending also gets rid of the harsh, drawn line around the edge of the bag.

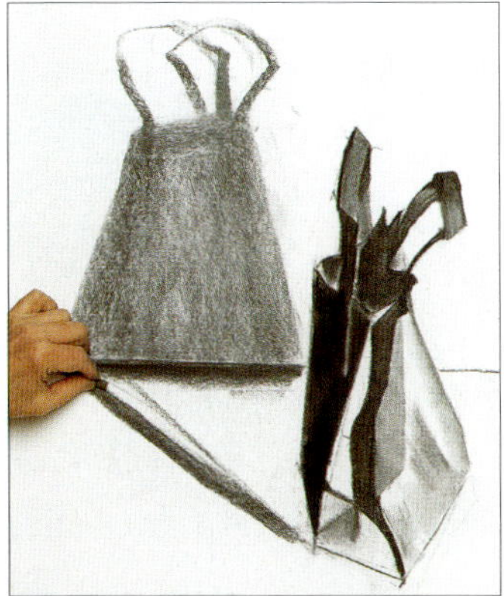

5 Using the side of the charcoal stick, block in the cast shadow on the wall. Block in the cast shadow on the table top, making it darker than the shadow on the wall.

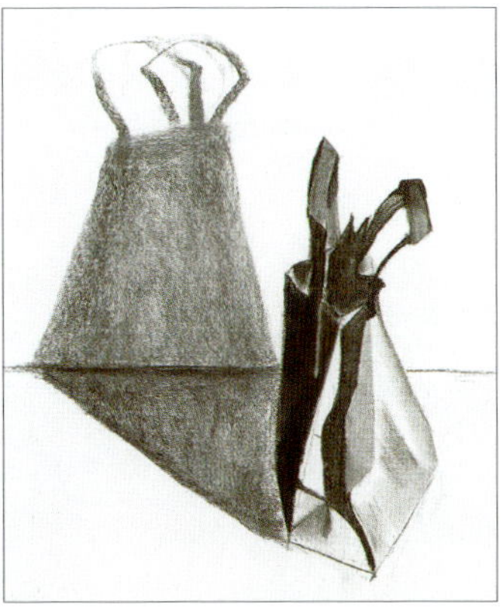

6 Using your fingertips, smooth out the cast shadow on the table top to create an even tone. Do not blend the cast shadow on the wall: the texture of the paper adds interest to the drawing.

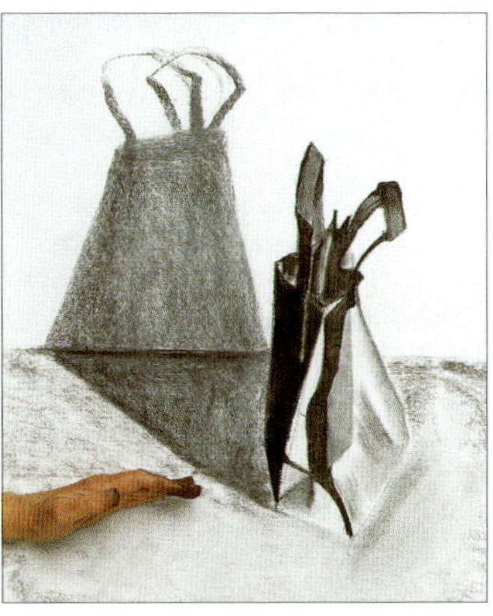

7 Using the side of the charcoal, apply a very thin covering over the table top. Blend it with the side of your hand, using a circular motion, to create an even, pale grey tone.

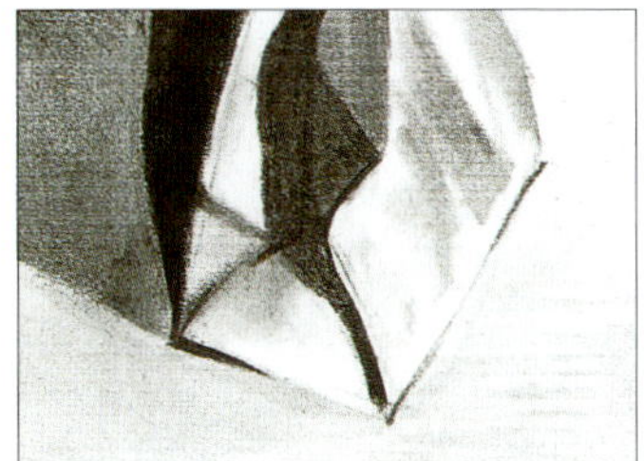

8 Draw in the very thin cast shadows underneath the bag on the table top to anchor the bag and prevent it from looking as if it is floating in space.

The finished drawing

The drawing looks convincingly three-dimensional, and the tones range from a very dense black on the back of the bag to a very pale grey (barely darker than the paper) in the most brightly lit areas. Note the use of finger blending – a good way of creating areas of smooth tone when using a powdery medium such as charcoal or soft pastel.

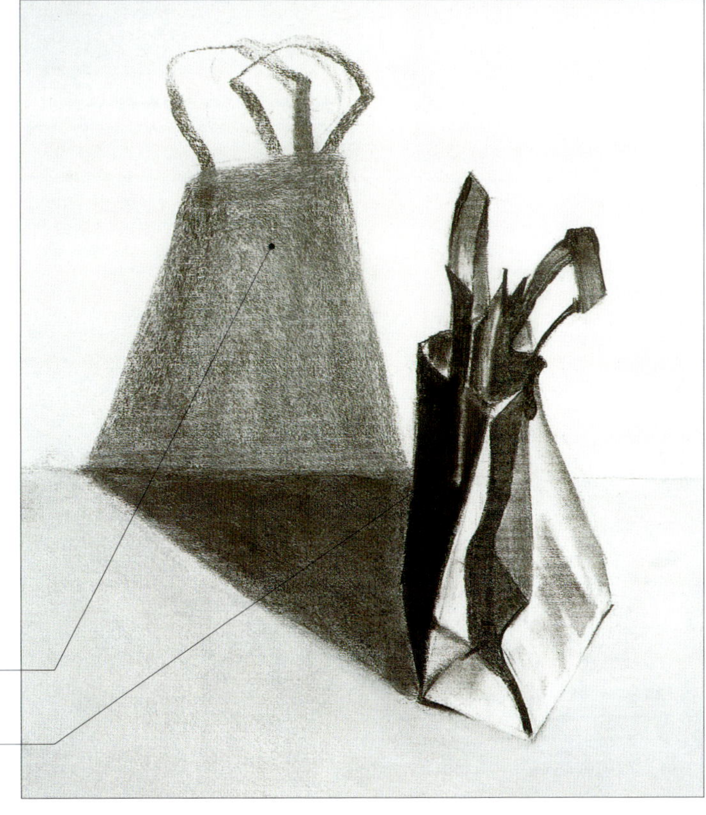

The texture of the paper is visible in parts, adding interest to the drawing.

In a tonal drawing, the darks are almost always darker than you expect them to be. The darkest areas are a very dense black.

Practice exercise: **Shading rounded objects**

Straight-sided objects have very clearly defined planes and it is easy to see the sudden fall-off of light. With rounded objects it is much more difficult, as there is no immediate transition from one tone to another. Nevertheless such a transition does occur, even though it happens very gradually. Look for the extremes of tone – the very lightest and darkest areas – and then let your eye travel over the rounded form to assess the degree of change that will be required.

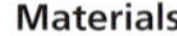

Materials

- *Smooth drawing paper*
- *Graphite pencils: HB, 4B*
- *Graphite stick*

The set-up

The overall composition of this grouping is triangular in shape. The wedge of cheese and the salami point towards each other, drawing the viewer's eye into the scene. The large, rounded loaf of bread balances the smaller objects.

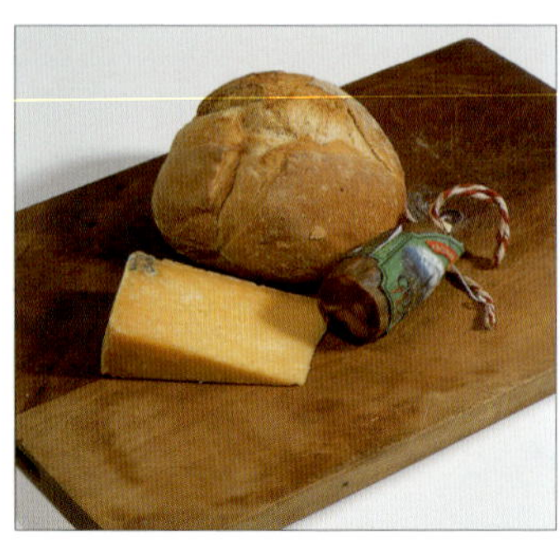

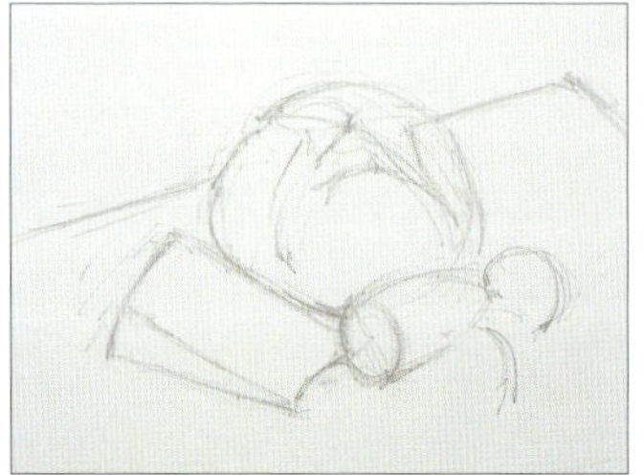

1 Using an HB graphite pencil, lightly sketch the composition. Don't attempt to put in any shading at this stage. Instead, think of the objects as simple geometric shapes and concentrate on getting the sizes and shapes right. Also put in the cracks in the top of the loaf of bread.

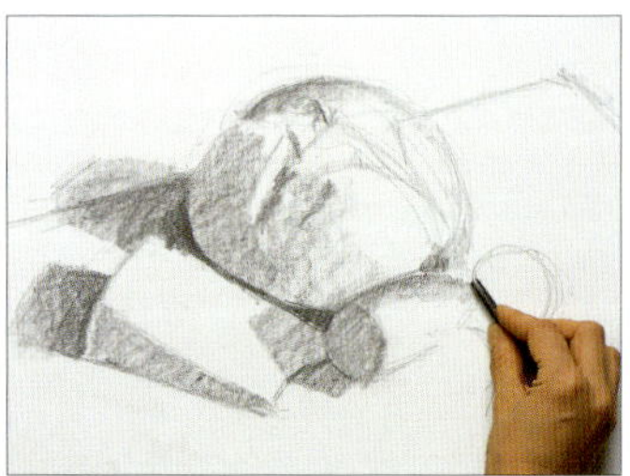

2 Using the side of a graphite stick, block in the mid-tones on the items and the cast shadows. As the loaf is rounded, the transition in tone from the front to the back is gradual. Putting the mid-tones in at this stage makes it easier to judge how light and dark the rest of the drawing needs to be.

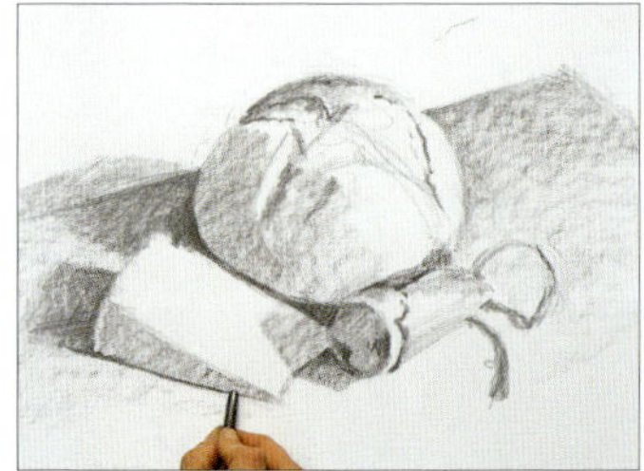

3 Still using the side of the graphite stick, shade the darkest parts of the wooden board behind the bread. Using the tip of the stick, reinforce the dark cracks in the top of the bread and put in the string of the salami and the deep shadow under the wedge of cheese.

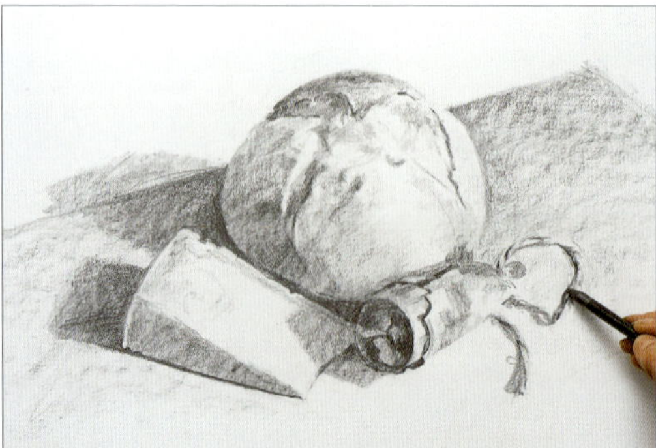

4 Using the tip of the 4B pencil, carefully darken the shaded areas between the objects. In addition to telling us about the quality and direction of the light, these areas also help to anchor the objects on the surface. Put in more linear detail on the salami and its string.

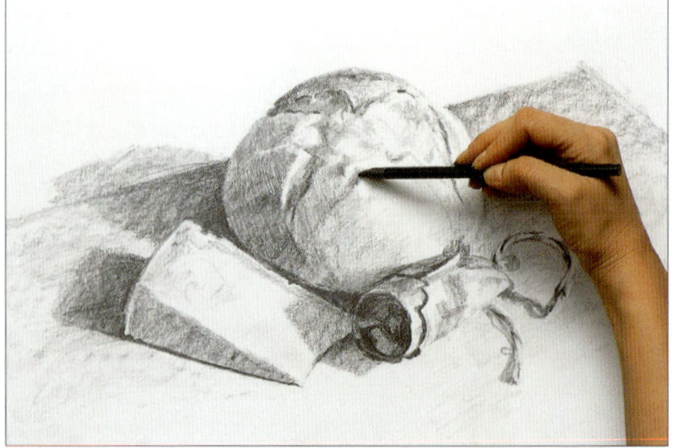

5 Shade the wooden board within the loop of string. Note that this area is lighter in tone than the board behind the bread. Go over the darkest part of the bread again, drawing fine hatching lines close together. Don't bring the lines too far forwards, as the front of the bread is very light in tone.

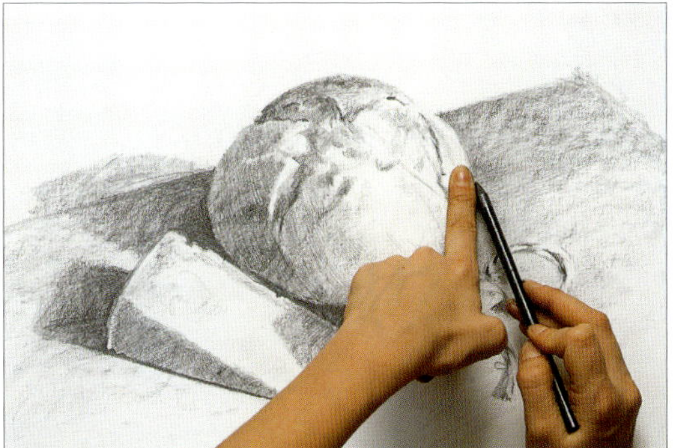

6 Repeat the hatching process on the shaded side of the cheese. Darken the board up to the edge of the bread by placing your finger on the curve of the bread and shading right up to your finger. This allows you to maintain the curve of the loaf without having to draw a harsh line around the edge. (You will have to move your finger around the loaf, following the edge very carefully.)

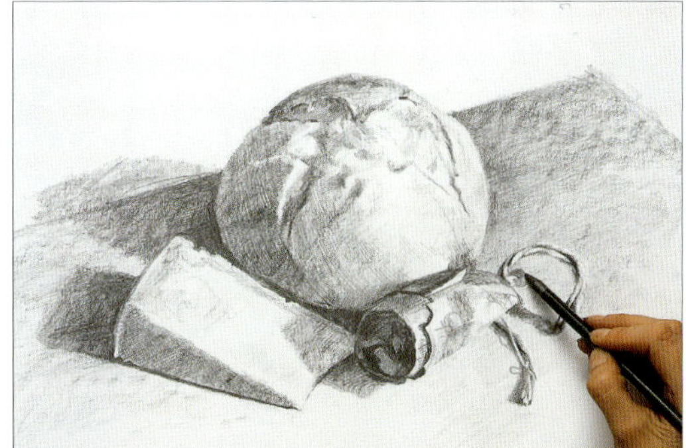

7 Put in any final linear details on the salami wrapper and its string. Finally, use the 4B pencil to put in the small shadow cast by the string on the wooden board, so that it is clear that the string forms a loop that is raised up above the surface of the board.

The finished drawing

A number of shading techniques have been used in this drawing, including loosely scribbled tone using the side of a pencil or graphite stick on the wooden board and cheese, and hatching on the darkest areas of the loaf. There is a very marked difference in tone between the light and the shaded sides of the wedge of cheese. The transition from dark to light tone on the rounded objects (the loaf and the salami) is much more gradual, but it has been very carefully observed to make them appear convincingly three-dimensional.

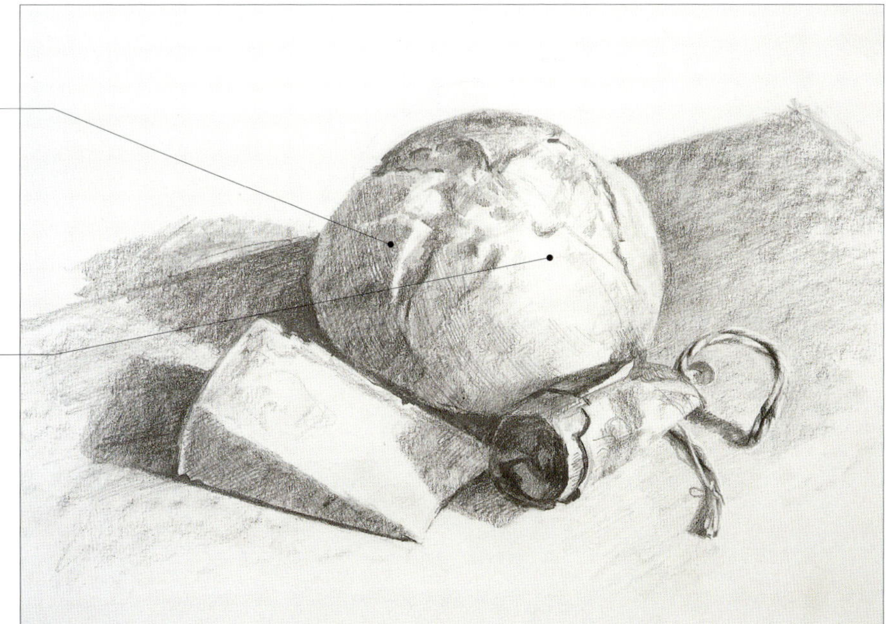

Parallel lines hatched close together form a dark tone on the shaded side of the bread.

The very brightest areas on the front of the loaf contain hardly any tone; the paper is left blank.

Measuring systems

Getting the proportions and relative size of your subject right is essential in representational art and, unless you have some means of checking measurements, it's almost inevitable that you will make some mistakes. There are a number of well-established measuring systems that you can use and two of the most common are described here.

The most important thing is to learn to trust your measurements rather than your instincts or prior knowledge of a subject. You may be surprised to find when drawing a portrait, for example, that the base of the eye socket is generally about halfway down the face – but if you don't actually measure the distance, you'll probably draw the eyes too high up.

Your viewpoint in relation to your subject and the angle at which the subject is positioned can also make a huge difference to how things appear. Say, for example, you're drawing an avenue of trees receding away from you into the distance. They may be roughly the same height and spaced the same distance apart, but the ones that are furthest away will appear to be smaller and the gaps between them will appear to decrease with distance – so you must measure the relative sizes and follow your measurements. Similarly, if you look at something like a table, you might be tempted to draw it as a rectangle, because you know that's what shape it is – but if you're looking at it from the other side of a room, you'll be seeing it in perspective, rather than from above, and so its shape will be very different.

Get into the habit of taking measurements of everything you draw, whether landscape, still life or portrait. It may seem complicated at first, but as you gain experience measuring techniques such as these will become second nature. It's also important to keep re-checking measurements as you work on your drawing. As you refine a drawing it is very easy to emphasize one element at the expense of another, but a little time spent double-checking that the proportions are still correct could save you a lot of trouble in the long run.

Using a grid

When working from a photograph this is relatively easy. Simply divide the photograph into a grid of squares, and divide your paper into the same number of squares, making the squares larger if you want your drawing to be larger than the photograph and smaller if you want it to be smaller than the photograph.Then copy the image one square at a time.

You can use the same principle when working from reality. Cut a rectangle out of the middle of a piece of card (stock) and stretch a series of rubber bands across the aperture to form a grid, spacing them evenly. Draw the same grid on your paper at the size you wish the drawing to be, and then position the grid so that you can look through it at your subject. In order for this to work, you must position the grid so that it lines up with the subject in exactly the same way every time you look through it.

1 Using a craft (utility) knife and steel rule on a cutting mat, cut a rectangle out of the middle of the card (stock).

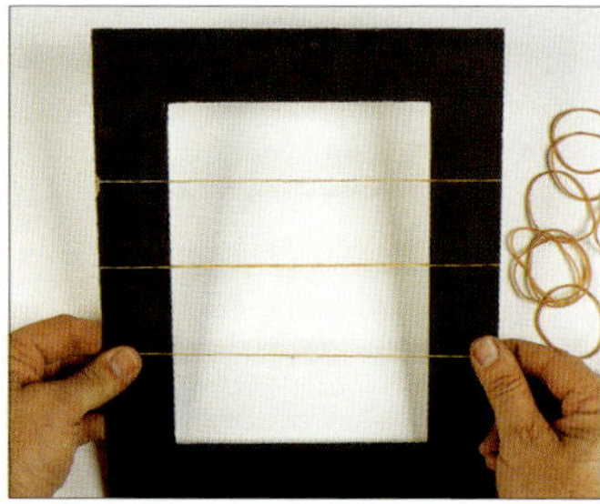

2 Stretch rubber bands across the width of the aperture, making sure they are evenly spaced.

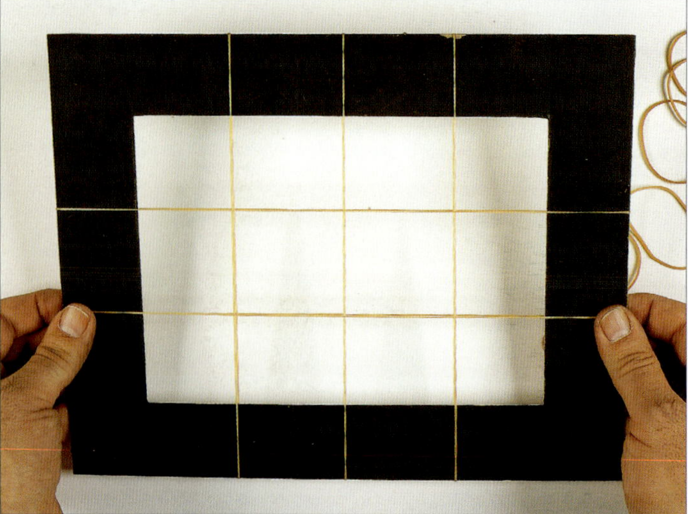

3 Do the same across the height of the aperture, spacing the bands the same distance apart as in Step 2.

Using a pencil to measure

An alternative method is to use a measuring device – usually the instrument with which you are drawing. Hold the pencil out at arm's length, so that you can see past it to your subject. Choose a part of your subject to measure; this can be the whole length or width of the subject or just a small section. Align the top of the pencil with one end of the distance you are measuring and move your thumb up or down the shaft of the pencil until it is level with the other end of the distance being measured. Now transfer these measurements to your drawing; a small guide mark is sufficient, as you will add detail later once you are sure the proportions are correct. For your first attempts at measuring using this method, work so that you can put marks down directly on the paper at their actual size, without having to scale them up or down to fit.

When using this method, it's absolutely vital that you keep your arm straight, so that the pencil remains a constant distance from the subject. Close one eye to make it easier to focus, and concentrate on looking at the pencil rather than at the subject.

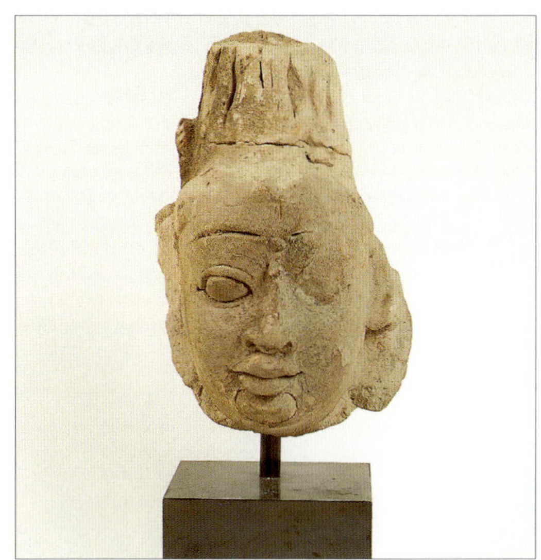

The subject
Here, we used a small statue as the subject, but the principle remains the same whatever subject you are drawing.

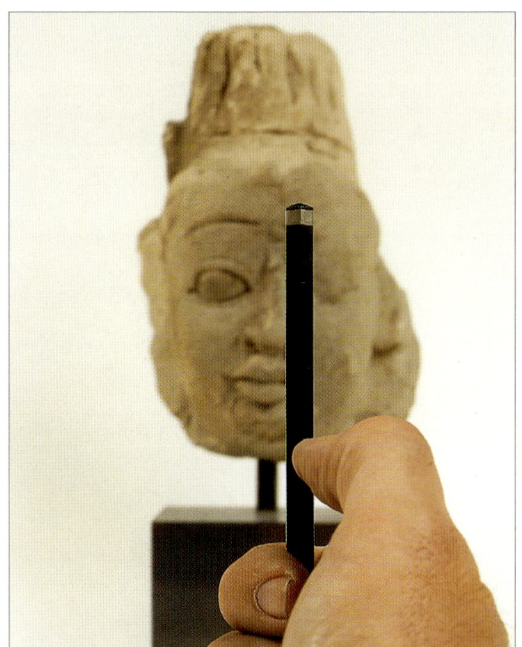

1 Holding the pencil at arm's length, measure the chosen section of your subject – here, the distance from the statue's eyebrows to the base of the chin. Then transfer this unit of measurement to the paper.

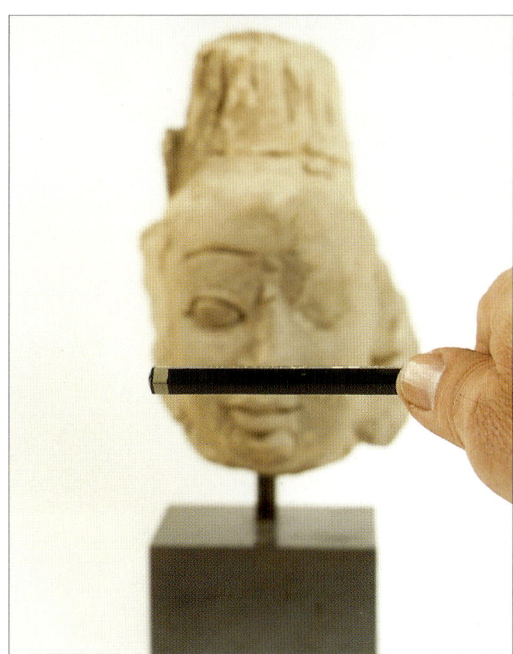

2 Use the same unit of measurement to compare the size of other parts of the subject. Here, the distance across the widest point of the statue is the same as the measurement taken in Step 1.

Negative shapes

The term 'negative shapes' is used in art to mean the spaces between objects in a composition or between different parts of an object. But how does this help you when drawing? It's all about making yourself really look at your subject, rather than relying on your preconceptions about how things should look.

A lot of this has to do with the way that the different hemispheres of the brain work. The left side of the brain is concerned primarily with verbal skills, and it is this side that is dominant in many adults, as we're brought up to express ourselves verbally rather than visually. This means that when we look at something we tend to concentrate on the things we can name – the 'positive' shapes. So if we're looking at a tree, our brain registers things like the trunk and the branches rather than the spaces between the branches, which have no name.

Looking at the negative shapes forces us to switch our thinking from the left side of our brain (the verbal side) to the right side (the visual side). Instead of concentrating on the things we can give a name to and thinking, for example, 'I'm going to draw that square table', we have to say, 'I'm going to draw that straight-sided shape'. So we're much more likely to observe and put down correctly the relative shapes and sizes if, instead of being distracted by our knowledge of the fact that all four legs of the table are the same size and shape, we really look at the shapes of the spaces between the legs. Because we're looking at the table in perspective, they appear to be different sizes and positions in relation to one another – and you need to get this across in your drawing in order for it to look realistic.

In the following exercises, you will draw by looking only at the negative shapes. To prepare for them, spend plenty of time looking at the subject before you put pencil to paper. Really force yourself to look at the spaces instead of at the objects. It takes a lot of concentration, but if you try hard you'll find that these negative shapes suddenly 'pop' out at you – rather like a camera lens shifting focus from subject to background.

Practice exercise: **Drawing a straight-sided object using negative shapes**

In this exercise, your task is to draw using only the negative shapes – the spaces around and between the different parts of the chair. It's an artificial way of working (in practice one would alternate between the negative and positive shapes), but it will help fix the principle in your mind. It doesn't matter whether you draw the negative spaces around the outside the chair first and then those within it, or vice versa.

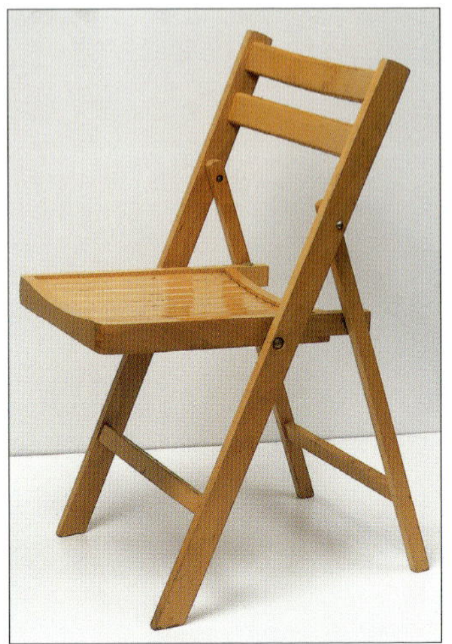

Materials

- *Smooth drawing paper*
- *Graphite stick*

The subject

With a straight-sided subject such as this folding chair, the negative shapes are relatively simple to draw.

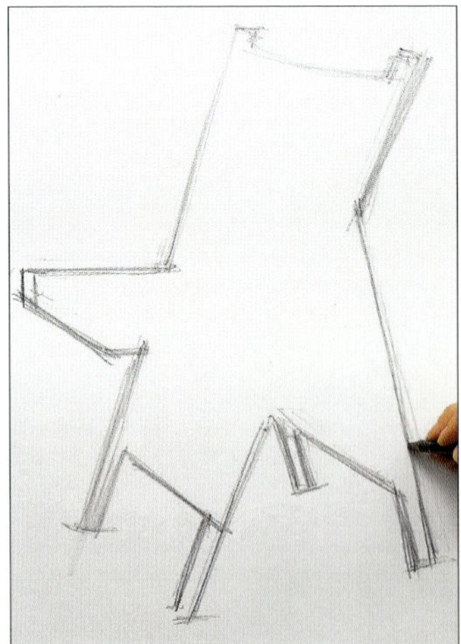

1 Look at the space to the left of the chair and concentrate until you feel you are able to see it as a shape in its own right, rather than an area of nothingness with the chair along one edge. Then begin drawing the outline of the negative shapes that you can see, concentrating on getting the angles of the shapes and the length of each side of each shape right.

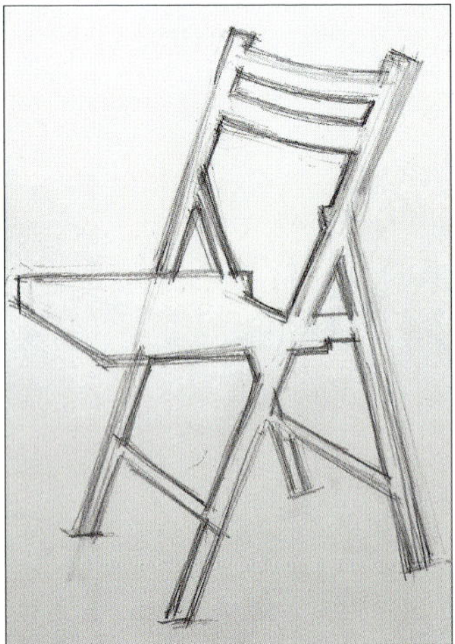

2 Now move on to the negative shapes within the chair itself – the spaces between the bars of the backrest, the space between the backrest and the seat, and the spaces under the seat between the supporting side bars. Provided you've made your measurements accurately, drawing the negative spaces defines the shape of the subject – the chair.

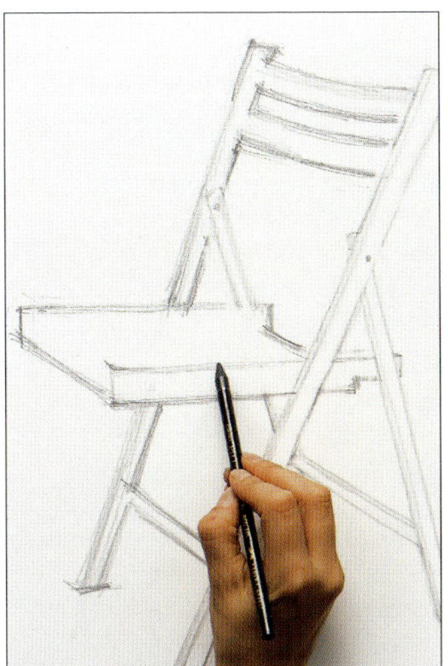

3 When you've laid down the basic negative shapes, you can begin to refine the drawing and look at the positive shapes – the different planes of the seat of the chair, for example.

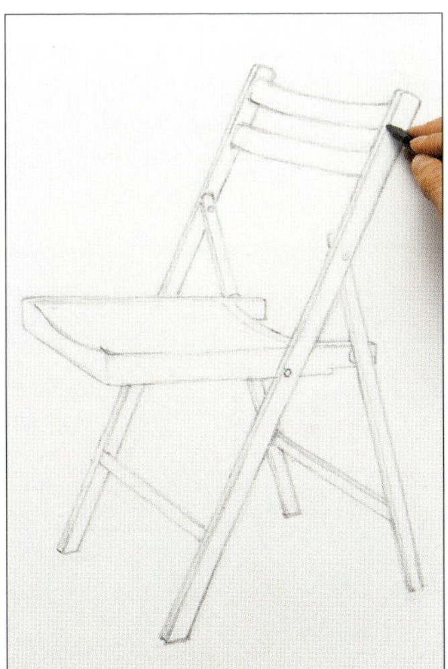

4 Put in the remaining positive shapes, such as the rivets that connect the side supports to the seat, and detailing, such as the tongue-and-groove effect on the seat. Also carefully draw in the different facets of the side bars and the connecting struts so that the chair looks three-dimensional.

The finished drawing

The subject is simple, but it still requires concentration to draw the relative angles and sizes of all the components accurately. As the chair has straight sides the negative spaces, too, are straight-sided – which makes it easier to see and measure them accurately. Even though no shading or tone has been used, careful measuring of the different elements has resulted in a drawing that looks three-dimensional.

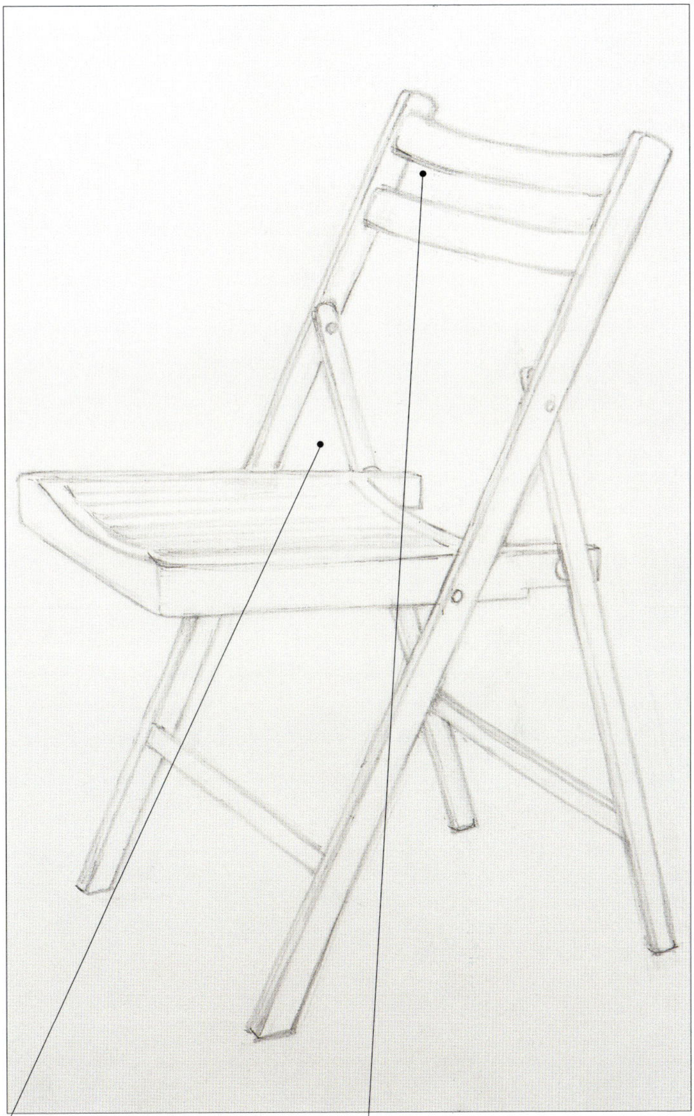

The negative shapes are mostly four-sided or triangular, which makes them simple to measure.

Drawing the negative shapes makes it easier to get slopes and angles right.

Perspective

One of the major challenges in learning to draw is how to create the illusion of spatial depth on the flat, two-dimensional surface of a piece of paper. For example, if you're drawing a landscape with a boulder in the foreground and a mountain range in the distance, how do you make it look as if the boulder is near by and the mountains are far away?

Over the centuries, many different drawing systems have been devised to help create the illusion of spatial depth. One approach is to employ a vertical arrangement, with the most distant elements of the scene at the top of the picture space. For example, traditional Chinese brush-drawn landscapes place mountains at the top, with forested lower slopes under the peaks and a lake or river, perhaps with a boat, in the lower portion.

In Western art, changes in tone and scale are usually employed to create the impression of distance. Whole books have been written about the technicalities of perspective, but the basics are relatively easy to understand. Keen observation of your subject is the key to success.

Aerial perspective

Aerial, or atmospheric, perspective exploits apparent differences in tone between nearby and distant objects to create a sense of depth and recession. When seen from close by, dark-coloured objects or areas cast in shadow appear strong in tone. In the middle distance, darker areas appear less sombre. Further off, rich darks will be perceived as more muted; and from a great distance, they will acquire a pale, bluish tinge. This filtering effect is caused by the dust, motes, moisture particles and other pollutants in the atmosphere, which cloud the air with tiny particles and partially obscure the far distance. This phenomenon has been much exploited in Western art.

Tonal differences for distance
Note how effectively differences in tone create the impression of distance in this drawing. Looking along the strand, the nearest beached boats are the darkest in tone. Further along the foreshore, distance softens strong tonal values, and most distant still, the coastline and ocean are much lighter in tone.

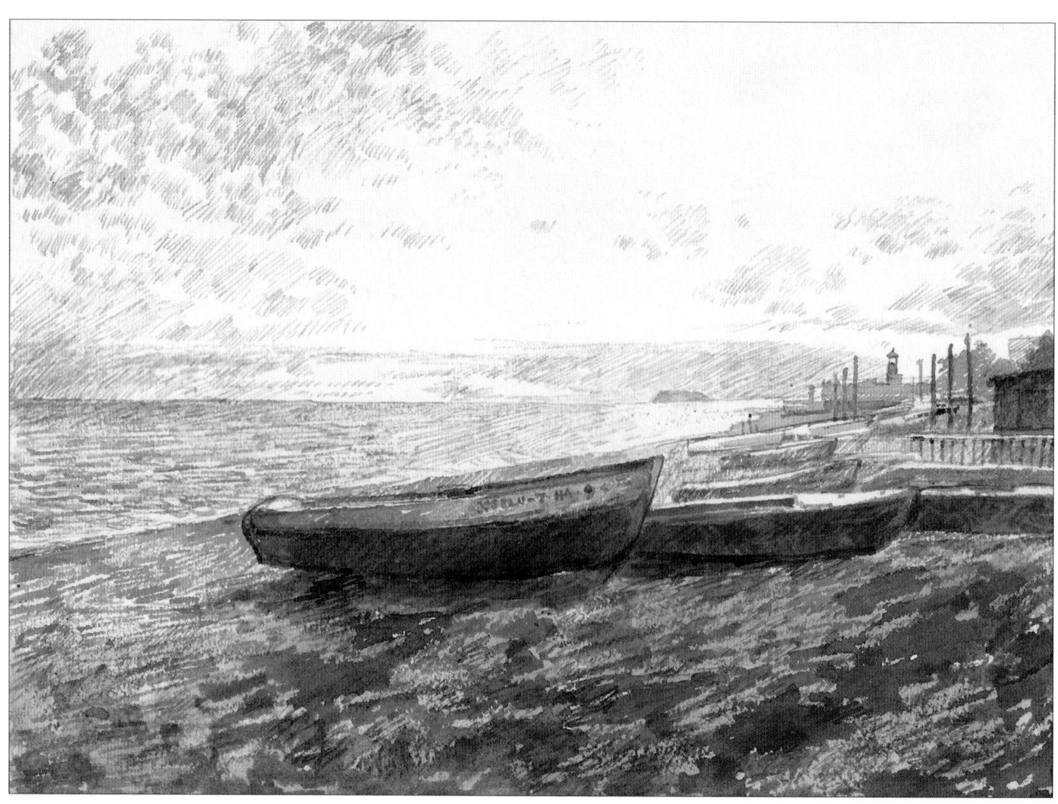

Softly-toned haze

In damp, misty weather, or when a heat wave has drawn moisture up as a heat haze, landscapes will show the softening, or blueing, of distant strong tones. In this scene the shadowed trees and foliage framing this old house which would appear sombre were they close at hand, are seen as relatively softly toned in the middle distance and pale when viewed from afar. The transitions in tone are subtle, but essential in creating an impression of distance.

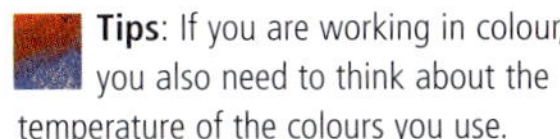

Tips: If you are working in colour, you also need to think about the temperature of the colours you use.

- Distant objects tend to look 'cooler' and bluer in tone than those that are nearer.
- Skies generally appear paler near the horizon of a scene.
- Include more texture in the foreground of a scene – for example, spiky grasses in the foreground of a landscape; the viewer will assume that the textured areas are in front.

Vertical perspective

In this sketch, after the Japanese artist Hiroshige's *Winter: Scene on the Sumida River*, the illusion of depth is created by means of vertical perspective, or placing the most distant elements at the top of the picture space. The boatman is placed on a raft low on the torrent, creating the impression that he is in the foreground, while the near-distant trees are higher in the picture and the far-off mountain is above them, conveying a plausible sense of recession.

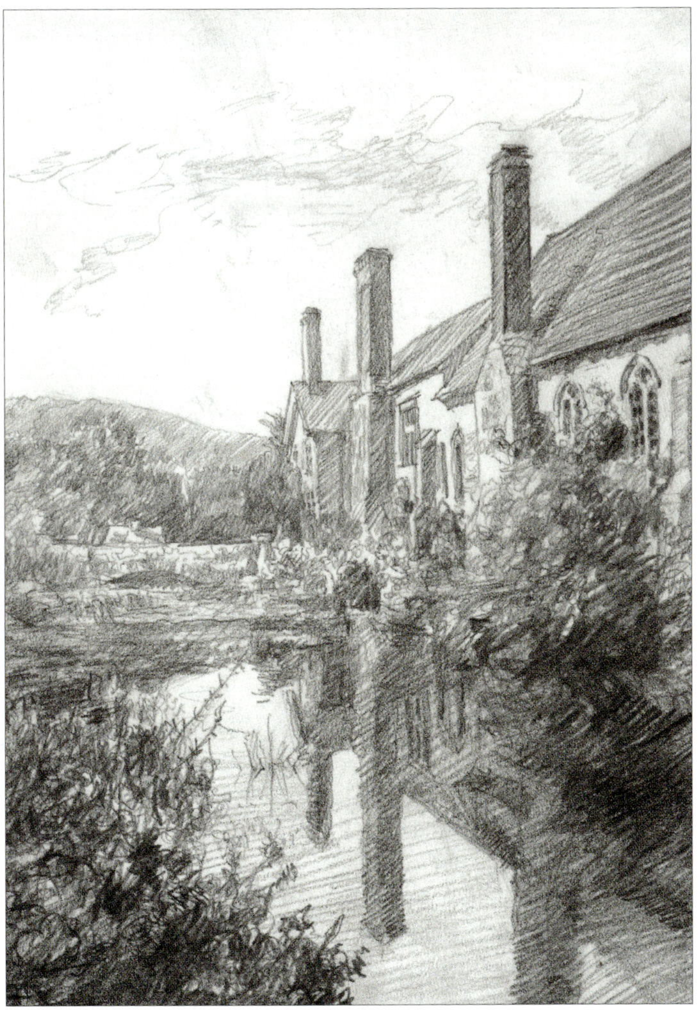

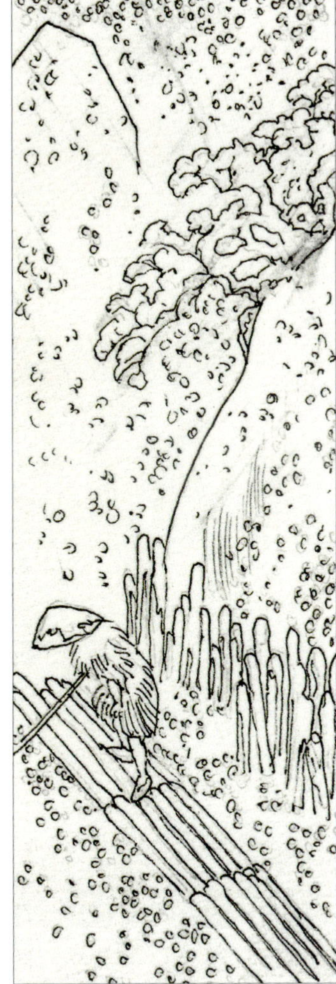

Linear perspective

Objects appear to be smaller the further away from you they are. You can use this effect in your drawings to create the illusion of distance.

Linear, or one-point, perspective applies when all the receding planes are aligned and parallel. To see this, look straight down a road where only one façade of the buildings on each side is visible. The horizontal planes of the upper floors above eye level will appear to slope down through the length of the street, although, in fact, they do not get lower. Horizontal lines below eye level will be seen to slope upwards, while in reality the planes remain level. These are the illusions that must be reproduced if the viewer of the picture is to be convinced that the road is receding into the distance.

To determine the correct slant for the horizontal planes, one-point perspective may be plotted to a notional spot known as the vanishing point. A person of average size, looking straight ahead on the flat, will see the horizon at about 5km (3 miles) away. To make a perspective drawing, plot the imaginary horizon at eye level and mark on it the vanishing point – the place at which all the horizontal lines would meet if they were extended as far as the horizon. Adhere carefully to the plotted lines and you will create the effect of recession. Note that this rule affects only the horizontal elements: verticals must remain upright.

Street scene in single-point perspective

In this scene, all the horizontal elements above eye level (for example the roof lines and the tops and bottoms of the windows) appear to slope down towards the vanishing point, while those below eye level seem to slope up – although, in reality, the planes remain level along the road. If the houses were shown with equidistant planes (that is, without the lines of the roof and road appearing to slope towards the vanishing point), the viewer would not perceive them as parallel.

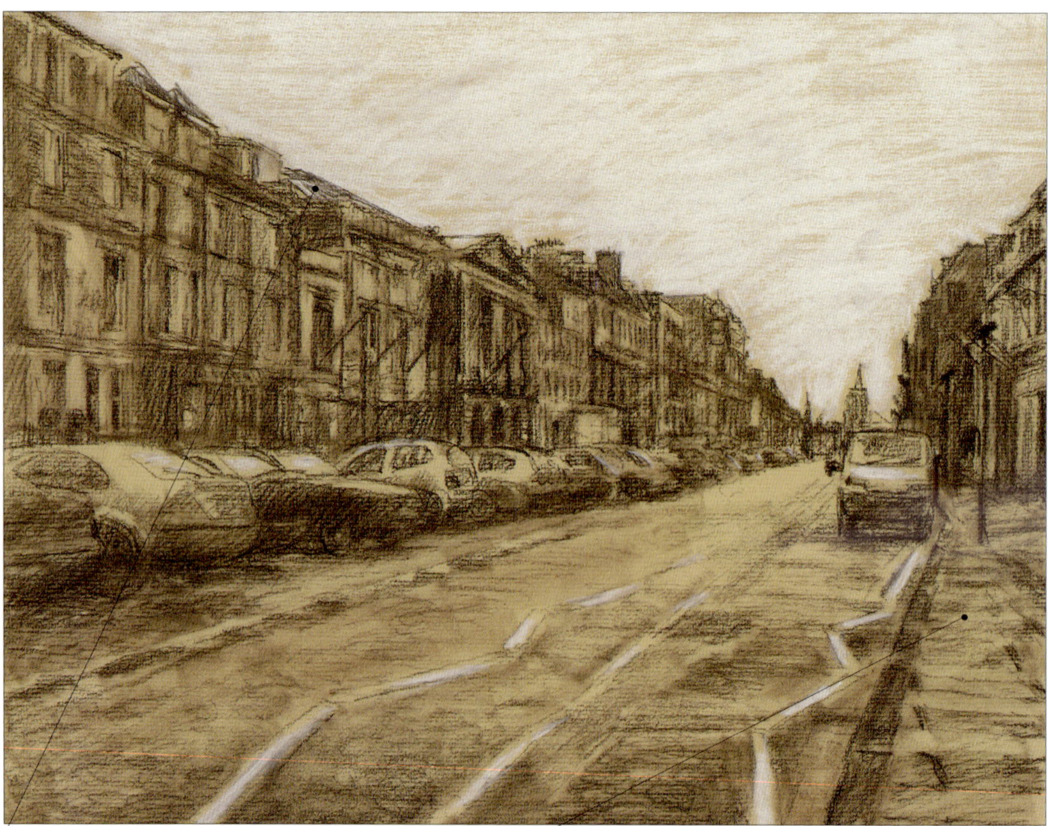

The roofs and many of the windows are above eye level and appear to slope down as the street recedes.

The pavement is below eye level and therefore appears to slope upwards as the road recedes.

Single-point perspective with right angles

Here, too, single-point perspective is used to plot the lines of the buildings and indicate distance. The people furthest away are also drawn smaller than those in the foreground. At the end of the road, another street runs at right angles to the street on which the drawing is made; as this second street is parallel to the picture plane, it has no vanishing points. If the sides of the neoclassical-style building on this second street were visible, the extensions of the horizontal planes would converge on the same single vanishing point as the road from which the scene is viewed. If further streets at right angles to the road were visible, decreasing size and softer tones would also give clues to distance.

Vertical elements remain vertical: only receding horizontal lines converge on the notional vanishing point.

This road is parallel to the picture plane and therefore has no vanishing points.

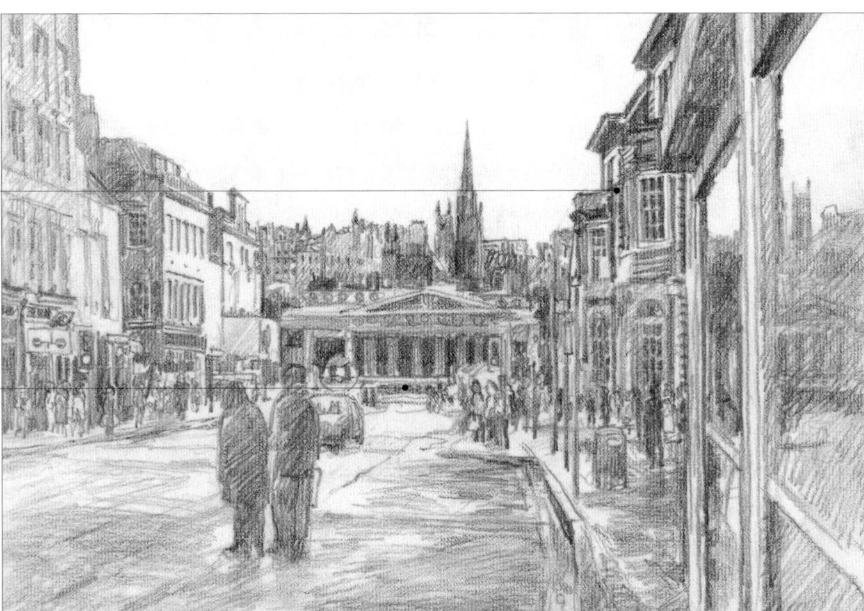

The single point pespective combined with a larger structure.

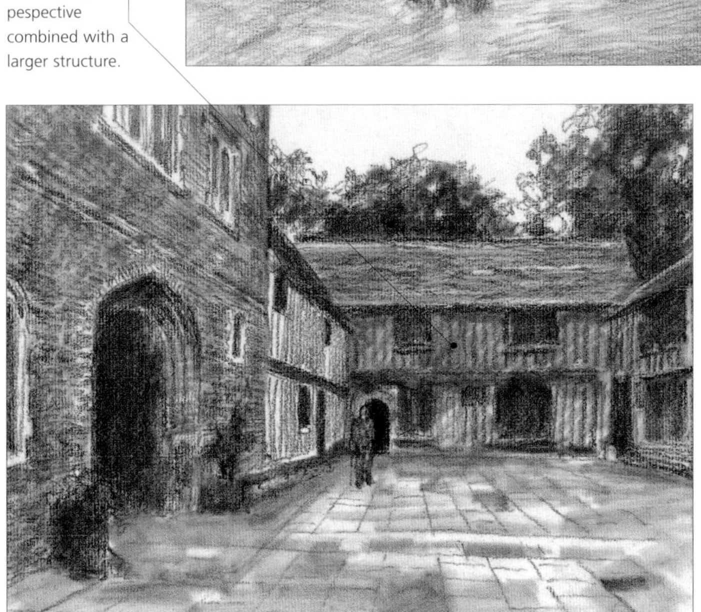

Creating drama

Dynamic compositions can be achieved when single-point perspective is combined with larger structures that are parallel to the picture plane. In this example (left), the design focuses attention on the junction between the brick-and-timber gatehouse wing, on the left of the picture, and the half-timbered block at the back of the courtyard.

The courtyard background appears four-square to the viewer, while the sloping lines of the gatehouse wing (which is seen in single-point perspective) help to direct the viewer's eye through the scene.

In a similar fashion, the lines of the courtyard paving stones, which are also drawn in single-point perspective, help to guide our eye to the figure standing towards the far end.

Two-point perspective

Few constructed environments make interesting compositions unless they involve more than one vanishing point. Once you have tried and understood single-point perspective, you will soon find that multi-sided buildings, or those whose elevations are not all in the same parallel plane, hold more exciting design possibilities. In single-point perspective, the apparent size of forms reduces evenly, as do the spaces between. While this is also true of two-point, or multi-point, perspective, different avenues of vision receding in less depth or at differently oblique angles may appear to diminish to differing degrees.

Remember that in plotting the vanishing points in two- or multi-point perspective, not all the points will fall within the picture space. Clearly, those that are four-square to the picture must be drawn as rectilinear, but those close to square on will have vanishing points far beyond the edge of the image. To discern these, you may need to make a preliminary sketch on a small scale and affix it to a large sheet on which you can plot the angles of recession to the vanishing points. You can then transpose the correct angles from the thumbnail sketch on to the larger-scale support on which you intend to draw the finished work.

Several vanishing points in the same scene

Multi-point perspective will be used if a building is viewed at a tangent, as the different sides of the building on view will have horizontal planes that extend to different vanishing points. In this example, both vanishing points are out of the picture; the moat façade, diminishing sharply, has a vanishing point close by, but the front elevation with the bridge is viewed at a less oblique angle and has a vanishing point that is further out, far to the left of the picture area.

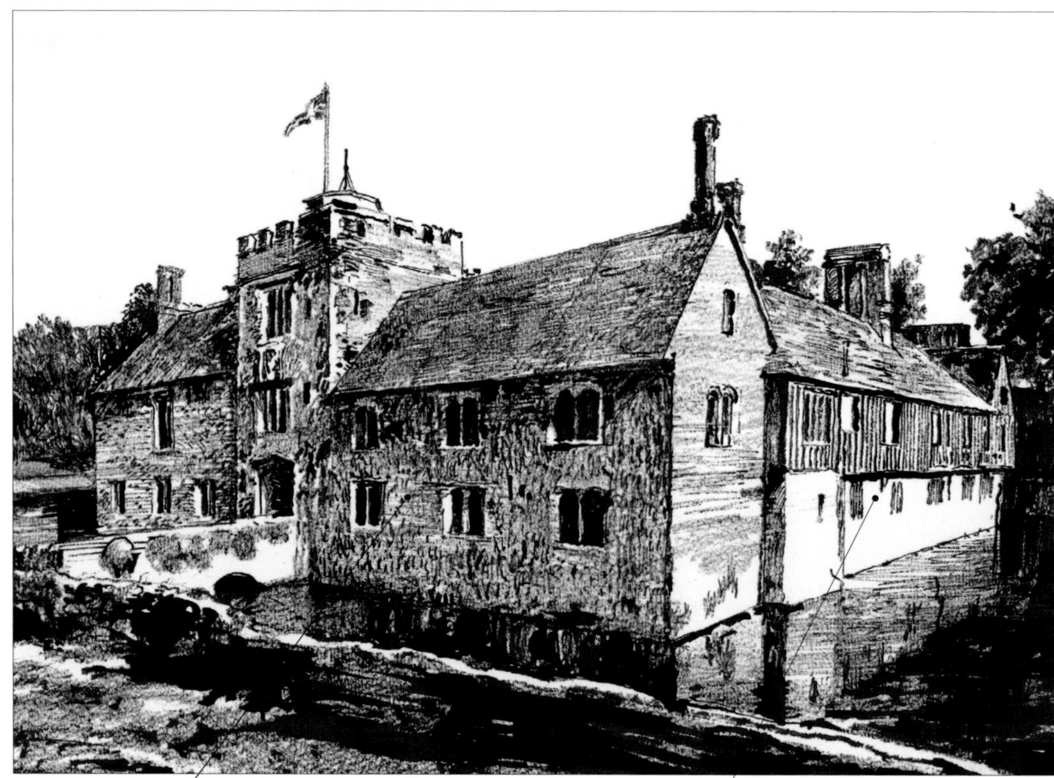

This side of the building is viewed from only a slight angle and so the horizontal lines recede only very gradually towards the vanishing point; the vanishing point iteself is far outside the picture area.

This side of the building recedes into the distance; the horizontal lines recede much more steeply, but the vanishing point is still outside the picture area.

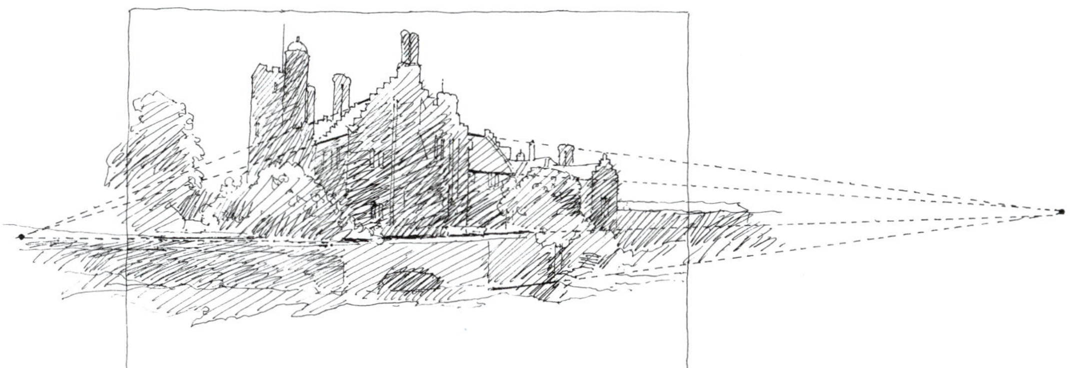

Sketch plotting the vanishing points
The sketch above shows the horizontal planes extended to the vanishing points, which are not visible within the image itself. The greater the angle at which a plane is turned from the vertical, the further out the vanishing point will be. Only horizontal planes angled relatively close to vertical are likely to have vanishing points within the picture space.

Different vanishing points on each side of the subject
To make the drawing shown below, the artist selected a viewpoint that enabled her to see two sides of the building, as this creates a much more dynamic and interesting image than a flat façade viewed square on. Note how the line of the roof, which is above eye level, appears to slope downwards on each side, while the wall, which is below eye level, seems to slope upwards – just as in the examples for single-point perspective on the preceding pages. The difference here is that each side disappears to a different vanishing point (see the sketch above).

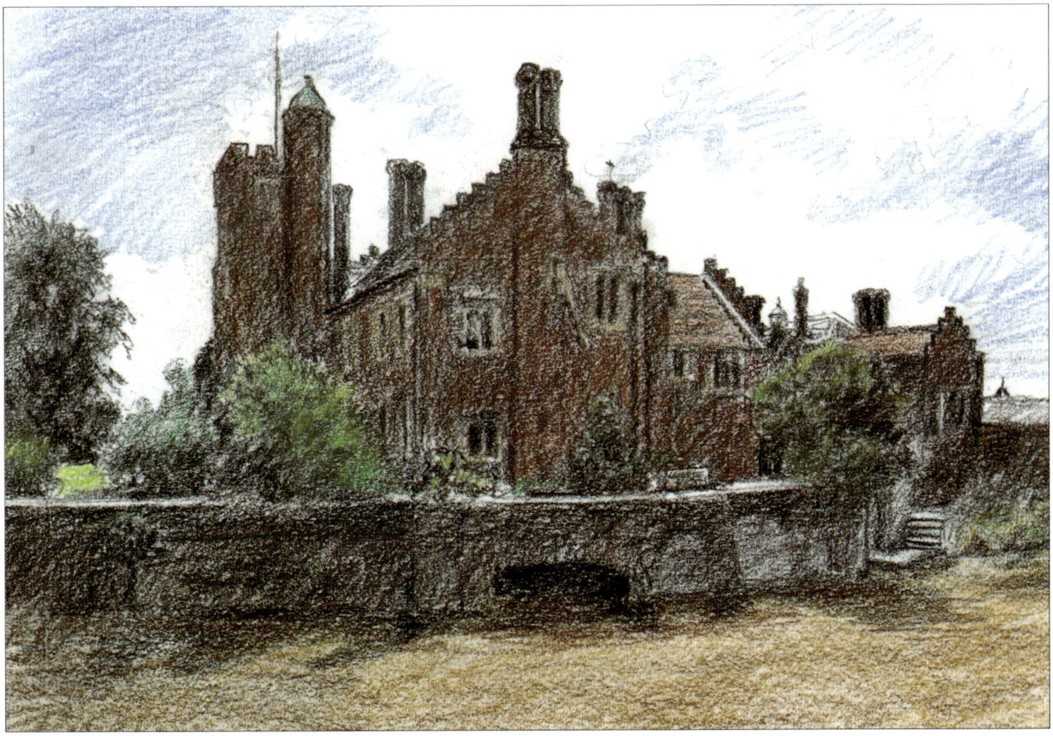

Multiple vanishing points

Multi-point perspective is also used when not all the horizontal elements in view could have their planes extended to the same single vanishing point. In architectural drawings, this may occur if there are several structures built at various different angles to the picture plane. If one large structure – for example, a country house – has wings or outbuildings added at disparate angles to the main building, the planes are also extendible to multiple vanishing points.

However, it is very easy to get so caught up in the technicalities of perspective that you lose sight of your drawing as a whole. Although you could choose to plot every single horizontal line to its notional vanishing point, the chances are that you would produce a very tight, laboured drawing as a result – it would become a technical exercise rather than a spontaneous response to your subject. Once you've mastered the basic principles of perspective, learn to trust your observational skills. Hold a pencil out in front of you to assess the angle of any horizontal lines as they recede towards their vanishing point. Now measure the distances between different elements of your subject carefully, ignoring any preconceptions that you may have about the relative sizes of things.

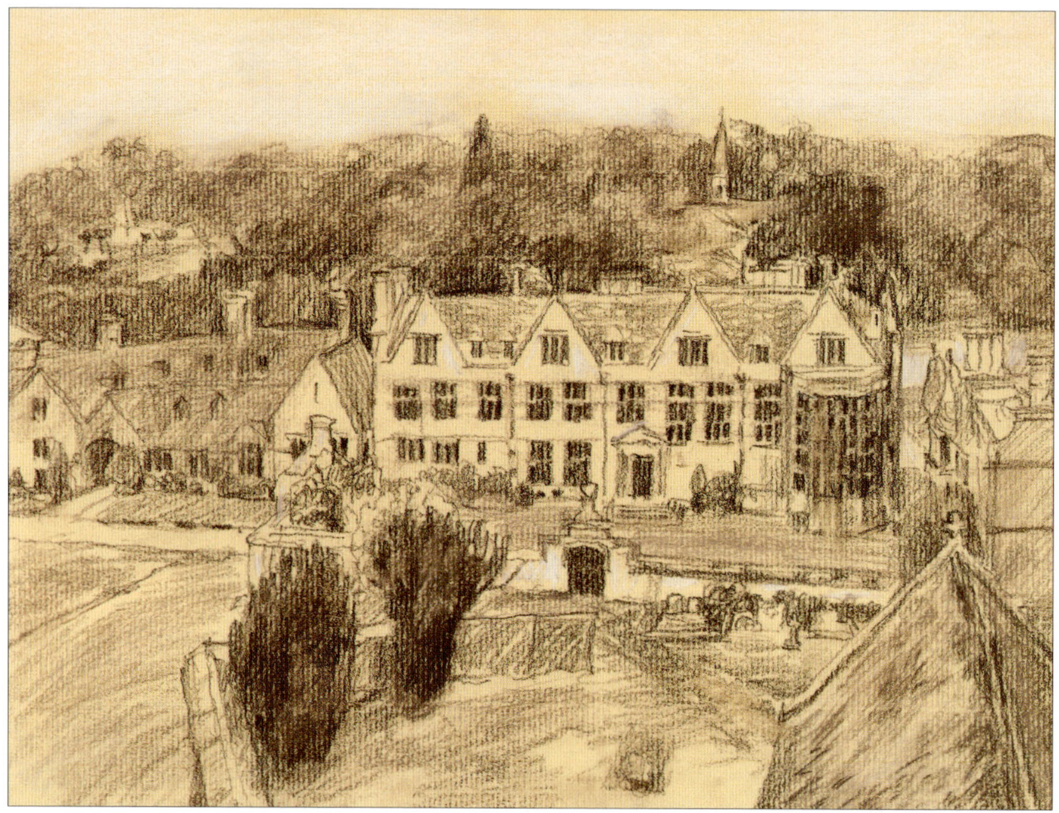

Check – and check again

Careful observation and measuring are the only ways you will be able to tackle a complicated, multi-point perspective subject such as this. We are looking down on the scene; the horizontal lines of the roofs of the foreground buildings appear to converge inwards towards a vanishing point, while those of the buildings on the far side of the street slope upwards. Note, too, how the inclusion of buildings at different angles to the main house adds interest to the drawing: as well as creating a sense of depth, they also help to lead the viewer's eye towards the main centre of interest.

Foreshortening

You must also gauge the phenomenon of foreshortening in perspective drawing. This term is used to describe the effect of looking along a subject at a tangent, where the length appears shortened but the width is seen as relatively unchanged. Long spans appear much curtailed from the foreshortened viewpoint. For example, viewing a tall person reclining from a vantage point just beyond and above the head shows the long legs and torso taking up little vertical space, while the trunk and limbs are relatively wide. Different degrees of foreshortening may be evident in all the various directions in landscape multi-point perspective work, especially if elements are not on the level.

Foreshortened figure

Figure work often calls for the rendering of foreshortening, as the head, body and limbs are seldom all viewed in profile together, except in simple standing poses. Note that, when seen at a tangent, any element will appear diminished in length or telescoped, while the width is little affected along the span. With extreme foreshortening, you can expect to see some overlaps: for example, a foreshortened head seen from above might show the chin overlapped by the nose. Initially, you may find that it helps to draw a faint box, or cube, in perspective around your subject and plot the vanishing points, just as you would in an architectural drawing.

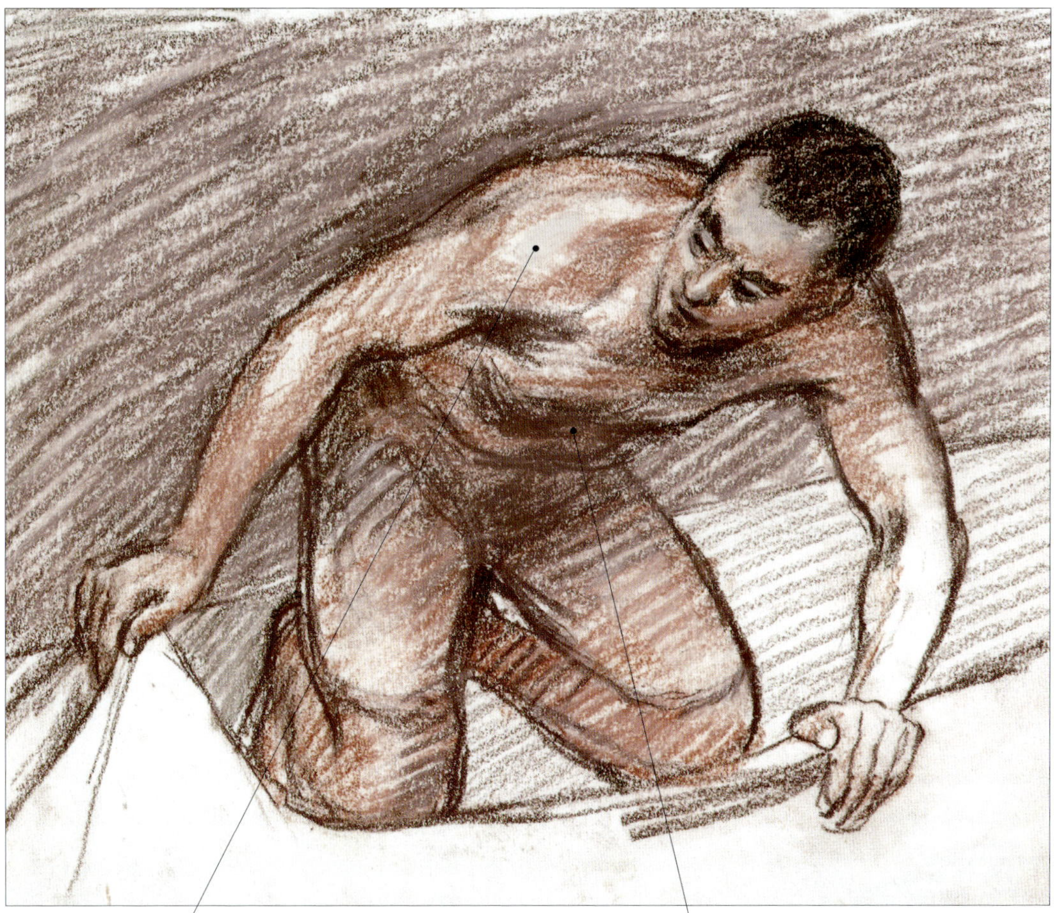

From this viewpoint, the model's right shoulder appears much broader than the left – though they are, of course, the same size.

Viewed from a relatively high eye level, the torso appears shortened in relation to the legs.

Curved forms in perspective

The eye level of the observer determines the distance to the horizon on which the vanishing point or points are fixed. This is the boundary of the visible land or sea, marking the point at which the curvature of the earth turns away so that the continuing surface is no longer seen. Although it is possible to look for some distance on flat land, an even greater vista is possible from a height – for example, a hill or mountain top. From an aeroplane, vast tracts of land are visible before the horizon.

Eye level determines the way circular objects are seen, too. Viewed from above, they appear completely round. When you lower your viewpoint, the same circular form appears to be elliptical, because the span across it is foreshortened, decreasing the apparent length of the diameter in relation to the width. The lower your viewpoint, the narrower the ellipse will appear, but at the extremes the edges are always curvilinear. This is because no round form can have sharp corners, so a curve always defines the width, however tight the turn. Only when the eye level coincides with the profile view of circular objects will the shapes appear flat and show angles at the periphery. Test this for yourself by placing a glass on a table and viewing it from different eye levels – first standing directly overhead so that the top of the glass appears as a complete circle, then sitting down so that the top of the glass appears as an ellipse, and finally crouching on the floor, so that your eyes are level with the top of the glass.

Tall curved forms in real space also appear flatter at eye level and more curved when above or below it. Castles, lighthouses or buildings with circular towers demonstrate this: the base appears flat when viewed at ground level and the upper floors show increasing curvature as they rise above. Knowledge often impairs perception, so guard against the tendency to flatten the bases of smaller circular objects when seen from above, as the base will display more curvature than the top if it is viewed from a higher point.

Circular perspective in wine glasses

The perspective of circular forms is easier to see if the objects are transparent and the full ellipses, in perspective, are visible. Clear glass is an excellent example and if the glass, dish or vase contains liquid, this too will have to conform to the length and width of ellipse required at that level. Remember that any contents such as flower stems may appear distorted by the curved glass and should be drawn as seen.

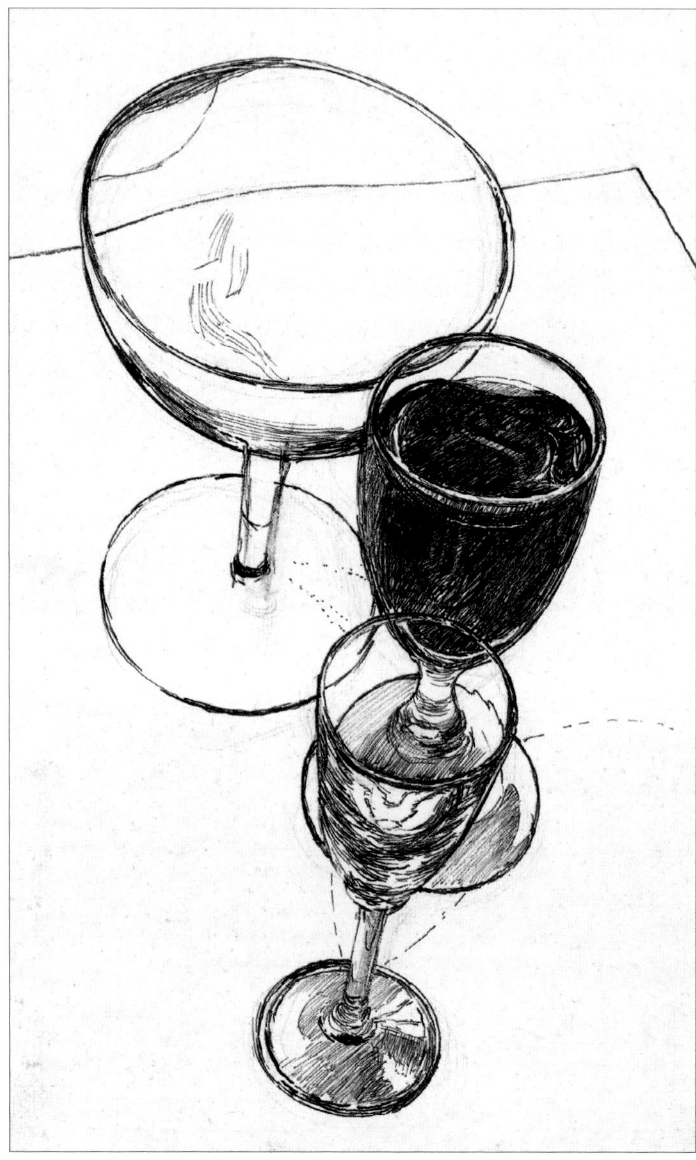

Large circular forms in perspective

Exactly the same principles apply when drawing large circular or cylindrical forms: when they are viewed in perspective, they will appear as ellipses. How flat or round the ellipses are depends on your viewpoint, or eye level – and in a large-scale subject such as the one shown below, the ellipses will vary in different parts of the image because some parts of the subject are above your eye level while others are below it. Here, the round towers of the castle are seen as nearly flat at water level; the bases appear as shallow ellipses. When looking up from the moat, the round tower battlements appear to be most curved, with the stonework between showing gradually increasing curvature as the courses rise. All the rectilinear horizontal planes of the walls and towers in between have vanishing points to the left, far out of the picture space.

Tip: One common mistake that people make when drawing ellipses is to make the ends pointed.

- To avoid this, lightly sketch (or at least imagine) a square enclosing the ellipse.
- Then find the centre of the square by drawing diagonal lines from corner to corner; the two halves of the square will be different measurements, because the parallel lines of the square will converge towards the notional vanishing point.
- Draw a horizontal and a vertical line through the centre of the square in perspective to work out the halfway point along each side of the square.
- Finally, draw the ellipse, using the intersection as a guide to drawing the curve accurately.

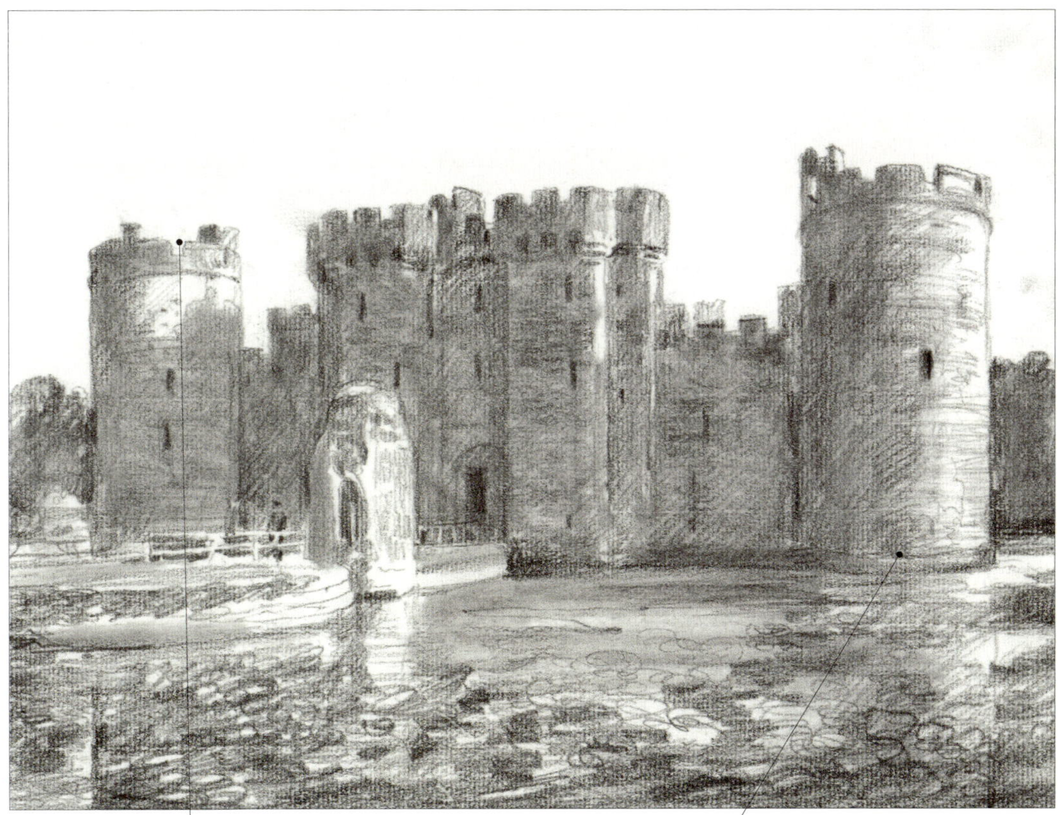

The tops of the towers are above eye level and the curves of the ellipses appear more pronounced.

The bases of the curved towers, which are only slightly below eye level, appear as very shallow ellipses.

Sketching

While a drawing can be a finished work with its own pictorial aims, the word 'sketch' implies a quick study. There is, however, a difference between sketching for its own sake – for pleasure – and making studies to be used as reference for another work, whether that is a finished drawing or a painting.

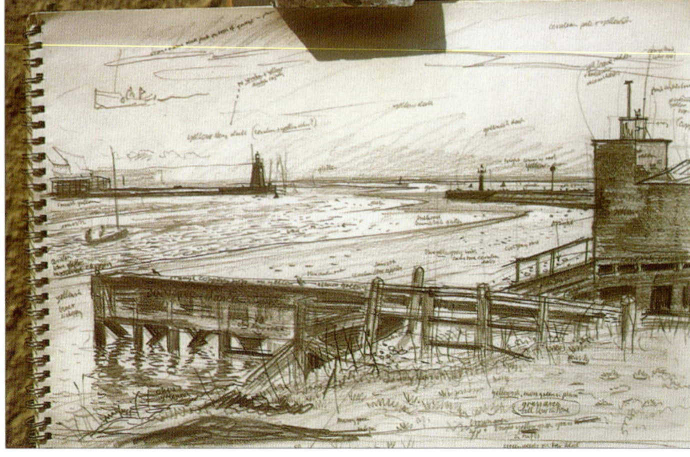

▲ Sketching for painting
This sketch by Stephen Crowther was made as the first stage in planning an oil painting, and the artist has made copious written notes to remind him of the colours. Using a large spiral-bound sketchbook enables him to remove the sheet and pin it up near his easel.

Collecting visual material

Sketching helps to polish up your observational skills, and artists often go through their sketchbooks to get ideas for compositions or simply to refresh their memories on some detail of a scene. The more you sketch, the more reference material you will have.

In some cases, however, sketches are made not randomly but to gather material for a composition, in which case it is necessary to consider the kind of visual notes required. You may need sketches in colour and tone as well as in line. Trying to make a painting from a line sketch in pencil or pen and ink is virtually impossible; you will have no idea what colour the sky was or which areas were dark and which ones light.

It is wise to make a habit of including all the information possible on your sketches – if you don't have time to sketch in colour, make written notes about the colours. Do not simply write 'blue' or 'green', but try to analyse the colours; this can be more valuable than sketching in colour, particularly if you intend to use a different medium for the painting. A sketch in coloured pencil, for example, would be very difficult to translate into watercolour or oil.

Materials

For sketching you can use any media with which you feel comfortable. Pencil is a good all-rounder, as it allows you to establish tone as well as line. Pen and ink is useful for small sketches, but less so for tonal studies. Coloured pencils are tailor-made for colour sketches, and so are pastels and oil pastels, although neither of the latter is suitable for small-scale work.

You can buy large pads containing different colours of pastel paper, or clip paper to a drawing board. Sketchbooks, usually containing cartridge (drawing) paper, can be bought in many sizes. Unless you like to work small, don't be tempted by a tiny address-book size, as you may find that it restricts and frustrates you.

▼ Choosing a sketchbook
The kind of sketchbook you require depends on your method of working and the kind of visual notes you wish to make. Some artists have two or three in different sizes and formats. John Townend uses a large book for coloured-pencil drawings like this, and a smaller one for pen-and-ink drawings.

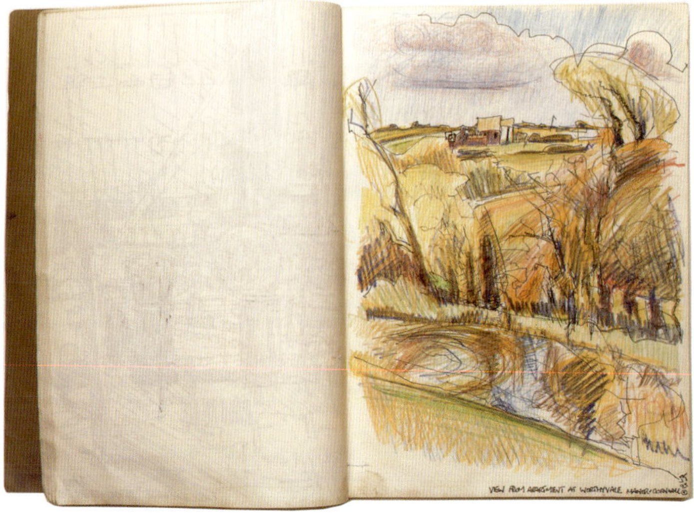

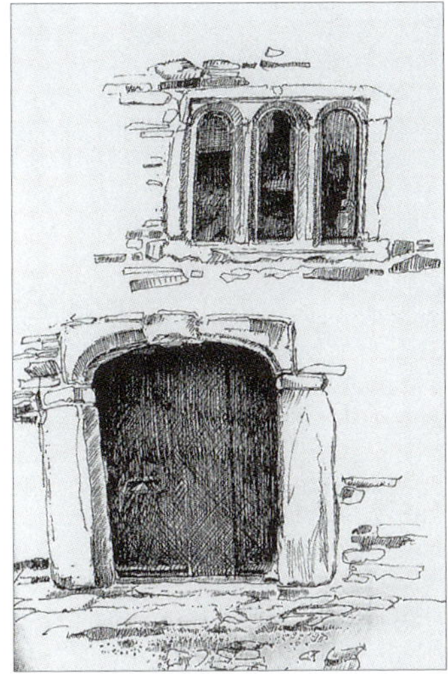

▲ **Choosing the medium**
When you are out sketching it is wise to take a selection of different drawing media, as you may find that a particular subject is better suited to one than another. John Townend likes coloured pencil for landscapes, but prefers pen and ink for architectural subjects, where colour is less important than line.

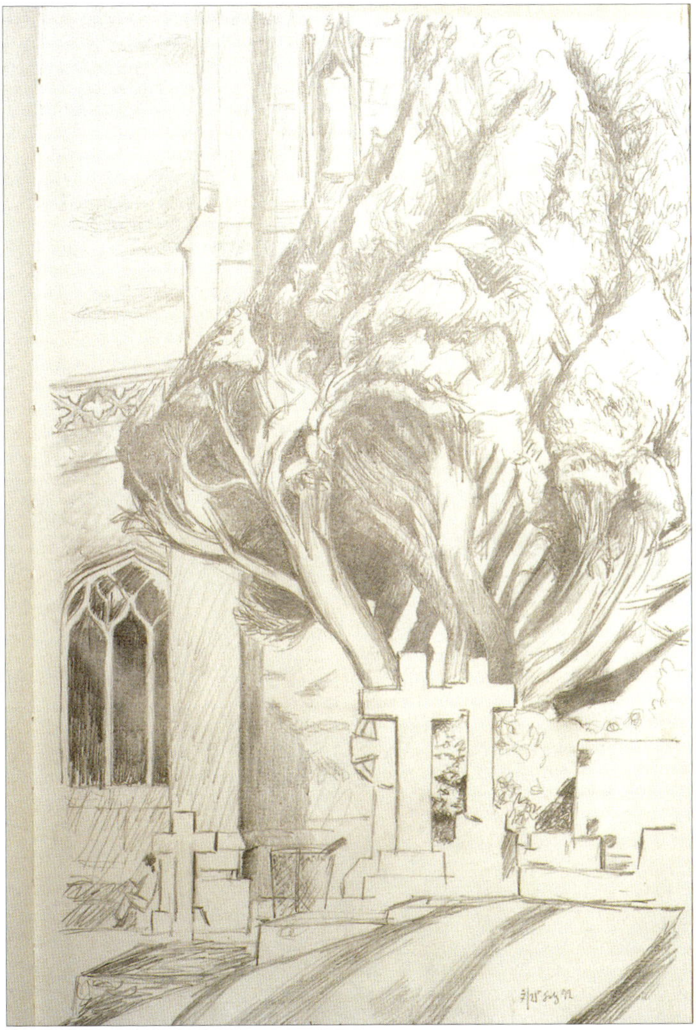

▶ **Collecting ideas**
David Cuthbert does not make sketches with a specific painting in mind, but he has several sketchbooks in which he notes down anything he sees, often taking photographs at the same time so that he has a store of possible ideas to hand when planning a new work.

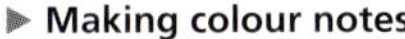

▶ **Making colour notes**
Gerry Baptist works mainly in acrylic, using vivid colours, and his sketches in watercolour reflect his artistic preoccupations; preparatory monochrome sketches in pencil would not provide the information that he needs for his paintings.

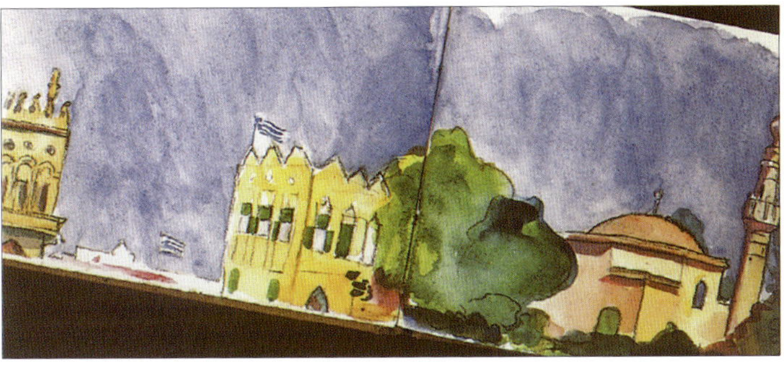

Drawing figures

The old saying, 'If you can paint people you can paint anything,' reflects the fact that the human figure is one of the most challenging of all subjects, whether you are drawing or painting. The importance of figure study as a training ground for aspiring artists was recognized in the past, when drawing from life formed an important part of any art student's education. Nowadays there is less emphasis on it, at any rate in art schools, but amateurs continue to flock to life classes, and many professionals return to them at stages during their careers to brush up their skills.

Joining a life class is not essential if you intend to restrict yourself to the clothed figure or to portrait studies; you can usually find someone you know who is willing to pose for you, or you can draw yourself by looking in a mirror. However, for nude studies you must have a model, so, as friends are unlikely to be willing to pose naked, a class is the best answer and they are held in many locations. Alternatively, you could share the cost of a model with friends or colleagues.

The proportions of the figure

In the main, drawing is learned by practice, not from books, but books can provide some advice and point out things you may overlook when drawing. Figure drawings often go wrong because the proportions are not properly understood, and, although human figures vary greatly, it is helpful to bear in mind some basic rules. These will prevent you from making heads and feet too small – a common error – and help you to analyse what is special about the body you are drawing.

In figure drawing, the head is always used as the unit of measurement, enabling you to make comparative measurements. Allowing for individual differences, the

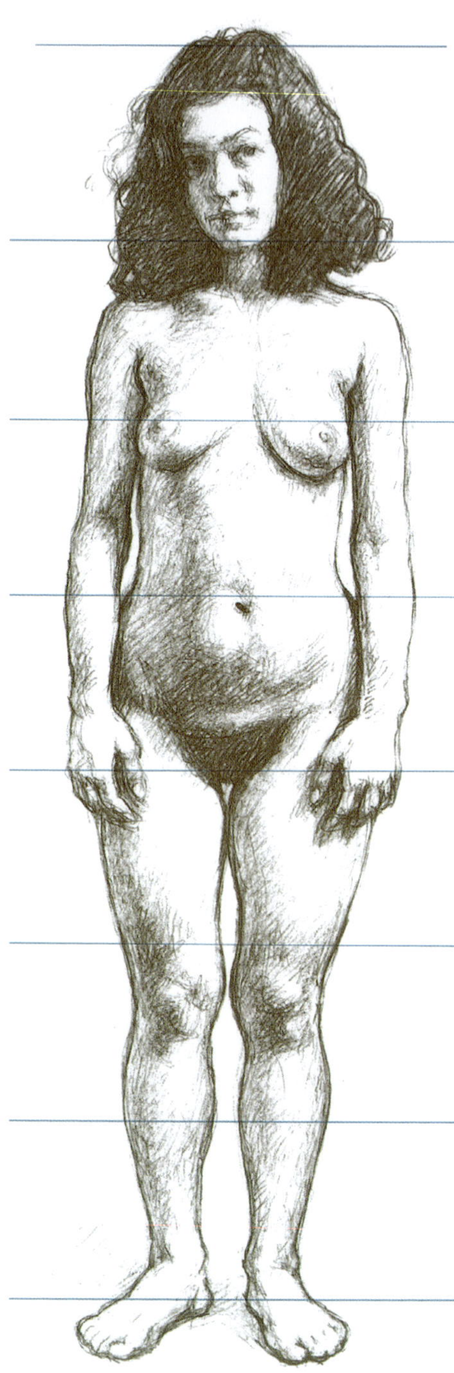

▶ **Proportions**
Although the general rule is that the body is about seven-and-a-half heads high, it is essential to remember that there are variations; this model's head is relatively large. Observing these individual differences will give authenticity to your drawings.

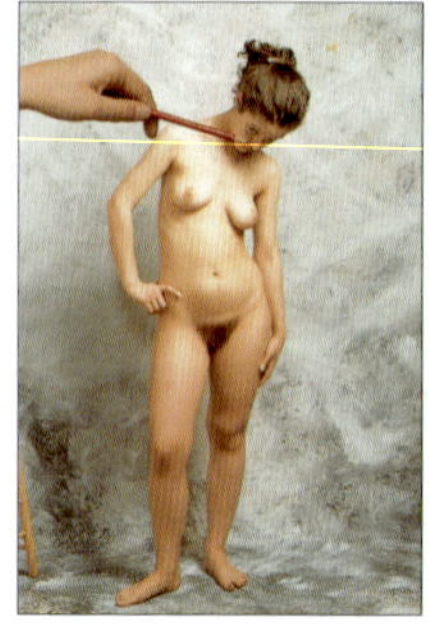

▲ **Checking angles**
In a pose like this it is important to represent accurately the slope of the shoulders and hips. Establish the precise angle by holding your pencil at arm's length and adjusting it until it coincides, then take it down to the paper and mark in the line.

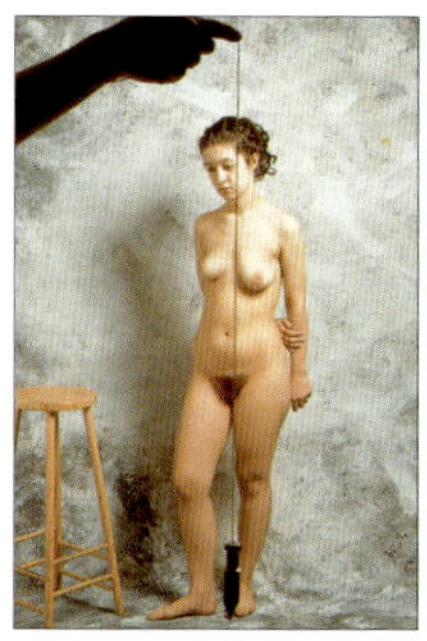

▲ **Checking balance**
The centre of balance is vital in a standing pose, and you can check this either with a pencil or a plumbline, as shown here. This is a slightly laborious method, but is more accurate than holding up a pencil, where there is a danger of tilting it away from the vertical.

human body is about seven-and-a-half heads high. The mid-point of the body is slightly above the genital area, with one quarter point above the nipples and the other just below the knees. If arms are hanging loose by the side of the body, the wrists will be below the mid-point of the body, with the fingertips reaching to mid-thigh. The hand is about the same length as the face, from chin to forehead – try this out by covering your own face with your hand – and the length of the foot is approximately equal to the whole height of the head.

Foreshortening

Measuring systems become particularly important when the figure, or any parts of it, are foreshortened. Foreshortening is the perspective effect which causes things to appear larger the nearer they are; in a reclining figure, seen from the feet end, the feet will be large and the legs very short. It can be difficult to assess the effects of foreshortening accurately, partly because you know a leg is a certain length and find it hard to believe what you see, and partly because the forms themselves often change depending on the pose. For example, in a seated figure seen from the front the thighs will be wide and short, because the flesh is pushed out by the body's weight.

Some degree of foreshortening is generally present in any figure drawing and, because the effects created are often surprising, it is vital to take measurements. As you draw, hold your pencil out at arm's length to check the relative lengths and widths of the limbs and body, always returning to the head as the basic unit of measurement.

Balance and weight

You can also use the outstretched pencil method to check the angles of different parts of the body, another problem area. The angle of the shoulders or the tilt of the hips often provides the key to the pose. In a standing figure with the weight on one leg, for example, the shoulders and hips slope in opposite directions; whenever one part of the body moves, another does so in compensation, to maintain the balance. Hold out your pencil and align it with the shoulder or hip line and

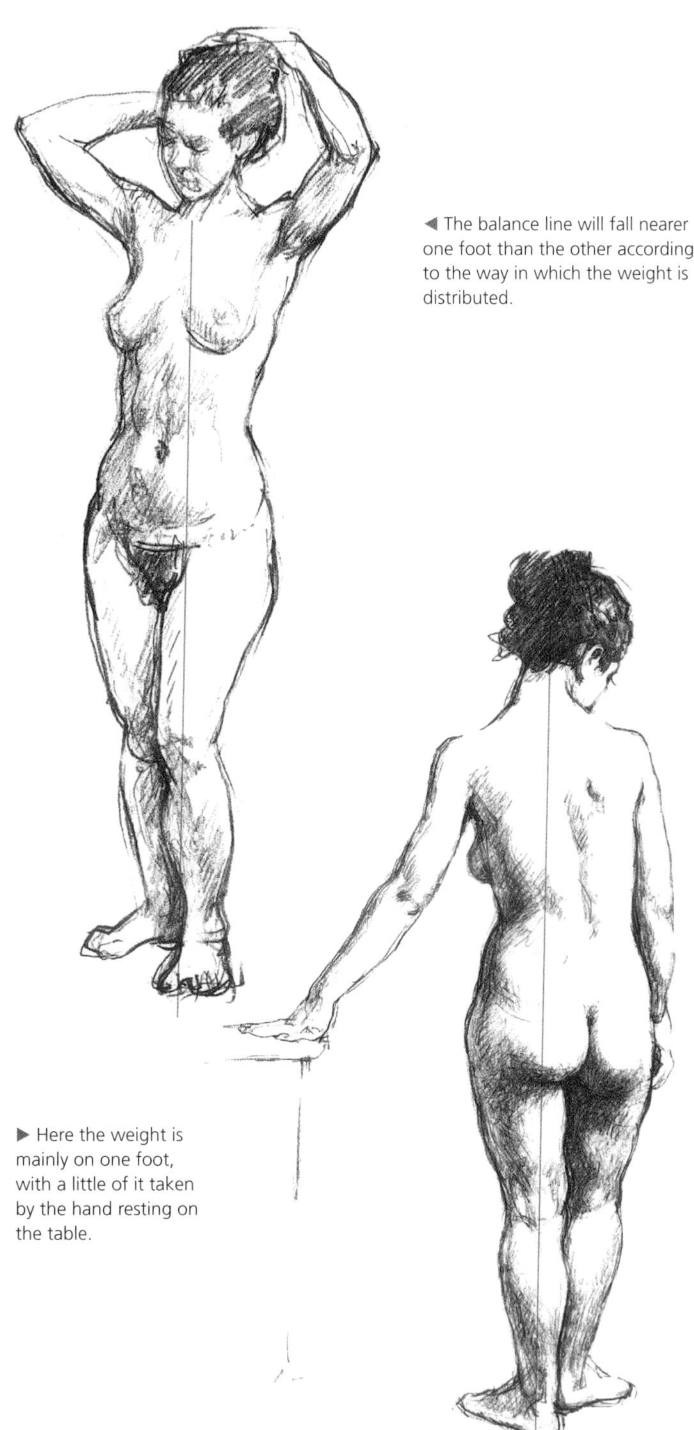

◀ The balance line will fall nearer one foot than the other according to the way in which the weight is distributed.

▶ Here the weight is mainly on one foot, with a little of it taken by the hand resting on the table.

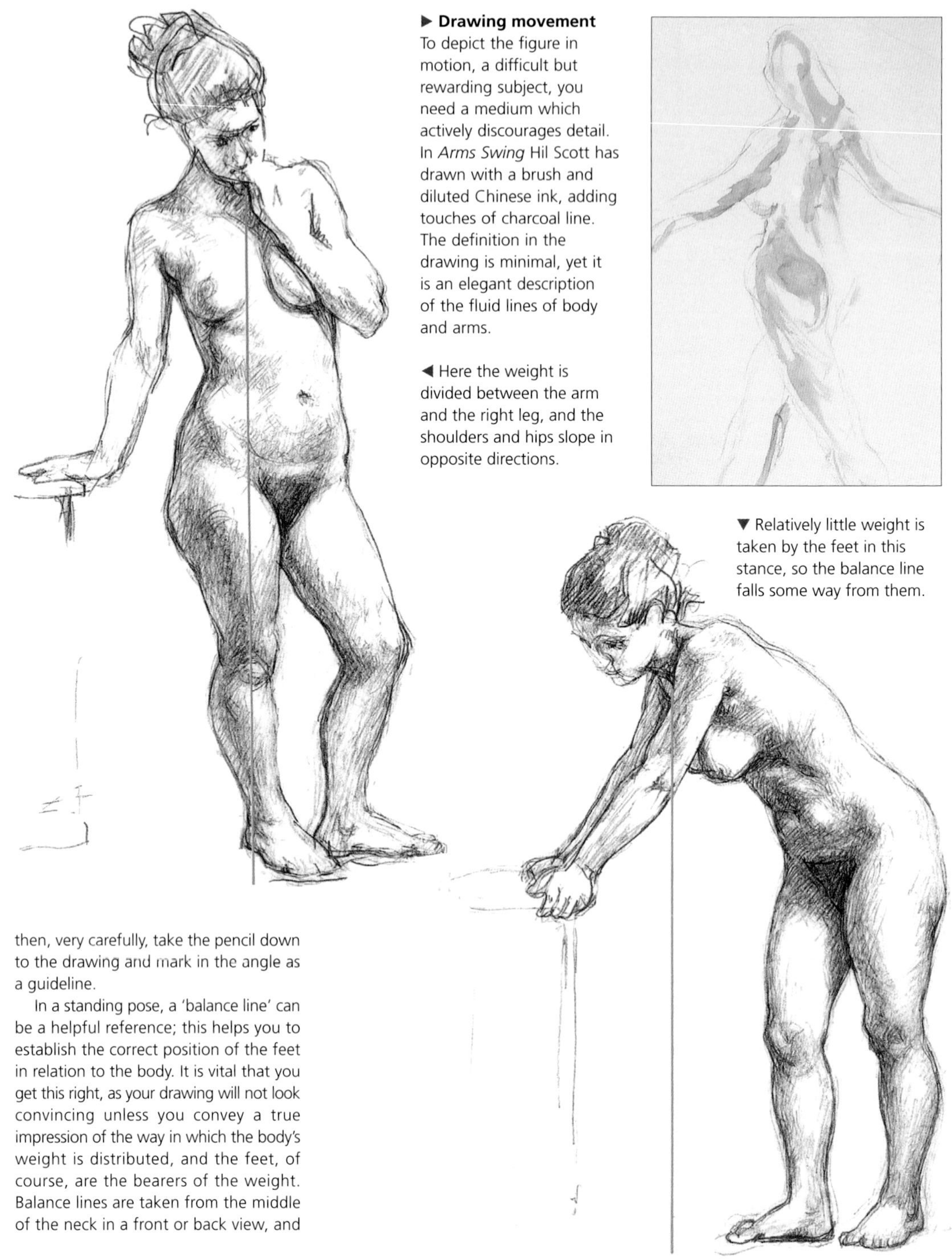

▶ **Drawing movement**
To depict the figure in motion, a difficult but rewarding subject, you need a medium which actively discourages detail. In *Arms Swing* Hil Scott has drawn with a brush and diluted Chinese ink, adding touches of charcoal line. The definition in the drawing is minimal, yet it is an elegant description of the fluid lines of body and arms.

◀ Here the weight is divided between the arm and the right leg, and the shoulders and hips slope in opposite directions.

▼ Relatively little weight is taken by the feet in this stance, so the balance line falls some way from them.

then, very carefully, take the pencil down to the drawing and mark in the angle as a guideline.

In a standing pose, a 'balance line' can be a helpful reference; this helps you to establish the correct position of the feet in relation to the body. It is vital that you get this right, as your drawing will not look convincing unless you convey a true impression of the way in which the body's weight is distributed, and the feet, of course, are the bearers of the weight. Balance lines are taken from the middle of the neck in a front or back view, and from the ear in a side view, down to the feet. If the model is standing with the weight evenly distributed, the balance line will fall between the feet, but if most of the weight is on one leg it will be considerably nearer the weight-bearing foot. The most accurate way to provide yourself with these vertical references is to check your view of the model using a plumbline, which simply consists of a piece of string with a weight at one end.

The way in which the distribution of weight affects the body is less obvious in a seated pose, but it is equally important to identify it, or the drawing will look stiff and unnatural. Here again it is essential to check alignments, either with a pencil or a plumbline. You can either use the same system of balance lines or mark in a central vertical line to which you can relate the position of the feet, head and various parts of the torso.

▶ Choosing the right medium
Children are notoriously restless and usually have to be drawn very fast. It is thus wise to choose a medium which enables you to work quickly and broadly. Ted Gould has used brown Conté crayon for his lovely *Mother and Child*, suggesting both form and detail with a few deft touches.

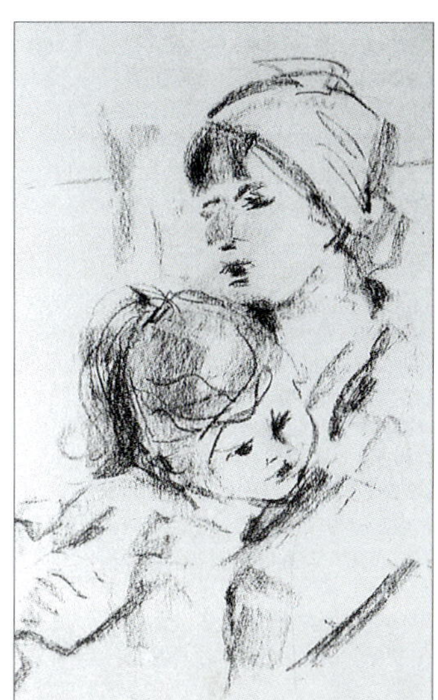

▼ The standing figure
As explained on the previous pages, it is vital to analyse the pose and to understand how the weight is distributed and how the whole body is affected by any movement. In his two brush-and-wash drawings James Horton captures beautifully both the swing of the body, and also its three-dimensional quality of mass and weight.

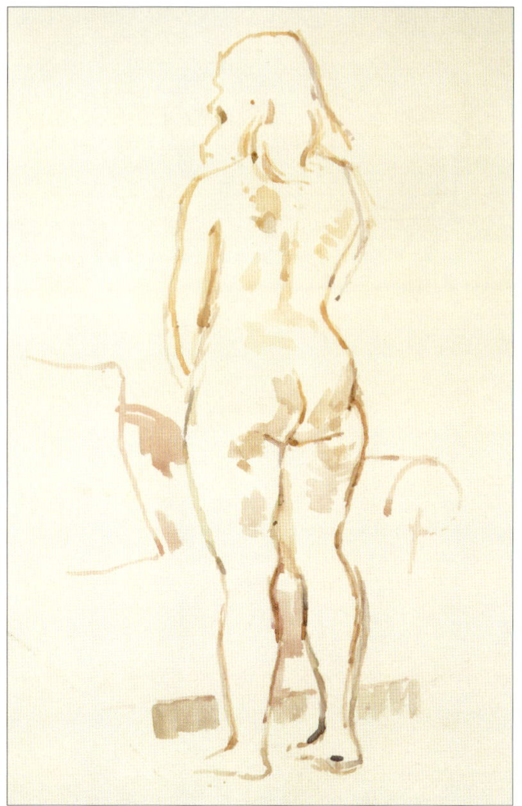

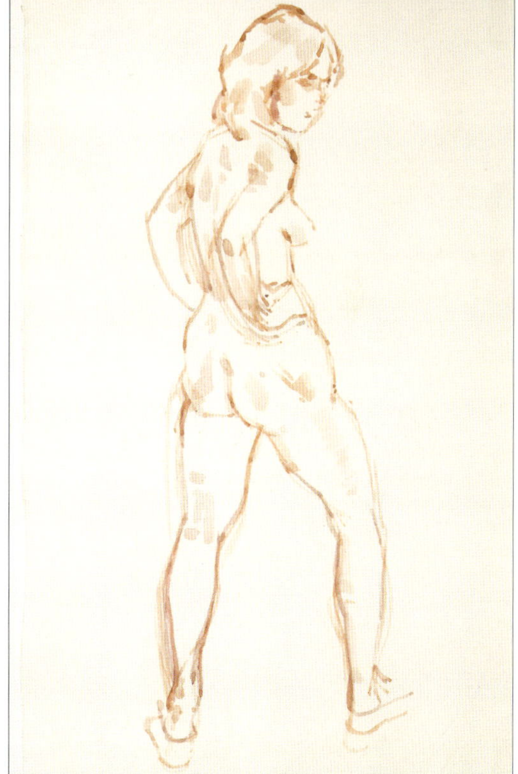

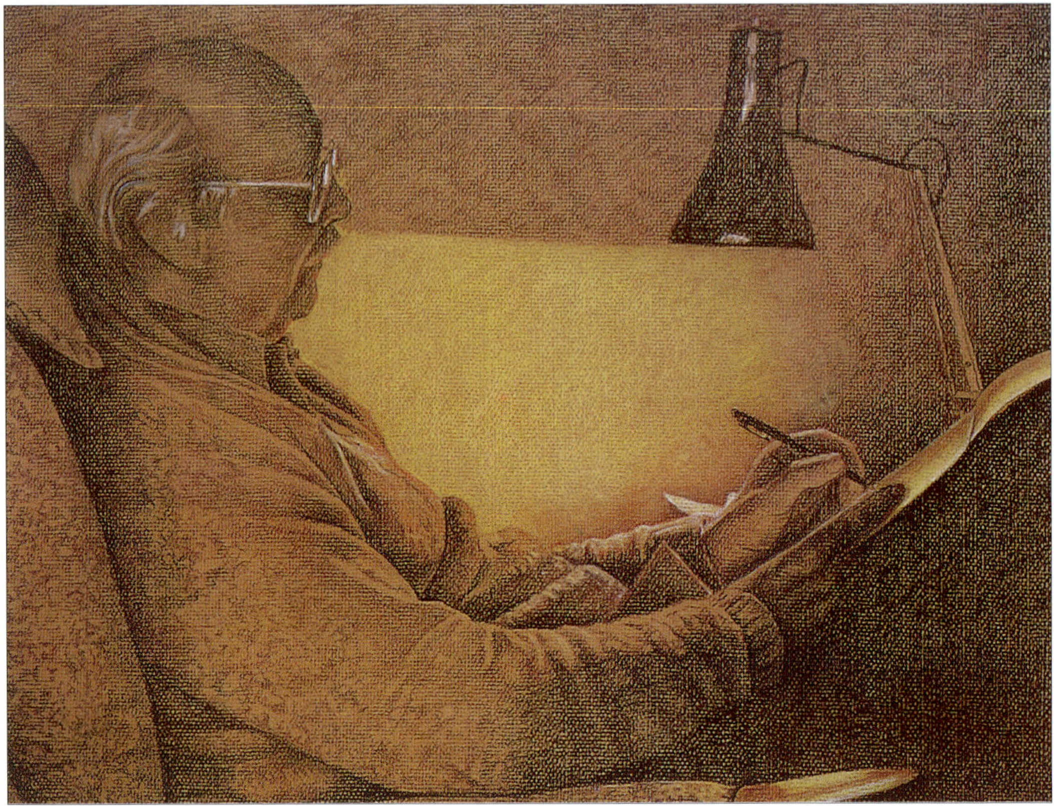

The clothed figure

Drawing people with their clothes on is perhaps slightly easier than drawing the nude, if only because there is far more opportunity to practise. You don't need to hire a professional model because you can draw people anywhere as long as you restrict yourself to quick sketches. If you get into the habit of carrying a sketchbook with you, you can find interesting subjects as you go about your daily life – sitting at a café table, waiting for a train or playing in the park.

For more thorough and detailed studies, however, you need to persuade someone to hold a pose for a reasonable length of time. Your friends or members of your family may oblige – indeed many people are flattered to be asked to pose. When you are deciding on a pose for your model, they will be more co-operative if you choose a position that is comfortable for them and easy to stay in. If they can read a book or do a crossword while posing they are less likely to fidget.

Clothing can be helpful in defining the forms beneath it, providing a set of contour lines, but it can also disguise form and confuse the issue in a bewildering way. A thin garment, for example, reveals the body, while a heavy overcoat gives little idea as to the shapes beneath or to the way its wearer is sitting or standing. In such cases you must look for clues, such as the angle of a protruding wrist and hand, the bend of an elbow or the slope of the shoulders.

The clothing itself can be difficult to draw; it often forms complicated shapes of its own and you can become so involved with drawing folds, or the pattern on a fabric, that you fail to make sense of the figure itself. You need to analyse what is causing the creases and

▲ Composing the drawing
Drawings can be made for practice, or they can simply be sketches of something which happens to take your fancy. A drawing, however, can also be carried out with the intention of producing a finished work, in which case you must consider composition. Paul Bartlett's *Father with Lamp* is as carefully composed as any painting, with the sweeping curves of the figure, chair and writing pad balanced by the table and the dark upright of the lamp.

▶ **Rounded forms**
This simple pencil drawing by Elisabeth Harden concentrates on the rounded nature of the female form. The relaxed pose and raised left leg are depicted in a flowing outline, with no sharp angles.

▼ **Composing with shapes**
In his pastel drawing, *Elly*, David Cuthbert has made an exciting composition by reducing detail and concentrating on the interplay of shapes – the curves of the limbs counterpointing the more geometric shapes of the clothing and chair.

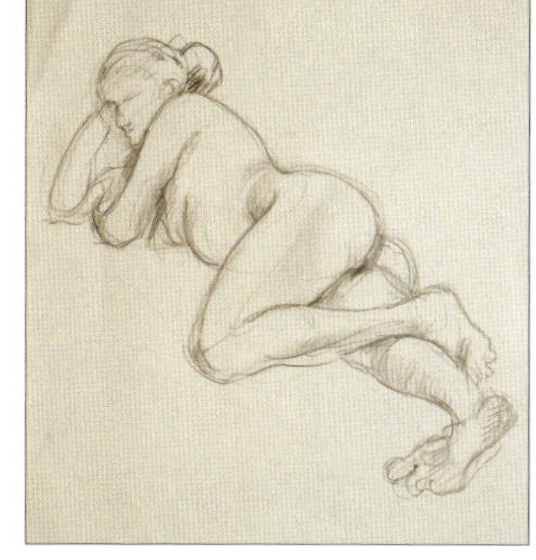

▼ **Drawing light**
Forms are described by the way in which the light falls on them, so in life drawing or portraiture it helps to have a fairly strong source of illumination. In Gerry Baptist's simple but powerful charcoal drawing, the light comes from one side, slightly behind the model, making a lovely pale shape across the shoulders and down the hip and leg.

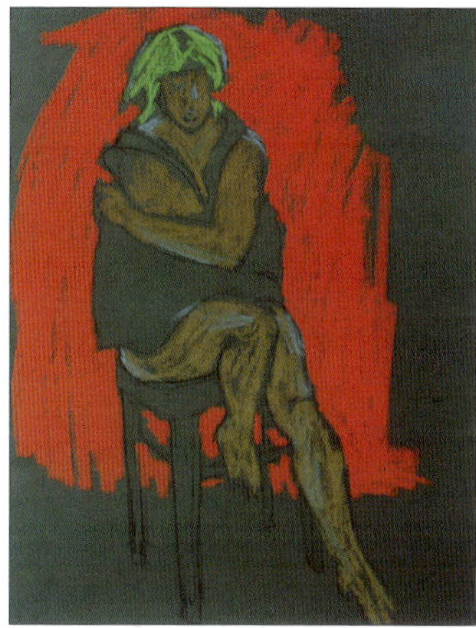

wrinkles – whether it is being stretched by a part of the body beneath, such as a knee or hipbone, or by the way the model is bending or twisting – and convey its soft texture by subtle variations in tone. Patterns such as checks and stripes present a challenge, but can also be used to accentuate form, and the way a loose garment folds, drapes and swings can be very useful if you are attempting to convey movement in a figure drawing,

Whatever kind of garments your subject is wearing, try to visualize the body beneath as you start to sketch out your drawing. Analyse the pose just as you would in a nude study, taking measurements and checking alignments of head, shoulders, feet and so on, and perhaps drawing in some light guidelines to indicate key points on the body, even if you can't see them.

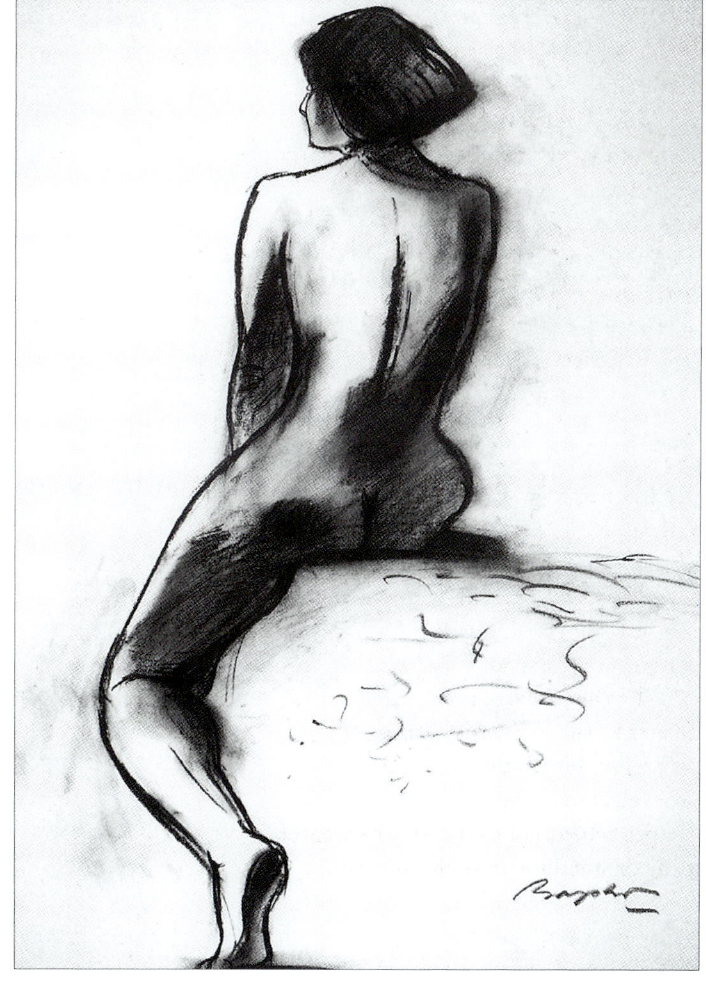

Drawing animals

As subjects, animals can be rewarding and frustrating in equal measure. Whether they are wild creatures, farm animals or household pets, animals make wonderful subjects, but unfortunately they are not the most co-operative of models. Even cats, which generally sleep for long periods, tend to wake up and walk away as soon as you reach for your sketchbook. However, many artists have portrayed animals successfully because they were fascinated by them, and this should be your sole criterion in choosing your subjects.

Observation and sketching

As with any branch of drawing, the secret lies in careful observation of detail, the determination not to be put off by failures and, most important of all in this context, the ability to tailor your methods to your subject. You will not be able to produce the kind of finished drawing you might achieve with a figure or an architectural subject, but you can make quick sketches, and a good sketch often says more than any amount of detail and polish.

You may find it difficult at first, because it does require some practice to be able to grasp the essentials of a subject and get them down on paper in a few minutes, or maybe just a few seconds. However, you will find that even your first, perhaps not very successful sketches will have sharpened your observational skills, and the next ones will be better for this reason. Sketching is a knack, and it really does become easier the more you do it. Use a medium you know you can control well and one that enables you to work quickly in both line and tone, such as soft pencil or Conté crayon.

Repeated movements

There is an element of memory involved in drawing anything in motion, particularly if the movement is rapid, because our eyes simply can't keep up with it. There is no one split second in which you can say, 'Ah, that's what the legs are doing.' Even the great eighteenth-century British artist George Stubbs, who specialized in horses, was unable to portray them convincingly in motion. It was not until the era of photography that the sequence of

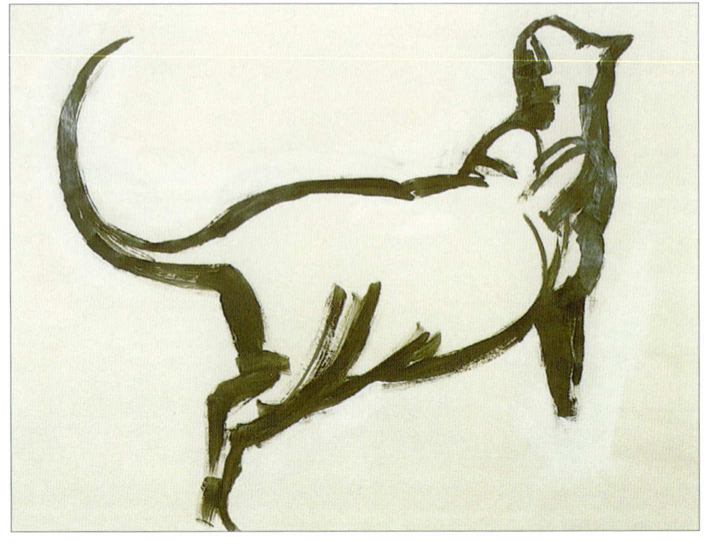

▲ **Rhythm and movement**
In an animal drawing, as in a figure study, it is important to convey the living quality of the creature and the way it moves, so choose a medium which allows you to work rapidly and freely. Judy Martin's *Cat Study* is a large-scale drawing: she likes to work 'from the elbow', and has drawn directly with a brush and acrylic paint. The diagonal placing of the animal on the paper, together with the sweeping curve of the tail, give a strong sense of movement.

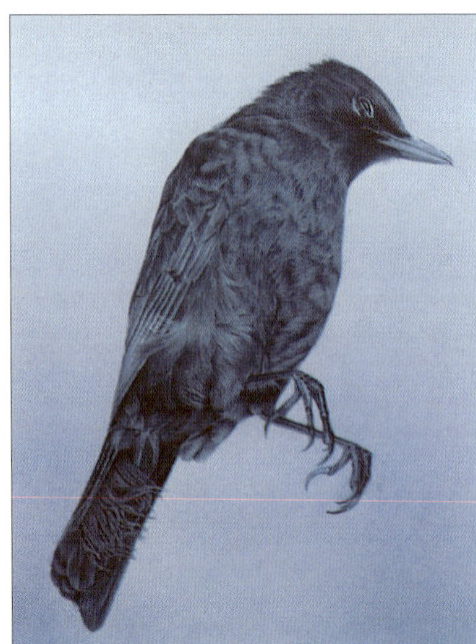

◀ **Drawing texture**
Texture, whether it is the rough, shaggy coat of a dog, the soft fur of a cat or the lustrous plumage of a bird, is one of the most attractive features of animal subjects, but you cannot concentrate on these qualities when you are trying to draw animals in motion so you will often have to work from photographs or museum specimens. In this pencil drawing, *Dead Bird*, Robert Maxwell Wood has taken advantage of the mortality of all creatures to give himself an excellent subject for close study.

movements made by a galloping horse was fully understood, making it much easier to comprehend the repetitive nature of most animals' movements. Look for these repeated movements when you are sketching, making several small sketches on the same page so that you have a complete visual record of all the different positions of the legs and body.

Photographic reference

The advent of photographs was invaluable to the nineteenth-century painters in correcting misconceptions about movement, and they still play an important part in providing reference for drawings and paintings. If you want to draw wild animals in their natural habitat – where they seldom even appear to order, let alone stay still – photographs are generally the only option available for reference.

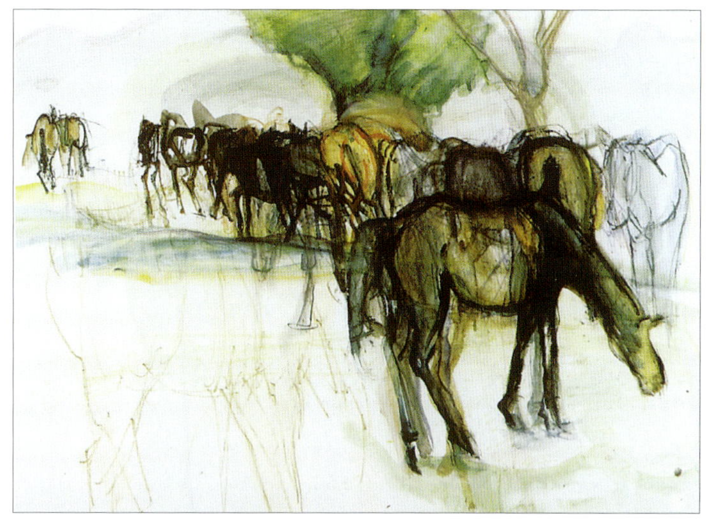

▼ Shape and pattern
This pencil drawing is a preliminary design for a print, a medium in which three-dimensional form is less important than the arrangement of shapes. What first attracted Elisabeth Harden to the subject was the shapes of the animals' markings, which she has stressed with firm outlines and shading.

▲ Keeping up with movement
Even when quietly grazing, animals will shift their weight and make other small movements. Karen Raney, in her coloured-ink drawing *French Horses*, has begun with light lines and washes, and delayed finalizing the positions of limbs and feet with more positive colours until the later stages.

▼ Multiple drawings
As animals tend to repeat their movements, another approach is to make several drawings simultaneously, as Vicky Lowe has done in her brush-and-wash studies of rabbits. This means you can work on different drawings as the creature moves, and creates the feeling of an animated cartoon.

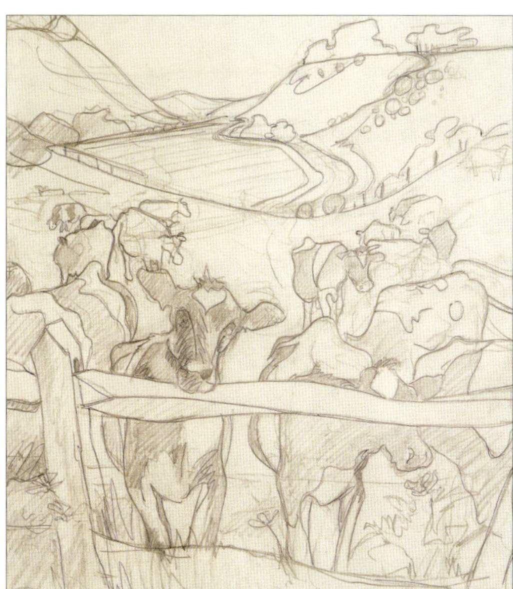

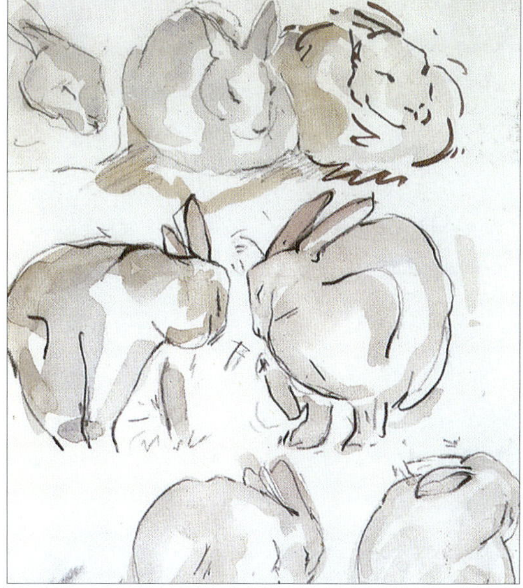

Drawing buildings

The man-made environment of cities, towns and villages provides a wealth of varied and exciting drawing subjects, whether you are interested in architectural styles or simply in atmosphere. It is sometimes thought that drawing buildings is a special skill, but, although detailed 'architectural renderings' are specialized and have a particular purpose, buildings and townscapes present no more of a problem than any other subject, and are almost certainly easier than drawing the nude human figure. What puts many people off is the word 'perspective' – most of us know that linear perspective is based on mathematics and, for those of us who failed to grasp the principles of geometry at school, that can be quite enough to cause alarm and despondency.

Converging parallels

It is true that the laws of perspective were arrived at originally through mathematics, but it is not true that they cannot be understood by non-mathematical people. The basic rules are really very simple, and they always bear out the evidence of your own eyes. Most people must at some time have walked or driven down a straight road and noticed how the two sides appear to converge in the distance. This apparent meeting of receding parallel lines is one of the many tricks the eye plays with reality – the lines don't really meet, but in visual terms they do, and drawing is concerned with what we see. Without perspective it would be impossible to create the illusion of our three-dimensional surroundings on a flat piece of paper.

As parallel lines appear to come closer and closer together until they meet, it follows that all objects appear smaller the further away they are. Imagine a row of identical buildings along the road. If you were to draw one line through the top of the roofs and another below the doors, they would be receding parallel lines too, and would meet at the same place on the horizon, known as the vanishing point, as those for the sides of the road, with the houses becoming smaller and smaller. Again, the effect of this law of diminishing size is something that everyone must have observed.

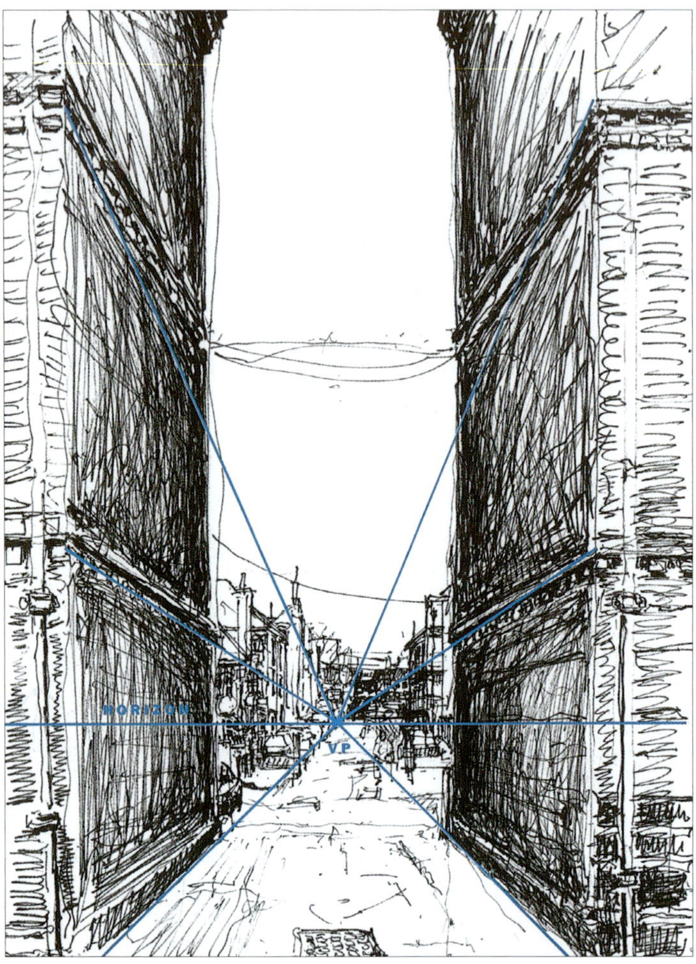

Perspective by eye

Although the horizon is an imaginary line, it is not arbitrary – it is your own eye level. This is why perspective changes as soon as you move your own viewpoint, even from a sitting to a standing position. You have changed the horizon, the vanishing point and the direction of the parallel lines.

There is, of course, the further complication that there are often two or more different vanishing points. In an old town or village, for example, houses may be set at odd angles to each other, resulting in many different vanishing points. In such

▲ Central vanishing point
The drawing has been done from a central position, so the vanishing point is also in the centre, with the receding parallel lines sloping down to the horizon line, which is at the level of the artist's eye. In fact the receding lines at the top of the drawing are not entirely correct – they should slope more steeply – but drawings can often be the better for small inaccuracies in the perspective provided they still make visual sense. All three drawings on these pages, by John Townend, are in pen and ink.

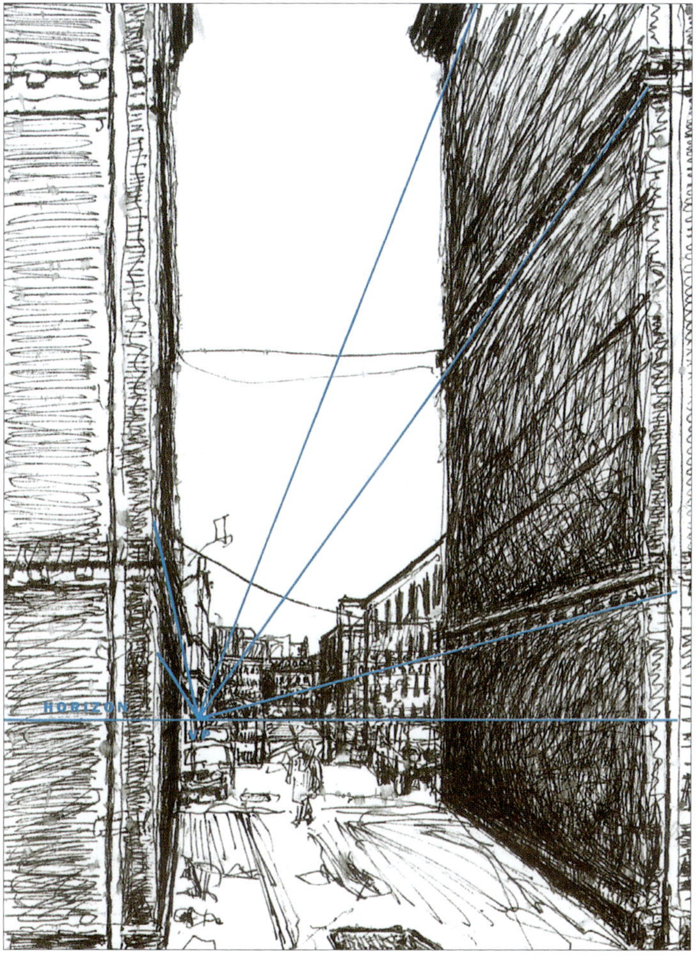

cases you cannot possibly establish the exact position of each vanishing point, but it is important to mark in the horizon line and, if possible, the vanishing point for one key building in the scene before you. You can work out the correct angles for the other receding lines by holding up a pencil or ruler and tilting it until it coincides with the edge of the roof, the window tops or other features, as explained in the section on figure drawing.

You do not have to get all the vanishing points exactly right – indeed this will be impossible, as some of them may be far outside the picture area – but do make checks from time to time if you see something that doesn't look right. If you misjudge one angle and try to relate all the others to it the drawing will become distorted. And if you are bad at drawing straight lines don't be afraid to use a ruler, at least at the start of a drawing. Vertical lines really do have to be vertical in architectural subjects.

Scale and proportion

Proportion is every bit as important as perspective – perhaps even more so. While it is correct (or reasonably correct) perspective that ensures that a building does not look as if it is about to fall over, it is well-observed proportion that conveys character. You would not expect to draw a portrait without paying attention to the size of your sitter's eyes in relation to his or her face, but it is surprising how many people ignore the importance of the size of windows and doors, or the heights of roofs in relation to walls.

▲ Moving position
The artist has now moved to the left and the vanishing point has changed position. The horizon, however, remains constant, as this drawing was done from the same level as the first one.

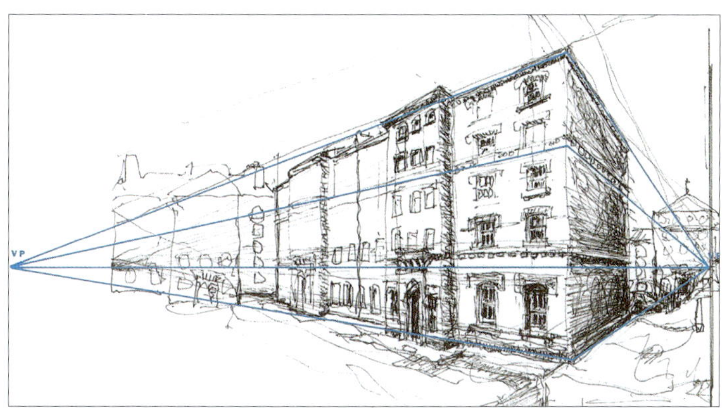

▶ Two vanishing points
The majority of architectural subjects have at least two different vanishing points, depending on how many planes there are and the angle from which they are viewed. Here there are two, with the converging parallels sloping more sharply down to the horizon line on the right.

When drawing a prominent designed building such as a historic cathedral or a fine country house, such factors are naturally taken into account, because the grand scale of the building or the carefully planned balance of the architectural features are the principal attractions of the subject. But scale and proportion are always important, even when your subject is an old wooden barn or a higgledy-piggledy collection of cottages or town houses; these are the characteristics that will give your drawing a convincing 'sense of place'.

▼ Interiors
The inside of a building is as interesting and rewarding to draw as the exterior, and you have the additional bonus of being protected both from the weather and inquisitive eyes. In his pen-and-ink drawing *The Church Organ Before Renovation* John Townend has made an exciting composition based on the interplay of curves and diagonal lines.

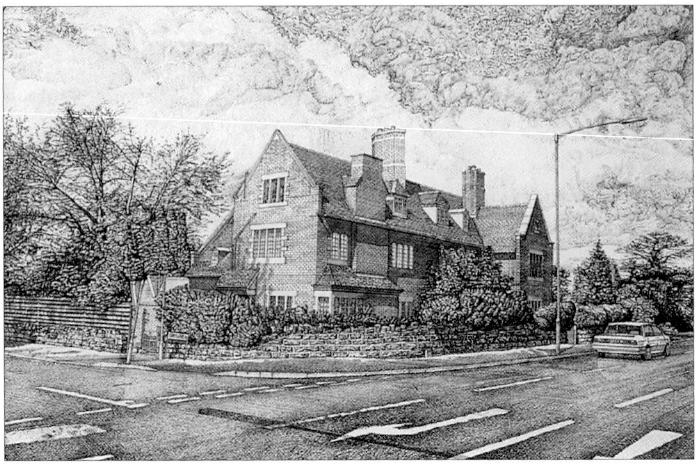

▲ Perspective and proportion
In Paul Bartlett's pen-and-ink drawing, a study made for a painting, the perspective is impressively accurate, as is the observation of the building's proportions. Notice the care taken over the number of bars in each window and the exact size of each brick and roof tile.

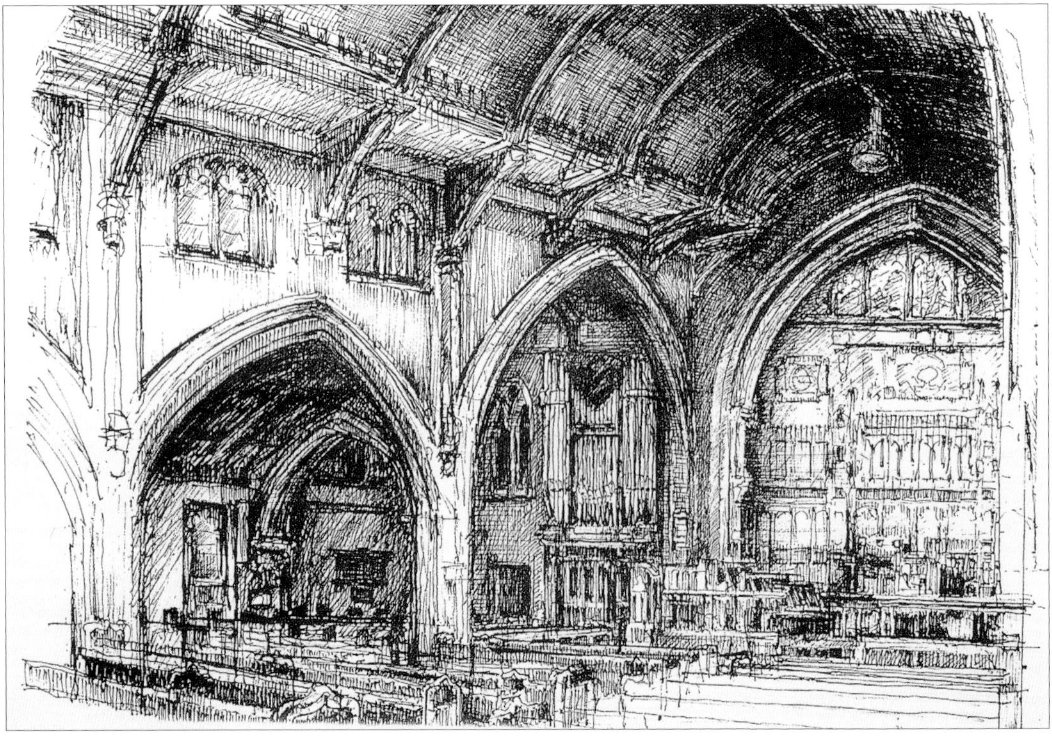

Relative sizes can be measured by holding up a pencil at arm's length and moving your thumb up and down it, but if you are drawing sight-size (that is, at the scale at which you are looking at the building) you can be more accurate by using a ruler to read off the actual measurements. Work out the height of the building in relation to its width, the proportion between wall and roof, and the number and size of the windows. Don't forget that the laws of diminishing size make the spaces between the windows become smaller as they recede, as well as the windows themselves – this is a trap for the unwary. Be particularly careful with doors, as they will look structurally impossible if they are too small, and bizarre if they are too large – doors are designed so that the average person can pass comfortably in and out without having to stoop or walk in sideways. Drawing people in a townscape gives an indication of scale as well as creating a feeling of atmosphere, but make sure that the doors you draw in the buildings can accommodate them.

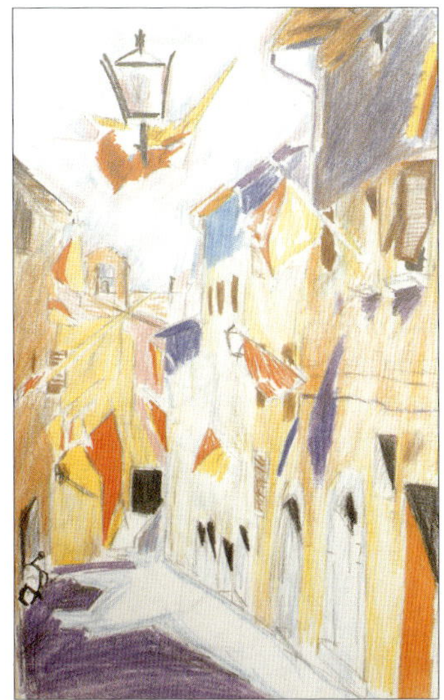

▲ **Shapes and colours**
Town scenes provide an opportunity to explore contrasts of shape, texture and colour. In his sketchbook study in coloured pencil, David Cuthbert's interest is primarily in the lively patterns made by the buildings, street furniture, flags and shadows.

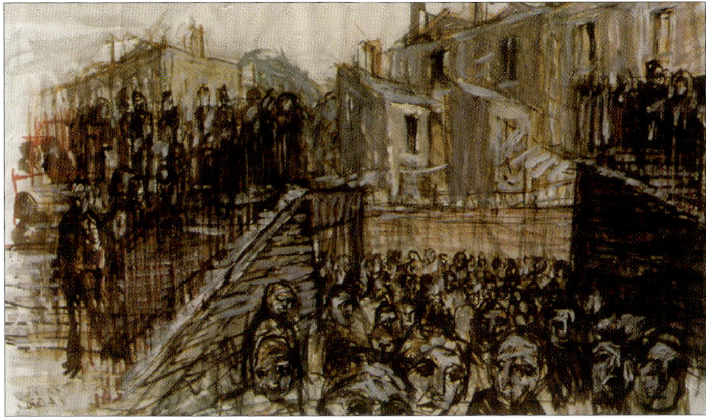

▲ **Buildings as a setting**
In Gerald Cains's mixed-media drawing *Open End, Ashton Gate* (in acrylic, watercolour and ink) it is the people who claim attention rather than buildings, which merely provide an urban setting. He has created a very powerful and rather sinister effect by playing with scale; the foreground figures on the steps dwarf their surroundings.

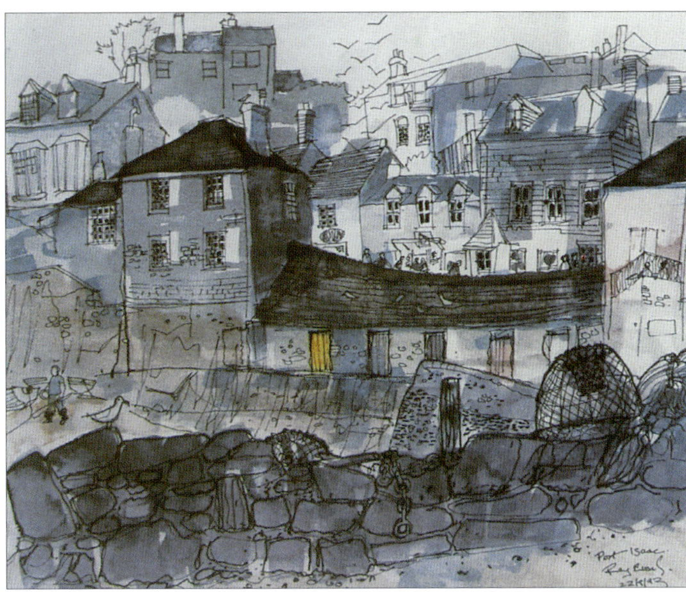

▶ **Composition**
Making a finished drawing from sketches or photographs gives you more opportunity to adjust reality. Ray Evans sketches continually to amass a store of visual information, and when he makes finished drawings he often combines elements from several sketchbook studies. His *Port Isaac* is in pen and watercolour.

Blending with coloured pencils

The hues of coloured pencils cannot be mixed physically. Each colour keeps its integrity when applied, so the only way to blend or mix colours is to allow this to happen optically.

This can be achieved in several ways, and a combination of techniques may be used in the same image. One way is to apply the colour so that it sits in layers, one over the other, rather like a thin watercolour wash or glaze. The reason for applying thin layers is that coloured pencils contain wax, which can build up on the paper surface and make it difficult to apply further layers. Colour can be applied dark over light or light over dark; the resulting effect and colour mix will differ depending on whether the darker or the lighter colour is applied first.

Colour can also be applied as a series of crosshatched lines – parallel lines that run across one another at an angle. Where the colour comes into contact with the support, it remains bright; where it crosses another colour, the two mix optically. Colours can also be scribbled loosely on to the support, in an action that mixes the first two techniques.

Depth of colour is achieved by increasing the density of the marks – by making them closer together or increasing the amount of pressure on the pencil.

Finally, coloured pencil marks can be made to mix and blend together optically on the support by adopting a technique used by the Pointillists, whereby colour is applied as tiny individual dots. It is the proximity and density of these marks that gives the depth and quality of the colour. This technique is time-consuming and is best used on relatively small drawings.

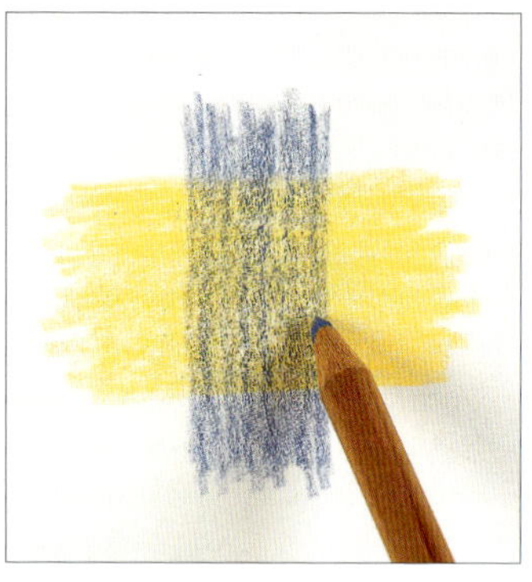

Dark over light
A layer of blue applied over yellow results in a dark green.

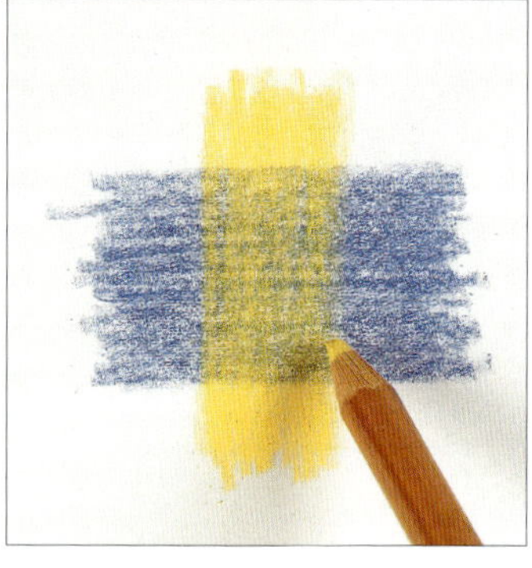

Light over dark
A layer of yellow applied over the same blue results in a light green.

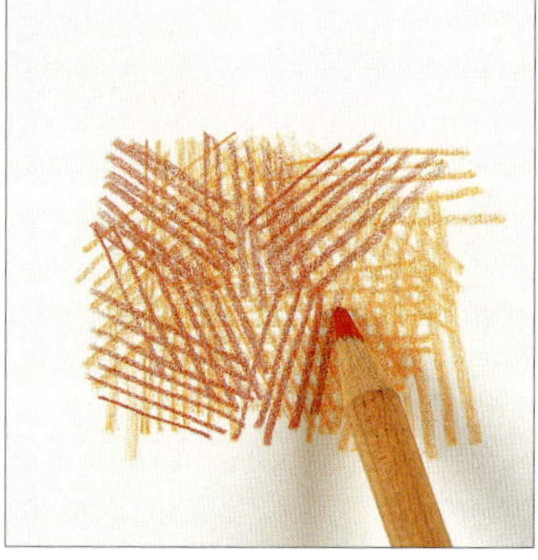

Crosshatched lines in two colours
Red lines crosshatched over yellow mix optically to make orange.

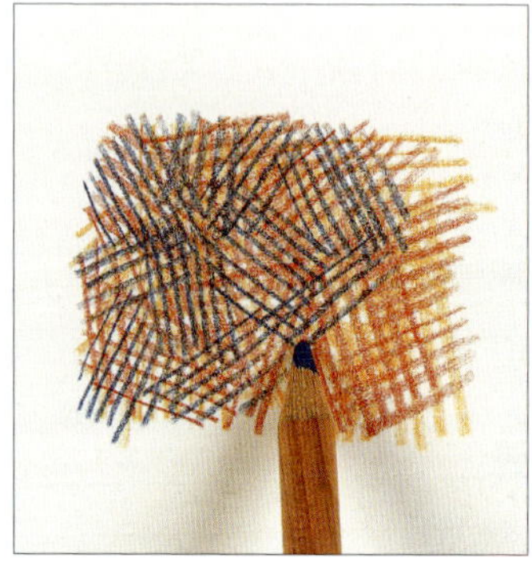

Crosshatched lines in three colours
Add blue and the overall effect is that the swatch appears brown – yet all the applied colours have kept their individual integrity.

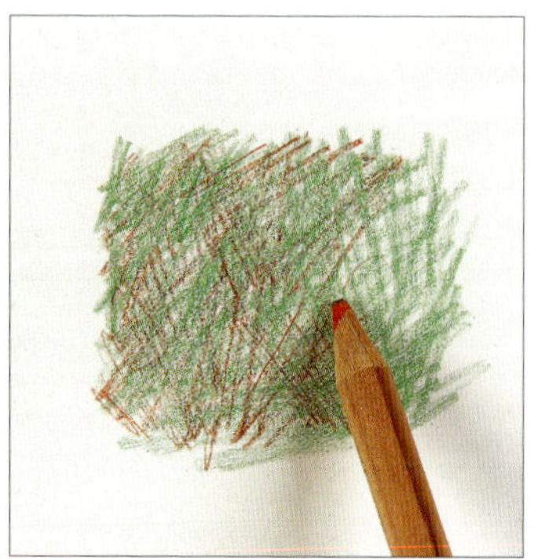

Loose scribbles
Colours can also be mixed optically by loosely scribbling one over another. Here, red is applied over green to make a brown.

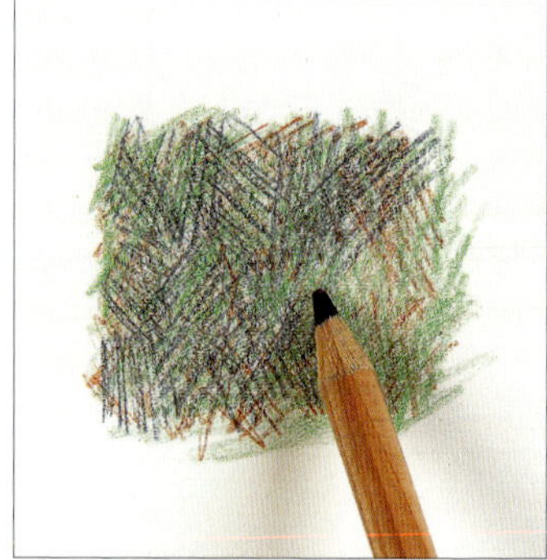

Rich optical blends
As each colour retains its integrity when blended in this way, the result is likely to look much more lively than an application of a single colour.

Practice exercise

To practise blending coloured pencils, choose a simple subject that contains a limited range of colours. Here, the artist selected a red and green apple – a good subject to begin with, as the colour and surface texture are naturally uneven, so you need not be as precise as you would when drawing a very smooth, evenly coloured surface.

Spend plenty of time looking at your subject to work out where one colour shifts into another. Above all, apply the colour loosely and lightly so that underlying colours can show through, creating lively and interesting optical mixes. To build up the necessary depth of colour you will need to apply a number of thin, light layers – a slow process, but one that merits the effort.

Materials

- *Heavyweight smooth drawing paper*
- *2B pencil*
- *Coloured pencils: zinc yellow, bright green, pale vermilion, deep vermilion, deep cadmium yellow, raw umber, Vandyke brown, olive green*

The subject

The greens in this apple range from a very yellowy green on the right-hand side to quite a bright mid-toned green in the centre. Similarly, the reds range from a delicate blush to a rich red at the top and side.

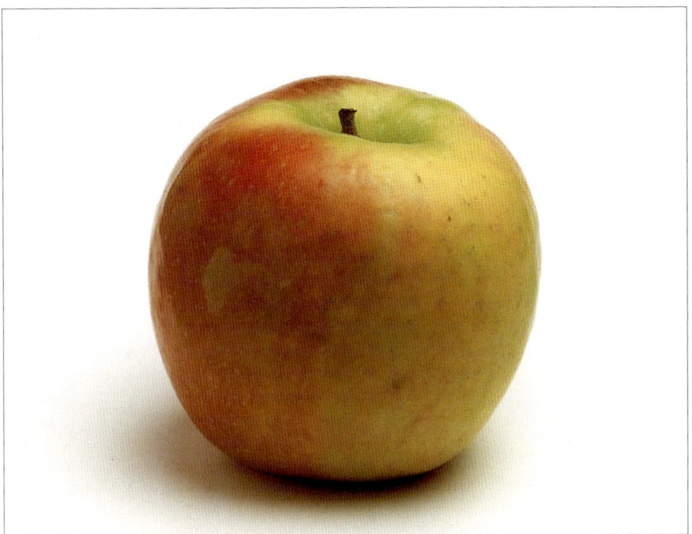

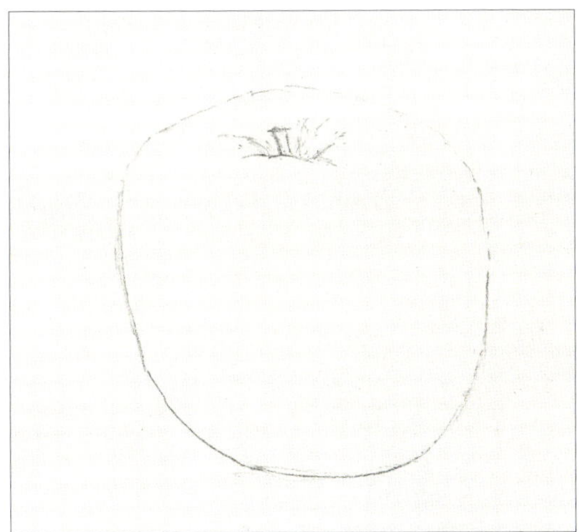

1 Using a 2B pencil, outline the shape of the apple, remembering that it is a rounded form. Put in the stalk, observing the angle. The stalk forms a central axis that runs all the way through to the base of the apple; if you bear this in mind you will find it easier to get the shape at the base right. Also put in the recessed area around the stalk.

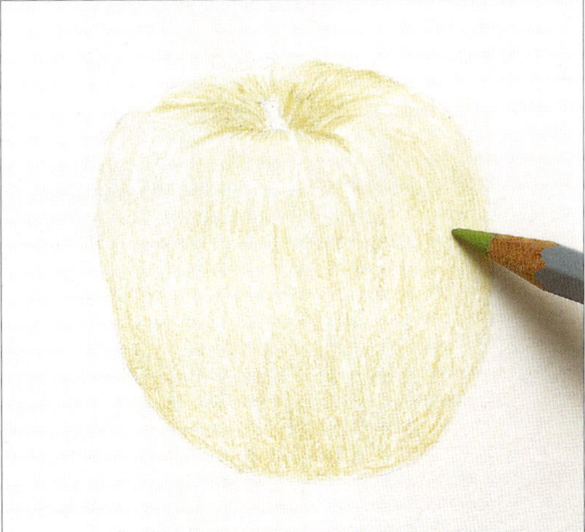

2 Lightly fill in the whole of the apple, using a zinc yellow pencil. This colour will stand for even the brightest highlights; leaving the paper white for the highlights would look too stark. Apply a bright green over all the areas that will be green in the final image. Use light strokes that follow the form of the subject.

▶

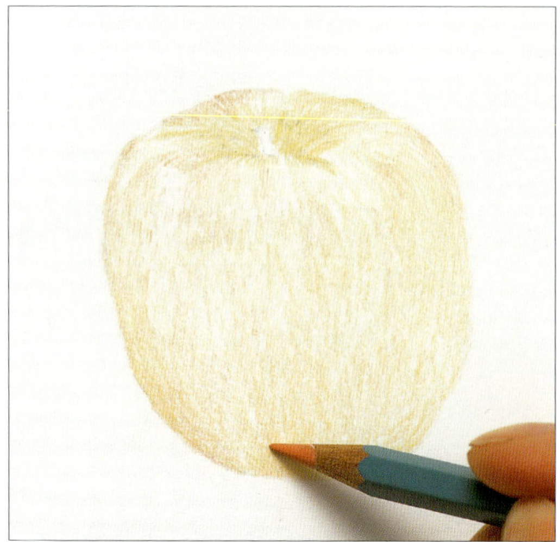

3 Using a pale vermilion pencil, lightly put in the first reds on the apple. Note that the apple itself is not completely smooth in texture or even in tone, so apply the colour unevenly, allowing some of the underlying yellow and green that you applied in Step 2 to show through. Again, make sure your pencil strokes follow the form of the apple.

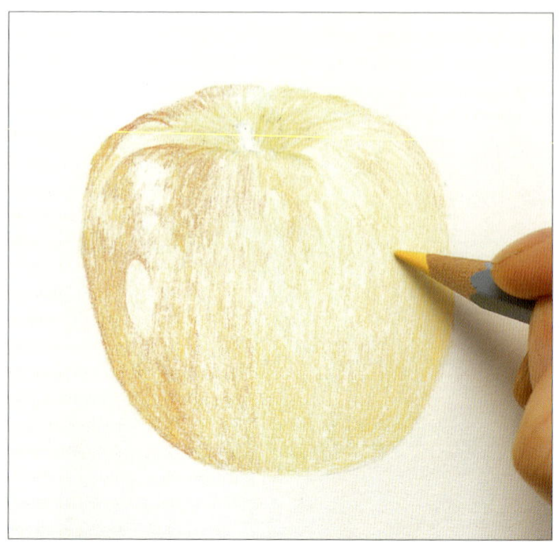

4 Working around the very brightest highlights, strengthen the reds by applying deep vermilion, noting how the colour combines optically with the underlying zinc yellow to make an orangey red. Now look for the more yellow areas of green on the apple, and go over them with a deep cadmium yellow pencil.

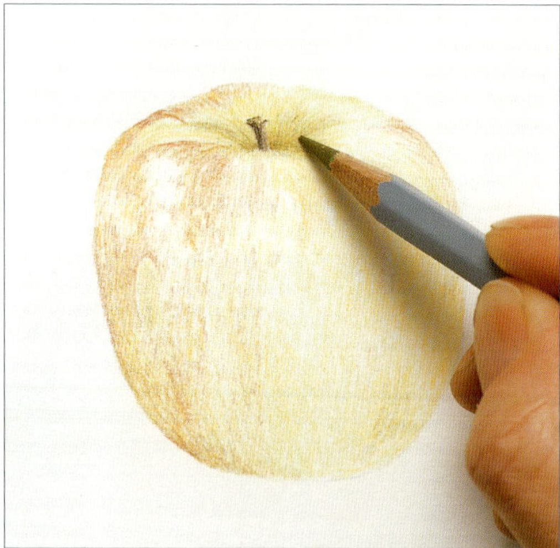

5 Now colour in the stalk. It is a darker brown on one side than the other, because of the way the light hits it, so alternate between raw umber for the paler brown areas and Vandyke brown for the darker areas. Using an olive green pencil, lightly draw the indentations in the skin around the stalk. As a result of this shading, the apple is beginning to develop some form and depth.

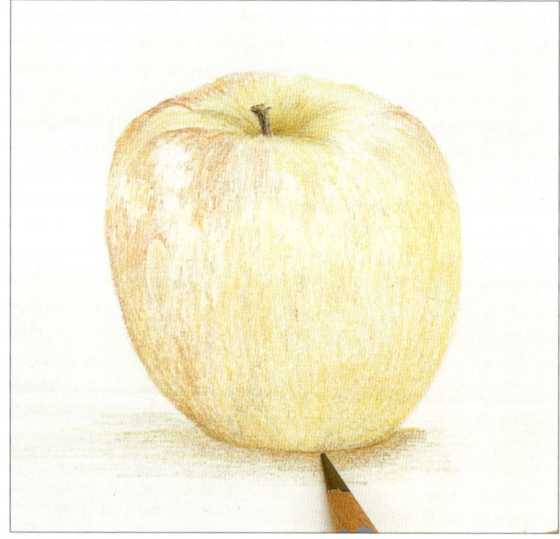

6 Still using the olive green pencil, put in the darker areas of green on the apple and the shadow underneath it. The shadow helps to anchor the subject on a surface: it no longer looks as if it is floating in mid-air. Some colours from the apple (red and brown, in particular) are reflected in the shadow, so put these colours in very lightly to give some visual continuity to the picture.

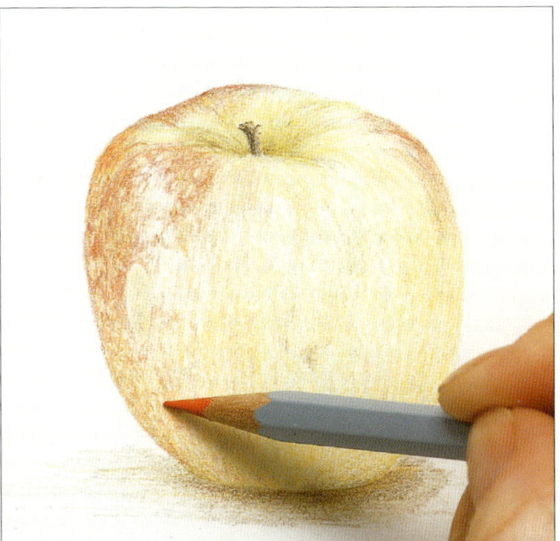

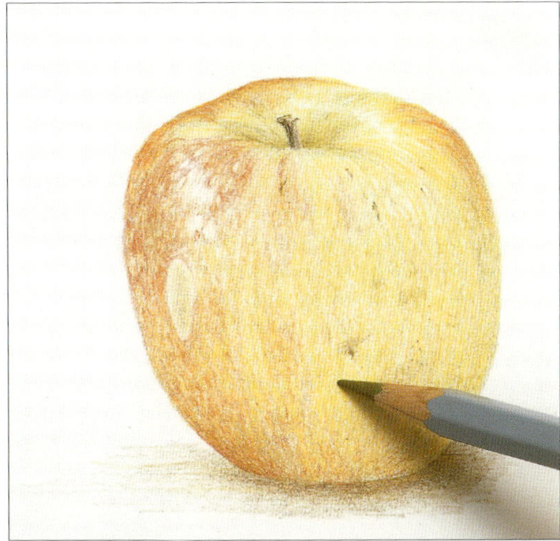

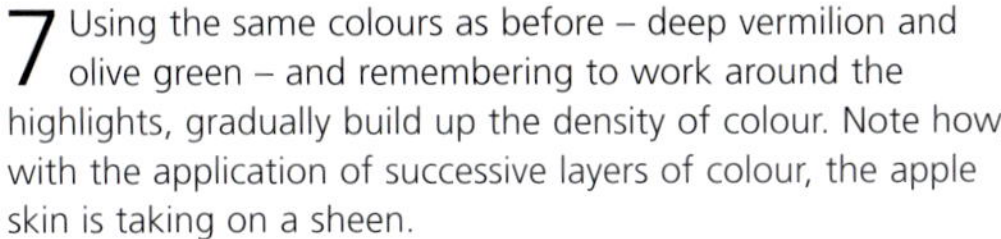

7 Using the same colours as before – deep vermilion and olive green – and remembering to work around the highlights, gradually build up the density of colour. Note how, with the application of successive layers of colour, the apple skin is taking on a sheen.

8 Working slowly and methodically, continue building up the density of colour, using the same colours as before and light pencil strokes. Finally, use the olive green pencil to put in the dark, mottled patches on the apple skin and add some texture to the drawing.

The finished drawing

At first glance, this is a deceptively simple drawing – but note how effectively the artist has built up the layers of colour to create a beautifully textured surface in which the colours combine optically into a seamless whole. Coloured pencils are the perfect medium for conveying the mottled coloration of the apple skin: they can be used to cover both broad areas and precise points of detail.

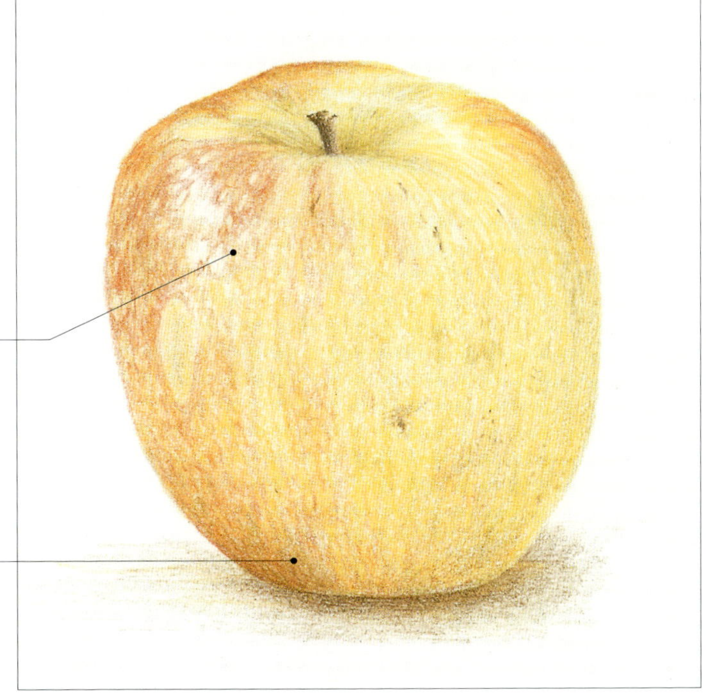

The contrast between the very bright highlight and the dark red of the apple skin helps to make the fruit look shiny.

Thin strokes of the pencil allow the underlying colours to remain visible.

Blending with water-soluble pencils

Water-soluble coloured pencils behave in exactly the same way as non-soluble coloured pencils and you can use exactly the same techniques of scribbling, hatching and glazing to blend them. The difference is that when you apply water, the dry pigment breaks down and becomes liquid colour – and then behaves in the same way as watercolour paint.

Applications of colours look clean and bright when applied dry, because each applied colour, in effect, remains separate from those around it. Once water is applied and the colours mix together physically, however, the colour may look dull and dirty. The answer is to keep to simple, two-colour mixes.

Remember that once water has been applied and the colours blended, the image can be dried and further applications of dry colour applied over the top. These, in turn, can be worked into and the process repeated several times, just as when painting in watercolour.

An alternative way of applying water-soluble pencils is to apply a wash of clean water to the support and work into it, taking care not to damage the surface by digging the sharp pencil tips into the softened paper fibres.

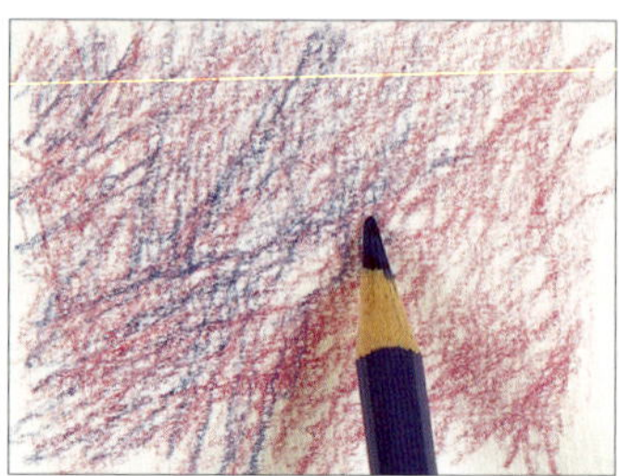

Applying water-soluble pencils
Water-soluble pencils are applied in exactly the same way as conventional coloured pencils.

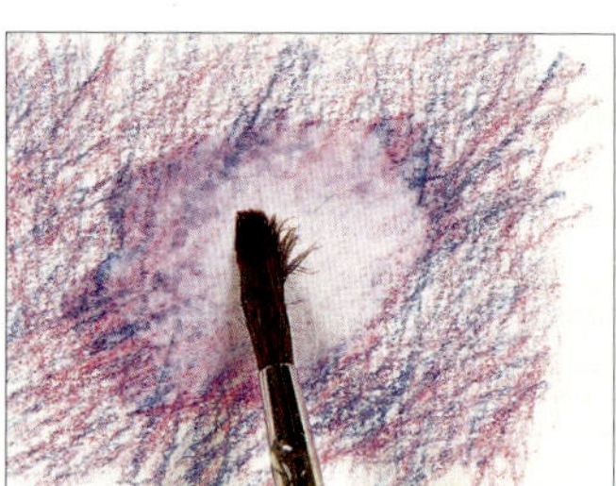

Applying water
When water is applied, the coloured pencil work is converted into watercolour.

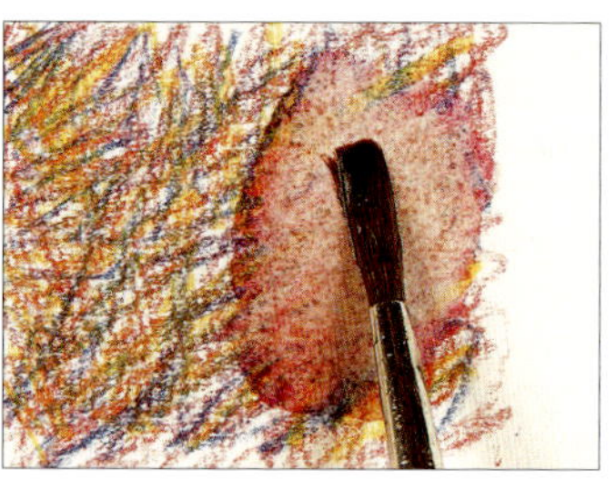

Muddy mixes
Beware of combining too many colours, as the mixes can look dirty when water is applied.

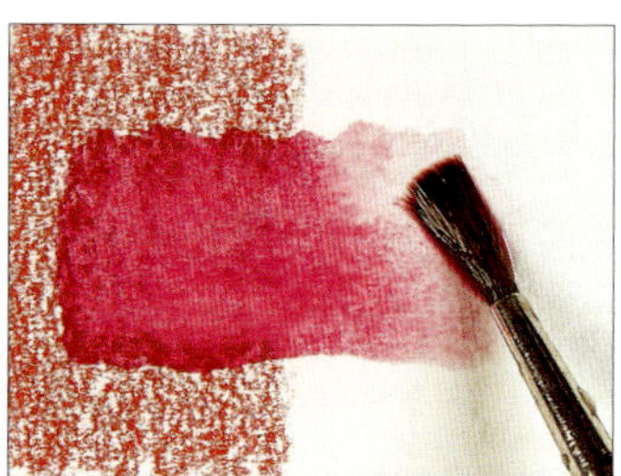

Varying the tone
To lighten the tone, add more water or lift off wet pigment with the brush or a piece of kitchen paper.

Practice exercise: **Bananas**

This exercise allows you to use water-soluble pencils in a linear fashion to draw the shape and facets of the bananas, and as a kind of watercolour, by brushing with clean water.

When you set up an exercise like this at home, the key is to keep it simple! If you choose a complicated group of objects with too many colours, the chances are that when you add water to the pencil work, your washes will look muddy.

Materials

- *HP watercolour paper*
- *Water-soluble pencils: yellow ochre, mid-green, burnt sienna, bright yellow, dark brown, violet*
- *Brush*
- *Clean water*

The set-up
A plain background provides a contrast in colour without detracting from the main subject. Here, a light was placed to one side of the bananas so that some facets were in shadow. The difference in tone between the light and the dark facets is what will make the subject look three-dimensional.

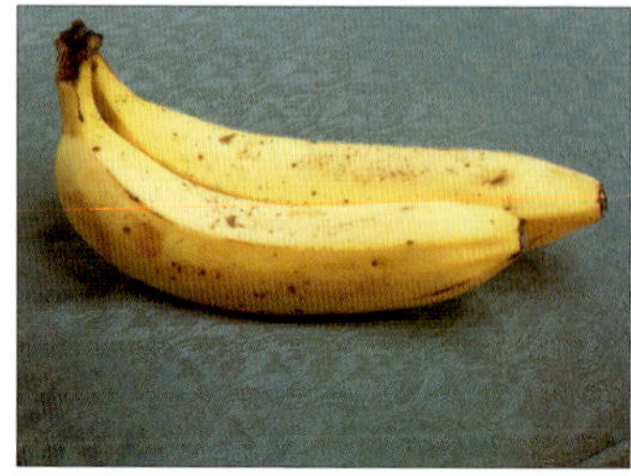

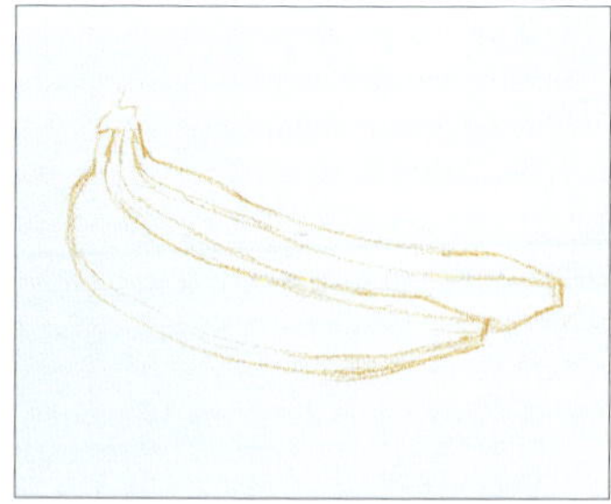

1 Lightly sketch the bananas using a yellow ochre water-soluble pencil. (This is the mid-toned yellow of the bananas. The hard line will disappear when you brush over clean water in the later stages of the drawing.) Indicate the different facets of the fruit as well as the outline shape.

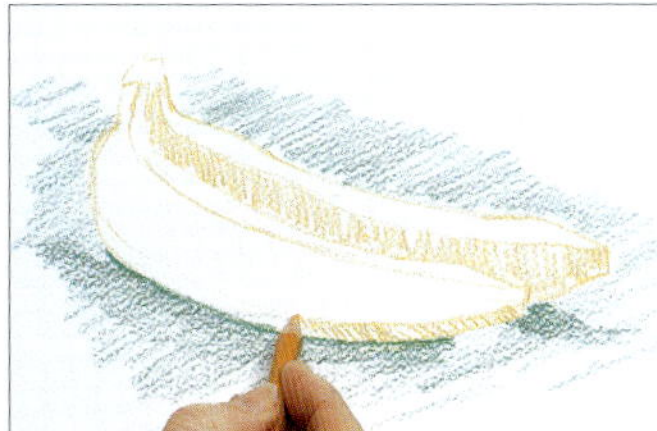

2 Block in the background with a mid-green water-soluble pencil, applying more pressure for the shaded area under the fruit. Apply yellow ochre to the shaded facets of the bananas.

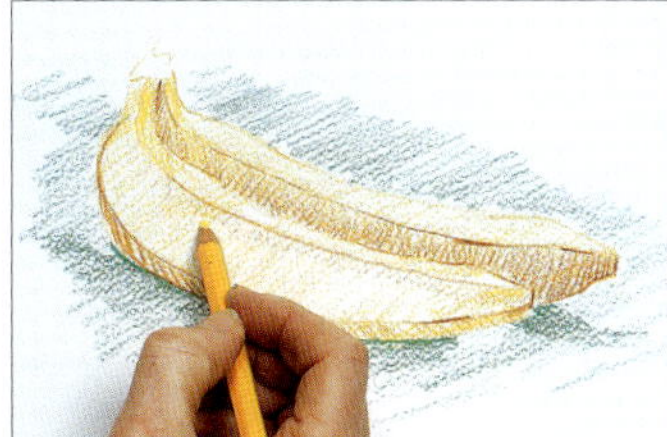

3 Loosely hatch the darkest parts of the bananas with burnt sienna, allowing some of the underlying colour to show through. Apply bright yellow loosely all over the bananas.

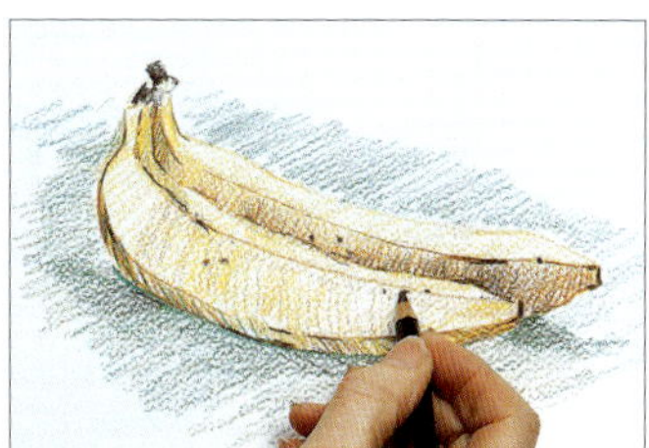

4 Draw the stems with a dark brown water-soluble pencil and dot in some dark marks on the bananas. Apply more burnt sienna over the most deeply shaded facets.

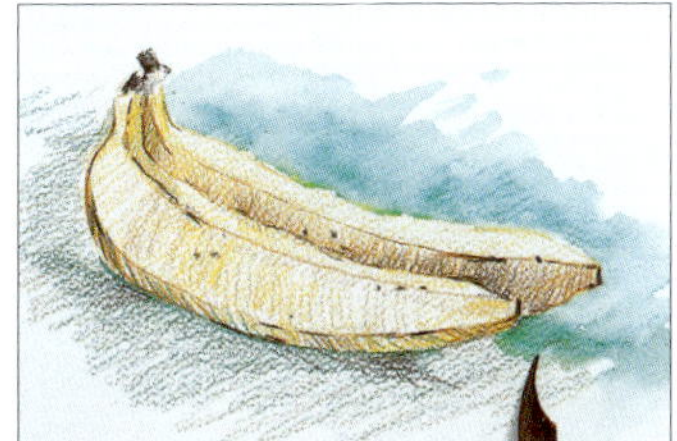

5 Dip a brush in clean water and carefully brush over the background, making sure you do not brush any of the background colour on to the bananas. You can move the pigment around on the support in exactly the same way as you can with watercolour paint. Leave to dry. (If you wish, you can use a hairdryer to speed up the drying process.)

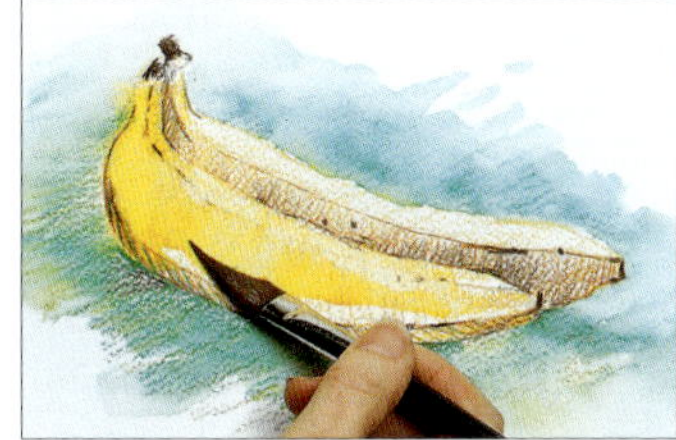

6 Clean your brush and brush over the bananas. Take care not to apply too much water, or it may spread on to the background.

Tip: If you want to vary the tone in parts, dab off pigment with a piece of kitchen paper.

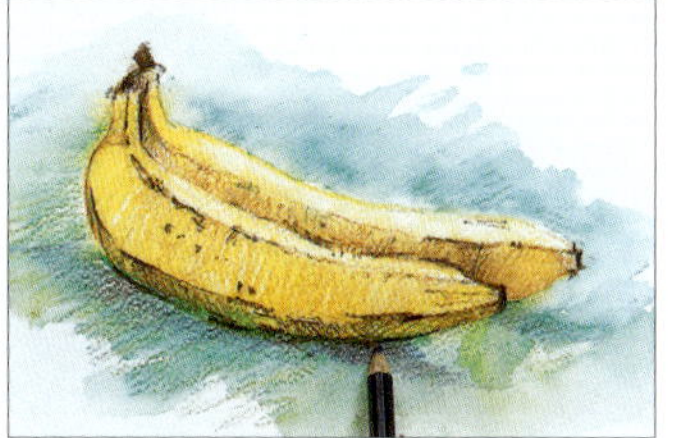

7 While the paper is still wet, take a dark brown pencil and darken the stem. Also dot in some stronger marks on the bananas. The pencil marks will blur a little on the damp paper, so you end up with a soft spread of colour rather than a sharp point. Add a touch of violet in the most deeply shaded area and put in more of the shadow cast by the bananas in the same colour.

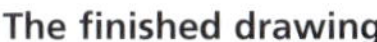

The finished drawing

This simple little study demonstrates the potential of water-soluble pencils very well by combining linear marks with simple washes. By limiting the number of colours used, the artist has kept the colours bold and bright.

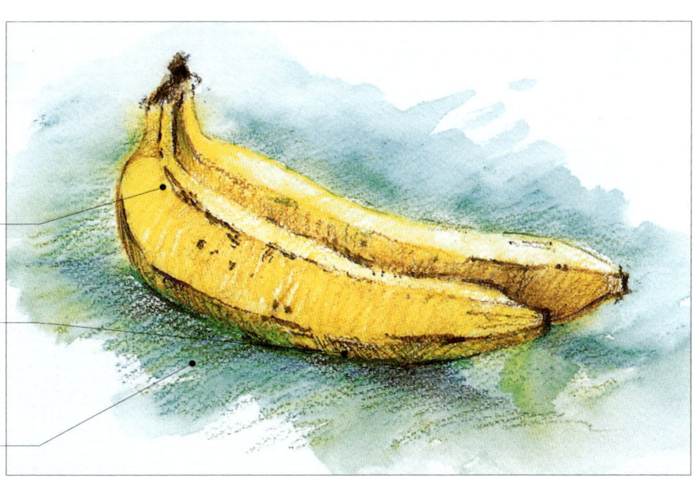

Linear detail is still visible. If you accidentally destroy linear marks that you want to keep, draw them again once the water has dried.

Washing over the hatched lines of burnt sienna with water has softened the marks to create a darker tone on the shaded facets.

The background is a soft wash of colour, against which the bananas stand out clearly.

Brush drawing

Although we tend to associate brushes with painting techniques, they are extremely versatile drawing tools and are capable of producing tremendously expressive lines.

Soft-haired brushes, of the kind used in watercolour painting, are best for this kind of technique. You can also use Chinese brushes, which are designed for calligraphy. They hold a lot of ink or paint, so you don't need to keep stopping to re-load the brush, and the tip comes to a fine point so you can vary the width of the line with ease. The hairs of both Chinese and watercolour brushes are very flexible, making it easy to alter the direction of the line you are making; with a brush, you can round corners smoothly in situations where you might falter with a pen or pencil. Experiment with different types of brush and compare the marks that you can create with each one.

Also experiment with the way you hold the brush. If you hold it on or near the ferrule (the metal part that holds the hairs of the brush in place), you will have a great deal of control. This is great if you are making small, short marks, but longer marks may look tight and laboured, as you control the brush primarily with your fingers, which can move only a limited distance. Holding the brush about halfway down the shaft, or even near the end, allows you to make longer, sweeping strokes from your wrist, so you get a much more flowing line. Similarly, try the side of the brush as well as the tip to see what difference that makes.

You can use either ink or paint with this technique. Waterproof ink can be brushed over once it is dry without the risk of it spreading, but the blurring that occurs with water-soluble ink is an attractive effect in its own right; the choice is yours. If you want to use paint, watercolour, gouache or acrylic (all of which are water-soluble) are all suitable.

You can make brush drawings on virtually any support – paper, board or canvas. If you use ordinary drawing paper, opt for a reasonably heavy type so that the wet ink or paint does not soak through and tear the support. However, unlike watercolour painting, there is no need to pre-stretch the support; you are not flooding it with water or paint, so it is not likely to cockle.

One key drawback of brush drawing is that if you make a mistake in paint or ink, it is much harder to erase than a pencil mark. For this reason, it is always a good idea to map out the main lines of your subject first by making a very light pencil underdrawing – at least until you feel confident enough of your drawing skills.

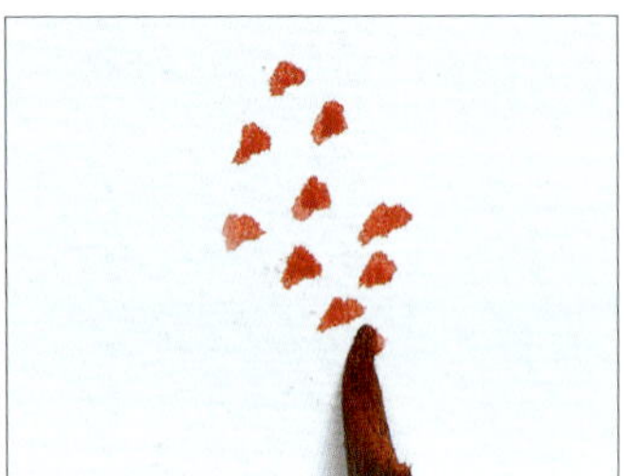

Short marks and dots
Hold the brush perpendicular to the paper and touch the tip on to the surface.

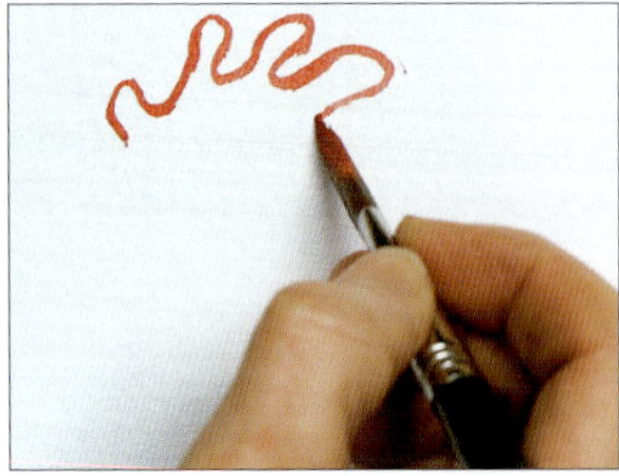

Short, undulating lines
For greater control, hold the brush on the ferrule; you can change the direction of the brush simply by moving your fingers slightly.

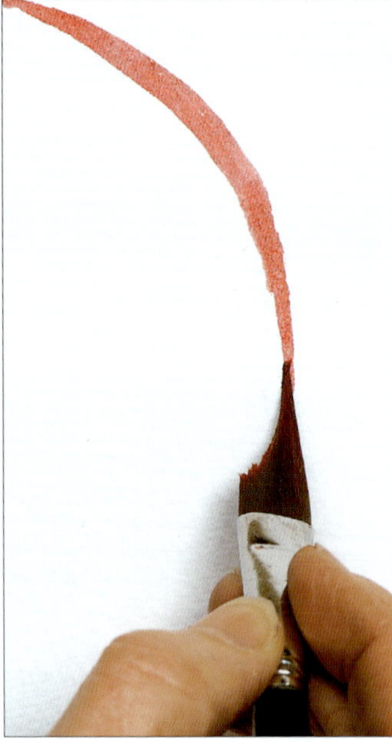

Thin curves
For thin, relatively short curves, hold the brush on the ferrule so that you can control it easily and apply only the tip to the support.

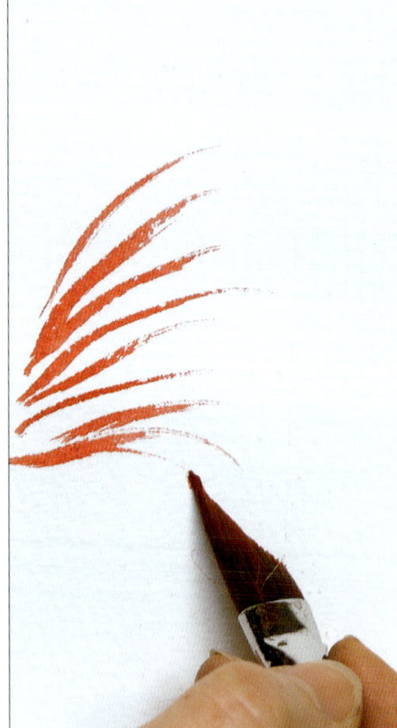

Short lines that tail off
Lift the brush up from the support as you near the end of the stroke so that only the tip is touching when you reach the final part of your mark.

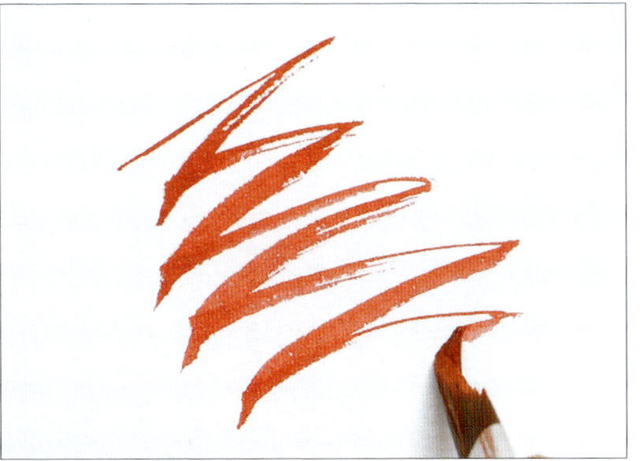

Lines of varying widths
Use the side of the brush, pressing the hairs on to the support, to make broad strokes; on the upstroke, lift the brush so that only the tip is touching the support to create a thinner line.

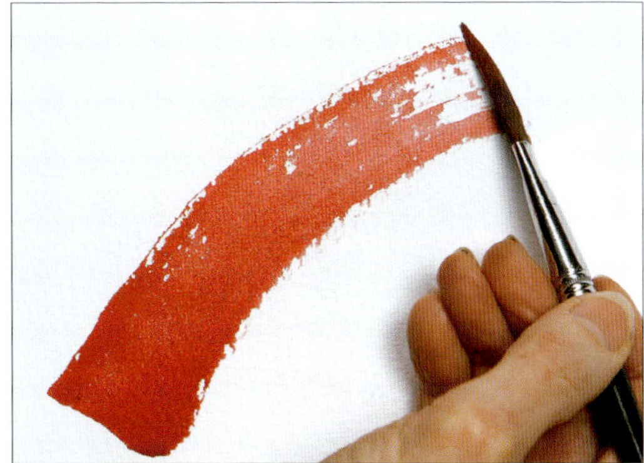

Broad strokes
Hold the brush further up the handle, press the full length of the hairs on to the support and use a sweeping motion to pull the brush across the paper.

Practice exercise: **Poppies**

These flowers are a wonderful subject for brush drawings. When the flower heads are fully open they are floppy, with slightly frilled edges, which you can depict by means of flowing, expressive lines. The stalks, too, twist and turn in interesting ways. They are covered in tiny hairs and, while it is neither possible nor desirable to draw them all, you can convey the texture with a few swift flicks of the brush. The leaves give you the opportunity to make spiky, linear marks of different thicknesses, using the tip of the brush for the veins.

Materials

- *Watercolour paper*
- *2B pencil*
- *Watercolour paints: cadmium red, olive green, ivory black, ultramarine blue*
- *Brush*

The set-up
Fresh poppies wilt quickly so, for this exercise, the artist used artificial poppies. She decided to simplify the composition to include just one full bloom, one bud and a few leaves. This gives an uncluttered picture that allows us to appreciate the shapes of the flowers to the full.

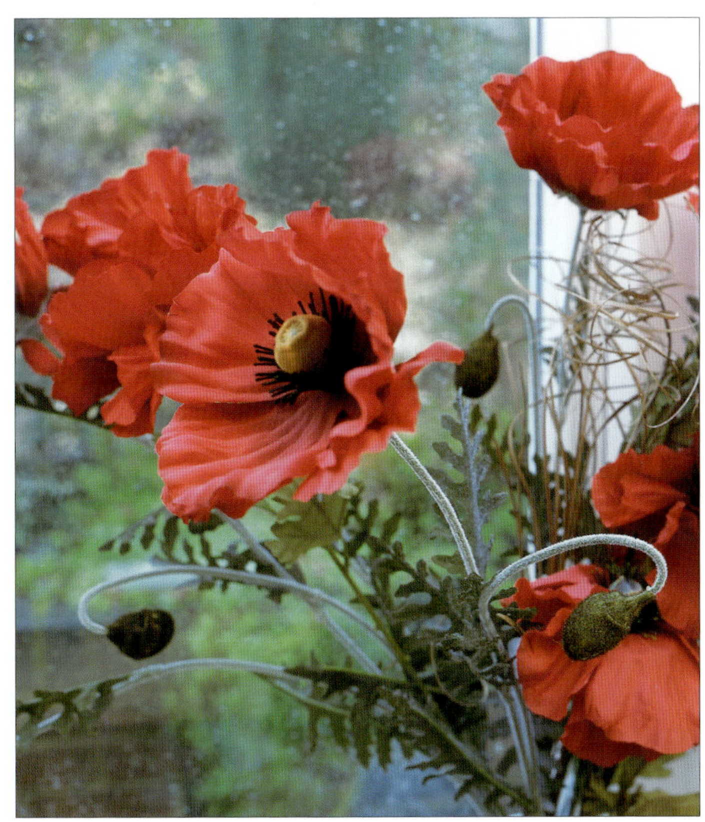

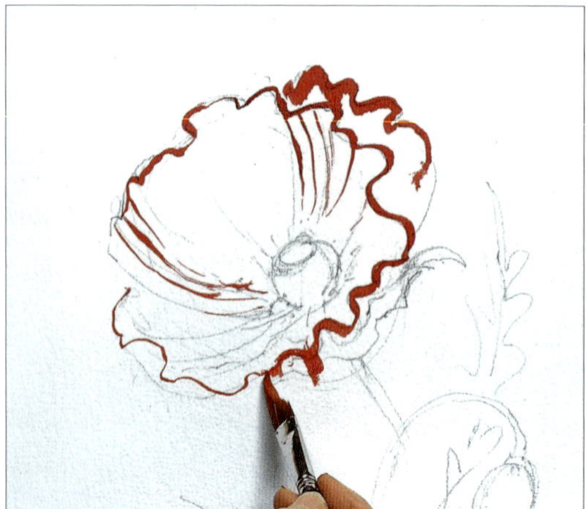

1 Lightly sketch your subject in pencil. If you're confident, you could omit this stage and put in the initial lines of the flowerhead using a brush and paint – but to begin with, it's best to ensure you get the basic structure right. Use a medium-size brush and cadmium red watercolour paint to outline the shape.

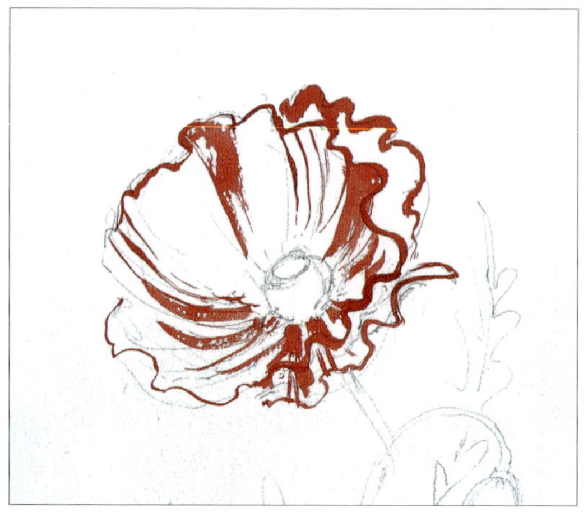

2 Put in the main striations in the petals of this large flower. The flowerhead consists of several overlapping layers of petals. Indicate the petal overlaps by giving them thicker brushstrokes, using the side of the brush to achieve this effect rather than resorting to painting them using just the tip.

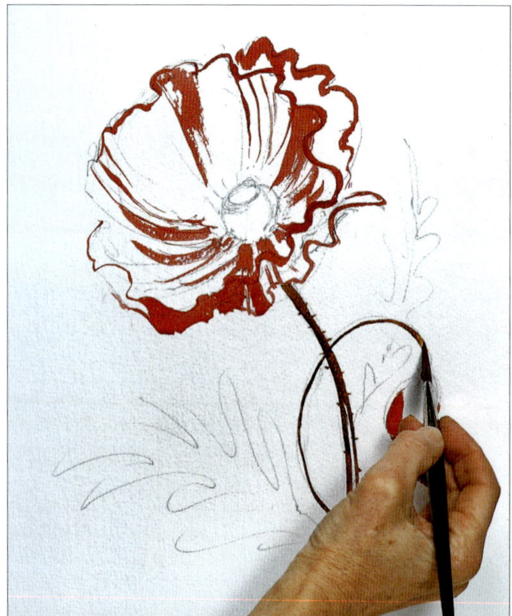

3 Rinse your brush in clean water. Using olive green paint and the tip of the brush, draw the stem. Flick the tip of the brush sideways to draw the tiny hairs along the stem. To get a lighter shade of green, add a little more water.

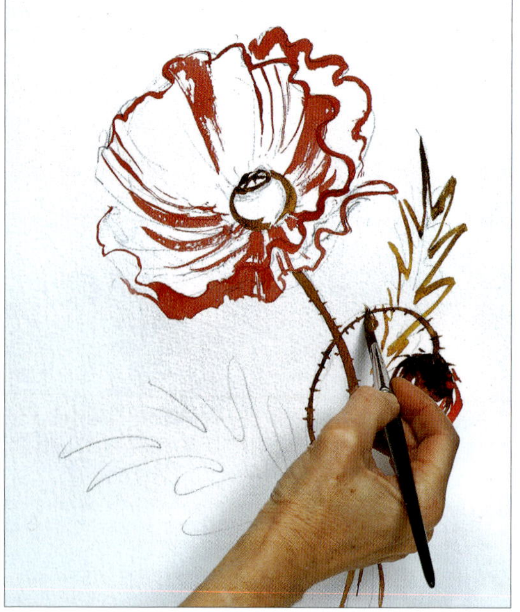

4 Block in the olive green of the poppy bud and the centre of the main bloom. Outline the leaves. Draw the stalk of the bud in the same way as in Step 3, again adding a few little hairs along its length to create a different texture.

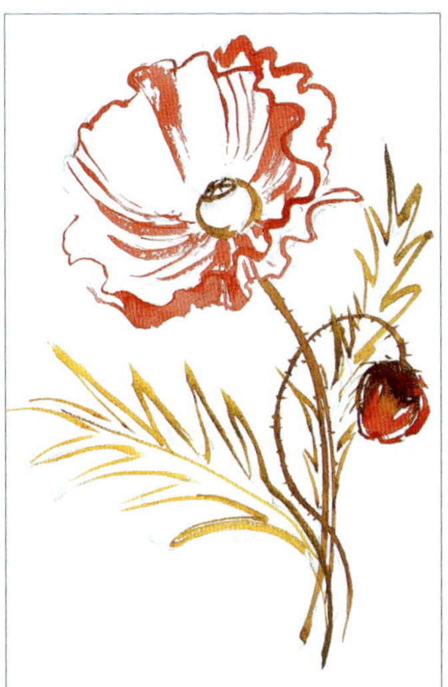

5 Complete the outline of the leaves and put in the vein that runs down the centre of the largest leaf.

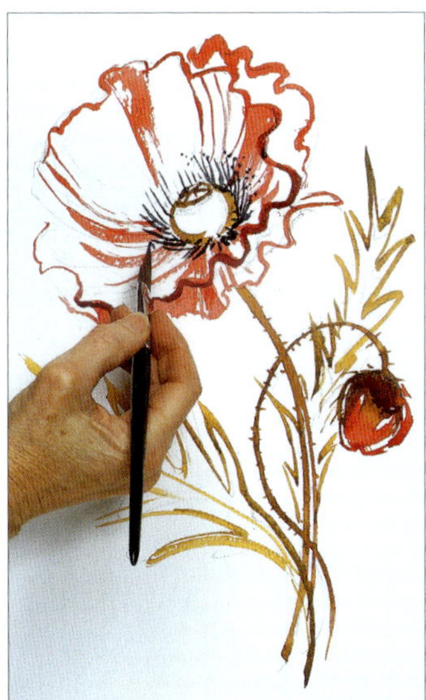

6 Mix a dark blue-black from ivory black and ultramarine blue (black on its own tends to look 'dead'). Using the tip of the brush, draw the tiny stamens around the centre of the large flower. Load the brush sparingly so you don't flood the paper.

The finished drawing

This is an energetic brush drawing, full of flowing lines that capture the characteristics of the flower extremely well. The artist has used a wide range of brushstrokes, from delicate flicks of the brush for the hairs on the stems to lines of varying width for the spiky leaves and broad marks for the overlapping petals. Even though much of the paper is left white, she has put in just enough detail to convey the shapes and textures.

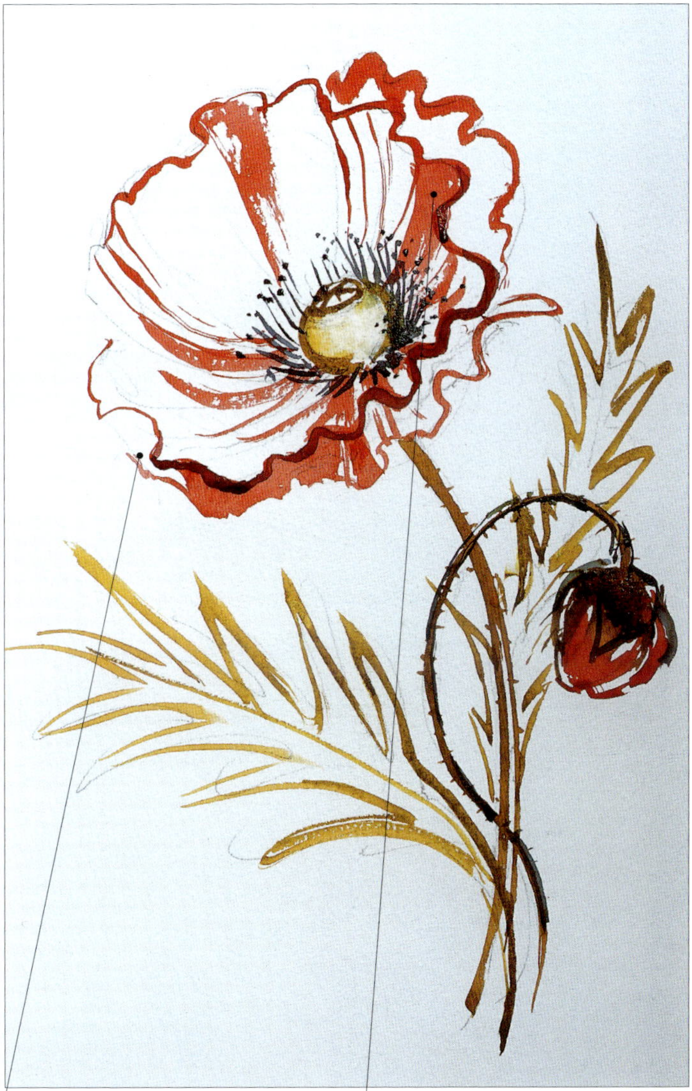

Thin, flowing lines made using the tip of the brush convey the attractively frilled edges of the petals.

Broader strokes, made using the side of the brush, imply the way petals overlap one another in this large flower.

Line and wash

The term used to describe a combination of pen-and-ink work and watercolour or ink washes is line and wash. Pen and ink is often employed for subjects that contain a lot of linear detail, such as buildings and architectural details, but can result in a somewhat mechanical feel – particularly if you are using a technical drawing pen, which does not allow you to vary the width of the line. The advantage of using line and wash is that by brushing clean water over water-soluble ink to dissolve the lines, or applying a wash of dilute ink or watercolour paint over lines drawn in permanent ink, you can soften the overall effect and create areas of tone that contrast well with the detailed pen work.

The key is not to make your work too detailed. The best line-and-wash drawings allow the viewer to infer much of what is being shown. Be selective and pick out the essential details of your subject – a good discipline, whatever medium you are working in.

Think, too, about the quality of line that you want to create and choose your pen accordingly. Technical drawing pens give a very even, regular line, but can be too rigid and regular for some people. Dip pens give a lovely quality of line, and you can vary the width by turning the pen over and drawing with the flat back of the nib – but you do have to keep stopping to re-load the pen with ink and some find this disruptive to their drawing. Many artists prefer so-called sketching pens, which are loaded with a cartridge that holds a considerable amount of ink.

Finally you need to choose whether to use waterproof or water-soluble ink. Once it has dried waterproof ink, as the name implies, will not run if a wash is applied on top of it. With water-soluble ink, on the other hand, you can brush over the marks with clean water to dissolve them and create an area of tone. You can, of course, use both types of ink in the same picture, provided you plan things in advance and work out which areas you want to blend with water and in which ones you want to retain the detail of the line work.

Brushing over waterproof ink

When you brush over dry waterproof ink with clean water, the linear work remains and the quality of the drawing is not altered in any way.

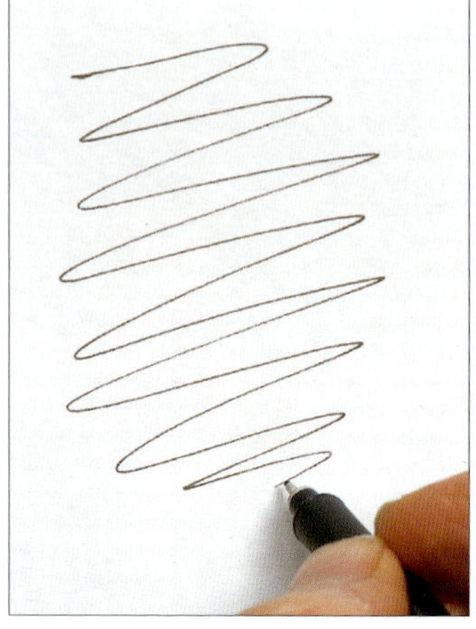

1 Scribble a few lines using permanent ink, and allow to dry.

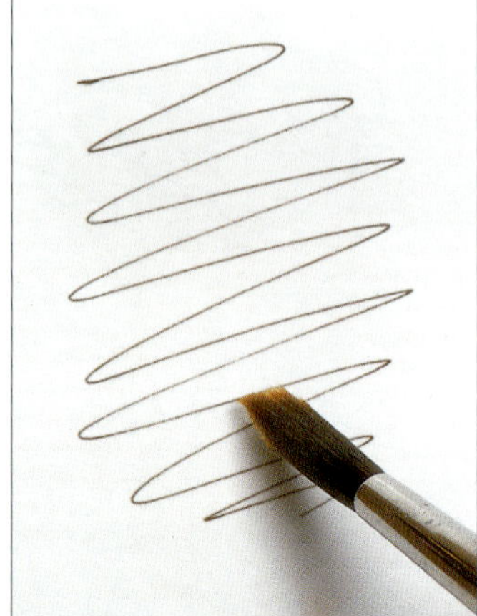

2 Brush over the lines with clean water. The lines will remain.

Brushing over water-soluble ink

When you brush over dry water-soluble ink with clean water, the linear work is dissolved to create an area of tone.

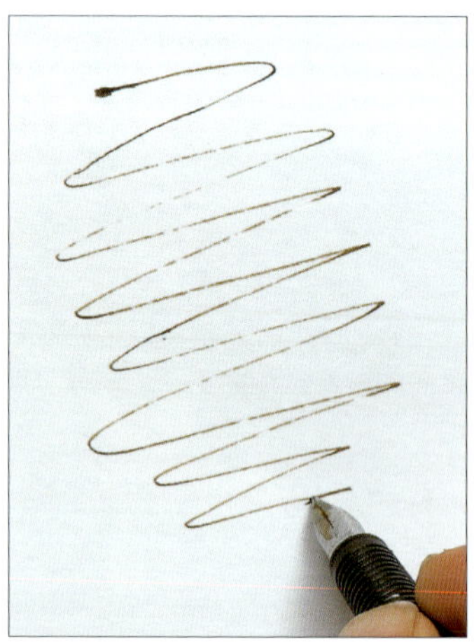

1 Start by scribbling a few lines using water-soluble ink, and allow these lines to dry.

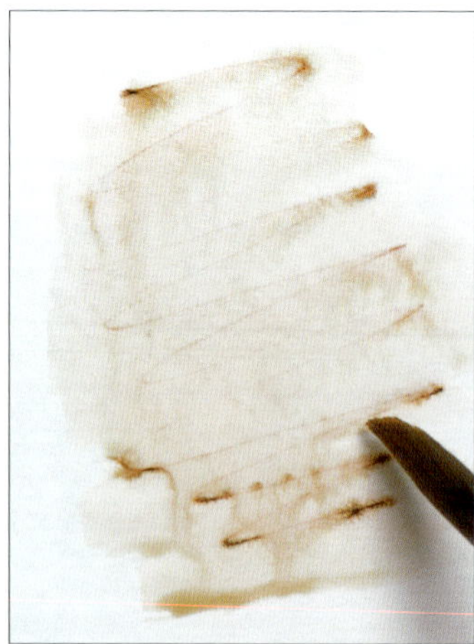

2 Brush over the lines with clean water. The water will dissolve the ink, creating an area of pale tone.

Creating dark tone

To create a darker area of tone, simply apply more ink to the paper by making the lines closer together.

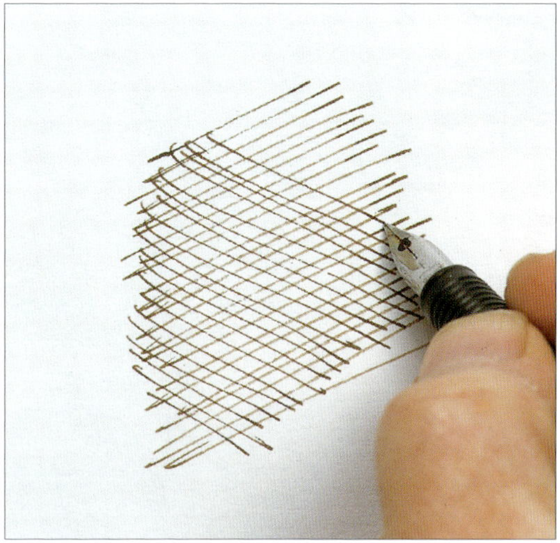

1 Hatch, or crosshatch, a series of lines close together, using water-soluble ink.

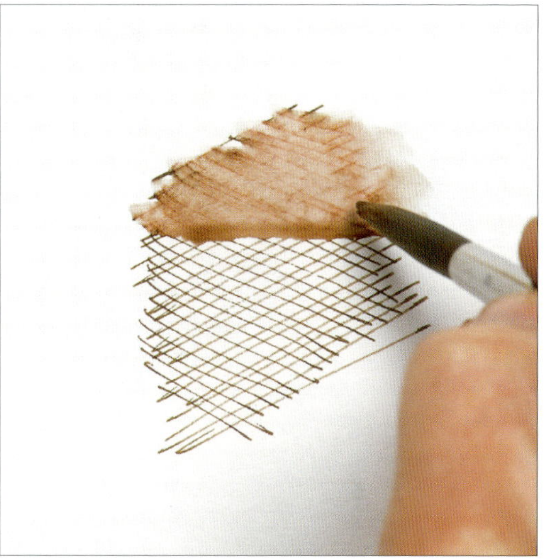

2 Brush over the lines with clean water. As before, the water will dissolve the ink – but because the lines were drawn close together, more ink has been applied to the paper and the resulting area of tone will be darker.

Practice exercise: **Combining permanent and water-soluble inks in the same drawing**

This exercise uses crisp, permanent ink work for the details of the wrought-iron gate and some areas of foliage, and water-soluble ink brushed over with clean water to create areas of tone in the foliage and brickwork.

Take plenty of time over your initial pencil sketch to make sure you've got the elaborate scrollwork details and proportions right. Only then should you start going over the lines in pen and ink. Much of the right-hand side of the gate will be obscured by foliage in your final drawing, but a good underdrawing will ensure you've got the structure right and the gate symmetrical.

Materials

- *Heavy drawing paper*
- *HB pencil*
- *Technical drawing pen loaded with permanent black ink*
- *Sketching pen loaded with water-soluble black ink*
- *Brush*

The scene

This late nineteenth-century wrought-iron gateway is partially covered by greenery and it is hard to see the intricate detail. In a drawing, however, you can subdue certain elements and emphasize those on which you want to focus attention.

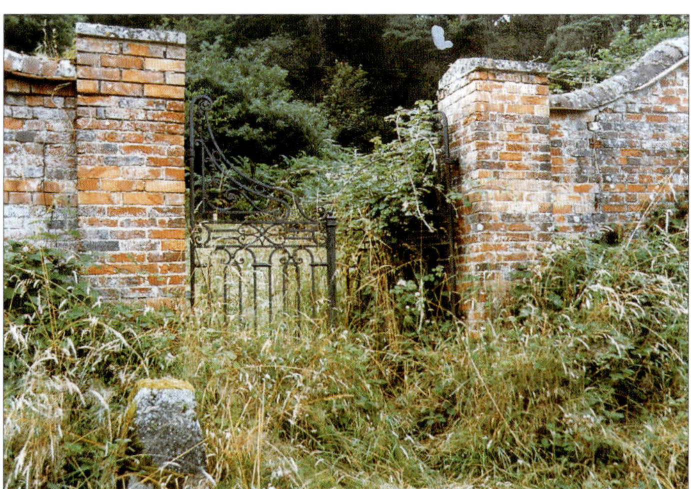

▶

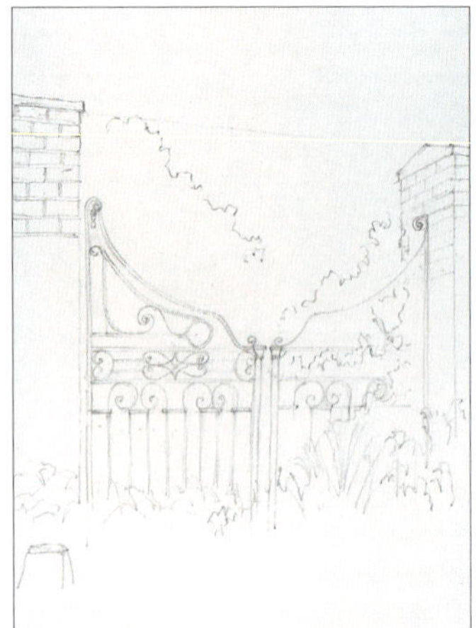

1 Using an HB pencil, lightly sketch the scene, using single lines for the bars of the gate to be sure you've got the placement and proportions right. Once you've got this stage right, you can go over the gate in pencil again, putting in a double line for each bar. A loose impression of the foliage shapes is sufficient. Similarly, you don't need to draw every individual brick.

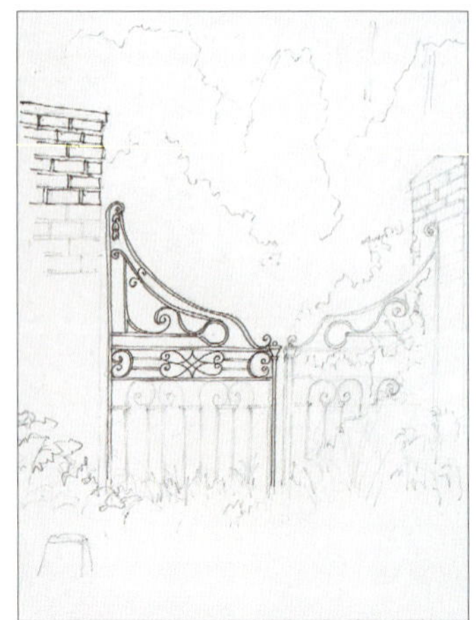

2 Using permanent black ink, go over those areas of the gate in which you want to retain detail. Draw the bricks in permanent ink, too.

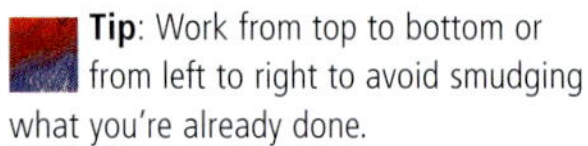

Tip: Work from top to bottom or from left to right to avoid smudging what you're already done.

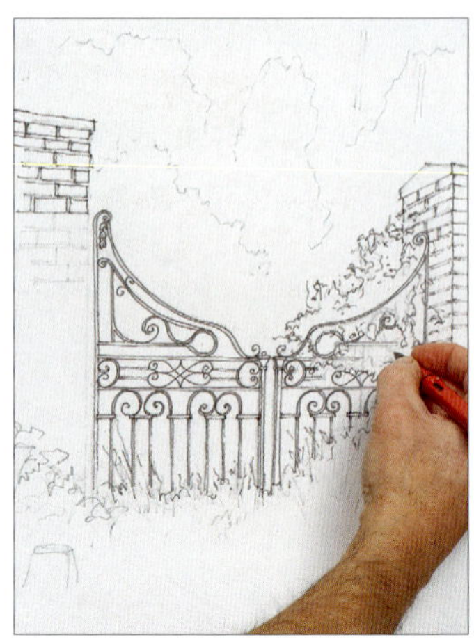

3 Continue working on the gateway, using permanent black ink. Loosely scribble in the top of the grasses below the gate in permanent ink. Switch to water-soluble ink and begin outlining the tendrils of foliage that hang over the gate. Working on the foliage will make it clear which parts of the gate are obscured by leaves and do not need to be drawn in permanent ink.

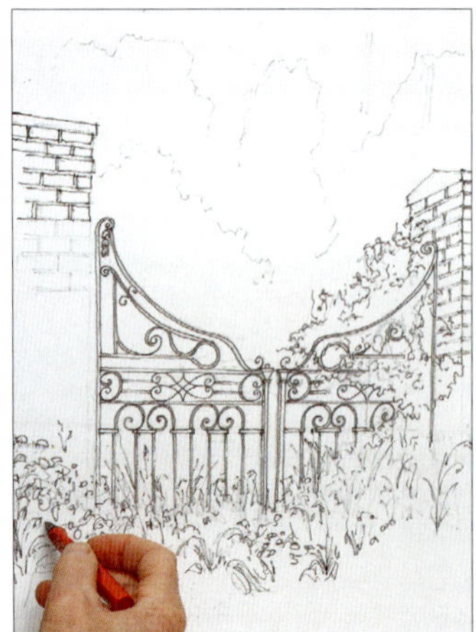

4 Continue working on the foliage and the vegetation in front of the gateway, using both permanent and water-soluble inks for the foreground area. Try to capture the general pattern of growth, without putting in every detail.

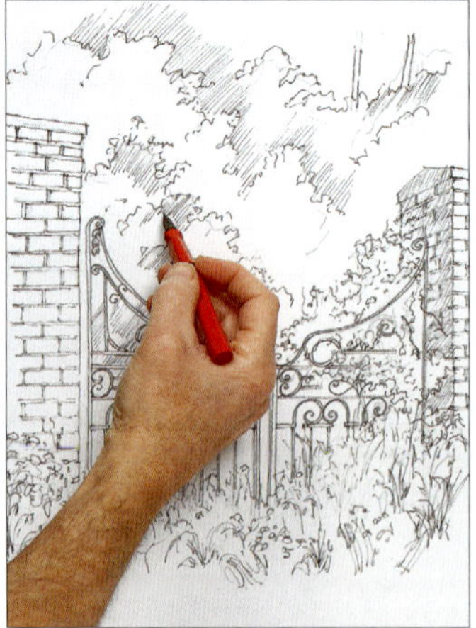

5 Using water-soluble ink, lightly shade the left-hand side of the right-hand brick pier to show which direction the light is coming from. Hatch the darkest areas of foliage in the background trees so that you begin to develop some form in this area.

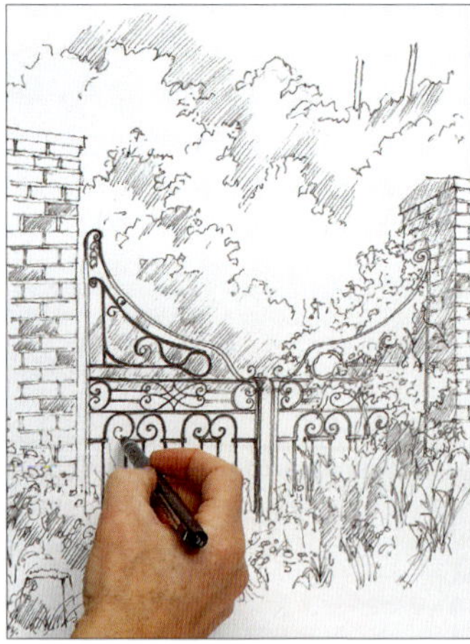

6 Hatch the darkest areas of the foreground vegetation, in front of the gate, in the same way. Erase any remaining pencil marks. Using permanent black ink, fill in the the scrollwork on the wrought-iron gate so that it stands out from the background.

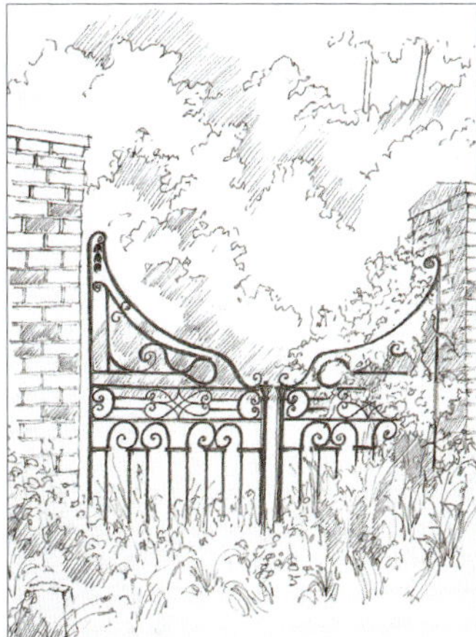

7 Thanks to the loose hatching done in the previous stages, the drawing is now starting to look three-dimensional. Stand back and assess whether any areas need to be darkened with more hatching before you go on to the next stage.

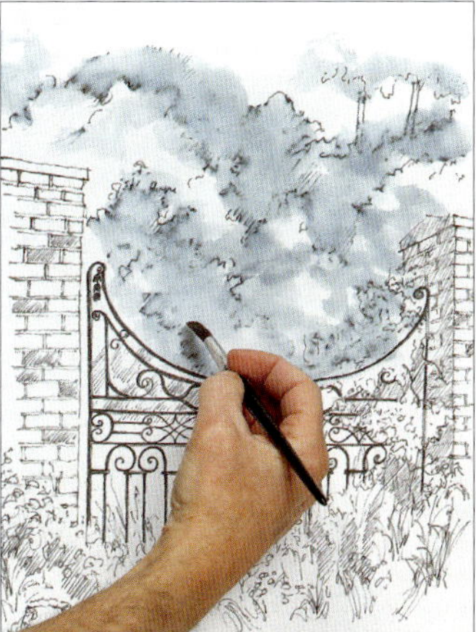

8 Load a paintbrush with clean water and lightly and rapidly brush over the foliage area behind the gate, leaving some areas untouched. The water-soluble ink will dissolve, creating areas of tone that contrast well with the linear work on the gate.

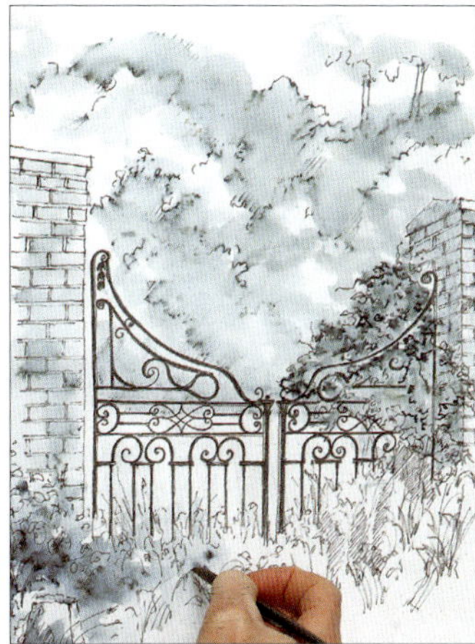

9 Repeat the process on the foreground vegetation and gently pull some of the wet ink (across) on to the brickwork to make it look less stark. If necessary, go back over some of the foliage in pen and ink (once dry) to create more texture and density of tone.

The finished drawing

If this drawing had been made using pen and ink alone, the result would have been very harsh. It would also have been hard to differentiate between the different parts of the image, as the foliage and gate are very similar in tone. Brushing clean water over carefully selected areas of water-soluble ink has softened the image, allowing the gate – which is the main focus of interest in the drawing – to stand out clearly. Although black ink was used throughout, the artist has created a number of tones by varying the density of the hatching and by working back over the washes to add more detail.

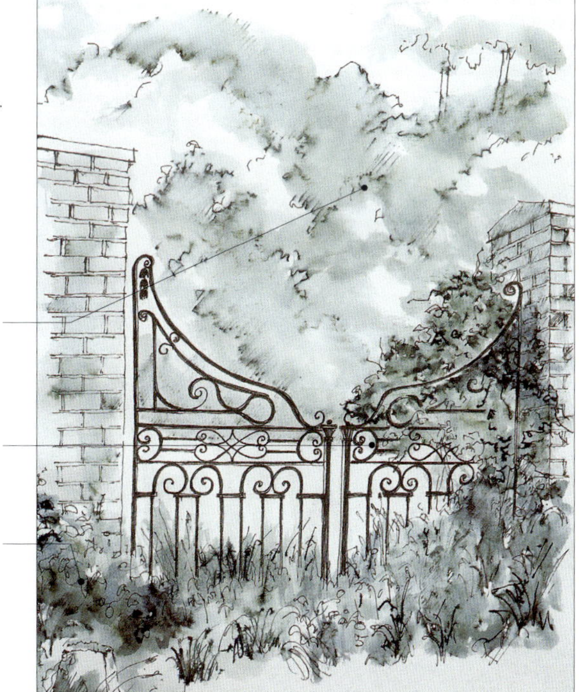

The background foliage to this gateway is suggested, rather than drawn in detail.

Permanent black ink was used for the gate; even if water was accidentally brushed on to these areas, the lines would remain.

The foreground vegetation was darkened and given more texture by drawing back over the wash.

Mixed-media demonstration

Karen Raney is an artist who enjoys experimenting with different media and different techniques, in both her drawings and her paintings. Her subject matter is as varied as her methods, but as a city dweller she is particularly interested in the challenge and stimulation of urban scenes. She uses photographs as a starting point when it is not possible to work direct from the subject – which can be difficult in towns and cities – but does so selectively, rejecting any elements in the photograph which she does not require for her composition.

Practice exercise: **Combining pencil and crayon**

In this exercise the artist intends to use a version of the sgraffito technique in combination with pencil and Conté crayon. The colourless oil bar used to prepare the surface resembles an application of linseed oil. This can subsequently be blended with the Conté crayon where required to produce a mixture rather like paint, which can then be moved around and scraped away where required. Fine details applied with a pencil also bite into this soft layer, creating a richly textured surface.

Materials

- *Heavy watercolour paper*
- *Colourless oil bar*
- *Conté crayon: black*
- *Plastic card*
- *Pencils: 6B and 2B*
- *Gouache paint: white*
- *Paintbrush*

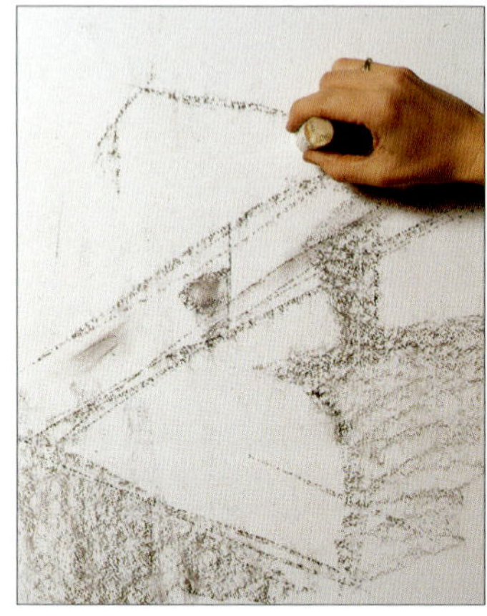

1 The artist has begun by scribbling all over the paper with an oil bar, which is similar to a thick, soft oil pastel. Having drawn over this with Conté crayon, she now applies more oil in selected areas.

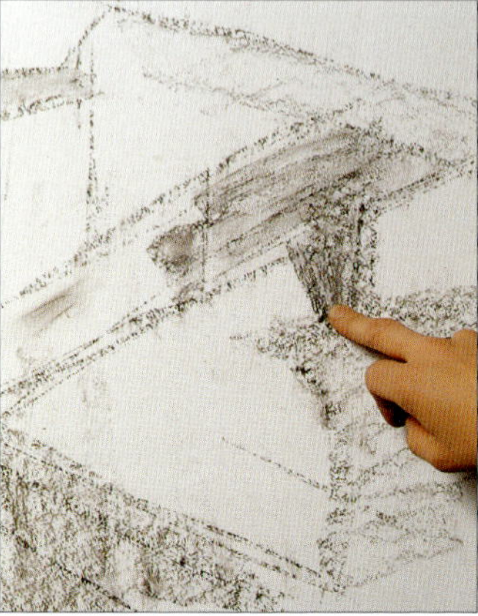

2 The Conté crayon is smudged with a finger so that it mixes into the layers of oil bar beneath. The oil and the texture of the heavy watercolour paper have broken up the Conté marks, creating a nice soft effect.

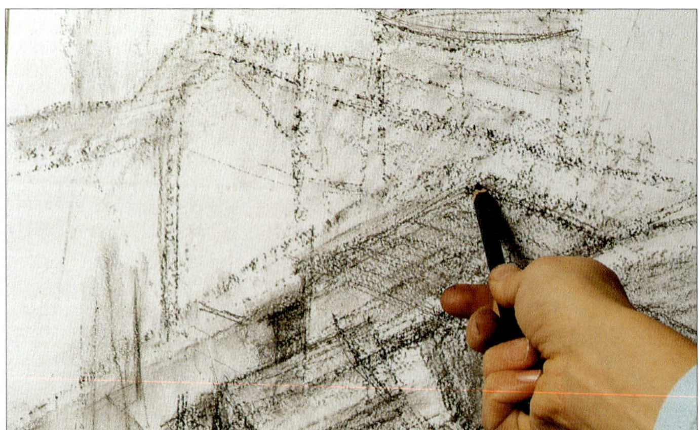

3 Conté crayon is now inscribed more heavily over the first applications of oil and crayon. The drawing is kept loose and free at this stage, with the shapes evolving very gradually.

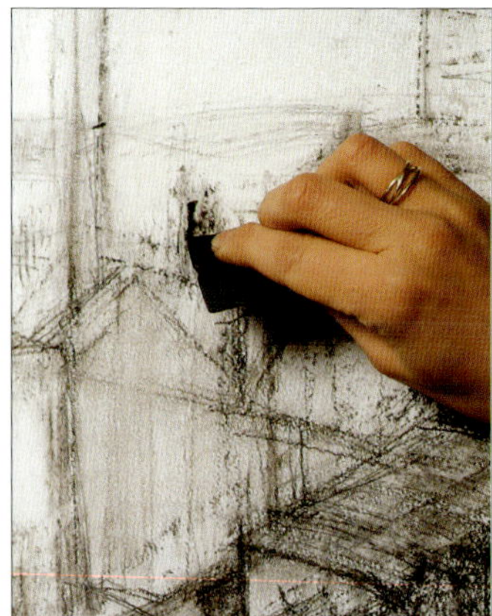

4 The corner of a plastic card is used to scratch into the surface and then re-apply the mixture of oil and Conté.

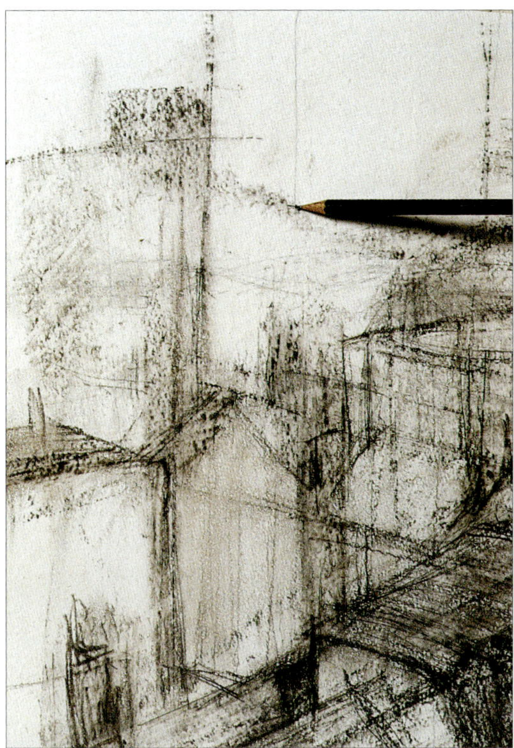

5 The composition is allowed to emerge gradually, with the foreground established first. The artist now uses a soft pencil to mark the side of a more distant building.

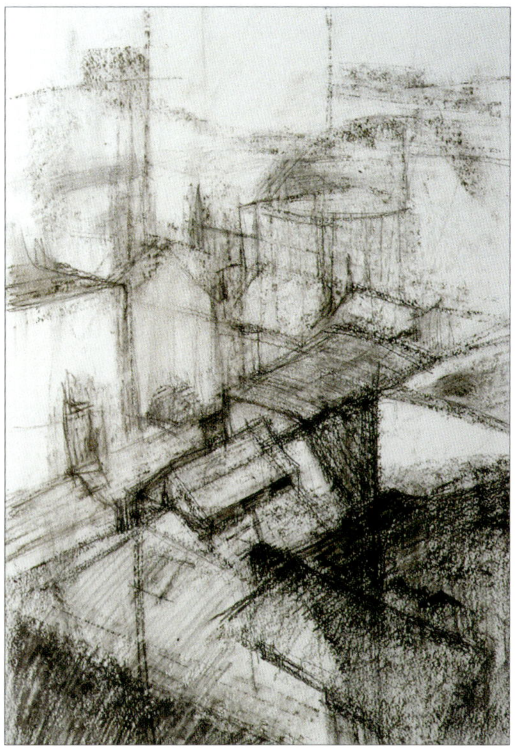

6 Detailed definition will be left until the final stages; concentration now is on the composition, the main perspective lines and the distribution of lights and darks.

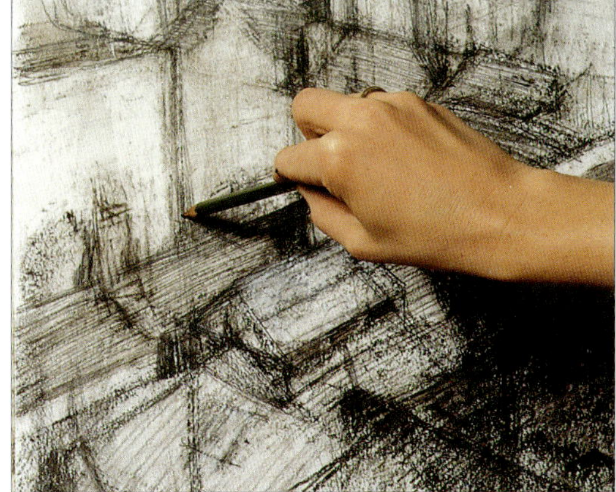

7 Some lines are strengthened with soft pencil. The effect of scratching and scraping with the plastic card can be clearly seen here, particularly in the foreground.

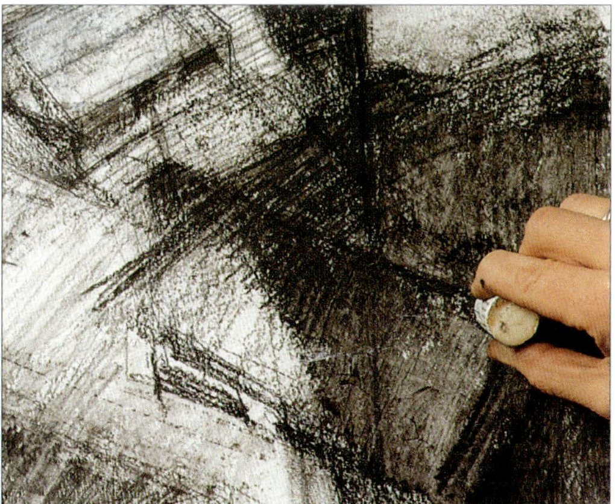

8 A further application of oil bar again mixes with the Conté crayon beneath to produce a soft paste that can be manipulated and moved around.

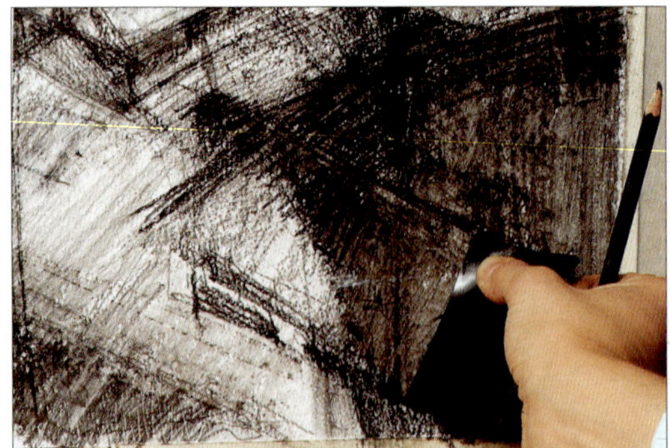

9 The card is used to draw into the paste-like substance. The effect resembles brushmarks in a painting, with the corner of the card making a positive dark line.

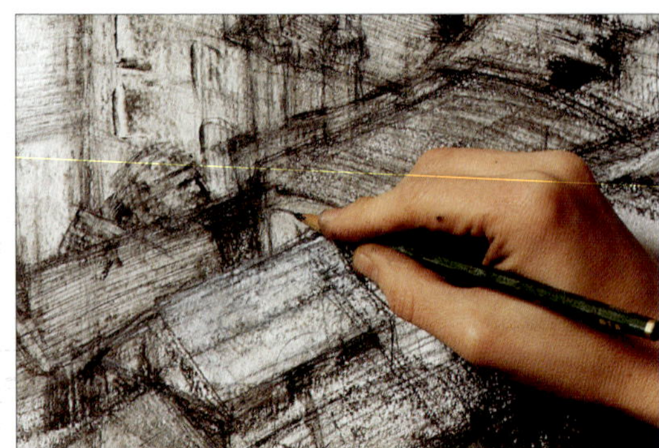

10 The picture is sufficiently advanced for the artist to begin work on the details, and here she uses a 2B pencil, applying pressure to bite through the thin layer of oil.

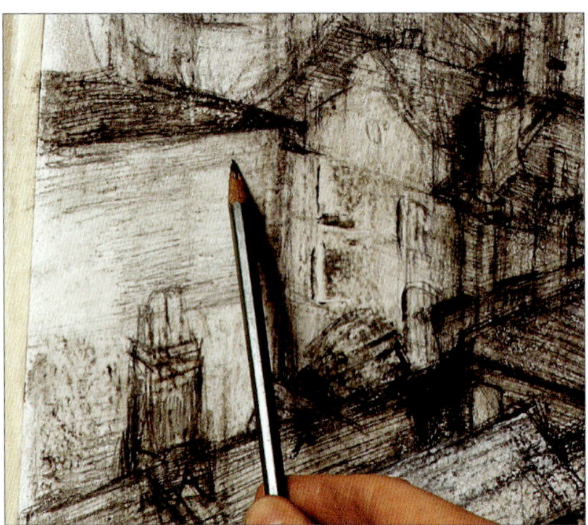

11 To suggest the texture of the building on the left, she has applied a further layer of oil bar and now draws into it, using the pencil lightly so that it only partially dislodges the oily underlayer.

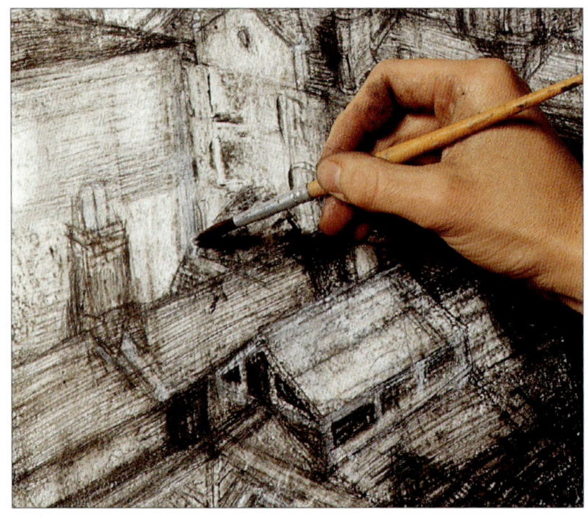

12 A further hint of texture is given by painting over the lines of oil and Conté with white gouache. This also lightens an area that was previously rather too dark.

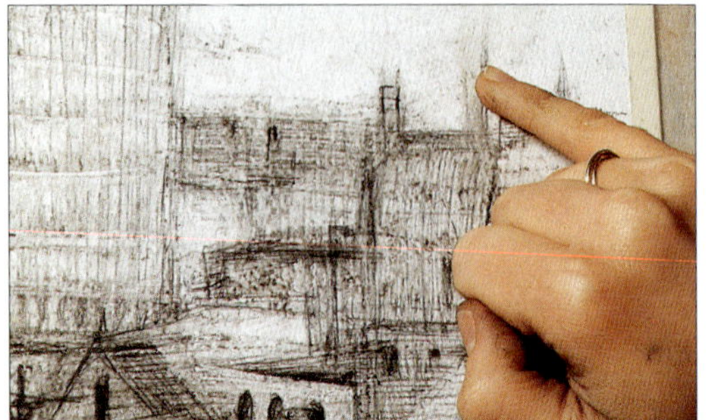

13 With all the details of the foreground buildings now completed, the artist turns her attention to the details in the background. Here she needs a soft effect to suggest distance, so she smudges the Conté-and-oil mixture with her fingertip.

The finished drawing

This piece is not only an exciting evocation of a cityscape, it is also fascinating in terms of technique. The repeated layering and scraping of the Conté crayon and oil have produced a wonderful surface texture and density of tone, which give the drawing something of the richness of an etching.

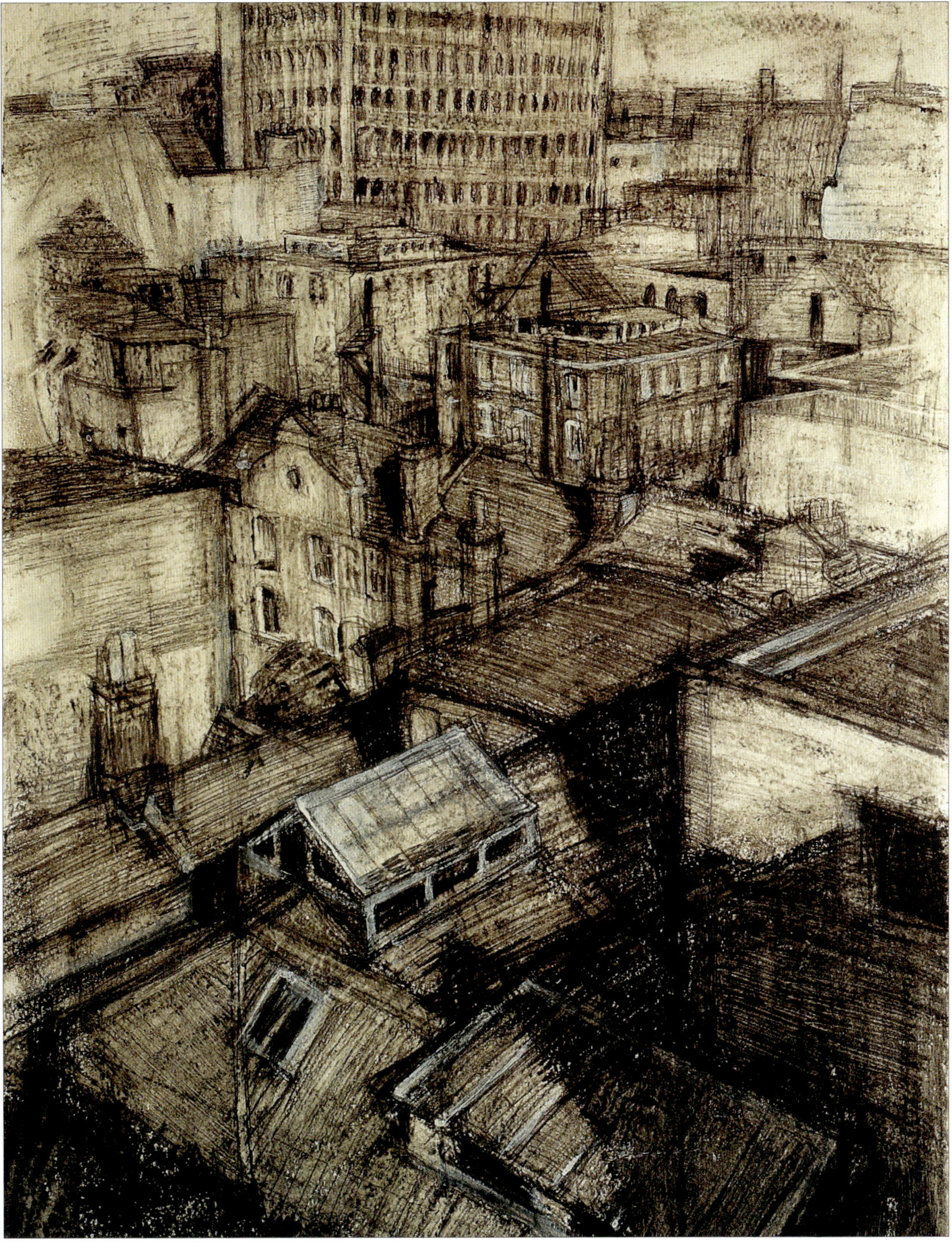

Masking

Although it is usually associated with painting and the application of fluid colour, masking can be put to excellent use with dry drawing materials. One of the traditional uses of masking in painting is to prevent paint from getting on to an area where it is not wanted. Masks can be used in this way in drawing, too.

The main application of masking in drawing, however, is to create an interesting edge that might be difficult to achieve by other means. The technique can be used with all drawing materials.

There are a number of materials that can be used as masks. Perhaps the most common and well known is masking tape, which can be cut or torn to the required shape. Take care when removing it from the paper, however, as it can easily tear soft-surfaced papers. It is also difficult to apply masking tape over areas that have been worked on using powdery materials, such as pastel or charcoal. Masking film (frisket paper) is another option.

Paper and card (stock) can easily be cut or torn to shape. Thick watercolour paper makes an excellent mask, as it tears in interesting ways. For straight edges, nothing is as quick as scribbling colour or tone up to the edge of a thick piece of card, although you can also use the edge of a ruler in the same way.

Paper and card masks can either be held in place or fixed with masking tape. But even if you tape the mask in place, it is a good idea to take the added precaution of holding it down while you are working so that there is no chance of it slipping out of position.

Masking to create straight lines

There are many occasions when you need to apply colour or tone right up to the edge of a straight-sided subject – when blocking in a sky behind a building, for example. Holding a mask along the straight edge allows you to work right up to the edge without risking accidentally applying colour over the area you want to protect.

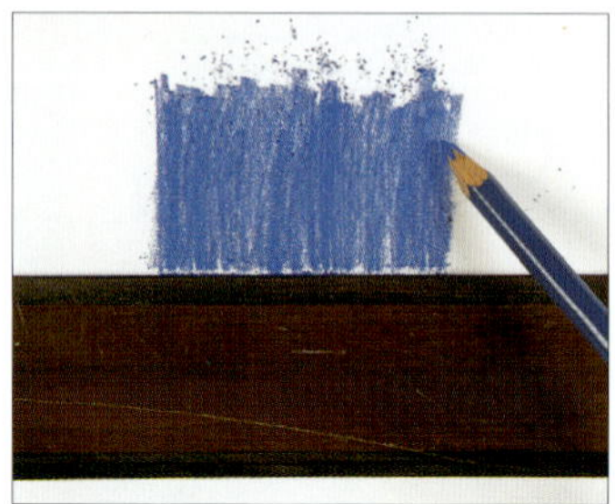

1 Hold the edge of a ruler or a cut piece of card along the straight edge and apply colour or tone. It doesn't matter if you scribble over the mask as the mask is there to protect the area underneath.

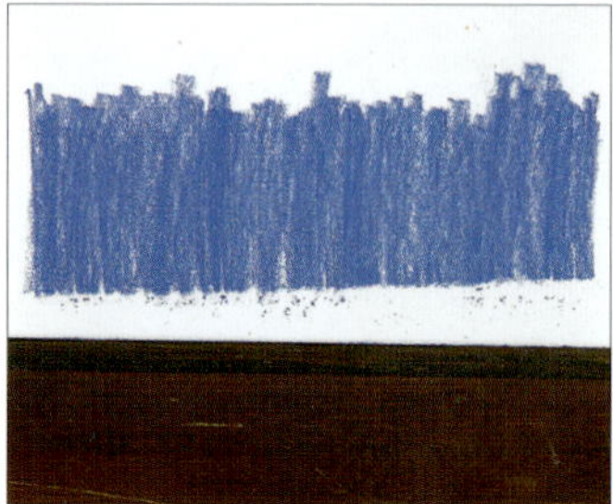

2 When the ruler is removed, the straight edge along the base of the area of colour is evident. It would be difficult to achieve such a crisp edge working freehand, and you can work much more freely with this technique.

Using a mask to create a shaped edge

Masks can also be cut or torn to create interestingly shaped edges.

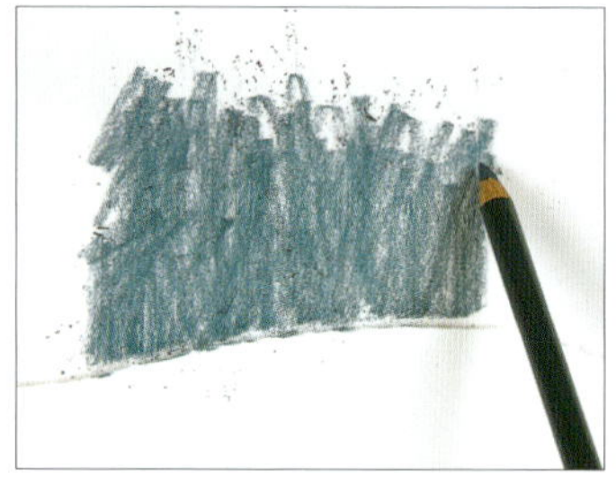

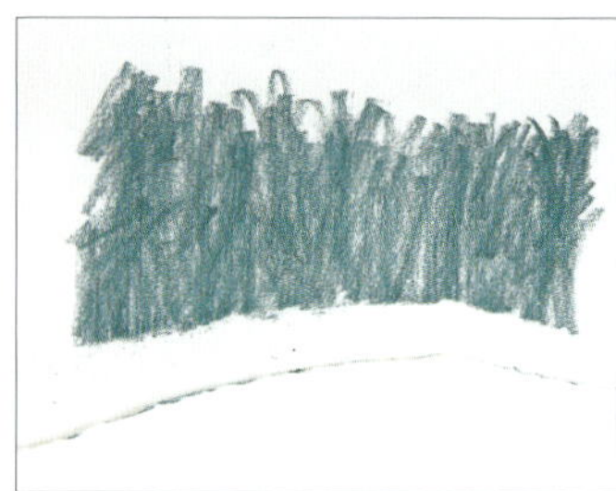

Practice exercise: **Using torn and cut masks**

This is a fun exercise in using masks made from torn and cut paper to make a sketch of broccoli stems and florets. You don't need to be terribly precise about the shape of the mask as the florets have irregular edges.

Materials

- *Smooth drawing paper*
- *Scrap paper*
- *Thin charcoal stick*
- *Scissors*

The set-up

Place a stalk of broccoli on a white tablecloth or a piece of white paper and adjust the leaves and stem until you have an attractive composition. This particular variety of purple sprouting broccoli has attractive leaves with serrated edges, which add another texture to the drawing. Position a small table lamp to one side to create shadows that you can incorporate into the composition.

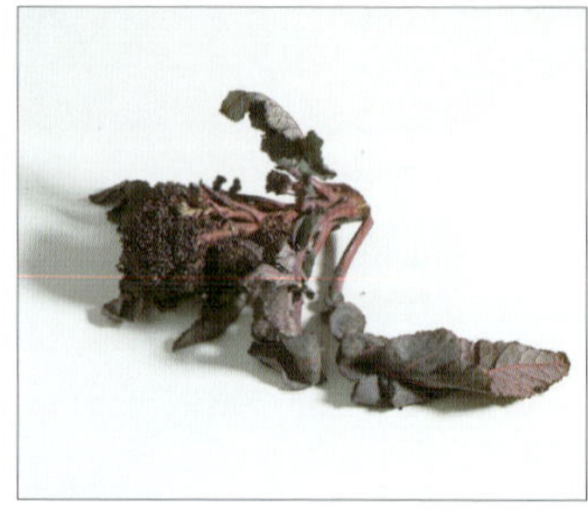

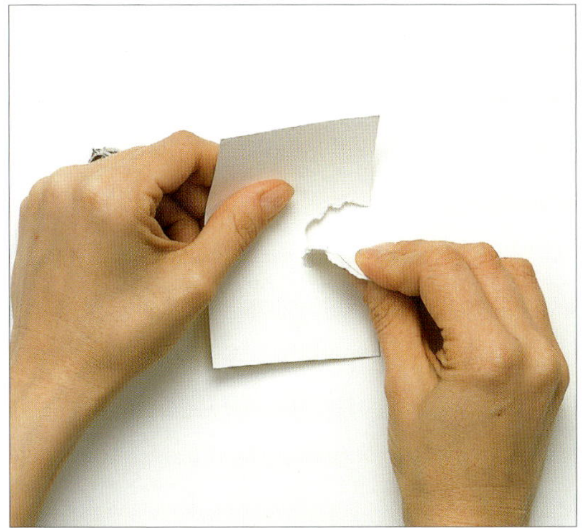

1 Take a piece of scrap watercolour paper and roughly tear a jagged, curved shape for the broccoli florets. Watercolour paper is fairly heavy and tearing it produces lovely, irregular edges that are perfect for this kind of subject.

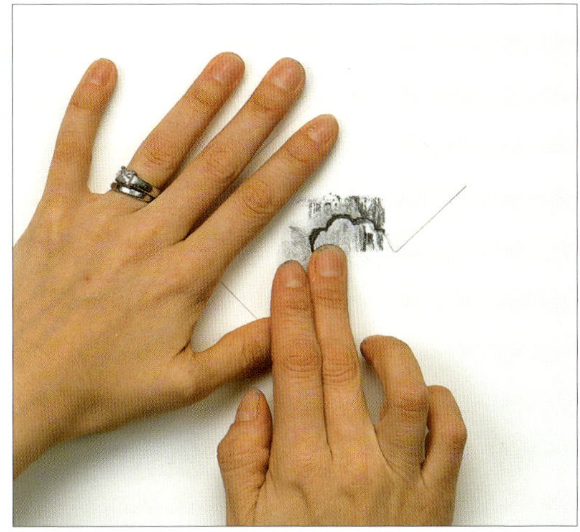

2 Hold the mask firmly in position on the paper and, using a thin stick of charcoal, make a series of short, vertical marks around the torn edge. With the mask still in place, blend the marks with your fingers.

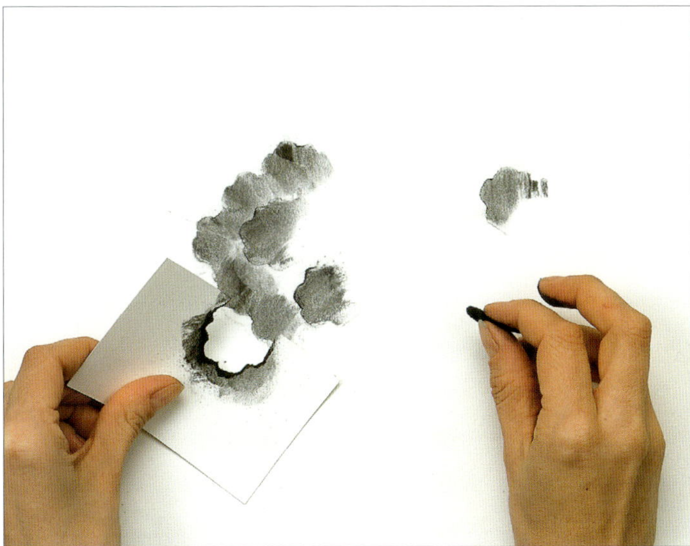

3 Remove the mask. You will see that you have made a semi-circular shape with irregular edges. Move the mask further along the paper and create a second floret in the same way. Continue working around the broccoli, creating a series of overlapping florets, until you have completed the head.

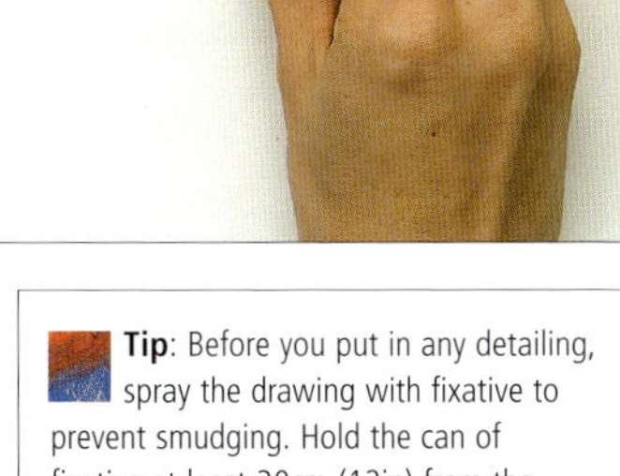

Tip: Before you put in any detailing, spray the drawing with fixative to prevent smudging. Hold the can of fixative at least 30cm (12in) from the paper and work back and forth, from top to bottom, without stopping.

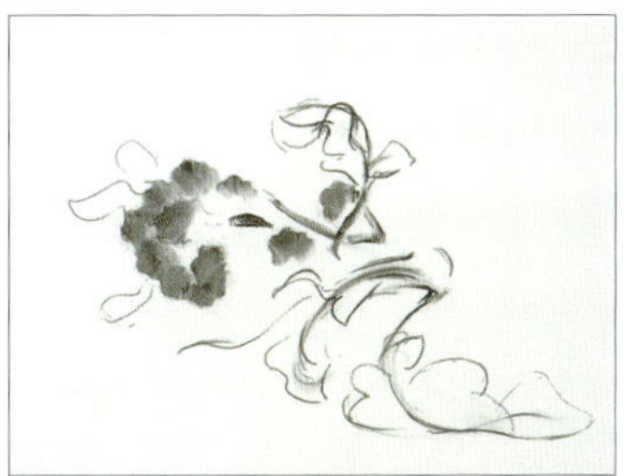

4 Outline the leaves and stem. Put in the leaf veins with long, flowing strokes and blend with your fingertips.

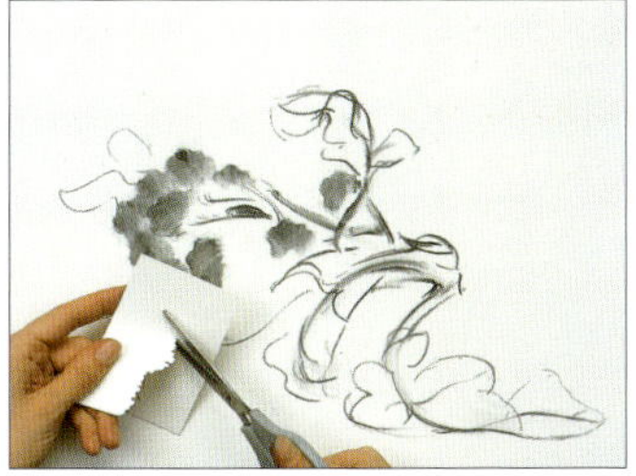

5 The edges of the leaves are slightly jagged – unlike the more rounded forms of the broccoli florets. Cut a second mask for the leaves, keeping the cuts random in shape and size.

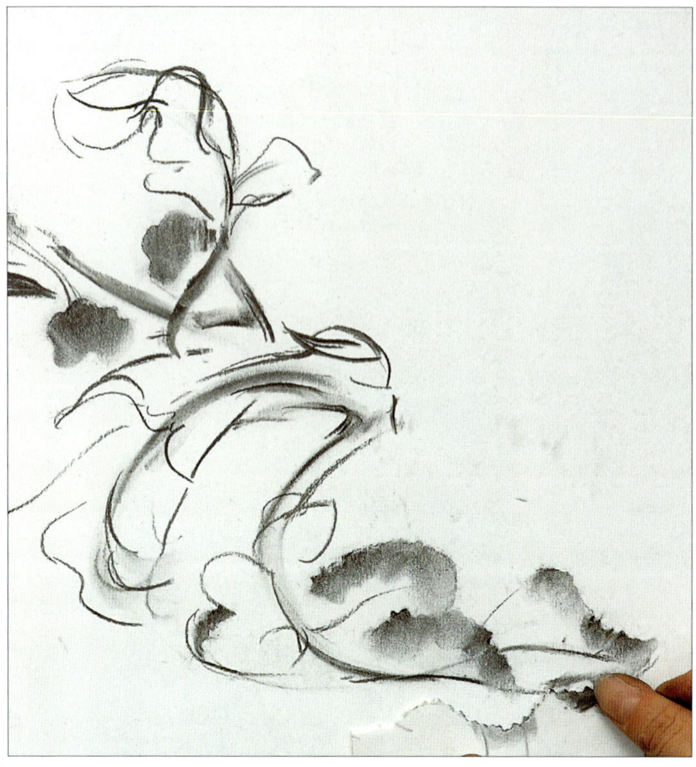

6 Place the leaf mask in position and apply charcoal up to and over the edge, as in Step 2. Use different sections of the mask, or turn it upside down, to create the shapes you want, lifting and replacing it further along the stem as you work around the leaves.

> **Tip**: Use a kneaded eraser to clean the mask at regular intervals, so that you don't accidentally transfer smudges to the drawing.

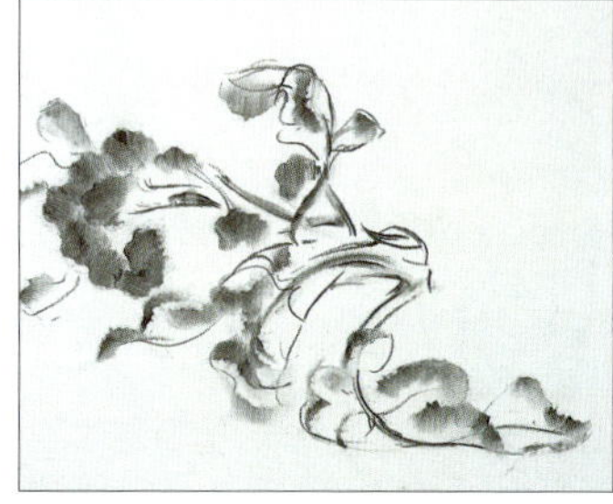

7 Continue working around the stem of broccoli until all the leaves are in place. Note how the leaves flop and twist over one another and the stalks.

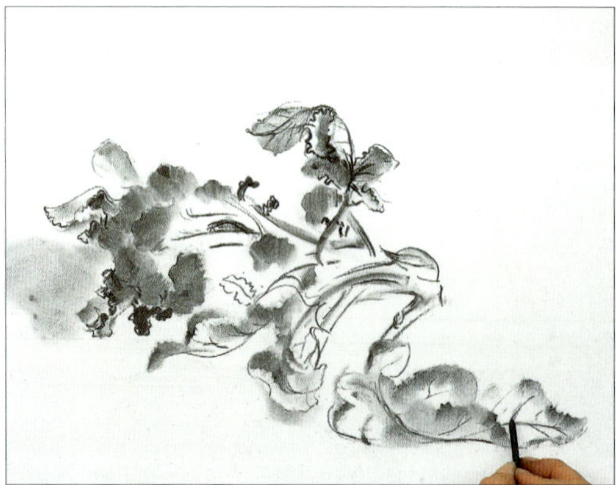

8 Use the side of the charcoal to block in more tone on the leaves where necessary, gently blending the marks with your fingers as before. With confident, flowing strokes, using the tip of the charcoal stick, put in the most prominent veins on the leaves. These strong, linear marks contrast nicely with the blended tone on both the leaves and the florets. The drawing is really taking shape now.

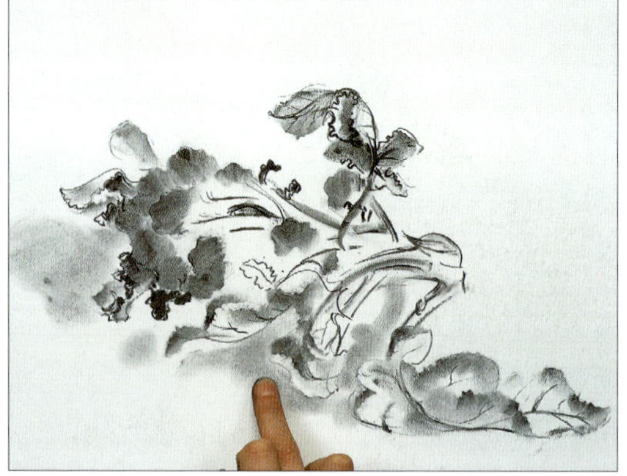

9 Very lightly stroke charcoal on to the background, following the shape of the cast shadows, and blend with your fingers. The shadows need to be much softer and lighter in tone than the broccoli, so you will not need to apply much charcoal; you may even find that your fingers are already covered in so much charcoal that you can use them as a drawing tool in their own right!

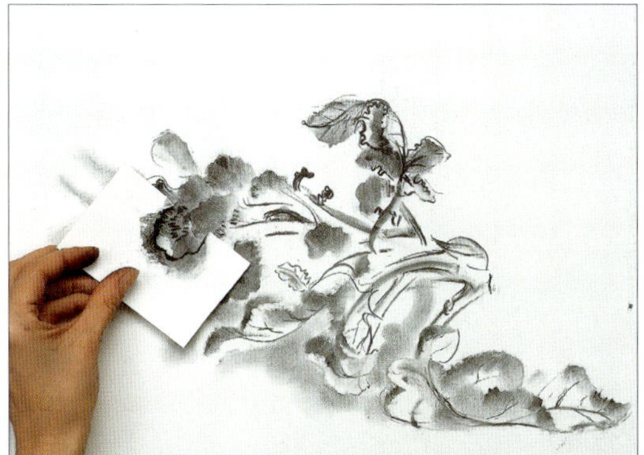

10 Place the broccoli floret mask that you used in Steps 2 and 3 in position again and go back over the shapes, making a series of small dots and dashes to create some texture. Don't blend the marks this time.

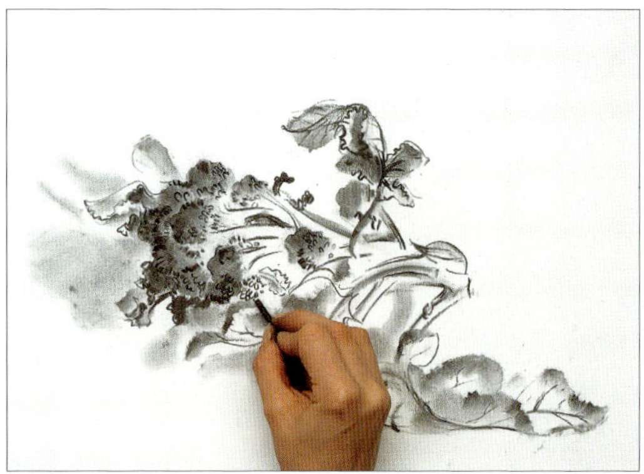

11 Add more detailing and texture to the broccoli florets by making a series of short, hook-shaped marks with the tip of the charcoal. These dark marks stand out well against the smoothly blended charcoal base.

The finished drawing

This is a very lively drawing, full of vitality and movement. Masks have been used to create random, irregular edges on both the florets and the leaves, complementing the flowing, calligraphic-style lines of the stems and veins.

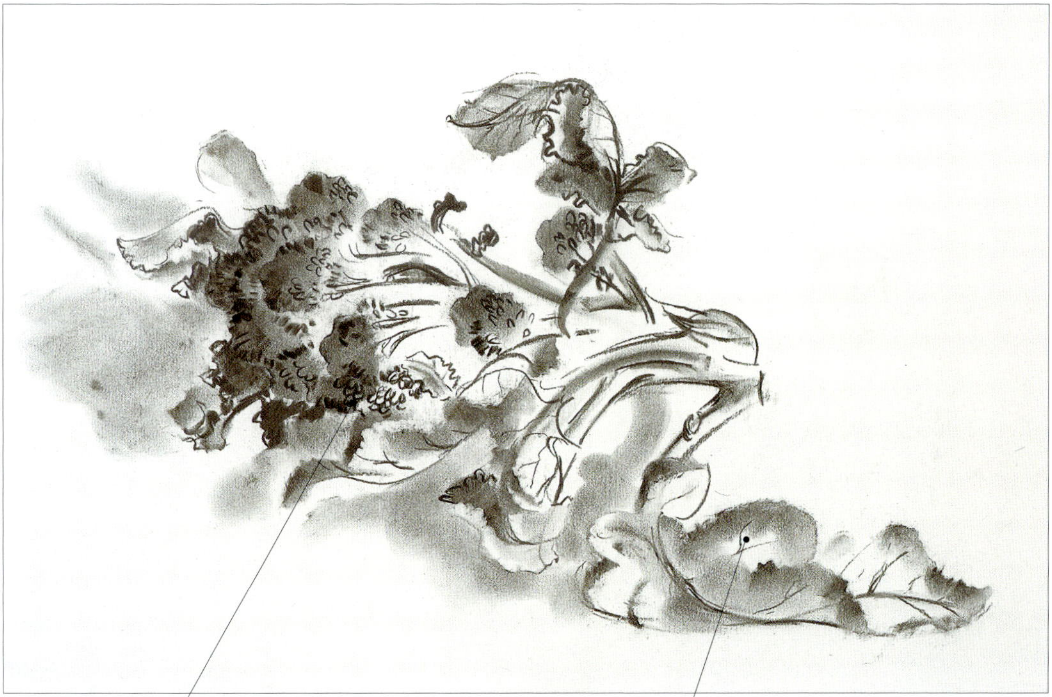

Short, linear marks on top of the smudged charcoal create the texture of the broccoli florets.

The mask was turned upside down to create leaves of different shapes.

Eraser drawing

Erasers can be used for far more than simply making corrections: they are also a powerful drawing tool in their own right. The difference is that they are used to remove marks, rather than to add them. The technique works best with high-contrast subjects that contain both very dark and very light tones. It is also a good way of picking out highlights as by using the tip of the eraser or a cut edge, you can wipe out very precise marks.

Erasers can be used with graphite, coloured pencils, charcoal, pastel and chalks, as well as with all types of pigmented artists' pencils. Different erasers produce different marks, and some perform less well than others with certain materials. Kneaded erasers can be moulded to shape, making it possible to work into tight, precise areas. However, they become dirty very quickly and are of limited use with pastel or charcoal. Vinyl and plastic erasers are harder and do not become dirty so quickly. They can be used with softer drawing materials without becoming completely clogged and unusable. Use only clear or white erasers, as coloured erasers can leave a mark on white paper. When an eraser does get dirty, you can clean it by rubbing it on a scrap piece of paper or by cutting away the dirty edges with a craft (utility) knife. Use the sharp edges of a cut eraser to draw sharp, precise lines and the blunter edge for working into wider areas of colour or tone. If the eraser picks up colour or pigment as you use it, take care not to transfer that colour on to an area where it is not wanted.

You can also use masking techniques with erasers, by working up to the edge of a piece of card (stock) to create a precise edge or by working over torn paper to create a more random edge. As an alternative to commercially available erasers, try rolling a piece of soft, white bread into a ball and using it to clean up white areas of paper or lighten an area of tone.

Practice exercise: **Still life**

In this exercise, erasers are used to wipe out highlights and enhance the three-dimensional feel of the drawing. The papery skin of the garlic is full of tiny crinkles, the ridges of which catch the light. If you were to draw these individually, the chances are that your drawing would look somewhat laboured and tight – but using the cut edge of an eraser allows you to wipe out a line that is slightly uneven and much more sympathetic to the subject. For broader highlight areas, the flat side of the eraser is used. As with all textural techniques, your eraser strokes should follow the form of the object.

As a variation on this exercise, cover the paper with graphite or charcoal and use an eraser as a drawing tool.

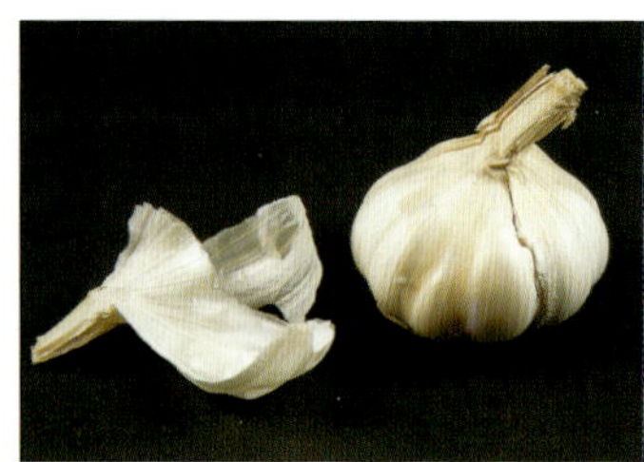

Materials

- *Smooth drawing paper*
- *9B graphite stick*
- *Plastic and kneaded erasers*

The set-up

In this simple set-up, a bulb of garlic and a twisted section of peeled garlic skin were arranged on a dark marble background, creating a composition that contains strong contrasts between very dark and very light areas. The stalks were carefully angled to create a diagonal line that makes a dynamic composition.

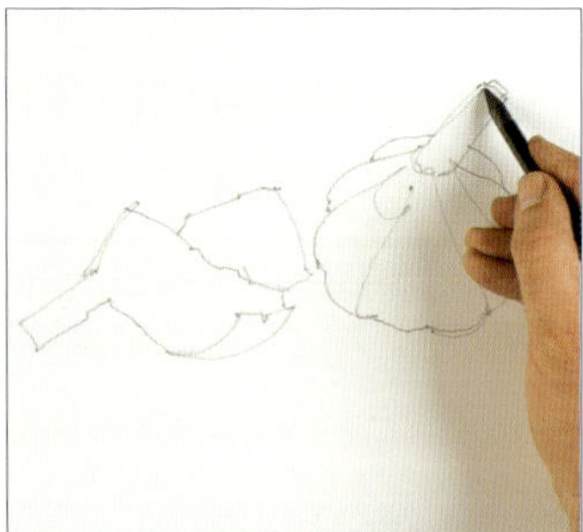

1 Using a 9B graphite stick, outline the bulbs of garlic.

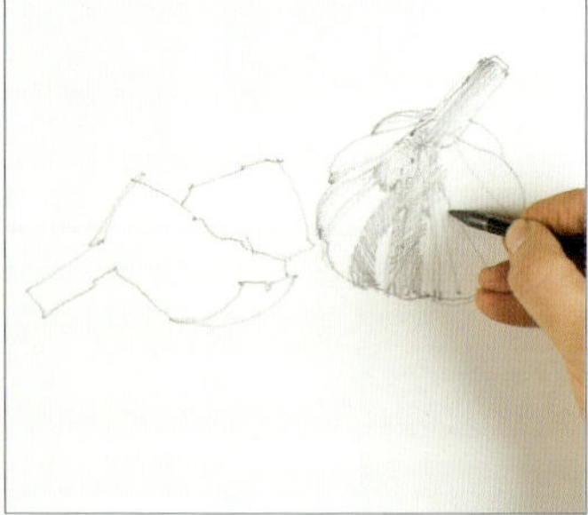

2 Put in the internal lines in the garlic skin, following the contours of the individual cloves beneath. Using loose hatching marks, apply some tone.

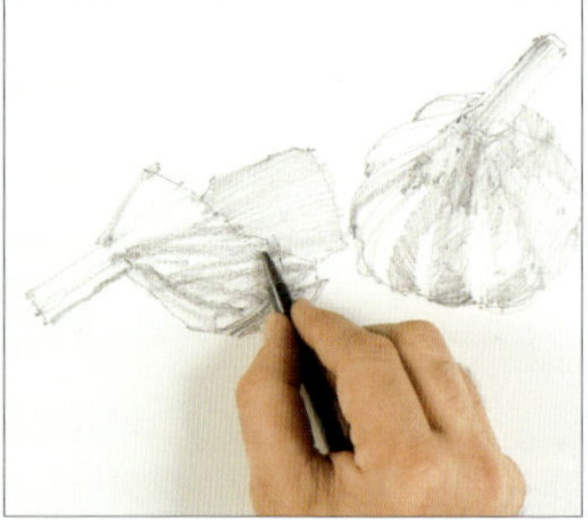

3 Continue adding tone to the garlic. Note how its form immediately becomes more evident, as the more deeply shaded areas reveal both the contours of the individual cloves and the ridges in the papery outer covering.

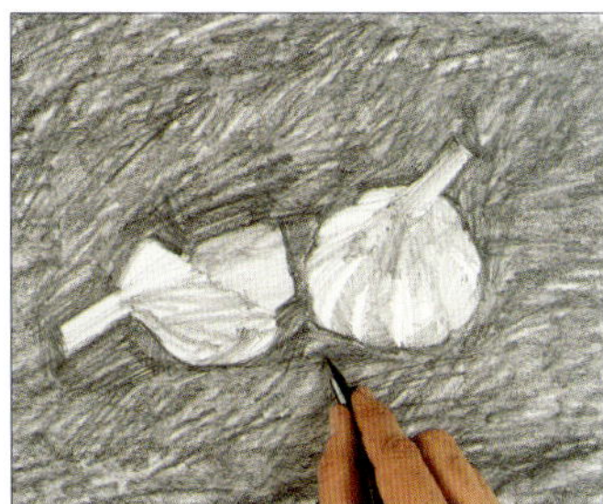

4 Applying reasonably heavy pressure to the graphite stick, scribble in the dark background. Work carefully up to the edge of the garlic, redefining its shape as you work.

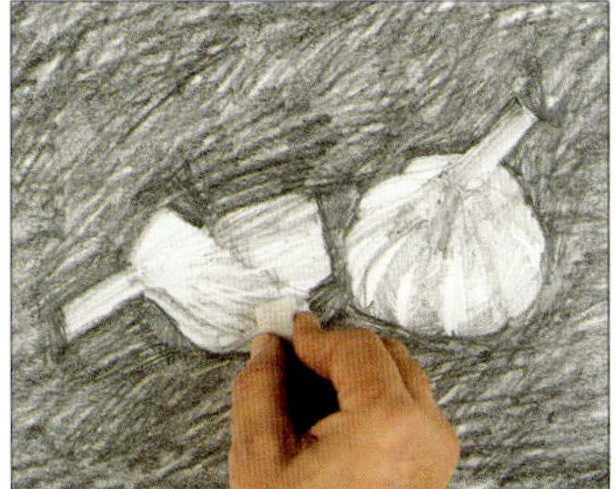

5 Using the sharp, cut edge of a plastic eraser, wipe out fine lines on the garlic skin. These thin, bright lines help to show the crinkled, papery texture of the skin.

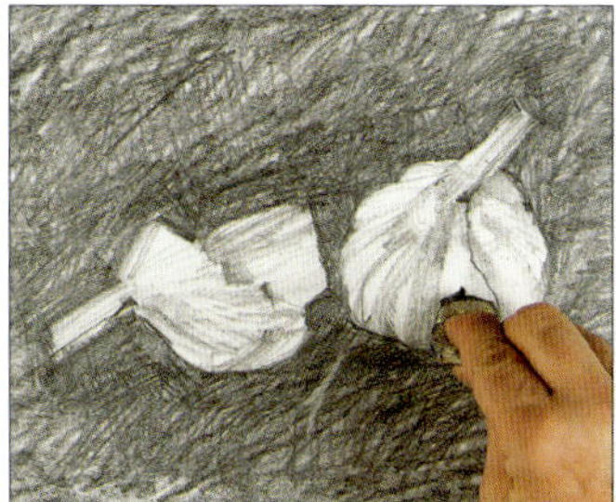

6 Using the flat side of a kneaded eraser, wipe out larger areas of tone to reveal the highlights on the garlic. If you accidentally wipe off too much, just hatch over the affected area again.

The finished drawing

This simple still life relies for its impact on the contrast between very dark and very light areas. Using an eraser to wipe out the highlights has resulted in loose, natural-looking lines that capture the crinkled texture of the garlic skin, and has produced a more integrated drawing than could be achieved by positive applications of pigment alone.

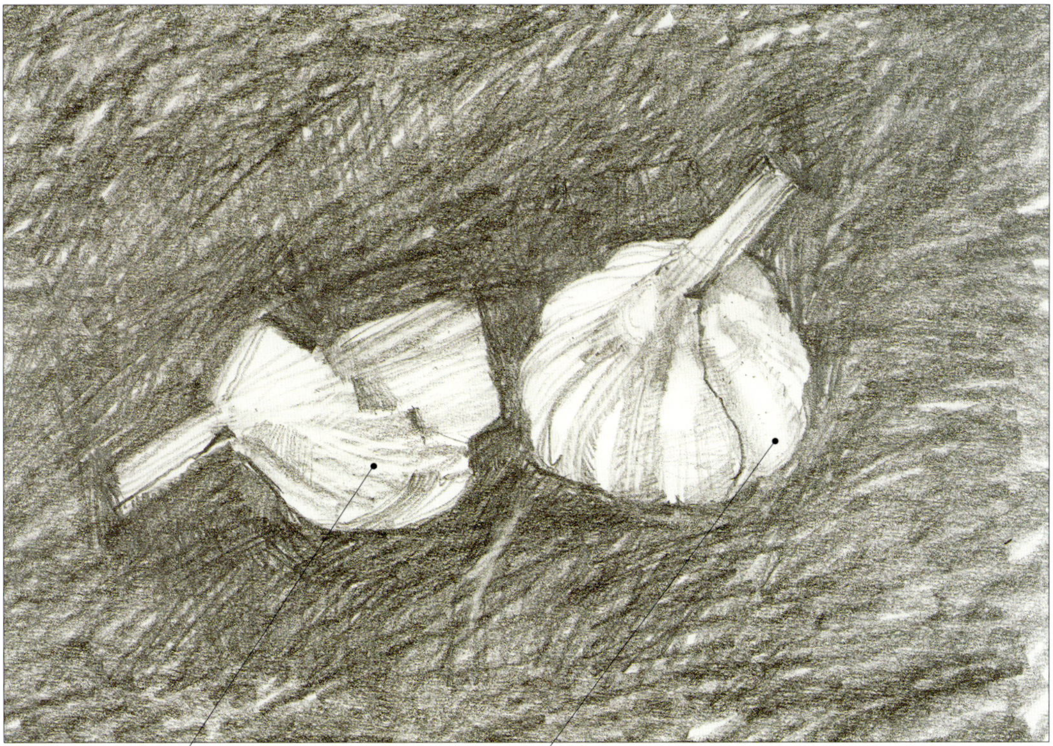

The sharp, cut edge of the eraser creates fine highlight lines.

Broader areas are wiped out using the flat side of the eraser.

Drawing hard lines

Although drawing is concerned with lines, they are more often used to create the illusion of three-dimensional form and texture than to put down solid outlines. The edges of hard objects require precise delineation, and this is best achieved by the accurate rendering of sharp shadows and highlights.

Practice exercise: **Stainless steel olive oil pourer**

When you're drawing metal, remember that it is a hard substance and that the edges of metal objects, even if they are irregular in shape, are very clearly defined. Metal is a highly reflective surface, although the reflections may be distorted. Metal tends to pick up very bright highlights, which will help you to convey the form of the object you are drawing. Finally, remember that all metals (and metals such as silver and stainless steel in particular) take much of their colour from objects that are reflected in the surface – so look at the surroundings as well as at the objects that you are drawing.

Materials

- *Smooth drawing paper*
- *Charcoal pencil*
- *White chalk*

The subject

In terms of its shape, this is a relatively simple subject to draw – but in order for it to look convincing you will need to recreate the smooth, shiny texture.

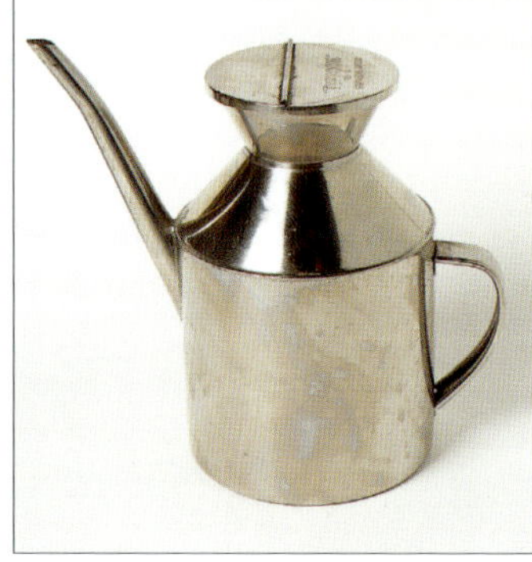

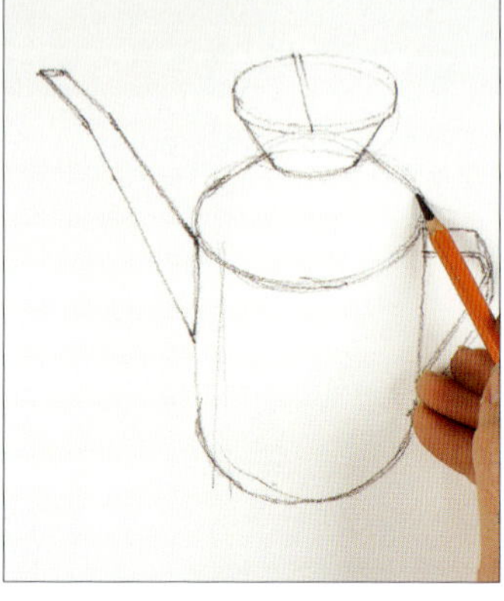

1 You need to establish first the shape of the olive oil pourer using relatively light lines made with a charcoal pencil.

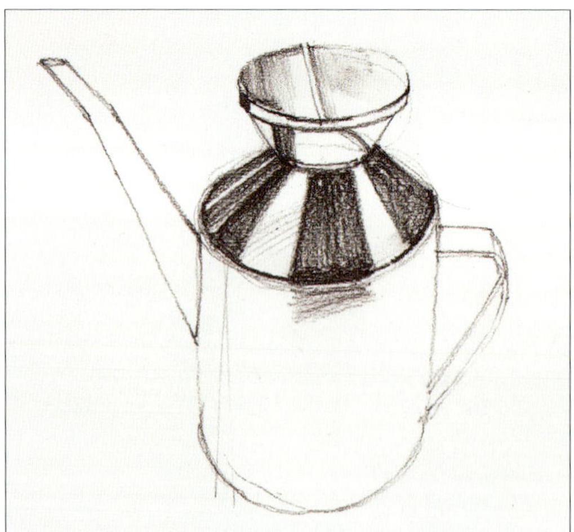

2 Establish the darkest reflections using heavy charcoal work, carefully working around any areas that reflect the light. Note how putting in these dark reflections immediately tells us something about the shape of the object: although the lid of the oil pourer is not faceted, the shapes of the reflections do help to imply that it is gently curved.

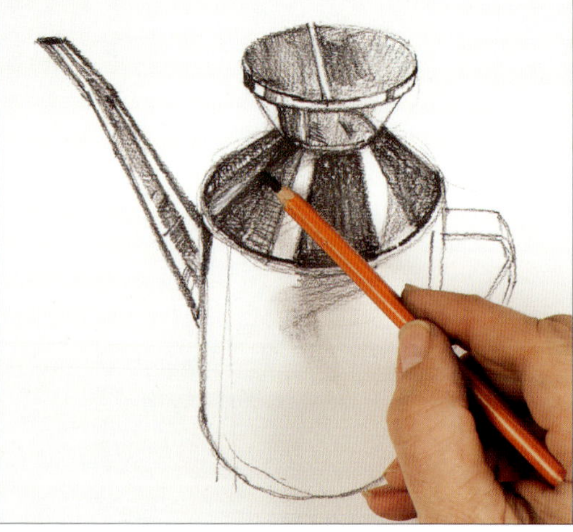

3 Consolidate the darkest areas, such as the very dark lip of the lid and the inside of the tip of the spout, and begin to draw in the mid-tones using light pencil work. Blend the pencil marks by using your fingertips or a paper torchon: the surface of the oil pourer is smooth, so try to ensure that no pencil marks are visible.

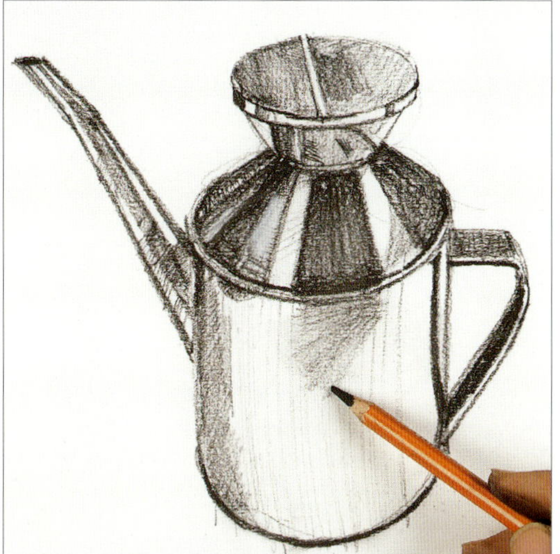

4 Continue to work the mid- and light tones on the cylindrical body of the pourer, using pencil marks that follow the contours of the object.

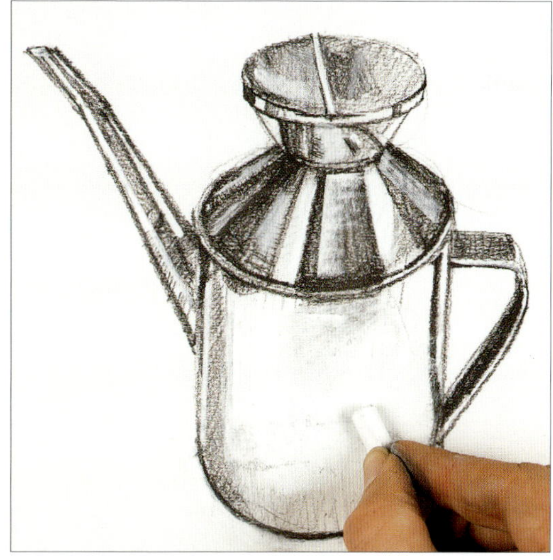

5 In order for the hard, shiny, reflective surface to read correctly, the marks need to be precise and sharp. Use a white chalk to sharpen the highlights.

The finished drawing
This metal's smooth and shiny surface is achieved by building up the layers gradually and by observing the shape, position and tone of the highlights carefully.

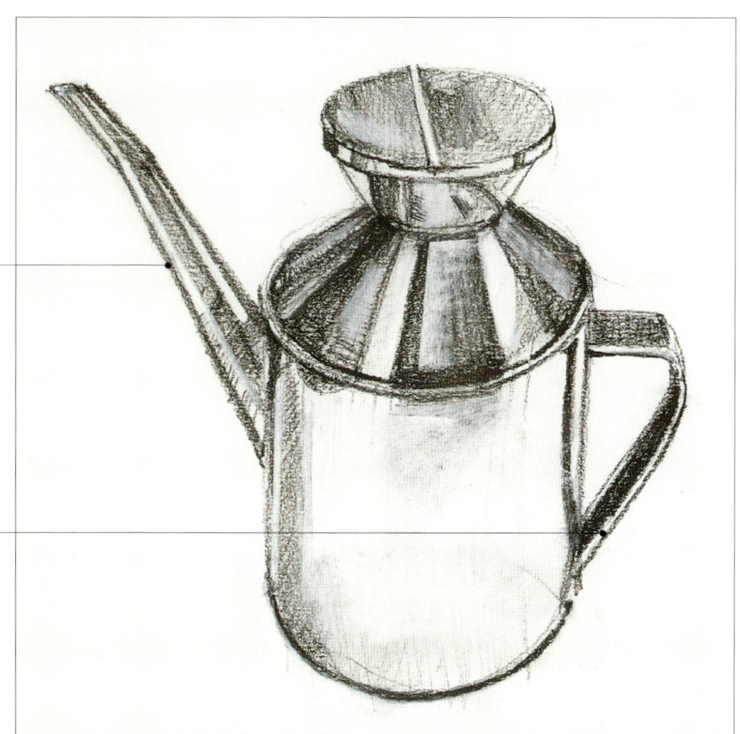

Note how the edges of the metal object are very clearly and crisply defined.

The light catches the outer edge of the handle, creating a very bright highlight, while the inside of the handle is in deep shadow.

Drawing rough textures

For an artist, rough textures are perhaps the most fun to draw as they allow you to use a whole range of calligraphic and textural marks. The types of rough surface that you will come across include pitted stone and rock, brickwork, weathered wood and bark, certain animal skins such as elephant and rhino, and some types of coarse fabric.

With a rough-textured subject, working on a surface that has some texture to it will help the mark-making process – but beware of choosing a support in which the texture is too dominant, as no amount of mark-making will prevent it from showing through.

Many rough textures are repetitive over a large area – but this does not mean that you have to draw in the texture so that it covers the area. You can suggest the texture in places and, if this is done successfully, the viewer will mentally fill in the missing bits. In fact, it can be a mistake to draw in textures too comprehensively as they can easily overpower a drawing and make it appear lifeless.

The degree to which a rough texture shows up depends very much on the quality and direction of the light. In bright light that hits the object at an angle, the texture will appear to be quite pronounced; in flat light, the same texture will appear less evident.

Practice exercise: **Weathered driftwood**

With a subject such as this, you can explore a wide range of marks to convey the texture – flowing, linear strokes for the main lines of the wood grain, short dots and dashes for little indentations in the surface, and smudged marks for dark areas of tone.

Materials
- *Rough watercolour paper*
- *Charcoal stick*

The subject
This piece of weathered driftwood has lots of tiny cracks and crevices within it, as well as a deeper recess in the centre. Lighting it from the left casts a shadow to the right of the wood and also helps to reveal the texture.

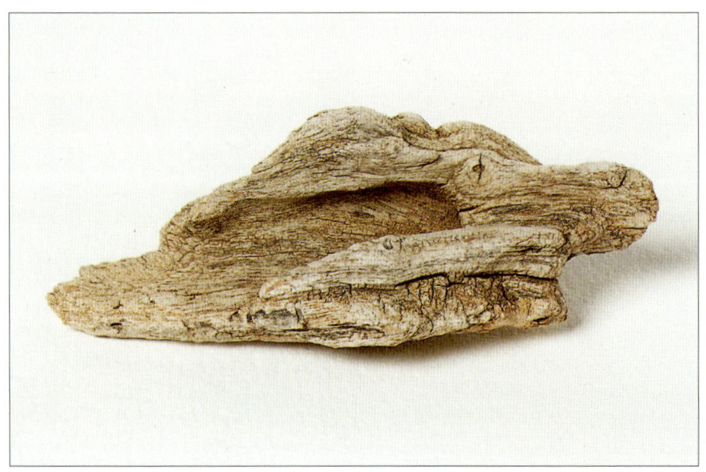

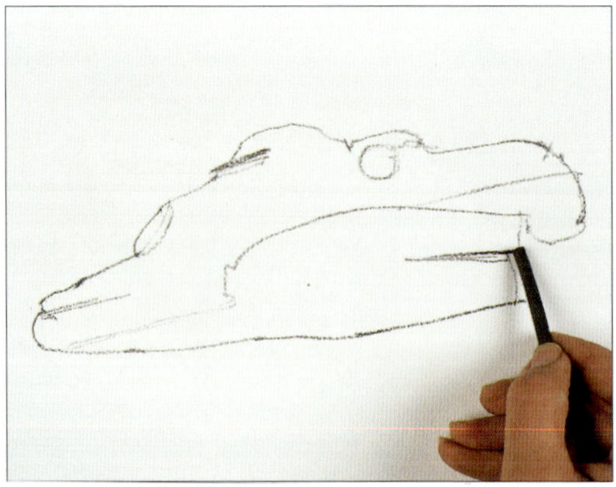

1 Establish the shape of the piece of driftwood using stick charcoal on a sheet of rough watercolour paper. It helps to put in the most obvious cracks as guidelines.

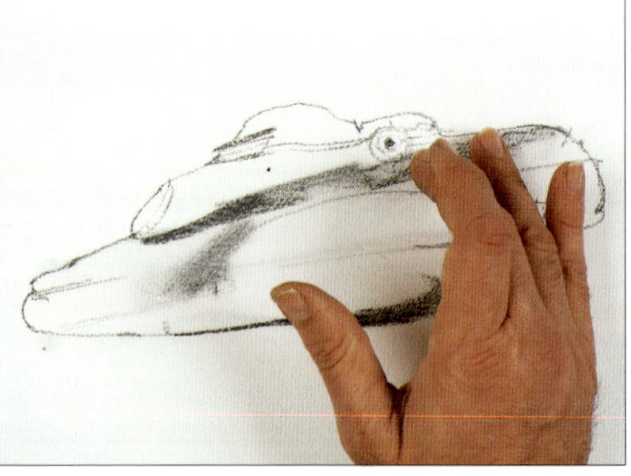

2 Once you have drawn the main shape, put in the darker areas of tone using the side of the stick. Blend the pigment and push it into the paper surface using your finger.

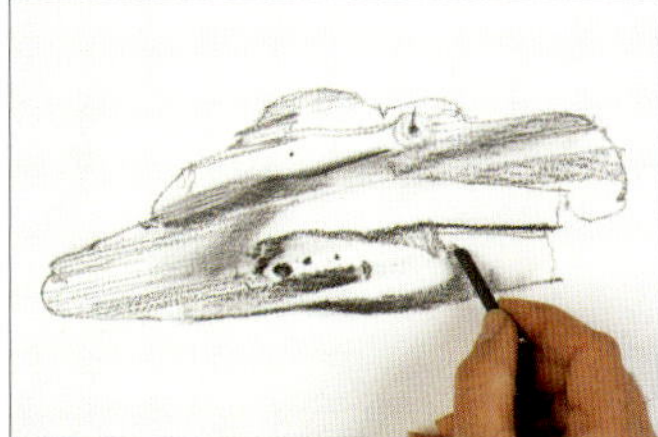

3 Continue building up lines and tones on the driftwood surface. Note how the texture of the paper reads through these marks and helps suggest the pitted, weathered surface.

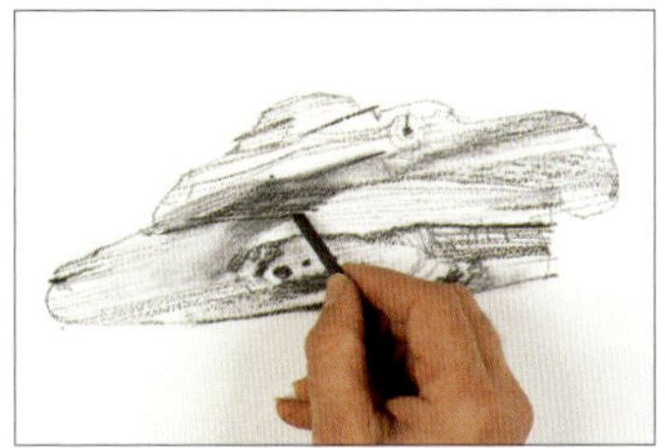

4 Once you have drawn the main tones and flowing lines of the wood grain, put in the darker areas deep in the splits and holes using heavy pressure and firm, deliberate marks.

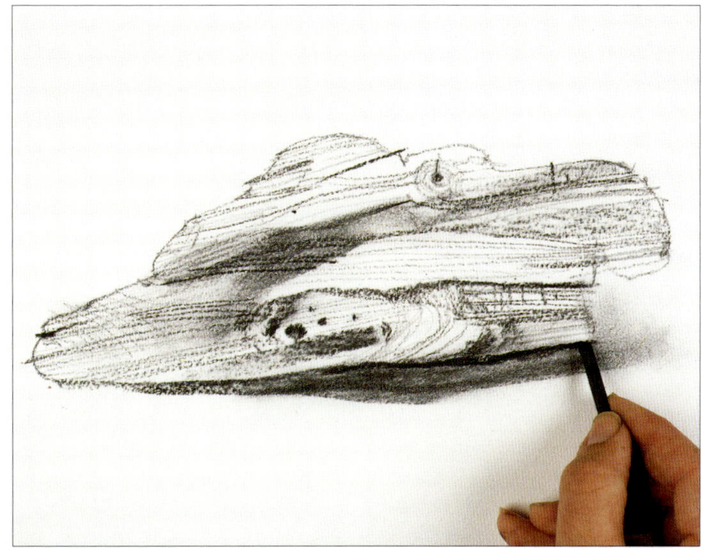

5 Complete the sketch with light, flowing texture lines and put in a dark shadow beneath the object, smoothing out the marks with your fingers.

The finished drawing
This is a lively drawing in which a combination of confident linear marks and soft blending of the charcoal creates the texture of the wood. Note how the linear marks follow the direction of the wood grain. The cast shadow anchors the piece of wood on the surface and provides an interesting shape in its own right.

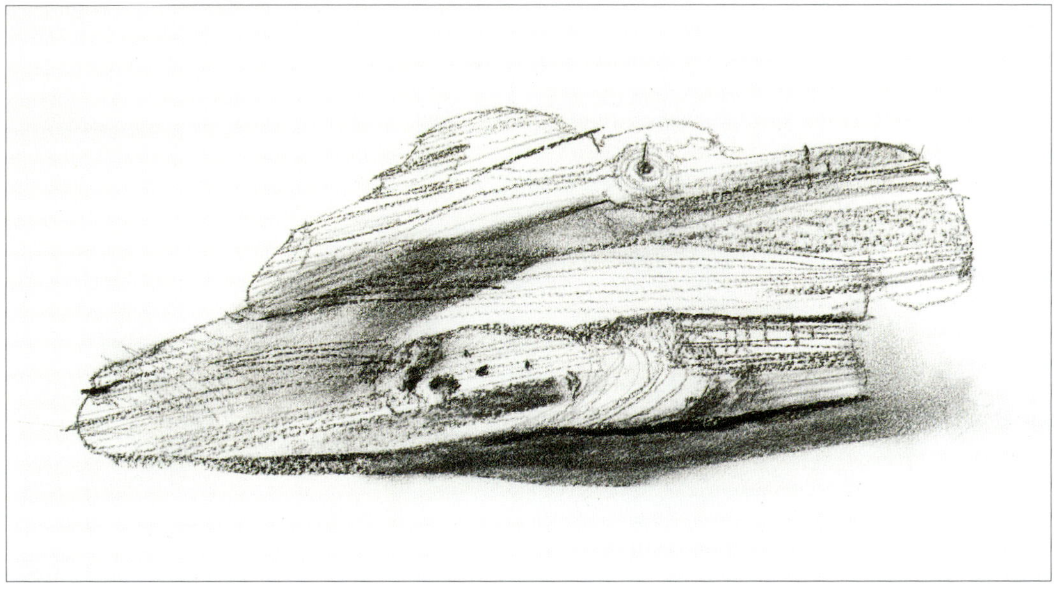

Drawing soft textures

Soft textures include skin, animal fur and feathers, and fabrics. These types of texture are often affected by an underlying structure (for example, the skeleton in the case of an animal or bird). Sometimes, they are covered in a design, and the design or pattern on a surface can tell us about the shape of that object, as the way lines flow or a pattern is distorted indicates the structure that lies underneath.

The texture of soft objects is, more often than not, relatively smooth. Even animal fur and birds' feathers, when viewed from a distance, appear smooth and unruffled.

As with rough textures, when you are drawing fur or feathers it is neither necessary nor advisable to put in every hair and every feather. Skin needs to be treated with care, as any texture is barely noticeable; even in elderly people, where the inevitable wrinkles can be seen, you should take care not to overdo the effect.

Unless they are really coarse, the texture of fabrics is virtually imperceptible from all but the closest distance. More often than not, it is revealed by the quality of any surface pattern or decoration. It also depends on the quality of the lighting: strong, directional light will make the surface folds and creases far more apparent than flat, even lighting.

Practice exercise: **Folded fabric**

Most fabrics are soft in texture. Sometimes you can use the distorted lines of the pattern to show how the folds and creases in the fabric fall; at other times, particularly if the fabric is a uniform colour, they are revealed by variations in tone. Look for both these things when drawing fabric.

Materials
- *Smooth drawing paper*
- *2B pencil*
- *Soft eraser*

The subject
Here, a man's handkerchief was folded and rucked up slightly at one side to create interesting creases and shapes within the fabric.

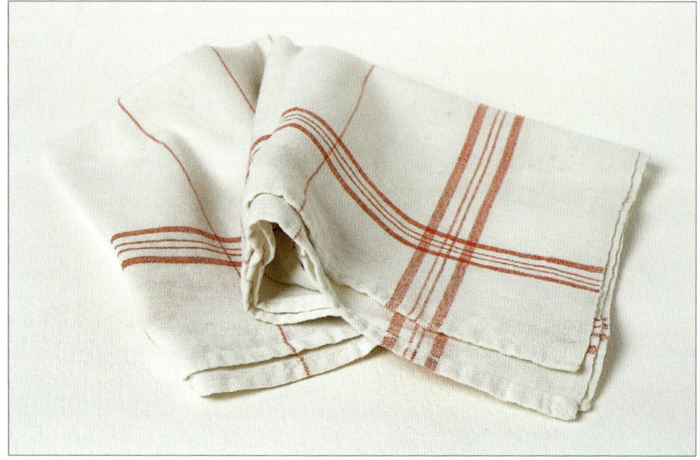

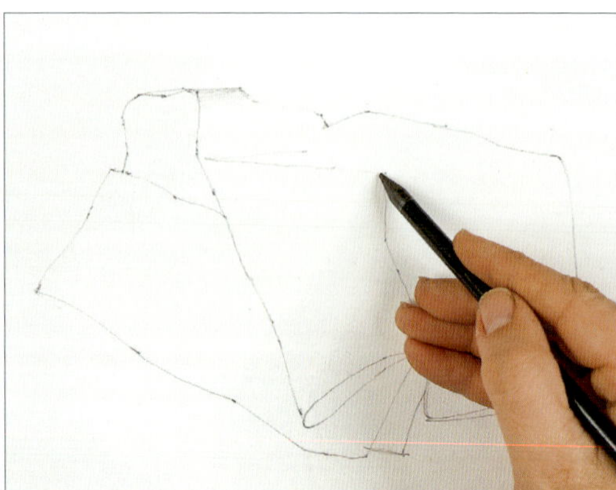

1 Establish the shape of this crumpled handkerchief using a 2B pencil. Use light, flowing lines to suggest not only the shape but also the position of any shadows.

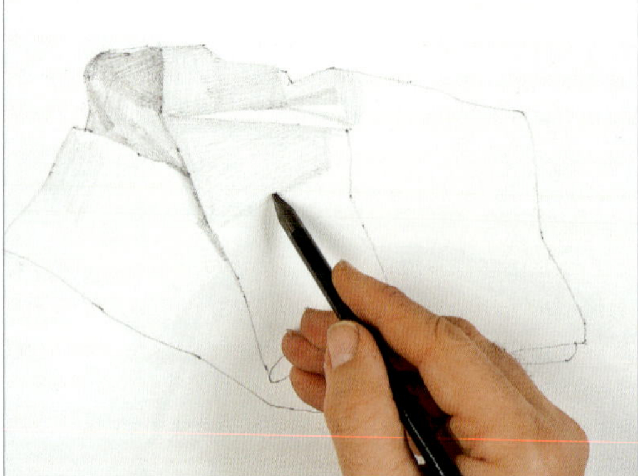

2 Begin to put in the tones, using scribbled pencil marks that follow the contours of the fabric. Use light pressure for the very light tones, holding the pencil high up the shaft.

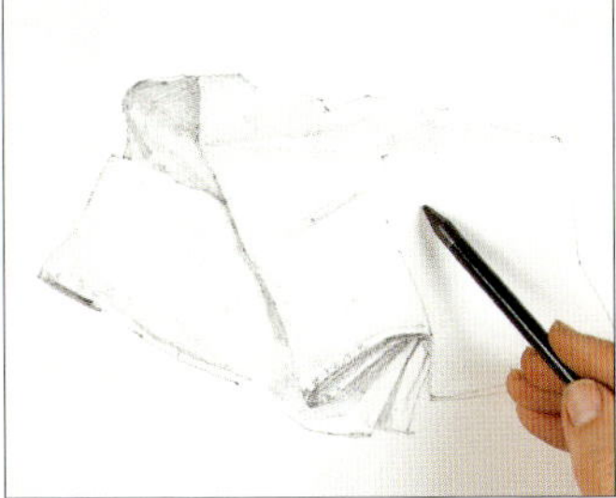

3 Continue steadily searching out the contours and the relevant tones. Gradually the form of the object becomes apparent.

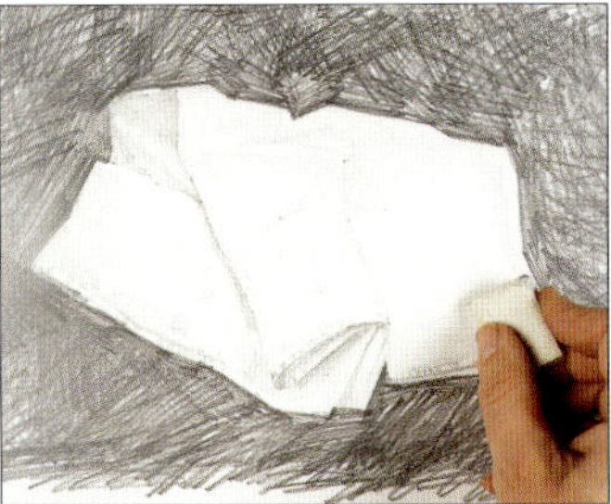

4 Give the area surrounding the handkerchief a dark tone. 'Draw' in any light creases on the fabric using a soft eraser.

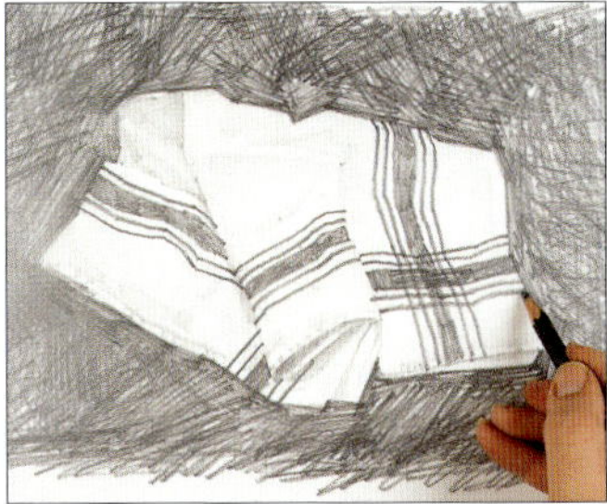

5 Finally, draw the patterned lines that are woven into the fabric of the handkerchief, carefully following the shape of the contours.

The finished drawing

Note how careful observation of the subtle differences in tone, from the white of the paper for the most brightly lit areas to a pale covering of grey elsewhere, reveals the gentle folds in the fabric. More abrupt folds are indicated by the changes in direction of the pattern woven around the edge of the handkerchief.

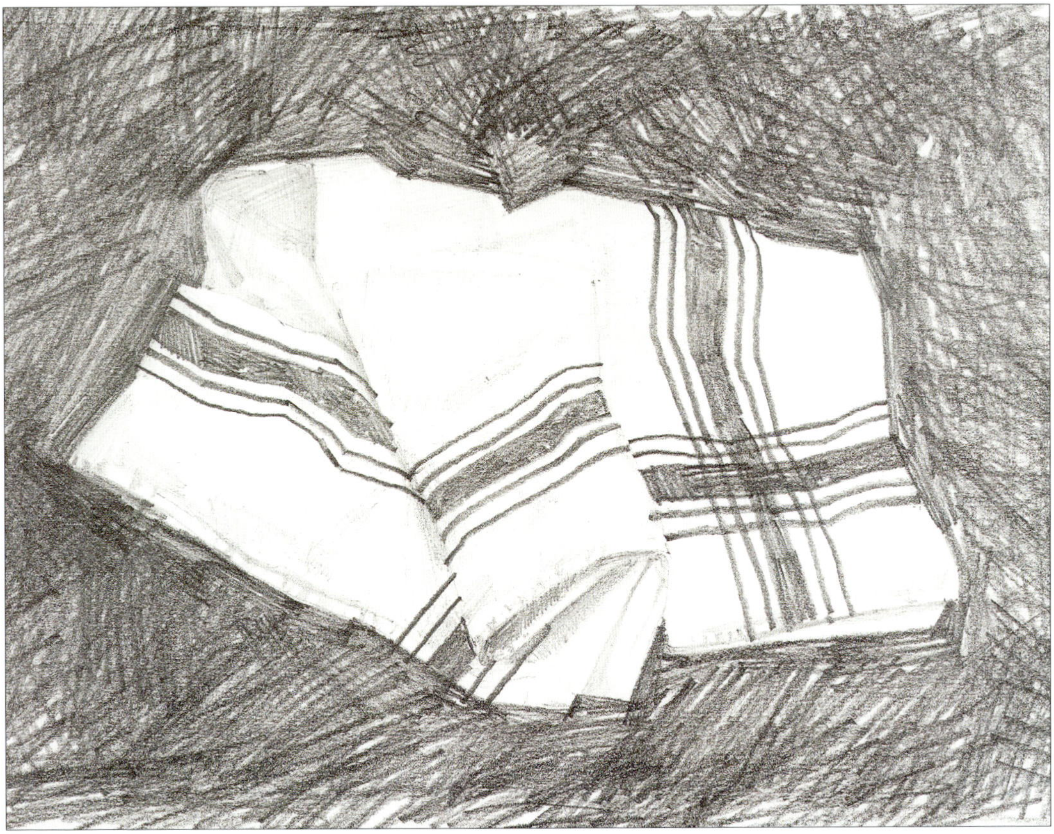

Practice exercise: **Feathers**

When you are drawing a bird, it is neither necessary nor advisable to put in every single feather – particularly if you are drawing a front view, as the chest feathers tend to be relatively small. Look instead for the blocks of feathers and think about their function: are they strong, primary feathers that are used for steering and to produce the power of flight as the wing is brought down through the air, or the softer, more pliable secondary feathers that lie above the primary feathers? Also think about the skeleton that lies underneath the feathers, as this will make it easier for you to get the shape of the body and head right.

Materials

- *Smooth drawing paper*
- *Fine liner pen*

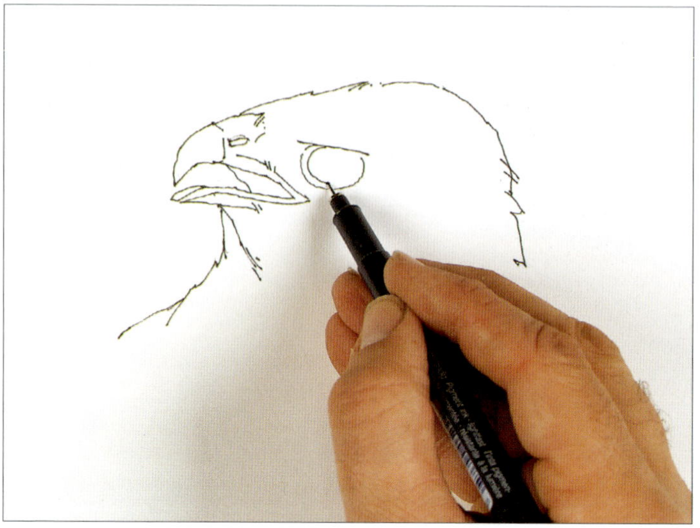

1 Using a fine liner pen, map out the main shape and features of the bird of prey's head. Use small, jagged strokes around the edge to convey the texture of the facial and neck feathers.

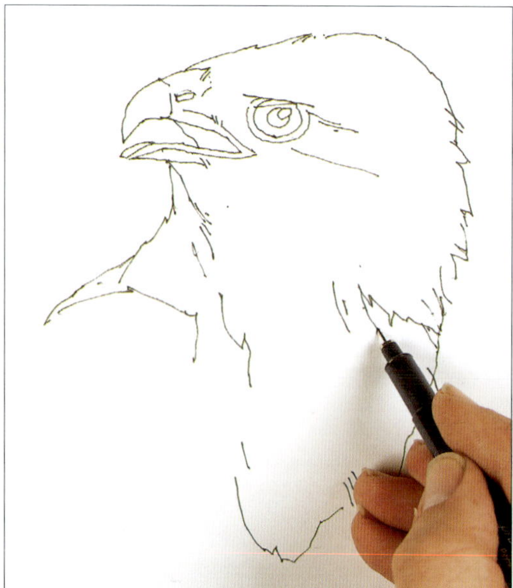

2 Draw in the position and shape of the main feather groups – the feathers at the base of the head and on the bird's chest.

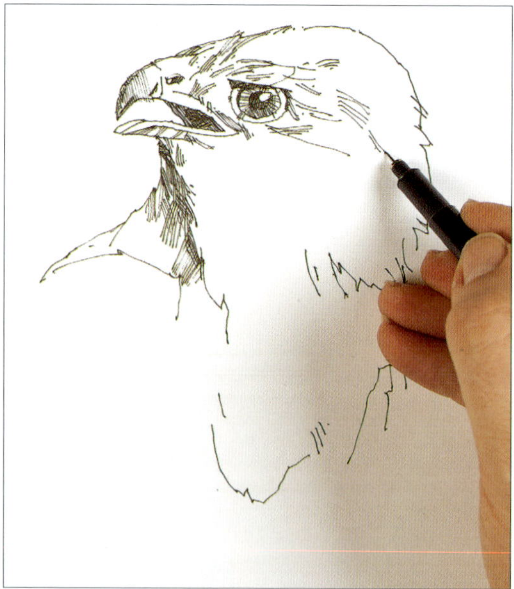

3 Elaborate the main feather groups, defining some feathers more clearly than others. Colour in the eye, remembering to leave the highlight untouched.

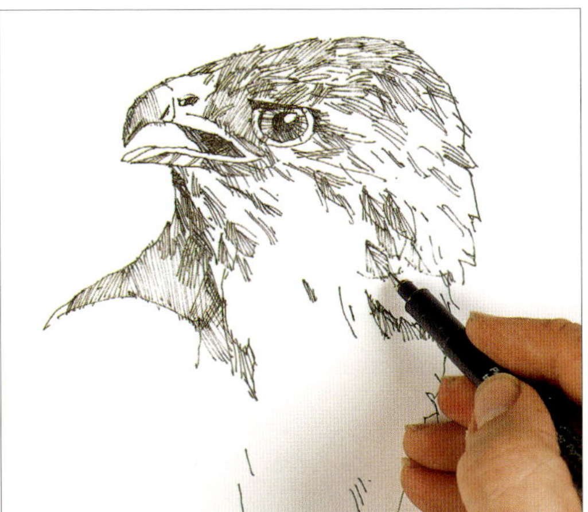

4 Build up the tones by increasing the density of the pen lines, carefully following the surface contours of the underlying body structure.

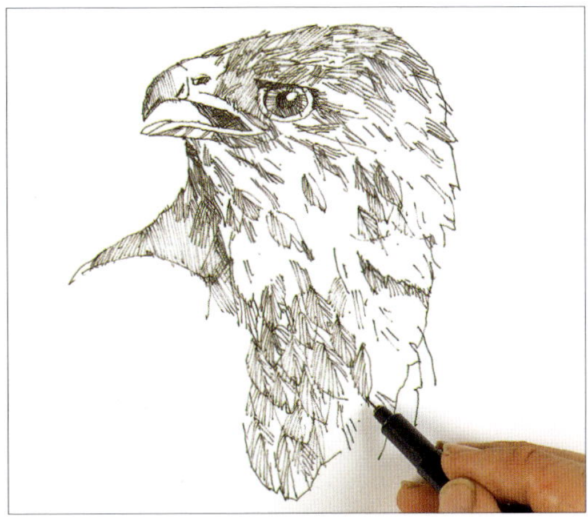

5 Finally draw the cluster of feathers that runs from the bird's neck over its chest. They help to give the subject a sense of solidity.

The finished drawing
Using a liner pen can give a drawing a rather mechanical feel if you're not careful, and the trick is not to put in too much detail. Here, the artist has created the soft texture by drawing pen lines that follow the direction of the individual strands within the feathers.

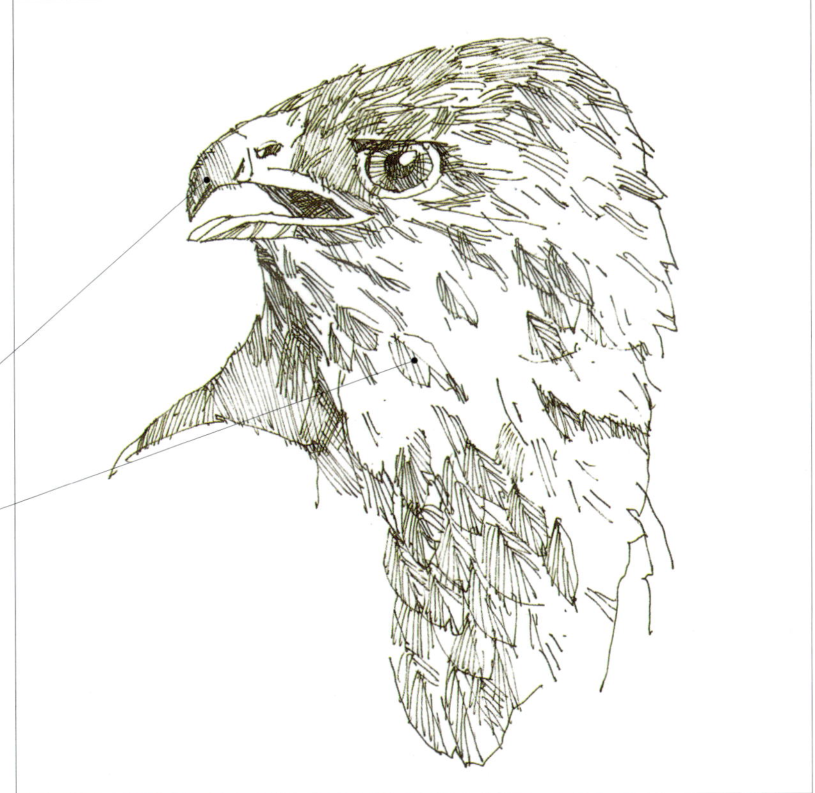

Make sure the beak looks hard and slightly shiny.

Even though some areas are left almost blank, the viewer's eye fills in the missing details.

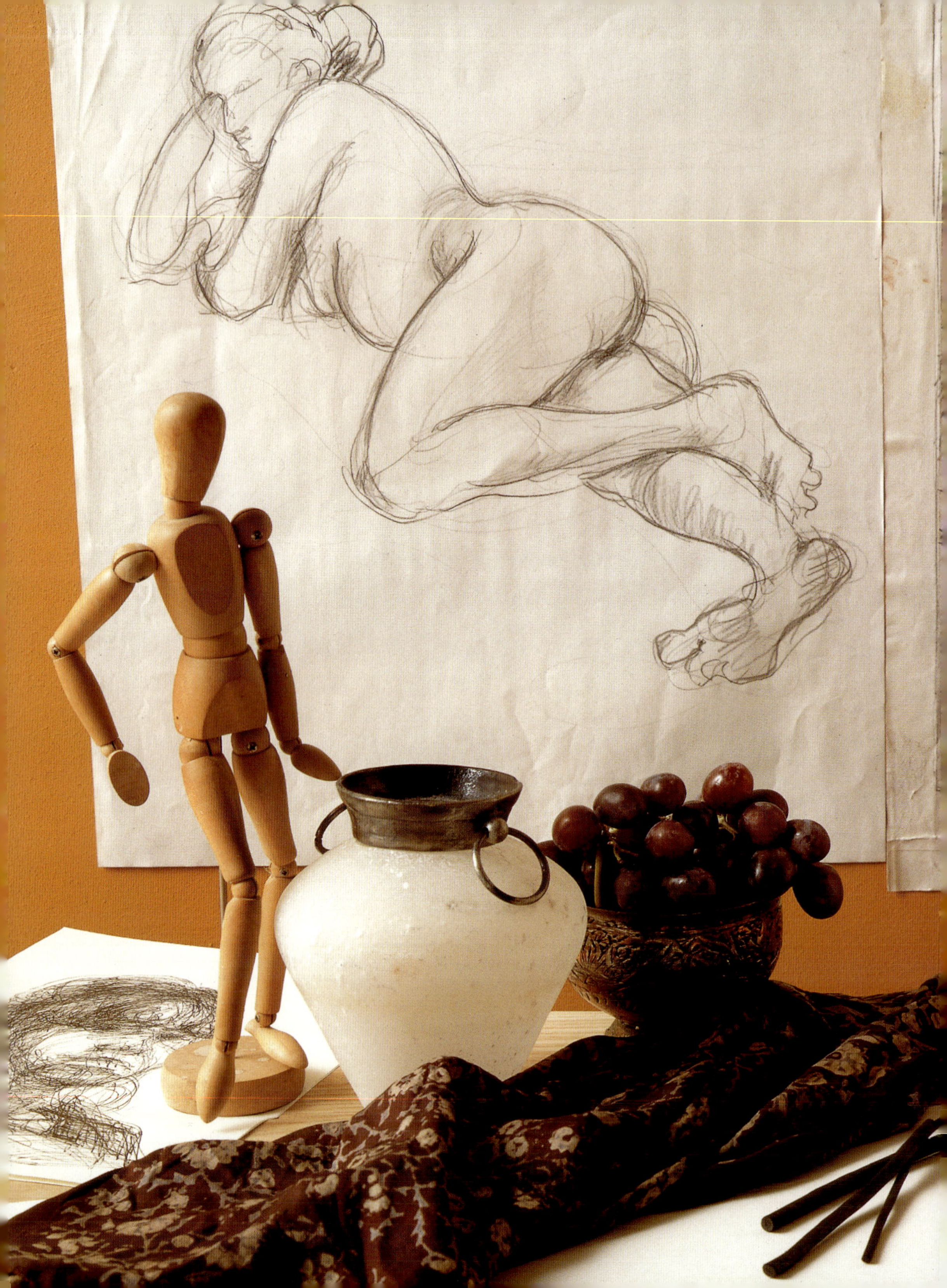

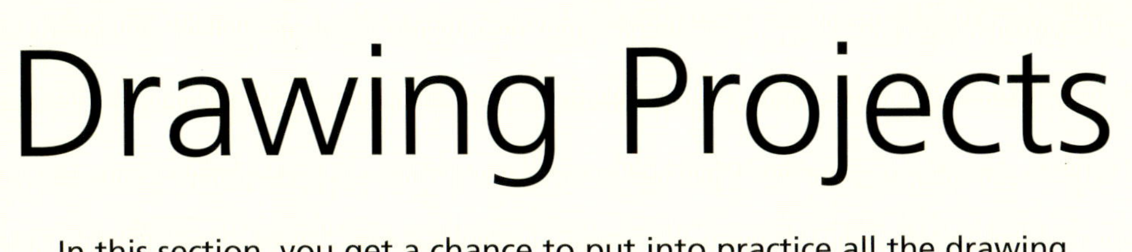

Drawing Projects

In this section, you get a chance to put into practice all the drawing skills you have learned, in a series of step-by-step projects specially commissioned from leading professional artists. Each project begins with a full list of the materials you will need and a photograph of the scene that the artist chose to draw – so you can either copy the project exactly or use it as a starting point for your own artistic explorations. Packed with useful tips, it is full of ideas that will inspire you to create works you will be proud to hang on your wall.

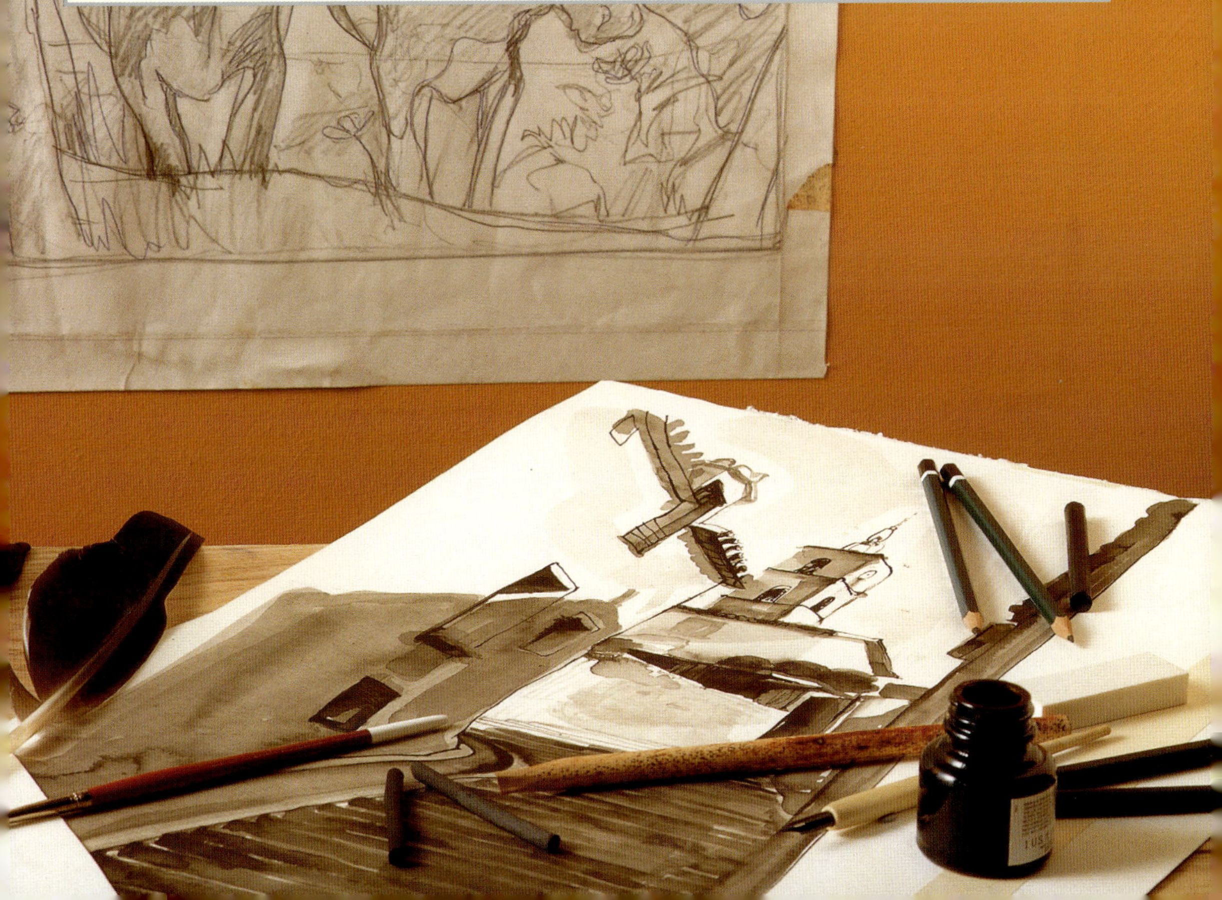

Quick sketches of trees: Damaged tree

Trees are a delight to draw – particularly old trees that have gnarled bark and twists and splits in their trunks – as they allow you to explore a wide range of textural techniques and approaches to making marks. Monochrome sketches are perhaps the most interesting and satisfying of all as, without the distraction of colour, the textures and shapes really start to come into their own.

It's important to try to convey a sense of trees as living, growing organisms, and you should always examine the shapes of the trunk and branches carefully before you start to draw: some trees, such as the silver birch, have thin, relatively smooth trunks, while others, such as ancient olives that have been cultivated for many decades, have gnarled trunks with distinct grooved patterns in the surface. If you're sketching *in situ*, try running your fingers over the trunk to get a feel for the texture and the pattern of the bark: does the pattern run up and down in fairly straight lines or does it go round in nobbly circles?

Look at how the branches grow out of the main trunk: do they spread out straight, or veer upwards in a v-shaped pattern on either side of the trunk, or droop downwards? Finally, think about how you're going to draw the leaves. For small leaves, a few loose dots and dashes may be sufficient; for larger leaves you may need to be more precise about the shape – but don't overdo the leaf detailing, or you'll detract from the shape of the tree as a whole.

The scene

This tree was badly damaged in a winter gale. The artist came across it when she was out for a walk in the country and was attracted by the shapes made by the broken and contorted branches and by the gnarled texture of the bark.

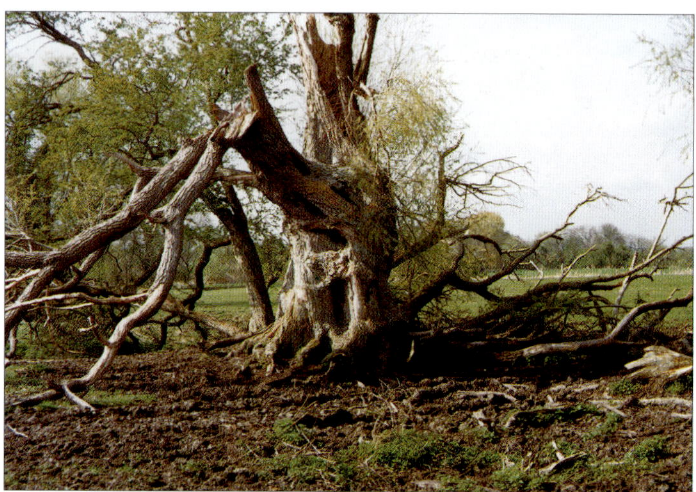

5-minute sketch: graphite pencil

After putting down the outline with slightly jagged pencil strokes, the artist then scribbled in the darkest areas of tone, such as the undersides of the branches and the shaded interior of the split in the trunk. Even in a quick 5-minute sketch such as this, you can begin to capture something of the form of the tree.

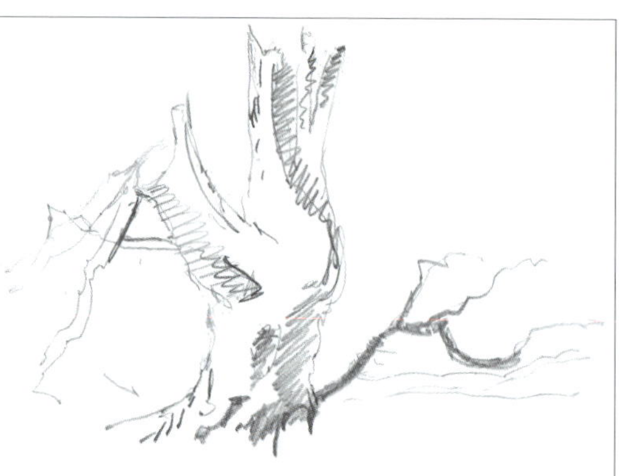

10-minute sketch: graphite pencil

In a slightly longer sketch, you can begin to refine the detail, putting in tones that range from a mid-grey on the shaded parts to a much denser black in the hollowed recess near the base. In addition to providing information about the light and shade, the tone is applied in such as way as to hint at the pattern of the bark.

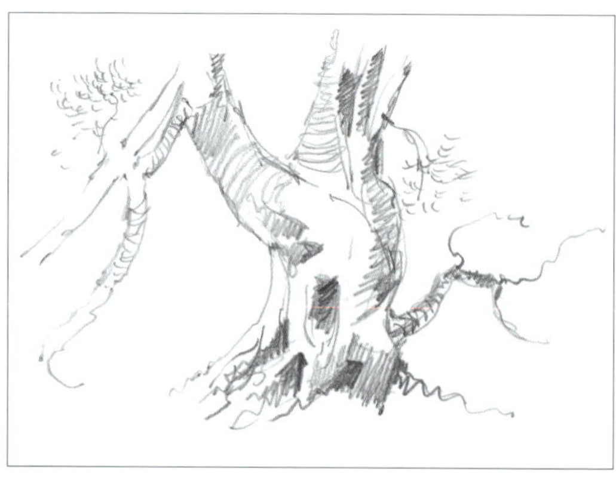

15-minute sketch: graphite pencil
The shading is more highly developed in this sketch and the tree looks more three-dimensional. Although the background has not been drawn in detail, putting in the horizon and blocking in generalized shapes for the trees and bushes in the distance sets the tree in context.

25-minute sketch: graphite pencil plus pen and ink
Confident, scribbled pen lines over an initial pencil sketch give this drawing a real sense of energy and capture the character of the tree very well. Note the use of a wide range of marks, from simple hatching on the trunk to tiny flecks and dashes for the small leaves.

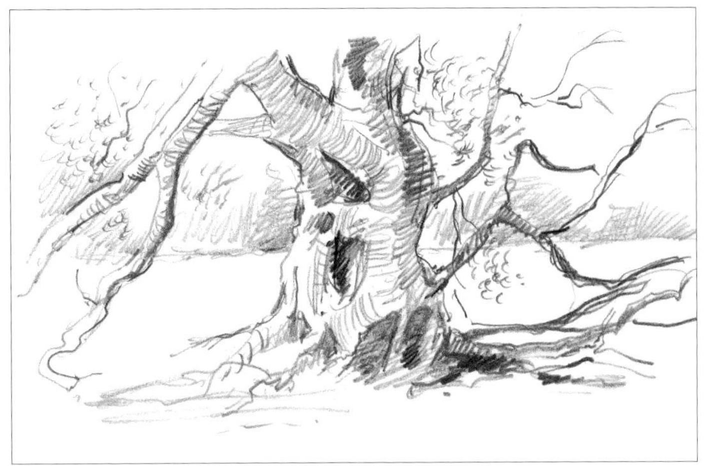

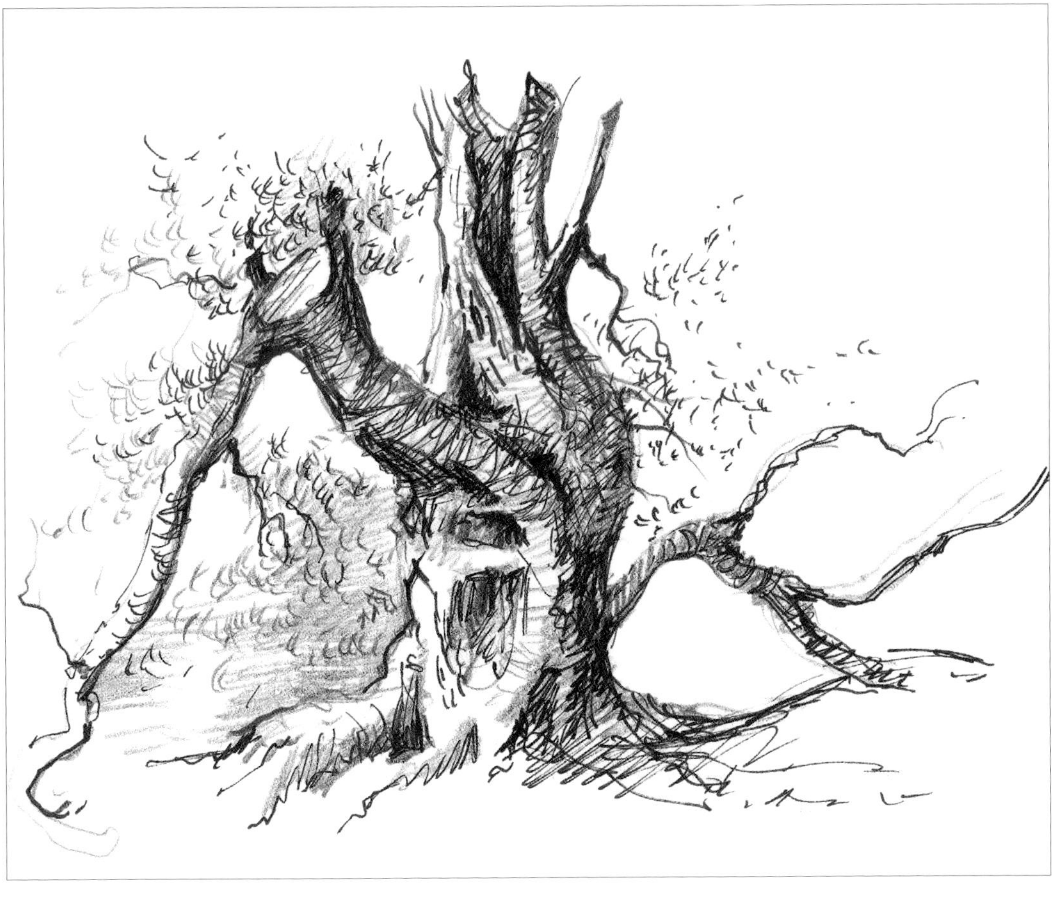

Quick sketches of trees: Foliage masses

Trees form an important part of many landscapes and can also be used as a compositional device, to lead the viewer's eye into the scene or to provide a natural 'frame'. Different types of foliage, however, require different artistic approaches. One of the most common mistakes is to attempt to put in too much detail. Start by looking at the shape of the tree: is it conical or rounded? Then look at the shapes of the leaves within the foliage mass: are they large with a distinctive shape, such as a maple or horse chestnut, or are there many small leaves clustered tightly together, as in the example on these pages? Finally, look for the differences in tone that will make the foliage masses look three-dimensional. Even in dull lighting, as here, some areas will be lighter than others; half closing your eyes as you look at the scene will make it much easier to assess this.

The scene

The dark mass of the tree on the left forms a natural 'frame' for the mountainous, wooded landscape beyond and helps to give a sense of scale. The artist elected to make a number of studies of this single tree in order to capture its character.

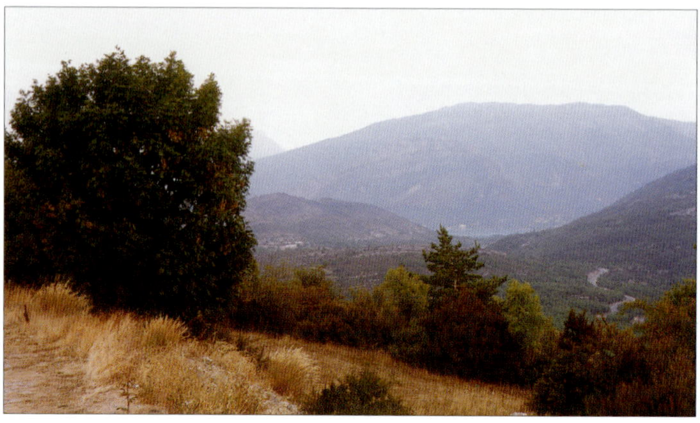

5-minute sketch: charcoal

Start by loosely blocking in the overall shape using the side of the charcoal stick, then work into this shape with the tip of the charcoal, scribbling and dotting in the darkest parts of the foliage mass to create some variation in tone so that the tree begins to look three-dimensional. Smooth out the charcoal with your fingertip or a torchon.

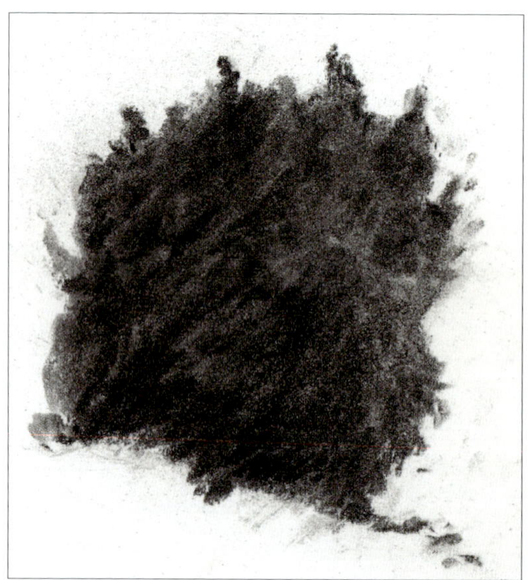

15-minute sketch: 4B pencil, black ballpoint pen

Graphite pencils and ballpoint pens are perfect for reference sketches on location as they are easily portable and not messy. The artist roughly blocked in the shape with a 4B pencil, which makes a lovely, dense mark, before hatching in the darkest areas with a black ballpoint pen. The closer together the hatched lines, the darker and denser the tone will be.

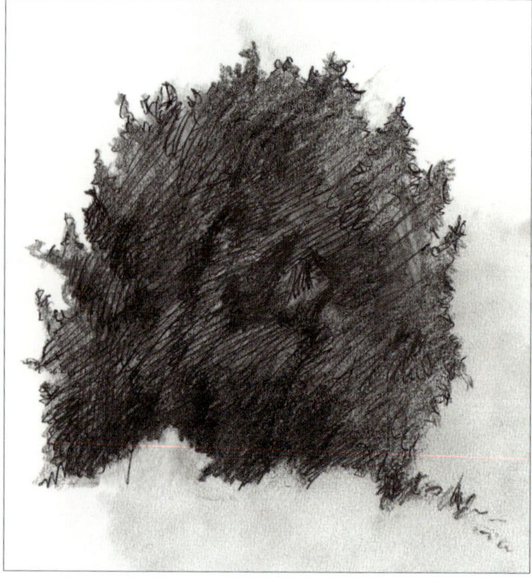

30-minute sketch: coloured wax pencils

With wax pencils you can quickly build up areas of broken colour and create lively optical mixes that capture the full range of tones within the foliage mass. Start with the lightest colour first – a pale, yellowy green. Then add progressively darker greens until you achieve the effect that you want, using a carefully controlled scribble. Some areas are very dark indeed, but beware of using a solid black as it can 'deaden' the overall effect; instead, use dark, reddish browns that complement the greens and give some warmth to the scene. (Look closely at any subject and you will often see that the shadow areas contain a dark colour that is complementary to the colour of the main subject.)

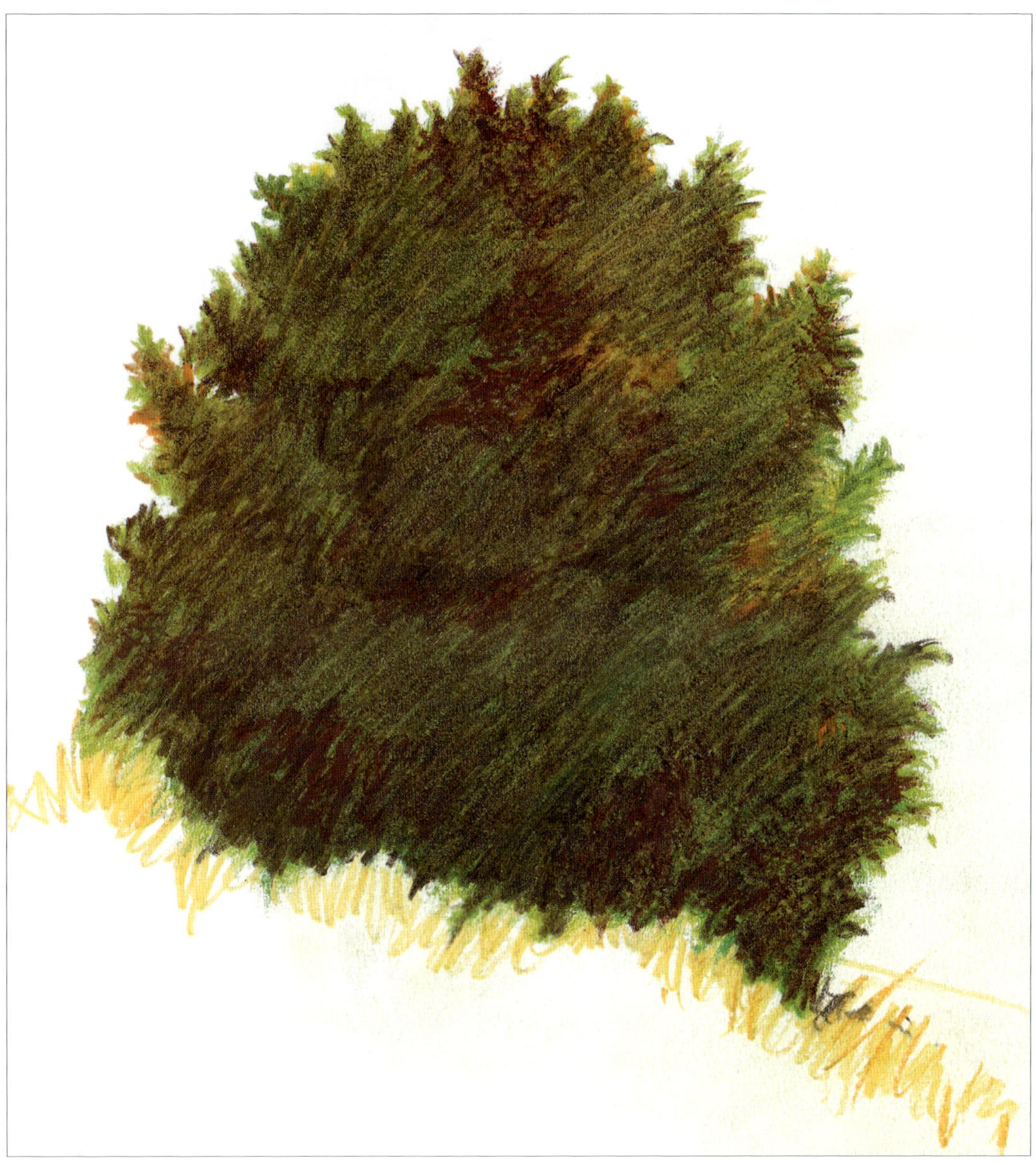

Quick sketches of flowers: Poppies

Some flowers, such as bedding plants in a municipal park, grow in straight, regimented lines. Others grow in untrammelled profusion, their stems twisting and turning over one another, the flower heads flopping in all directions. When you draw or paint flowers, allow the natural growth pattern to dictate your artistic approach so that you can capture the essential character of the plant.

These poppies seem to rise and pop up almost at random. Artistically, the rich colours and ruffled shapes call for a free, impressionistic approach. The translucent petals provide plenty of opportunity to explore tonal contrasts and colour mixes, as deeper tones are created where petals overlap or cast shadows on neighbouring petals. Powdery media such as charcoal and soft pastel are perfect for this subject. The black centres and seed heads offer interesting contrasts of colour and shape; here, you can make stronger, linear marks.

The scene

The artist came across this patch of poppies growing in a corner of her garden and wanted to create the feeling of random, spontaneous growth. Deliberately cutting off the edges of some of the poppies in her sketches helps to convey this: such a subject should not appear too neat and tidy!

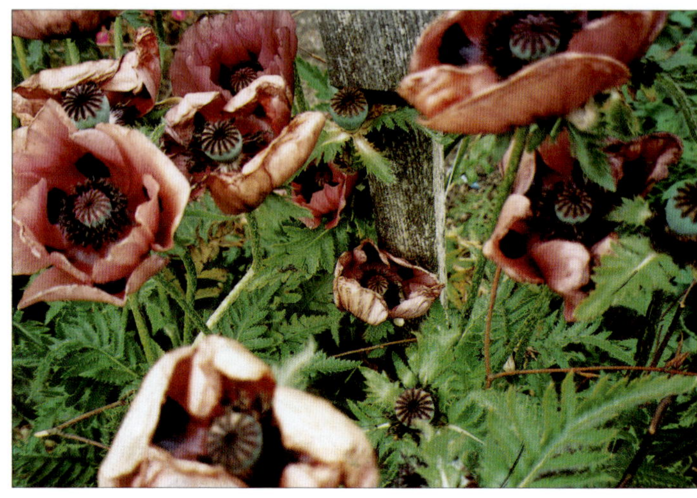

5-minute sketch: black and white soft pastels

If you only have 5 minutes or so to spare, you will not have time to sketch more than one or two individual blooms. Nonetheless, this is a good loosening-up and observational exercise. Here, loose, light white pastel lines recreate the frilly edges of the poppy petals, with more controlled marks being made for the seed heads. Finally, the artist has scribbled in black pastel for the very dark flower centres.

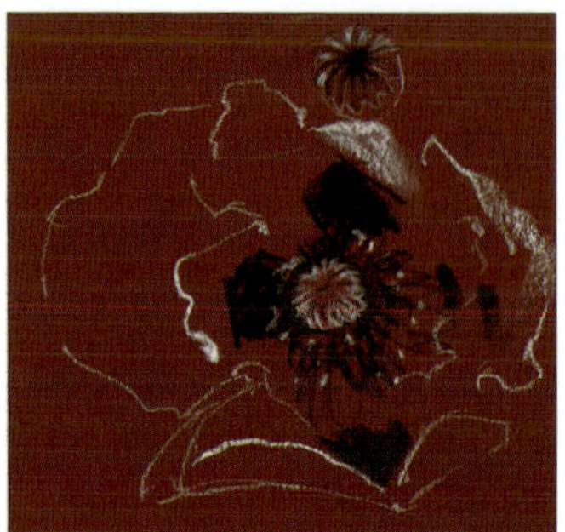

10-minute sketch: charcoal

In a very quick sketch like this one, you need to concentrate first on capturing the shapes of the flowers and the individual petals within them. At the same time, try to keep your marks loose and spontaneous. Don't worry if the shapes are not completely perfect because the main aim is to get the general feeling right. Here, the artist used free-flowing, calligraphic marks to delineate the shapes of the petals, smudging the charcoal to create the darkest tones on the flowers.

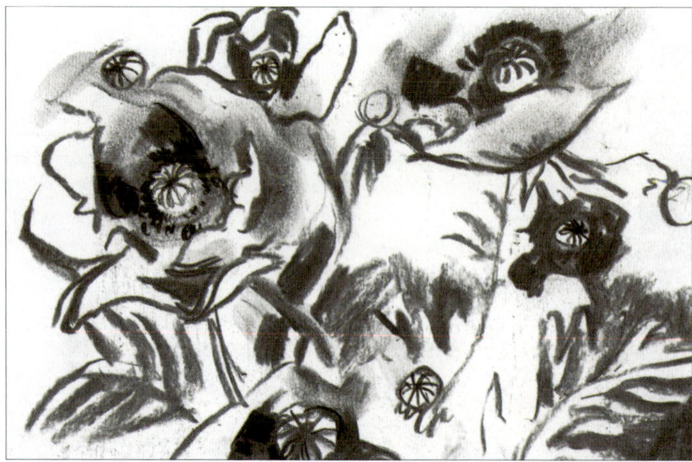

15-minute sketch: inks, dip pen and brush, and rollerball pen
Pen and ink is a good medium for sketching the spiky texture of the poppy leaves – but again, in order to create a feeling of spontaneity, you should try to keep your pen marks fairly loose and jagged. The artist first sketched the outlines with the dip pen. Then she brushed varying dilutions of coloured inks over the top, to create the petals, with the darker tones being used where the translucent petals overlap one another. She used a rollerball pen for details such as the stamens, as it gives a less crude line than the dip pen. Note how effective it is to leave much of the image uncoloured. Blocking in every single petal could easily have produced a rather tight and laboured image that failed to capture the character of the flowers.

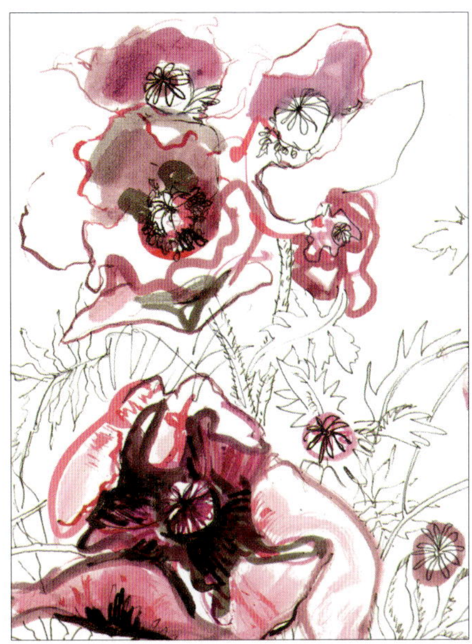

30-minute sketch: soft pastels
Soft pastels are a lovely medium for the translucent petals, as you can blend the colours to create lively optical mixes and subtle transitions in tone. At the same time, you need to make sure that the edges of the petals are clearly delineated, which you can do using the tip of a slightly lighter-coloured pastel. The artist used a cool blue pastel paper because this is an appropriate colour for the background and allows the flowers themselves – which are much warmer in tone – to come forwards in the image. Flowing, calligraphic marks capture the character of the flowers in a similar vein to the other quick sketches on these pages.

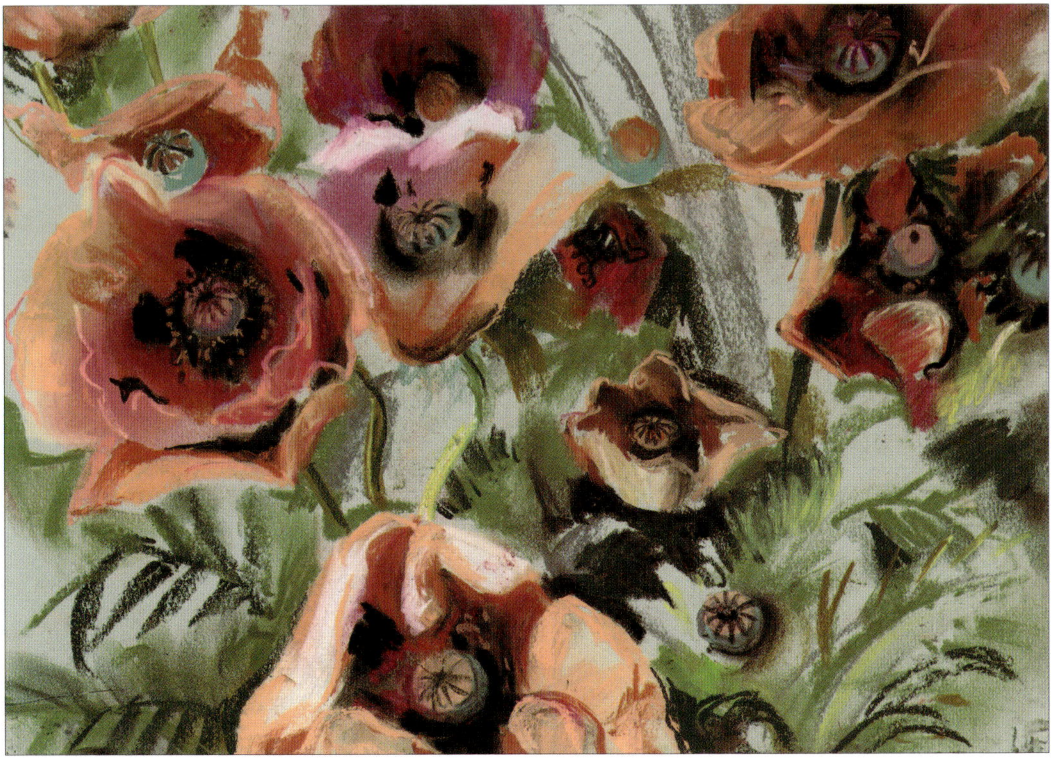

Trees in winter

Monochrome media such as charcoal or graphite are perfect for wintry scenes; there is relatively little colour so you can concentrate on tone and texture. With the coming of winter the underlying shape of deciduous trees, which is largely disguised by leaves in other seasons of the year, becomes apparent. In some species such as willow, the main boughs droop down; chestnut trees spread in a gentle arc, while some pine trees are basically conical in shape. It's a good idea to look for the overall geometric shapes first and sketch them in very lightly before you add any detail.

One of the most important things to remember when drawing trees is that the branches are not mere appendages, stuck on as an afterthought in the way they might be in a young child's drawing, but an organic part of the tree as a whole. Look at each tree in its entirety, instead of drawing the trunk first and adding the branches later. Look at the negative shapes – the spaces in between – as well as at the positive shapes of the branches.

Branches are such solid, heavy things that it may strike you as odd to draw them in outline and leave them as white shapes, as the artist does here. Look closely at this scene, however, and you will see that they are actually lighter in tone than the mass of ivy leaves behind. If you were to block them in with a mid-tone of grey, they would not stand out clearly. In areas where they are silhouetted against the bland white sky, you can use dark pencil marks.

Materials

- *Smooth drawing paper*
- *6B pencil*

The scene

A group of trees is starkly silhouetted against the white sky and the snow-covered ground, with just a few exposed patches of earth adding texture to the foreground. The trees are very near the centre of the image, which is generally not considered advisable, but in this case, the central placement is one way of conveying the calm, still mood of the scene.

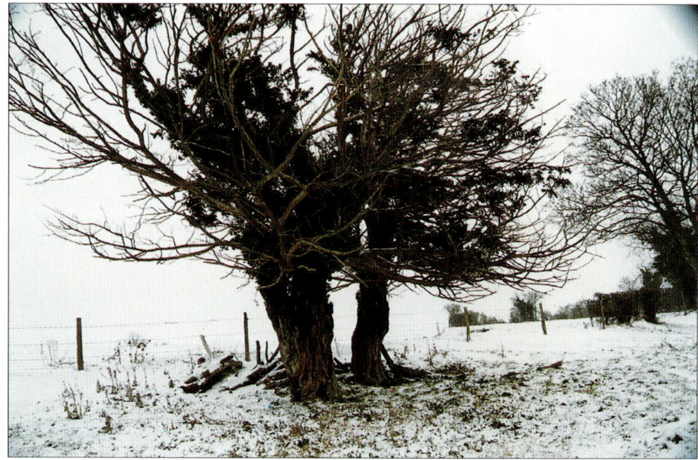

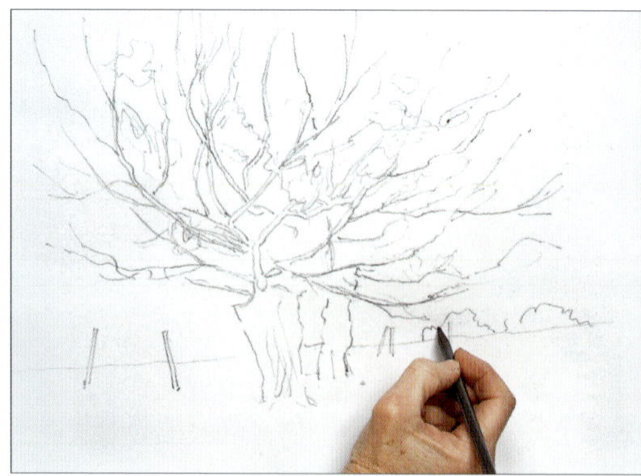

1 Using a 6B pencil, which makes a strong, dense mark, put in the main lines of the trees. Remember to look at the negative shapes – the spaces between the branches – as well as at the branches themselves. Also indicate the fence posts and a few small bushes in the middle distance, remembering to make the posts smaller as they recede.

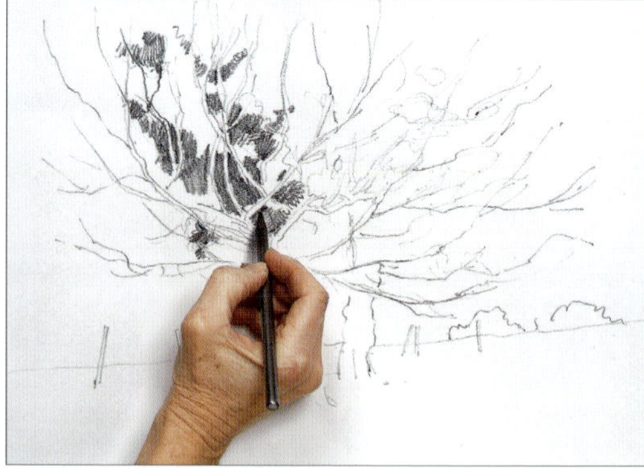

2 Loosely block in the main areas of ivy so that you begin to establish the structure of the trees. Don't try to put in individual leaves or any texture at this stage – this will come later. Remember to leave spaces where the branches lie over the top of the ivy and keep checking to make sure you're not covering any major branches that need to be left white.

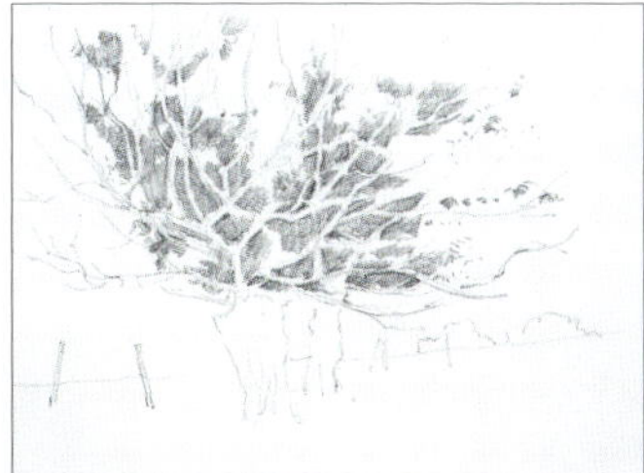

3 Continue working on the negative spaces between the branches of the trees until you have blocked in all the clumps of ivy.

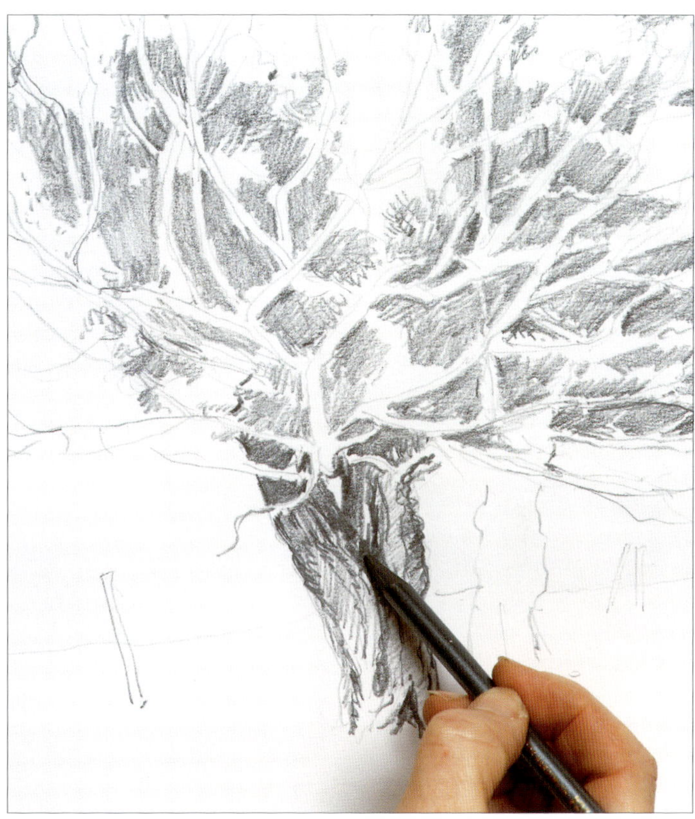

4 Now shade in the trunks, making short, jagged pencil marks with the tip of the pencil to convey the texture of the bark. Note that the trunk of the foremost tree is split; darken one side of the split to make it clear that one part of the tree stands in front of the other part. Even though there is no textural detail in the foliage, and the branches have simply been left as white shapes, the trees are already beginning to take shape.

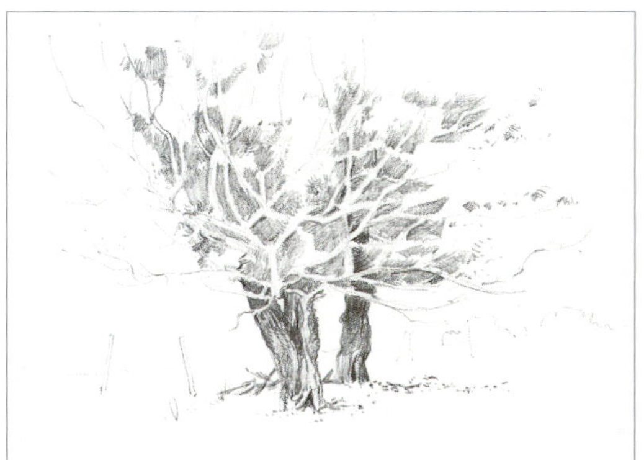

5 Block in the trunk of the second tree in the same way and dot in fallen leaves and exposed clumps of earth in the foreground. As you work, pay careful attention to where the main branches jut forwards in front of the trunk; allow them to remain white so that their position in relation to the dark trunk behind is clear.

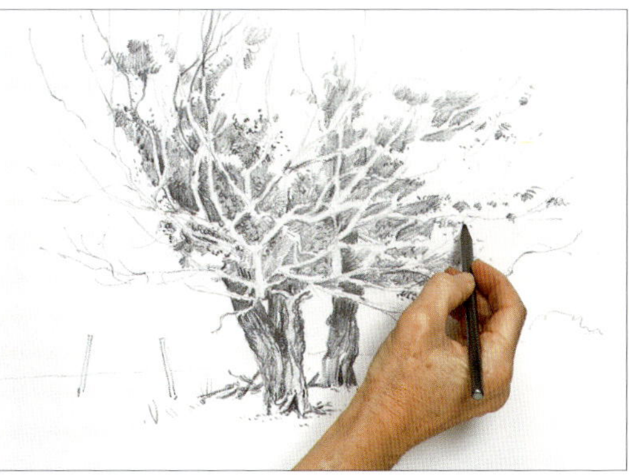

6 Now that the clumps of ivy have been blocked in, you can begin to put in more texture, by adding loose scribbles over the main blocks and dotting in some of the smaller clumps and individual leaves towards the extremities of the branches. Don't be too precise about the placing of the leaves – try to create a general impression of the way the ivy grows.

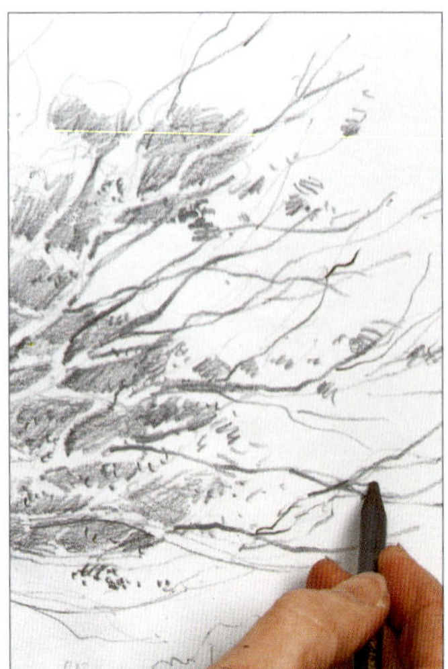

7 At the extremities, reinforce the lines of the branches in front of or parallel to the trunks with strong pencil marks, applying more pressure than you have done so far. There are lots of kinks and twists in the branches; make sure you convey this in your line work. Leave the largest branches in front of the trunks as white negative shapes so that they stand out against the darkness of the bark and the ivy.

Assessment time

The trees are taking shape well and the differences in tone help us to see where one trunk or branch is positioned in relation to others, with the darker elements appearing to advance towards us while lighter ones appear to be farther away. However, at this stage the trees seem almost to be floating in a void; you need to anchor them within the landscape by adding more detail to the fence posts and the bushes in the middle distance.

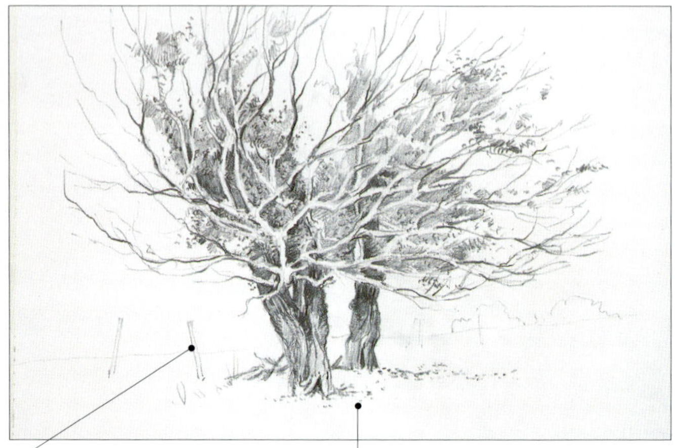

Strengthening the fence posts will make the setting clearer and help to lead the viewer's eye through the picture.

Adding more texture to the ground in front of the trees will help to set them in the context of the landscape.

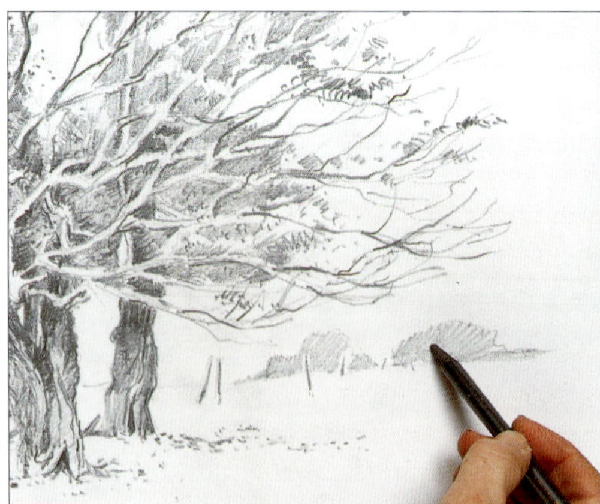

8 Because the bushes in the middle distance are further away than the trees, they appear to be lighter in tone. Block them in, applying medium pressure to the pencil so that you create a mid-tone rather than the very dense, solid greys and blacks used for the trees.

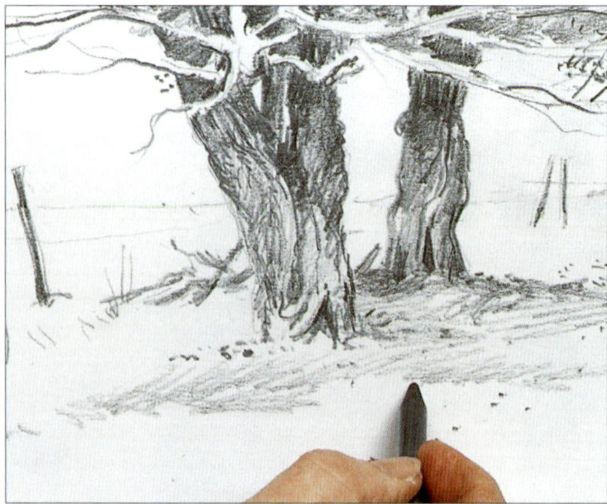

9 Block in the fence posts, making the two posts on the left of the image very dark and the others less so, so that you create a feeling of recession. Put some light shading in the foreground; even though it is covered in snow, the shadows reveal the undulations in the ground.

The finished drawing

Against the white sky, the starkness of the trees makes for a bold, graphic image. With flowing, confident pencil lines, the artist has created an image in which the branches grow organically out of the tree trunks, twisting and turning over one another. There is just enough detail around the trees, in the form of the fence posts, a few small bushes, and some textural detail in the immediate foreground, to hint at the landscape in which they are situated.

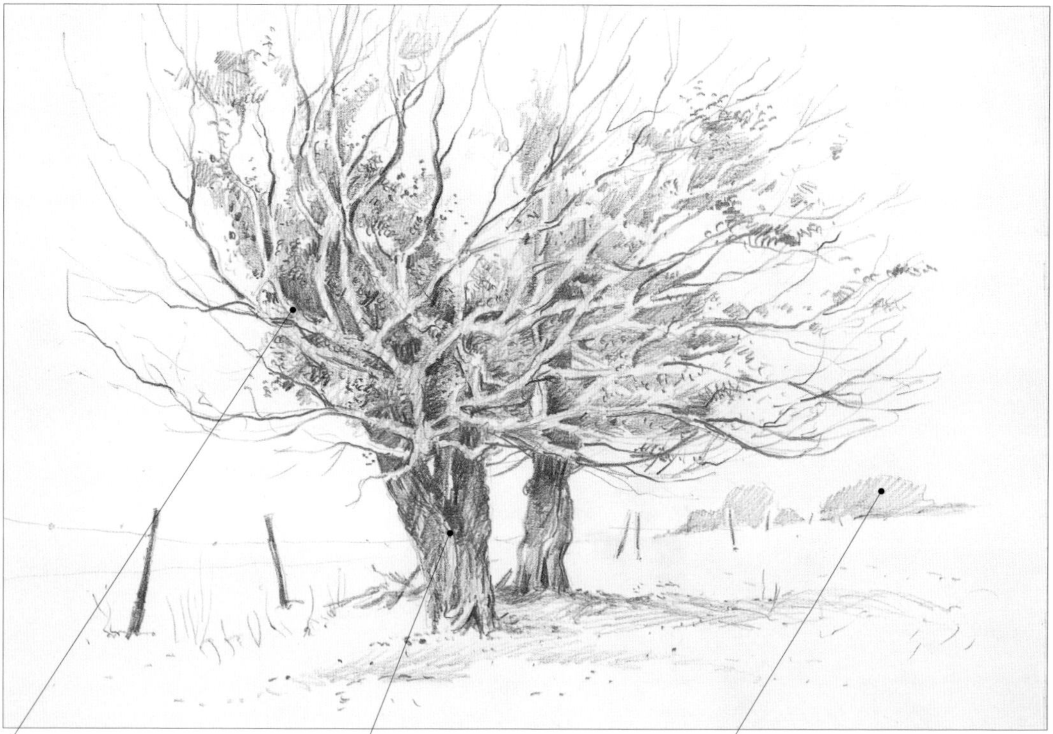

Confident, flowing lines capture the trees' growth pattern beautifully.

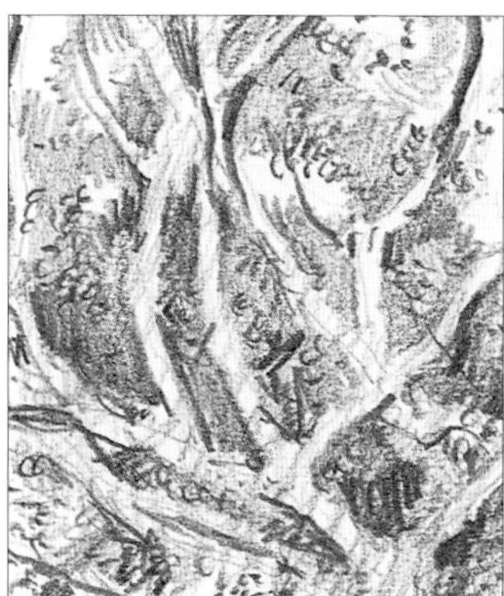

Jagged pencil marks convey the texture of the bark.

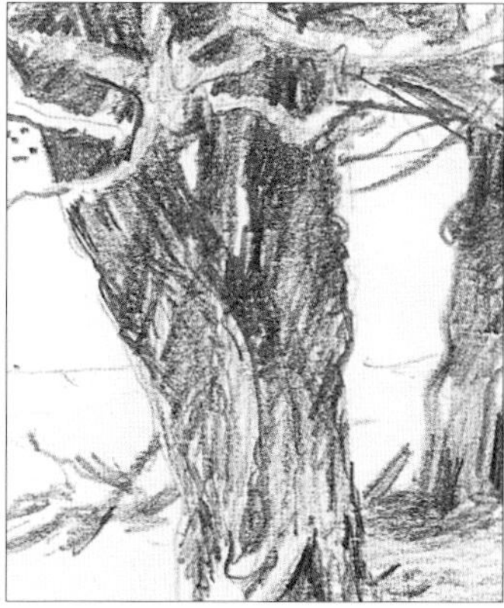

Soft mid-tones in the middle distance help to create a sense of recession.

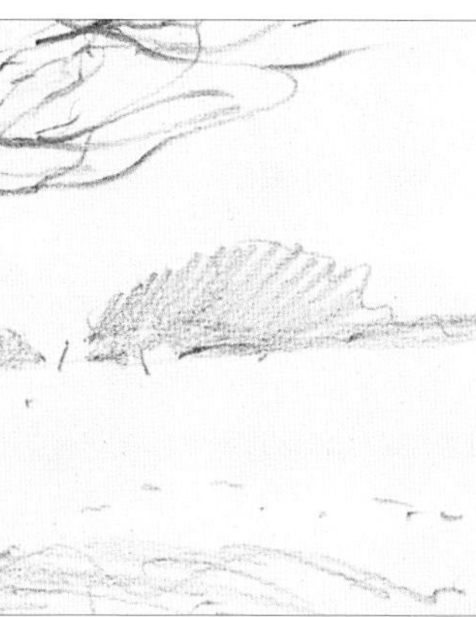

Field of sunflowers

A field of bright yellow sunflowers in full bloom is a dazzling sight and one that has attracted many artists and photographers. But although the colour is the first thing that attracts your eye, it isn't necessarily enough to make a successful drawing: you also need to make sure that there's a focal point to the image, so spend plenty of time choosing the right viewpoint. Select a place where some flowers are face on and others are partially turned away, as this allows you to examine the structure of the flowers and introduce some variety into the way that you draw them. Also make sure that the flower heads are at different heights, so that you don't get a straight line running across the image.

The background is important, too – both the fields in the distance and the spaces between the plants. Although it's relatively indistinct in this scene, it sets the sunflowers within the context of the landscape. Half-close your eyes to assess which tones and colours to use – and don't be too literal in your rendition. Aim, instead, to create lively mixes of colour on the support by applying several layers of thin colour. Also make sure that the background hangs together as a whole and that no one part jumps forwards too much in the scene.

This is a complicated scene, with lots of different elements. To prevent yourself from getting bogged down in too much detail, concentrate on the negative shapes between the flowers. It's often easier to see these shapes than it is to draw the positive shapes (the flowers themselves).

Materials

- *Good-quality drawing paper*
- *Coloured pencils: a selection of pale, mid-toned and dark blues and greens, burnt sienna, canary yellow, lemon yellow, yellow ochre, light brown and lilac*

The scene

Although this scene might look a little confusing on first glance, the artist selected her viewpoint carefully to ensure that the sunflower heads made interesting shapes and were positioned at different heights within the picture area.

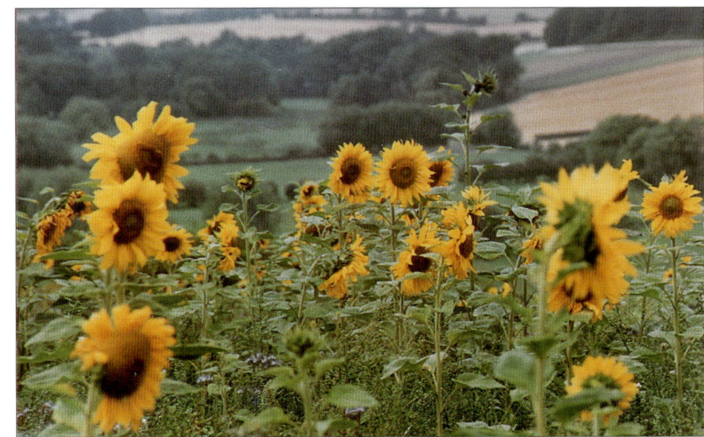

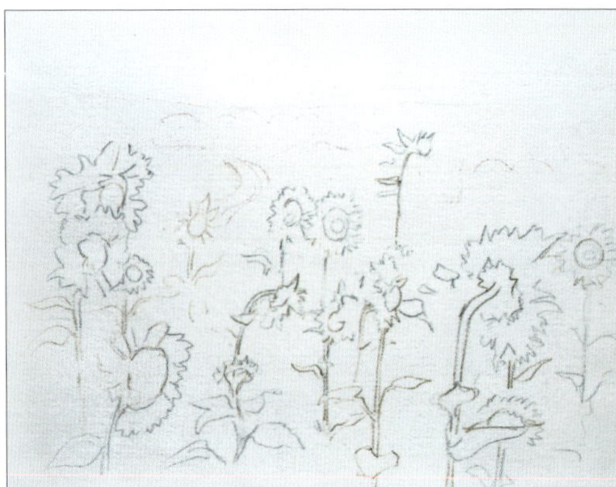

1 When you've chosen your viewpoint, lightly sketch the scene using burnt sienna for the sunflowers and pale blues for the shapes of the fields in the background. Look at the spaces between the flowers, and at where they overlap one another, as well as at the individual flower heads.

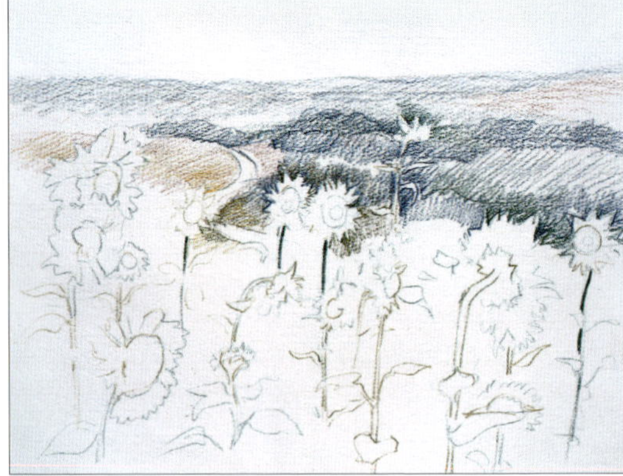

2 Loosely colour in the background fields with a range of blues and greens, with touches of burnt sienna in places for the exposed patches of earth, getting slightly darker as you move towards the foreground. As you reach the sunflower field, begin to fill in the negative shapes between the stems.

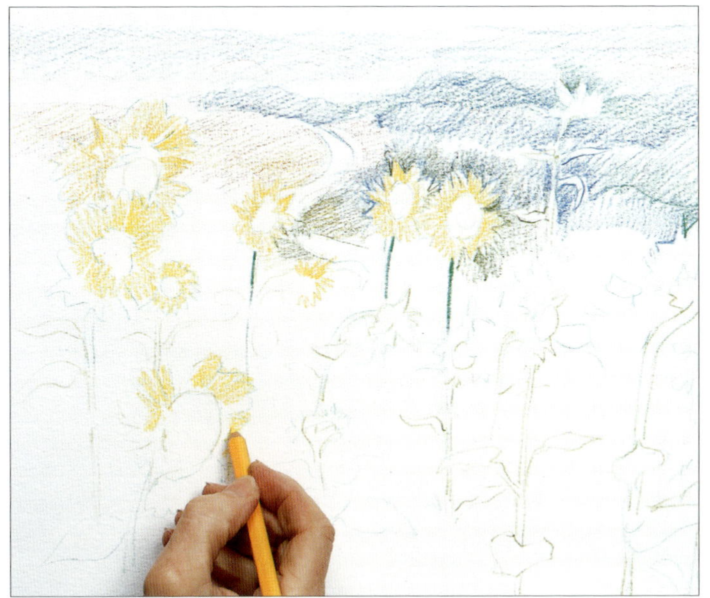

3 Start blocking in the yellow petals of the largest sunflowers using a canary yellow pencil for the darker yellows and lemon yellow for the brighter yellows.

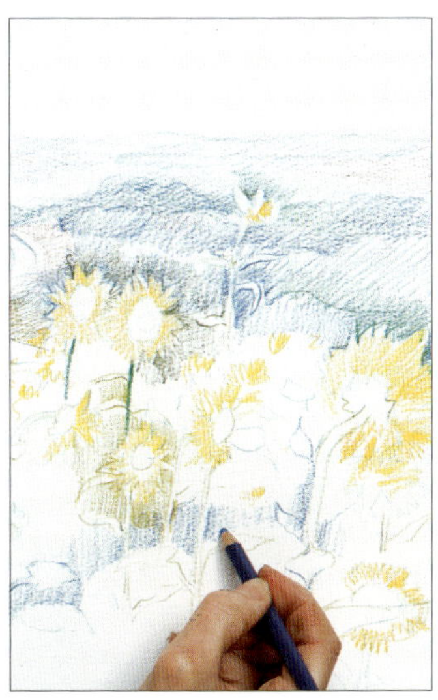

4 Continue blocking in the yellows, varying the tones as appropriate. Block in the negative shapes in the immediate foreground in blue, using loose scribbles.

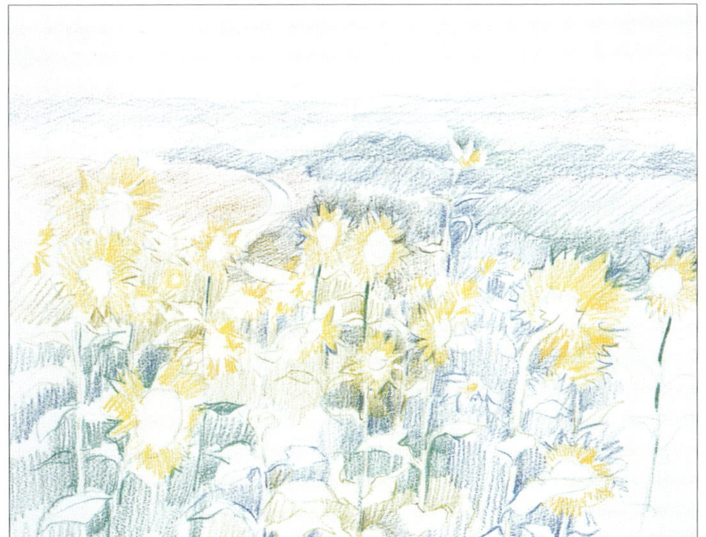

5 Continue the process of blocking in the negative spaces between the sunflowers that you began in Step 2, using a range of blues and greens as appropriate. Note that the colour is not uniform: look for differences between the warm and the cool tones, as some areas are cast into shadow by the sunflower leaves and flowers while others are in bright sunlight.

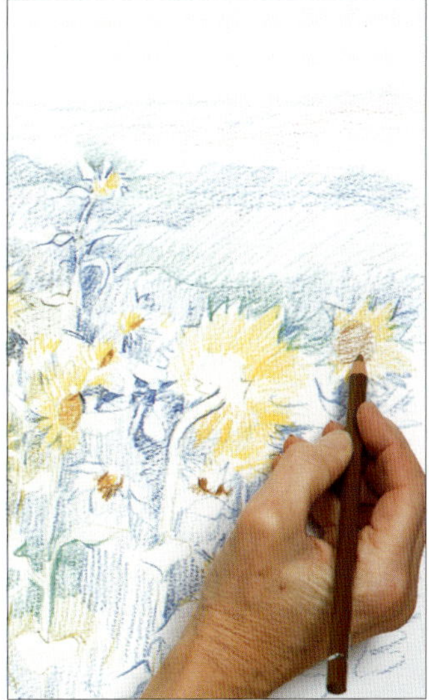

6 Work over the background fields again, gradually darkening them. Colour in the flower centres. Note that some are darker than others: alternate between yellow ochre and burnt sienna.

▶

Assessment time

Achieving the correct tonal values is a gradual process and one that cannot be rushed, but now that all the elements are in place you should take the time to stand back and look at the drawing as a whole to assess how much more needs to be done. You can see that the drawing is too pale overall and that more contrast between the lightest and darkest areas is required. In addition, more modelling is required on the main subject – the sunflowers.

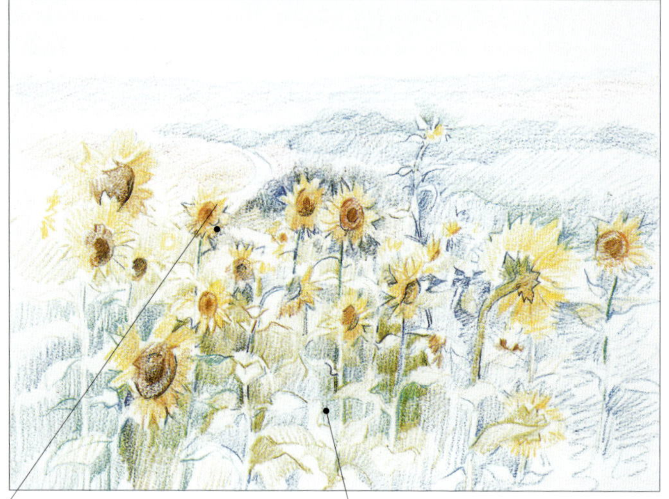

The sunflowers look rather flat and somewhat two-dimensional.

The leaves do not stand out clearly against the background.

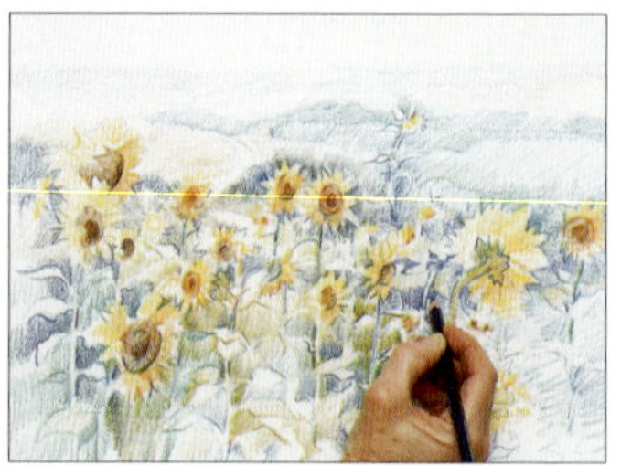

7 Using dark blue block in the bluer tones of the background fields with vertical scribbles, getting darker as you come towards the foreground.

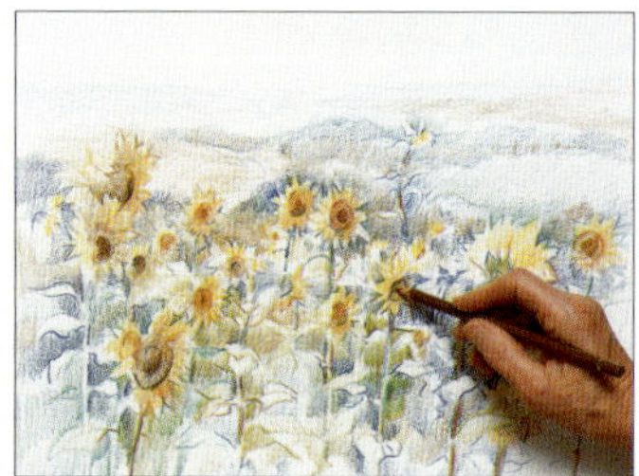

8 Apply brown over some of the brighter background greens to soften them. Block in some of the brown stalks. Some flowers are partially turned away from the sun: apply brown pencil over these areas.

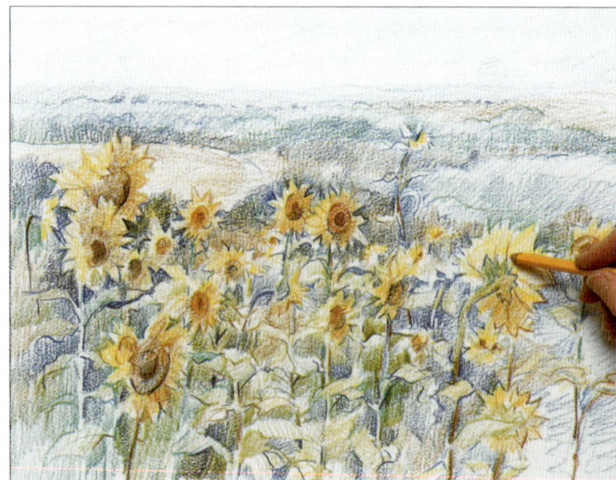

9 Loosely scribble blue over the sky. Work on the background, trying to develop some texture and a range of shapes and tones. Work on the negative spaces between the flowers again, delineating the edges with dark greens and blues, and darken the yellows of the sunflowers.

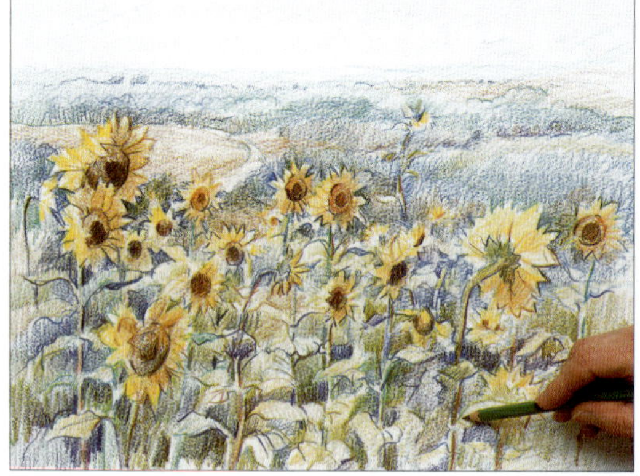

10 Adjust the colours and shading across the image as a whole, applying touches of warmer colours such as lilac in the foreground to make this area seem closer to the viewer. Using the tip of the pencil, apply some veining to the leaves in the immediate foreground.

The finished drawing

With the flower heads and leaves turning and twisting at different angles, this drawing is full of interest. There is just enough of the landscape in the background to convey something of the setting, while the spaces between the plants in the foreground provide a darker backdrop against which the leaves and flowers can stand out.

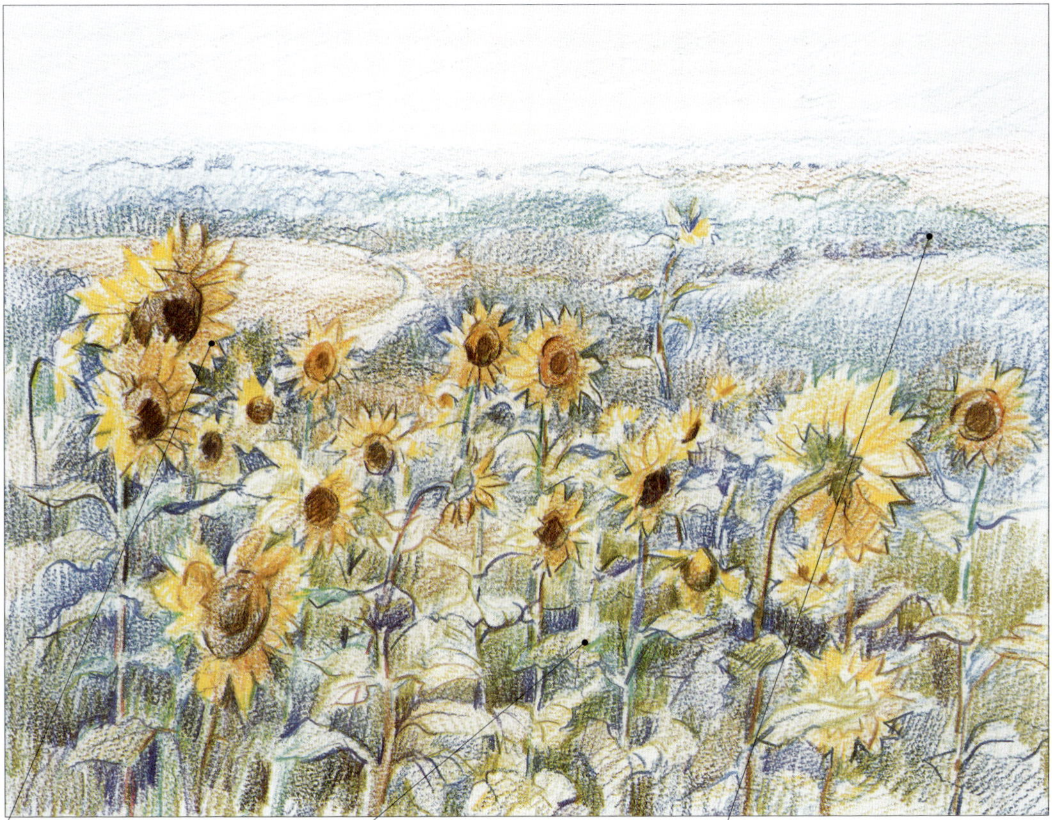

Simple shading makes the flowers look three-dimensional.

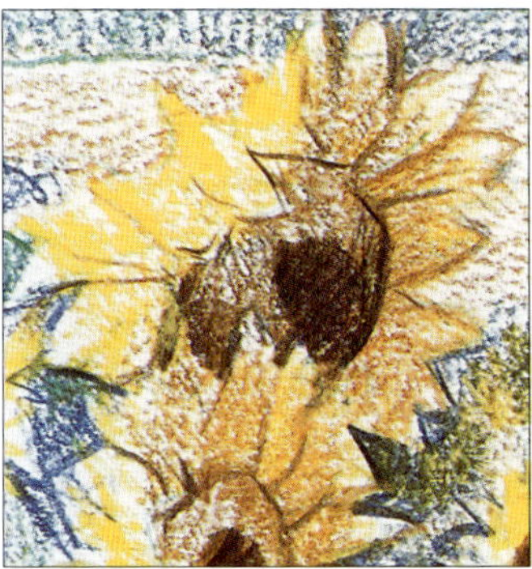

The leaves stand out well against the dark negative spaces between the plants.

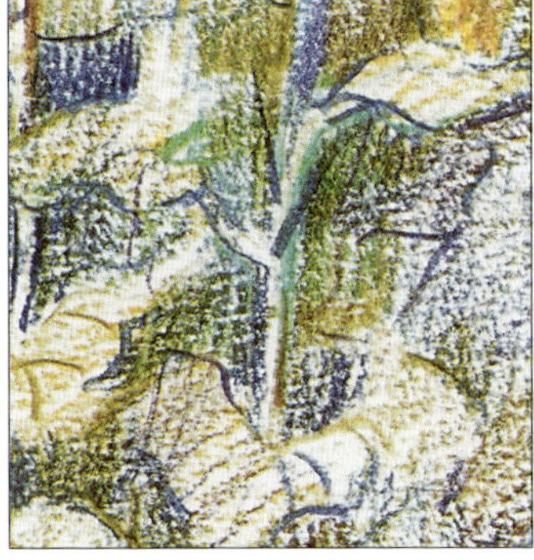

The colour is paler on the distant fields, creating a convincing sense of recession.

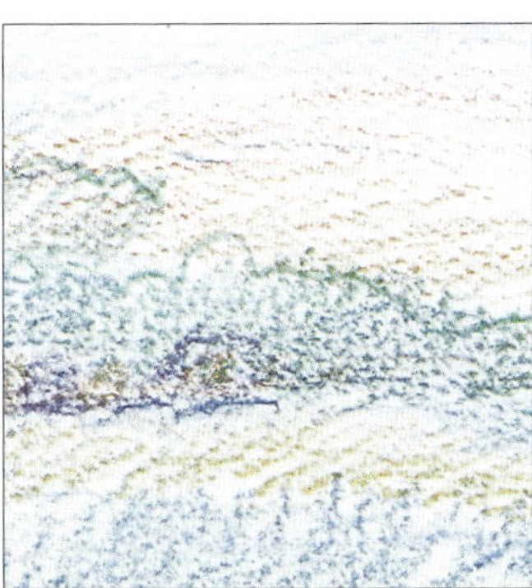

Quick sketches of landscapes: Riverbank

A riverside setting has lots of potential for interesting landscape sketches. If the river runs swiftly, there will be splashes and swirling eddies as the water breaks around rocks and other objects. Gentle ripples create a different mood, slightly distorting any reflections. Occasionally, you come across a hidden pool in which the water appears to be completely still, where the reflections are sharp and crisp. Each requires a different approach, from dynamic, energetic marks for rapidly flowing water to a more measured, controlled approach for very still water and reflections.

Whatever the mood of the river, it is often a good idea to use it as a compositional device to lead the viewer's eye through the picture. Bear this in mind when you position yourself on the bank to take a reference photo or make a sketch. A view along a river, so you can see how it meanders its way through the surrounding area, is almost always more satisfying in compositional terms than one looking straight across from one bank to the other as, in the latter case, the river will form a broad horizontal band that cuts the composition in two and blocks the viewer's eye from moving any further through the scene.

When you're drawing water, always remember that it takes its colour from surrounding objects – although the colour is generally slightly more muted in the reflection than it is in the object itself. In a riverside setting the greens and browns of nearby trees may be reflected in the water; alternatively, there may be patches of sky that are so bright that you need apply virtually no colour whatsoever.

The scene
Here, the river forms a gentle curve that leads our eye through the scene to the buildings on the horizon. The sky is very bright and bland, with no dramatic cloud formations to add interest to the scene, so the reflections of the trees along the bank provide a feature in what would otherwise be a completely empty area.

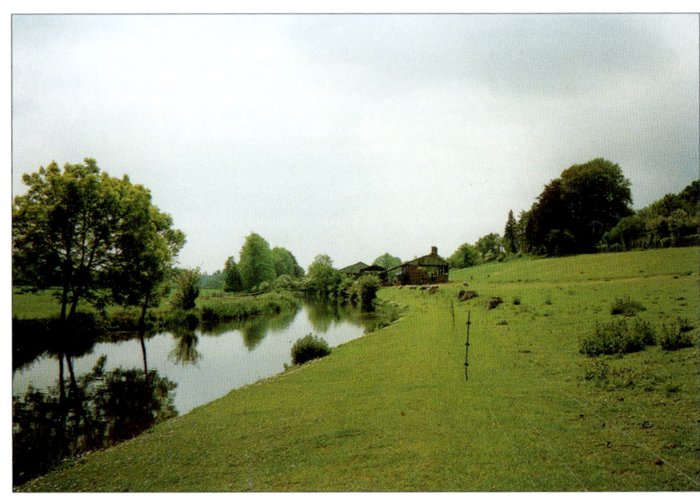

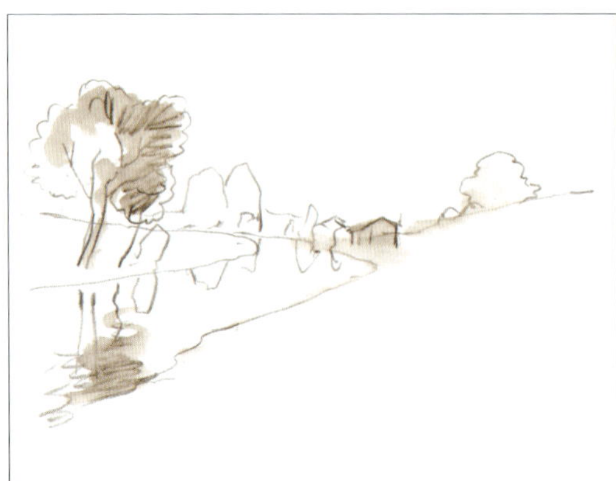

5-minute sketch: sepia water-soluble pencil
Five minutes is plenty of time for you to work out a composition for a larger drawing. Make a quick thumbnail sketch, roughly outlining the shapes of the main elements (including the reflections).

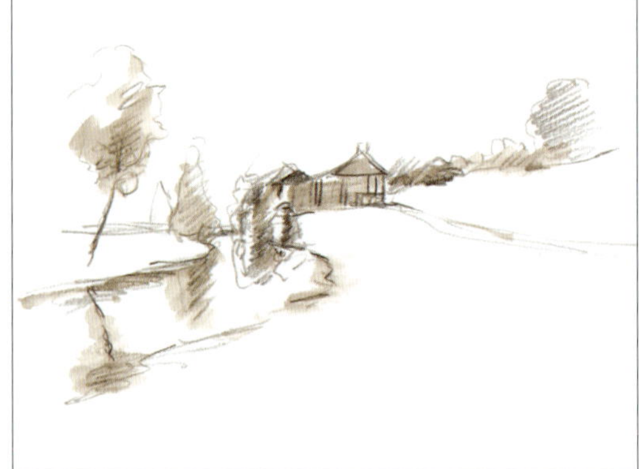

10-minute sketch: sepia water-soluble pencil
A tonal study will require a little more time. Here, the artist lightly brushed a little clean water over some of the pencil marks to blend them to a tonal wash, leaving the brightest areas untouched.

15-minute sketch: sepia water-soluble pencil
In this sketch, more textural detail is evident. It is created by using the water-soluble pencil dry (on the grass on the near bank, for example) and on slightly damp paper, so that the marks spread a little (on the large tree on the far bank).

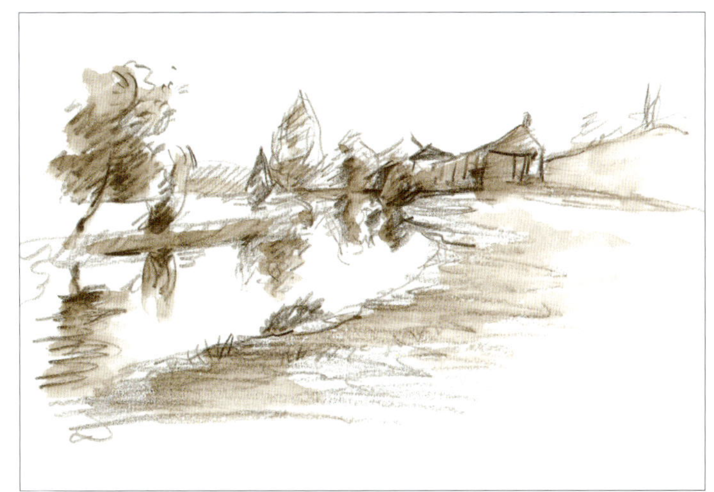

30-minute sketch: sepia water-soluble pencil
In the longest sketch of the series, the scene is beginning to look more three-dimensional. Note how some elements, such as the large tree on the far bank and the grass in the foreground of the near bank, are given more textural marks, which helps to indicate that they are nearer the viewer and create a sense of recession in the scene.

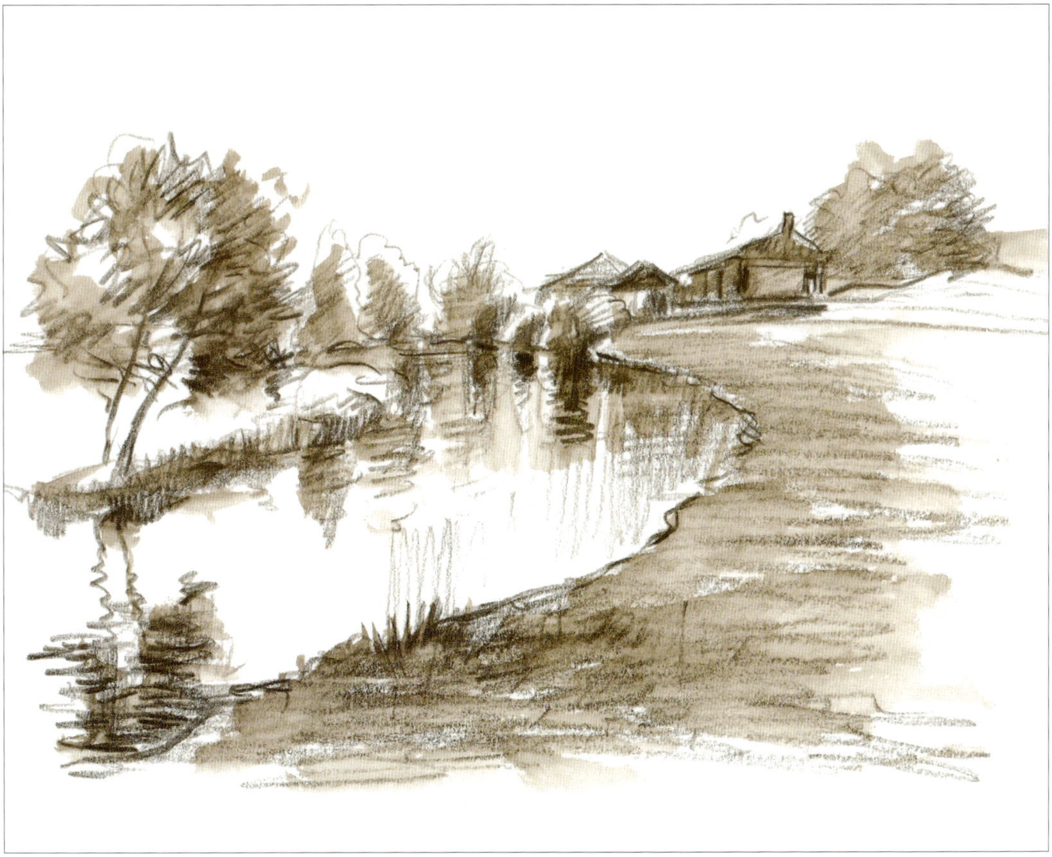

Quick sketches of landscapes: Mountain track

When you're drawing or sketching on location, particularly when you're faced with a panoramic view, it's very easy to get carried away by the grandeur of the setting and lose sight of the fact that your image needs to work as a composition. Always look for something that you can use as a focal point, such as a large boulder or a tree, and place it at a strong point in the picture space so that the viewer's eye goes immediately to it. Look for lines (real or imaginary) that lead the viewer's eye through the scene – maybe a wall or a fence, a line of bushes or, as here, a stony track leading into the distance.

To convey the scale of the scene and create a convincing sense of recession, you must also remember the rules of aerial and linear perspective: objects that are further away should appear smaller and paler in tone than those that are close by. Having more texture and detail in the foreground is another way of making this part of image appear closer.

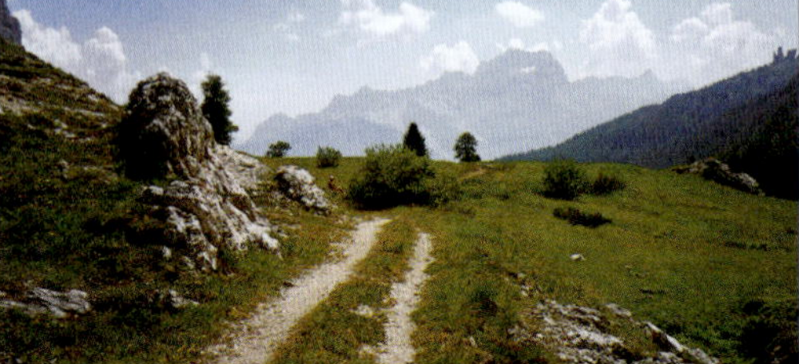

The scene

The track directs our attention to the mountains in the distance, while the rocks on the left provide a much-needed focal point.

5-minute sketch: charcoal

Compositionally, the track is an obvious way of drawing our attention to the backdrop, as are the wedge-shaped slopes on the left and right. Once she had worked out the composition, the artist scribbled down some very rough, linear marks for the pebbly track and rocks, and smudged charcoal to create broad areas of dark and mid-tone. The mountains were largely left untouched, so that they are paler than the foreground areas, which helps to create a feeling of recession.

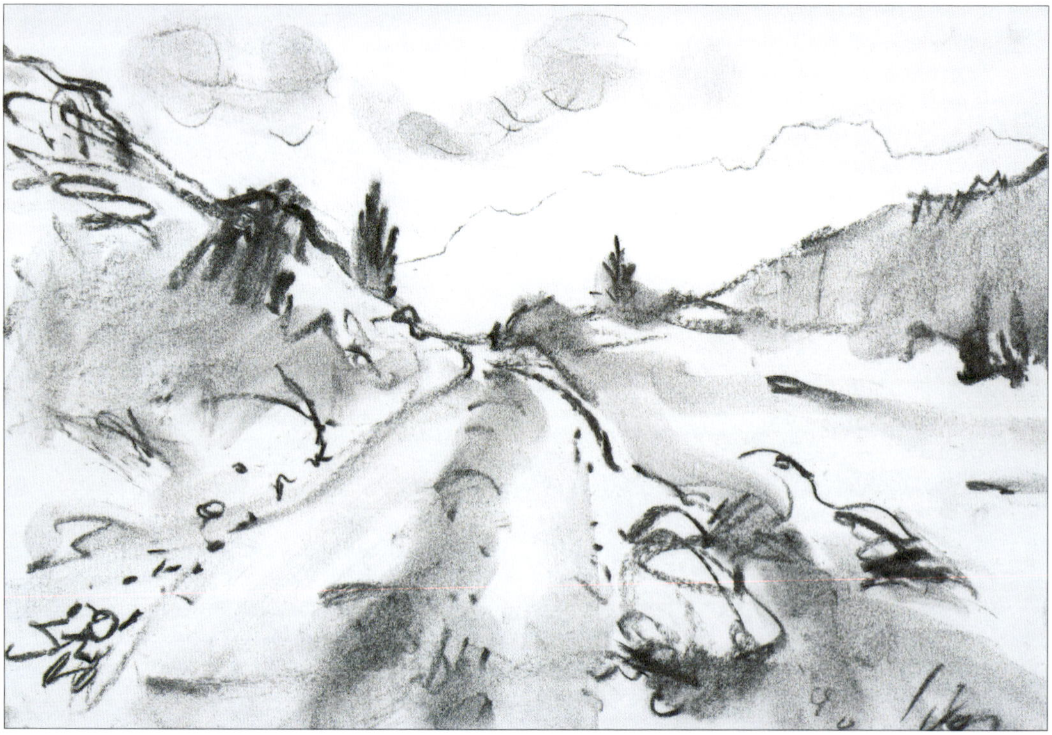

15-minute sketch: chisel-tip pen

You may never have thought of using an ordinary fibre-tip pen as a drawing tool but, although it is not the most sophisticated of implements, it can be very useful for making quick sketches on location as it is easily portable and clean to handle. By adjusting the angle at which you hold it and by applying differing amounts of pressure, you will also find that it can make a surprisingly varied range of marks. Here, the artist used spiky vertical marks to convey the texture of the grasses, while rough circles describe the pebbles on the track and wispy curves imply the fluffy clouds overhead. The chisel-shaped tip of the pen was used to block in larger elements such as the trees, bushes and boulders, creating a convincing sense of solidity in these areas. Note how the amount of visible detail decreases with distance: apart from a few sketchy lines to indicate the contours, the distant mountains are left blank.

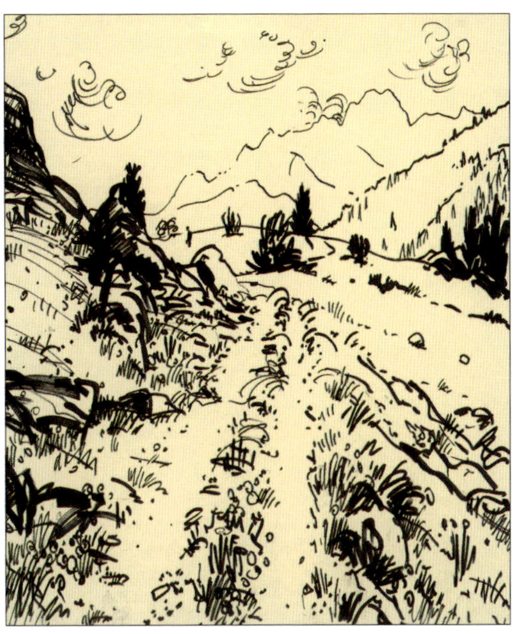

30-minute sketch: soft pastels

A cream pastel paper gives an underlying warmth to the image; the tooth of the paper also has an effect, as it helps to convey the texture of the pebble-strewn ground. Note how many different greens and yellows the artist has used. She has overlaid them to create lively colour mixes and blended them in parts so that areas of soft grass contrast effectively with the hard texture of the rocks. (Turn to page 212 for pastels.)

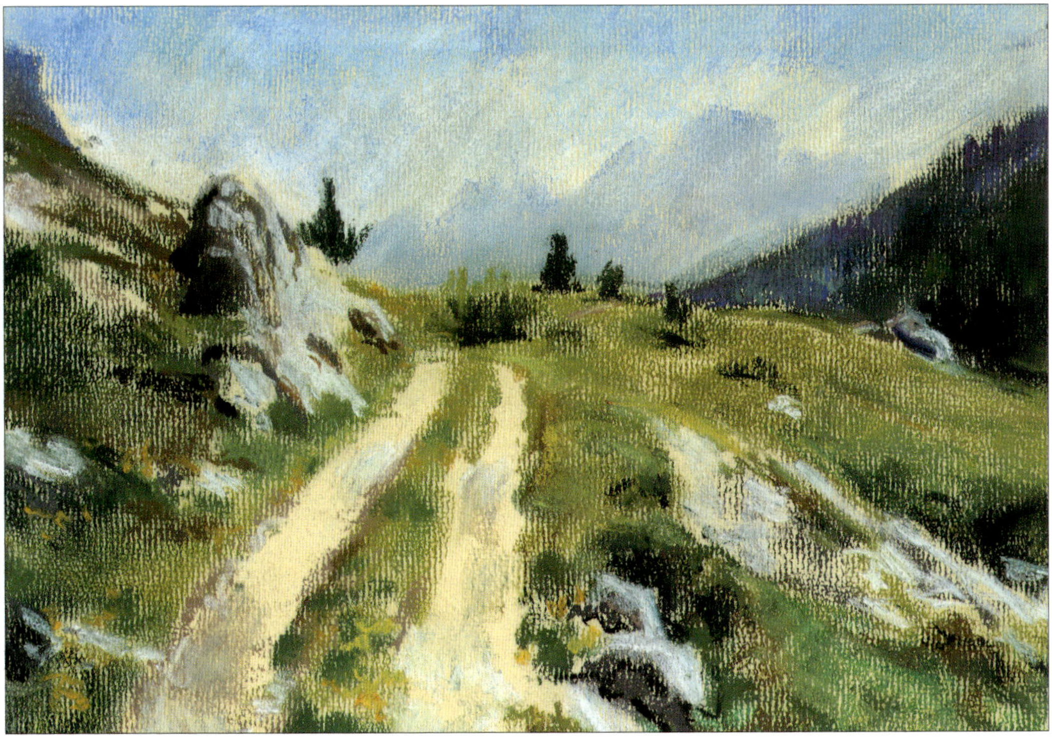

Quick sketches of landscapes: Field of rape

Don't ignore the potential of man-made landscapes such as arable crops: they can provide you with subjects that are every bit as colourful and intriguing as wild, rugged scenes. Start by looking for something that you can use as the main centre of interest in your drawing – a lone tree, farm machinery rusting away in a corner, or a distant farmhouse, for example – and place it at a strong position in the picture space. If there is no obvious focal point, as in the images on these two pages, decide what it is that makes you want to draw the scene. Here, it is obviously the mass of brightly coloured flowers. In a situation such as this, where almost all the plants are the same height, select your viewpoint carefully and pay attention to the negative spaces in between the plants in order to create a well-balanced composition.

5-minute sketch: ballpoint pen

This is a compositional sketch: the converging lines of the hedgerow on the left and the line of trees in the background create strong, dark lines against which the lighter flowers will stand out clearly. The artist has indicated the darkest areas within the flowers by means of swiftly hatched lines, leaving the paper white for the densely packed mass of flowers in the bottom left of the image.

The scene

Meadows and fields of crops such as this rape in flower make colourful subjects for landscape drawings and paintings. Here, the artist selected a relatively low viewpoint, which gave a large mass of flowers in the bottom left of the image. The hedgerow on the left and the line of trees in the background jut up above the field, providing much-needed vertical elements in the composition. Their dark, straight lines also help to concentrate the viewer's attention on the flowers.

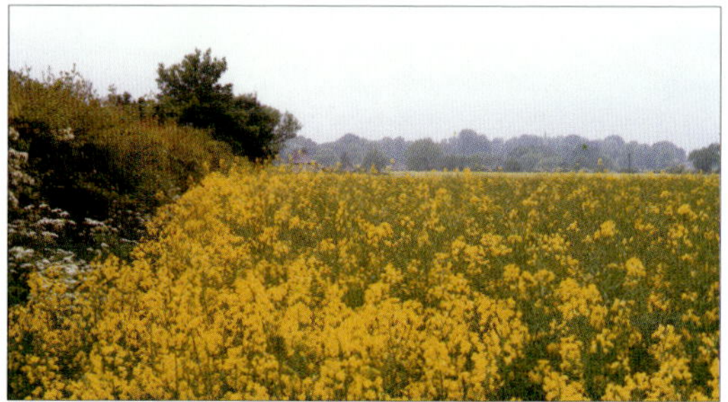

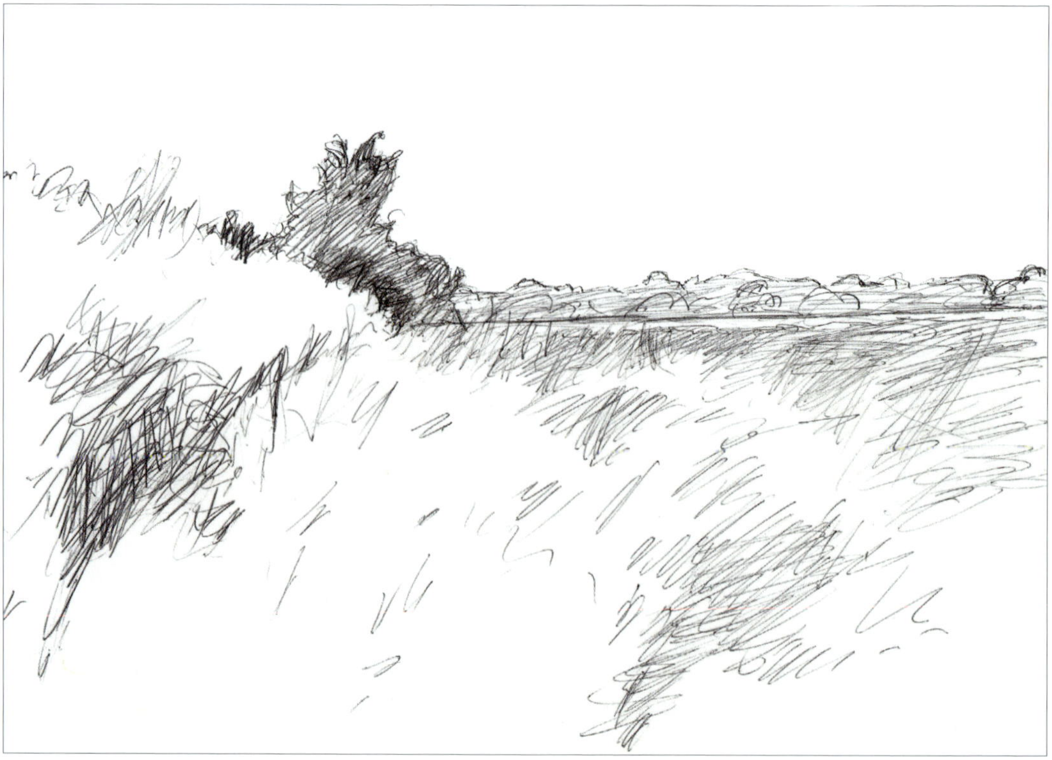

15-minute sketch: 4B graphite stick
This is a slightly more elaborate sketch than the one on the previous page: the artist had time to begin exploring the range of tones within the scene. Once he had established the dark, solid lines of the hedgerow and trees, he concentrated largely on the negative shapes – the dark spaces between the stems – scribbling them in with the tip of the graphite stick.

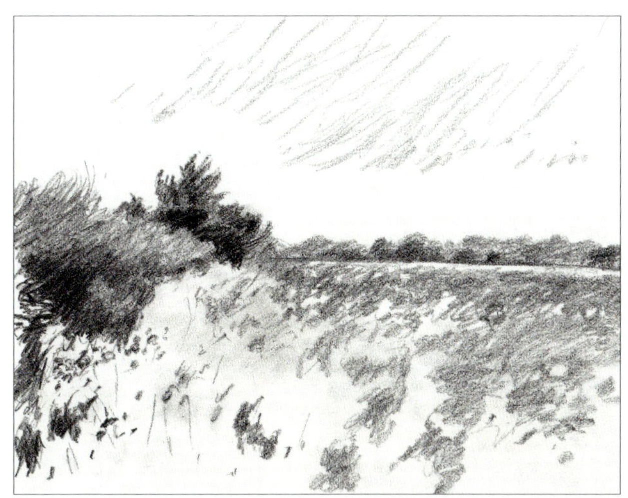

30-minute sketch: pastel pencils
Pastel pencils are a lovely medium for this subject, as the pigments can be blended both optically and physically. Look carefully at the scene and you will be amazed at how many different greens and yellows you can discern. Here, the artist has created an impression of the stems blowing in the breeze. Note how the warm, orangey yellows in the foreground make this area seem closer to the viewer.

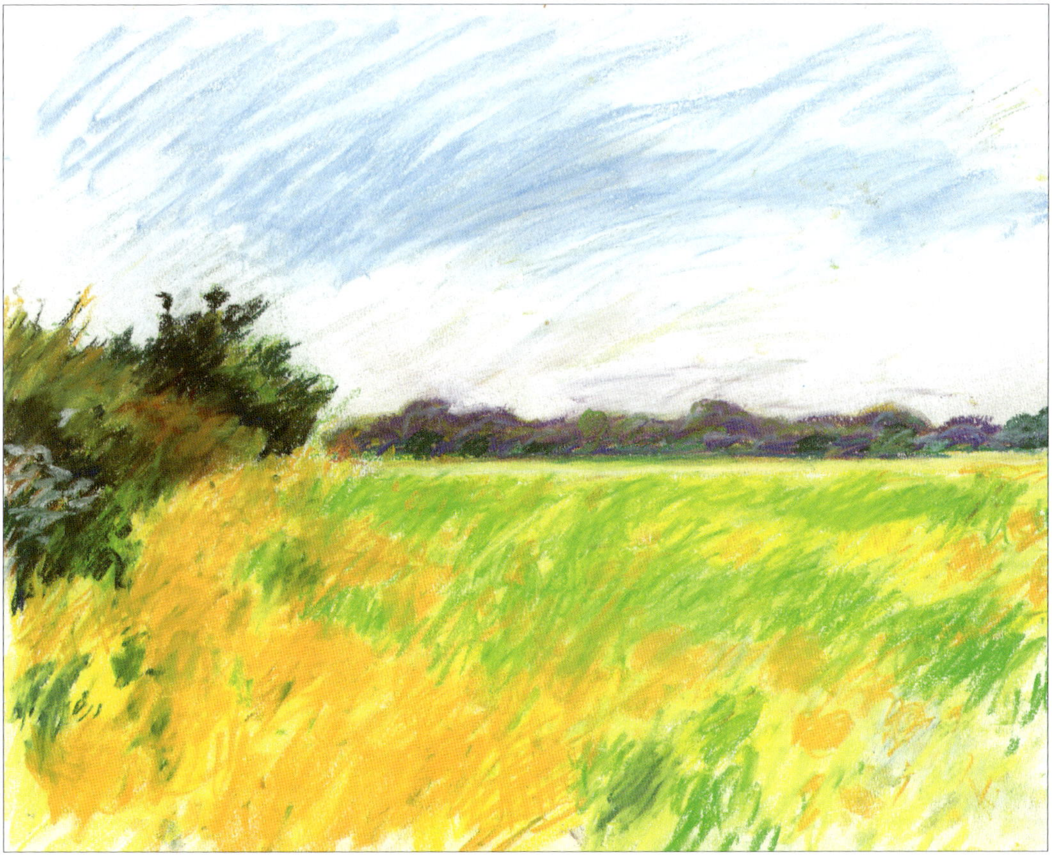

Snow scene

Here's an interesting challenge: how do you draw a bright, white subject such as snow using charcoal, which is one of the densest and darkest drawing media available? The answer is not to attempt to draw the snow at all: allow the white of the paper to stand for the brightest parts of the snow and use the charcoal for the mid- and dark tones. Focus your attention on the clumps of earth that poke up above it and the thicket of trees on the right of the image, rather than on the powdery, white covering on the ground.

Also, note that the snow is not a uniformly pure, unsullied white. The ground undulates, forming little peaks and shaded troughs. Tones of grey are required to make this distinction – smooth, pale tones without any sharp edges. To give the drawing impact, you also need to contrast the heavy, solid forms of the trees and background ridge with the much softer and less substantial shapes of the clouds and shadows. Use all the blending techniques at your disposal: smudge lines with your fingertips or (for larger areas) the side of your hand, or blend marks with a torchon, a sponge or a piece of tissue paper, as this allows you to build up areas of tone without creating a hard line.

If you get accidental charcoal smudges, don't worry. This is an unavoidable part of charcoal drawing and you can always wipe off powder with an eraser. A kneaded eraser gives a soft, smooth finish; for sharp edges, cut a plastic eraser or pull a kneaded eraser to a fine point. For an cheaper alternative, try small pieces of soft white bread.

Materials
- *Smooth drawing paper*
- *Willow charcoal sticks – thin and medium*
- *Kneaded eraser*
- *Compressed charcoal stick*
- *Large torchon*
- *Plastic eraser, cut to give a sharp edge*
- *Small sponge*

The scene
Here is a typical winter scene across a ploughed field. The thicket of trees on the right provides a focal point while the clumps of earth poking up through the snow form diagonal lines across the field that lead the viewer's eye through the composition.

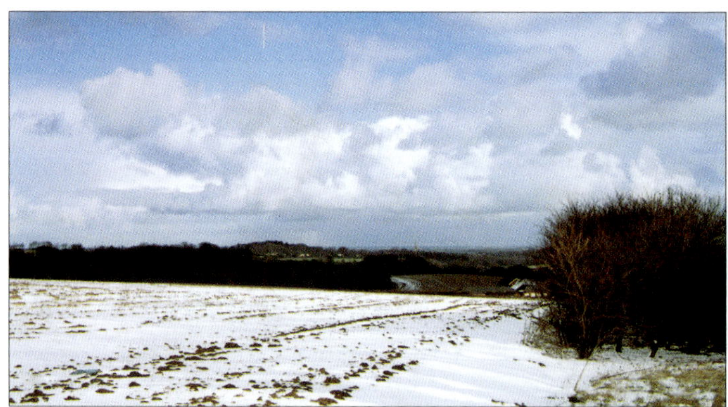

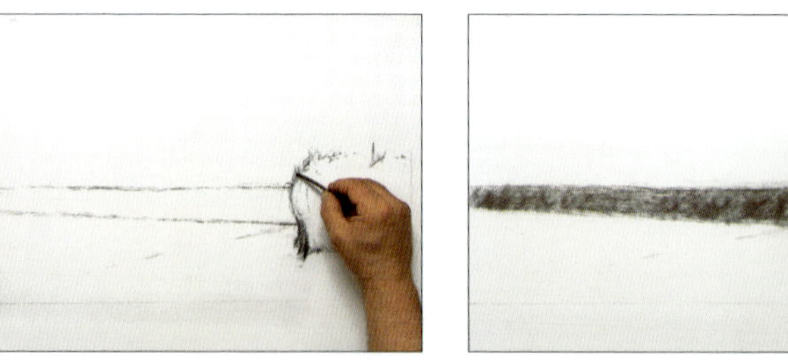

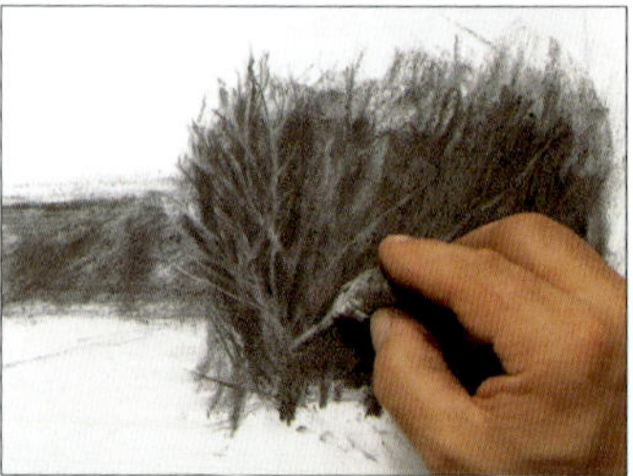

1 Using a thin charcoal stick, map out the proportions of the scene. Look for specific points from which you can measure other elements. Here, the artist used the clump of trees as a starting point. When he measured it, he discovered that the distance from the base of the clump to the base of the ridge in the distance is roughly the same as the distance from the base of the trees to the base of the image.

2 Using the side of the charcoal, roughly block in the wedge-shaped area of land in the middle distance and the thicket of trees on the right. Make jagged, spiky marks for the top of the thicket to convey the texture of the trees. Note also that some areas are darker in tone than others; although you will elaborate this later, it's a good idea to get some tonal variation into the drawing even at this early stage.

3 Using the tip of a medium charcoal stick, draw the darkest areas within the thicket of trees. Look for the negative shapes – the spaces between the branches rather than the branches themselves. Switch to a thin charcoal stick for the branches that stick out at the sides and top of the main mass. Using a kneaded eraser, lightly stroke off charcoal for the lighter-toned branches within the clump.

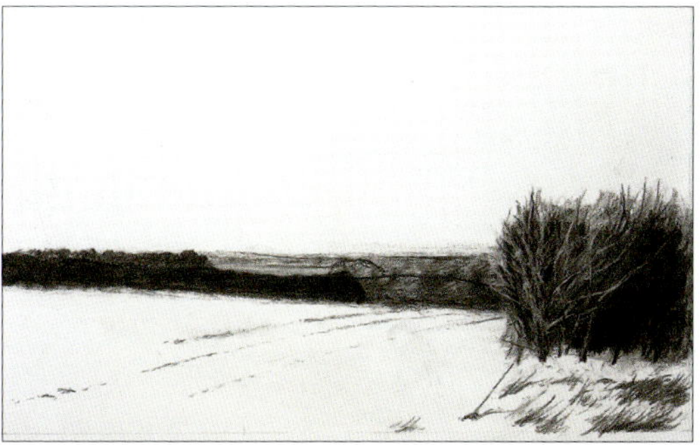

4 Start to introduce some form into the wedge-shaped area of land in the middle distance. The trees at the front of this area are very dark in tone, so build up the tone with heavy, vertical strokes. Use a thin charcoal stick to start dotting in the exposed clumps of earth peeping up above the snow in the field and make thin vertical strokes for the grasses on the right-hand side of the image.

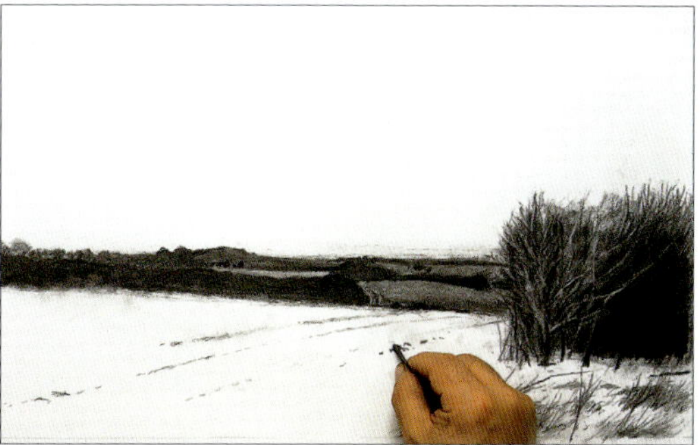

5 Using a stick of compressed charcoal, put in some very dark blacks in the trees in the middle distance so that you gradually begin to build up texture and tone. Also use the compressed charcoal to draw more of the exposed clumps of earth that run across the field, making small, dotted marks of varying sizes and making the marks darker as you come towards the foreground.

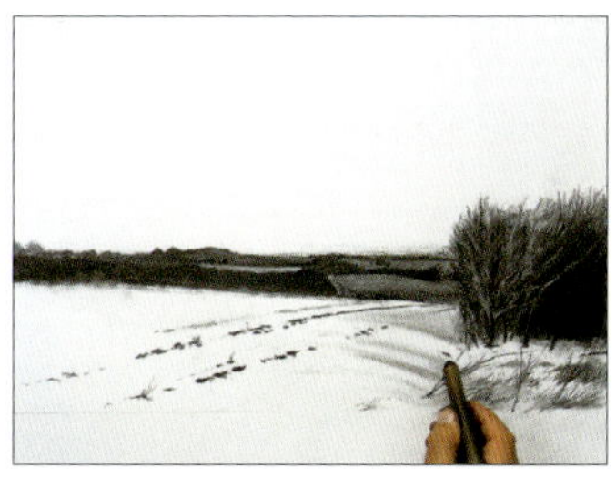

6 Rub some charcoal on to a scrap piece of paper and press the end of a large torchon into the resulting powder. Gently stroke the torchon over the snow that leads down to the clump of trees to create soft shadows.

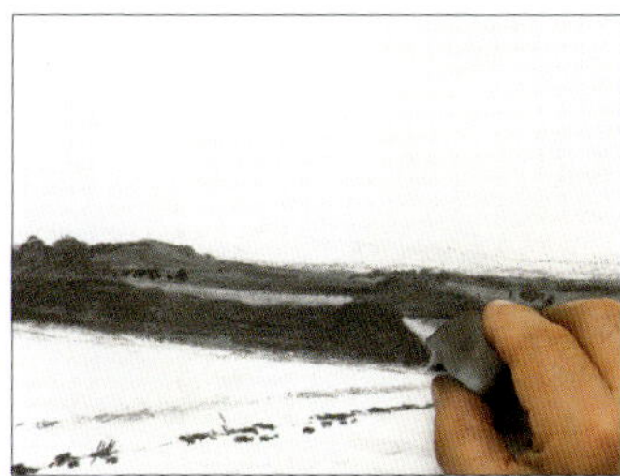

7 Using a plastic eraser, wipe off some of the charcoal to create the snow on the edges of the fields in the middle distance. By cutting the eraser you can get a crisp, sharp-edged line.

Assessment time

The main elements of the composition are in place, but the contrast between the sky (to which no charcoal has been applied so far) and the dark, dense tones of the trees is too extreme. Even so, the thicket of trees on the right still needs to be darkened in places. Your task now is to develop texture and tone across the whole image. In order to do this, you will need to continually assess the tonal balance of the drawing as a whole, to ensure that no one part becomes too dominant.

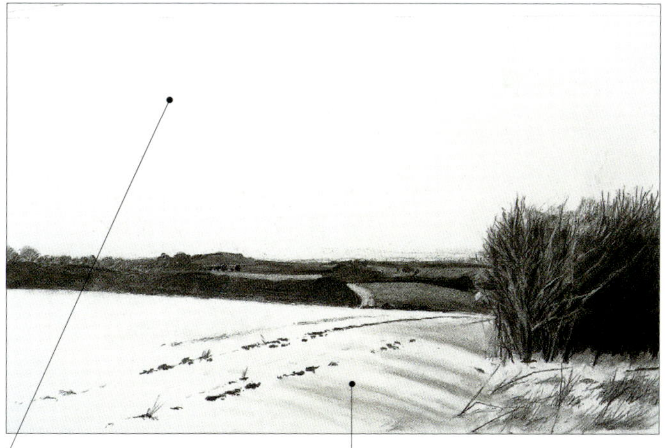

As yet there is no detail in the sky, which forms roughly half the image.

With the exception of a few foreground shadows, there is no texture or detail in the snow areas.

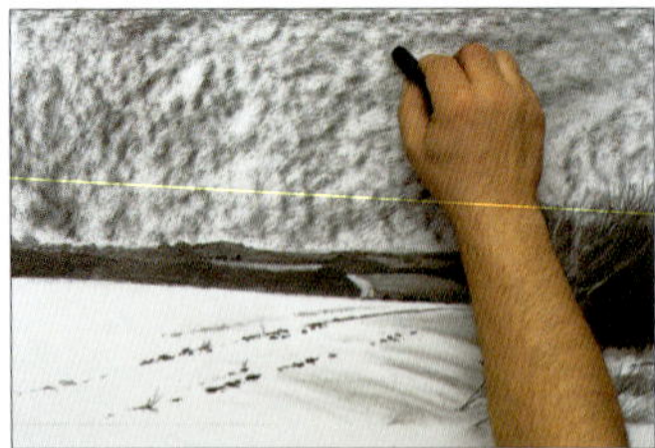

8 Wipe the side of a medium stick of charcoal over the sky area. Note how the coverage is uneven, creating lovely dappled marks.

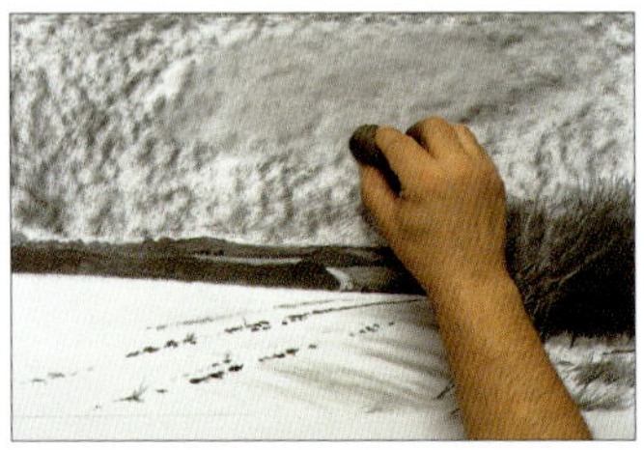

9 Using a circular motion, vigorously rub a small sponge over the sky to smooth out the charcoal marks.

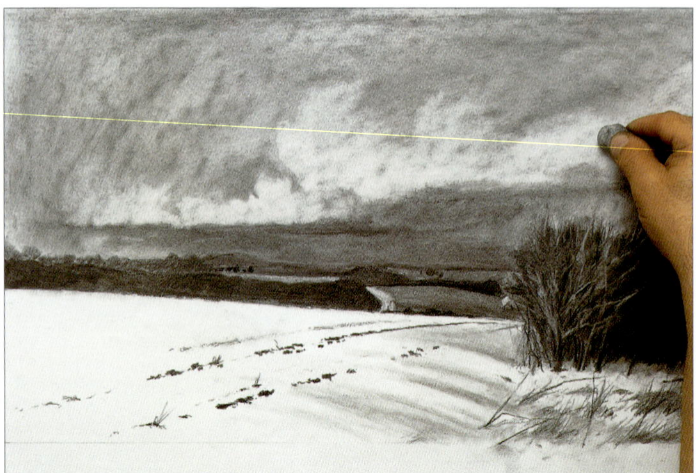

10 There is a band of blue in the sky above the land and below the mass of clouds. Block this in using the side of a medium charcoal stick and blend it to a mid-grey with a torchon, making it darker in tone than the rest of the sky. Using a kneaded eraser and a vigorous circular motion, lift off shapes for the looming storm clouds. Don't worry about the tones within the clouds at this stage; just try to get the approximate shapes. Note how putting some detail in the sky has changed the mood of the drawing from a tranquil winter scene to something much more dramatic, in which the threat of a storm is imminent.

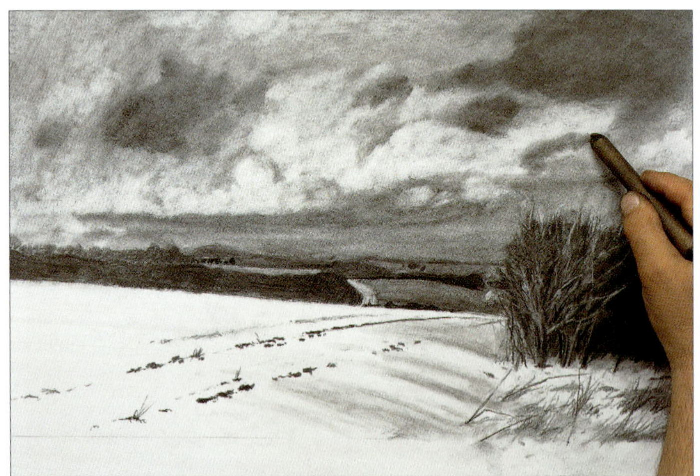

11 Put in some very dark storm clouds and blend the charcoal with your fingertips or a sponge. Immediately, the scene looks much more dramatic; note how the dark areas of sky balance the thicket of trees on the right of the image. Scribble some charcoal on a piece of scrap paper to get some loose powder, as in Step 6. Dip a torchon in the powder and gently stroke it over the sky to create softly blended areas of mid-tone between the clouds. This allows the white areas of the clouds to stand out more clearly.

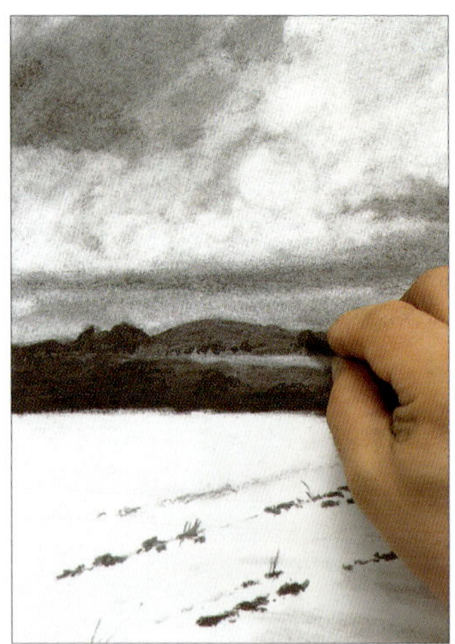

12 The sky is now quite dark, so you may need to darken the land mass to make it more dominant. Compressed charcoal gives a very rich, intense black. Note how the snow also seems to sparkle and stand out more once the land mass has been darkened.

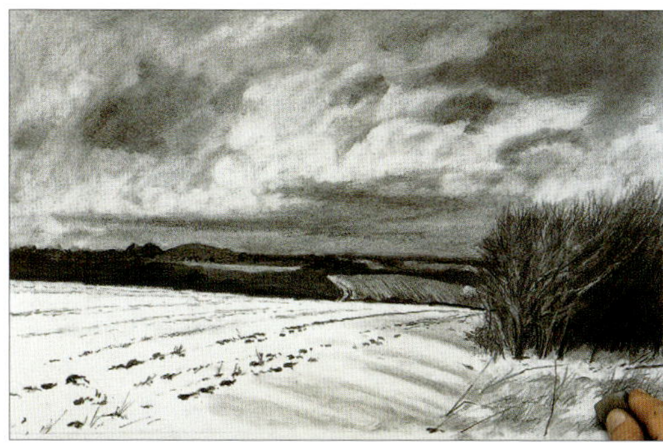

13 Using a thin charcoal stick, put in any remaining exposed clumps of earth on the field. Re-assess the whites in relation to the rest of the image. You may need to use a kneaded eraser to lift off some charcoal in the grasses on the right.

The finished drawing

This drawing demonstrates the versatility of charcoal. It can be blended to give a smooth, even coverage, as in the mid-toned areas of the sky, or used to create bold, highly textured marks, as in the clump of trees. The success of the image is due largely to the contrast between the very light and the very dark areas. In scenes like this, the key is often to darken the dark areas rather than to lighten the lights.

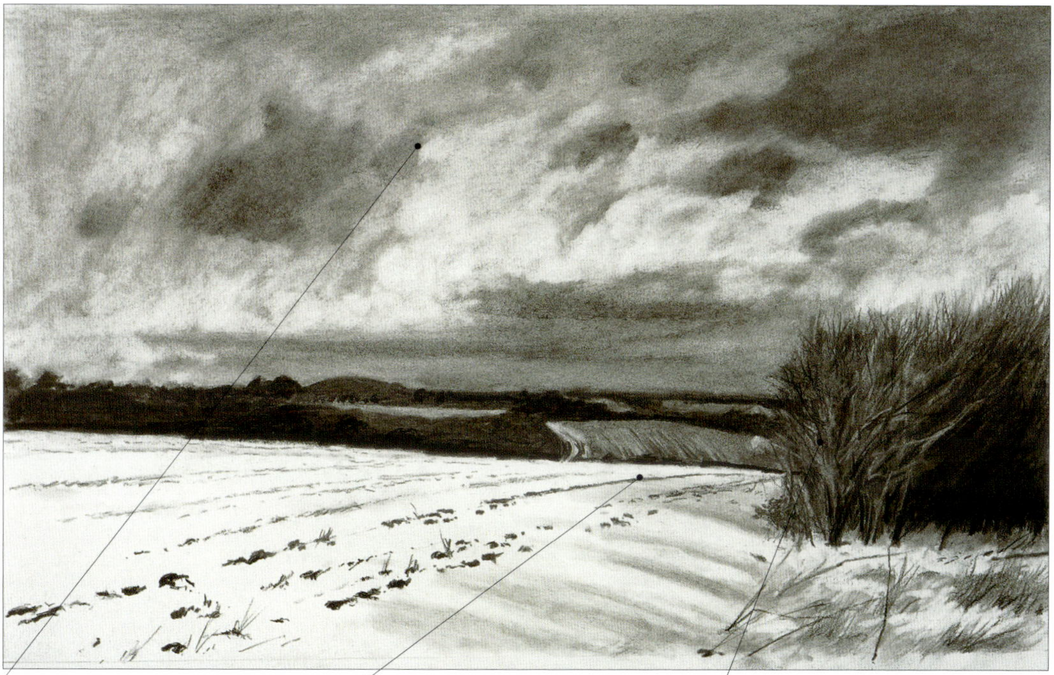

Charcoal is softly blended with a sponge to create the clouds.

The exposed clumps of earth are paler in the distance, creating a sense of recession.

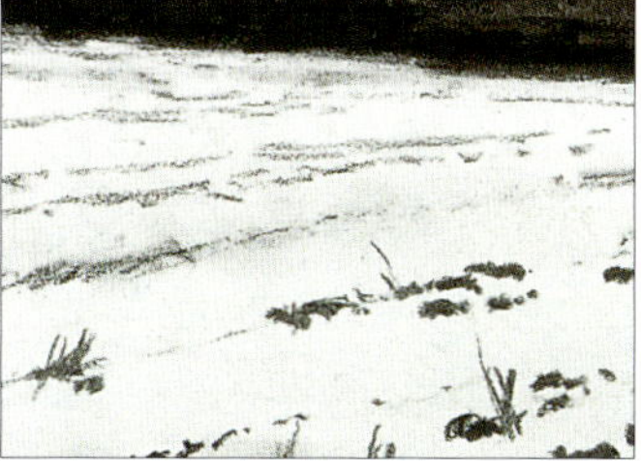

'Drawing' some of the branches with an eraser creates fine, crisp-edged lines.

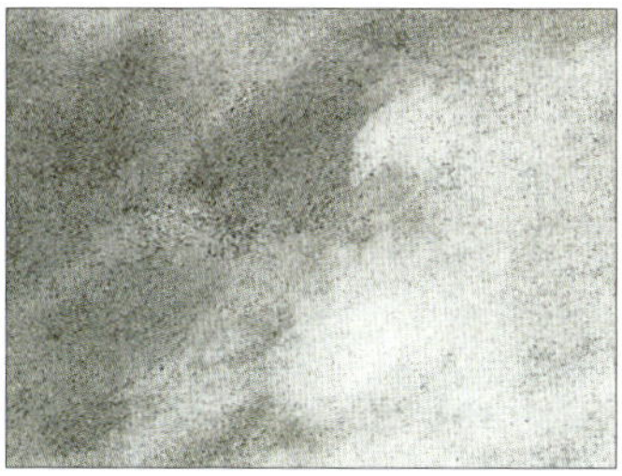

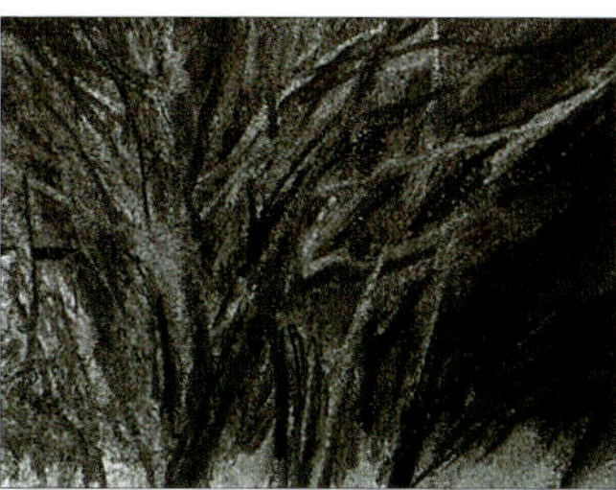

Reflections in rippling water

Shimmering reflections are great fun to draw. Perfect reflections, however, do not necessarily make the most interesting subjects, as part of the fascination lies in seeing how familiar shapes and objects are distorted when reflected. In this project, your challenge is not only to draw the reflections convincingly but also to capture a sense of movement in the gently rippling water.

Before you start drawing, spend time looking at both the shapes and the sizes of the ripples. There are two distinct types of ripple in the scene – horizontal ripples, which are caused by a very slight breeze, and circular ripples in front of the ducks as they move through the water. Look out for these shapes and alter your pencil strokes accordingly, using a curving or swirling motion for the circular ripples. And remember the rules of perspective: in order to create a sense of distance, foreground ripples need to be larger and further apart than those in the background.

Coloured pencils are used for this project – the perfect opportunity for you to practise optical colour blending. The water, of course, takes its colour mainly from the trees and foliage on the bankside – and even though the trees are not actually included in this scene, you need to provide enough information for the viewer to be able to infer something of the country park setting.

The first stage is to colour in the background. This makes it easier to gauge how to treat the birds. If you were to colour the birds first, you could easily find that you'd made them too dark – an irreversible mistake. When you're drawing white objects, remember that they are never pure white, even though our eyes perceive them as such. Some shading, however slight, is essential for them to look three-dimensional.

Materials

- *Smooth drawing paper*
- *Coloured pencils: turquoise-green, range of greens, yellow, dark blue, pale blue, violet, light orange, dark red*

The scene

Placing the birds almost in the centre of the image helps to create a calm, peaceful mood that is appropriate to the subject. The rippling water adds interest to what might otherwise be a fairly bland scene.

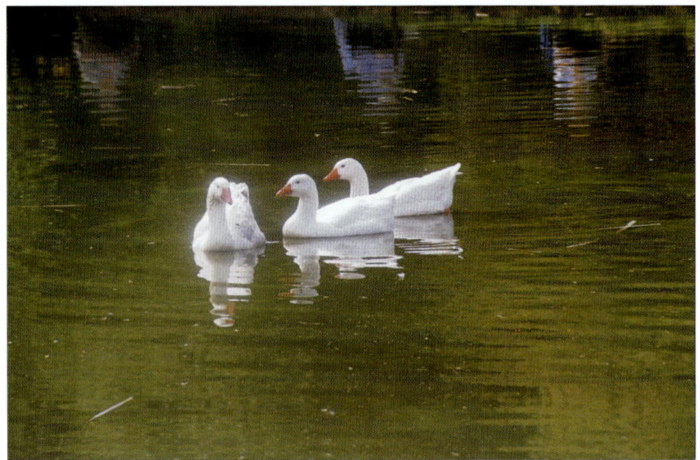

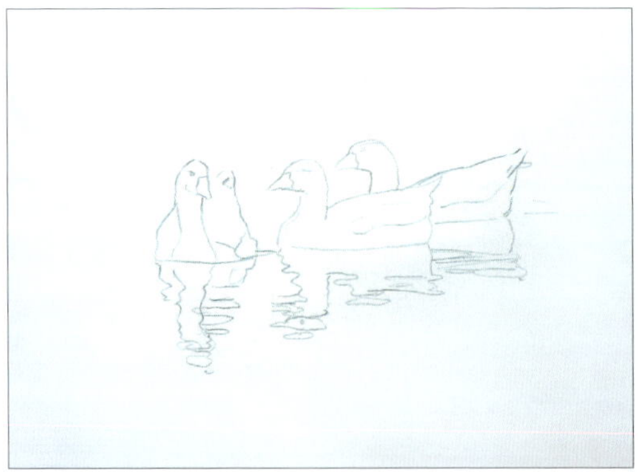

1 Using a turquoise-green pencil, outline the ducks and their reflections and indicate the main ripples. If you're worried about colouring in the birds when you start to work on the water in Step 2, use masking fluid for the outlines.

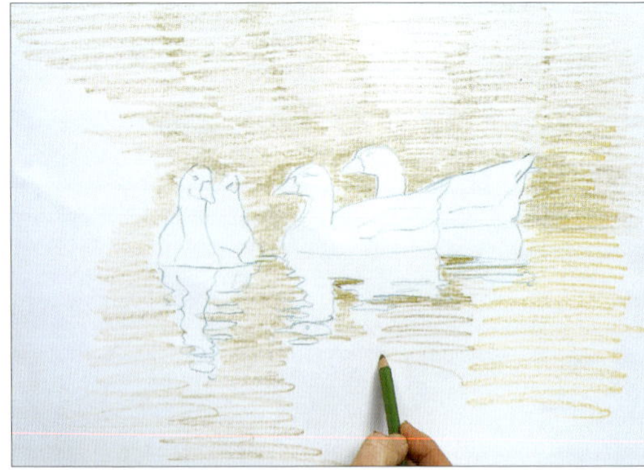

2 With green and yellow pencils (yellow for the right-hand side, which receives a little more light than the rest of the scene), lightly colour in the water around the birds, using a zig-zag motion to echo the shape of the ripples.

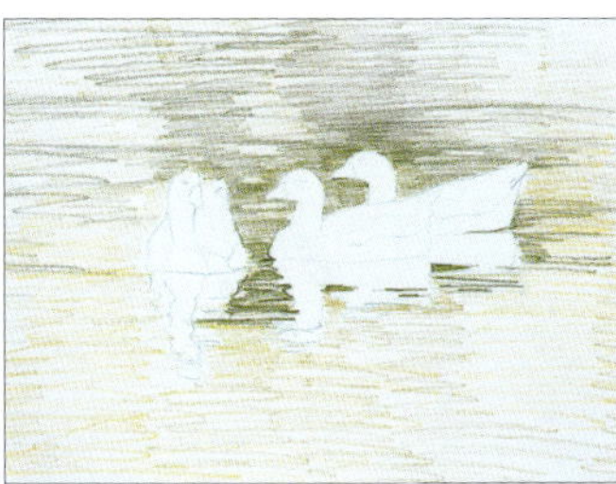

3 Apply more yellow over the lower half of the water, below the birds, and dark green behind them, again using a zig-zag motion of the pencil and leaving some gaps so that the underlying colours remain visible. Note that the water that lies between the birds is very dark indeed, so you can afford to apply a little more pressure with the pencil here.

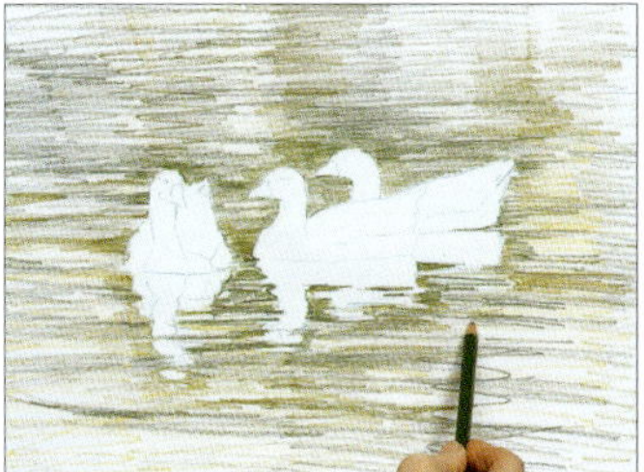

4 Apply dark green in front of the birds. Now that you've established much of the base colour of the water, you can begin to create more of a sense of movement – so switch from a zig-zag motion to curved marks and swirls to capture the ripples. Remember the rules of perspective: make the foreground ripples larger and further apart than those in the background.

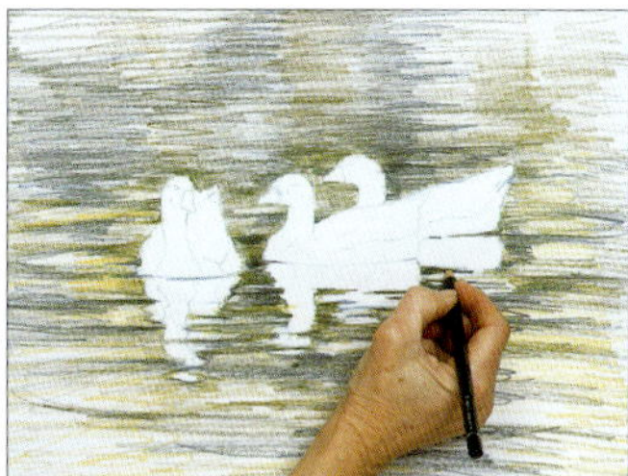

5 In areas where the foliage is reflected in the water, apply more yellow over the green, still using curved marks and swirls to maintain the movement of the ripples in the water. Apply dark blue in the very darkest areas – particularly under the birds. Remember to maintain an even but light pressure so as not to give too much emphasis to one particular area.

Assessment time

The water takes its colour from the things that are reflected in it – the trees on the bankside. Already we can see a range of colours, but the water is still too light overall. We are also beginning to get a feeling of movement, as the ripples flow outwards from the birds, and this needs to be enhanced. Finally, of course, the birds themselves need to be drawn in detail – something that is much easier to do now that we have a clearer idea of how dark the darkest areas need to be.

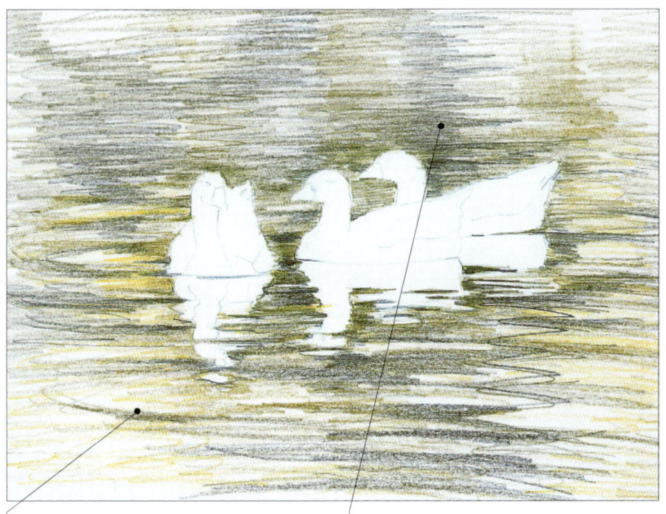

Curved pencil marks create the ripples in the water.

The water needs to be darker overall, but the base colours have been established.

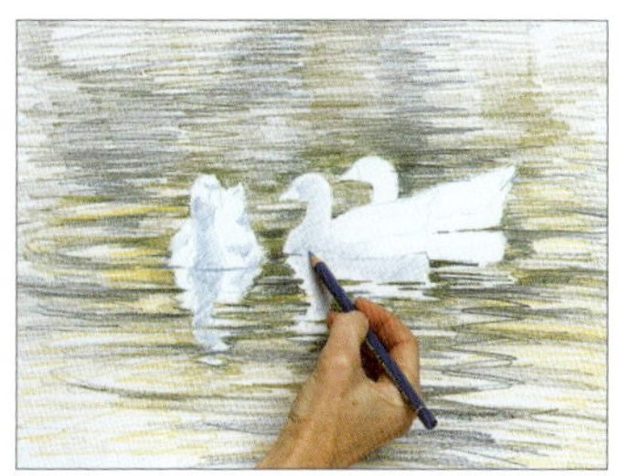

6 Using a pale blue pencil and horizontal strokes, lightly put some shading on the birds' white feathers.

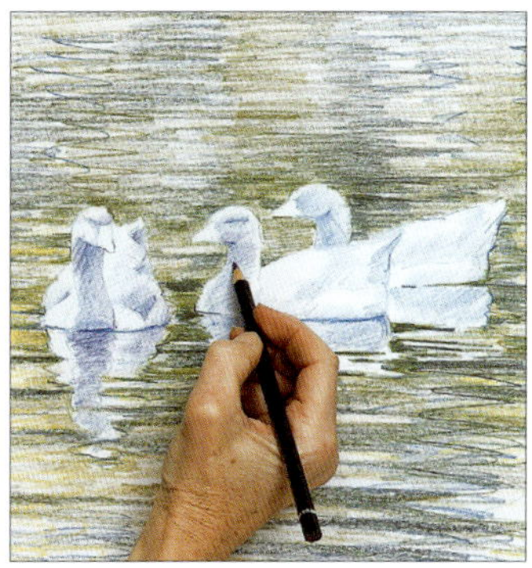

7 Using a violet pencil, lightly hatch over the blue to darken it slightly. Lightly indicate the position and angle of the birds' eyes.

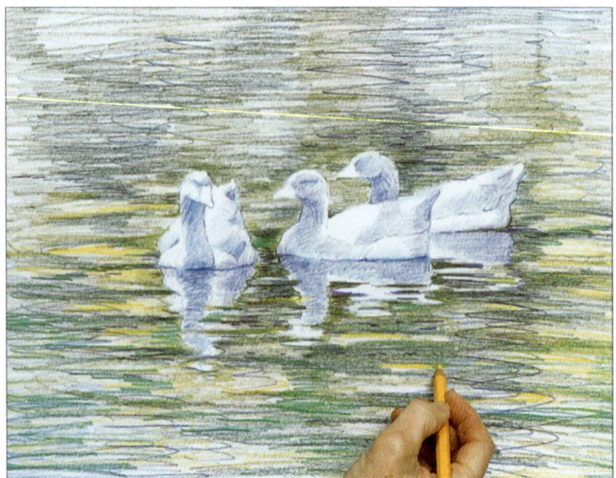

8 Continue working on the foreground water, putting in dots and dashes of violet, bright green and yellow. Keep referring to your reference photo to see where the yellow highlights, which are formed where the lightest bits of foliage are refected in the water, occur and what shape and size the ripples need to be.

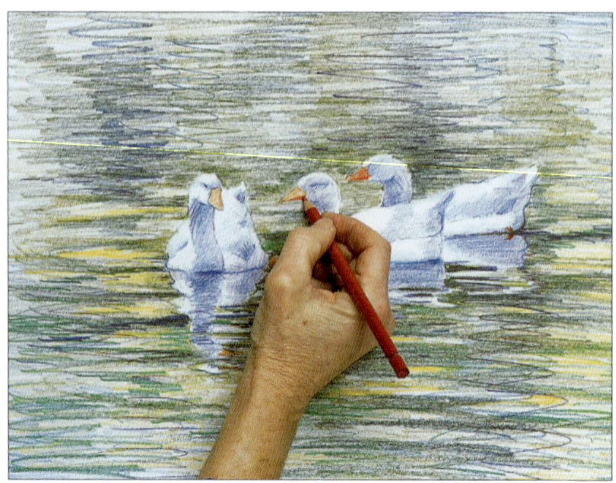

9 Darken the water with a dark blue pencil, still using zig-zag and swirling motions so that you don't lose the ripples and the sense of motion in the water. By bringing the blue right up to the birds, you can sharpen their outlines. Colour in the beaks and reflections with a light orange and overlay with dark red on the lower beaks.

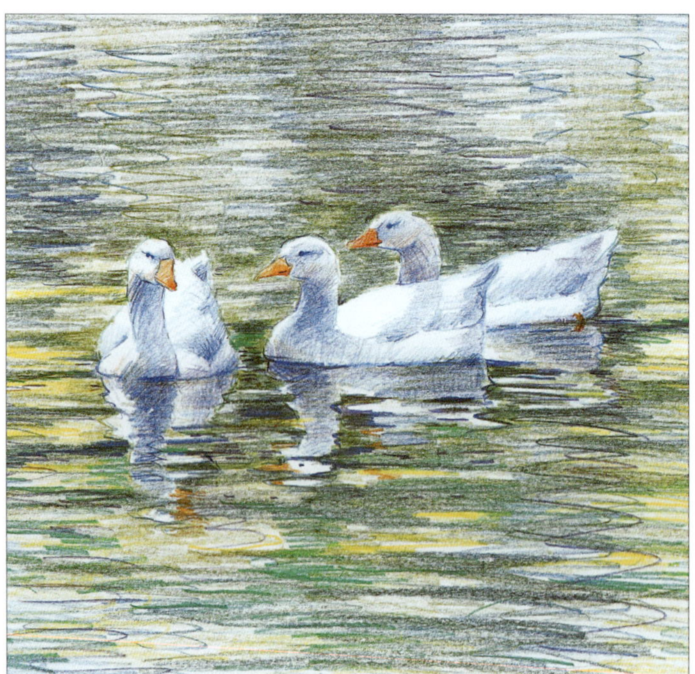

10 The divide between the birds and their reflections is not clear. Gently stroke dark green over the reflections to subdue them and push them back into the water. Using a dark blue pencil, draw around the backs and necks of the birds so that they stand out from the water.

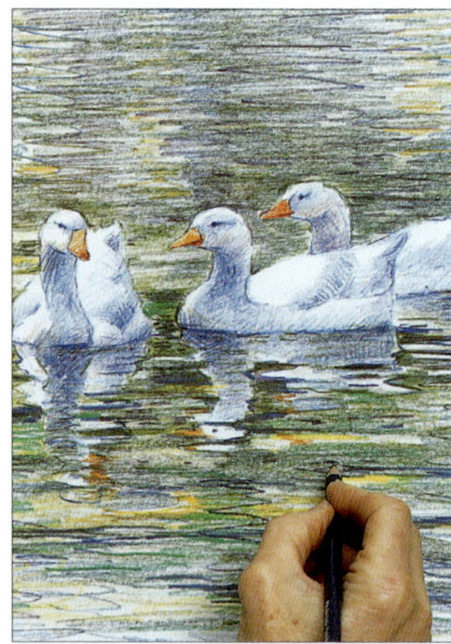

11 Adjust the colours in the water until you feel you've got the balance right; it helps to take a short break from the drawing at this point, as it will enable you to look at your work more objectively. Make sure the darkest parts are dark enough (add more blue if necessary), and that the yellows are not too bright (yellow ochre is a less harsh alternative). Note that the reflections are broken by the ripples in the water – but the overall shapes are still very clear.

The finished drawing

By using curved and zig-zagging pencil strokes for the ripples, the artist has created a lovely sense of movement in the water. Note that the ripples are larger in the foreground than in the background, which helps to create a sense of distance. The reflections are slightly broken by the ripples and more subdued in colour than the birds themselves.

The artist has also made the scene slightly sunnier than it was in reality, by using brighter colours and including more yellow. Although the birds are centrally placed in the picture area, the two birds on the left have their heads turned towards one another, which helps to draw our attention in to the centre of the scene.

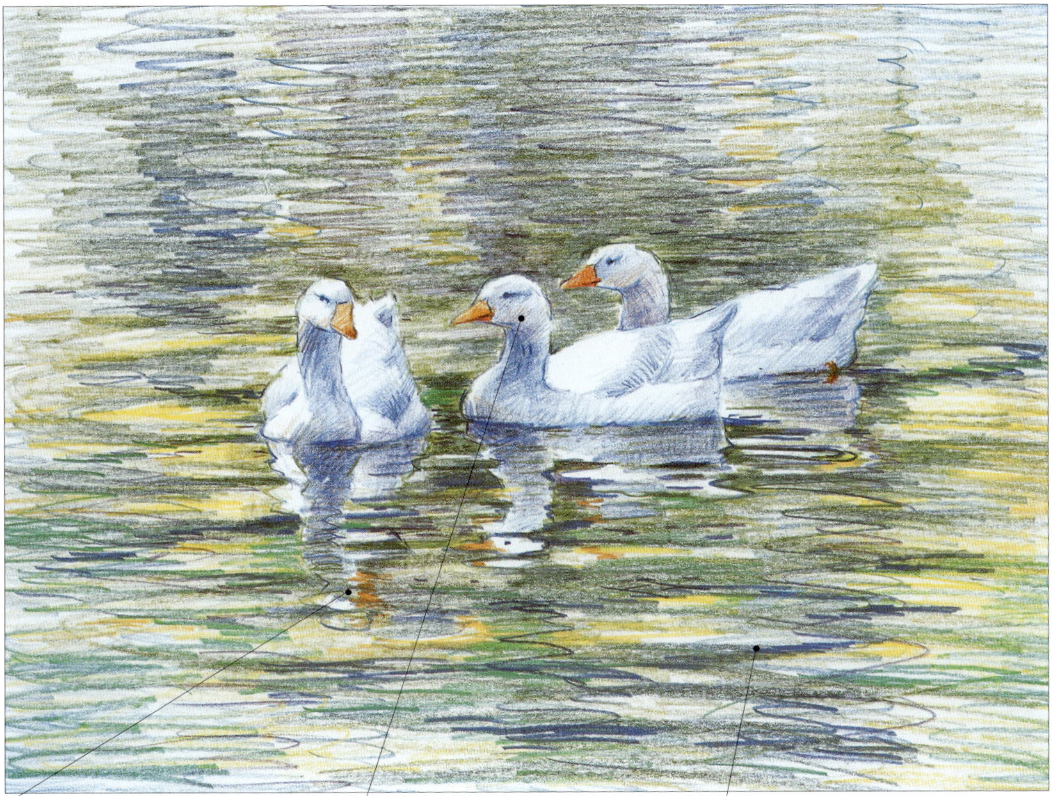

The reflections are broken by the ripples and more subdued in colour than the birds.

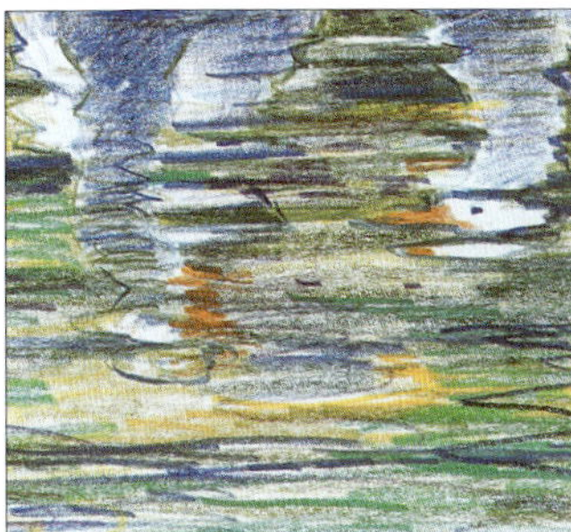

The angle of the birds' heads directs our attention to the centre of the scene.

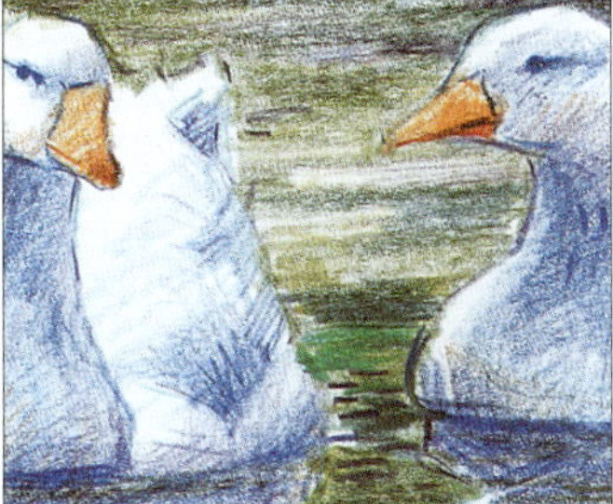

The foreground ripples are larger than those in the background.

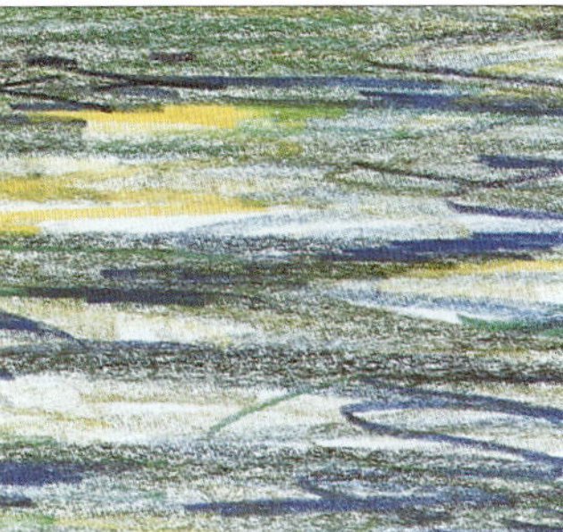

Landscape on a large scale

Drawing on a large scale is very liberating, both physically and mentally. Physically, it allows you to use the full stretch of your arm and hand to make bold, sweeping marks that are full of energy. Mentally, you have to simplify things and stop yourself getting bogged down in unnecessary detail. Try to get back to the essence of the scene – the aspects that made you want to draw it in the first place.

Charcoal is the perfect medium for a project such as this, as it is so versatile and easy to apply. You can drag the side of the charcoal across the support to cover large areas quickly, blend it using a variety of techniques, or use the tip to make expressive, linear marks.

If you can't find sheets of purpose-made drawing paper large enough, a roll of lining (liner) paper from a DIY store makes an inexpensive alternative. Pin it to a drawing board (or attach it with masking tape), and then place the drawing board on a studio easel or hang it on a wall.

The composition of large-scale drawings needs careful thought and planning. Before you embark on the actual drawing, it's a good idea to make a schematic sketch of the composition, working out where the centre of interest falls and making sure that the viewer's eye is led to that point.

Materials

- *Drawing paper 1 x 1.25m (3 x 4ft)*
- *Charcoal: thick and thin sticks*
- *Kneaded eraser*

The scene

The rocky escarpment is surmounted on the left by a wooded area that echoes the bands of trees at the base of the escarpment and in the fields below. In the foreground, a narrow track leads the eye into the scene along the line of trees and up to the rocks.

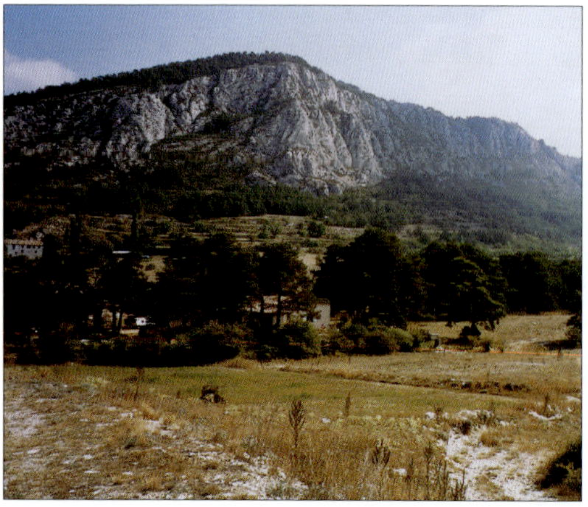

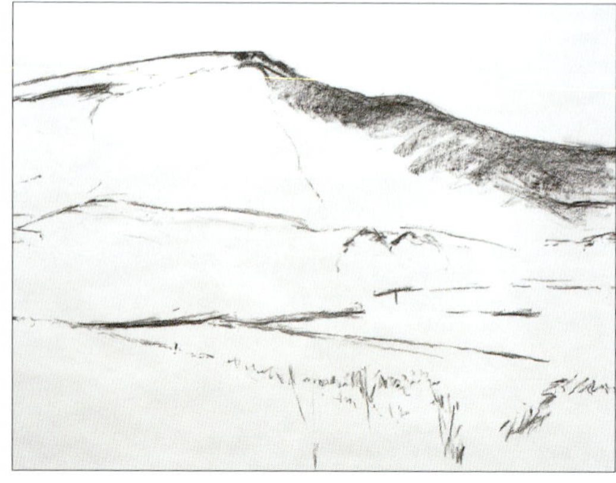

1 First, decide how much of the scene you want to include in your drawing and map out the positions of the main elements. To make this process easier, divide the scene into quarters (either mentally or by making light marks at the edges of the paper) and mark out where things fall in each square. Use light marks at this stage, just to establish where everything goes. Lightly block in the slope of the cliff to give yourself a visual guide to where to position the trees that stand at its base.

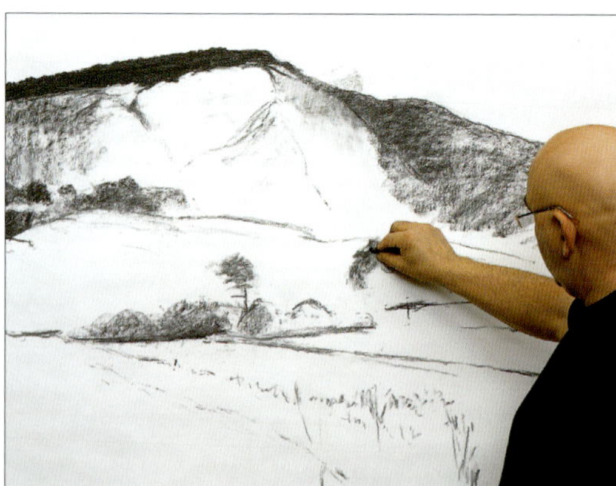

2 Work out where the darkest areas of tone are going to be and roughly block them in with a thick charcoal stick. The wooded mass on the top of the cliff is very dark, so you can apply a lot of pressure to the charcoal for this area. However, it's not a solid, straight-edged wedge shape: look closely and you will see that the tops of the trees are gently rounded. Outline groups of trees at the far side of the fields with light dots and dashes, then block them in with the side of the charcoal stick.

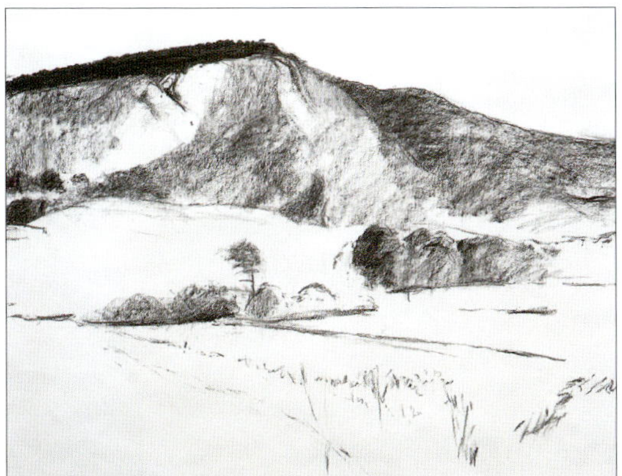

3 Turn your attention back to the cliffs and look for differences in tone: the contrasts between dark, shaded gullies and crevices and the more brightly lit areas that are in full sunshine give the cliffs some sense of form. Block in the larger areas of tone using the side of the charcoal stick and moving your whole arm, not just your hand, keeping the coverage fairly uneven so that some of the paper texture shows through. Note that the brightest areas are barely touched by the charcoal. Continue blocking in the band of trees at the back of the fields, putting in nothing more than generalized shapes at this stage.

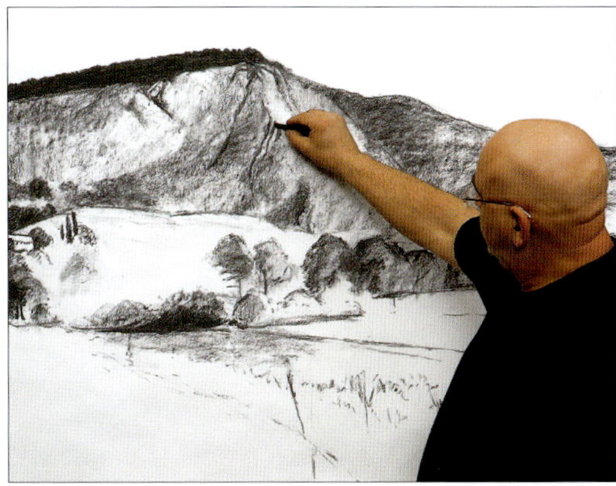

4 Outline the trees at the base of the cliff, then sketchily develop some tone within them. Note the number of different shapes – the tall, elongated cypress trees and the more rounded shapes elsewhere. Start to put in some jagged, linear marks on the cliff to create some texture.

Tip: Continually check the size of the trees and the distances between them and other elements of the scene. It's very easy to make the trees too big and destroy the scale of the drawing.

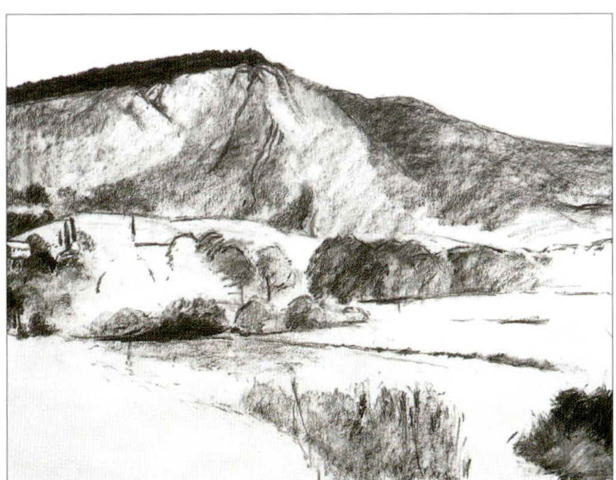

5 Finish outlining the shapes of the band of trees that runs across the middle of the drawing. Now you can begin to develop the foreground a little. Put in the foreground grasses, using both the tip of the charcoal and the side.

Tip: Work across the drawing as a whole, rather than concentrating on one area. This makes it easier to get the tonal balance of the drawing right.

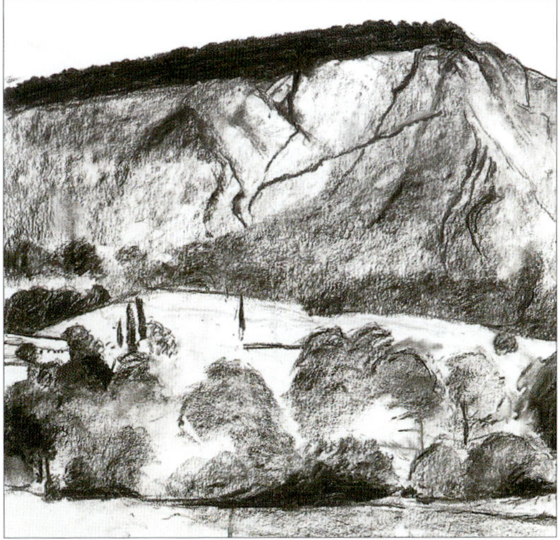

6 Continue working on the trees in the middle of the drawing, concentrating on the overall shapes. Add more tone to the trees at the base of the cliff so that they begin to stand out more. Using the tip of the charcoal, put in more jagged, linear marks on the side of the cliff. These dark fissures help to create a sense of form and texture.

Assessment time

Details in the image are taking shape, but it requires much more tonal contrast and texture. The trees are little more than generalized shapes at this stage and do not look truly three-dimensional; you need to develop more tone within them and also to put in the shadows that they cast. We are beginning to see the different facets of the cliff, but the darkest marks are not yet dark enough to give us any real sense of form.

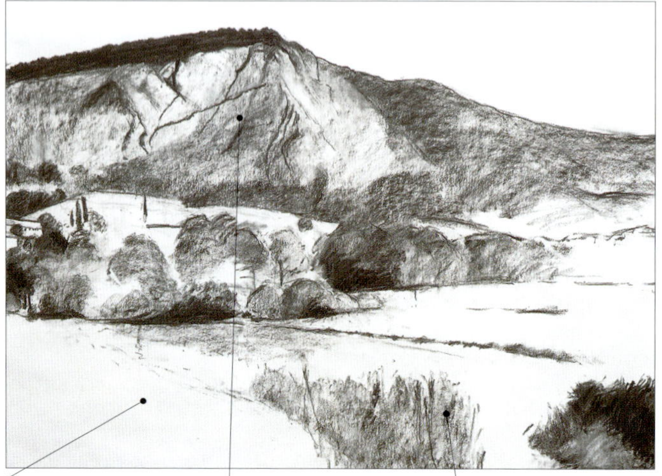

Very little work has been done on the foreground. It is too bright in relation to the rest of the image.

The linear marks on the cliff need to be developed further to create a sense of form.

The foreground grasses are too indistinct. More texture is needed here.

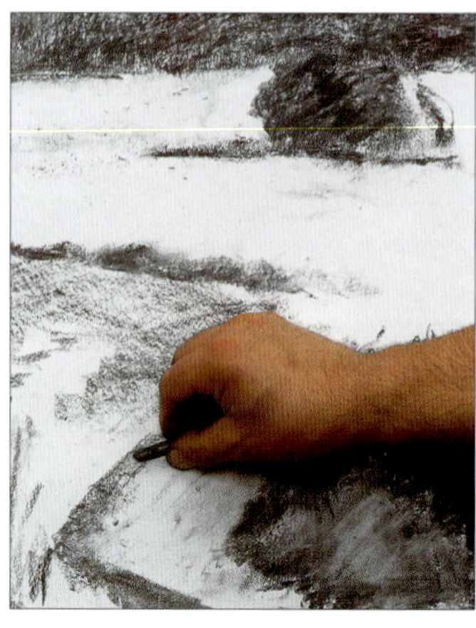

7 Very gently stroke the side of a thin charcoal stick over the foreground to create some tone and texture. Note how using the charcoal in this way gives a slightly uneven coverage. Press slightly harder on the charcoal to put in the sides of the track that zig-zags its way through the scene. Also indicate the shadows cast by the trees.

Tip: Smooth out the long cast shadows with your fingertips, in order to make them less textured than the trees themselves.

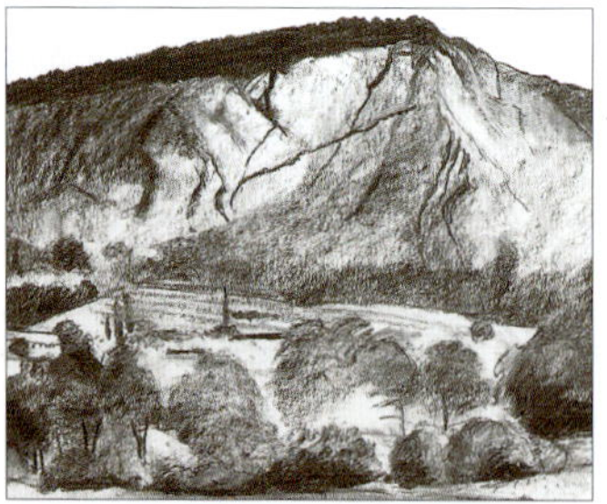

8 Very gently make a series of horizontal marks over the fields immediately below the cliff, pulling the full length of the charcoal stick over the paper to create the effect of ploughed furrows. Using the tip of the charcoal and pressing down firmly, put in the dark trunks of the trees in the centre of the image.

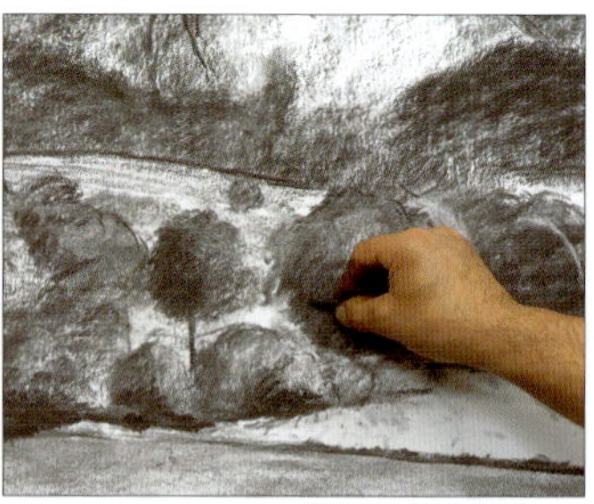

9 The trees are now taking real shape. Look at how the light catches them. Darken the shaded sides, using the side of the charcoal to create broad areas of tone. Immediately the trees begin to look more three-dimensional as you add the shadows they cast. Developing this tone takes them away from generalized shapes.

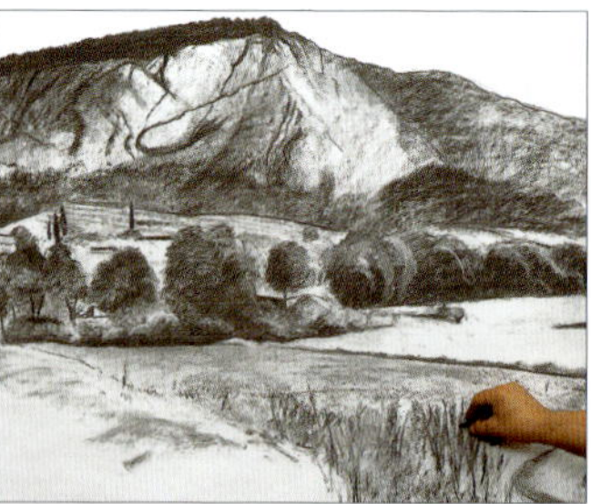

10 Using a kneaded eraser, gently lift off some of the charcoal from the side of the trees that catches the light. If you lift off too much, simply go over the area in charcoal again. Using the tip of a thin charcoal stick, introduce more texture into the foreground grasses by making crisp, dark, vertical marks.

The finished drawing

Working on a large scale has allowed the artist to use the full stretch of his arm to make bold, sweeping marks that give the drawing a very energetic, lively feel. He has concentrated on the essentials of the scene, rather than trying to put in every single detail, but his clever use of tonal contrasts gives the image a convincing sense of form. The foreground track leads our eye through the scene to the trees and cliff beyond – a classic compositional device.

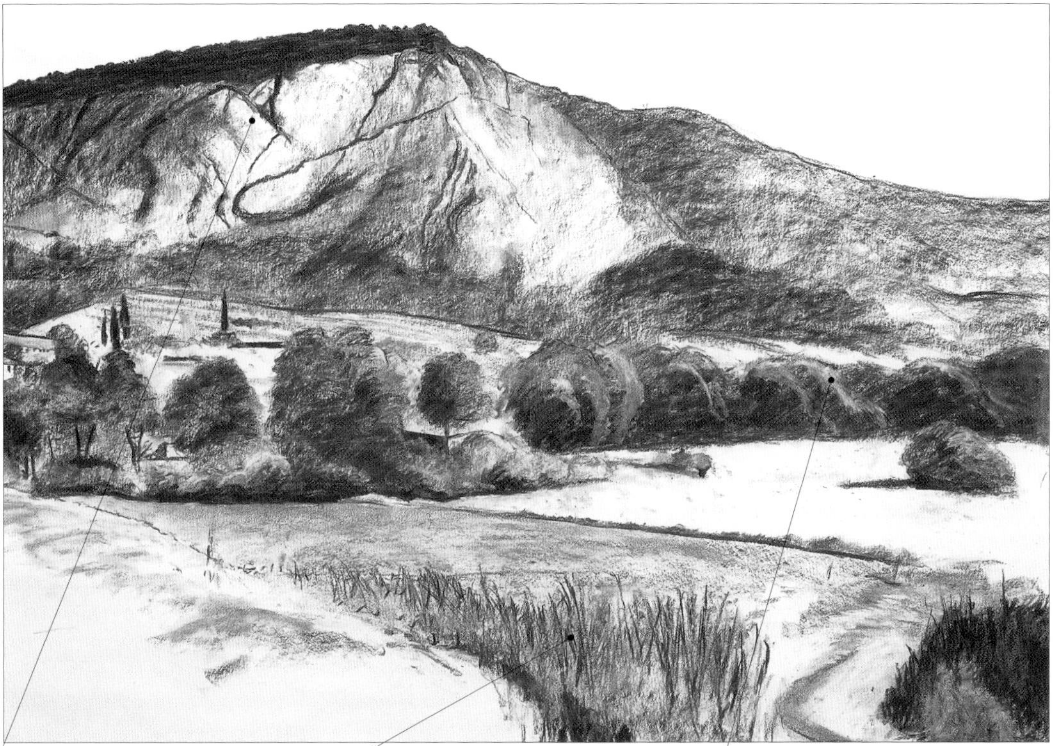

Note how the contrasts between light and dark areas reveal the different facets of the cliff face.

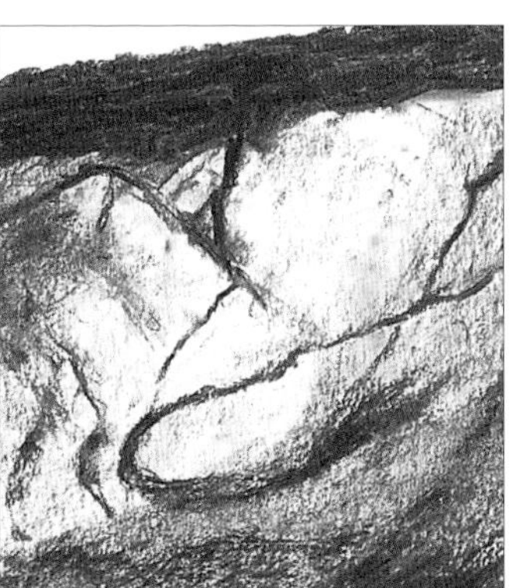

Detail diminishes with distance; the amount of detail that we can discern in the grasses tells us that they are in the foreground.

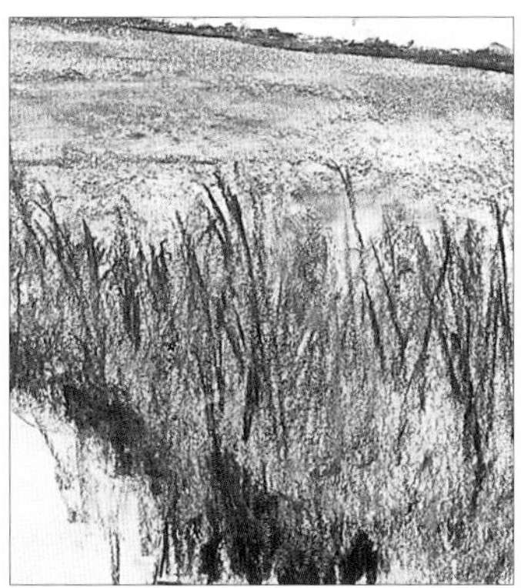

Lifting off charcoal from the most brightly lit sides of the trees shows us which direction the light is coming from.

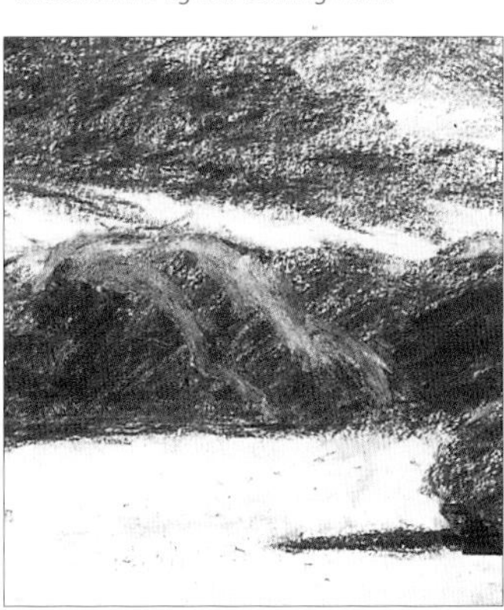

Quick sketches of still lifes: Potted plant

Although we normally think of a still life as being an item, or a group of items, that the artist has deliberately arranged, there are also what are known as 'found' still lifes, which are things that the artist has come across by chance.

As with any subject, you need to think about your viewpoint and position carefully. If the object is heavy, it may not be possible to move it – but you can easily adjust your own position to give a more pleasing composition. Your eye level is important, too: in the examples shown on these two pages, the artist's eye level was above the plant, enabling her to look inside the pot and see how the leaves grow out of the main stem. If the pot had been at eye level, so that she was looking at it horizontally, this kind of information would have been hidden from view.

The background is also an important element of a still life and you need to decide how to treat it. One of the delights of drawing and painting is that you have the freedom to interpret things as you wish, and to omit or alter things that you do not like. If you find that the background detracts from the subject, or prevents the subject standing out clearly, simplify it to a tonal wash.

The scene
Here, the artist discovered a potted plant in a corner of a friend's garden and was intrigued by the sculptural shapes of the leaves and the arching shadows that they cast on the gravel beneath the pot.

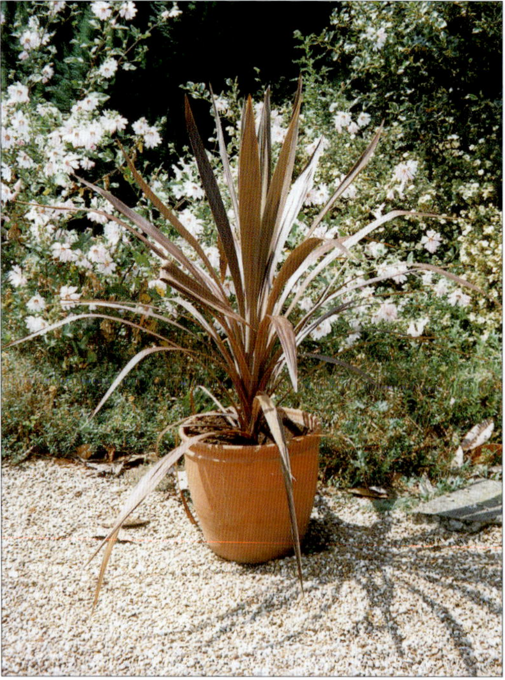

5-minute sketch: graphite pencil
In a 5-minute sketch, you can only explore the basic shapes of the subject. Looking at the negative shapes can be a great help when you are drawing objects that are irregularly shaped. Here, the artist blocked in the negative shapes on the left with loose scribbles, as this made it easier to see the shapes of the leaves themselves. A context and three-dimensional feel were also suggested by sketching in the cast shadow.

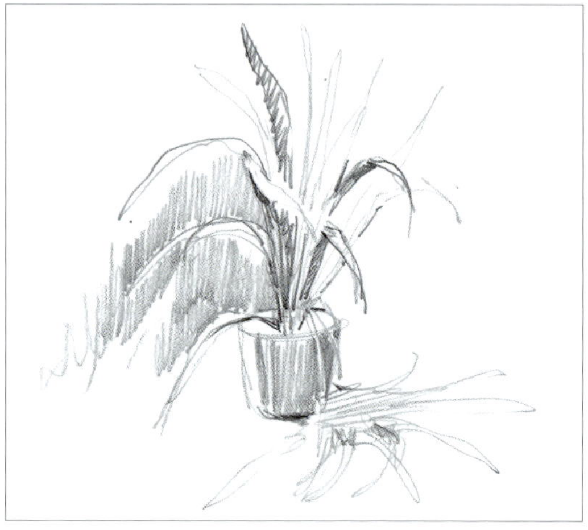

10-minute sketch: graphite pencil and water-soluble sepia ink
In this sketch, the artist explored ways of treating the background, using both washes of water-soluble ink between the leaves to provide a dark background and loose pen-and-ink shapes to imply the presence of other plants.

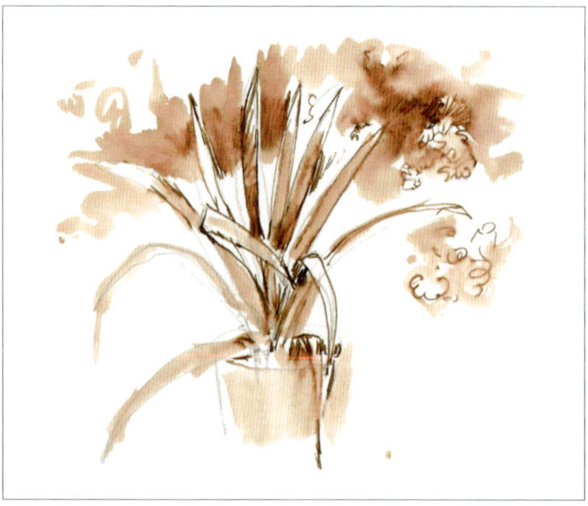

15-minute sketch: graphite pencil, water-soluble sepia ink and water-soluble pencils
The plant itself was treated in the same way as in the 5-minute sketch, opposite. While the ink was still damp, water-soluble pencils were used to add detail on the pot and shadows. As the paper was damp, the colours spread.

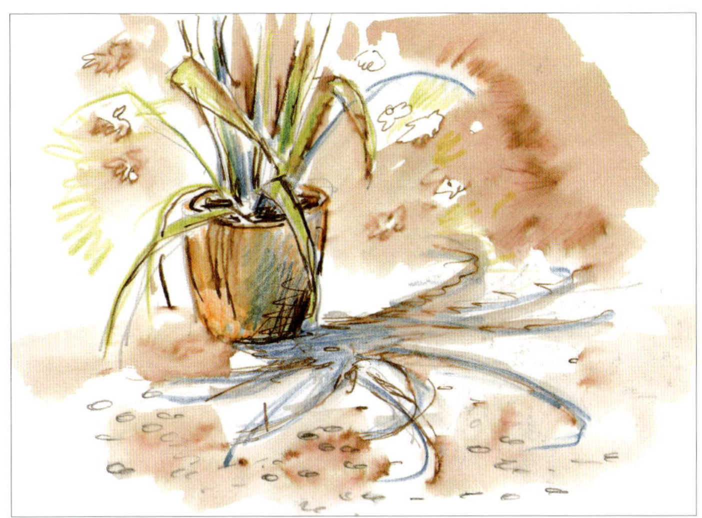

25-minute sketch: graphite pencil, masking fluid, water-soluble sepia ink and water-soluble pencils
Here, masking fluid protected some of the daisy-like flowers in the background from the washes of ink. When the other details were complete, the masking fluid was removed and the centres of the flowers drawn in with an orange water-soluble pencil.

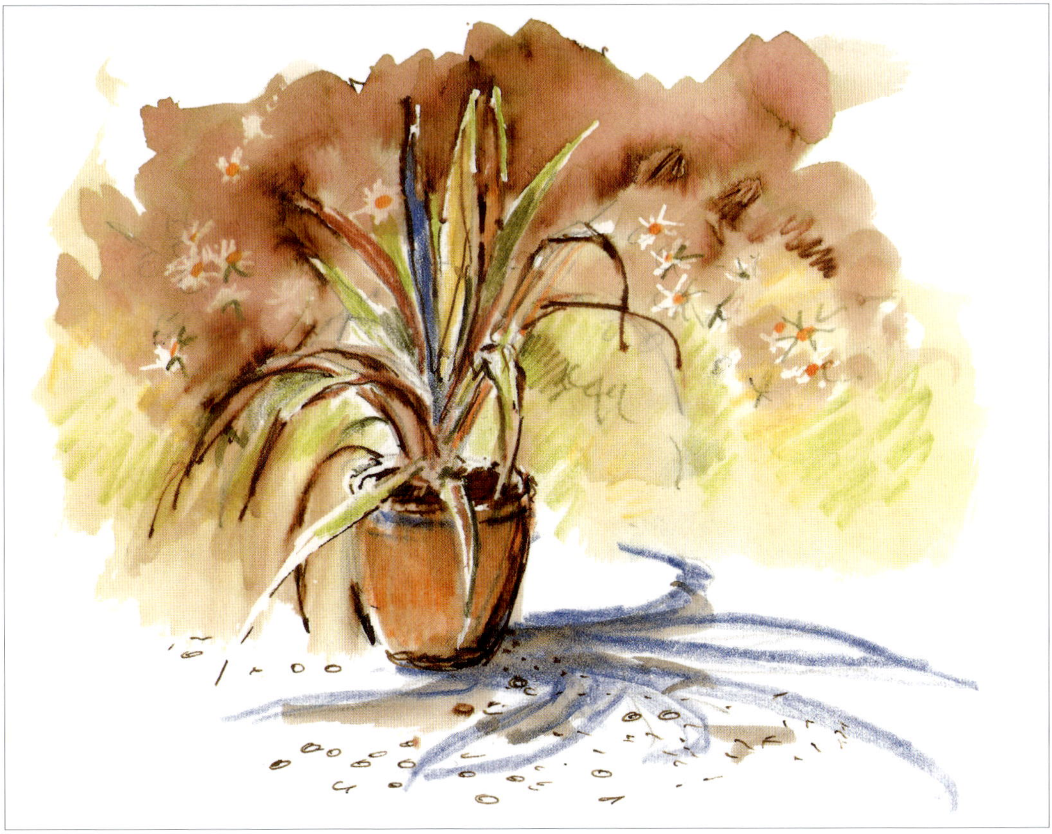

Quick sketches of still lifes: Patio table

Still lifes can sometimes benefit from a helping hand. If you find a potentially interesting subject, take time to think about ways you might improve on it. You could perhaps rearrange the different elements so that they make a more balanced, or a more dynamic, composition. Look at the spaces between the objects, as well as at the objects themselves, and experiment with different combinations, adding or removing items until you are happy with the way things look. Also think about the relative scale of the objects: although you can create some dramatic images by extreme contrasts, it is usually better if the items in a still life are on a similar scale.

When sketching glassware, remember that it takes on the colour or tone of objects around it. Look at the background and at nearby objects before you sketch the glass itself. Against a pale background, the edge may not be entirely visible. For example, look at the glass on the left in the sketch below.

5-minute sketch: water-soluble sketching pencil

Once she was sure she had drawn the ellipses of the glasses correctly, the artist blocked in tone for the red wine, paying careful attention to the highlights reflecting off the glasses in order to convey their smooth shininess. The shadows on the metal table were created by brushing clean water over the water-soluble pencil marks, providing an effective contrast with the linear marks used for the hard glass.

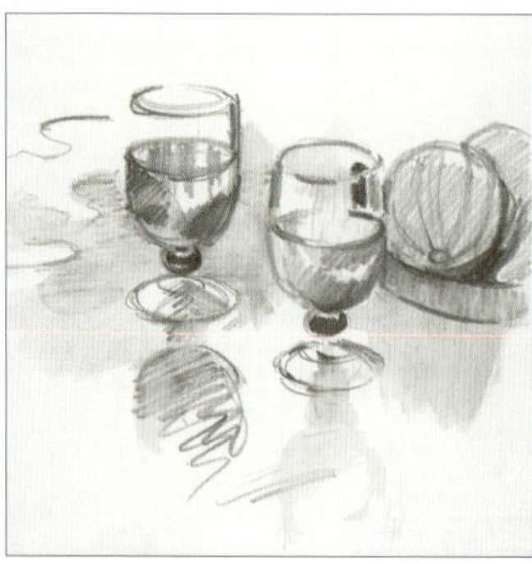

The scene

The artist was attracted by the lovely dappled light on the table and the colourful gourds and grapes, but felt that something was missing. She decided to add the two glasses of wine to provide some extra colour and to introduce a vertical element into the composition. They also give the still life more of a story, linking the wine with the grapes from which it was made.

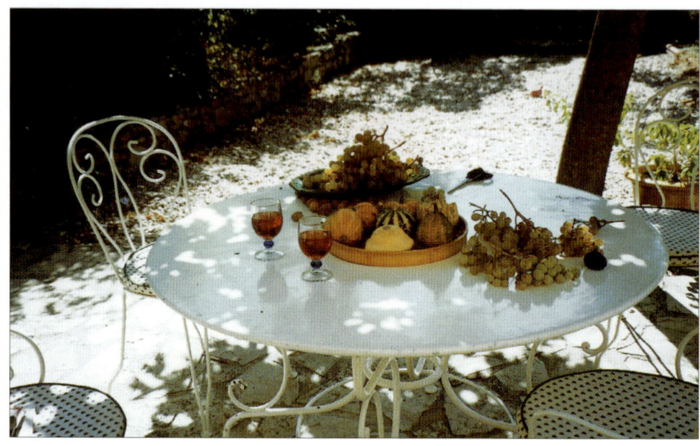

15-minute sketch: chalk and charcoal pencil

In a scene full of contrasts such as this, where there are very bright highlights and dense shadows, it often helps to use a toned ground so that you can start from a mid-tone. Here, the artist worked on dark-blue pastel paper to create a simple but effective tonal study. White chalk was used for the wrought-iron chair and table, with the side of the chalk being used for the tabletop and the highlights scribbled in with the tip of the chalk. The darkest elements of the still life – the bottle, glasses and fruit – were sketched in charcoal pencil.

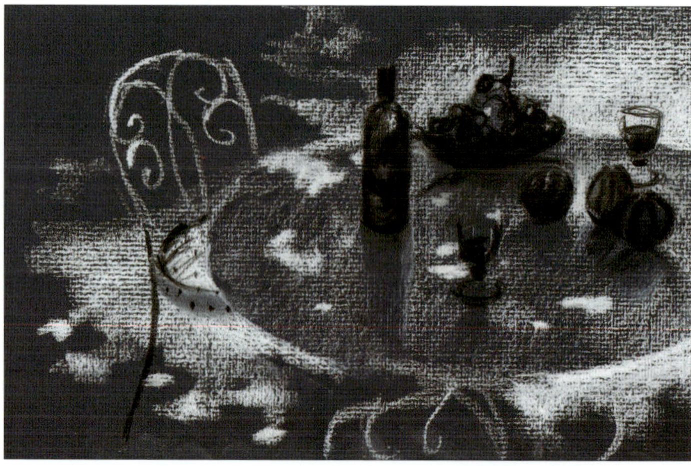

15-minute sketch: ballpoint pen
For this sketch, the artist removed some of the grapes to give a less cluttered arrangement and positioned the glasses on opposite sides of the table to create a more balanced composition. Although you cannot vary the width of the lines you make with a ballpoint pen, you can create a surprisingly wide range of marks and tones by hatching and cross-hatching. Note how the tones range from the very dark fig on the right to the very bright tone of the table in areas where no shadows are cast. Note, too, how shading the background allows the lines of the white wrought-iron chair on the left to stand out.

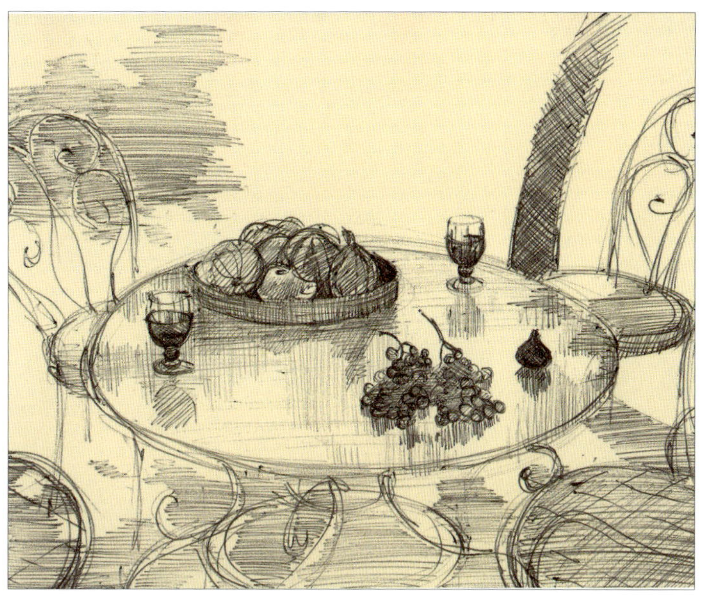

30-minute sketch: oil pastel
To create the reflective surface of the wrought-iron table, the artist applied colour with oil pastels and softened the marks with a rag dipped in turpentine.

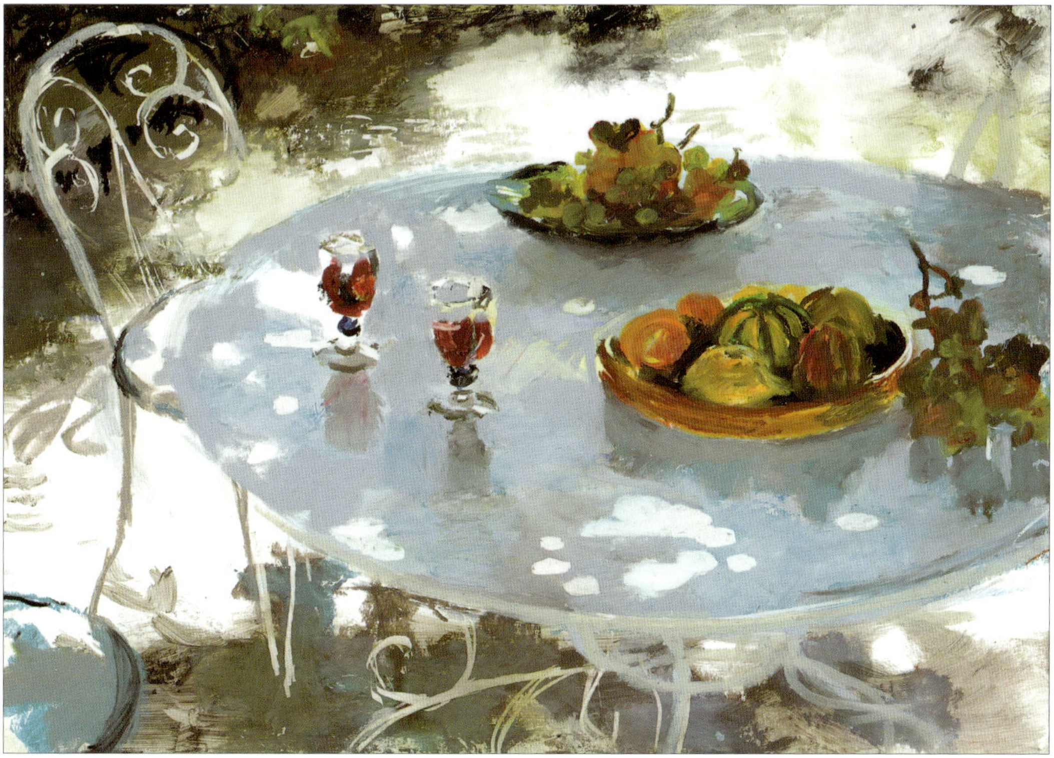

Quick sketches of still lifes: Old tools

Still lifes don't have to be 'pretty'. Functional items, such as old tools, kitchen utensils or garden implements, can make a graphic composition. The more time you spend working out the arrangement, the better. Think about the relative scale of the objects: something like a tiny nut or bolt will simply have no impact if it's placed next to a large object such as a mechanical vice or other large industrial tool. Think about the background, too: it's generally best to go for something fairly neutral, which doesn't detract from the subject. A plain, painted wall or a scratched wooden workbench, grimed through years of use, will both make good backgrounds for this kind of still life.

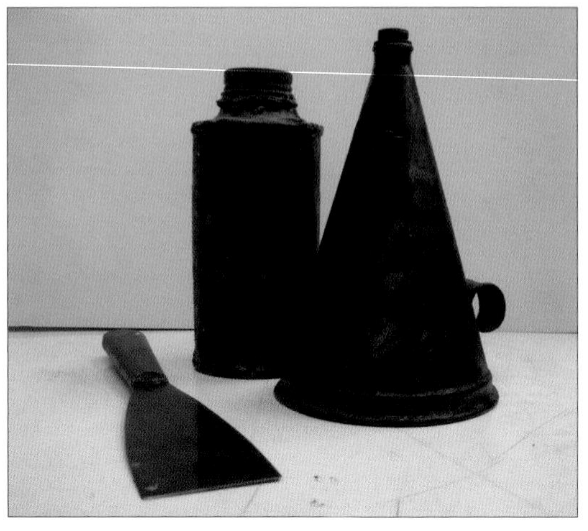

The set-up

Here, the artist selected a few battered items from his workshop and set them up against a plain white background to allow the shapes to stand out clearly. He chose three items of similar size, as odd numbers of items tend to work compositionally. The composition is well balanced, with both the scraper and funnel placed 'on the third'.

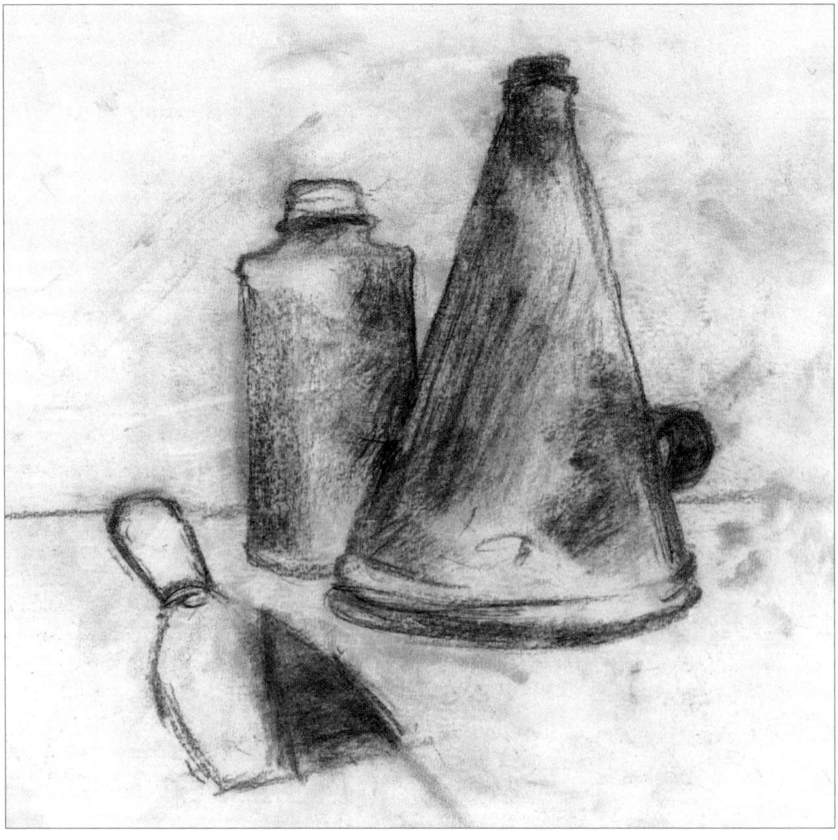

5-minute sketch: charcoal

Here, the artist began by outlining the shapes of the objects before blocking in the darkest areas, such as the reflection of the old bottle in the metal scraper, with the side of the charcoal stick. He then smudged the marks on the scraper and funnel with his finger to soften them and create the effect of a smooth, metallic surface. Note how the charcoal is applied roughly and unevenly, helping to convey the texture of the rather battered funnel and bottle.

15-minute sketch: ballpoint pen
You can't cover large areas quickly with a ballpoint pen, so any subject that requires a lot of shading, as here, is likely to take longer. Here, the shaded areas were hatched, with the lines being drawn closer together or even cross-hatched for the darkest sections. As always with a subject such as this, it is essential that you observe the highlights accurately in order to convey the form; it's easy to get so engrossed in the rather mechanical and repetitive business of shading that you lose sight of the drawing as a whole.

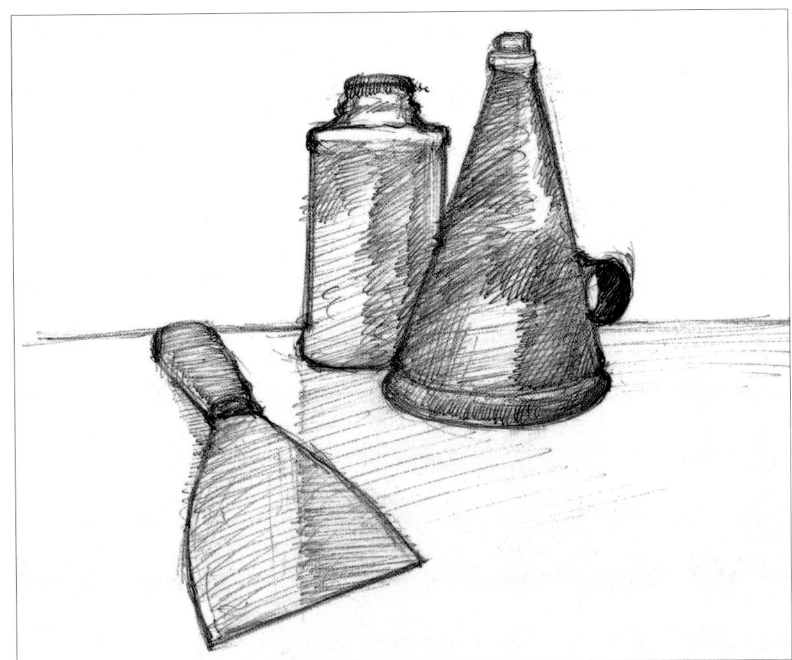

30-minute sketch: pencil
As in the ballpoint pen sketch, above, the artist made use of hatching to shade the darkest areas – but the beauty of using a soft pencil is that you can combine linear work (to outline the shapes and get crisp edges) with softly blended areas that convey the smooth metallic surfaces. The result is a less mechanical-looking sketch than the ballpoint pen version shown above. And, with more time at your disposal, you can concentrate on subtle changes in tone that convey the somewhat pitted surface of the funnel and bottle.

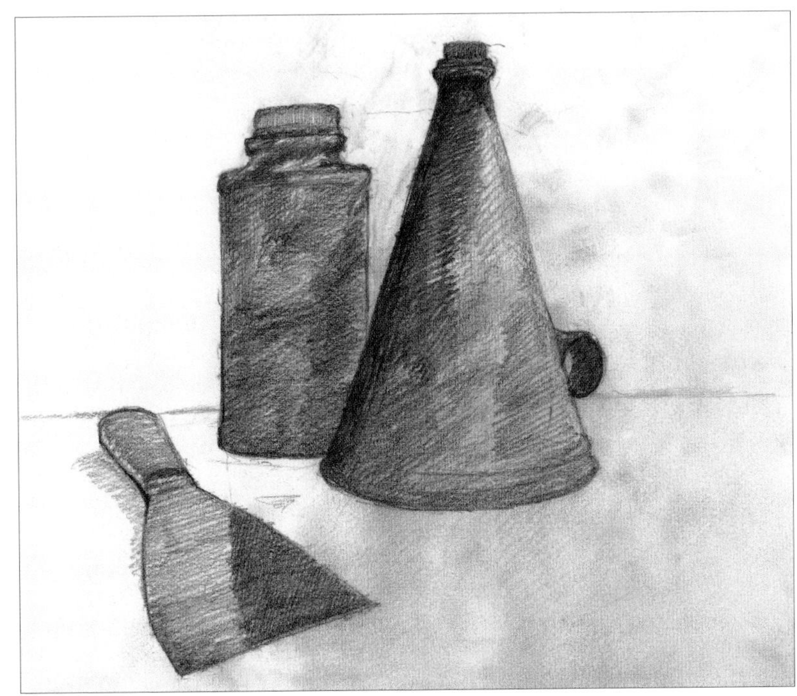

Metal detail

In this project, coloured pencils are used to draw the distinctive Rolls-Royce 'Spirit of Ecstasy' motif, creating a smooth, metallic-looking sheen. As always with this kind of detailed coloured-pencil work, you need to put down a number of very light layers of pigment. If you apply too heavy a layer, the wax in the pigment clogs up the tooth of the paper so subsequent layers of colour will not go on as smoothly or as evenly.

Try to maintain an even pressure, using the side of the pencil so that the coverage is perfectly smooth and there are no obvious pencil marks. You can get away with a few imperfections when you are drawing a more uneven surface, but not when you are trying to convey perfectly smooth metal.

It is also very important to assess the tones carefully. The figurine is smooth and rounded, and it's sometimes hard to work out exactly where changes in tone occur – but these changes in tone are the only real clue you have to the form of the object. Look for a darkening of tone as the figure curves away from the light. It happens so gradually that it may seem barely perceptible when you first look at a subject like this, but at some point a darkening does occur and you need to render it in your pencil work.

The surface is also highly reflective. There are many different facets in the figurine, so you don't see complete reflections in the same way that you would in a flat plate-glass window, for example. Nonetheless, the green of the foliage and the red of the car can be seen in the silver of the figurine. Details like this, tiny though they may be, add verisimilitude to your work.

Materials

- *Smooth, heavy drawing paper*
- *HB pencil*
- *Craft (utility) knife and cutting mat*
- *Masking film (frisket paper)*
- *Kitchen paper or clean rag*
- *Coloured pencils: bottle green, olive green, mineral green, scarlet lake, gunmetal grey, blue-grey, burnt umber, indigo, geranium lake, deep vermilion*

The subject

The viewpoint has been chosen so that the head and wings of the 'Spirit of Ecstasy' figure stand out against the dark background foliage and the distinctive Rolls-Royce logo is clearly evident.

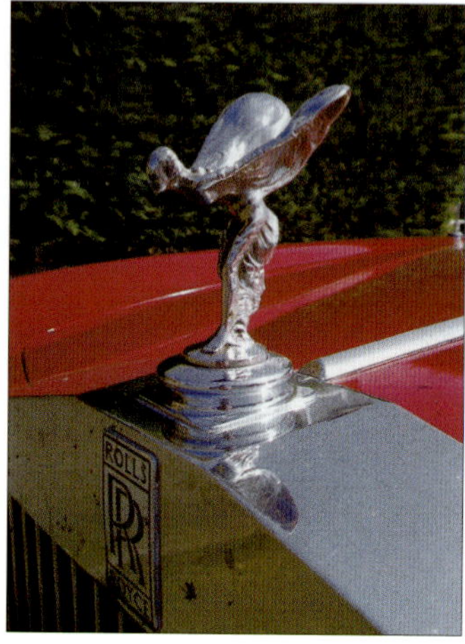

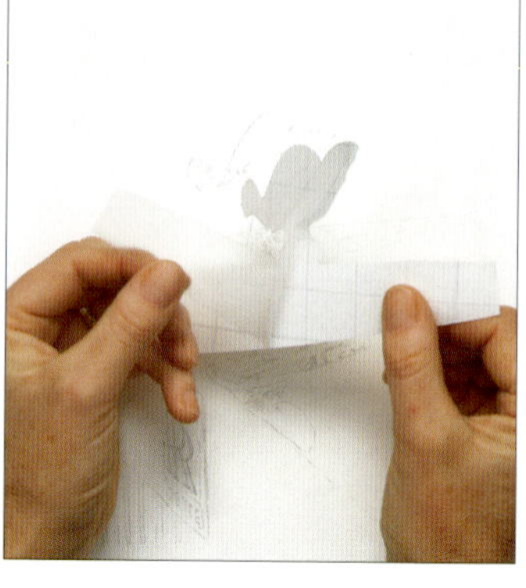

1 Using an HB pencil, lightly sketch the car indicating the main area of mid-tone within it. Using a craft knife on a cutting mat, cut a mask out of masking film to place over the metal figurine and the car bonnet (hood). Peel off the backing paper and stick it in place, smoothing out any wrinkles by rubbing over it with a piece of kitchen paper or a clean rag.

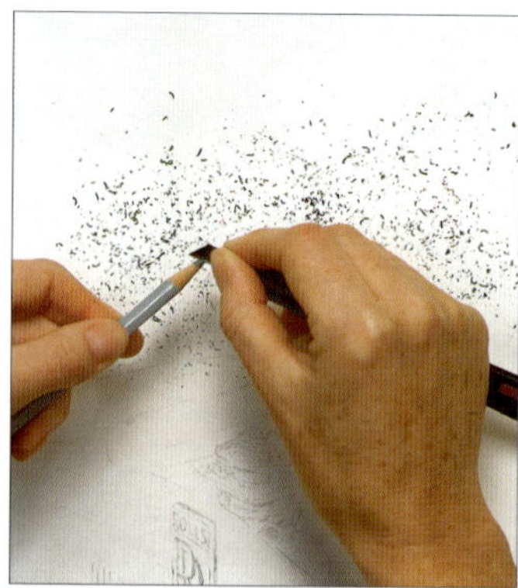

2 Using a craft knife, shave tiny slivers of pigment off a bottle-green pencil over the foliage background. Repeat with olive and mineral greens so that you get a number of shades of green in the foliage. Finally, add a few flecks of scarlet lake; a complementary colour to the green, this gives more variety to the foliage and provides a subtle visual link with the colour of the car bonnet.

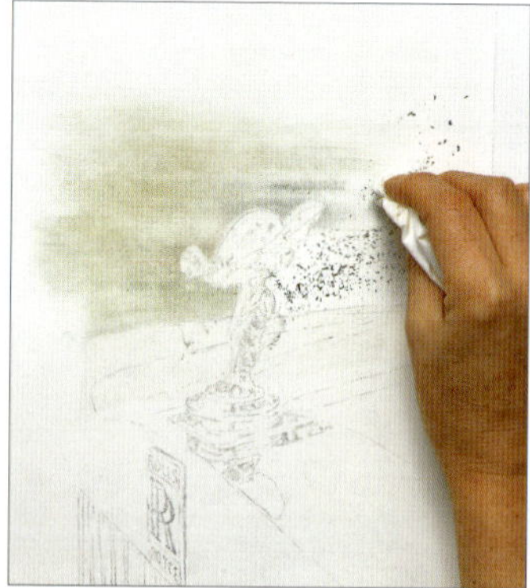

3 Take a piece of kitchen paper, scrunch it up, and gently wipe it over the pencil shavings to blend them on the paper. This is an effective way of covering a large area quickly.

Tip: Make horizontal strokes. This creates a streaked effect, which gives the impression of movement.

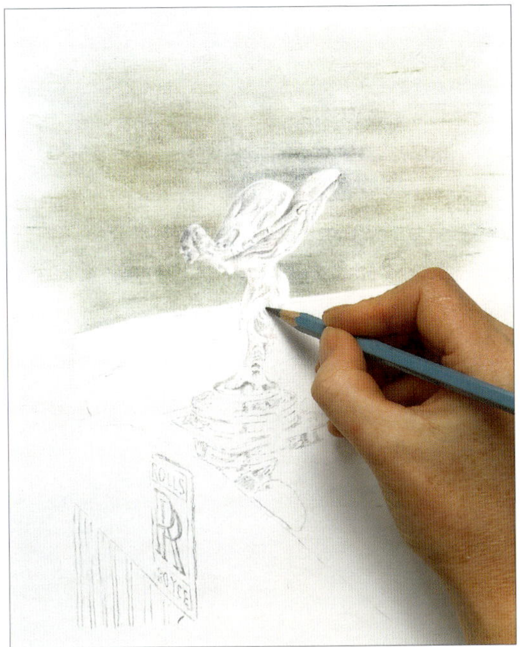

4 Remove the mask. (You may need to use the tip of a craft knife to lift up the edge.) Alternating between a gunmetal grey and a blue-grey pencil and using very light strokes, put in the darkest parts of the metal figure. You may find it easier to assess the tones if you half-close your eyes.

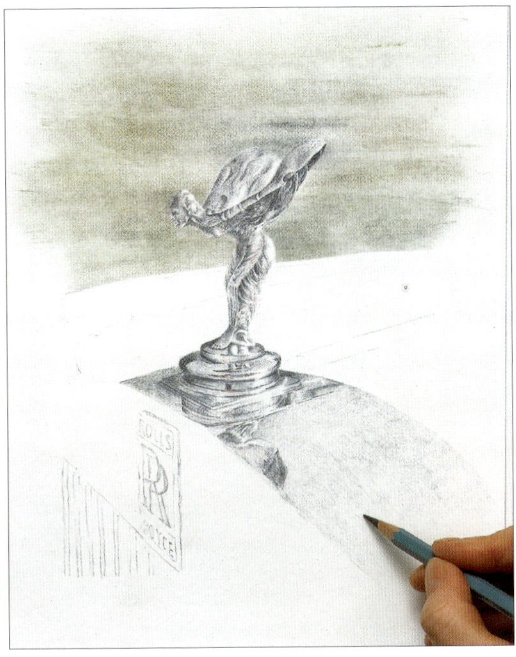

5 Continue the process on the base of the figurine and the top of the radiator grille, still using very light strokes. Note that some of the foliage is reflected in the metal towards the back of the base; put this in using whichever greens you feel are appropriate.

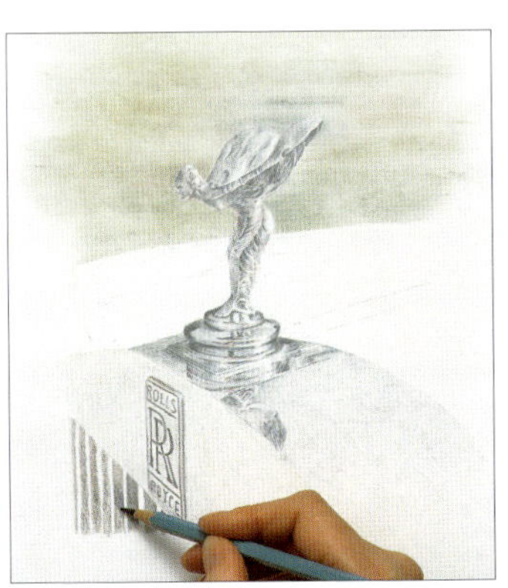

6 Go over the lettering in gunmetal grey. Block in the most deeply shaded parts of the radiator grille in burnt umber, then overlay indigo in the same area. The optical mix creates a richer, more varied colour than you could achieve using only black.

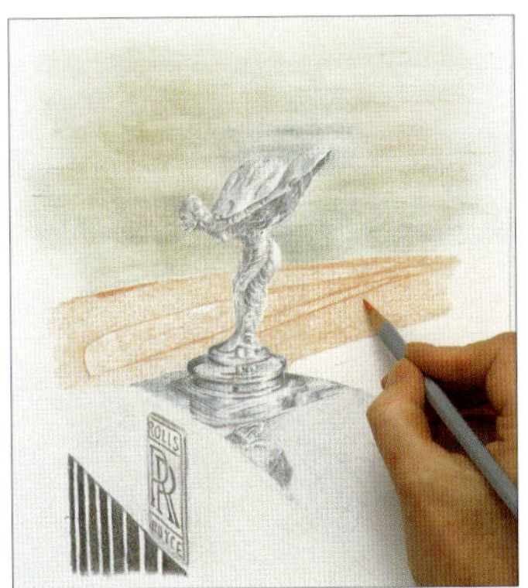

7 Using a scarlet lake pencil and horizontal strokes, apply the first thin layer of colour to the car bonnet, leaving the very brightest highlights untouched. Where there is a change of plane, define it with a slightly heavier pencil line.

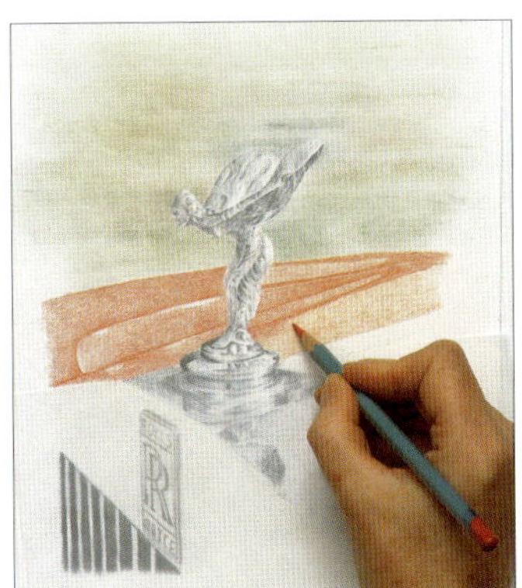

8 Go over the scarlet with geranium lake. With the application of this second layer, the colour is beginning to look closer to the way it should look, as the two reds mix optically on the paper. The coverage is also more dense and is beginning to take on a metallic sheen.

▶

Assessment time

The red section of the car needs to be more intensely coloured. Go over it again with a deep vermilion pencil. We can see how smooth the metallic front and top of the car is, but it does not yet look shiny enough. We are beginning to see the different planes of the image, but more differentiation is needed between them. Building up the layers of a coloured-pencil drawing is a slow, meticulous process that needs to be done.

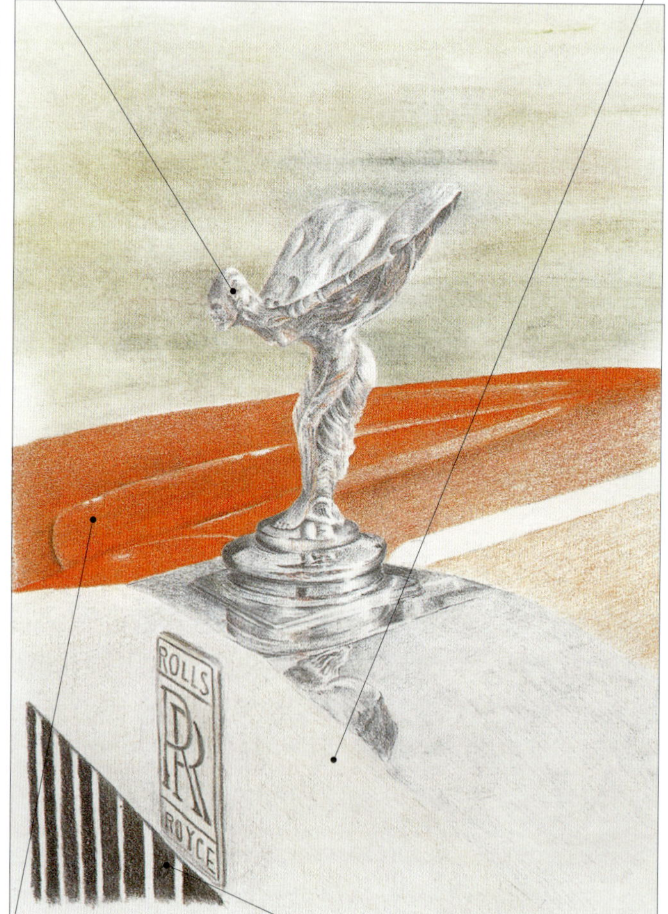

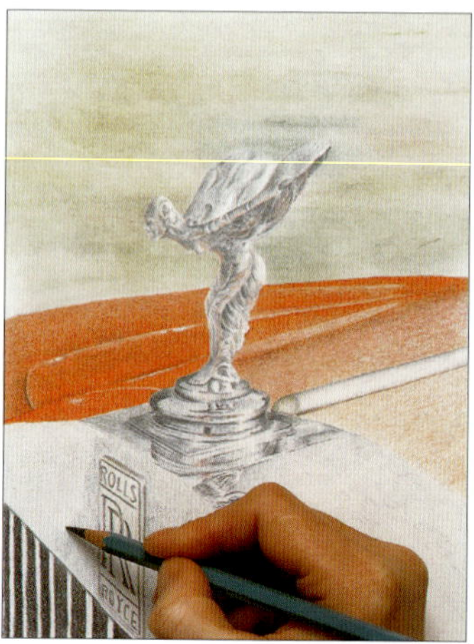

9 Apply a light layer of gunmetal grey to the thin metal strip that runs along the length of the bonnet, behind the figurine. This strip catches the light, so only a little colour is needed. Overlay very pale olive green on the rounded end, which is slightly in shadow. Darken the tone on the front of the radiator panel with a blue-grey pencil, using the side of the pencil rather than the tip.

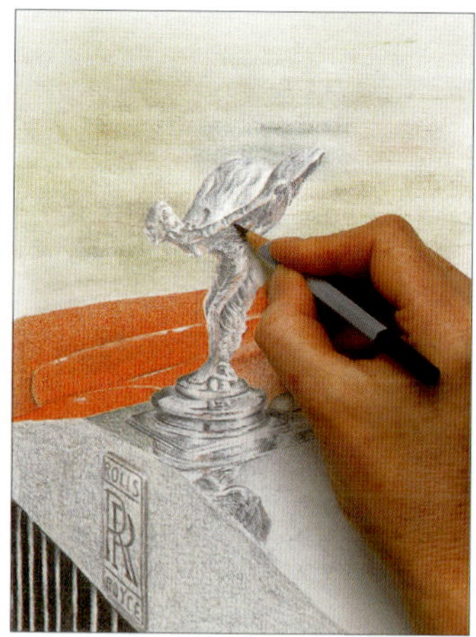

10 Re-assess the tonal values of the picture as a whole, reinforcing the darks wherever necessary. Also continue building up the red of the bonnet, alternating layers of scarlet lake and geranium lake, until you reach the right density of colour.

The finished drawing
In this drawing the metalwork looks so smooth that you almost feel you could reach out and touch it! The artist has paid very careful attention to the highlights and shadows, as these are what convey the form of the object and make it look three-dimensional. She has built up the colour by applying several thin layers, allowing them to mix optically on the support to create a rich finish. You could put more detail into the background if you wish, but this simple approach allows the subject to stand out.

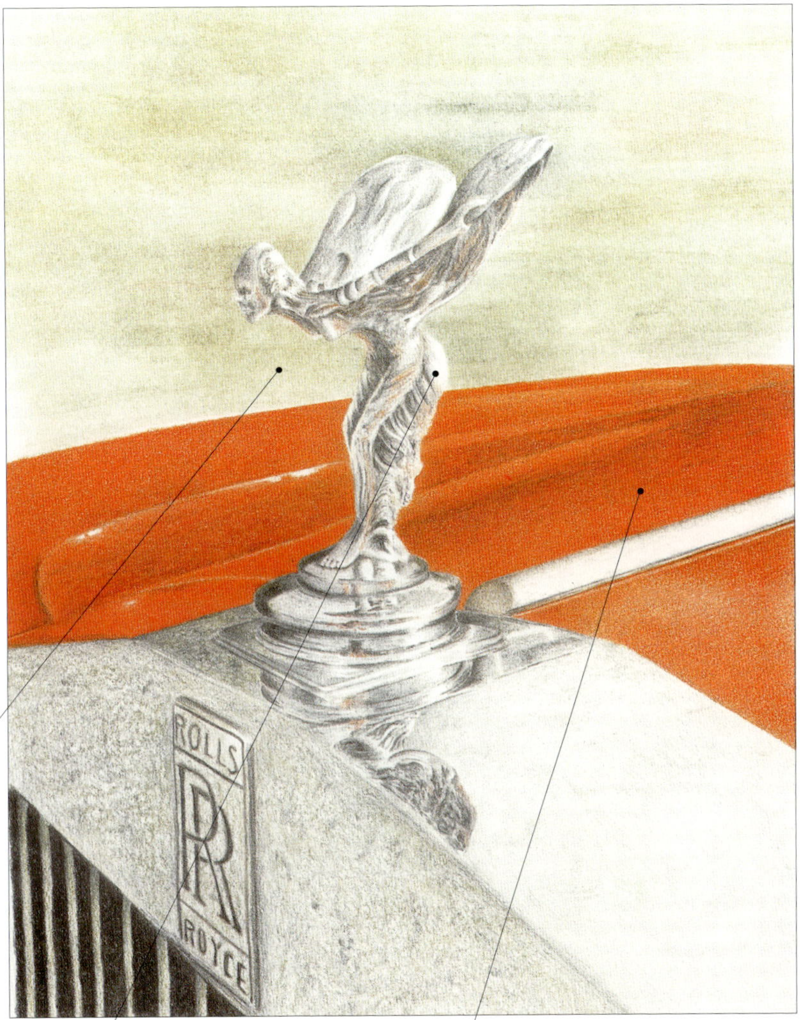

The plain background allows the subject to stand out.

Bright highlights on the figure tell us which direction the light is coming from.

Variations in the density of the red convey the curve of the bonnet (hood).

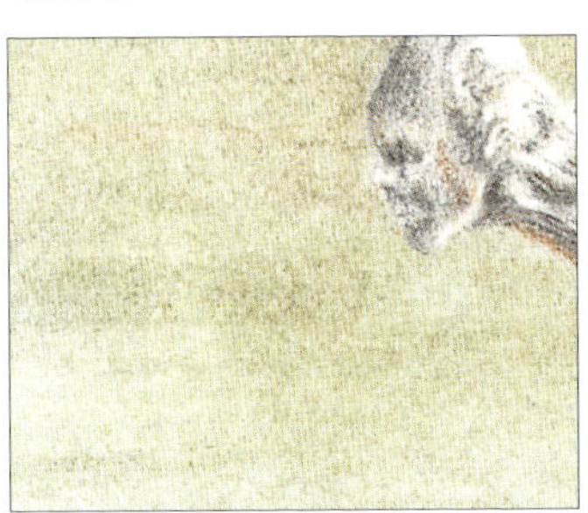

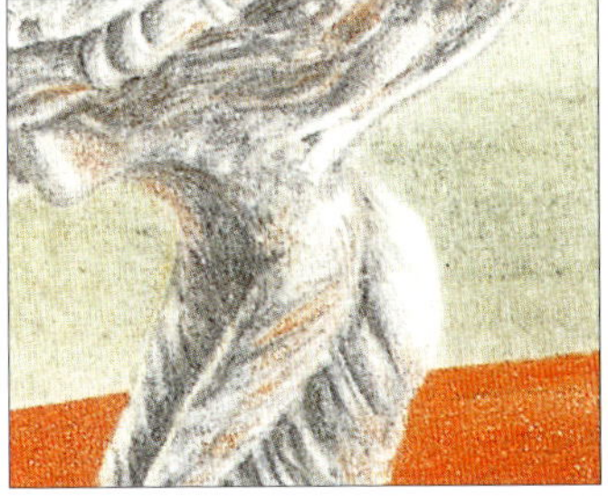

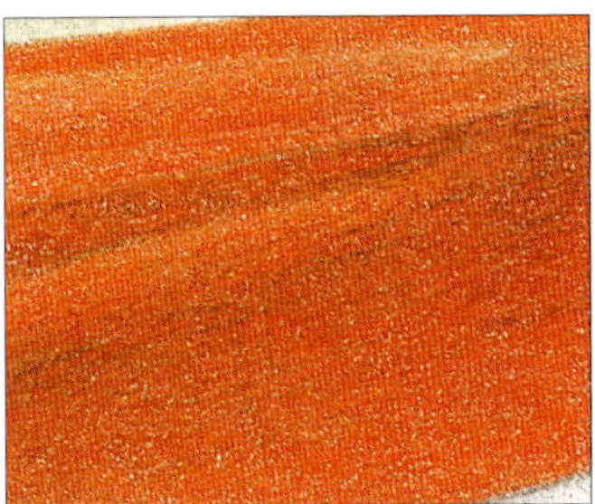

Still life with garlic and shallots

Try to get into the habit of drawing every day – even if it's only for ten minutes during your lunch break. One of the most wonderful things about drawing is that you can create images anywhere, from anything that you have to hand. Paper clips and a pencil sharpener from your desk at work, a piece of fruit that you're going to eat for your lunch, a coffee cup or a few children's toys – anything will do, so long as you spend time observing and drawing.

The project shown here is a good example of this approach. The artist constructed a simple still life using nothing more than a wooden chopping board, a bulb of garlic and a couple of shallots from the kitchen. For drawing equipment, he deliberately restricted himself to just two graphite pencils and a torchon. It's well worth setting yourself an exercise like this one, as limiting the number of drawing tools that you use allows you to experiment and become familiar with the range of marks that each one can create. Here, for example, the torchon is used not only to blend graphite marks but also to 'draw' soft marks that add an interesting texture to the image.

No doubt you've heard it before, but we make no excuse for repeating it here: odd numbers of objects (three, five, seven) invariably make more satisfying still-life compositions than even numbers. When you're setting up a still life, look at how the objects relate to one another. Look at the overall shape that the assembled objects make, as well as at the shape of each item within the group. Remember that the spaces between them are, compositionally, as important as the objects themselves, as are any shadows. Try different viewpoints: the spatial relationships will change if you look down on (or up at) your subject. Above all, try out different arrangements until you find one that seems to work.

Materials

- *Smooth drawing paper*
- *Graphite pencils: HB and H*
- *Torchon*
- *Kneaded eraser*

The set-up

Shadows almost always make a scene more interesting, as they allow you to exploit the differences between the light and the shaded areas of your subject. Here, the artist set up a table lamp to one side of his still life, so that the objects cast strong shadows to the left of the image.

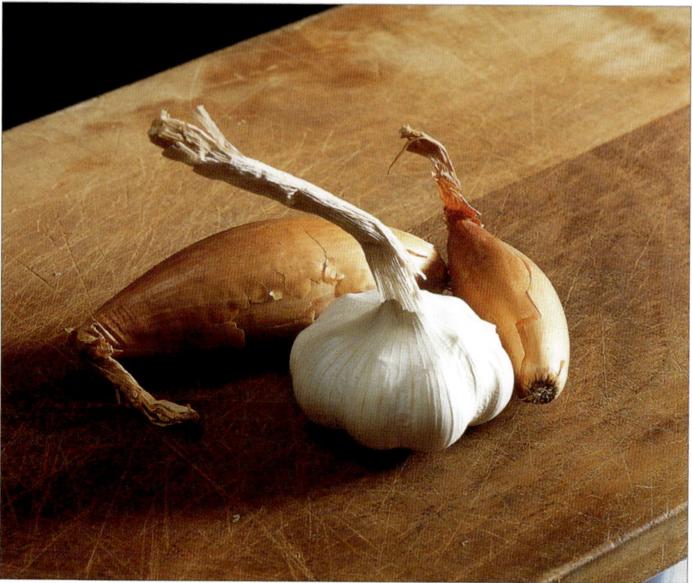

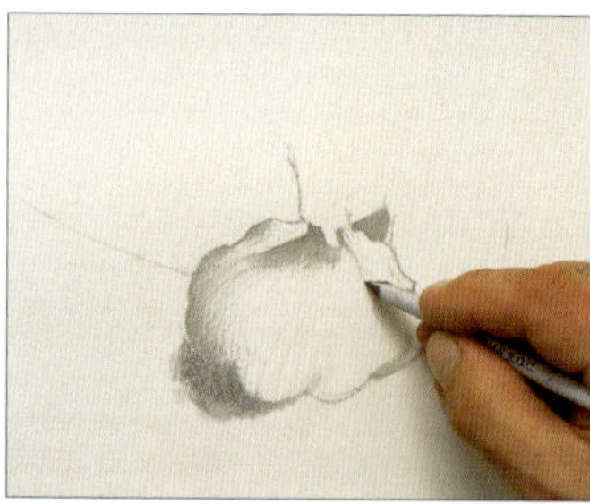

1 Lightly sketch your subject. Start from the base of the garlic stalk and work outwards: this will enable you to establish the relative positions and sizes much more easily than an outline drawing would. Lightly shade the darkest areas of the garlic bulb and indicate the cast shadow to the left. Use a torchon to blend the graphite and create smooth areas of tone. Also use the torchon to 'draw' the individual cloves of garlic.

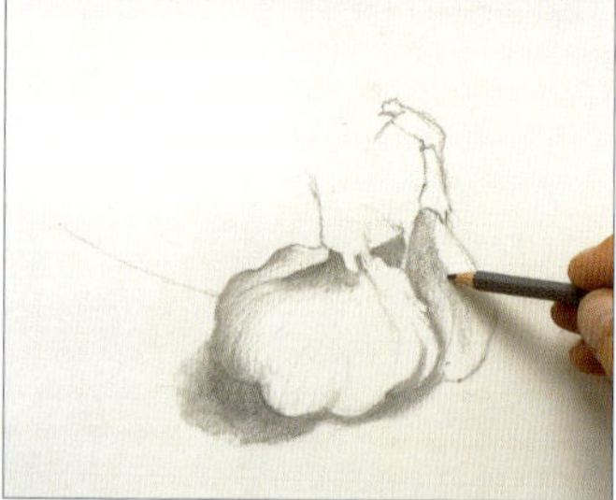

2 Using an H pencil, outline the shallot on the right and its papery stem. Start to shade underneath the garlic bulb and put in the deep area of shadow that lies between the garlic and the shallot. Using the side of the pencil, begin shading the darkest side of the shallot. Try to make sure your pencil strokes run in the same direction as the striations in the skin of the shallot.

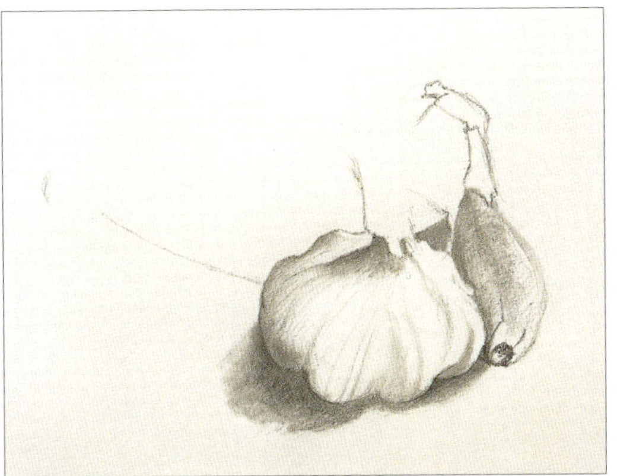

3 Working downwards (and making sure you keep within the outline), smooth out the graphite on the shaded area of the shallot with a torchon.

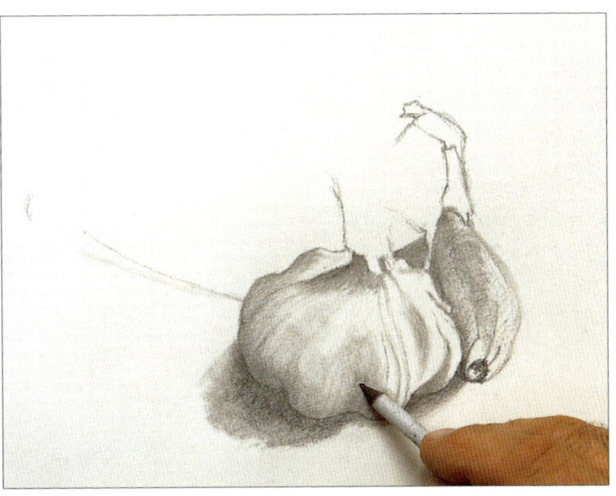

4 Using an H pencil, draw the veining on the papery outer covering of the garlic. Put more shading on the dark areas of the garlic and smooth out the marks with a torchon.

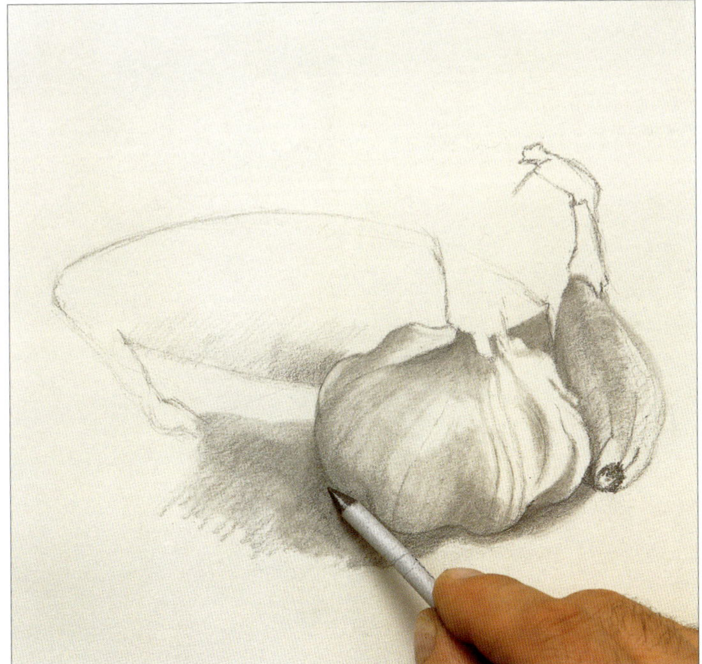

5 Outline the stalk and the lower part of the shallot on the left, where it cuts across behind the garlic, and shade in the underside of the shallot. Lightly hatch in more of the shadow cast by the garlic and blend with the torchon. (Shadows need to look considerably less substantial and solid than the objects that cast them.) Make sure, however, that you retain the crisp line around the edge of the garlic so that there is a clear distinction between it and the shadow; if necessary, reinforce the outline.

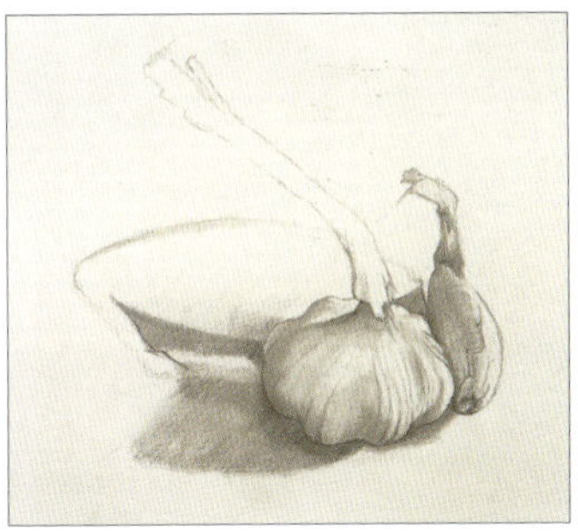

6 Reinforce the twisting line of the garlic stalk, using an irregular, slightly broken line which helps to convey the texture.

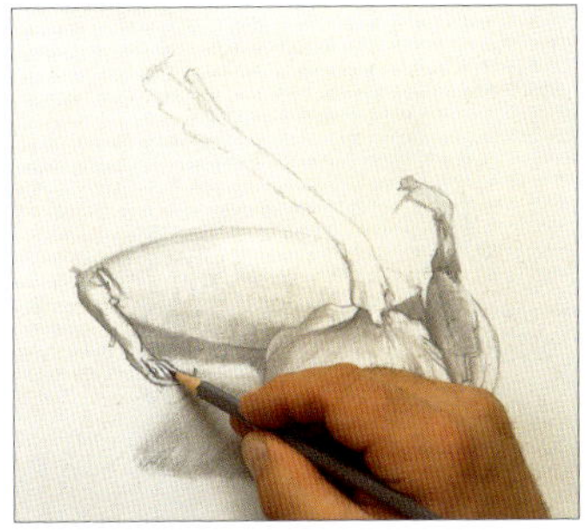

7 Using an HB pencil, put in the linear detailing around the top of the stalk of the shallot on the left. It almost looks like a small claw reaching forwards.

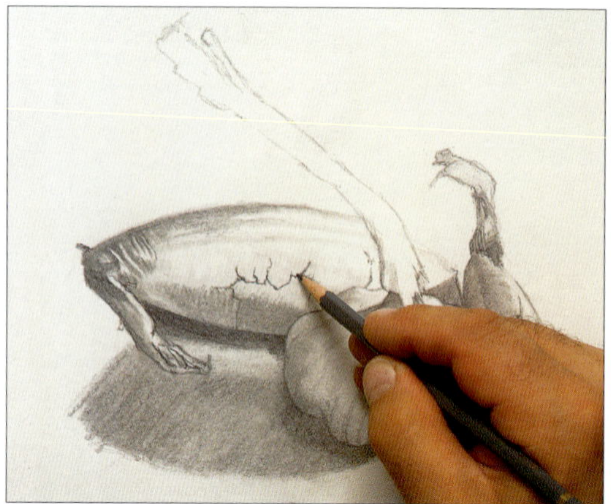

8 Shade the stalk of the shallot on the left and darken the shadow underneath. Use the torchon to 'draw' soft horizontal lines across the shallot, and then the H pencil to put in sharper, linear marks on the shallot's papery covering.

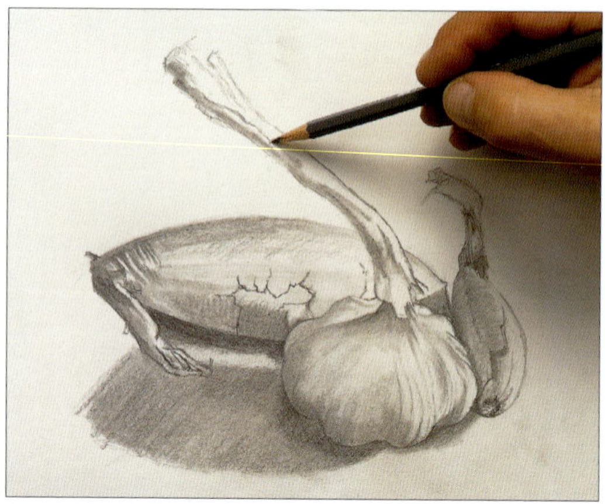

9 Shade the left-hand side of the garlic stalk, which is furthest away from the light. Note how the stalk twists and turns, and is irregular in width; convey this in the way that you shade it.

Assessment time

The drawing is progressing well, but the objects do not stand out clearly enough in relation to each other or to the shadows. More tonal contrast is needed, as is more contrast of texture.

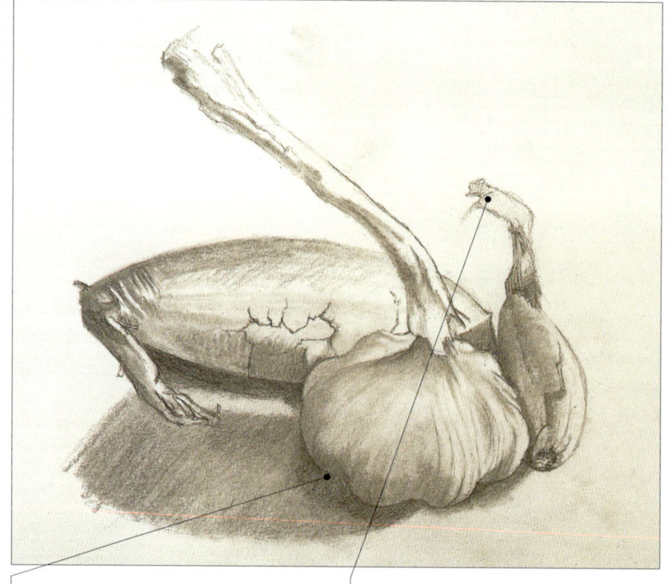

The shadow is almost as strong in tone as the object that casts it.

The stalks of both the shallot and the garlic are not strong enough.

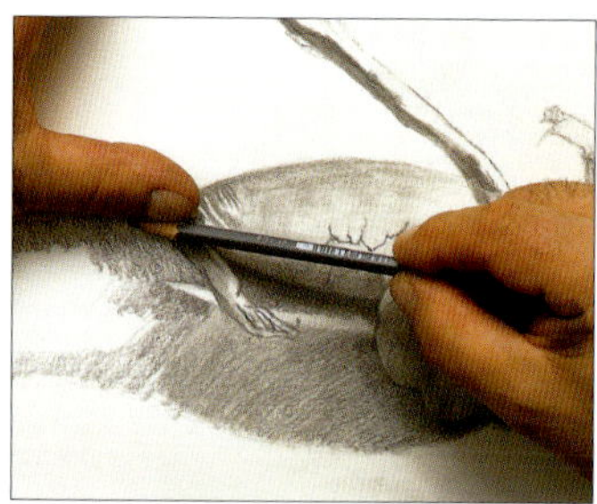

10 Extend and darken the shadows cast by both the garlic and the shallot on the left. Blend the marks to a soft shadow using a torchon.

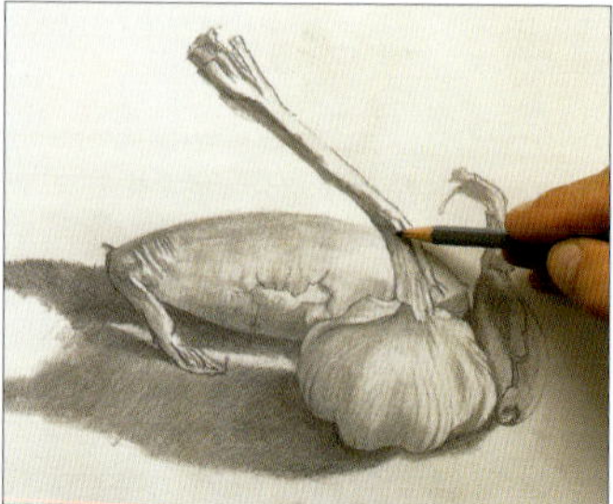

11 Darken the shaded areas of the shallot on the right and complete the linear detailing on the garlic. Clean off any smudges with a kneaded eraser.

The finished drawing

Objects in this still life are not particularly interesting in themselves, but they have been carefully arranged so that the stalks lead our eye around the picture in a circle. The soft shadows anchor the subjects on the surface. The artist used a range of pencil techniques, from crisp linear detailing on the stalks to soft shading using the side of the pencil, and smooth blending of the graphite using a torchon. He also used the torchon as a drawing tool in its own right, to put in the segments of the garlic that can be seen under the papery outer covering. The result is a simple but effective still life.

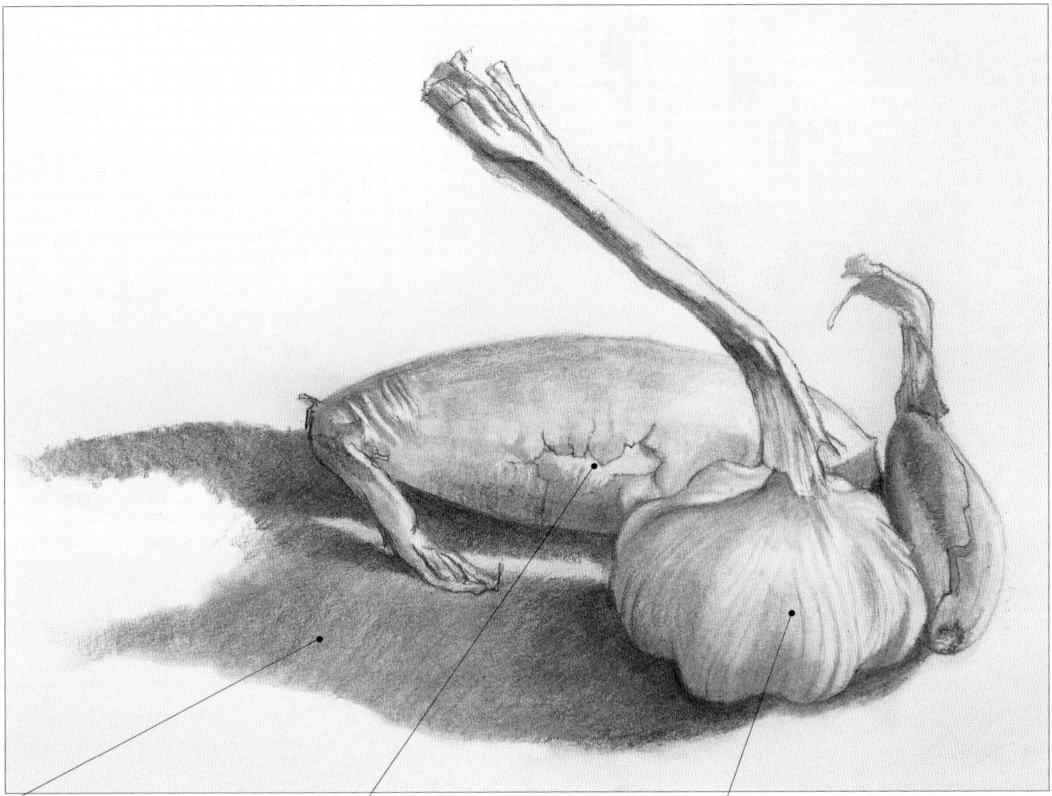

The shadow has been blended and softened so that it appears less substantial than the object that casts it.

Linear details, such as this split in the covering of the shallot, add a contrast in texture.

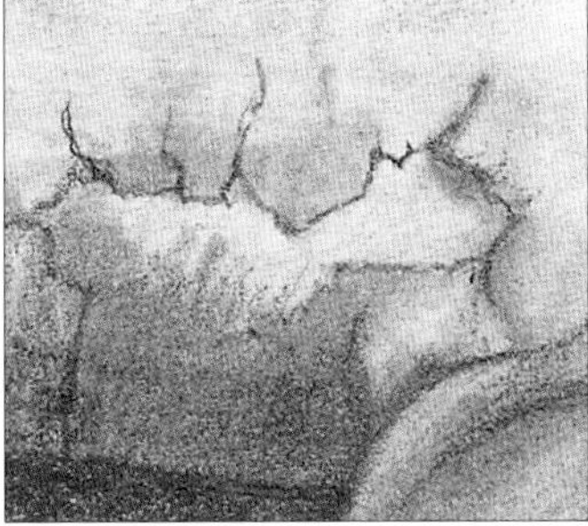

These subtle striations in the papery outer covering of the garlic are made by 'drawing' lines with the torchon.

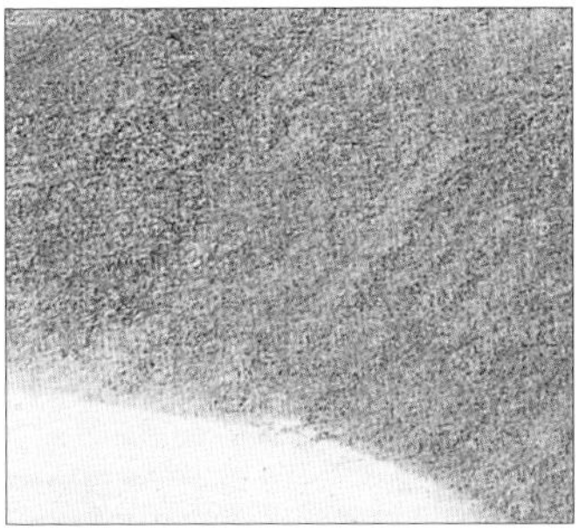

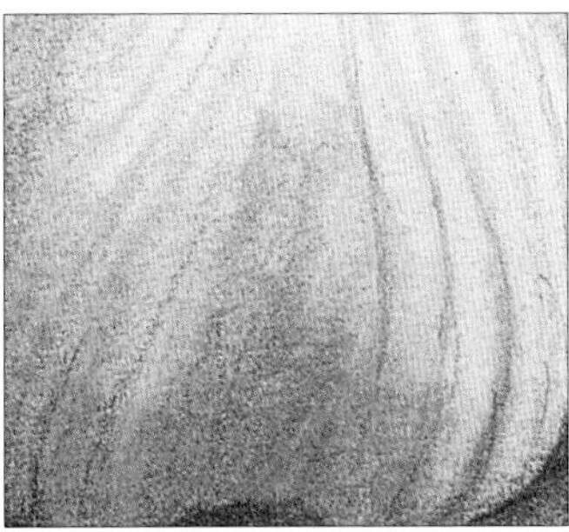

Still life with pears

Fruit is ideal for still-life drawings, with simple shapes and subtle textures and colours that are perfect for rendering in coloured pencil. Select fruit that is not over-ripe, as any blemishes will soon start to deteriorate and you will be in a race against time to complete the drawing before the fruit starts to shrivel. This particular project uses slightly under-ripe pears with smooth surfaces that have a few marks and blemishes to add texture, and a soft blush of warmth on the skin. To keep the arrangement simple, the artist placed the pears on a plain, dark-blue background which contrasts effectively with the pale-green fruit and adds depth to the shadows.

The key to the success of this drawing is to work slowly, carefully building up the tones and textures of the fruit with gentle pencil marks. The depth and range of colours found on the pear skins are achieved through several layers, starting with the lightest tone and adding light pencil strokes on top, with any spots or blemishes added at a later stage to enhance texture and emphasize the rounded shapes. When working with a group of objects, keep checking their relationships and use their cast shadows to create a convincing visual link.

Materials

- *Smooth drawing paper*
- *HB pencil*
- *Coloured pencils: pale yellow, bright green, warm yellow, olive green, dark brown, raw umber, burnt umber, pale brown, bronze, mid-brown, mid-blue, dark blue, rich dark blue, ultramarine blue*
- *Eraser*

The set-up

A rich blue fabric background complements the yellow-green of the pears. Try out different arrangements to find what works best. Here, the shadows cast by the foremost pear add interest to the composition. The foremost pear is also laid on its side so that we can see the dimpled base, adding variety to the composition.

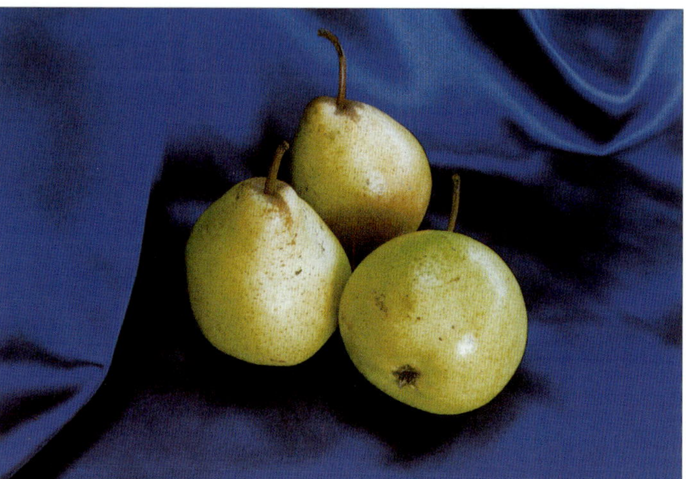

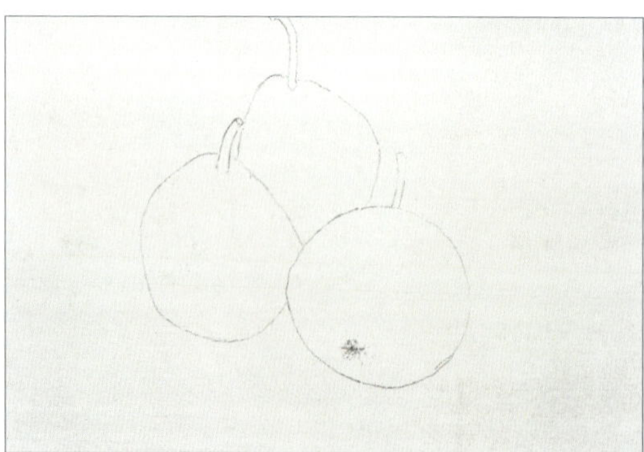

1 Using an HB pencil, lightly sketch the outlines of the pears, making sure you allow enough space on either side for the folds in the background fabric. Map out the positions of the stalks and the corresponding base on the pear at the bottom right of the composition. To make it easier, look at the angle of the stalk. This helps you to establish the central axis that runs all the way through the fruit.

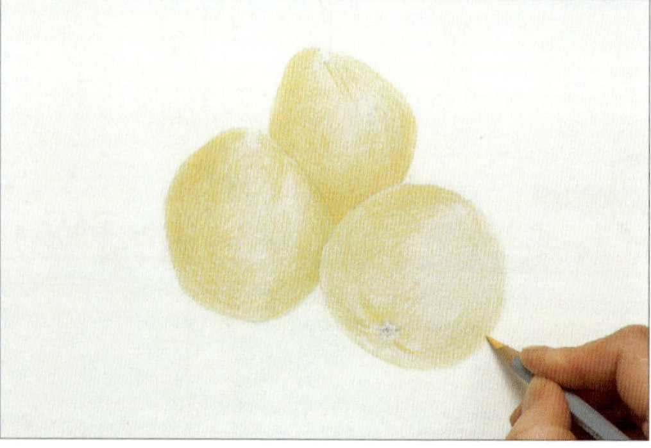

2 Very lightly apply a layer of pale yellow over all the pears, including the highlight areas. Apply a bright green over the green areas of the pears, using gentle pressure and loose strokes. Reapply the pale yellow and then add a warmer yellow, such as Naples yellow, around the edges of the back pear where it is tinged with pink. Use the same colour where the cast shadow falls on the middle pear.

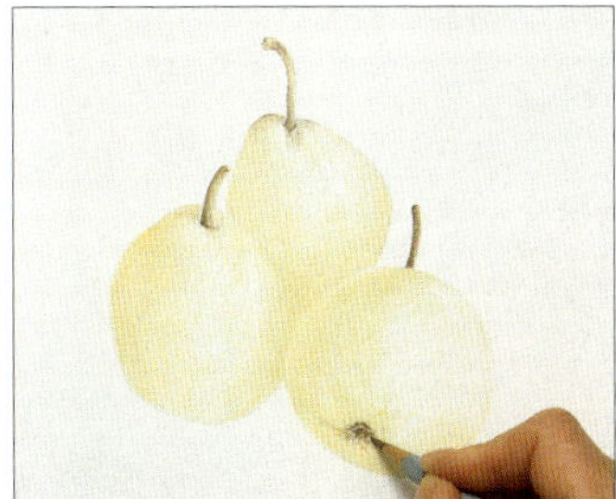

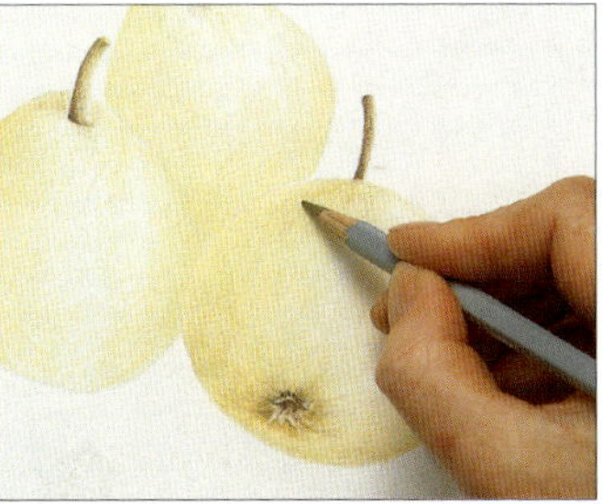

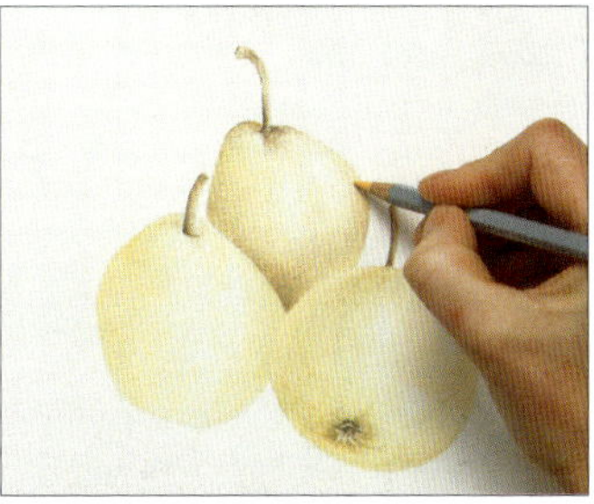

3 Start to build up tones to develop the form of the pears. Use a combination of pale yellow and bright green on the foreground pear to add the darker tones. Use loose strokes when applying the bright green so that the underlying yellow shows through. Combine pale yellow and an olive green to fill in the colour of the stalks, using darker browns, such as raw umber and Vandyke brown, on the shadow side. Use the same browns to sketch in the details of the dimple at the base of the foreground pear, using olive green for the darker areas of skin surrounding it, and a dark brown such as burnt umber for the darkest areas.

4 Continue gradually building up the colours and tones on the foreground pear. Use loose, light scribbles of olive green to develop a sense of texture as well as colour. To give an impression of the rounded form of the fruit, apply the strokes in the same direction as the curves.

Tip: Don't make the stalks too dark at this stage, as they will need to stand out against the background.

5 Next, build up the colours and texture on the background pear. Use pale brown to define the edge where the foreground pear overlaps it, then apply loose, even strokes of the same colour, following the form of the pear. Work around the highlights and add a light layer of bright green with a slightly darker brown on top. Define the outer edge in olive green to ensure that it will stand out against the background. Add a hint of a warm pink glow by combining bronze and mid-brown on the lower half of the pear, fading out to a soft edge on the shadow area. To bring all the colours together, apply a layer of pale yellow.

6 Finish the back pear by adding green along the edges where the shape curves. Use short marks to add texture, avoiding the highlight areas. Emphasize the shadow with light touches of dark brown. Start to build up the colour on the middle pear, with an olive green for the area of shadow cast by the foreground pear, following the form of the pear with more upright, vertical strokes. Add brown along the edges with yellow over the top to knock it back. With a dark brown, such as Vandyke brown, add the details at the base of the stalk, using tiny strokes to follow the contours of the recess to give the impression of a dip. Add any tiny blemishes or rough patches of skin using the same dark brown.

Tip: Use a sheet of tracing paper beneath your hand to protect the lower half of the drawing.

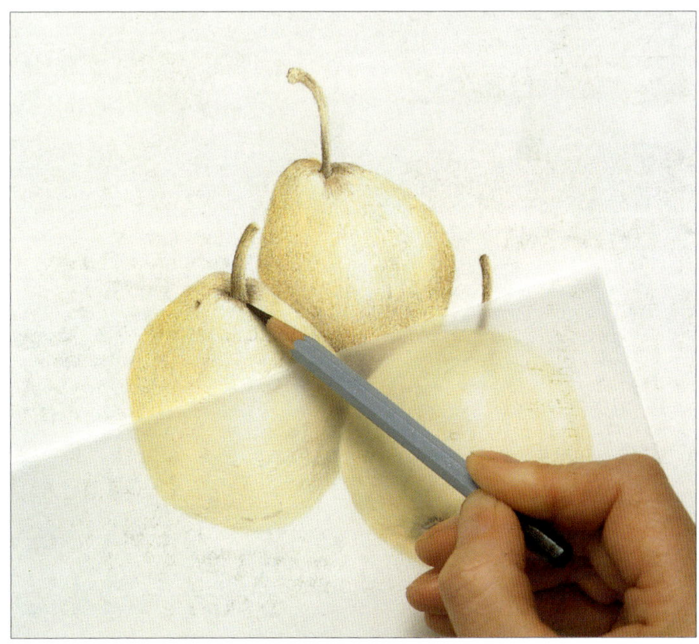

Assessment time

At this stage the pears appear to have form and texture, defined by the light highlights and the darker shadows. To complete the subtleties of the pears' skin colours, you need to build up more layers of pale yellow and green.

Fill in around the highlights to finalize their shape with a light yellow. Use mid- to dark browns to add any blemishes or areas of rough skin, keeping the pencil marks light.

Work over all the pears with a final layer of yellow and a little olive green on the darker tones. You can then start to add in the blue background; this will be a long, slow process, as you need to apply several layers, but it's worth taking your time over it in order to achieve the right density of colour.

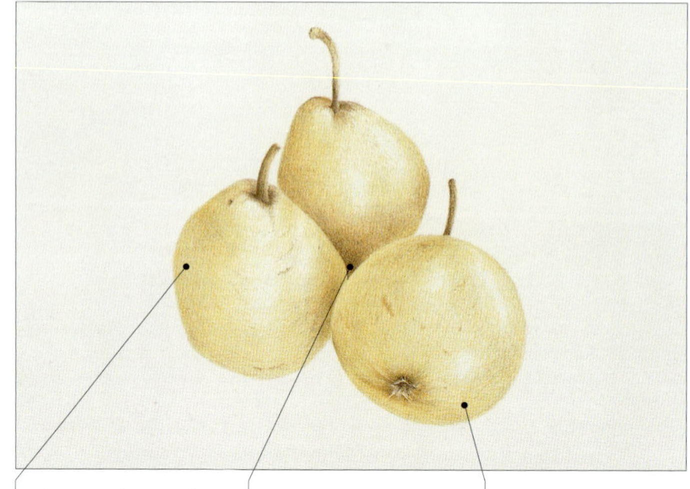

Using a pencil on its side gives broader strokes that bring out the tooth of the paper.

The intensity of the dark shadow area has been built up very gradually with light strokes.

A combination of pale yellow and bright green gives depth to the base of the pear.

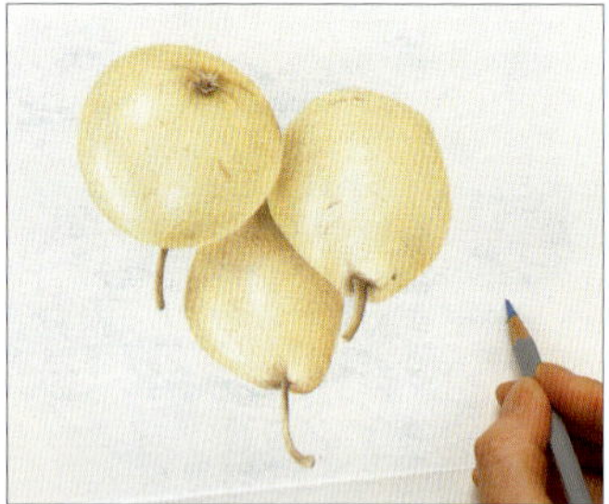

7 Start to add the blue background using a mid-blue, such as Prussian blue, applied with very light strokes using the tip of the pencil. Try to achieve an even layer of colour with no variations, working from the outside in to the edge of the pears for better control. Turn the drawing as you work, but keep the pencil strokes running in the same direction.

Tip: Use a soft eraser, or a piece of reusable putty adhesive, to soften or remove any hard edges along the folds.

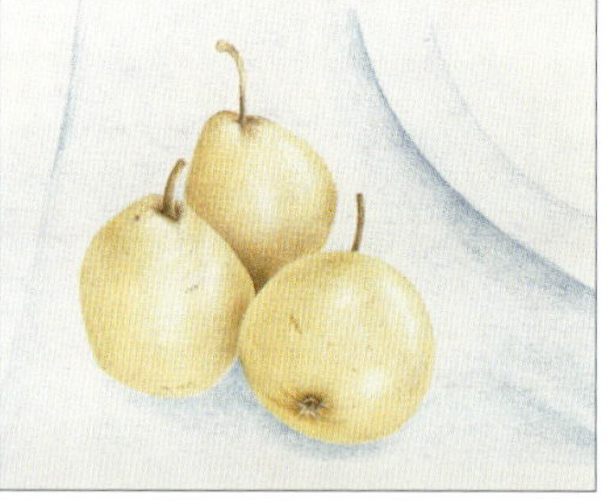

8 Using a slightly darker blue, continue to build up the colour, mapping out the folds of the material. Roughly sketch in the edge of the long vertical fold on the left, a soft diagonal fold in the lower right-hand corner, and swathes of fabric in the top right-hand corner. To emphasize the way the fabric is draped, build up the colour on the shadow side of the folds using strokes that follow the drape. Build up the shadows at the base of the pears with the same colour, to establish a visual link between the pears and the background fabric, and apply a crisp line around each pear with a very sharp pencil point.

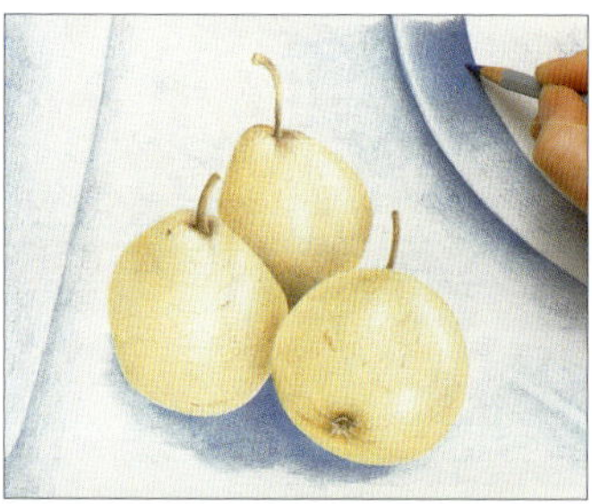

9 With a dark, rich blue, such as indigo, start to intensify the colour of the background, applying more pressure in the deepest shadows. To accentuate the folds, build up colour on the edge of the fold, turning the paper if necessary to follow the direction of the curve. Where the light hits the top of the fold leave a lighter edge, using a rich blue such as ultramarine with a mid-blue underneath. The lines of the folds should give a sense of the weight of the fabric and the effect of gravity. Use a very dark blue in the darkest shadow areas between the two foreground pears and the recessed fold on the left.

The finished drawing

With the background completed, an intensity is added to this subject which brings the pears to life. The pleasing composition is enhanced by the subtle effect of the contrasting colours of blue and green. To ensure that the pears aren't overshadowed by the rich blue of the fabric, the artist reassessed the whole drawing, adding more strength to the fruit to reinforce any light areas. The stalks and blemishes or shadows on the top of the pears were also redefined with a dark brown to give them a crisper edge, and the texture of the skin was further highlighted with some additional speckles.

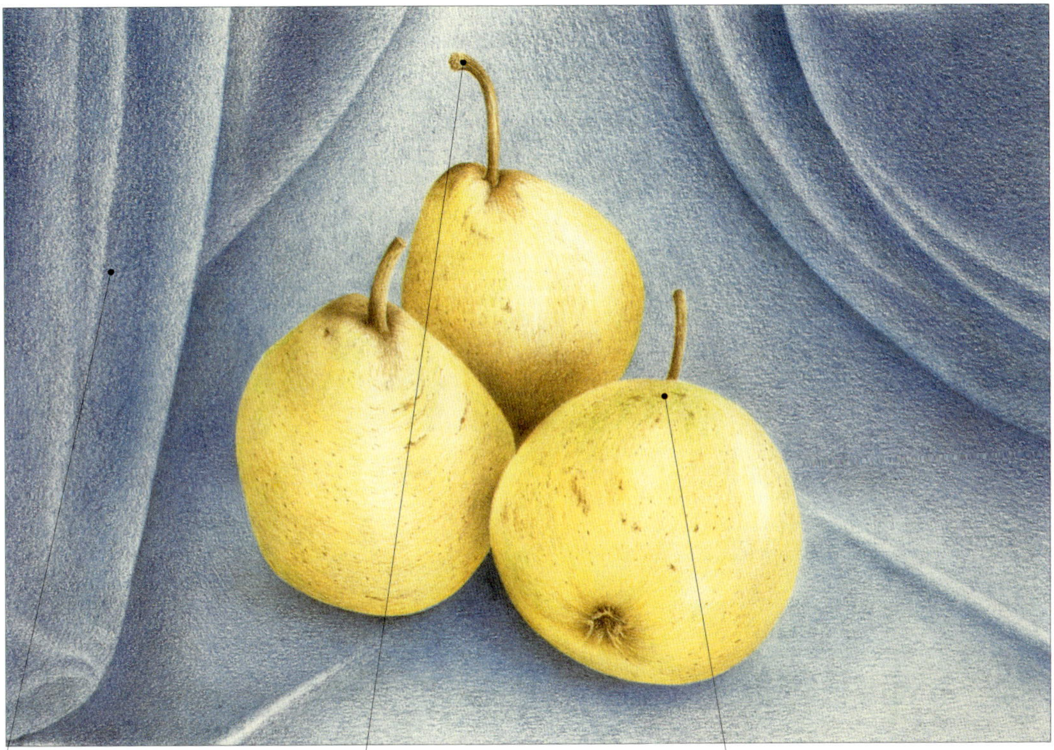

The folds of fabric are created by leaving a bright highlight with soft edges that blend to a deep blue in the recess of the fold.

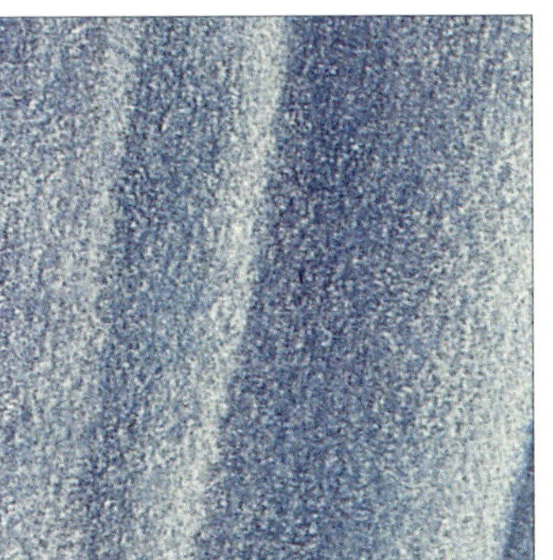

A dark brown has been used to define the stalks so that they stand out against the blue background.

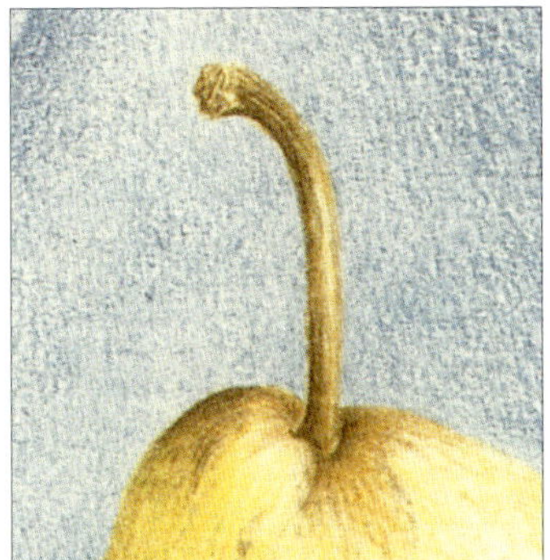

The brown speckles on the fruit are closer together on the edges to give the impression of rounded form.

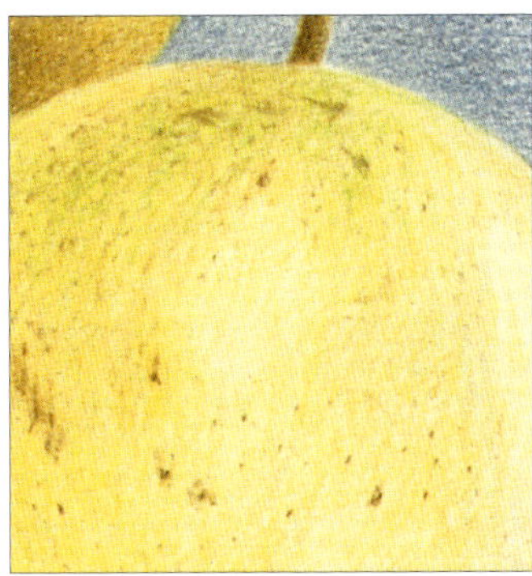

Small objects drawn large

This project, which uses everyday household objects such as keys, nuts, bolts and screws, is easy to replicate at home and produces a graphic, contemporary-looking image that would look wonderful hung on a plain white wall.

The point of the exercise is two-fold. First, although the arrangement appears random, when you set it up you really have to think about the negative shapes in the composition – that is, the spaces between the objects. Compositionally, the spaces help the viewer's eye to move through the composition to alight on the positive shapes – that is, the metal objects themselves.

Second, this is an exercise in loosening up and freeing both your eye and your hand. When you are drawing small objects, there is sometimes a tendency for your hand to tighten up as you try to put in every tiny detail, and this can make a drawing look very dull and lifeless. Drawing things larger than life size, as here, forces you to move your hand and your wrist as you work, producing a looser, freer image. It also makes you look at your subject in a different way: you're more likely to view the composition as a whole, instead of getting bogged down in individual items, and to concentrate on the overall shapes and how they relate to one another.

To give you some idea of the scale involved, the large key towards the bottom of the image was about 7cm (just under 3in) long in reality, whereas in the finished drawing, it is about 15cm (6in) long – so the objects were drawn at roughly twice life size.

Materials

- *Smooth drawing paper*
- *Thin charcoal stick*
- *Charcoal pencil*
- *Kneaded eraser*

Tip: To make the measuring easier, imagine lines running horizontally and vertically through the composition and work out where the small household objects intersect them.

The set-up

Scatter your chosen objects loosely on a white background, such as a large piece of paper or a white tablecloth. You'll find you get a better result if you just throw the objects down and see what shape they make rather than attempting to place each one precisely – although you'll almost certainly need to spend time creating the right balance and adjusting the positions before you start drawing. To create some modelling on the objects, place a table lamp to one side.

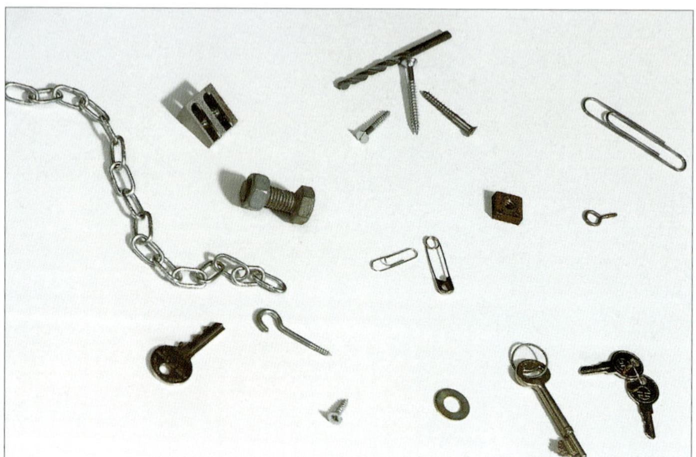

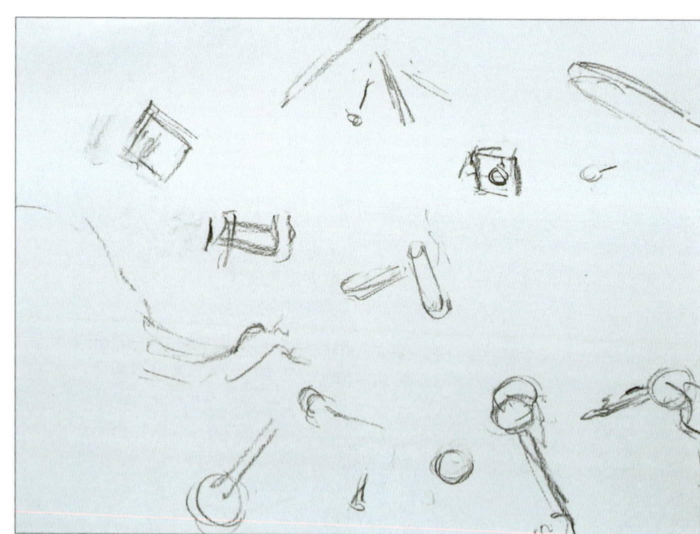

1 Using a thin charcoal stick, map out the shapes, carefully measuring both the objects and the spaces between them. Here, the artist decided to allow some of the objects to disappear off the edge of the paper, as she felt this created a more dynamic image than keeping everything within the rectangle of the paper.

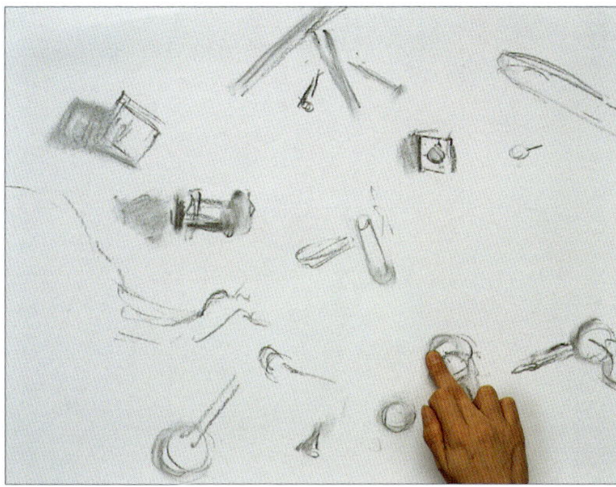

2 Using the side of the charcoal stick, block in the shapes of the shadows cast by the objects and smooth out the charcoal with your fingers. Putting in the shadows helps to give the objects solidity.

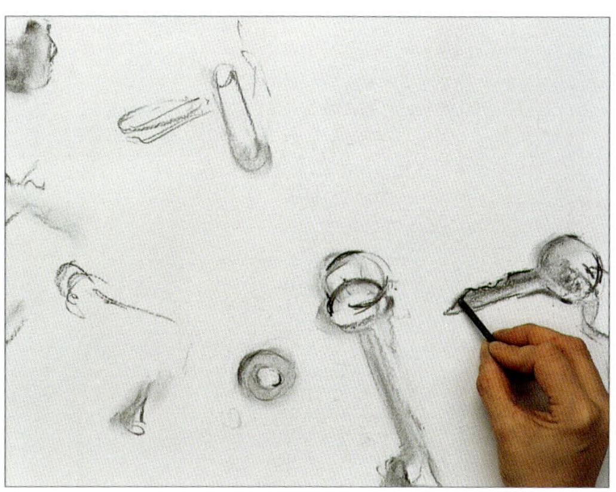

3 Gradually begin to refine the shapes of the objects, sharpening the edges with darker, linear marks. Blend the marks with your fingers, as before, to create the smooth, metallic finish.

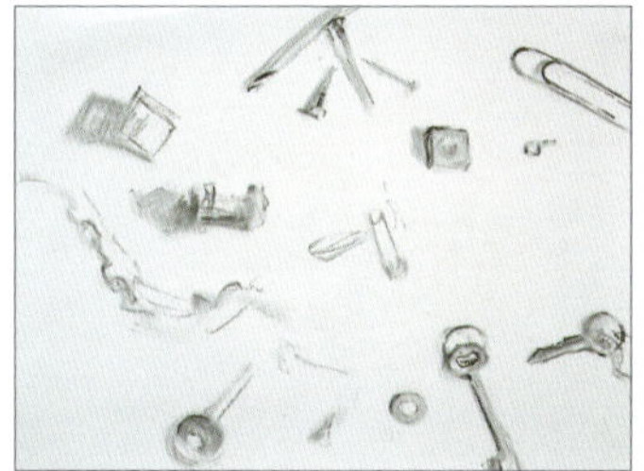

4 Continue refining the shapes. This is a gradual process, but the objects soon begin to 'emerge' from the paper as three-dimensional forms.

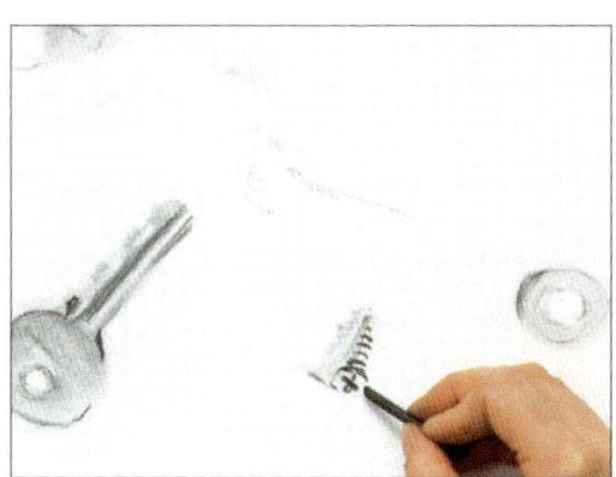

5 Using the tip of the charcoal, introduce some detailing, such as the threads of the screws and the notches on the keys. Work across the drawing as a whole, so that you can continually assess each object in relation to its neighbours.

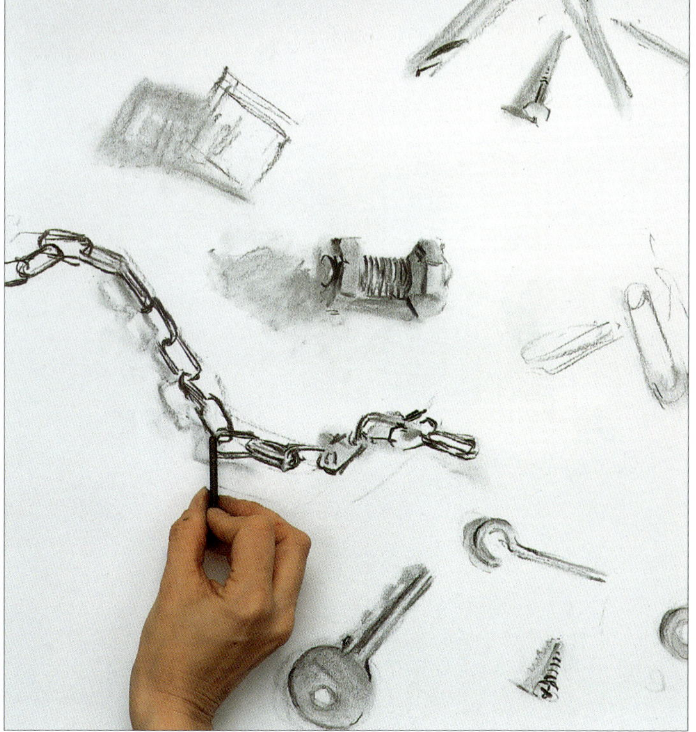

6 Continue the process of refinement and detailing. The process is akin to a photographer zooming in on his or her subject: initially you're looking at just the overall shapes, but as you add detailing the subject pops into sharper focus.

Assessment time

The shapes of the objects and their shadows are in place, but they still look rather indistinct. The edges, in particular, need to be more clearly defined. Overall, the tone is too uniform. Increasing the contrast between the dark and the light areas will make the objects look more three-dimensional.

Much crisper detailing is required on some objects.

Although the basic shape is there, some objects are too pale and lack the contrast that is needed to make them look realistic and three-dimensional.

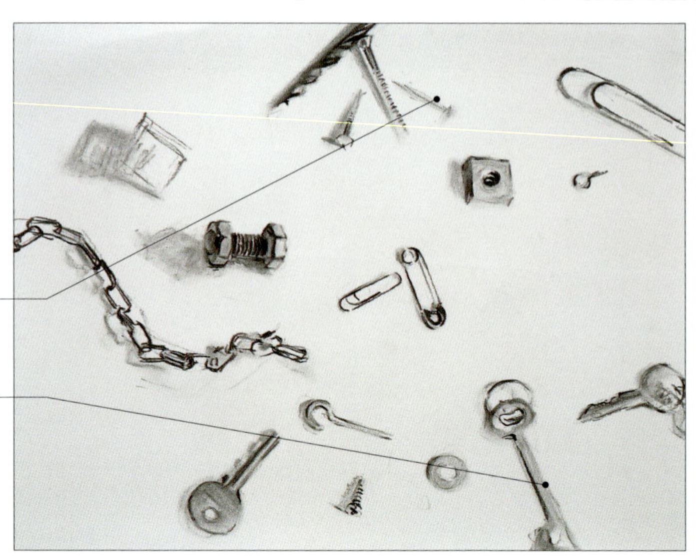

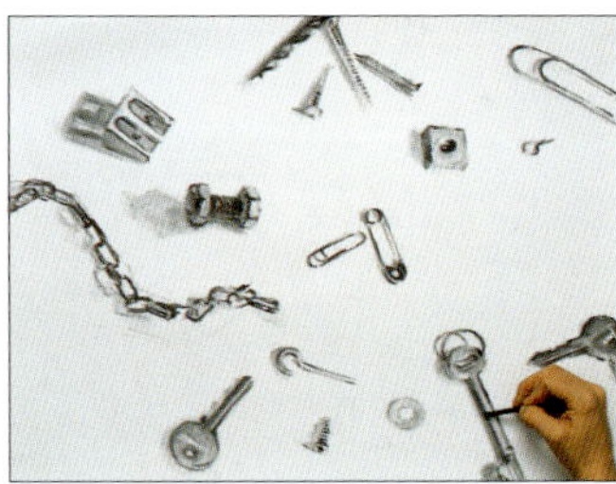

7 Working over the drawing as a whole, continue defining the edges of the objects and blending to create smooth, metallic surfaces.

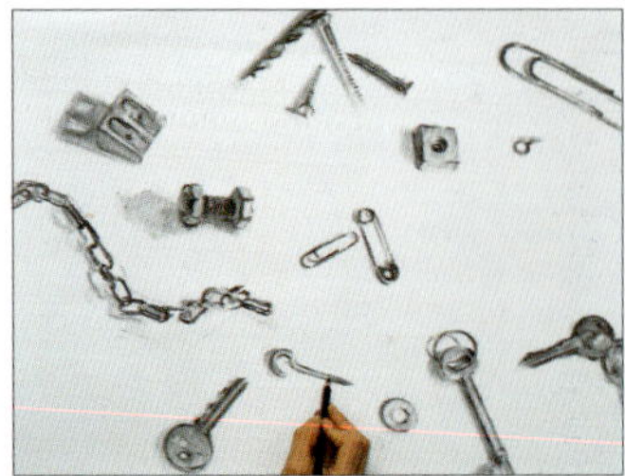

8 Use the tip of a charcoal pencil to sharpen up the edges of the objects and put in very fine details such as the screw threads.

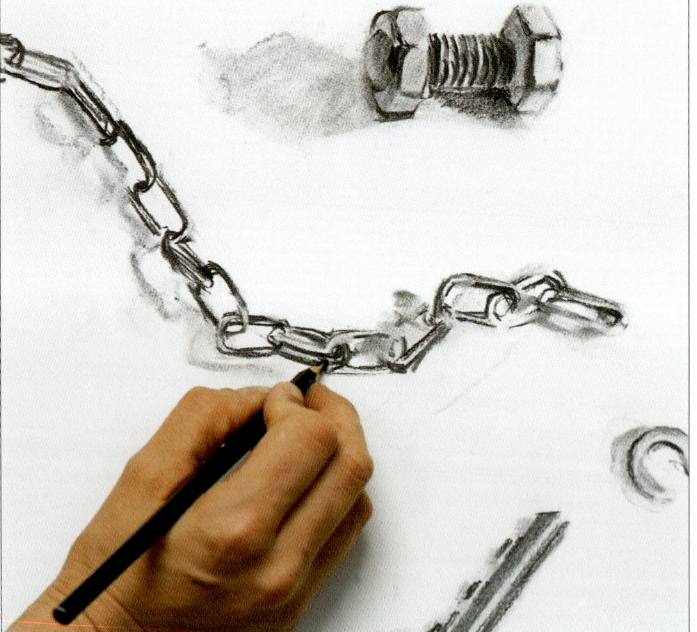

9 The chain is one of the few objects that look rather indistinct. Define the edges with the charcoal pencil, observing carefully how the links are connected. Remember to note where the highlights fall on the chain and allow the white of the paper to show through here. Clean up any smudges with a kneaded eraser.

The finished drawing

This is a graphic and realistic drawing that shows how even the most humble of objects has potential as an artistic subject. The composition has been carefully planned: note how all the objects are placed diagonally on the paper so that they lead the viewer's eye into the picture. Although all the objects are small, some, such as the bolt and pencil sharpener, are deeper than others and cast shadows that add interest and another texture to the image. Crisp, linear marks and soft blending of the charcoal combine to depict the hard-edged metal objects and the smooth surfaces.

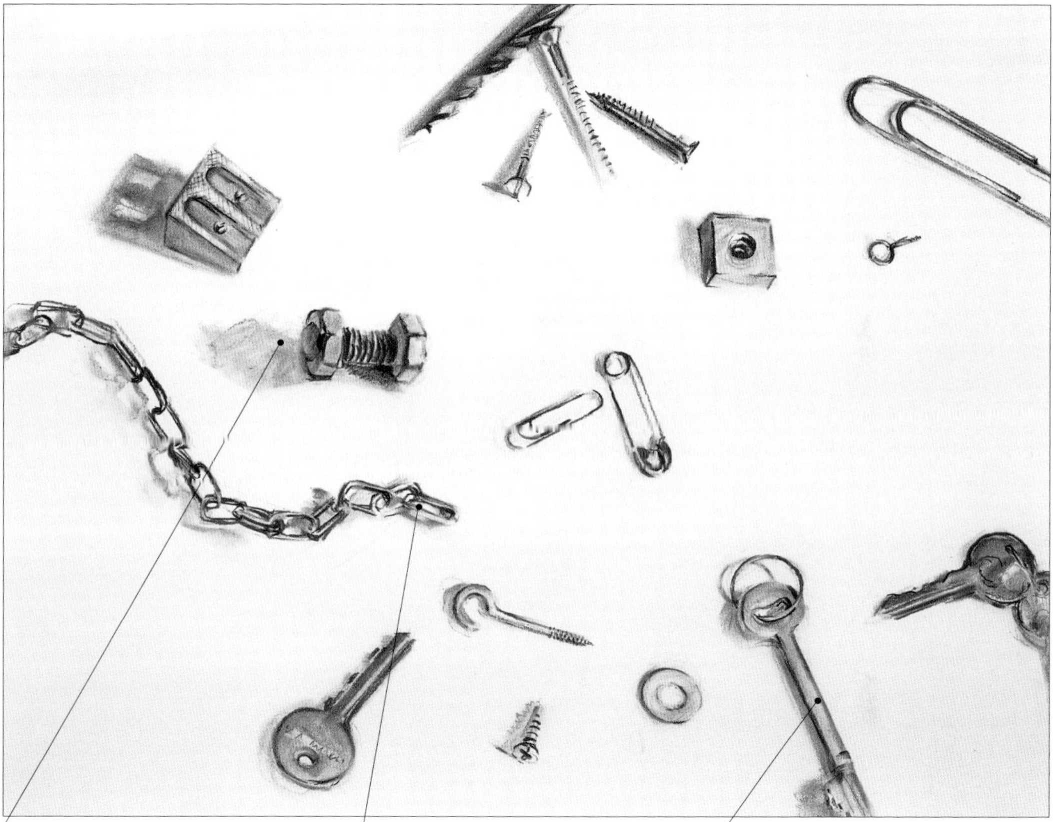

The cast shadows reveal that some objects are deeper than others.

The highlights on the twisted metal chain reveal the direction of the light.

Blending charcoal with the fingers creates a smooth texture.

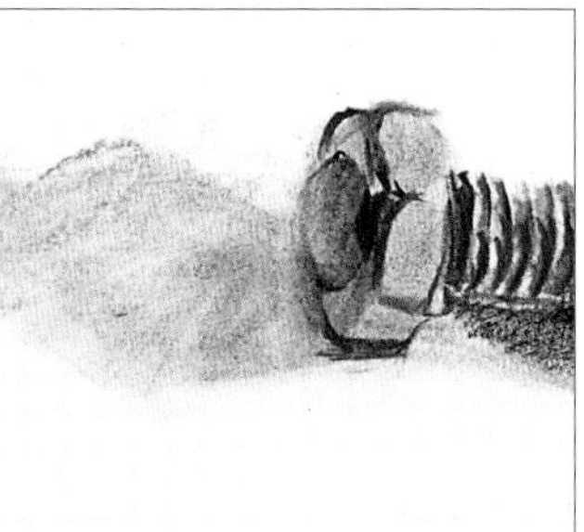

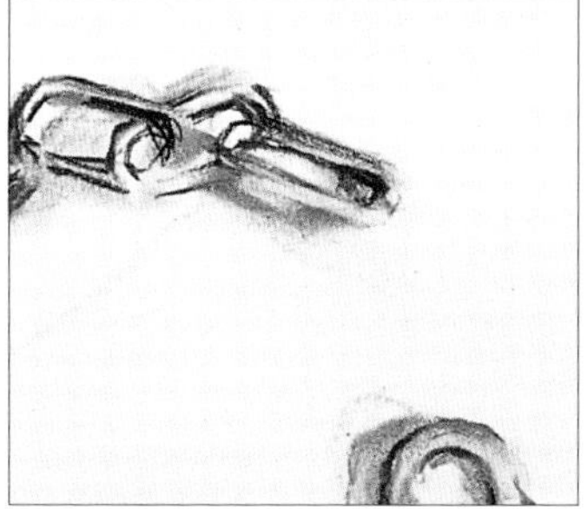

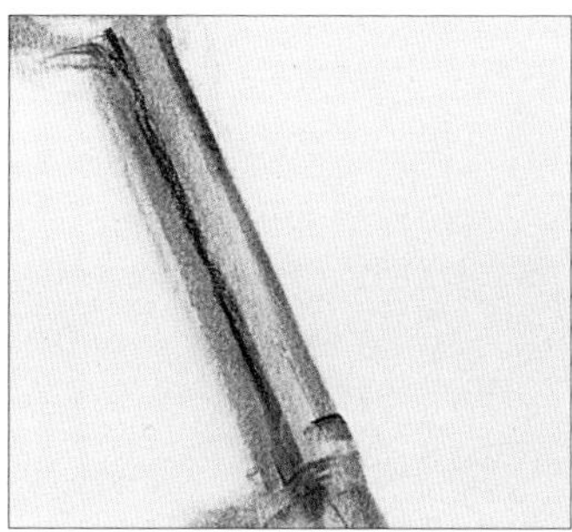

Quick sketches of buildings: Church façade

Drawing a façade is a good way to start sketching buildings as, since you're only dealing with one side, there is no need to get involved in the complications of two-point perspective. Here, the light and shade on the building and the lovely rough texture of the stonework provide plenty of interest. Beware of putting in too much textural detail, though, as it can make a drawing look dead and lifeless; a suggestion of the texture in a few key parts of the image is normally sufficient.

These sketches were made in pen and ink, or pen and ink plus water-soluble pencils. Pen and ink is a popular choice for architectural studies, as fine lines are often required. Ink is difficult to erase if you make a mistake – so it's a good idea to start in pencil and then reinforce the lines in pen once you're sure the measurements and proportions are correct. Though the water-soluble pencils were used dry on this occasion, blending the colours of the stonework with water would be very effective without destroying the textural pen-and-ink work.

The scene

This viewpoint offers several possible compositions: the façade of the church, the details of the arches on the left, and even textural studies of the stonework.

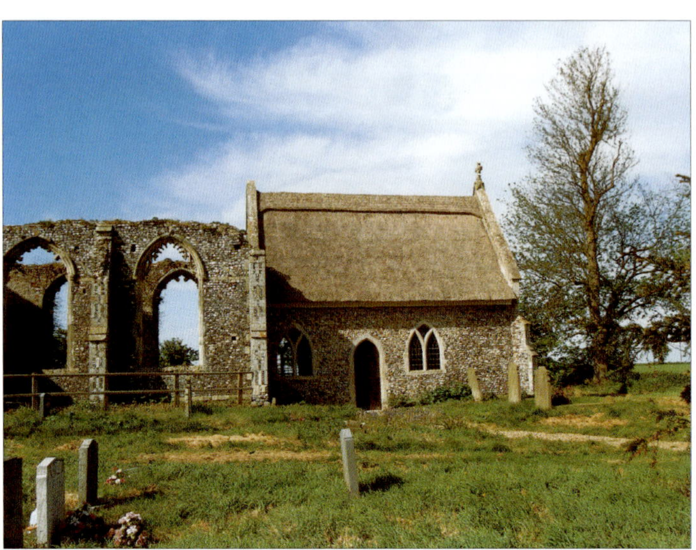

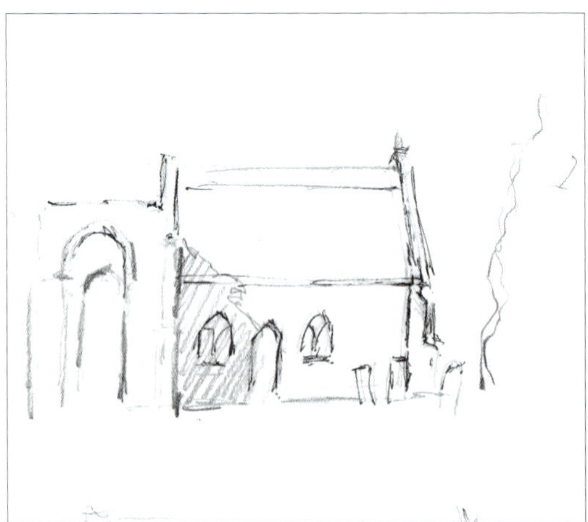

5-minute sketch: pen and ink

With a relatively simple shape like this church, you should be able to map out the basic structure of the building in a matter of minutes. The key, of course, is to measure all the elements and their relative positions very carefully. A thumbnail sketch like this is a good warm-up exercise when you're drawing on location. It also gives you the chance to work out the composition of a larger drawing.

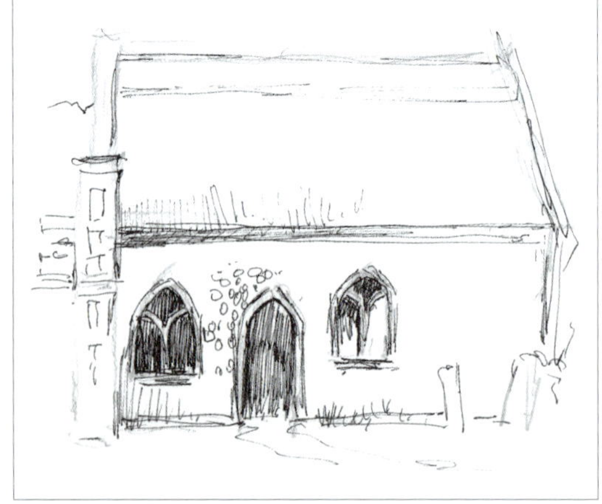

10-minute sketch: pen and ink

In 10 minutes, you have time to indicate the texture of the stonework and the heavy wooden door. A few simple pen lines are enough to show the shape of the stones set into the walls; don't overdo it or you'll deaden the overall effect. A sketch made *in situ* like this provides very useful reference material for a larger drawing that you can work up in more detail at a later date.

15-minute sketch: pen and ink, plus water-soluble pencils
Here, the artist decided to concentrate on the arches to the left of the church. With a little more time at your disposal, you can explore the effects of light and shade and try to capture more of the texture and character of the stonework. As in the other sketches on these two pages, the basic composition was mapped out in pencil before any pen-and-ink work was done, with hatched pen lines indicating the most deeply shaded parts of the scene. Finally, water-soluble pencils were used to block in the colour of the stonework. Sketches such as this are a very good way to explore the tonal relationships in a scene.

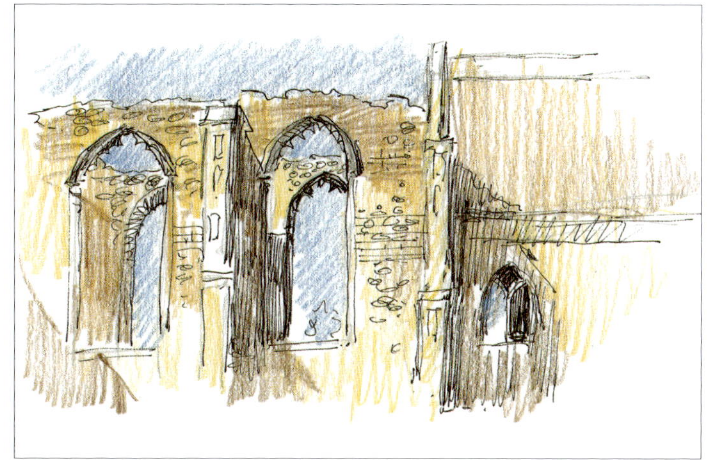

25-minute sketch: pen and ink, plus water-soluble pencils
This is a more elaborate version of the sketch above, and shows the relationship between the church and the ruined building next to it. The artist was able to get closer to the true colours of the scene, using warm, purplish blues for the shadow areas. There was also time to place the building in a setting by including trees and foreground grass.

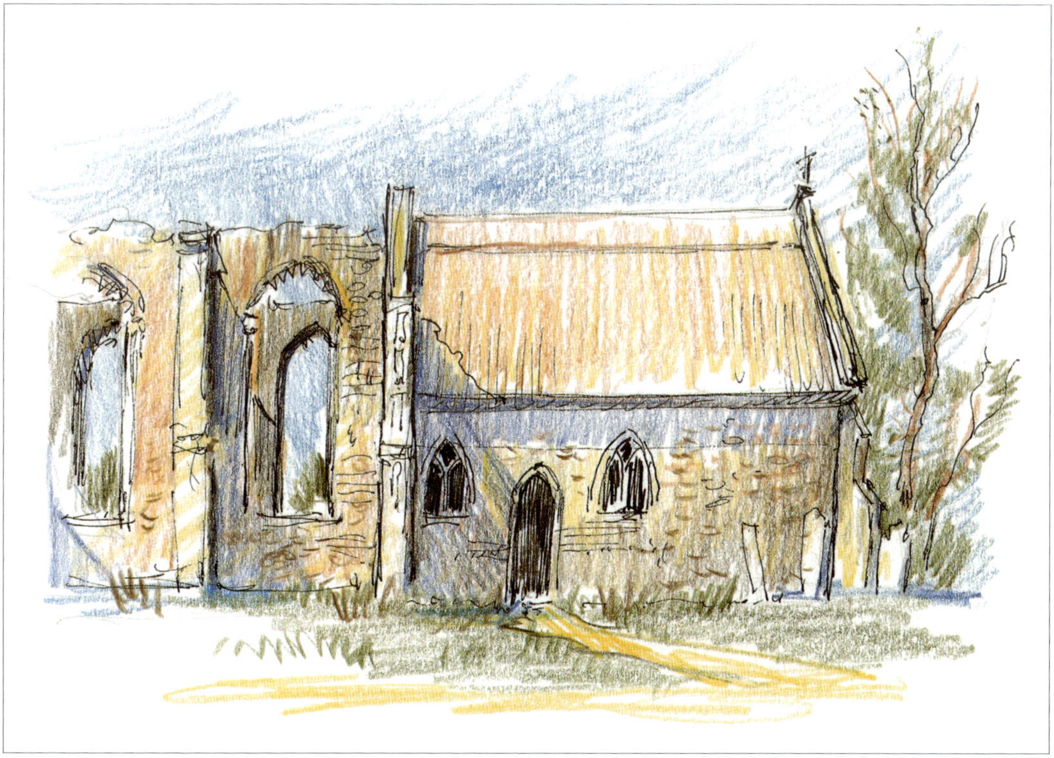

Quick sketches of buildings: Doorway

Old, dilapidated buildings provide a great opportunity to practise sketching different textures. Crumbling stonework and tiles, sun-bleached wood with the grain exposed, worn carvings: all are full of texture for the artist. And if the building happens to be in an exotic location, so much the better. When it comes to capturing the essence of a foreign country, architectural styles are as evocative as costumes or landscapes. Look for interesting details when you're on your travels. You'll be amazed at how effectively a few quick sketches made *in situ* can bring back memories.

When you are sketching textures, do not put in too many details or they will dominate the image. Imply the textures rather than putting in every single brick and crack. Allow the shapes and textural contrasts to speak for themselves.

The scene

Coming across this doorway into a courtyard in Beijing, China, the artist was attracted by the contrast between the rather grandiose entrance and the much more humble-looking abode within. Although the subject is almost monochromatic, it provided enough visual interest to prompt her to make a few quick sketches.

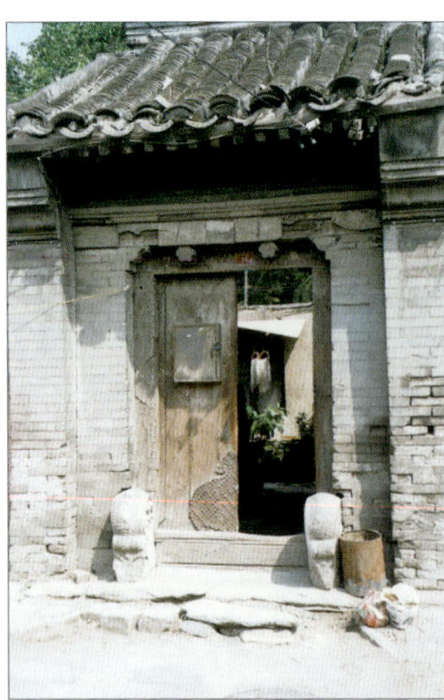

5-minute sketch: charcoal

In this sketch, the artist has managed to create a convincing impression of depth through her use of tone. Strong linear marks for the shaded undersides of the arch and doorway combine with smudged charcoal for the shadow areas. The artist has put in just enough linear detail to hint at the shapes of the bricks and roof tiles, without detracting from the tonal study.

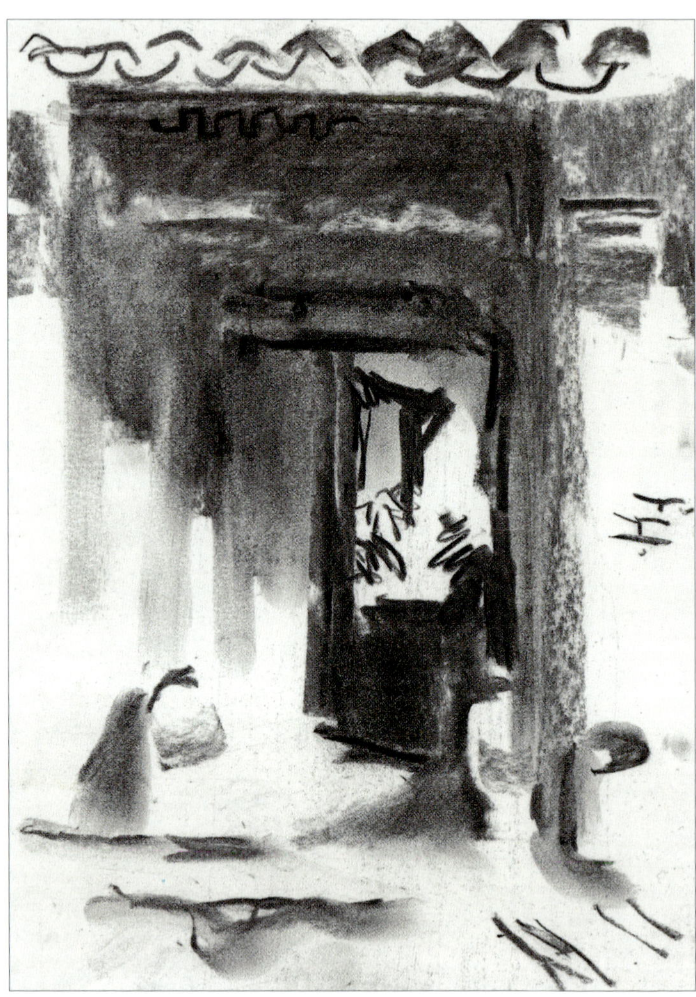

Tip: If you don't measure up carefully, the proportions will look wrong – particularly if you can see two sides of the building and want to use two-point perspective. Imagine lines running horizontally and vertically through the image and work out where the different elements, such as a window, or a decorative detail such as a door knocker, intersect them.

15-minute sketch: pen and ink, plus brush
Overlapping roof tiles make an attractive graphic study. Here, the scratchy, irregular lines produced by using a dip pen seem appropriate for the rather rough-textured, handmade tiles. The artist wanted to retain the lines of the tiles, so she drew them in waterproof ink before applying a dilute wash of ink over the top for the shadow areas.

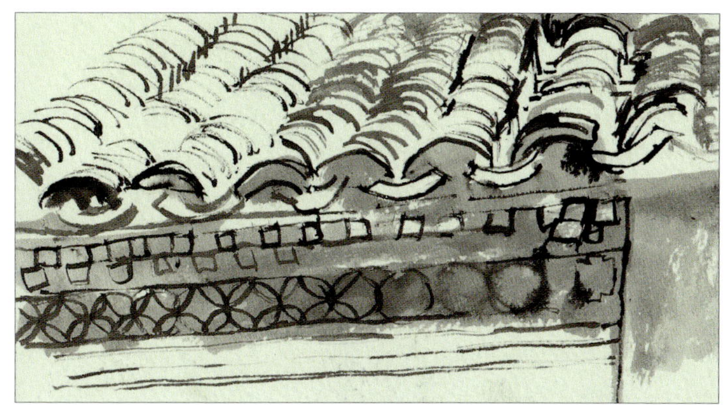

25-minute sketch: pastel
This sketch is built up of blocks of colour and tone which get progressively lighter the nearer they are to the foreground of the scene. The tooth of the paper helps to convey the texture of the stonework.

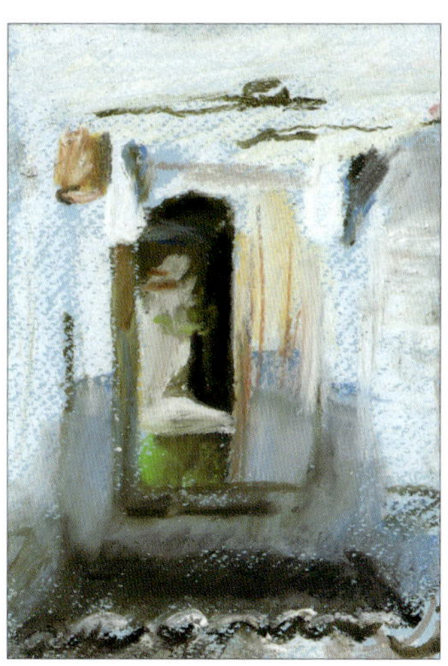

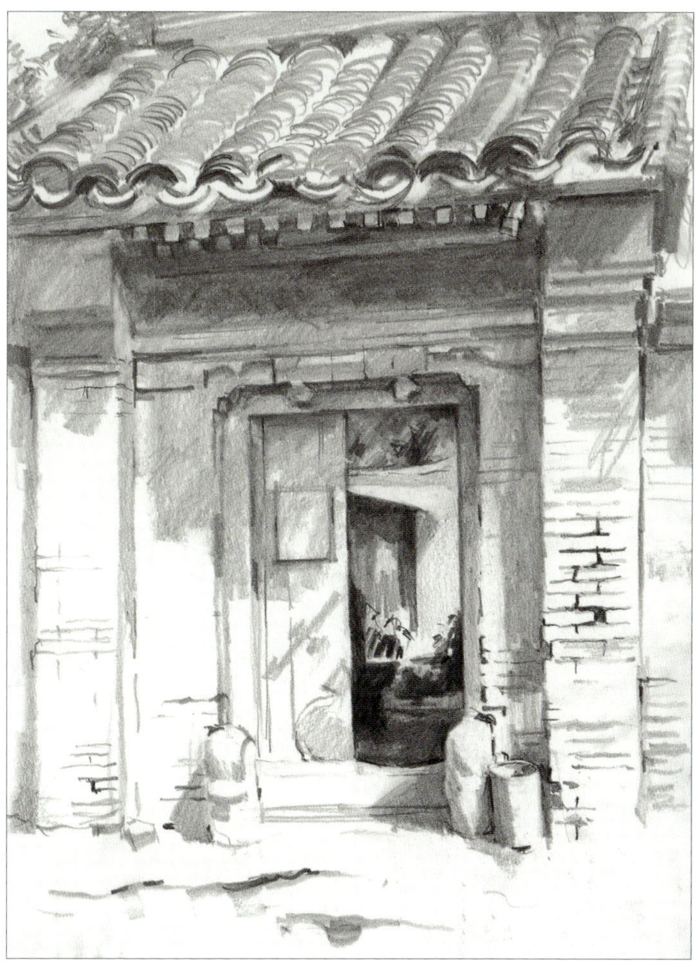

40-minute sketch: pencil and graphite
Having explored the composition of the scene and some of the textures in the previous two sketches, the artist then settled down to making a more detailed sketch. She used a 6B pencil for the darkest parts, including the deep cracks in the bricks on the right, and a graphite stick (blended with a torchon) for the areas in shadow. Note how much of the brickwork is left untouched: nonetheless, the texture is conveyed very effectively.

Quick sketches of buildings: Farmhouse

A viewpoint that shows two sides of a building almost inevitably creates a more interesting drawing than one that shows only the front façade. It also allows you to exploit contrasts of light and shade, as one side will be more brightly lit than its neighbour. Bear in mind the rules of two-point perspective. You can plot the perspective lines to their vanishing points if you wish, but careful observation and measuring are generally sufficient.

5-minute sketch: 2B pencil

Here, the artist drew the farmhouse from a slightly higher eye level than that from which the photo on the right was taken. As a result, the front façade of the house is virtually square on and the line of the roof does not slope downward. When you're drawing a building, it's well worth making a quick sketch such as this simply to measure and check the placement of the different elements.

The scene

In this winter scene, the dark hedge in front of the building and the skeletal trees by the side stand out well against the snowy ground and provide a contrast of texture with the flat stonework. The hedge also echoes the shape of the building, as the lines of the hedge run more or less parallel to the building's sides. In this instance, the artist chose to make a series of monochrome sketches – but the bright red door and little outbuilding or porch would provide an uplifting splash of colour in a study made in coloured pencil or chalk.

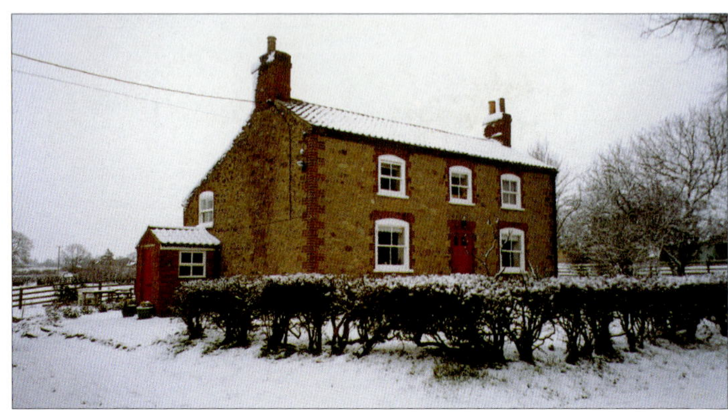

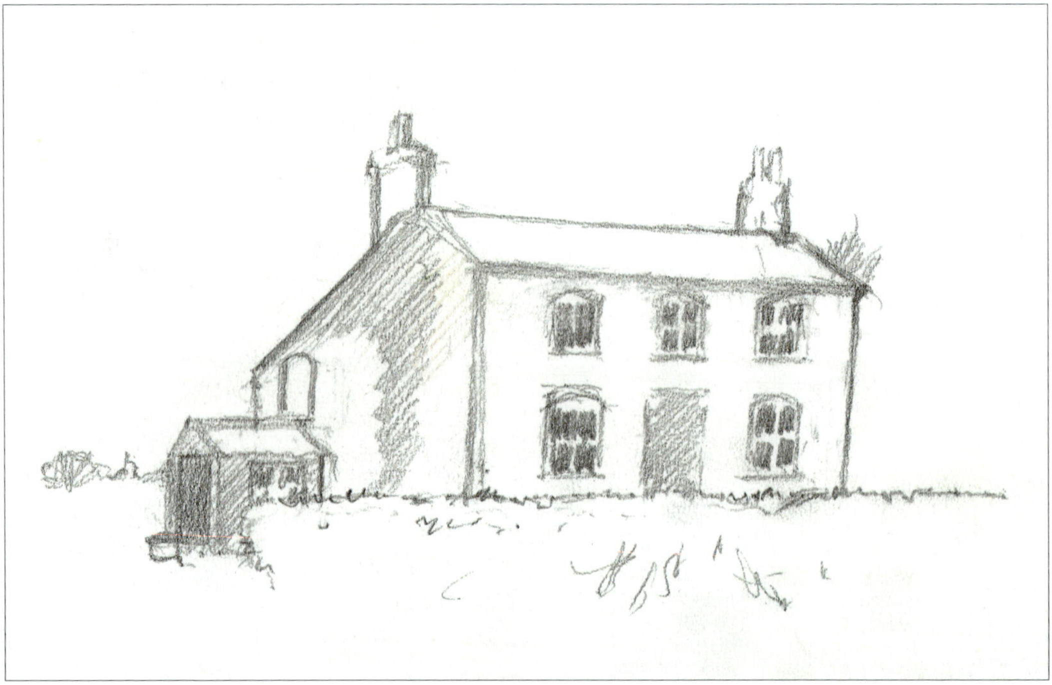

15-minute sketch: burnt umber coloured pencil
When you've established the basic lines of the composition, you can begin to explore the tonal relationships in more detail. Here, we've shown the tonal study as a separate sketch; in reality, you might choose to make this the second stage of the sketch shown on the opposite page. The artist has also begun to put some detail into the stonework, being careful not to overdo things and deaden the overall effect.

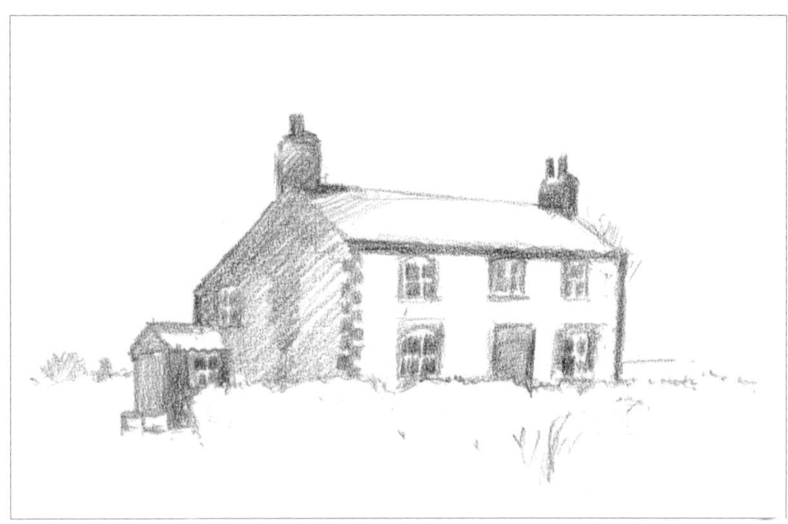

30-minute sketch: ballpoint pen
Although only the cornerstones are drawn in any detail, the artist has nonetheless created the texture of the building very well by means of simple shading. One of the most common mistakes that beginners make is to underestimate the tonal range in a scene; make sure that the darkest areas, such as the window recesses, are really dark, as this will make the snow-covered areas really sparkle. The brightest parts, such as the roof, can be left virtually untouched.

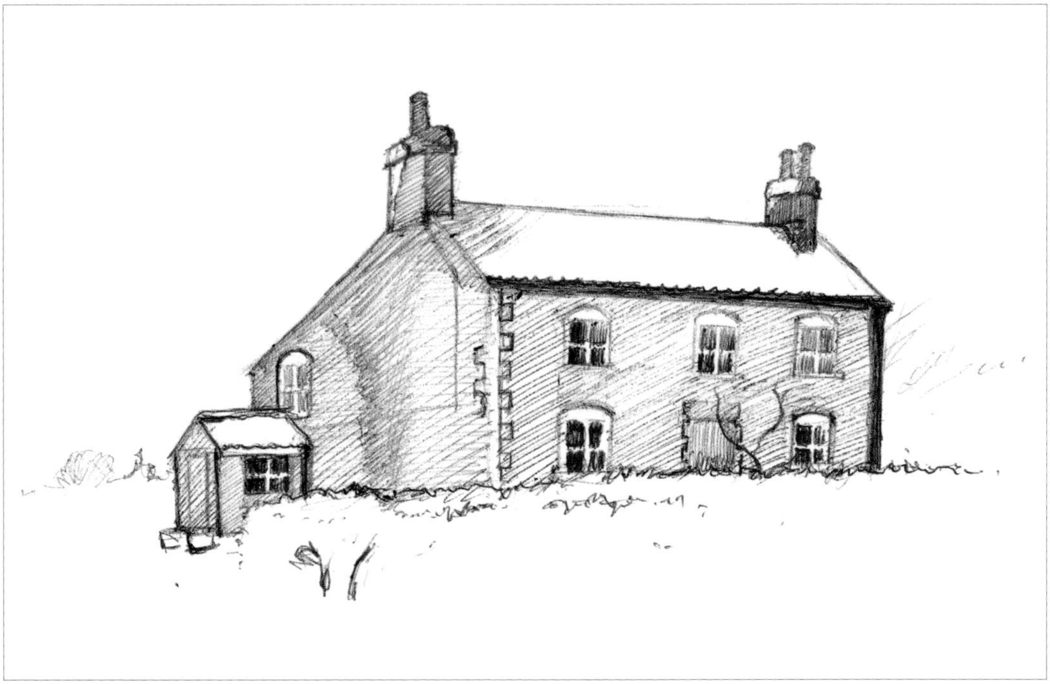

Venetian building

This project is an exercise in perspective. The bottom of the balcony is more or less at the artist's eye level – so this is the horizon line. If you look at the initial pencil sketch in Step 1, you will see that the artist has drawn the bottom of the balcony to form a straight, horizontal line across the centre of the image. Any parallel line above this point (such as the line of the roof) will appear to slope down towards the vanishing point, while anything below it (such as the base of the building) appears to slope upwards. Take time over your initial pencil sketch to make sure you get the angles and proportions right. Texture is important, too, and the rough texture of the ancient brickwork is very pleasing to the eye. Don't try to draw every single brick, as this would make the image too 'busy' and detract from the overall effect. Leaving some areas empty gives much-needed contrast of texture and implies the smooth render that would once have covered the whole façade of the building.

Pen and ink is an ideal medium for architectural drawings, as it allows you to make very precise marks. Here, both permanent and water-soluble inks are used, creating a combination of crisp, linear details and ink washes, which soften the overall effect. For this project, the artist chose to use sepia ink, rather than black, as it is a much softer colour and helps to give the drawing a rather nostalgic, old-fashioned feel.

Materials
- *Heavy drawing paper*
- *HB pencil*
- *Permanent and water-soluble sepia inks*
- *Steel-nibbed pens*
- *Fine paintbrush*
- *Gouache paint: white*

The scene
Old buildings such as this one, with the canal lapping at its foundations, are common in Venice, and can evoke a strong sense of the past. The decorative lines of the balconies are not overly ornate, but they hold our interest, and the beautiful arched doors and windows form a repeating pattern that runs through the whole image.

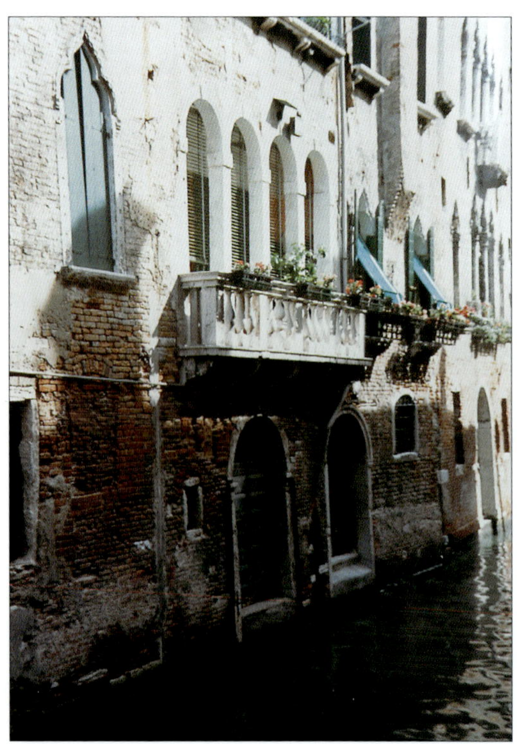

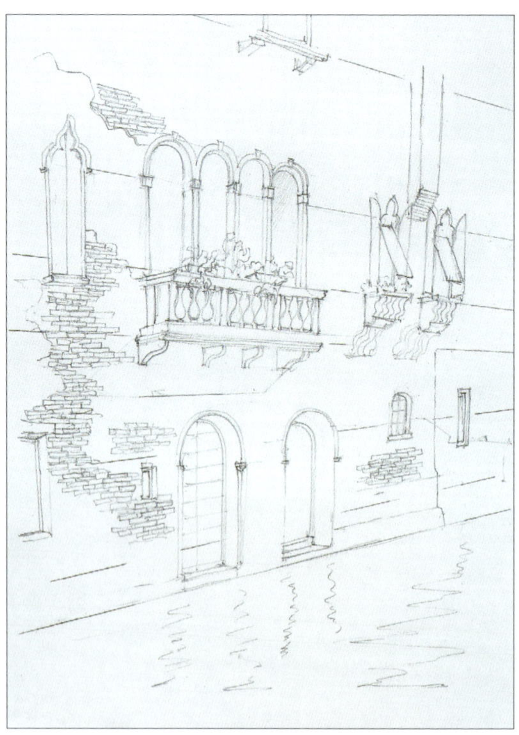

1 Using an HB pencil, make a light, detailed sketch of the scene, making sure you measure all the different elements.

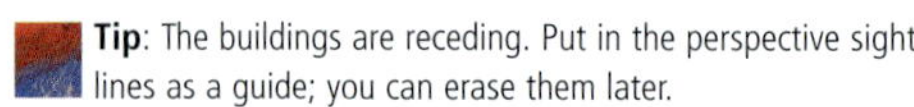

Tip: The buildings are receding. Put in the perspective sight-lines as a guide; you can erase them later.

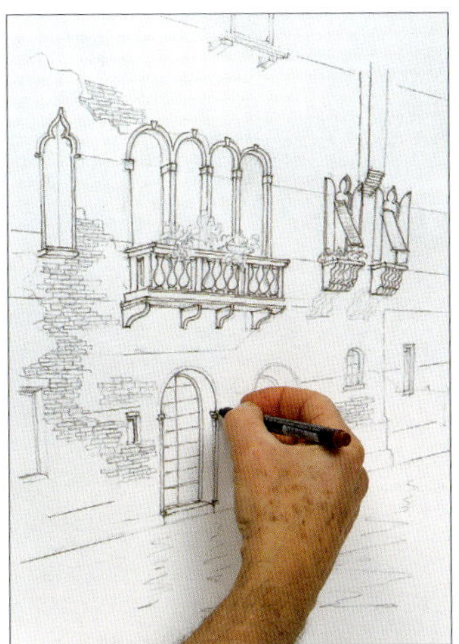

2 Following your pencil lines and using permanent sepia ink, carefully ink in the windows and balconies. It is very important not to use water-soluble ink here, as you want to retain all the crisp detail of these lines in the finished drawing.

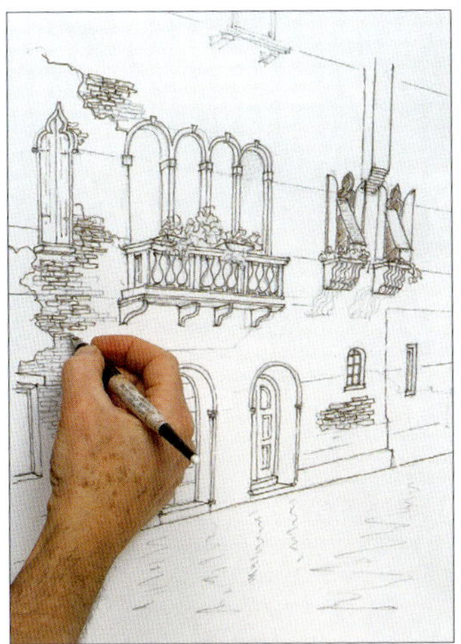

3 Continue with the ink work, using water-soluble sepia ink for the foliage and brickwork. Also hatch the windows behind the open shutters on the top right of the drawing in water-soluble ink, drawing the lines close together as this area is very dark.

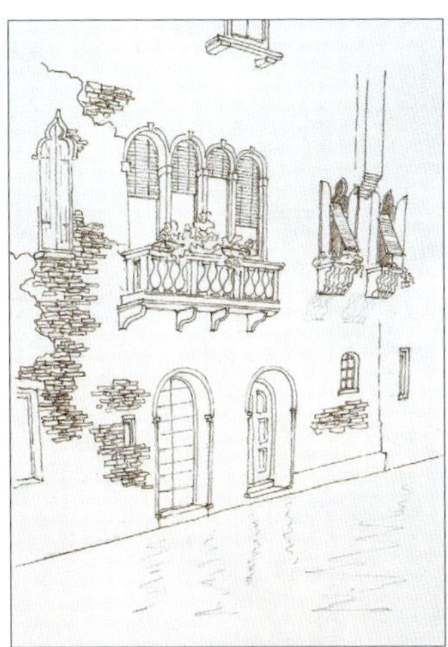

4 Continue working on the brickwork, alternating between permanent and water-soluble sepia inks. Put in the lines of the Venetian blinds in permanent ink. Here the artist has put the blinds in at different heights to add interest.

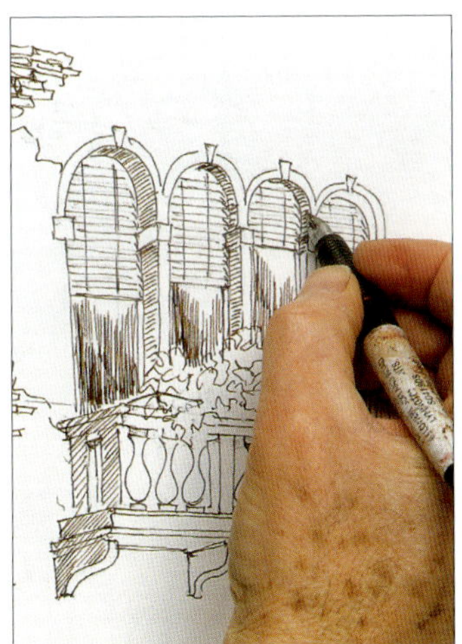

5 Using water-soluble ink, put in some light hatching around the window recesses, in the windows below the blinds, and under the balconies to introduce some shading. (The ink will be washed over at a later stage, so that the hatching marks blend together to create an area of solid tone.)

Assessment time

The main lines are now in place. However, although there is some indication of the shading around the windows and balconies, the image overall looks rather flat and two-dimensional. From this point onwards, concentrate on creating more depth and texture.

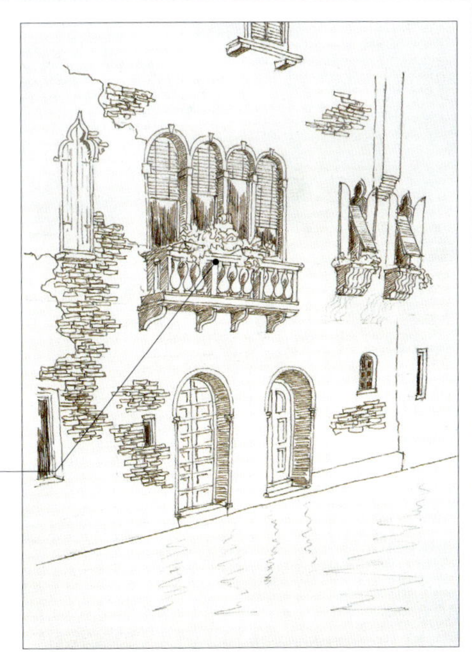

Although there is some texture and detail, the image as a whole is rather lifeless. Washes of colour will help to counteract this.

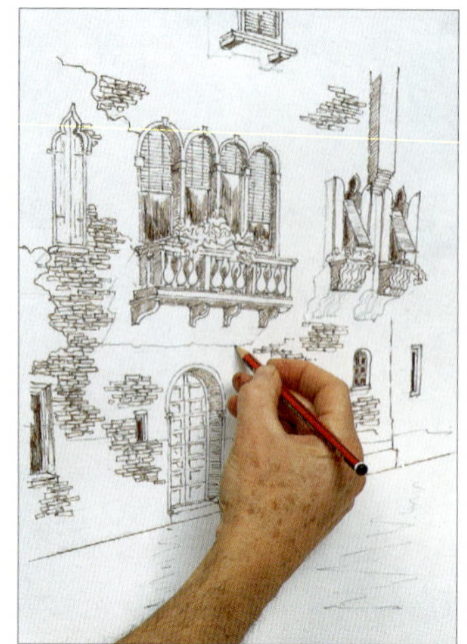

6 As the light is coming from the right of the scene, the balconies cast oblique shadows on the façade of the building. Put them in lightly, using an HB pencil. (The pencil lines act as a positional guide – they should be covered up by washes of ink later.)

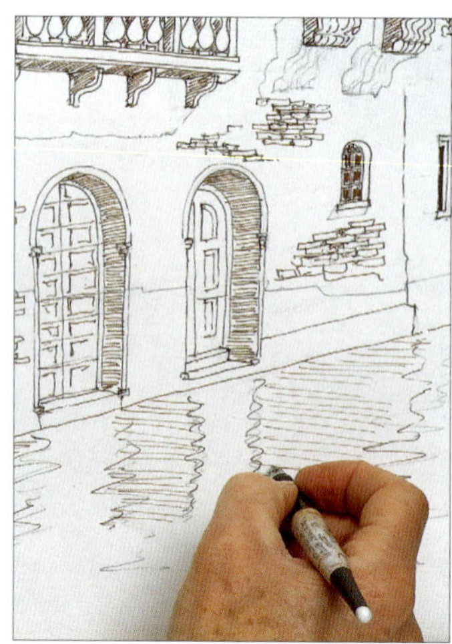

7 Using permanent ink and zig-zagging vertical lines, draw the ripples in the water. Hatch the darkest areas of the water, using water-soluble ink. The ripples will remain visible when a wash is applied, while the hatching will blend to an area of solid tone.

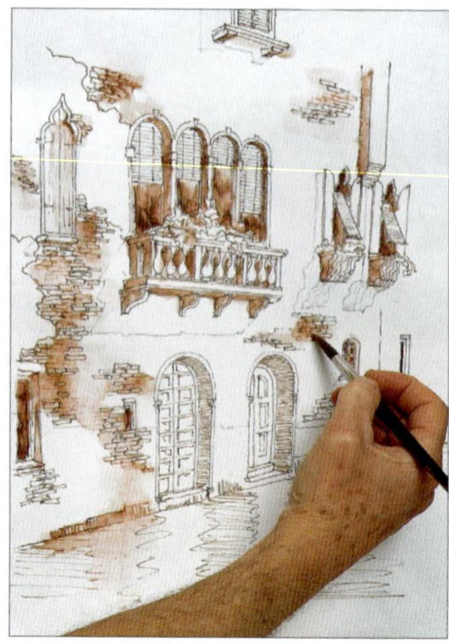

8 Erase all the remaining pencil lines, apart from the cast shadows that you put in in Step 6. Load a paintbrush with water and brush over the shaded parts of the building. The lines drawn in water-soluble ink will dissolve, allowing you to create areas of solid tone.

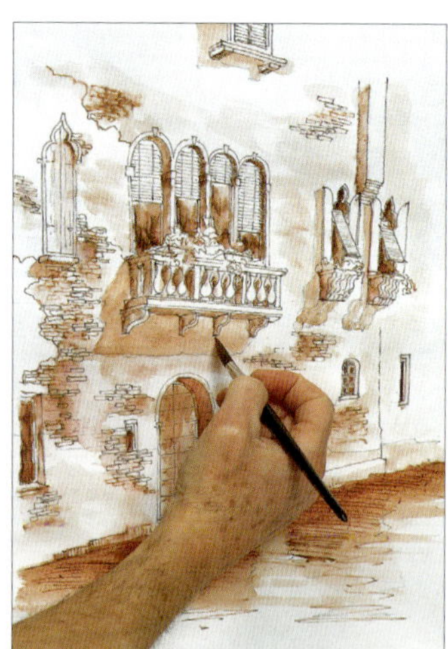

9 Continue brushing water over the water-soluble ink, including the canal. Brush colour over the doors, darkening them with more ink if necessary. Dilute some sepia ink (or use sepia watercolour paint) and brush it over the cast shadows on the building, keeping within the pencil marks.

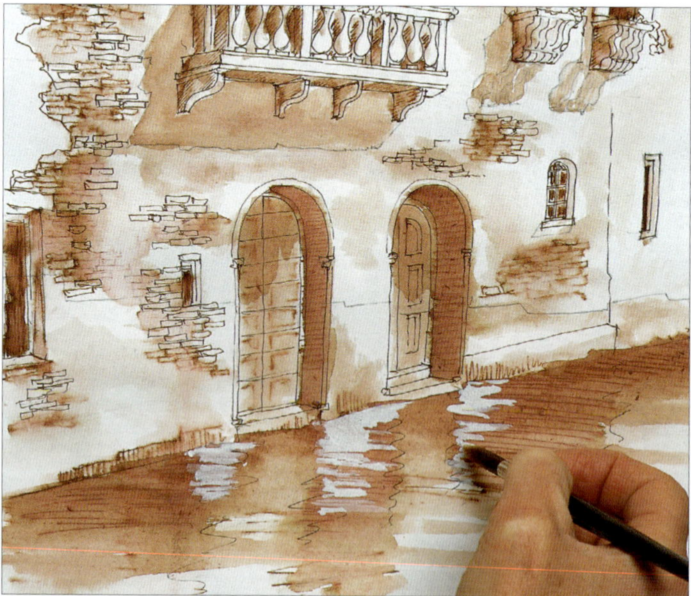

10 Using a fine paintbrush and white gouache, paint in the reflections of the doors in the water. Gouache paint used straight from the tube can be quite thick so only dip the tip of your brush into it.

The finished drawing

This is an evocative and elegant pen-and-ink study of a classic Venetian building. Permanent ink was used for the linear details in the most important areas, while brushing water over the water-soluble ink has helped to create areas of tone that soften the harshness of the pen work, transforming an architectural study into something much more picturesque. Although only one colour of ink was used, a good range of tones was created by washing water over different densities of hatched marks.

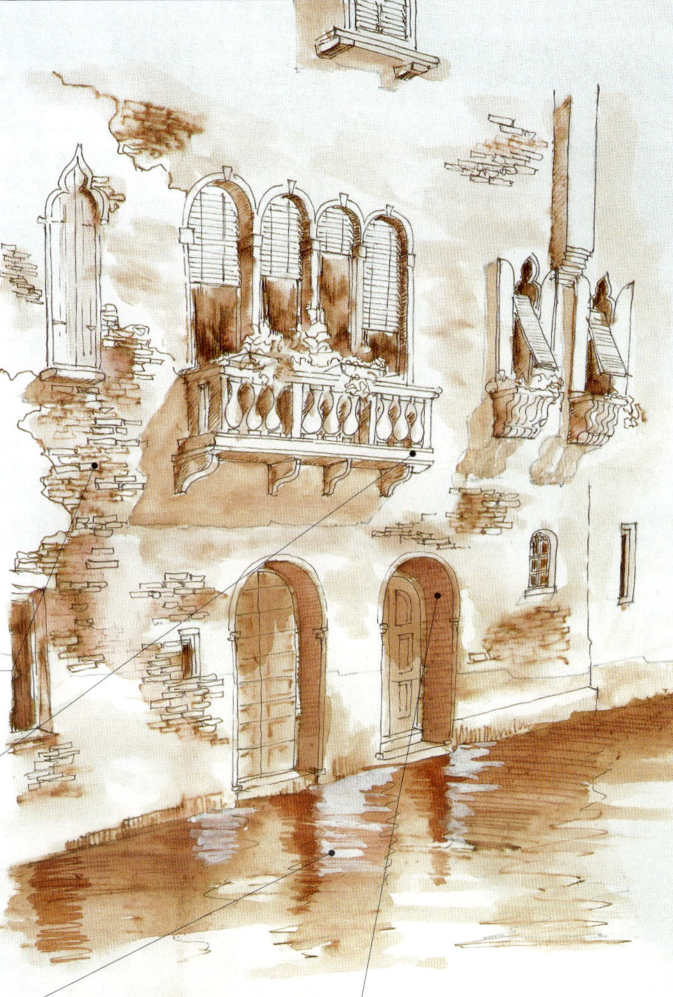

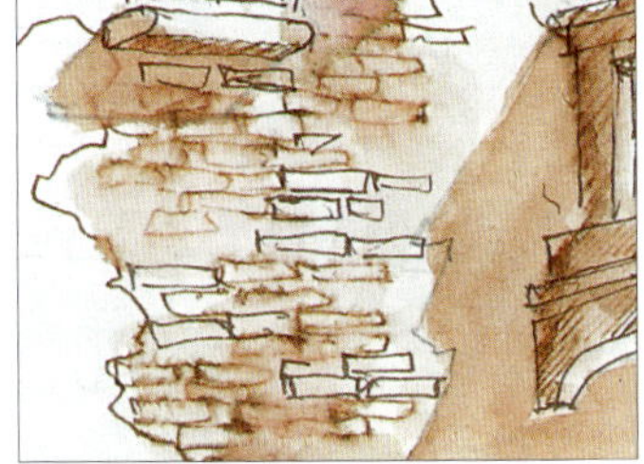

Both permanent and water-soluble ink were used here, creating a combination of linear detail and soft tonal washes.

The linear detailing of the building, as in the balcony, was drawn using permanent ink.

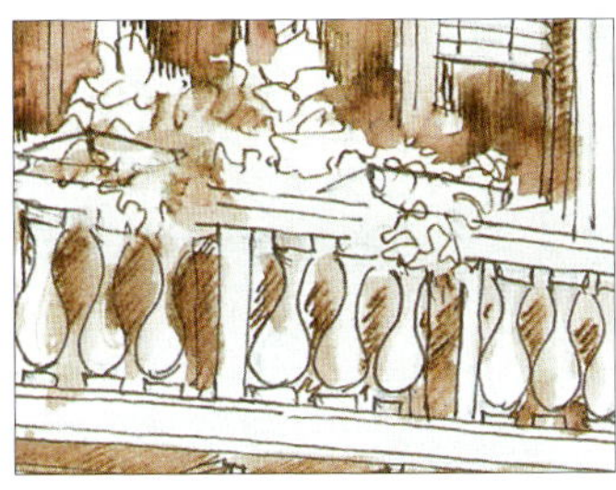

White gouache paint, which is opaque, is used to paint the light reflections on top of the dark patches of water.

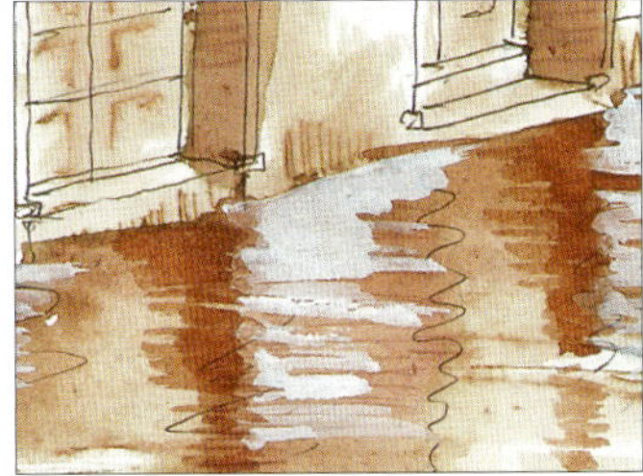

Washing water over hatched lines produces an area of solid tone – the closer together the lines, the darker the tone.

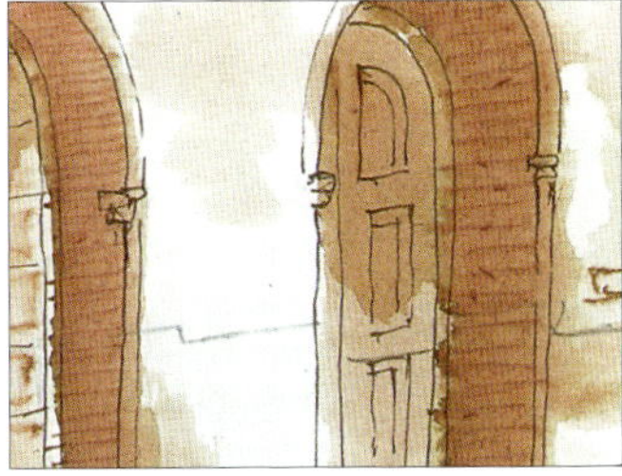

Sunshine and shadow

When you're drawing buildings, you can opt either for a very detailed approach that captures every single element, rather like an architectural drawing, or for something more atmospheric, as here, where the effects of light and shade are as important a part of the image as the buildings themselves.

In this project, the light is very strong and is illuminating the front of the buildings. If the light were coming from the side, the differences in tone between the shaded and brightly lit areas would be more pronounced. Nonetheless, there are still areas of deep shadow within the scene, particularly around the arched doorway – and it is these shadows that give depth to the façade. There is also a large shadow on the left of the scene, cast by a building behind the artist's viewpoint. This shadow occupies almost one-quarter of the drawing. Although it is dark, some detail is still visible within it so don't allow it to dominate the image completely.

Creating a strong enough contrast between very bright and very dark areas is the key to this drawing. As this is a charcoal drawing, the white of the paper is left untouched for the brightest areas. You can't make the light areas any lighter than they already are so, in order for the brightest areas to look really bright, you need to make the dark areas really dark.

Because the light on the brightest parts of the buildings is so strong, much of the detail is subdued. In many ways this is a bonus: when you're drawing a complicated subject like this, it's very easy to get obsessed with detail and put in so much that it detracts from the essential elements of the scene – the lively interplay between light and shade.

Materials

- *Smooth, heavy drawing paper*
- *Thin willow charcoal stick*
- *Clean rag or kitchen paper*
- *Kneaded eraser*

The scene

There is an interesting balance between light and dark in this scene, with the top of the buildings bathed in sunlight and the bottom half deep in shadow.

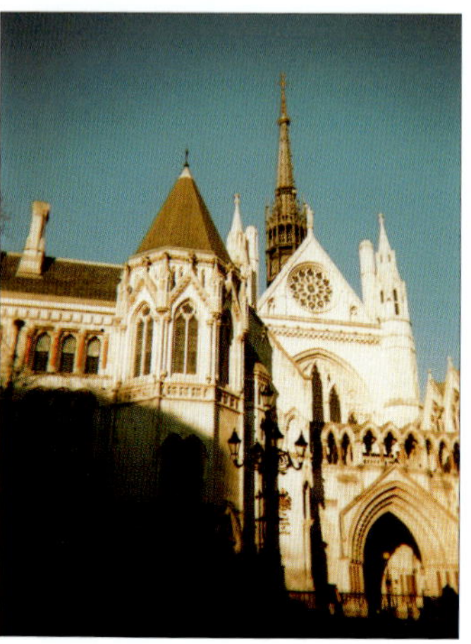

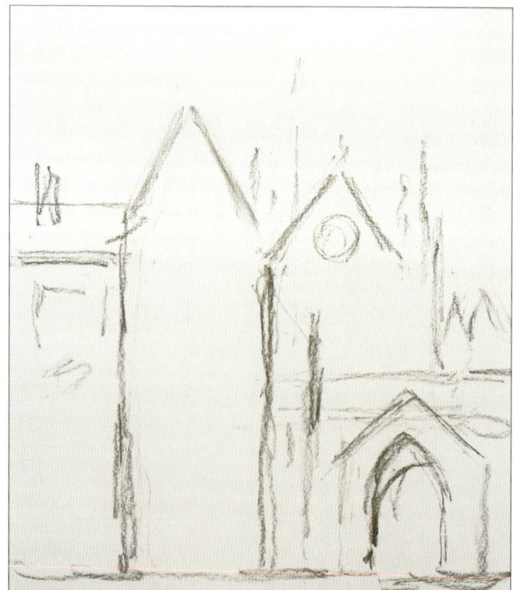

1 Using a thin charcoal stick, map out the shapes and proportions of the buildings, checking your measurements as you work. Use line only: there is no point in putting in any shading until the basic structure has been established.

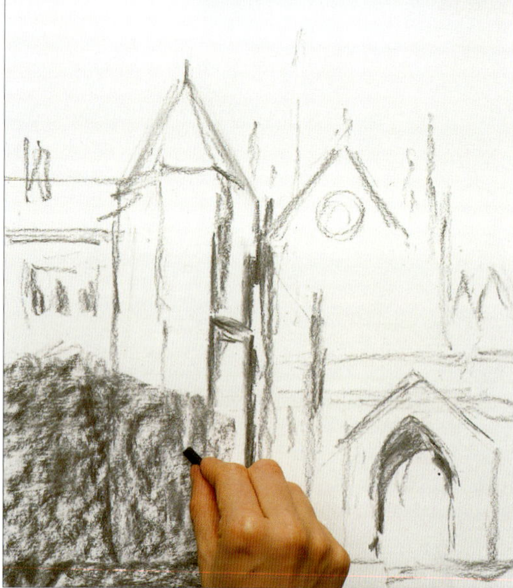

2 Block in the dark recesses of the windows and the arched main door. Using the side of the charcoal stick, block in the shadow on the left-hand side, which is cast by a building behind the artist.

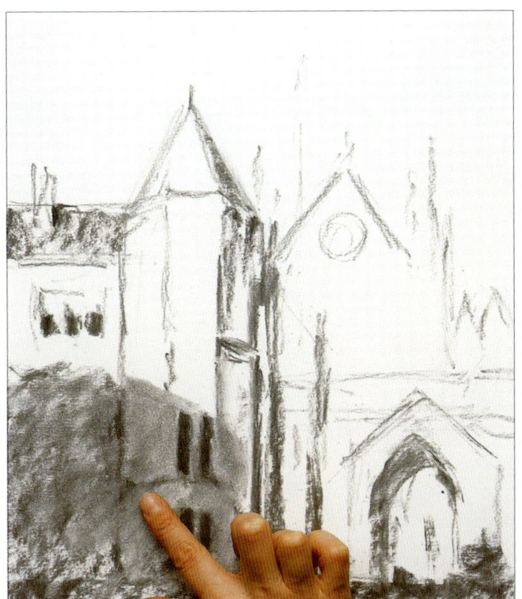

3 Using the tip of the charcoal, lightly block in the windows on the left-hand building. At this stage you are still establishing the basic shapes of the different architectural elements; refining the dark and light areas will come later. Smooth out the cast shadow with your fingertips.

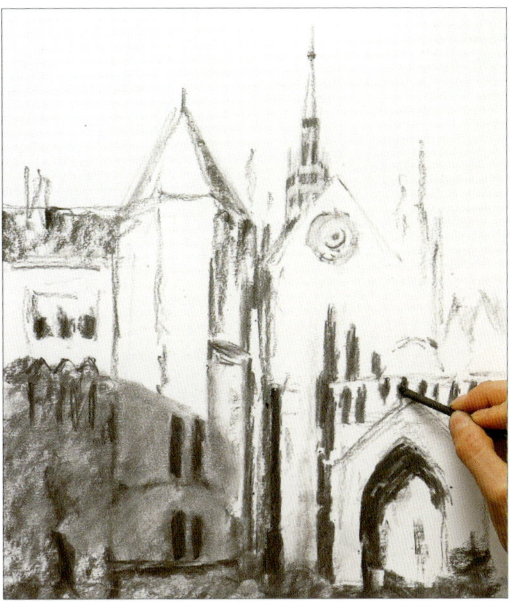

4 Begin to put more detail on the buildings, such as the windows above the arched doorway and the rose window on the front façade. The windows above the arch are among the darkest areas, so you can afford to press quite hard on the charcoal as you block in the shapes of these elements.

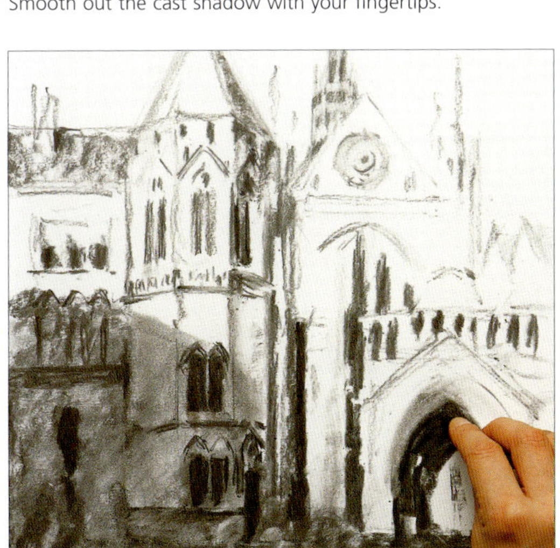

5 Continue adding dark details to the buildings. Using the side of the charcoal stick to get a broad, even coverage, darken the shadows at the base of the image and in the archway, and then gently smooth out the charcoal with your fingertips.

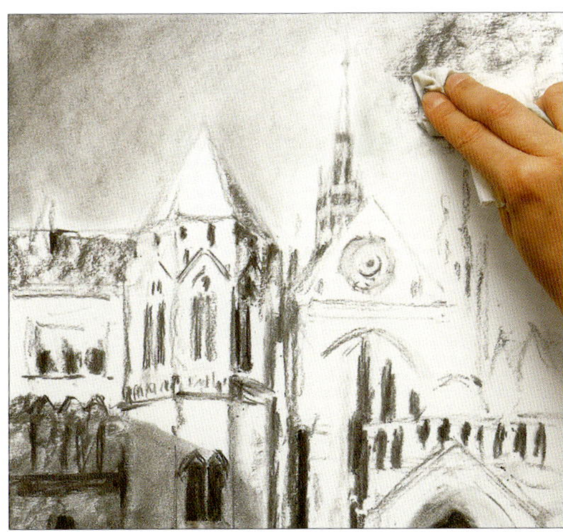

6 Lightly sweep the side of the charcoal stick over the sky area. Using a clean rag or a piece of kitchen paper and a gentle circular motion, smooth out the charcoal to give a soft tone. Note how the brightest parts of the right-hand building are beginning to stand out against the darkened sky.

▶

Assessment time
This is the time to stand back and assess the tonal values, as the drawing depends for its success on there being sufficient contrast between the very dark and the very light areas. You can't make the lightest areas any lighter, because the white of the paper is as light as you can get – so the only way to make the light areas really stand out is to darken the darks.

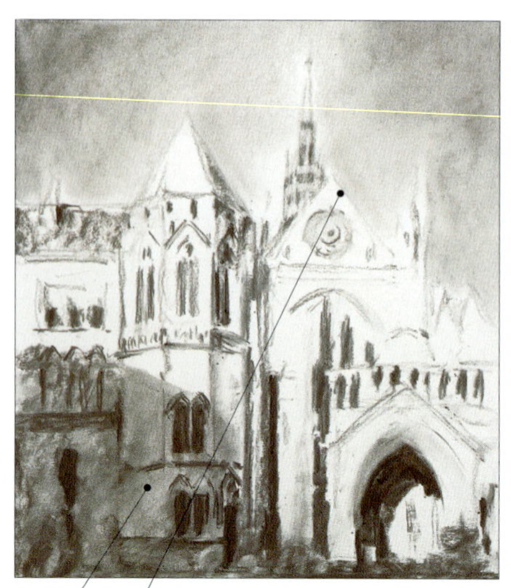

The shadows on the building look too light and hazy.

The lightest parts of the buildings are almost lost against the sky.

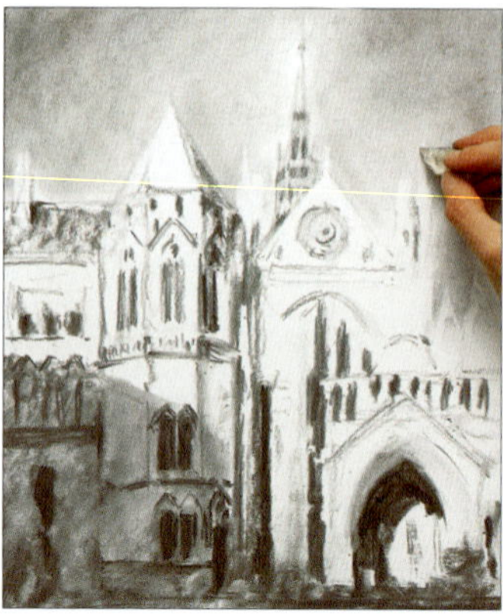

7 It's almost inevitable that you will have muddied the edges of the buildings when putting in the sky so, using a kneaded eraser, gently wipe around the edges of the buildings to give them a sharp outline. If your eraser is worn, shape a section with your fingertips to create a clean, sharp edge.

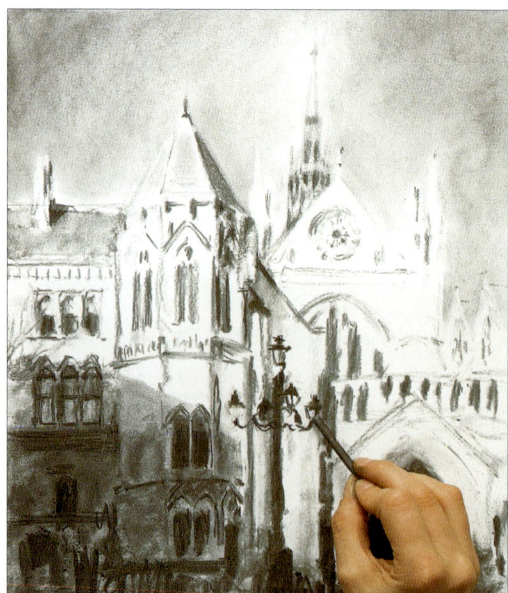

8 Adjust the tones across the image, darkening the sky slightly if necessary so that the buildings stand out more. The shadows in the bottom left need to be really dark, too. Draw the lamppost in the foreground, making it very dark so that it comes forwards in the image.

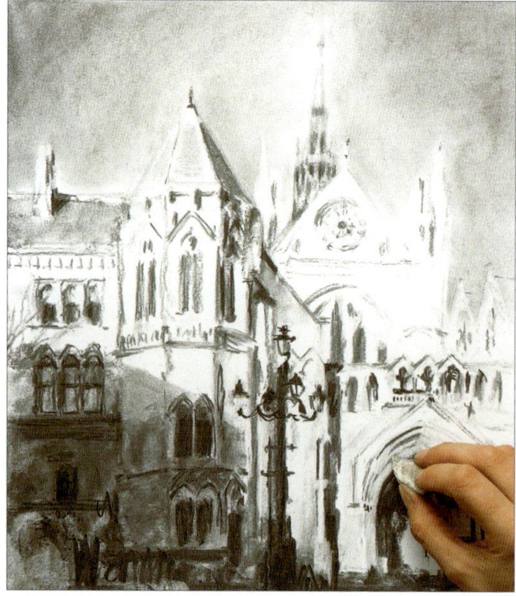

9 Continue refining the lights and darks across the whole image, and use the kneaded eraser to accentuate highlights and sharpen edges. The adjustments are minor at this stage, but you need to keep assessing the tonal values of the drawing overall.

The finished drawing

This is an atmospheric drawing that captures the fleeting effects of light and shade extremely well. The contrast between the solidity of the buildings and the smoothed-out, insubstantial-looking shadow areas is particularly effective. The artist has used the white of the paper to good effect for the brightly lit parts of the buildings; they are almost dazzlingly bright when compared with the deep shadows in the bottom left of the image. Although much of the detail is subdued because of the lighting conditions, we can see enough to know how grand and imposing the buildings are.

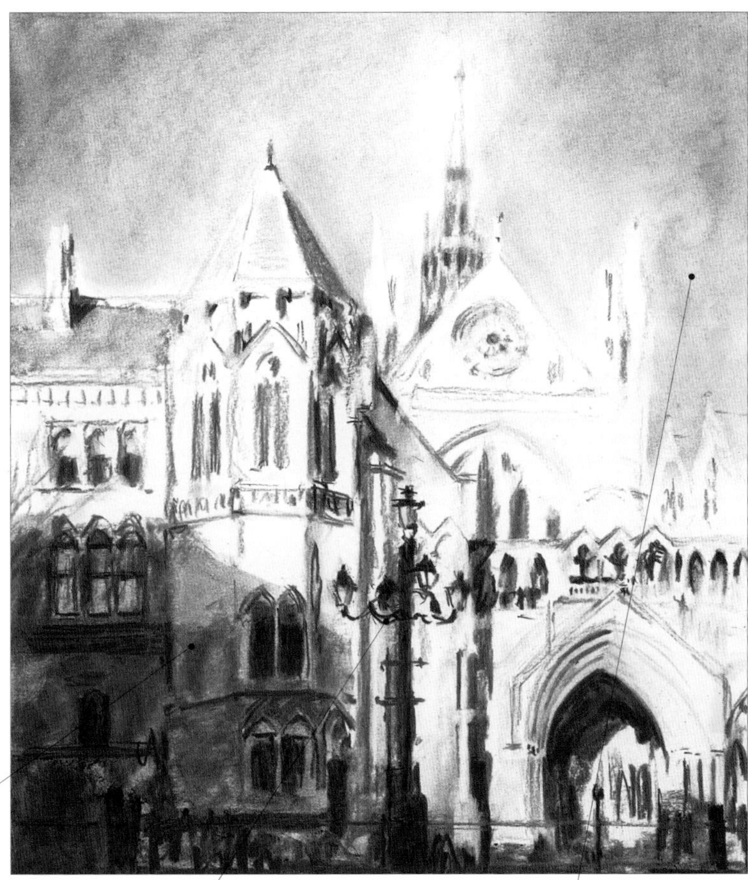

Smoothing out the shadow areas makes them appear less solid.

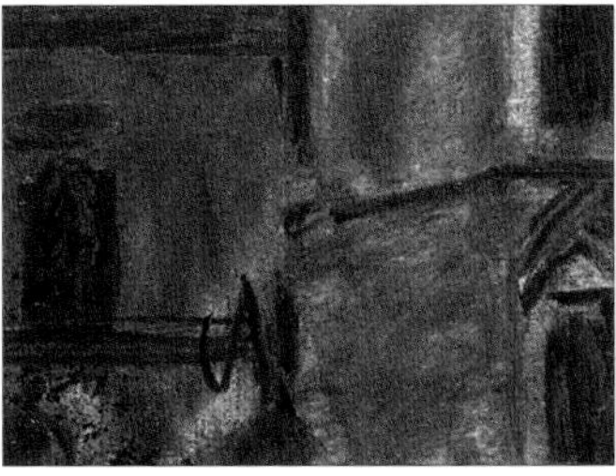

The lamppost is very dark, which brings it forwards in the image.

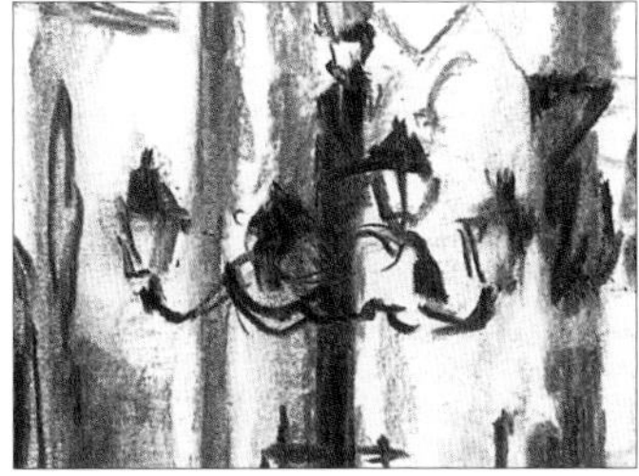

There is just enough tone in the sky to allow the brightly lit buildings to stand out.

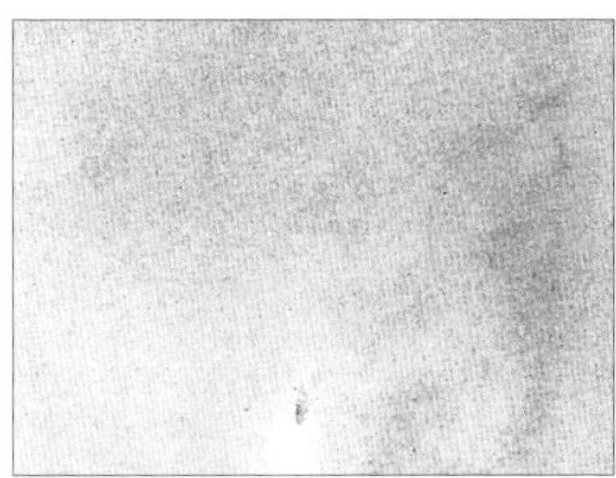

Quick sketches of animals: Cows in a field

Of all the domesticated animals that one could draw, cows are probably the most docile – and, particularly when there's a plentiful supply of fodder, the most likely to stay in the same place for a reasonable amount of time. With luck, therefore, you may have time to work up a reasonably detailed sketch before they amble off to pastures new.

When you're drawing any group, be it a group of animals, people, or objects in a still life, you need to observe the spatial relationships between the different elements very carefully. Use grid lines (real or imaginary) to work out where things should be positioned, and remember to look at the negative shapes (the spaces between different elements), both to get the shapes right and to make sure that your composition is balanced.

One of the difficulties of working on location is that the light can change dramatically in the course of a few hours, so it's a good idea to make a note of the direction from which the light is coming. In the 10-minute sketch (below), the artist drew a small arrow to remind herself of the direction and angle of the sun.

The scene

Within a large group such as this, there are a number of potential scenes to draw. Rather than drawing the whole scene, try isolating different elements, as the artist has done in the sketches shown here, to find a grouping that you like. Remember that you may have to reposition other elements, such as the fence posts, in order to get the composition to work.

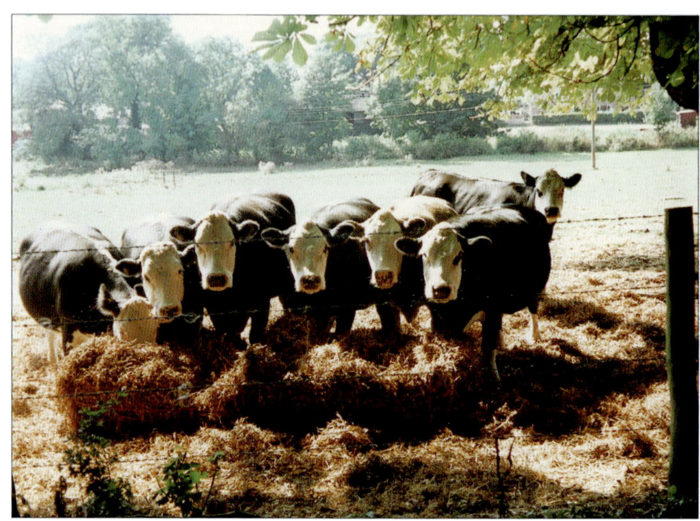

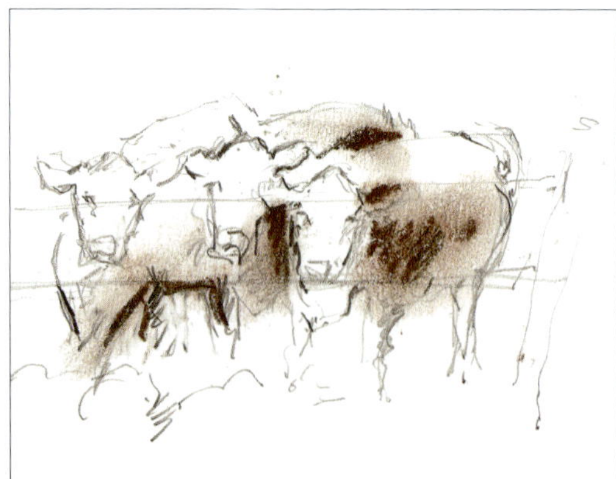

5-minute sketch: graphite and pastel pencils

Look for elements within the scene that you can use to help yourself position things. Here, the line of the barbed wire fence is a useful guide: the top wire is level with the eyes of the cow on the left while the bottom wire is level with the nose of the cow on the right. Even in just a few minutes, you can apply some colour to the basic shapes – either as a colour note to refer to later or simply to block in areas of dark tone.

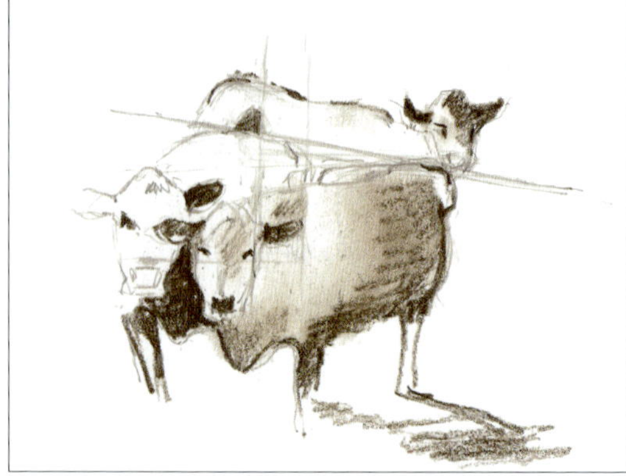

10-minute sketch: graphite and pastel pencils

When you draw a line across the rumps of the two foreground cows, you can see that it runs parallel to the back of the cow in the background. (Guidelines would be rubbed out but have been left in here to show what was done.) Also, if you look down from the tip of the right-hand cow's left ear, you will see that it's level with the animal's left foreleg: by drawing in a faint line, you can place the leg accurately.

15-minute sketch: graphite and pastel pencils

Even though the cows' bodies are a single colour, look for differences in tone that will tell us about the form of the animal. In this scene, the sun is quite high in the sky and is hitting the animals' backs. By blocking in the tops of the backs in a lighter tone than the flanks, the artist has created some modelling that conveys the rounded shape of the cows' bellies.

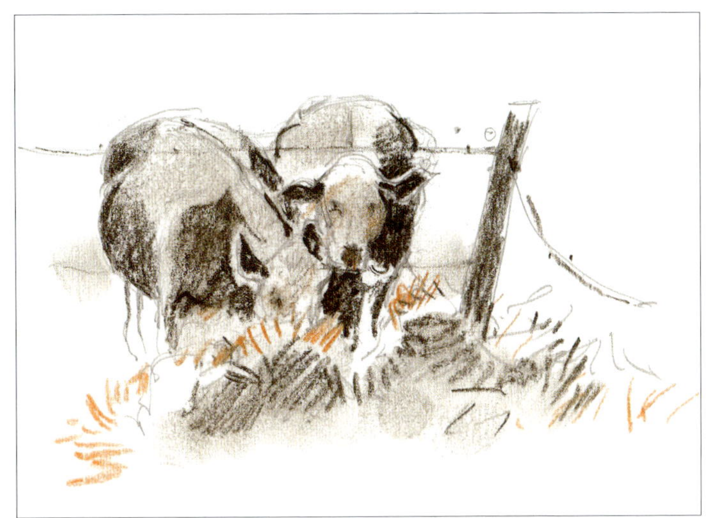

20-minute sketch: graphite and pastel pencils

Building on the previous three sketches, this sketch conveys more of the texture of the animals' coats. Vigorous scribbles of pastel pencil hint at the semi-rough texture and indicate the direction in which the hairs grow.

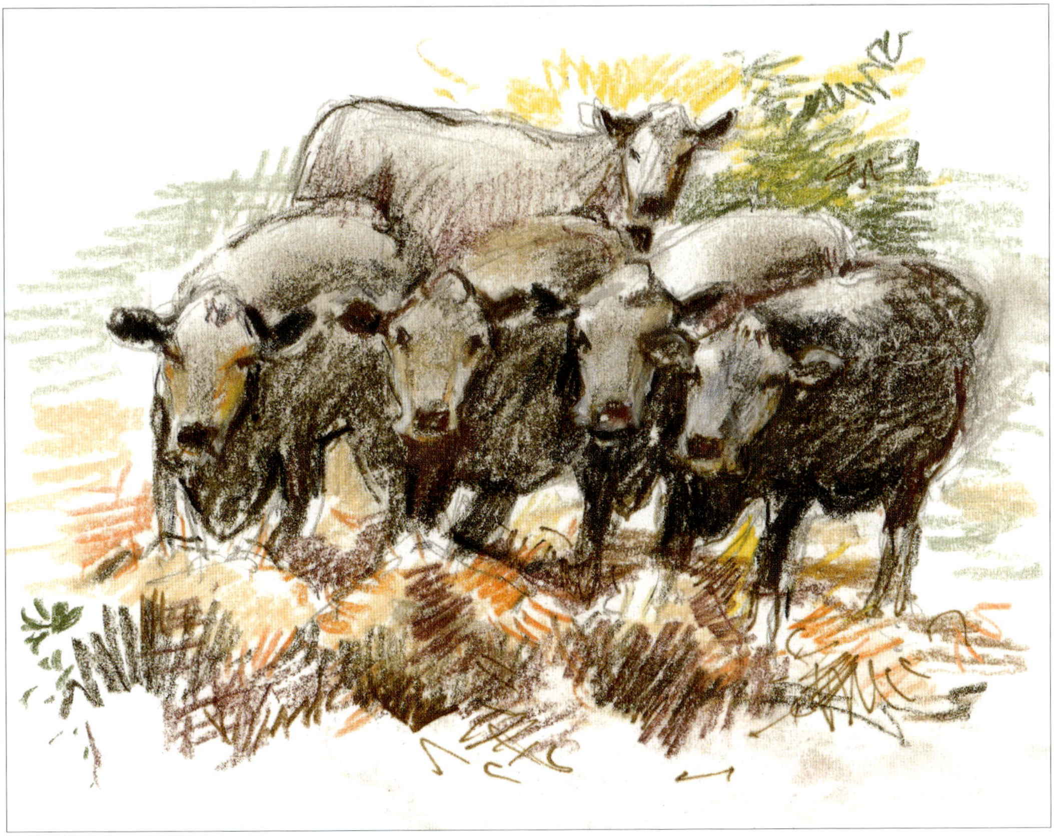

Quick sketches of animals: Leopard

Whatever your views on the morality of keeping animals in zoos, they certainly give you the opportunity to study at first hand animals that are extremely difficult to get close to in the wild. Just like domestic cats, big cats spend a lot of their time drowsing or sleeping, which is the perfect time to sketch them. Even in this situation, however, you need to convey a sense of their strength and power – so think about the skeleton underneath the fur and about where the largest muscle groups are situated. And as in any portrait, human or animal, the eyes are vital in conveying the character.

When you are drawing fur or hair, always look at the direction in which it grows and make sure your pen or pencil marks run in the same direction. Think about the quality of the fur and alter your marks accordingly: are the hairs small and tightly compacted, as on the top of the animal's head, or longer and farther apart, as around the bridge of the nose? Remember that you do not need to put in every single hair: a suggestion is enough, as the viewer's brain will fill in the missing details.

10-minute sketch: soft pastels
Soft pastels are a wonderful medium for portraying the beautiful markings and the soft texture of the fur, as you can overlay one colour on top of another and blend the marks with your fingertips to create subtle optical mixes, while also putting down stronger marks for the dark spots. If you are pushed for time, try sketching just part of the face as a practice exercise, as the artist did here. Note how including just one eye immediately brings the 'portrait' to life.

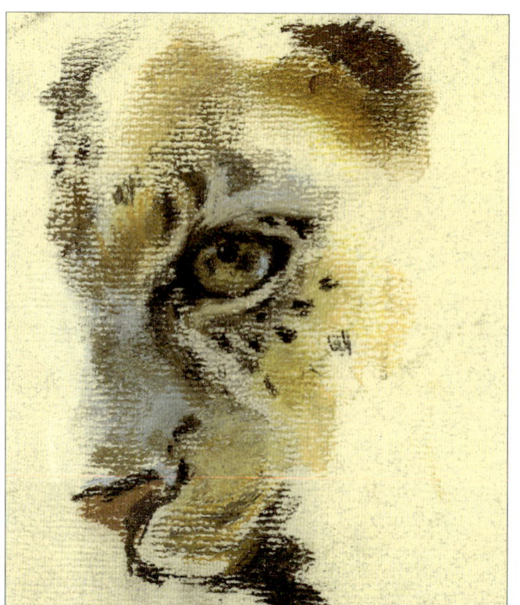

The 'relaxed pose'
This apparently relaxed pose, with the leopard draped over the branch of a tree from where it can survey its surroundings, is characteristic of this large cat – and there's no mistaking the alertness in the eyes or the power of those huge neck muscles and jaws.

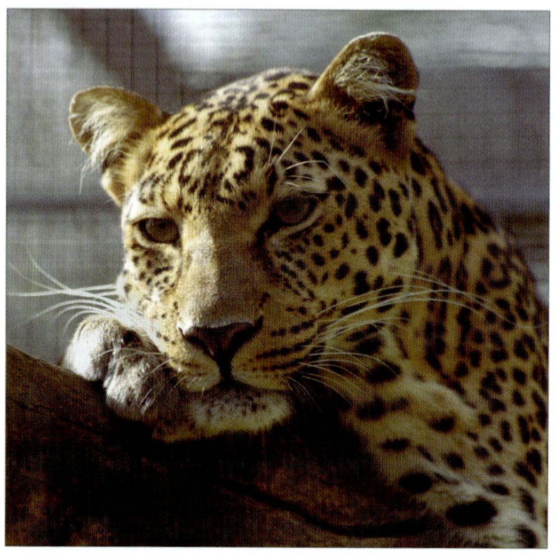

15-minute sketch: pen and ink
This is an exercise in creating the texture of fur using the harsh, linear medium of pen and ink. The sketch is incomplete, which is fine for a quick practice exercise in which you want to concentrate on just one aspect – but note how the artist has put in faint pencil guidelines marking the position and shape of the eyes. Getting the eyes right is critical in any portrait, human or animal.

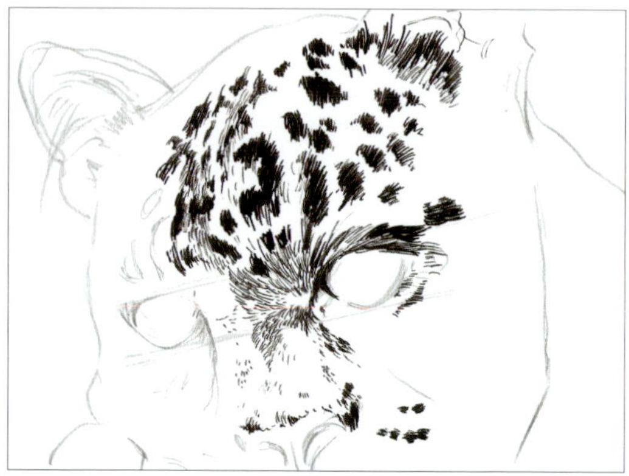

30-minute sketch: charcoal

Like soft pastels, the powdery medium of charcoal is perfect for rendering the texture of fur. Here, the artist worked on a pale but warm-toned grey pastel paper, so that she could start from a mid-tone. A brilliant white paper would have been too stark and unsympathetic. Note how she has captured the shape and form of the animal's skull through her use of shading: the left-hand side of the head and what we can see of the body are in shade, while the left eye is more deeply recessed still. As in the pastel drawing opposite, the artist has blended the charcoal marks with her finger or a torchon to create the softness of the fur, while adding dark scribbles on top for the actual markings.

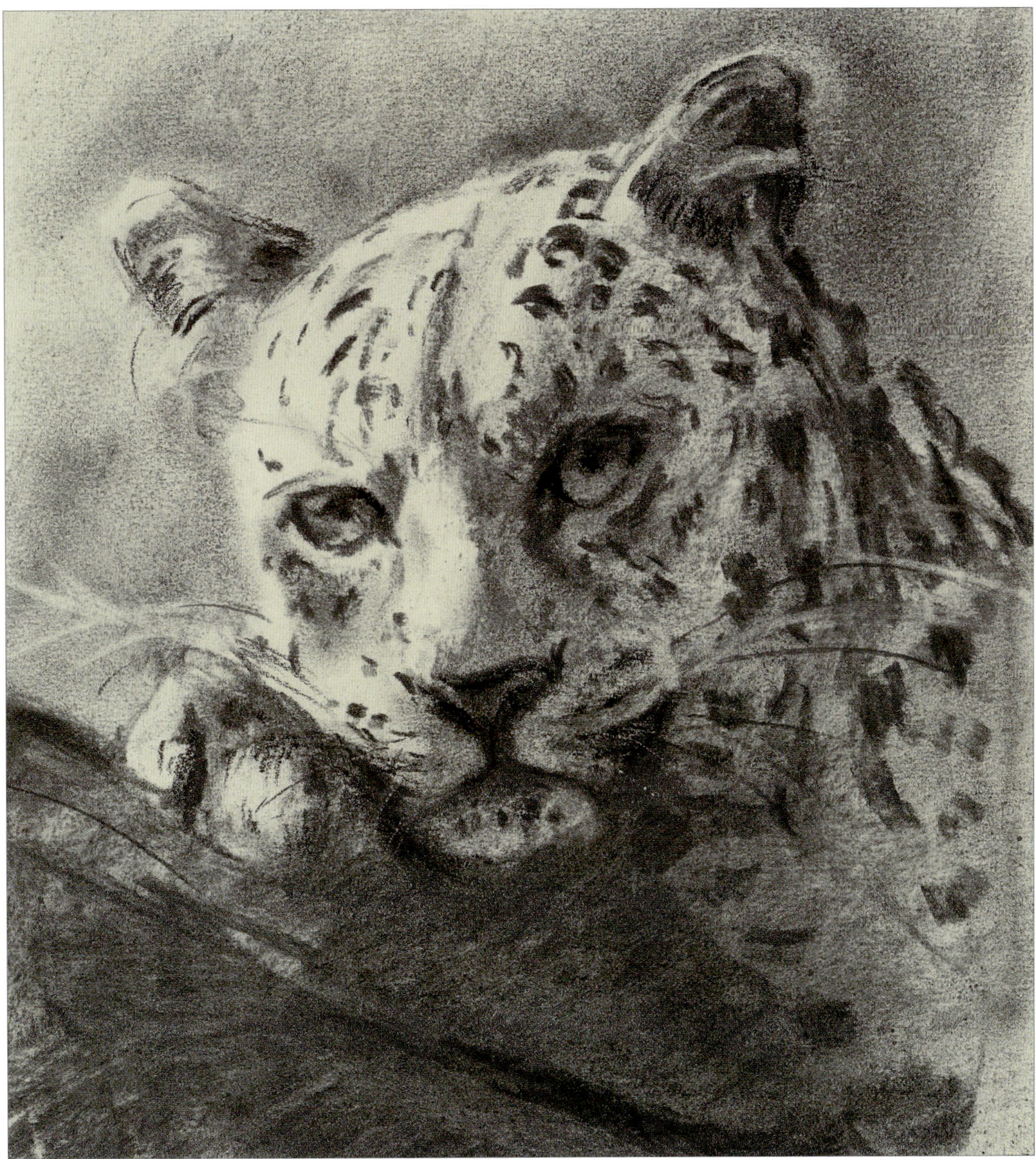

Quick sketches of animals: Short fur

This breed of dog has relatively short fur, which means that the muscles and bone structure are more obvious than in long-haired species. But the fur is also quite thick and you need to convey a sense of this in your drawing. The best way to achieve this is to build up the texture gradually, using light, short pencil or pen strokes until you have the desired effect.

As for colour and tone, even areas that, on first glance, appear to be pure white or a solid black will contain other tones. Observe this carefully: the fur follows the contours of the animal, so capturing changes in tone will help you to convey the shape of the animal, be it a stocky body, as here, or the streamlined silhouette of a greyhound.

Start from the eyes because once you have placed the eyes, it is easier to map out the rest of the head and its features. When you have completed the head, you can use it as a guide to work out how big the body is in relation to the head.

The 'pose'

This alert stance, with head and tail erect and feet planted squarely on the ground, is typical of the breed. The side-on viewpoint gives you the opportunity to study both the anatomy of the animal and the markings and texture of the fur, while the lolling red tongue adds a splash of colour to an otherwise muted range of browns and blacks.

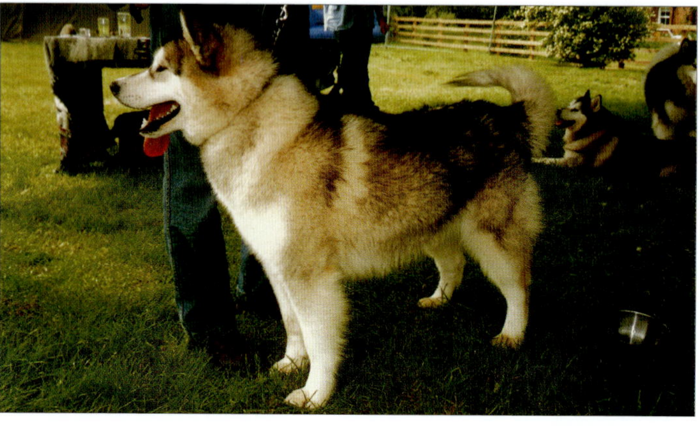

5-minute sketch: B pencil

Even in a very short space of time, you can put down the essentials of the animal's 'pose'. Look at the dog's stance: here the legs are planted four square on the ground, but in a moving animal the balance would be very different. Measure the size of the head and legs in relation to the body and roughly scribble in the darkest patches of fur to give some indication of the position of the markings.

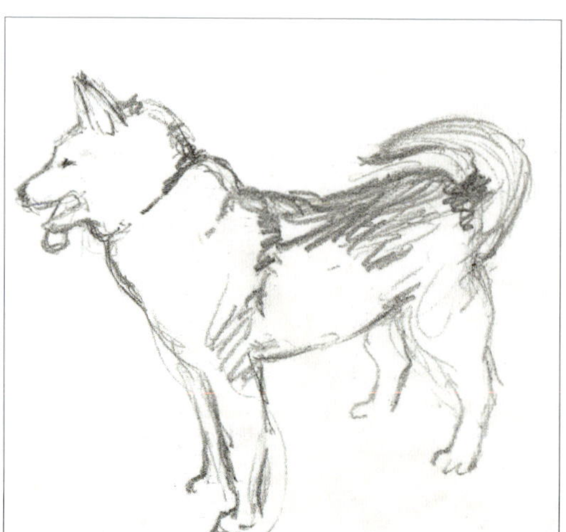

15-minute sketch: coloured pencils

Here, the artist has added more texture and detailing to the animal's fur (as well as adding colour to the dog's tongue). Note the short, jagged strokes around the edges, rather than a smooth outline, and how the pencil marks follow the direction in which the fur grows. A range of browns was used in this sketch, starting with the lightest and moving on to the darkest in order to build up the colours and tones gradually.

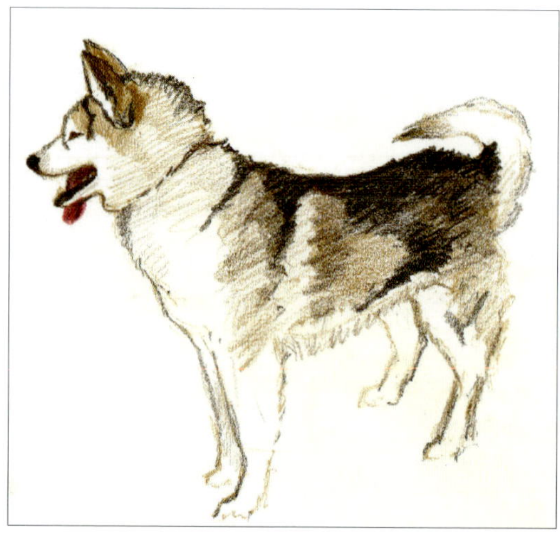

30-minute sketch: black ballpoint pen

Even with an ordinary ballpoint pen, which does not allow you to vary the width of the line that you produce, it's amazing how much variety of tone you can achieve if you take the time and trouble to build up the drawing gradually. Note how much more textured the fur is in this sketch than in the ones on the opposite page. It also has depth: light marks in the brightest areas (on the dog's shoulder, for example) indicate the shadows within the fur and tell us that the individual hairs are relatively short.

Tips: When drawing fur, make sure that your pencil or pen marks follow the direction in which the fur grows.

- Remember that fur rarely, if ever, lies completely flat: use sharp, spiky marks around the edge of the animal's body to convey the texture and length of the fur.
- Within areas that appear at first glance to be a single tone, look for subtle differences that will help you to convey the underlying shape of the animal and the direction of the light.

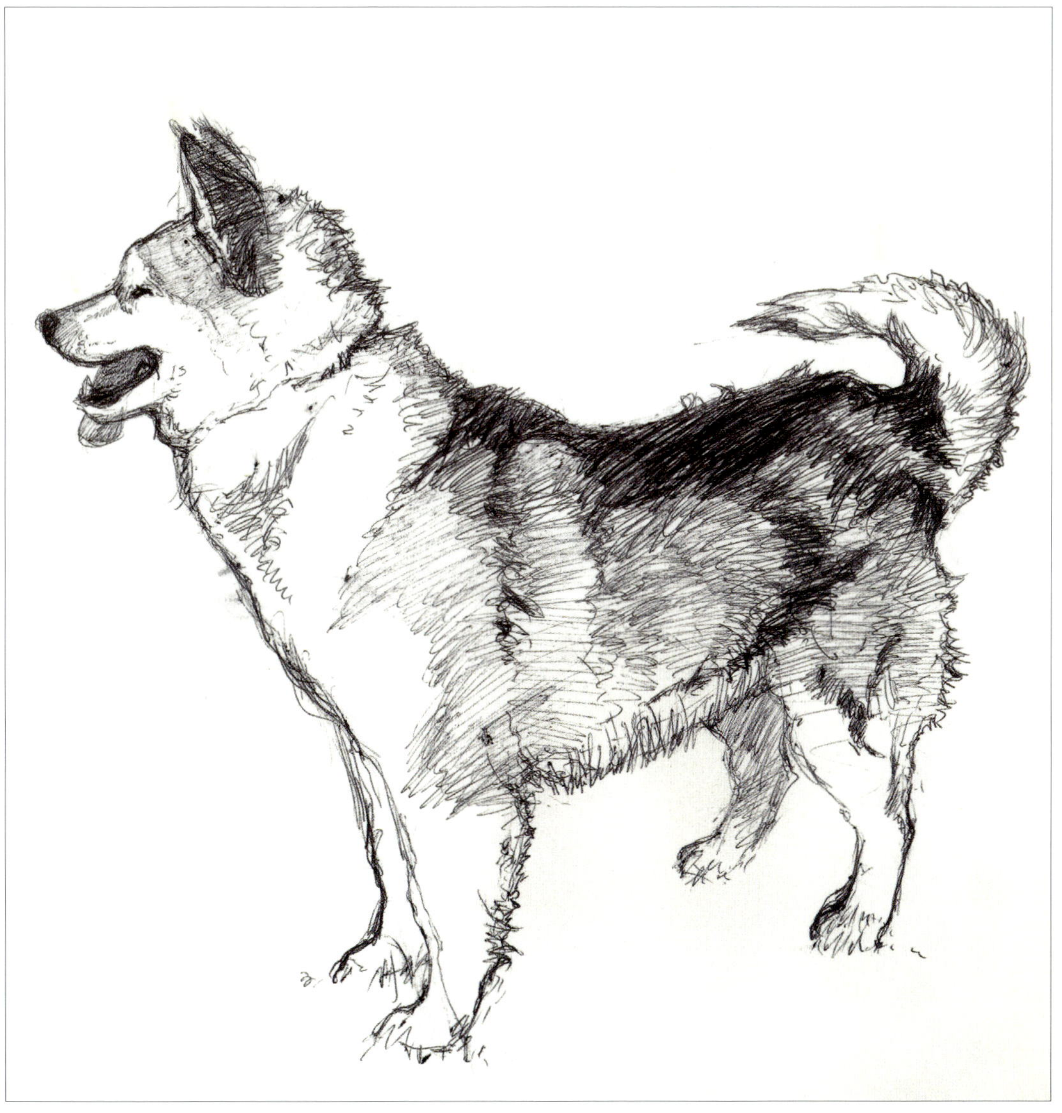

Old English Sheepdog

The Old English Sheepdog is a delightful breed and their faces (or the little that you can see underneath the animal's shaggy hair) are full of character. A textural study seems particularly appropriate for this breed, whose whole character is defined by its long, flowing fur. For a short-haired breed such as a Whippet or a Great Dane, a more linear drawing that emphasizes the muscles might be more suitable.

When you're drawing long-haired animals such as this, however, it's very easy to be seduced into concentrating on the wispy, flyaway fur and to forget about the bone structure of the animal underneath. Always start by establishing the underlying structure, and then add the decorative and textural detail on top. The way to do this is to start by drawing prominent features such as the eyes, nose, mouth and any bony protuberances near the surface. Once you've got their shape, size and position right, the rest will follow much more easily.

When drawing any kind of portrait, be it human or animal, it is a good idea to begin by positioning the facial features. Think of the eyes and nose as an inverted triangle: establish the outer point of each, as this will make it easier to get the rest of the features in the right place. If you start by drawing the outline of the head, you may find that you haven't left enough space to fit in the features.

In a monochrome drawing, you also have to think carefully about tone. Monochrome might seem ideal for an animal whose coat consists almost entirely of white and grey tones, but a very common beginner's mistake is to make the greys too light: consequently, the whole image can appear to be lacking in contrast. Reassess the tones continually, and be prepared to adjust them as you work and to darken the darks in order for the light tones to sparkle and shine through.

Materials

- *Smooth drawing paper*
- *Graphite pencils: HB, 6B*
- *Torchon*
- *Plastic eraser*

The subject

When you're drawing an animal (or a person, for that matter) always look for a characteristic pose or expression. The lolling pink tongue is typical of this breed of dog and gives the animal a quizzical, slightly comical expression that is very appealing. You can't rely on animals to stay still for long, however, so (unless you're an experienced artist and can draw quickly) you'll probably find it easiest to work from a reference photograph.

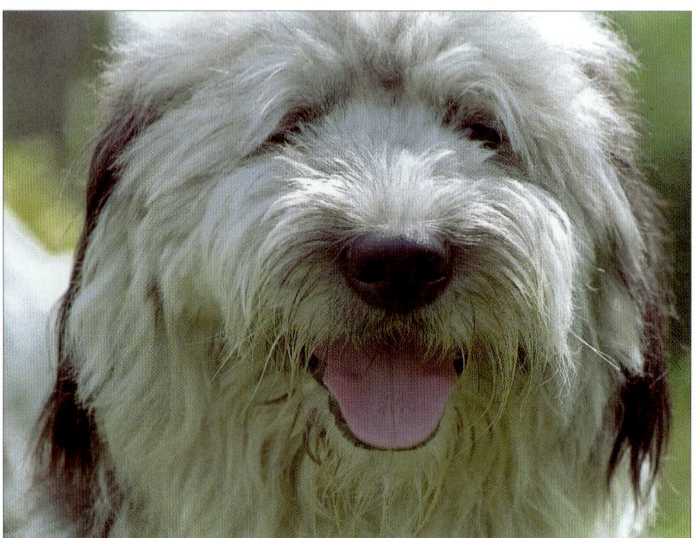

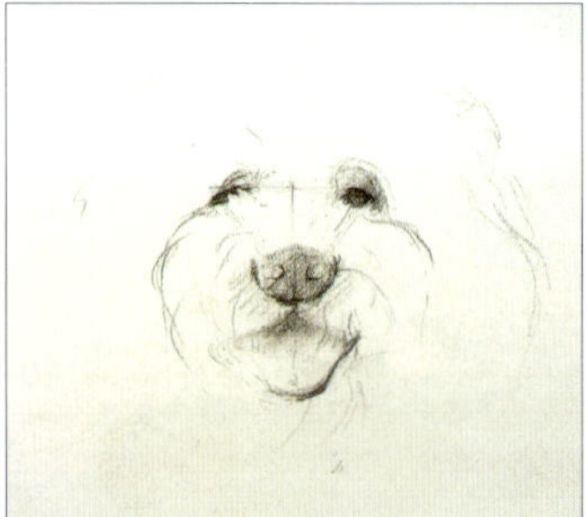

1 Using an HB pencil, lightly sketch your subject. Start with the facial features, as once you get these right, the rest will follow relatively easily. Note that the eyes and nose form an inverted triangle and begin by putting down the outer points of each as a guide. Roughly shade the eyes, nose and tongue, and indicate the direction in which the fur grows around the head.

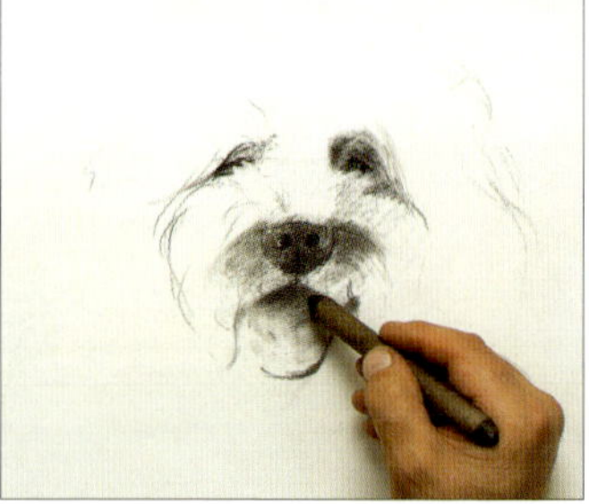

2 Using a 6B pencil, darken the nose and the sockets of the eyes. Note that, because the dog's head is turned ever so slightly to one side, one eye appears to be fractionally larger than the other. Use a torchon to blend the graphite on the nose and tongue to get a smooth, soft coverage. Also use the torchon as a drawing tool to apply some tone to the fur around the nose.

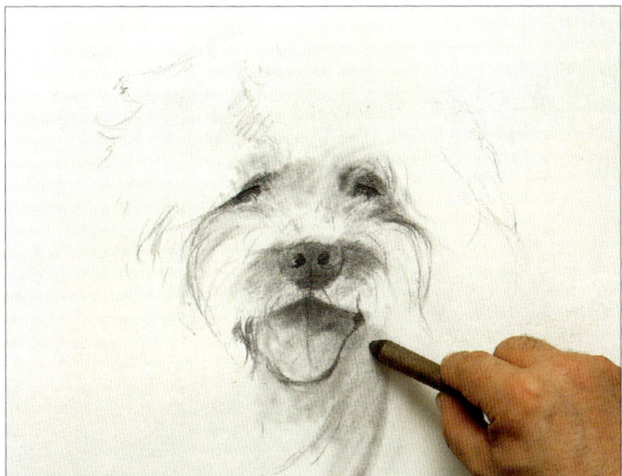

3 Again using the 6B pencil, draw the mouth (which can just be glimpsed around the tongue) more clearly. As in the previous step, use the torchon as a drawing tool to apply some tone to the fur on the dog's face and body. Your strokes should follow the direction in which the fur grows.

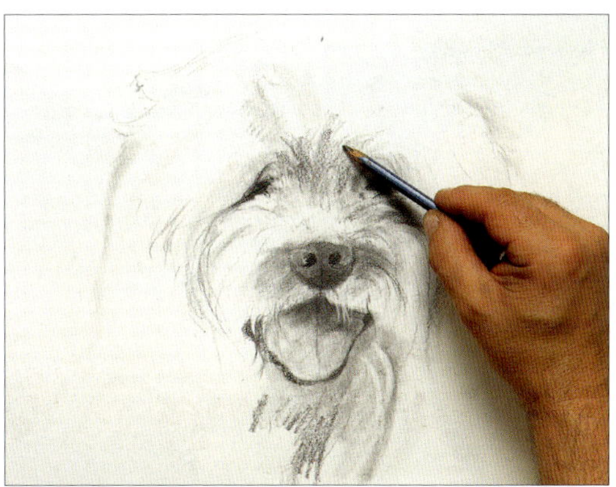

4 Loosely define the outer limits of the fur around the head to give yourself a boundary towards which to work. Using a 6B pencil, put in the darkest areas of fur on the dog's face, always making sure your pencil strokes follow the direction in which the fur grows.

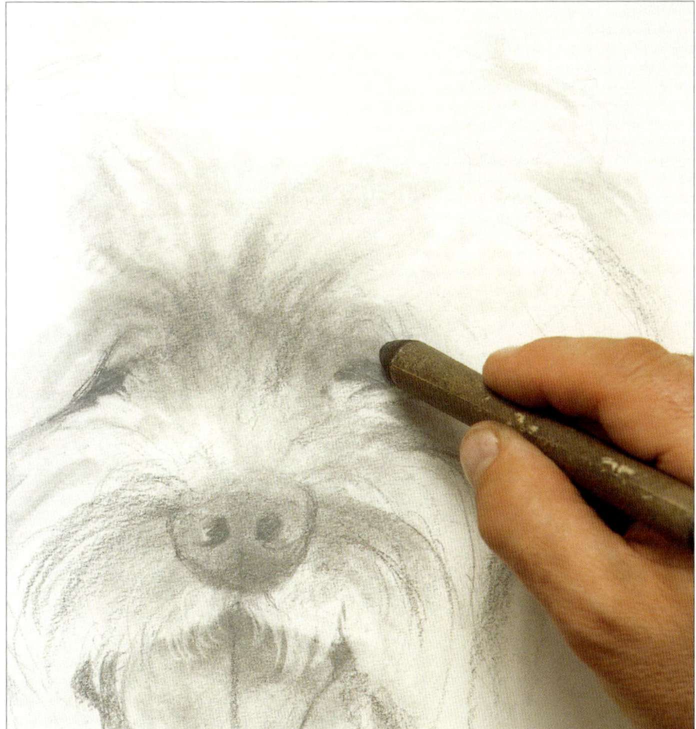

5 Blend the graphite marks with a torchon to create smooth areas of tone between the eyes and on the face.

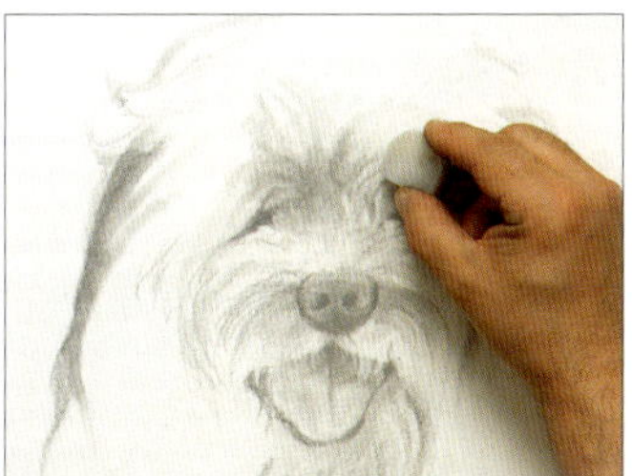

6 Using the edge of a plastic eraser, wipe off fine lines of graphite to create the white hairs around the eyes. (It is easier to wipe off white details than to apply dark tones around them.)

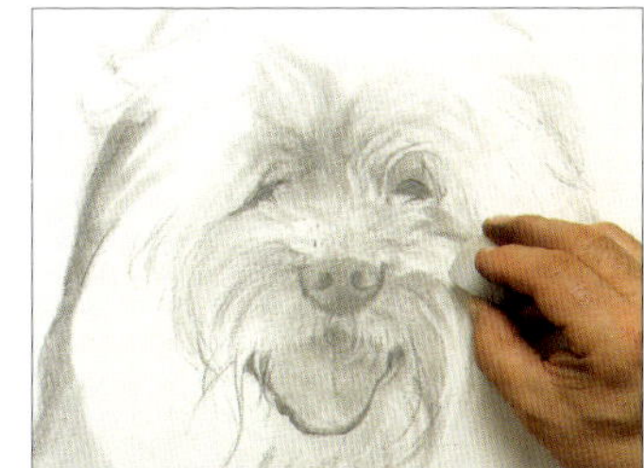

7 Using an HB pencil, draw more mid-toned hairs around the mouth. Wipe the eraser across the dog's face above the mouth to create the lighter-toned fur in this part of the face.

Assessment time

The sheepdog's eyes, nose and mouth areas are prominent points that establish the structure of the dog's skull; the surrounding shaggy fur, by comparison, can be regarded as little more than decorative detail. For the rest of the drawing, concentrate on looking at the tones within the fur. Your shading in this area will convey the colour of the fur and also, because of the way the fur falls, imply the bony structure of the skull underneath.

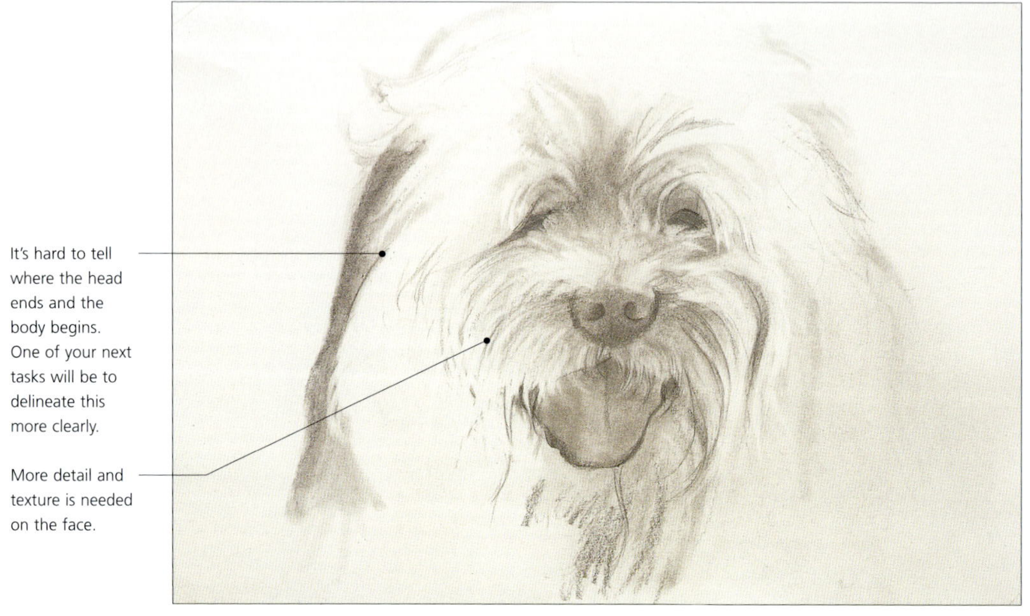

It's hard to tell where the head ends and the body begins. One of your next tasks will be to delineate this more clearly.

More detail and texture is needed on the face.

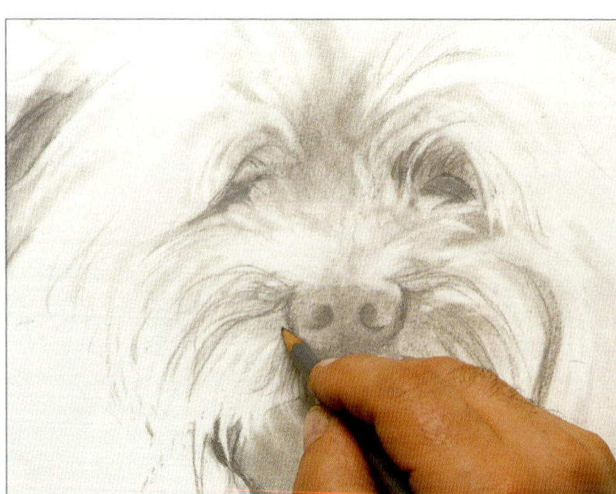

8 Now you can complete the textural detail of the fur. Using an HB pencil with a fine point, draw more individual wispy hairs – particularly around the nose and eyes. Beware of applying too much detail to the body; this would detract from the head, which is the most important part of the drawing.

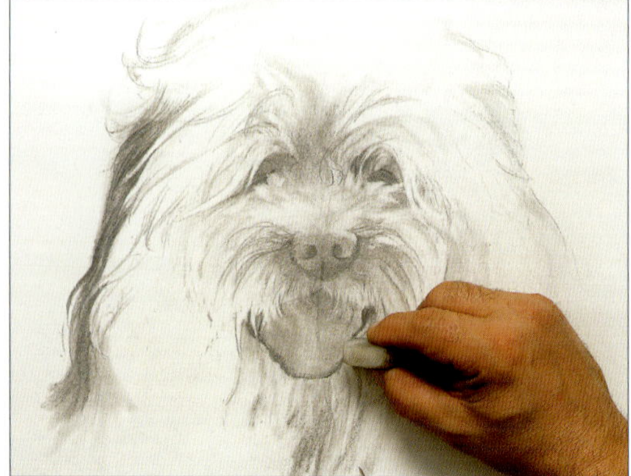

9 Using a 6B pencil, reinforce the dark line on the left-hand side to try to make it clearer where the head ends. Assess the drawing as a whole and readjust tones by blending graphite with a torchon or lifting out tone with an eraser wherever you judge it to be necessary.

The finished drawing

This is a charming study of a well-loved family pet, and an interesting exercise in texture. The texture of the fur is created through a combination of softly blended pencil marks and more linear strokes for individual hairs on the face. The fact that the dog is looking directly at us immediately engages us in the portrait.

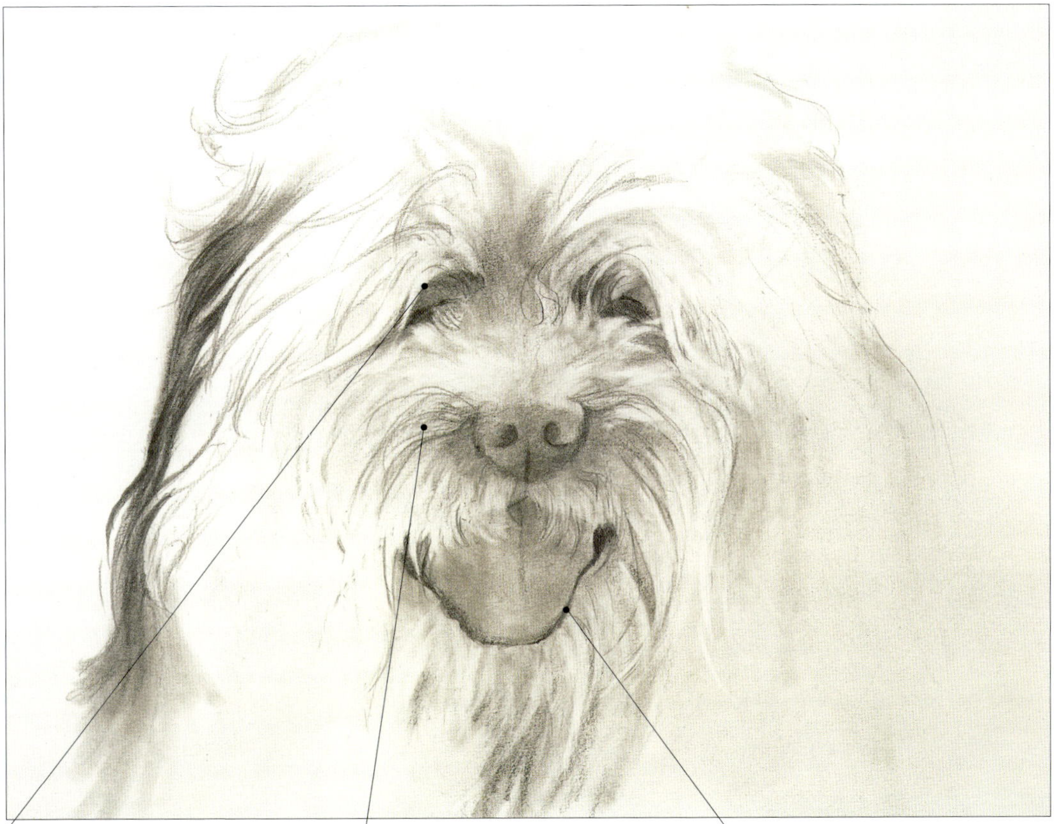

The eye socket has depth; it appears as a rounded form rather than a flat circle on the surface of the face.

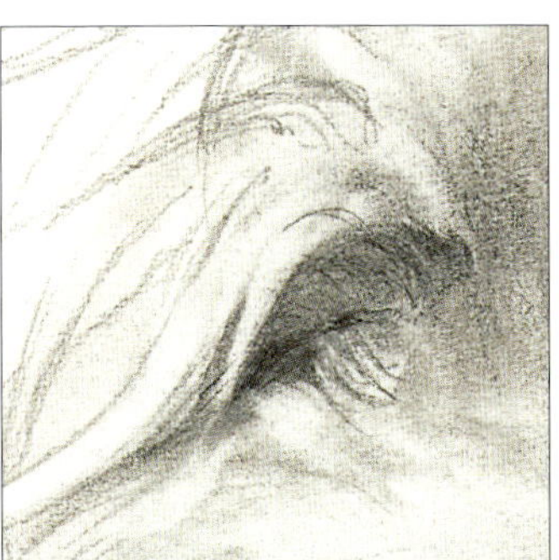

The texture of the fur is created through a combination of marks blended with a torchon and individual linear strokes.

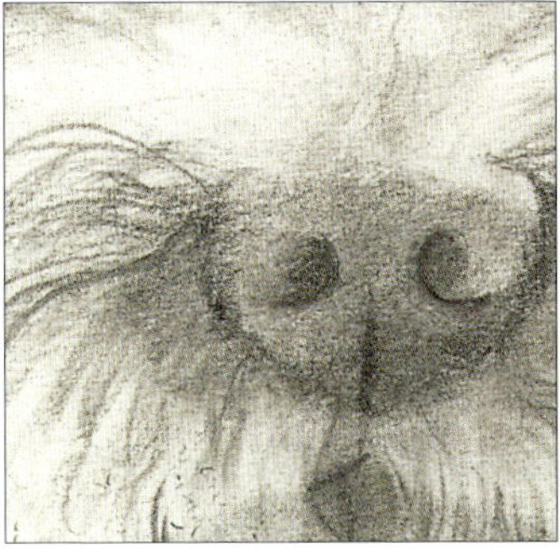

The dark line of the lower lip helps to make the lolling tongue stand out more clearly in the drawing.

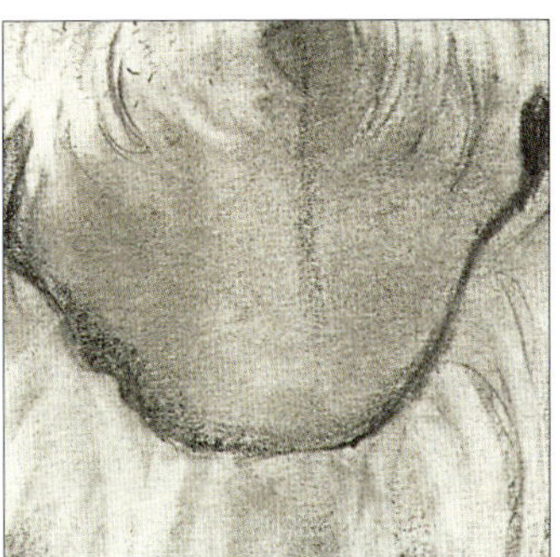

Short-eared Owl

Feathers and fur make wonderful subjects for a drawing. You don't even need to draw the whole animal: close-up details concentrating on the wonderful colours and patterns can make very striking semi-abstract works of art.

This drawing is made using coloured pencils, the fine tips of which enable you to capture the subtle coloration to perfection. Although on first glance it looks as if the bird is predominantly white and brown, there are many different colours within the dark areas – blue-greys and blacks as well as a range of browns. Paying attention to these differences will give your drawing depth and form, as they reveal the shaded areas within the feathers. Beware of using pure black for the very darkest areas, however: it's a very harsh, unforgiving colour and a combination of indigo and a very dark brown will give you a softer, more sympathetic result.

Take plenty of time to build up the texture. Get it right and you'll almost feel as if you could ruffle the feathers with your fingertips. Use short pencil strokes that follow the direction in which the feathers grow. The highlights are not very obvious in the reference photo, so you need to work out where they would appear: as any light source is likely to be above the subject, they are normally in the upper part of the eye. Note also that the owl's head is turned slightly to one side, so we can see more of one eye than the other.

The most important thing in a drawing like this is to keep referring to your reference photo to ascertain the lights and darks. Stand back from your drawing at regular intervals and assess it as a whole. It's easy to get caught up in detail and concentrate on the tip of your pencil rather than on the overall effect.

Materials

- *Smooth, heavy drawing paper*
- *2B pencil*
- *Coloured pencils: primrose yellow, olive green, gold or mid-yellow, gunmetal or charcoal grey, blue-grey, indigo, chocolate brown, sepia,*
- *Tracing paper*
- *Pencil sharpener*
- *Kneaded eraser*

The subject

You'd have to be very lucky to get so close to such a magnificent bird in the wild. This owl was photographed at an owl sanctuary. Whatever you think about zoos and wildlife parks, they do provide an opportunity to admire and draw specimens that might otherwise be difficult to see.

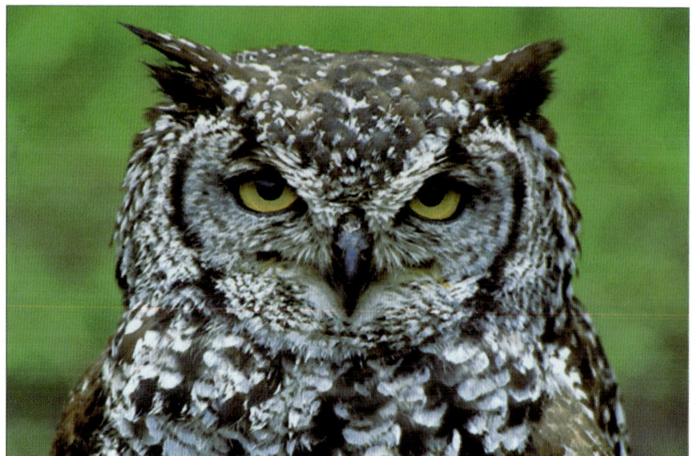

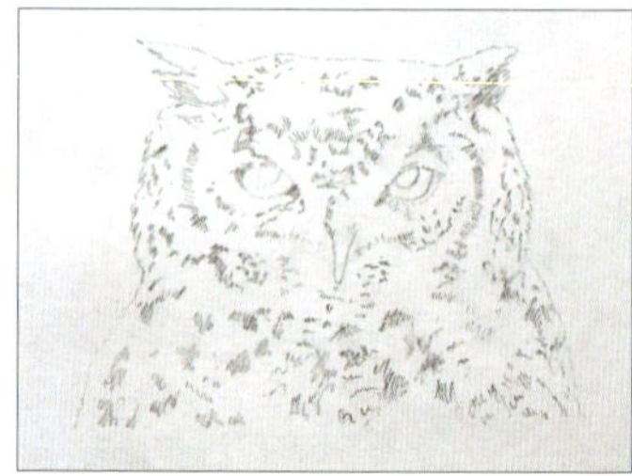

1 Using a 2B pencil, lightly sketch the subject. Map out the blocks of dark-coloured feathers across the bird's head and body with light, gentle strokes.

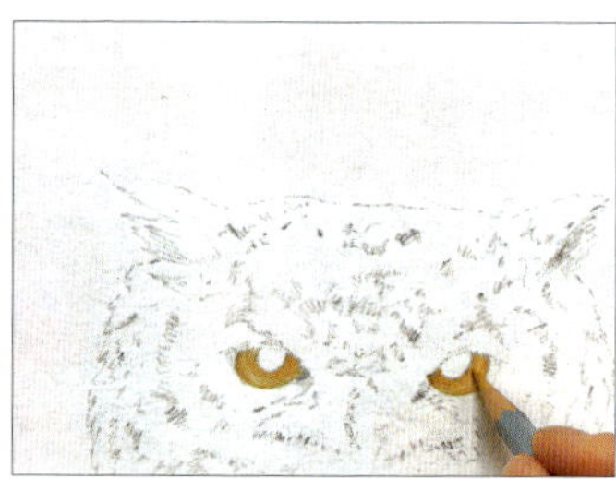

2 Using a primrose yellow pencil, colour in the iris of the eye and put tiny strokes of olive green over the darkest part (the part immediately below the pupil) to darken the yellow. Go over the iris again with gold or a mid-yellow pencil.

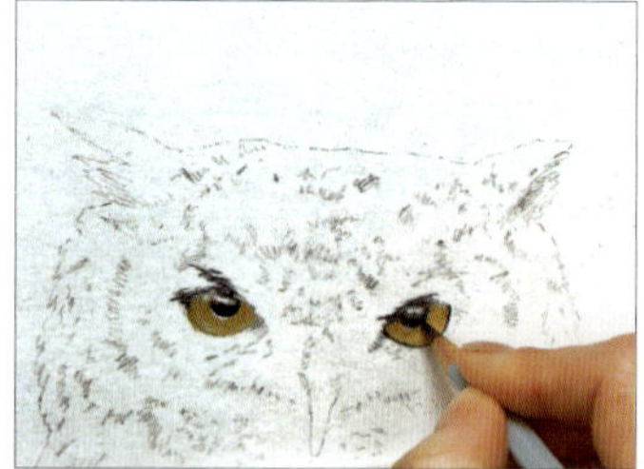

3 Colour in the pupils of the eyes, using a gunmetal or charcoal grey pencil and leaving a highlight in each pupil untouched. Go over the pupil again with a blue-grey pencil. Using an indigo pencil, put down the first indication of the feathers that grow around the eyes.

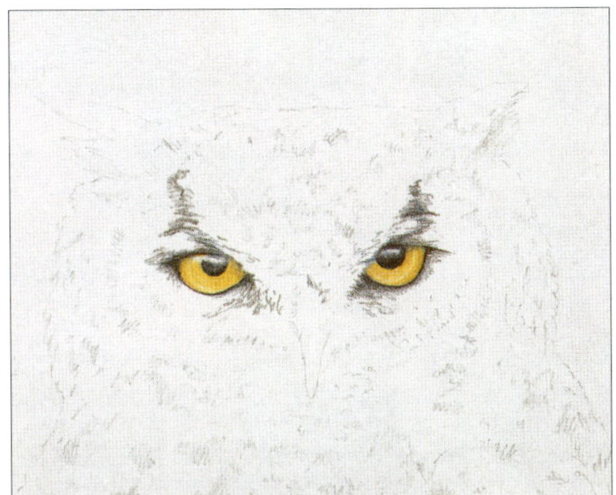

4 Go over the pupil again with indigo and the iris with mid-yellow. Note how these successive layers build up, creating a smooth, almost glossy surface colour. Outline the eyes with an indigo pencil and put in some of the feather detail around the eyes with the same colour.

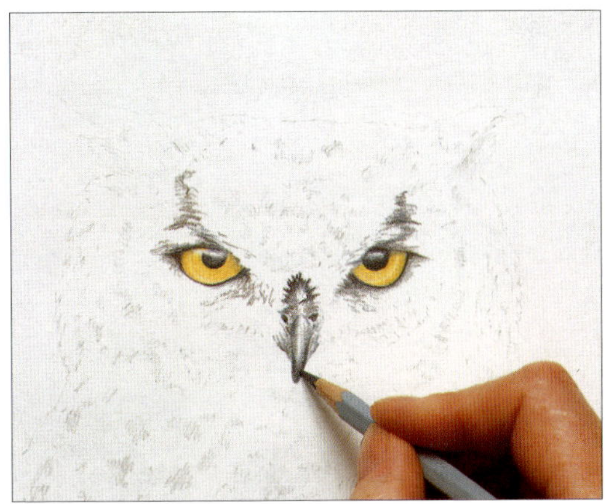

5 Put in the beak with a blue-grey pencil, leaving the bright highlight untouched. Go over the darkest part with a chocolate brown pencil. Use tiny pencil strokes for the feathers that overlap the top of the beak. Take care not to make the beak too dark or it will overpower the whole image.

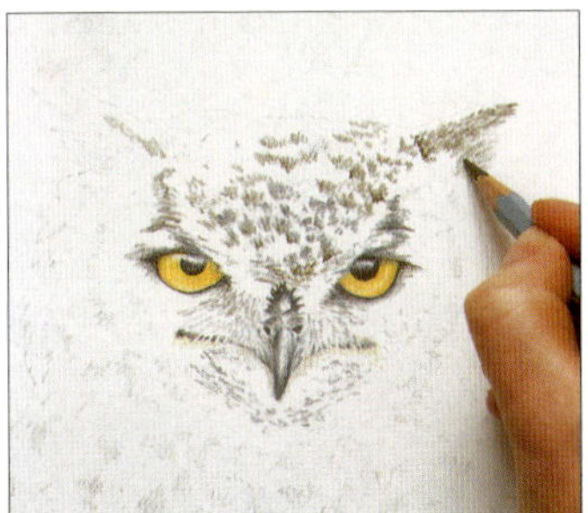

6 Using a sepia pencil, put in the dark feathers on the owl's face and head. Use little, jagged scribbling strokes that follow the direction in which the feathers grow so that you begin to get some realistic-looking texture into the feathers. Look at the relative length of the feathers, too: those around the ears are longer, so make long pencil strokes, using the side of the pencil rather than the tip.

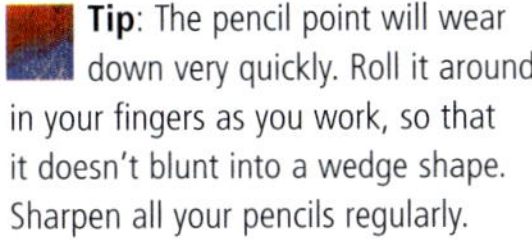

Tip: The pencil point will wear down very quickly. Roll it around in your fingers as you work, so that it doesn't blunt into a wedge shape. Sharpen all your pencils regularly.

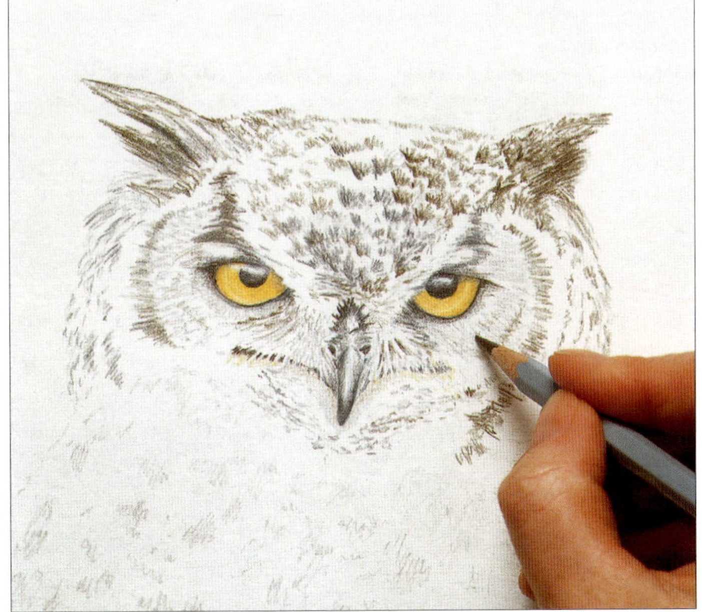

7 At this point you need to define the outline of the bird without creating a rigid line. Use short, wispy, horizontal strokes around the edge of the face and vertical strokes for the body behind, as the difference in direction helps to define the form, and leave some gaps around the outline for the white feathers. Continue mapping out the dark areas of feathers on the face, using blue-grey and sepia pencils as before.

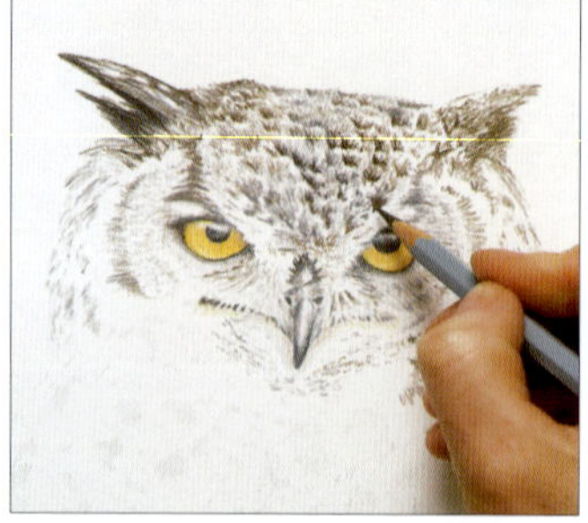

8 Continue working around the top of the head, using jagged, scribbling strokes as in Step 6 and alternating between charcoal grey and sepia pencils as appropriate. For the very darkest feathers, use chocolate brown. This immediately gives the feathers more depth and we can begin to see the different layers.

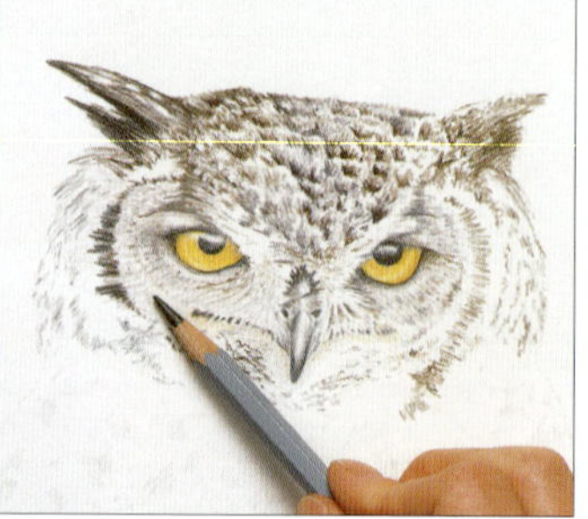

9 Darken the side of the face with sharp, jagged strokes of indigo, so that it stands out more clearly from the body. Some areas within the face are still completely empty of pencil marks. Using the side of the pencil, make light strokes for the feathers in this area. Although the feathers are largely white, you need to introduce some tones of pale grey here as there are shadows within them.

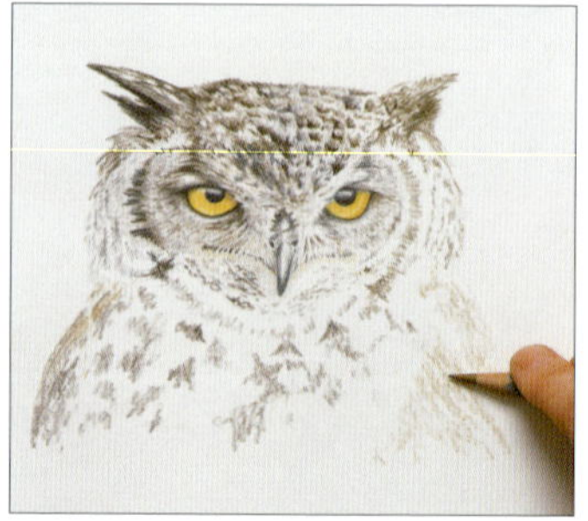

10 Build up the colours on the owl's face using the same pencils as before – indigo and chocolate brown for the very darkest areas, and blue-grey and charcoal grey elsewhere. The area around the eyes is particularly important: build up the dark feathers here so that you see the eyeball as a rounded form rather than as a flat circle on the surface of the face. Begin mapping out the darkest blocks of feathers on the body, using the side of a chocolate brown pencil. The feathers are bigger here than on the face, so you can be less precise about their placement and shape.

Assessment time

The drawing is progressing well, but more detailing is needed on the side of the head and the body. Work slowly and deliberately: it is amazing how much texture you can create by building up the layers of pencil work.

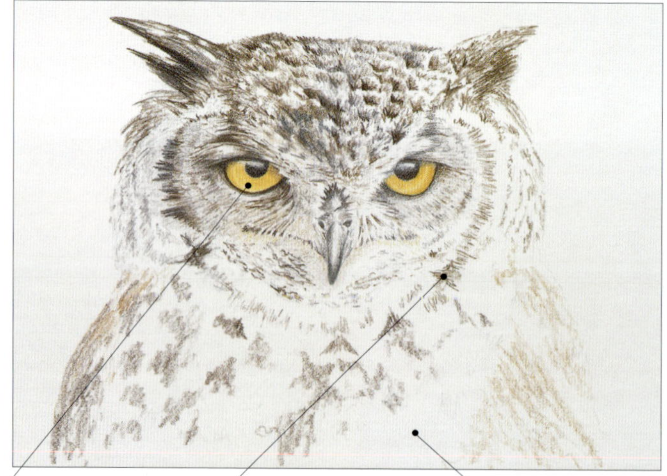

Our attention is drawn to the eyes, but the vivid yellow needs to be still more vibrant.

The face is in danger of merging into the body and needs to stand out more clearly.

Only the main blocks of feathers have been put in on the body. More detail and texture are required.

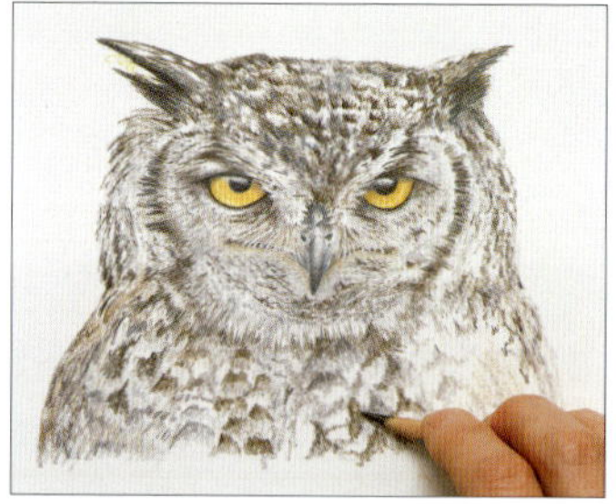

11 Go over the irises again with another layer of primrose yellow and olive green to intensify the colour and create a smooth, glossy surface that contrasts well with the soft ruffles of the feathers. Reinforce the dark feathers on the owl's face with indigo and chocolate brown. Repeat the process on the body, using the side of the pencil rather than the tip to create broader marks. (The clumps of feathers are larger here, so you can be less precise with your marks.)

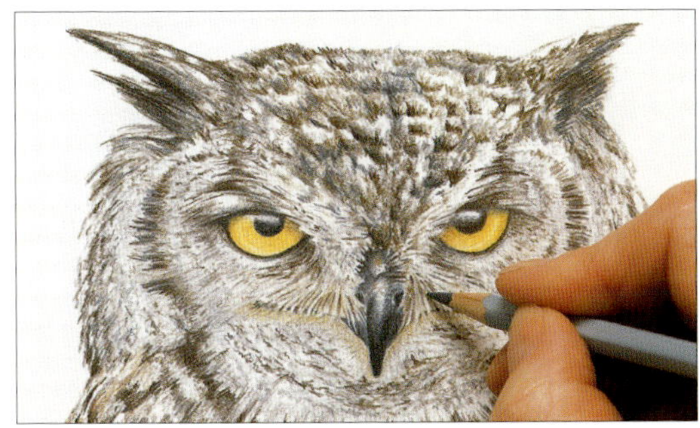

12 Darken the beak with indigo, so that it stands out from the feathers, taking care not to obliterate the highlights. Use long, smooth pencil strokes to create the hard, bony texture. Reassess the feathers on the face, and add more definition if necessary.

The finished drawing

This drawing is a perfect demonstration of how successive layers of coloured pencil marks can create detailed textures and depth of colour. The key is patience: if you rush a drawing like this, you will not achieve such subtlety and detailing. Contrasts of texture – the hard, shiny beak versus the soft, ruffled feathers and the shiny, moist eyes – are vital.

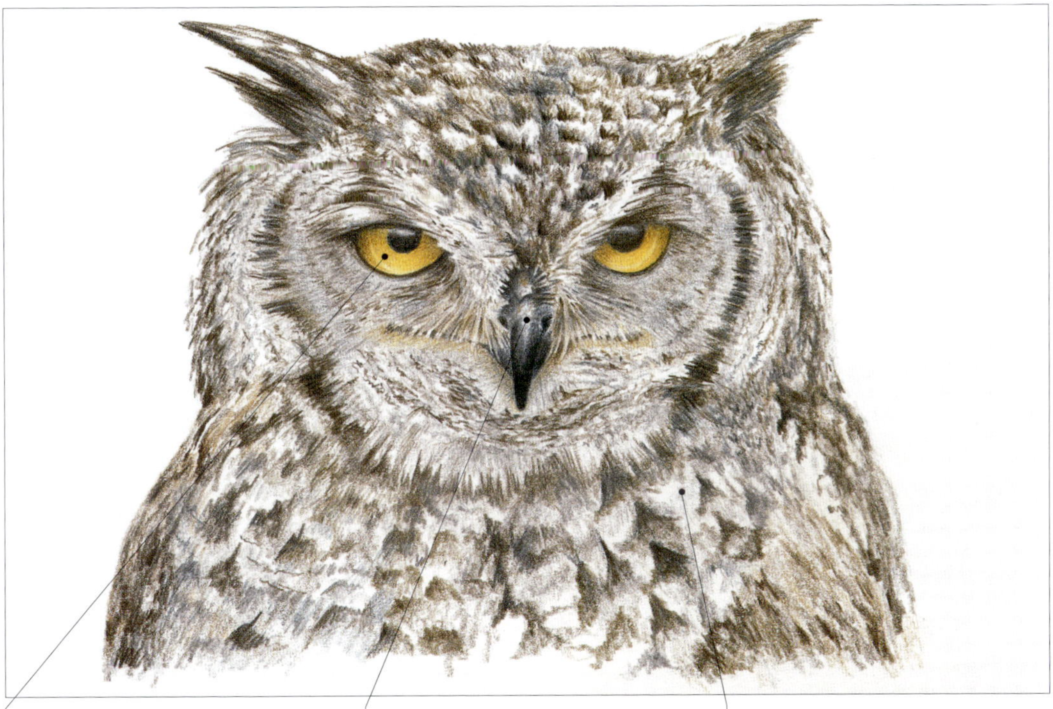

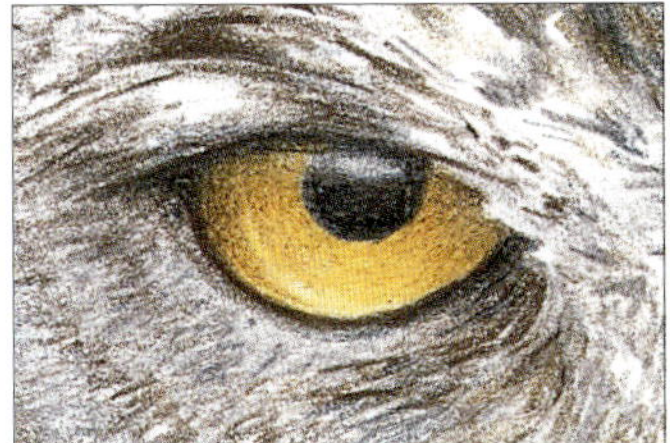

Note the intensity of colour created by gradually building up successive layers of different colours.

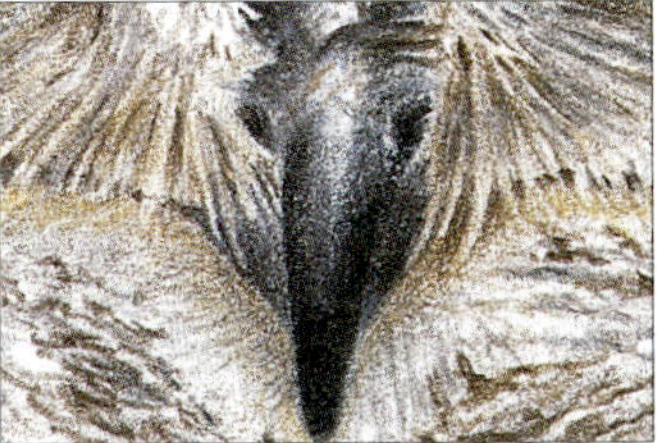

The highlight on the beak helps to indicate its curving shape, hard, bony texture and slightly shiny surface.

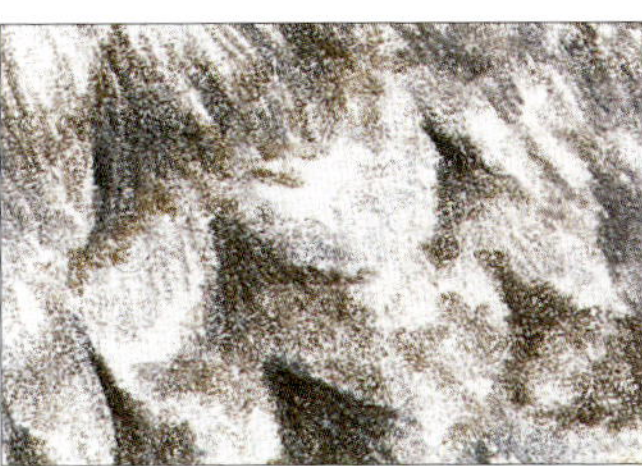

The face stands out well from the body, thanks to the jagged pencil marks used for the feathers in this area.

Tabby cat

Lovers of cats invariably find them fascinating subjects for their drawings and paintings, and the fact that they are often content to sit quietly near you as you work makes them unusually appealing animal models. Even so, it is generally easier to work from photographs than from life, interpreting the pictures in order to create your own compositions and colours. For this drawing a photograph was used as the reference for the cat, but the background and foreground were devised to contrast effectively with the vivid markings and texture of its fur.

Materials
- *Watercolour paper*
- *Water-soluble pencils: black, Naples yellow, mid-green, red, ultramarine, raw umber, raw sienna, mid-grey*
- *Gouache paint: white*
- *Paintbrush*

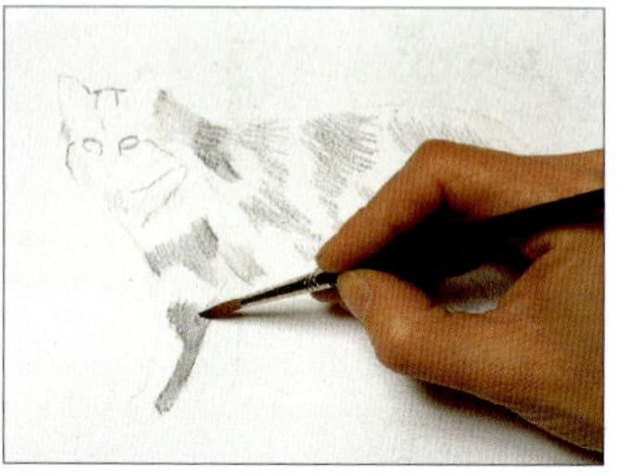

1 Begin by laying some light pencil lines to establish the form and then wash over them. This releases some of the colour and softens the pencil marks without disturbing them.

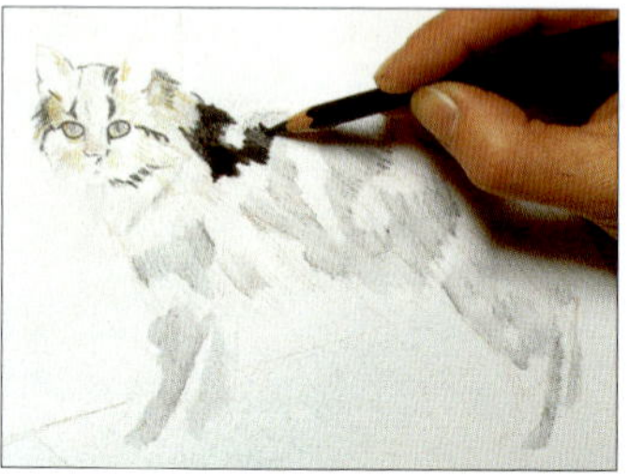

2 A different effect is created by dipping the water-soluble pencil into water before applying it. As you can see, this produces a more solid area of colour.

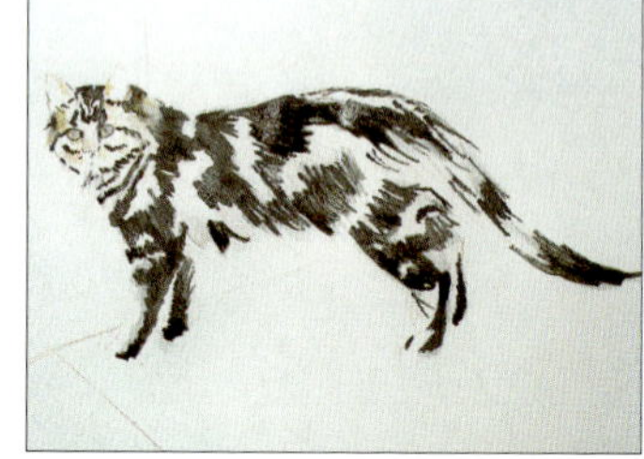

3 With dry coloured pencils, dark colours have to be deepened gradually, but water-soluble pencils make it easier to establish the dark tones at an early stage.

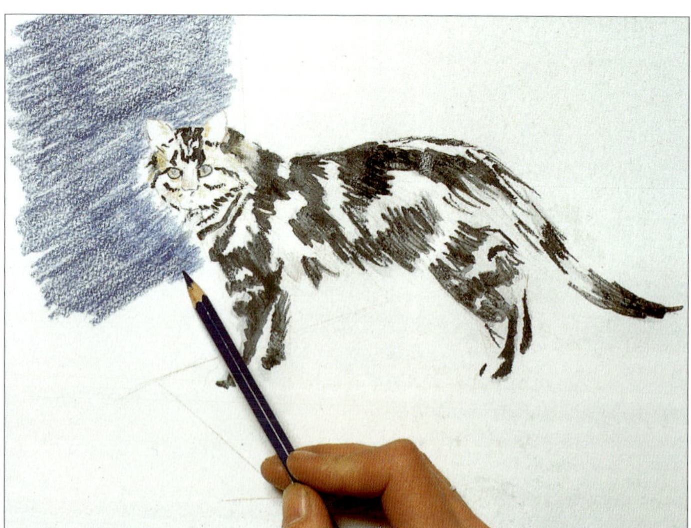

4 With the dark and light tones of the cat established, you can now consider the background. A solid area of colour on the left is needed to provide a balance for the animal, plus a contrast of textures, so use the pencil dry here.

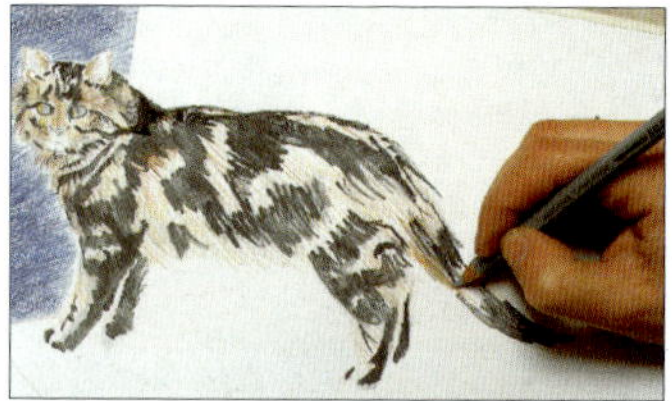

5 Introduce warm reddish browns, using the pencils dry, to suggest the texture of the fur. A wet grey pencil creates a soft effect on the tail.

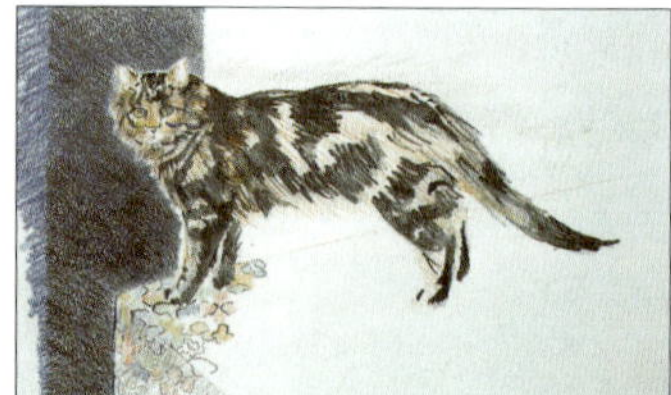

6 Complete the dark background with black crosshatched over the blue. A patterned cloth (which was not in the photograph) has been invented here to create some interest in the foreground of the picture.

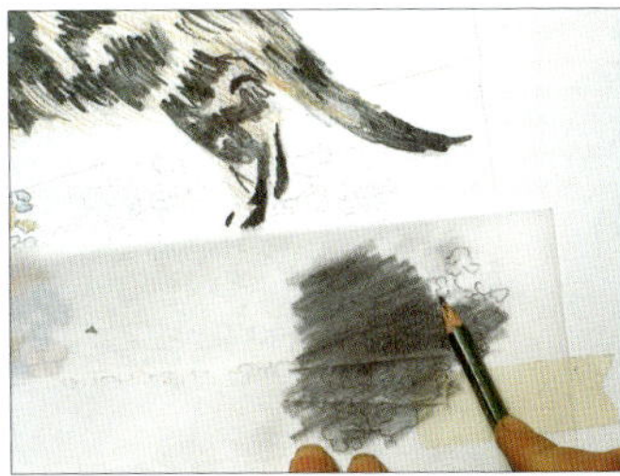

7 Building up a complex pattern is a slow process and it is easy to make mistakes; to guard against this, you can make a tracing from a completed area of the pattern and transfer the lines to the working surface.

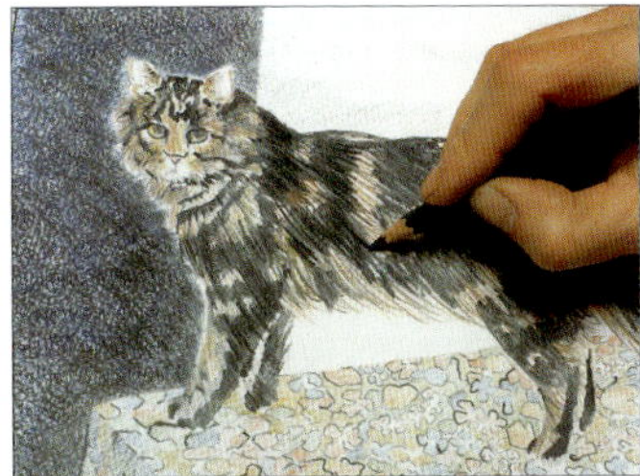

8 With the background and patterned cloth finished, return to the focal point of the picture, and build up the detail and texture of the cat's fur with a combination of wet-and-dry applications of pencil.

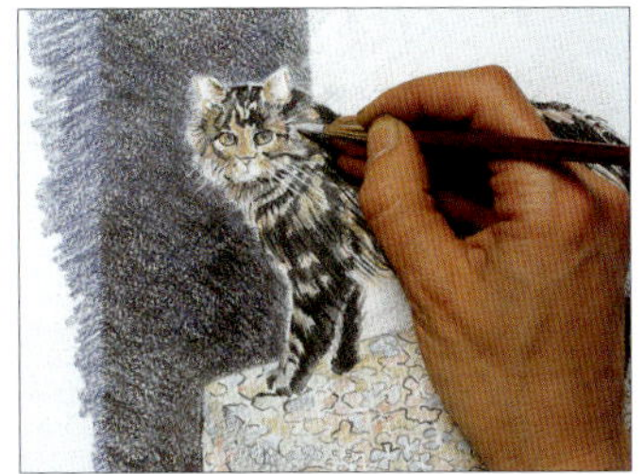

9 Finally, use white gouache paint and a fine brush to touch in the whiskers. Coloured pencils are not opaque, so clear whites cannot be produced by drawing over dark colours with white pencil. Gouache has the required opacity for this last detail.

The finished drawing

In any drawing, the composition is as important as the representation of the subject; here careful planning has balanced the elongated shape of the cat's body with the patterned cloth on the table, and placed the dark rectangle in the background behind the animal's head, to focus attention on the face.

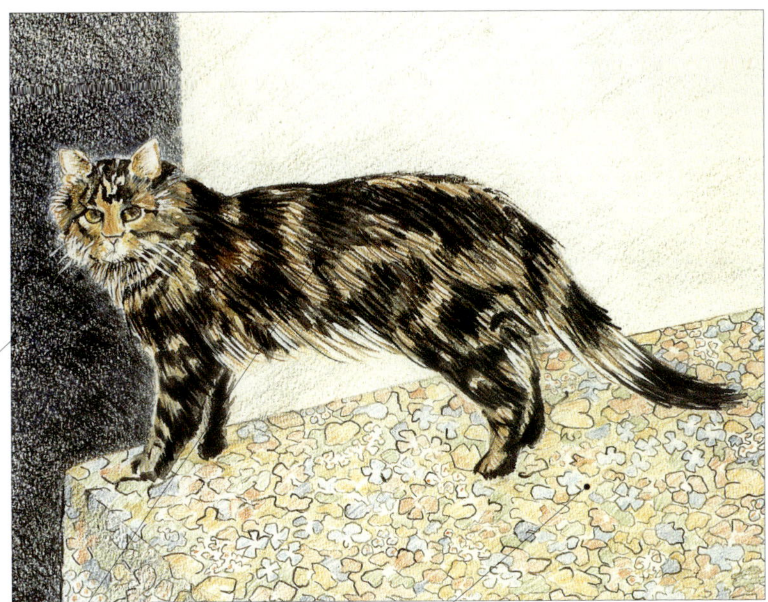

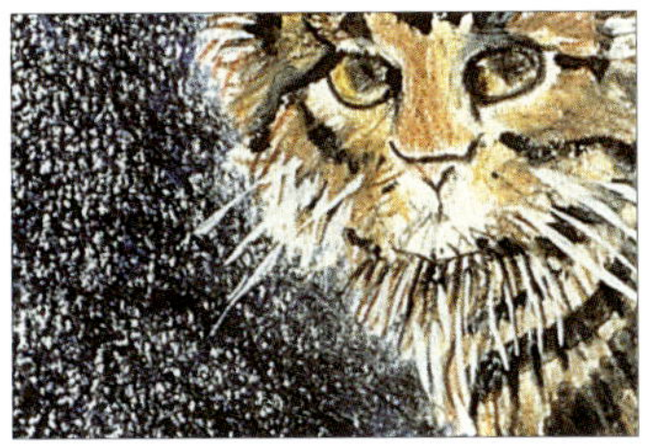

The finest detailing is reserved for the face, emphasizing it as the focal point

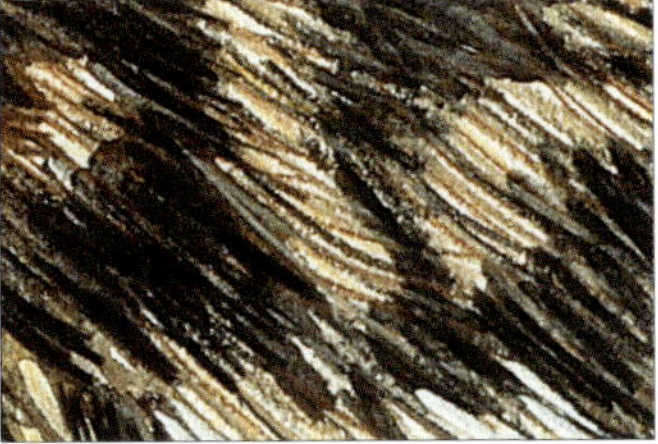

A combination of tone and line conveys the texture and thickness of the fur.

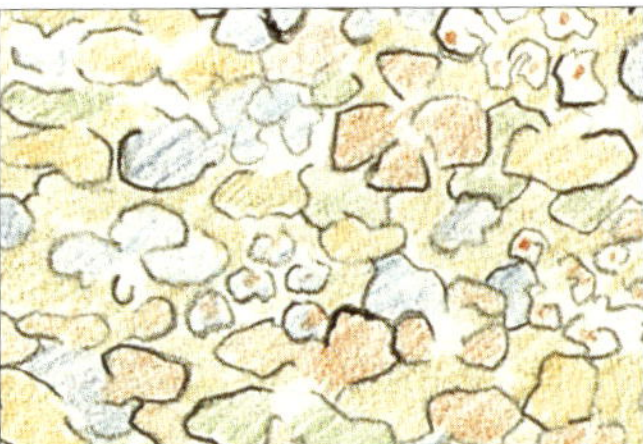

A real piece of fabric was used as reference for the invented foreground pattern.

Swimming fishes

This colourful project combines elements of both drawing and painting. In the early stages, water-soluble pencils are used in a linear fashion as drawing tools; later, they are washed over with clean water, so that the pigment spreads on the support just like watercolour paint. You can also apply dry water-soluble pencil over wet washes to deepen the colour, either by using the pencils directly or by brushing water over the tip of the pencil so that the brush picks up a little pigment. The benefit of this technique is that you don't create hard edges.

As you'll be applying water to the paper, use watercolour paper, which is absorbent enough not to tear under the weight of the water. When you start applying water, work on one part of the image at a time – first the fishes, then the water – so that the colours don't all blur together.

One of the most attractive aspects of this project is the sense of movement in the water. Observe how the ripples catch the light as this will help you to convey the movement. Use curved pencil strokes that follow the ripples and look at how the water breaks around the fishes.

Materials

- *Watercolour paper*
- *Water-soluble pencils: orange, bright yellow, dark blue, olive green, yellow ochre, warm brown, reddish brown, red, blue-green*
- *Masking fluid and old dip pen*
- *Paintbrush*
- *Kitchen paper*

The subject

The colouring on the fishes is spectacular – strong, saturated reds, yellows and oranges. Note how the shape of the fishes is slightly distorted by the ripples in the water. The ripples themselves catch the light from above, which creates a glorious sense of movement and shimmering light.

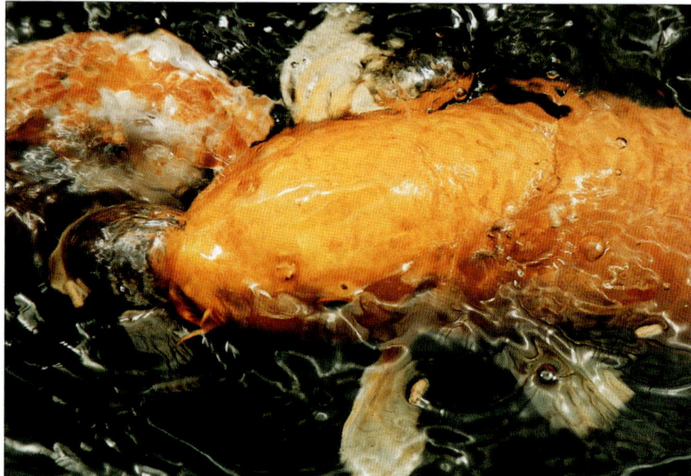

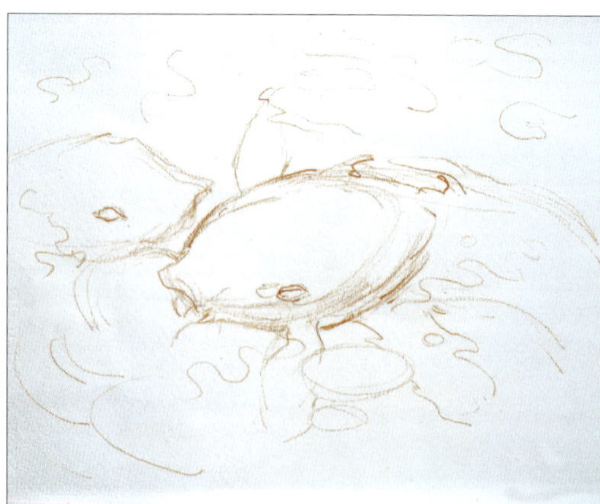

1 Using an orange water-soluble pencil, lightly sketch the outline of the fishes, making a clear distinction between the top of the larger fish's head, which is just poking out of the water, and the rest of the body. Draw a few of the largest ripples in the water, too.

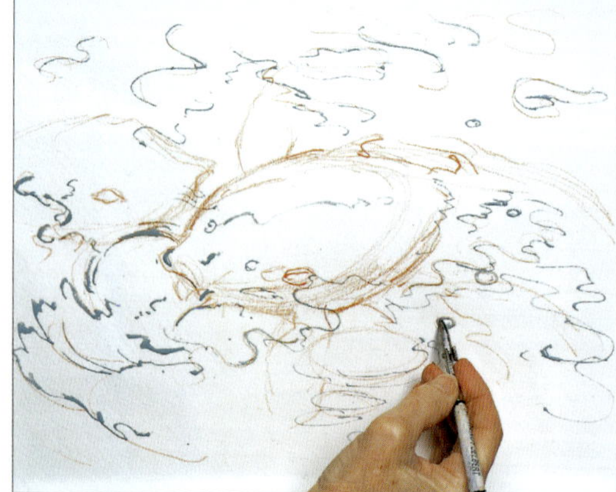

2 Using masking fluid and an old dip pen, mask out the white highlights on the water and the fishes. Leave to dry.

Tip: You can speed up the drying process by using a hairdryer.

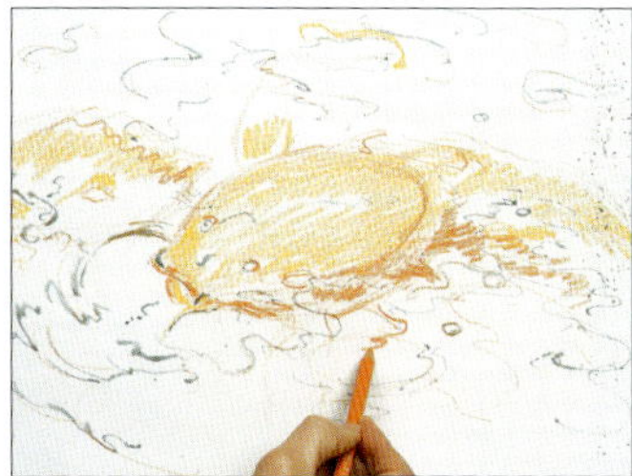

3 Lightly scribble bright yellow over all except the white parts of the fishes. Apply orange to the reddest areas, pressing quite hard on the pencil.

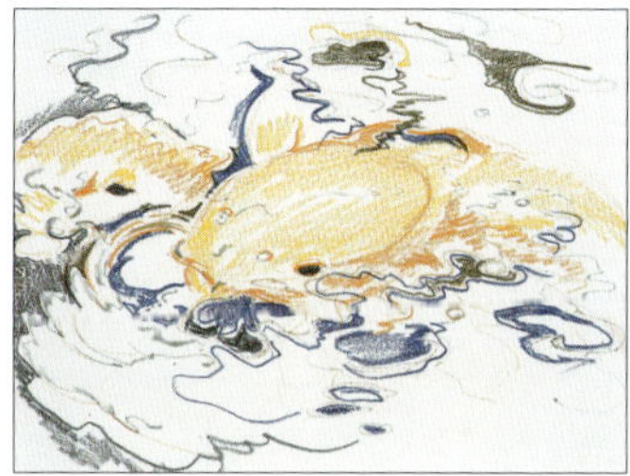

4 Now start putting some colour into the water, using dark blue with a few touches of olive green for the very darkest parts.

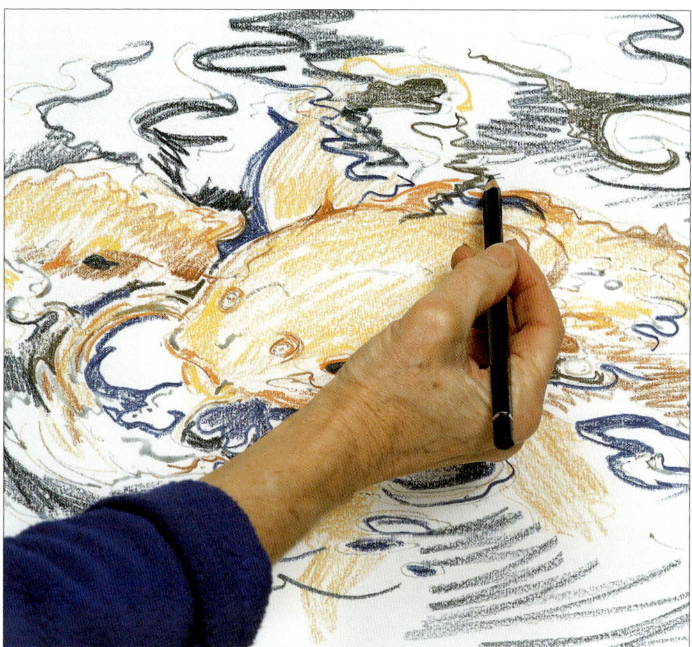

5 Colour in the submerged fins of the large fish using a yellow ochre pencil and go over the reddest part of both with a warm brown. Continue adding colour to the water, using the same colours as before and making curved strokes that follow the shape of the ripples.

Assessment time

You've now put down virtually all the linear detail that you need. Once you start applying water, however, there's a risk that you might lose some of the detail: it's important, for example, to retain some of the ripples in the water – so decide in advance where you want the pigment to spread and, if the colours run into areas where you don't want them to go, be ready to mop them up with a piece of absorbent kitchen paper.

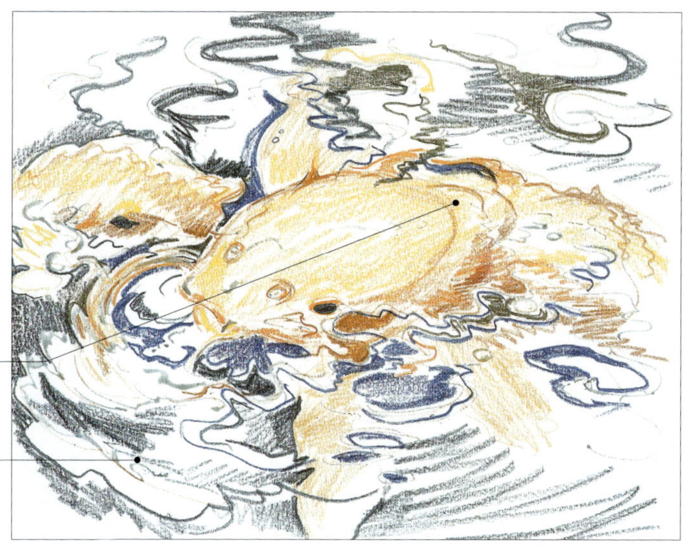

Although the shape of the fish is clear, it's hard to tell which parts are submerged and which are above the water.

Confident, flowing linear marks capture the ripples in the water – and at least some of these marks should be visible in the finished drawing.

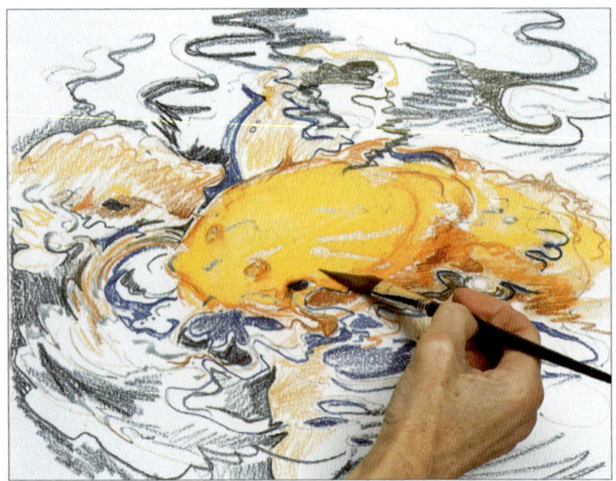

6 Dip a paintbrush in water and gently brush over the large fish. Note how intense and vibrant the colour becomes.

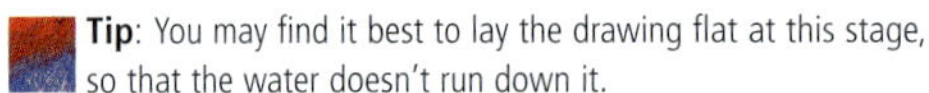

Tip: You may find it best to lay the drawing flat at this stage, so that the water doesn't run down it.

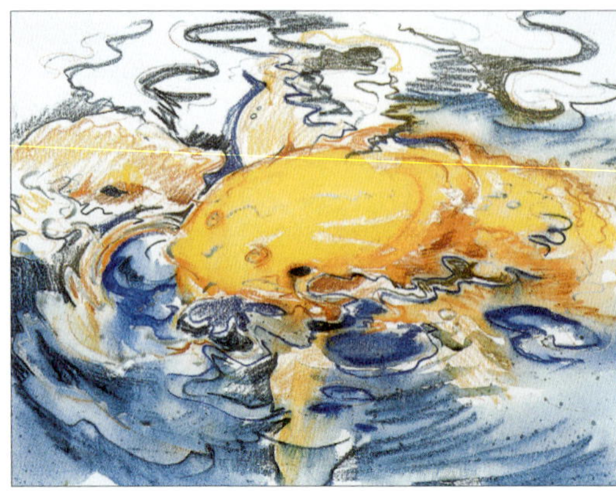

7 Brush clean water over the painted water, following the lines of the ripples and leaving some highlight ripples white.

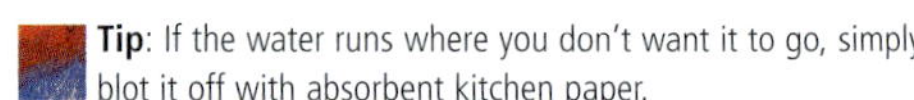

Tip: If the water runs where you don't want it to go, simply blot it off with absorbent kitchen paper.

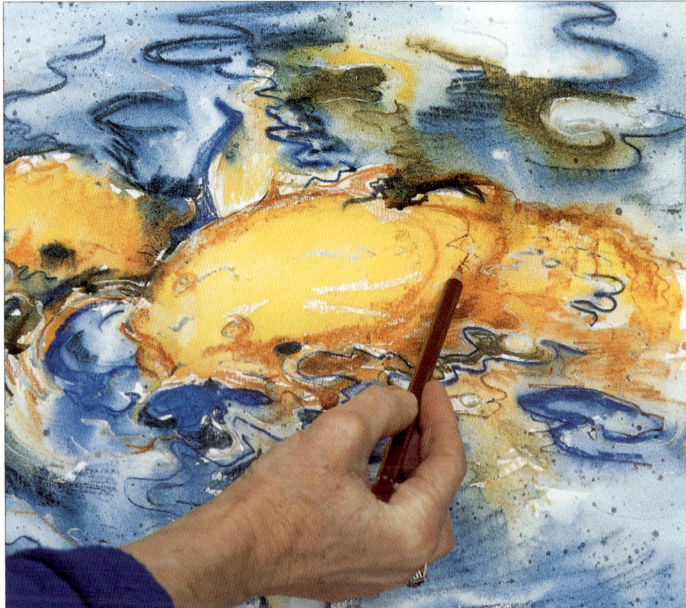

8 Brush clean water over the small fish. Allow the support to dry slightly, but not completely, and go over the reddest parts of the fishes with a reddish brown pencil. The colour will intensify. It will also blur and spread, so you won't get any hard edges. The blurred orangey-red will look as if it is under water – so it will become clearer which parts of the large fish are jutting up above the water's surface.

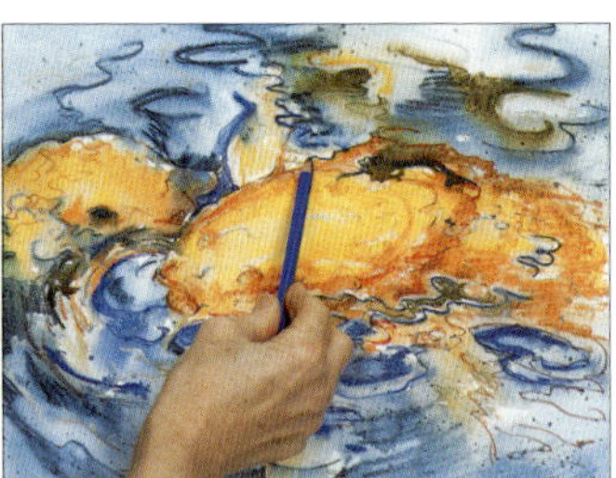

9 Darken the red of the fishes and reinforce the outlines of the fishes with a blue pencil. Leave to dry.

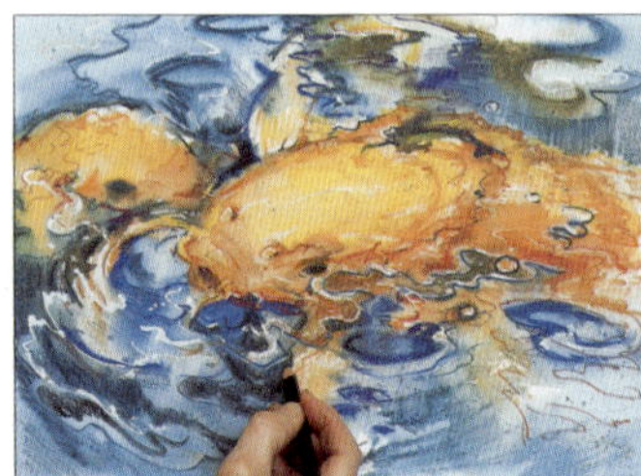

10 Rub off the masking fluid. Scribble blue-green into the darkest parts of the water, pressing quite hard with the pencil to create the necessary depth of colour.

The finished drawing

This drawing demonstrates the potential and versatility of water-soluble pencils and combines linear detailing with lovely, fluid washes that intensify the colours and blend them together on the support.

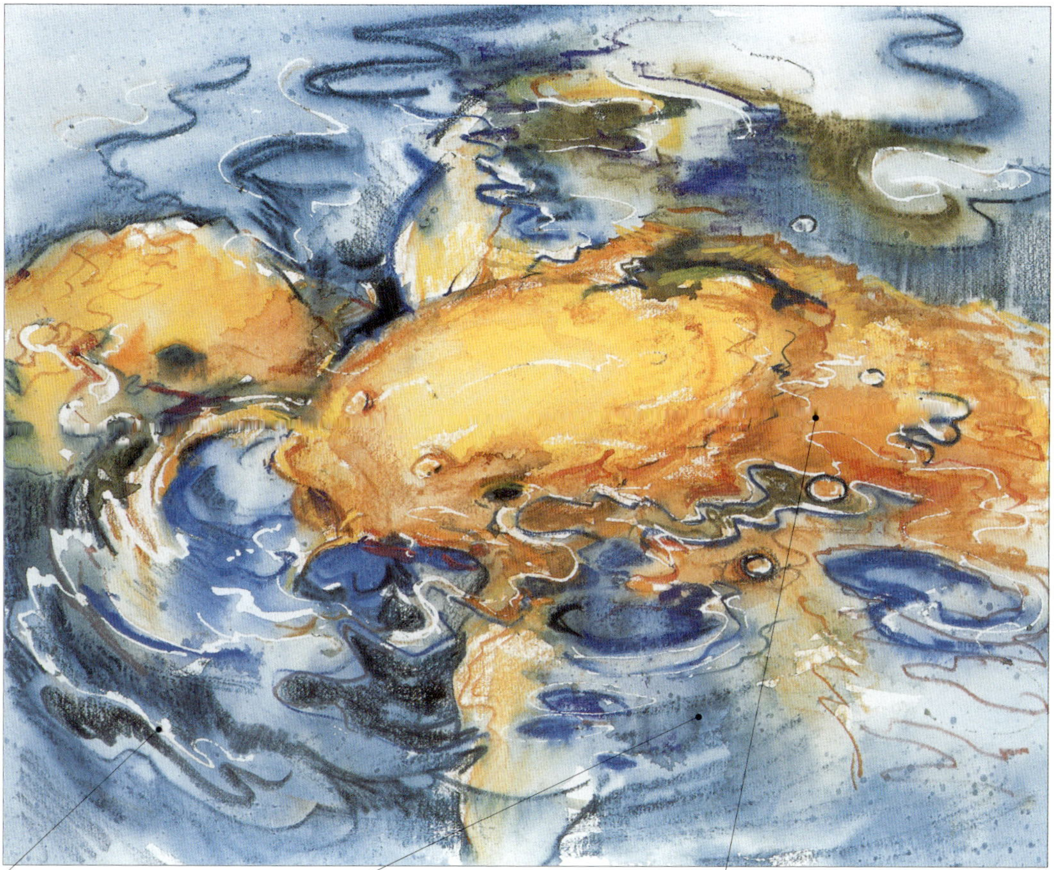

Masking fluid can be used to keep the highlights white.

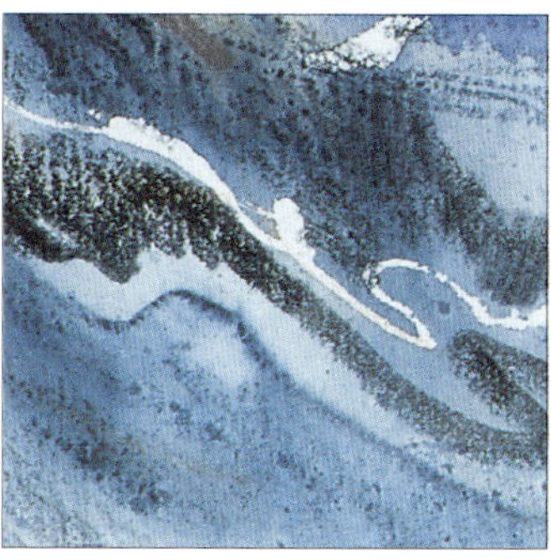

Curved pencil strokes create a sense of movement in the water.

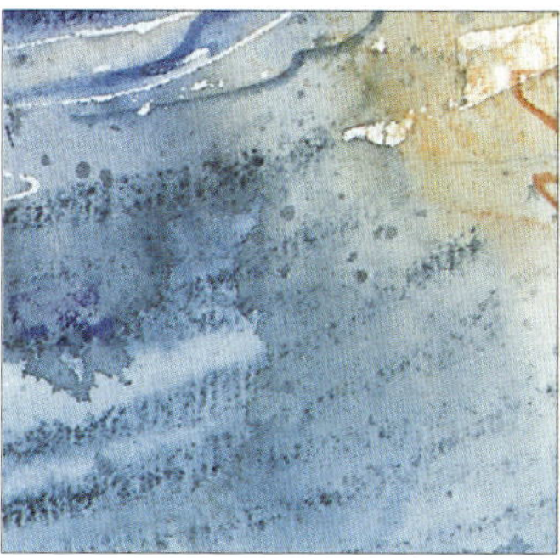

The transition from one colour to the next is almost imperceptible.

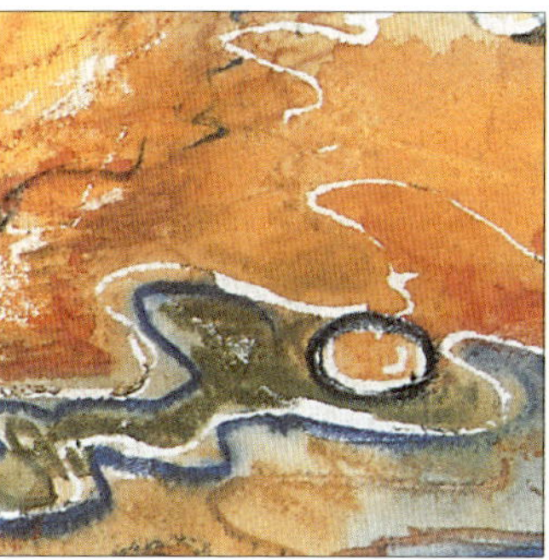

Quick sketches of people: Artists at work

People who are engrossed in what they're doing make great subjects, as they'll probably be unaware that you're drawing them – a far less daunting prospect than asking someone to pose for you.

When you're drawing people, remember that the limbs are not separate entities: they're part of a linked, articulated skeleton. Even when your subjects are fully clothed, you must try to get a sense of the underlying structure and form of the body and of how the different parts interconnect. Creases in the fabric and distortions in any printed pattern on the cloth will give you clues about the shape of the body underneath.

When it comes to getting the proportions right, the only way to do it is to measure. You may have read that the head of an adult is equal to one-seventh of the total height. This is a generalization: the head is a useful unit to use to work out the height of the torso, but the proportions can vary considerably from one person to another – so always measure things for yourself.

The scene

The sketches on these next two pages are of some of the artist's students hard at work in an outdoor painting class.

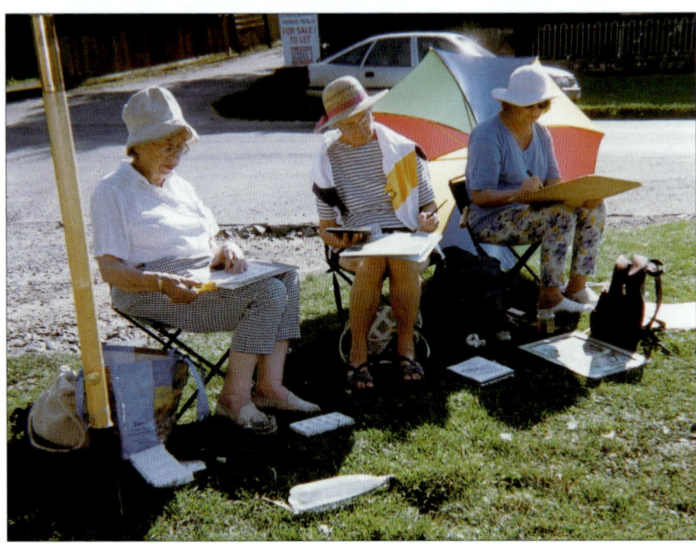

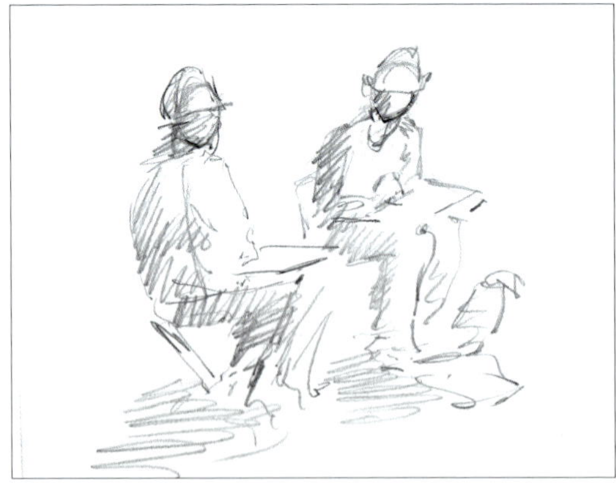

5-minute sketch: HB pencil

The artist here chose to draw just the outer two figures. You might be tempted to start by drawing the outlines of the figures, but you'll get a much better result if you think of the forms that lie under the hats and clothes. Lightly draw the whole oval of the skull, for example, and then superimpose the hat on top. Look at the tilt of the shoulders, the curve of the back and the angles at which the knees and arms are bent, as these will give you the dynamics of the pose. Loosely indicate which areas are in shadow.

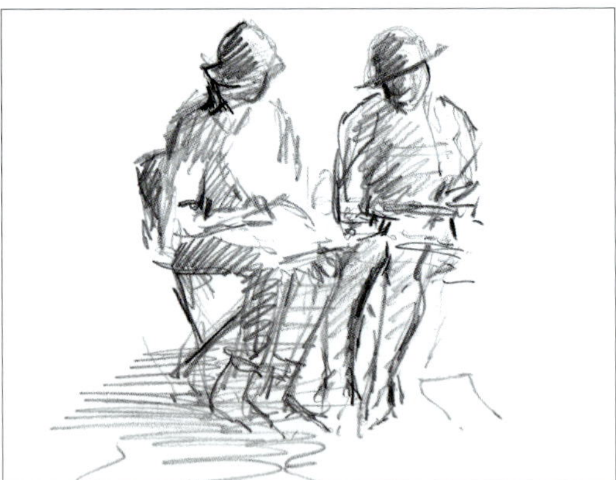

10-minute sketch: HB pencil

In a slightly longer sketch (this time of the two left-hand figures), more detail is introduced, such as more precise shaping of the legs and an indication of where the sleeves and trouser legs end. You can take a bit longer to assess the shading so that the figures begin to look more rounded. It's often a good idea to make a monochrome sketch first, before you attempt to do the same thing in colour – otherwise you can find that you're distracted by the colours and don't properly assess how light or dark the tones need to be.

15-minute sketch: HB pencil, watercolour pencils and pen and ink
This sketch is a nice combination of pen-and-ink work for linear details, such as the lines of figures and the sketching stools, and coloured pencil for some simple patterning and shading on the clothes. Note the use of a cool blue for the areas of white clothing that are in shadow. The artist has also blocked in the background, allowing the figures to stand out more.

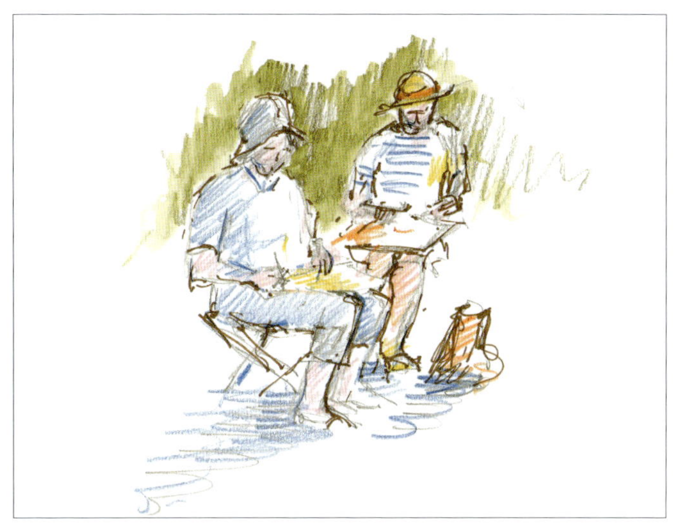

25-minute sketch: HB pencil, watercolour pencils and pen and ink
In 20 minutes or more, you have time to put more pattern on the clothes and to make the figures look rounded by indicating creases in the fabric of their clothes or through differences in tone. Here, the artist brushed over the water-soluble pencil work to create areas of soft tone.

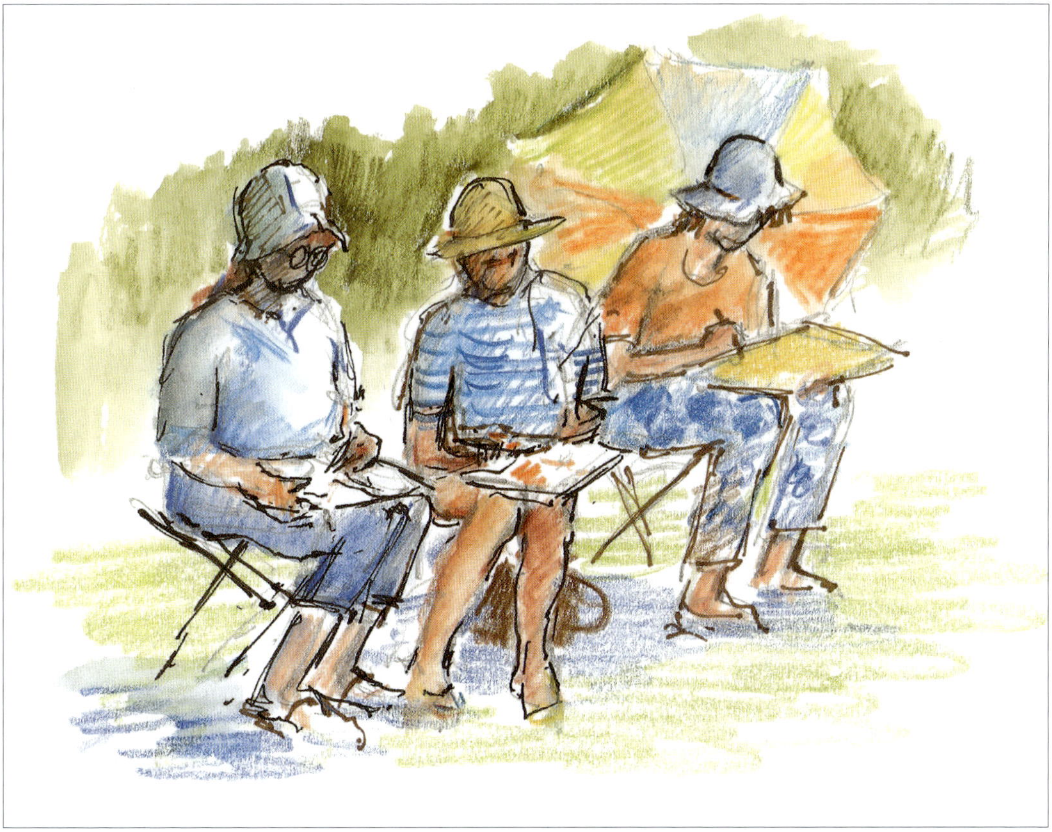

Quick sketches of people: At the beach

The idea of sketching in public might seem rather daunting at first, but a beach or park is a great place to start. It's easy to find a quiet corner to hide away in – and there is usually so much going on that no one takes any notice anyway. In addition to drawing the whole scene, try pulling out individual figures from the crowd, too, for quick practice sketches. This is a great way of sharpening your observational skills.

When you are sketching people quickly, look for the essence of the 'pose' – the tilt of the head, the curve of the back, the angle of the shoulders. Remember this subtle but important clue to get a stance right: a movement in one part of the body is counter-balanced by a movement on the opposite side, in the opposite direction. So, if someone rests their weight on one leg, the opposite hip and shoulder will be thrust slightly upwards.

5-minute sketch: pencil
This is a preliminary compositional sketch for a painting. The curving path naturally leads our eye through the scene. The foreground umbrella and the lamp on the left balance each other; both are placed on the third, which is a strong position for features of interest in a drawing, and together they form a strong diagonal line across the composition.

The scene
This artist selected a viewpoint from the esplanade above the beach. Looking down on a crowded scene makes it much easier to separate the different elements from each other and to work out a pleasing composition. Drawing the same scene from beach level would have resulted in a confusing jumble of shapes and figures.

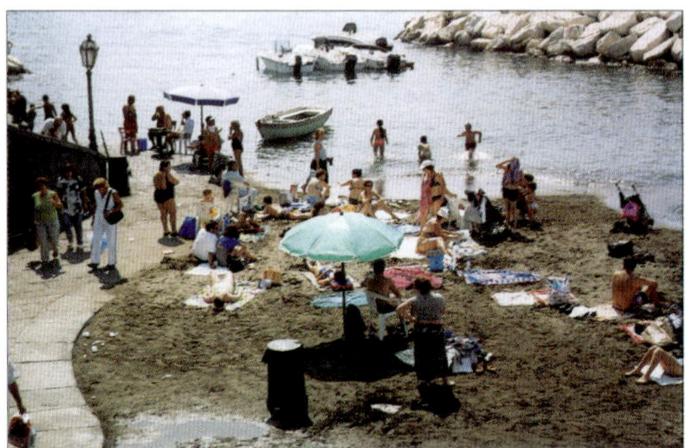

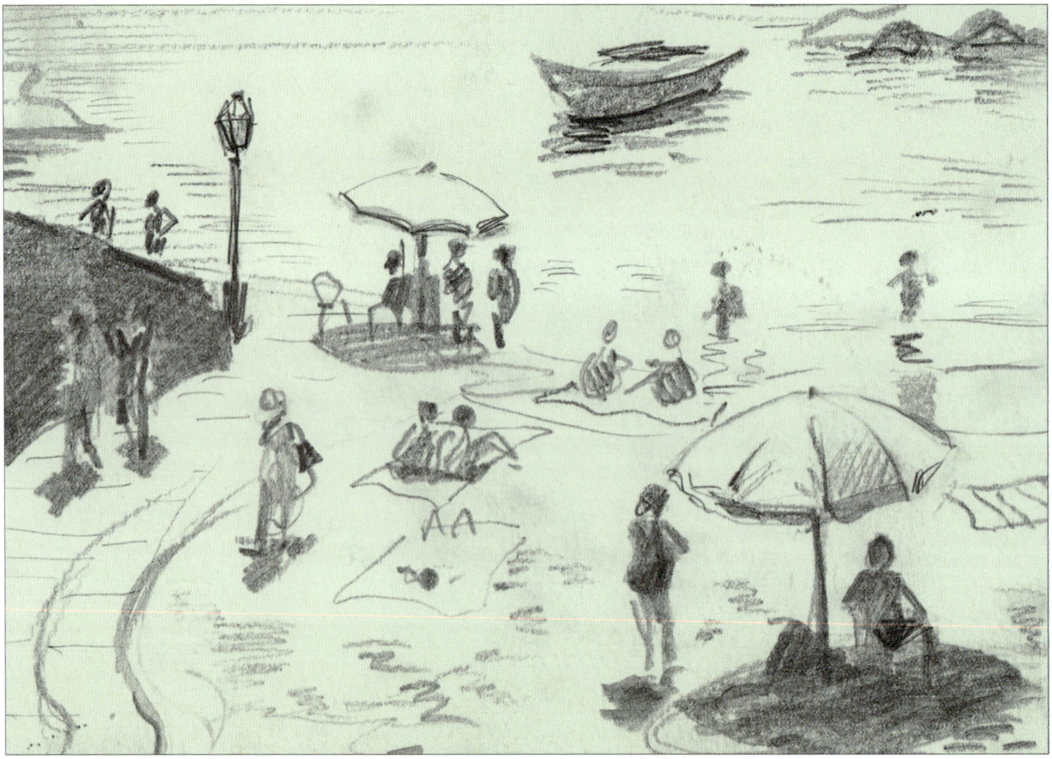

10-minute sketch: oil pastel

This sketch was made in oil pastels on beige-coloured pastel paper, which is similar to the colour of the sand. It imparts a warm mood to the image while a loose smear of blue hints at the sea beyond. Oil pastels are a handy tool for making quick sketches: although they're fairly chunky, which means you cannot make very fine, detailed sketches, they enable you to block in large areas quickly. Note how the artist has captured the young woman's stance with just a few swift marks: the brown marks laid over the pale blue of her T-shirt show how the fabric creases and give important information about her posture. The colour is smudged to create the shadows beneath the figures. The shadows give the image immediate depth and help to 'anchor' the figures.

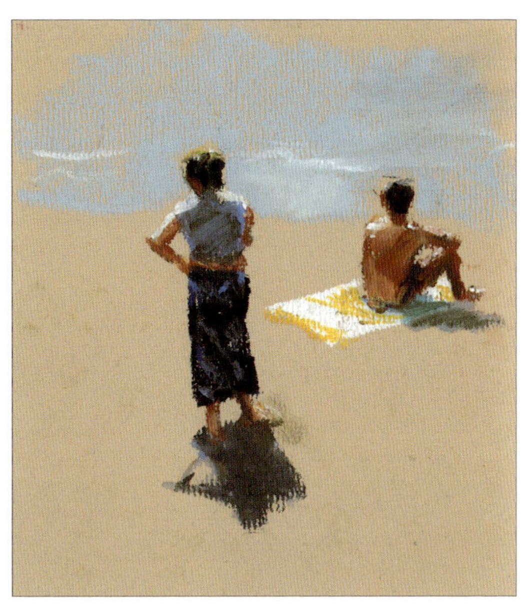

25-minute sketch: pen and ink, wash

This sketch was made using a dip pen – which gives a fresh, spontaneous quality of line – and waterproof ink. Washes of dilute ink are used to create areas of tone, such as the shadow under the umbrella and the boat, the wedge-shaped wall on the left and the flesh tones. Note the different textures created by using different kinds of line: straight horizontal and vertical lines for the hard stonework and paving, small circles and squiggles for the soft sand.

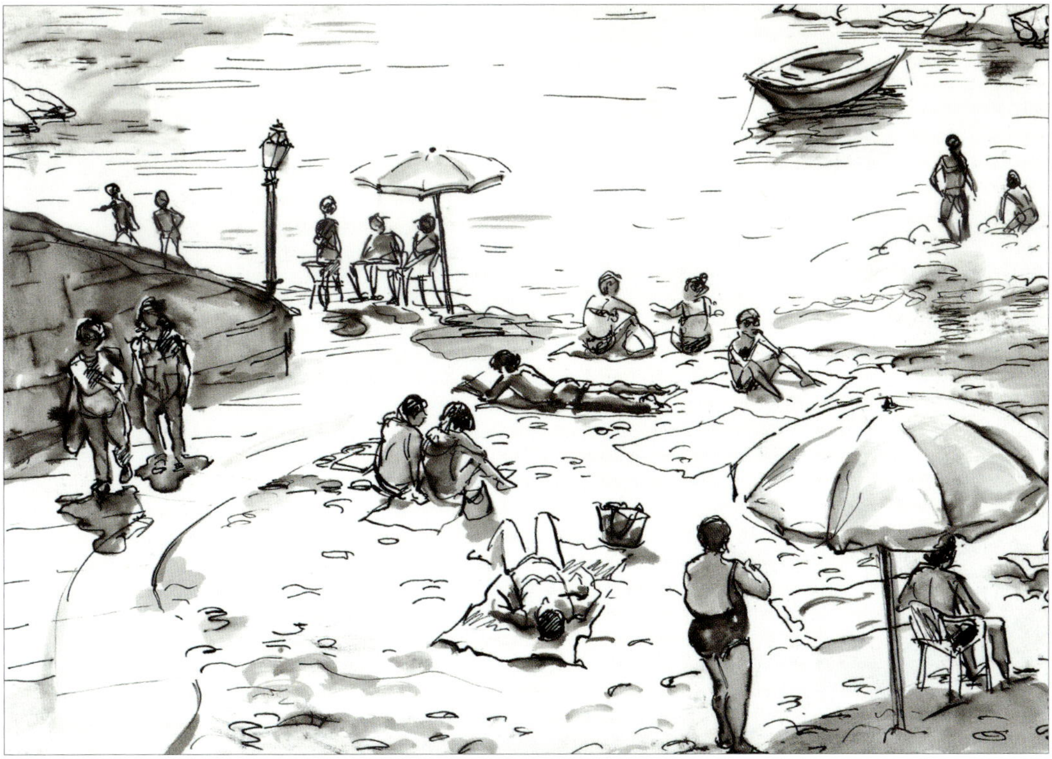

Quick sketches of people: Al fresco lunch

Informal gatherings of family and friends are a great place to sketch people, as the atmosphere is relaxed and people behave naturally – but if you're nervous about sketching in front of other people, use the opportunity to take a few photos that you can use as reference material and then make your sketches later. With a large group, you may find that you need to direct the proceedings, in much the same way as a photographer at a wedding, in order to get the composition that you want. Don't feel intimidated about doing this – but remember that the people are there to enjoy themselves, not to pose for long periods of time while you try to capture their likeness on paper!

The scene

Here, the artist selected his viewpoint carefully to create a balanced composition, with none of the heads overlapping. He felt that if everyone was looking directly at the camera the image would look too self-conscious and posed, so he asked the man and woman on the far left and right to look at each other, rather than at the camera. There is a good mix of full-face views (the three people at the back of the group), side profiles, and three-quarter views, giving you the chance to practise placing the facial features with the head turned at different angles.

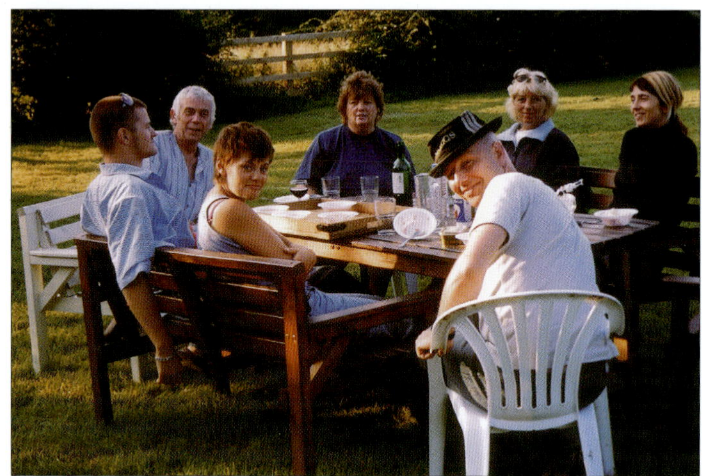

5-minute sketch: ballpoint pen

With a large group it can be hard to know where to start. Here the artist began by sketching the man in the hat, positioned just off centre, and then worked outwards in each direction. This helps to avoid the risk of making the first figure too big and running out of paper for the remaining figures.

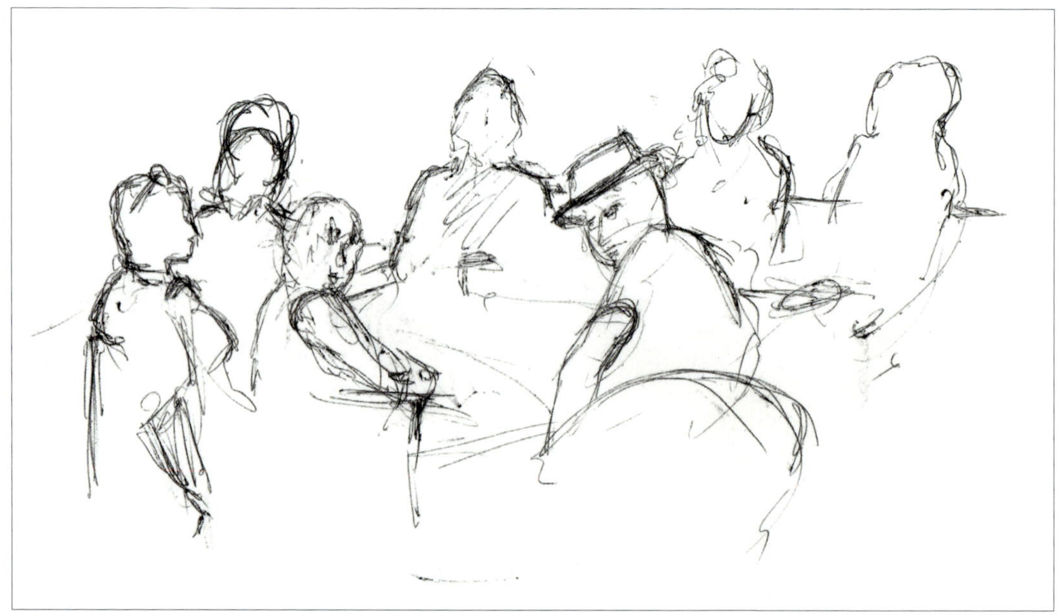

15-minute sketch: pencil
Here, too, the artist began with the man in the hat. He then used the straight lines of the hat as a guide to help him assess the angles at which the sitters' heads were tilted. Light shading, done using the side of the pencil, introduces some tone into the image, while stronger crease lines in the clothing suggest the folds in the fabric and begin to give the image some form.

15-minute sketch: coloured pencils
This was made to provide the artist with rough colour notes that he could elaborate on later in a more detailed drawing. Note how the intensity of the blue in the men's shirts varies, with a deeper tone being used for the shaded creases. Even the white T-shirt of the man in the hat contains a surprising amount of blue, as his back is largely in shadow and there are many wrinkles in the fabric.

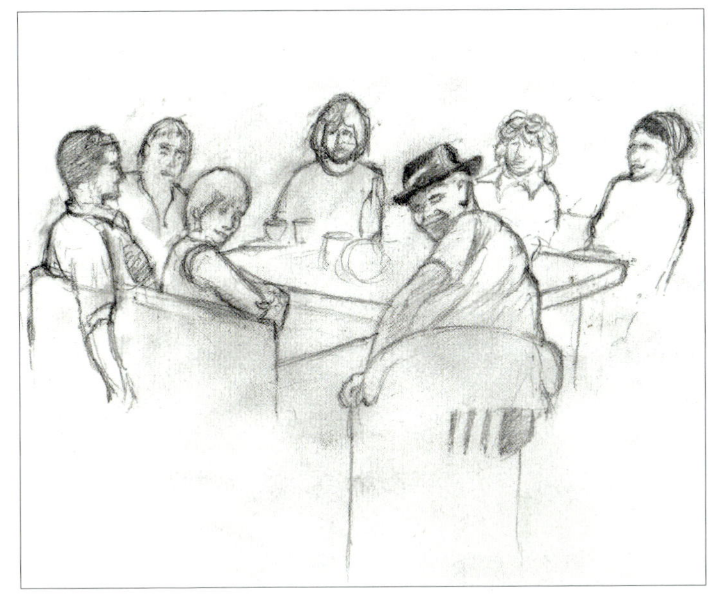

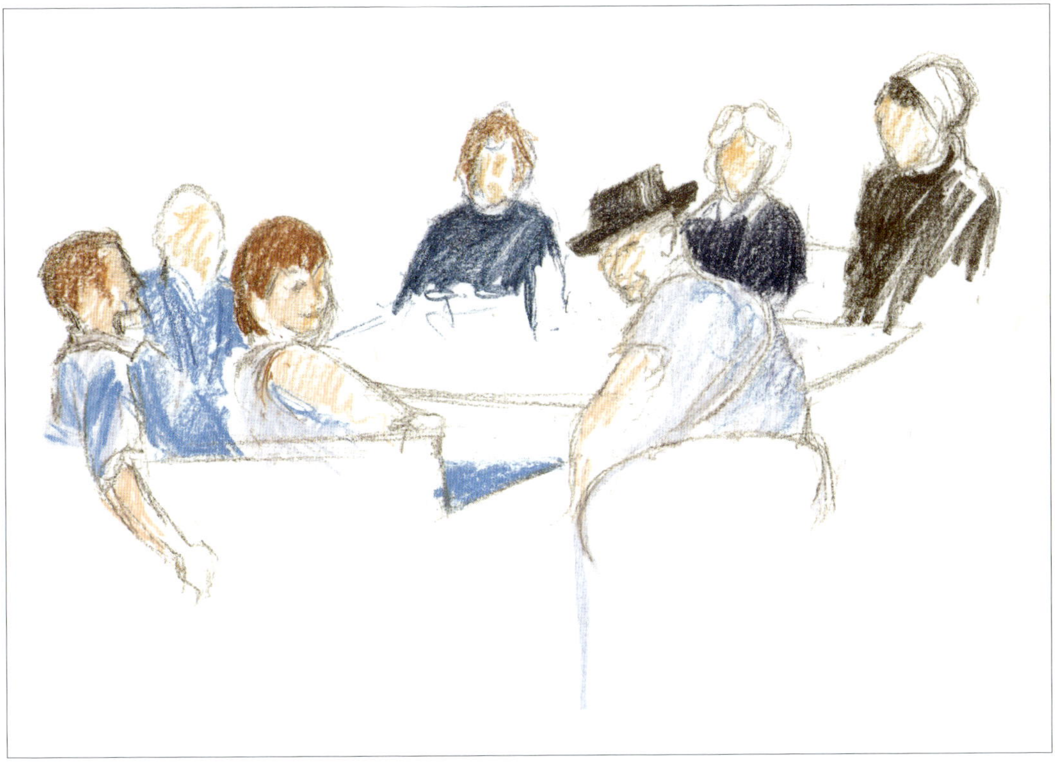

Character portrait

Markets are a great place to make quick sketches or take snapshots of people going about their daily business, which you can then work up into more detailed portraits at a later date. People are so engrossed in what they're doing that they're unlikely to take much notice of you – so your photos and sketches may be much more informal and natural.

Here, the artist decided to omit both the background and the woman on the left and to concentrate on making a character portrait of the man – although you could, of course, include the setting, too, provided you keep the main emphasis of the drawing on his face.

This particular portrait gains much of its strength from the fact that there is direct eye contact between the subject and the artist, which immediately brings the portrait to life and makes the viewer feel involved in the scene. His gaze is quizzical, perhaps even slightly challenging, and even without the inclusion of the market setting, his slightly hunched pose and wrinkled face indicate that he leads a hard life.

Charcoal is a lovely medium for character portraits and, like black-and-white reportage or documentary-style photographs, a monochrome drawing has a strength and immediacy that works particularly well with this kind of subject. The same drawing in colour would have a very different feel – and probably far less impact. Why not try the same project in coloured pencil, too, to see the difference?

Materials

- *Fine pastel paper*
- *Thin charcoal stick*
- *Compressed charcoal stick*
- *Kneaded eraser*

The pose

In this scene two market traders in Turkey were spotted by chance rather than asked to pose formally. So these are character portraits. The artist concentrated on the man on the right, as the three-quarters pose, with direct eye contact, is more interesting than the head-on view of the lady. He has a strong profile, while the woman's face is more rounded and her features less clearly defined. The plastic sheeting could be confusing so it was omitted.

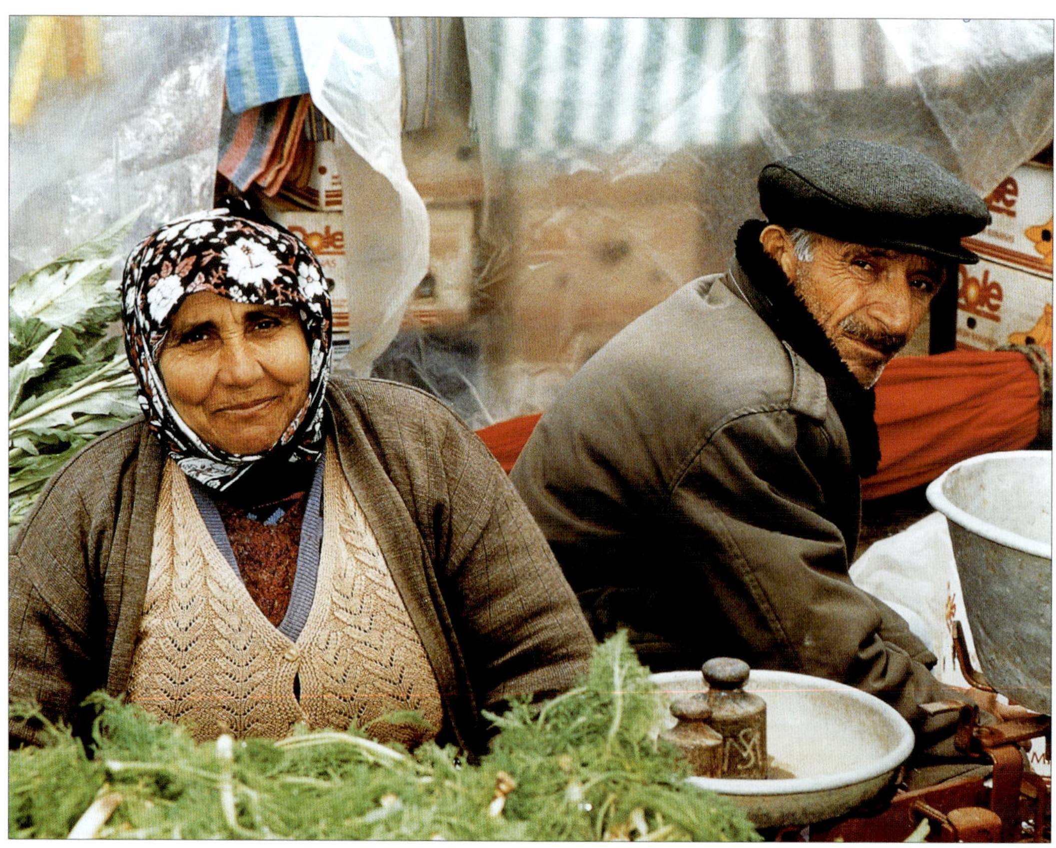

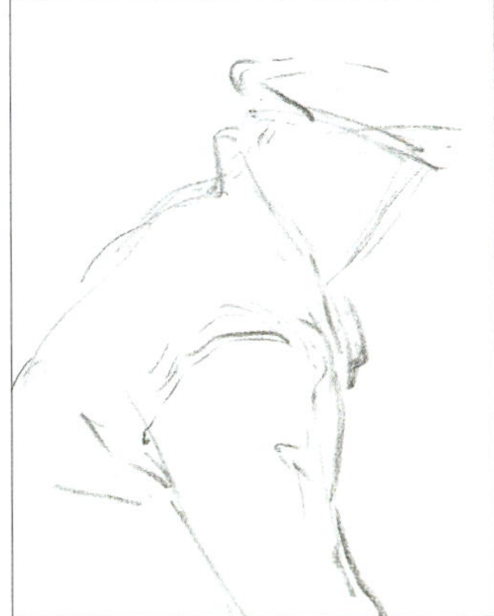

1 Using a thin stick of charcoal, map out the lines of the pose. Look at the angle of the shoulders and back and at where imaginary vertical lines intersect, so that you can place elements correctly in relation to one another. Here, for example, the peak of the man's cap is almost directly in line with his wrist.

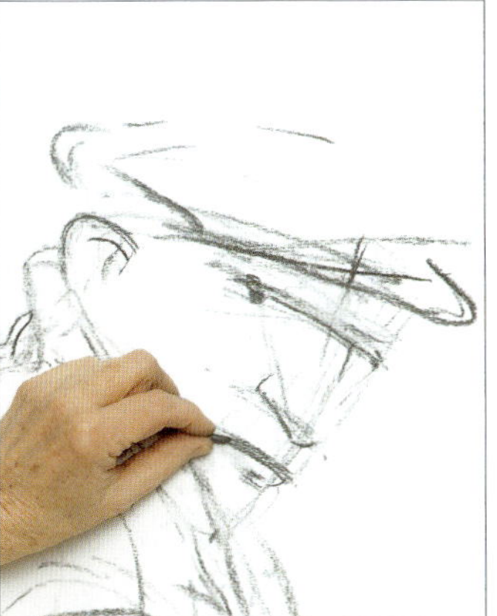

2 Still using the thin charcoal stick, lightly put in guidelines to help you place the facial features. Draw a line through the forehead and down to the bottom of the chin, lines across the face to mark the level of the eyes, the base of the nose and the mouth, and an inverted triangle from the eyes down to the nose.

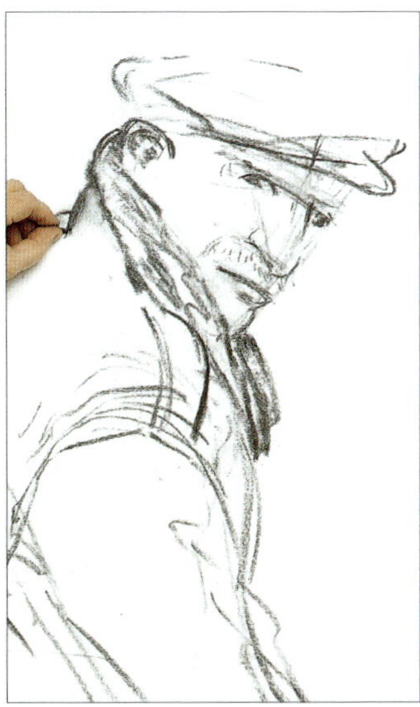

3 Refine the facial features and roughly block in the fur collar on the man's jacket. (It provides a dark frame for the face.)

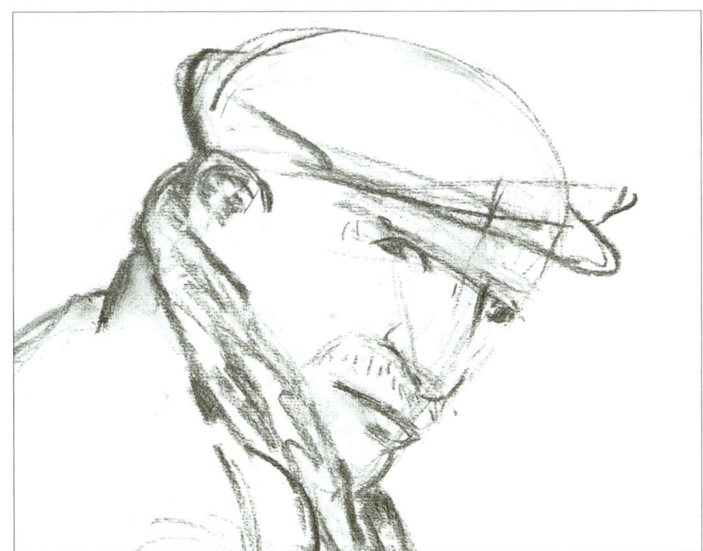

4 Lightly draw the curve of the top of the skull. Although you can't actually see the skull beneath the cap, you can use the tilt of the head and the features you've already put in to work out where it should be. Remember that the base of the eye socket is generally about halfway down the face, so the top of the skull is likely to be higher than you might think.

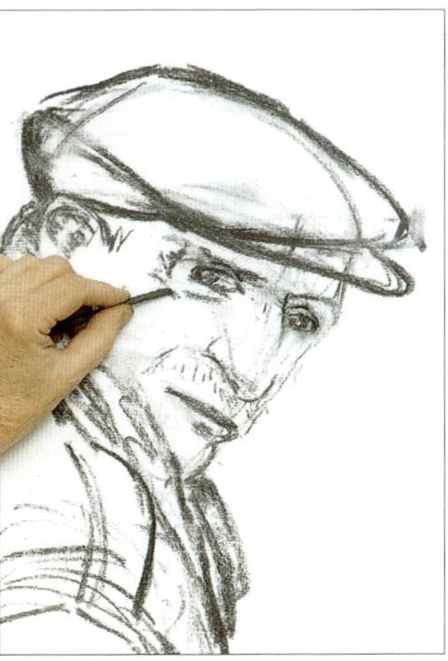

5 Now you can draw the cap. Without the faint guideline of the skull that you drew in the previous step, you'd probably make the cap too flat and place it too low on the head. Draw the eyes and eyebrows and the sockets of the eyes. Already you can see how the form is beginning to develop.

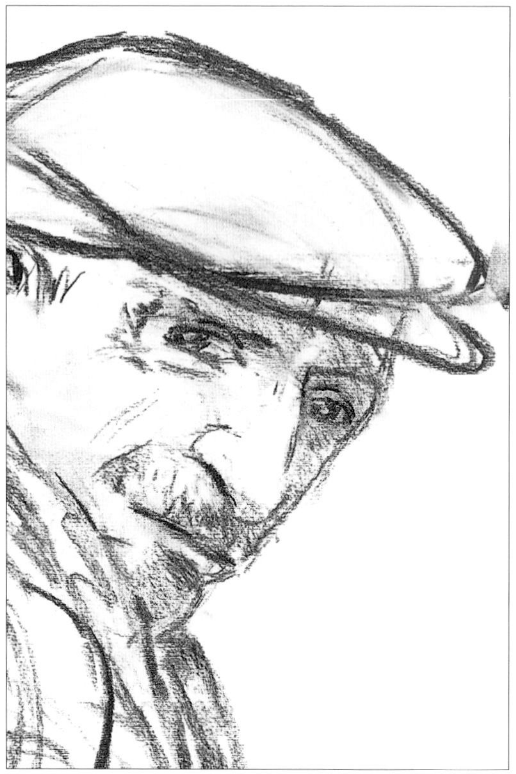

6 Sharpen the line of the far cheek and apply loose hatching on the far side of the face (which is in shadow) and on the forehead, where the cap casts a shadow.

Assessment time

The facial features are in place and most of the linear work has been completed, although the details need to be refined and the eyes darkened. Now you can begin to introduce some shading, which will make the figure look three-dimensional and bring the portrait to life.

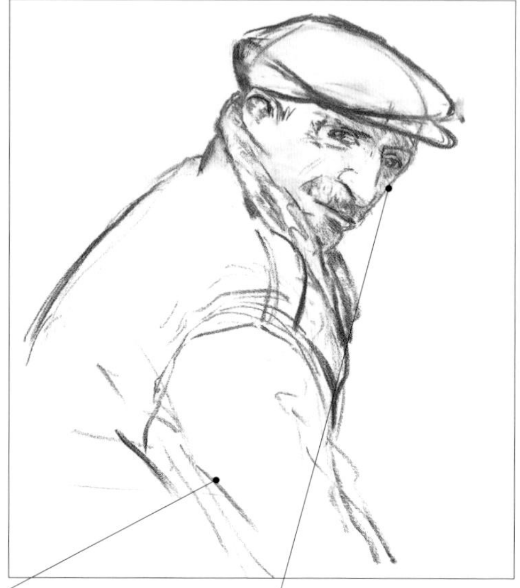

The jacket looks flat. There is nothing to tell us how heavy it is or what kind of fabric it is made from.

Shading has introduced some modelling on the far side of the face, but more is needed.

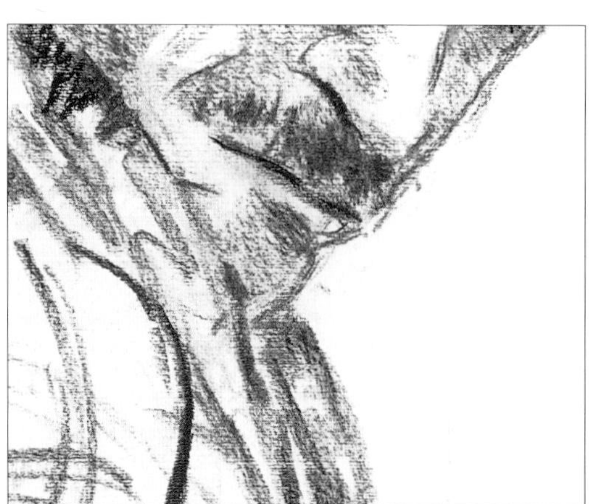

7 Using a compressed charcoal stick, which is very dense and black, put in the line of the mouth.

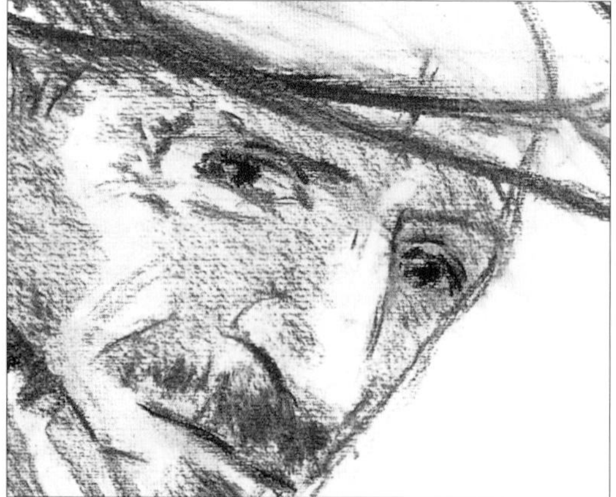

8 Again using the compressed charcoal stick, put in the pupils of the eyes, remembering to leave tiny catchlights.

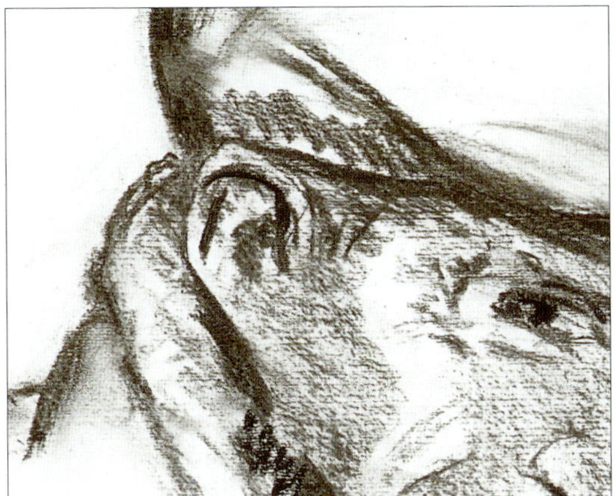

9 Using the side of a thin stick of charcoal, very lightly shade the right-hand side of the man's face. The shadow is not as deep here as on the far side of the face, but this slightly darker tone serves two purposes as it helps to show how tanned and weatherbeaten his face is and also creates some modelling on the cheeks.

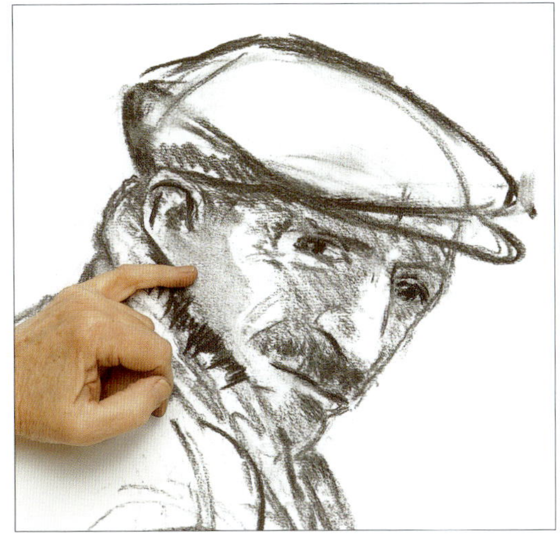

10 Using the tip of your little finger, which is the driest part of your hand, carefully blend the charcoal on the right cheek to a smooth, mid-toned grey.

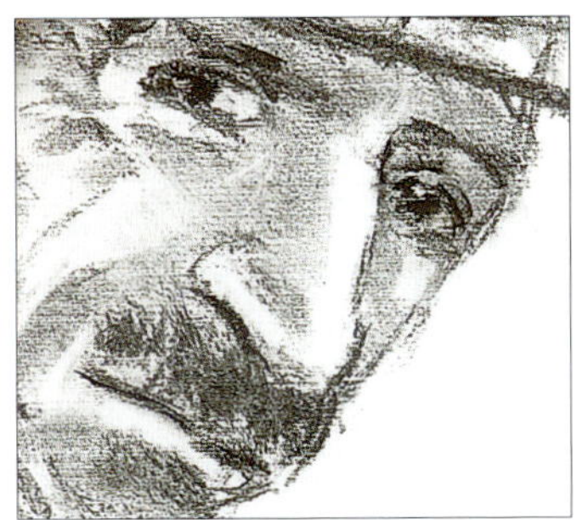

11 Using a kneaded eraser, pick out the highlighted wrinkles on the face, and the whites of the eyes.

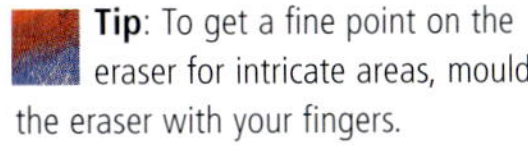

Tip: To get a fine point on the eraser for intricate areas, mould the eraser with your fingers.

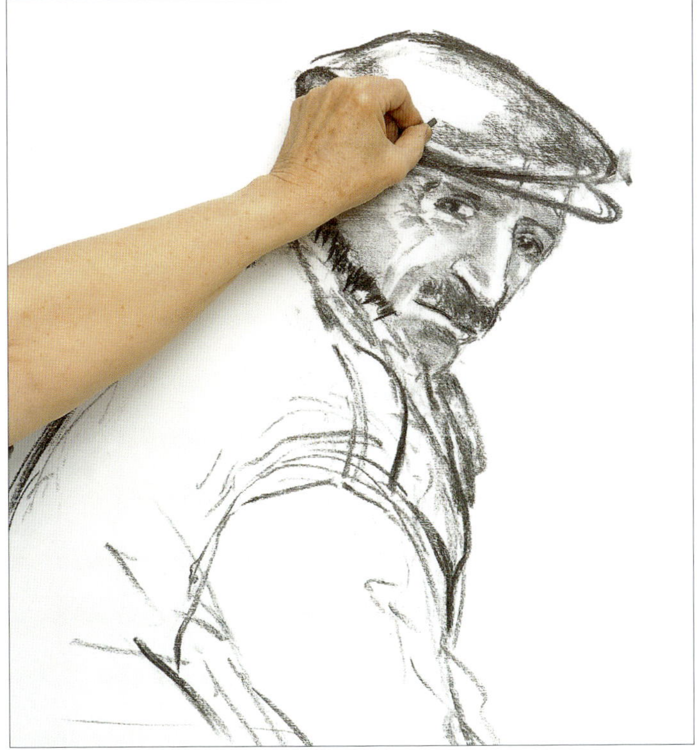

12 Block in the dark, shaded side of the cap, using the side of the charcoal stick. Note that the cap is not a uniform shade of black all over: leave areas on the top untouched to show where the highlights fall.

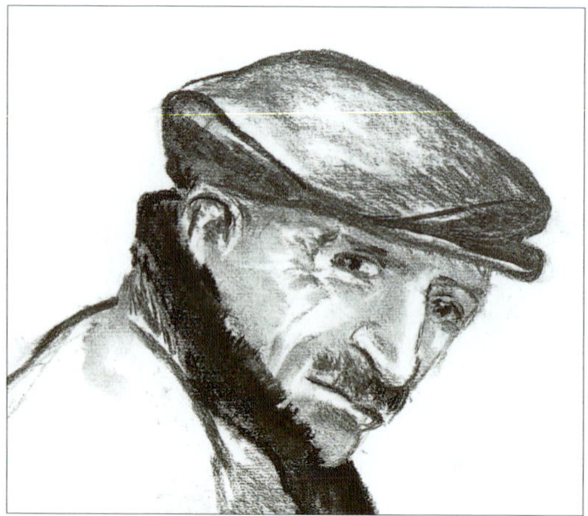

13 Using compressed charcoal, block in the fur collar on the jacket and smooth out the marks with your fingers. By making slightly jagged marks, you can suggest the texture of the fur. Note how the face immediately stands out more strongly when framed by the dark fur.

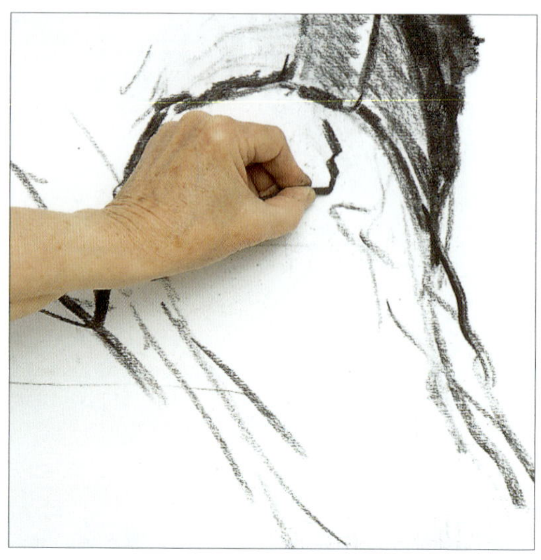

14 Put in the dark crease lines of the folds in the jacket. The deep creases help to show the weight of the fabric.

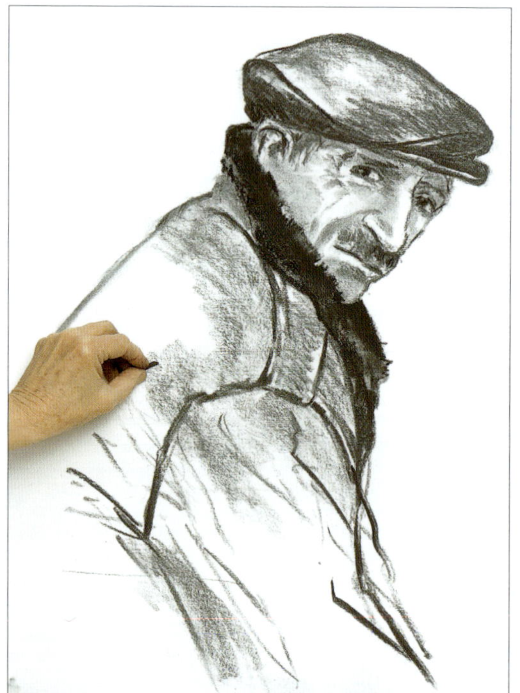

15 Using the side of the charcoal, apply tone over the jacket, leaving highlights on the sleeve untouched.

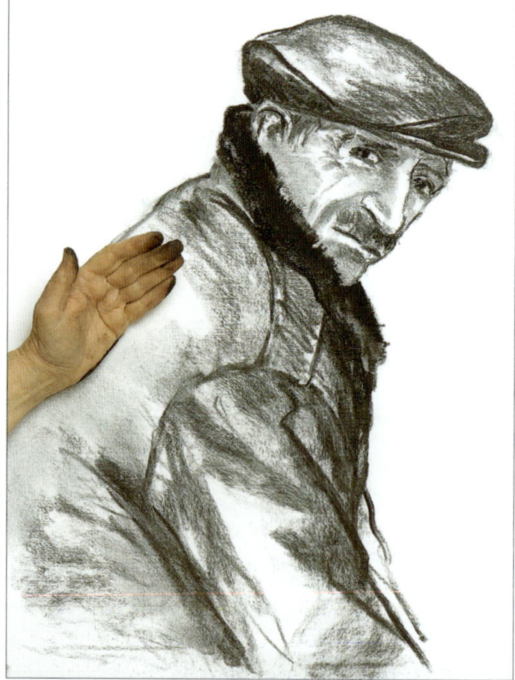

16 Using the side of your hand in a circular motion, blend the charcoal to a smooth, flat tone.

The finished drawing

This portrait is full of character. Note the classic composition, which draws our attention to the face. The overall shape of the portrait is triangular, with the strong line of the back leading up to the face and forming the first side of the triangle, and a straight line down from the peak of the cap to the arm forming the second side. In addition, the face is positioned roughly 'on the third' – a strong placement for the most important element in the drawing.

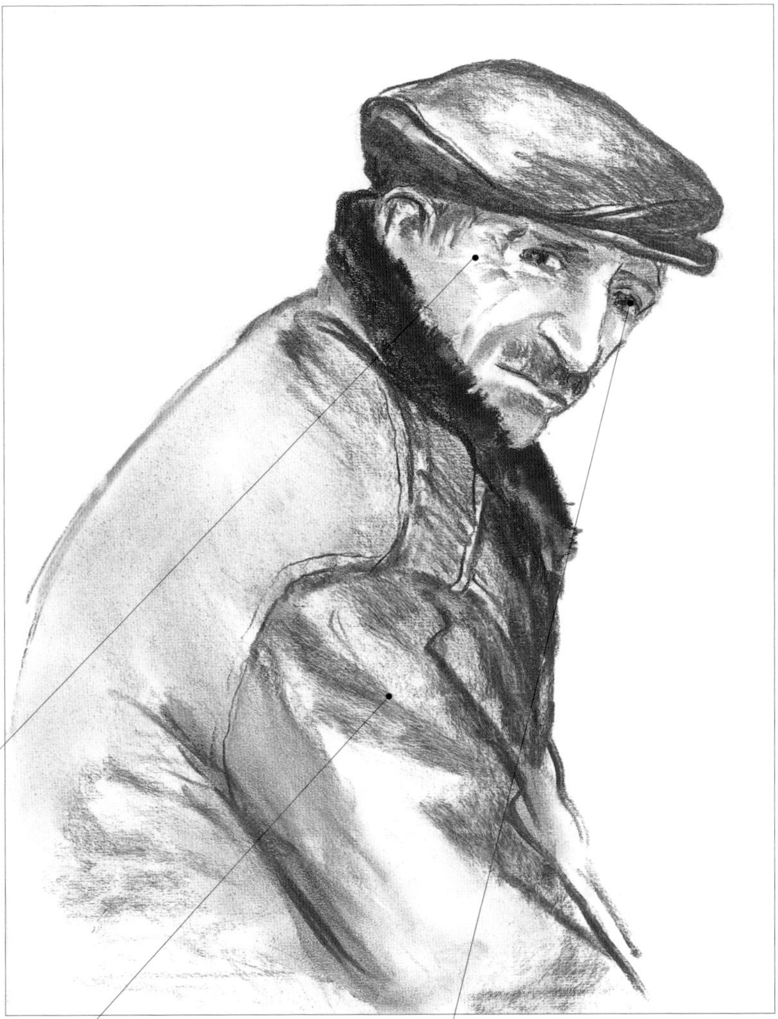

Wrinkles in the skin are picked out using the sharp edge of a kneaded eraser.

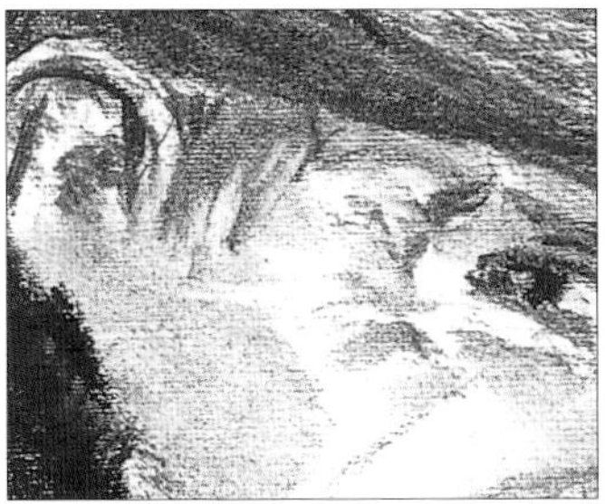

The crease lines and variations in tone show the weight and bulkiness of the fabric.

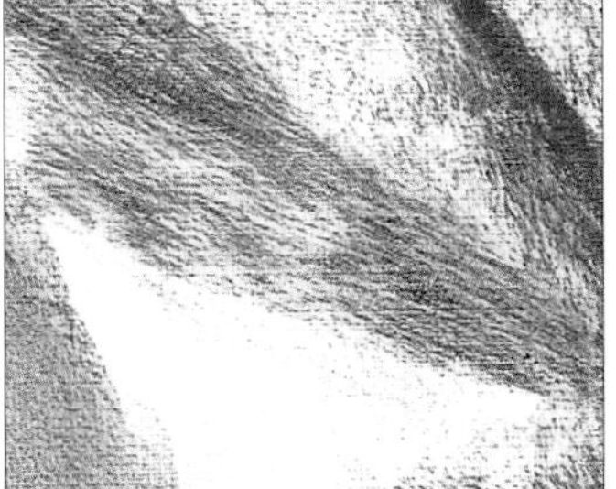

The direct eye contact between sitter and viewer makes this a very strong portrait.

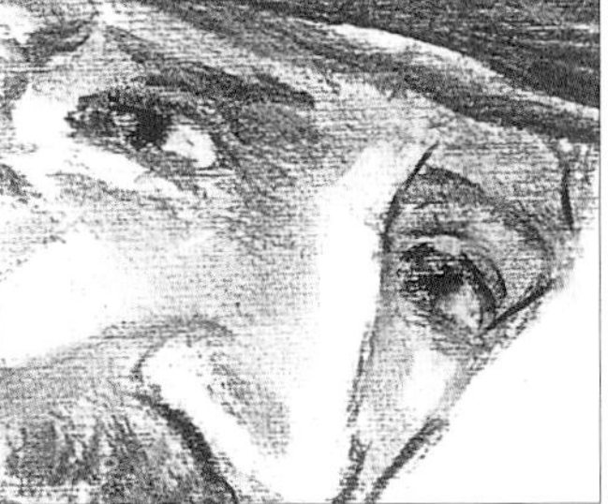

Male nude

People come in all kinds of shapes and sizes! Nonetheless, we can make some generalizations about the differences between men and women and you should bear these in mind when drawing a male nude. The main differences to note are that, generally, men have less fat tissue than women and look more angular. Men's shoulders are usually broader and their hips narrower. Typically, a man's neck looks shorter than a woman's and his feet and hands are larger in proportion with the rest of the body.

When making your initial sketch, it's tempting simply to outline the pose – but if you imagine the skeleton of the body underneath the skin as you draw, you will undoubtedly find it much easier to get the shapes right.

Materials
- *Grey pastel paper*
- *Thin willow charcoal stick*
- *Kneaded eraser*
- *Soft pastel: pale cream*

The pose
This sofa provides support, making the pose easy to hold for a long time. Even so, it's a good idea to mark the position of the feet and hands with pieces of masking tape, in case the model moves. The back is slightly bent and the stomach is convex, creating interesting shading on the torso. Note the slight foreshortening: the legs are closest to the viewer and so appear slightly larger than they would if the model were standing up.

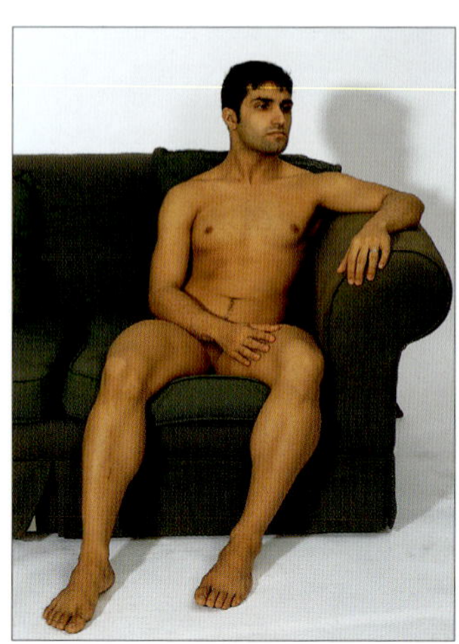

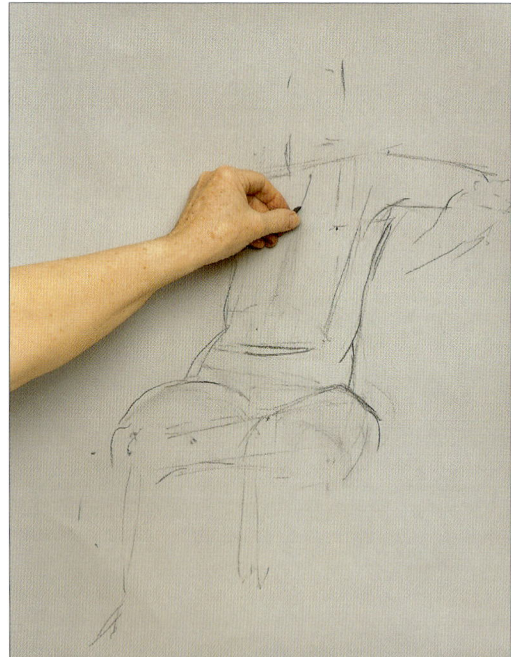

1 Sketch the figure using a thin stick of charcoal, making sure you allow space for the sofa on either side. Measure and mark where each part of the body is positioned in relation to the rest; the face, for example, is in line with the model's left knee. Also look at the slope of the shoulders and at where the elbow is positioned in relation to the chest.

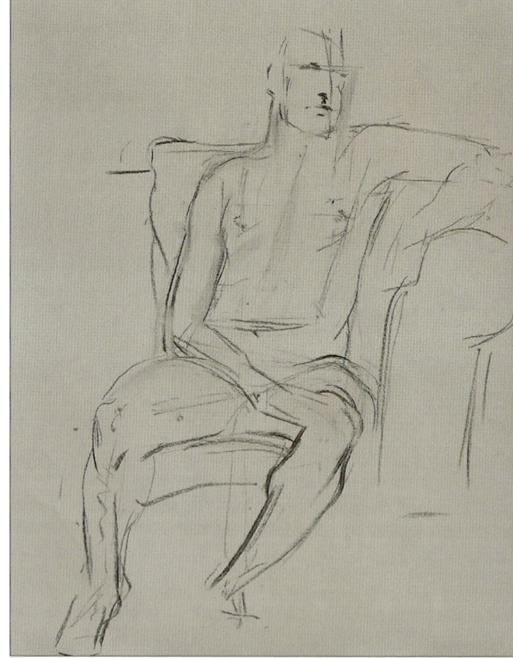

2 Begin searching out the form, making angular marks that establish the three-dimensional shape of the head and torso. Put in faint guidelines running vertically and horizontally through the centre of the face to help you position the facial features. Lightly mark the shape of the sofa – the curve of the arm and the cushion behind the model.

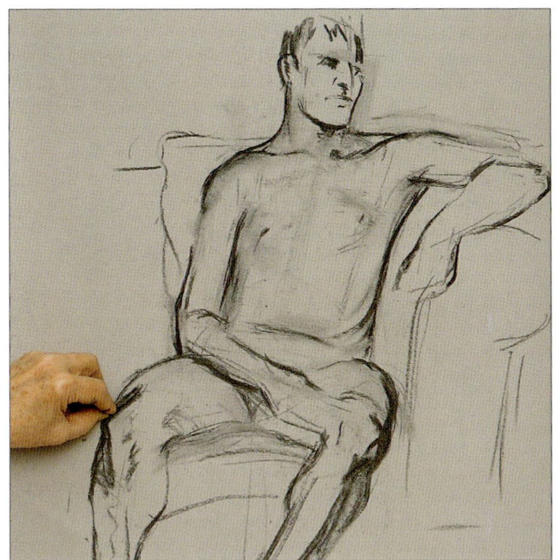

3 Once you've mapped out the basic composition, you can begin to strengthen the lines and put in the facial features in more detail. Draw the eyes, noting how the upper lids fold over the lower ones at the outer corners and how the line of the nose obscures the inner corner of the far eye. Roughly scribble in the hair line. Put in some shading under the chin, on the legs and arms, and on the left of the torso.

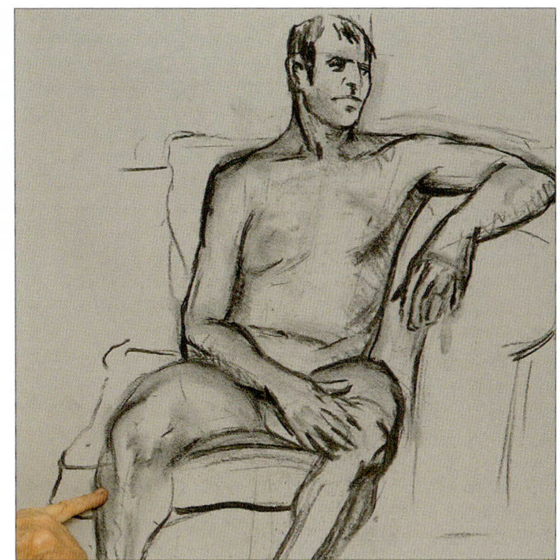

4 Using the tip of the charcoal, draw the muscle that runs diagonally along the side of the neck. This is a very strong, pronounced muscle and putting it in helps to emphasize the tilt of the head. Using the tip of your little finger, smooth out some of the shading on the torso and legs to create more subtle modelling. The figure is already beginning to look more three-dimensional.

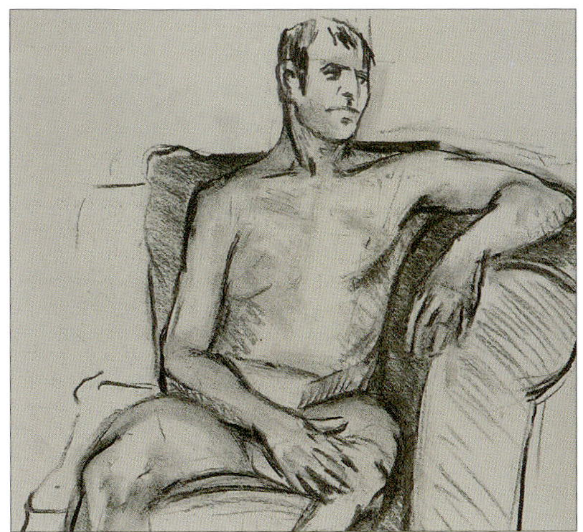

5 Loosely scribble over the sofa, so that the figure stands out. Look at the negative shapes – the shape the sofa makes against the body – rather than at the body itself. This makes it easier to see if any adjustments need to be made to the outline of the body. Alter the direction of the hatching lines to make the different planes of the sofa more obvious.

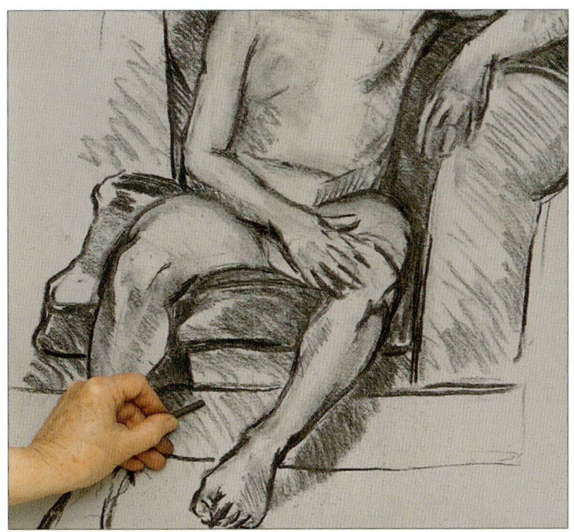

6 Draw the model's left foot. (Try to think of it as a complete unit rather than a series of individual toes.) Shade one side, and indicate the spaces between the toes with very dark marks. Loosely scribble in the shadow cast on the base of the sofa by the model's legs, and hatch the different facets of the cushions.

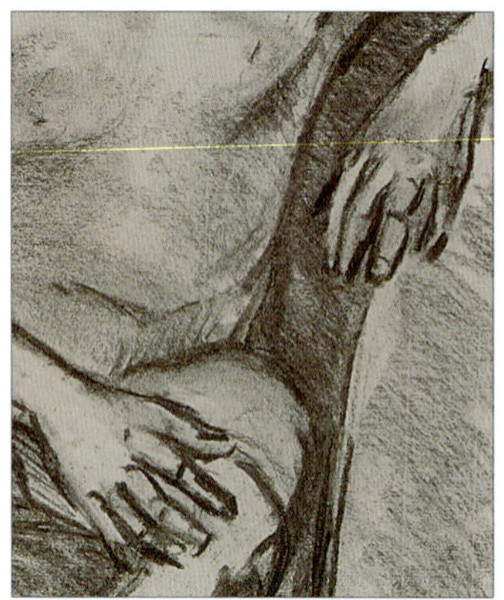

7 Use a kneaded eraser to gently clean up and create more contrast between the lightest and darkest parts. Darken the spaces between the fingers and indicate the segments of the fingers to show how they articulate.

Assessment time

Assess the tonal contrast of the figure as a whole to see where more shading or highlights are needed. For example, the lower part of the torso is slightly shaded by the ribcage as the model slumps back on the sofa, and this area needs to be darkened.

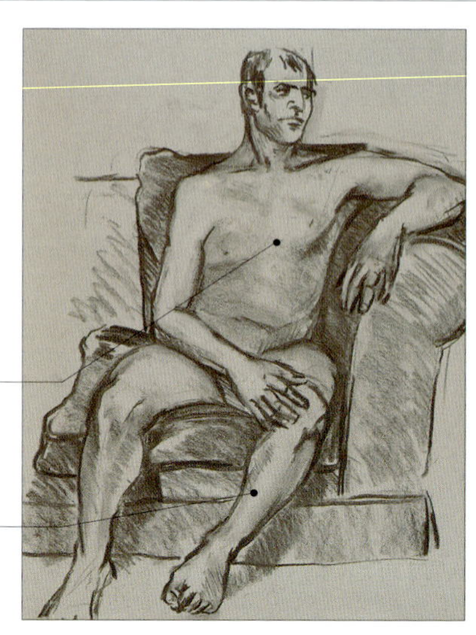

The upper part of the torso is a little too bright.

More shading is needed on the model's left leg.

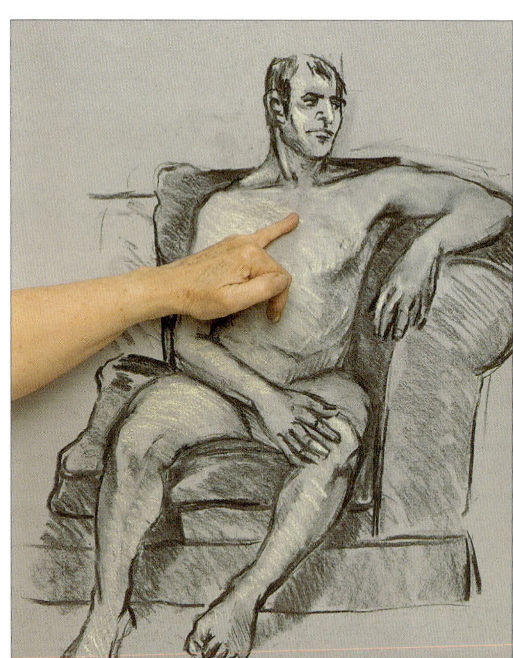

8 Using a very pale cream pastel, put in the highlights on the face, right arm and leg. (Cream is a more sympathetic colour for flesh tones than a stark white.) Even though the limbs are rounded forms, the highlights help to define the different planes. Blend the pastel marks with your fingertip.

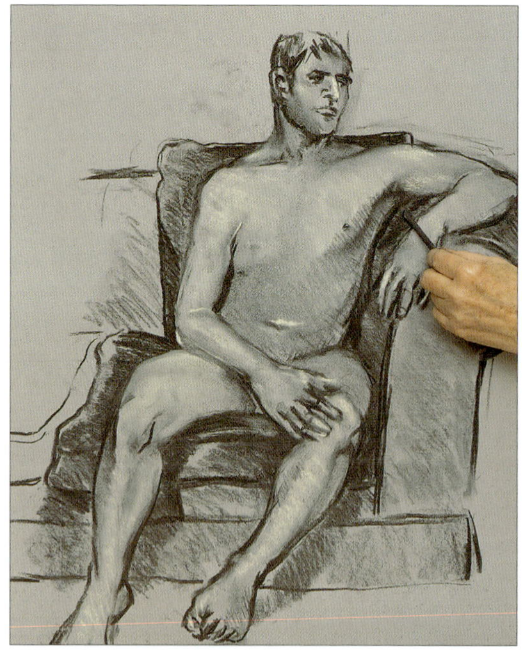

9 Apply more charcoal shading on the lower part of the torso, again blending the marks with your fingertip. (Use your little finger for blending, as it is the driest part of the hand and the risk of smudging the charcoal is reduced.) Darken the sofa under the model's arm, so that he stands out more.

The finished drawing
Although this is not an overly elaborate drawing, it conveys the muscular nature of the model's body. The calves and thighs, in particular, are well developed (this particular model is a professional dancer). Subtle shading reveals the different planes of the body and the combination of dark, intense charcoal marks and soft pastel works well.

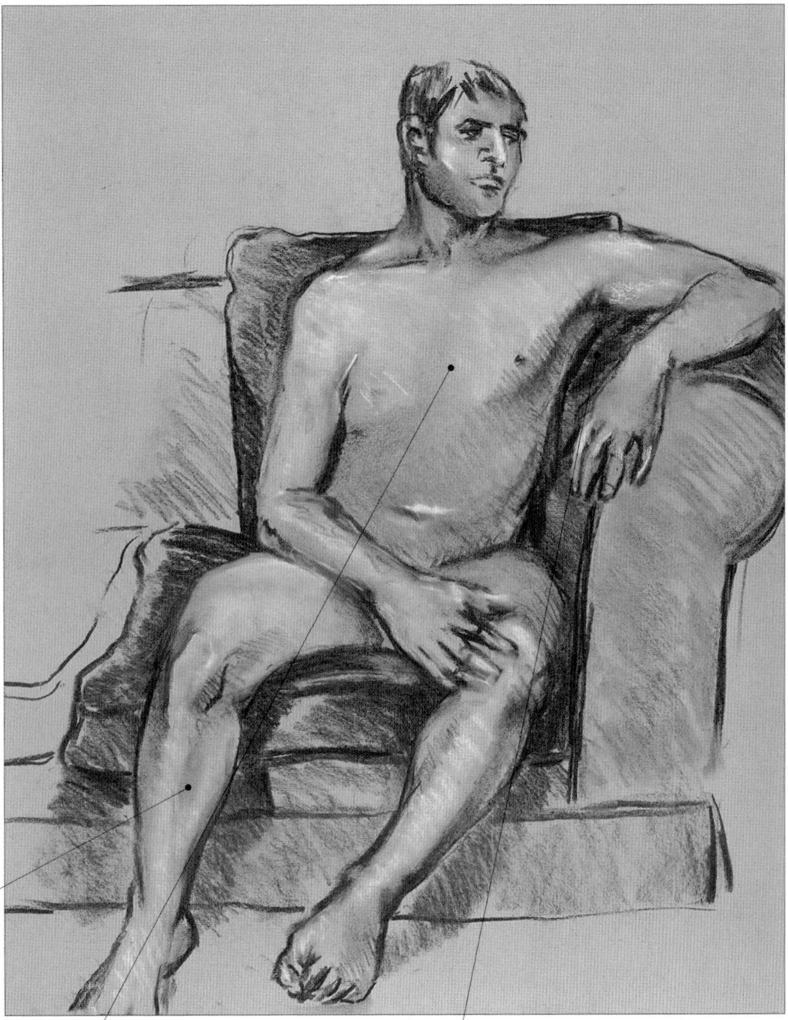

Note how effectively shading conveys the muscles in the calf.

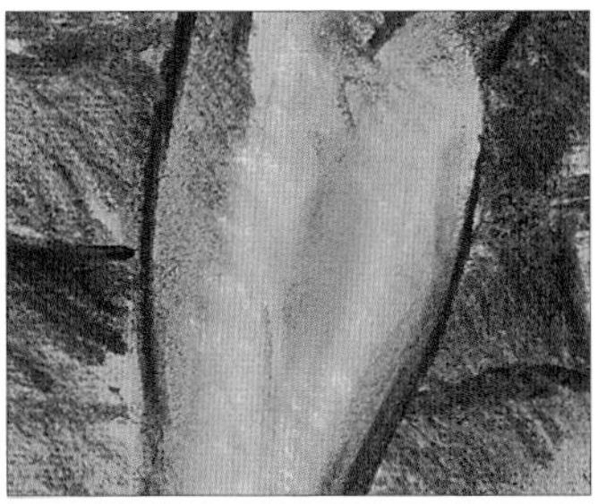

The pastel marks on the torso are blended to convey the smooth skin texture.

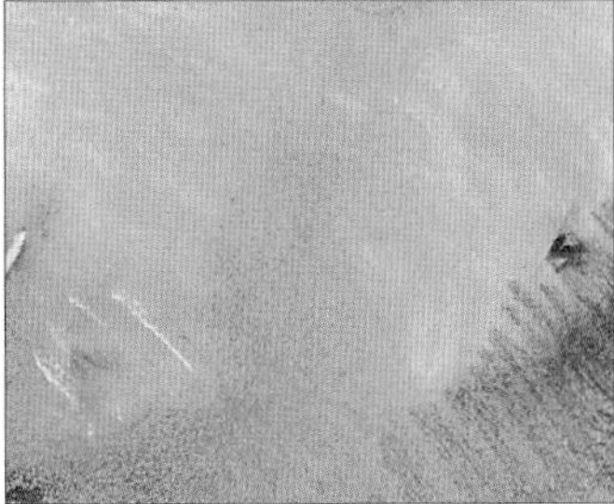

The figure stands out well against the dark background of the sofa.

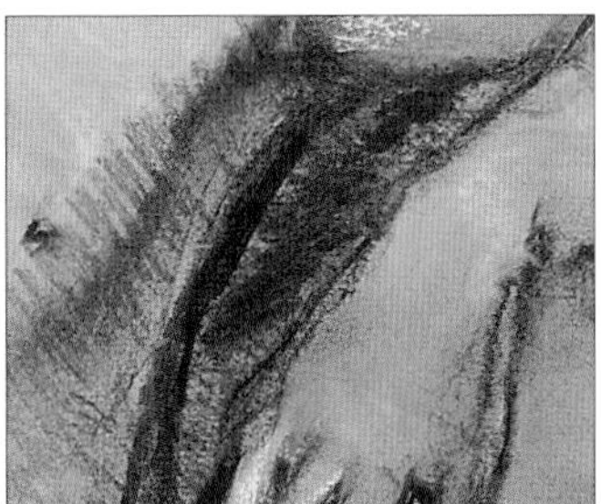

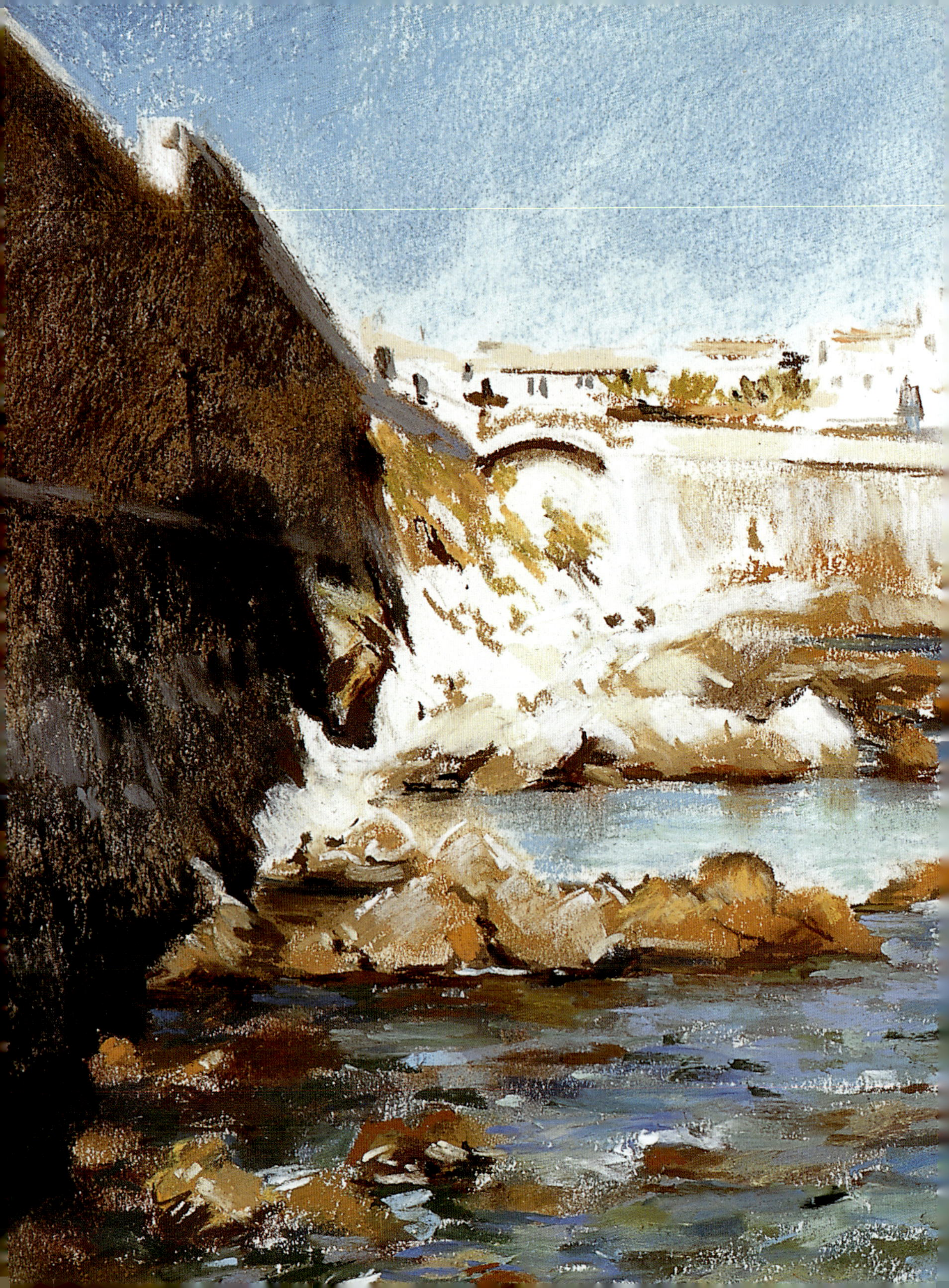

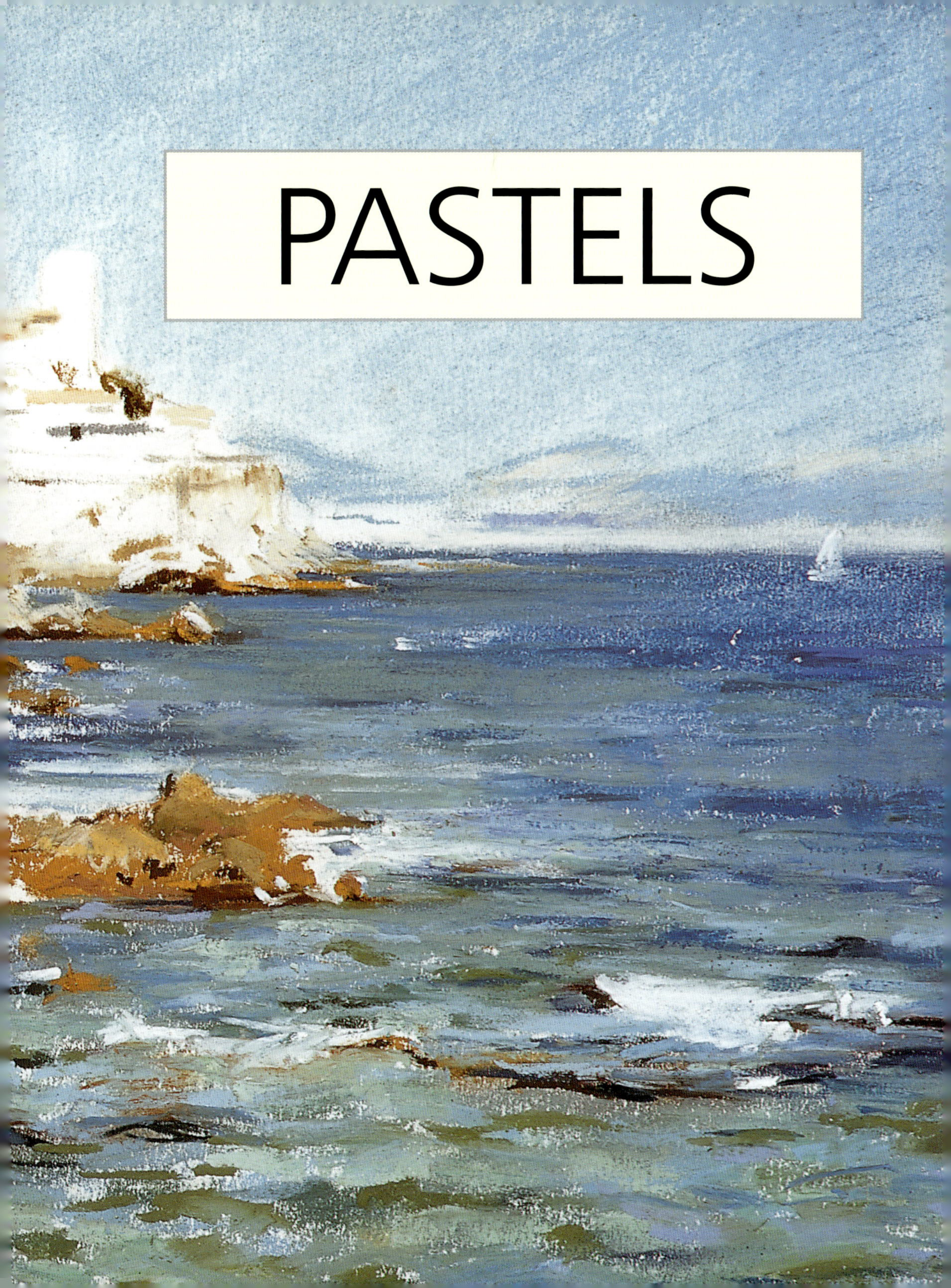

PASTELS

Introducing pastels

Pastel is unique in that it is both a drawing and a painting medium. It tends to be associated with drawing because the colours are not applied with a brush, but the medium's malleability and richness of colour invite a painterly approach. Many of today's artists exploit this effect in pastel to produce works that at first sight look almost like oil paintings.

Pastel is rapidly becoming one of the most favoured painting media, vying with watercolour for popularity. One of the reasons for this is probably that pastel sticks simply look so beautiful – open one of the boxed sets of pastels in an art shop and you will see a rich array of colours, which seem to offer a direct invitation to the artist. A tube of paint is a poor thing by comparison because you can't see the colour until you have squeezed it out.

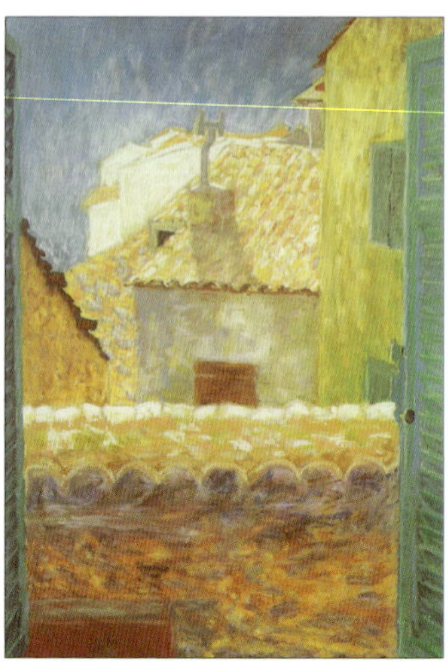

▶ **'Window in Provence'**
The colours are built up thickly here, using short pieces of pastel to make broad marks. To create the gentle but luminous colours, the artist has restricted himself to light and mid-tones, controlling them carefully, and changing the direction of the strokes for the different surfaces.
Patrick Cullen

▼ **'Summer Hillside'**
Pastel is often associated with delicate colours, hence the term 'pastel shades', but this powerful landscape shows that considerable depth of tone can be achieved. The artist has created a lovely feeling of energy, handling the pastels like brushstrokes in an oil painting.
James Crittenden

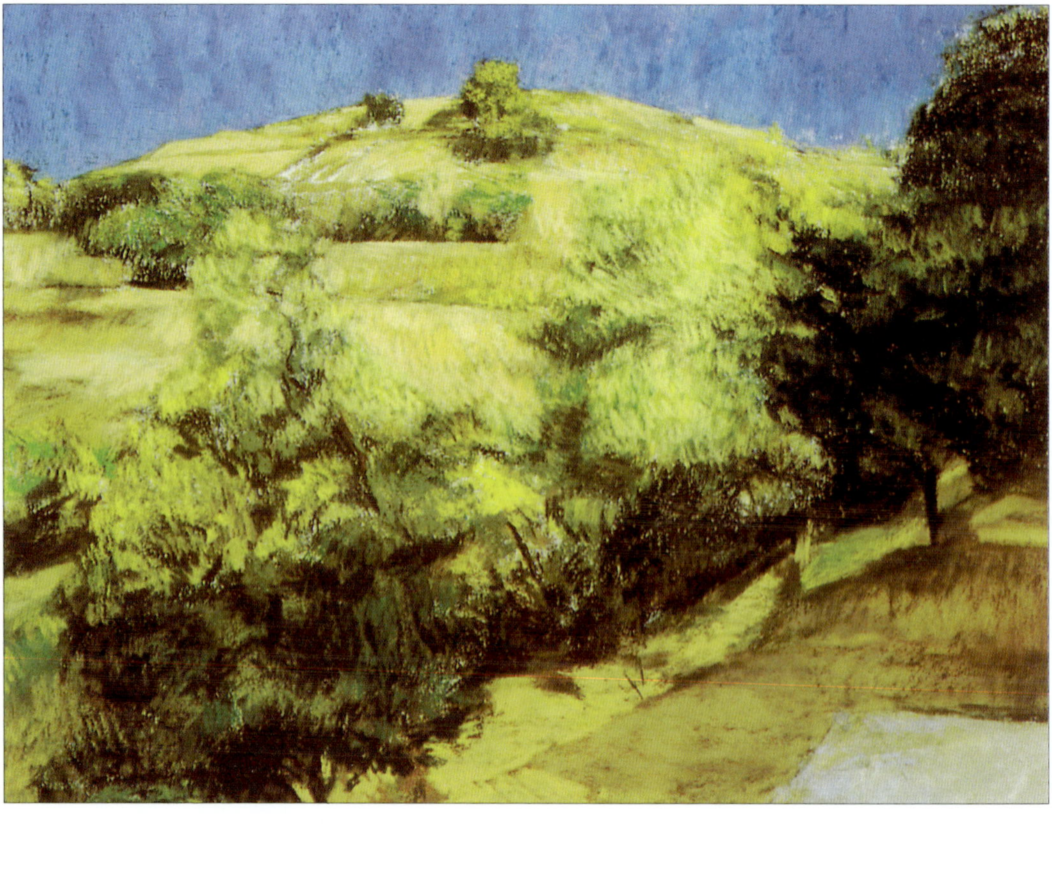

Pros and cons

The immediacy of pastel is also appealing. These sticks of colour form a direct link between your hand and the paper. You don't have to mix colours on a palette and you need no brushes. Like any drawing medium, pastels are responsive, easy to manipulate and quick to use, which makes them ideal for outdoor work and rapid effects; but because of their loose, crumbly texture and brilliance of colour – pastels are almost pure pigment – they can also be built up thickly in layers just as paints can. As you will see from the small gallery of paintings shown here, pastels are a versatile medium and there are many different ways of using them.

No medium is perfect, however, and those who are not accustomed to pastels may experience some problems until they become familiar with the techniques involved, and learn what pastels can and cannot do. One of the advantages – that you do not have to pre-mix colours – can also work against you. Any mixing has to be done on the working surface but, because it is not possible to try out mixes in advance as you can with paints, it is all too easy to make mistakes. You cannot erase pastels easily, although you can correct mistakes to some extent by laying more colours on top. If you do too much of this, however, you will clog the paper surface and may end up with a tired-looking, muddy result.

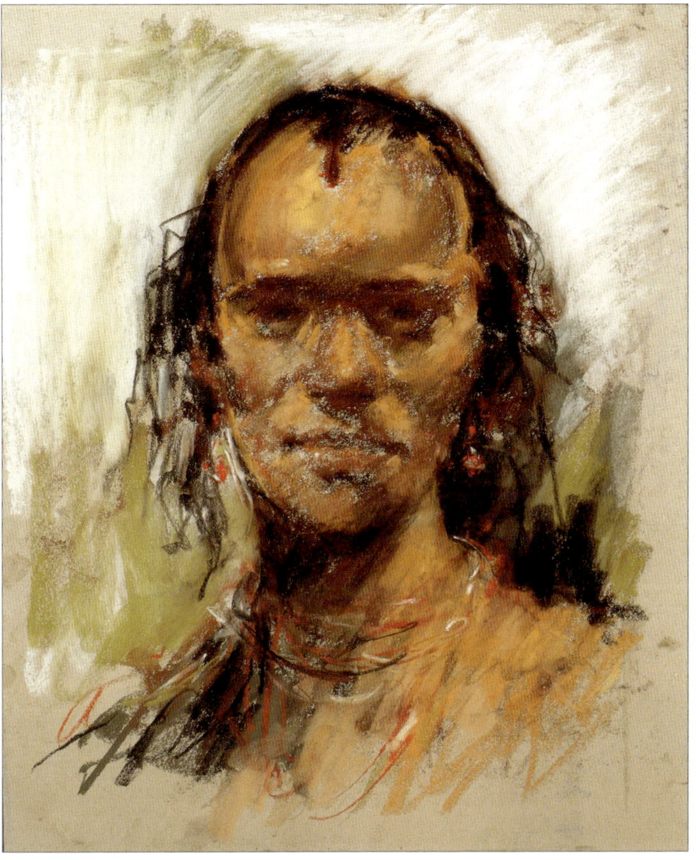

▲ **'Head of a Young Woman'**

This artist exploits the directness and expressive qualities of pastel in his portraits. He works with great rapidity, usually beginning by building up the tonal structure with a monochrome 'underpainting' made with broad strokes of short lengths of pastel. Linear definition and bright colour accents are left until the final stages. The coloured paper is still visible in areas.

Ken Paine

◀ **'Rose and Geranium Textures'**

The artist has exploited the whole range of pastel techniques in this vivid and lively picture, combining solid, thickly applied colour, blended in places, with fine line drawing to pick out individual flowers and petals. In the foreground, an area that can be dull in a floral group, a series of strong, decisive marks creates its own pattern and interest.

Maureen Jordan

One of the greatest exponents of pastel, the eighteenth-century portrait painter Maurice Quentin de La Tour, mentioned the possibility of spoiling work in this medium by over-mixing colours; he had one or two other complaints, too – about the dust generated by working with pastels, for example. It has to be admitted that it is not a medium for those who like to keep their floors clean, and one of the advantages of using pastels outdoors is that dust is not such a problem. Pastels are hard on the hands too, as they become covered with colour as soon as you pick up a stick.

A more serious problem is the fragility of pastels, in particular soft pastels. The sticks break very easily under pressure, added to which it is very easy to smudge areas that you are happy with, or the finished work. Even when sprayed with fixative, the pigments tend to fall off the paper, especially if they rub up against another surface. Unless you can frame and glaze your work immediately, it is vital to store it carefully, laying it flat with pieces of tissue paper on top.

Despite these minor problems, pastel is a wonderful medium to use. Few who have taken it up, whether amateur or professional, feel inclined to abandon it.

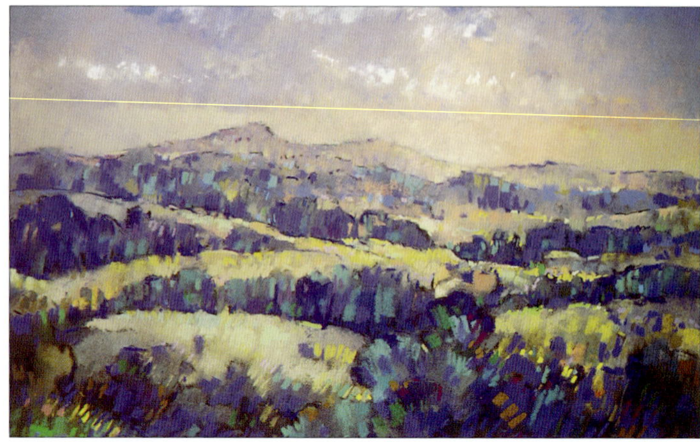

▲ **'Landscape in the Auvergne'**
When he first took up pastels, Geoff Marsters was determined to use the medium as a painting rather than a drawing technique, and through constant experiment he has evolved his own methods of working. He achieves his rich, dense colours by working on sandpaper, rubbing the pastel into it, fixing and then applying further layers on top.
Geoff Marsters

▼ **'Still Life with Blue Spanish Glass'**
In this gentle and tranquil picture the artist has made clever use of pastel's capacity for creating a variety of textures. For the glass, deep blues have been blended to imitate the smoothness of the material, but the central area of the plate has been left slightly rough, while in the background several colours have been dragged lightly over one another.
Jackie Simmonds

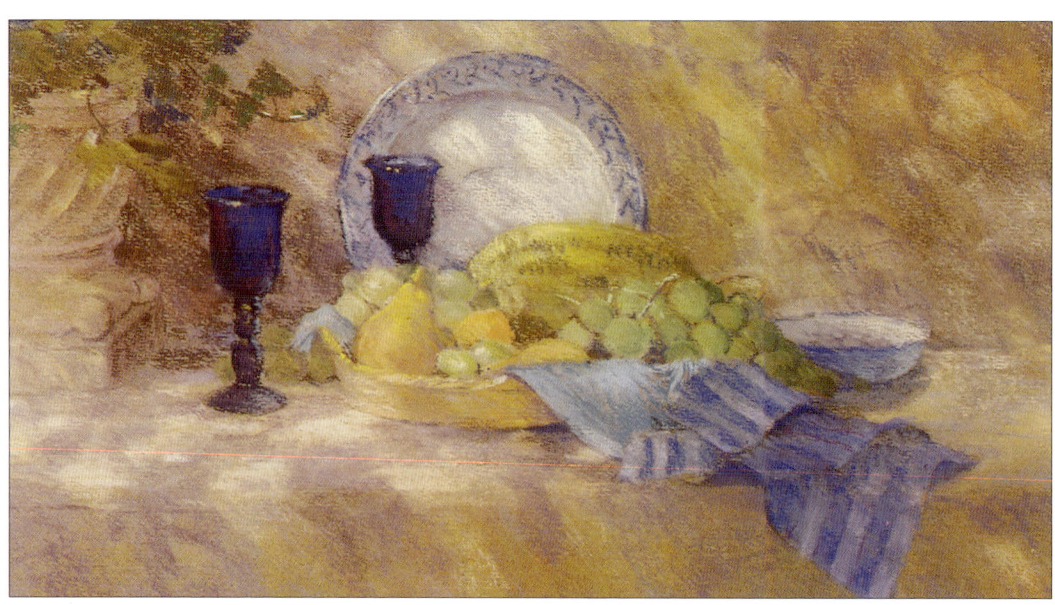

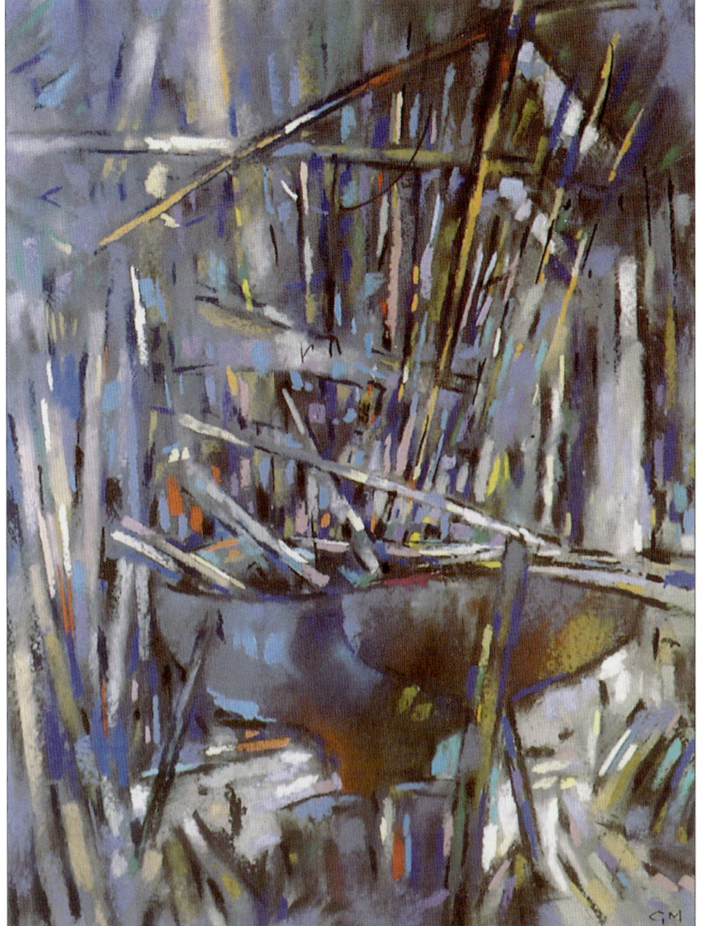

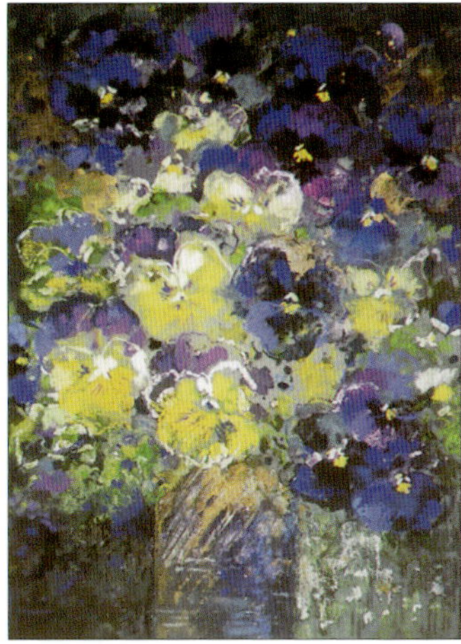

▲ **'Pansy Textures'**
The crumbly texture of pastel can benefit from contrast with a smoother medium, and here the artist has used it with acrylic. The underpainting has allowed her to establish rich colours without a heavy build-up of pastel.
Maureen Jordan

▼ **'Casa de Lido'**
In this atmospheric work, the approach to colour is more naturalistic than in the landscape opposite, but there are some similarities in technique. Patrick Cullen usually works either on sandpaper, or on heavy watercolour paper on which he first lays a ground of watercolour.
Patrick Cullen

▲ **'Interior of Boathouse'**
This subject, with its angularity and profusion of detail, might not seem suitable for a soft, crumbly medium such as pastel, which is usually considered better when aiming for broad effects, but the artist has treated it with great assurance. If you look closely you can see that the lines and edges are in fact quite loose and free; the impression of sharp linearity is created by the strong contrasts of tone and colour.
Geoff Marsters

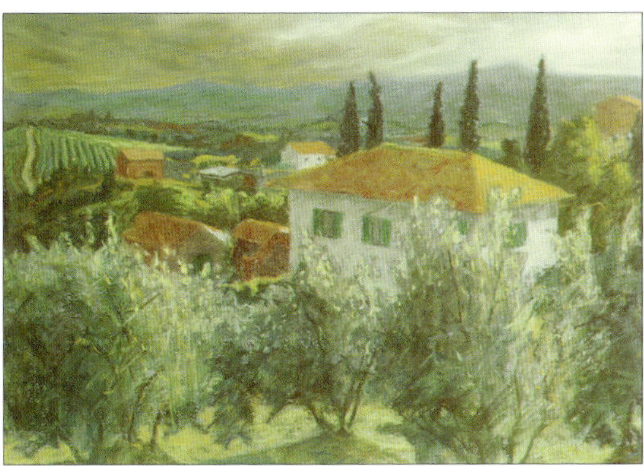

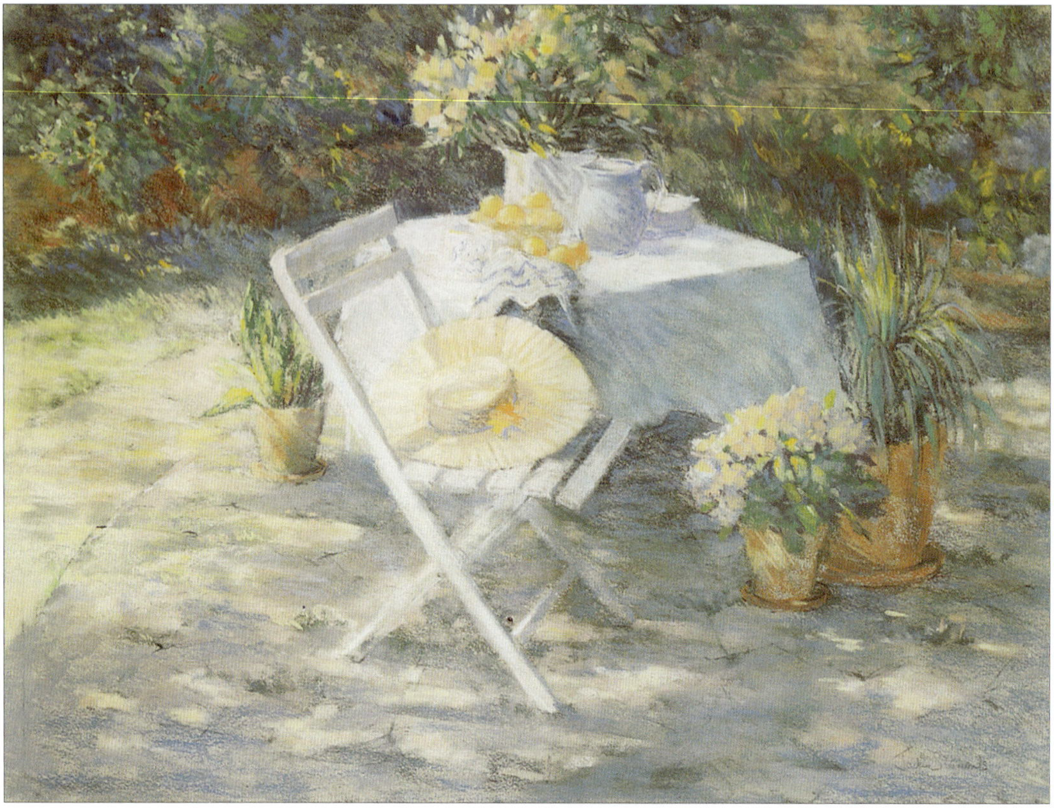

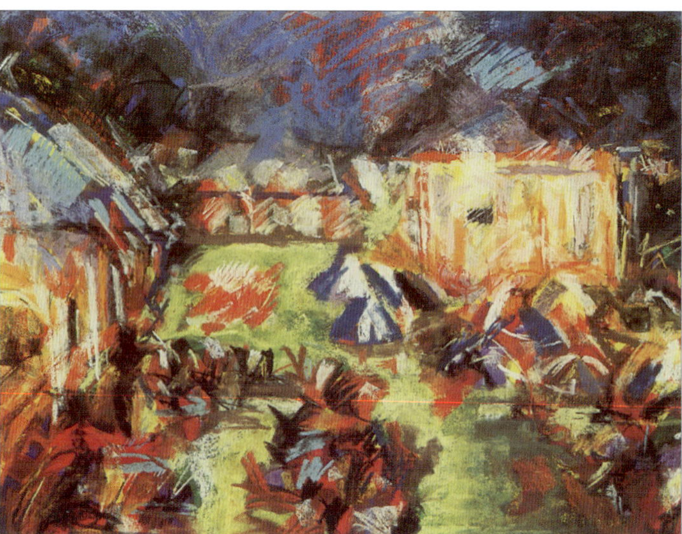

▲ **'Tea on the Patio'**
This delightful picture probably comes closest to most people's idea of pastel – the colours are light and fresh, in keeping with the airy subject, and the handling is delicate. The medium needs a light touch and a sound knowledge of both colour and technique to achieve such effects.
Jackie Simmonds

◀ **'Bandstand Series'**
Vivid colour was of primary importance in this work, and acrylic has been used in combination with pastel. The underpainting, which set the colour key, was mainly in shades of red and yellow, with contrasting colours of pastel applied on top. You can see this effect clearly in the sky, where strokes of blue pastel overlay bright red paint.
Judy Martin

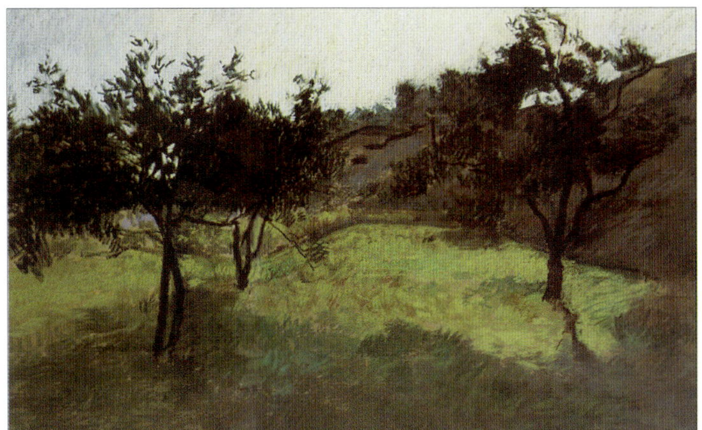

◀ **'Orange Grove in the Evening'**
As in most of his pastel works, this artist skilfully combines the drawing and painting qualities of pastel to produce an interpretation of the landscape that is both realistic and highly personal. What appear at first glance to be solid areas of colour – the sky and grass – are in fact a complex network of overlaid lines and marks made with the tip of the stick, while the leaves of the trees are expressed by rapid calligraphic dashes and squiggles.
James Crittenden

▶ **'The Sun-Dappled Table'**
This piece, worked on a dark, greenish paper, gives the initial impression of oil pastel, but in fact is soft pastel pressed hard into the paper and fixed between stages to allow one colour to be laid over another. The artist was particularly excited by the effect of the light on the different surfaces – the volume of the fruit and the flat plane of the ornamental iron table.
Pip Carpenter

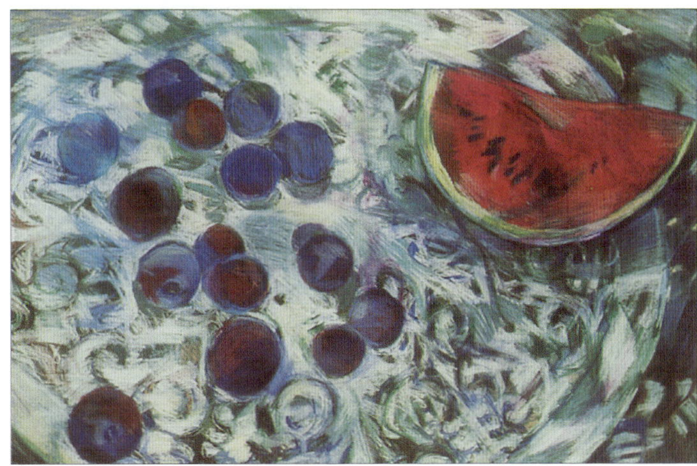

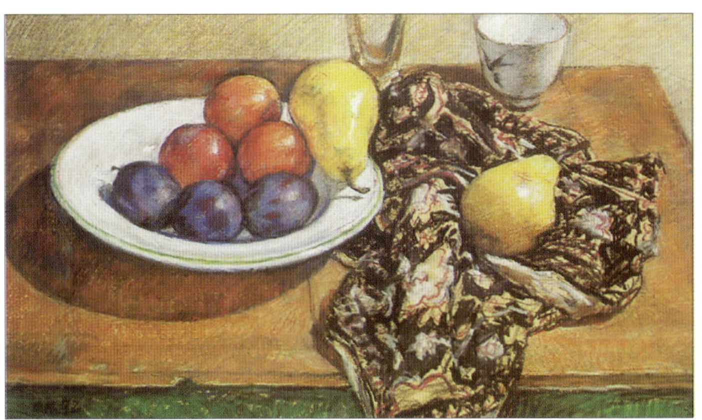

◀ **'Still Life With Pears and Plums'**
For this still life, the artist has worked in oil pastel, which she likes because it is related to oil paint, the medium she uses most frequently. She also finds it more controllable than soft pastel. Here it has allowed her to build up deep, rich colours as well as very subtle effects, notably the bloom on the plums.
Elizabeth Moore

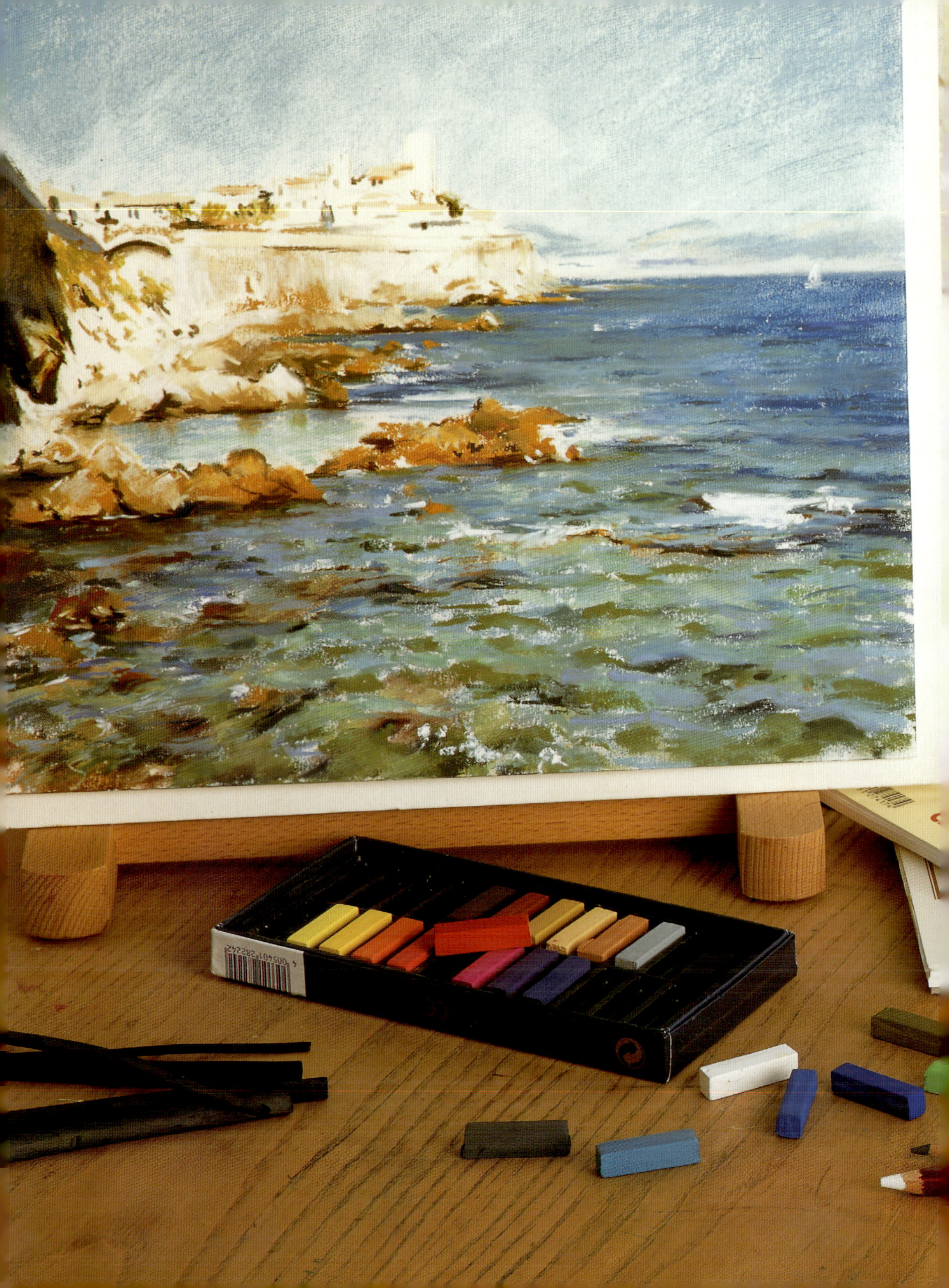

Getting Started in Pastels

While it shares some of the characteristics of both drawing and painting, pastel work uses a unique range of techniques, which are outlined on the following pages. This section begins with a look at the materials themselves and suggests tips and tricks for choosing and handling them. Pastels can be used on a wide range of papers, from watercolour paper to velour and sandpaper, which has a really rough texture that will hold deep multiple layers of colour. Your choice of support depends on your personal drawing style.

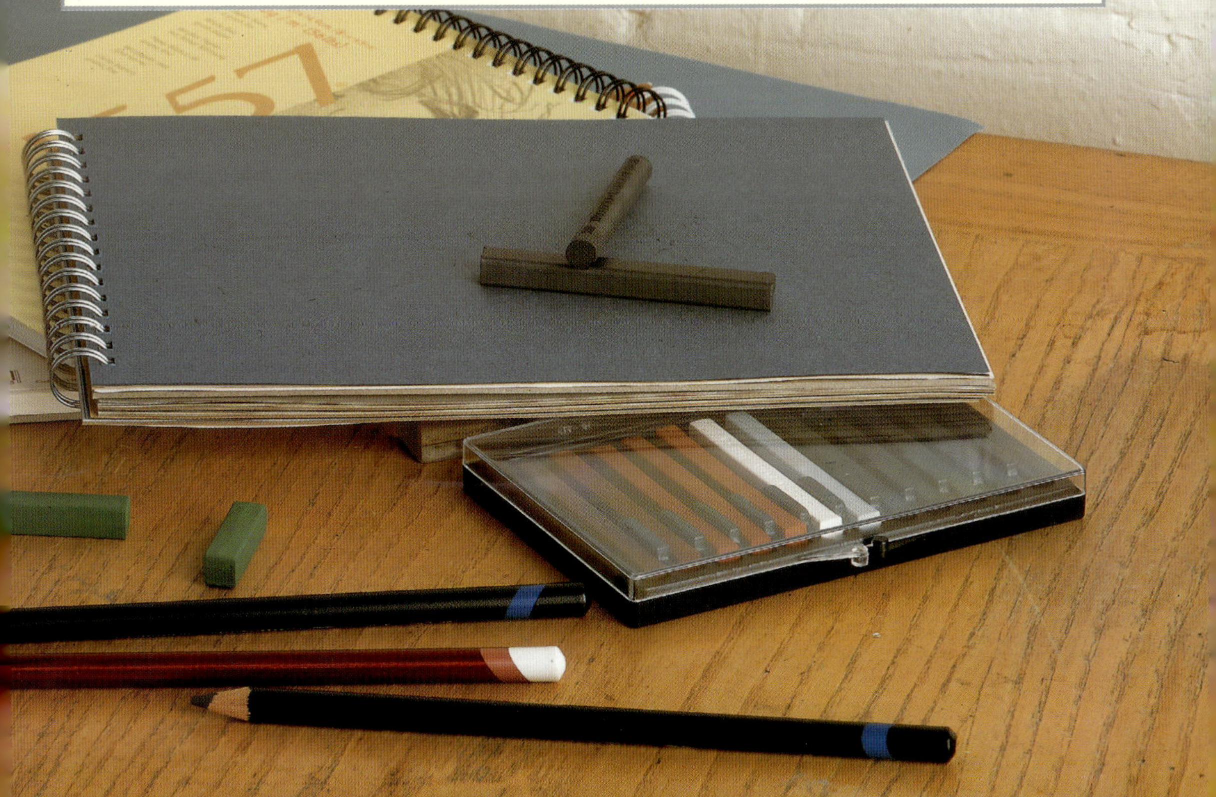

Pastels

Pastel work is often described as painting rather than drawing and it is an unusual drawing medium in that the techniques used are often similar to techniques used in painting. Pastels are made by mixing pigment with a weak binder (usually gum tragacanth) to hold the mixture together. The more binder in the mix, the harder the pastel. Various amounts of titanium or zinc white can be added to the pure pigment, resulting in a range of pastels of slightly different tints.

Soft pastels

Usually around 6cm (2½in) long and about 1cm (½in) in diameter, soft pastels can also be purchased in half-lengths (shown below), as well as a limited range of much thicker pastels that are ideal if you want to work on a large scale.

As soft pastels contain relatively little binder, they are usually quite delicate and prone to crumbling, so they are wrapped in a paper wrapper to help keep them in one piece. Even so, dust still comes off the pastels, and can easily contaminate other colours near by. The best option is to arrange your pastels by colour type – all the blues together, all the greens together, and so on – and store them in boxes with shallow drawers. Some artists recommend putting dry rice in the drawer, too, so that any dust comes off on to the rice rather than on to the other pastels.

Because soft pastels are so crumbly, you will find that small pieces break off as you draw. Often the pieces are so tiny that they are very difficult to hold comfortably for drawing – but don't discard them. Even tiny fragments can be used to block in areas of colour: simply put your finger over the piece of pastel and gently rub it on to the paper.

In some ways, the small amount of binder in soft pastels is a bonus, as it means they are almost pure pigment and hence the colours are very fresh and immediate.

Pastels are mixed together on the support either by physically blending them or by allowing colours to mix optically. The less blending that is done, the fresher the image looks. For this reason, pastels are made in a range of tints and shades that runs into the hundreds.

Pastels are coded for strength and colour. All brands can be mixed and used together, although the coding system used is not consistent across the different brands. The degree of softness also varies between brands, so it's a good idea to try out a few pastels from one manufacturer's range to see whether or not you like the feel of them before you spend a fortune on buying a large set.

As pastels are a dry, powdery medium, the paper on which you draw must have enoughtexture to hold the particles of pigment in place. Pastel paper is specifically designed to do this, allowing you to build up several layers of colour.

Remember to spray any soft pastel drawing with fixative to prevent the colours from smudging. You can fix (set) work in progress, too – but there is a risk of the colours darkening, so don't overdo it.

Box of pastels ▼
When you buy a set of pastels, they come in a compartmentalized box so that they do not rub against each other and become dirtied.

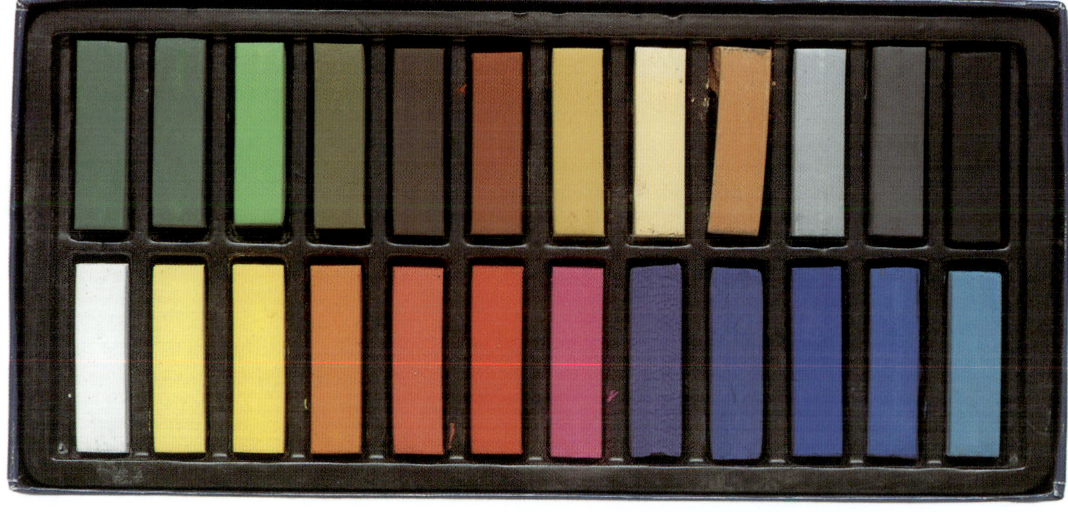

Hard pastels

Formulated slightly differently to soft pastels, hard pastels contain less pigment and more binder. They are easier to control than soft pastels and have the added advantage that they can be carefully sharpened to a point. They are found in a reasonably comprehensive range of colours, but the selection is nowhere near as great as that for soft pastels and the colours are not as pure or brilliant.

One advantage of hard pastels is that, in use, they do not shed as much pigment as soft pastels, and so they do not clog the texture of the paper as quickly. For this reason, they are often used in the initial stages of a work that is completed using soft pastels. Hard pastels can be blended together by rubbing, but not as easily or as seamlessly as soft pastels.

Pastel pencils

A delight to use, the colours of pastel pencils are strong, yet the pencil shape makes them ideal for drawing lines. If treated carefully, they do not break – although they are more fragile than graphite or coloured pencils. The pastel strip can be sharpened to a point, making pastel pencils ideal for describing detail in drawings that have been made using conventional hard or soft pastels.

Pastel pencils ▼
Available in a comprehensive range of colours, pastel pencils are clean to use and are ideal for linear work. They can be used with both hard and soft pastels.

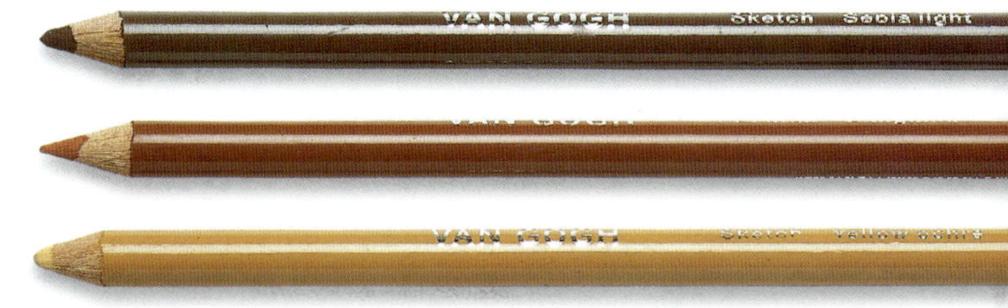

Oil pastels

Made by combining pigment with fats and waxes, oil pastels are totally different to pigmented soft and hard pastels and should not be mixed with them. Oil pastels can be used on unprimed drawing paper and they never completely dry.

For bold, confident strokes, oil pastels are perfect – so make a point of exploiting their textural qualities and work on a large scale, using vigorous strokes and building up rich colour.

Oil-pastel marks have something of the thick, buttery quality of oil paints. The pastels are highly pigmented and available in a reasonably comprehensive range of colours. If they are used on oil-painting paper, they can be worked into using a spirit solvent such as turpentine or white spirit (paint thinner), which you can apply using either a brush or a rag. You can also smooth out oil-pastel marks using your fingers. Wet your finger first: as oil and water are not compatible, a damp finger will not pick up colour.

As with the other types of pastel, oil pastels can be blended optically with one colour on top of another.

You can also create a wide range of textural effects by scratching into the pastel marks with a sharp implement – a technique known as sgraffito.

Water-soluble oil pastels have an additional ingredient such as glycol that allows you to thin and blend the colours using a water wash. You can experiment with wet and dry pastels – dip them in water, use a wet paint-brush over the lines you have drawn, or use a dry pastel on wet paper.

Oil pastels ▼
Less crumbly than soft pastels, and harder in texture, oil pastels are round sticks and come in various sizes. They are sold in a paper wrapper, which helps to keep the pastel intact and the artist's hands clean. Tear away the wrapper as the pastel wears down.

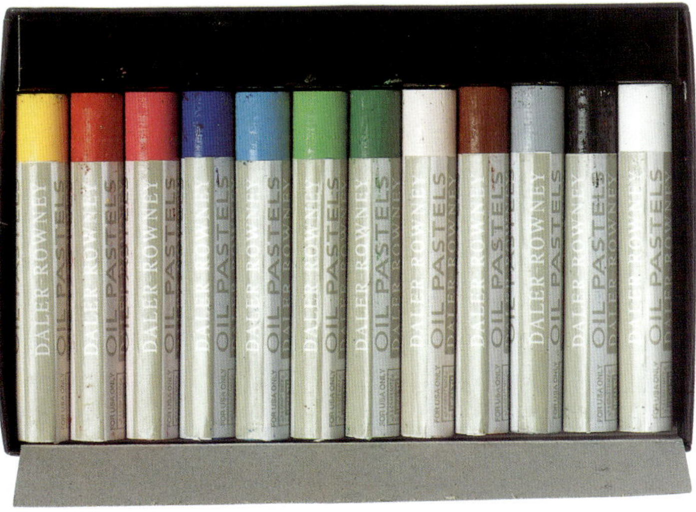

Line strokes

Pastel is a drawing medium as well as a painting one in as much as the pastel stick, like a pencil, is the direct intermediary between your hand and the paper. Although it is possible to blend all the colours smoothly with no visible lines or marks, this is something of a lost opportunity, as the way in which pastel bridges the gap between drawing and painting is one of its major attractions. In the eighteenth century, when pastel painting became very popular, artists such as Jean-Etienne Liotard and Maurice Quentin de La Tour produced works whose smooth finishes emulated contemporary oil paintings. However, nowadays most artists prefer to exploit the mark-making aspect of pastel, to give free rein to its energetic, linear quality.

In order to do this successfully, you need to develop your own 'handwriting' in pastel. The tip of a pastel stick can produce a wide variety of different marks, depending on how much pressure you apply, the sharpness or bluntness of the point and how you hold the stick. To practise mark-making, don't try to draw actual objects, but just doodle or scribble as the mood takes you. Try applying heavy pressure at the start of a line and then tapering off towards the end, or twisting the stick in mid-stroke so that it trails off in a narrow tail.

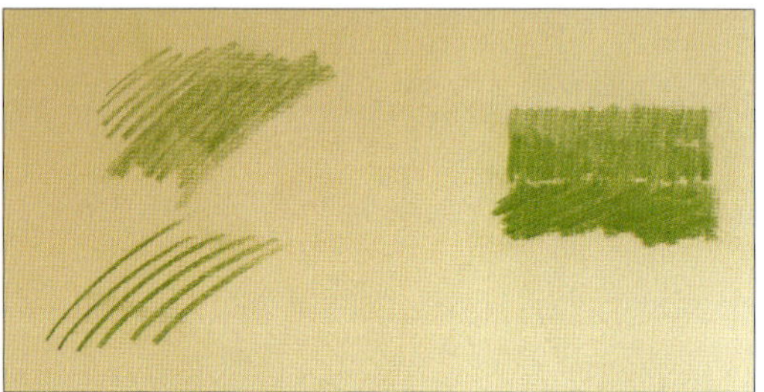

◀ ▶ ▼ These swatches show the variety of marks that you can make with the tip and side of a pastel stick.

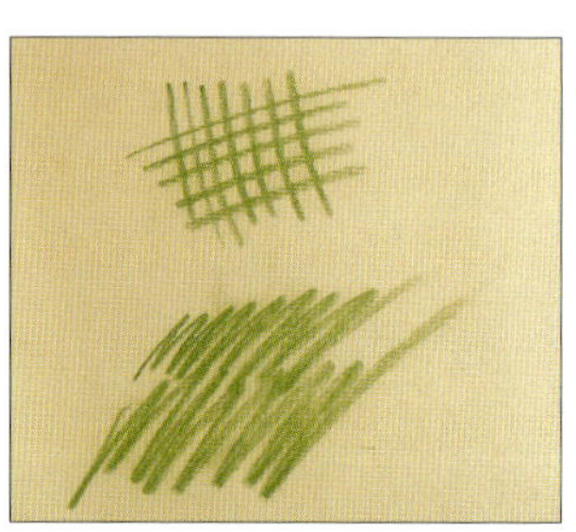

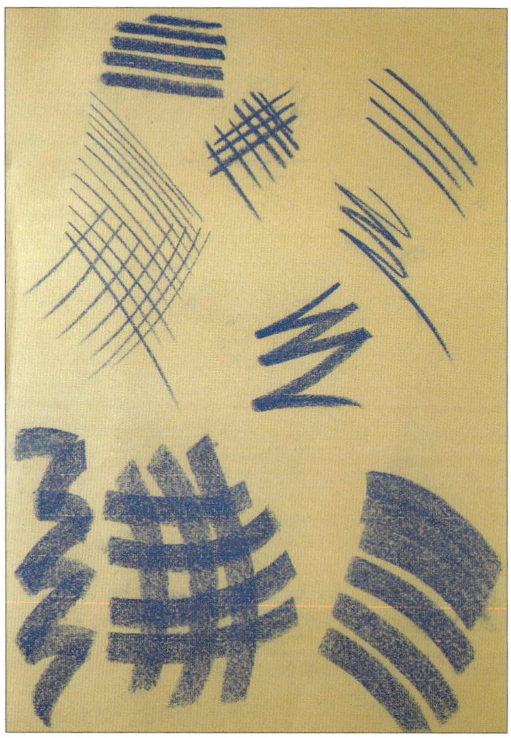

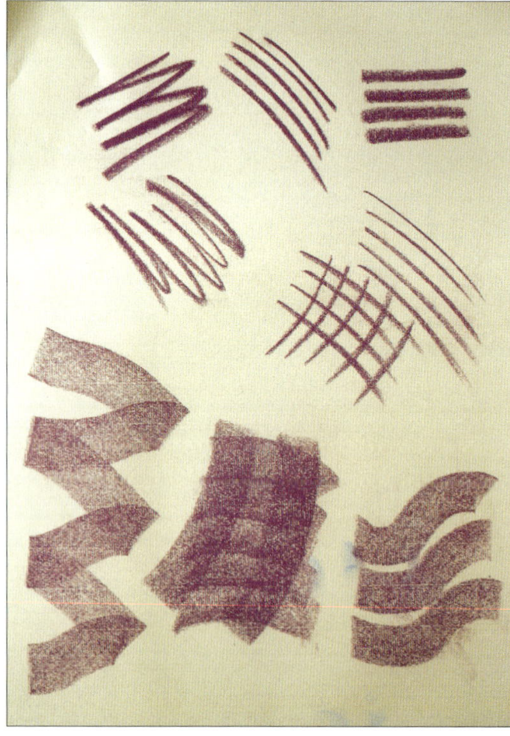

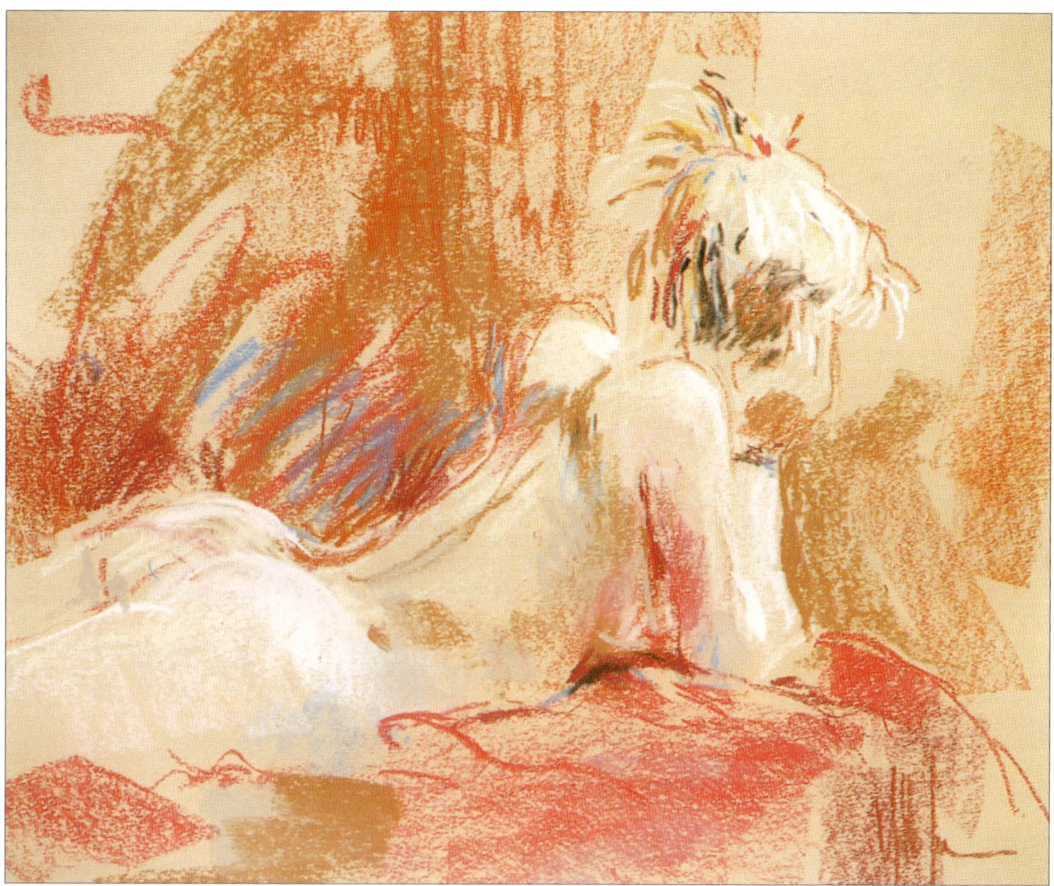

Although pastel is soft and crumbly, you will find that you can make surprisingly fine lines if you break a stick in half and use the edge of the broken end. However, hard pastels are the ones for really crisp details, so if you have these, experiment with them too.

Side strokes

The way to cover large areas of the paper in pastel work is to sweep the side of the stick across the paper, thus depositing a broad band of colour. Side strokes can, however, be much more than just a means of 'blocking in' – they can be as varied, beautiful and expressive as line strokes. Many different effects can be created by varying the pressure and direction of the stroke, by laying one stroke over another, by blending in some areas and by laying one colour over another.

The length of the pastel stick also affects the kind of stroke you make. Unless you are using hard pastels, which are relatively tough, you will nearly always have to break the stick. If you try to make side strokes with the whole length of the stick, it will probably break under pressure anyway, added to which a short length is more controllable. Usually the length should not be more than 5cm (2in), but you can use much smaller pieces of pastel than these to make short, jabbing strokes, similar to linear marks.

The other factor that affects side strokes, even more than linear ones, is the texture of the paper. A heavy texture such as watercolour paper will break up the stroke, producing a grainy effect, with the colour deposited only on the top of the weave. On smoother paper, the colour will be denser and, if you apply the pastel heavily, it will cover the paper thoroughly. Be warned that, if you intend to use side strokes as a means of colour mixing, with one colour laid over another, the pressure should be kept light initially, or the paper will quickly become clogged.

▲ **'Nude Against Pink'**
A classic combination of line and side strokes can be seen in Maureen Jordan's lively figure study. Notice how the artist has used pastel sticks in a descriptive way, following the directions of the shapes and forms.

Mixing pastels

Variations of tone (the lightness and darkness of colours) are produced by controlling the amount of pressure you apply to the pastel stick – the more pressure you put on it, the more solid the colour will be. But however large a collection of pastels you build up – and professional pastel artists may work with hundreds of different colours – you will nearly always have to mix them to reproduce the colours you see in life. Nature provides far more subtle and varied nuances of colour than could be matched by any manufacturer of artist's pigments.

Lightening and darkening colours

As mentioned earlier, all pastel colours are available in light and dark versions, but you will frequently have to lighten or darken colours further by mixing them on the support. A pale blue sky, for example, may call for a combination of blue and white, or blue and pale grey; dark areas of foliage or heavy shadows may need a mixture of dark blue or black with green and other colours, and gradual variations of tone are essential to the modelling of three-dimensional objects in drawing.

Black is particularly useful in pastel work, as the colours themselves are brilliant and generally not very dark, so it is hard to achieve any depth of colour without using black.

Lightening

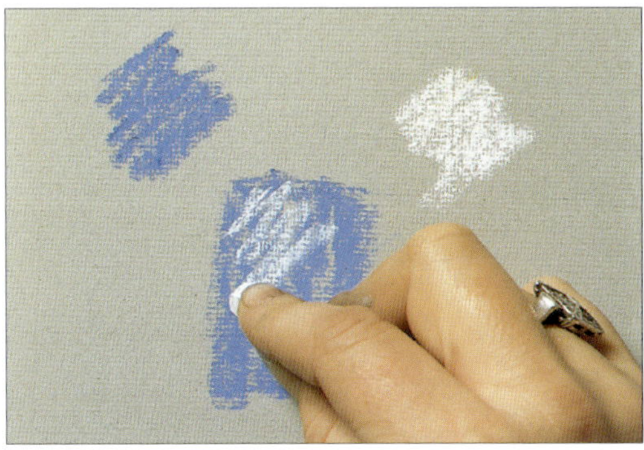

1 When very pale pastel colours are required, such as when creating highlights on a solid object, it is sometimes necessary to mix on the paper surface by adding white. Here white is laid over a mid-blue.

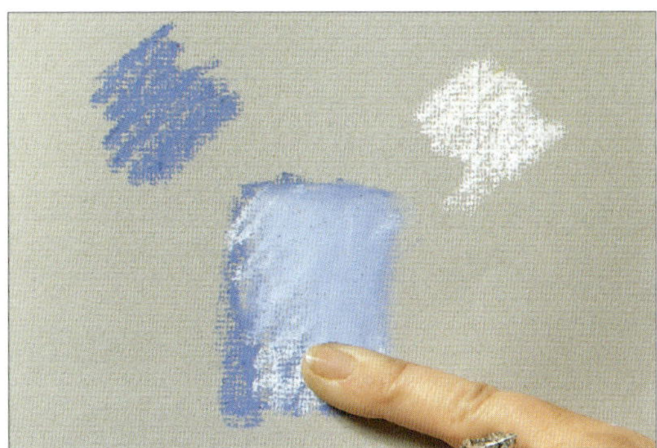

2 The pastel pigments are gently blended together with a fingertip. Be prepared to use your fingers a good deal in pastel work; they are the best 'implements' for blending in relatively small areas.

Darkening

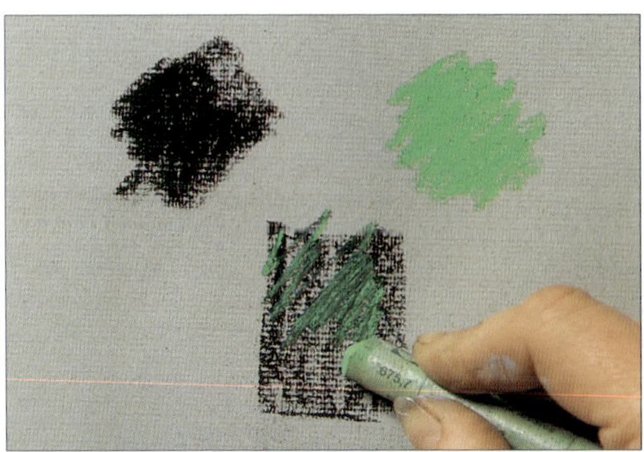

1 Black is a useful colour in pastel work, as it can be difficult to achieve really dark colours without it. The black has been laid down first here, with the colour applied on top.

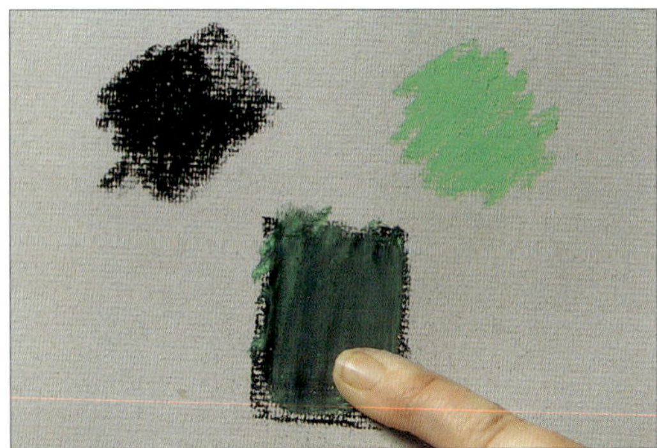

2 With experience you will discover which colours can be successfully darkened with black. This mixture is rather muddy and the light green has lost much of its character.

Mixing greens

To reproduce the wide range of greens in nature, you generally need to mix colours to some extent. Here, ultramarine is laid over a lemony yellow. The two colours are blended lightly to produce a strong green. Yellows and blues can also be added to ready-made greens to modify them.

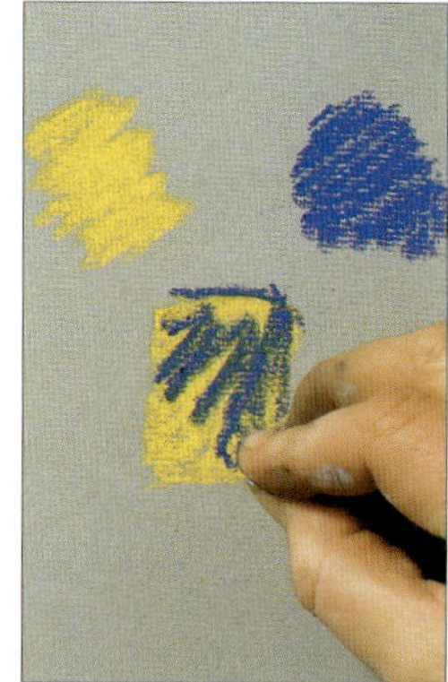

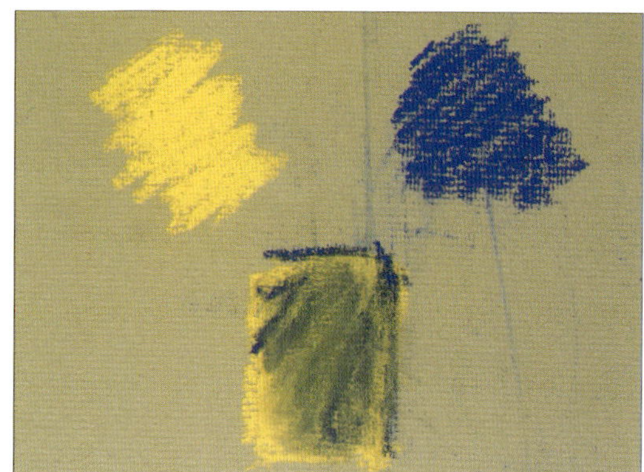

Mixing oranges

To mix a pure orange, choose the strongest red and yellow in your pastel set, and lay the yellow over the red. Even when the two colours are blended, the darker colour will dominate if it is laid over the lighter one. Experiment to discover the effect of light-over-dark and dark-over-light mixtures.

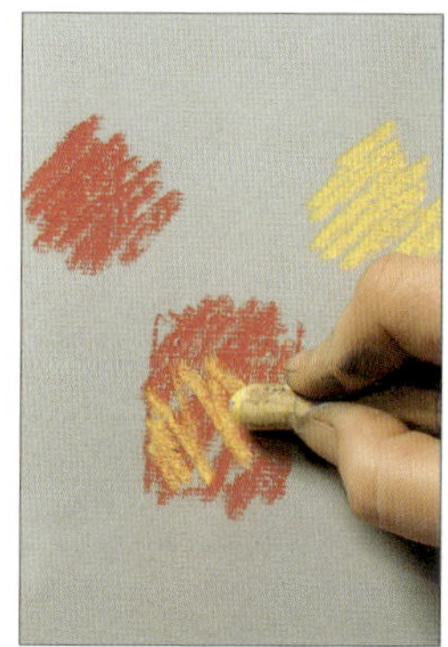

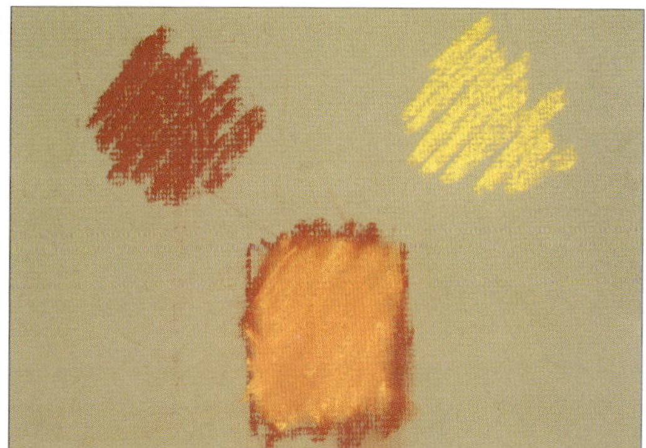

Mixing greys

Most pastel ranges include a good selection of greys, but they can easily be mixed from black and white. Other colours, such as blues and greens, can be added for interest. The result will be affected by the order in which the colours are laid: white over black will produce a lighter mixture, particularly if the colours are blended only gently.

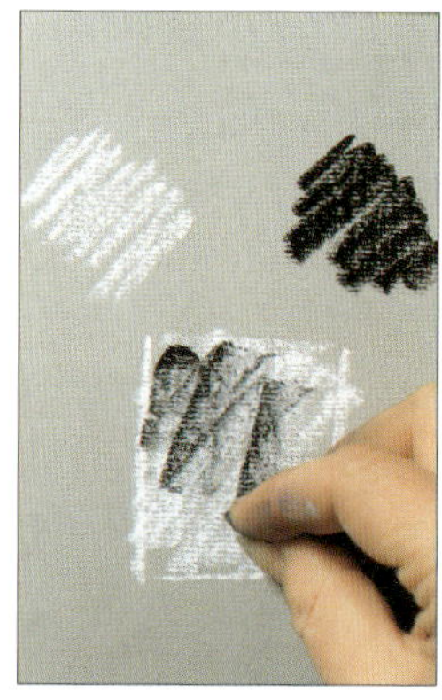

Methods of mixing

The main technique for colour mixing is blending. Colours are applied to the working surface and rubbed together with the fingers, a rag, a piece of cotton wool or a torchon (a rolled paper stump made specially for the purpose). With care, you can achieve almost any colour and tone in this way. However, although blending is ideal for areas where you want a soft effect, you should not rely on it too much, as over-blending gives a bland result.

A light, unblended application of one colour over another is a more vibrant and exciting alternative because the first colour shows through the second, producing an attractive sparkle. Pastels are opaque, and so light colours can be laid over dark ones as well as the other way round, to modify the tone of colours.

For many artists, one of the main attractions of pastel is its vigorous linear quality, with the marks of the pastel stick forming an integral part of the image (like brushwork in painting). For this reason, colours are sometimes mixed by building up a network of linear strokes, which merge when seen from a distance. A related method is feathering, which is often used to revive an area of colour that has become flat and dull through over-zealous blending. It involves dragging light strokes of colour over the offending area with the tip of the pastel stick and provides a useful means of modifying colours that do not look quite right. For example, a solid area of red that seems too bright in the overall context of the work can be feathered over lightly with strokes of green, or a too-blue sky can be transformed with greys or pale mauves.

Choosing paper

When one colour is laid over another it produces a third colour – yellow over blue makes green; red over yellow makes orange and so on. Thus it follows that the colour of the paper will influence the applied colour. If you choose a neutral mid-toned paper the effect will not be dramatic, but a light application of yellow on a rich blue paper has a similar effect to laying yellow over blue pastel. It is important to remember this, as the paper always acts as a third colour in any two-colour mixture, unless the pastel is applied heavily. On the following pages you can see some of the effects of the paper colour on mixtures.

▼ 'Fen Light'

In this piece, Geoff Marsters' rich painterly effects have been achieved by laying one colour over another, with the work fixed between stages.

For the bright patches of highlight in the fields, Geoff has used the tips of the pastel sticks, applying thick colour over softer blends.

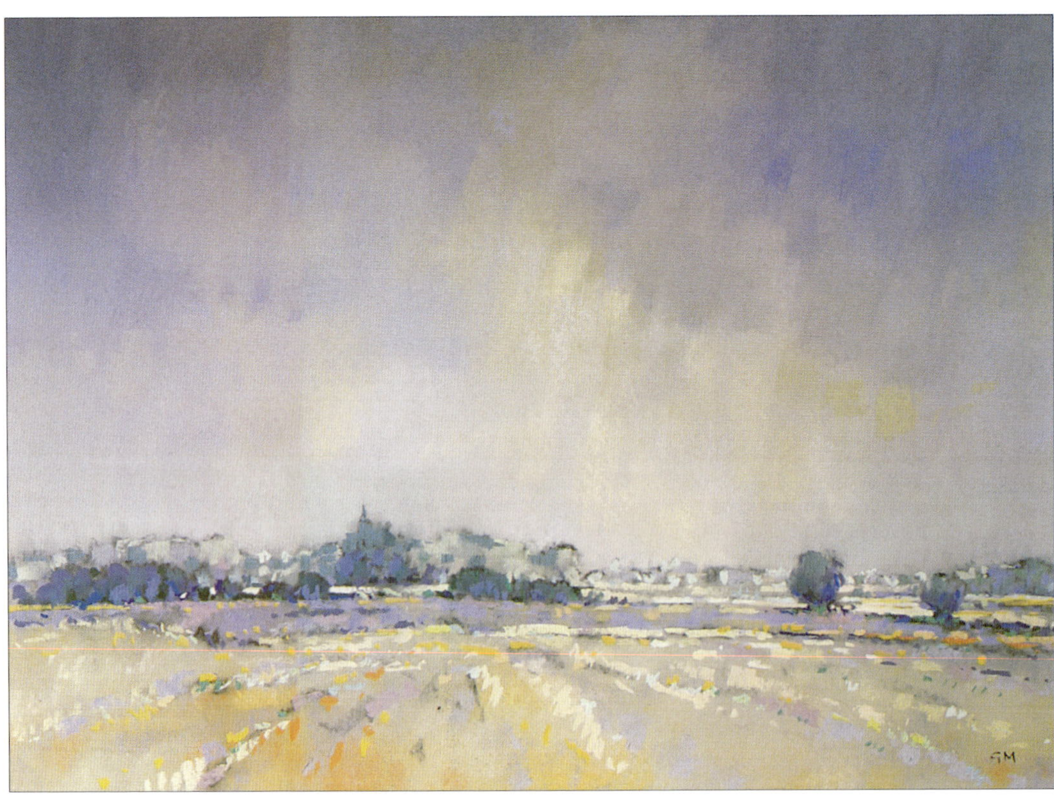

Blending large areas

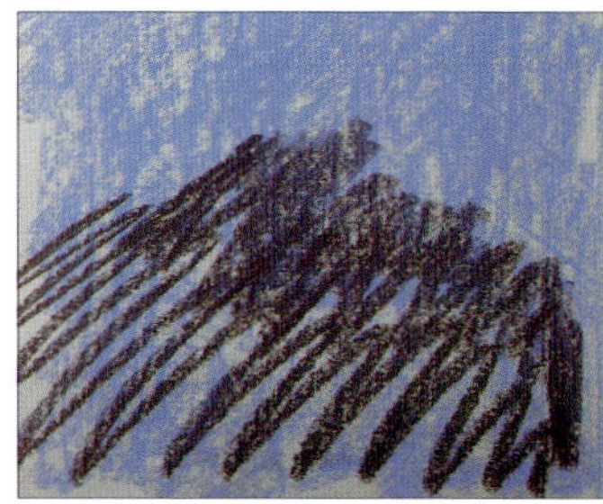

1 For a subtle blend that would be suitable for a large area of dark sky, for example, blue and black are first lightly scribbled together.

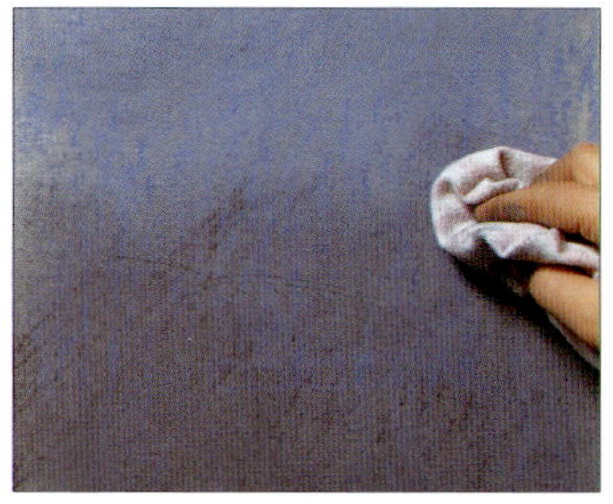

2 Using a rag to blend the colours knocks some of the particles of pastel off the paper, producing a lighter mixture than finger blending, which pushes the pigment into the paper.

Feathering

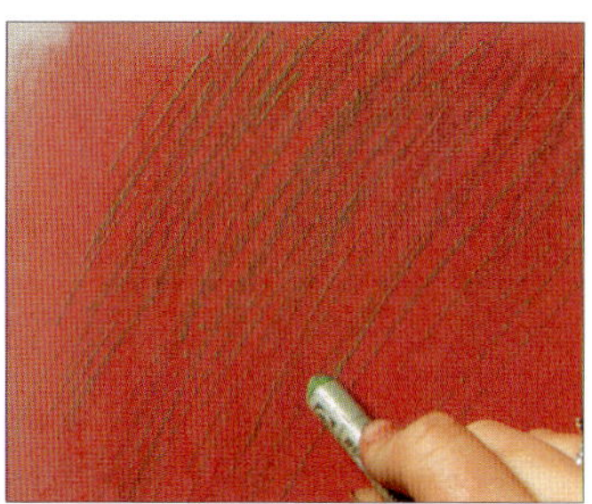

This is a useful method for rejuvenating an area of colour that has become flat and dull, or for toning down a bright colour. Here light feathering strokes are made in green over an area of red.

Overlays

Thoroughly blended colour mixtures may be necessary in certain areas of a picture, but the effects of unblended colours are often more interesting and exciting. In the examples below you can see how one colour shows through another applied over it to produce a lively, sparkling effect.

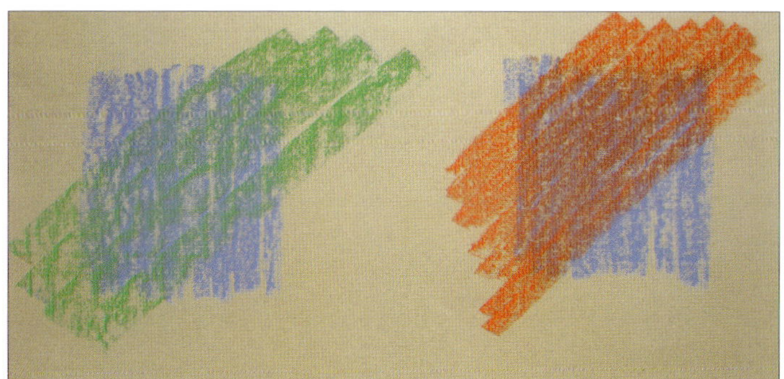

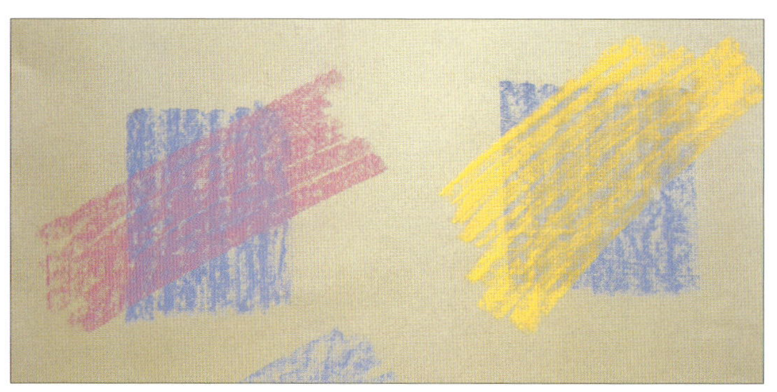

Using the paper colour

Even when pastel is applied thickly, some paper will show through and affect the applied colour. Paper colour acts as the 'key' against which you must judge the first colours you put on, so at first it is wise to choose mid-toned neutral colours to avoid the possibility of the base colour working against you.

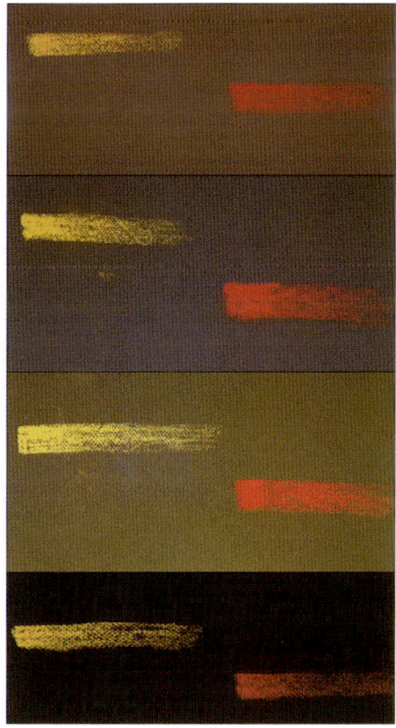

Blending with soft pastels and oil pastels

Soft pastels can be blended both physically and optically; more often than not, a combination of techniques is used in a drawing. The dusty, loose pigment that is left on the support after a mark has been made can be manipulated in a number of ways. The handiest tool for blending colours is your finger – but make sure that your hands are clean and free from grease. Your little finger is usually the coolest and driest part of the hand and hence the best one to use. For larger areas such as skies, you can use the side of your hand in a light, circular motion. A rag or piece of kitchen paper can be used in the same way and a cotton bud (cotton swab) is ideal for intricate areas. However, the tool intended for the job is the torchon. Made from rolled or compacted paper pulp, it is used to move the pigment around the surface of the support. Torchons get dirty very quickly, but you can clean them by rubbing them on fine abrasive paper.

Harder pastels and chalks can be used in the same way, but they can be sharpened to a point so you can mix colours by using scribbled and hatched marks, as with coloured pencils. Both hard and soft pastels can also be blended by lightly glazing one colour over another. Success depends on how much loose powder is already on the support; you may find it advantageous to apply a thin layer of fixative between applications of pastel, to prevent the colours from smudging.

Oil pastels can be blended with the finger, but the results are not as satisfactory as with soft pastels. They can also be mixed simply by working one colour into another. Take care not to build up too much pastel on the support, as this can prevent you from applying more. Oil pastel drawings made on oil paper or on a paper prepared using gesso can be blended together using a solvent such as white spirit (paint thinner) or turpentine.

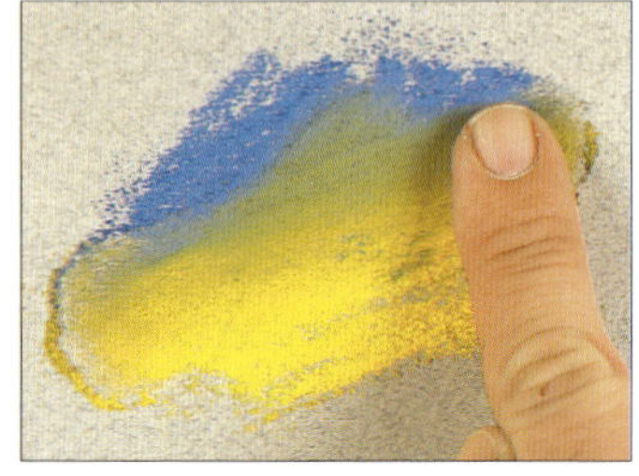

Finger blending
The easiest and most convenient way to blend soft pastels is to use your finger.

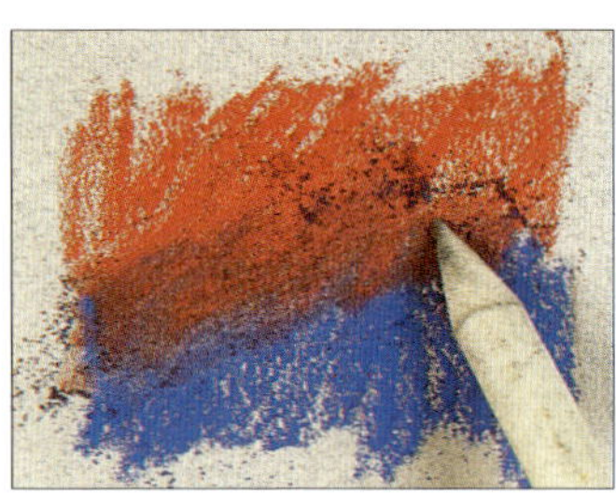

Blending with a torchon
A torchon can be used to blend soft pastels in the same way. As it has a pointed end, it is good for small areas.

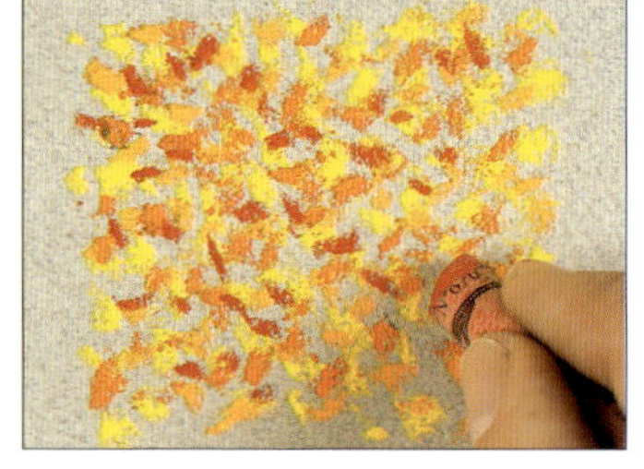

Pointillist approach
Optical mixes can be achieved by applying dots of pure colour, in the same way as the Pointillist painters.

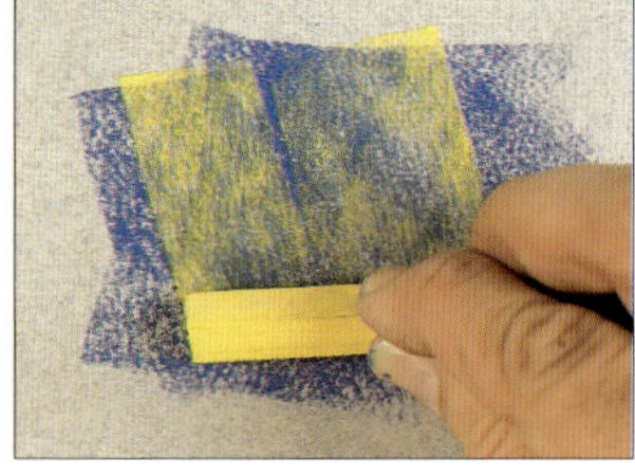

Applying a glaze
Soft pastels can also be mixed by applying a thin glaze or covering of another colour.

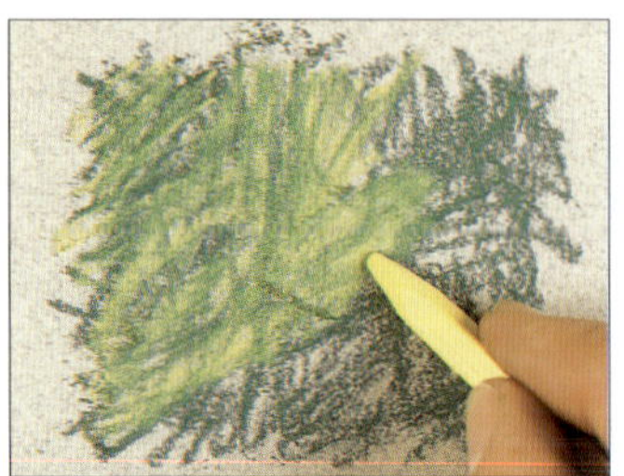

Crosshatching
Hard pastels can be sharpened to a point and used to create mixes by scribbling in layers and hatched or crosshatched lines.

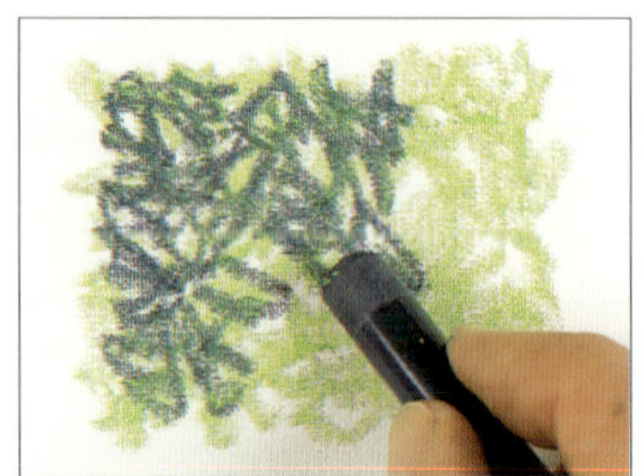

Layering
The colours of oil pastels can also be mixed and blended by working in scribbled layers. Don't make the layers too thick.

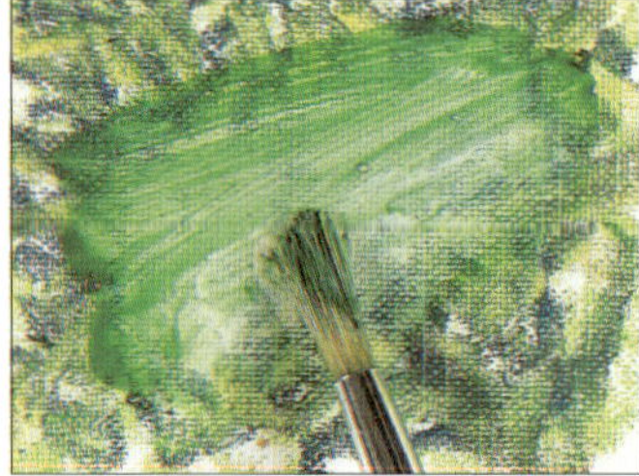

Blending with a solvent
Oil pastels can be blended by working into the applied colour with a spirit solvent such as white spirit (paint thinner) or turpentine.

Practice exercise: **Seascape in soft pastels**

Drawing skies and clouds is the perfect way to practise blending techniques in a powdery medium such as soft pastel or charcoal: because the precise shapes are not important, you can practise moving the pigment around on the paper without having to worry about getting the detail exactly right.

This exercise is also a good lesson in restraint. If you overblend the colours in the water and clog up the tooth of the paper with pigment, you will end up with a flat, lifeless image. Similarly, if you overblend the colours on the rocks you will end up with a muddy-looking mess with no discernible tonal variation. The rocks will appear as silhouettes against the brightness of the sea.

Materials

- *Pastel paper*
- *Grey pastel pencil*
- *Soft pastels: mid-grey, dark grey, black, reddish brown, mid-green, pale grey, mid-blue, dark brown, fawn, pale yellow*

The scene

This is a moody and atmospheric seascape, with storm clouds billowing overhead and sunlight glinting on the water. Although the colour palette appears limited at first glance, there are a number of different tones within the clouds and rocks and these need to be blended smoothly. Two reference photographs were used for this exercise – one for the detail of the foreground rocks and one for the stormy sky and sunlight sparkling on the water.

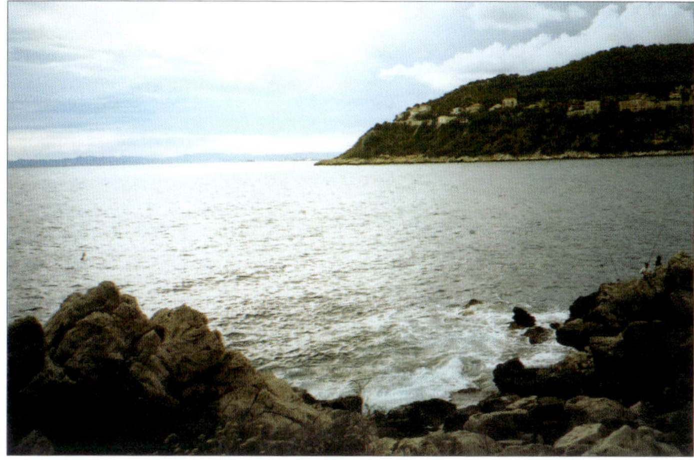

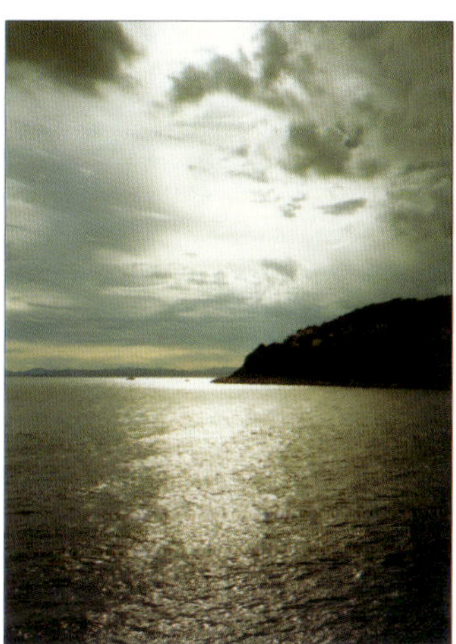

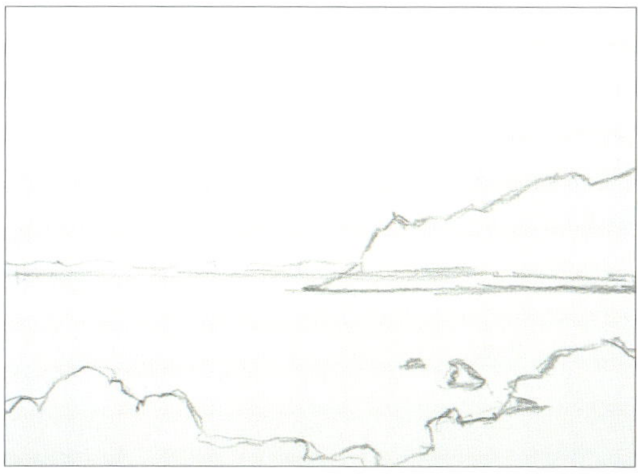

1 Using a grey pastel pencil, outline the headland and foreground rocks. The artist has changed the composition to make it more dynamic: in the photo, the horizon line is in the centre – but here it is positioned lower down.

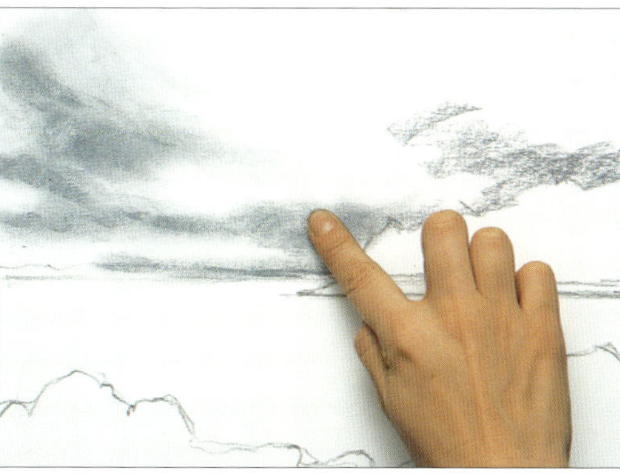

2 Using the side of a mid-grey soft pastel, block in the darkest tones in the sky and blend with your finger. Allow some areas to remain darker than others, as there is a lot of tonal variation in the clouds.

▶

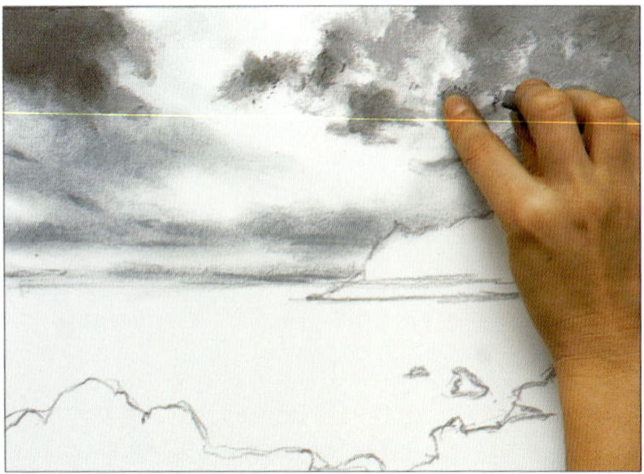

3 Apply a darker grey pastel for the clouds immediately overhead. (The difference in tone helps to convey a sense of distance, as colours tend to look paler towards the horizon.) Build up the very darkest areas of cloud with more dark grey and black, blending the marks with your fingers as before. Remember to leave some gaps for the white of the paper to show through, to create the impression of sunlight peeping out from behind the clouds.

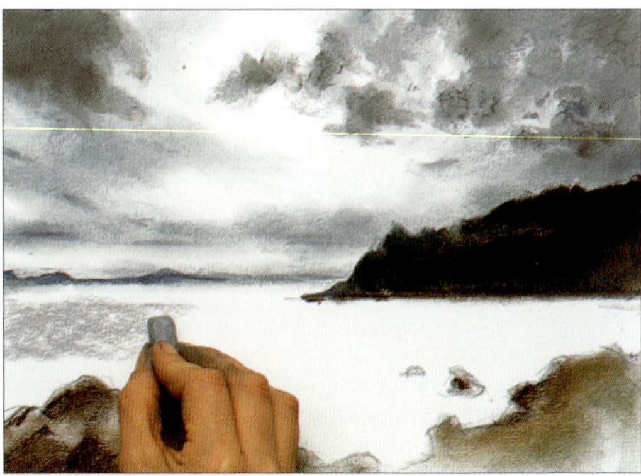

4 Block in the headland with a dark reddish brown and smooth out the pastel marks with your fingers. Use the same reddish brown for the foreground rocks, then overlay the brown in both areas with a mid-green, blending the colours only partially with your fingers so that both colours remain visible. Gently stroke the side of a pale grey pastel across the water area, leaving the central, most brightly lit, section untouched.

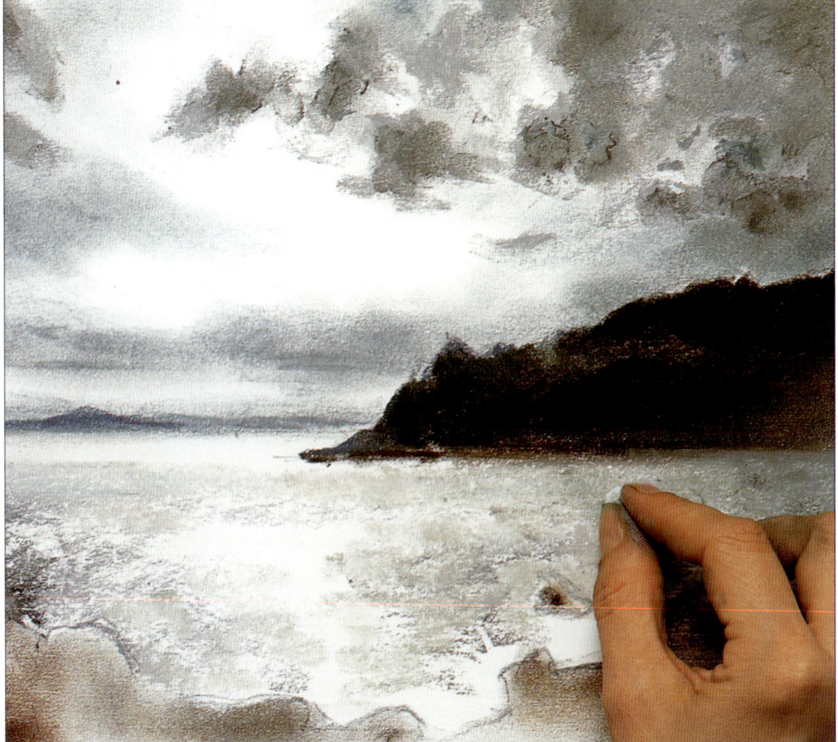

5 Darken the water by overlaying touches of a dusky mid-blue, green and black. Do not overblend the marks or apply them too heavily: it's important to see some differences in colour within the water and to allow some of the white of the paper to show through to create the impression of light sparkling on the water.

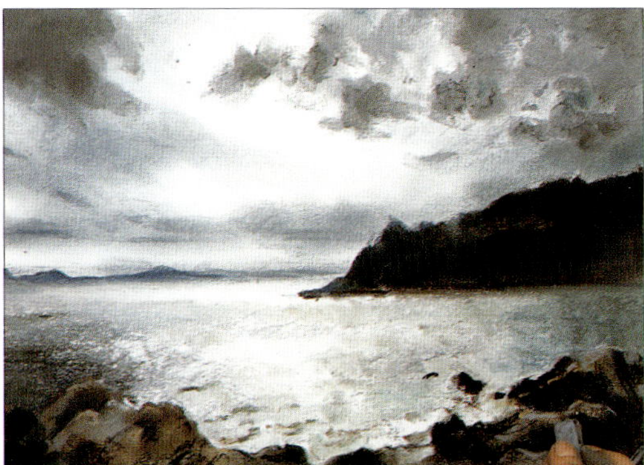

6 Now build up more of the texture on the foreground rocks. Loosely block in the darkest areas (the shaded sides of the rocks) in reddish brown, then overlay dark brown and green and blend the colours slightly with your fingers. For the lighter sides of the rocks, use greys and fawns. Immediately the rocks begin to look three-dimensional.

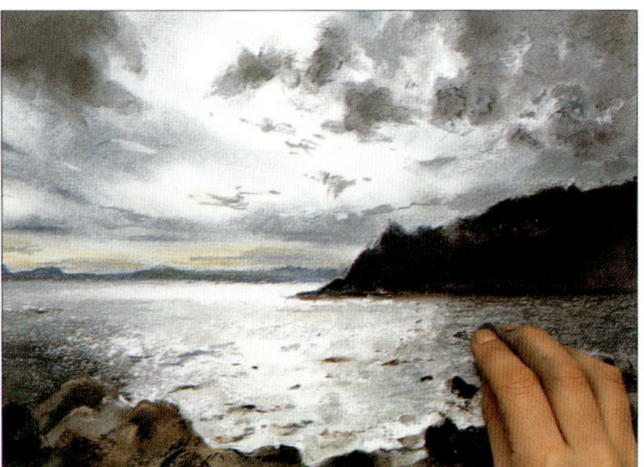

7 Lightly draw a pale yellow line along the horizon and add touches of yellow in the sky to warm it up, blending the marks with your fingertips or a clean rag. Using the tip of a mid-grey pastel, put tiny dashes and dots for colour into the sea to create the impression of wavelets and a sense of movement in the water.

The finished drawing

This drawing uses a number of blending techniques. In the sky, softly blended marks create the impression of swirling clouds. The texture and form of the rocks in the foreground are achieved by overlaying several colours, allowing each one to retain its integrity, and adding a few linear marks as the finishing touch. Our overall impression of the water is that it is a dark blue-grey, but on closer inspection we can see a number of different colours and tones within it – optical mixes that enliven the scene and also imply the movement of the waves in the sea.

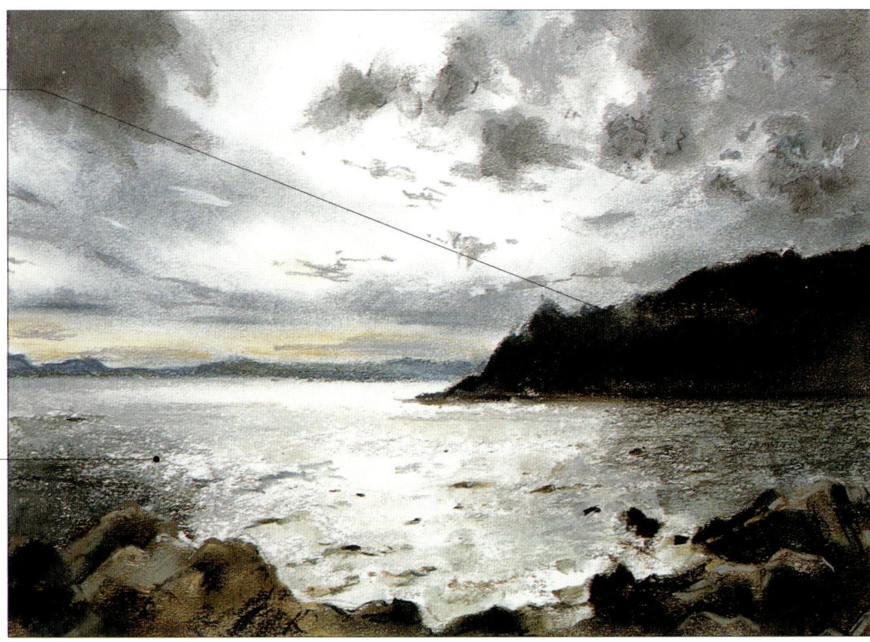

Although little detail is discernible in the distant headland, some tonal variation is essential in order to prevent it from appearing as a solid silhouette. The tonal variations also tell us something about the form of the land.

It is important not to overblend the marks in the water or to obliterate the white of the paper completely.

Practice exercise: **Still life in oil pastels**

In this exercise, you can practise two very different ways of blending oil pastels – by using your fingers and also by working colours on top of one another so that they blend optically. In the final stage of the drawing, you will also see how to brush a tiny amount of solvent over oil pastel to dilute the colour and create a smooth texture.

The range of oil pastel colours is not as extensive as that for soft pastels, so you can't always achieve realistic-looking colours. Instead of worrying about it, go for a more decorative approach.

Materials

- *Oil painting paper*
- *Oil pastels: pale grey, yellow, dark green, pink, purple, dark red, orange, bright green, pale green, blue, dark blue*
- *Craft (utility) knife*
- *Flat brush*
- *Turpentine or white spirit (paint thinner)*
- *Kitchen paper*

The set-up

This simple still life of a mango and two figs contains lively colours and interesting textures. The fruits were arranged on a white background and lit so as to cast shadows on the table, which stops them looking as if they're floating in thin air.

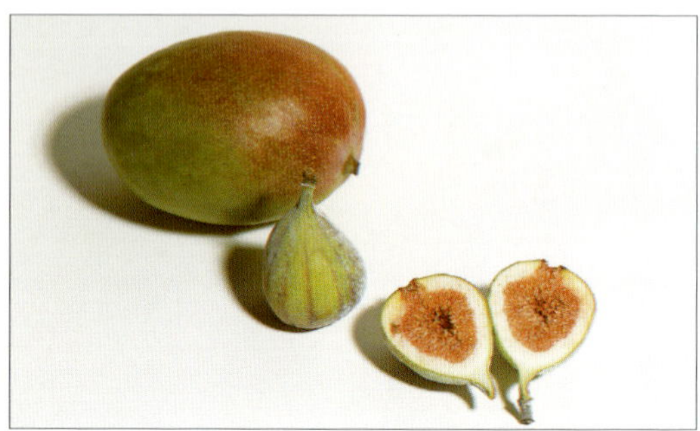

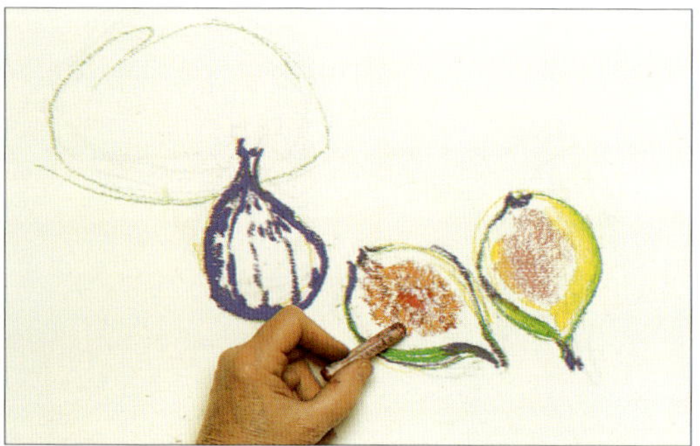

1 Using a pale grey oil pastel, outline all the fruit, then outline the figs in yellow and green and lightly block in the inside of the cut fig in pink. Put in the purple markings on the skin of the uncut fig. Apply a little yellow around the edge of the fleshy interior of the cut fig. Dot dark red on to the cut surface and add some orange around the edge.

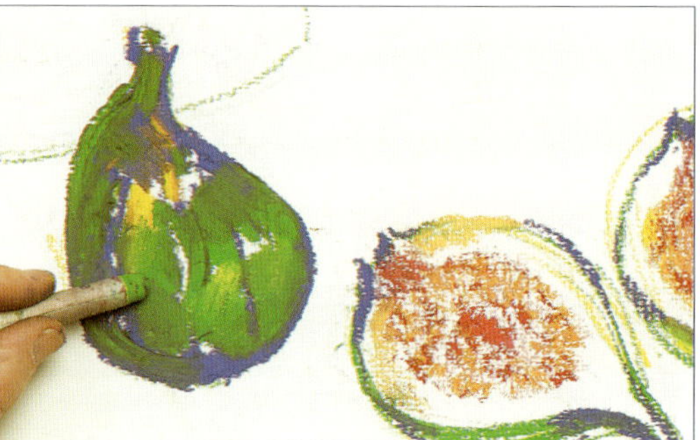

2 Apply very bright green oil pastel over the purple of the uncut fig and a little yellow in the brightest parts, making sure you leave a few small areas of white paper for the highlights. Then add some pale green over the top, again reserving the highlights. Note how the colours blend together optically, creating a very lively-looking mix.

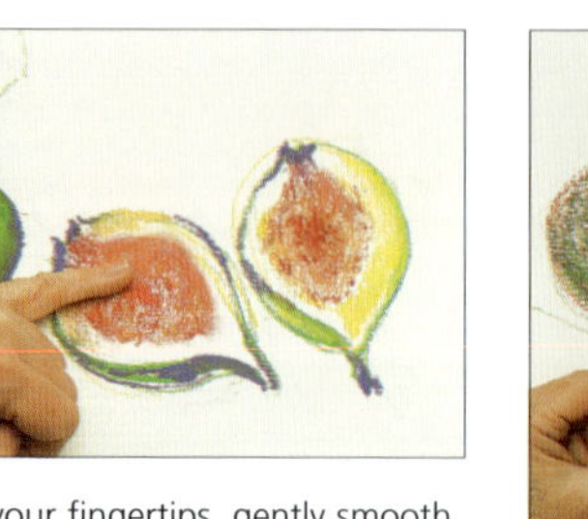

3 With your fingertips, gently smooth out some of the pastel marks on the pink interior of the cut fig.

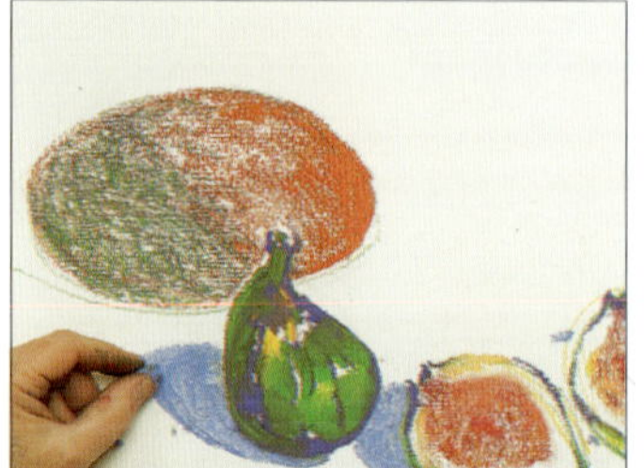

4 Roughly scribble red over the mango, allowing some of the white of the support to show through. Apply a little more pressure on the top half of the mango for a more dense coverage. Although the bottom half of the mango is green, some red can still be seen in this area – so lightly scribble dark green over the red, making sure you don't obliterate the red completely. The two colours combine optically to give a dark, red-tinged green. Lightly block in the shadows cast by the figs in blue.

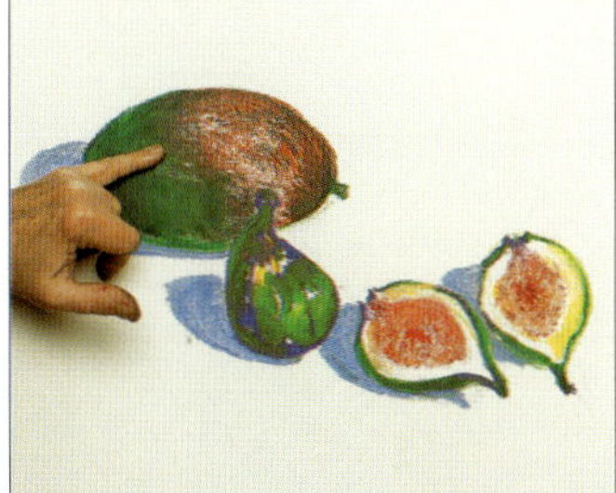

5 Apply more dark green over the bottom half of the mango, still allowing some of the red pastel and the white of the paper to show through. Add a little dark blue, as some of the red is so dark that it is almost purple, and a little pink over the centre, to soften the transition from green to red. Blend the marks just a little; it is easy to end up with a flat, muddy mix that retains none of the liveliness of individual colours.

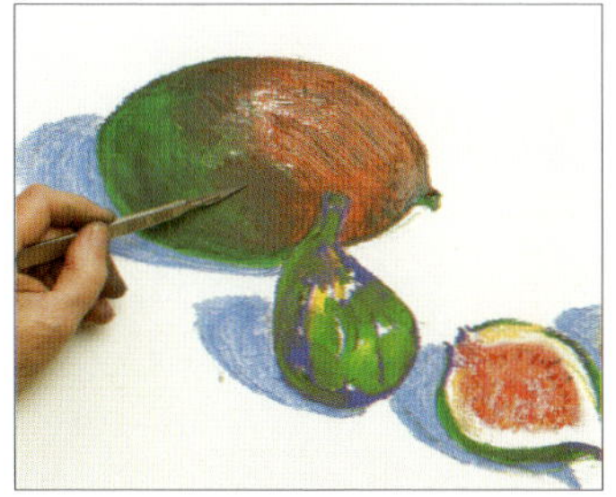

6 Using the tip of a craft knife or other sharp-tipped object, lightly scratch a series of thin, parallel lines over the mango to create the soft bloom on the surface of the fruit. 'Draw' the lines close together and angle the knife so that you don't dig into the paper and damage the surface. Apply tiny dots and dashes of red oil pastel around the interior of the cut fig to create the rich, red seeds and add more texture.

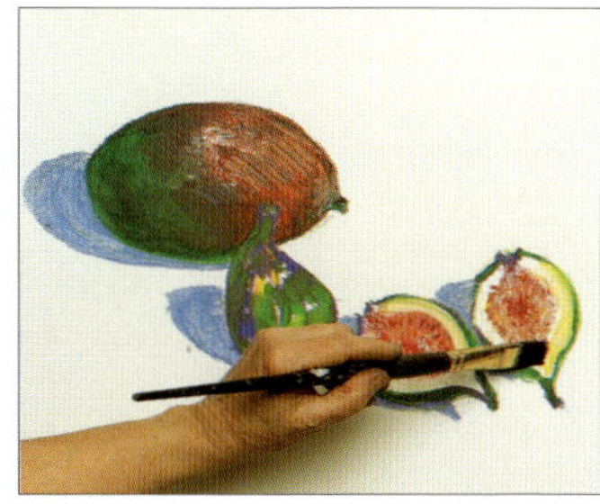

7 Dip a flat brush in turpentine or white spirit, dab off any excess on kitchen paper and carefully pull down a little yellow oil pastel from around the edge of the cut figs to reduce the starkness of the paper.

Tip: Keep dabbing the brush on kitchen paper or a rag between strokes to avoid dirtying the support.

The finished drawing

This is a simple still-life exercise, but it demonstrates the different effects that can be created using oil-pastel blending techniques. The optical colour mixes on the mango are much livelier than a flat application of a single, physically mixed colour could ever be. Finger blending and scratching into the oil pastel with a knife create lovely textures.

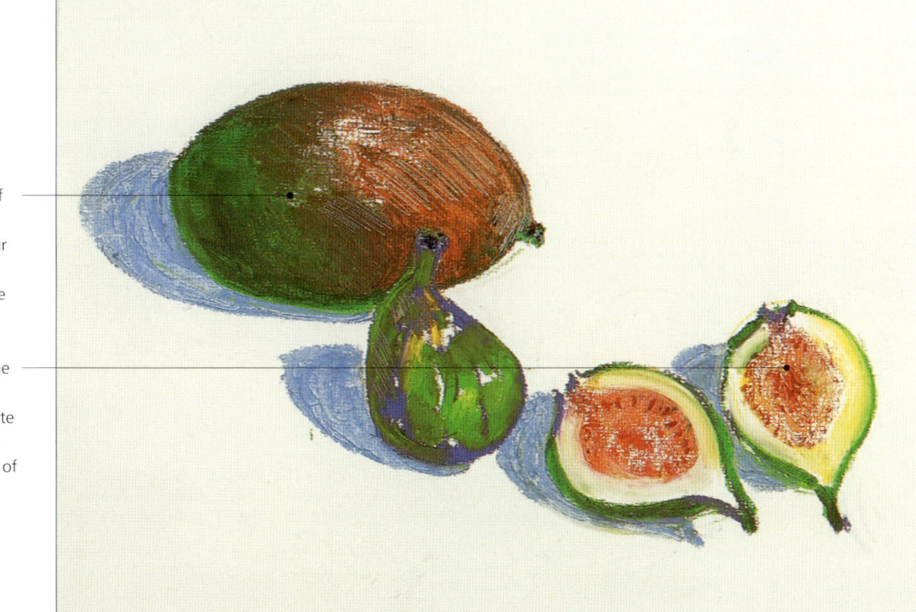

A combination of finger blending and optical colour mixing enlivens the surface of the mango.

Solvent dilutes the colour, while the brush marks create a smooth texture for the soft flesh of the fruit.

Experimenting with different papers

It requires a good deal of experience to know which colour of paper to choose, so it is not a bad idea to start by drawing the same subject on two different colours. Set up a simple still-life group, making sure that whatever objects you choose have a predominant colour theme. You might decide on blue, in which case you could draw a bunch of blue flowers, perhaps with one or two yellow ones for contrast. Or you might set up some green bottles, again with one other colour for contrast – perhaps an orange or apple.

Draw the still life first on a colour that is the opposite of the main colour in the group. This is orange-yellow if you have chosen blue as the predominant colour, and red or red-brown if you have decided on green. These opposite colours are called complementaries; there are three pairs of them: red and green, blue and orange, and yellow and violet. For your second drawing, choose a paper that matches one of the colours in the subject. For the blue flower group you could use a dark or mid-toned blue, or a blue-grey. You should find that you don't have to cover the entire paper with pastel colour.

Some artists always use a complementary coloured paper, while others prefer one that tones with the key subject colour.

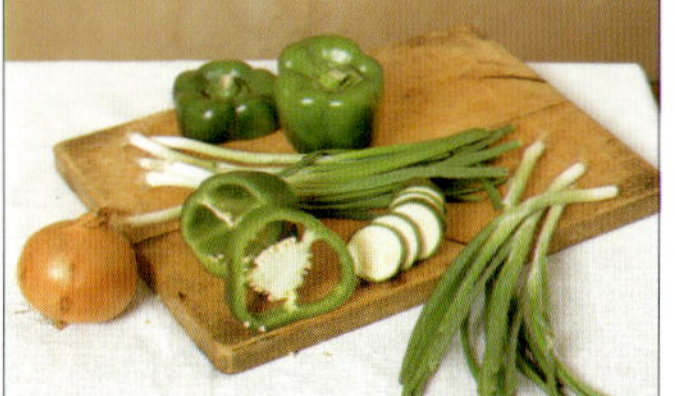

Materials

- *Pastel paper: dark green, light brown*
- *Soft pastels: red-brown, brown, warm yellow, lime green, mid-green, white, black, pale blue*

The set-up

Some of the vegetables in this simple arrangement were sliced to increase the range of textures and tonal contrast.

Practice exercise: **Working on toning paper**

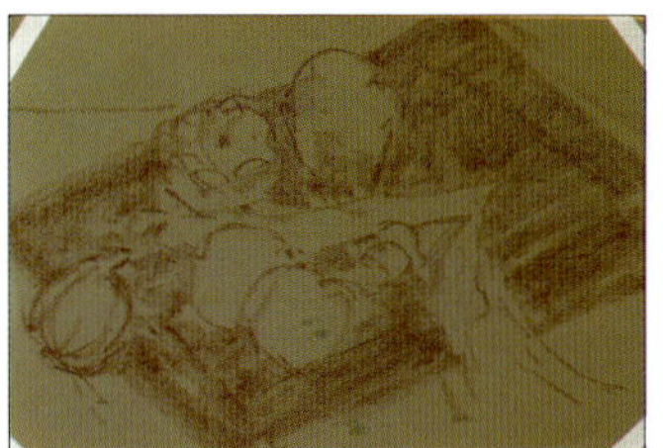

1 Working on dark green paper, chosen in order to represent the dominant greens, make a light drawing in red-brown pastel.

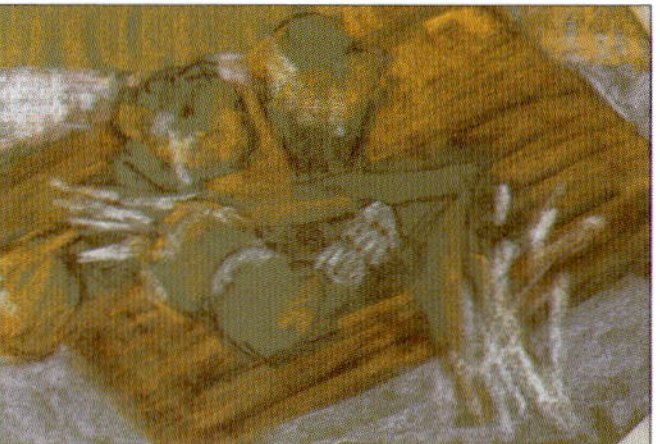

2 Initially, concentrate on covering the green paper in the non-green areas, establishing the contrasting warm browns and blue-whites.

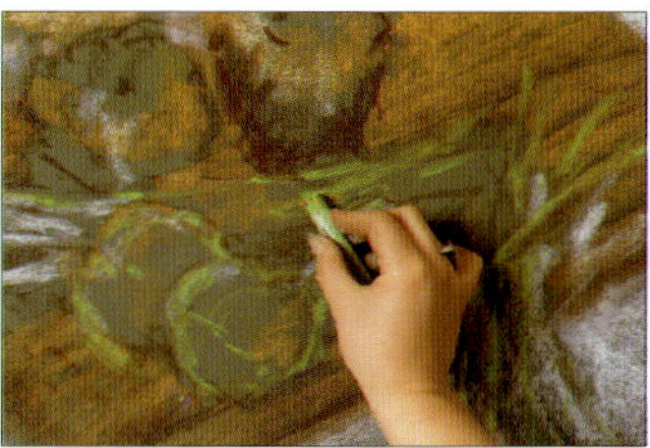

3 Leaving the paper colour to stand for the mid-tones of the vegetables, build up both the dark shadows (the pepper in the background) and the brighter green highlights. Touches of the warm browns and yellows used for the chopping board also need to be introduced into the vegetables, so that the green-brown theme runs through the picture.

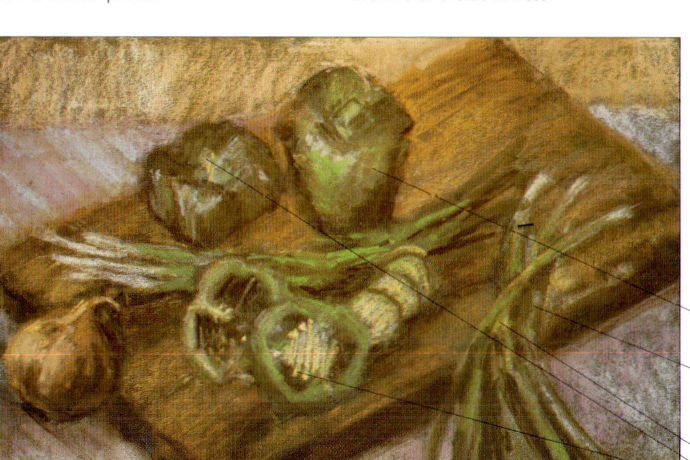

The finished drawing

Choosing the right colour for the paper and pastels is essential:

Large areas of paper show through.

Streaks and flecks of the green paper are visible under light pastel strokes.

Repeating colours makes a series of visual links, and creates an overall untiy in the picture's composition.

Practice exercise: **Working on contrasting paper**

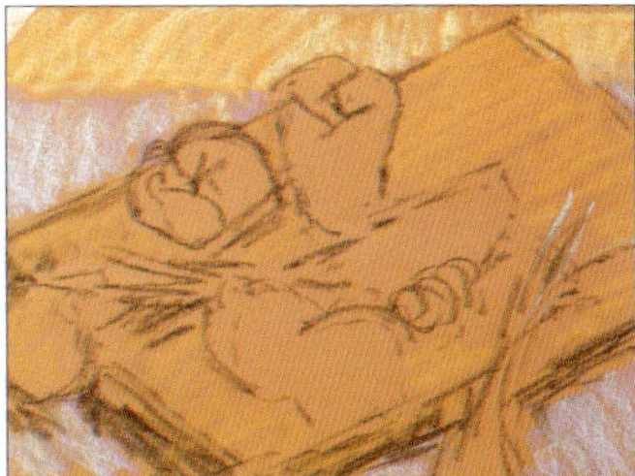

1 In this case the paper is much lighter and warmer in tone. It picks up the yellow-brown of the board and background, but is in opposition to the greens of the vegetables.

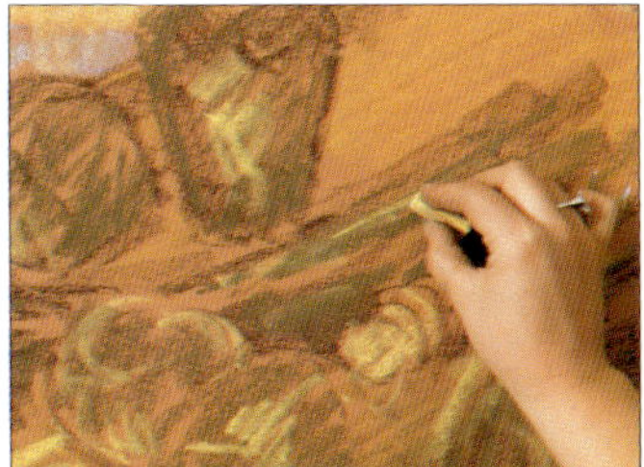

2 To counteract the colour of the paper, you will need to use a different selection of greens and yellows from those chosen for the first version. Here the colour scheme is warmer and the greens are less dominant.

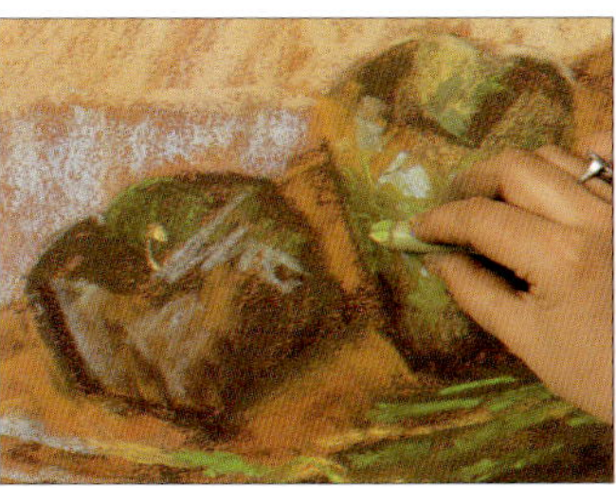

3 In the first drawing, the greens of the vegetables were applied quite lightly because the paper did not need to be covered completely. Here, however, the greens have to be built up heavily to prevent too much of the paper from showing through.

The finished drawing

There are a number of differences between this and the first version of the still life. The method of working has also been affected by the need to build up the greens heavily; the vegetables look darker and more solid, forming a stronger contrast with the wooden board. The denser treatment of the vegetables helps to focus attention on them as the main subjects. The smoother side of Mi-Teintes paper was chosen for both drawings.

The dominant colour is orange-brown rather than green, with the paper colour showing most clearly on the board and background.

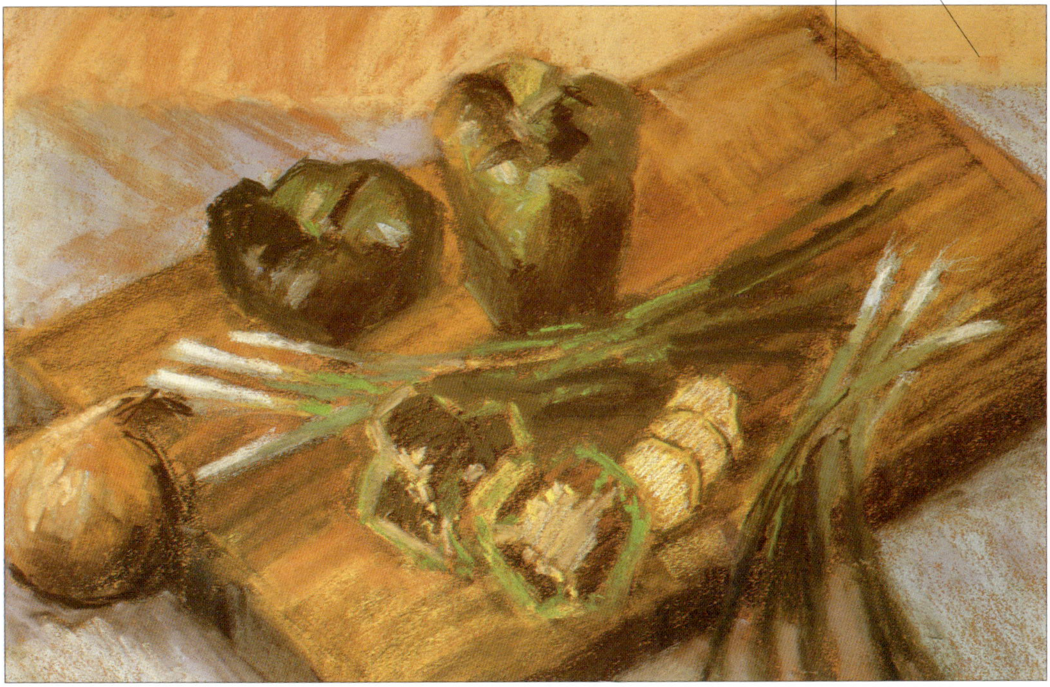

Tinting your paper

The two standard pastel papers, Ingres and Mi-Teintes, are produced in a vast range of colours. However, some artists, particularly those who like to build up their colours thickly, prefer to work on watercolour paper, which has a distinctive texture, and which they generally tint in advance with their chosen colour.

There are two ways of laying a tinted ground. One is by laying a wash, either of watercolour or thinned acrylic paint, which is quick and easy. However, if you work exclusively in pastel you won't have these paints to hand, in which case you can prepare the paper with what is called a dry wash of pastel. Dry washing may be an even spread of one colour, for example for a blue sky, but it is also a useful method for creating hazy effects of a number of soft background colours. If you intend to work over the wash, however, spray it with fixative first. The advantage of the watercolour or acrylic method is that you need not do this.

Practice exercise: **Laying a dry wash**

The effect is created by wiping powdered pastel over the paper, and to do this you need to scrape some dust from a pastel stick. If you want an all-over colour, spread the dust evenly across the paper, but the method also allows you to introduce tonal variations by applying colour more thickly in some areas. You can also use more than one colour, perhaps using a blue dry wash for a sky in a landscape and a brown or yellow ochre one for the ground.

Materials

- *Soft pastels*
- *Small dish for each colour*
- *Craft (utility) knife*
- *Cotton wool (cotton ball) or rag*
- *Watercolour paper*

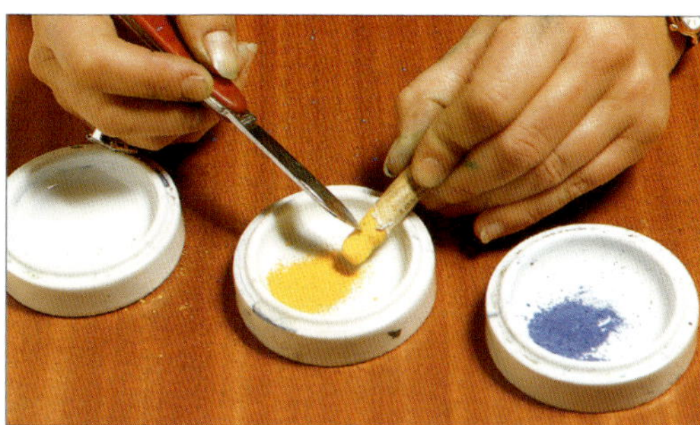

1 Hold the pastel stick over a dish or palette and scrape down the side with the knife blade, producing a fine dust. The method may seem wasteful, but in fact you don't need a great deal of colour.

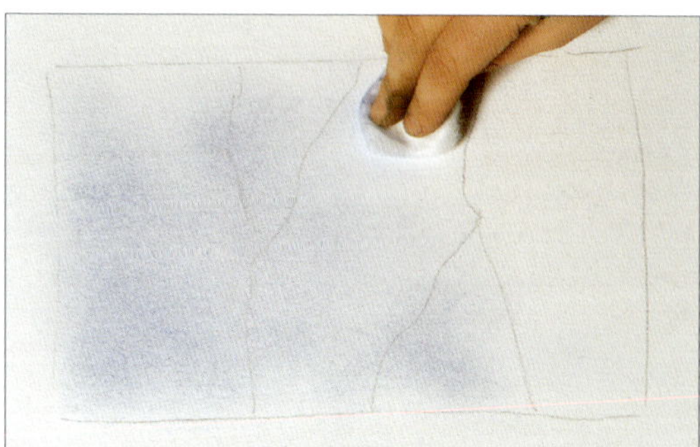

2 This dry wash is for a landscape, using two colours: blue for the sky and yellow for the land. Using a piece of cotton wool, apply the blue powder lightly to watercolour paper, spreading it with an even pressure.

3 Take some of the blue into the land area, and apply the yellow on top, so that the two colours overlap to produce a yellow-green mixture. Before starting the drawing proper, the dry wash should be sprayed with fixative.

Practice exercise: **Wet brushing with a bristle brush**

If you go over soft pastel marks with a brush dipped in water, it releases some of the colour while leaving the pastel strokes clearly visible. You can use this technique only on watercolour paper, as standard pastel papers are quite thin and would buckle. If you like to work on watercolour paper, wet brushing is a useful alternative to tinting the paper in advance. It allows you to colour the surface quickly, obliterating the distracting white specks you see between strokes on white paper.

Wet brushing over side strokes produces a granular wash, which is ideal for suggesting rough textures. Over linear strokes, the effect is somewhat similar to that of line and wash in watercolour, with the wash a paler version of the original line. Wet brushing is often used to 'pull together' lines and marks made with soft pastel or pastel pencil; it can also create light and shade effects to suggest form. Edgar Degas took to pastel painting when his eyesight began to fail and was one of its greatest technical innovators. He would make a paste of his pastels, sometimes steaming his board or spraying warm water over the colours and then working into them with stiff brushes, before overlaying further linear marks.

Materials

- *Watercolour paper*
- *Soft pastels*
- *Bristle brush*
- *Water*

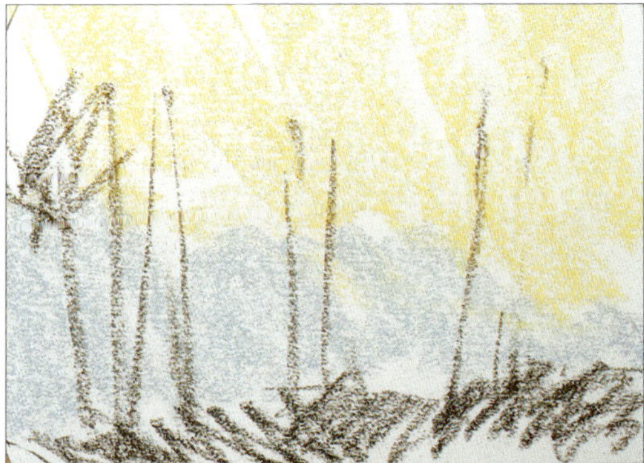

1 Working on watercolour paper, begin by sketching out the main lines of the composition. Having blocked in the large areas with side strokes, use a pastel tip to sketch in the shapes of the trees.

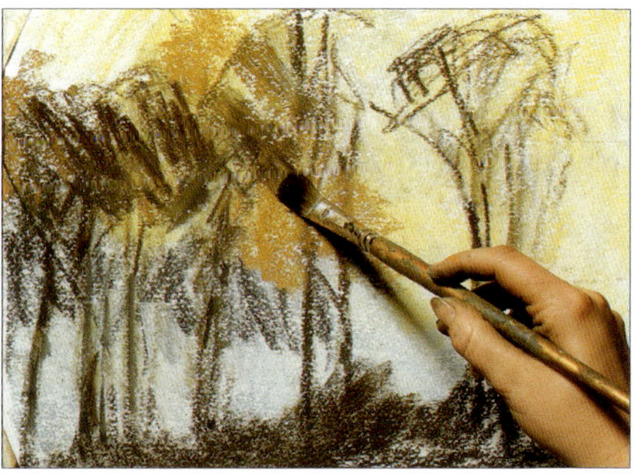

2 Use a bristle brush dipped in water to spread the colour. This type of brush, being harder than a watercolour brush, creates a more thorough spread of colour, dislodging more particles of the pastel.

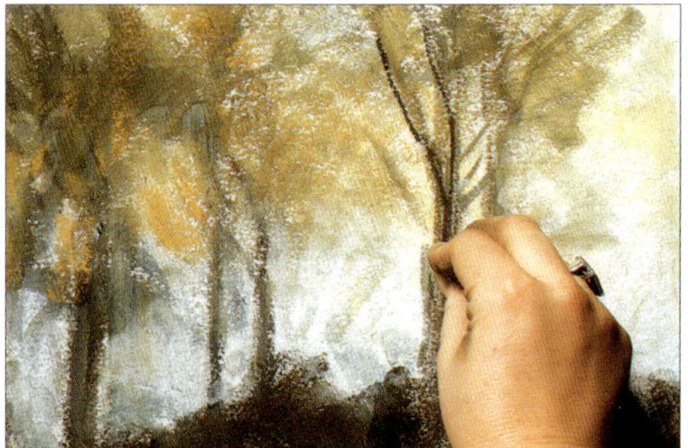

3 You can draw over the wet-brushed areas with the tip of the pastel stick to add touches of crisp definition to the tree trunks and branches. In places, try drawing on still-damp paper to create softer lines and strokes.

▼ Wet brushing with a soft brush

Clean water taken over pastel marks with a soft brush releases some of the colour to form a watercolour effect, leaving the marks of the pastel stick intact. Watercolour paper rather than pastel paper should be used for this method, as the latter may buckle.

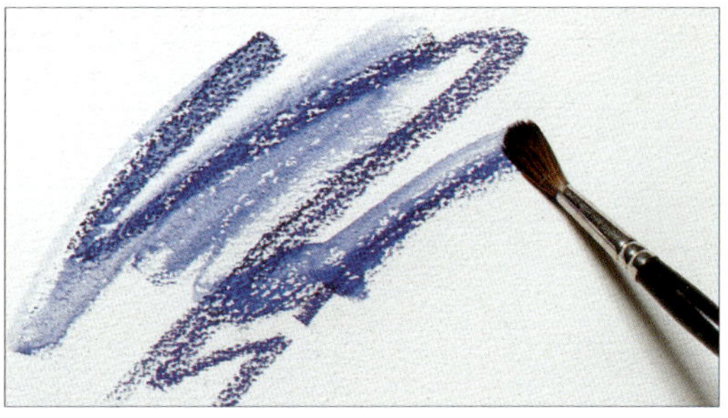

Underpainting

The practice of working over an underpainting, which is usually done in either watercolour or acrylic, is rapidly gaining acceptance in pastel-painting circles. It stems from the same idea as colouring the paper in advance, but goes several steps further. By making a full-scale underpainting, you can introduce as many colours as you like before laying on any pastel, and so relate the colours of the painting to the planned shapes in your picture. Alternatively you can make a monochrome underpainting to establish the drawing and main tonal structure of the painting, perhaps choosing a colour that contrasts with the overall colour key of the subject.

The advantage of a multi-coloured underpainting is that you can carry out at least some of the colour mixing at the painting stage. This helps to avert one of the potential dangers of pastel painting: overmixing and clogging the surface of the paper. You can also work on smoother paper than usual; as you will not be laying so many layers of pastel colour, there will be less risk of the pastel pigment slipping off the surface. As a general rule pastel paper should be textured, but it can be exciting to work on a smoother surface, such as Hot-pressed watercolour paper. This does not break up the pastel strokes as much as the medium-surface (NOT, or CP) paper normally used for watercolour work, thus allowing you to lay thick, solid areas of smooth colour.

Practice exercise: **Pastel over paint**

Some knowledge of watercolour techniques is needed for this exercise, but if this is a medium you have some experience of, the addition of pastels can produce exhilarating effects, as they allow you to introduce a new range of textures and linear strokes. The spontaneity of pastels makes them very effective in suggesting the movement of foliage, for example.

Materials
- *NOT watercolour paper*
- *Watercolours*
- *Paintbrush*
- *Soft pastels*

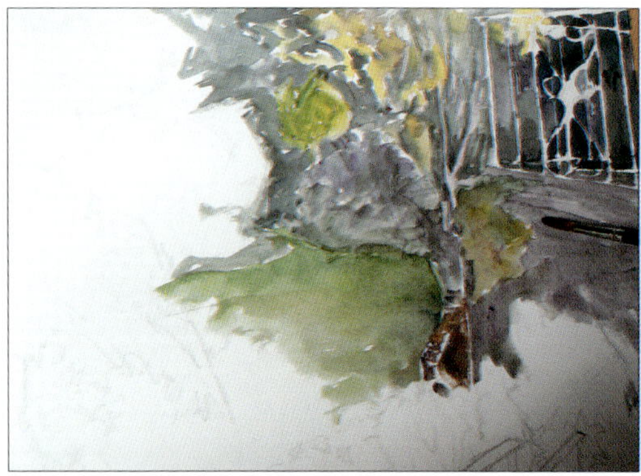

1 Having lightly sketched in the main lines of the composition, lay down the main blocks of colour with watercolour washes, leaving the paper exposed for highlights.

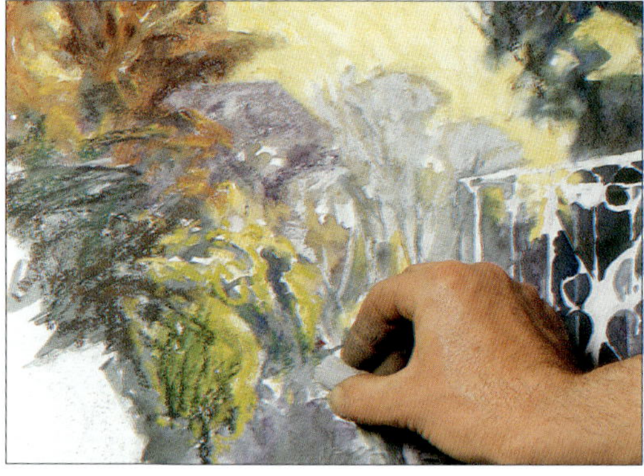

2 When the washes are dry, use light pastel marks to overlay the paint in the foliage and sky areas, and pale grey to draw into the darker blue-greys.

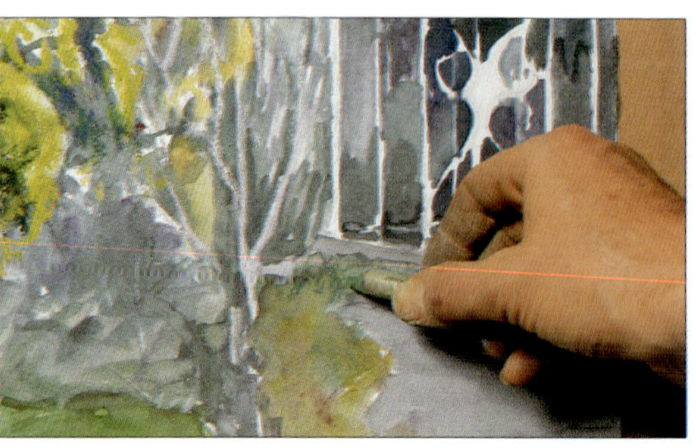

3 As the intention in this exercise is to achieve a blend of the two media, the pastel colours chosen are close to those of the watercolour beneath. There is no need to cover the first colours completely.

Tip: There is no need to cover the underpainting completely with pastel work. Allowing the brushmarks to show in the initial painting will complement the pastel strokes. You can leave the paint to dry before applying the pastel, or experiment with working the pastel into the still-damp paper. You could also wash over the pastel to blend the colours into the painting.

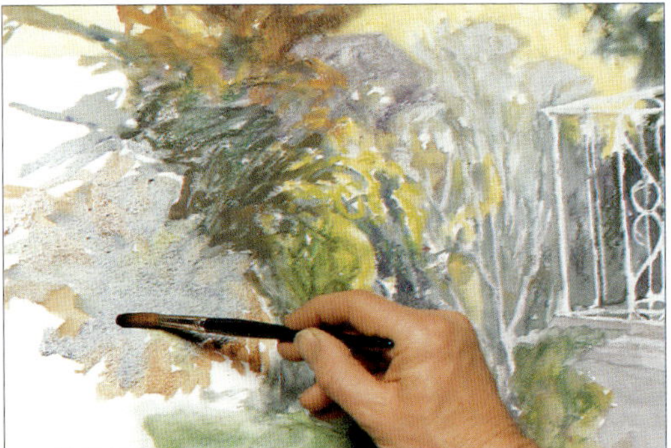

4 Working from the centre of the picture outwards, you can now lay down more watercolour, again using brushstrokes that suggest the movement of the foliage.

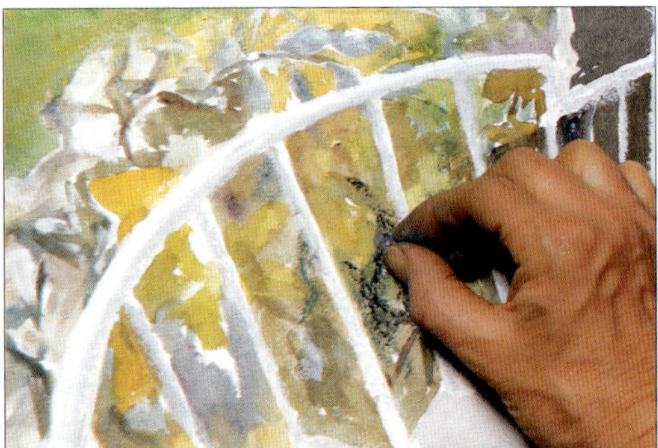

5 The railings have been reserved as highlights, and light applications of grey pastel on the shadowed side give a suggestion of modelling. Darken the central area of foliage so that the whites stand out clearly.

The finished drawing
Some artists use a watercolour underpainting much as they would a coloured ground, covering most of it with pastel. In this case, however, the two media work together, with the watercolour playing an important part in the overall effect.

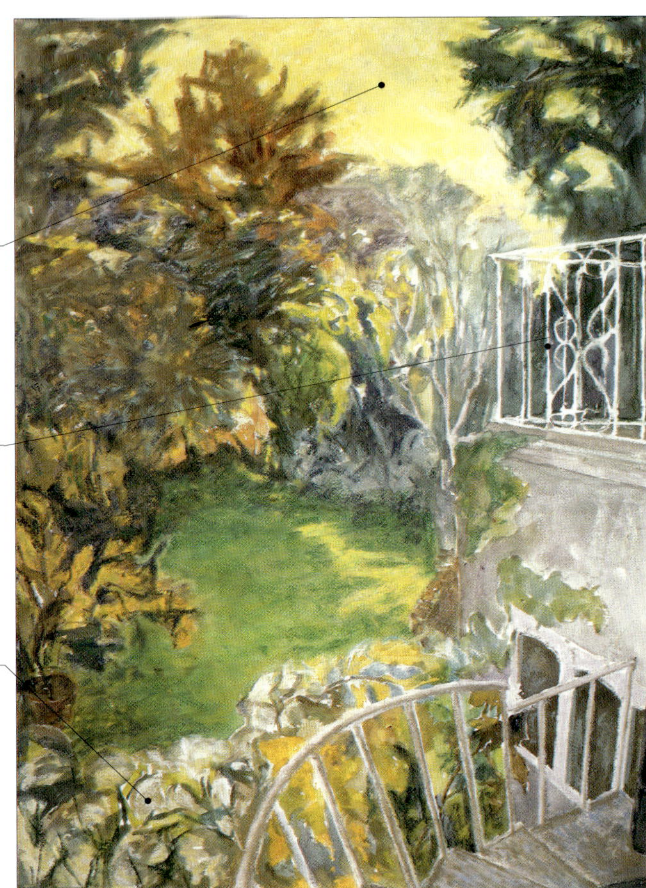

The gentle colouring of the initial watercolour wash is left partly exposed in the sky area.

The white paper, which is the whitest white in the finished picture, is left untouched for the highlights on the sunlit railings.

The delineation of the foreground foliage is emphasized with broad linear pastel strokes, strengthening the painted colours.

Wet brushing oil pastel

Oil pastel is an exciting medium to use, although it is very different in character from soft pastel, being bound with oil rather than gum. Its dense, rather greasy quality means that it fills the grain of the paper relatively quickly, making it less suitable for colour mixing by layering.

However, this is only true if the medium is used 'dry' like conventional pastel. The great advantage of oil pastel is that the colour can be melted with an application of turpentine or white spirit (paint thinner) and spread with a brush or rag over the paper. (Canvas or oil-sketching paper are possible alternatives.)

Oil pastels come in a more limited colour range than soft pastels, but this wet-brushing method allows you to achieve very subtle colour mixes on the working surface. As with paints, you can even mix colours on a palette before putting them on. Simply moisten the tip of a pastel stick with a brush dipped in turpentine or white spirit to release the colour and transfer this to the palette.

As oil pastels are quick to use, easy to correct and, best of all, do not need fixing they make an ideal medium for outdoor sketching. However, they do have a tendency to melt under a hot sun, becoming very soft and buttery, which makes them hard to manage; it is best to work in the shade wherever possible.

Practice exercise: **Oil pastel and white spirit**

This technique allows you to lay broad areas of colour very quickly. You can then work over these with more linear strokes, building up the picture with a succession of wet and dry layers. If the paper becomes clogged, you can remove whole areas of colour by applying more white spirit and rubbing gently with a rag. On oil-sketching paper you can make as many such corrections as you like, without harming the surface.

Materials

- *Oil-sketching paper*
- *Oil pastels*
- *Bristle paintbrush*
- *Turpentine/white spirit (paint thinner)*
- *Rag*

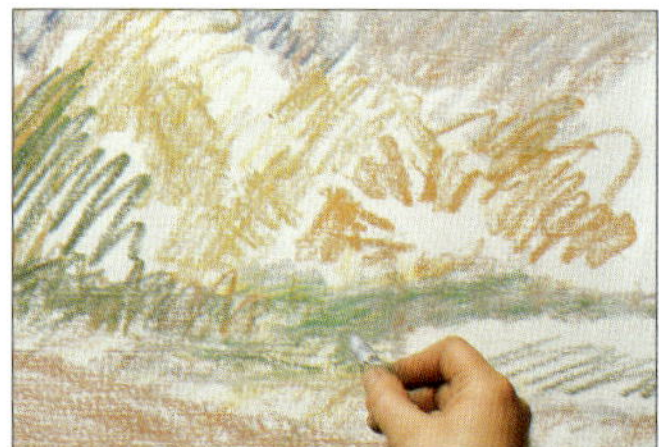

1 Working on oil-sketching paper, block in the composition lightly with very soft oil pastels, using broad strokes. (You can also work on ordinary pastel paper, such as Ingres, but there is a slight possibility of the oil in the pastels causing deterioration over time.)

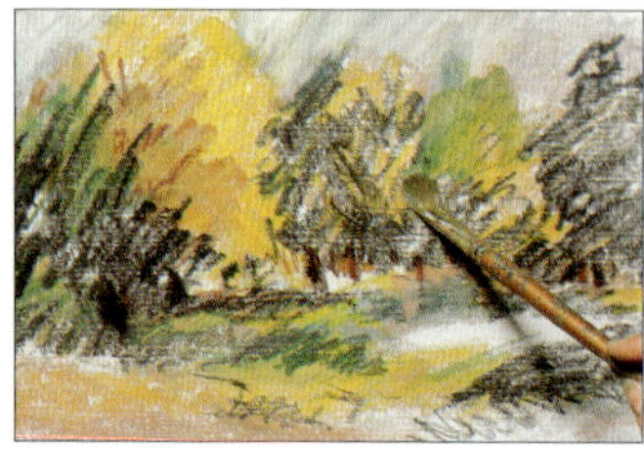

2 Dip a bristle brush in white spirit and spread and mix the colours. Aim to keep the mixture relatively transparent by applying the first colours lightly, otherwise it can become muddy.

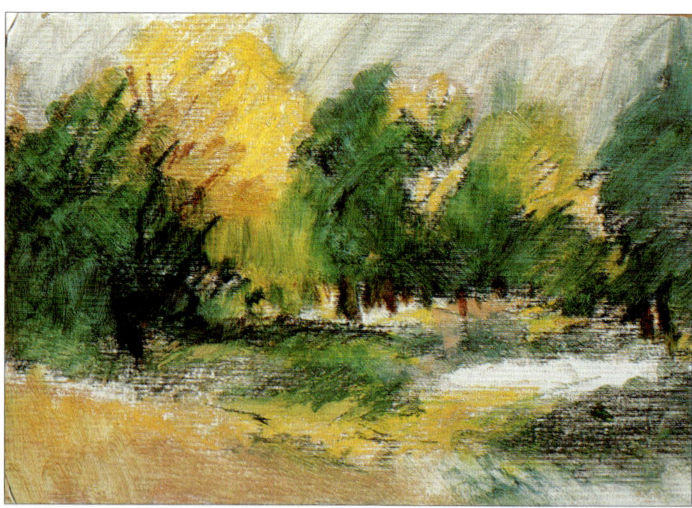

3 With further brushwork over the whole picture you can firmly establish the form and colours of the trees. Again, it's important to avoid over-mixing and churning up the colours; in this example, the blues and yellows can be clearly distinguished in the dark and light green areas.

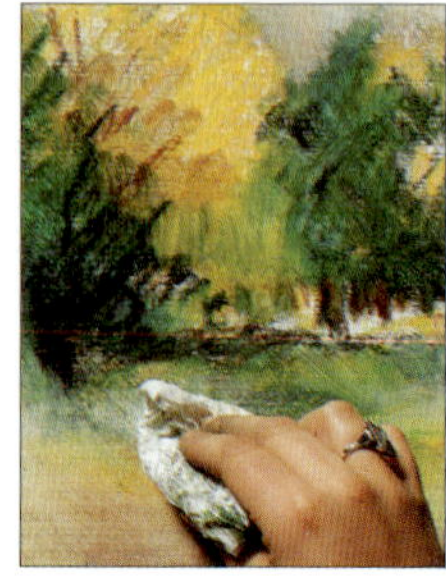

4 The beauty of this method is that amendments can be made simply by wiping off colour with a rag dipped in white spirit. Here, the foreground needs to be softened, so the whole area is wiped down prior to re-working.

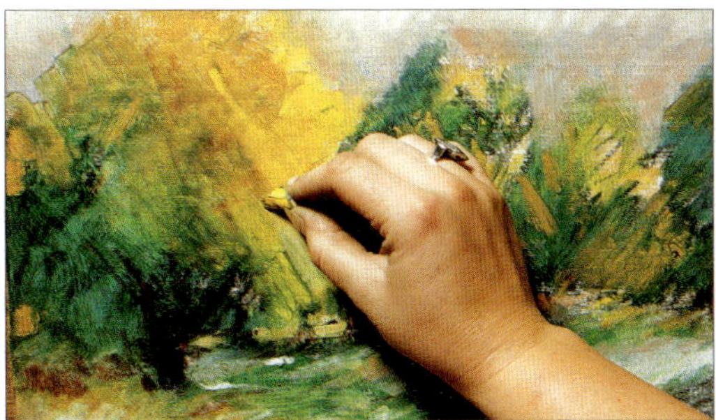

5 To produce a textured effect on the foliage, work into a still-wet area with firm strokes of the pastel stick. This creates distinctive marks and slight ridges, rather similar to the effects of sgraffito.

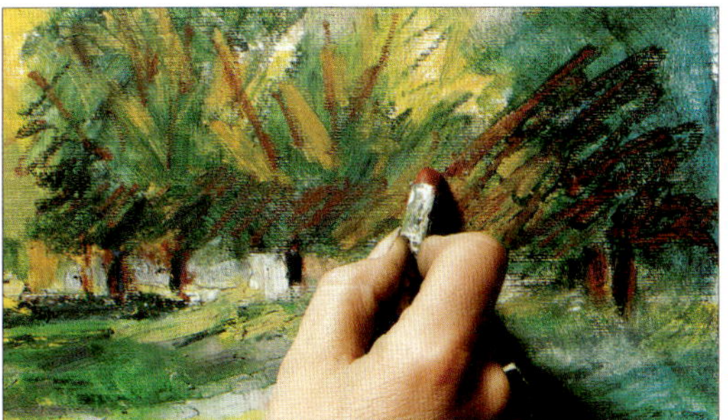

6 For colour contrast and a suggestion of the trunks and branches, use a dark red oil pastel to draw over the earlier colours. Keeping these marks very broad and free produces an impressionistic effect.

The finished drawing

As the oil pastel has been applied in a series of thin washes, rather like glazing in oil painting, the colours in the completed work are beautifully luminous, an effect enhanced by the white paper reflecting through the colours. For this reason, when using oil pastel in this way, white paper can be a better choice than coloured.

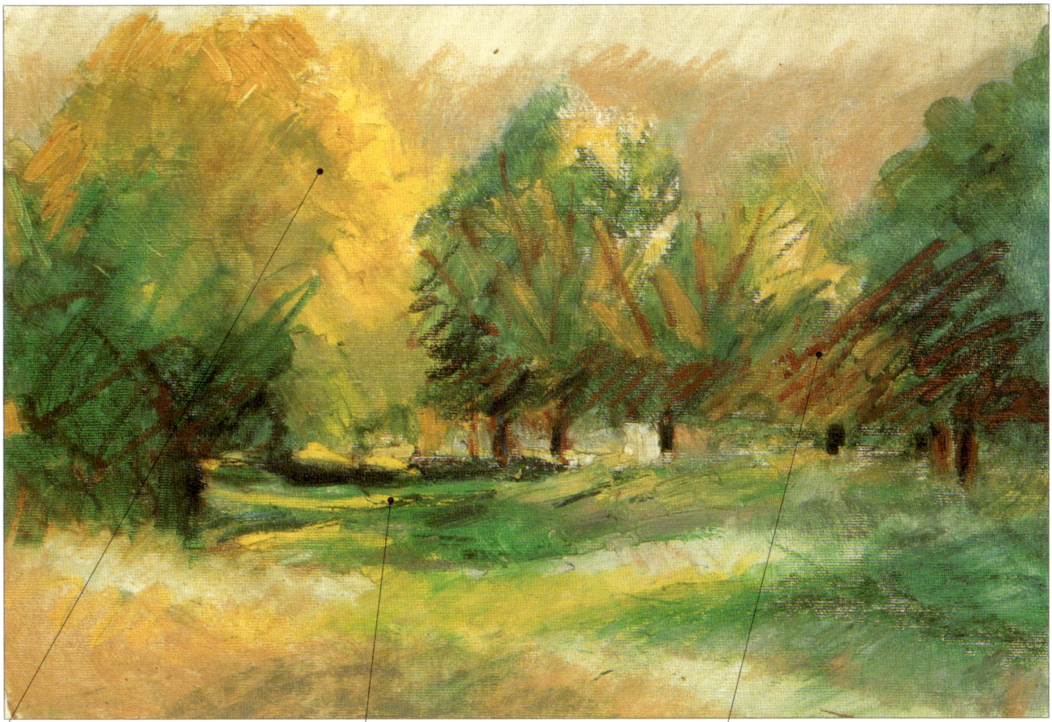

In places the oil pastel has moved around on the paper while wet, creating a textural, ridged surface.

Strong yellow in the centre of the scene evokes patches of sunlight between the trees to attract the eye.

Final touches of dark red strengthen the shadow tones and add a sense of drama to the landscape.

Charcoal and pastel

Charcoal and pastel are frequently used together; they are natural partners because both have a similar texture. Charcoal is routinely used by pastel artists to make a preliminary underdrawing, as in the exercise below.

However, the combination of pastel and charcoal can also be used in a more positive way, with the charcoal complementing the pastel colour. As charcoal gives a crisper line than pastel, it is sometimes used to define detail and provide a linear structure, with the pastel used for the broader colour areas (in a way similar to line and wash in watercolour painting).

Another approach, which is sometimes used for figure work and portraiture, is to make a tonal underdrawing, using the side of the charcoal stick to establish the light and dark areas of the work. This is suitable only when the artist's intention is to produce a work that is relatively 'low-key' in colour, as, even when the charcoal is fixed, the pastel laid on top picks up a little of the black dust. This has the effect of muting the pastel colours, particularly in the areas of darkest tone, which can be very effective for certain subjects.

Charcoal can also be used hand in hand with pastel colours and, because it is less dense than black pastel, it is particularly useful for the subtle mid-toned colours that are often hard to mix successfully. The grey-greens or grey-blues seen in the middle distance of a landscape, for example, can often be achieved by mixing charcoal and green or blue pastel, or by dragging a light veil of charcoal over a pastel colour to tone it down.

Practice exercise: **Making a charcoal underdrawing**

Because underdrawings for pastel work should never be done in pencil – the greasiness of graphite repels the pastel colour – charcoal is often used to make the preliminary line drawing. Any loose dust is then brushed away and the charcoal is sprayed with fixative before the pastel colour is applied on top. Charcoal may also be used to darken the tone of pastels, but here it is largely obliterated by the overlaid colours and plays no part in the finished work.

Materials

- *Mauve-blue pastel paper*
- *Charcoal stick*
- *Bristle paintbrush*
- *Fixative*
- *Soft pastels*

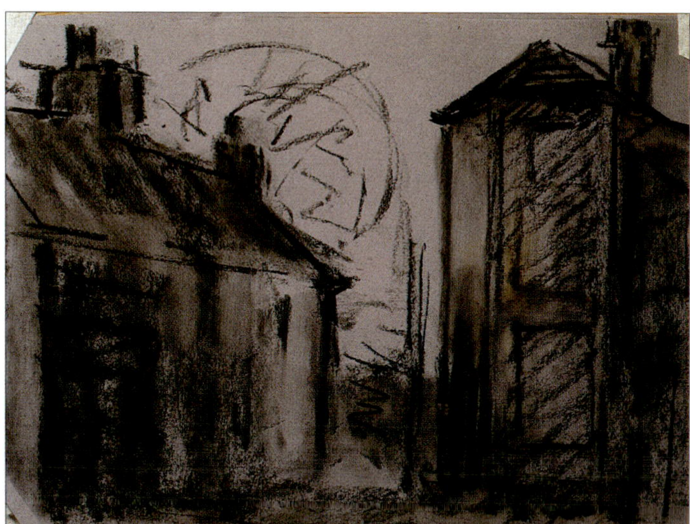

1 The colour scheme planned for this picture is relatively sombre, with a predominance of dark tones, so a mauve-blue paper sets the key for the later colours. The paper chosen here is Mi-Teintes, used on the smoother side. Using a thick charcoal stick, sketch the main lines of the composition, keeping the outlines light for the trees in the centre, which will be the lightest part of the drawing. Use the side of the stick to block in the shadowed areas, smudging the charcoal to create areas of smooth tone.

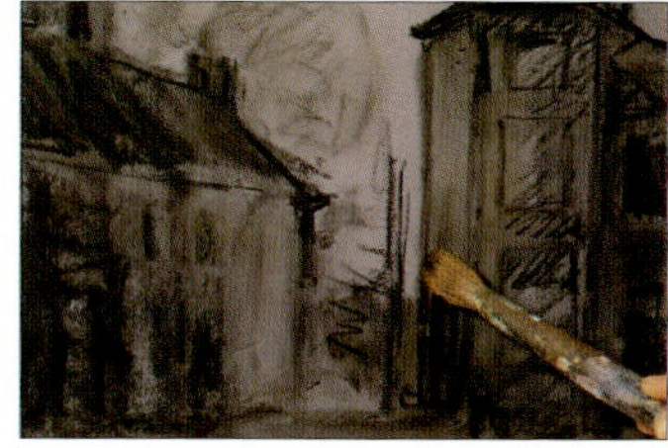

2 Flick off the excess charcoal dust with a bristle brush and spray the drawing with fixative to prevent the charcoal muddying the colours.

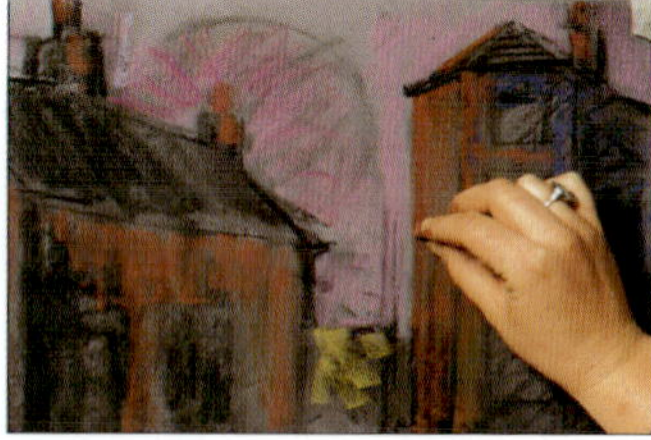

3 Build up the colours gradually with a series of overlays. The bright pink used for the sky at this stage will be modified by later applications. Although dark in tone, the colours chosen for the buildings are very rich.

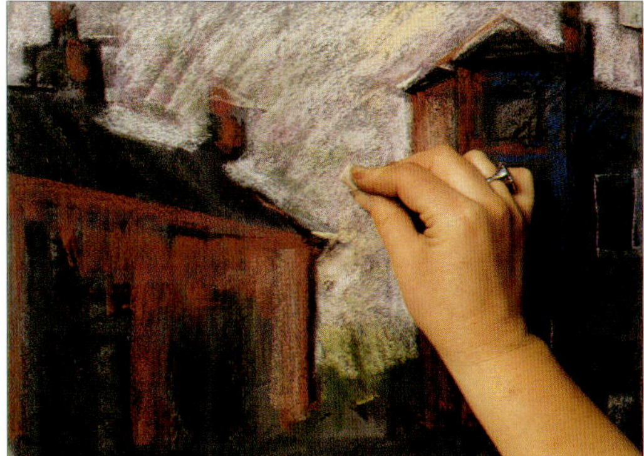

4 Drag the side of a short length of white pastel lightly over the earlier pink, leaving some of this visible as well as some of the paper colour. The sides of the buildings nearest to this sky area also need to be lightened slightly.

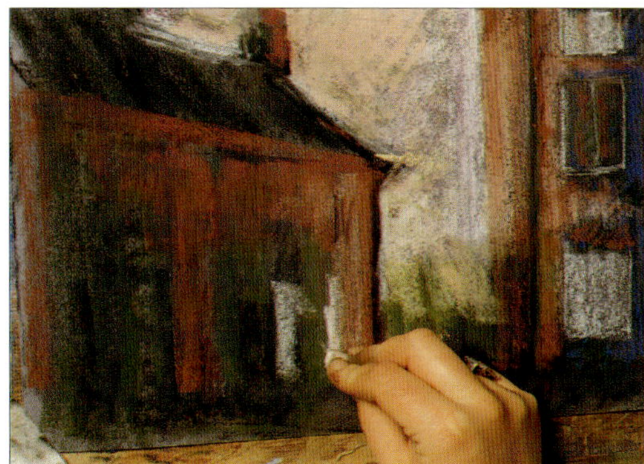

5 Leave the highlights until last, because pastels are opaque and it is possible to cover dark colours with light ones. The walls of the houses are rendered in a variety of colours from deep greens to reds and pinks, plus a mauve produced by the paper showing through the original charcoal drawing.

The finished drawing

Finishing touches have been added to define the details of the buildings with fine lines (made with the edge of a broken pastel stick), and to suggest the large tree behind the houses on the left. Both trees are important to the composition, but play a minor part, so they have been treated lightly, with smeared strokes, to merge them partially into the sky.

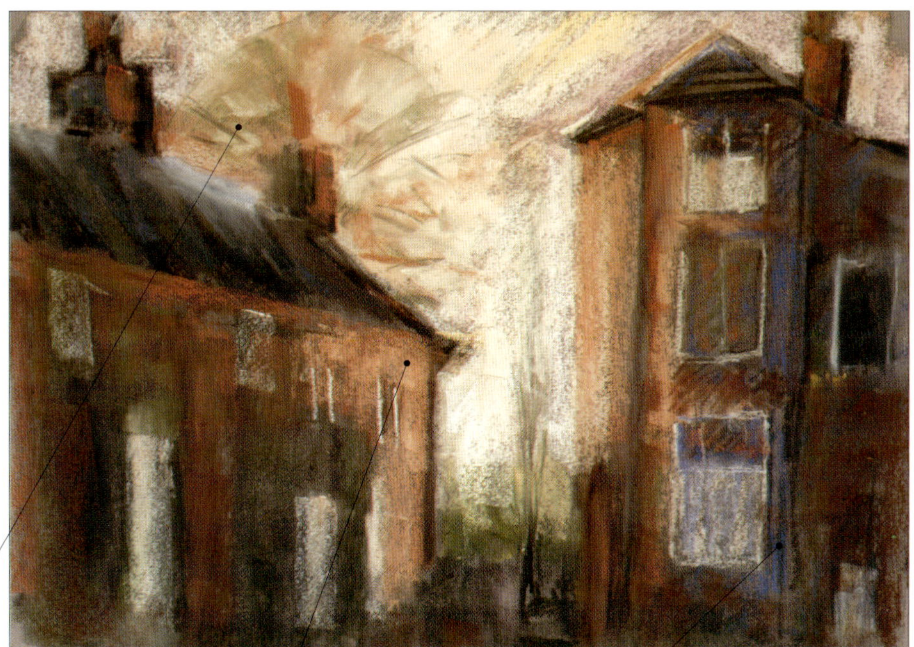

The light charcoal drawing of the tree is completely covered by the pastel colour.

Overlays of progressively lighter colours on the house walls produce a rich effect.

Fine details on the houses are drawn in using the edge of a black pastel stick.

Building up pastel

Although the standard pastel papers such as Canson Ingres and Mi-Teintes are versatile and allow for a certain amount of layering, you cannot build up colours really thickly on them. For those who like truly painterly effects, it is worth trying one of the special papers produced for pastels, such as sandpaper, velour paper and Sansfix paper.

These papers handle very differently from the normal pastel paper. Sandpaper in particular grips the pastel pigment so firmly that it is virtually impossible to blend colours by spreading them with either your fingers or a rag; for the same reason you cannot move colours around on the surface. However, the paper's firm hold on the pastel pigment means that you can go on layering colours more or less indefinitely. This allows you to create very subtle mixtures and great depth of colour as well as effects similar to that of impasto in oil painting, where the brushstrokes stand proud of the surface. In fact, some pastel paintings on sandpaper look very much like oil paintings.

These papers all have one disadvantage: they are very 'greedy' with the pastel colours and you will get through your pastels at a faster rate than when working on Ingres or Mi-Teintes paper. This problem is partially balanced by the fact that you won't need much – if any – fixative, which is fairly expensive.If you find the paper beginning to clog you can use fixative, but it is not usually necessary. If you do use it, remember that it tends to darken the colours, so you may need to allow for this when creating the work.

Practice exercise: **Working on Sansfix paper**

Sansfix paper grips the colour more firmly than the standard papers and is ideal for creating painterly effects in pastel. It allows for a considerable amount of building up by layering of colours. Conversely, it is not suited to very delicate approaches or to blending techniques, as the pastel cannot be moved around on the surface once it has been applied.

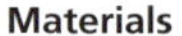

Materials

- *Dark grey Sansfix pastel paper*
- *Soft pastels: white, black, mid-brown, pale grey, ochre, pale blue, pale yellow, red*

1 Having sketched in the figure, work on the lightest areas, using short, decisive strokes like brushstrokes in oil painting to fill in the window, before doing further detail on the figure.

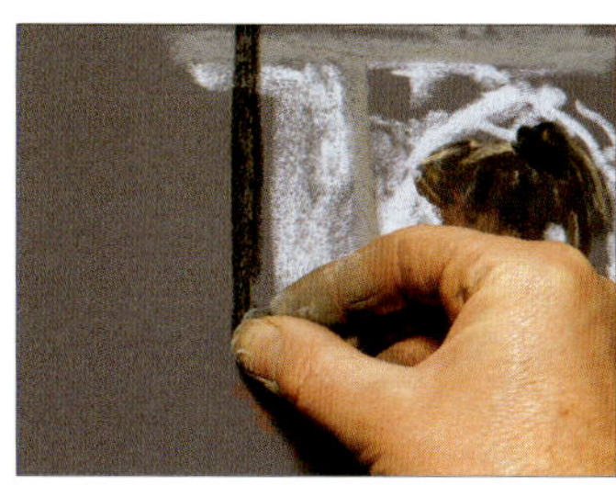

2 A solid line of black is now pulled down the paper to define the pole leaning against the windowsill, which provides a visual balance for the artist's easel.

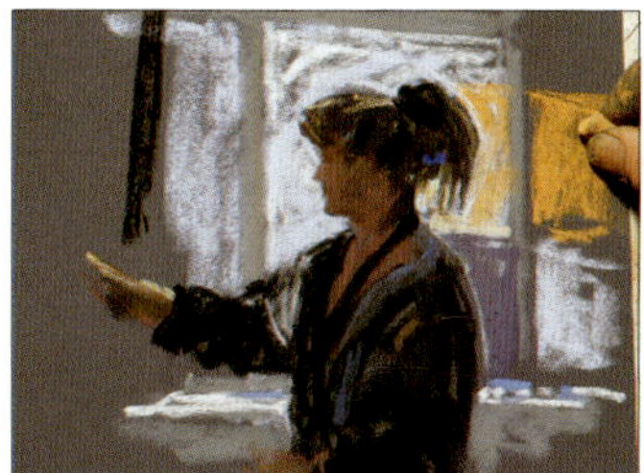

3 Create the subtle tones and modelling of the face and body by building up thick layers of colour in these areas, and tone down the white windows by adding warm yellow.

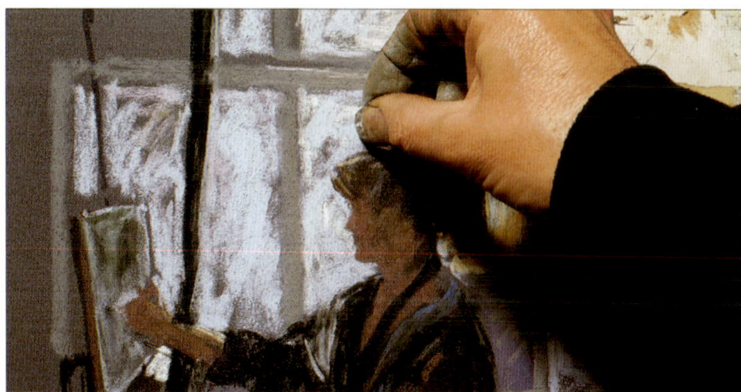

4 Using a small piece of pastel, lay light grey over the white. Allowing small patches of the dark grey paper to show through creates a lively broken-colour effect.

▶ **The finished drawing**

The finished picture, with its thick and heavy pastel marks, is reminiscent of an oil painting. The many layers of distinct colours, applied in bold strokes on the rough paper, create an appealingly textured surface.

Patches of the dark grey paper left showing in the windows enliven the treatment of the glass.

Most of the figure is in deep shadow, but the window behind her casts highlights along her arm and in her hair.

The background is only vaguely suggested, in colours that complement those used for the central figure.

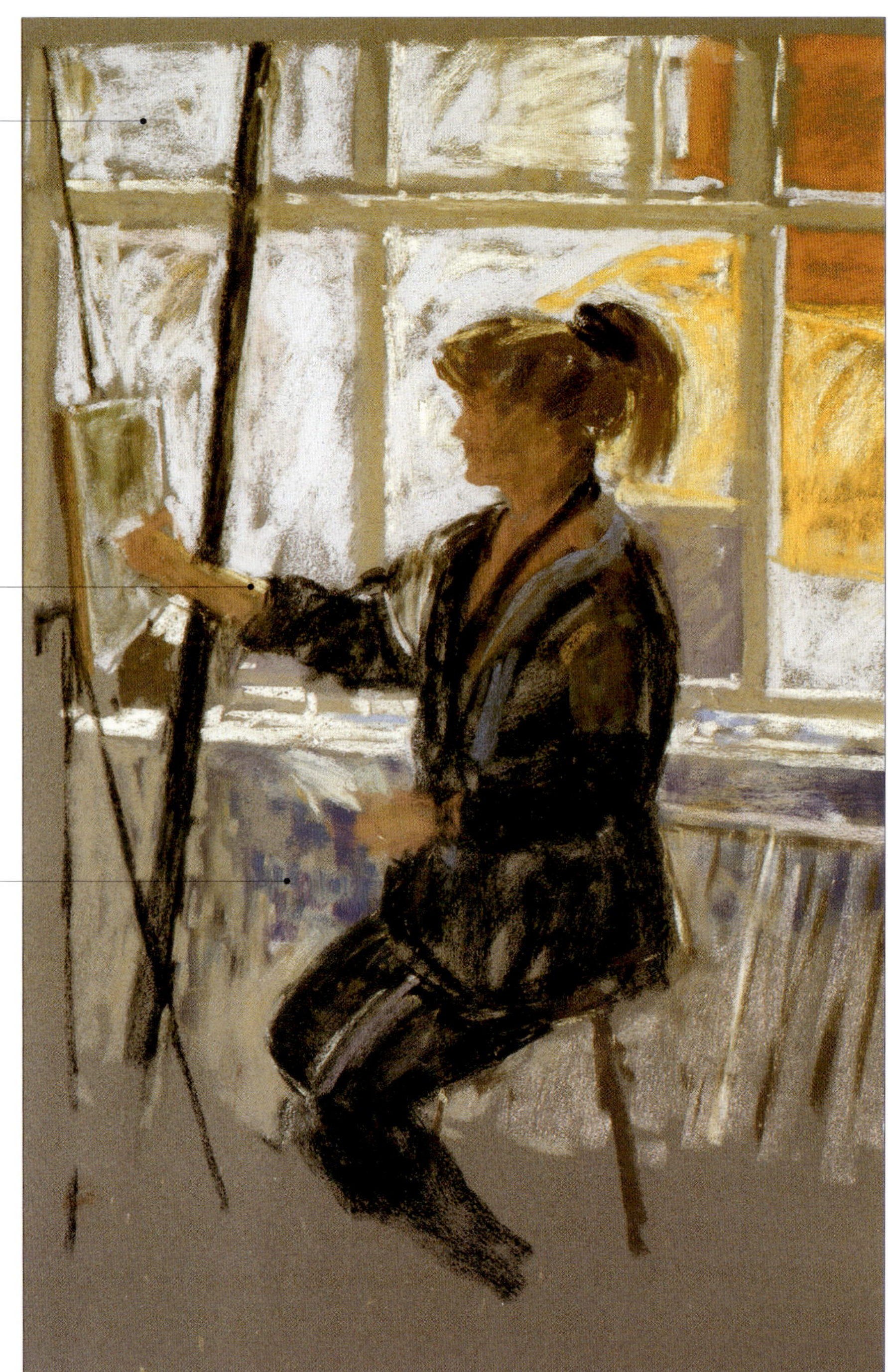

Laying a textured ground

The underlying texture of the paper is always an important factor with pastels. Some artists like to work on a texture of their own making, rather than relying on the mechanically produced texture of the paper. A 'home-made' texture can take any form you like, but the most usual one is a series of irregular diagonal or vertical brushstrokes, which give a directional emphasis to the overlaid pastel strokes. Such grounds can be laid with acrylic paint, used fairly thickly so that it holds the marks of the brush, with acrylic gesso, or, for a really heavy texture, with a substance called acrylic modelling paste, thinned with water. The latter is sold in large pots, however, and is quite costly, so make sure you like this way of working before you invest in it.

The advantage of using acrylic paint is that you can colour the ground as well as texturing it. You can even combine the texture element with a coloured underpainting, varying the colours and textures from one area of the painting to another. Don't overdo this, as you don't want to introduce too many different elements before you begin to apply the pastel. This method is best suited to thick applications of pastel; you need to work on a tough paper, such as heavy watercolour paper – don't try it on ordinary pastel paper, as it will buckle under the weight of the paint.

Practice exercise: **A tinted and textured ground**

Acrylic gesso, which is sold primarily for preparing boards and canvases for oil and acrylic painting, makes an excellent textured ground for pastel work. It is slightly thicker in consistency than tube acrylic and it dries fast. This is a method that is best suited to broad, impressionistic approaches; with a heavy underlying texture it is not possible to achieve fine detail. Mixing a little paint into the gesso allows you to add broad variations of tone.

Materials

- *Acrylic gesso*
- *Black acrylic paint*
- *Watercolour paper*
- *Bristle paintbrush*
- *Soft pastels*

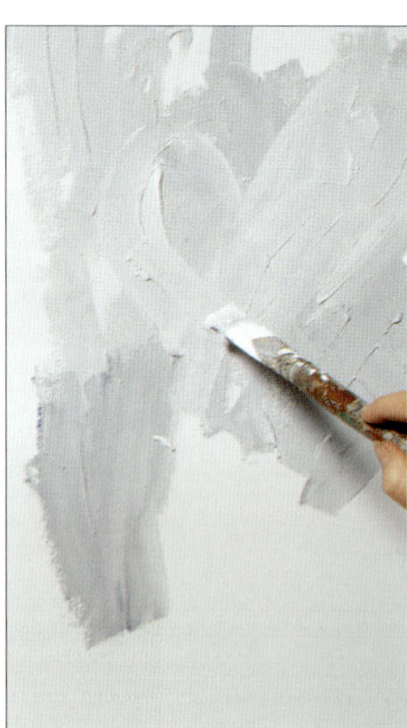

1 Mix the acrylic gesso with a small amount of black acrylic paint and apply it thickly to heavyweight watercolour paper with a large bristle brush, using broad strokes. As the subject of this work is to have a vertical emphasis, the strokes generally follow this direction.

2 The deliberately uneven application of the ground creates a surface that will break up the pastel strokes in interesting ways. This gives an exciting element of unpredictability, allowing you to exploit semi-accidental effects. The tone is also varied, so that the ground will be darker behind the brightest of the flowers.

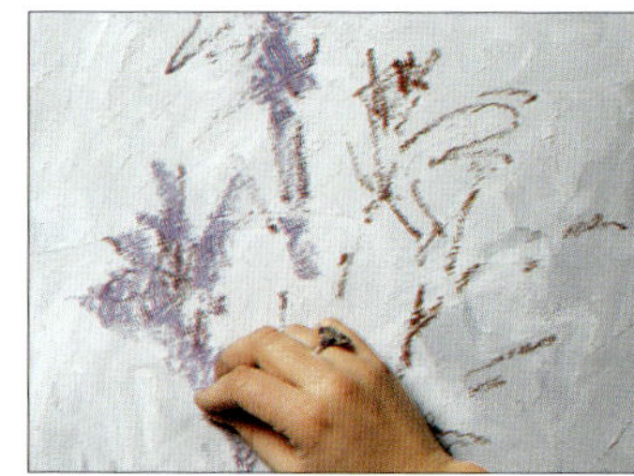

3 When you begin to scribble colour over the brushstrokes of acrylic gesso, it catches only on the raised areas, creating a series of strongly textured marks. This means that lines will be interrupted and diverted, making fine detail impossible.

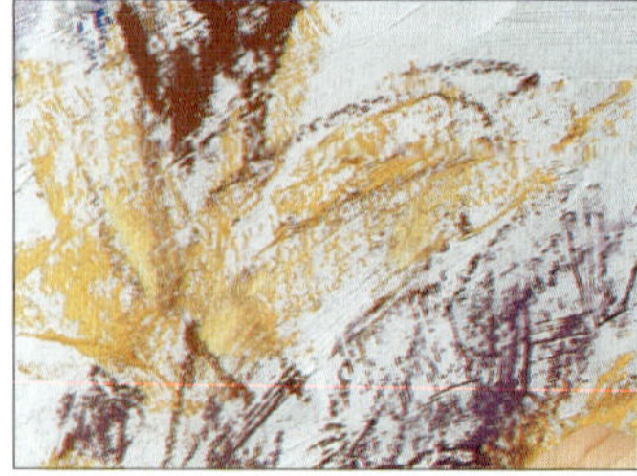

4 Use broad strokes of pastel to capture the essential colours and shapes of the flowers.

The finished drawing

The finished work has a broad painterly effect. In the final stages the artist used a painting method, dipping a brush into gesso and painting over the pastel. This enabled him to completely cover the brushmarks of the gesso ground, which cannot be done with pastel. By mixing the pastel colour it can be spread like paint.

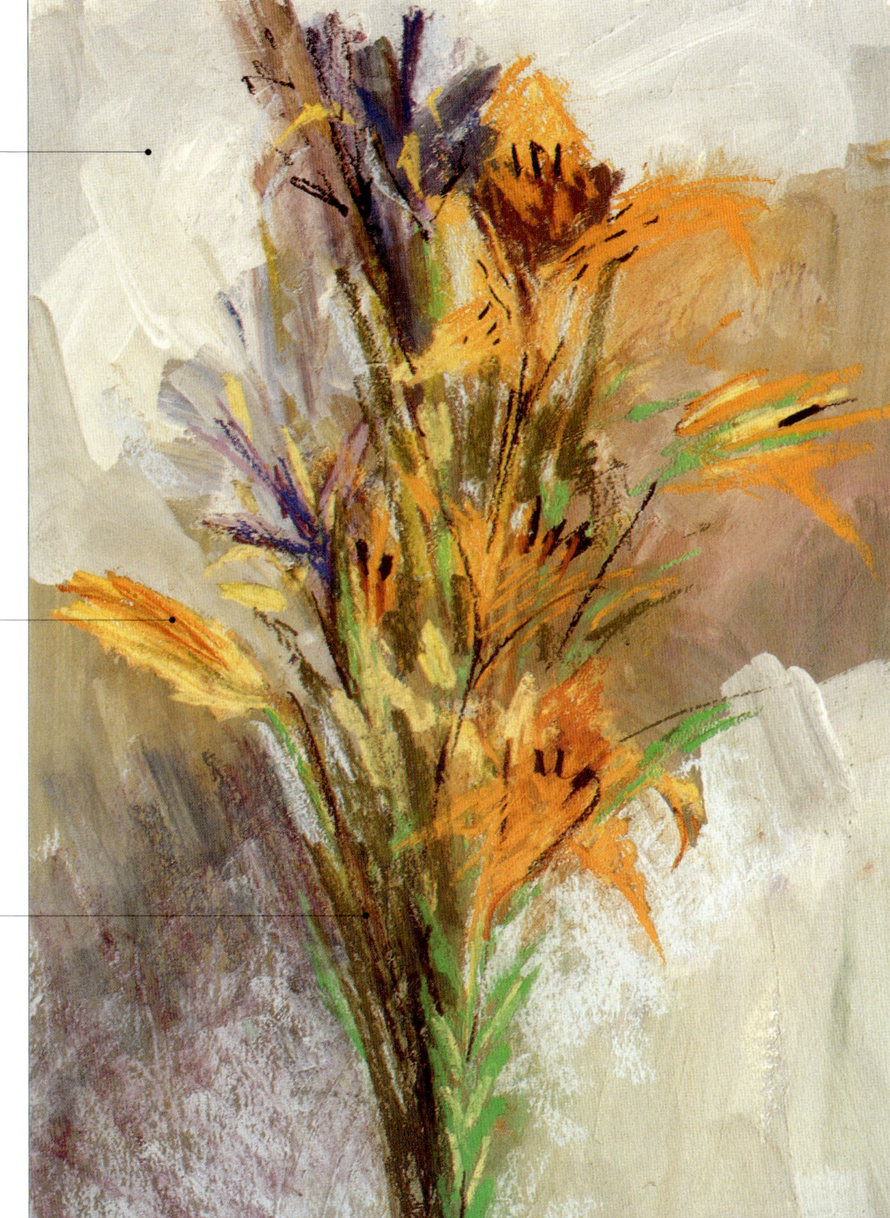

Thick vertical strokes of gesso create a lively texture in the background.

Mixing the pastels with gesso creates vibrant strokes of colour.

The flower stems are suggested by swiftly drawn pastel lines.

Sgraffito

The technique of using a sharp implement to expose an underlying layer of paint or pigment, or the support, is called sgraffito. Although it is perhaps more commonly associated with painting, it can also be used with certain drawing materials as a way of creating texture.

Sgraffito is especially successful with thick applications of soft pastel or oil pastel. You can use any sharp implement to make the marks – a craft (utility) knife, scissors, paper clips, even your fingernails. If you want to scratch through just one layer of soft pastel to reveal the layer beneath, fix (set) the lower layer before applying the top one.

Work confidently and quickly to create a sense of energy in your work, but remember to scratch through the pastel rather than cut into it, otherwise you risk damaging the support.

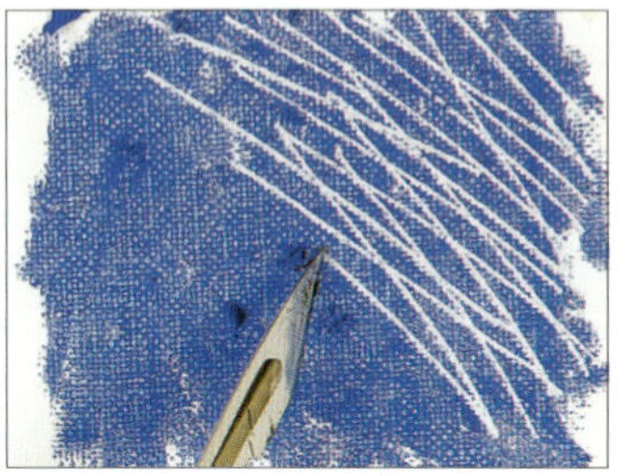

Scratching into oil pastel
Oil pastel on oil-sketching paper can be removed or scratched into using a sharp craft (utility) knife.

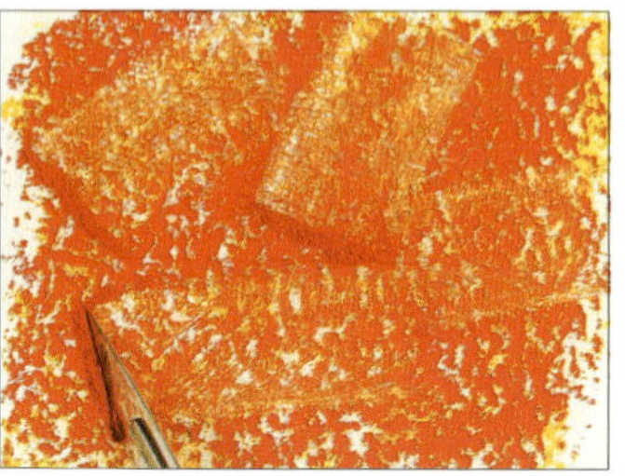

Scratching into soft pastel
To remove one layer of soft pastel to reveal the layer underneath, use the flat of the blade.

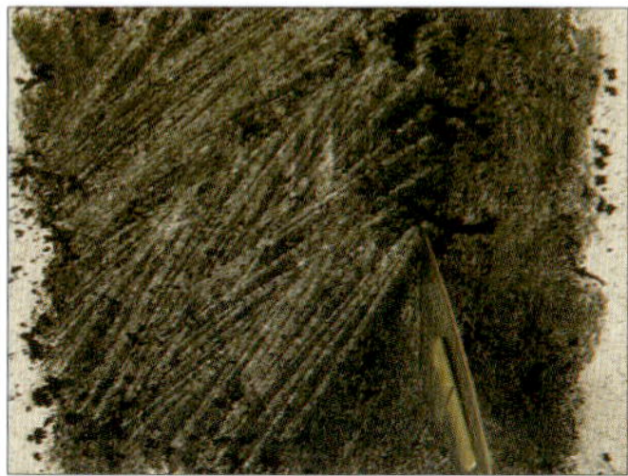

Scratching into charcoal
Any soft, pigmented drawing material can be scratched into. Here, linear sgraffito work is made into charcoal.

Practice exercise: **Woodland scene**

Woodland thickets, which are full of tangled undergrowth and spiky twigs and branches, are the ideal subject for practising the sgraffito technique, as you can scratch off pigment to reveal underlying colours and create thin, energetic lines that capture the profusion of growth to perfection.

For this exercise, the artist chose a dark brown oil pastel paper the same colour as the branches of the trees and scratched off pigment to reveal the colour of the support. She also used sgraffito in other areas, scratching off only the top layer of pigment to create interesting textural effects and colours in the foliage and grasses.

The scene
Here the artist selected elements from two photographs. Don't follow your reference photo too closely: try instead to capture the spirit of the scene and the direction of growth. Woodland scenes can look very jumbled and confusing, so always make sure there is a strong centre of interest. Here, it is provided by the large, solid tree trunk towards the left of the image, which is positioned 'on the third'.

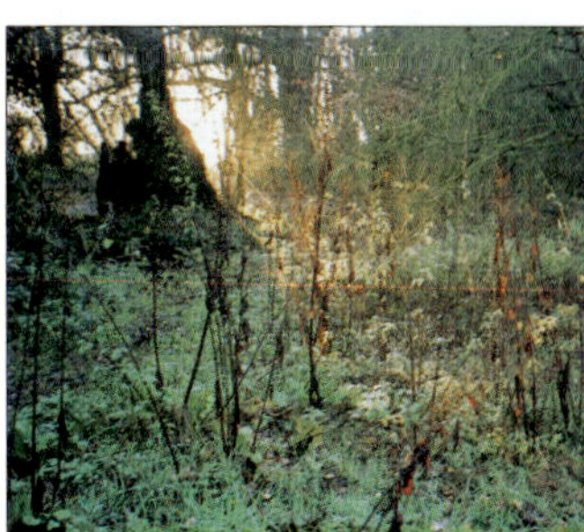

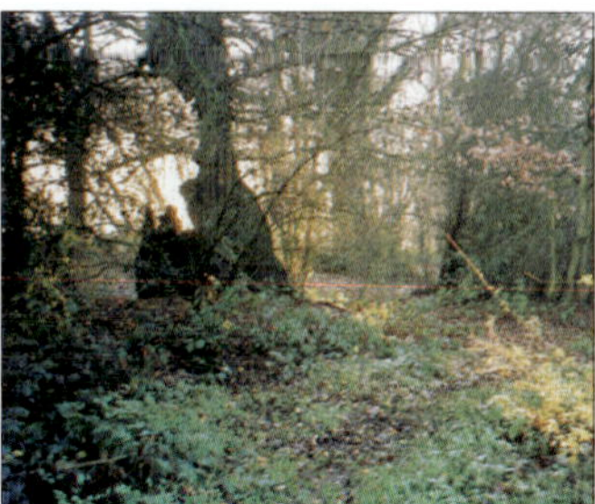

Materials
- *Dark-toned oil pastel paper*
- *Oil pastels: dark brown, black, violet, dark green, white, bright yellow, dark blue, reddish-brown*
- *Scraperboard tool*

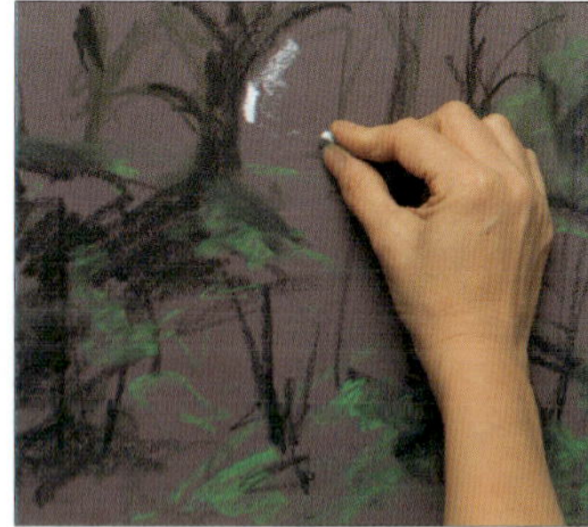

1 Roughly indicate the main trunks and branches, using dark brown, black and violet oil pastels. Scribble in the main patches of foliage in dark green. Using the side of a white oil pastel, block in the light areas of sky between the trees.

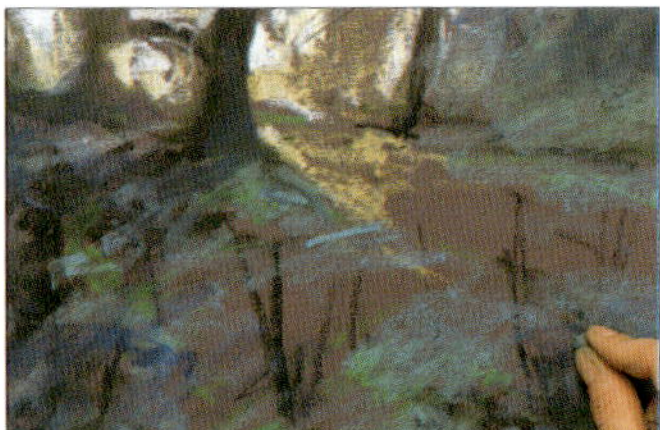

2 Put in the areas of very yellow foliage with a bright yellow oil pastel. Now look for the shadows: using dark blue, scribble in the deepest shadow areas on the ground and the shaded sides of the tree trunks.

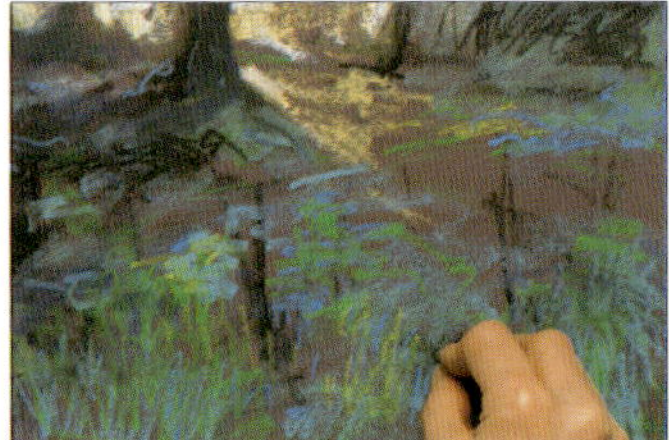

3 Put grasses in the foreground using jagged, vertical strokes of bright, warm colours to help bring this area forwards and create some sense of recession. Cover the support and get plenty of pigment down.

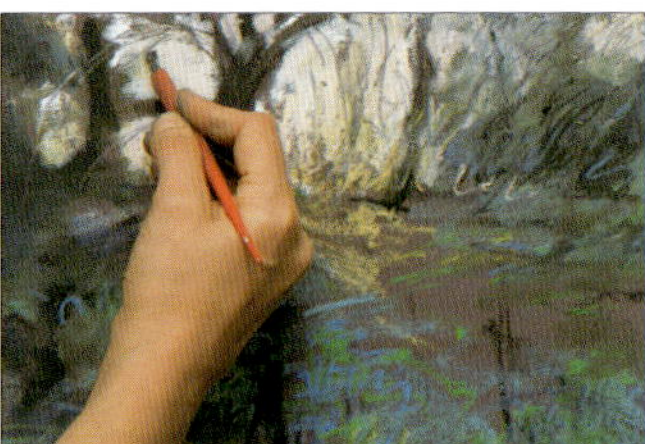

4 Using a scraperboard tool, scratch off thin lines across the white of the sky to reveal the underlying paper colour and create the thin and spindly branches of the background trees.

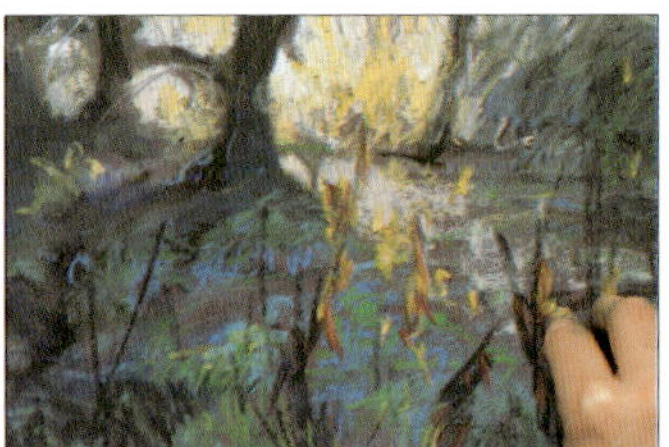

5 Add the sunlit, dead foliage in reddish brown, and patches of sunlight in yellow. Continue building up the colours in the foreground.

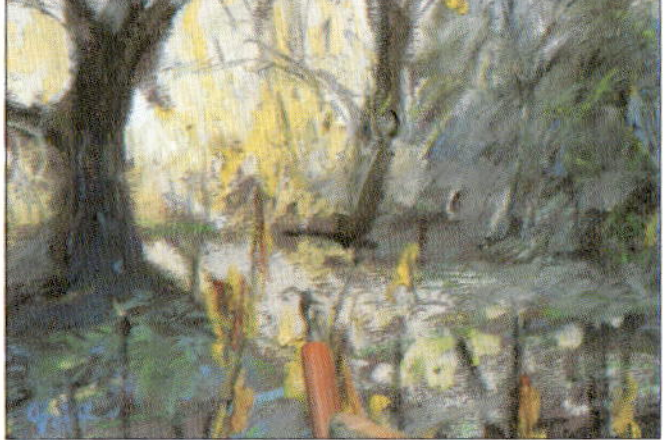

6 Scratch to create the impression of tall, thin grasses and stalks. Follow the direction in which the grasses grow, and use a scribbling motion to create a tangle of leaves and twigs.

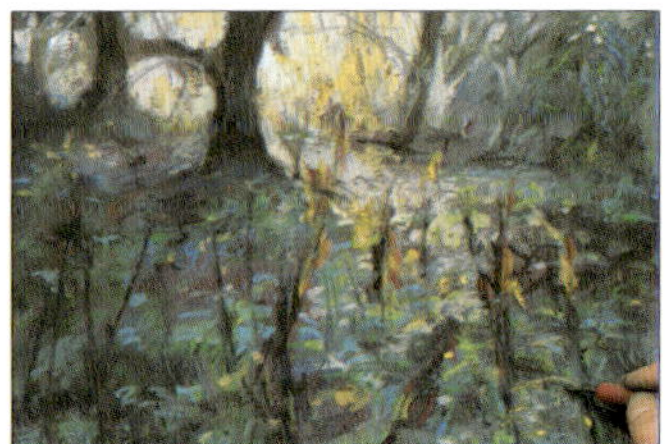

7 Use a variety of strokes to suggest different patterns of growth. For dark shadow, you can use the scraperboard tool to smear thick oil pastel across the support.

The finished drawing

Here, the artist has used the sgraffito technique to create a lively, highly textured drawing that captures the tangled undergrowth and the spindly branches to perfection. There is a good balance between marks made with the oil pastels, such as the larger trunks and branches, and sgraffito marks used to represent freer growth such as the spiky grasses and twisted stems.

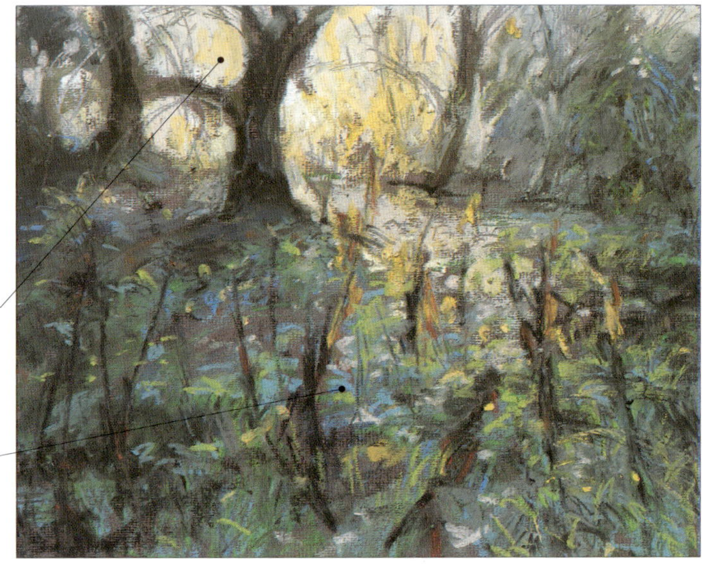

Lines scratched into the white of the sky reveal the underlying support and create the impression of thin branches.

Energetic, vertical scratches reveal the colour of the underlying layer of oil pastel and create movement.

Drawing smooth textures

Smooth surfaces are often hard and include things such as glass and plastic, metal, polished wood, stone and marble. Hard, smooth surfaces are often reflective. They may not always be mirror-like, but they do reflect any directional light source and pick up and reflect colours from objects that are near by.

Hard surfaces can cover extremely complex shaped objects such as a corkscrew or a coffee percolator. On curved surfaces, reflections are often distorted, which can make the smooth surface appear far more complex than it really is. Some smooth-surfaced objects such as polished marble also have a surface pattern, and in order to reproduce the true quality of the object, this will need to be rendered, too.

Work on a paper that is appropriate to the subject. Hard, smooth objects have a clean, smooth outline with clearly defined crisp edges, and a smooth, hot-pressed or NOT paper will help you to achieve the correct feel.

Practice exercise: **Smooth leather ball**

In this exercise, the smooth surface of the ball is created by building up layers of soft pastel and blending out the marks with either your fingertips or a torchon.

Although it is not highly reflective, the leather ball is shiny enough to reflect the light source. Such highlights can be drawn by leaving the paper white or, when working in a soft, powdery medium such as the pastel pencils used here, by wiping off pigment with a kneaded eraser.

Materials

- *Smooth drawing paper*
- *Pastel pencils: ochre, red, dark brown*
- *Torchon (optional)*
- *Kneaded eraser*

The subject

A ball was lit from the front to create a bright highlight near the top. Note the gradual change in tone from the front of the ball to the back, as the light falls off.

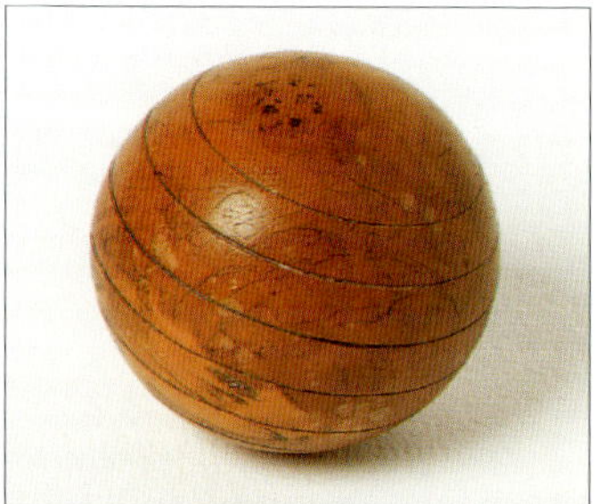

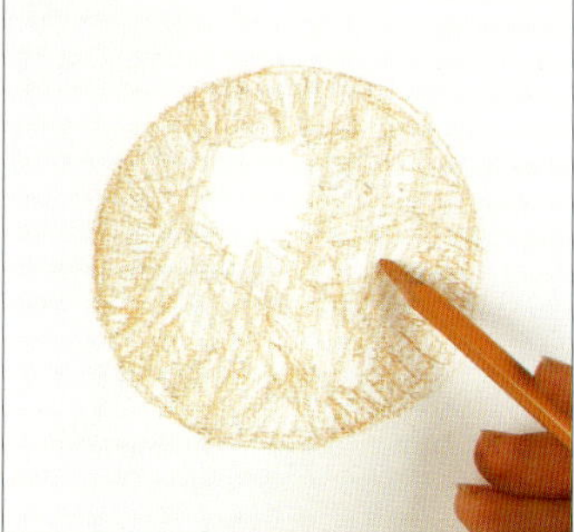

1 Apply the lightest colour first. Using an ochre pastel pencil, scribble on the pigment using multi-directional strokes. Leave the white paper to represent any highlights.

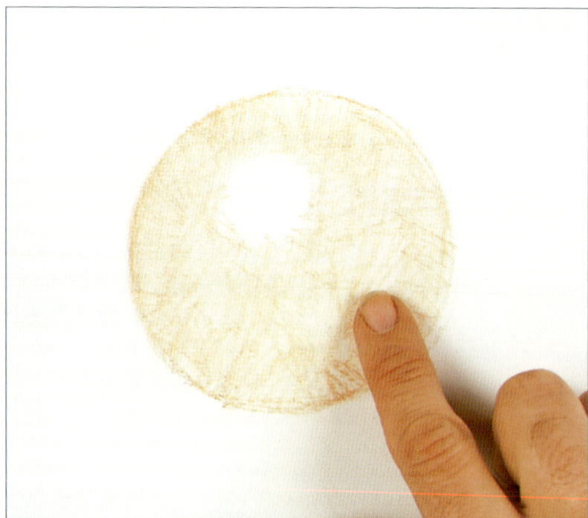

2 Blend the pastel pencil work, using your finger or a paper torchon. The pigment does not have to be completely smooth; blend it just enough to soften any of the scribbled lines that show too clearly.

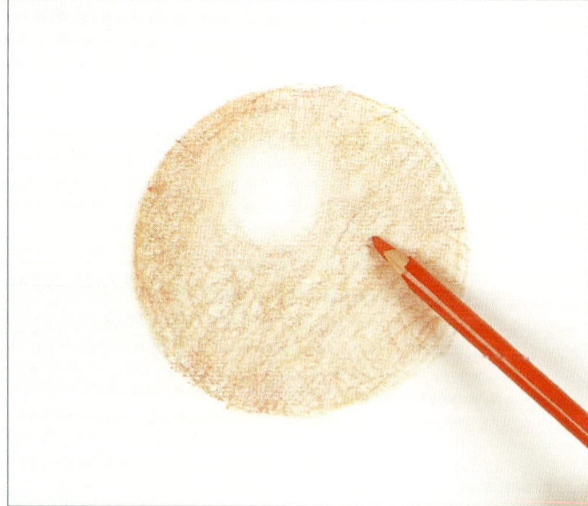

3 Repeat the process, using a red pastel pencil; the two colours blend together to create the rich, reddish-brown of the leather. Apply lighter strokes around the highlights and blend the colour slightly using your finger or a torchon.

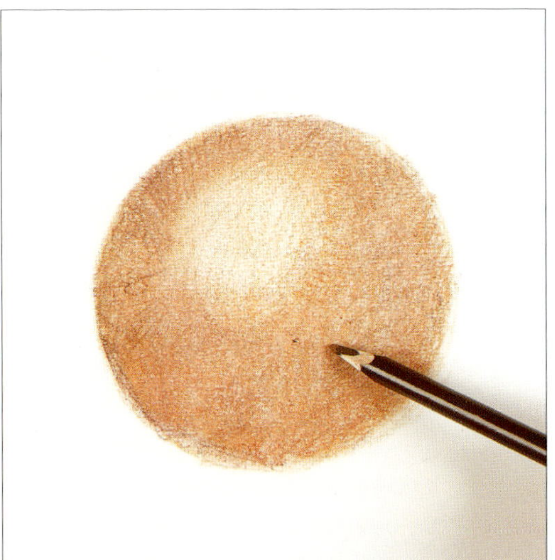

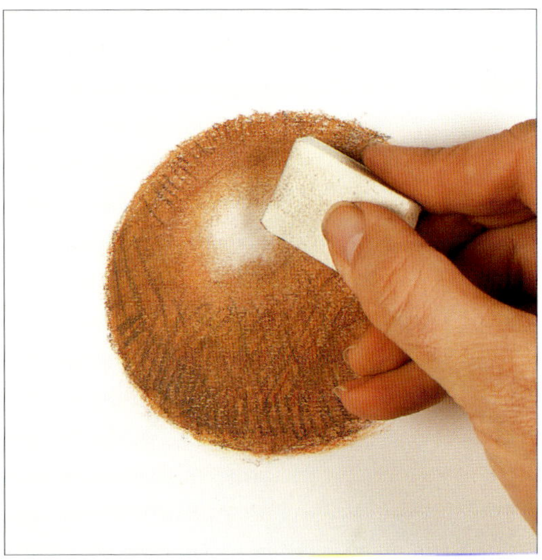

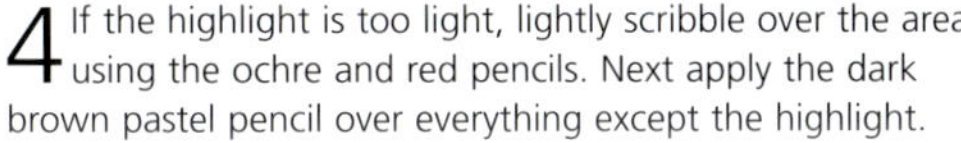

4 If the highlight is too light, lightly scribble over the area using the ochre and red pencils. Next apply the dark brown pastel pencil over everything except the highlight.

5 Once you have applied all the colour, you can re-establish the highlight if necessary by gently lifting off pigment with a kneaded eraser.

The finished drawing

Leather reflects the light that is positioned above it, so careful observation of the size and shape of the highlight is the key to the success of this drawing. Working on a smooth paper also helps, as does blending the pastel marks to obtain a smooth, even coverage.

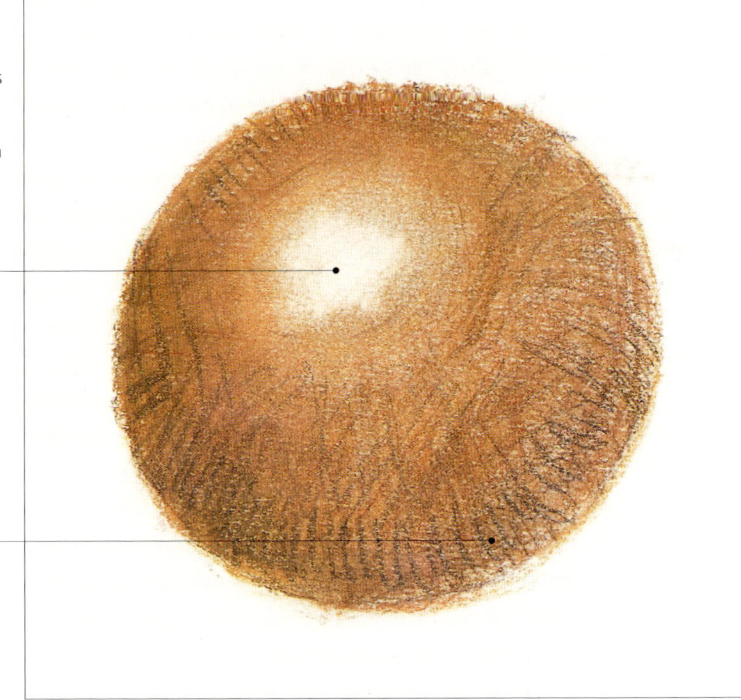

The bright highlight tells us that the subject is both smooth and shiny.

The smooth surface texture of the ball is conveyed by means of light, blended pastel strokes.

Drawing rough textures

Pastel is ideally suited to the rendering of rough surfaces such as weathered stone. With this kind of subject you can make full use of the rough surface of pastel papers – even of extreme surfaces such as sandpaper, on which you can build up many layers of different colours, leaving specks of underlying pigment showing through. Texture is made visible by the way light hits it, so shadows and highlights, as well as outlines, should be jagged and broken to indicate a rough surface.

Practice exercise: **Pitted stone**

The stone has very obvious indentations of differing sizes in the surface and this irregularity is something that needs to come across in the drawing. At the same time it is hard and unyielding, so your marks need to convey this. Blend the colours to create the overall background colour and then apply dabs of oil pastel on top for the holes.

Materials

- *Oil-sketching paper*
- *Oil pastels: dark brown, ochre, mid-grey*
- *White spirit (paint thinner)*
- *Paintbrush*

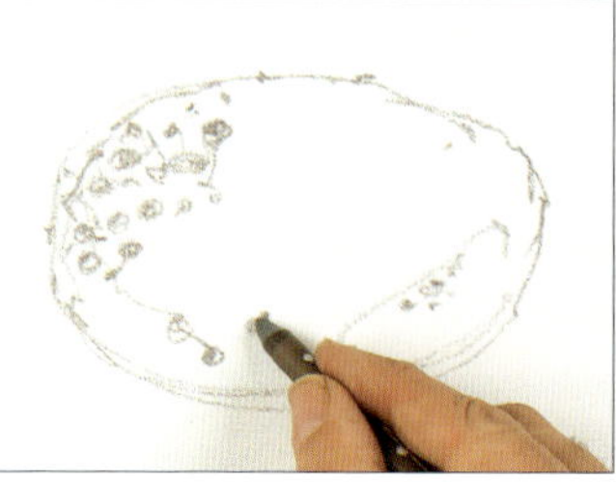

1 Establish the shape of the stone and the position of the pitted marks using a dark brown oil pastel.

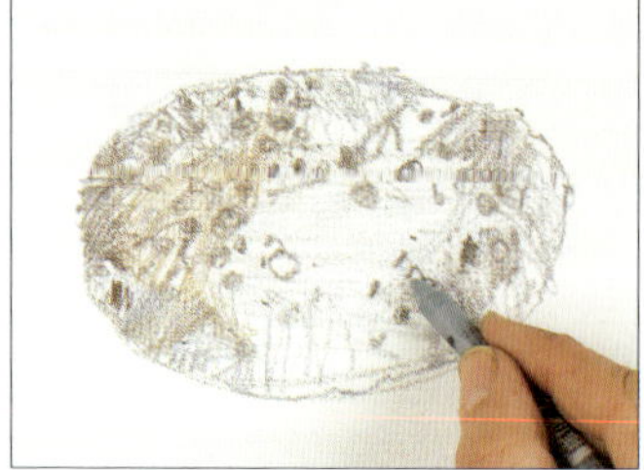

2 Build up the colours within the rock using an ochre and a mid-grey pastel. Make loose, directional strokes that follow the contours of the stone.

The subject

Note the slightly jagged, irregular outline of the stone – very different from the smooth outline of surfaces such as metal. This is one of the keys to conveying its rough texture.

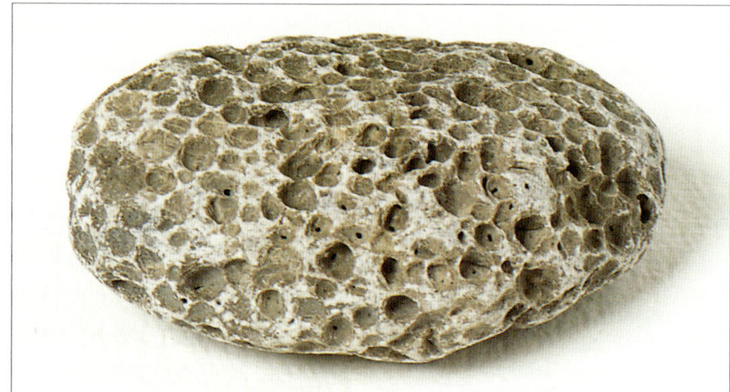

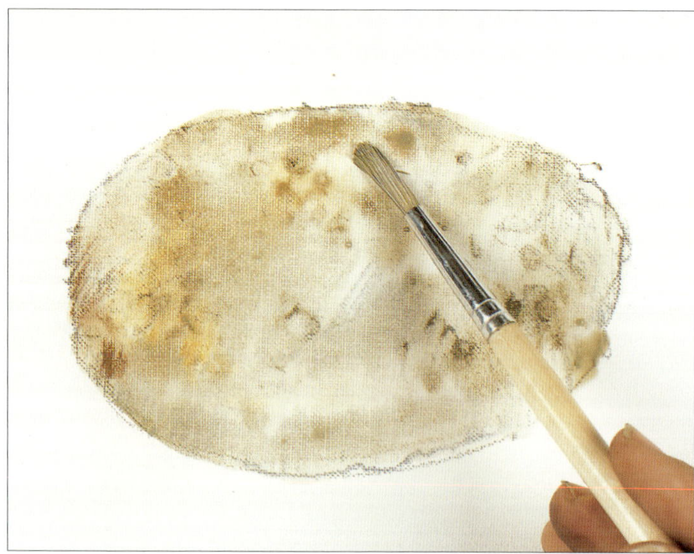

3 Apply white spirit to dilute the pastel work and distribute it over the image surface, allowing some of the linear work to show through in places.

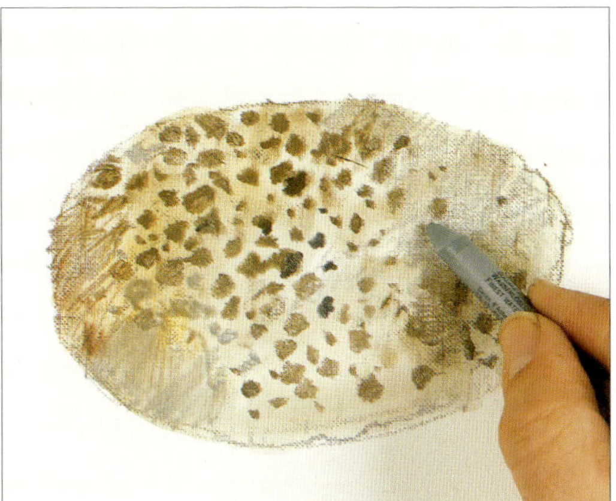

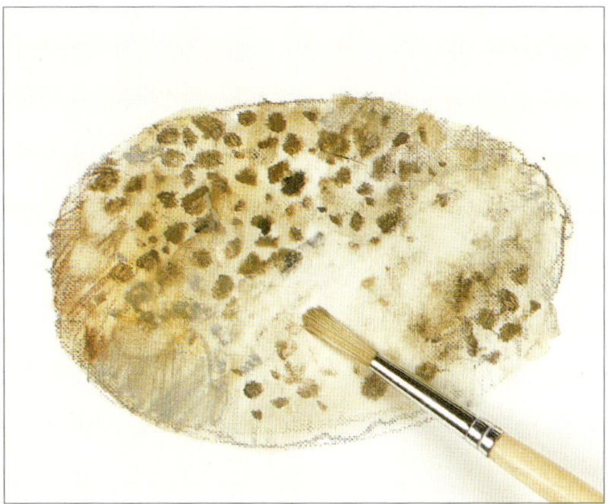

4 While the surface is still wet, use various colours to re-establish the contours and dark holes on the stone's surface, keeping the work fluid and loose.

5 Finally, work into areas of the stone that are still smooth, brushing on a little more white spirit to blend the pastel colours together where necessary.

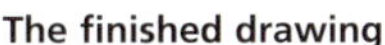

The finished drawing

Blending the oil pastel with white spirit enabled the artist to smooth out the tone to create the relatively even coloration of the stone, while stronger dots of colour on top effectively convey its hard, pitted texture.

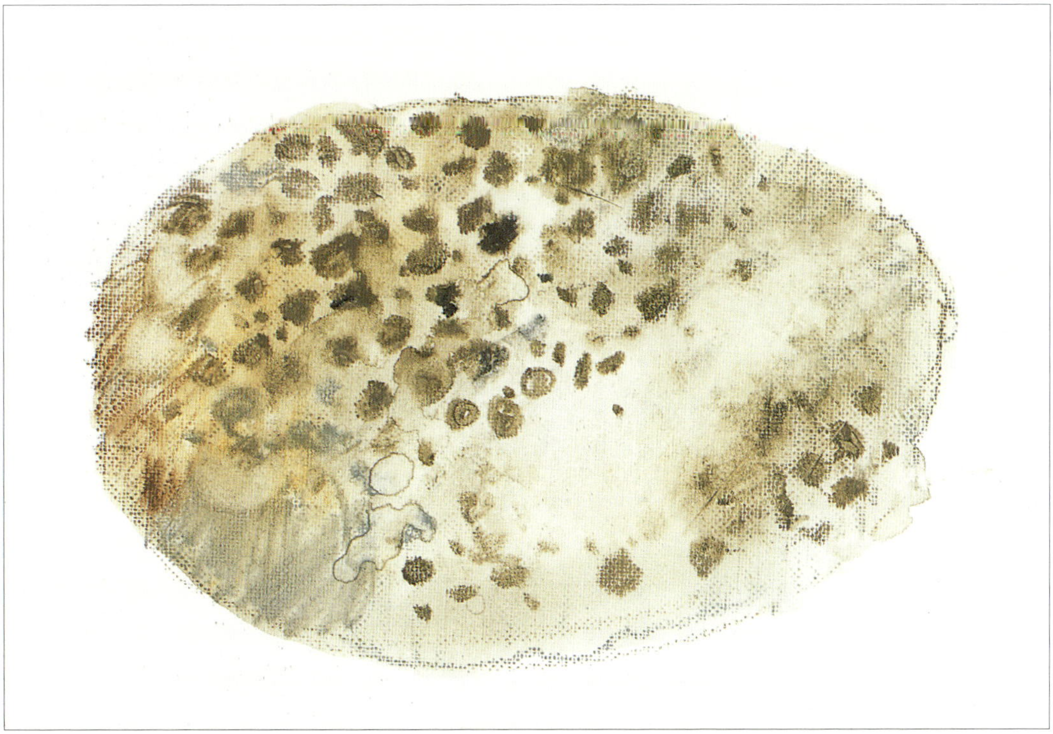

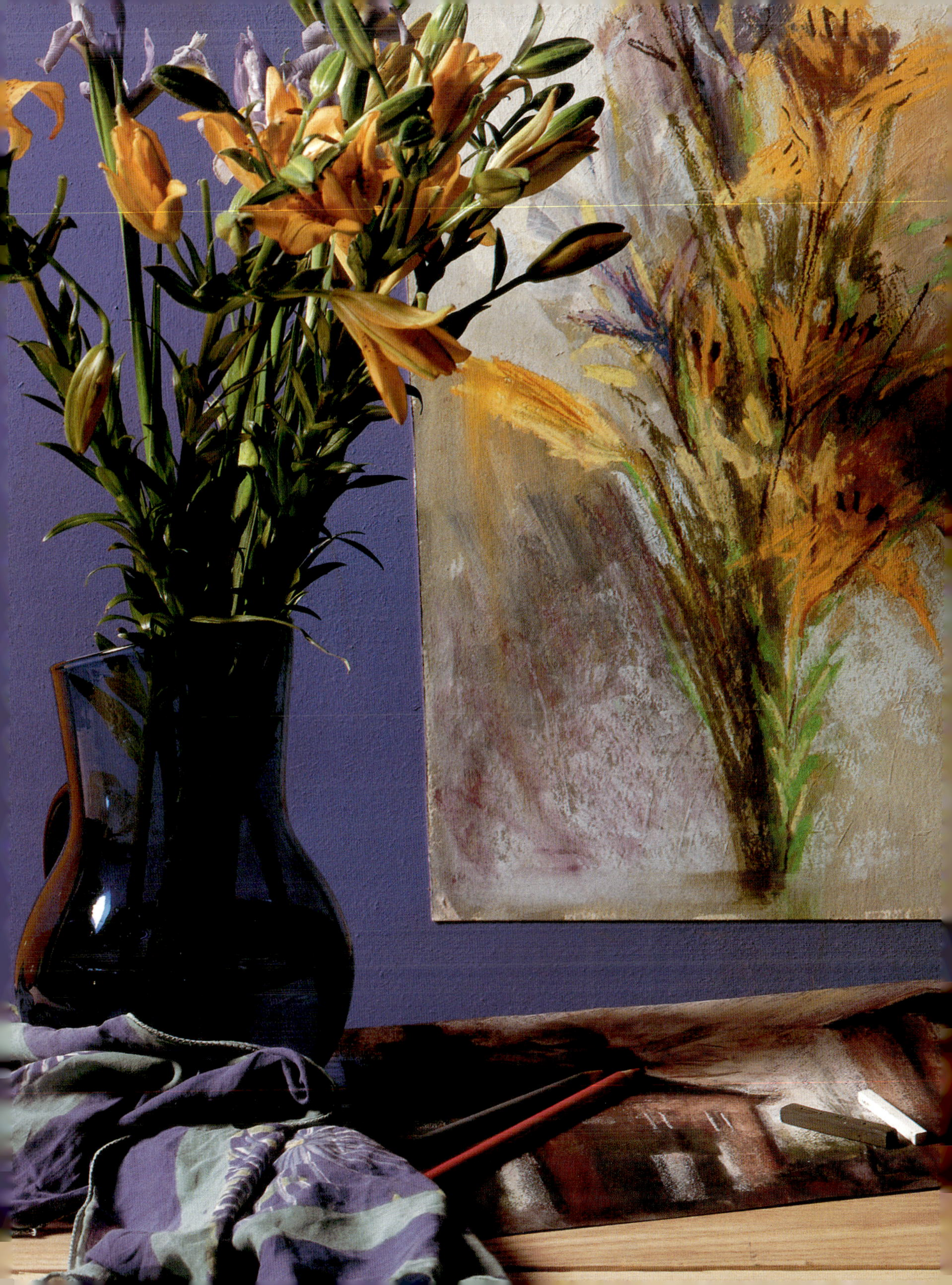

Pastel Projects

This section features a series of pastel pictures analysed step-by-step, from the first outlines to the finished works. If you are a newcomer to this very expressive medium you can follow the steps and learn how to get the best from your materials. Others who have more experience of pastels can pick up useful hints and tips to improve their technique. The works are by different artists and represent a wide range of styles, from precise flower drawings and endearing animals to impressionist landscapes and powerful portraits. Whether you choose to copy each stage line by line, or use the ideas as starting points for your own drawings, you are bound to find inspiration here.

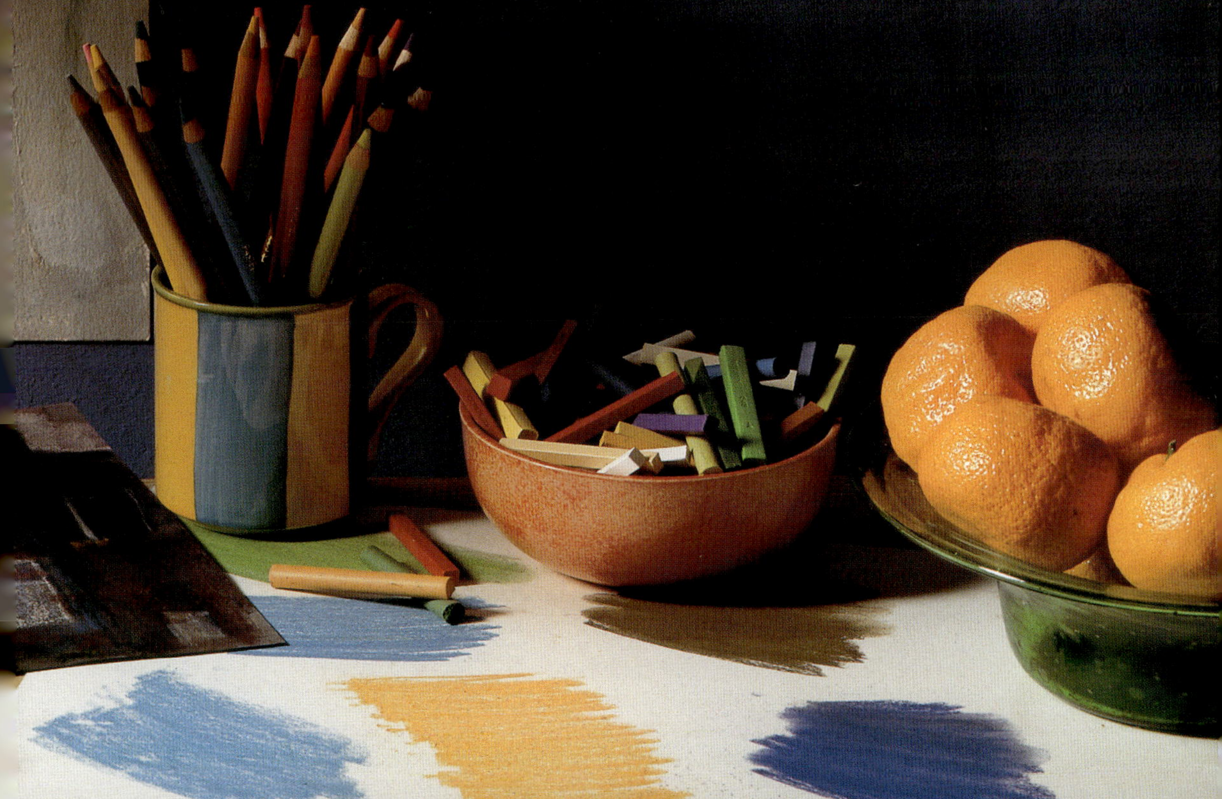

Flower-filled alleyway

Scenes of alleyways with whitewashed buildings adorned with brightly coloured plants are commonplace in Greece, Spain, Portugal and other Mediterranean countries and are the perfect reminder of an enjoyable holiday.

When drawing flowers you have to choose between a very detailed drawing that is botanically accurate in every respect, or a more impressionistic approach that captures the mood of the scene, as the artist does here. Oil pastels are an excellent medium for this approach. With their broad tips they are not suitable for precise linear details, but they can be used for bold spots of colour.

The key to this scene is to make sure there is enough contrast between the very dark and the very light areas. Here, the brightest areas are created by using the white of the support: as you can't make the light areas any lighter than this, the only way to ensure sufficient contrast is to make the darks really dark. At the same time, you need to maintain some textural detail in the areas of shadow.

Materials

- *Oil-sketching paper*
- *Oil pastels: pale grey, turquoise blue, mid-brown, purplish blue, bright green, reddish-brown, orange, grey-black, dark green, crimson, cadmium yellow deep, mid-green, black, white, olive green*
- *Turpentine or paint thinner and clean rag*

The scene

A wedge-shaped shadow on the left directs the viewer's eye towards the flowers scrambling up the wall on the right-hand side. The pale-coloured stonework acts as a foil for the bright flowers and adds an interesting contrast of texture.

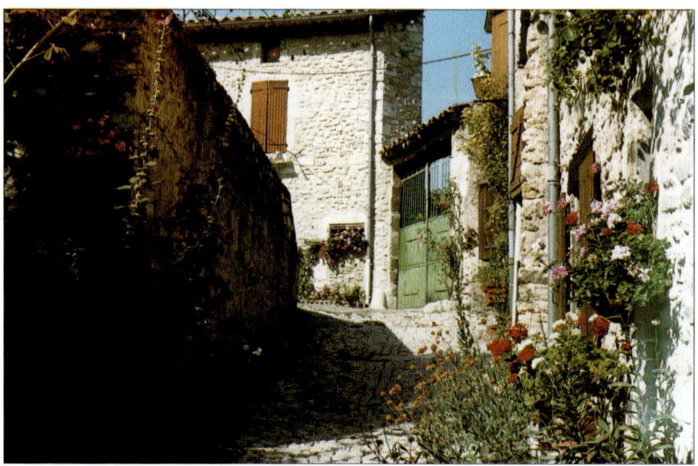

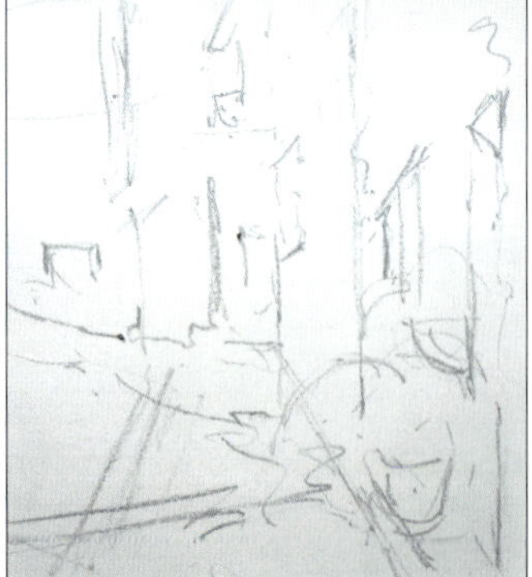

1 Using a pale grey oil pastel, sketch the main lines of the scene – the buildings, with their windows and doors, and the large wedge-shaped shadow that juts across the alley from the left. Measure the proportions and angles carefully; if you're unsure, put in the lines lightly in pencil first, as pencil is much easier to erase than oil pastel.

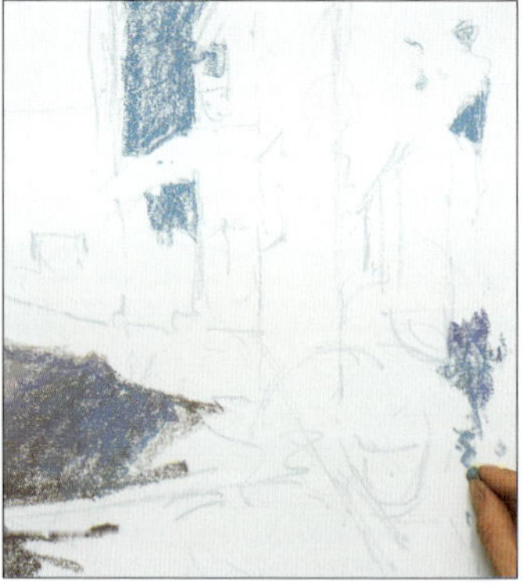

2 Using a turquoise blue oil pastel, block in the sky. Block in the shadow with a mid-brown oil pastel and go over it with purplish blue and turquoise. (Shadows are never a single, uniform colour.) Using the purplish blue and turquoise pastels, block in the shadows cast on the right-hand wall by the flowers.

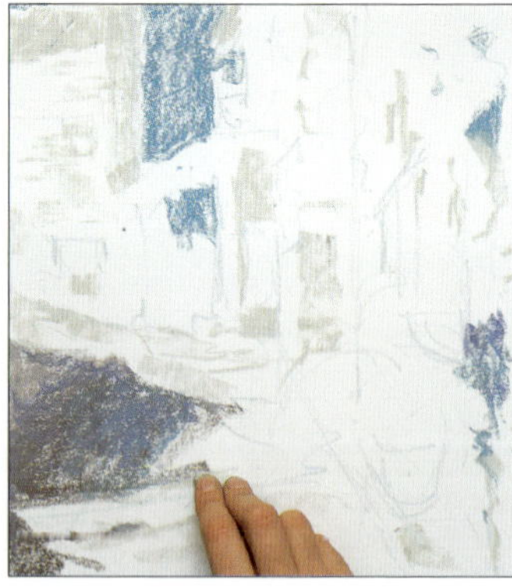

3 Using the side of a pale grey pastel, loosely block in the sides of the buildings that are in shadow and the long, thin shadows that run across the foreground. Don't press heavily on the pastel or the coverage will be too thick, making it difficult to apply subsequent layers and achieve lively, interesting colour mixes in the shadows.

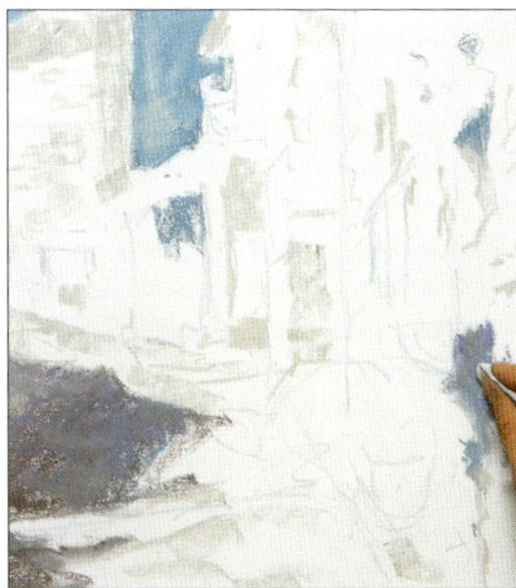

4 Dip a rag in turpentine and rub the rag gently over the sky and shadows to blend the pastel marks to a smooth colour.

Tip: Use a clean section of rag for each area that you blend, so as not to muddy the colours.

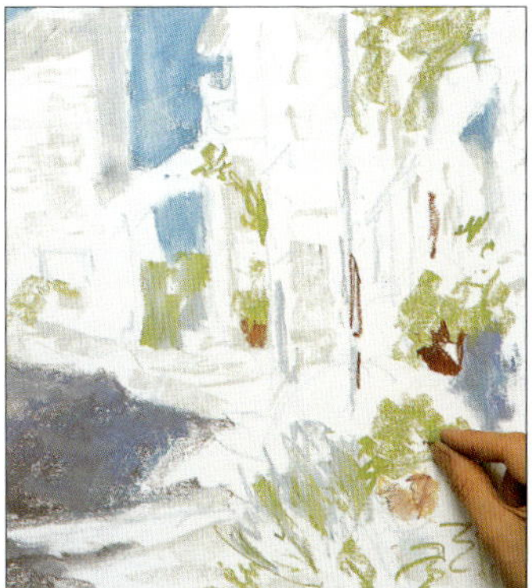

5 Using a bright green oil pastel, loosely scribble in the lightest green of the foliage and the iron gates at the end of the alleyway. Don't make your marks too specific, as you will refine the shapes and colours later; these loose strokes give the impression of uncontrolled growth. Use a reddish-brown pastel to block in the shape of the large terracotta pot on the wall.

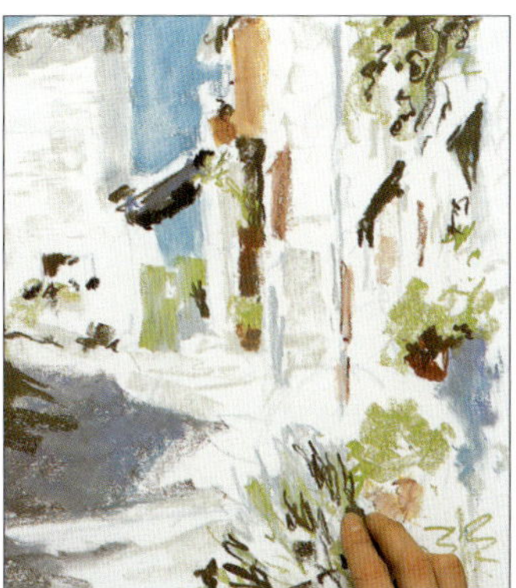

6 Using a reddish-brown oil pastel, put in the door and woodwork. Soften the colour in places by adding a little orange over the top, blending the colours on the support by rubbing them together. Add grey-black for the tiled roof between the buildings. Scribble in very dark green throughout the scene for the darkest foliage. The image is now beginning to take on some depth.

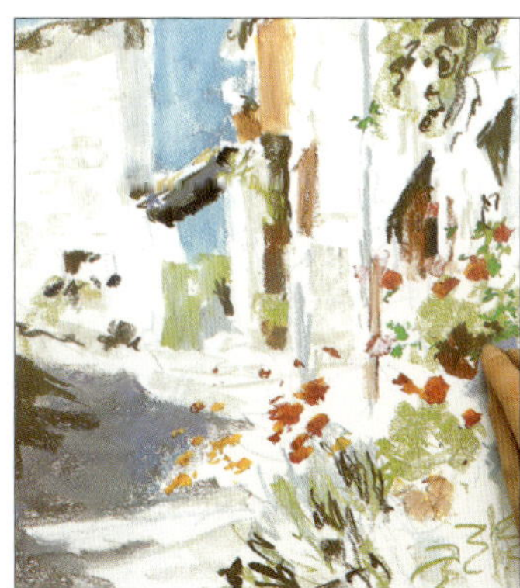

7 Block in the red flowers in crimson and the lighter flowers in cadmium yellow deep. Both are warm colours, so the flowers immediately jump forwards in the scene. Scribble in the mid-tones of the foliage using a bright mid-green. The range of foliage tones helps to give the image depth as the light and dark tones hint at shadow areas within the leaves. Although the leaves are not drawn in detail, the use of different colours shows that there are several types of foliage in the scene.

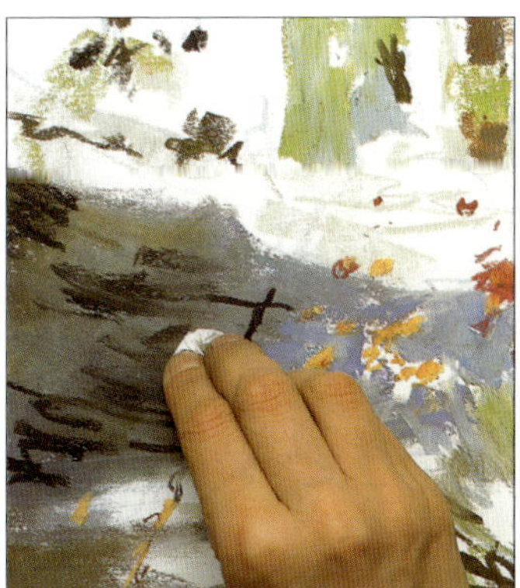

8 The large shadow on the left is an important part of the composition, but now that the rest of the picture is beginning to take on some form, it appears too pale and flat. Add a little blue, green and purple to this area and blend the colours with a rag soaked in turpentine. Keep the coverage patchy, however, to help create the texture of the ground. Draw the cracks in the paving in black oil pastel, making strong linear marks of varying degrees of intensity.

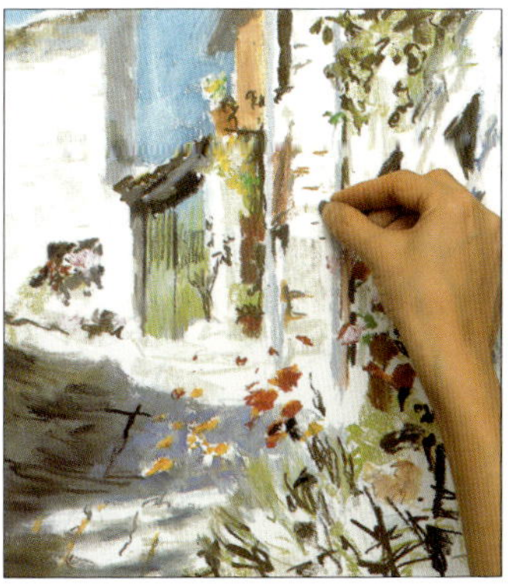

9 Block in the metal gate in the background in mid-green and use fine vertical lines of dark green for the individual bars. Draw the flowers on the background building, dotting in the general shapes and moving between light and dark tones to create a sense of form. Lightly apply pale grey over the shaded side of the background building. Indicate some of the horizontal courses in the stonework using grey and orange overlaid with white for a pinky terracotta colour.

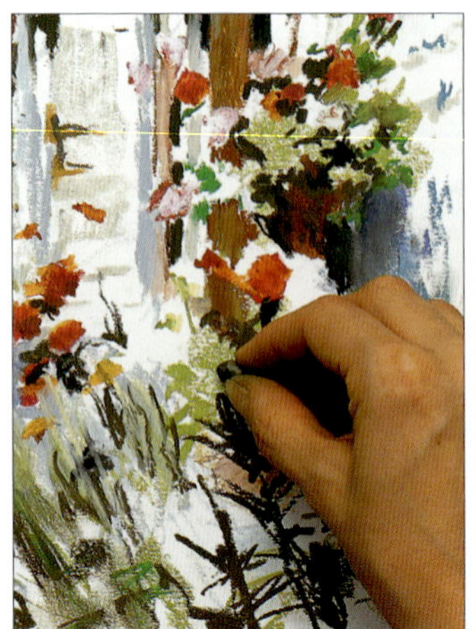

10 Using the tip of the pastel and making jagged, spiky marks that jut out from the main stems, apply strokes of dark olive green to the stems in the foreground.

Tip: These spiky, linear marks create more detail and texture in the immediate foreground, which is one way to create a sense of depth in a drawing.

Assessment time

Now that the drawing is very nearly complete, you should take some time to assess the overall balance. Ask yourself, for example, if there is enough contrast between the very bright sunlit patches on the ground and the very dense shadows. Is there enough detail in the flowers and stems in the immediate foreground? Even very small adjustments at this stage can make a difference.

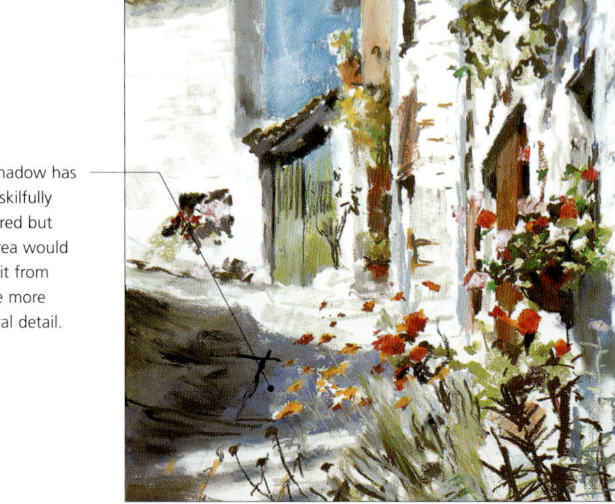

The shadow has been skilfully rendered but the area would benefit from a little more textural detail.

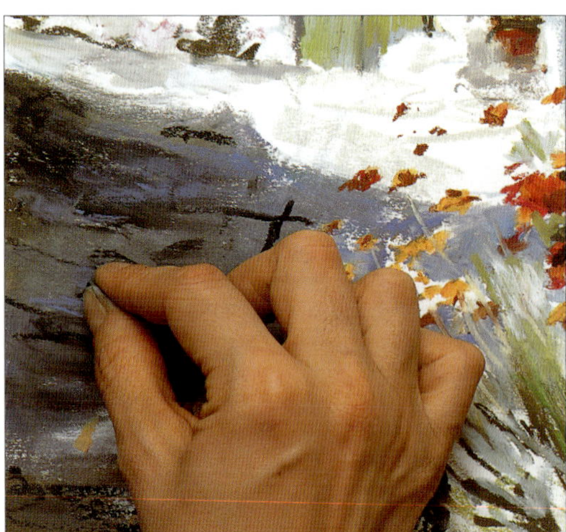

11 Even within an area that appears, at first glance, to be very dark, some texture should be evident. Where necessary, add a few small linear marks using a black pastel – but take care not to overdo it.

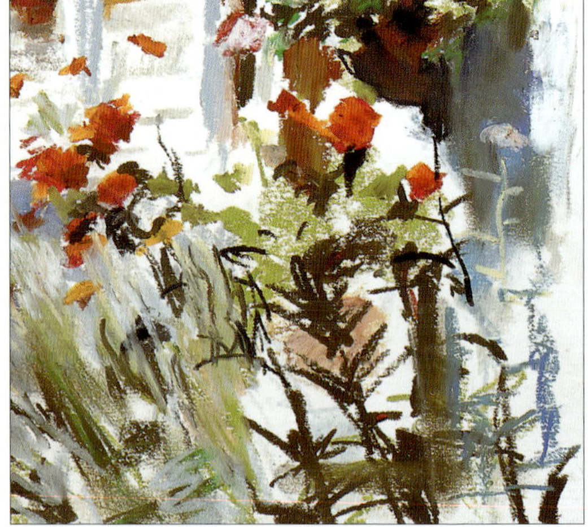

12 Working lightly and quickly, add very thin vertical strokes of white, grey and yellow to the grasses in the immediate foreground to create more depth and enhance the spiky texture.

The finished drawing

There is a lovely sense of light and shade, and of warm and cool areas, in this drawing. Note how the artist has left some areas of the paper almost untouched, so that the white of the support is allowed to stand for the dazzling patches of sunlight. Bold dashes of colour for the flowers and leaves combine with smoothly blended passages such as the sky and the large foreground shadow, creating a generalized impression of the scene, rather than a detailed rendition in which every flower or crack in the wall can be seen. The overall effect is very lively and appealing – almost inviting the viewer to step into the scene.

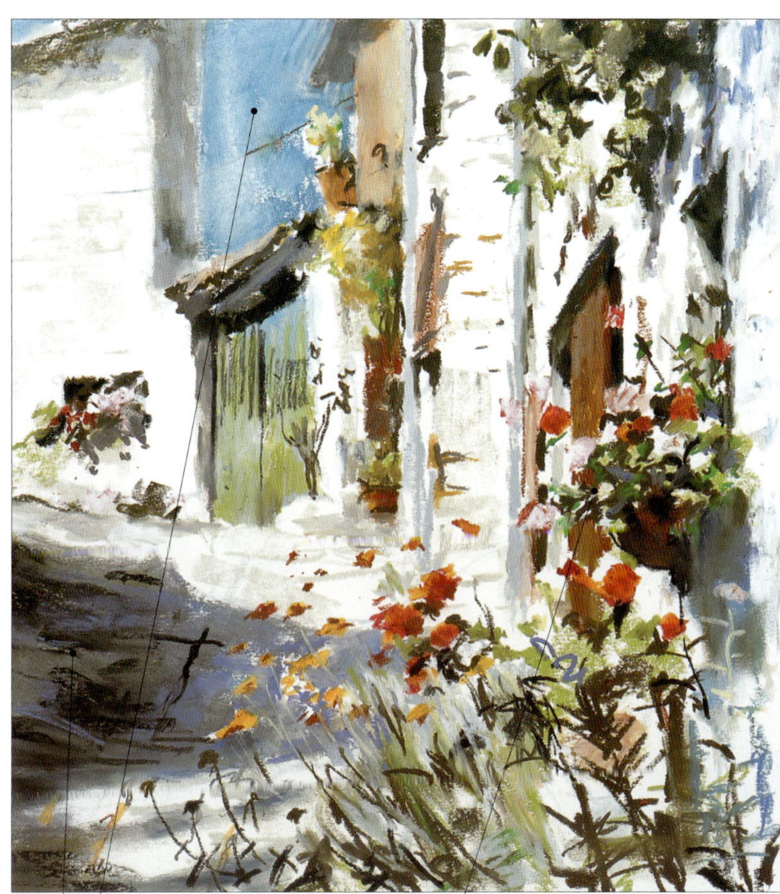

Although we cannot see the building on the left, its presence is implied by the very strong shadow, which also serves to lead the viewer's eye into the scene.

The smoothness of the sky (created by blending the pastel marks with a rag dipped in a solvent) contrasts well with the texture of the buildings and plants.

Although the individual leaf and flower shapes are not drawn precisely, the use of a range of tones creates a convincing three-dimensional feel.

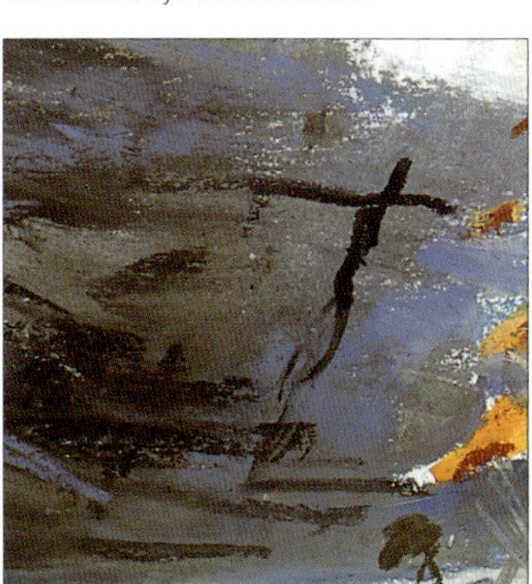

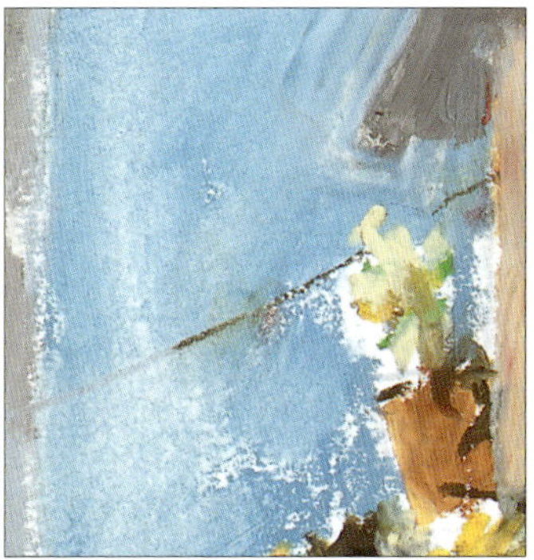

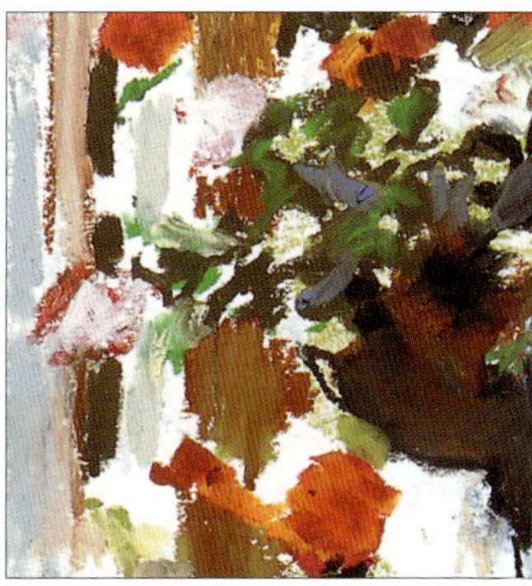

Exotic flowers

Many exotic flowers are readily available from good florists' shops. They are wonderful things to draw and make a simple still life to set up at home. The bright yellow or orange flowers of *Strelitzia* burst out of a boat-shaped bract like head feathers on an exotic bird, giving rise to one of the flower's common names – the bird of paradise flower.

This project gives you the opportunity to exploit the potential of soft pastels. The colours are vibrant and perfectly suited to this subject, and soft pastels have a smooth texture which is ideal for the flowers and leaves. The bold, graphic shapes of the flowers and leaves require strong, flowing marks, which can be easily blended.

Materials

- *Paper or board*
- *Soft pastels: pale green, yellow ochre, bright yellow, greyish green, reddish brown, dark green, grey, pale pink, ultramarine blue, cadmium yellow, cadmium orange, bright green, vermilion, deep red, Naples yellow*
- *Hard pastel: cadmium red*
- *Pastel pencil: Hooker's green*
- *Rag or kitchen paper*

The set-up

The *Strelitzia* and amaryllis were placed in a tall vase, with the leaves acting as a dark background. The vase does not form part of the final drawing, but it keeps the flowers upright.

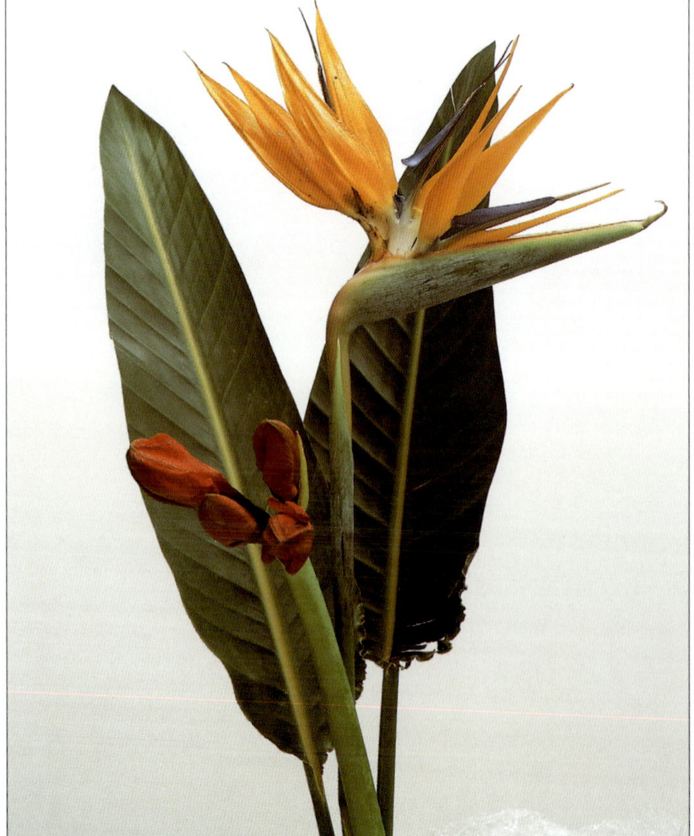

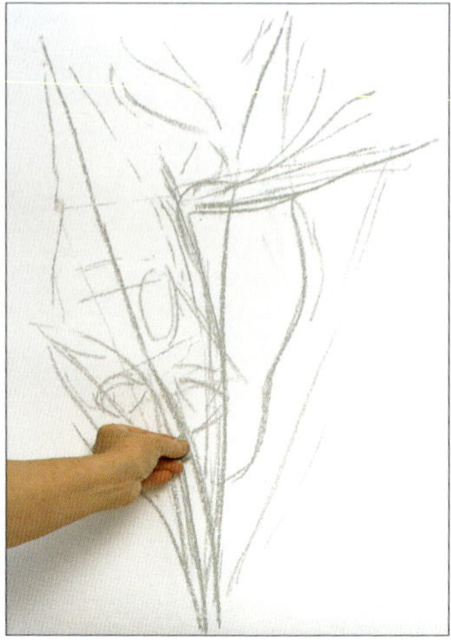

1 Using a pale green soft pastel, map out the main lines of your subject, including the main veins of the two large leaves.

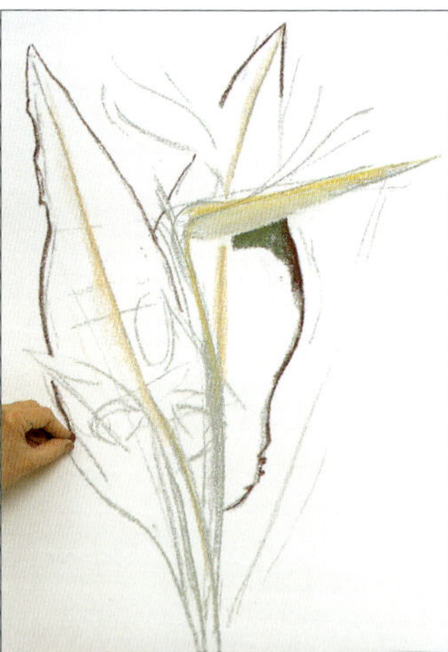

2 Put in the main veins of the leaves with a yellow ochre pastel. Use a bright yellow and a greyish green pastel for the *Strelitzia* bract, smoothing out the join between the colours with your fingers. Outline the leaves in reddish brown (the colour will barely be visible in the finished drawing, but the edge of the leaves needs to be clearly defined).

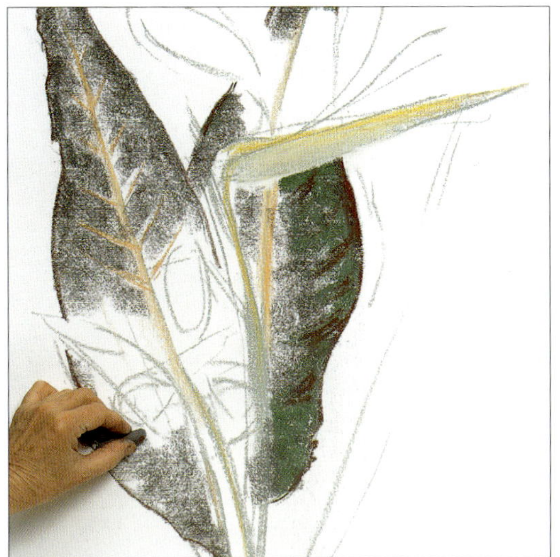

3 Draw the veins on the background leaf in the same reddish brown. Fill in the spaces between them with a dark green, using the side of the pastel. Repeat the process on the foreground leaf, using yellow ochre for the veins and filling in the spaces in grey.

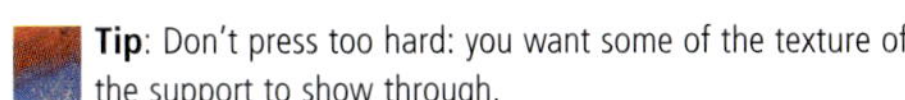

Tip: Don't press too hard: you want some of the texture of the support to show through.

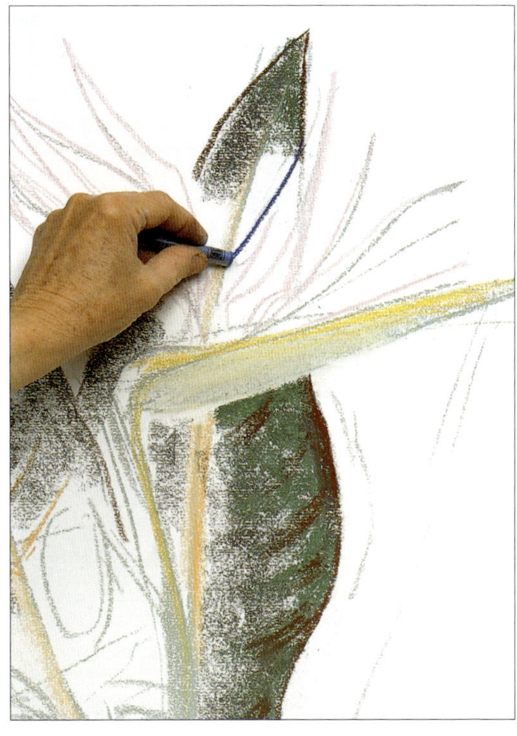

4 Outline the individual *Strelitzia* flowers in pale pink and the tongues in ultramarine blue.

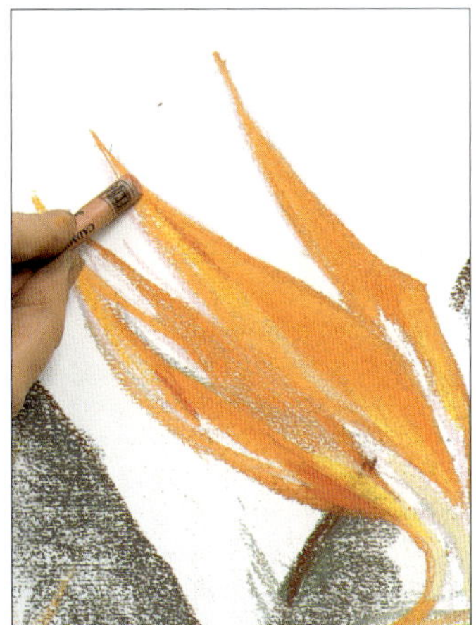

5 Fill in the flowers in cadmium yellow and cadmium orange soft pastel, and define the line between the petals with a cadmium red hard pastel.

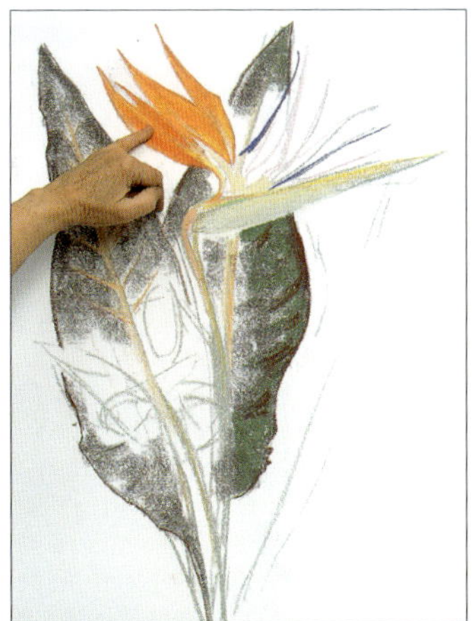

6 Blend the flower colours with your fingertips to give a smooth, waxy texture, making sure you don't pull any colour on to the background.

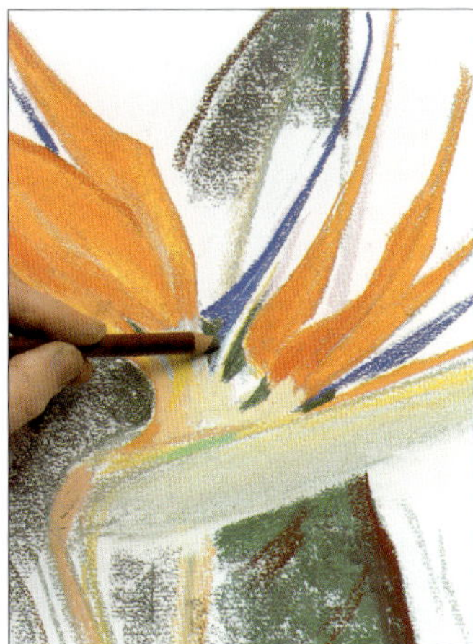

7 Use a Hooker's green pastel pencil to define the tiny triangular areas of leaf that lie between the bases of the flowers.

▶

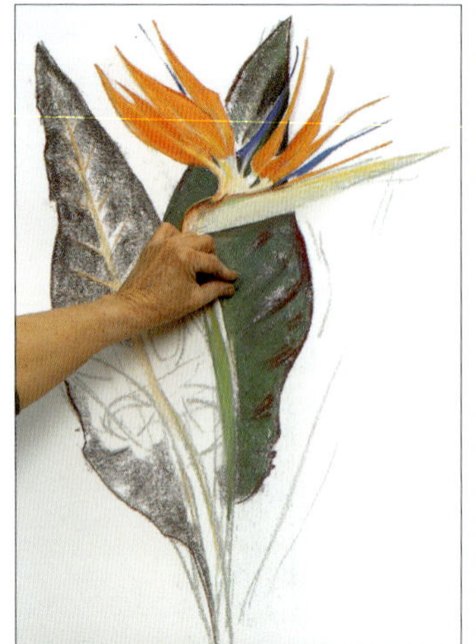

8 Block in the stem of the *Strelitzia* flower with a light, bright green, overlaid with a little cadmium yellow in places for the highlights. Block in the rest of the background leaf in dark green, using the side of the pastel.

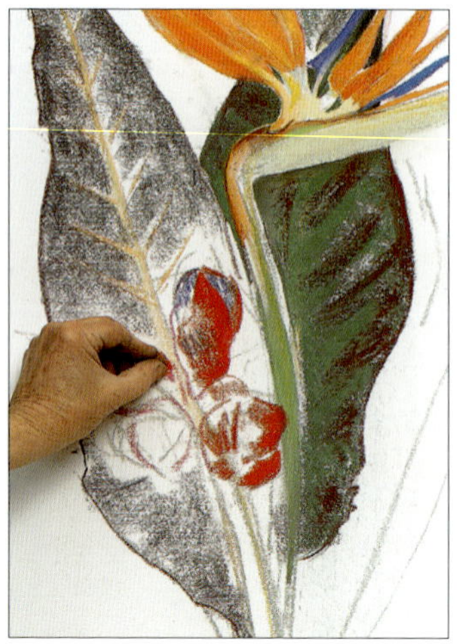

9 Leaving the brightest highlights in the drawing untouched for the moment, block in the red flowers with vermilion and ultramarine blue. Use ultramarine blue for the dark, shaded parts of the flowers.

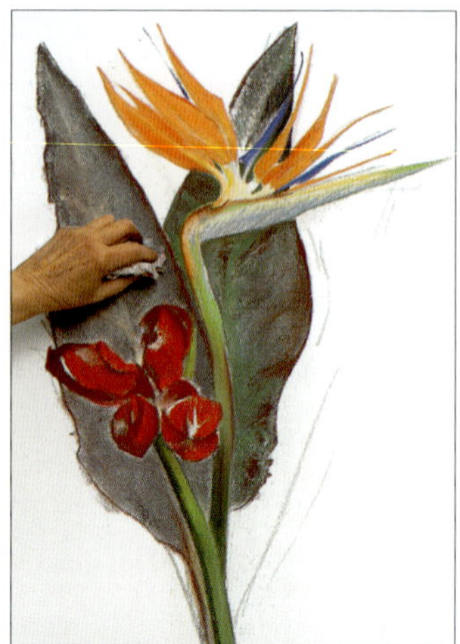

10 Still working around the highlights, overlay deep red on the ultramarine blue to create a rich, almost black, red. Carefully blend the colours on the leaves with the side of your hand or a clean rag, smoothing out the pastel marks to give a waxy finish to the leaves. Work on one section at a time, making sure you retain something of the linear marks of the veins.

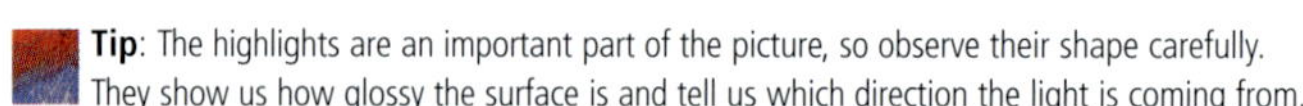

Tip: The highlights are an important part of the picture, so observe their shape carefully. They show us how glossy the surface is and tell us which direction the light is coming from.

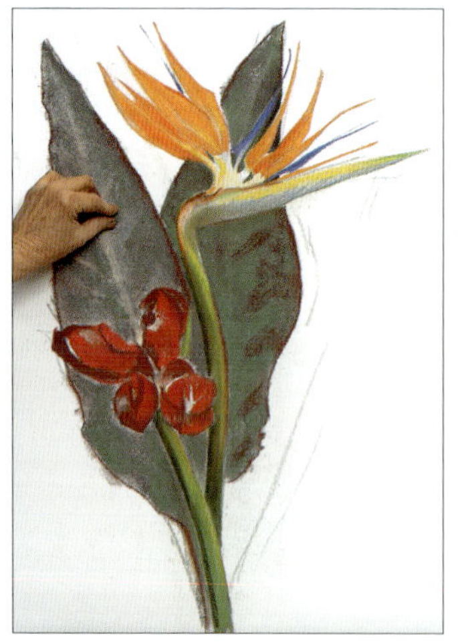

11 Using the side of the pastel, apply dark green to the foreground leaf between the veins to begin to add texture to the plant.

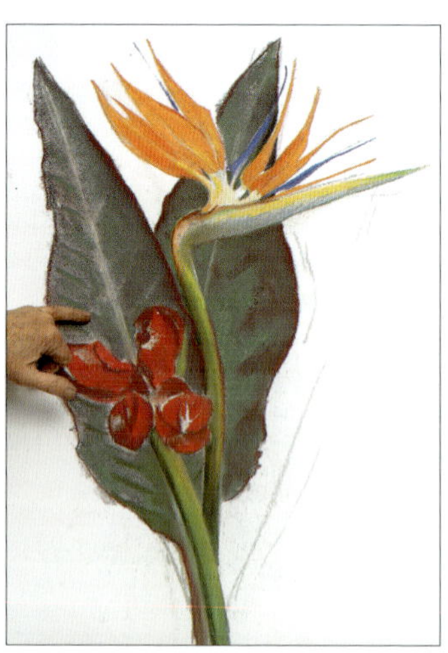

12 The leaves are firm and waxy in texture, so blend the dark green with your fingertips to get a smooth, even finish.

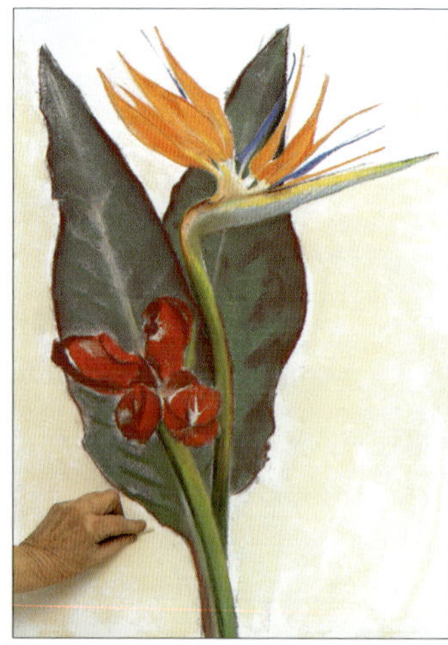

13 Using the side of the pastel, apply pale Naples yellow over the white background so that it does not look so bright and stark.

The finished drawing

This is a vibrant and colourful drawing that exploits the characteristics of soft pastels to the full. They are the perfect choice for this subject: the colours are very vibrant and the thick sticks ideal for covering large areas, while blending the marks creates the smooth, almost waxy texture of the flowers and leaves. Note how the foreground leaf is lighter and more textured than the background one, which helps to bring it forwards in the image.

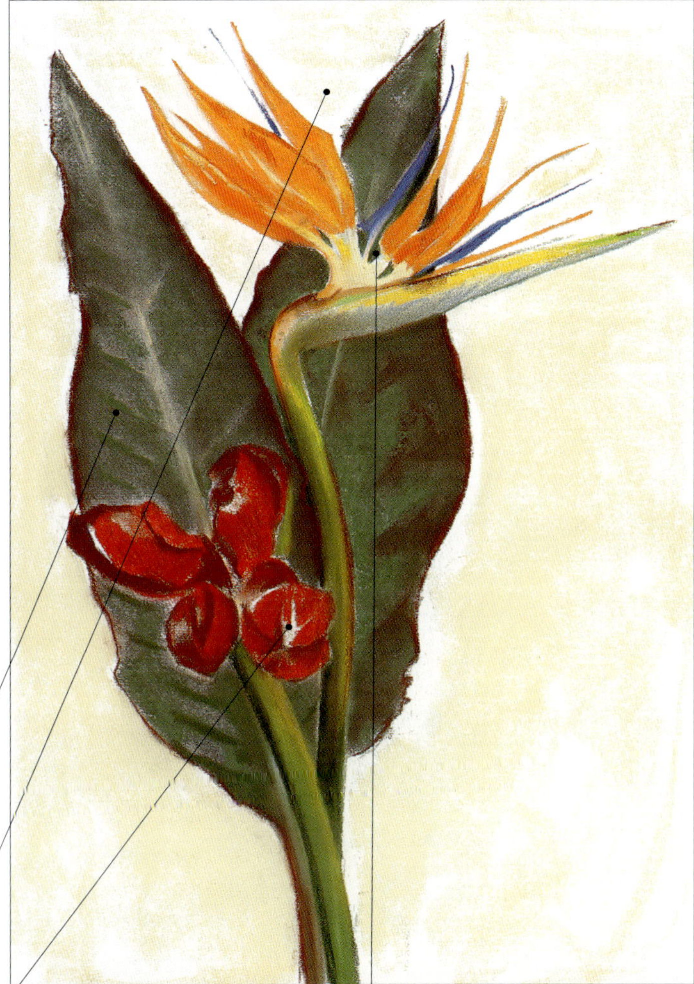

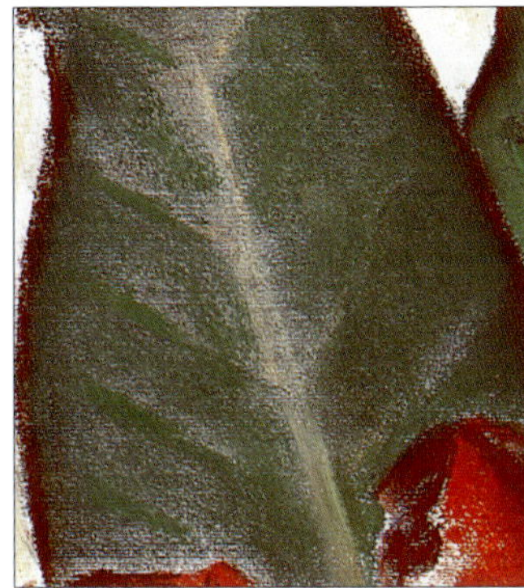

Soft blending of the marks makes the veins an integral part of the leaf.

The warm yellow background complements the orange flowers, which look striking against the dark green of the leaves.

The untouched white highlights reveal the direction of the light.

The sharp tip of a pastel pencil is used for small areas where precision is required.

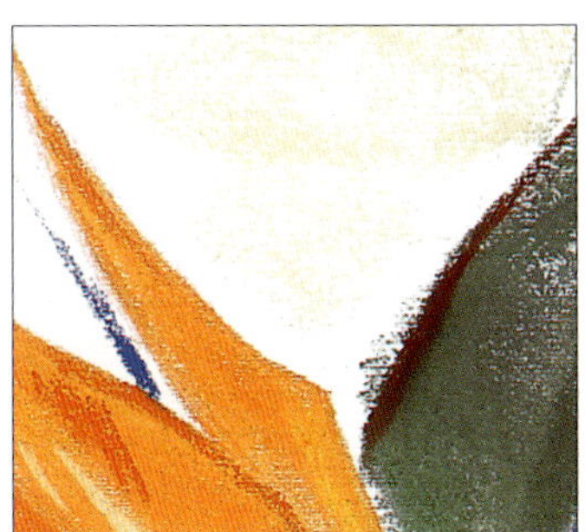

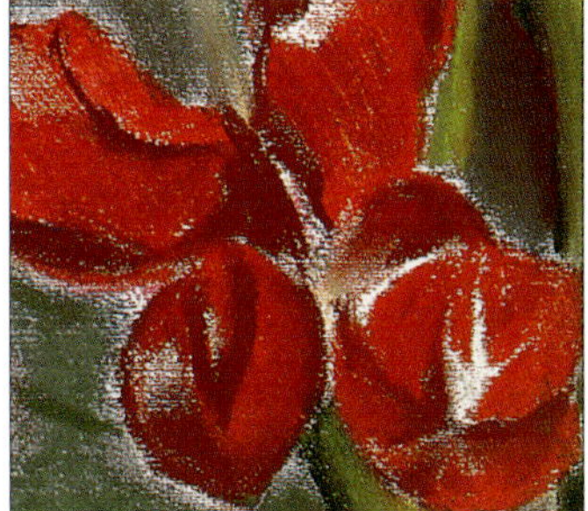

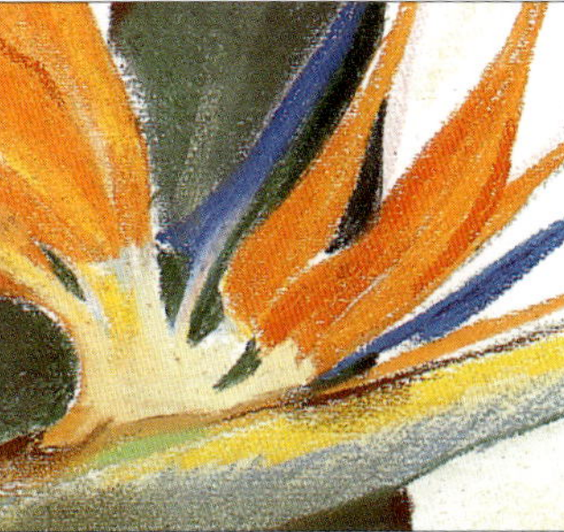

Autumn leaf

From delicate yellowy-golds through to rich russets and reds, autumn leaves contain a wonderful range of colours. Even a single leaf can make a very attractive study. If you're new to working in soft pastels, this is the ideal project to start with. As the colours merge together in a random way, you can practise blending colours without having to worry too much about exactly where you place each one.

Use some artistic licence when it comes to drawing the background. You can choose between lightly sketching some generalized leaf shapes or laying down an overall colour, rather like out-of-focus leaf litter. Whatever you decide, try to get some variety and interesting blends into this area as a flat application of a single colour can look very bland and boring.

Pastel papers come in a wide range of colours. Here, the artist has used a pale peach-coloured pastel paper, which is much more sympathetic to the glowing autumn leaf than stark white paper.

Materials

- *Pale peach pastel paper*
- *Soft pastels: pale cadmium yellow, lemon yellow, cadmium yellow, light red, burnt sienna, burnt umber, cadmium orange, white, yellow ochre, ultramarine blue*

The leaf

It is the lighting that makes this leaf so interesting: it allows the veins on the leaf to stand out prominently. Note how the stem is on the diagonal, which makes the image more dynamic than if it were straight.

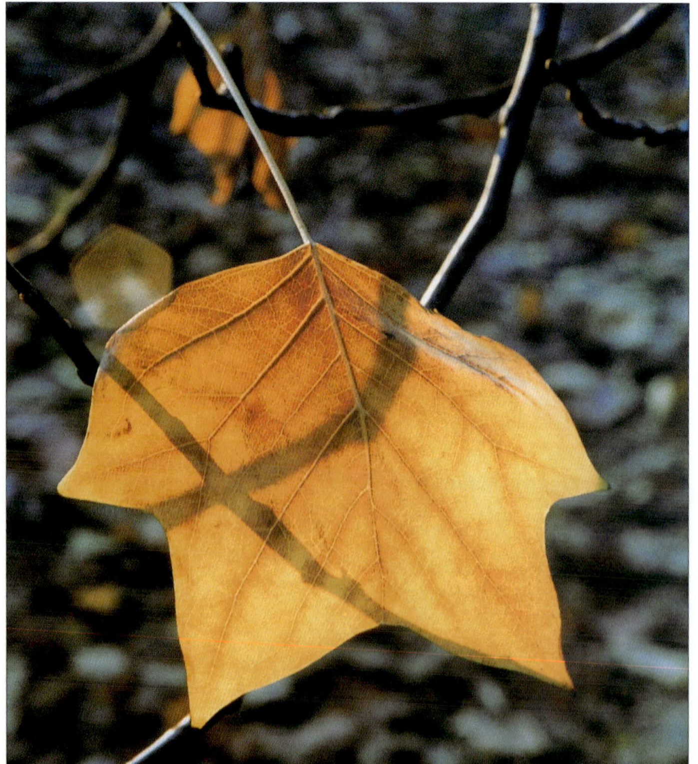

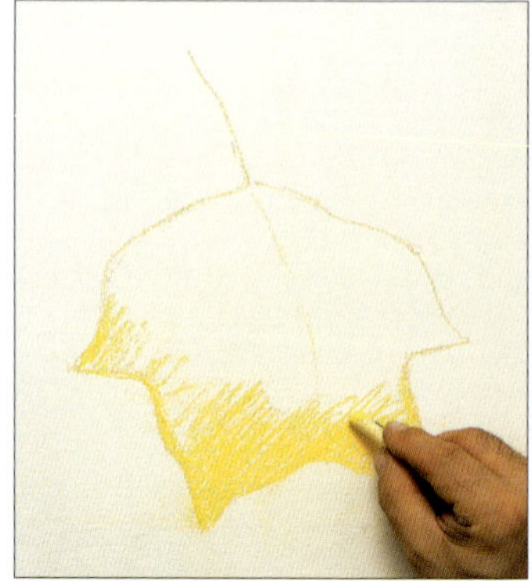

1 Draw the outline of the leaf and its stem in pale cadmium yellow pastel, putting in the central vein as a guide to help you judge where things are. Using a lemon yellow pastel, loosely scribble over the whole leaf. Although this will be modified by subsequent colours, it establishes the overall base colour.

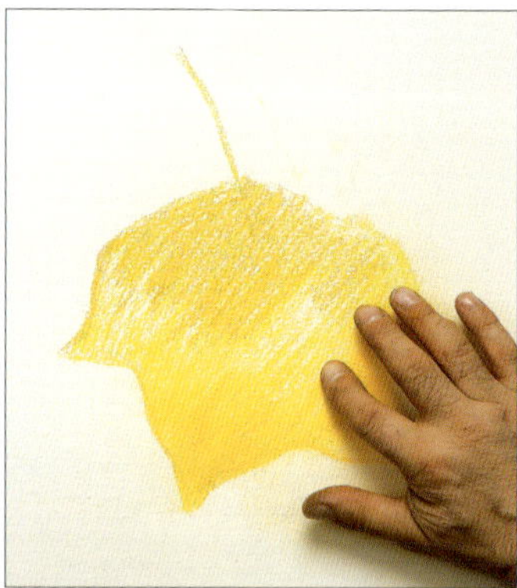

2 Make the lemon yellow pastel coverage looser in the centre. Scribble cadmium yellow (be aware this is poisonous) around the edges and blend with your fingers so that the individual pastel strokes cannot be seen.

Tip: Use the tip of your finger and work inwards, towards the centre of the leaf, so that you don't push pastel on to the background.

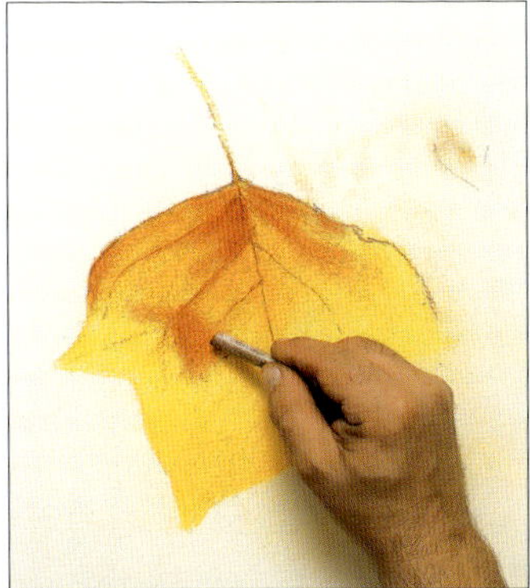

3 Stroke light red over the top of the leaf, where the reddest tones occur, and blend with your fingers. Touch burnt sienna into the darkest areas at the top of the leaf and blend. Draw the veins in burnt sienna.

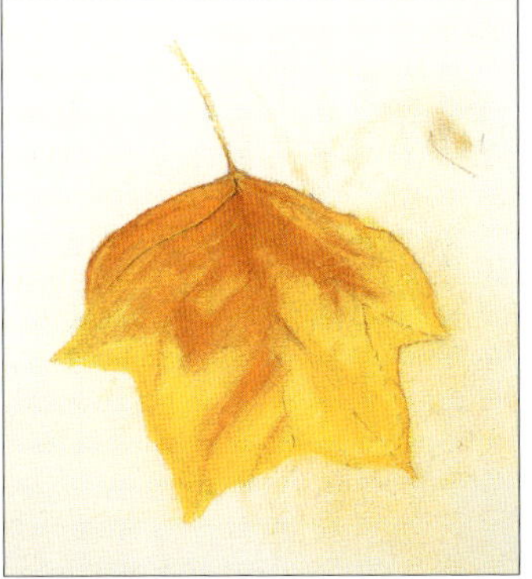

4 Continue using burnt sienna at the top of the leaf, blending the marks with your fingers as you go. Reinforce the veins with burnt umber. Blend cadmium orange over the top of the leaf and around the veins.

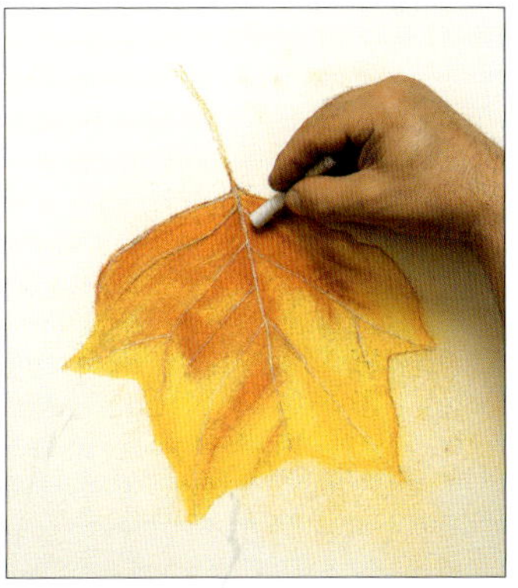

5 Now that the main colours are in place, you can start to add some detail. Using the tip of the pastel, carefully draw along the veins in white to begin to highlight the leaf's delicate framework.

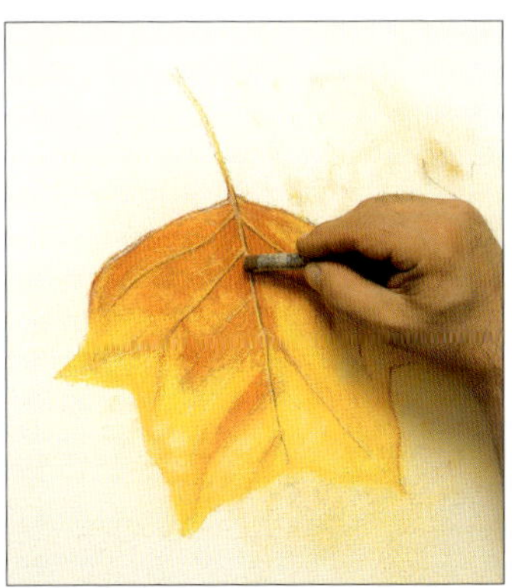

6 Apply pale yellow over the lightest parts of the leaf and the main veins. Blend small spots of lemon yellow over the lower half of the leaf so that it starts to take on a rich, warm glow. Using the tip of the pastel, draw along the shaded sides of the veins in burnt umber. Note how the veins are beginning to stand out from the rest of the leaf.

Assessment time

Draw around the edge of the leaf in burnt umber to define it. This helps to make the shape clearer, but the leaf still looks a little flat and two-dimensional. You need to build up the form and put in some kind of background so that the leaf really comes forward in the scene.

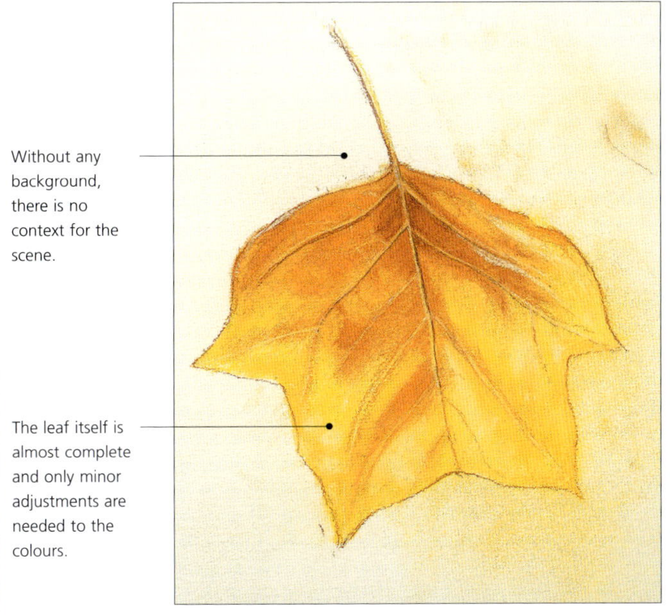

Without any background, there is no context for the scene.

The leaf itself is almost complete and only minor adjustments are needed to the colours.

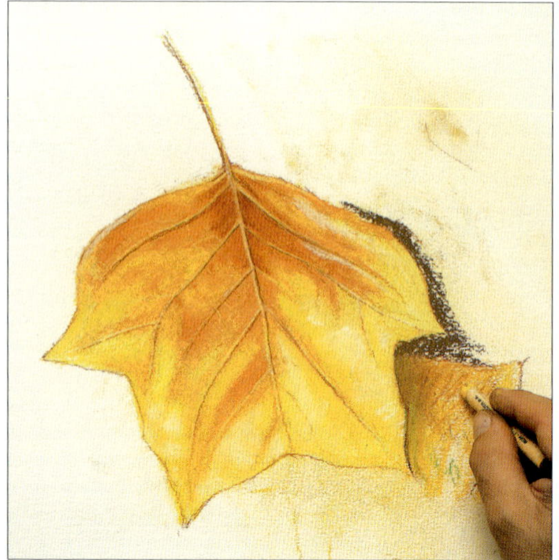

7 Start to put in the background by roughly sketching the shape of other leaves behind. Draw around the top right of the leaf in burnt umber to imply the bark of the tree behind. Scribble yellows, oranges and reds over the background, making the colours next to the leaf quite dark so that it looks as if the leaf is casting a shadow on those behind.

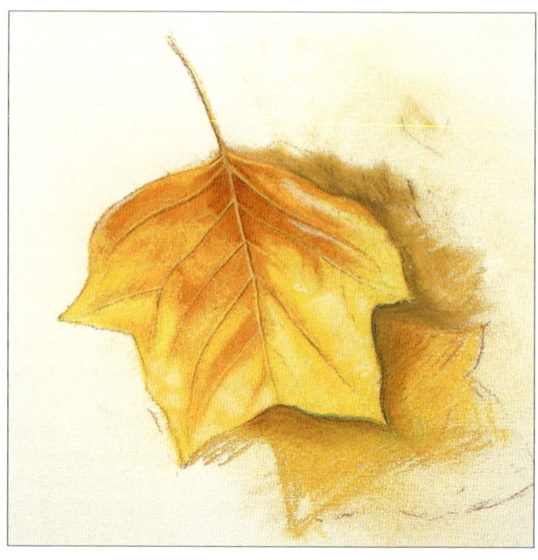

8 Your scribbles have helped to bring the leaf forwards in the scene. Now apply more colour to the background to imply that there are leaves in this area, too – yellow ochre, a little burnt umber, and any other colours in the same colour range. Blend the colours lightly with your fingers, so that the coverage is fairly smooth but some textural marks are still visible.

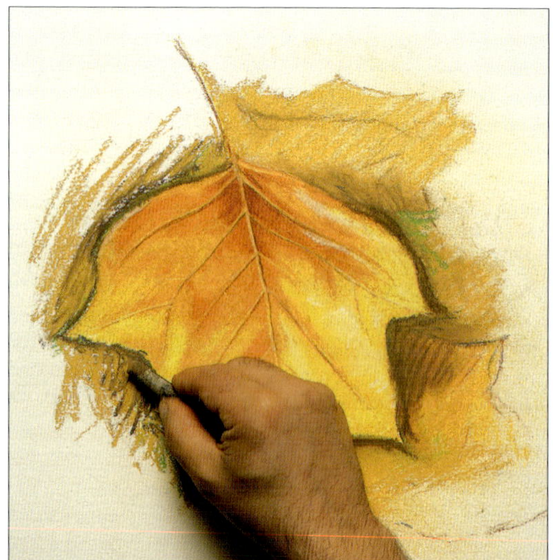

9 Continue blocking in the background with yellow ochre and other colours, and add a little ultramarine blue and burnt umber, so that the background is darker than the leaf. Blend the area with your fingertips.

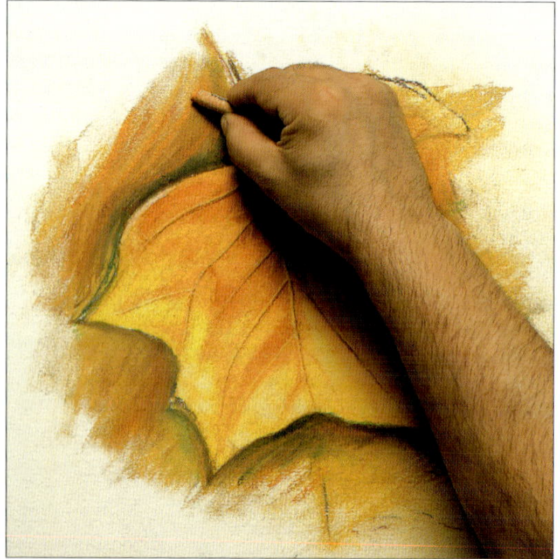

10 Continue working on the background, using the same range of colours as before and blending the marks with your fingers, until you're satisfied with the colours and the overall balance.

The finished drawing

This is a relatively simple exercise, but it demonstrates the potential and versatility of soft pastels. The pastel marks have been smoothed out to create almost imperceptible transitions from one colour to another, and the leaf has a luminous glow that is characteristic of late-afternoon sunlight in autumn. The careful application of light and dark tones on the veins has made them look convincingly three-dimensional and these crisp, unblended lines add another texture to the study.

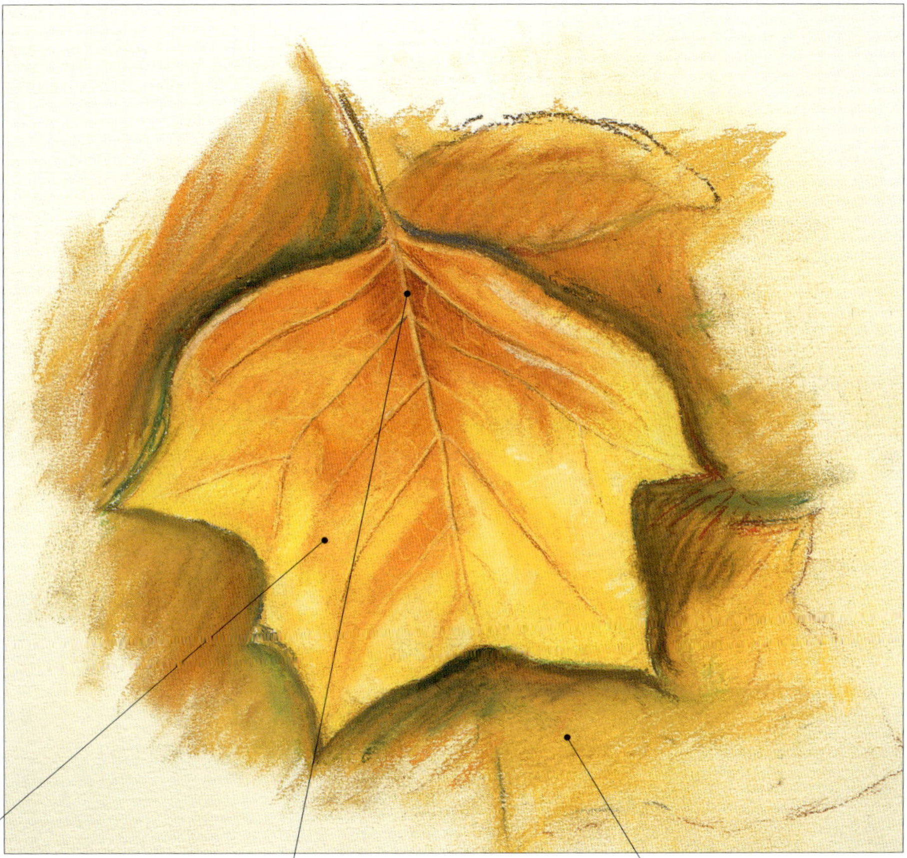

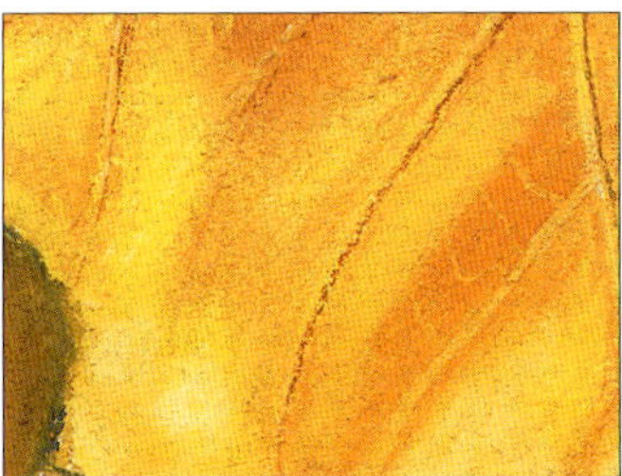

The pastel marks on the leaf have been blended on the support to create smooth areas of colour.

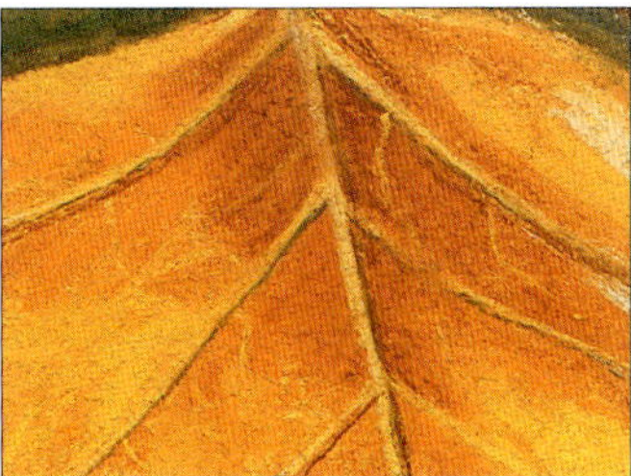

The crisp detail given to the leaf veins adds contrasting interest and a focus to the leaf structure.

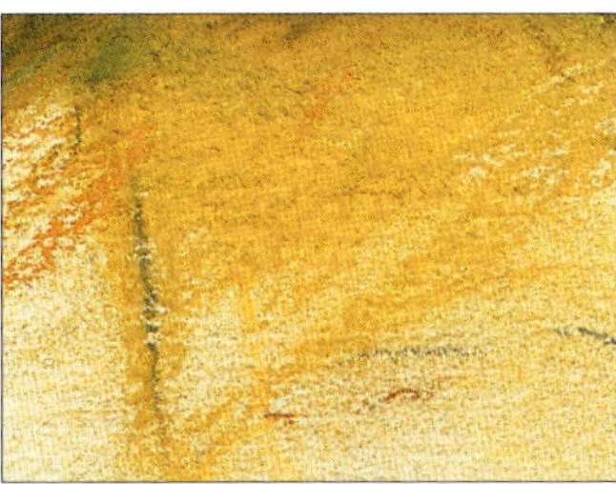

Vague leaf shapes in the background suggest the natrual woodland setting that lies beyond.

Vase of flowers

A light and delicate pastel style is well suited to this elegant and colourful arrangement of tall flowers. It is drawn on smooth-surfaced watercolour paper, which does not break up the strokes to the same extent as medium-textured pastel paper, thus allowing for clear, crisp lines. The paper has been tinted to give a warm ground for the brilliant colours of the flowers, and a soft yellow was chosen as it is the dominant colour in the subject. The tones of the undefined background have also been chosen to complement the flowers. Leaving a few blooms lying on the table provides foreground interest and introduces the contrasting, crisp texture of the crumpled wrapping paper.

Materials

- *HP watercolour paper, tinted soft yellow*
- *Charcoal stick*
- *Soft pastels: mid-blue, bright pink, white, grey, dark green, mid-green, pale yellow, warm yellow, red*
- *Hard pastel: white*

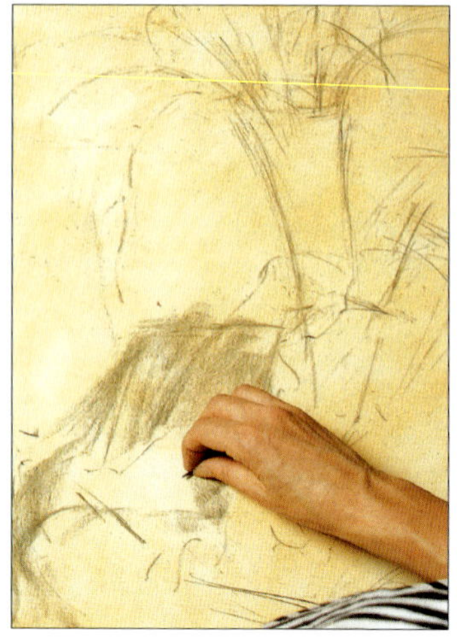

1 Having tinted the paper yellow using the dry-wash method, draw the main shapes lightly in charcoal. Using the side of the stick, lightly block in the deeper tone of the table.

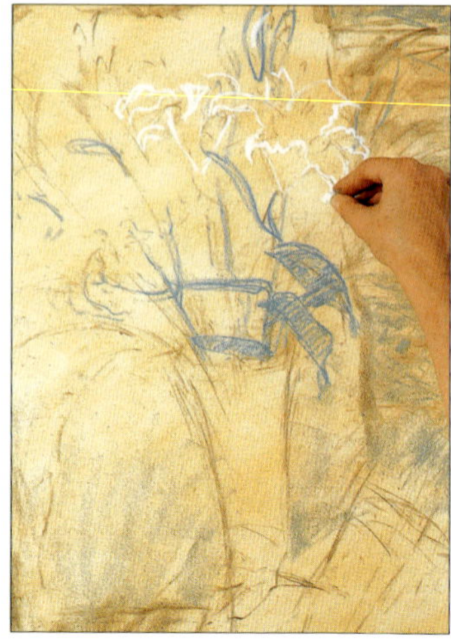

2 Sketch the leaves lightly with linear strokes of blue – the blue leaves will be modified later using other colours – then draw the outlines of the two pink-and-white lilies with the tip of the pastel stick.

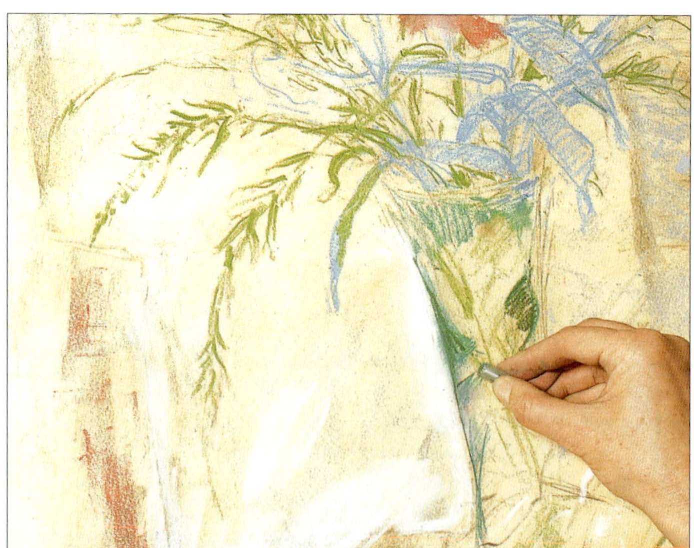

3 It is important not only to define the shape of the vase at an early stage but also to establish a balance of light and dark colours. Work with the tip of the pastel in this area. In the background, which will be only vaguely defined, softer effects are needed, and tonal variations can be introduced using light side strokes.

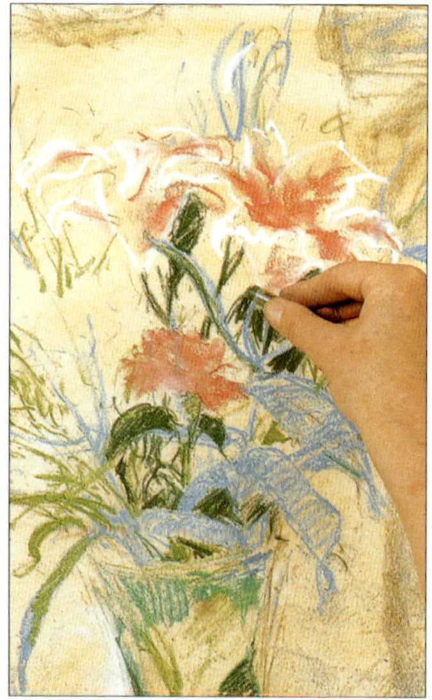

4 These dark leaves play an important part in the picture, as the light-dark contrast between them and the flowerheads draws the eye to this central area.

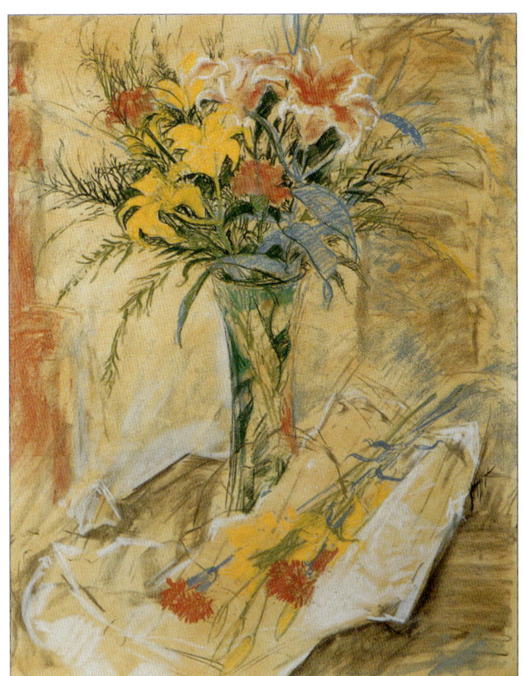

5 The painting has now reached approximately the halfway stage, with all the colours blocked in. Continue to work lightly and loosely to allow for later applications of colour and refinements of detail.

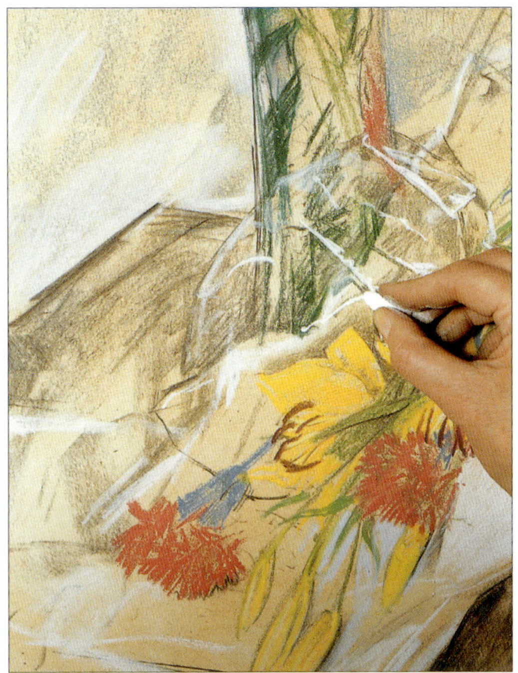

6 The foreground remains relatively undefined. Sharpen up the detail here with a crisp drawing of the piece of crumpled wrapping. The transparent upper layer is defined by drawing in the highlights along its folds.

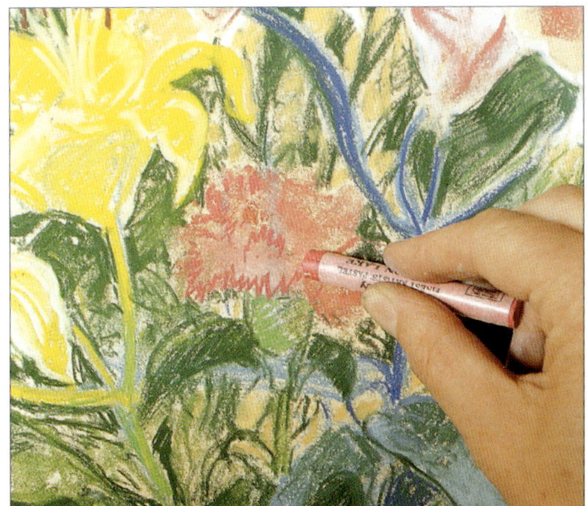

7 Suggest the frilly-edged petals of the carnations by adding jagged linear marks drawn with a darker version of the original pink.

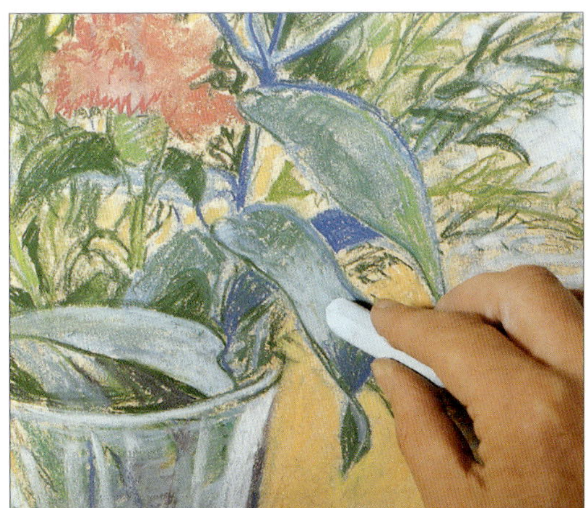

8 Overlay the original blue used for the leaves with other colours, blending slightly to imitate their smooth texture. The pale grey, here used thickly for the highlights, also appears on the vase.

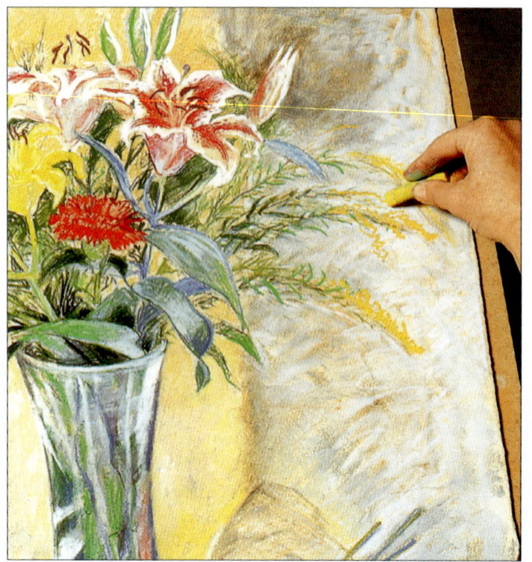

9 The dominant colour, yellow, is carried right through the painting, appearing in a paler version in both background and foreground. The pale grey background allows these small flowers to stand out, but they are treated lightly because the central flowers are the main focus for the eye.

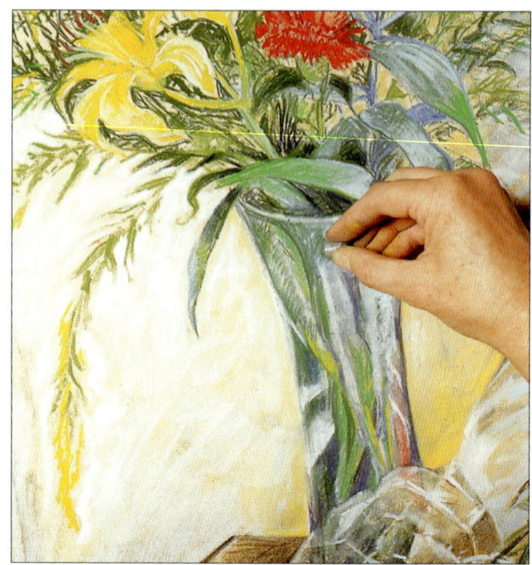

10 If colours are too smoothly blended they may lose their liveliness and freshness. To remedy this, lay small linear strokes on top. Here, this treatment is used for the vase, and it sets up a relationship between the vase and the grey-green carnation leaves above.

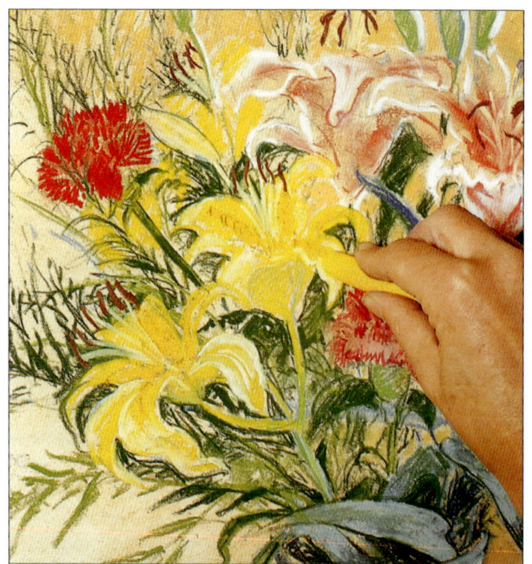

11 Build up the flowers with layers of colour. An occasional soft outline in hard pastel helps to define their shape. Work a soft deep yellow pastel carefully within the paler yellow edges of the petals.

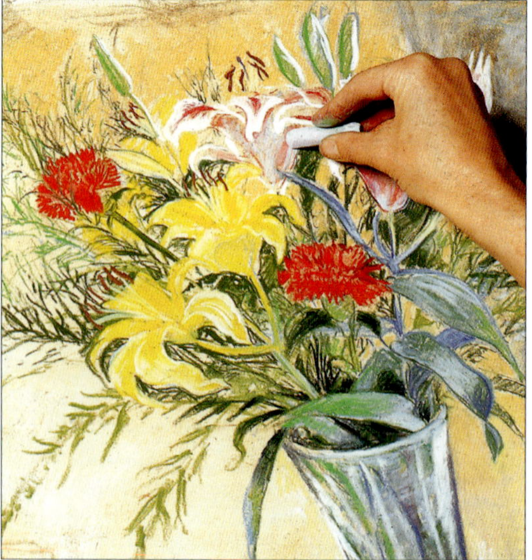

12 Use hard pastel to create a series of little broken lines on the petals of the pink-and-white lily and tone down the underside of the petals with grey, which mixes with the underlying pink to form a delicate mauve.

The finished work

Painting a group of tall flowers can cause problems of composition unless there is something in the foreground to create interest and to balance the shape of the vase. The artist has solved this by using the table top and the shape made by the wrapping paper as positive elements. The background, although lightly treated, is also carefully contrived, with the grey and red shapes at either side both balancing and enclosing the flowers and vase.

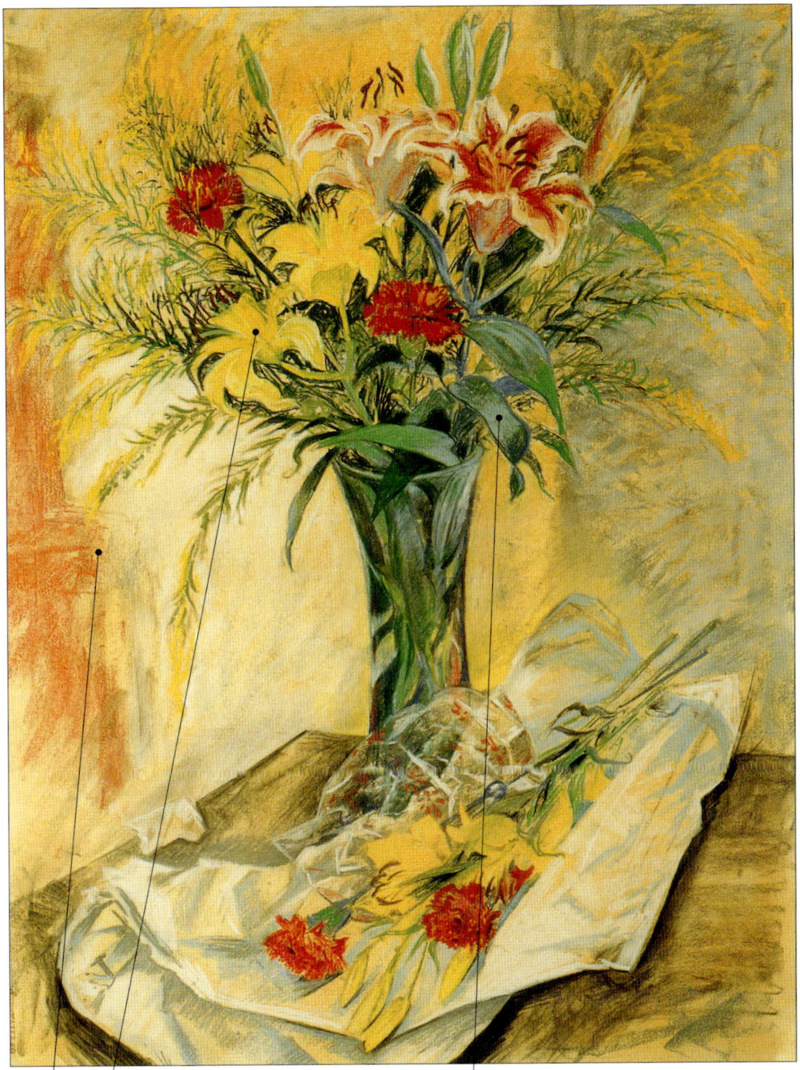

The background is simply indicated with sweeps of warm colour.

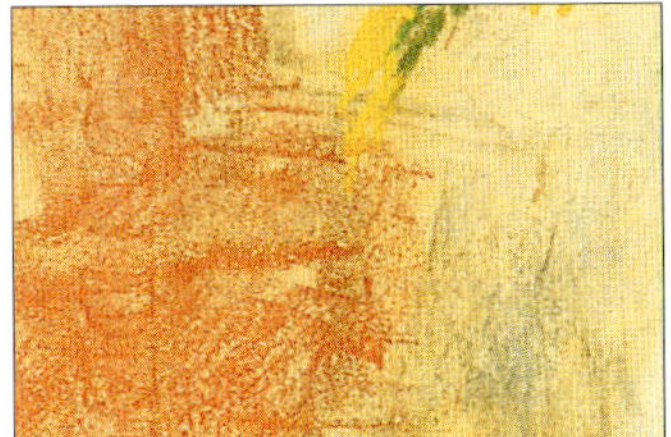

The colours of the flowers are gradually built up with a series of light overlays.

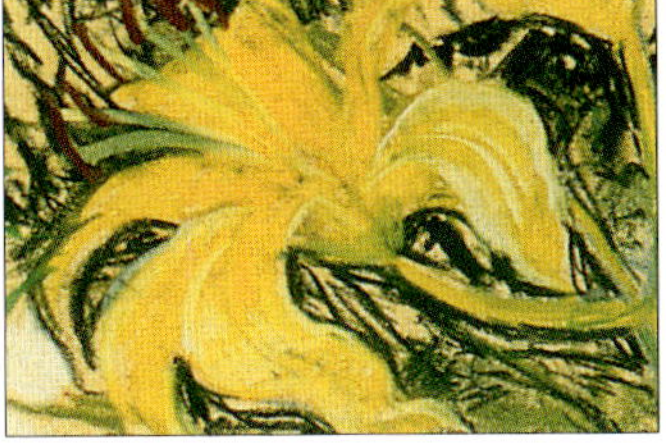

Smoothly blended greens and greys in the leaves tone with the vase.

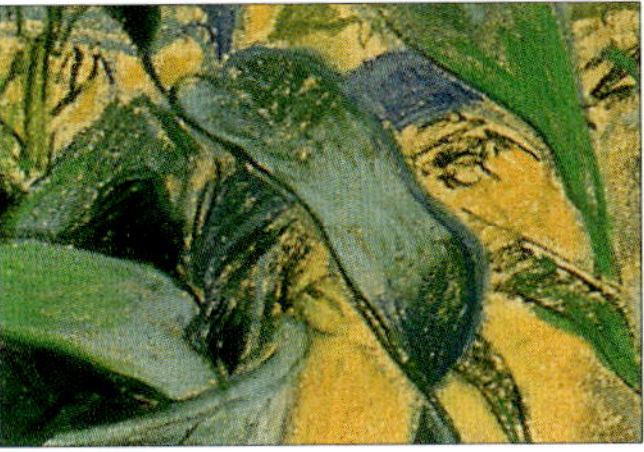

Rocky landscape

This pastel composition depicting a mountainous landscape in Tuscany is made on sandpaper and drawn on a large scale. As marks cannot be erased or blended on this very highly textured kind of support, it is vital to plan the picture carefully before you begin. In this case a large charcoal 'working drawing', the same size as the finished work, was used as reference, together with colour sketches made at the scene. Where a smooth effect is required, such as in the sky, a bristle brush can be used to work into the surface of the paper to blend the colours slightly.

Materials

- *Sandpaper*
- *Pastel pencil: white*
- *Soft pastels: white, pale grey, mid-grey, black, chrome yellow, pale yellow, pale blue, reddish-brown, dark brown, dark green*
- *Bristle paintbrush*

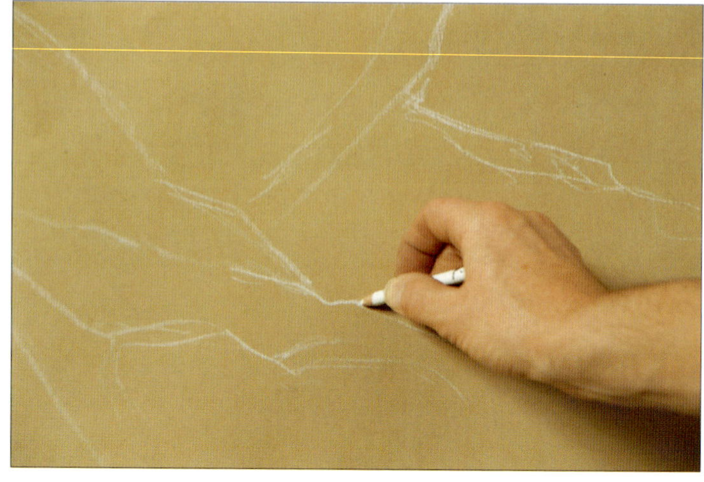

1 Referring to the reference drawing, begin by mapping out the composition in pastel pencil. This needs to be done lightly and carefully, as it is impossible to erase pastel marks on sandpaper.

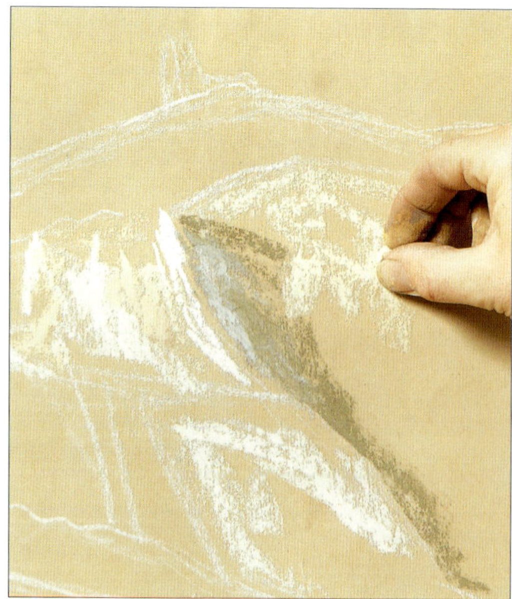

2 Sandpaper is unlike the standard pastel papers in that colours cannot be moved around to any great extent on the surface. Instead, they need to be built up in layers. This can be done on individual sections of the picture, beginning with the mountains in the centre.

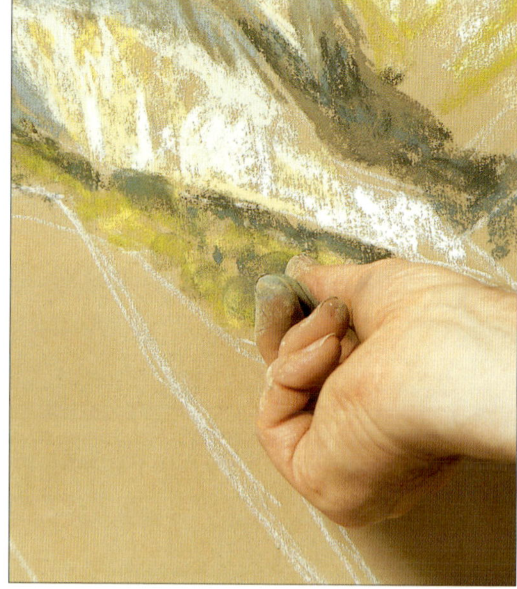

3 To create the textured effect of the foliage, push your thumb into the pastel colour and twist it. While the colours remain distinct, this will push the various shades into rounded forms.

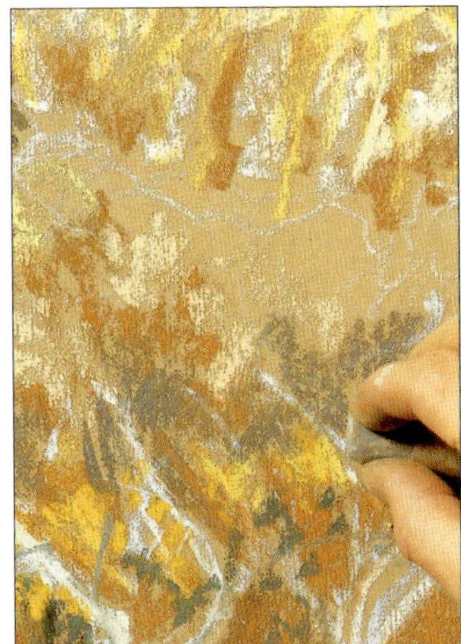

4 The marks made by the pastel sticks are as important as brushwork in an oil painting; here you can see a wide variety of different strokes, from short jabs to tapering side strokes and crisp linear marks. These impart a lively energy to the picture as well as suggesting shapes and textures.

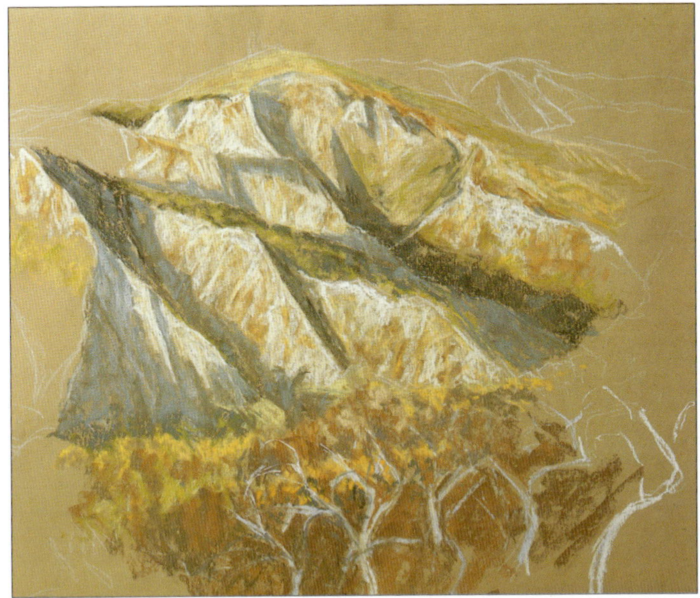

5 The piece-by-piece approach of working from the centre outwards, which has been adopted for this work, is unusual: it involves having a clear vision of how the finished picture will look.

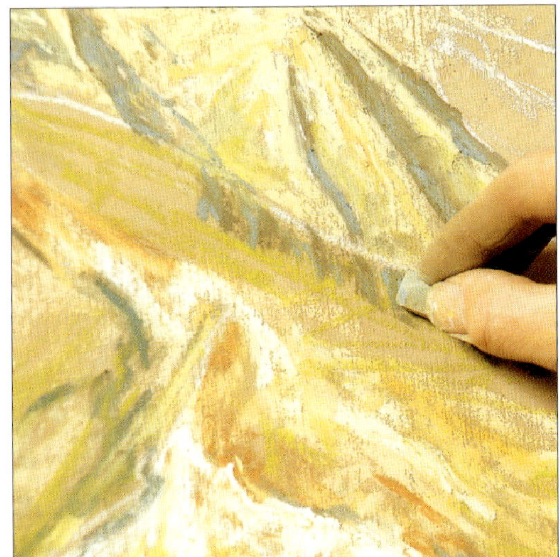

6 Short, jabbing marks, made with the edge of a broken pastel stick, contrast with the long sweeping strokes used elsewhere. Leave some of the paper showing through between strokes, to contribute to the overall colour effect.

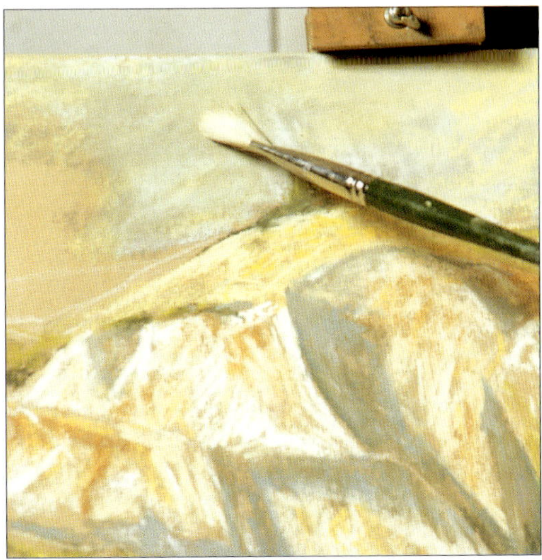

7 By leaving the sky until a late stage, you can assess it in the context of the whole work. In this case, yellows and pale blue-greys have been chosen to echo the colours of the mountains. Use a bristle brush to blend the colours together slightly on the sandpaper.

▶

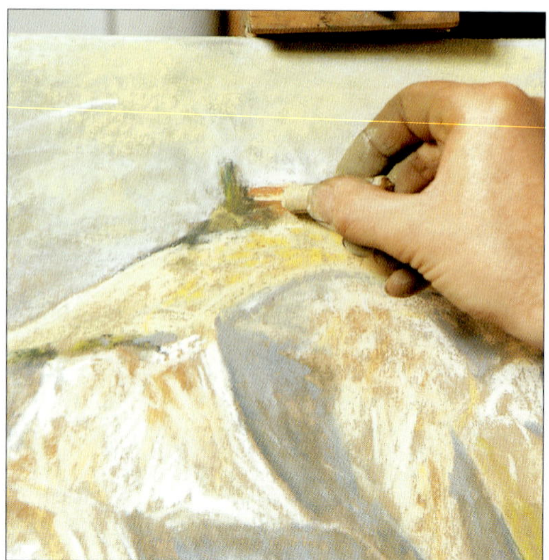

8 Drag further pale colours lightly over the original ones in the sky area, and draw in the building on the top of the mountain with the tip of a pastel stick. Although small, the building is important to the composition because it provides a focus for the eye.

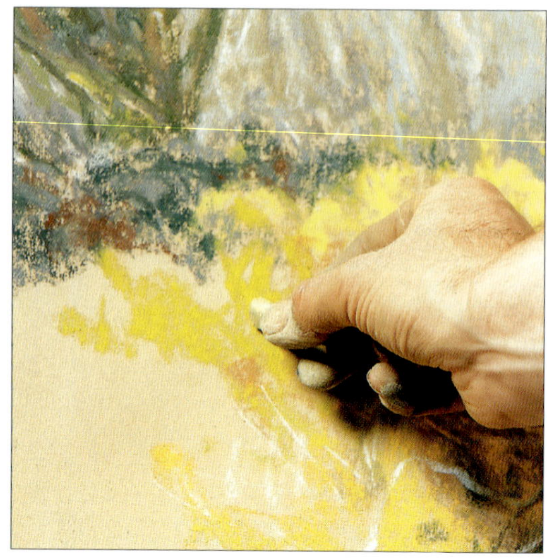

9 On the right-hand side of the painting, develop the area above the bare white trees with short strokes of green and yellow, following different directions to create a sense of movement.

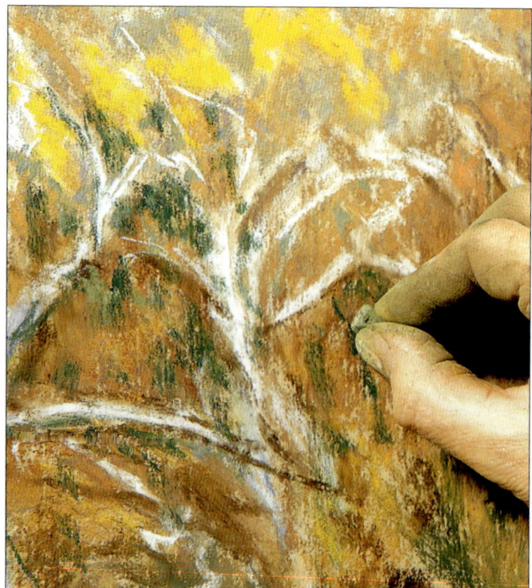

10 The composition is now nearing completion, but requires some crisp touches and bright colours in the foreground to bring it forward in space. Use vivid green both to suggest leaves and to outline some of the branches.

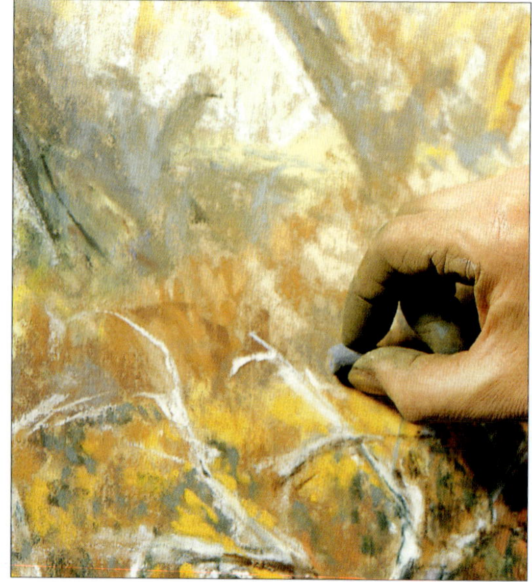

11 With the side of a short length of pastel, drag colour lightly above and around the branches, creating soft areas of colour that contrast with the sharper lines of the branches.

The finished work

Although the painting was virtually completed in one working session, the artist re-assessed it a day or two later and made some adjustments. The most significant of these was to increase the height of the trees on the right so that the white branches lead the eye in towards the dark tree-clad crevice, thus creating a visual link between foreground and distance.

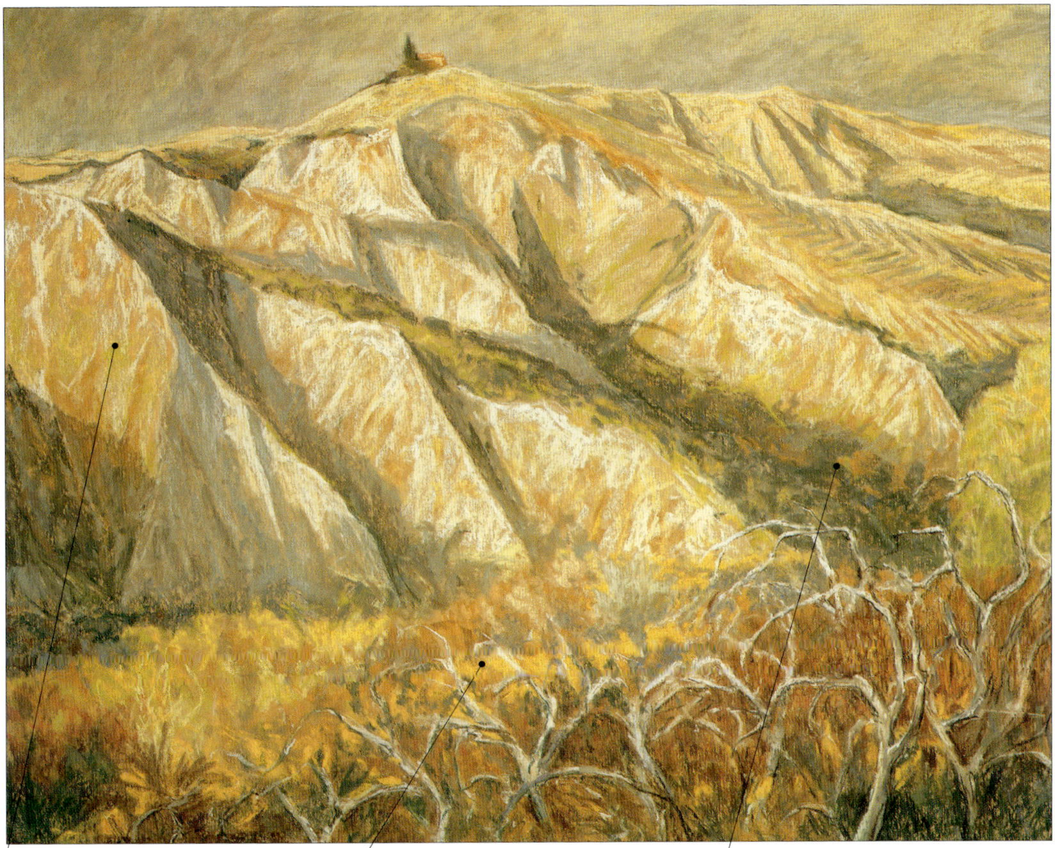

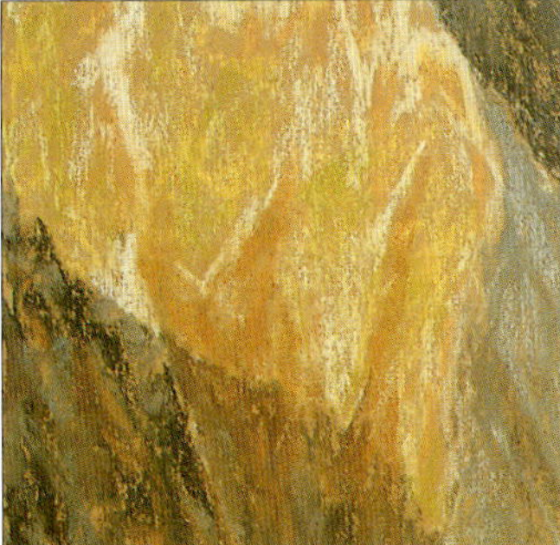

The rough texture of the support echoes that of the rock face.

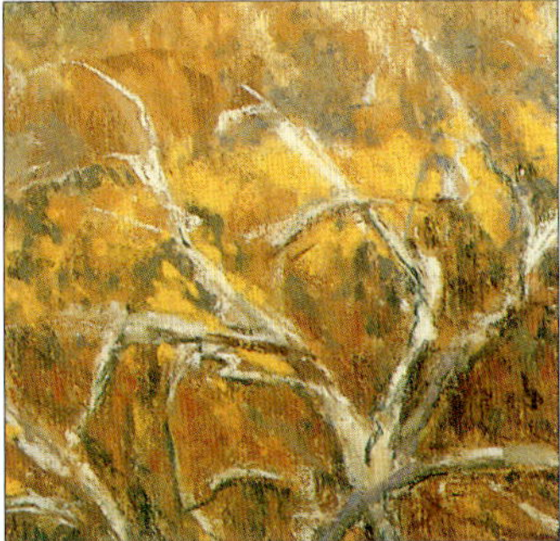

Well-defined linear strokes bring the foreground subjects forward.

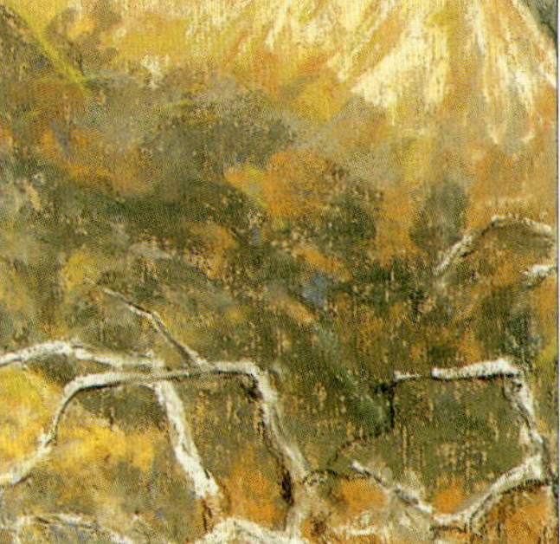

The dark wooded valley provides a sharp contrast with the foreground trees.

Mediterranean seascape

This tranquil scene of waves lapping a Mediterranean shore is full of sunshine and light. Although the composition is simple there is plenty to hold the viewer's attention, from the partially submerged rocks in the foreground through to the town in the distance.

The main interest, of course, is the rippling sea itself, with its myriad tones of blue, green and even violet – and soft pastels are a wonderful medium in which to portray this. It's surprising how many colours you can see in the water. Water takes its colour from objects in and around it – the sky, rocks, seaweed and algae, and so on – so look at the surroundings, as well as at the water, as this will help you assess which colours are required. Half-close your eyes when you look at the scene, as this makes it easier to assess the different colours and tones. It's hard to be precise about which colours to use in this project, as soft pastels are available in such a huge range of colours, but put together a selection of blues, greens, violets and browns, from very pale to very dark.

Remember that the rules of both linear and aerial perspective apply to sea and sky just as much as they do to objects on land. Distant waves, for example, appear smaller than those close at hand. Colours also appear lighter with distance and texture is less pronounced – so smooth out your pastel marks on the sky and the most distant part of the sea by blending them lightly with your fingers or a clean rag.

Observe your seascape very carefully before you draw. Look at any sea scene for a while and you will see that the waves follow a regular pattern, with incoming waves building to a peak and then falling back. Note how high they go and how far back they fall when they break around a rock or crash on to the shoreline.

Materials

- *Cream pastel paper*
- *Neutral brown or grey pastel pencil*
- *Soft pastels: a selection of blues, greens, blue-greens, turquoises, violets, browns, oranges, ochres and white*
- *Soft rag*

The scene

The dark wall on the left forms a diagonal line at its base which directs the viewer's attention towards the town in the distance. The town itself is positioned roughly 'on the third' – a strong position in any composition.

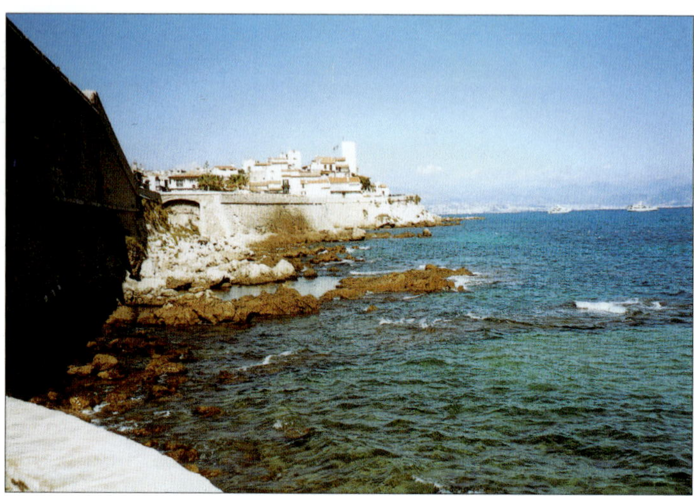

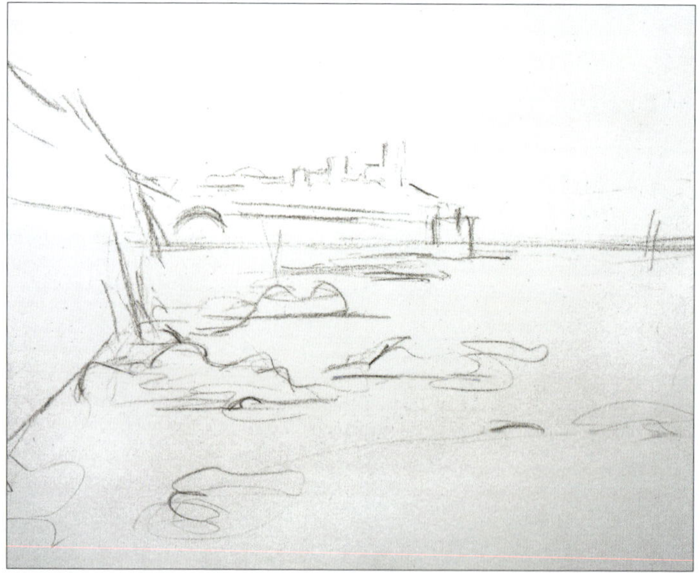

1 Using a neutral-coloured pastel pencil, put in the lines of the headland and horizon and the dark, submerged rocks in the water. Note that the artist decided to make the headland and rocks more prominent in the scene and omitted the light-coloured concrete walkway in the bottom left of the reference photo.

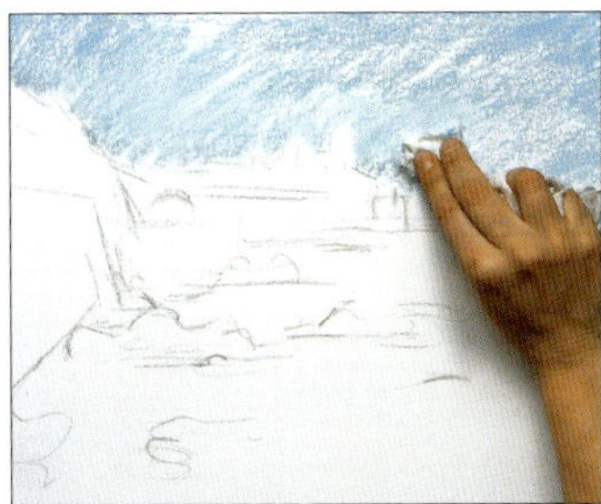

2 Roughly block in the sky with a mid-blue pastel and blend with a clean rag to smooth out the marks.

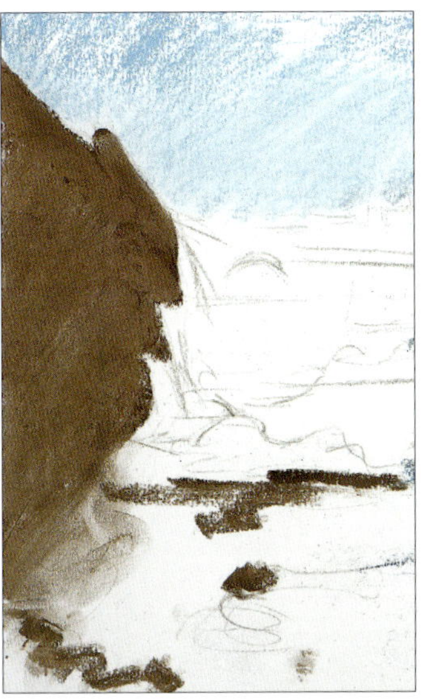

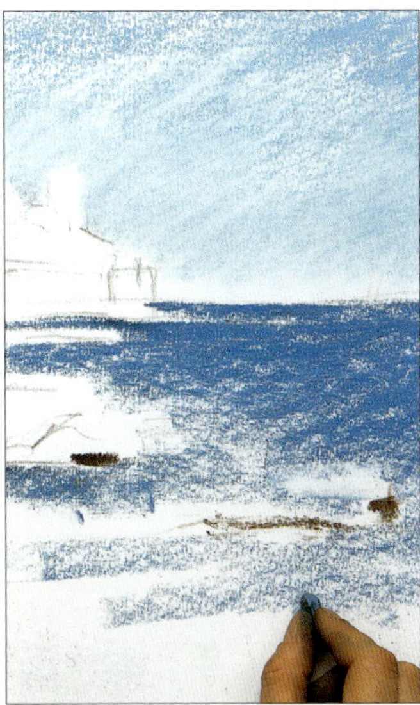

Tip: Keep the coverage slightly uneven, to give some texture to the sky. If the colour is completely flat and uniform, it will look rather boring.

3 Block in the wall on the left with a mid-brown pastel and smooth out the marks with a rag or your fingers. Scribble in the partially submerged rocks using the same colour.

4 Block in the sea using a turquoise pastel, leaving some spaces for the breaking wavelets. Note that the sea has some areas that are lighter than others, so apply less pressure here.

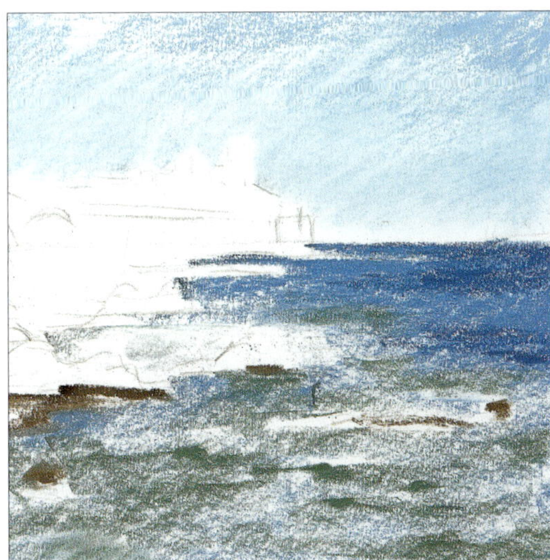

5 Apply a few light touches of a darker turquoise to the darkest parts of the sea in the background. Loosely scribble jade green over the foreground water to pick up the green tones, varying the amount of pressure you apply to get some variety of tone.

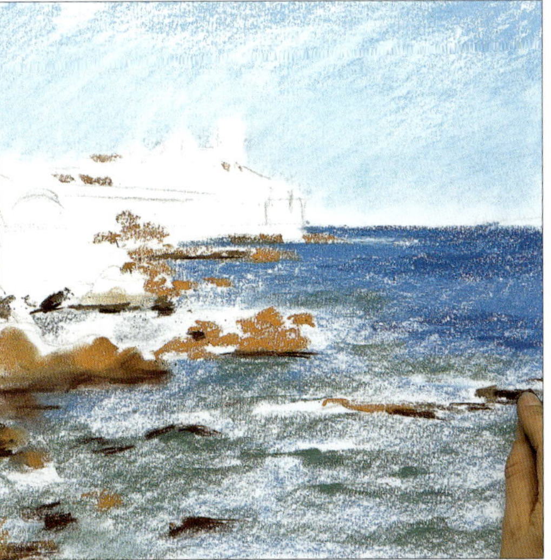

6 Looking carefully at their rough, uneven shapes, apply burnt orange over the tops of the exposed rocks in the sea near the base of the wall, switching to a reddish brown for their bases. Blend the marks gently with clean fingertips.

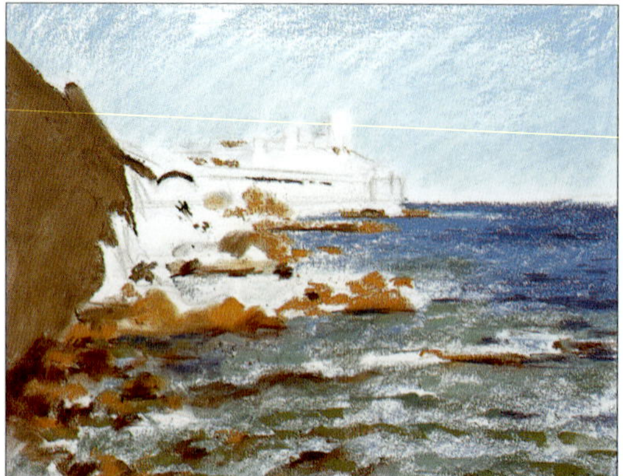

7 Look at the colours in the water. The underside of breaking wavelets contains some surprisingly dark greens and blues. Stroke these in lightly, making sure your strokes follow the direction in which the waves are moving. Gently smooth the marks a little with your fingertips – but don't overdo the blending, as allowing some of the underlying paper colour to show through helps to create a sense of movement in the water.

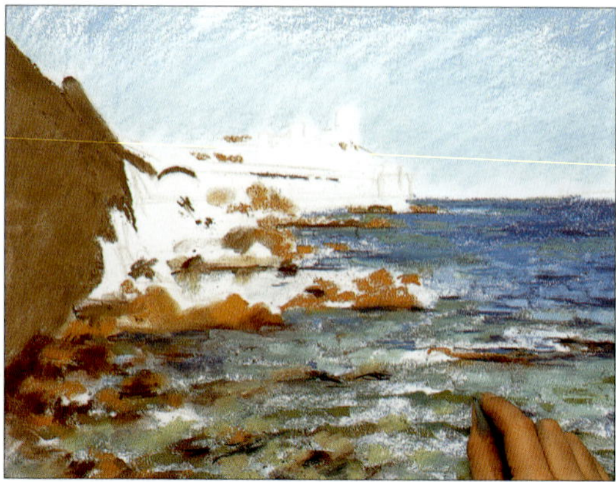

8 Continue building up different colours in the water, using dark greens and blues and dots of light spring green.

Tip: Remember to keep referring to your reference photo. It's easy to get carried away with building up the colours and forget to look at the shades that are actually there.

Assessment time

There is a lovely sense of movement in the sea and a good range of different tones and colours. However, the rocks themselves are nothing more than flat blocks of colour and need to be made to look three-dimensional.

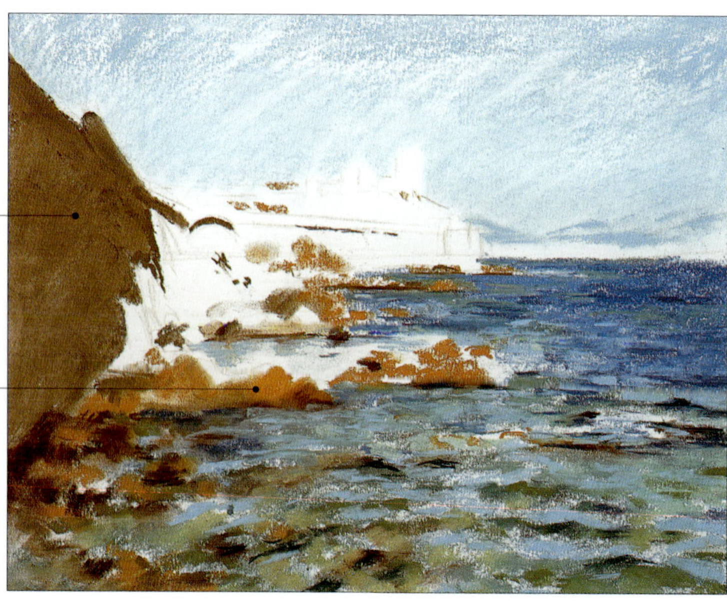

The wall is a flat expanse of brown – it needs to look rough in texture and three-dimensional.

The rocks are little more than patches of colour and lack form.

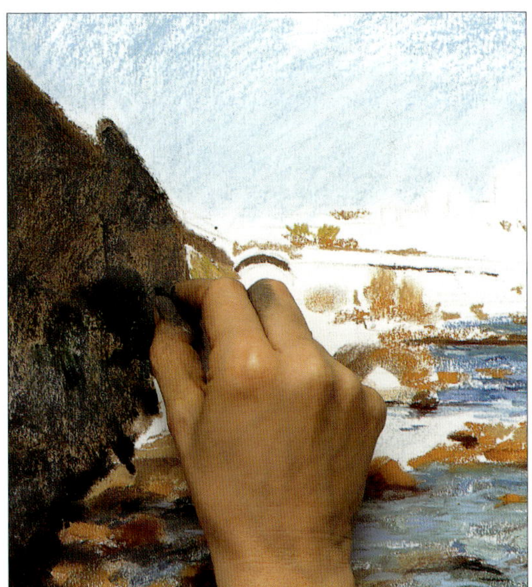

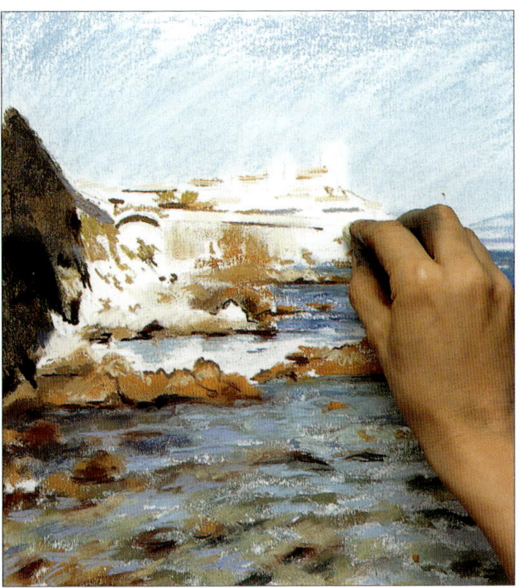

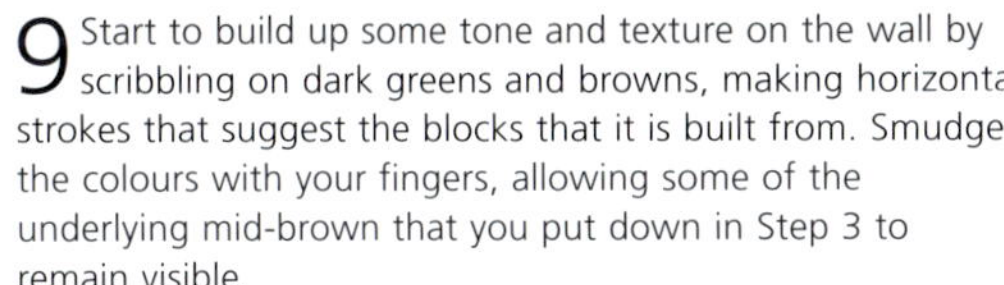

9 Start to build up some tone and texture on the wall by scribbling on dark greens and browns, making horizontal strokes that suggest the blocks that it is built from. Smudge the colours with your fingers, allowing some of the underlying mid-brown that you put down in Step 3 to remain visible.

10 Repeat the process on the rocks surrounding the partially enclosed still pool, scribbling a reddish brown over the orange to build up the form. On the distant headland, put in the darkest colours of the buildings – the browns and terracottas of the roofs. Apply pale yellow ochre to the white of the headland so the paper doesn't look so stark.

11 Dot some light and mid-toned olive greens into the headland for the distant trees. Apply pale blue and mid-tone turquoise over the sky to darken it towards the top (skies generally look paler close to the horizon).

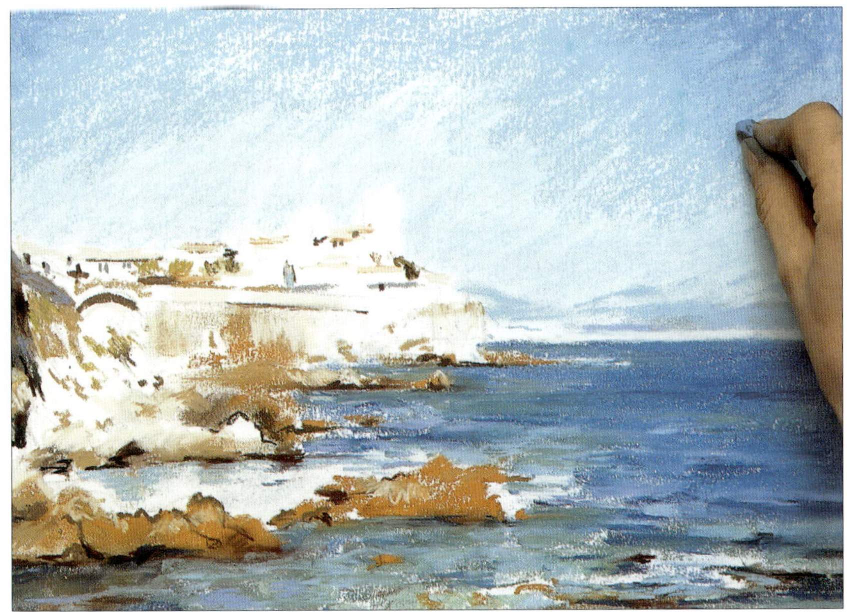

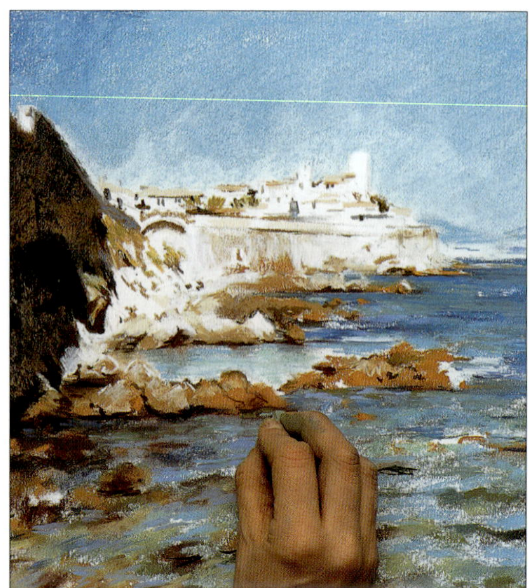

12 Although little detail is visible in the distant town, you need to give some indication of the buildings. Look for the dark tones under the eaves of the roofs. Making small horizontal strokes, apply pale blues and greens over the most distant part of the sea and smooth them out with your fingers. Apply thin lines of dark brown around the bases of the partially exposed rocks.

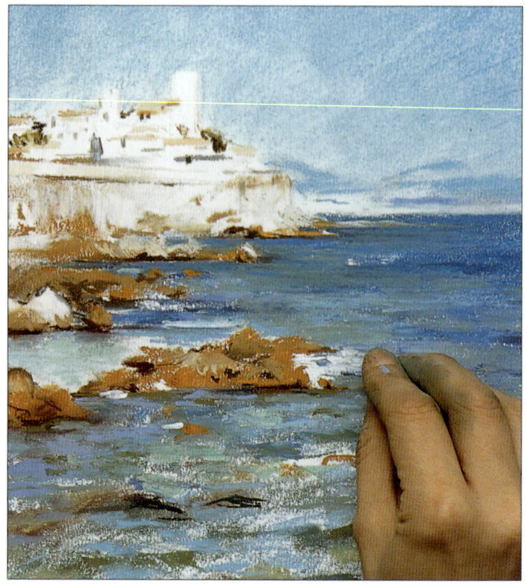

13 Having now given the rocks some solidity, return to working on the foreground seascape again, and put in the white of the wavelets as they break around the partially exposed rocks. Use the tip of the pastel and dot in white here and there around this area. The softly lapping sea has only a gentle swell, so take care that you don't make the wavelets too big.

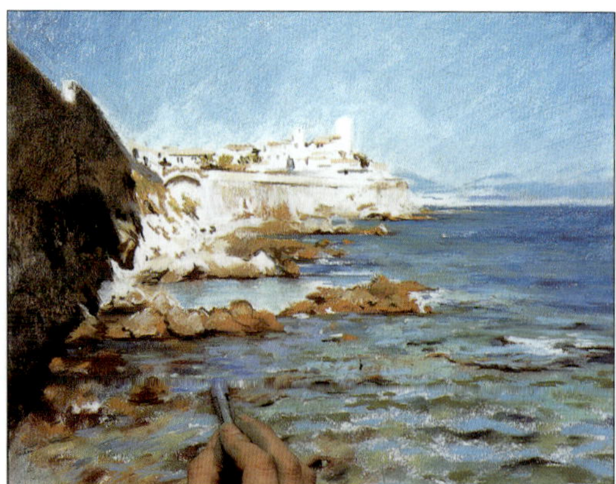

14 Continue adding texture to the foreground sea, making sure that the dark greens, blues and purples in this area are dark enough. Don't smooth out your marks too much: it is important to have more texture in the foreground of a scene than in the background, as this is one way of creating a sense of recession.

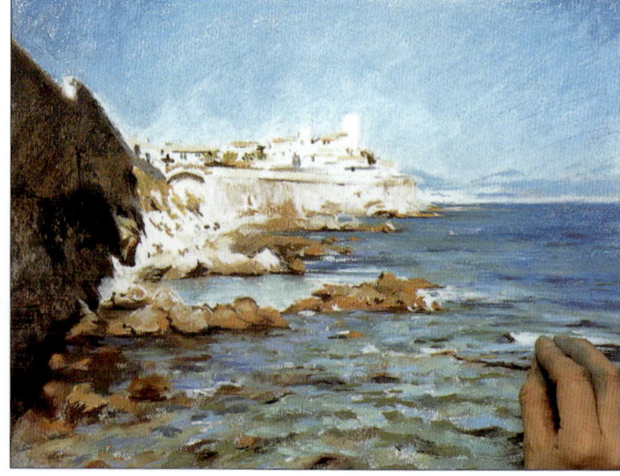

15 Continue building up form on the exposed rocks, using a range of dark oranges and browns as before. It is now time to put in the final touches – more tiny strokes of white for the breaking wavelets and horizontal strokes of dark greens and blues in the foreground sea, wherever you judge it to be necessary.

The finished drawing

There is a lively sense of movement in the sea: one can almost feel the ebb and flow of the waves and hear them lapping around the rocks. Note how allowing some of the paper to show through the pastel marks creates the effect of sunlight sparkling on the water. There is just enough detail in the distant headland for us to know that there is a town there; more detail, however, would draw the viewer's attention away from the sea in the foreground and destroy the illusion that we are looking almost directly into the sun, our eyes dazzled by its brilliance.

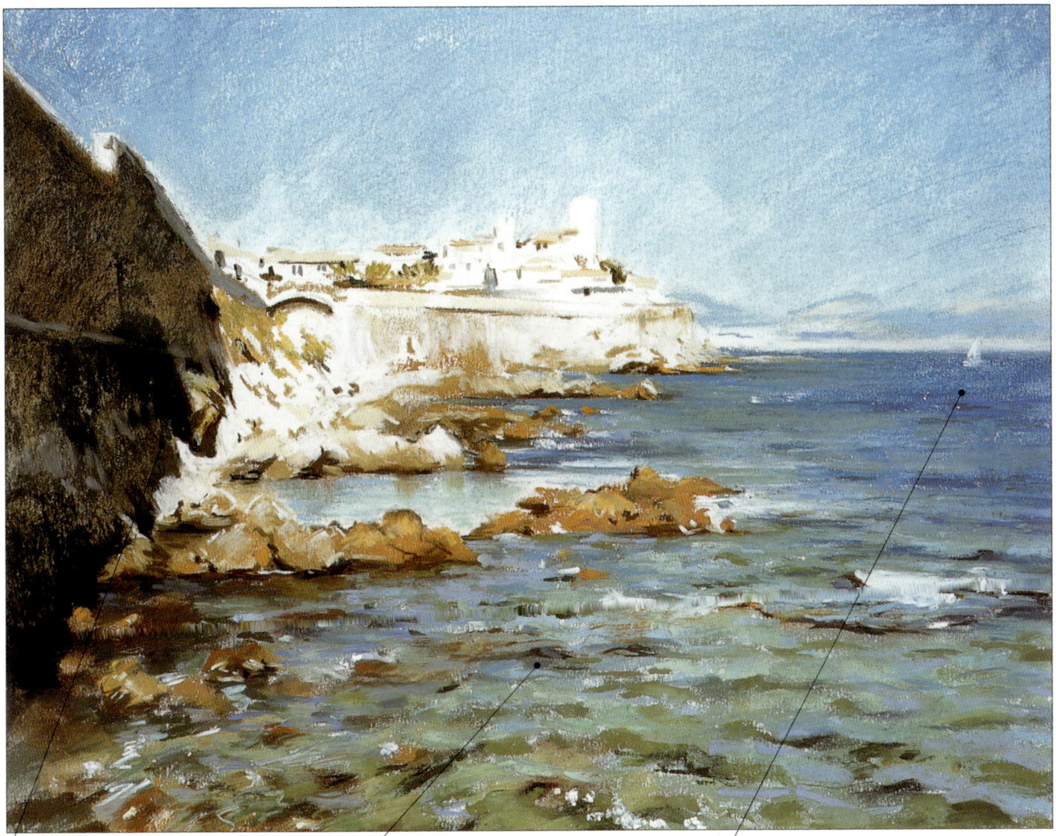

The wall provides solidity at the edge of the picture area and helps to direct the viewer's eye through the scene.

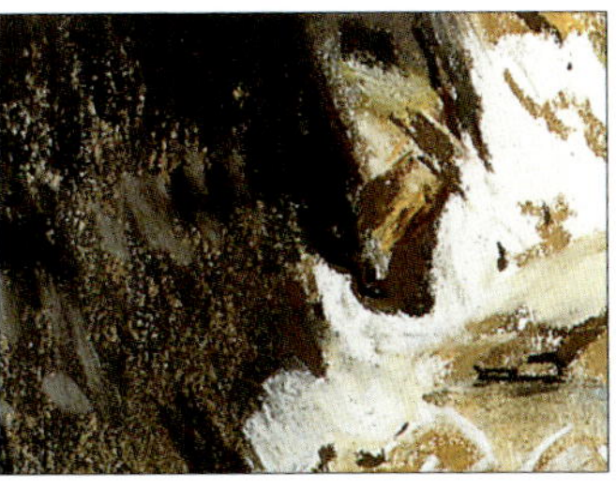

Small horizontal strokes of blues, greens and purples are used to convey the many different shades in the water.

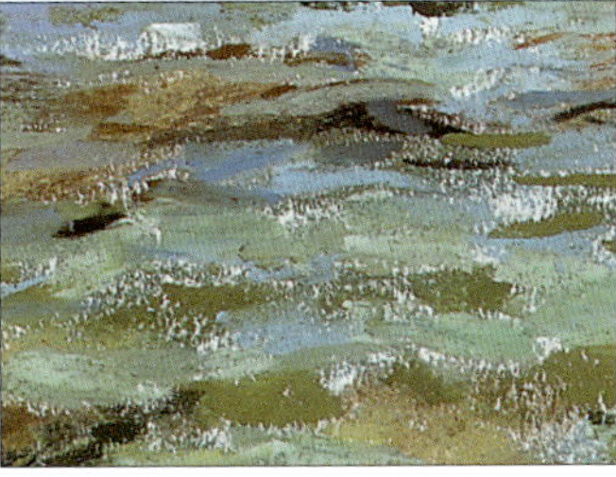

Detail diminishes with distance, and so the pastel marks in this area of the sea are smoothed out to give less texture.

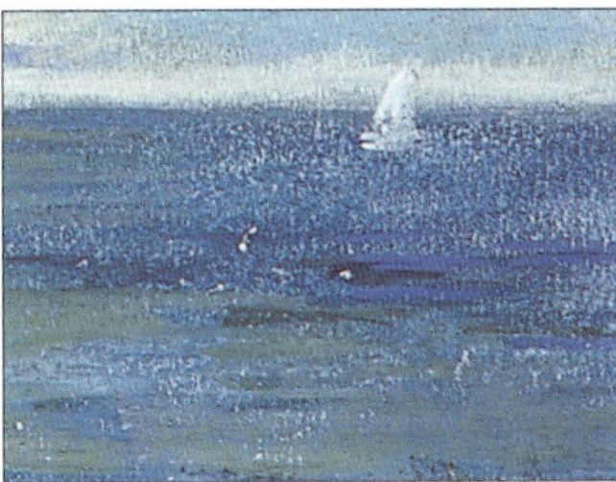

Rocky canyon

This is one of the best-known and most distinctive of all landscapes in the USA – Bryce Canyon in south-western Utah. The colourful rock formations, a series of eroded spires, are best viewed in early morning and late afternoon, when they glow in the sunlight.

When you're drawing formations such as these, look for tonal contrast within the rocks as this is what shows the different planes and makes it look three-dimensional. If a rock juts out at a sharp angle, there is a clear transition from one plane to another and the difference in tone between one side and another is very obvious. If the rock is smooth and rounded, the transition in tone is more gradual.

Drawing the many fissures and crevices also shows the form of the subject. If the shadows in these crevices are very deep, you might be tempted to draw them in black – but black can look very stark and unnatural. Instead, use a dark complementary colour for the shadows – so if the rocks are a reddish-brown, as here, try opting for a purple-based shadow colour.

Materials

- *Pastel paper*
- *Thin charcoal stick*
- *Soft pastels: pale and dark blue, grey, violet, browns, cadmium orange, pale pink, greens, yellow ochre*
- *Clean rag or kitchen paper*
- *Kneaded eraser*
- *Conté stick: brown*
- *Blending brush*

The scene

Trees in the foreground provide a sense of scale: without them, it would be hard to estimate how tall the rocks are.

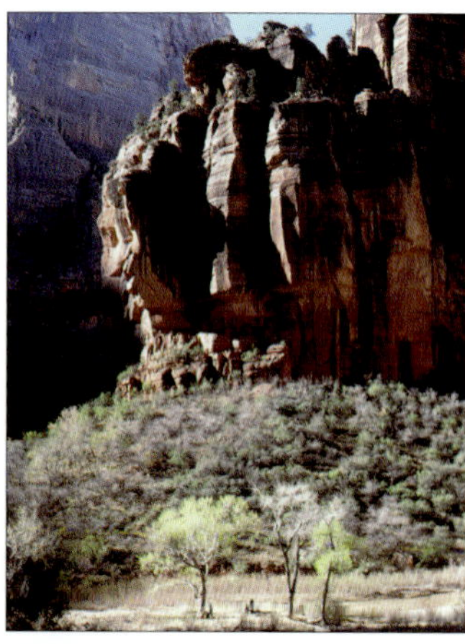

Tip: If you're working from a photograph, you may find that it helps to grid up both the photograph and your drawing paper and then work systematically one square at a time until all the elements are in place.

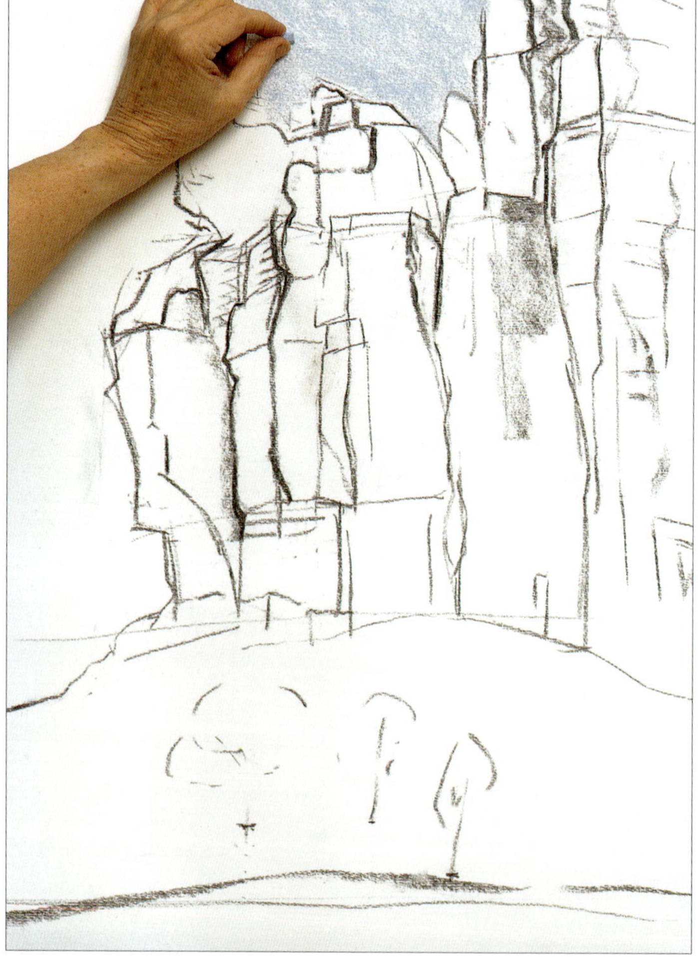

1 Using a thin charcoal stick, draw the rock formations and lightly indicate the main areas of shade. Using the side of a pale blue pastel, block in the small patch of sky that is visible above the rocks.

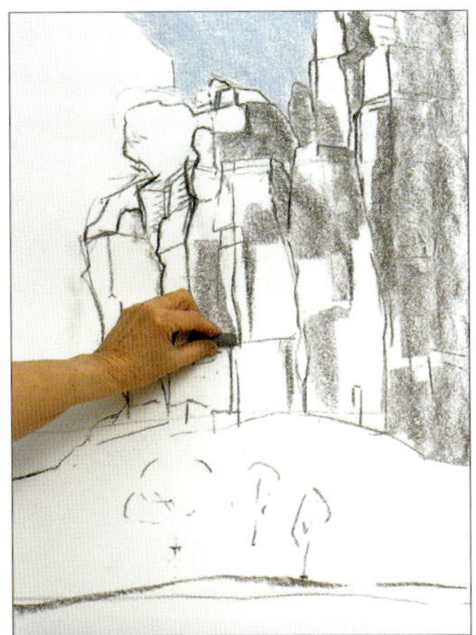

2 Using a cool grey pastel on its side, block in the darker, shaded areas of the rock formations. This gives the rocks some form and establishes the direction from which the light is coming.

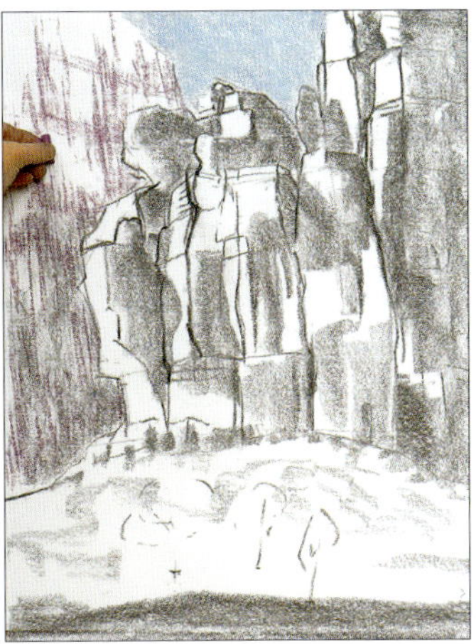

3 Using a violet pastel on its side, put in the strata of the background rock-face. Note how the diagonal lines within this rock-face reveal the structure and add drama to the composition.

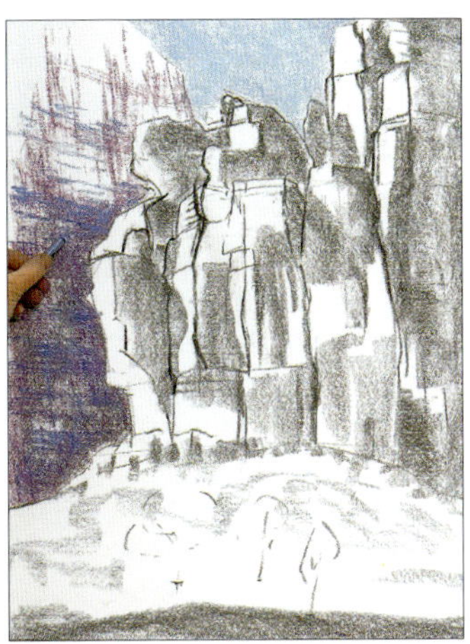

4 Again using the side of the pastel, strengthen the horizontal strata on the background rock, applying light blue at the top of the rock and a darker blue at the base.

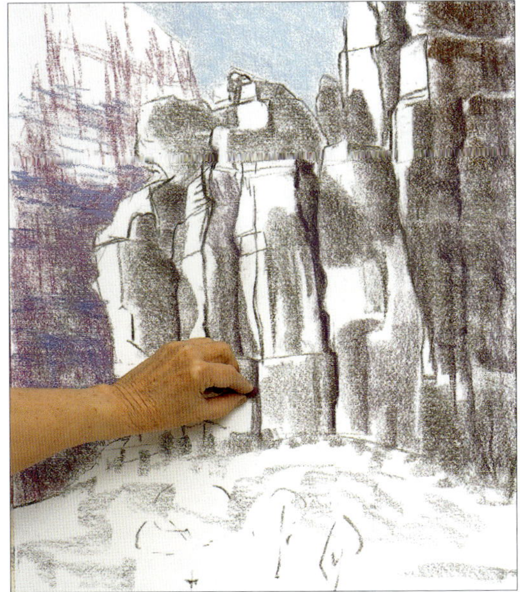

5 Begin applying colour to the rock formations, using brown and dark violet in the shadow areas, using the edge of the pastel to define the divisions between the sections. The crevices between the rocks are dark and deep: a deep violet provides the necessary dark tone and is a warmer and more lively colour than black.

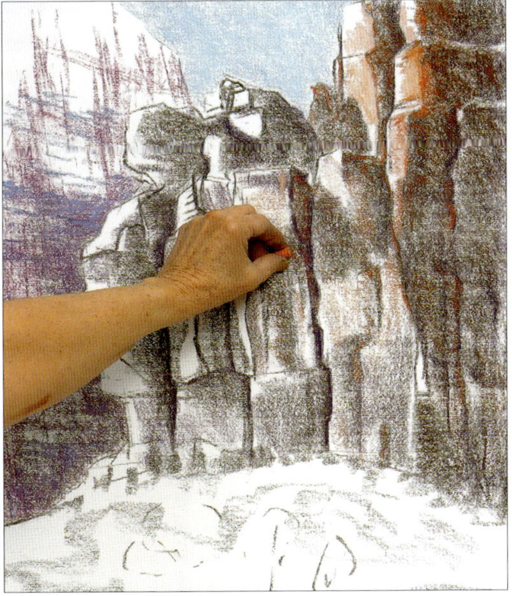

6 Apply cadmium orange to the rock formations. On the shaded facets, where the orange is overlaid on the violet, a rich optical colour mix ensues. On the more brightly lit parts of the landscape, the orange represents the naturally warm, sun-kissed colour of the rock. The colour combination is sympathetic but striking.

▶

Assessment time

The structure of the rock formations is beginning to emerge, but the contrast between the shaded and the more brightly lit facets is not yet strong enough. The rock formations also need to be brought forwards in the scene, so that they stand out from the background cliff.

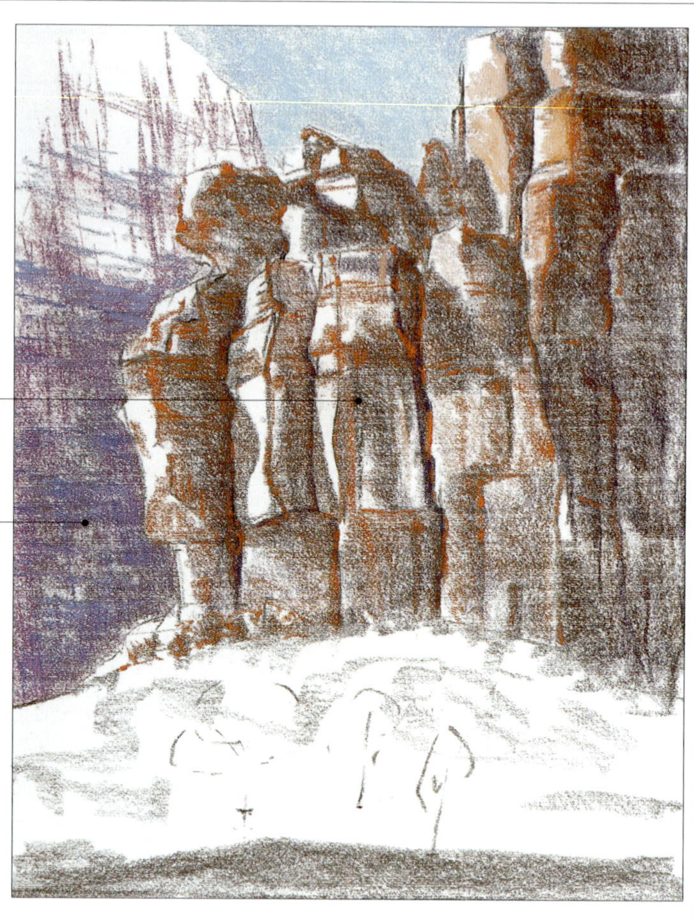

The main rock formations look rather flat.

It is hard to tell that this cliff is some distance behind the main rock formations.

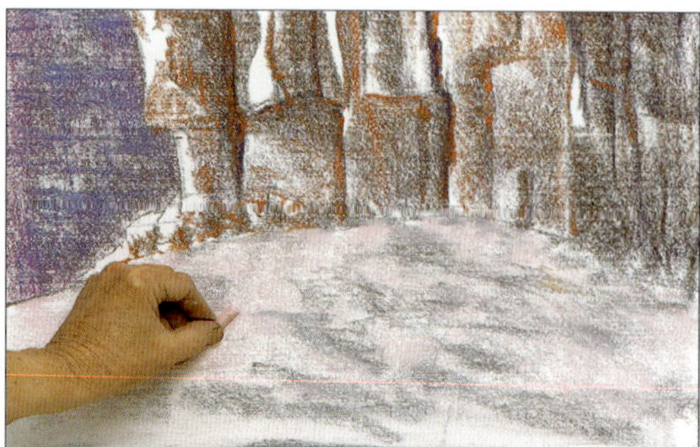

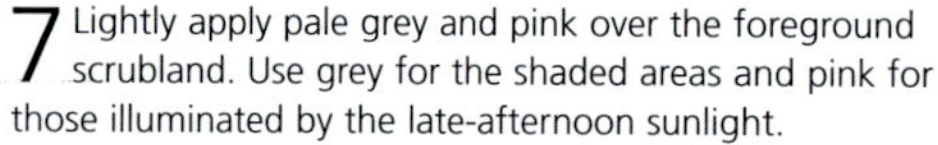

7 Lightly apply pale grey and pink over the foreground scrubland. Use grey for the shaded areas and pink for those illuminated by the late-afternoon sunlight.

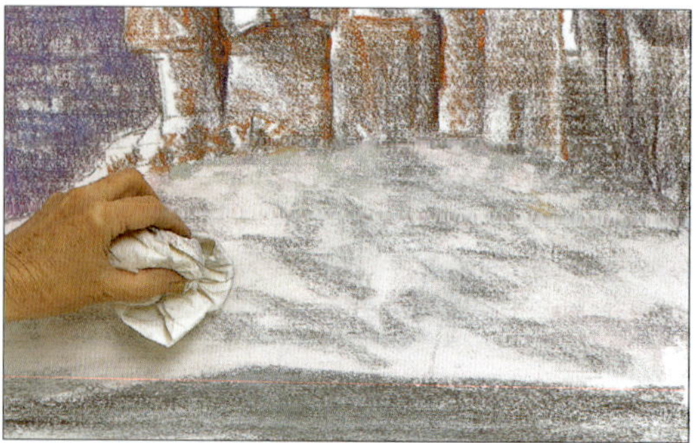

8 Apply touches of pale green to the scrubland, then soften the whole area by blending the colours with a clean rag or piece of kitchen paper, using a gentle circular motion.

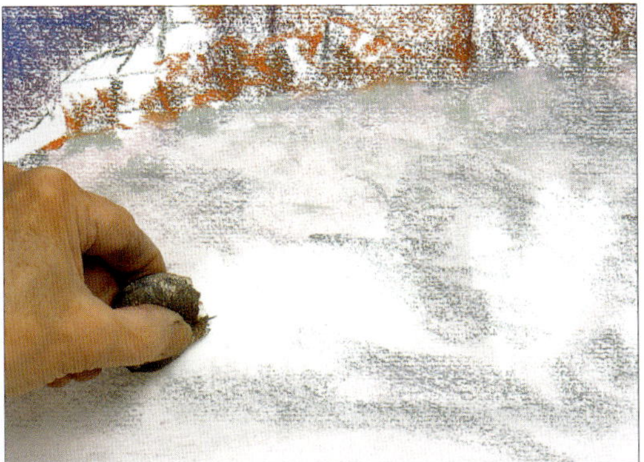

9 Using a kneaded eraser, wipe off the shapes of the trees in the foreground. If you accidentally wipe off too much, simply repeat Steps 7 and 8 for the right background colour.

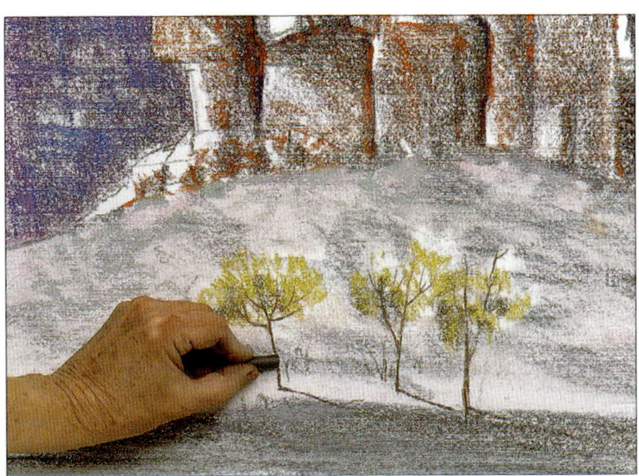

10 Draw the trees, using a brown Conté stick for the trunks and their shadows, and bright green to roughly block in the masses of foliage.

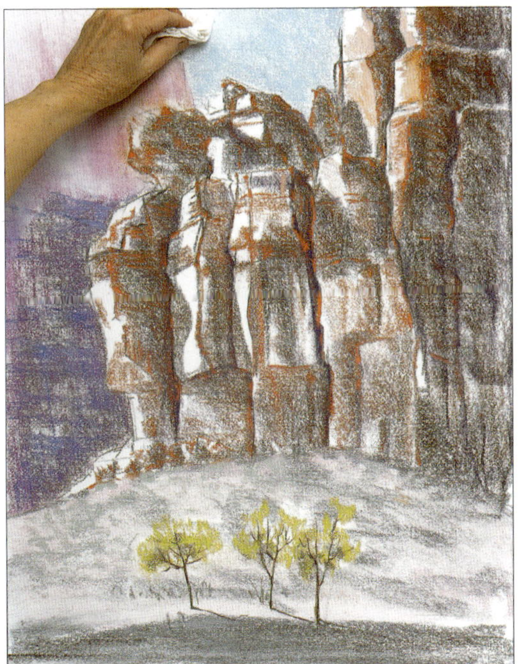

11 Wipe a clean rag or a piece of kitchen paper over the top of the background rock-face and the sky to lift off excess pastel dust and soften the colour.

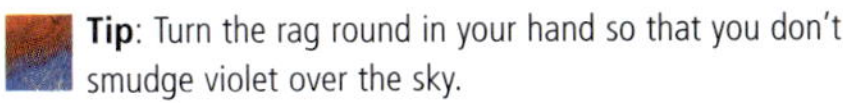

Tip: Turn the rag round in your hand so that you don't smudge violet over the sky.

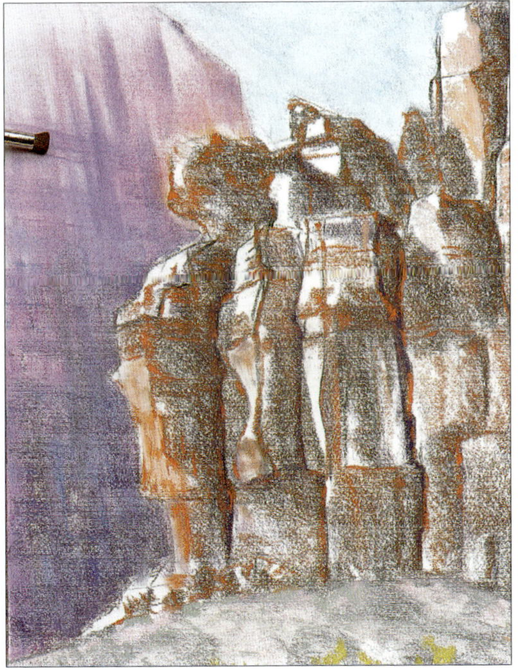

12 Soften the violet on the lower part of the background rock-face by using a blending brush, brushing it both horizontally and vertically. If you haven't got a blending brush, you could use your fingers or a torchon, but the bristles of the brush create very fine lines in the pastel dust, which are perfect for the striations in the rock. Although this rock-face is in the distance, it is important to create some subtle texture here.

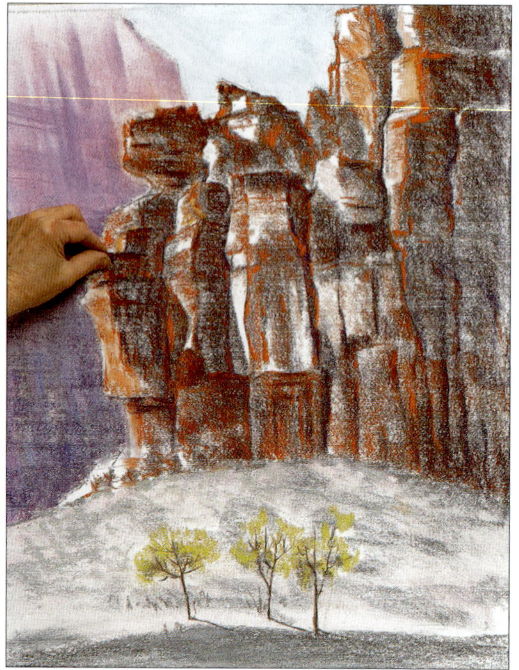

13 Add more detail to the main rock-face, using the side of the deep violet pastel to overlay colour and the tip to draw on short horizontal and vertical lines to emphasize the different facets within the rock.

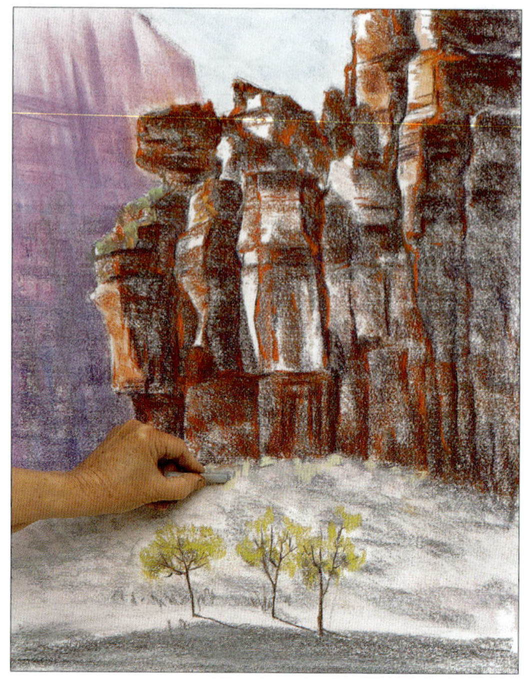

14 Now start working on the foreground scrubland. Using a pale green pastel on its side, roughly scribble in the base colour of the scrubby bushes that cover the ground immediately below the rock-face.

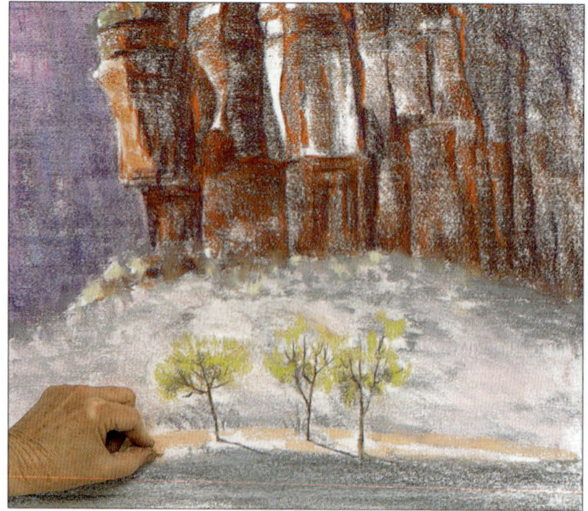

15 Build up the foreground foliage, using a range of pale and mid-toned greens and grey-greens. A general impression of the shapes is all that is required. Put in the roadway with a warm ochre pastel.

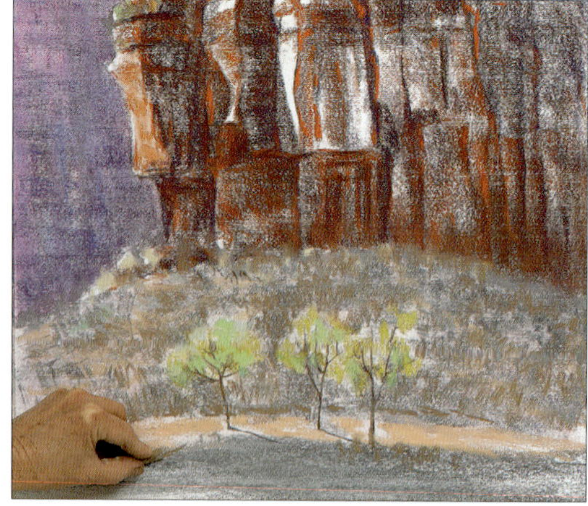

16 Define the edges of the roadway in brown. Also add a range of browns to the scrubland, using jagged, vertical strokes of dark brown for the thickest stems and branches. Make sure your pastel strokes follow the direction of growth.

The finished drawing

This colourful drawing captures the heat and the mood of the scene very well. Warm oranges and purples predominate and are perfectly suited to the arid, semi-desert landscape. The artist used bold linear strokes to capture the striations and jagged texture of the rocks and the drawing is full of energy. Although some texture is evident on the background cliff, blending out the pastel marks in this area has helped to create a sense of recession. For the foreground scrubland, the artist opted for an impressionistic approach, describing the overall shapes and textures with dots and dashes of greens and grey-greens. This contributes to the liveliness of the scene and concentrates attention on the rocks, which are the main point of interest.

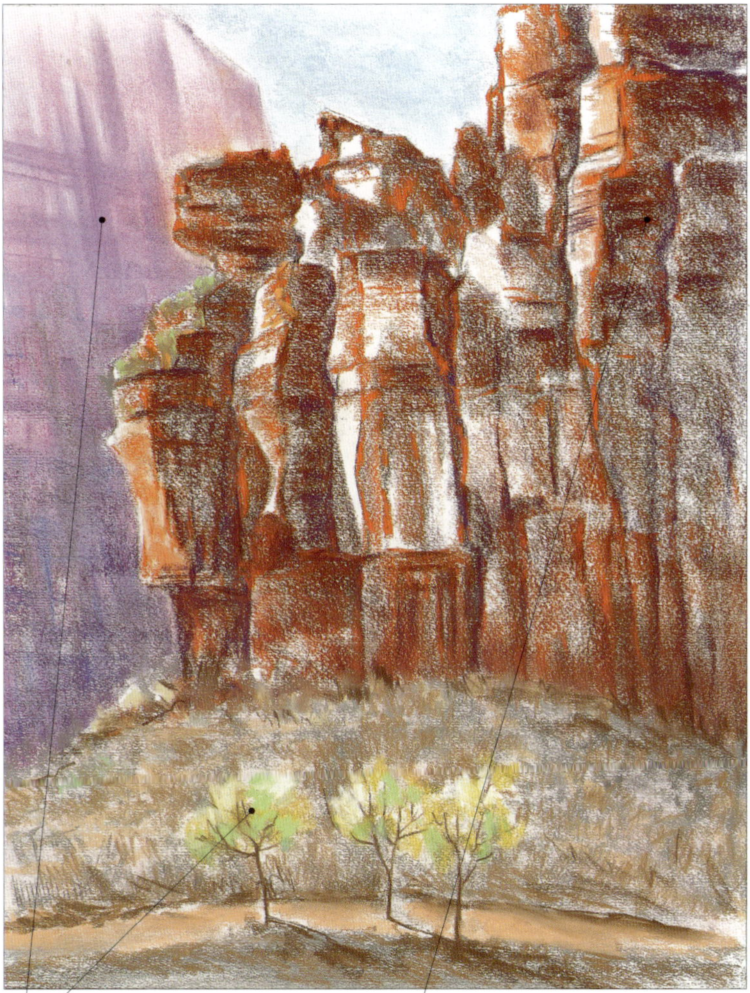

As the background cliff is less textured, it appears to be further away.

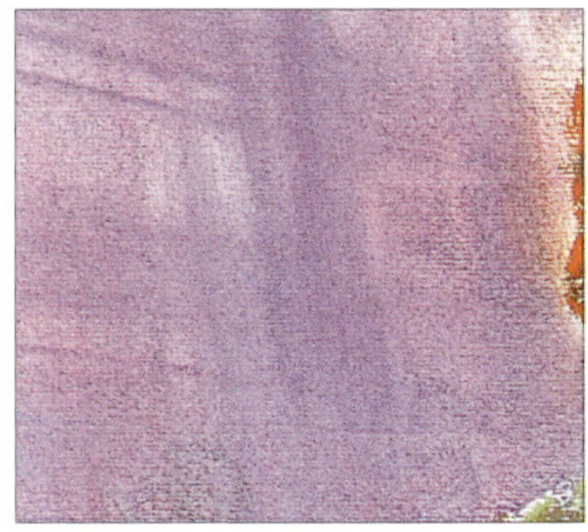

The trees are dwarfed by the rocks that tower above, and give a sense of scale.

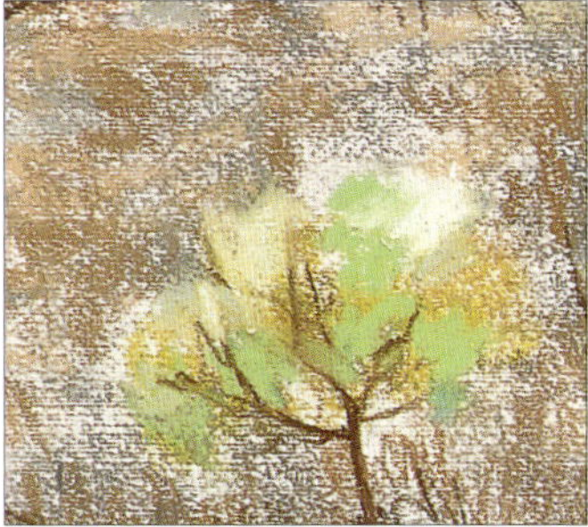

Tonal contrasts reveal the different facets of the rocks.

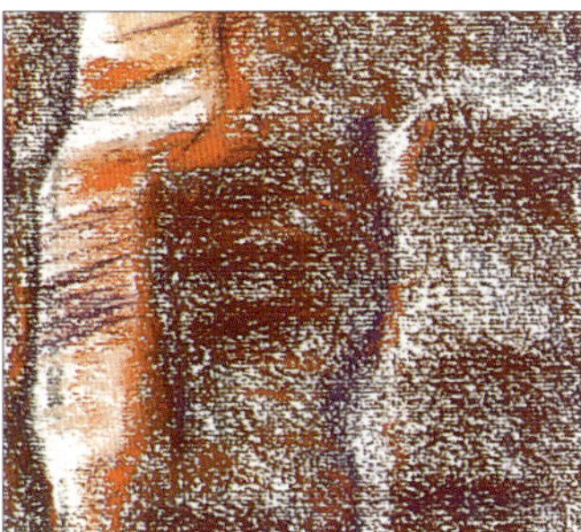

Cup and saucer

Pastel artists work in an amazing diversity of styles, and the simplest subject can be turned into a sophisticated and stylish piece of art. This work uses only a few colours and is almost diagrammatic in its delineation of simple geometric shapes, yet the subtle treatment of light, shadow and texture communicates atmosphere in a satisfying and complete way.

Materials

- *Watercolour paper*
- *Violet watercolour*
- *Paintbrush*
- *Charcoal stick*
- *Soft pastels: black, white, grey, mid-brown, light brown, yellow*

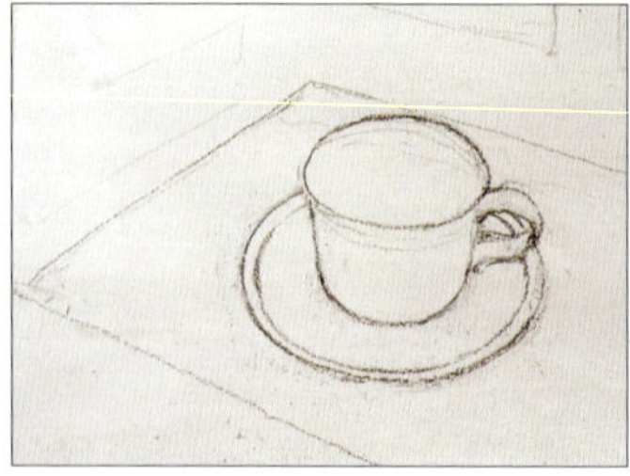

1 Begin by laying a light violet watercolour wash to tone down the white of the paper and make it easier to assess the first colours. When this is dry, make a charcoal drawing of the main components of the composition.

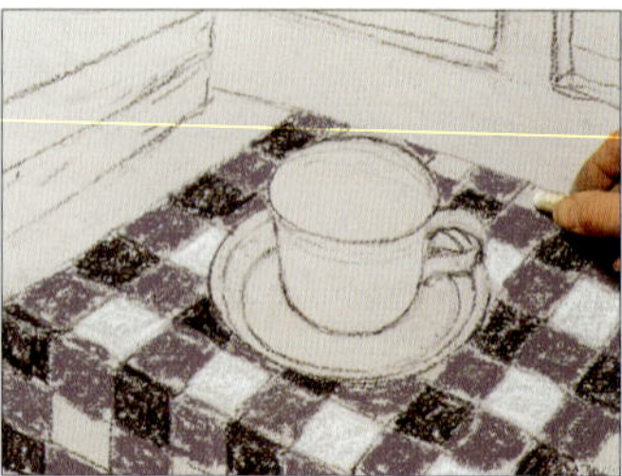

2 This artist's method of working is unusual as each area is treated separately, beginning with the tablecloth, which will provide a context for the other colours.

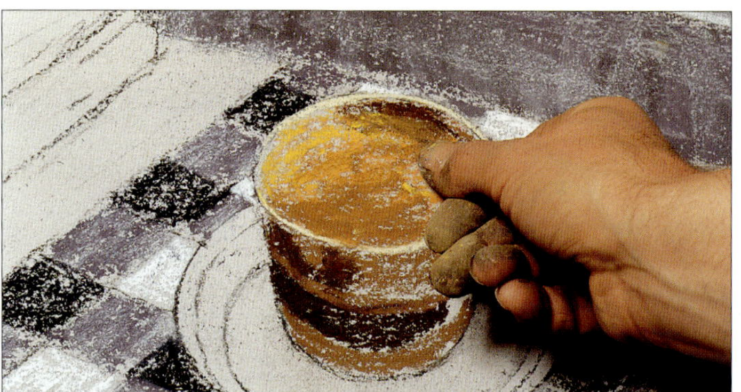

3 To link the tablecloth visually with the bottom of the windowframe, use the same grey. The cup and saucer provide the warmest colour area in the composition; begin by defining the ellipse at the top and then draw the interior of the cup and blend the colours to create a sense of depth.

Tip: The use of a very restricted palette can be instructive because it forces you to concentrate on close observation of textural and tonal variations in your subject.

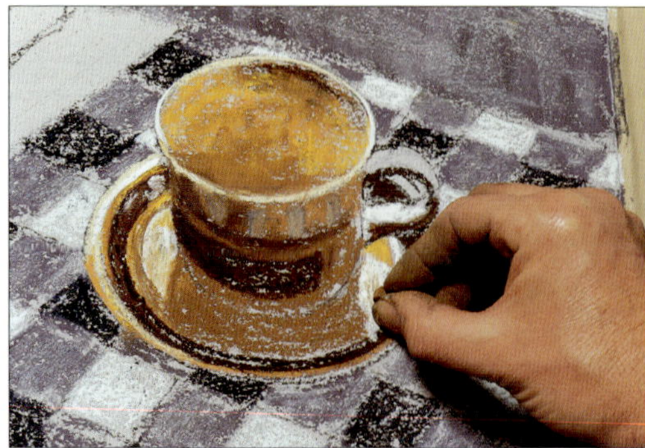

4 The highlights on the saucer, like the ellipse on the top of the cup, define its shape, so draw them in firmly in white. Few highlights are pure white, however, so they need to be modified with light strokes of brown laid on top.

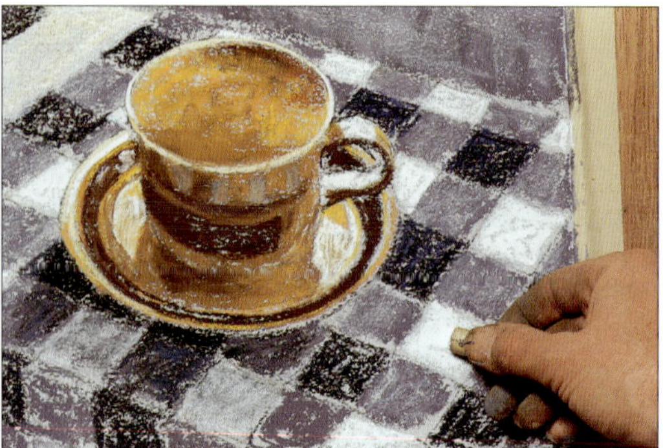

5 To increase the contrast between the shadowed area in front of the cup and the right-hand side of the tablecloth, where the light falls, lighten this area with pure white.

The finished drawing

In spite of the simplicity of the subject and the limited colour scheme, the picture is satisfying and well-balanced, with the dark shapes of the window and the boxes on the left making a frame for the cup and saucer.

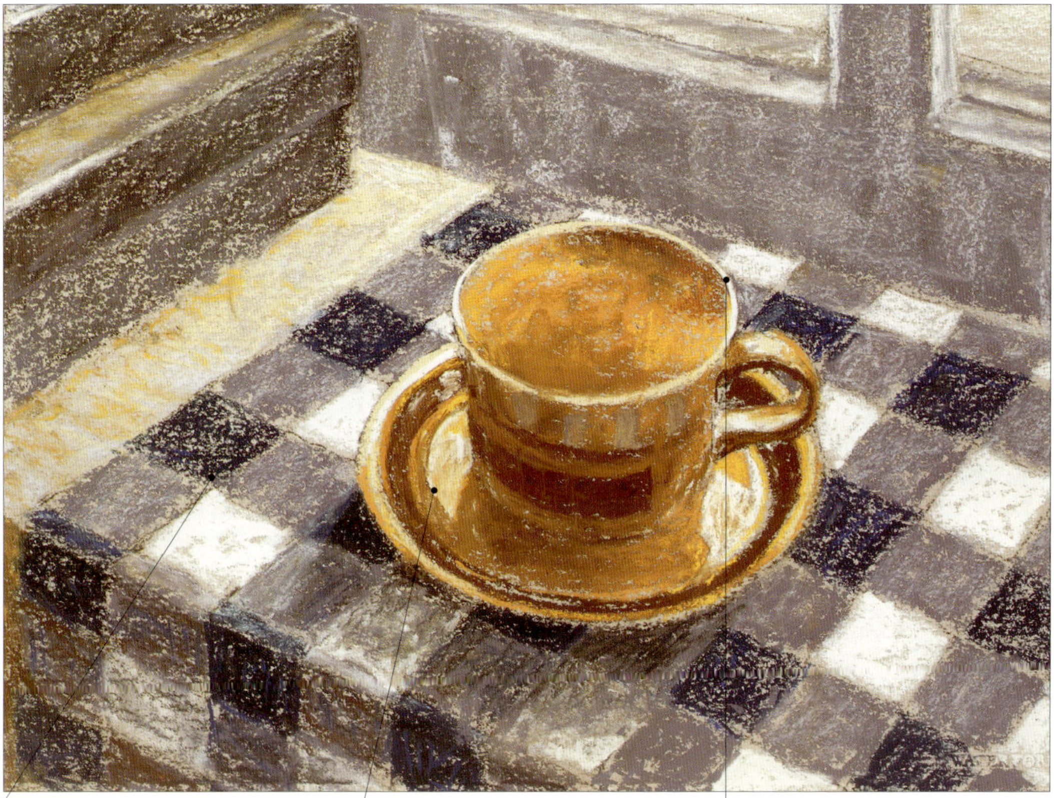

White specks of the paper showing through the pastel strokes help to convey the weave of the tablecloth.

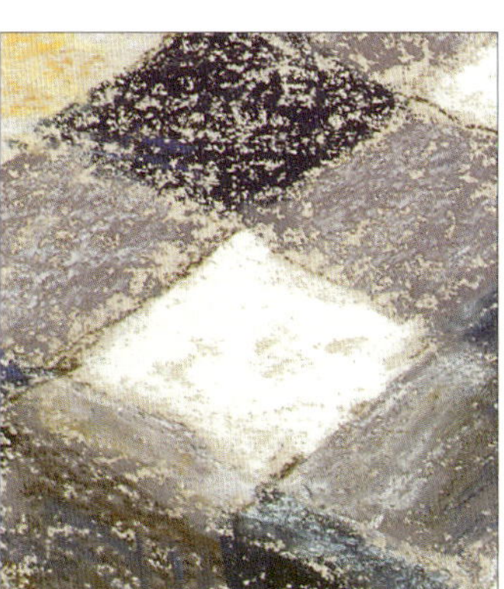

The smooth ceramic surface is indicated by the sharp, straight edge of the cup's shadow across the saucer.

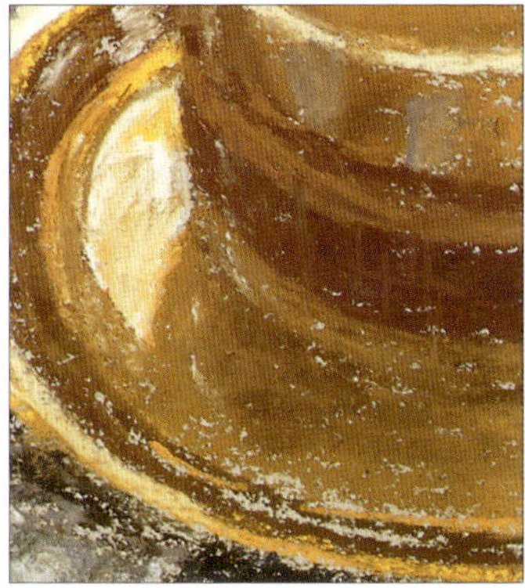

The brightly lit edge of the cup is finely drawn, and its smooth ellipse forms the focus of the picture.

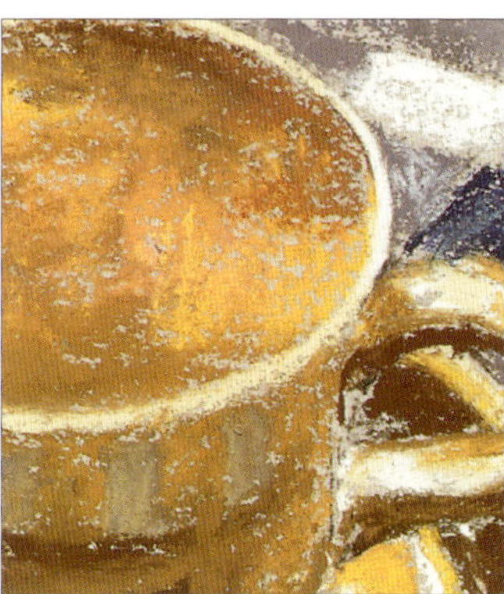

Cityscape

Although a construction site might not seem the most obvious choice of scene for a drawing project, if you choose your viewpoint carefully, the bold colours and graphic shapes can give you the chance to create a modern-looking, semi-abstract drawing. It will also test your ability to draw straight lines – always important when drawing buildings, whatever era they date from.

Scenes such as this can be found in towns and cities all over the world and recording a new building at all stages of its construction, from site clearance through to completion, makes an interesting long-term project. Moreover, many companies are waking up to the investment potential of buying original art – so who knows? If there's a prestigious building project going on near your home and your work is good enough, you might even be able to persuade them to buy it to display in the reception area or to use in promotional literature.

Oil pastels are not renowned for their subtlety of colour, but for a subject such as this, which relies on the bold, primary colours of the building cranes for much of its impact, they are ideal. You need to press quite firmly on the oil pastels, so use a heavy drawing paper or an oil-painting paper for this project to avoid the risk of tearing the support.

Materials

- *Heavy drawing paper or oil-painting paper*
- *4B pencil*
- *Oil pastels: pale greys (warm- and cool-toned), bright blue, red, yellow, white, lilac, Naples yellow, black*
- *Scraperboard tool or craft (utility) knife*

The scene

The brightly coloured cranes stand out dramatically against the cloudless blue sky, while the straight lines of the cranes and the buildings under construction create a graphic, almost abstract composition. The diagonal lines of some of the cranes make the composition more dynamic.

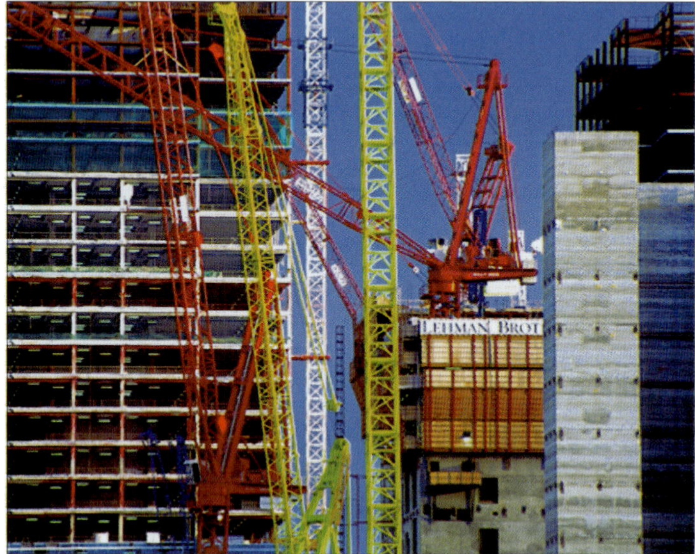

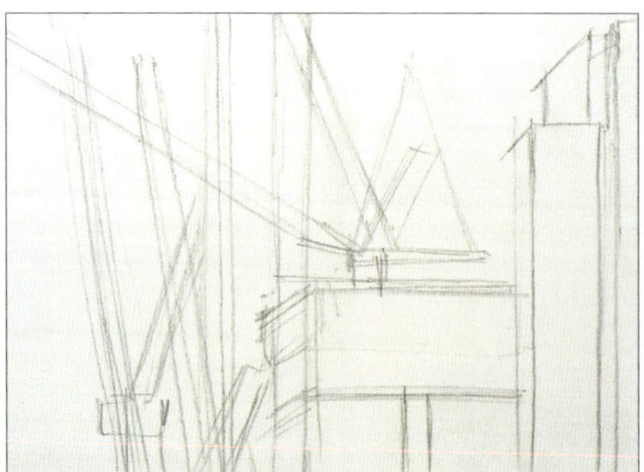

1 Using a soft pencil, mark out the lines of the cranes and the buildings under construction. There's no need to put in any of the internal lines at this stage, but do make sure you measure all the angles and distances carefully.

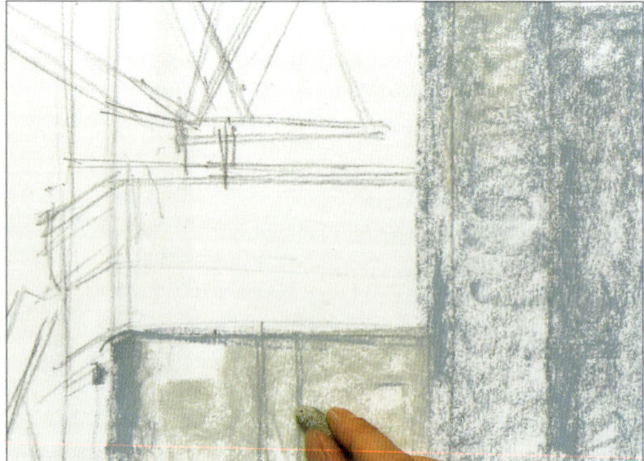

2 Using pale grey oil pastels, block in the building on the right. Note that the shaded sides are cooler in tone than those in full sunlight, so alternate between warm- and cool-toned greys as required.

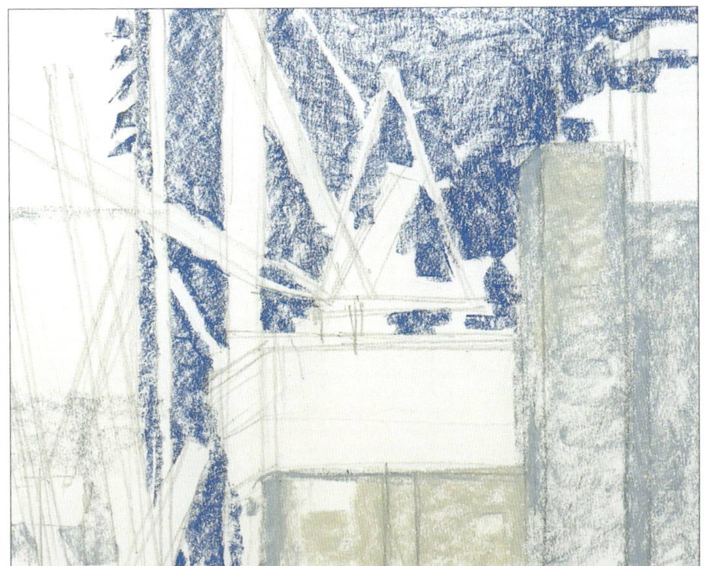

3 Block in the sky, using the side of a bright blue oil pastel and making sure you don't go over the lines of the cranes. Putting in the negative shapes of the background sky at this early stage makes it easier to see any thin lines of the cranes that you have not yet drawn.

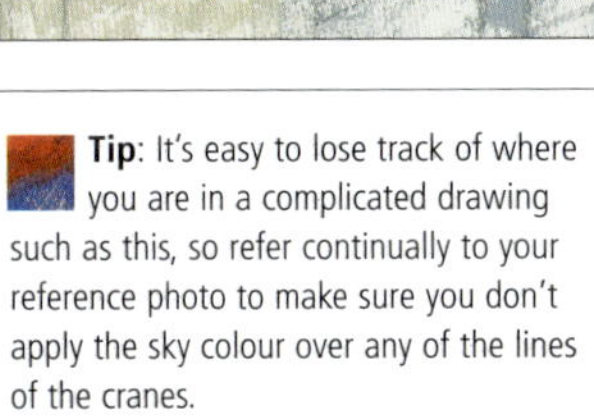

Tip: It's easy to lose track of where you are in a complicated drawing such as this, so refer continually to your reference photo to make sure you don't apply the sky colour over any of the lines of the cranes.

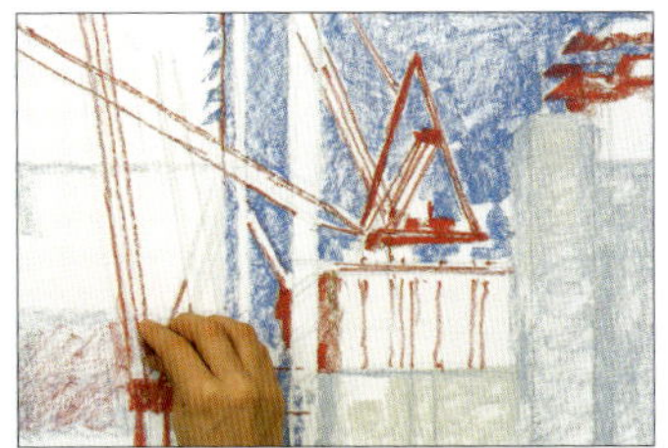

4 Begin putting in the red lines of the cranes, using bold, confident strokes and pressing quite hard on the tip of the pastel. Lightly stroke the side of the pastel over the warm-toned shadow areas of the buildings.

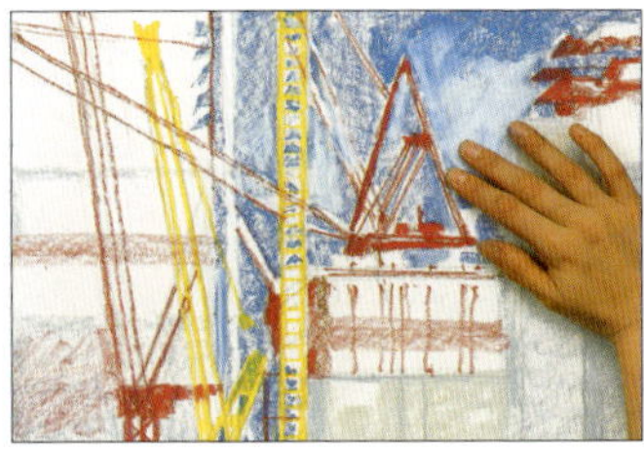

5 Now put in the bright yellow of the cranes, filling in the spaces between the rungs with blue. Work white oil pastel over part of the sky and blend it with your fingers.

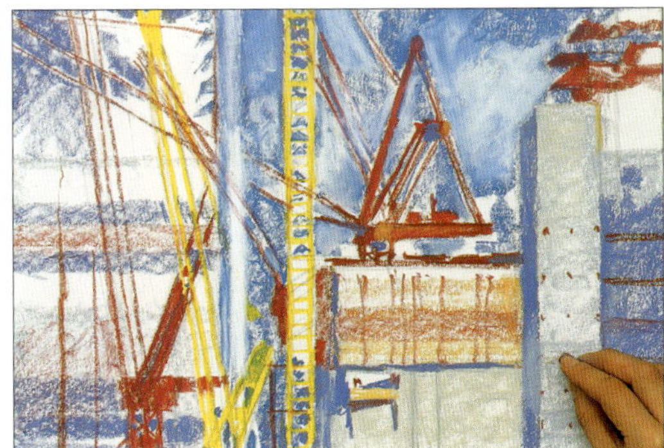

6 Using the side of a lilac oil pastel, roughly block in the shaded sides of the buildings on the right. (Note, in particular, the shadow cast on the building on the far right of the image.) Apply the same colour to some of the shaded interior floors of the building on the left. Work Naples yellow, which is a pale, warm yellow, over the warm-toned area of the building in the centre and add small dashes of red on the tall foreground building.

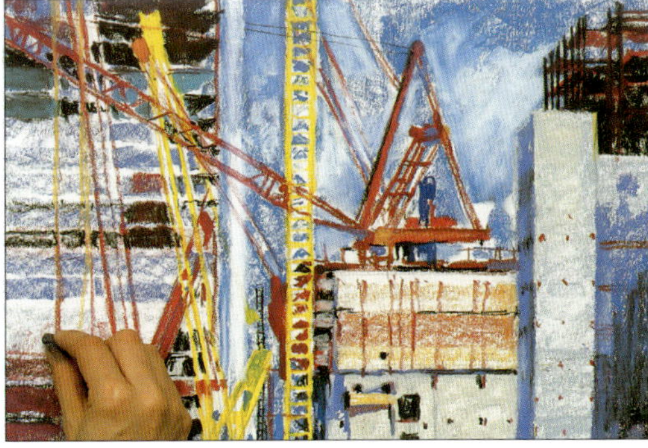

7 Using the tip of a black oil pastel to make strong, bold marks, draw the reinforced steel joists of the building in the background. Establish the different storeys of the building on the left, using a range of shadow colours (blue, lilac, black) as appropriate. Use the side of the pastels to make broad, lightly textured marks; you can then go over them with other pastels to blend the colours optically and create a more interesting shadow colour.

▶

Assessment time

The drawing is nearing completion and only a few minor adjustments are needed. In places, the cranes are lost against the building or the sky and need to be more sharply defined. Some of the shadows need to be darkened slightly.

This crane merges into the building behind it and needs to be a little more clearly defined.

The lines of the white crane are quite delicate and will be hard to draw with a thick oil pastel.

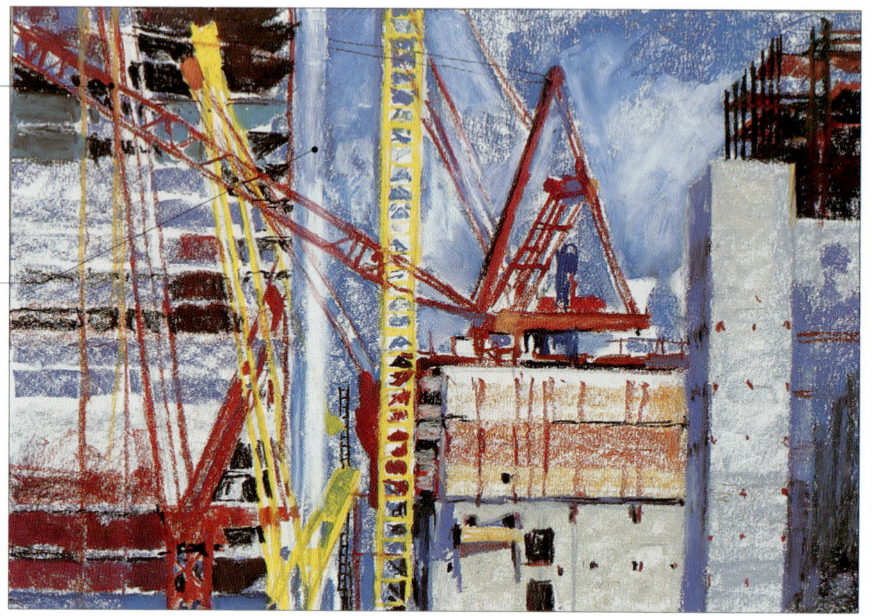

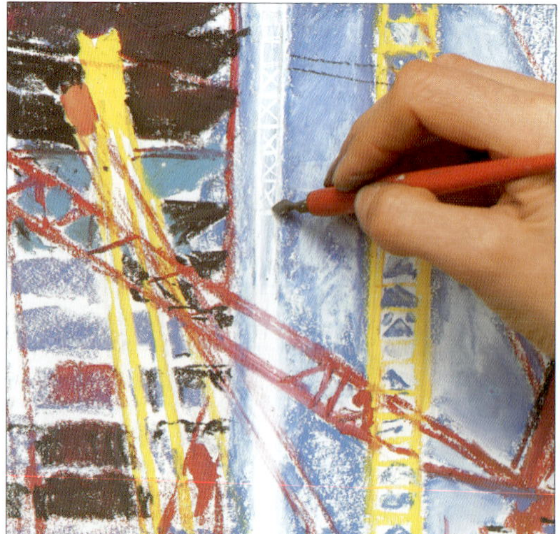

8 Using a scraperboard tool or the tip of a craft knife, scratch off blue oil pastel to create the lines of the white crane in the centre of the image.

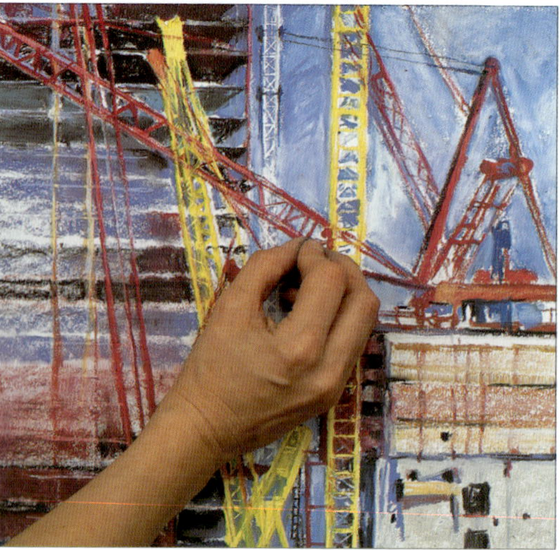

9 Scratch into the red crane on the left to create some highlight areas, and strengthen the red diagonal line so that the crane really stands out against the building.

The finished drawing

This artist has matched the medium to the subject beautifully. The bold, vibrant colours of oil pastels, which might be too brash and unsubtle for many subjects, are perfect for the bright, primary colours of the cranes and sky. Although it is difficult to draw fine details with oil pastels, they are the ideal drawing tool for the solid, graphic lines of this scene. Using the side of the pastels for the façades of the buildings brings another quality to the image and creates a lighter texture. Overlaying one colour on another, particularly in the shadow areas, has created interesting optical colour mixes that are much more lively and interesting than a flat application of a single colour could ever be.

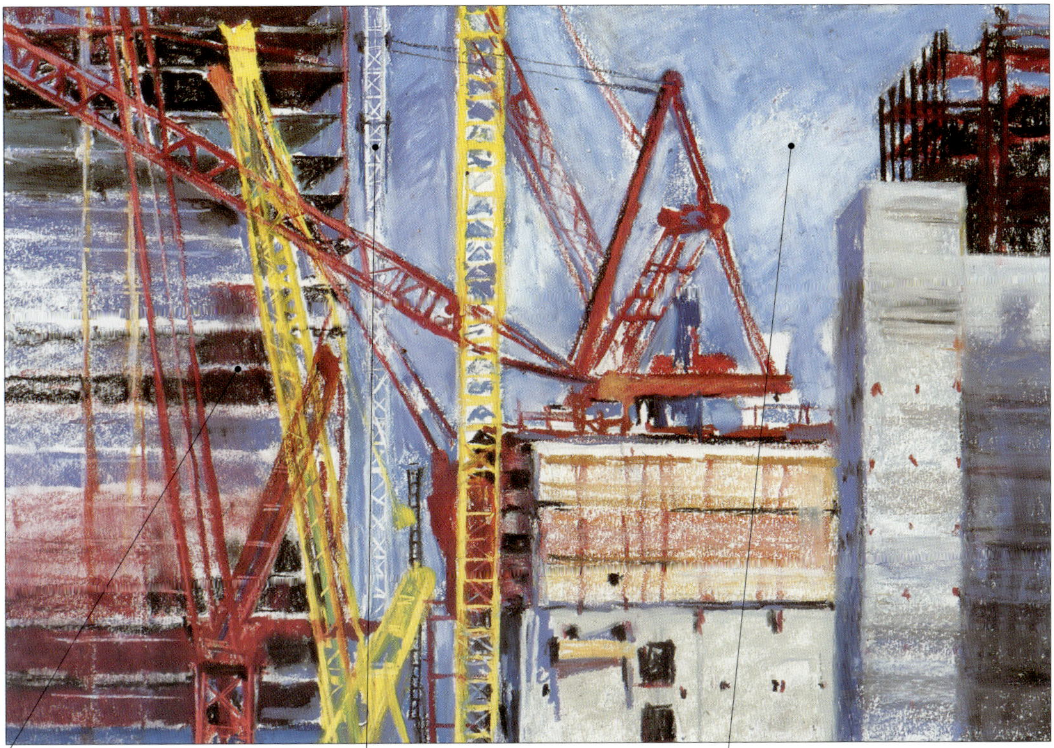

Optical colour mixes create lively shadow colours.

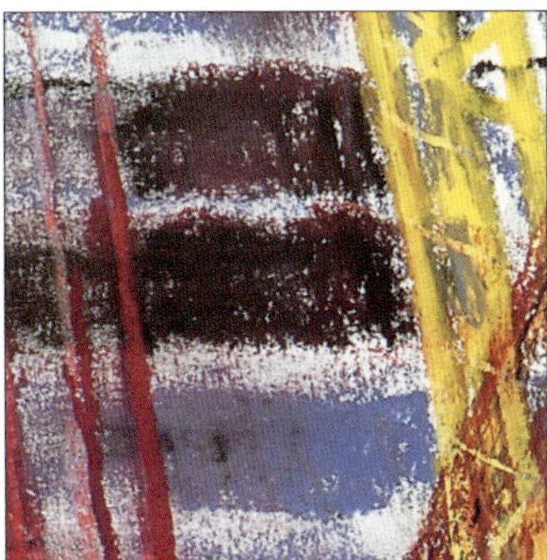

The sgraffito technique allows you to scratch off the pastel and create fine lines.

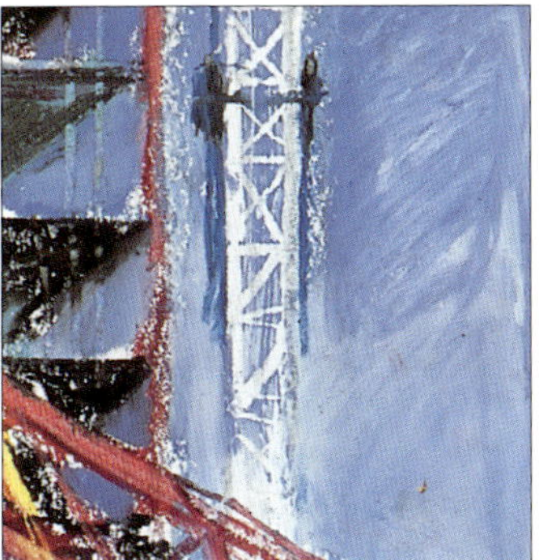

Finger blending in the sky softens both the colour and the texture.

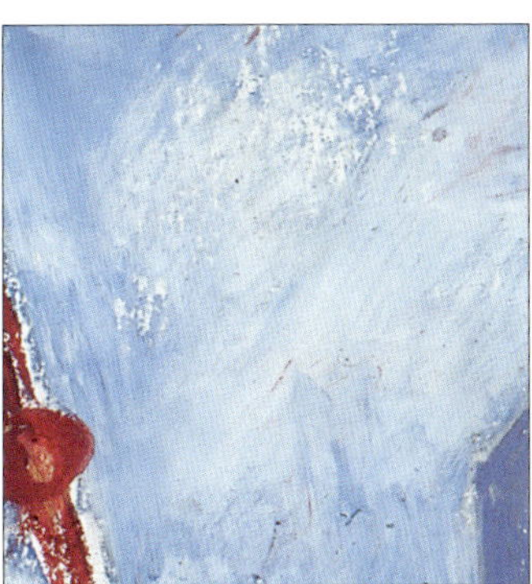

Old wooden gateway

There is something very appealing about drawing distressed wood and peeling paint. Rusting nails and bolts, differences in tone where the sun has bleached and faded the paintwork, the grain and texture of the wood underneath – all these things are far more interesting to look at than a pristine, gloss-painted surface. Perhaps part of the fascination is that, as the paint begins to peel away, we catch glimpses into the past and a hint of how the subject once looked.

Soft pastel is a lovely medium to use for a project such as this. By using the pastel on its side and lightly applying a thin layer of colour that does not completely cover the paper or a previous layer of pastel (a technique known as scumbling), you can create wonderful textures and optical colour mixes. By blending the pastel with your fingertips, you can produce smooth textures and even tones.

This particular scene is also a study in light and shade. The bright patch of sunlight that can be seen through the gateway is balanced by the area of shade to its left, with the wedge-shaped shadow helping to lead the viewer's eye through the scene to the buildings at the back of the courtyard.

A drawing of the gateway alone might result in a soulless study of an architectural detail: by including the yard, we can speculate about the daily routine and living conditions of the inhabitants and bring the scene to life. However, too much emphasis on it would detract from the gateway, so subdue the detail and draw the buildings as blocks of colour.

Materials

- *Terracotta-coloured pastel paper*
- *Soft pastels: reddish brown, black, white, pale mint green, dark mint green, greys, browns, yellow*

The scene
This old wooden gateway, covered in peeling paint and bleached by the sun, offers both interesting textures and colours and an intriguing glimpse into the courtyard beyond.

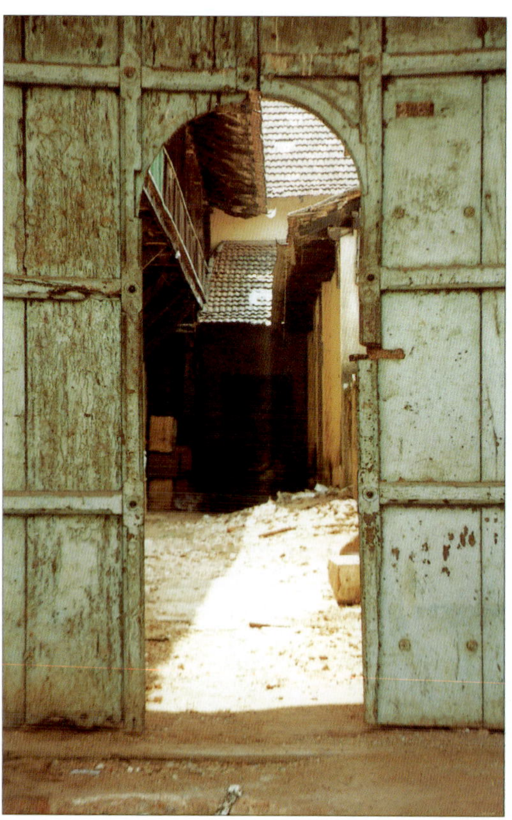

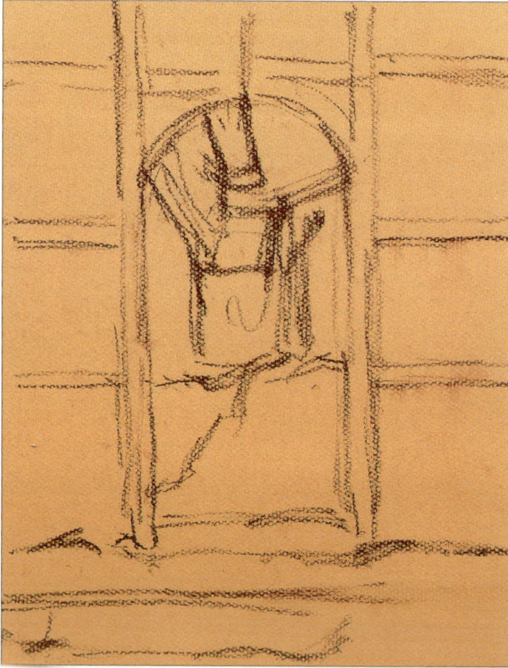

1 Using a reddish brown pastel on terracotta-coloured pastel paper, lightly sketch the main lines of the scene – the arch of the gate, the wooden panels, the roofline and the division between the shaded and sunlit parts of the ground that can be seen through the gate. The terracotta paper enhances the feeling of warmth and sunlight in the scene; it also provides the base colour both for the buildings in the courtyard and for the wooden gateway, which means that the paper does part of the work for you, without you having to apply the base colour separately.

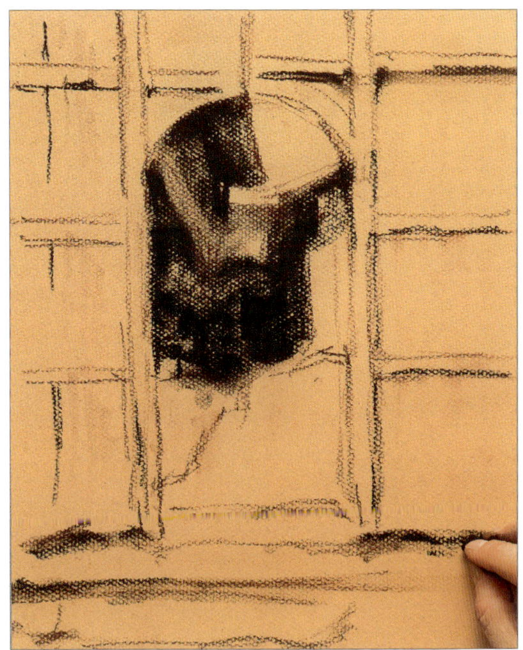

2 Using the side of a black pastel, block in the buildings. Note the differences in tone: some areas, such as the underside of the overhanging roof, are darker than others. Add the thin shadows cast by the wooden panels on the gate.

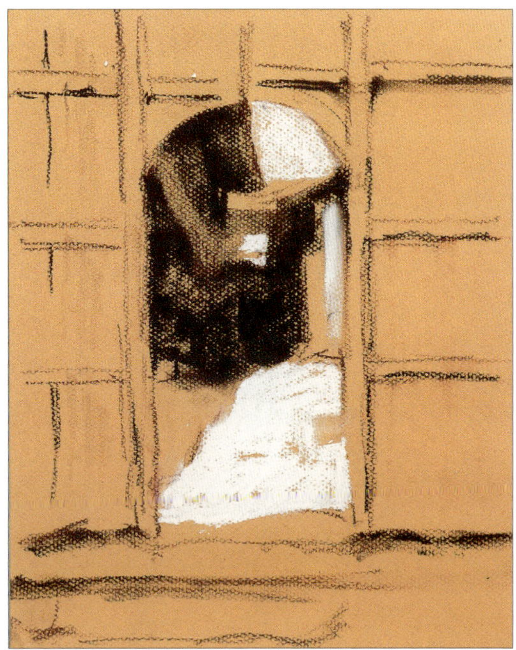

3 Using the side of a white pastel, block in the very bright highlight areas of the sunlit foreground and the sky above the building, as well as those parts of the building that receive the most light.

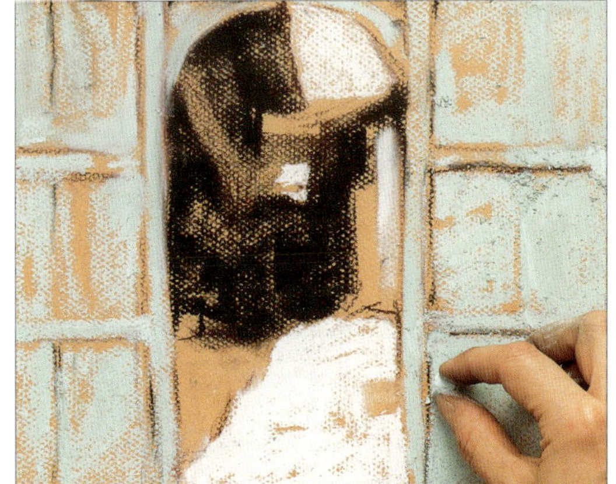

4 Using a pale mint green pastel (again using the side rather than the tip), block in the painted gateway. Allow some of the paper to show through so that it looks as if an earlier colour is showing through the peeling paint: with this kind of subject, it's important to keep the coverage loose and uneven so that you create the right kind of texture.

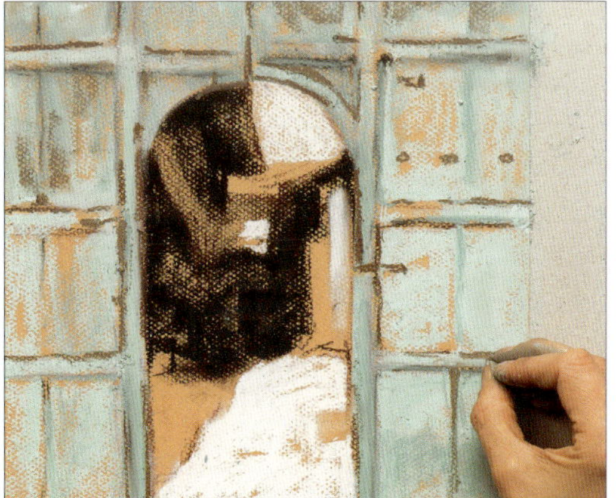

5 Use a reddish brown pastel to put in some of the exposed wood on the gateway, rubbing with your fingers to smooth out the colour. Roughly scumble a darker mint green over the paler green in places, allowing some of the lighter colour to show through. The successive layers of pastel help to develop more depth and texture on the gate.

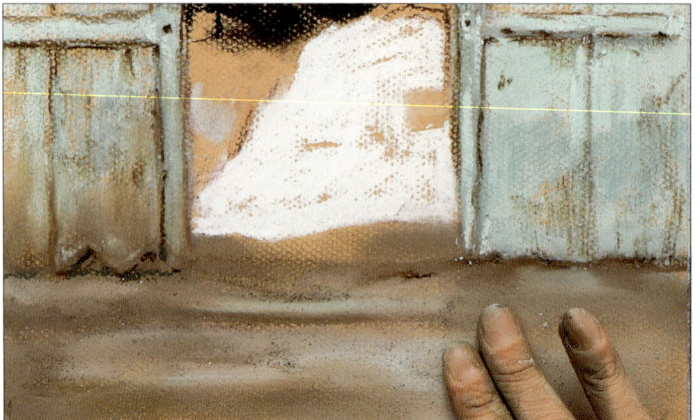

6 Stroke pale mint green followed by reddish brown over the foreground and blend the colours with your fingertips. Allow some of the mint green to remain visible: some parts of the foreground are cooler in tone than others.

Assessment time

Although the buildings in the courtyard are little more than blocks of colour, we can see the different facets: paying careful attention to the light and dark tones makes them look like three-dimensional forms. A little more depth of colour is needed on the gateway, as too much of the paper texture is visible.

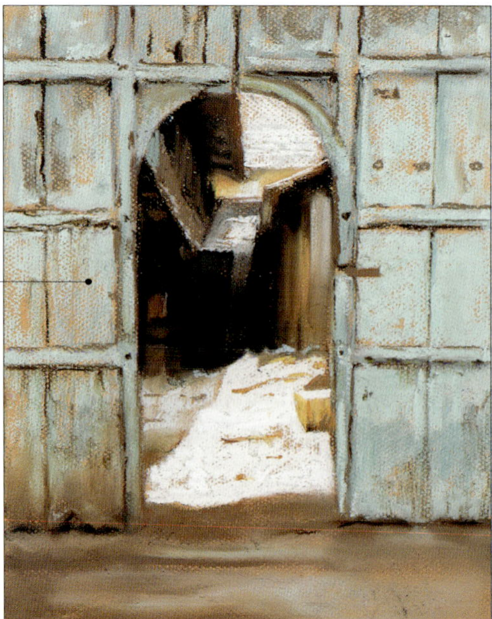

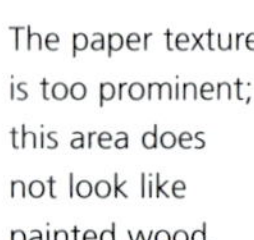

The paper texture is too prominent; this area does not look like painted wood.

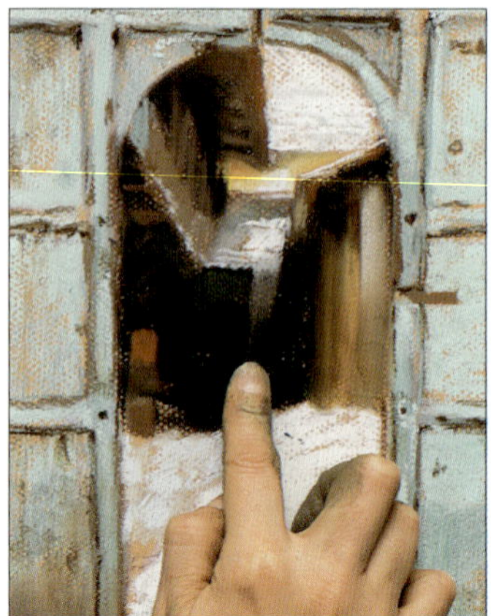

7 Block in the shaded part of the ground in the yard with pale grey and white, blending the colours a little with your fingers but taking care that they retain their individuality. Reinforce the different facets of the courtyard buildings using mid-browns and greys for the shaded sides and applying light touches of white, smoothed out with your fingers, for the more brightly lit parts and the shafts of light.

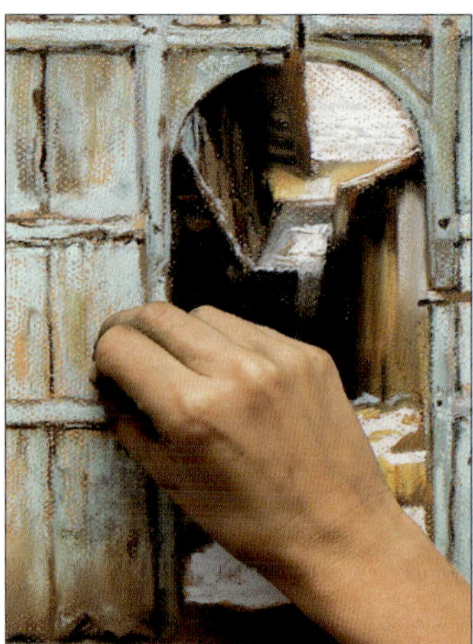

8 Apply light vertical strokes of mint green, with tiny touches of yellow, over the individual panels of the gate and blend with your fingers. Remember to allow a little of the paper colour to show through, to give the impression of underlying layers of paint.

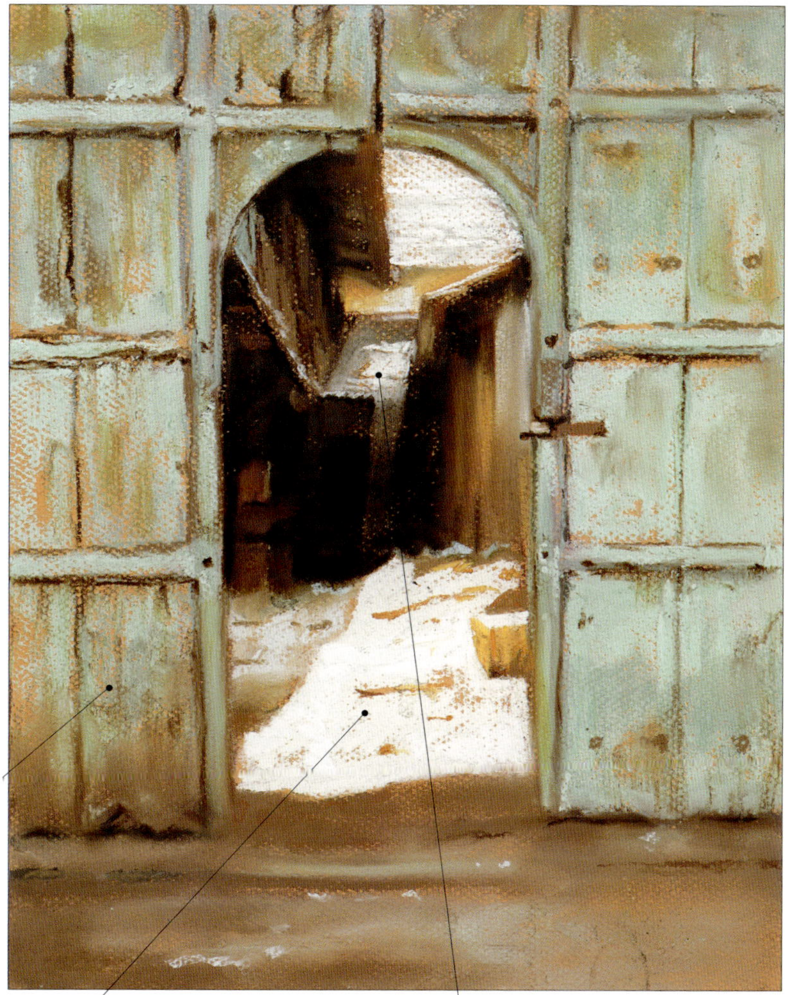

The finished drawing

This drawing exploits two important soft pastel techniques – scumbling and finger blending. The main focus of interest is the sun-bleached, painted gateway, which forms a natural frame for the scene of the courtyard beyond. Although detail is subdued and the buildings are little more than blocks of colour, there is a delightful sense of light and shade in the scene. The shafts of sunlight, which are created by stroking a thin line of white pastel across the paper, are balanced by blocks of shadow, so neither one dominates.

The arch of the gate is positioned almost centrally in the picture space, which creates a calm mood. However, this is balanced by the lines of the buildings and the wedge-shaped patches of sunlight and shadow, which help to break the symmetry and make the composition more dynamic.

Scumbling allows the paper colour to show through and, at the same time, suggests the texture of the wood.

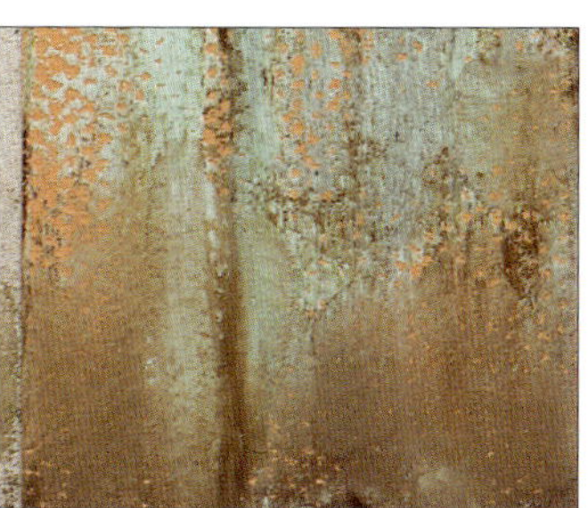

The bright, wedge-shaped patch of sunlight leads our eye through the picture to the buildings at the back of the courtyard.

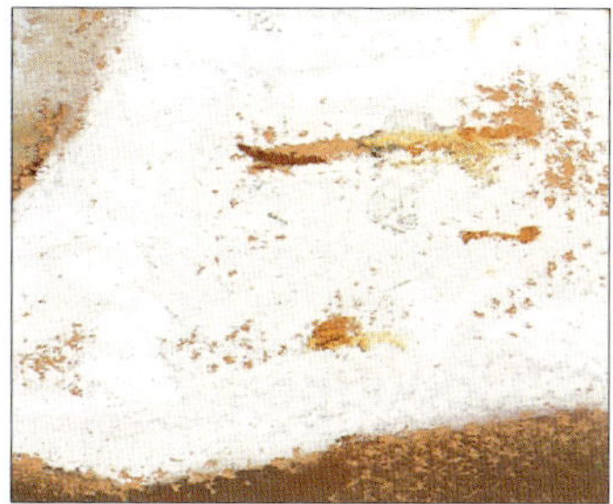

Blocks of tone – light versus dark – reveal the form of the buildings and the direction from which the light comes.

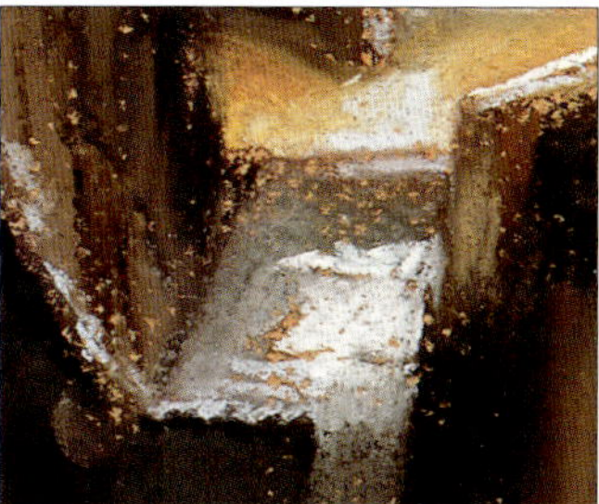

Chickens

When you're drawing birds, you can opt either for a very detailed and painstaking rendition of the feathers or for a more impressionistic approach that attempts to recreate the lovely sheen. This project takes the latter route and relies on a combination of building up layers of water-soluble oil pastel to give a rich sheen and making linear, textural marks with both oil pastel and water-soluble pencil.

The project also involves brushing water over the pigment in order to blend it on the support and create the right colour mixes – so use a medium-weight or heavy watercolour paper which will be absorbent enough for you to be able to apply water without it cockling. Work with your drawing board flat for these stages, so that the colour doesn't run where you don't want it to go.

Look carefully and you will see that, even in areas that at first glance appear to be a single colour, there are many different colours within the birds' feathers – rich browns, oranges and yellows, with blues and violets in the darkest, most shaded parts. The feathers also have a slight iridescence, which is very hard to convey accurately. However, applying layers of colour on top of one another creates lively optical colour mixes that give something of the effect.

Materials

- *Watercolour paper*
- *Water-soluble pencils: grey, dark brown*
- *Ruling drawing pen*
- *Masking fluid*
- *Water-soluble oil pastels: dark olive green, yellow ochre, grass green, pinkish brown, bright yellow, orange, burnt sienna, violet, bright green, red, blue, brown*
- *Paintbrush*
- *Kitchen paper*

The scene

This artist spotted these two chickens in a local farmyard and was attracted by the colourful plumage and lovely rounded shapes. She had to take a reference photo quickly, since the chicken on the left was about to walk away. She decided to swap the birds around in her drawing so that they would be facing one another, as this made a more pleasing composition.

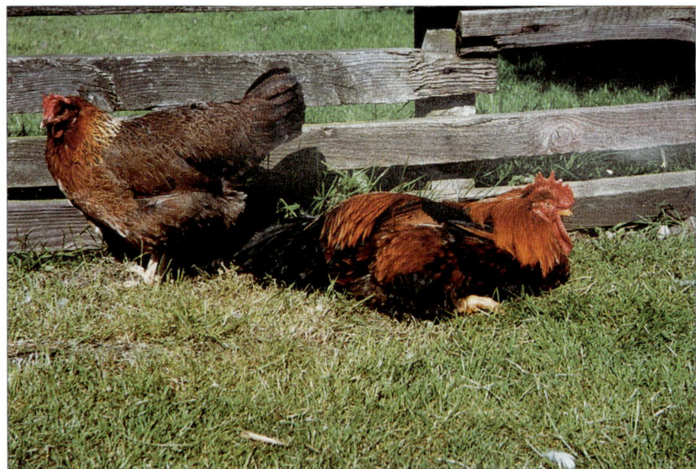

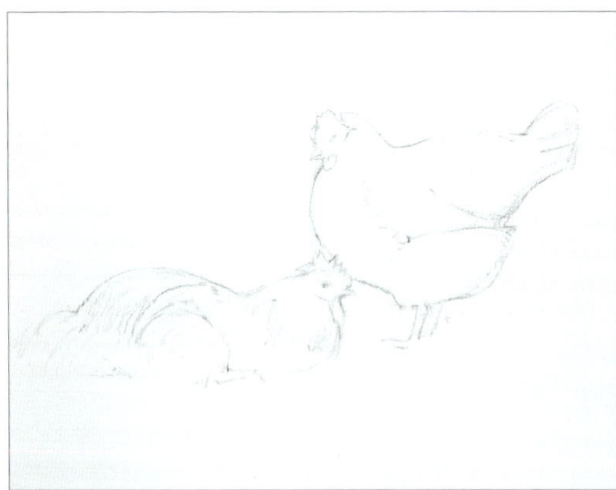

1 Lightly sketch the scene using a grey water-soluble pencil. To give yourself a guide when you apply the colour, draw some light lines within the outline of the birds to indicate the positions of the main blocks of feathers, such as the wings.

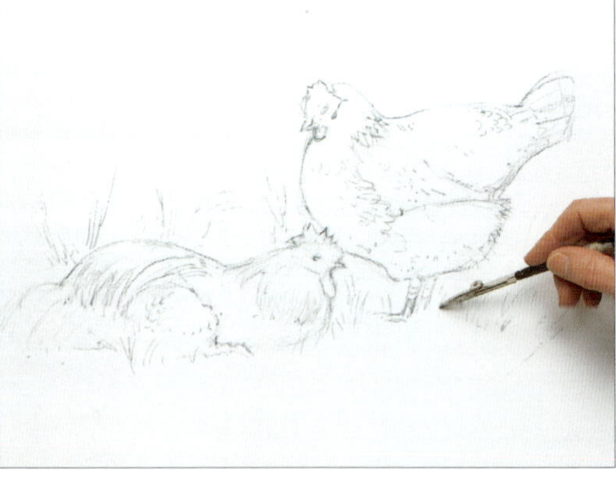

2 Using a ruling drawing pen, apply masking fluid over the lightest parts of the image, where you want to preserve the white of the paper – the white feathers, the chickens' legs and the tall stems of grass in the foreground.

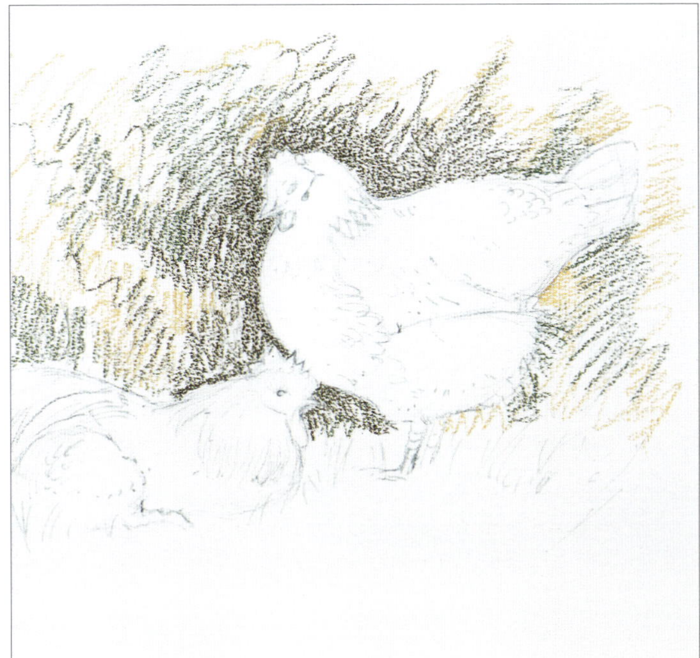

3 Loosely scribble dark olive green water-soluble oil pastel over the background, working around the chickens. Work some yellow ochre and grass green oil pastel over the top.

Tip: You need to press quite hard on the oil pastels, so take care not to dislodge the masking fluid.

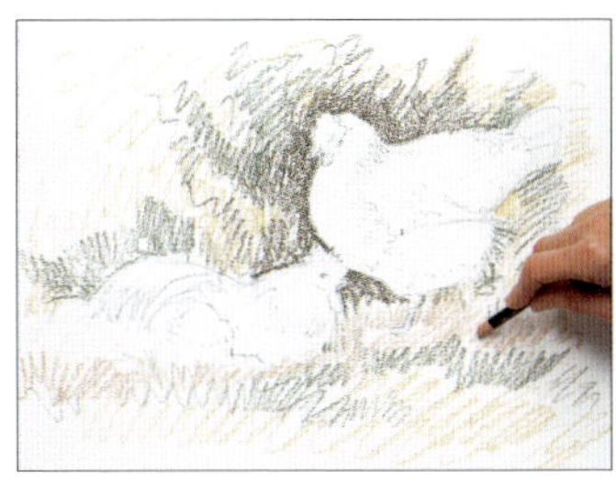

4 Scribble yellow ochre and dark olive green oil pastel over the foreground, adding pinkish brown oil pastel where the dry, dusty earth can be seen under the grass stems.

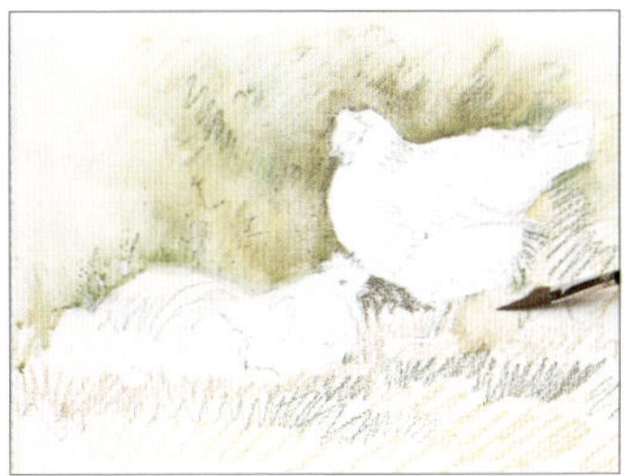

5 Brush clean water lightly over the foreground and background, blending the colours on the support and making sure that no colour spills over on to the chickens.

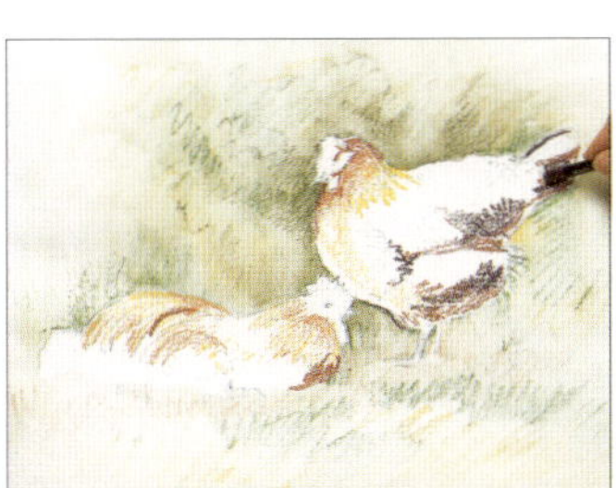

6 Now you can begin applying colour to the chickens. Work bright yellow water-soluble oil pastel around the neck and tail feathers, making vertical marks that follow the direction in which the feathers grow. Overlay orange oil pastel for the darkest orange parts. Use burnt sienna for the dark browns and add violet for the very darkest parts so that you begin to develop a sense of the depth of the feathers.

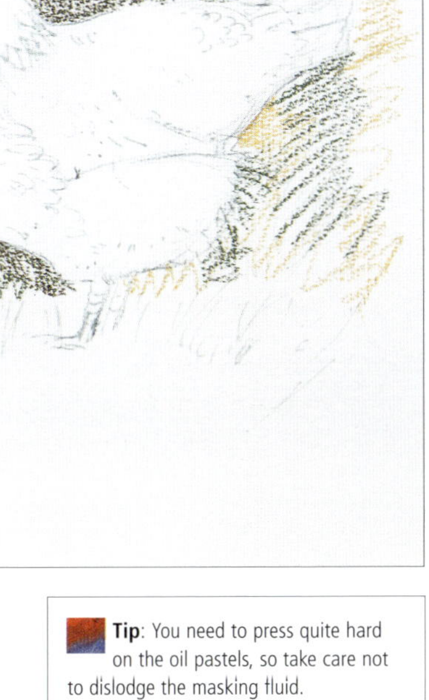

7 Darken the background behind the birds so that they stand out more, making jagged strokes of bright green to give a grass-like texture.

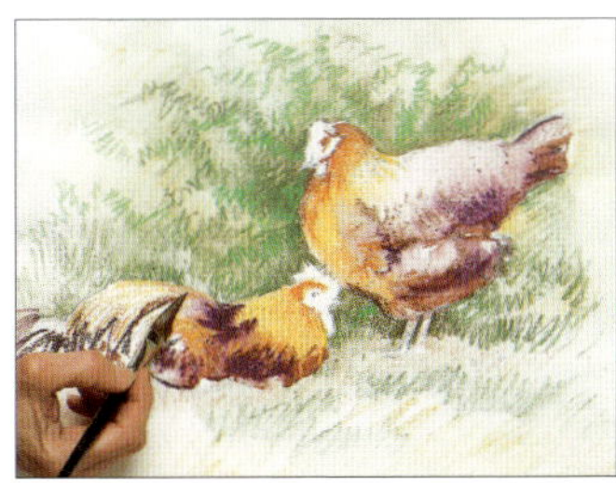

8 Carefully brush clean water over the birds. Keep a piece of absorbent kitchen paper to hand to dab off any excess water so that you can control where the colour goes.

Tip: Rinse your brush frequently so that you don't contaminate the light orange areas with dark violet or brown.

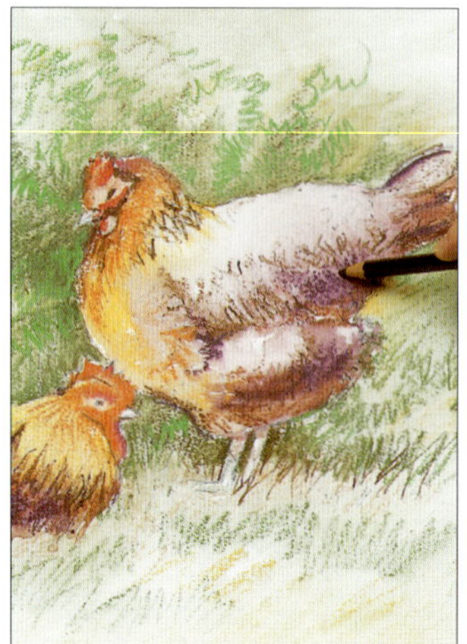

9 Put in the red combs, using both red and orange water-soluble oil pastels to get the right shade of orangey-red. Wash over with clean water to blend. Dip the tip of a dark brown water-soluble pencil in water and, using short feathery strokes, draw in the ruffle at the base of the neck and the large feathers that lie around the base of the wing. (Dipping the pencil in water intensifies the colour, while the linear pencil strokes add texture.)

Assessment time

The drawing is nearing completion and contains an interesting mix of linear marks, which create texture in the grass, and softly blended colour. However, more detail is needed on the chickens' feathers, both to add texture and to increase the depth of colour and create a realistic-looking sheen.

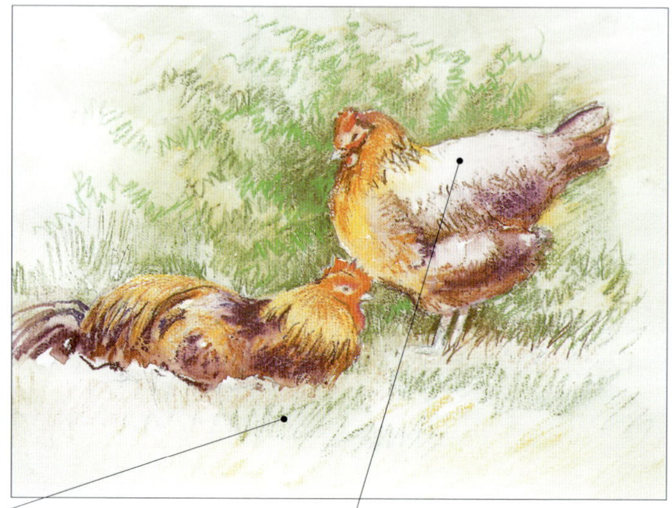

The grass in the foreground needs more colour and texture, as this will help to imply that it is closer to the viewer.

Although this area is the most brightly lit part of the chicken, it looks too stark at present; it needs more texture and detail.

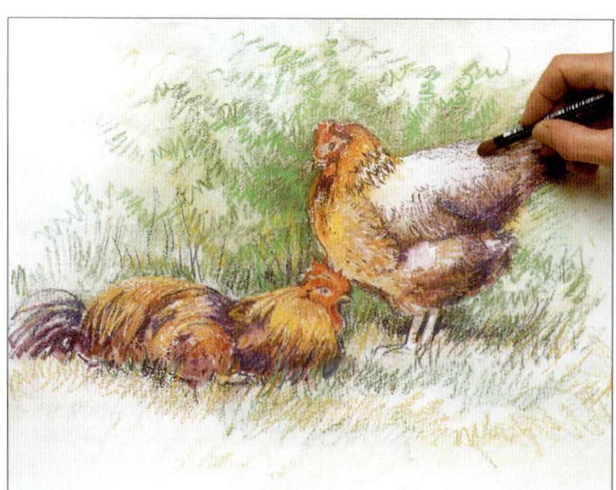

10 Gently rub over the drawing with your fingertips to remove the masking fluid that you applied in Step 2. Using the dark brown water-soluble pencil, put more detail into the feathers, as in Step 9. Scribble blue oil pastel into the darkest parts of the feathers. Darken the birds' upper bodies by applying short, linear marks with a brown oil pastel.

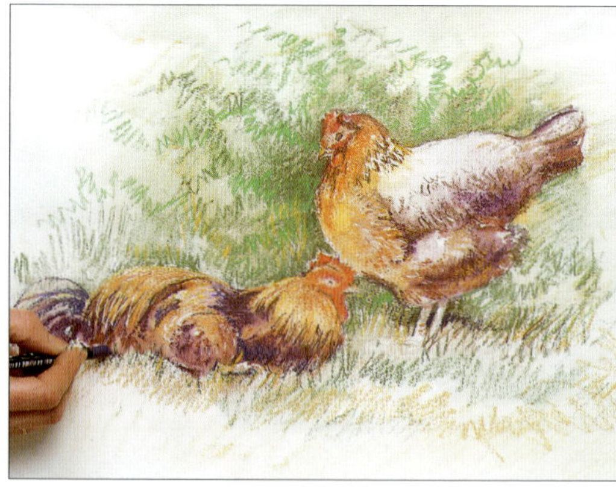

11 If any of the highlights look too big or bright now that you've removed the masking fluid, dot in any appropriate feather colours to subdue them and make them less obtrusive. Add any final linear detailing on the feathers, using the same colours as before in either oil pastel (for thicker marks) or water-soluble pencil (for fine lines).

The finished drawing

This is a colourful and lively drawing that demonstrates that you don't need to put in every minute detail to achieve a realistic-looking image. The artist has exploited the soft, buttery consistency of the water-soluble oil pastels to create blended layers that convey the sheen on the feathers, while linear marks made using both the oil pastels and water-soluble pencils convey the texture of both the feathers and the grasses.

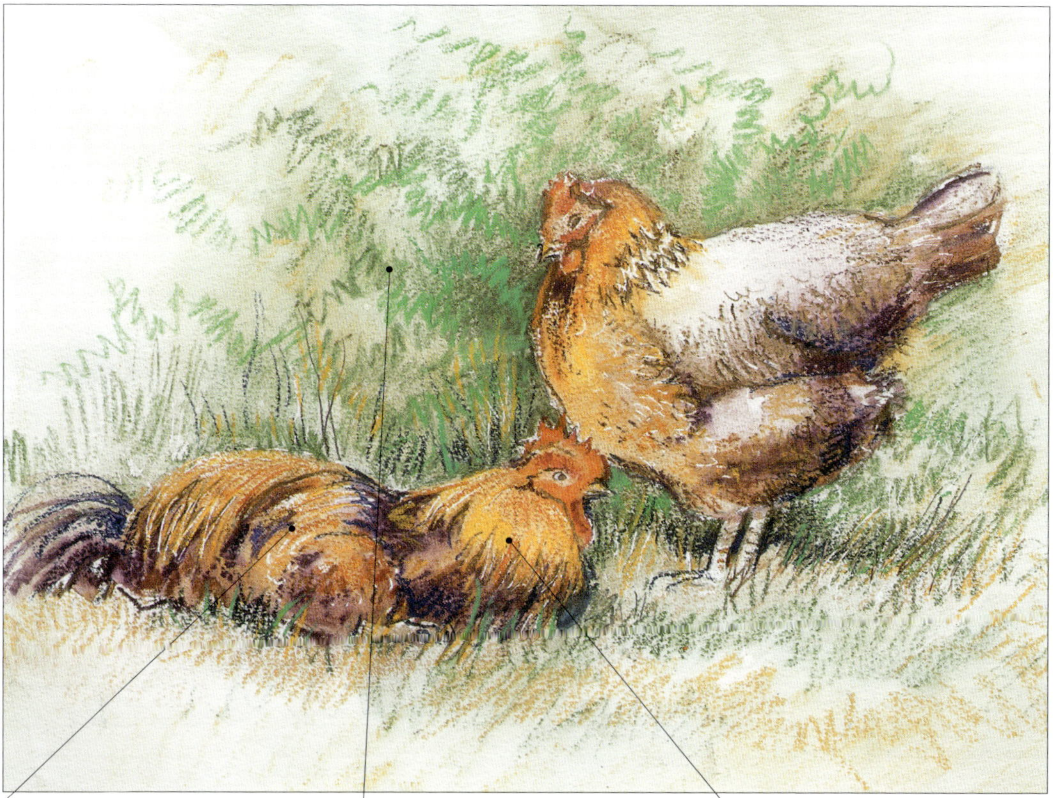

Masking fluid preserves the highlights on the feathers, allowing you to work freely without fear of covering them up.

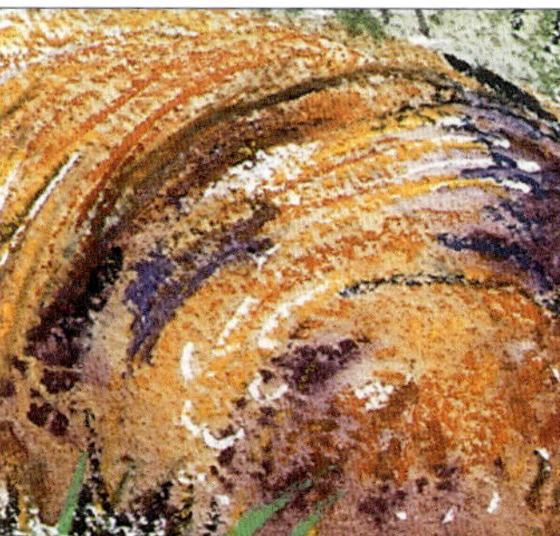

Linear marks overlaid on blended areas of water-soluble oil pastel create the texture of the grasses.

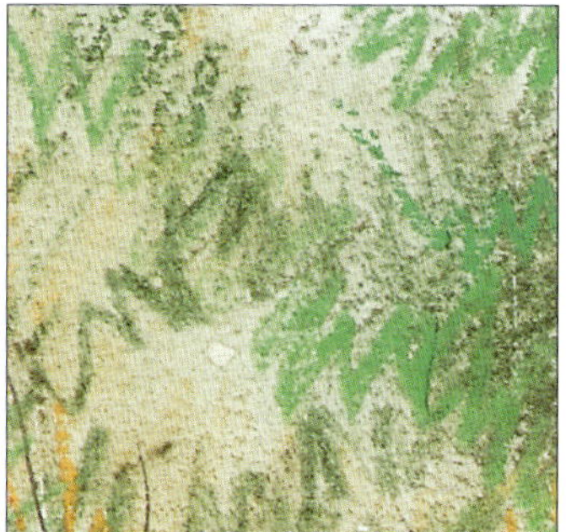

The waxy consistency of the oil pastels helps to create a rich, glossy sheen on the birds' feathers.

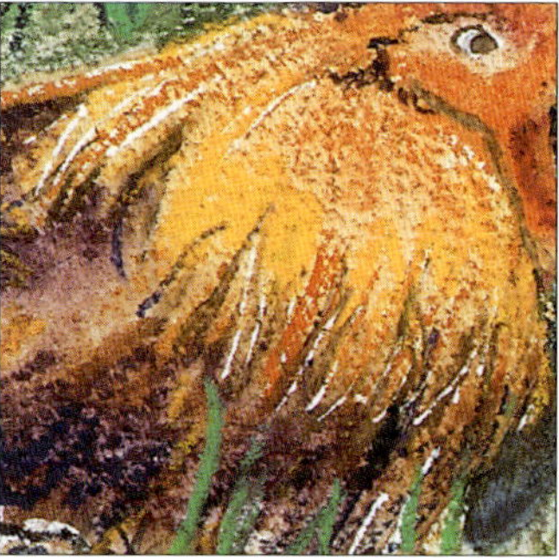

Grandmother and young child

Family portraits, particularly of very young children, are always popular – and a project like this would make a wonderful present for a doting grandmother. Soft pastels capture the skin tones beautifully, and you can smooth out the marks with your fingers or a torchon to create almost imperceptible transitions from one tone to another. Build up the layers gradually. You can spray with fixative in the latter stages to avoid smudging the colours, but be aware that this may dull or darken the colours that you've already put down. Soft pastel is also a lovely medium for drawing hair, as you can put down many different colours within the hair mass to create depth and an attractive sheen. When drawing hair, look at the overall direction of the hair growth.

Young children have very short attention spans and they certainly can't hold the same pose for the time it takes to draw a detailed portrait. You'll be lucky if they sit still for long enough for you to do anything more than a very quick sketch – so working from a photograph is almost certainly your best option. Even then, it's very hard to get a young child to do exactly what you want. If you try to tell them what to do, the chances are you'll either get a very stilted shot, with the child staring grumpily at the camera, or he or she will wriggle and squirm, making an attractive shot virtually impossible.

One simple solution is to make the photo session into a game by pulling faces, clapping your hands, holding up a favourite toy and generally interacting with the child so that he or she forgets all about the camera. Above all, take lots of shots so you have plenty of reference material to choose from. Then you can combine material from several shots – invaluable if you can't get a shot in which both sitters are smiling at the same time.

Materials

- *Pale grey pastel paper*
- *Soft pastels: pinkish beige, white, dark brown, mid-brown, orangey beige, pale yellow, pinkish brown, reddish brown, dark blue, red, pale blue, grey, pale pink, black*

The pose

This is a happy pose, with both child and grandmother smiling broadly. To help them relax for the shot, the photographer got them to make a little game out of clapping their hands together which, in addition to helping them forget that they're having their photo taken, imparts a sense of movement to the pose.

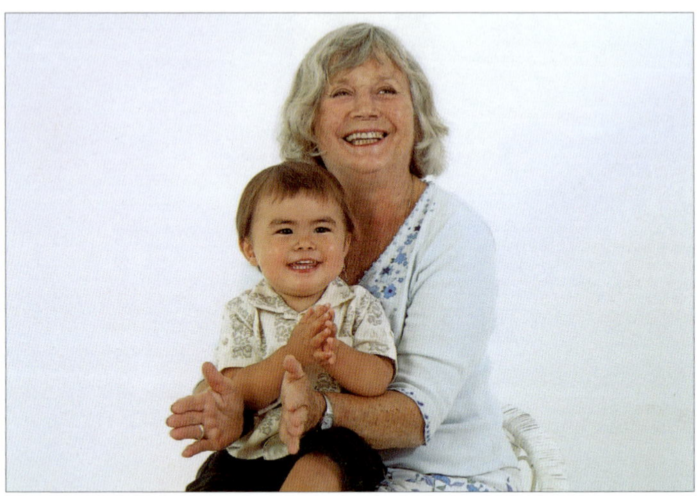

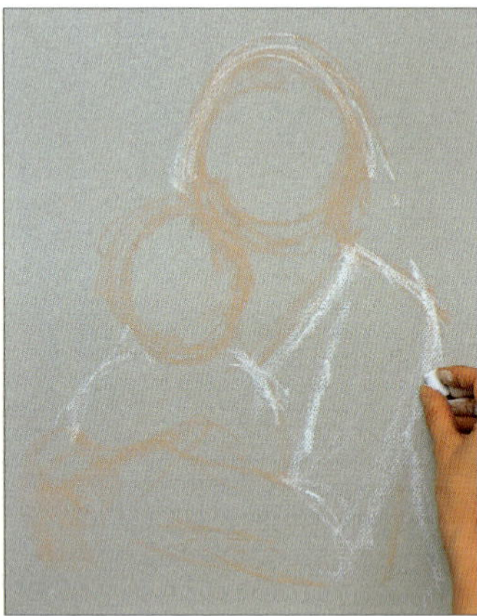

1 Using a pinkish beige soft pastel map out the basic shapes – the heads of the two sitters and the position of the arms. Draw the sleeves and neckline of the grandmother's sweater in white pastel, putting in the most obvious creases in the fabric, and put in the slant of the little boy's shoulders in white, too.

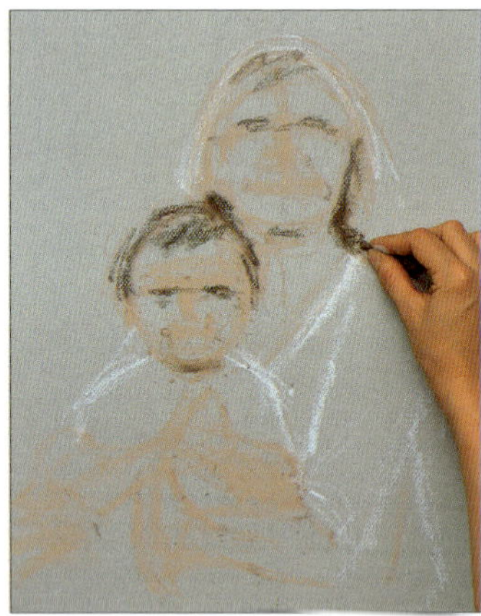

2 Using the pinkish beige pastel again, indicate the position of the facial features by marking a central guideline with the eyes approximately halfway down. The grandmother's head is tilted back, so her eyes are a little above the halfway point. Roughly block in the child's hair and the shadows in the woman's hair in dark brown.

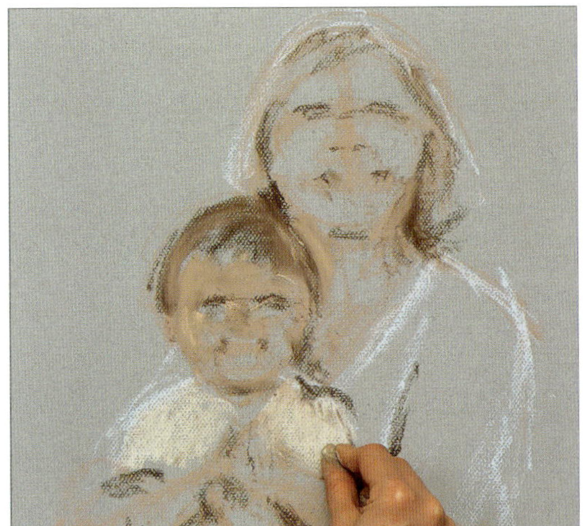

3 Still using the dark brown pastel, put in more of the hair, smudging the pastel marks with your fingers. Indicate the darkest parts of the facial features – the recesses of the eye sockets and nostrils. Apply some flesh tone to the child's face, using mid-brown for the darker parts and a more orange version of the beige used in Step 1 for the lighter parts. Using the side of a pale yellow pastel, roughly block in the base colour of the little boy's shirt.

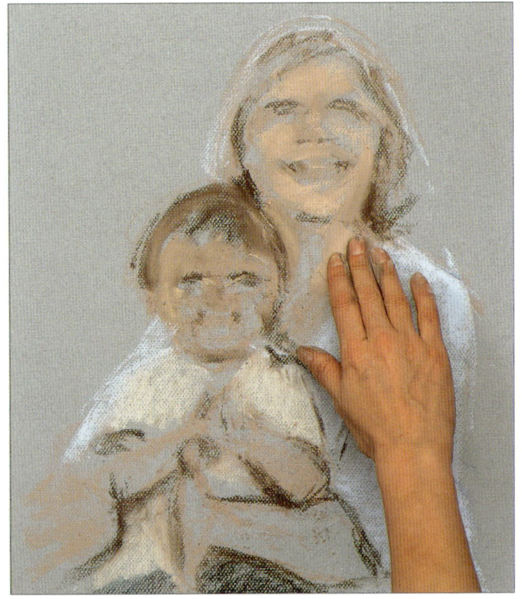

4 Using the side of a white pastel, block in the grandmother's sweater. Apply a pinkish beige to her face and neck, blending the marks with your fingers.

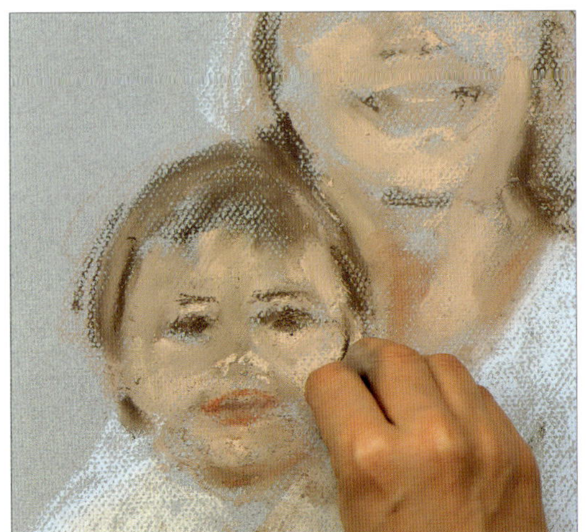

5 The grandmother's neck is slightly warmer in tone than her face. Use a reddish brown for the slightly darker tones in this area, again blending the marks with your fingers. Use the same colour for the child's lips. Using your fingertips, smooth out the mid-brown on the child's face, leaving the orangey beige for the lighter parts. Use a very dark brown for the child's eyebrows and eyes.

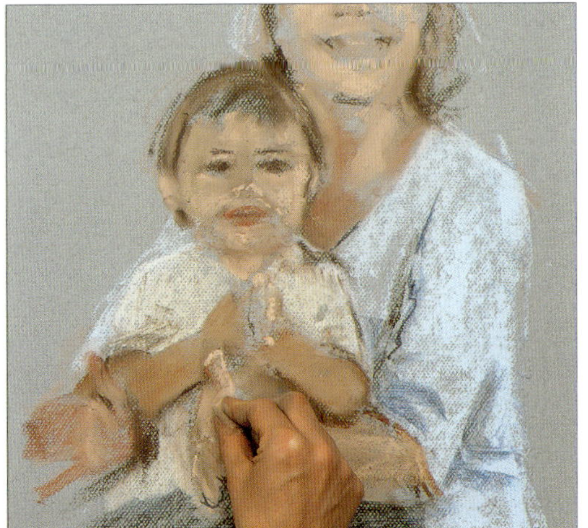

6 Using a dark blue pastel, put in the creases in the fabric of the grandmother's sweater. Block in the arms, using a pinkish brown for the grandmother and a reddish brown for the little boy. Overlay various flesh tones – pinkish beige, orangey beige, red – as appropriate, blending the marks with your fingers. Flesh is not a uniform colour; look closely and you will see warm and cool tones within it.

▶

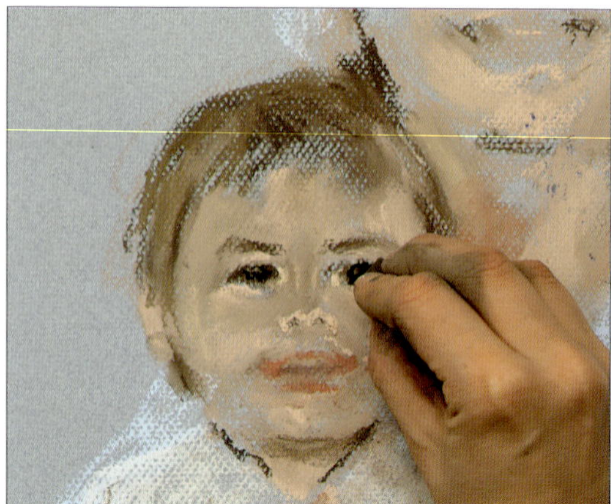

7 With a dark brown pastel, put in the shadow under the child's chin and around the collar of his shirt. Put in some jagged strokes on the hair so that you begin to develop something of the spiky texture. Darken the child's eyes.

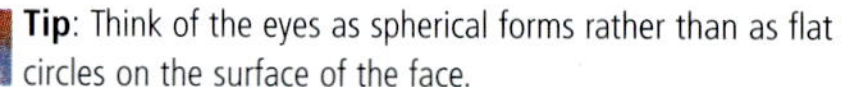

Tip: Think of the eyes as spherical forms rather than as flat circles on the surface of the face.

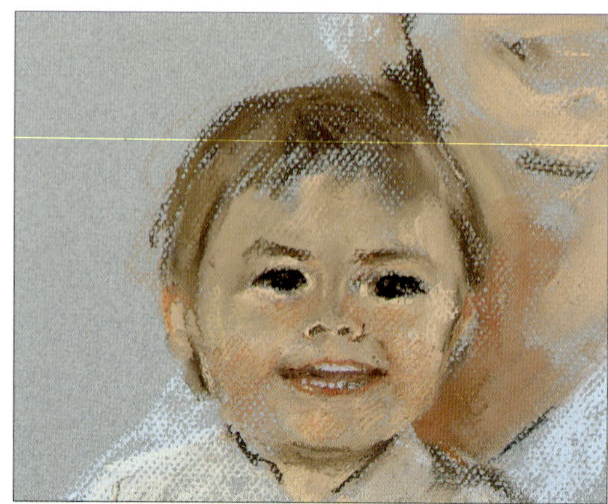

8 Using the same flesh colours as before, continue building up the modelling on the little boy's face. Add some red to the cheeks, blending the marks with your fingers. Like most toddlers, he has a fairly chubby face, so there are no deep recesses under the cheekbones, but with the mix of light and darker-coloured tones the flesh is starting to look more natural. Using the tip of a white pastel and dabbing on small marks, lightly draw his teeth and apply some tiny, glossy highlights to the lips.

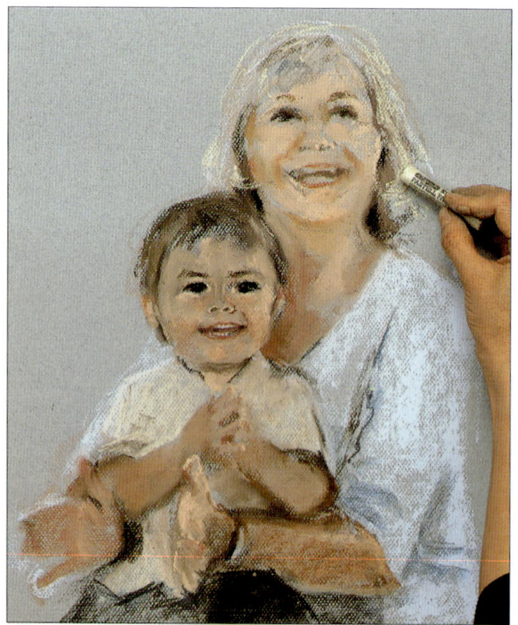

9 Repeat the process of building up modelling on the grandmother's face. Apply pale yellow to her hair.

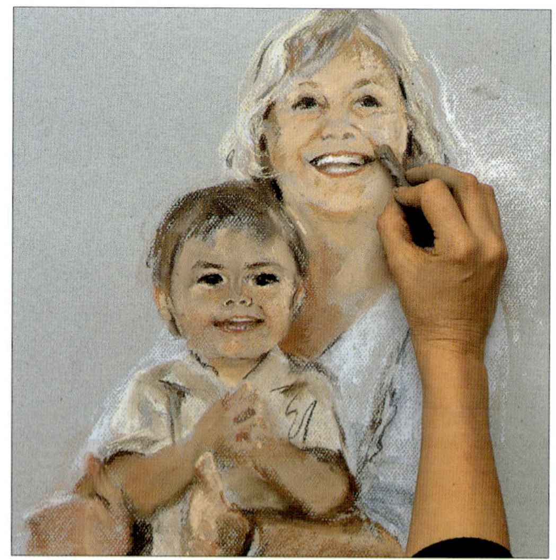

10 Continue working on the hair, putting in browns and greys to get some tonal variation within the hair. Note, too, how the hair casts a slight shadow on her face. Use a brown pastel to draw in the creases in the little boy's shirt. Draw in the crease lines around the grandmother's nose and mouth with a reddish brown pastel.

Assessment time

The expressions and pose have been nicely captured, but in places the skin tones appear as blocks of colour and need to be smoothed out more. A little more modelling is also needed on the faces and hands. The eyes need to sparkle in order for the portrait to come alive.

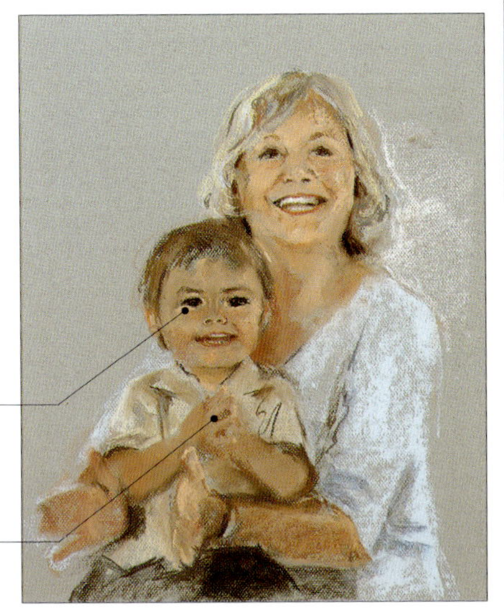

The pupils and irises have been carefully observed, but there is no catchlight to bring the eyes to life.

The child's hands, in particular, appear somewhat formless.

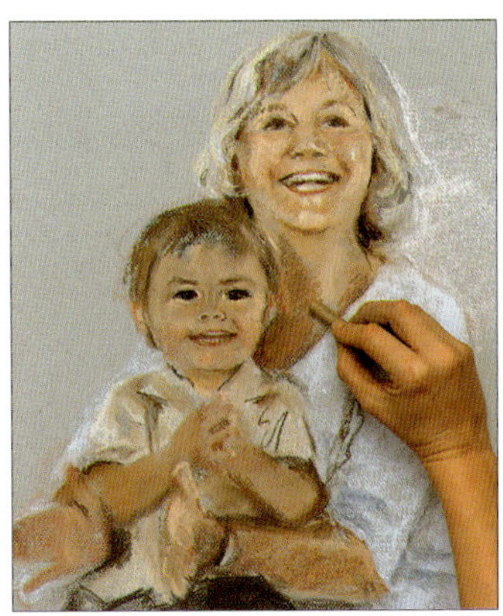

11 Continue the modelling on the grandmother's face and neck, gradually building up the layers and fleshing out the cheeks. Use the same colours and blending techniques as before. The adjustments are relatively minor at this stage.

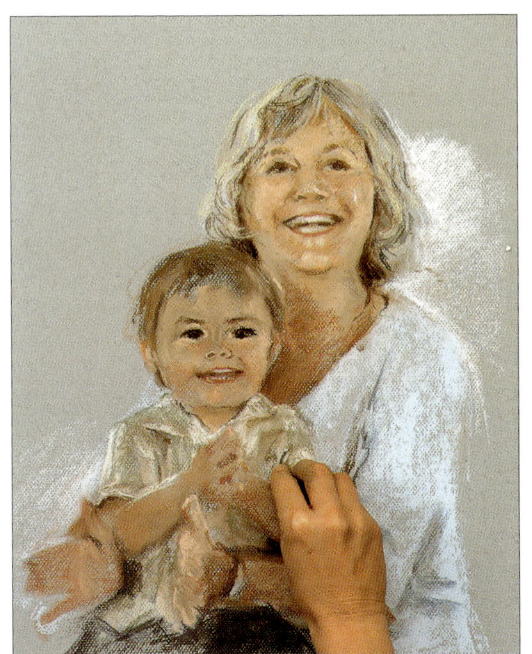

12 Apply more yellow to the boy's shirt, scribbling it in around the dark crease marks. Smudge more brown over the yellow for the stripes in the fabric. A hint of the pattern is sufficient; too much detail would detract from the face.

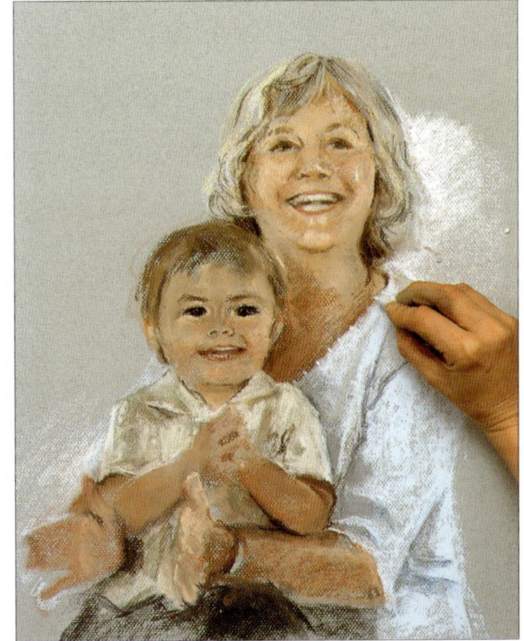

13 Using the side of the pastel, block in the grandmother's sweater with a very pale blue. Reinforce the dark blue applied in Step 6 to define the folds in the fabric. Apply tiny pale-blue dots around the neckline of the sweater.

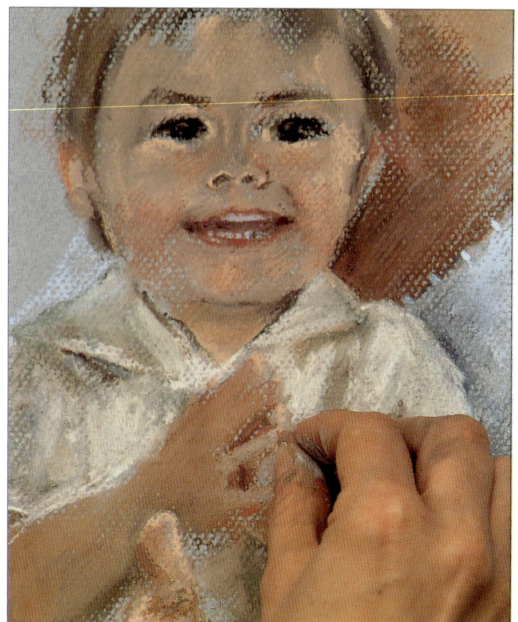

14 Draw the little boy's fingernails with a pale pink pastel and apply light strokes of reddish brown between the fingers to separate them. Like his face, the fingers are fairly chubby so you don't need to put too much detail on them. Blend the marks with your fingertips if necessary to create soft transitions in the flesh tones.

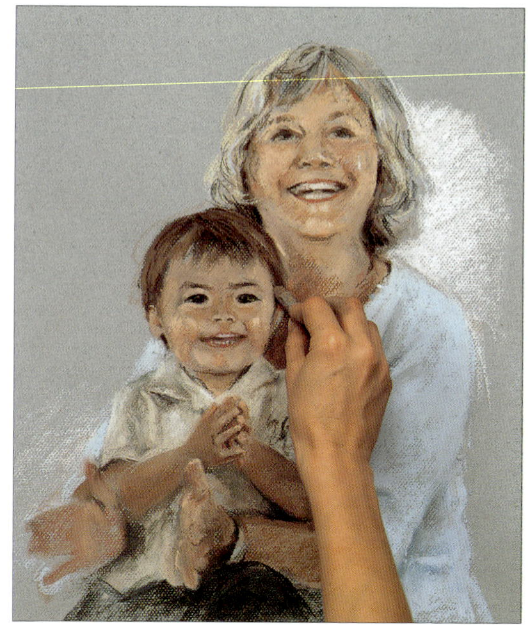

15 If necessary, adjust the flesh tones on the boy's arms and fingers. Here, the artist judged that the face was too dark, so she applied some lighter flesh tones – a very pale orangey beige – to the highlights to redress the balance. Apply a range of browns to his hair to build up the texture and depth of colour.

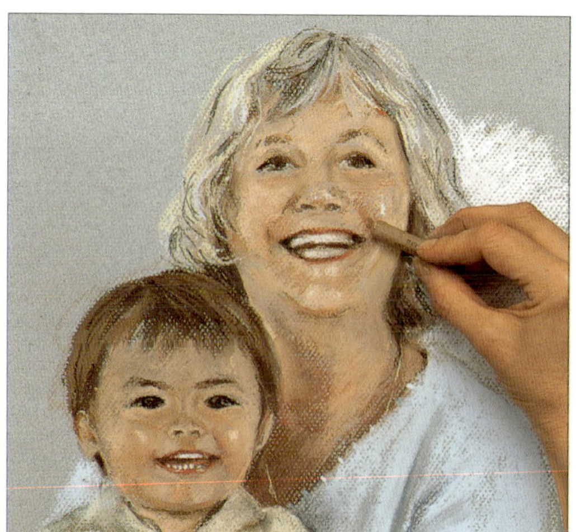

16 Add a thin white line for the grandmother's necklace. Darken her lips and inner mouth; adjust the flesh tones. Redefine the creases around the nose and mouth if necessary.

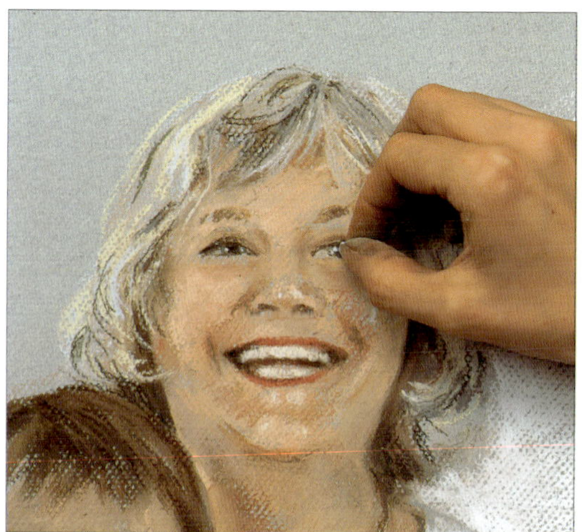

17 The final stage is to put in some detail in the eyes – the black pupils and some tiny dots of white for the catchlights.

The finished drawing

This is a relaxed and informal portrait that captures the sitters' moods and personalities. Using soft pastel has allowed the artist to build up the flesh tones gradually, achieving a convincingly lifelike effect. Leaving the grandmother's hands slightly unfinished helps to create a sense of movement as she claps her hands together – in much the same way as a blurred photograph tells us that a subject is moving.

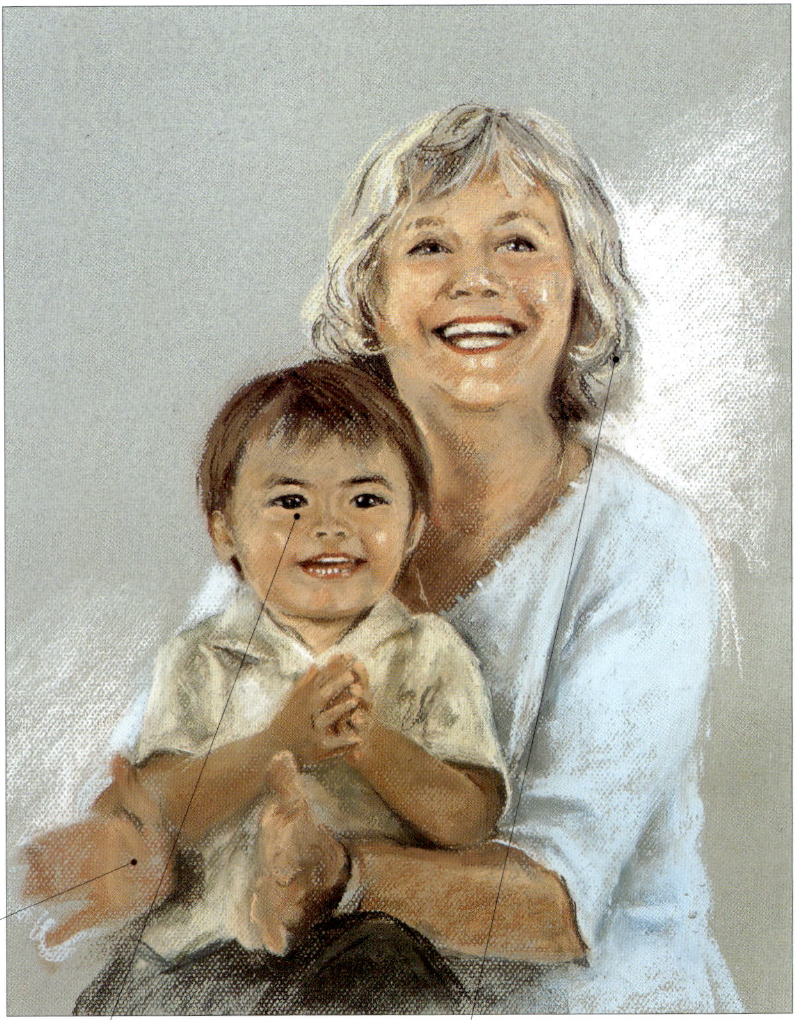

Leaving the hands unfinished creates a sense of movement.

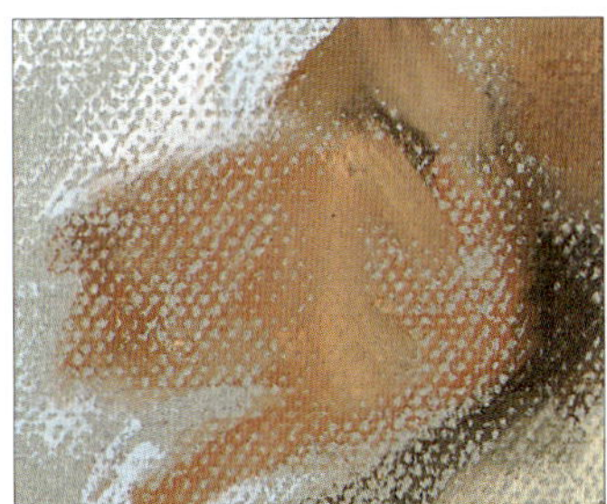

The eyes sparkle: a tiny dot of white is sufficient to bring them alive.

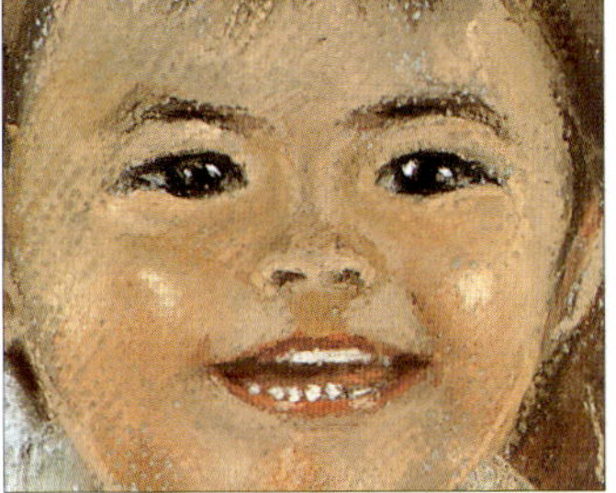

Note how many different tones there are within the hair.

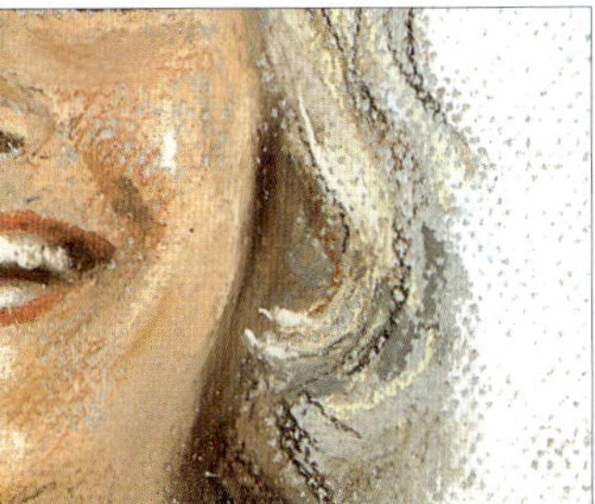

Male portrait

Drawing a portrait can be challenging but, as with all subjects, it helps if you can start by reducing things to basic shapes. Think of the face as an egg shape, with the wider end of the egg as the top of the head and the narrower end representing the chin.

The thing that beginners tend to find most difficult is placing the facial features accurately. Putting in a few guidelines – a central line through the forehead and down to the bottom of the chin, and lines across the face to mark the level of the eyes, nose and mouth – will help with this. As a general rule (although everyone is slightly different), the bottom of the eye socket is halfway down the face and the base of the nose is halfway between the eyes and the chin. The tops of the ears align with the eyebrows and the base of the ears with the base of the nose.

Remember that when the model's head is tilted slightly to one side, as here, you will be able to see more of one side of the face than the other – so the central line will not be centrally positioned. Moreover, as the head turns away, some features may overlap one another while others may be hidden from view altogether. In a three-quarters pose, for example, you will often find that the inner corner of the far eye is obscured by the top of the nose.

Rely on observation, not on your preconceptions about the relative sizes of features and where they sit in relation to one another.

Check your measurements, and then check them again, before you commit pencil to paper.

Materials

- *Drawing paper*
- *Thin charcoal stick*
- *Kneaded eraser*
- *Soft pastels: pewter grey, Naples yellow, dark brown, reddish brown, blue-grey, orangey brown, white*

The pose

This model has a strong profile, which the three-quarters pose (the head turned slightly to one side) shows off to advantage. As any portrait requires the same pose to be held for a long time, make sure your model is comfortable and, if he has to take a break, can resume the same position easily.

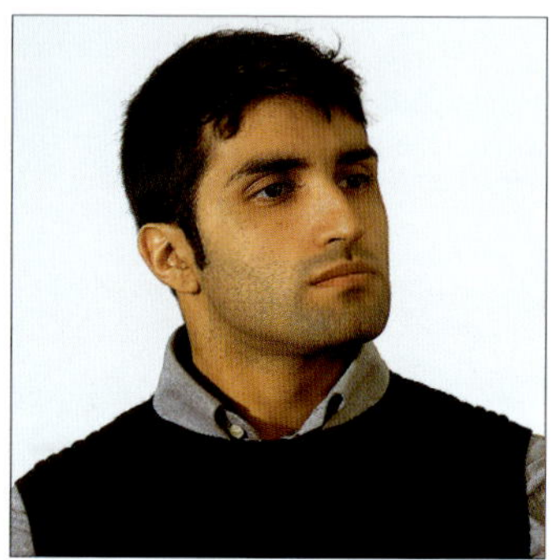

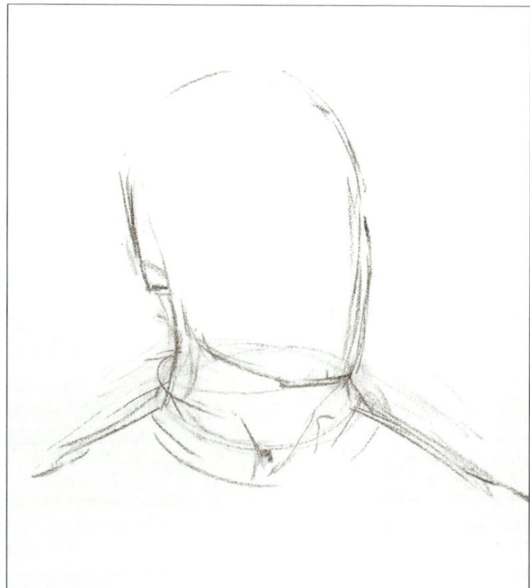

1 Using a thin charcoal stick, map out the head and shoulders. Think of the head as a three-dimensional geometric shape; all too often, beginners make the mistake of drawing a circular or oval outline for the face and forgetting that the head is a solid, three-dimensional form.

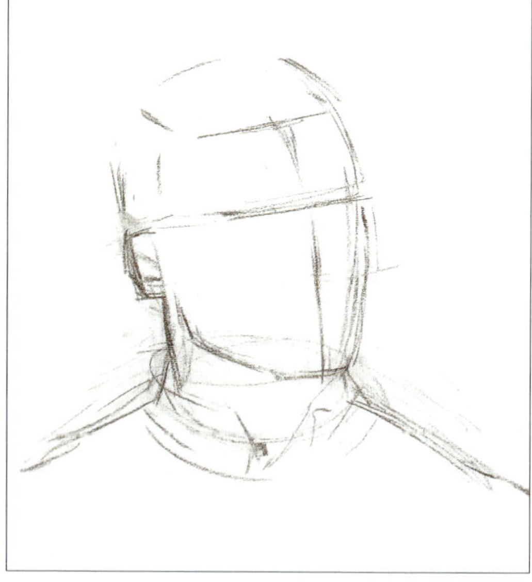

2 Draw a faint line down the centre of the face, from the top of the forehead to the chin. Then draw a line across the face to mark the level of the eyes. (Because of the tilt of the head, this line tilts up slightly here.) This line can also be used to indicate the level of the visible ear.

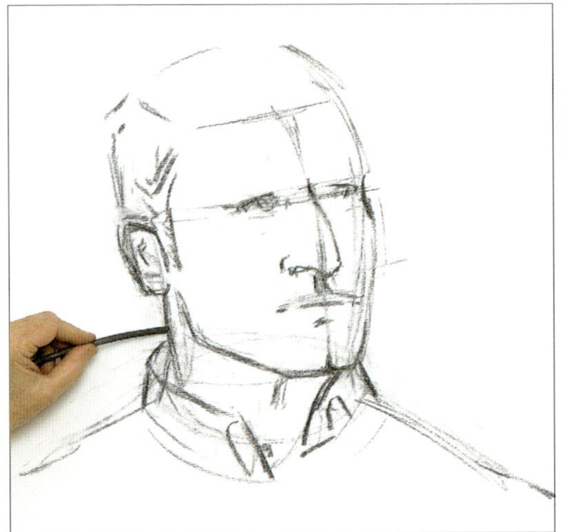

3 Establish the line of the nose, noting where it sits on either side of the central guideline, and the lips. You may find it helps to draw two inverted triangles – one from the outer edge of the eyes down to the tip of the nose and one from the outer edge of the eyes to the chin – as it is easier to judge positions within the triangles than by eye alone. Put in the eyes, remembering that the eyeballs must look rounded.

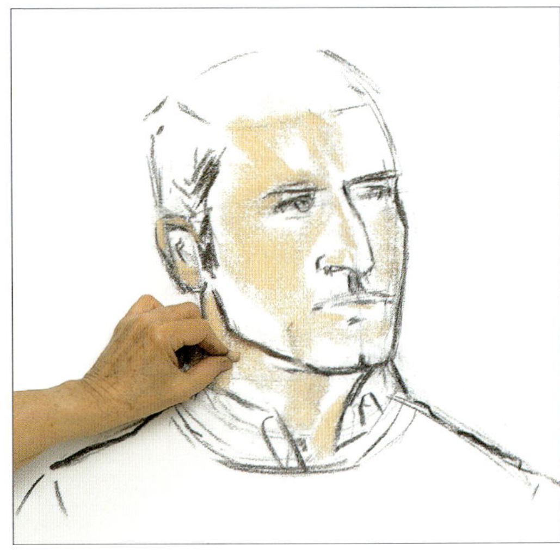

4 Now that you've established the positions of the features, you can erase your guidelines. Strengthen the line of the shoulders and the jaw. Using a pewter grey soft pastel, put in the eyebrows. Block in the lightest area of flesh tone – the cheek, the left of the forehead and the side of the neck – using the side of a Naples yellow pastel, which is a warm yellow well suited to this model's complexion.

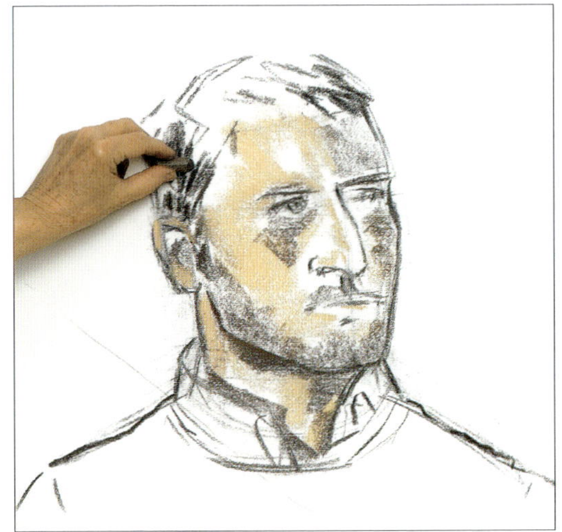

5 Using the side of a pewter grey soft pastel, lightly put in the stubble and shadows on the face and around the inner edge of the shirt collar. Now put in some of the hair, using a very dark brown pastel. Look at how the hair grows over the skull and make your pastel strokes follow the direction in which the hair grows.

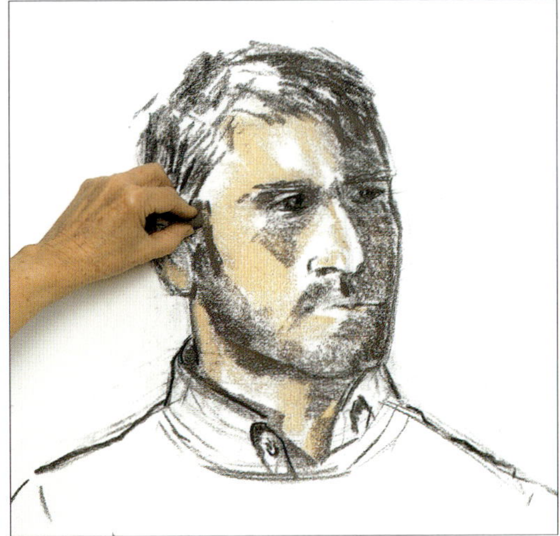

6 Continue working on the hair, noting that it grows in straight lines that go in different directions. Define the eyes more, noting how the lid wraps around the eye and preserving the catchlight – the lights reflected in the pupil. Using the pewter grey pastel again, introduce more tone on the shaded side of the face and in the hair.

▶

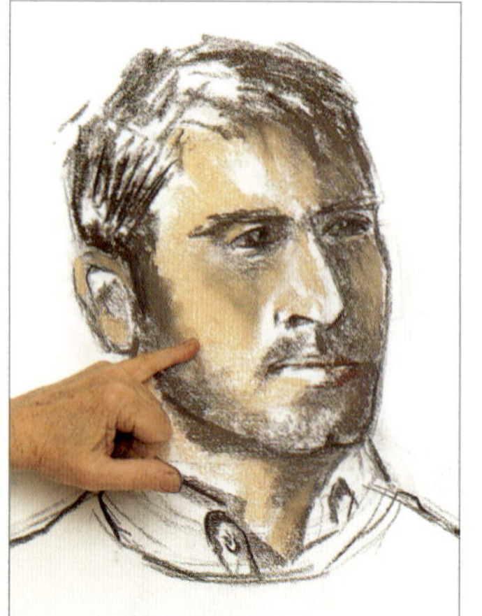

7 Use a dark reddish brown pastel to put in the lips. Use a thin charcoal stick to refine the shape of the nostril, the cleft in the chin and the overall line of the nose against the cheek. Using your fingertips, gently blend the grey charcoal on the areas of hair and stubble that are not quite as dark.

Assessment time

All the facial features are in place but more modelling is needed – particularly on the cheekbones as the shadows are not strong enough to reveal their form.

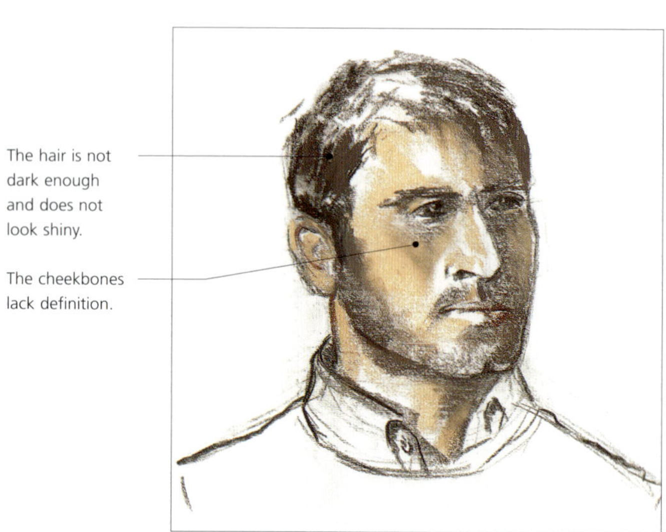

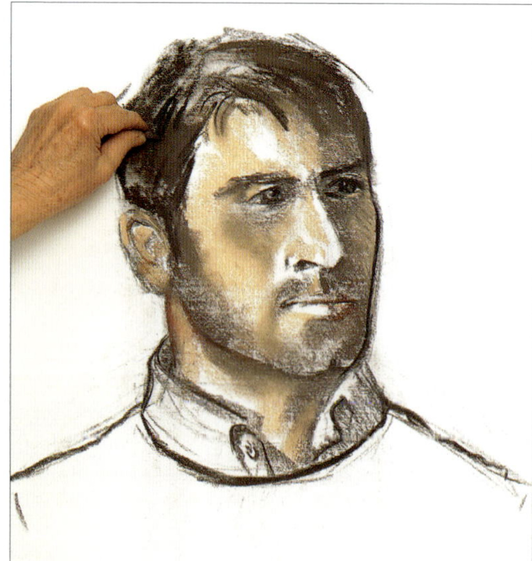

8 Roughly scribble in the hair, using a dark brown pastel. Remember to leave some areas lighter to show where the highlights fall and create a sheen on the hair. Lightly blend the marks with your fingertips, following the direction in which the hair grows.

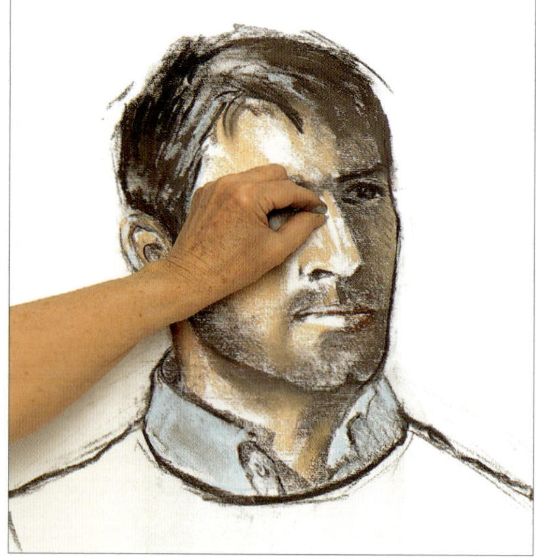

9 Using a blue-grey pastel, hatch and blend the blue collar of the shirt. Use the same colour on the hair to give a slight blue-black sheen. Shape the nose, using an orangey brown pastel for the dark, shaded parts and the tip of a white pastel for the highlights.

The finished drawing

A strong profile is enhanced by the side lighting, which throws one side of the face into shadow. Although only a limited range of pastel colours was used, subtle blending captures the evenly coloured skin tones very well. The same technique creates the modelling on the face. Here, the artist chose not to colour in the model's sweater as she wanted to concentrate the viewer's attention on his face, but you could put in more colour if you wish.

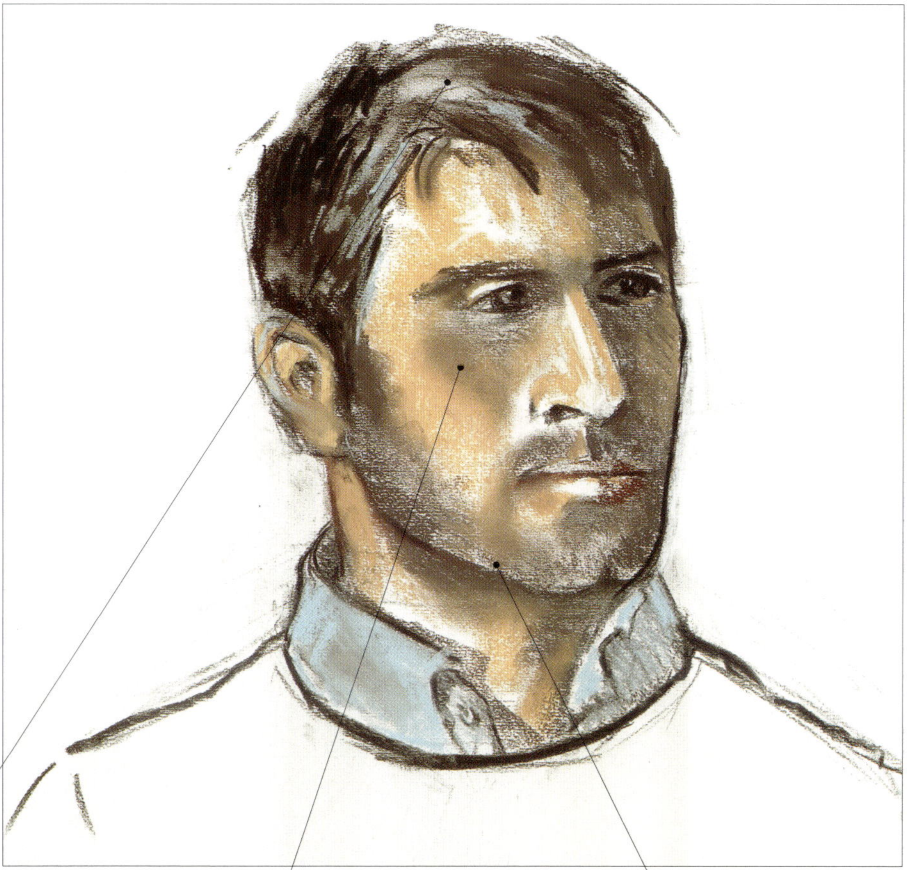

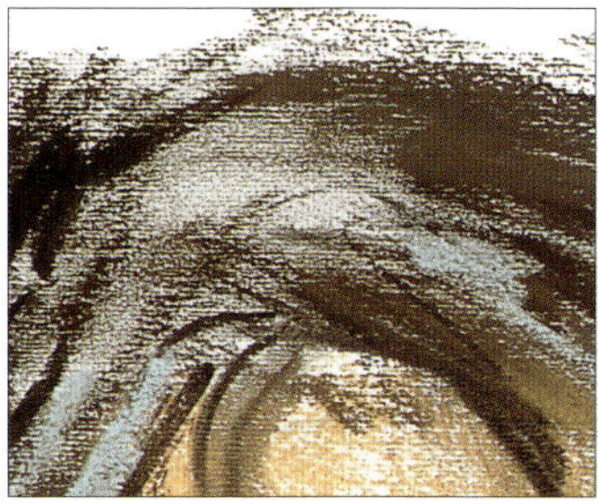

Touches of blue-grey give the hair a smooth, glossy sheen.

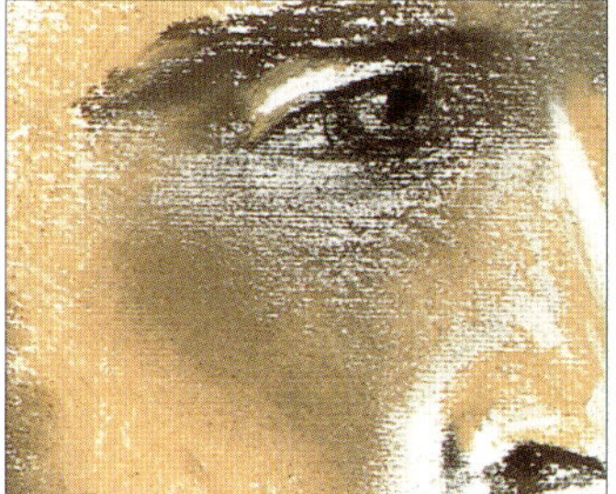

Blended pastel marks create shadows on the cheeks and neck and under the chin.

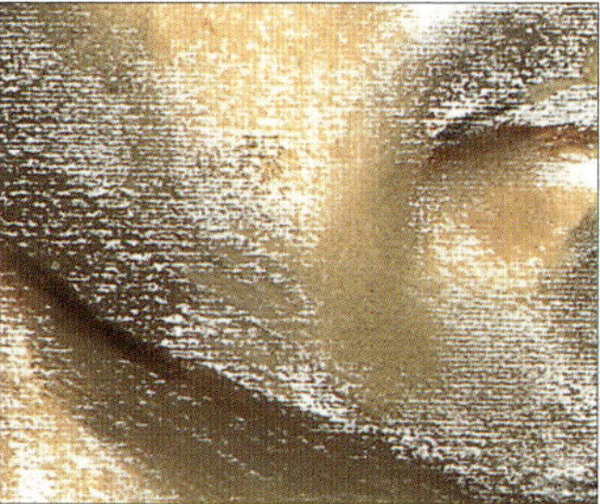

Linear charcoal work is used to define the jawline.

Dancing couple

When drawing a moving subject, it's helpful to take a photograph to use as reference. You have two options. You can use a fast shutter speed to 'freeze' the action and risk losing the sense of movement that you wanted to capture. Alternatively, you can use a slower shutter speed so that there is some blur in the photo – but then you risk not being able to see all the detail as clearly as you would like. Here the artist wanted to see the detail clearly and elected to freeze the movement in the reference photo.

The challenge in this scenario is how to create that all-important sense of movement. Sometimes, even when the action is frozen, we know that the subject must be moving because the 'pose' itself is so precarious that we know it simply couldn't be held for more than a second or two. (Think, for example, of a ballerina in mid-pirouette.) Here the dancers have both feet touching the ground and the movement is not obvious at first glance, so you need to find other ways of conveying a sense of movement.

In this drawing the artist used two techniques to give a sense of movement: a 'ghost' image, indicating the position from which the limbs have just moved, and curved lines in the background, which follow the contours of the bodies. The same techniques could be applied just as well to other moving objects, for instance a horse racing at full stretch, a rally car speeding past on a country road, or any sporting action.

Manikin
Also called a lay figure, a manikin (available from art supply stores), is a very handy tool for working out the lines of a pose. Use it to help you to work out the 'ghost' image.

Materials
- *Pastel paper*
- *HB pencil*
- *Pastel pencils: brown, spectrum orange, black, light sepia, pale brown, red, orange, pale blue, cream or pale yellow, red-brown*

The pose
Although the action has been 'frozen' in this photo, the woman's flowing hair and the fact that the right foot of both dancers is in the process of lifting off the ground indicate that they are, in fact, moving.

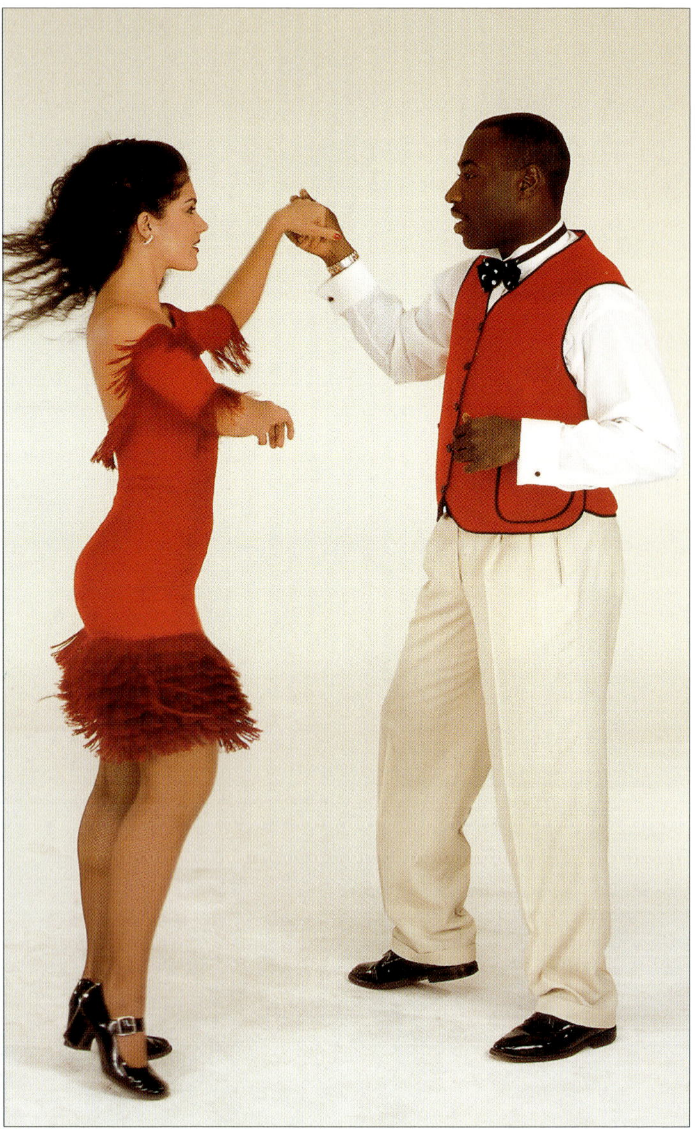

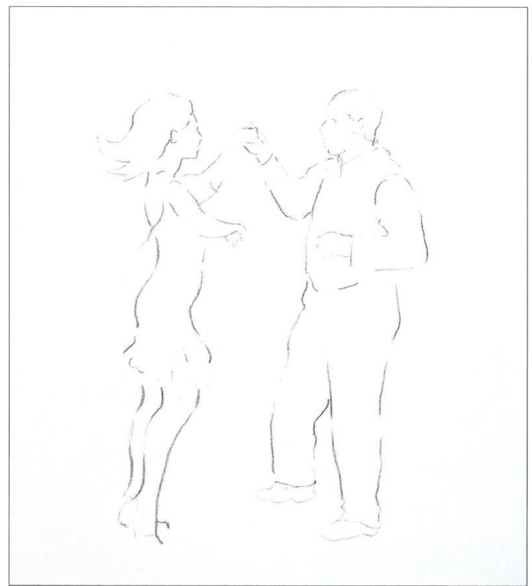

1 Sketch the scene, using an HB pencil. Imagine guidelines running across and down the image to help you: the man's left hand, for example, is roughly in line with his right heel.

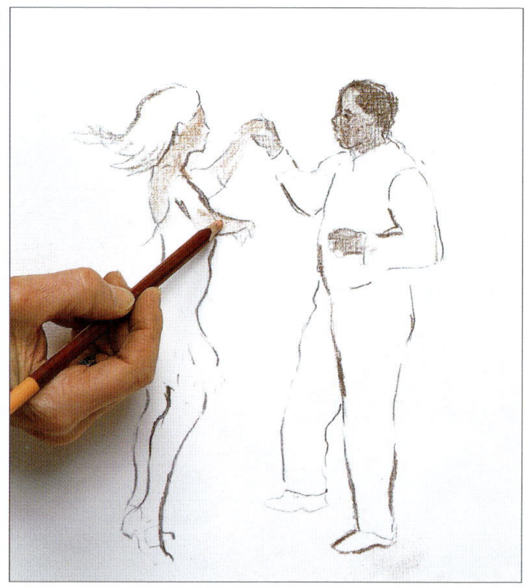

2 Block in the man's flesh tones and hair in brown and emphasize the strongest lines of the pose. Using spectrum orange, block in the woman's flesh tones.

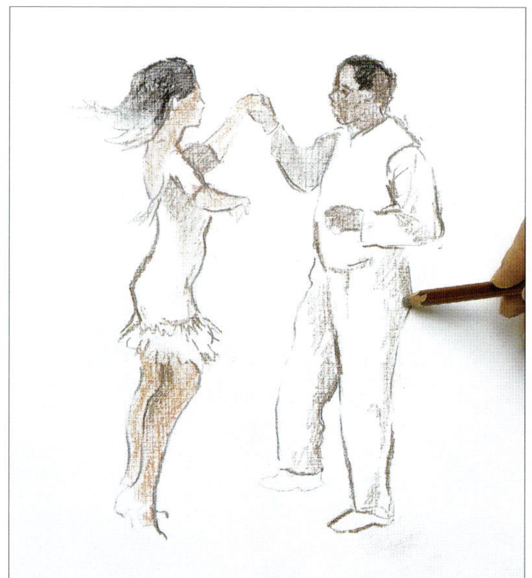

3 Block in the hair of both dancers in black. For the shaded parts of the man's trousers and shirt and the woman's dress, apply light sepia. Use the same colour to draw the frill around the bottom of her dress.

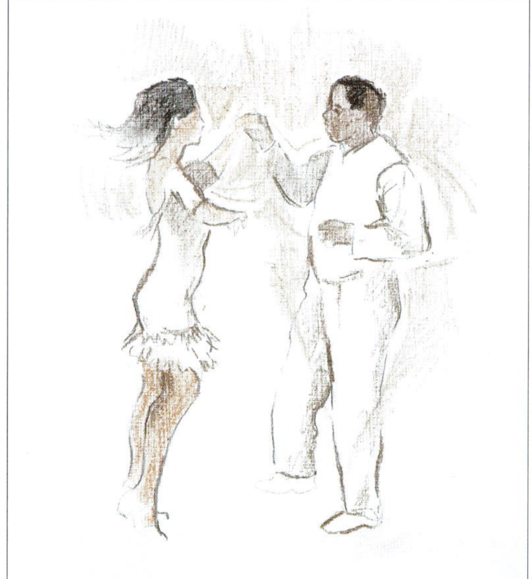

4 Using the side of a pale brown pastel pencil, block in the background. Begin to put in stronger, curved lines in the background to emphasize the movement of the figures, echoing the curves of the moving arms.

Assessment time
With the same pale brown pencil, put in a 'ghost' image of the moving legs and arms. This, along with the curved lines in the background which echo the shape of the woman's back, helps to give an impression of movement. Now that the main lines of the drawing have been established, you can begin to refine the detail and add some colour to bring the drawing to life.

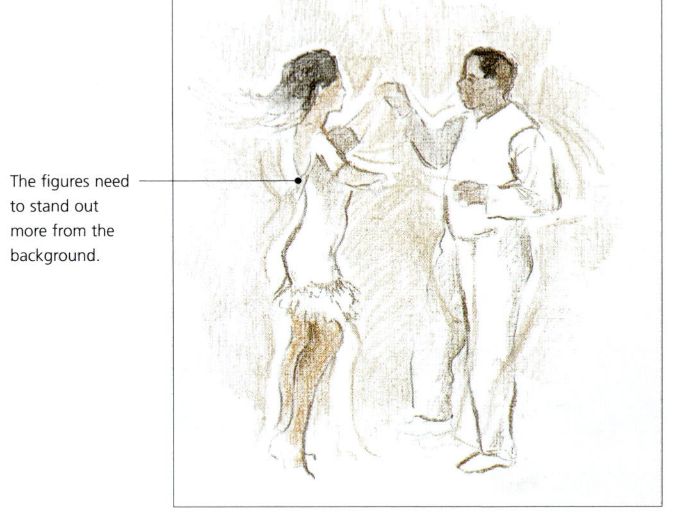

The figures need to stand out more from the background.

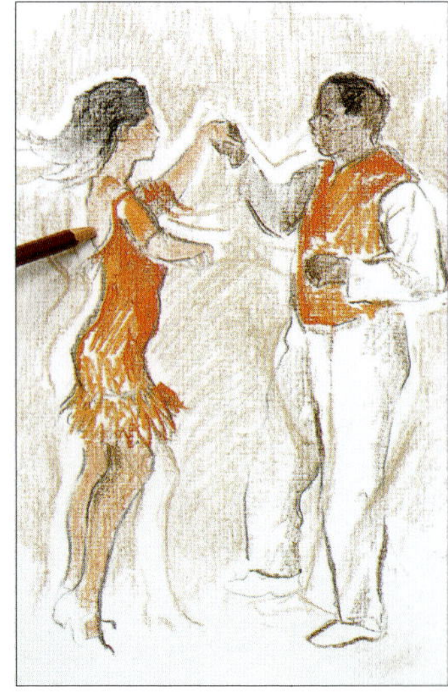

5 Using the same colours as before, darken the flesh tones so that the figures stand out from the background. Block in the woman's dress and the man's waistcoat in red overlaid with orange. (This optical mix of two colours creates a much more lively and interesting effect than a solid application of a single colour.)

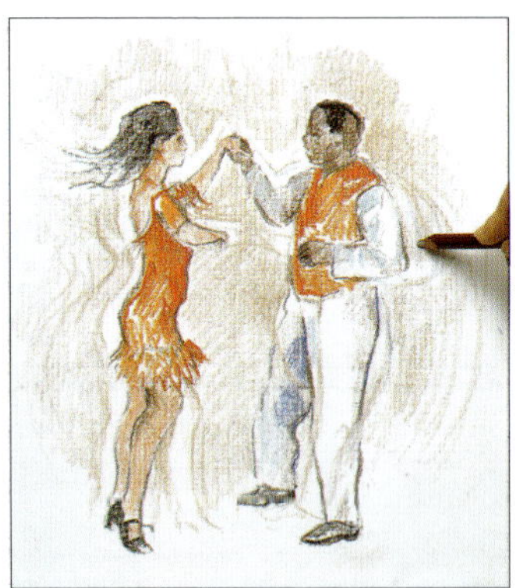

6 Using a very pale blue pencil, put in the creases in the man's shirtsleeve and shade his right leg. Block in the shoes in black, leaving the highlights. Working around the 'ghost' image, put in some stronger curved lines that follow the contours of the bodies to enhance the sense of movement.

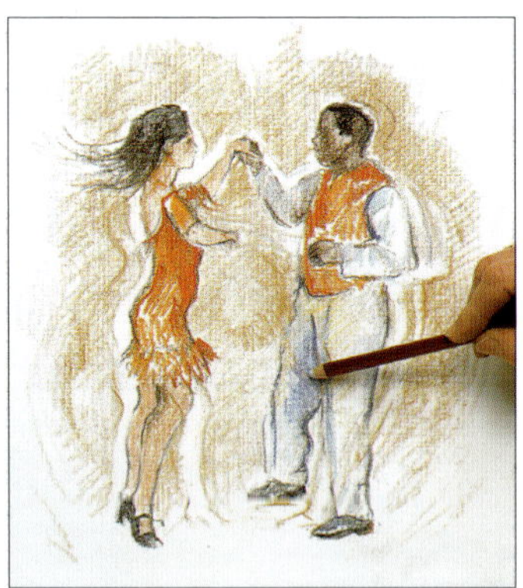

7 Darken the creases on the trousers and go over the trousers very lightly with a cream or very pale yellow pastel pencil. (Leaving the paper white would look too stark.) Draw the woman's hair, which is streaming out behind her as she moves, with quick flicks of a black pastel pencil.

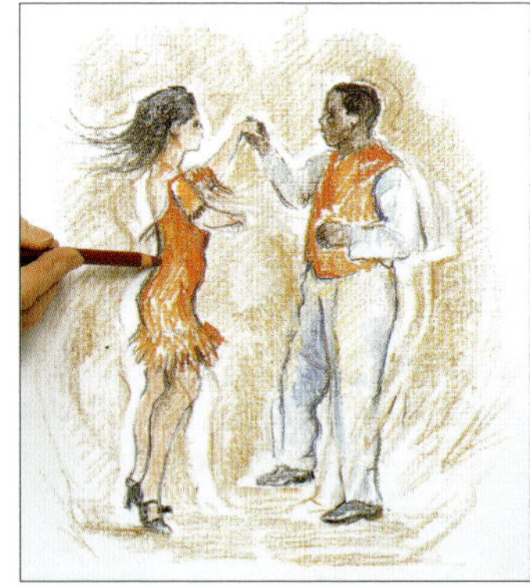

8 Using horizontal marks, put in the floor. It is on a different plane to the background and using horizontal, rather than vertical, strokes helps to make this clear. Using a red-brown pencil, sharpen the edges of the figures – the hands, faces, and the line of the woman's body and legs.

The finished drawing
The sense of movement in this drawing comes as much from the way the background has been handled as from the way the dancing couple has been drawn. The pastel pencil marks are light and free, which gives the drawing a feeling of energy.

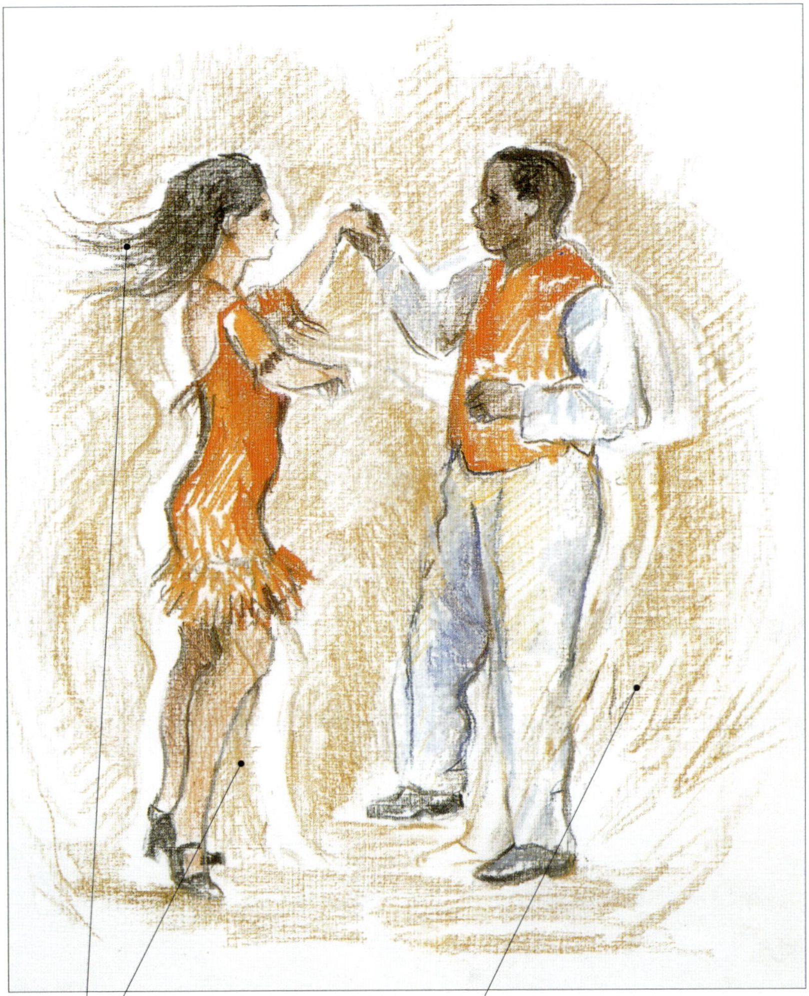

The hair streams out, making it obvious that the dancers are moving quickly.

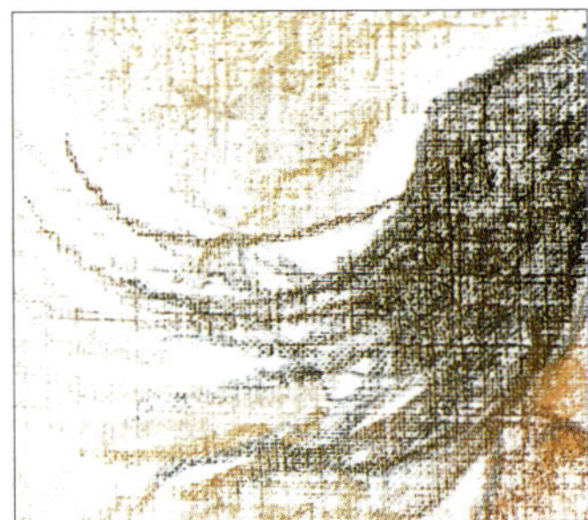

The 'ghost' images imply that this is the position the figure has just moved from.

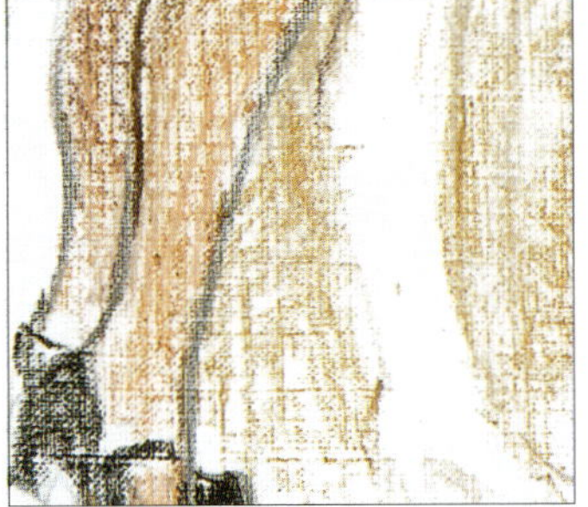

Curved pencil strokes in the background also help to imply movement.

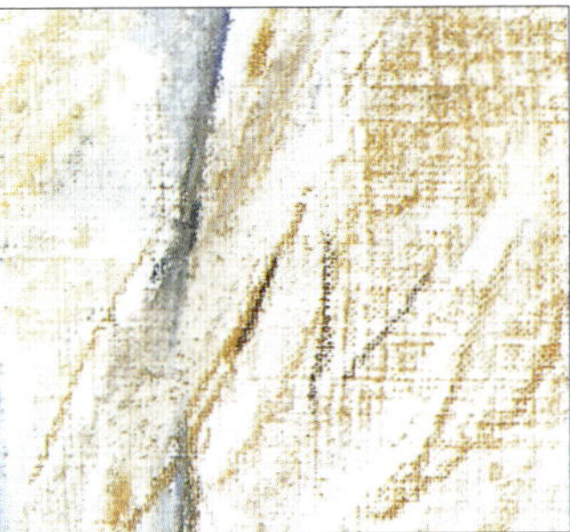

Character portrait

As a drawing medium, pastel sticks have a great directness; the artist's hand is in almost direct contact with the support, and the fingers themselves are often used to move and blend the pigment. Colour changes can be made swiftly as all the blending and mixing of colours is made on the work itself. This aspect of pastels can give rise to powerful works of spontaneity and immediacy, such as this remarkable portrait of great character and atmosphere. By building up the colours thickly, in a highly painterly technique, the artist has achieved an almost sculptural feeling of weight and solidity. For this demonstration he has worked on grey Mi-Teintes paper, using the 'right' side – that is, the more heavily textured one.

Materials

- *Light grey pastel paper*
- *Soft pastels: dark brown, white,reddish-brown, warm yellow, black*

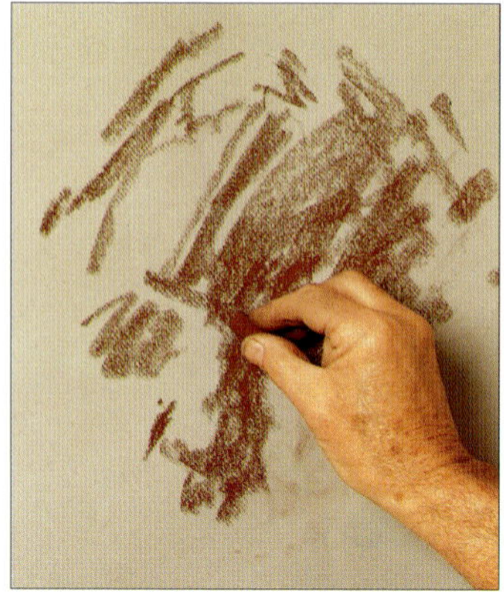

1 Begin the portrait in monochrome to provide a basis for the shadowed areas of the skin tones. The marks are heavily applied, appearing almost as random scribbles, but already the forms of the face are beginning to emerge.

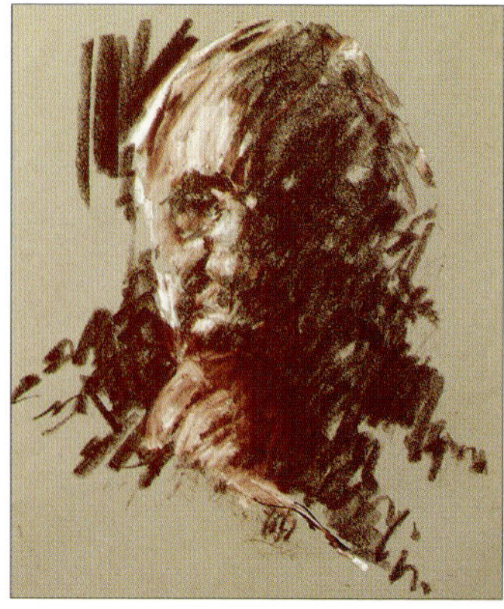

2 The monochrome underdrawing, which is now complete, will function as a basic tonal structure on which to build up the colours. This method is suitable only for work that uses a limited palette of relatively sombre colours.

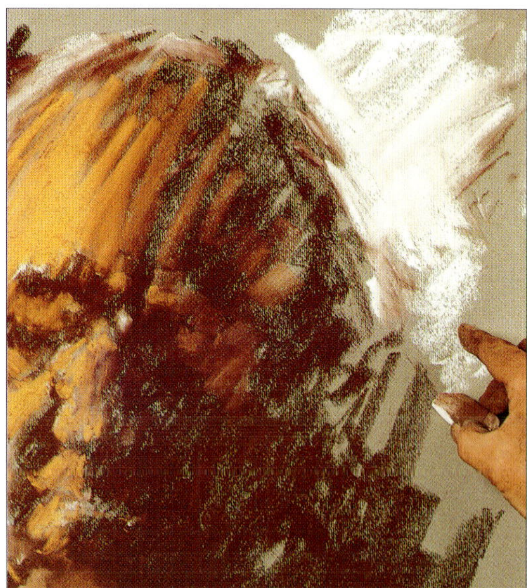

3 The shadowed side of the head will be considerably darkened as the work progresses, so lightening the background first enables you to judge the strength of colour needed. Tonal modelling is particularly important, and one tone must be continually assessed against another.

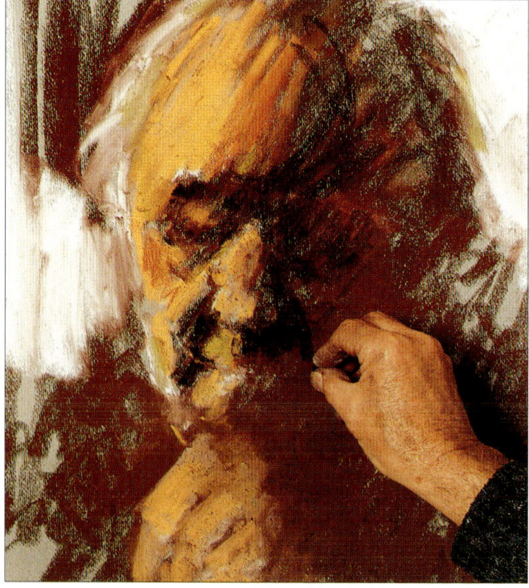

4 Now work blacks and darker browns over and into the red-brown underdrawing to build up the forms of the head. Short lengths of thick, soft-pastel sticks produce broad strokes and enable you to push the edges of the colours together as they are applied.

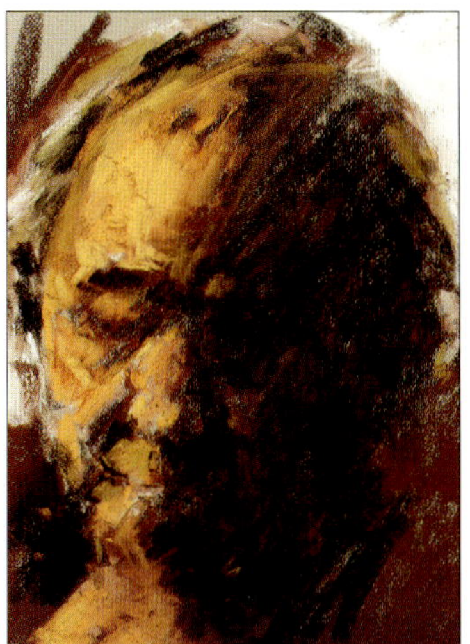

5 With the darker tones established, further work has been done on the lit side of the face. Notice that the pastel is much thicker here; this method is similar to that seen in many oil paintings, where the paint is thickest in the highlight areas, making them stand out from the shadows.

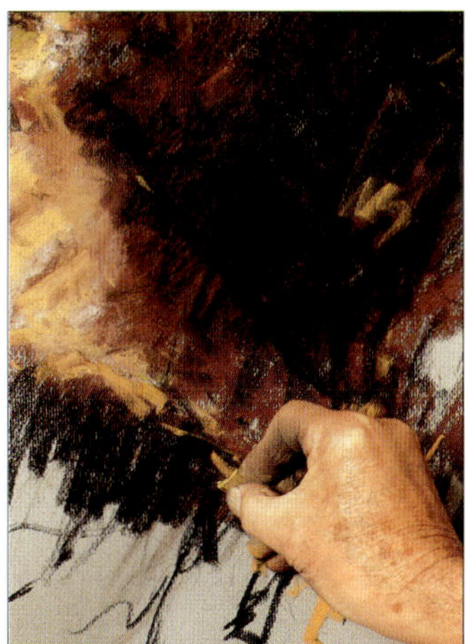

6 The artist had originally planned a hand and wrist as part of the composition (see step 2), and now gives some additional definition to this area. However, he then decided to make a dramatic change, eradicating the hand completely, as you can see in the finished piece.

The finished work

A complete transformation has now taken place – the hand has been painted out with heavy applications of dark green and red-brown, and suggestions of detail drawn in with an edge of white pastel (notice what fine lines can be produced in this way). The lighter colours below the chin, which suggest a shirt or cravat, balance the head much better than did the hand, and the composition is altogether more satisfactory.

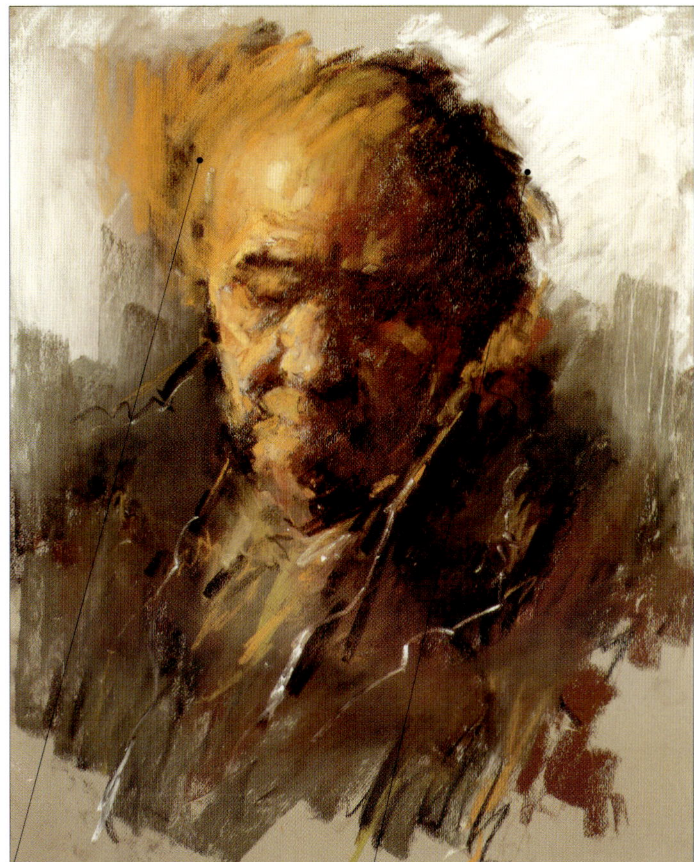

The lit side of the face emerges subtly from a background of similar tone.

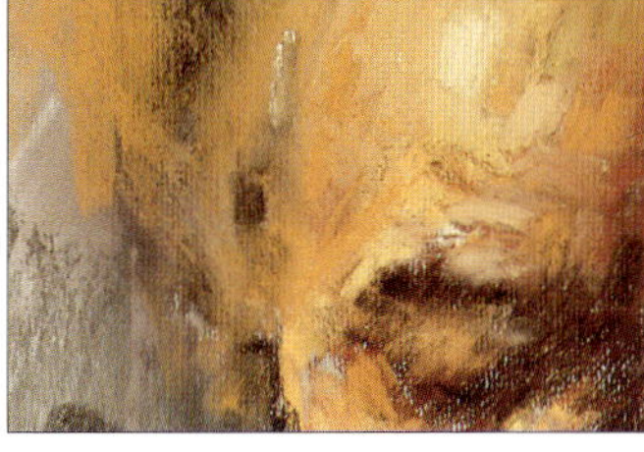

The hair is suggested by swift strokes against the pale background.

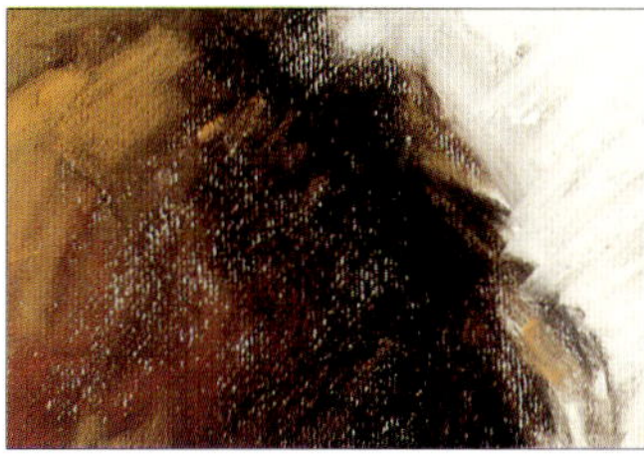

Female nude

Pastel is both a drawing and a painting medium, depending on how it is used, and this nude study exploits its linear qualities, building up colours with light layers of hatching and crosshatching so that each line remains distinct. This avoids the techniques that are most closely associated with pastel painting, such as side strokes, blending and overlaying layers of thick, solid colour.

Materials

- *Light brown pastel paper*
- *Compressed charcoal stick*
- *Soft pastels: white, light blue, purple, soft yellow, brown, reddish-brown, crimson, ultramarine*

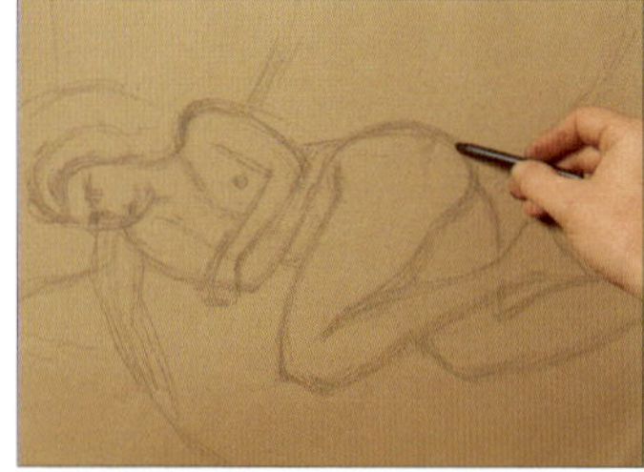

1 Because pastels cannot easily be erased it is important to begin with an accurate drawing. Use a stick of compressed charcoal for this; pencil should not be used for pastel work, as the slight greasiness of the graphite repels the pastel colour.

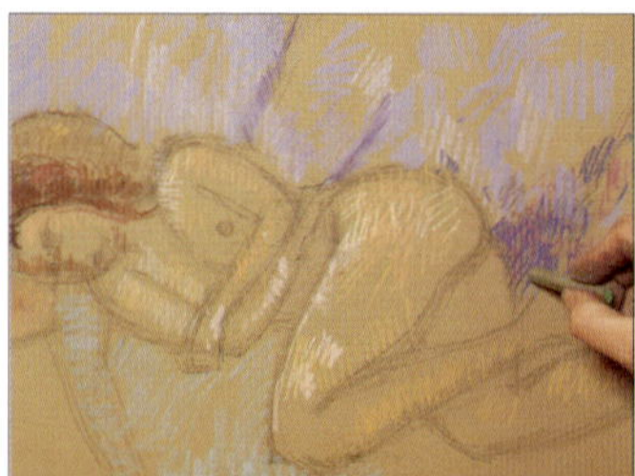

2 Begin by placing small areas of colour all over the picture, relating the rich background colours to the subtler flesh tints. The coloured paper provides a middle tone, making it easier to work up to the highlights and down to the darks.

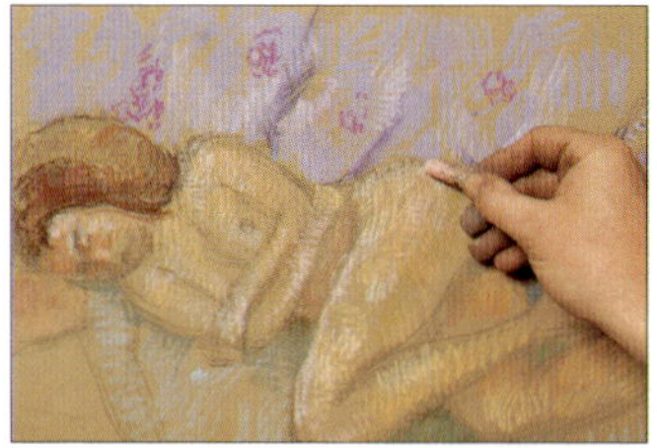

3 For this method of hatching and crosshatching, hold the pastel stick lightly and take care to vary the angle of the lines so that they do not all go in the same direction but follow the form of the body.

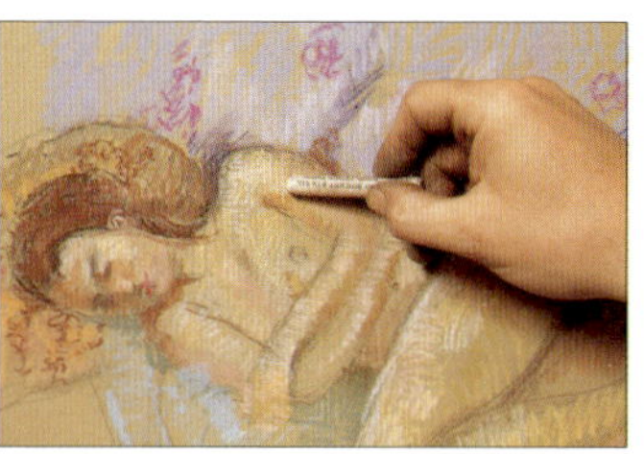

4 Build up the colours gradually, always allowing the first colours to show through succeeding applications. This creates a network of lines and marks that gives a livelier effect than smooth blends.

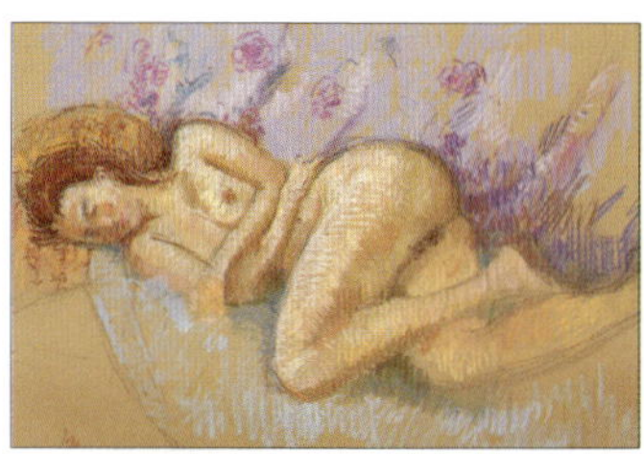

5 The light greenish-brown of the paper, which will not be completely covered, is very close to the colour of the shadows on the flesh. Build up the modelling with strong light and shadow areas.

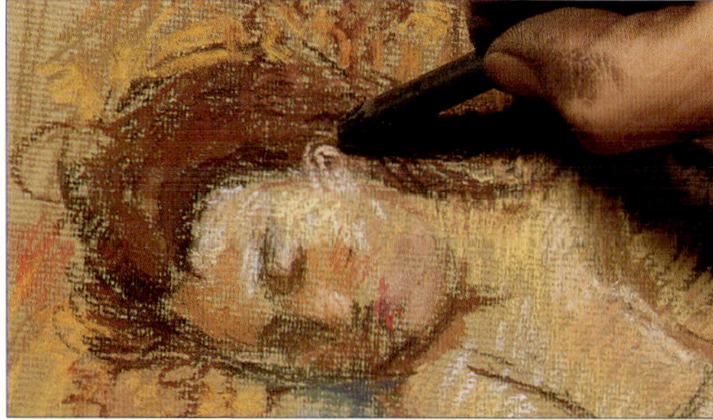

6 Use compressed charcoal again to darken and define areas of the hair and to sharpen up the drawing. Charcoal mixes well with pastel, and can be a better choice than black pastel, which makes solid and sometimes over-assertive black lines.

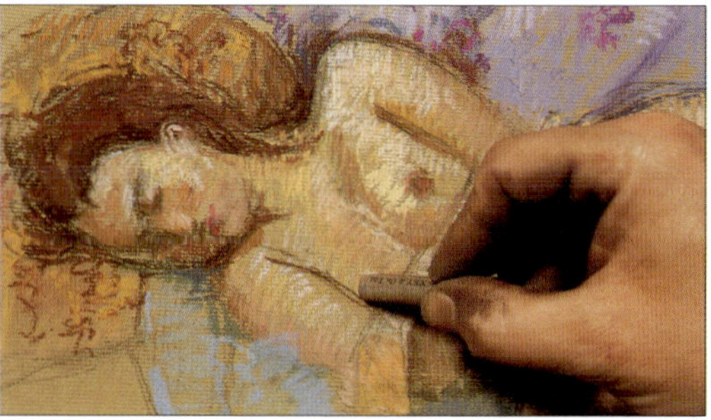

7 Continue to build up the darker colours and define details, using brown pastel lightly to draw the side of the arm. On the shoulder, some of the original charcoal drawing is still visible: it can be strengthened by curving lines of reddish-brown pastel behind it.

The finished drawing

The artist has not attempted to treat the background or foreground in detail, concentrating instead on the rich, golden colours of the body. This vignetting method, in which the focal point of the picture is emphasized by allowing the surrounding colours to merge gently into the toned paper, is a traditional pastel-drawing technique.

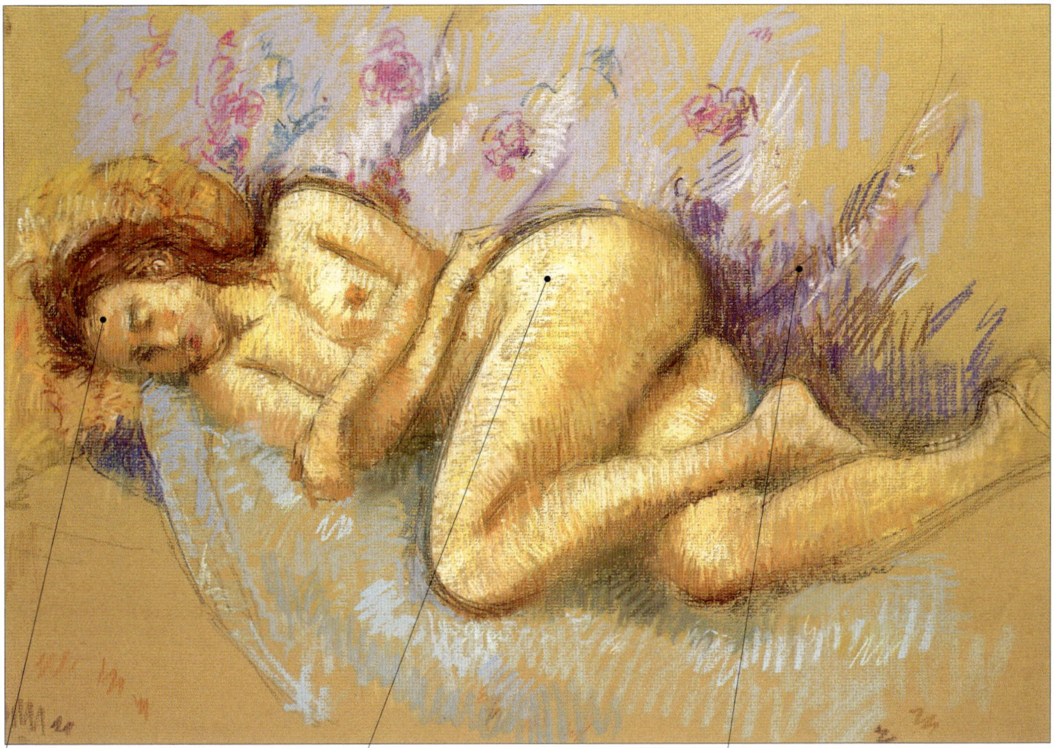

Delicate charcoal strokes are used to define the details of the face and hair.

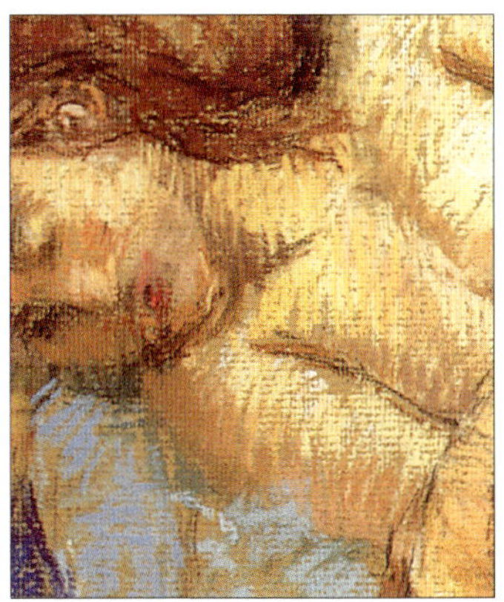

The crosshatching lines follow the contours of the body to bring out the three-dimensional form.

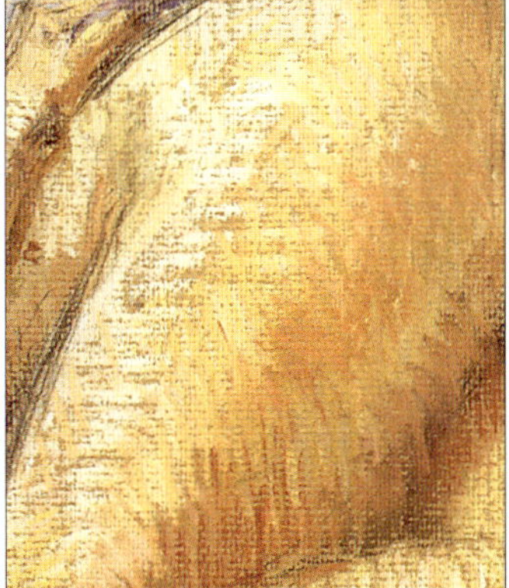

The background is only vaguely suggested around the figure, with much looser line work and much of the paper left exposed.

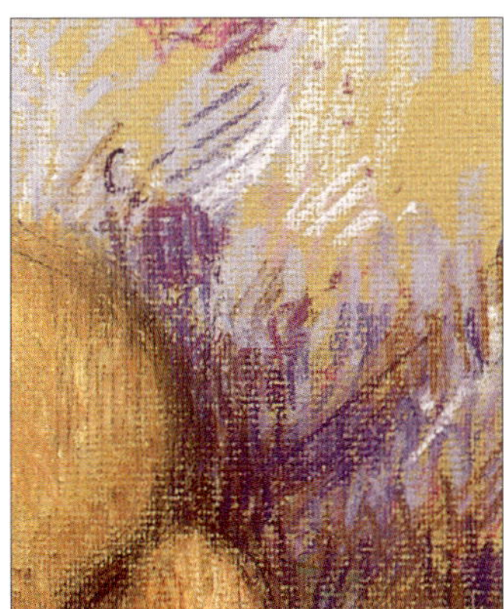

Grüße Grüße
Greetings
Saluti Voeux
Greetings
Grüße Grüße
Grüße
Grüße
Greetings
Saluti
Greetings

CALLIGRAPHY

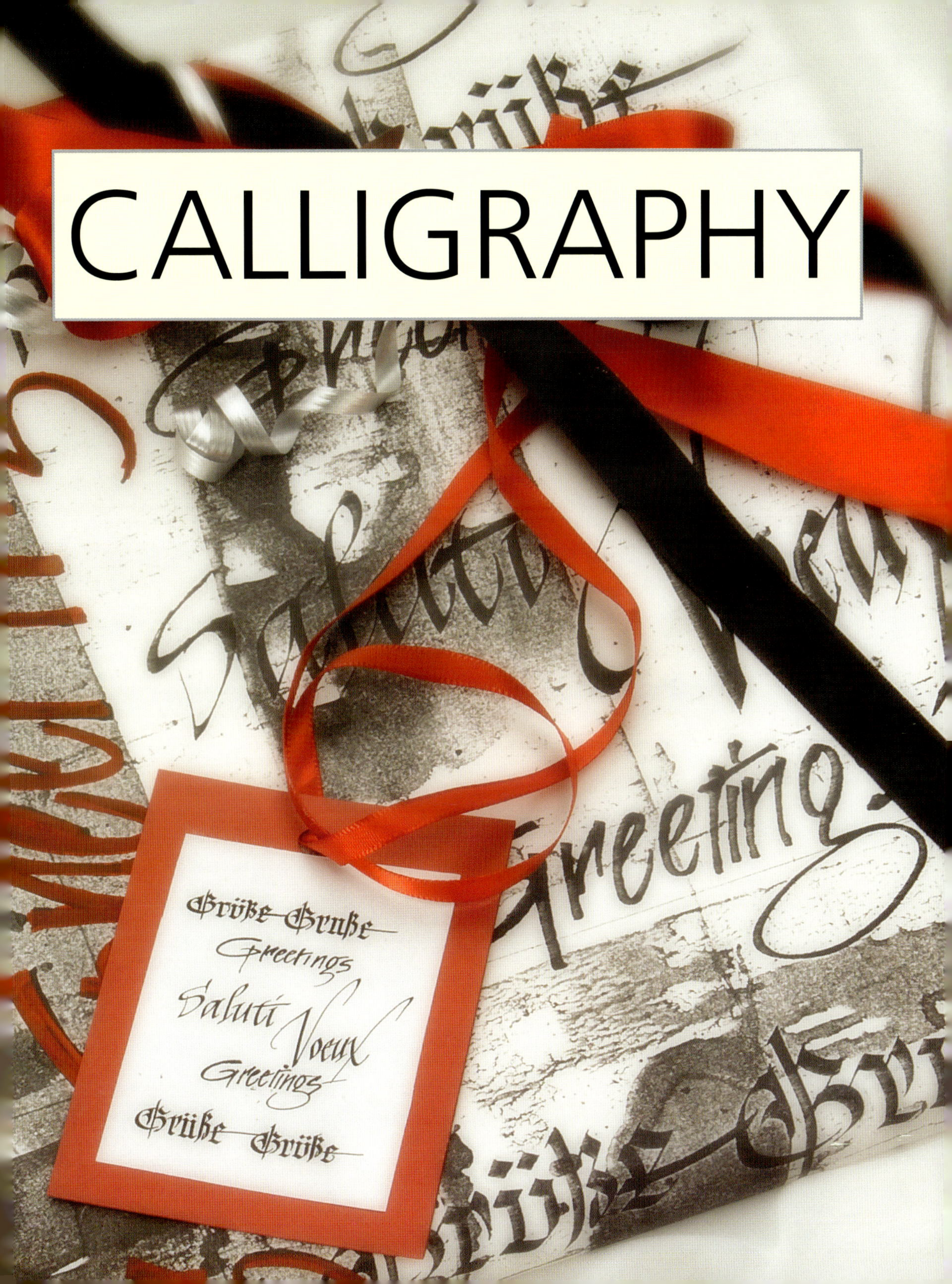

Introducing calligraphy

Calligraphy is a fascinating and absorbing skill, which is as fresh and inventive today as it was at the time of its origin in the earliest human civilizations. There is a rich calligraphic tradition, as well as modern technological advances, which informs and inspires all those with an interest in beautiful lettering. In these pages you will find instruction in the basic techniques and alphabets with practical exercises to reinforce knowlege. A variety of projects are designed to further the skills of the budding calligrapher as well as the more experienced lettering artist.

In order to fully appreciate the letterforms we use today, it is important to understand their origins. An insight into the development of writing, its historical roots, and the practical uses to which it has been put, is all-important. In the past, the calligrapher diligently recorded history, literature, documents and charters, but with the invention of printing by moveable type, his role was to change forever. Today, calligraphers, lettering artists and illuminators throughout the world are regarded not just as craftspeople but as artists. As well as taking writing to superb technical levels incorporating both new and old technologies, they also use words and calligraphic marks as images in their own right, creating a significant and exciting new art form. Examples of modern work offer inspirational ideas and illustrate the possibilities that are within reach of today's calligrapher.

Although mastery of the basic letterform is arguably the most important aspect of calligraphy, it is when this is combined with other skills that the true possibilities of calligraphy are revealed. The *Techniques* section features numerous ways to turn a piece of writing into a work of art, including an explanation and examples of brush lettering – which is a script in its own right. There are insights into useful skills including the use of colour washes, bookbinding techniques, cut letters and gilding. Each technique is accompanied by practical, step-by-step exercises.

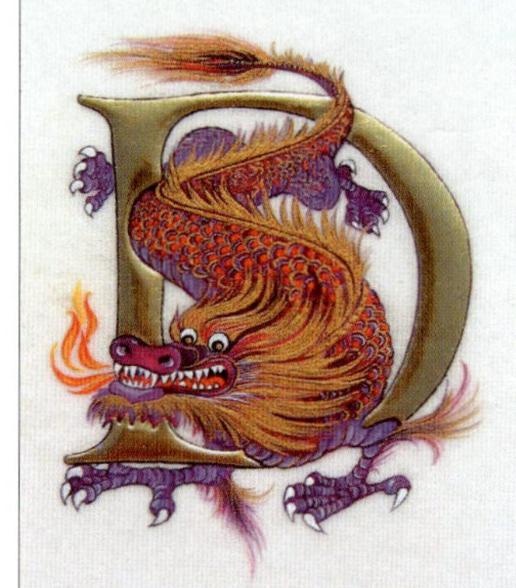

◀ **'Fire Dragon'**
Entwined letters and images give this design added impact. This dragon was painted on stretched vellum, using gouache, gilded with leaf gold on gesso.
Jan Pickett

▲ **'Autumn'**
A gilded Versal letter 'A' illuminates this miniature from a hand-written book on the poem *The Pageant of the Season and the Months* by Edmund Spenser.
Janet Mehigan

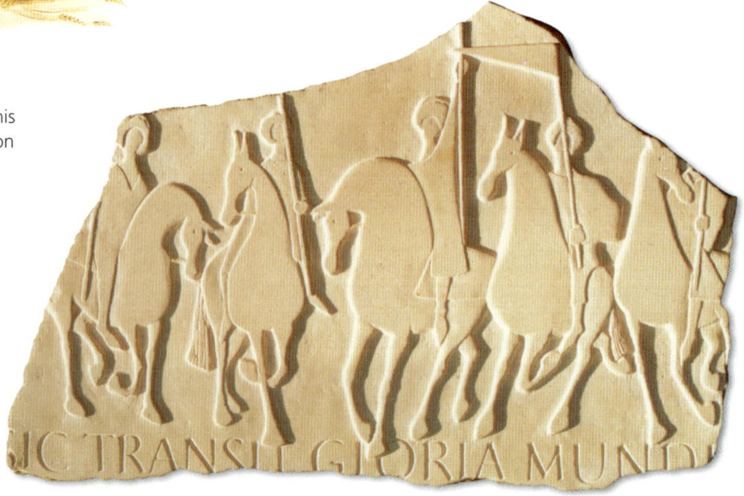

▶ **'Glory of the World'**
Carved in Portland Stone is the message 'Thus passes the glory of the world', echoing the broken stone.
Celia Kilner

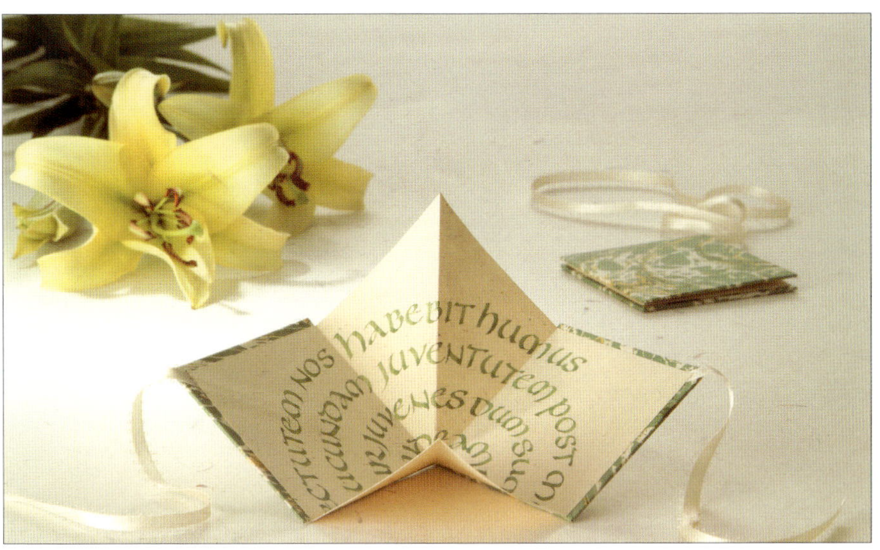

◀ **The perfect gift**
Calligraphic techniques can be employed to create a range of beautiful gifts and keepsakes such as this lotus book with a spiral script.

First, you need to practise the letterforms. Before embarking on a project, it is advisable to practise the chosen script until it can be written with some fluency and spontaneity – that is, until you can make letter shapes without continually referring to the alphabets. Good calligraphy relies primarily on well constructed letter shapes, secondly on freedom of execution and finally on individual expression.

Alternative scripts may be used on any of the projects given – change them to suit your own strengths. Work carefully from the step-by-step sequences trying not to cut corners. It is also worthwhile developing individual ideas and ways of working. However your skills develop, you will find calligraphy an immensely satisfying and rewarding pastime.

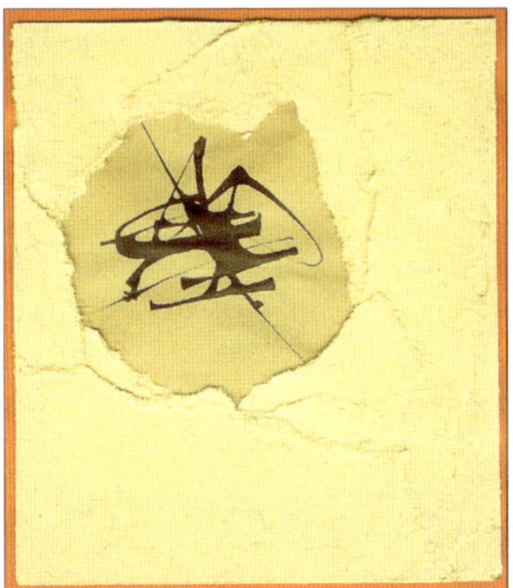

◀ **'Earth'**
Artist's own script and taken from a series on the four elements, using a ruling pen on torn handmade paper.
Penny Price

Creative projects to do ▼
Brown paper is transformed into stunning gift wrap with decorative lettering in white gouache paint.

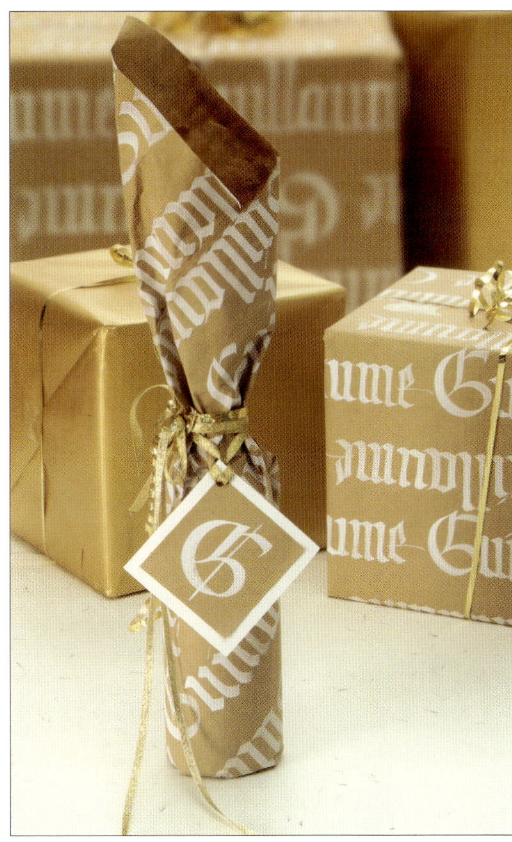

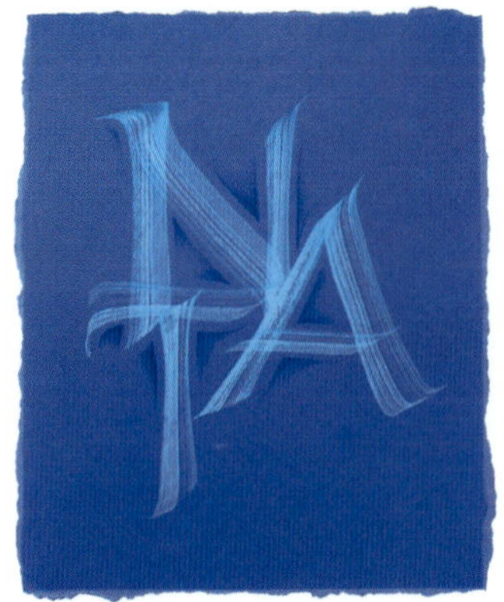

▲ **'The Deep Blue'**
Three Roman Capitals are blended in this haunting electric blue design, painted in gouache with an edged brush.
Jan Pickett

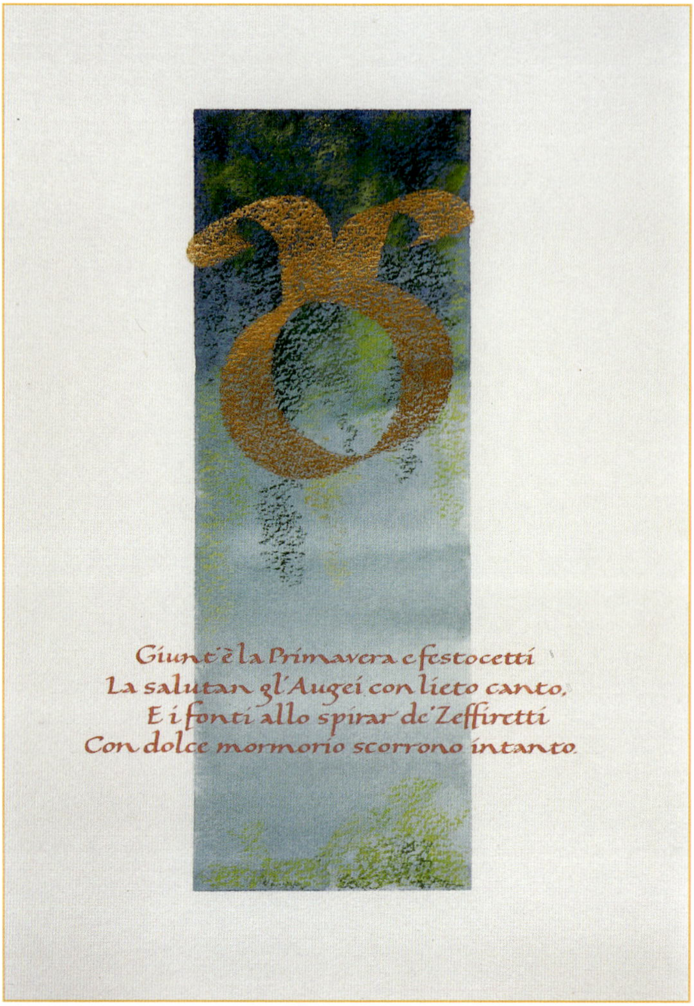

Giunt'è la Primavera e festocetti
La salutan gl'Augei con lieto canto,
E i fonti allo spirar de'Zeffiretti
Con dolce mormorio scorrono intanto.

▶ **'Spring'**
A piece from a series based on the four seasons in a hybrid Italic script using metal nibs on a textured background of acrylic paints, pastels and gold stencilling.
Penny Price

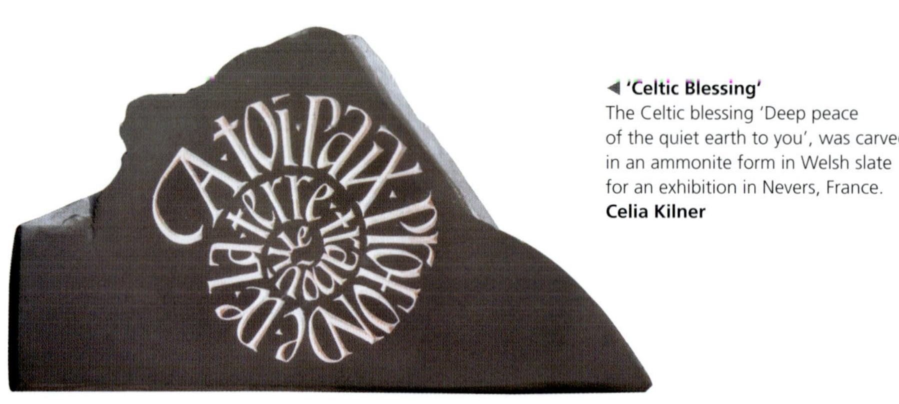

◀ **'Celtic Blessing'**
The Celtic blessing 'Deep peace of the quiet earth to you', was carved in an ammonite form in Welsh slate for an exhibition in Nevers, France.
Celia Kilner

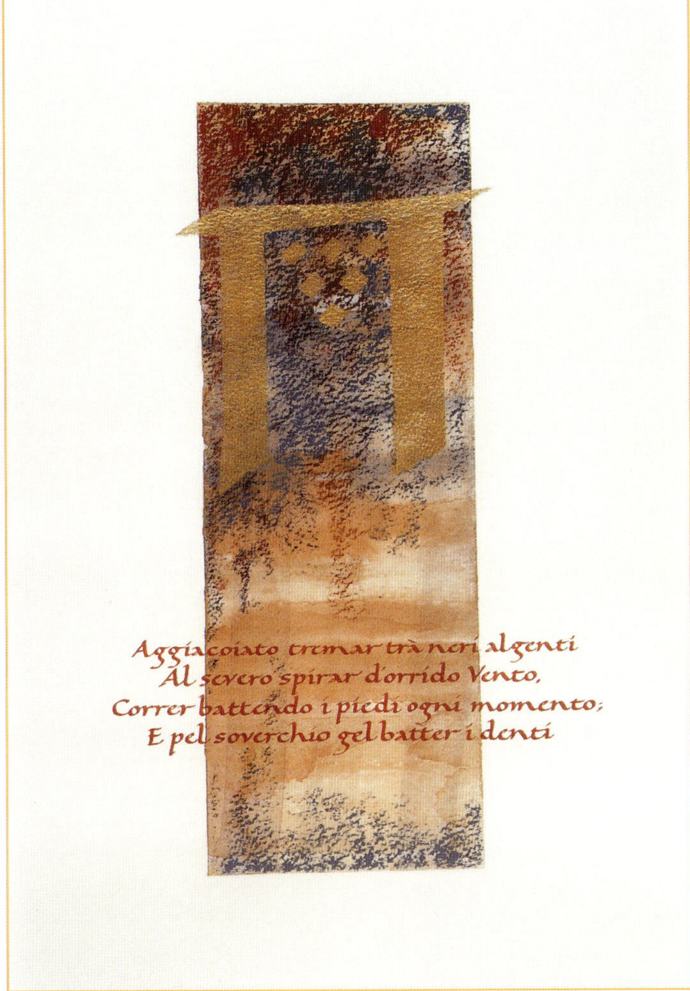

◀ **'Winter'**
A piece from a series based on the four seasons in a hybrid Italic script using metal nibs over a textured background of acrylic paints, pastels and gold stencilling.
Penny Price

▼ **'Letterform Exploration'**
Roman Capitals and Italic are created using broad-edged and pointed brushes with minimal pre-planning. Black Sumi ink was used on Khadi handmade paper with red gouache in the counter for extra embellishment.
Mary Noble

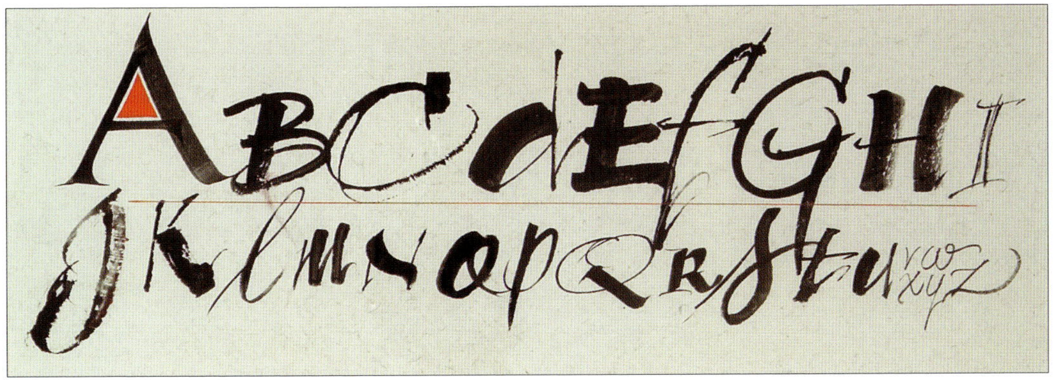

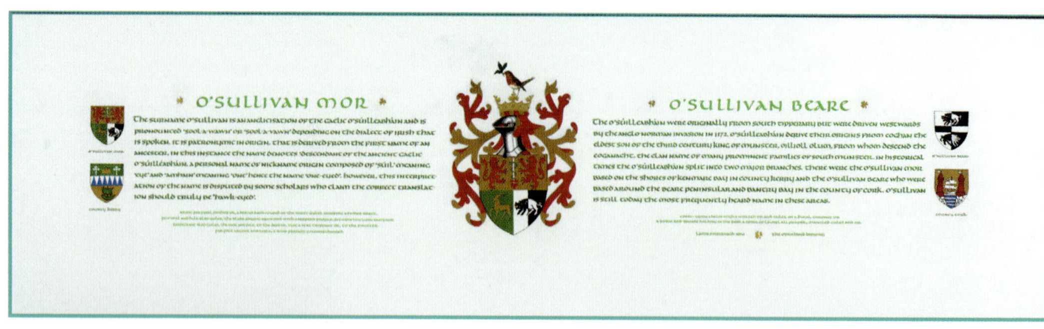

▲ **'Sullivan Family History'**
Uncials written in gouache on watercolour paper are used as a decorative means of showing the Sullivan family history.
Maureen Sullivan

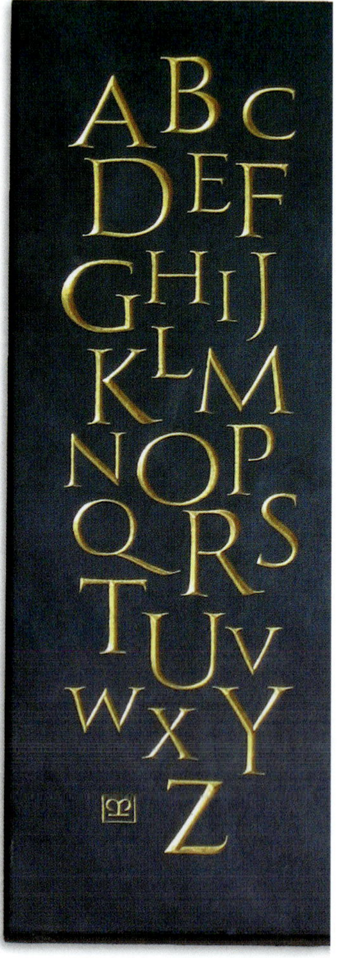

▲ **'Dancing Alphabet'**
Imperial Roman Capitals are used in this alphabet, incised and gilded in slate.
Rosella Garavaglia

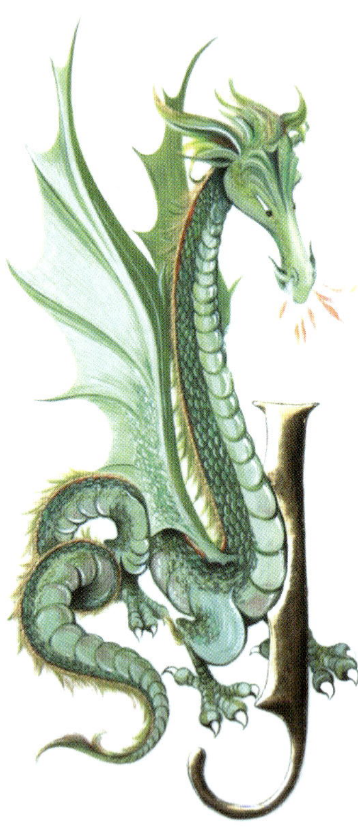

▲ **'Woodland Dragon'**
Gouache on stretched vellum with a gilded 'J', using leaf gold on gesso.
Jan Pickett

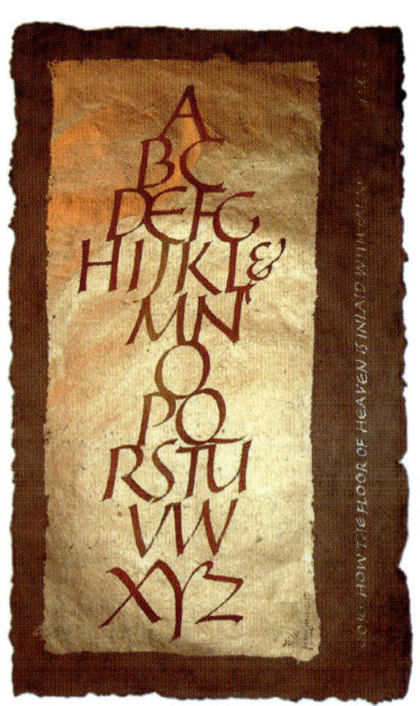

▲ **'Julian's Alphabet'**
This striking design on Nepali paper shows the effective use of gold leaf and oil pastel.
Peter Halliday

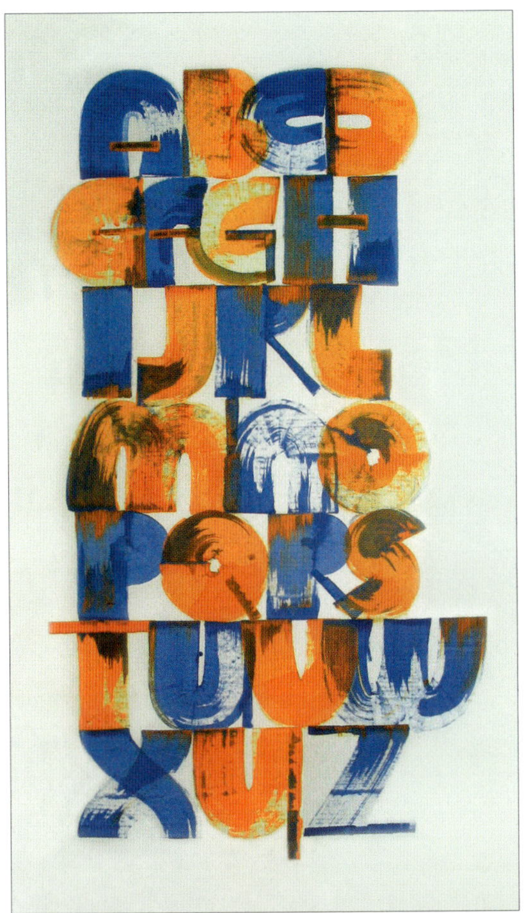

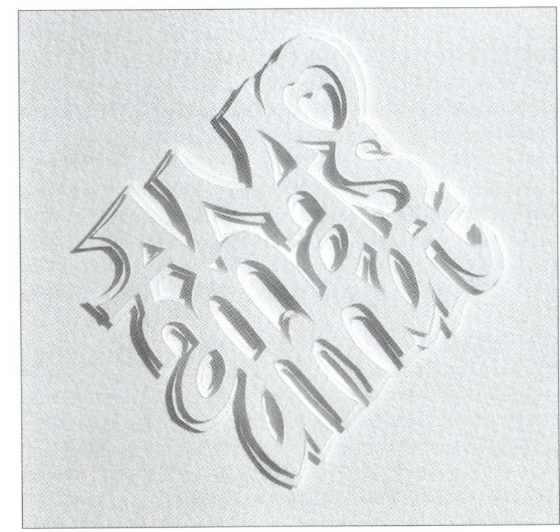

◀ **'Blue and Yellow Alphabet'**
Experimental script written with a piece of large heavy card and inks on Fabriano paper.
Rosella Garavaglia

▲ **'Amo, Amas, Amat'**
The design (meaning 'to love' in Latin) is cut from two layers of Bockingford paper and incorporates free majuscules, Foundational hand and Italic hand.
Viva Lloyd

▼ **'Digital Alphabet'**
A dark green backdrop provides an effective contrast with the gold lettering of this alphabet design. In an unusual twist on the conventional alphabet layout, the letter 'Z' has been made a focal point of the design. The alphabet is 'virtual' calligraphy in Italic to be viewed on screen.
George Thomson

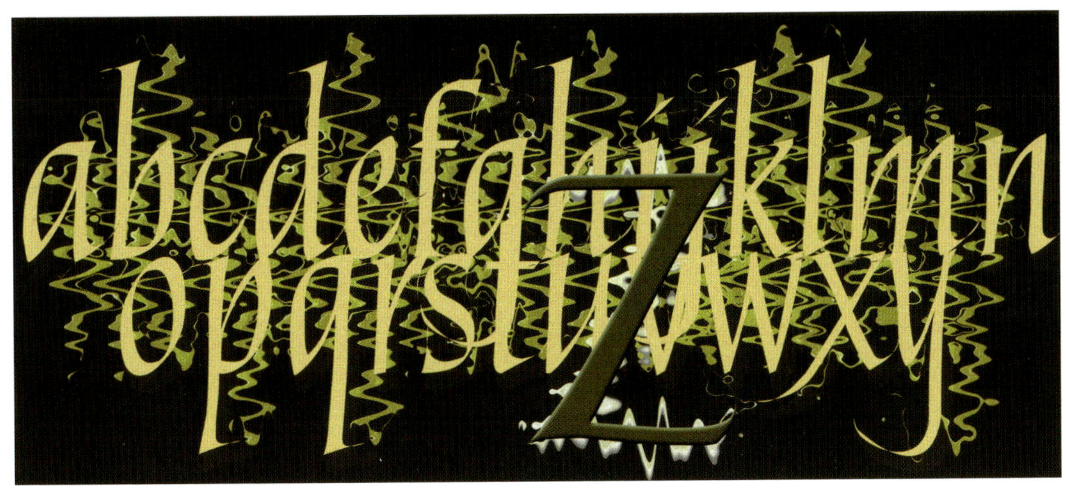

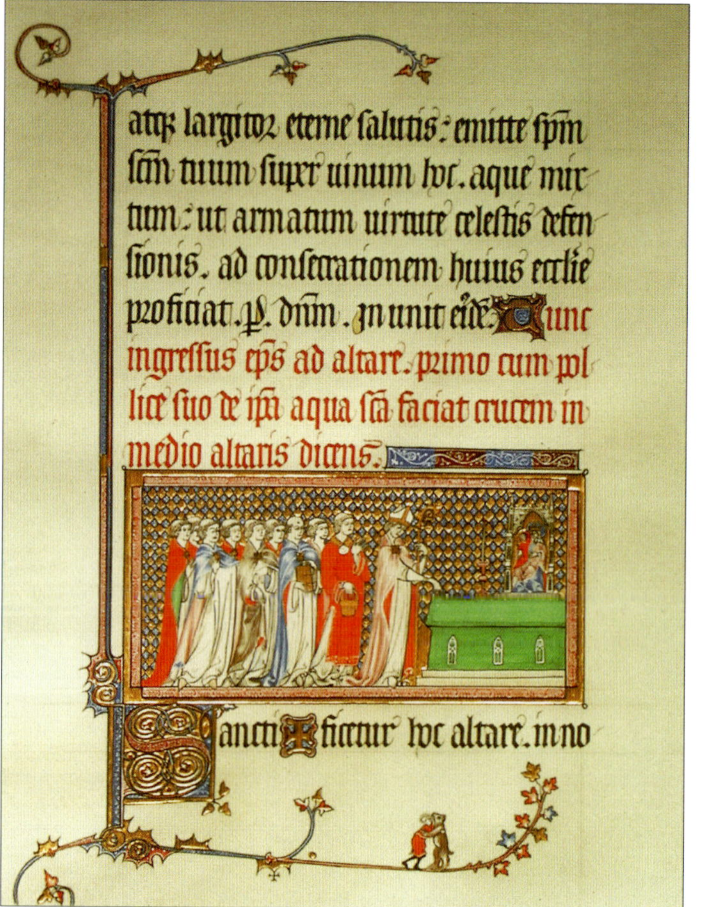

▲ 'Hebrew Alphabet'
Ashkenazi script has been created by carefully cutting out Hebrew letters from cream paper, which has then been mounted on dark green card.
Sylvie Gokulsing

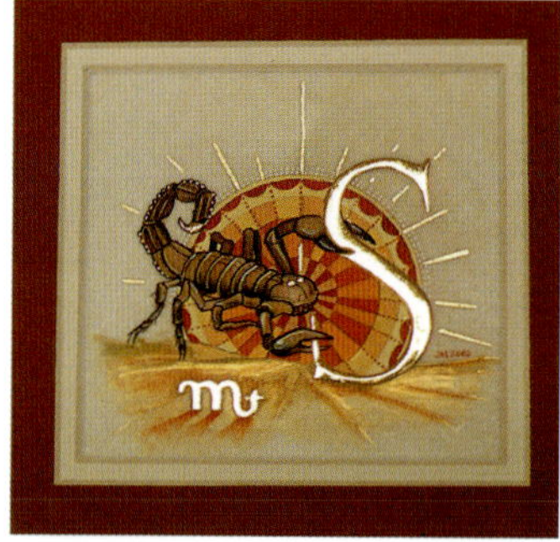

▲ 'Scorpio'
A gold Versal 'S' on raised gesso base. Painted using traditional egg tempera and watercolour washes on stretched vellum over wood.
Janet Mehigan

◄ 'Scene from Metz Pontifical'
This religious scene has been copied from the early 14th-century Metz Pontifical. It has been written on vellum using quills and iron gall ink in Quadrata Gothic script.
Penny Price

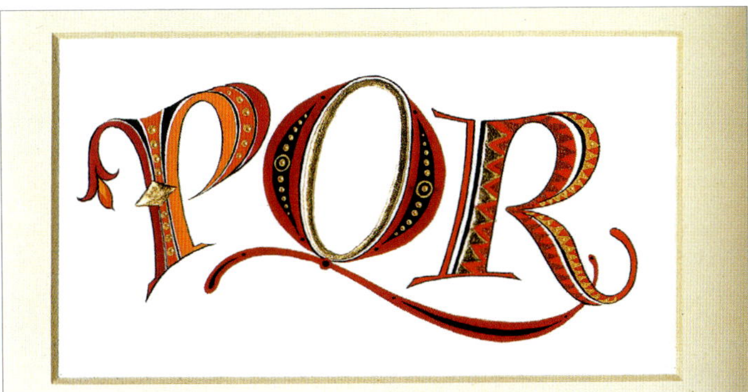

◀ **'Jester's Letters'**
Part of a complete alphabet book, initially painted in gouache then embellished using raised gold on gesso and shell gold.
Jan Pickett

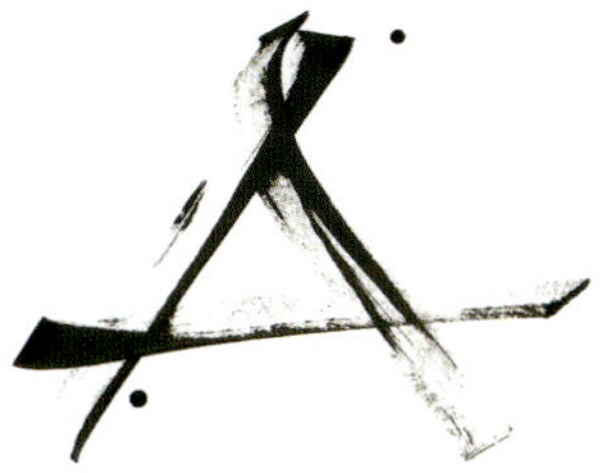

▲ **'Letter A'**
Using Chinese ink and an automatic pen this bold letter 'A' was created using several large sweeping movements of the hand and arm.
Michelle Goulder

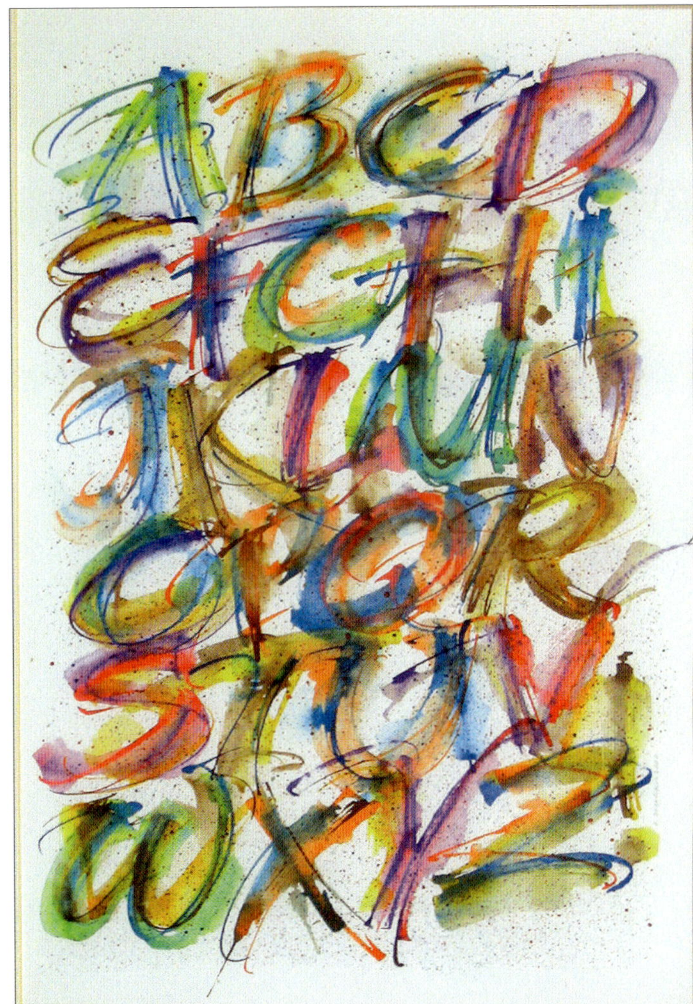

▶ **'Arlecchino'**
Experimental alphabet using a round brush and water, then inks, on Fabriano Artistico paper.
Rosella Garavaglia

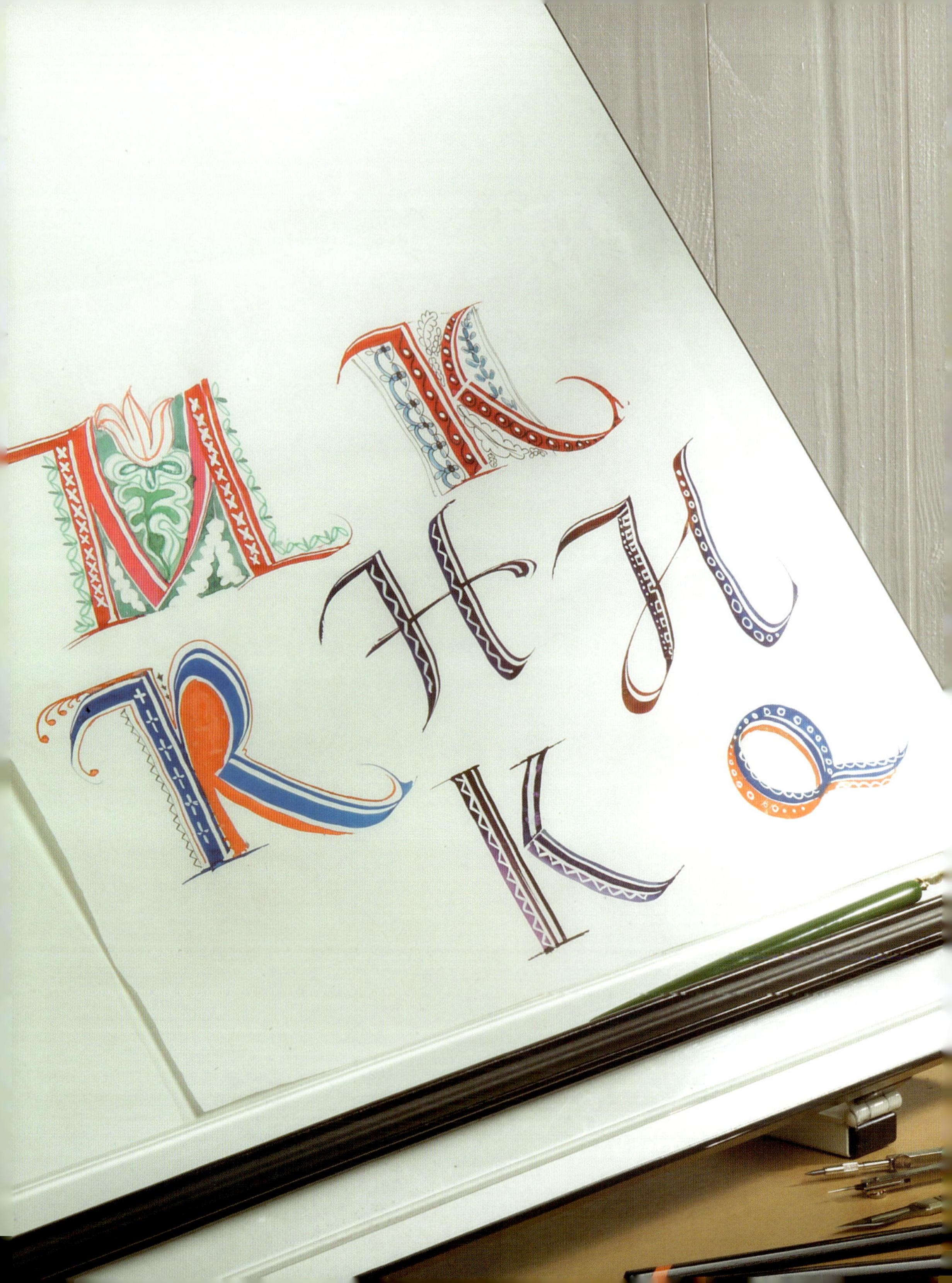

Getting Started in Calligraphy

Putting pen to paper, or beginning any form of calligraphy practice, requires some simple yet essential preparation. This section outlines the materials and equipment you will need to get started, explains the best way to set up your working space and teaches the fundamentals of penmanship, layout and design. As your enthusiasm grows, so will your interest in trying variants on the basics and this may require a variety of equipment. Visit a local supplier for art materials and before you buy be sure that the materials on offer will meet your needs. Use calligraphy suppliers' websites for details of more specialist tools.

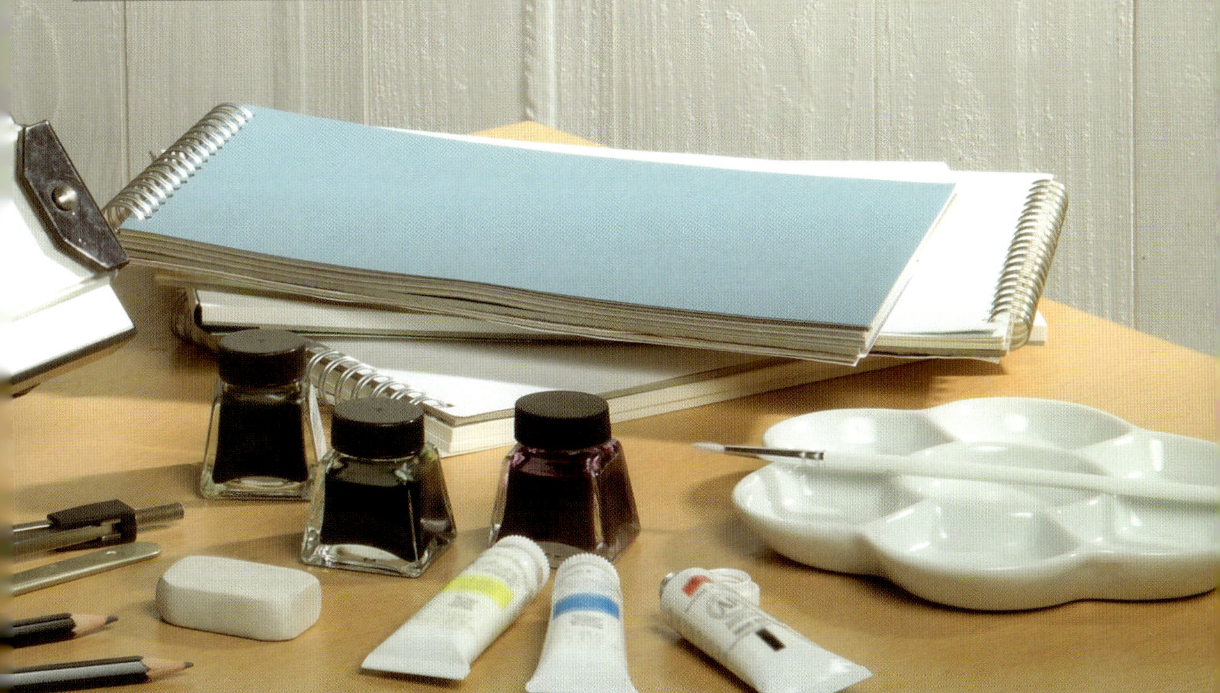

Pens

There are many different sizes and shapes of calligraphy pen, although the nearest supplier may only have a limited range. Check the pen has a wide nib at least 2mm (5/64in) in size. Left-handers should look for square-ended or left-oblique nibs.

Many calligraphers prefer a metal dip pen because it can be used with all kinds of paints and inks mixed to different colours and consistencies. While its name implies that it is dipped in ink, this is not always the case; feeding it with a paintbrush of mixed gouache paint allows good control of paint flow and consistency of colour density. The best metal nibs are modelled on the profile of the traditional quill, combining flexibility with sharpness. The dip pen is the nearest convenient equivalent to the quill, saving modern calligraphers the time and skill needed to cut and maintain that revered ancestor.

Pen sizes vary enormously, allowing large poster writing with perhaps a 2.5cm (1in) pen that demands a bold arm movement across the page; in contrast, small, delicate writing in a manuscript book would instead need a tiny nib, maybe just 1mm (3/64in) wide or smaller, and if choosing to write elegant Copperplate, then a flexible pointed nib is the only answer. In general, however, and certainly when starting out, it is best to begin in the middle range of these extremes, and study the letterforms at a size that allows you to see all the detail of construction, before going too small; a nib about 2.5mm (7/64in) is ideal. Other pens available to the calligrapher include larger poster pens, automatic pens, which come in many sizes, and ruling pens.

Felt-tipped pens and fountain pens are the most convenient of all calligraphic tools. They are available in bright colours and provide instant results with non-clogging inks. As the dye-based inks may fade in time they are best for practice and for short-term projects where the results will not be exposed to light for too long. The nibs flow well across smooth paper. Felt-tips will soften and lose their sharpness over time, so replace them frequently and before the writing suffers.

Pen manufacturers have not standardized their size coding, making instant comparisons difficult. One maker's smallest size is size 6, with its largest size 0, whereas most other makes increase their numbers with their size. This discrepancy only becomes apparent when working with different makes, so start with one complete set or just be prepared to make visual comparisons. Do not order by size number alone.

Dip pens ▶
A handle and a range of differently sized nibs make up the dip pen. There are several manufacturers. Some nibs have an integral reservoir, others have a slip-on version. Whatever pen collection is chosen, there will be a variety of nib sizes available, although the sizes may vary between manufacturers. Some makes are slightly right oblique, which will not suit left-handers, who should look out for square-ended or preferably left-oblique versions. Copperplate nibs are fine and can have a very distinctive elbow shape. For large, bold writing, explore the fun of enormous pens; they use a lot of ink, and dipping may be preferable to feeding with a brush.

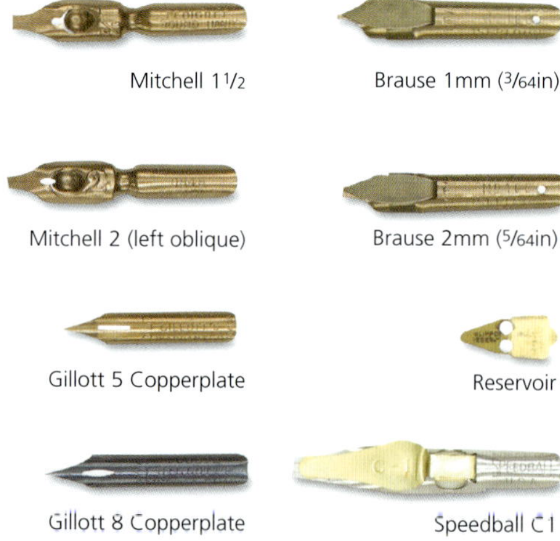

Mitchell 1 1/2

Brause 1mm (3/64in)

Mitchell 2 (left oblique)

Brause 2mm (5/64in)

Gillott 5 Copperplate

Reservoir

Gillott 8 Copperplate

Speedball C1

Mitchell Copperplate elbow

Speedball C2

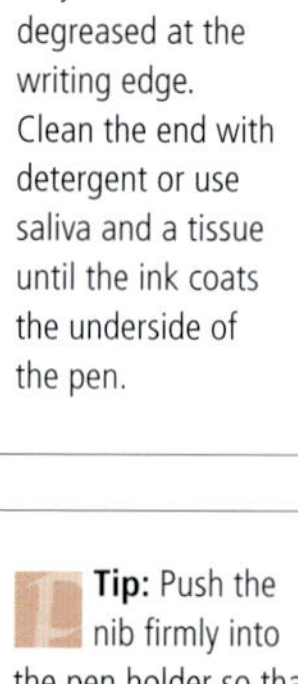

Tip: New dip pens may need to be degreased at the writing edge. Clean the end with detergent or use saliva and a tissue until the ink coats the underside of the pen.

Tip: Push the nib firmly into the pen holder so that the dip pen does not shake when you write. Ensure the nib sits securely between any metal prongs inside the holder, and its outer shell.

Handle of pen

Larger pens ▶
There are nibs that are designed for the large writing found on posters, which are sometimes called poster pens. Automatic pens can be moved in any direction with continuous ink flow, and produce both very thin and contrasting thick lines. Each pen nib has a serrated side and a smooth side, and is used with the smooth side against the paper. It can be used either full width, or when worked in can also produce lines by turning on its thin edge. Ruling pens were traditionally used for drawing straight lines against a ruler, but calligraphers also use them for freer writing and wider versions have been invented specifically for creative calligraphy. The screw adjustment allows for cleaning and for varying line width.

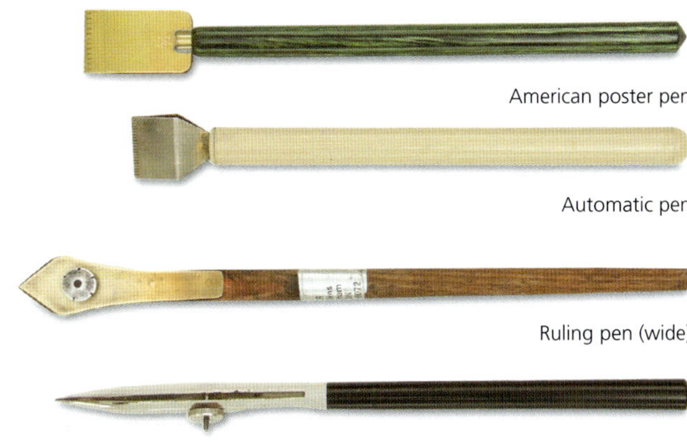

American poster pen

Automatic pen

Ruling pen (wide)

Ruling pen (technical drawing pen)

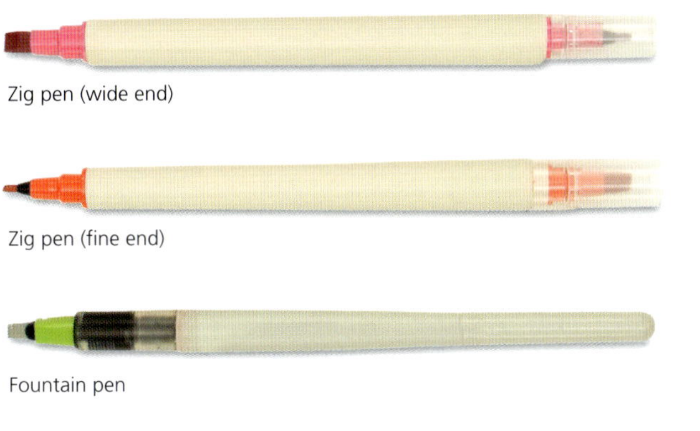

Zig pen (wide end)

Zig pen (fine end)

Fountain pen

Broad-edged brush

◀ Other types of pen
Personal taste will determine the other types of pen used. Felt-tipped pens are especially useful for quick work, and will travel well in a pocket. The ones with a nib at each end, in different sizes, are especially useful. Fountain pens are convenient; the ink is in cartridges so refilling is quick. Choose a make that supplies a flushing tool for washing out if the colours are to be changed frequently. Broad-edged brushes need to be nylon for springiness, not sable (too floppy) or bristle (too stiff).

Tip: If reading the nib size is a problem when changing nibs, buy a handle for every nib and label the handle with a sliver of paper fixed with transparent sticky tape.

Caring for your pens

Dip pens will last a very long time if they are cleaned after use. Do not allow them to rust. Store the spare nibs in a container that will allow some air circulation in case any are damp from cleaning. If nibs are kept attached to their handles, check them to see they have not rusted in. Store pens flat while drying, to prevent water causing rusting.

Materials
- *Water pot*
- *Old toothbrush*
- *Kitchen paper*

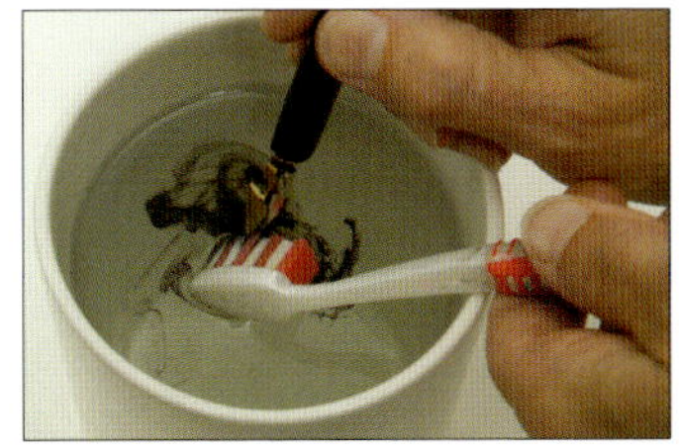

1 Clean the nib (while still attached to the handle) over your water pot, using a toothbrush, or water will run up the handle and cause rusting.

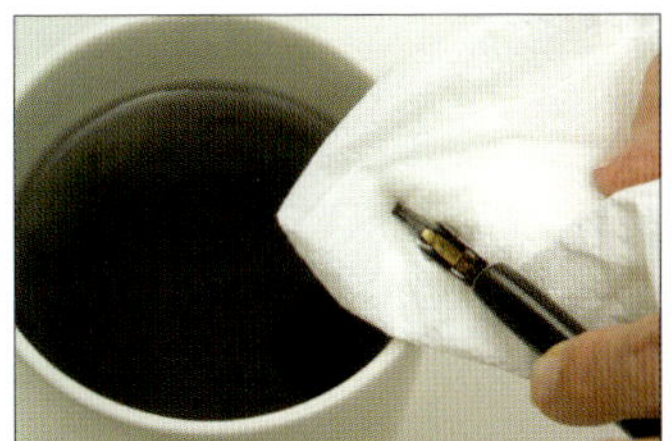

2 Once the nib has been cleaned, dry it (and the reservoir, if is a slip-on one) using kitchen paper.

Inks and paints

There are many inks available to the calligrapher. The most important quality of an ink or paint in the pen is that it should flow easily and not spread on the surface. Density of colour and light-fastness are important factors for finished work. Thus many calligraphers use Chinese or Japanese stick inks, or gouache paint, both of which are dense and opaque, or watercolours for more transparent effects. Bottled fountain pen inks are good for practising as they flow well. Waterproof inks are not recommended in the pen as they clog, and do not give sharp writing. They are better used much diluted for background washes. For beginners, fountain pens with broad calligraphy nibs provide inks in convenient cartridges and with a continuous flow. Felt-tipped pens are very successful for practising and have a range of calligraphy nibs. In both cases these inks are dye-based so they are free-flowing and translucent, but may fade on exposure to light.

Black inks

For black ink, Japanese or Chinese stick ink is recommended, purchased from a reliable source. Inks supplied for the tourist market will be for novelty value, not for ink quality. Be aware that whereas many stick inks are manufactured for the quality of their greys, Western calligraphers value black opacity in their inks. Some ink is supplied with helpful shade cards showing how black it is, and whether when thinner it is blue-grey or warm-grey. An alternative bottled version, known as Sumi Ink, is available for those who need their black ink constantly or instantly available.

Japanese stick ink ▼
Ready-to-use, Japanese stick ink comes, either in a bottle (water it down a little), or matured in a stick for grinding.

Tip: When starting a new tube of gouache, you should discard the first squeeze of paint if it oozes any transparent liquid, as this can interfere with smooth writing qualities.

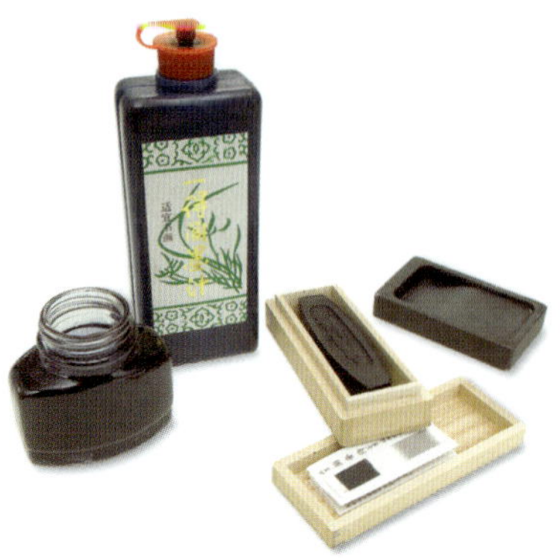

Gouache

Designers' gouache is an important choice when using colour. Gouache is opaque, so the colour will show up when writing on coloured backgrounds. Most colours are lightproof so ideal for finished pieces that will be on display. The choice of colours is vast, but by experimentation with mixing, only six colours are needed. They are: two reds – a pinkish one (magenta) and an orangey one (scarlet); two blues – ultramarine (makes purple with magenta) and cerulean, or a cheaper phthalo blue (makes bright greens); and two yellows – lemon (for bright greens) and a warmer hint of orange yellow. Imitation gold paint in gouache form is most successful for calligraphy; bottled versions will be fine for other applications but separate too quickly for pen work.

Colour wheel ▶
The three primary colours are red, yellow and blue. They are the only colours that cannot be made by mixing two other colours. The three secondary colours are green, orange and violet and they are each a mixture of two primary colours. The secondary colours are positioned between the colours from which they are made. The six tertiary colours (red-orange, red-violet, yellow-green, yellow-orange, blue-green and blue-violet) are made by mixing a primary colour with an adjacent secondary colour. The tertiary colours are positioned between the primary and secondary colours from which they are made.

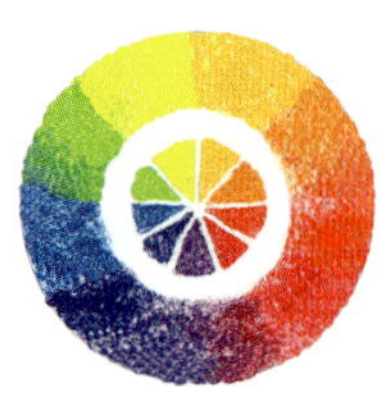

Tubes of gouache ▼
Designers' gouaches come in tubes. Squeeze out 1cm (1/2in) in a palette and add water by the brushful until a single (light) cream consistency is achieved, or until it flows well in the pen.

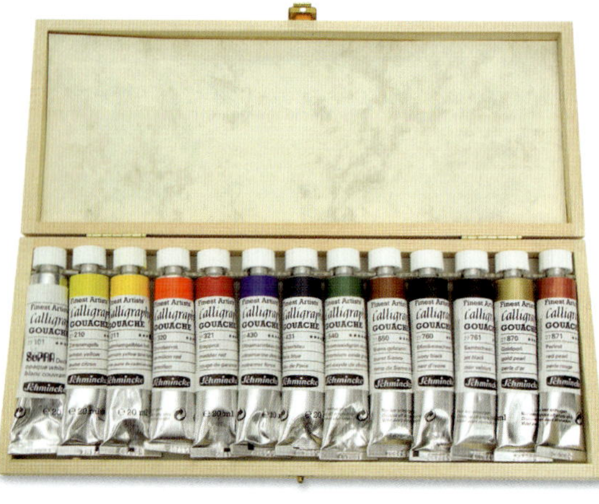

Watercolour paints

These paints are transparent and economical to use. Their transparency makes them ideal for use on white paper, which shows off their true colours. Watercolour paint can be effectively used when writing one letter on top of another. If a wet letter touches another the colours will blend. Writing in watercolour is easy to do because the paint flows easily from the pen. However, care should be taken when writing in watercolour on to coloured paper as its transparency will encourage it to disappear. As with gouaches, only six colours are required if they are mixed. In some watercolour paintboxes the selection has already been made.

Mixing watercolour paint ▼
Watercolours come in tubes and in pans. Tubes are useful when mixing up a large quantity, perhaps for a series of background washes. Brushes for fine painting need to keep their fine point, with no stray hairs. Choose size 0 or 1, springy acrylic or more absorbent sable.

Tip: Always replace the tops of paints immediately, as oxidation will occur and the paint will harden.

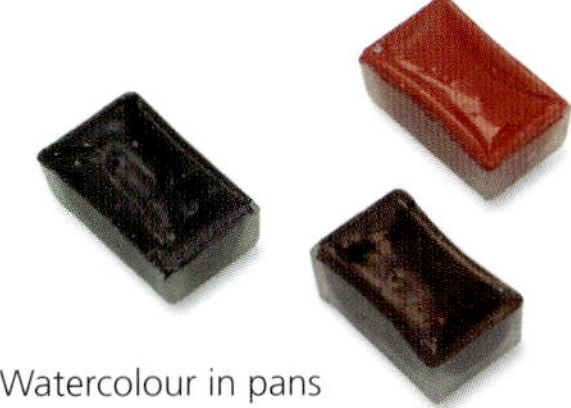

Watercolour in pans

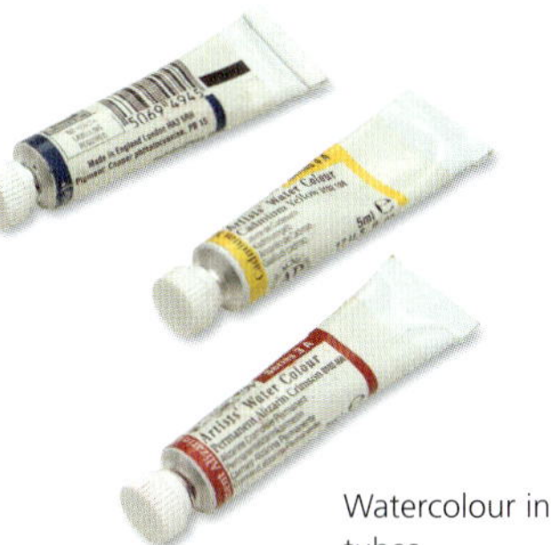

Watercolour in tubes

Other types of paint

Bottled acrylic inks are ideal for making wash backgrounds for calligraphy. This is because they dry waterproof, making a non-porous surface on which to write. Do not try putting acrylic ink in the pen, however, as it will not give sharp writing and the pen will need to be cleaned before it dries. Casein-based paints are bright colours that behave like household emulsion (latex) paint. Use these only as backgrounds. 'Bleedproof white' is like a gouache in a bottle and is very opaque. Once water is added it works well in a dip pen fed with a brush, producing very sharp writing.

Bottled acrylic ink ▼
This type of paint works well for creating wash backgrounds.

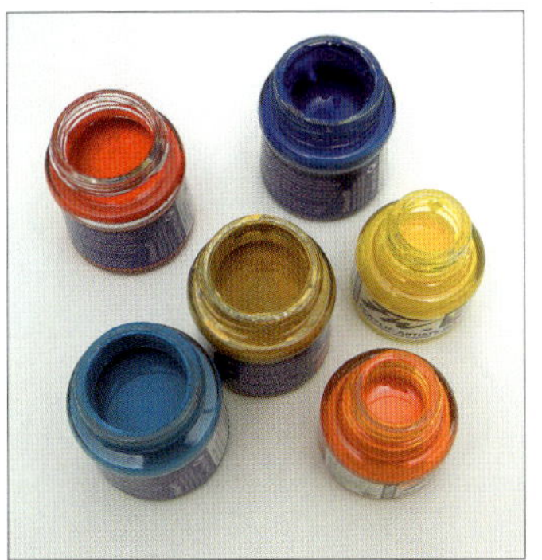

Practice exercise: **Using an inkstone**

An inkstone is a small sloping block with raised sides and a slightly abrasive surface. The ink is rubbed down with a stick and water to produce ink in small quantities as needed. In this way the calligrapher controls the density of colour and texture. The consistency of the ink can be controlled by fixing the amount of water and the rubbing time.

Materials

- *Water: distilled or boiled tap water*
- *Inkstone and stick*
- *Brush*
- *Cloth*

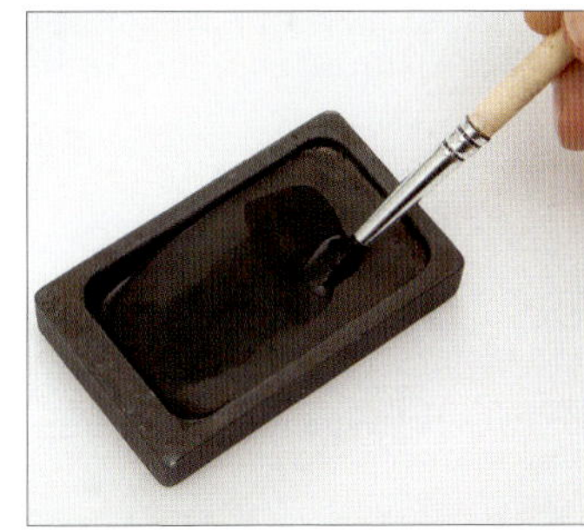

1 Put a few drops of water on the flat surface of the inkstone with a brush.

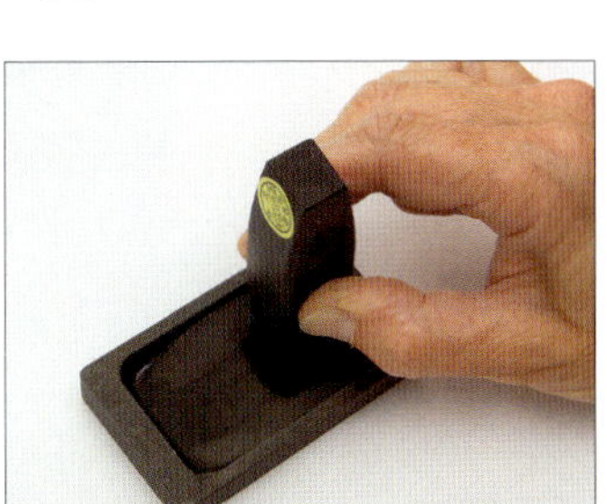

2 Rub the ink stick firmly in a circular motion for a minute or two to mix some of the ink with the water.

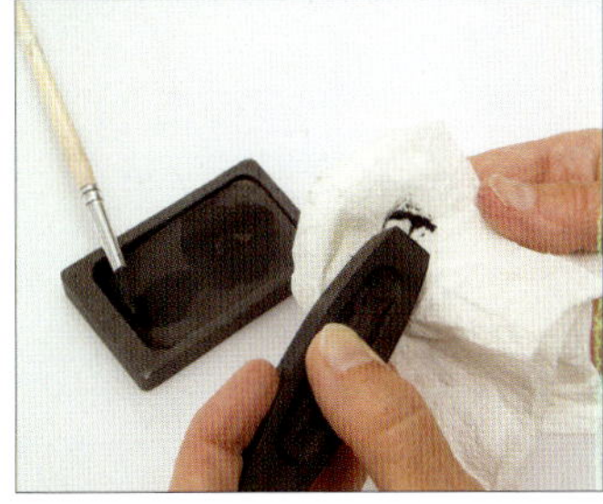

3 When it feels sticky, use a wet paintbrush to move the ink into the trough and repeat the grinding with fresh water until you have sufficient. Do not leave the stick to soak, or it will crack; dry it with a cloth.

Papers

There are many different papers on the market. They are intended more for watercolour artists than for calligraphers, so it is helpful to know which papers are most suitable for writing. A large supply of practice paper is probably the best investment, in order to try out designs and revise the writing many times before using 'best' paper.

Practice or layout paper conveniently comes in pads, in several sizes. Choose a size that has enough space to do paste-ups and expansive writing. Layout paper is very white and is about 50gsm (23lb). This is thin enough to see through and to have a grid of ruled lines placed underneath as guidelines. Photocopy paper is a good alternative that is available from office suppliers, and comes in large packs. It is 80gsm (39lb) making it thicker than layout paper, and therefore it may not be possible to see fine lines drawn underneath.

Paper for a final, 'best' piece needs to be thicker. Thicker paper will wrinkle less when written on, and will not be so easily bruised – thin paper poorly handled will show every little crease, and may take on more creases when erasing lines. A first 'best' paper might be cartridge, as this is available in pads and is very inexpensive. Choose at least 150gsm (71lb) and look for acid free, so it will not go brown.

Better quality papers have some rag content, with various surface treatments and a wide sizing range, which affects the absorbency. Thus, blotting paper is unsized. Hot-pressed watercolour papers are suitable for calligraphy as they have a very smooth surface and are well-sized so the ink will stay where it is placed, resulting in sharp writing. The paper accepts paint well when drawing or painting additional features. Choose 200gsm (95lb) or thicker, if planning to get the paper wet. Craft suppliers usually stock hot-pressed watercolour paper in a limited range. Internally sized print-making paper has a softer surface, accepts writing very well and is popular with calligraphers, but care should be taken when using an eraser because this disturbs its surface.

Papers with a texture, such as the more popular 'NOT' (meaning 'not hot-pressed') and 'rough' watercolour papers can impart an interesting broken effect to large writing but are an impeding factor when trying to write in small pens. As a general rule, look for smooth surfaced papers. These surfaces are, however, ideal for background washes as the texture gives added character. With experience, it becomes worth searching out more specialist suppliers with a wider range of papers that have different characteristics.

Types of paper ▼
From left to right: layout paper is thin, white paper used for practice. Cartridge paper is an inexpensive high-quality paper. Hot-pressed watercolour paper is a good quality paper used for finished work, while watercolour paper comes in a variety of qualities and may be textured.

Tip: If paper is absorbent and makes the ink bleed, try spraying it first with a cheap hairspray.

Other papers

There is a whole range of coloured papers which are useful for making small artefacts and for taking the place of coloured washes. Some surfaces have a 'laid' effect of parallel lines; one side will be smoother, check to see which is easier for writing. Pastel papers – bright and subtle colours for use with pastels – accept ink very well (but not small writing). Investigate handmade Indian papers – not all accept ink without bleeding but some are fun to try.

Practice exercise: **Removing a mistake**

It is worth investing in thicker, good quality paper for important work, as small corrections can be made by scraping and smoothing down.

Materials

- *Good quality paper*
- *Dip pen*
- *Ink*
- *Scalpel or craft (utility) knife*
- *Putty eraser or similar*
- *Fixative or hairspray*

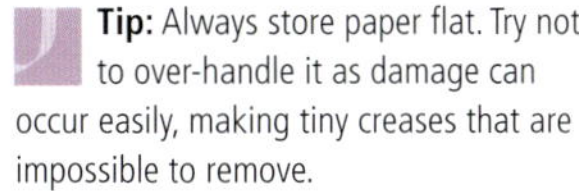

Tip: Always store paper flat. Try not to over-handle it as damage can occur easily, making tiny creases that are impossible to remove.

Tip: For washes, if paper is under 300gsm (142lb) stretch it. Soak it in water for 5–10 minutes, then smooth over a board with a sponge, before securing the edges with brown tape.

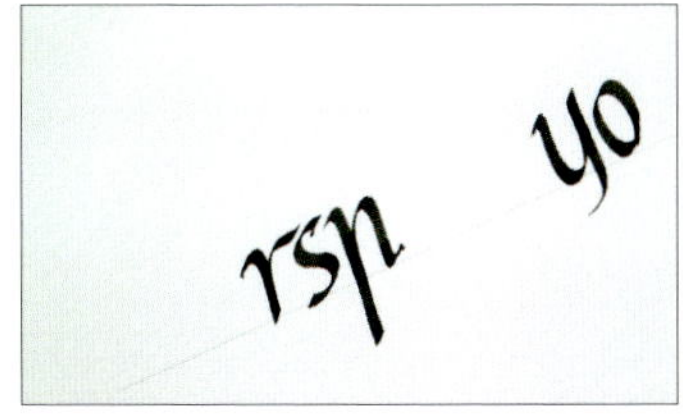

1 If a mistake has been made, all is not lost. First wait for the ink to dry completely.

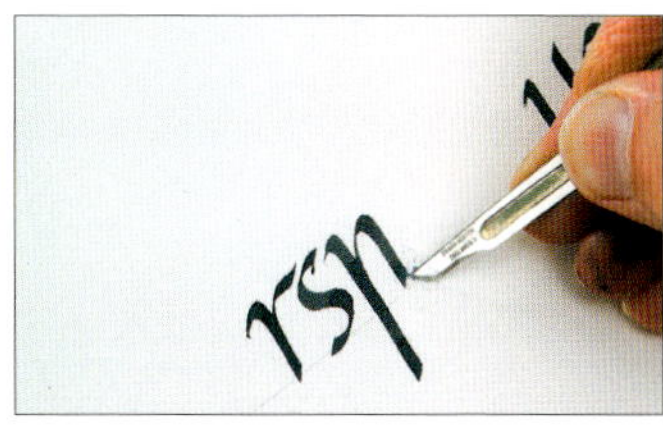

2 Gently scrape with a curved blade to remove the error.

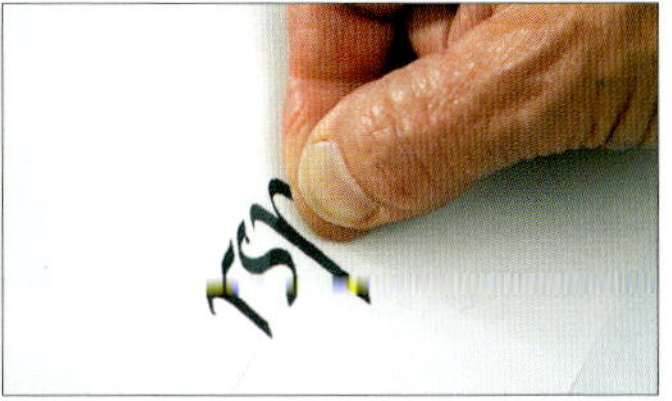

3 Lift off residue with a putty eraser or similar. Rub the surface with a hard smooth object or your fingernail to repair the surface, and lightly spray with fixative or hairspray to seal it.

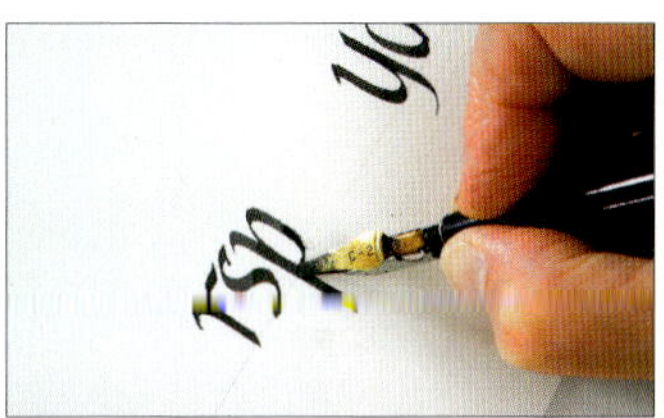

4 Rewrite when the repaired surface is completely dry.

Other types of paper ▼
Pastel papers such as Canson Mi-Teintes are heavy French papers in a series of colours, with a 'vellum' texture on one side and smooth on the other. Canson Ingres papers are a lighter weight than the Mi-Teintes and come in a series of colours. Khadi are heavy Indian handmade papers in a huge range of qualities and textures.

Vellum ▼
Writing material made from animal skins is called vellum. It costs more than paper, but offcuts can be found in specialist stores. This type of material is valued for prestige items such as illuminated manuscripts as it behaves well with gesso gilding. If you are using vellum for illumination it should need no extra preparation, but a final sanding with 400 grade 'wet and dry' abrasive paper may be necessary for sharp writing.

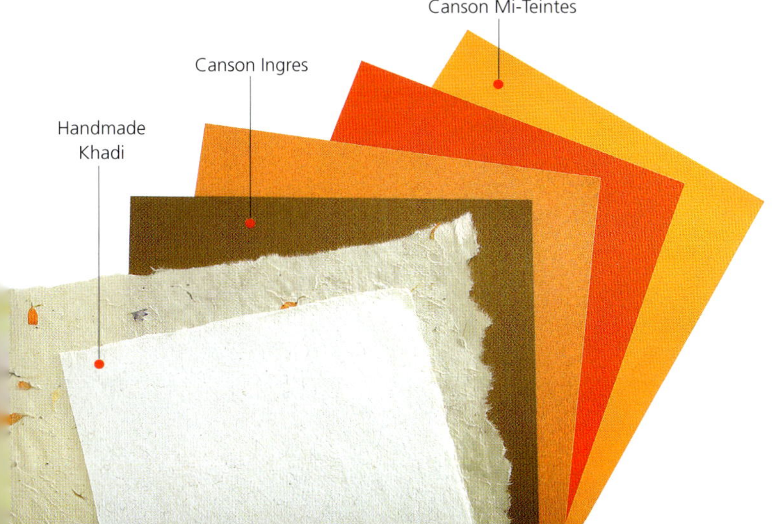

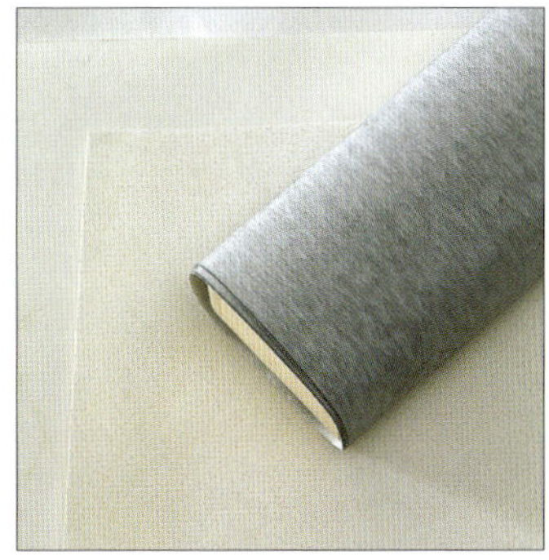

Abrasive paper block and vellum

Gilding materials

Gold leaf has a special attraction for calligraphers because it adds a sumptuous touch to lettering. It is useful to accumulate all the accoutrements available for developing this branch of decoration.

Loose leaf and transfer gold

A sheet of gold is thinner than paper and as delicate to handle as gossamer, so it is supplied interleaved in books of 25 leaves. The most flimsy to handle is the loose form ('loose leaf'). There is another version attached to a backing paper; most suppliers call this form 'transfer gold' but be aware there are differences between countries on this labelling. Gold leaf should be at least 23¼ carat as lower carats could tarnish with time. Gold also comes in two thicknesses, single and double (or extra thick). Double is useful for building up layers after the first layer has stuck to the base glue; layering will add depth to the shine. Gold leaf needs to be treated with care as it is expensive. It can be obtained from specialist art suppliers.

Other golds

Dutch metals or schlag are made from brass and other metals and are thicker, so they will not behave in the same way as gold leaf. They are much cheaper than gold and are available in unusual colours. They need to be applied with acrylic glues.

Gold and silver powders need to be mixed with glue and painted; imitation gold gouache can be very successful and works well in the pen, whereas bottled gold inks are only good for painting. Real gold for painting or writing comes as a tablet, originally supplied in a small shell and known as shell gold.

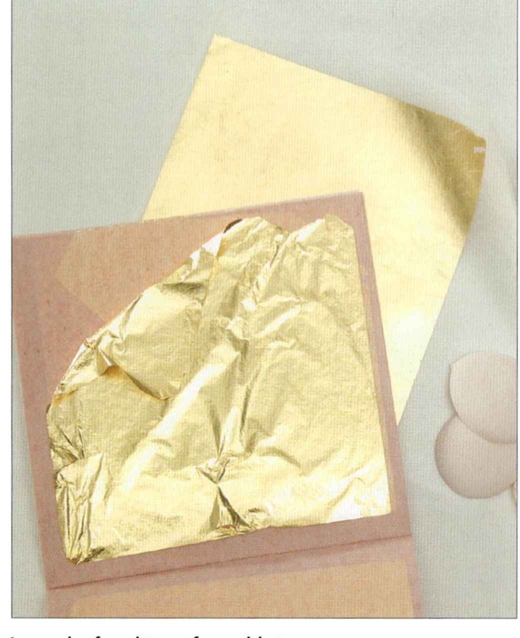

Loose leaf and transfer gold ▲
Laying gold leaf or gold transfer is a very delicate process as it is a fine, clinging material that needs to be placed on an adhesive background. Loose leaf or transfer gold is ideal for decorating a page with a highlighted initial letter or filling in an ornament.

Shell gold

Gold powder

Gold gouache

Dutch metals

Tip: It is useful to experiment with other forms of metallic leaf that are available. These include palladium leaf, derived from platinum, and silver leaf.

Gesso

Gold leaf needs a glue base in order to attach it to paper or vellum; the form familiar from historical illuminated manuscripts is gesso, which gives a cushioned or raised effect. The ancient skills for making and using gesso have been passed down through generations and remain the most successful and yet the most exacting of techniques. The gesso used for gilding is not the same as that manufactured for gilding wooden frames – the latter are oil-based and would stain paper or vellum. Gesso used in calligraphy may be applied with a quill or a brush. The substance has a slightly sticky surface once it has been activated.

Gesso is an ideal choice of platform for creating raised gold – by placing golf leaf on top of a raised surface to create a very shiny three-dimensional effect. It can take a while to prepare gesso if created from its raw materials but the results are well worth the effort.

Gesso ▶
Essentially a mixture of plaster and glue, gesso is solid but fairly flexible when dry. It is the ideal base for gold decoration, providing an even surface for gilding to take place.

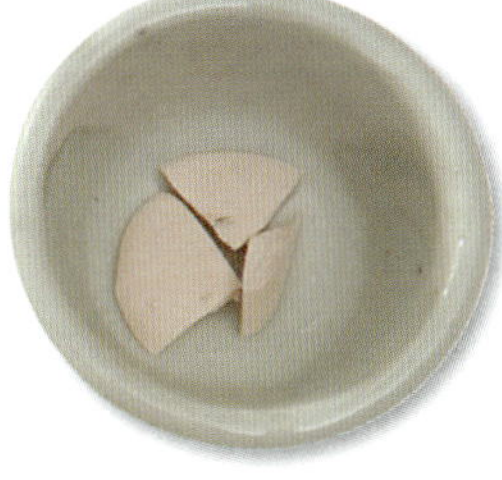

Gesso

Other glues

A number of other glues can be used for gilding. Gum ammoniac is a traditional sticky plant residue, sometimes available ready made. Modern glues include PVA or 'white glue', and acrylic gloss medium – a vehicle intended for extending and imparting shine to acrylic paints – but ideal as a glue base for gilding. Acrylic gold size stays sticky when dry (like adhesive tape), and is useful for sticking the Dutch metals.

Bases for gilding ▼
PVA (white) glue, acrylic gloss medium and water gold size can all be used as bases for gilding.

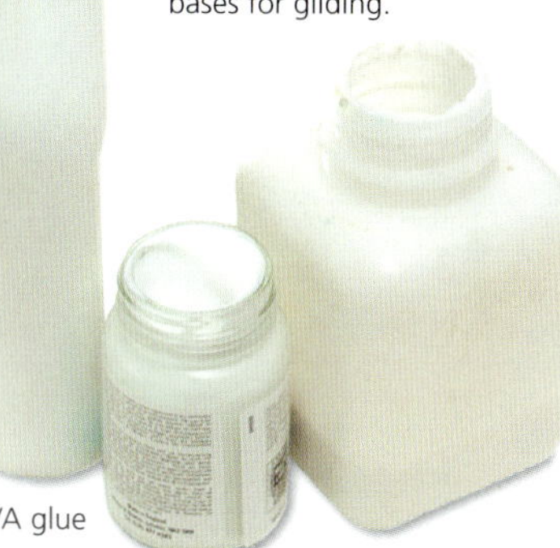

PVA glue

Water gold size

Acrylic gloss medium

Tools

A number of tools are needed for successful gilding, including a small pair of scissors (keep them polished and clean or they will stick to the gold), tweezers and a burnisher. Special burnishers are available with different shaped ends for polishing the gold and persuading it to stick in awkward corners. Agate burnishers, which are 'dog-tooth' in shape, are the most commonly available; their tips must be protected in a soft sleeve to prevent scratches, which would damage the gold. Psilomelanite burnishers have generally replaced the more valued haematite burnishers – a lipstick-shaped tool and the highest prized tool for getting the gold to stick and obtaining a good shine when polishing. Laying of the gold and the initial polishing is generally done through a sheet of glassine paper, which is a shiny paper sometimes seen in photograph albums. A dry, soft brush is useful for removing the excess gold leaf surrounding a gilded letter.

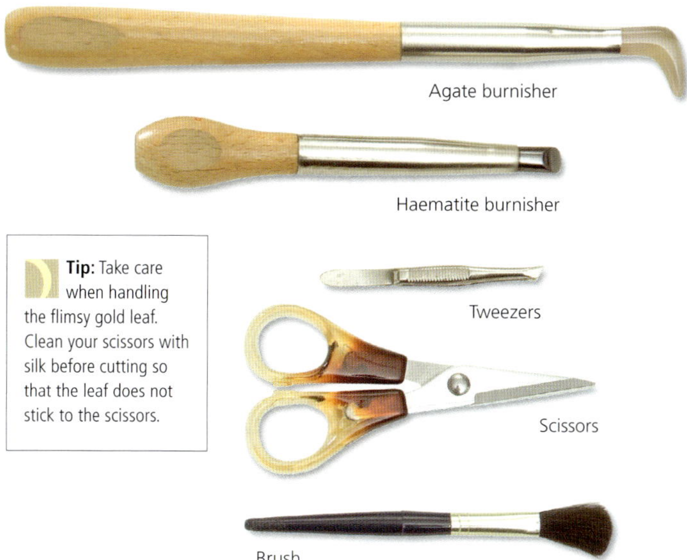

Agate burnisher

Haematite burnisher

Tweezers

Scissors

Brush

Tip: Take care when handling the flimsy gold leaf. Clean your scissors with silk before cutting so that the leaf does not stick to the scissors.

Setting up

To get the best results from calligraphy, a comfortable work surface is needed and a desk with a slope is the best option. Choose a chair that is the correct height so that it will support your back. A relaxed posture will encourage a consistent ink flow. Once you begin work, remember to take frequent breaks. You may find it helpful to do some stretches during this time.

The drawing board

Make a drawing-board out of a sheet of plywood, or MDF (medium-density fiberboard). Do not use hardboard as this will bend. Have it cut to size, if possible at approximately 60 x 45cm (24 x 18in). Customize this to your own needs by applying a padded writing surface. The simplest method is to iron at least six sheets of newspaper to remove all creases, attach this to the board with masking tape, then attach a final white cover of cartridge paper, or better still, white blotting paper. Tape the paper all around the board with masking tape, but ensure the tape does not go over the edges of the board, as this could hinder the use of a T-square.

There are many ways of positioning the board. It can be positioned on a table of comfortable height, propped up with some books. Alternatively, two boards hinged together with piano hinges can be used, so that the book props provide infinite adjustment without slipping.

If the single board slips on the table, try attaching it at the base with white-tack or a strip of non-slip rug underlay. If a steeper board is preferred, position the narrow side on your lap, rest it on the table edge, and adjust the distance between chair and table. If possible, sit near a window or good light source, with the light coming from the left if right-handed, or from the right if left-handed. For evening work, a lamp that can be adjusted to spotlight the writing area would be a major advantage. If intending to work at night using colour, consider using a daylight bulb as it will show the colours in a more realistic light.

The final refinement of the board is made by attaching a guard sheet. Take a strip of paper – fold a sheet diagonally to make it wider if necessary – and attach it left and right of the board so that the top edge sits where you would be writing. This ensures your hand will always rest on the guard sheet and not on the writing paper, preventing the paper from becoming greasy. If you forget to use a guard sheet, it may become harder to write – as you meet the greasier part of the paper, the ink will resist.

Prepared drawing board ▼
Whether using a simple sheet of wood, or a commerically produced drawing board, it needs to be well padded, with the padding taped down. Note the gap between the tape and the edge, allowing the T-square to operate. Attach the guard sheet or keep it free.

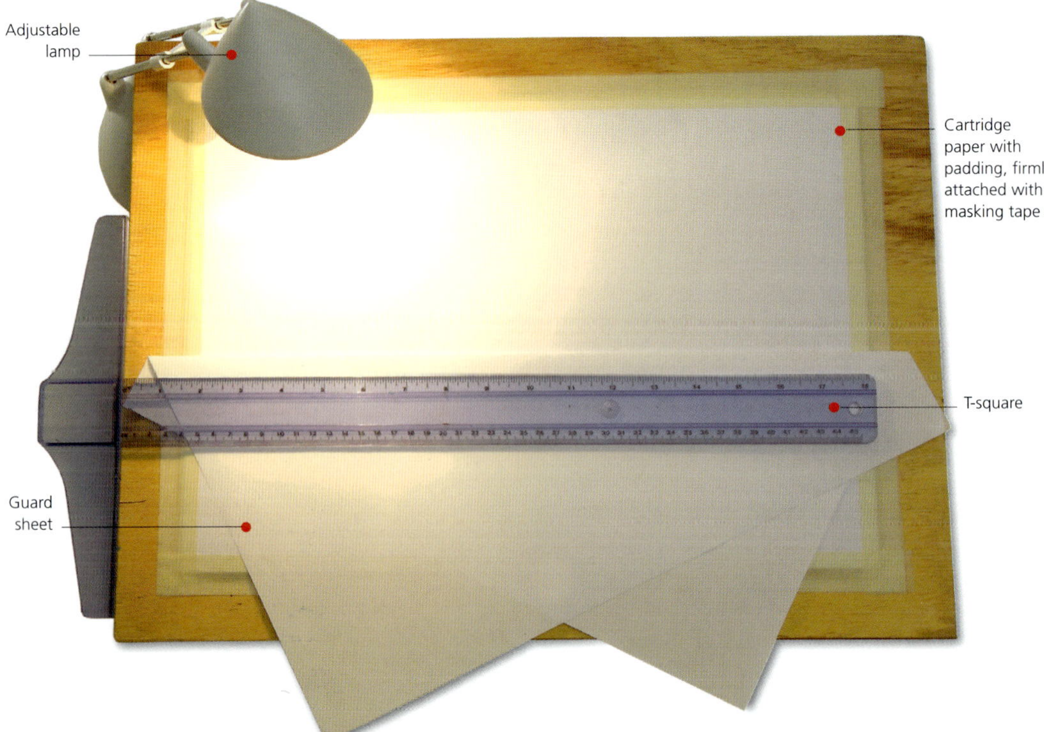

Useful tools

A ruler with clear markings for the accurate mark-up of lines is one of the most essential items. A metal edge is also a useful tool. A ruler or metal edge can be used when cutting paper; work on a self-healing cutting mat or use thick cardboard. Bone folders may be used for scoring and making crisp and accurate folds.

A T-square is a useful, time-saving luxury, as line markings need only be made down one side; parallel lines can then be ruled across. This is why the edge of the board should not be inhibited by masking tape. A set square (triangle) can be used to rule right angles and helps maintain pen angles of 45, 30 or 60 degrees. A protractor is used for measuring letter angles.

Masking tape can be used to attach paper to a sloping board to prevent it from sliding off. Tape can also be stuck in place to preserve a clean strip of paper when using colour washes.

It is useful to have a supply of 2H and 4H pencils for ruling lines and HB pencils for making notes. It is important that the pencils used for ruling lines are well sharpened. Always keep a soft eraser at hand.

Tip: Using scissors, cut a bottle-sized hole in a small bath sponge to keep your ink bottle safe from tipping. If ink does spill, some will be absorbed by the sponge.

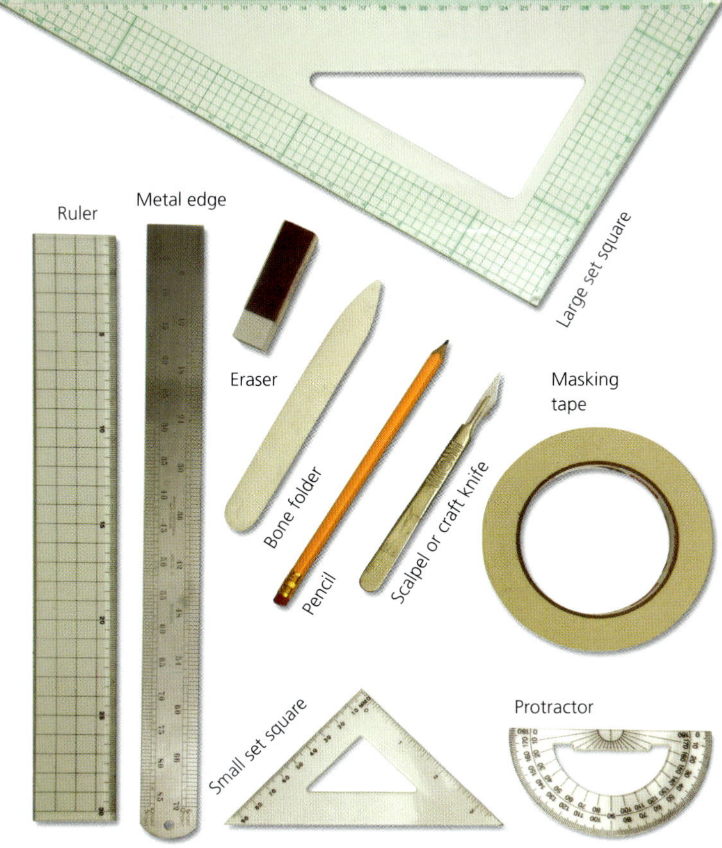

Basic techniques

These are techniques that you are likely to use repeatedly. It is important to do them correctly to avoid damaging materials and equipment.

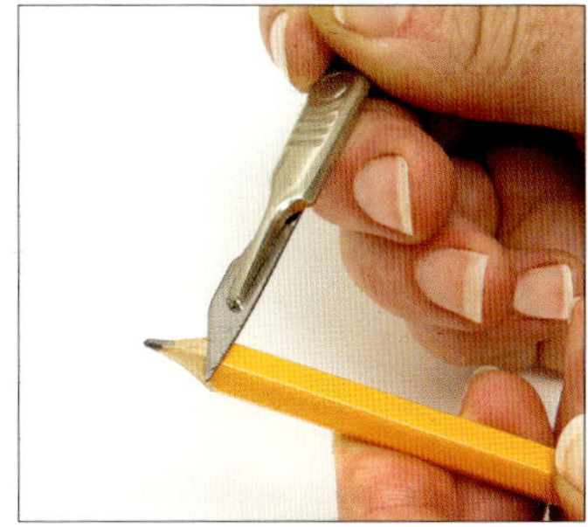

Sharpening a pencil ▲
Hard pencils (2H, 3H, 4H) will stay sharp for longer than soft pencils. Soft pencils (HB, B, 2B etc.) will break under pressure and become blunt quickly. A standard pencil sharpener will do most of the job (if it is new), but the final touch is to shave away the tip with a craft knife.

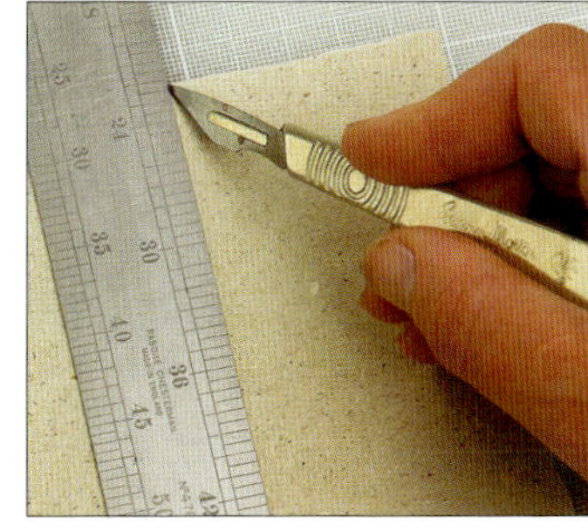

Cutting paper ▲
Always use a sharp blade. If it is blunt the blade will need to be pressed harder and the chances of it slipping are higher, with possible resultant injury. Cut against a metal ruler, or a plastic ruler with a cutting edge. Use a cutting mat or thick cardboard, such as the back of a layout pad. Cut with several light strokes rather than one heavy one, and arrange the paper so you can make cutting strokes towards your body. Cutting from left to right is less controlled and the knife may slip.

Basic penmanship

Once all the necessary equipment has been assembled, you can prepare to begin your calligraphy. To produce good work a relaxed posture is needed, as well as an arm position that encourages a steady flow of ink. Spend some time adjusting your position so that you are comfortable – learning calligraphy should always be an enjoyable experience, but it also requires much concentration. Work is more likely to be successful if calligraphy is practised on a regular basis and all the equipment is kept in one place. You may prefer to work on a drawing board resting on a table top, or secured to the edge of a table. Alternatively, the drawing board can be rested in your lap, or flat on a table, resting your weight on the non-writing arm so you have free movement with your pen. Remember to lay padding underneath your paper as this will help the flexibility of the nib, and prevent it from scratching on the paper. Make sure that the writing sheets are fixed to the board securely. Light should fall evenly on the working area, and although daylight is best, an adjustable lamp will illuminate the page.

Terminology

Calligraphy uses special terminology to describe the constituent parts of letters and words, and the way they are written. The style or 'hand' in which the writing is created is composed of letterforms. These are divided into capital, or upper-case letters, and smaller, lower-case letters (traditionally called majuscule and minuscule). Text is usually written in lower-case letters because they are easier to read than solid blocks of capital letters. The x-height is the term used for the height of the full letter in capitals (the space an 'X' occupies) and for the main body of the letter for lower case, excluding ascenders and descenders. In lines of text, the gap between x-heights, which accomodates ascenders or descenders, is known as the interlinear space. The spaces enclosed within letters are called counters.

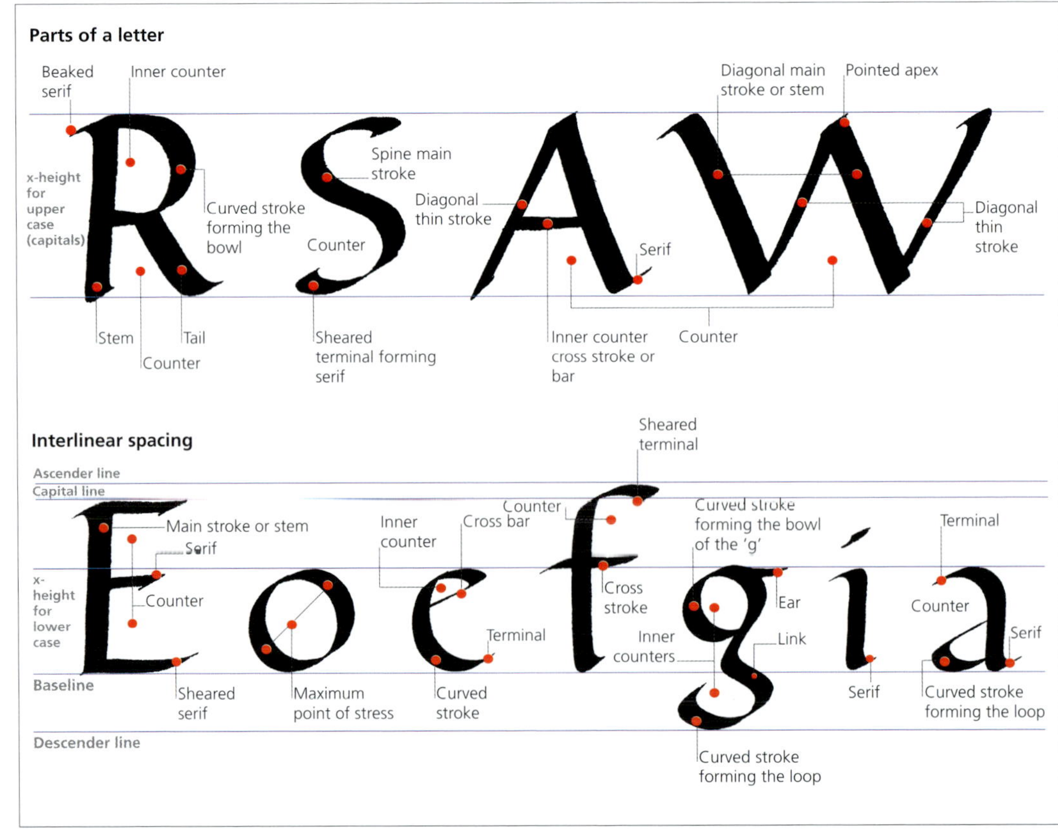

Essential techniques

The techniques detailed below are essential to creating good calligraphy. Carrying them out properly will ensure that letterforms are properly proportioned, well spaced and at the correct angle. It is important to practise some of these, such as using a broad nib and holding the pen at a constant angle, before you begin to write letters and words.

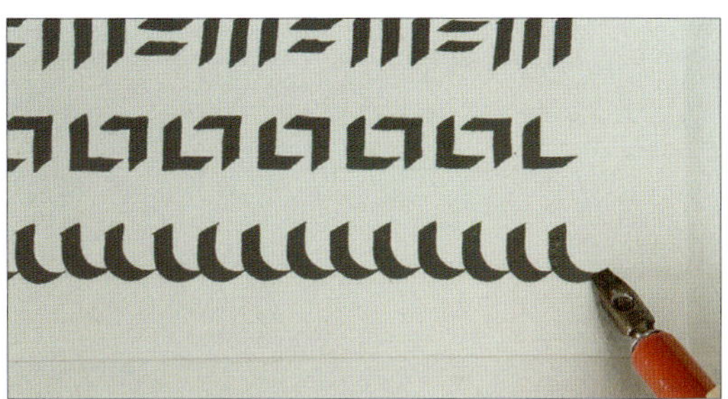

Using a broad nib ▲
A broad nib, pen or brush is the essential tool for calligraphy. When the pen is held in the hand it forms an angle to the horizontal writing line, known as the pen angle. It takes some adjustment to use this sort of tool after using pointed pens and pencils. It is helpful to pay careful attention to just keeping the whole nib edge against the paper when writing to avoid ragged strokes. Try some zig-zags – aim to create the thinnest and thickest of the marks by moving the pen along its side and along its width to appreciate its extremes.

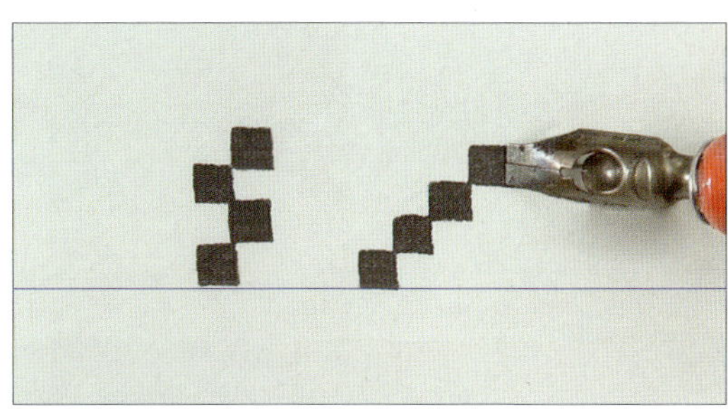

Measuring nib widths ▲
Whatever nib size is used, the height of the letter is determined by using a 'ladder' of nib widths. A baseline is ruled first and a broad-edged pen held at right angles (90 degrees) to the line. A clear mark should be made, long enough to be a square. The pen is moved upwards and marks are drawn so that they just touch; forming a 'stairway' shape or a 'ladder'. An alphabet exemplar will indicate the number of nib-widths needed for the x-height of a hand. Use that measurement for ruling all the lines.

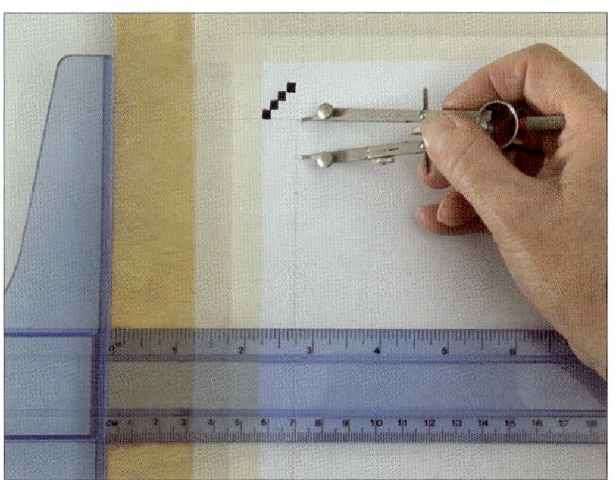

Ruling the lines ▲
The standard method is to mark repeat measurements (taken from the nib width exercise above) down both sides of the paper, then join them up with a ruler. Another way is to use a scrap of paper with a straight edge, mark a short series of accurate measurements and transfer these across (this is not suitable for measurements below 4mm (5/32in) but is accurate enough in larger sizes). Marking down just one side of the paper is sufficient if using a T-square. Attach the marked sheet to the board top and bottom to prevent movement. The T-square is used to rule parallel lines across the page.

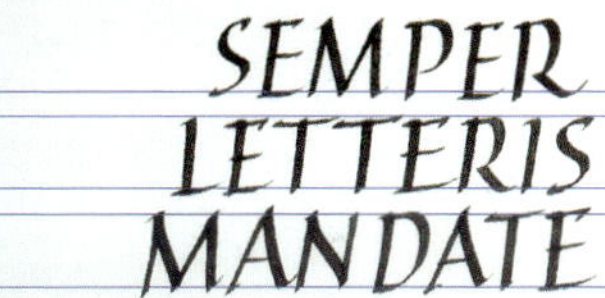

Leaving enough spaces ▲
Take the measurement of the required number of nib-widths for the x-height. For lower case letters such as Italic, rule all the lines to this measurement and leave two gaps between x-heights, to allow for ascenders and descenders. When ruling up for writing entirely capitals, it is sufficient to use a single gap, or even less, as there are no extensions.

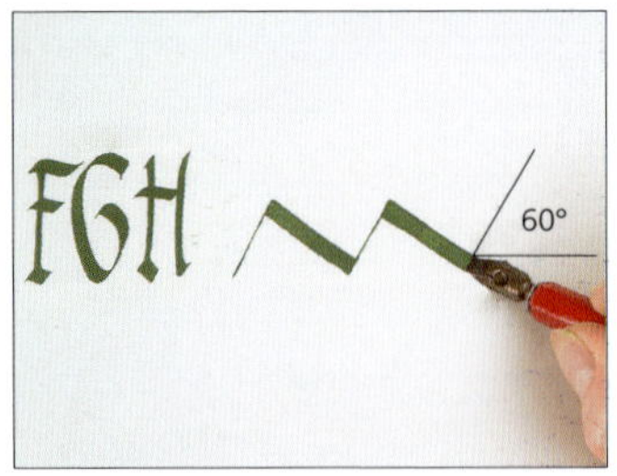

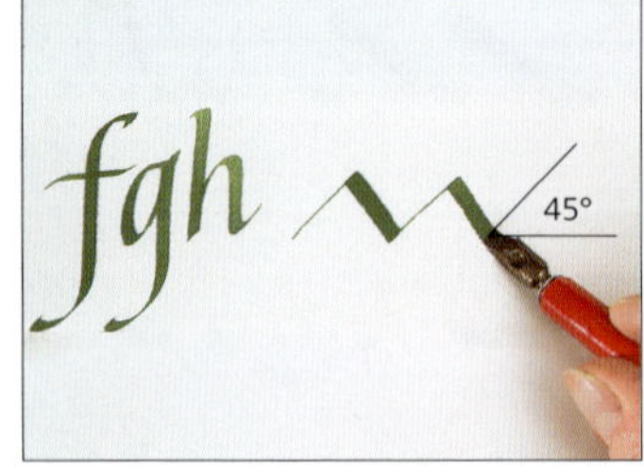

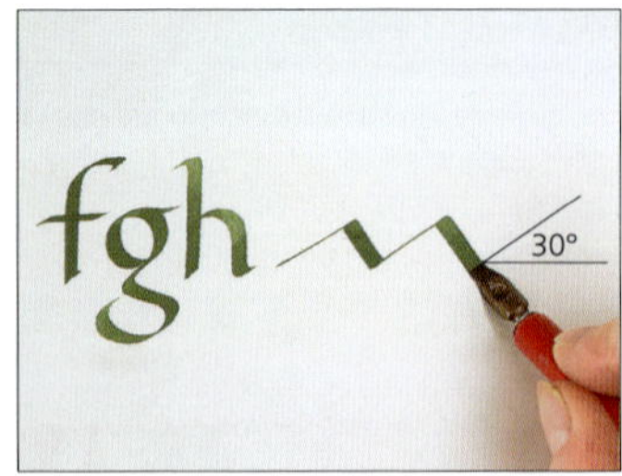

Pen angles ▲
Holding the pen at the same angle to the writing line for every letter is an essential discipline to create letters that work well together. Each alphabet exemplar indicates what angle is necessary, as they vary in different script styles. Resist the temptation to move the wrist as in standard writing. As the letter is completed, check it is still at the same angle – it is easy to change without noticing. Zig-zag patterns, made at whatever pen angle is indicated for the chosen alphabet style, can be a useful warming-up exercise.

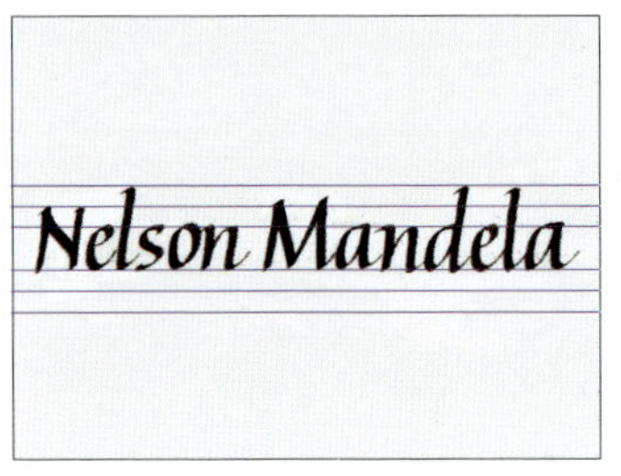

Allowing for the capitals ▲
When you are writing mostly lowercase with the occasional capital, rule the lines as for lower case, and gauge by eye how high to write the capital – often it is just two nib widths higher than the lower-case x-height, which will be lower than the height of the ascenders.

Left-handers

Left-handed calligraphers need to make some adjustments in holding the edged pen to mimic the natural position of the right-hander.

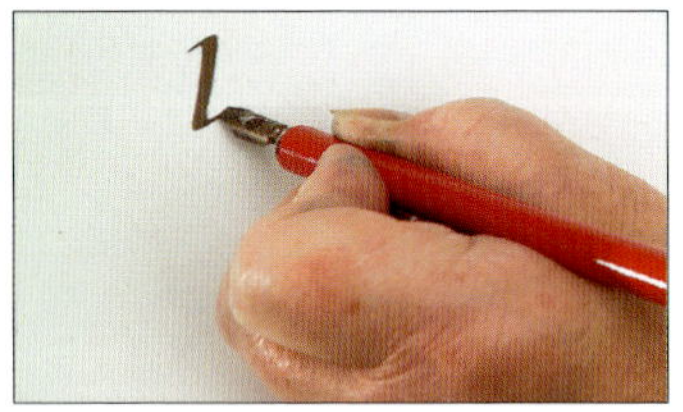

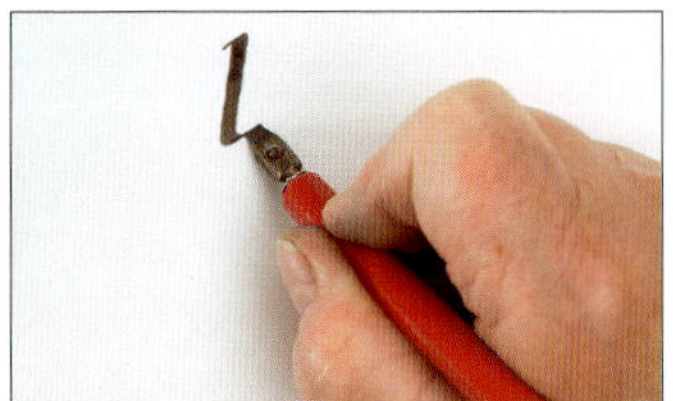

The left-hander should sit to the right of the paper, and tuck the left elbow into the waist, so that the wrist can be twisted a little to the left to hold the pen at the required angle. There are left-oblique nibs available to minimize the amount that the wrist needs to be bent, but if left-handers can cope with a straight-edged nib they will have a greater choice of nibs available to them.

Letter spacing ▶
Once you start to write words, it is important to be aware of letter spacing and awkward combinations. Aim to create an overall balanced texture in a page of writing. With lower-case letters, the space is generally regulated by a need for rhythm and an evenness of downstrokes, particularly noticeable in Italic and Gothic. Watch for rogue letters that already have a gap – they can cause problems when combined with the gap of an adjoining letter (such as with 'r' and 'a' in Foundational).

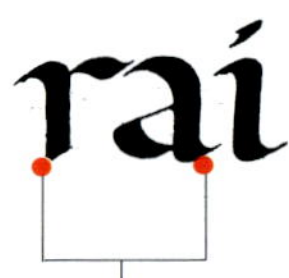

awkward combination of letters leaves a big space

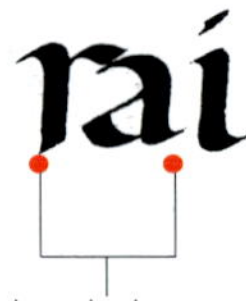

place the letters close together to create a more natural space

▼ The letter spacing below is helped to be more legible by spacing out the letters according to the shape and relationship of letters to each other.

Unspaced ▼

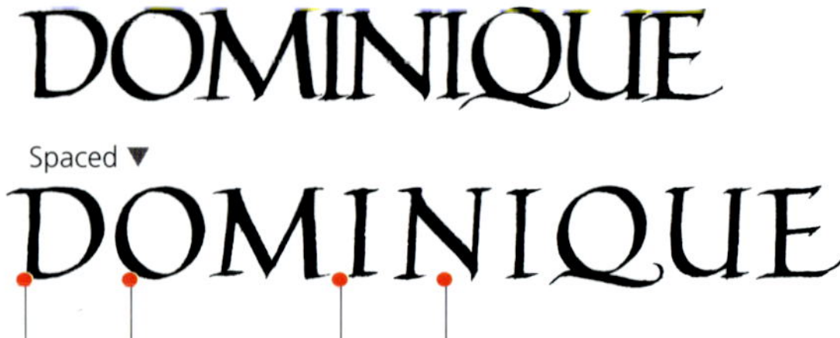

Spaced ▼

'DO' – two curves together require closest spacing

'IN' – two uprights adjacent – give these the most space

Alphabets

It is best to start by simply learning the alphabets and focusing on gaining a sound grasp of the principles. It is easy to get confused and create muddled hybrid letterforms when jumping from one style to another before understanding the family characteristics.

Learning the alphabets ▼

Study the proportion of the letters, their height and the width of the body of the letter. Capitals and lower-case letters are included for each alphabet where appropriate. Calligraphers normally establish the body height of the lettering by the number of pen widths it should contain. For example with Foundational hand, use four nib widths for the x-height, while the ascenders and descenders should be less than three quarters of the x-height (two or three nib widths). The capital letters should be just two nib widths above the x-height and do not look right if they are any higher. Serifs can embellish the end of the letter.

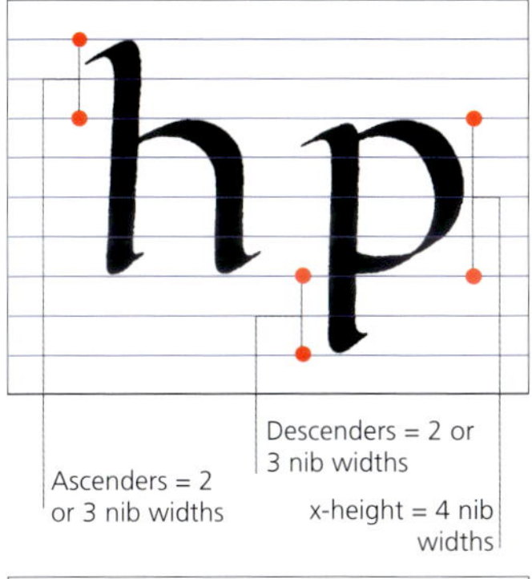

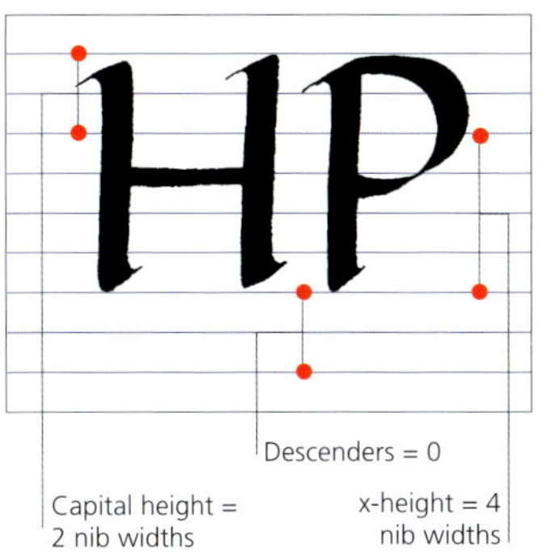

Basic strokes ▶

Every alphabet has a few basic strokes that are common to several letters. We think of them as 'family' characteristics, and understanding them is key to being able to accurately reproduce the alphabets. Thus in Uncials (capitals), many letters conform to the very rounded shape of the 'O'; in Italic, the branching nature of 'A' and 'N' is repeated in many other letters. In lots of cases, the family characteristics are also repeated in inverted versions. Thus, 'u' and 'n' in lower-case forms are upside-down versions of each other – so note how the arches are the same, and check you are properly reproducing this formation yourself. Note, too, whether upside-down ascender letters become their descender counterparts when inverted, and likewise check if your own rendering acknowledges this.

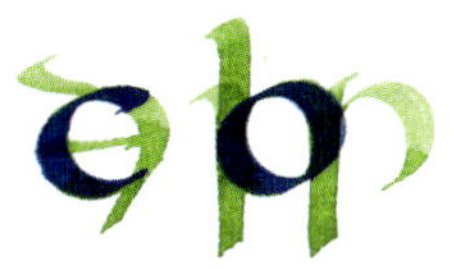

Uncial letters based on the 'o'.

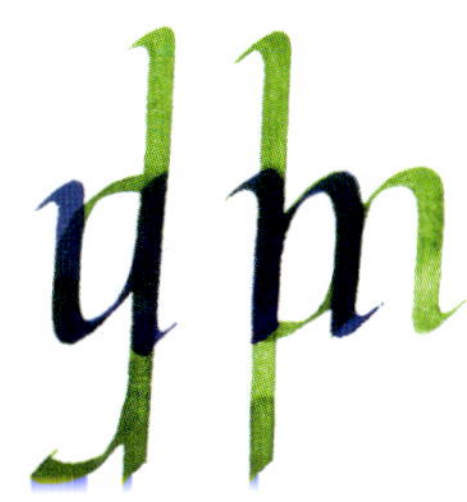

Inverted characteristics of 'u' and 'n' in other Italic letters.

Forming strokes

When writing with a normal pen, it can easily be moved round the page. When writing with a calligraphy pen this is not possible because the nib resists against the paper and may cause an ink blot or mark. This is the reason why letters are made by lifting the pen between writing separate strokes. For example the letter 'o' has a pen lift, and two strokes. Other letters of the alphabet are made up of one, two, three or four strokes. The pen strokes make writing in calligraphy much slower than normal writing. Pay close attention to the shape of the letter, and write slowly to start with.

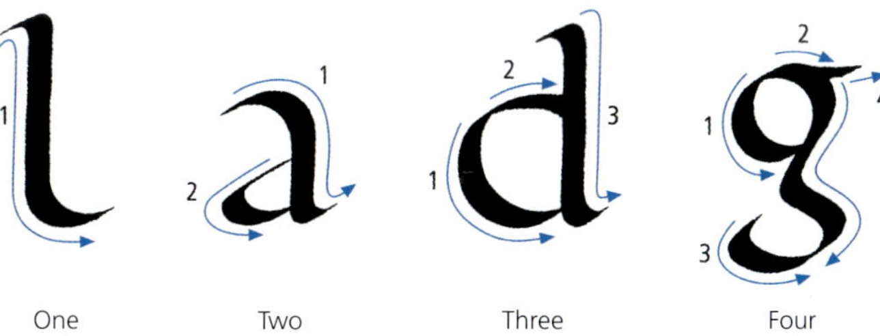

One stroke | Two strokes | Three strokes | Four strokes

Numerals

Numbers are frequently written at the same height as capital letters, with no extensions, and these are called 'ranging numerals'. They fit into the same x-height as capital letters. 'Non-ranging' numerals are modelled on the lower case x-height, with 0 and 1 confined to the lower-case x-height, whilst the others extend in imitation of ascenders and descenders, with even numbers above the line and odd numbers below. Numerals should match the family characteristics of the letters they accompany.

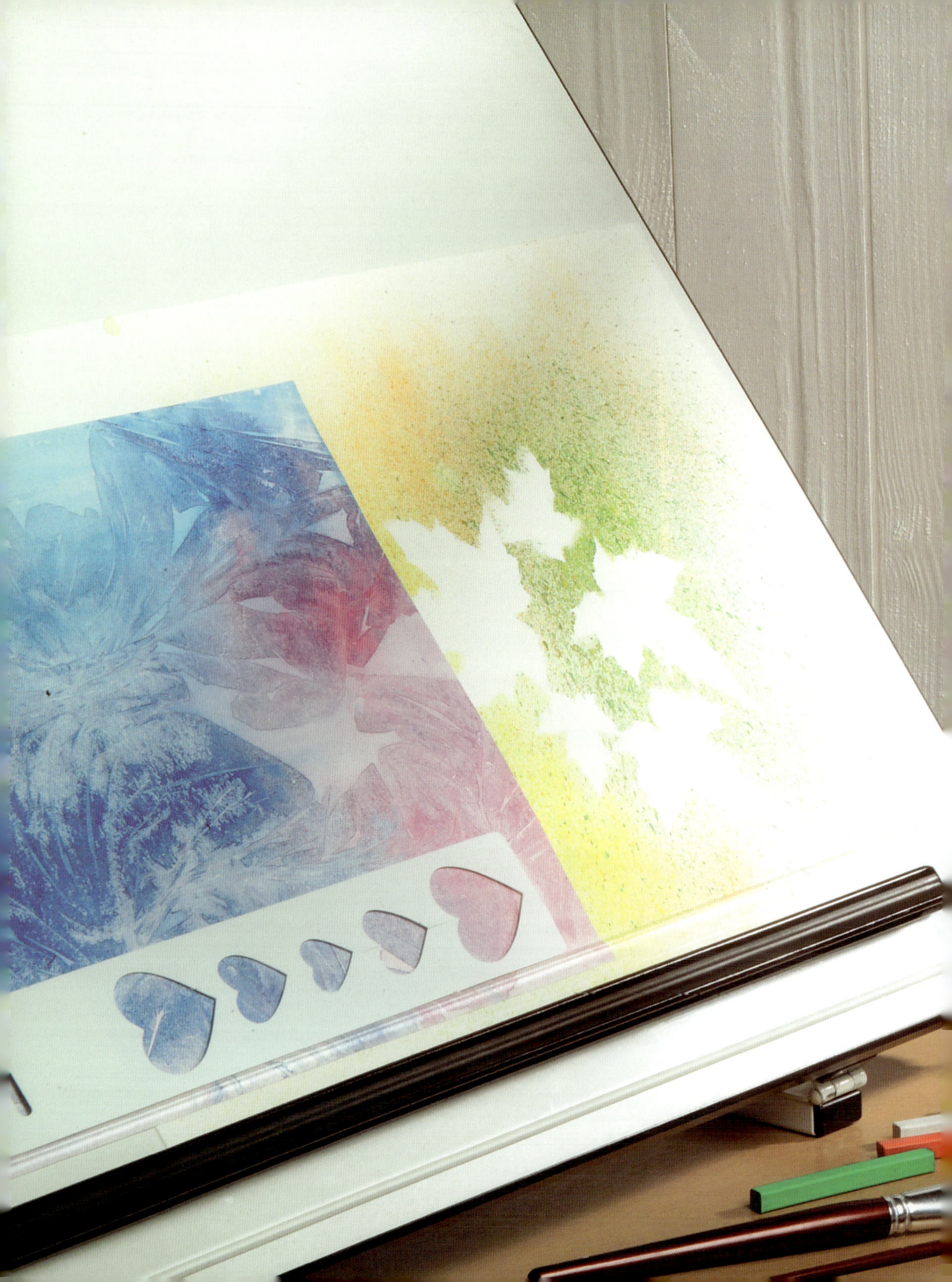

Calligraphic Techniques

There are numerous techniques, both traditional and modern, that can be combined with calligraphic lettering to create wonderful visual effects. This part of the book guides you through a number of these methods of decoration and embellishment, from the elegant simplicity of embossing to the more complicated but richly satisfying technique of gilding, and shows how they can be put into practice.

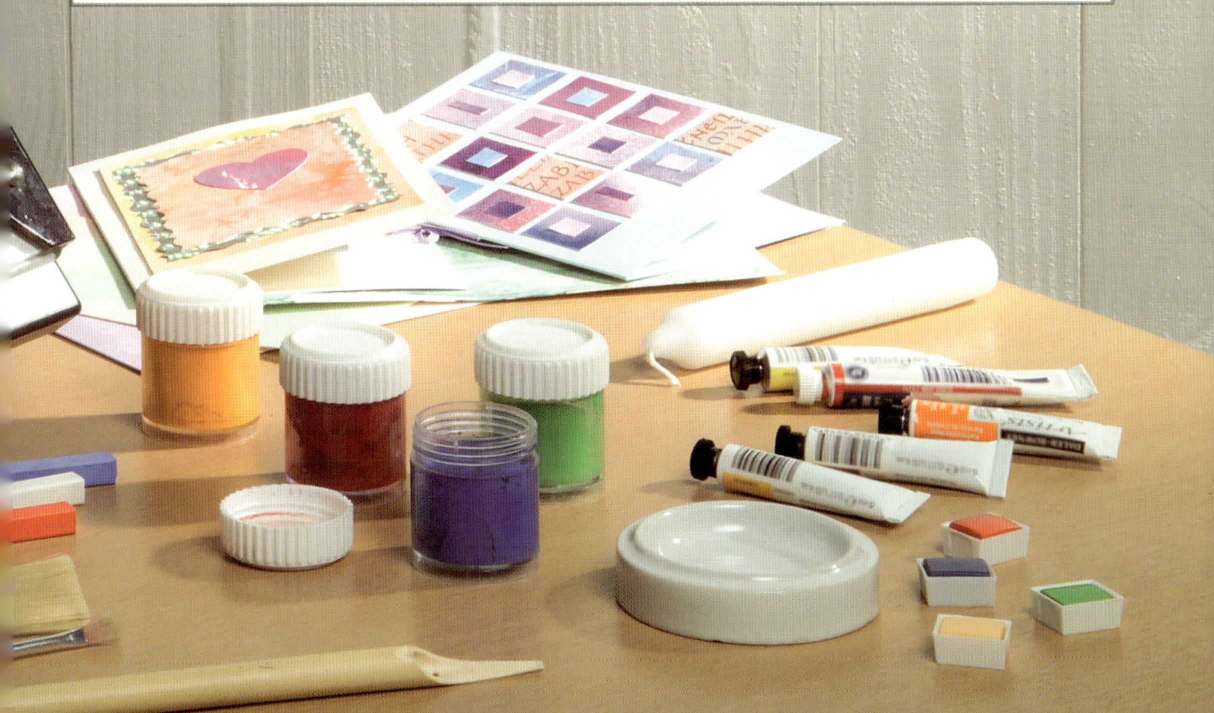

Flourished Italic and Italic swash capitals

Flourishes are extensions applied to the beginning and ending of letters. The variations produced by flourishing Italic letters are fun to do and the possibilities are endless. Practising will give you confidence in handling the pen. Some letters are easier to flourish than others, and there are some letters that cannot be flourished. Swash or flourished Italic capitals have simple extensions to the letter. A swash should be a simple flourish that is not too ornate, so as not to alter the character of the whole piece.

Practising letters

The letters are written and spaced as for formal Italic hand with the same x-height of 5 nib widths. The interlinear space will need to be greater to accommodate the flowing upward and downward flourishes. Care should be taken to keep a good basic Italic letterform throughout. The flowing movement of the letter extensions should not appear to be too constricted or too tight as flourished letters do not look good if they are too cramped. When deciding on the route of the extensions on the ascenders and descenders, a finely drawn pencil line is often helpful. Use a dip pen and keep it well loaded with ink as this helps the flow. Try writing the letters using some different sized nibs and a range of nib widths. Experiment with different letters of the alphabet to discover which flourishes work best.

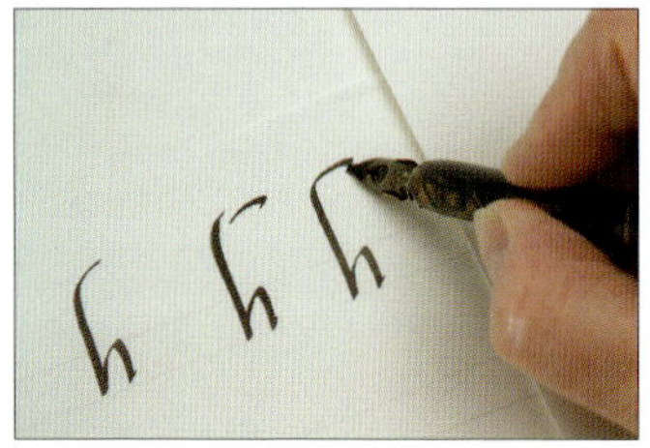

1 Rule writing lines as for formal Italic but make the interlinear space much larger to allow more space for the flourished ascenders and descenders. Begin flourishing by making the ascenders a little taller than usual. Try a simple lead-in stroke from the right of the letter 'h', completing it as normal. Go back to the top of the ascender and add the second stroke.

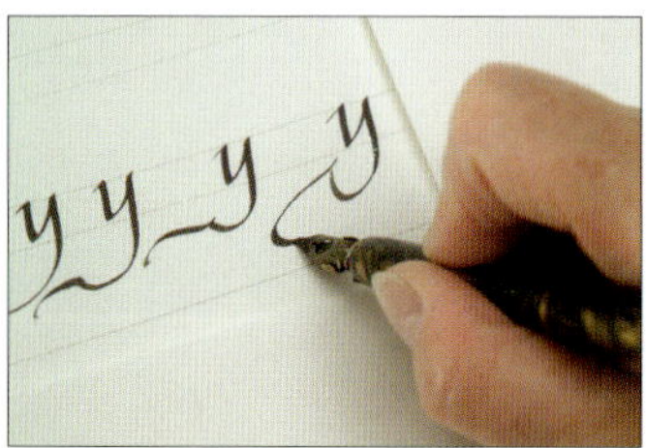

2 Try flourishing the letter 'y'. Remember to keep the underlying letterform. If the flourishes seem awkward to do then it is best not to pursue them. Practise the shapes that flow easily from the pen.

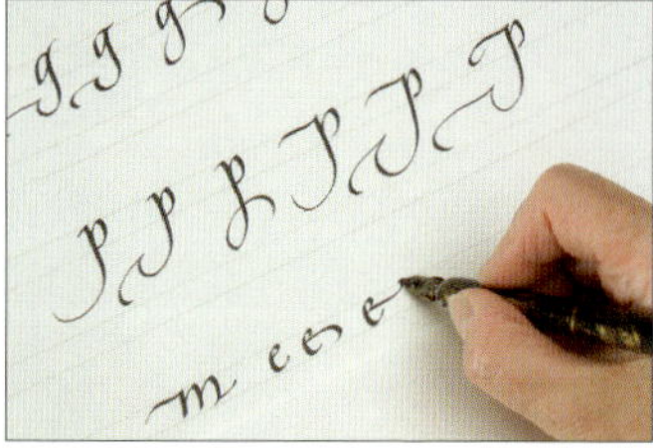

3 Try some different flourishes – be adventurous. Sometimes it is useful to extend the letter along the line (as in the case of 'm' and 'n'). Try elongating the central bar of 'e'. By trial and error you will discover which flourishes are the most successful.

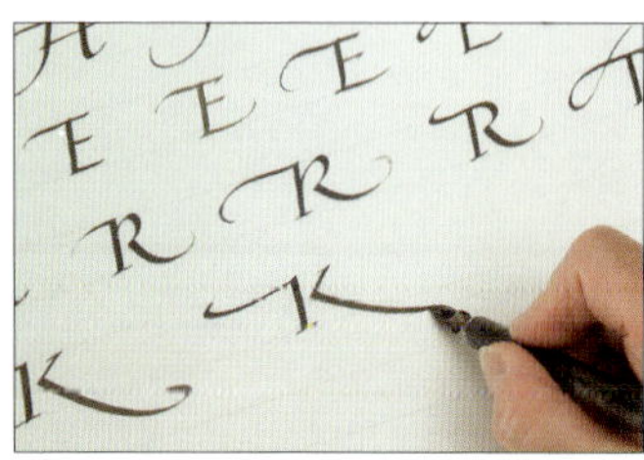

4 Flourished Italic capitals or swash capitals are also exciting to do and look very smart as a single letter to introduce a line of lower-case Italic writing. Practise adding some simple extensions first.

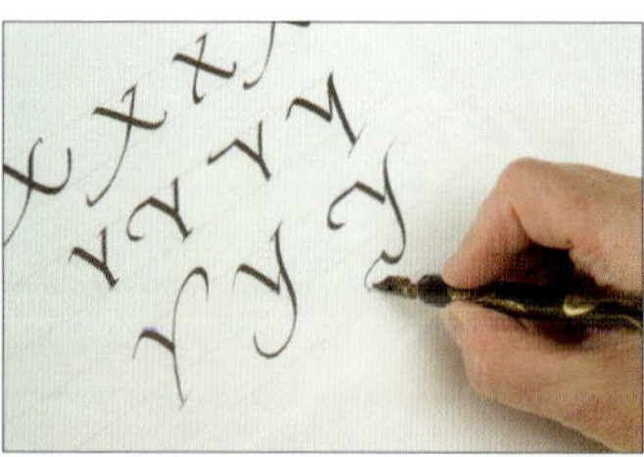

5 Try to relax when writing these shapes. The pen angle can change as you are working: moving from 40 degrees through to 5 degrees to enable you to manoeuvre the pen in a fluid way. Here the pen has been turned on its tip. It can be tilted on its side to add fine detail. This pen manipulation is quite acceptable.

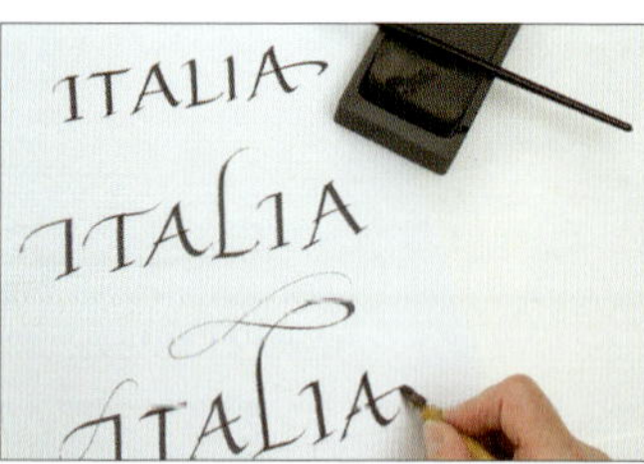

6 Practise three variations of Italic capitals with flourishes added. Note that not every letter is flourished. Less is better and has more impact.

Planning flourished letters

When flourishing letters, the action of the hand holding the pen should come from an arm movement rather than just the fingers or the hand. To practise these arm movements take a large sheet of practice paper and make some expansive, gestural movements with a loaded pen. This exercise will help you to create sweeping flourishes.

In a line of writing it is best to plan the letters that can be flourished. Resist the temptation to flourish every ascender and descender as this will look crowded and over ornate, making the writing unpleasant to read. On a short line of text, you should only flourish the first and last letter. Flourished capitals allow room for lots of creativity and can look very striking, but do not be tempted to use them for whole pieces of text – too many will not work well together as they make the text appear overly busy. Flourishes should always have a specific purpose – as decoration, to balance a design, or to emphasize the flow of the line. They should be lively but applied cautiously.

Practice exercise: **Name tags and place labels**

Show off flourished Italics and swash capitals by writing the names of friends and family for an event or party.

Materials

- *Layout or practice paper*
- *Black ink or gouache*
- *Good quality paper or thin card (stock), in a variety of colours*
- *Gouache paint in white*
- *Dip pens*
- *Scissors or craft (utility) knife*
- *Hole punch*
- *Ribbon*

Tip: Have fun writing in colour or adorn your place cards with flourished pen patterns.

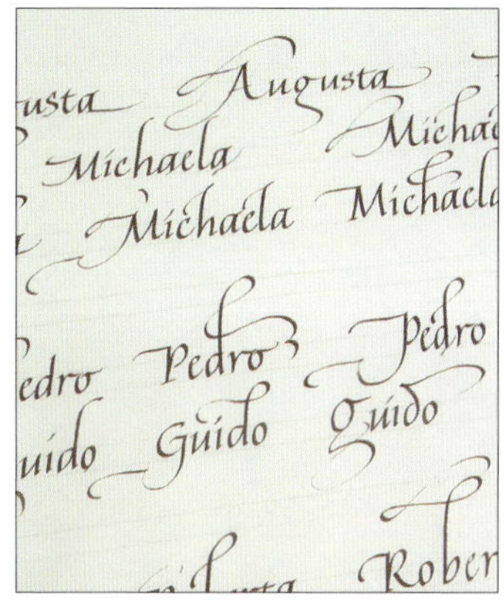

1 Name tags are a wonderful way to enjoy flourished Italic. Practise writing the names of people that you wish to invite on layout paper. Do a swash capital first followed by flourished Italic minuscules.

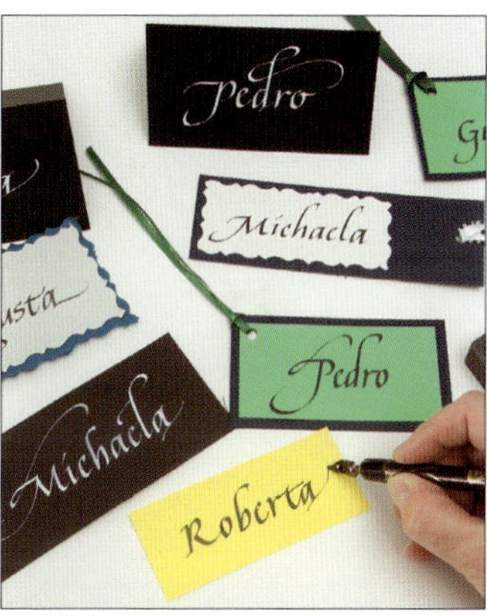

2 Make the gift tags by writing the names on coloured paper or thin card, then cut to size. Embellish decoratively and punch a hole to thread a ribbon, if required.

Practice exercise: **Quotation or poem**

Try writing a favourite quotation or poem and plan where the flourishes and swash letters should fall.

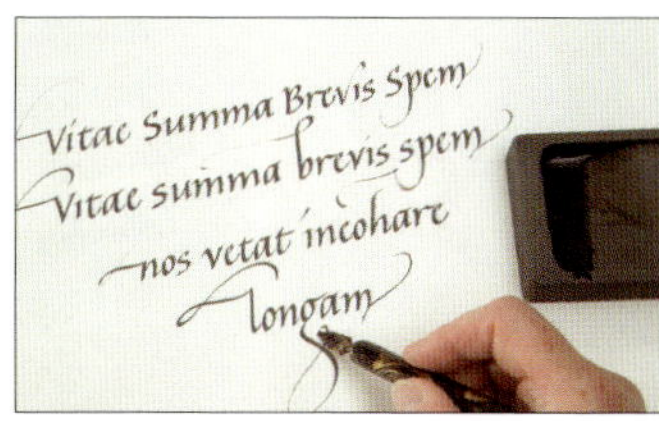

1 Practise writing the small quotation or poem and carefully plan the route of the flourishes to enhance and complement the layout of the design.

Materials

- *Layout or practice paper*
- *Black ink*
- *Dip pen*
- *Good quality paper*
- *Gouache paint in various colours*

2 Transfer to good quality paper. Decorate the project with colour, such as red and gold.

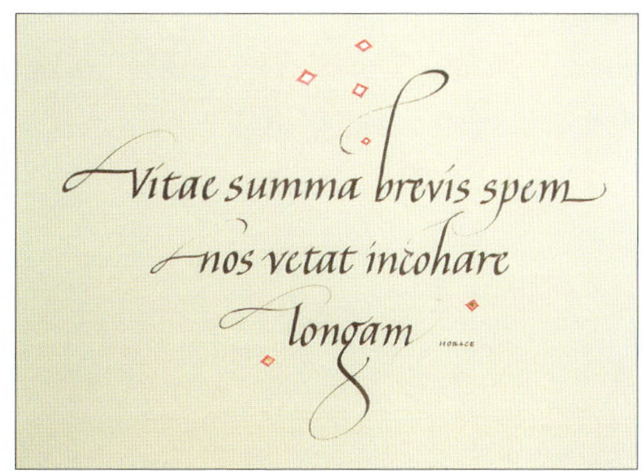

Pen patterns

Trying out different pen patterns is an excellent way to establish what your pen can do. These patterns help develop the skills that are required for calligraphy, as well as being an end in themselves. There are many decorative devices that can be copied and then developed as you build up a repertoire. The repetitive nature of pen patterns is also important because it enables you to build up a rhythm in writing.

Felt-tipped pens are ideal to use for pen patterns as they move freely across the paper without resistance. Choose two sizes of pen, in two colours, or the kind with a nib at each end in two sizes. This gives much more opportunity for variety in pattern-making at little cost. Once you are confident in using the felt-tipped pens, try creating the patterns using different sizes of broad-edged brushes.

Practising strokes

Many of the strokes that can be practised are parts of letterform strokes. Pen angles have to be consistent, or the pattern will be uneven, and this is a good discipline to learn. Notice any change in angle, and train your hand-eye coordination to maintain that angle. Measuring and ruling lines to accommodate the pattern is good practice for preparing lines for writing.

Tip: When using patterns try to achieve complete harmony throughout your work. Pattens should be planned before a piece of calligraphy is begun and not simply added in on a whim. By using a square grid at 45 degrees to the horizontal, you can create the diamond which forms the basis of the zig-zag pattern.

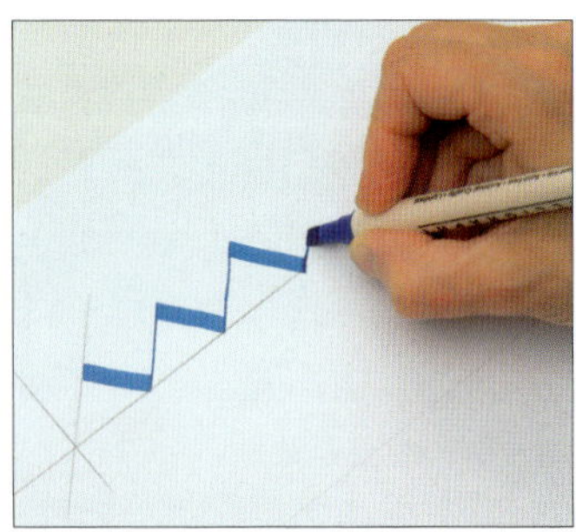

1 Practise holding the pen at a constant 45-degree angle. Control the pen by making equal-sized zig-zags. Practise making very thick and very thin lines in the zig-zags.

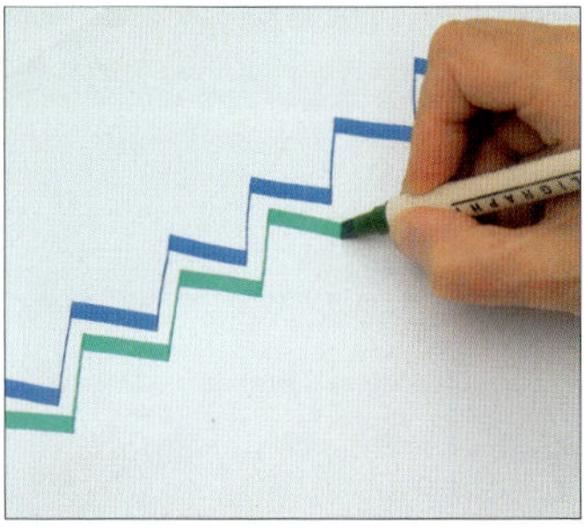

2 Put another row next to the first in a different colour to make parallel zig-zag marks. This will help develop co-ordination.

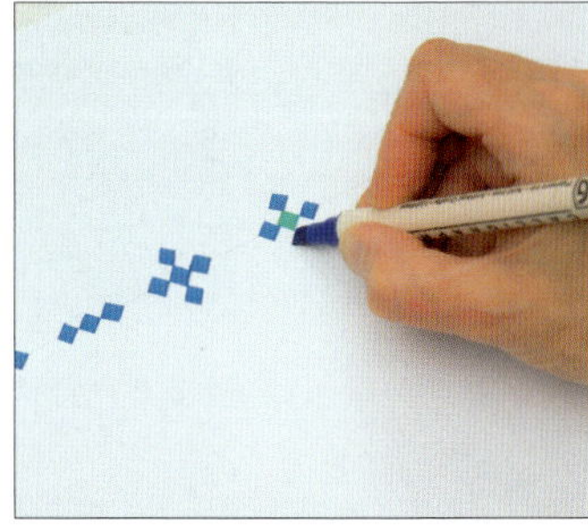

3 Make smaller, more concise marks just by making squares; make their edges touch – this takes more care.

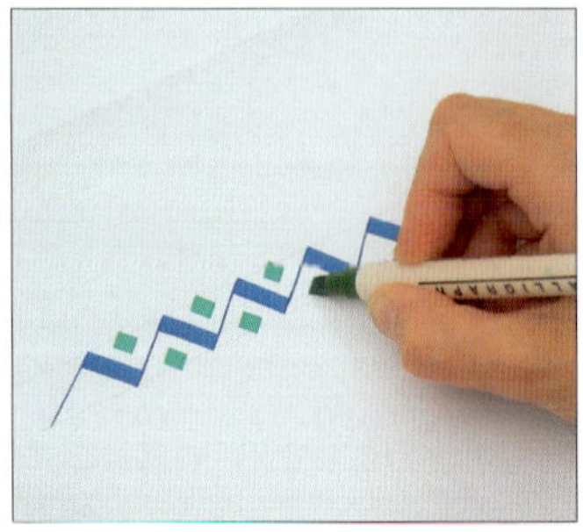

4 Do another zig-zag, then add squares using the other colour.

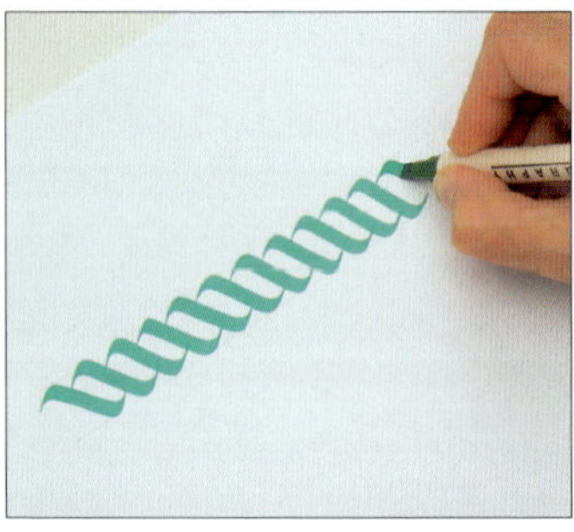

5 Curves are next; but do not be deceived, this is a small curve at each end of a straight stroke, which is repeated to build up the design.

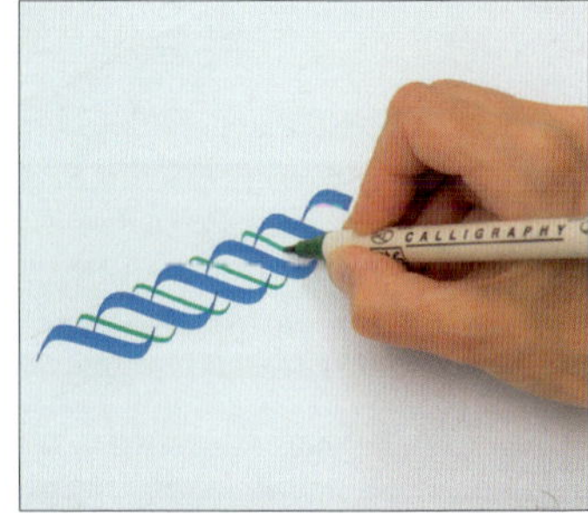

6 The appearance of the 'rope' created can be varied by opening up the white spaces between the curves and adding a narrower side stroke.

Practice exercise: **Building up pen patterns**

Continue to practise with more complex pen patterns created by using two colours of felt-tipped pen, each in large and small sizes, such as 5mm (1/4in) and 2mm (5/64in). Alternatively, use two sizes of broad-edged pen and two colours of ink. When you have perfected drawing the patterns in pen, try using brushes. Alter the pressure on the brush to change the thickness of the line.

Materials
- *Plain white paper*
- *Pens in two sizes*
- *Inks in two colours*

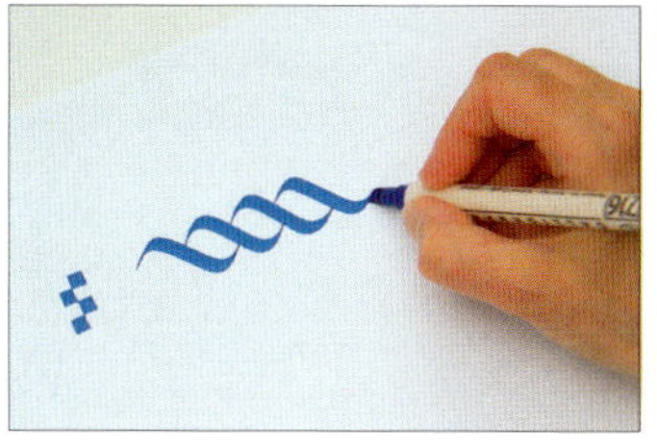

1 In one colour, make wide curves, paying attention to keeping the white spaces inside an even distance apart. Use a constant 45-degree pen angle.

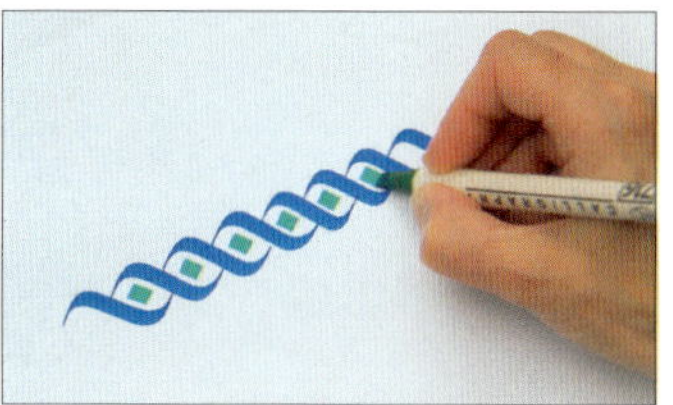

2 In another colour, add squares inside the curves, maintaining the 45-degree pen angle.

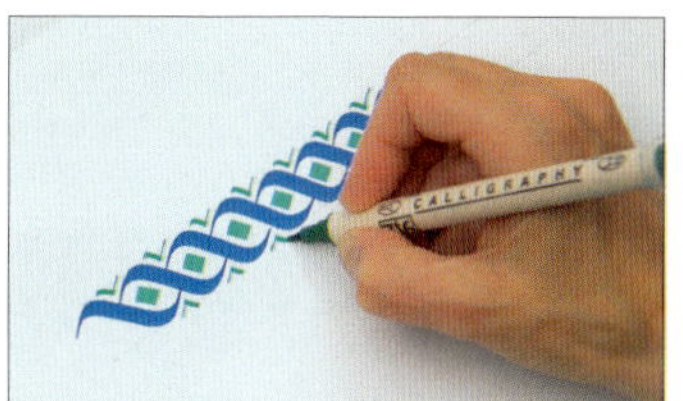

3 In one of the two colours already used, build up the pattern with a thinner pen on the outside.

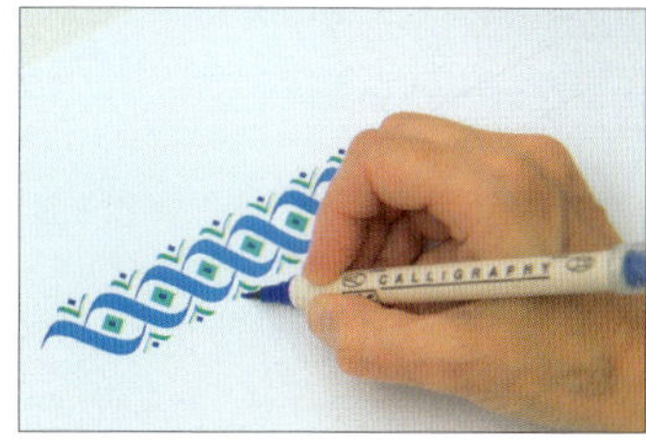

4 Complete the decoration with small squares using the narrower pen in the other colour.

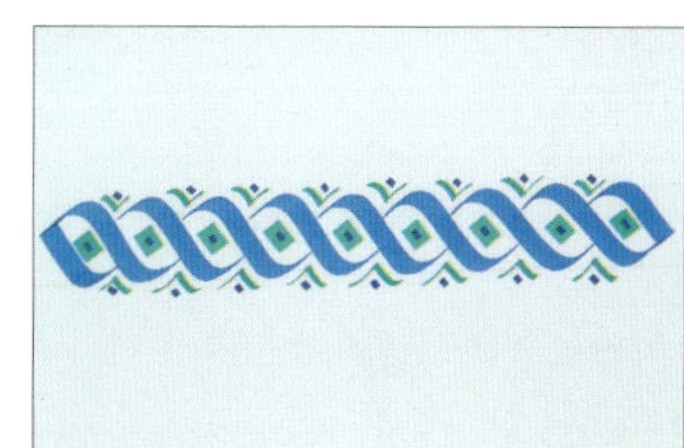

5 The finished design: repeated strokes develop a rhythm that makes a lively pattern. The two sizes add visual interest.

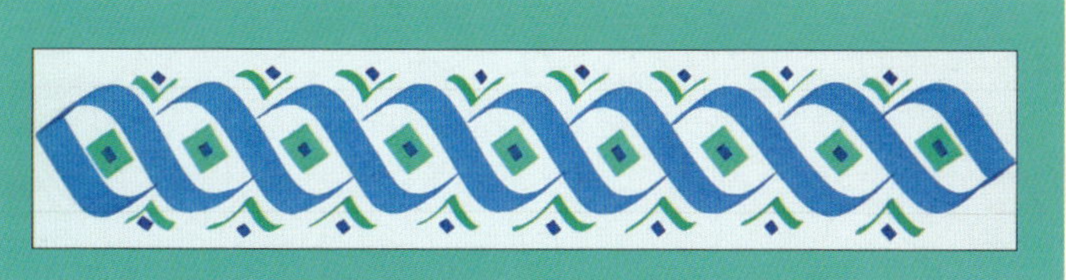

6 This would make an attractive border to a piece of work, or it could be given a frame and mounted by itself.

Other patterns

These decorative patterns will help you to practise different pen strokes.

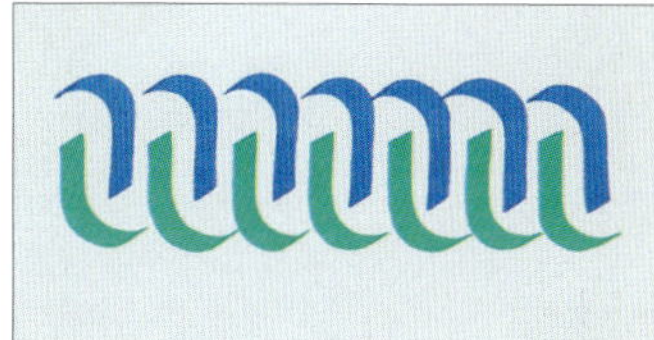

Curves ▲
It can be helpful to turn the page the other way up for the second row so that the marks are being repeated in the same way.

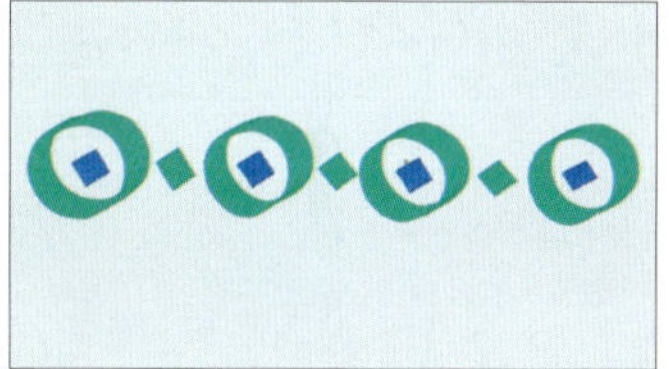

Circles and diamonds ▲
If all the circles are made first, judging the gap for the diamonds will be difficult, so make the diamonds as you progress.

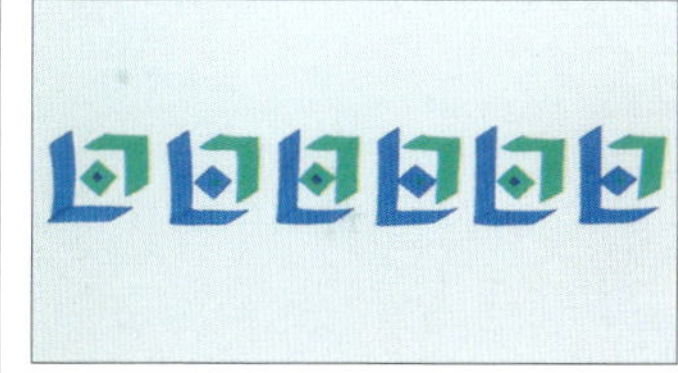

Build up 'L' shapes ▲
Make all the 'L's, then go back and make inverted 'L's in another colour. Add the diamonds last.

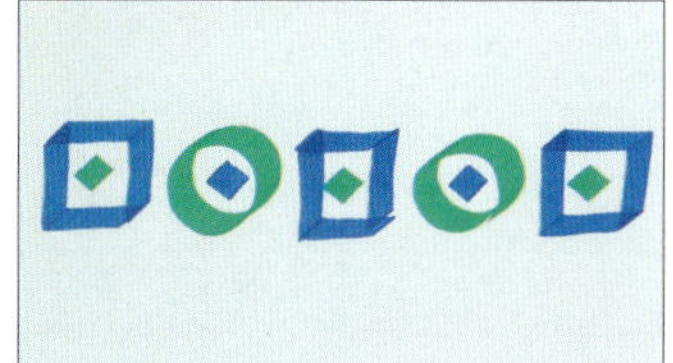

Squares and circles ▲
Alternate colours create added visual interest in this pattern.

Ruling pen

The ruling pen is a tool made up of a pen holder with two stainless-steel blades attached at the writing end. One of the pen's blades is straight and flat and the other bows slightly outwards. The tips of the pen almost meet and the space between them forms the reservoir for the ink or paint. The pen is loaded with ink or paint using a brush or the dipper that is supplied with bottles of ink. The thumbscrew on its bowed blade alters the distance between the tips and finely adjusts the amount of ink that flows, thereby changing the width of the line. The further apart the tips, the thicker the line made by the pen.

The original purpose of the ruling pen was for ruling accurate lines of uniform thickness. Technical drawing has now been overtaken by the use of technical pens, and in more recent years, by computer technology, which is able to produce ruled lines much more quickly. However, calligraphers have adopted the ruling pen as an artistic tool, and have found new ways to make marks, both conventional and more experimental. The attraction of this pen in calligraphy is its freedom of movement in any direction, unimpeded by a broad edge, which means it flows freely across the paper. Although the ruling pen is still frequently used for creating straight lines, it also presents possibilities for making calligraphy exciting for those who prefer expressive, gestural writing.

Practising ruling lines and making marks

Drawing neat straight lines is one way of using the ruling pen, but there is so much more that it can be used for. It is also an ideal tool for creating free, fine strokes for either writing or drawing, and if it is held in a less conventional way, flattened over the paper, with its open side pressed towards the paper, more ink will escape, making a thicker mark. When used in this way the ruling pen produces a heavy line rather like a brush. Once this technique has been mastered, the pen can be manipulated and bold marks of various thicknesses can be developed.

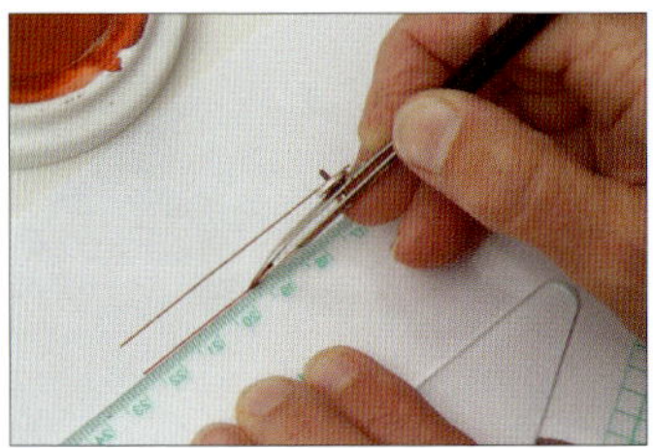

1 To rule lines conventionally, place the rule with its bevelled edge up, to prevent ink seepage. Dip the pen in ink and rule a straight line. Adjust the thickness with the screw thread.

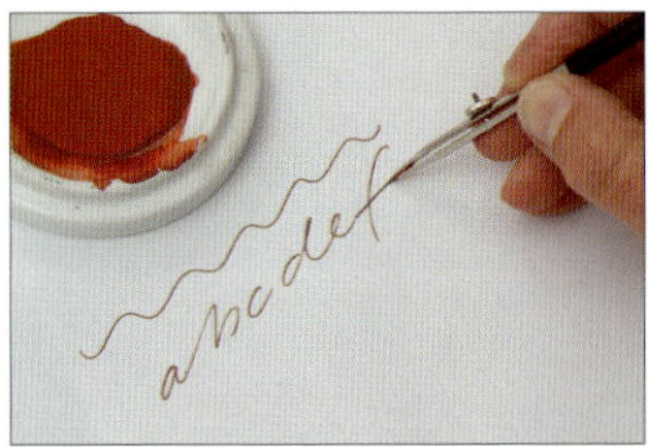

2 Without the ruler, use the ruling pen as an adaptable tool for sketching, scribbling, or writing a quick, flowing line.

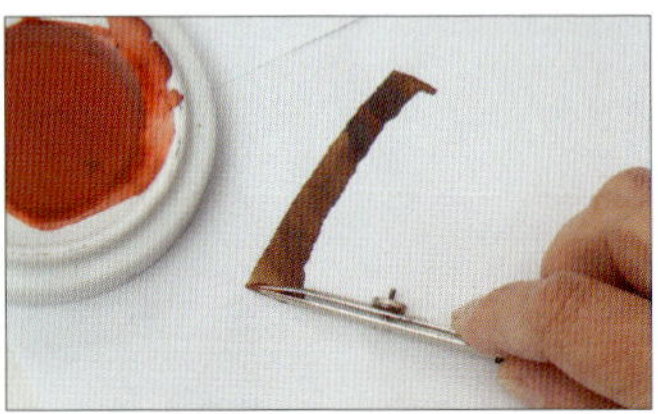

3 Held on its side, well charged with ink and with the open edge against the paper, the ruling pen will discharge its ink very dramatically.

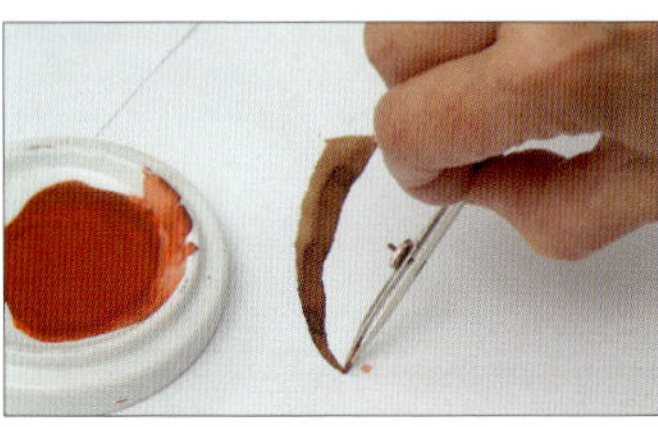

4 Make a more controlled mark from thick to thin, by changing the hold on the pen as you go down, moving from side to point.

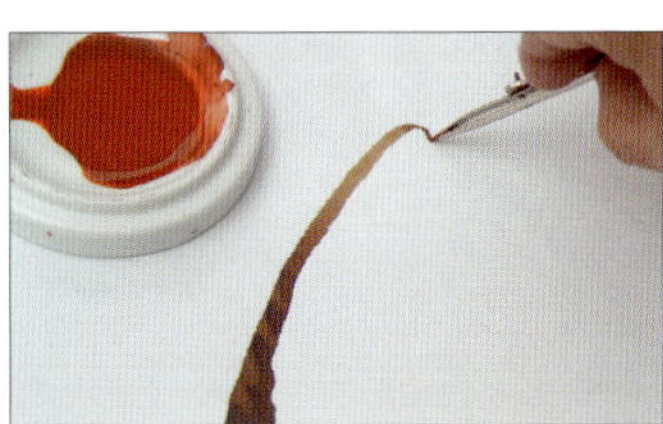

5 Dramatic upward strokes are also fun to try for lively ascenders.

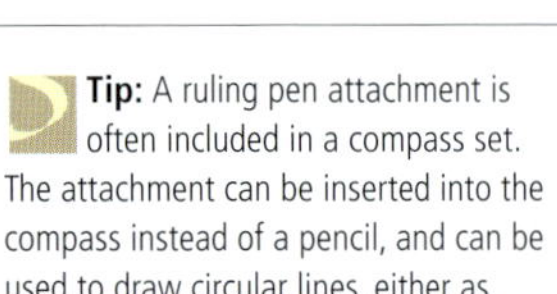

Tip: A ruling pen attachment is often included in a compass set. The attachment can be inserted into the compass instead of a pencil, and can be used to draw circular lines, either as guidelines for writing or as decoration.

6 Combining a thick stroke with a thin one takes a little more practice. Use a flick of the wrist as you change from holding the pen flat to riding back up to its point; thick stroke down, thin stroke up.

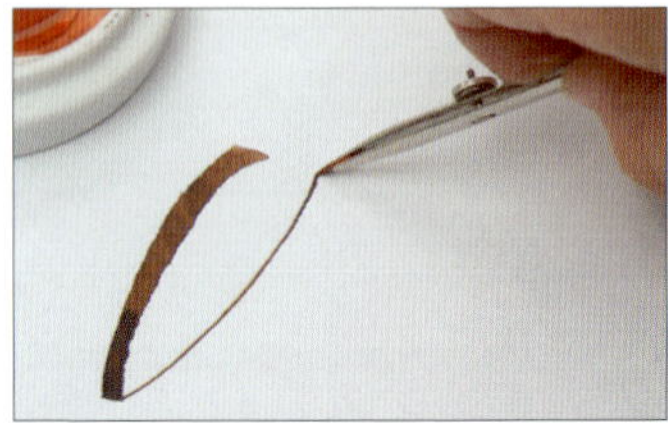

Practice exercise: **Core letters (a, b, c)**

Practise the first letters of the alphabet using contrasting thick and thin strokes.

Materials
- *Technical ruling pen*
- *Plain white paper*
- *Free-flowing ink or paint*

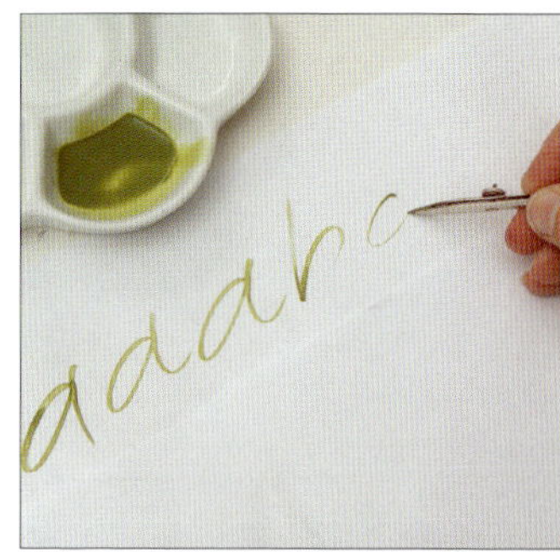

1 Write the core letter shapes in monoline first, holding the pen like a pencil and moving down, up, down to create this Italic form of 'a'.

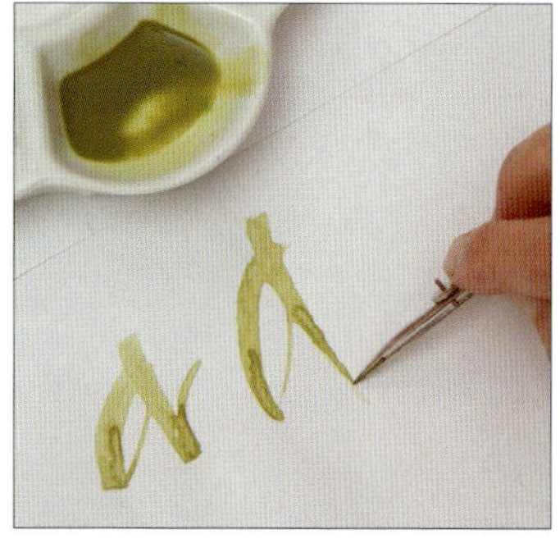

2 Repeat the structure of the letter, but this time manipulate the pen to create a thick downwards stroke and a thin upwards stroke.

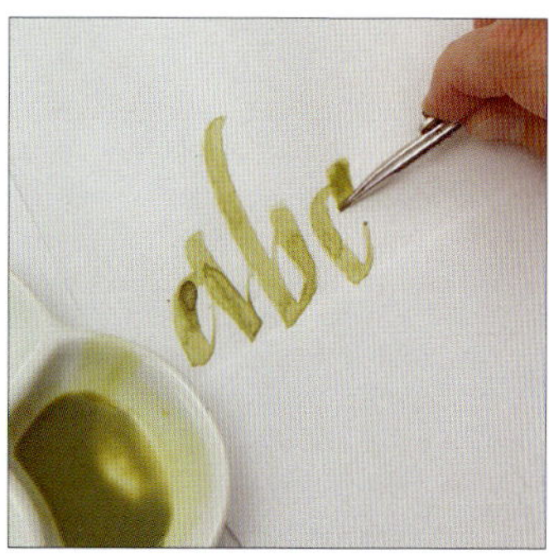

3 Follow the 'thick down, thin up' process for 'a, b, c' and keep writing these three letters until a successful set has been created.

Tip: Do not unscrew the ruling pen very much. Start with the points just touching, then loosen a hair's breadth – if the gap is too wide it will not allow for surface tension to hold the ink in place and it will not flow properly.

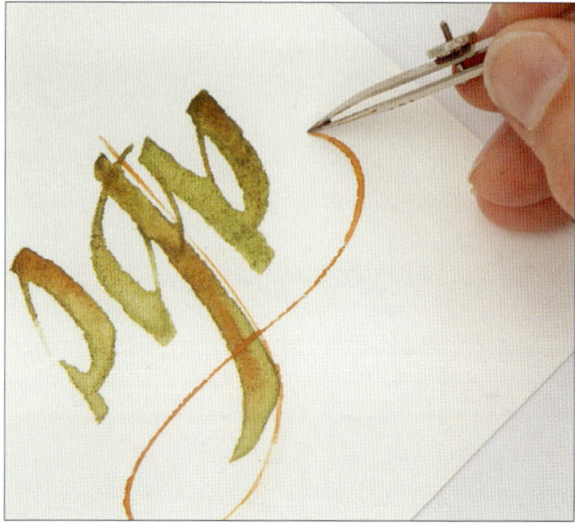

4 Make a thin-lined flourish to complete the design – it may help to complete this flourish by turning the work upside down.

Practice exercise: **Core letters (x, y, z)**

Just three letters create an attractive design in their own right. Placing any three letters together needs practice to avoid forming unsightly holes.

Materials
- *Technical ruling pen*
- *Plain white paper*
- *Free-flowing ink or paint*

Tip: Always make sure both tips of the ruling pen are on the paper, otherwise the ink will not flow.

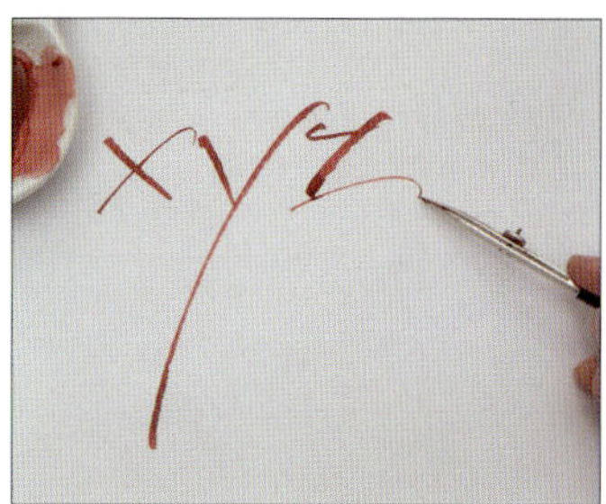

1 Write 'x, y, z' using all diagonals. Hold the pen flat to create the thick lines usually made by an edged pen.

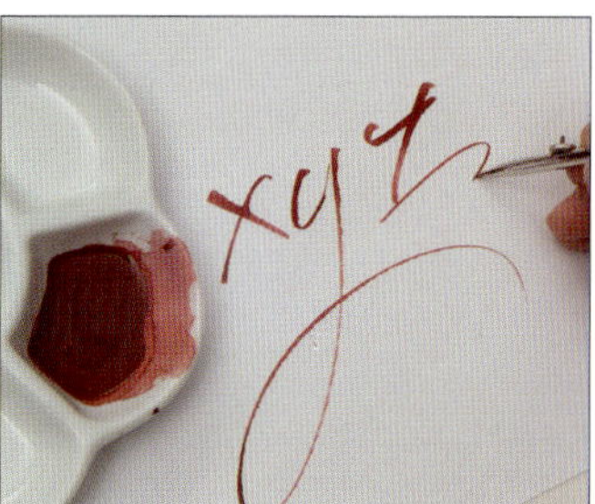

2 Try another version of the same letters, combining diagonals with curves and a bold flourish.

Brush lettering

The broad-edged brush is an underused calligraphic tool. The benefit of using a brush is that it allows writing to be carried out on surfaces that would be difficult for a pen. Brushes are also particularly useful for large-scale writing as they come in much larger sizes than pens. Beginners sometimes find the most difficult part of using the brush is controlling the hairs, as there is no definite pressure to be felt as when putting pen to paper. The secret is not to hold the brush in the same way as a pen. Instead, hold it perpendicular to the paper – this will feel unnatural at first. Position your fingers with the thumb one side and the first two fingers on the other; test if you can twist the brush with those fingers. Use the rest of your hand to steady the brush by resting on the paper. Slide your hand around to make the letterform – do not try to do it all using the fingers.

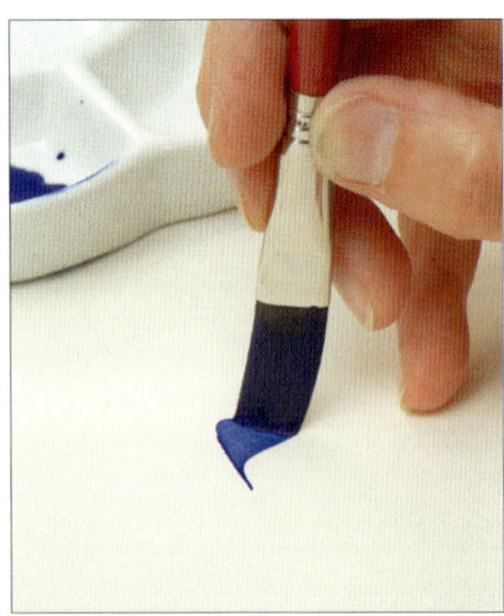

5 Check your fingers are either side of the handle and that you can twist the brush by moving your thumb, not your wrist. Try twisting a quarter turn.

Tip: Even if you make a mistake, do not stop work on a piece as it is good practice and helps you get used to the brush. With time, it will become easier to know the best brush to use in order to achieve the required effect.

Practising with the brush

The brush techniques shown here will help control lettering with the paint.

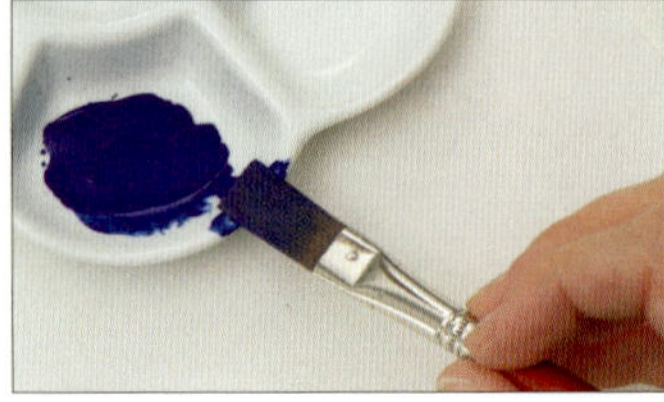

1 Practise preserving the chisel edge of the brush, by filling it with paint then wiping most of it off against the flat edge.

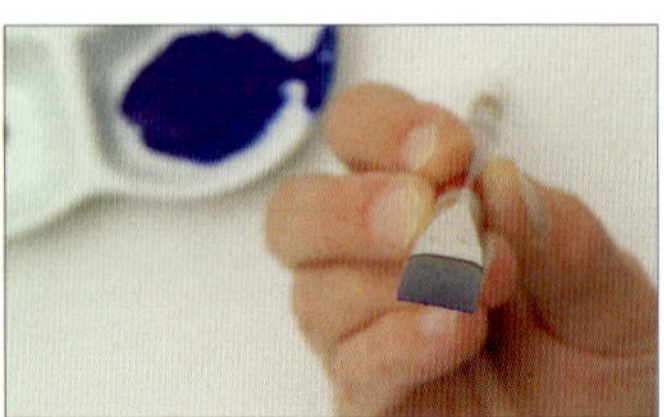

2 Get into the habit of checking closely that sufficient paint has been wiped off the brush to create a sharp chisel edge.

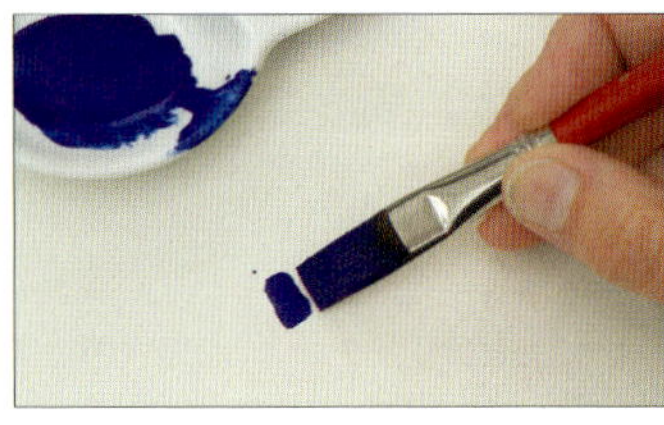

3 Keeping the brush overcharged with paint will result in an unattractive blobby mark.

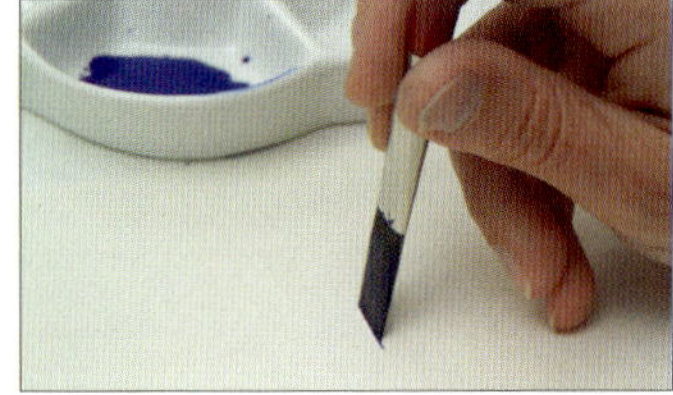

4 For best results, hold the brush perpendicular to the paper, not like a normal pen; this way you will be able to make fine lines as well as broad ones.

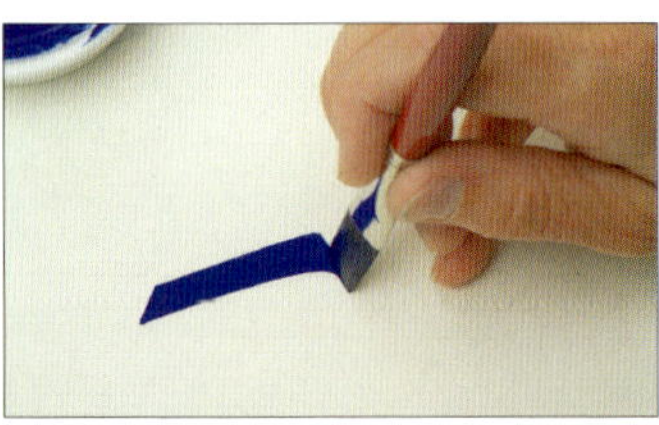

6 Twisting gives subtlety to strokes. Here the brush starts with its edge at 45 degrees to the writing line, then is smoothly twisted to 90 degrees.

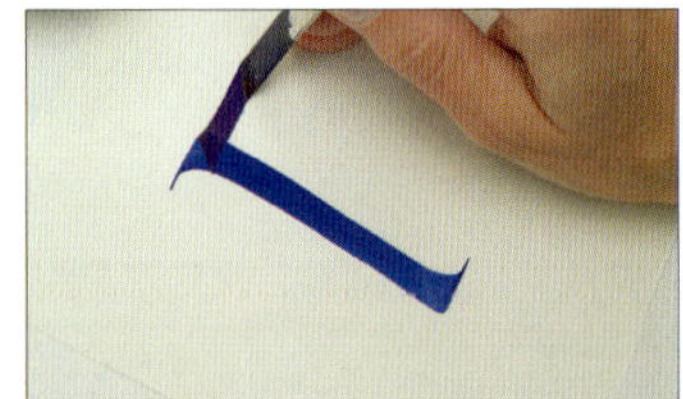

7 Blend adjoining strokes by starting the second stroke within the first. This is important with large letters, as thin joins weaken the structure.

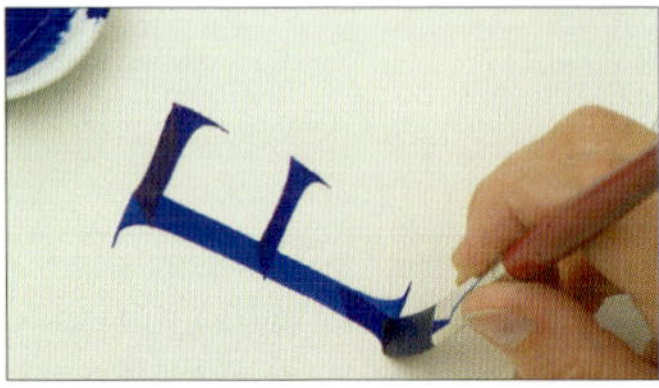

8 The final serif on this 'F' starts entirely within the upright stroke and twists clockwise as it emerges.

Practical exercise: **Making an Uncial 'E'**

This exercise uses the brush and two colours of paint to make an Uncial 'E'. Uncials are upper case letters and very rounded. Keep the brush at a flat angle or the letters will become too narrow.

Materials

- *Gouache paints e.g. ultramarine and magenta*
- *Paper with slightly rough surface*
- *Paint palette or saucers*
- *Water pot*
- *Broad-edged brush*
- *Handmade and Ingres papers*
- *Kitchen paper*

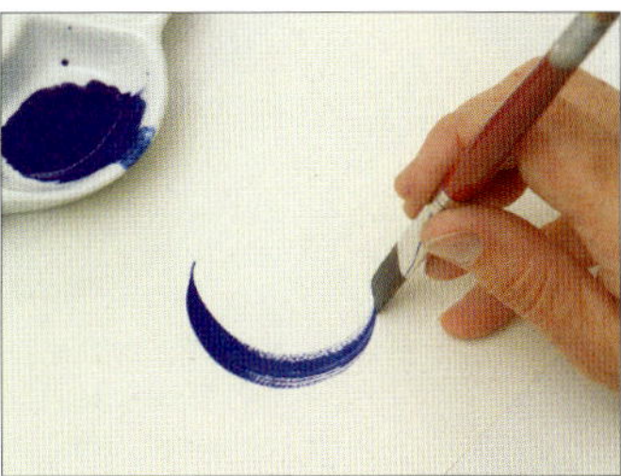

1 In the blue gouache, make a smooth half-moon curve by holding the brush perpendicular to the paper and moving your arm round in a sweeping movement.

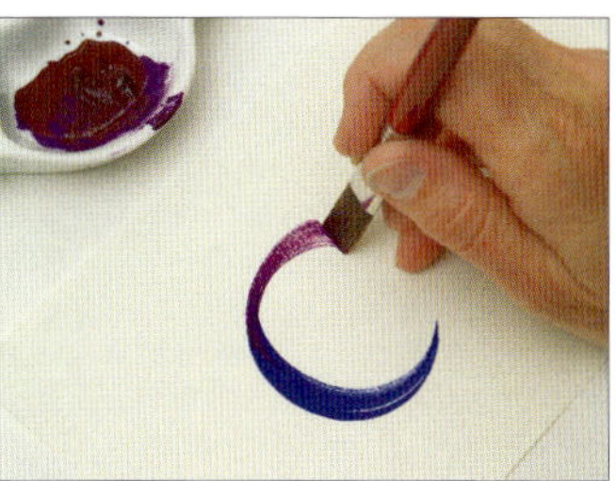

2 Without cleaning the brush, replenish with magenta paint at the same consistency; check you have wiped to a chisel edge. Start this stroke inside the first, and manipulate the serif by twisting.

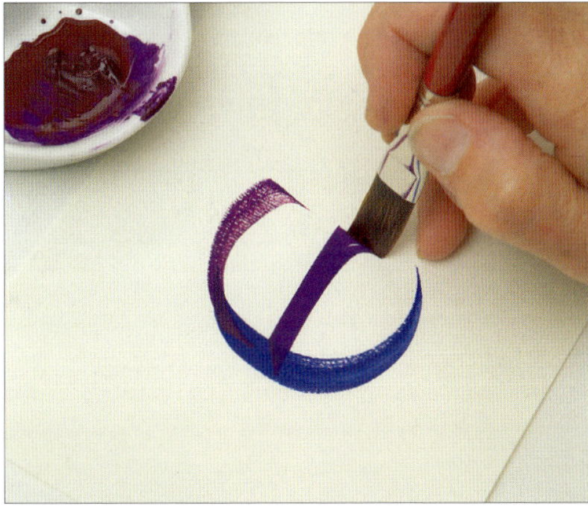

3 Replenish with more magenta (remember to wipe it sharp), hold the brush at 45 degrees to the writing line, pull a straight stroke and finish with a twist for the serif.

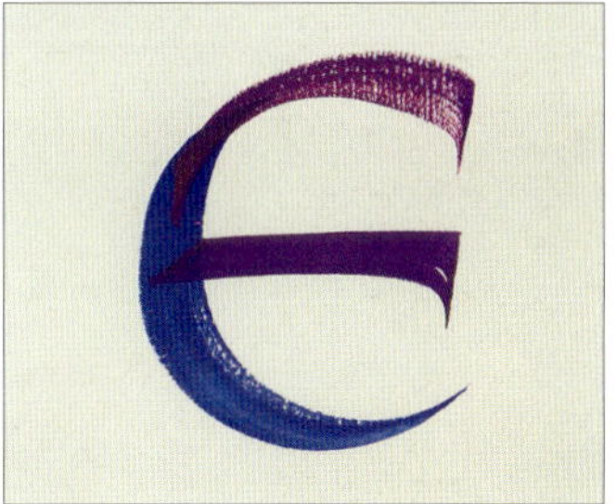

4 Using a large brush on paper with a 'tooth' can give a pleasing granular effect in places, adding texture. Here the colour changes highlight the structure of the letter, making it an object of visual interest.

Special surfaces

One big advantage of the brush is its ability to write on special surfaces such as quite rough-surfaced paper, which would be unsuitable for writing on with a metal pen. Experiment with any forms you can find.

Tip: Brush lettering is suitable for a huge range of designs and can be particularly effective when used as a headline. By placing a piece of paper underneath your working hand, you can help ensure the paper remains clean.

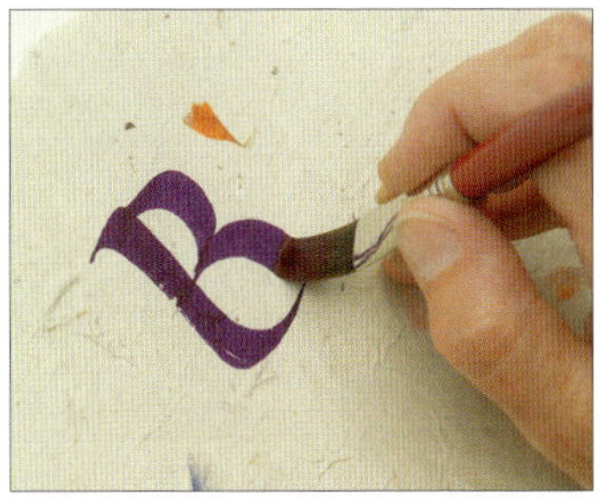

Handmade Indian petal paper ▲
This rough-textured paper has fibres and petals embedded in it which give the paint a slightly granular effect.

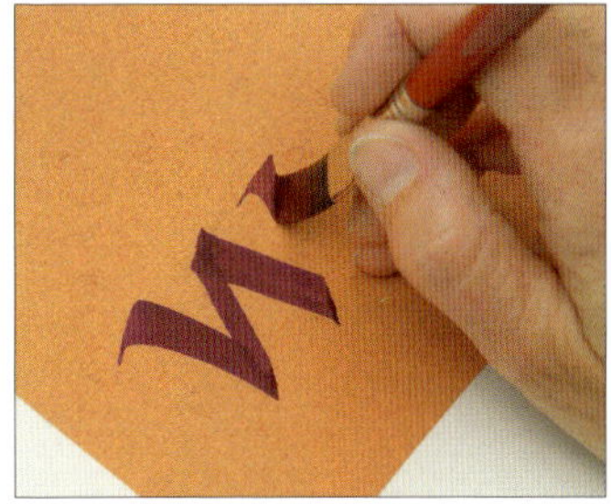

Ingres pastel paper ▲
This paper is lightly textured which creates plenty of 'drag', enabling controlled brush work.

Cutting balsa, reed and quill pens

Early writers used natural materials such as reeds and feathers for nibs. These materials have been used successfully for thousands of years as alphabets developed requiring a fine balance of thick and thin strokes. The modern calligrapher has access to an enormous range of modern equipment. However, elaborate effects may call for the use of more adventurous tools on traditional papers and surfaces such as vellum. It is well worth trying to create tools using traditional materials, and they are inexpensive to make and easy to replace.

Making a balsa pen

Balsa wood pens are enjoyable to use. They are quick and easy to make and many can be made from one sheet of balsa wood. Try a variety of sizes by varying the width of the pen. Balsa wood is a very lightweight wood and is often used in model-making because it is easy to cut and shape. There is a grain to the wood and it is best to follow the grain when cutting the length of the pen.

Materials

- *Sheet of balsa wood*
- *Self-healing cutting mat*
- *Scalpel and craft (utility) knife*

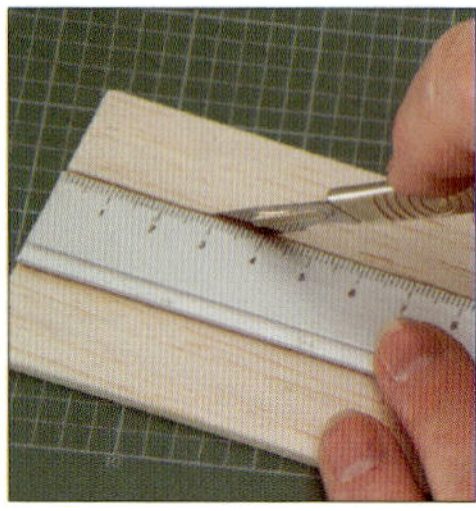

1 Cut the wood into a rectangle approximately 10–12cm (4½in) in length. The width can be varied to suit your needs, but about 2.5cm (1in) is a good guide.

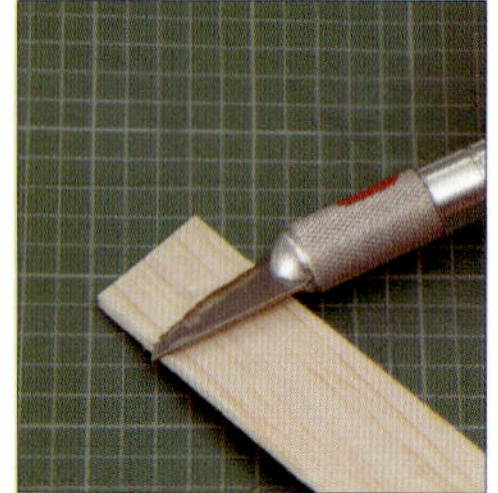

2 Starting 1cm (½in) away from one of the narrow ends, use a sharp craft knife to shave a bevelled cut. A left-hander should make a left-oblique cut.

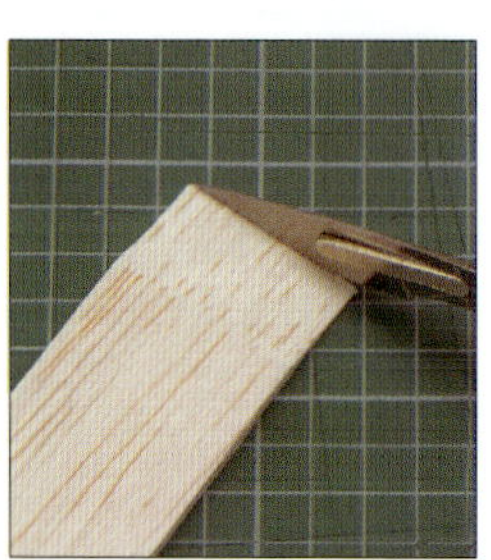

3 Make a cut straight down at 90 degrees, using the scalpel. The edge will need to be sharp to do this.

Making a reed pen

Reed pens date back even further in history than the quill. They were used by Middle Eastern scribes because reeds were in plentiful supply. They were sturdy and hollow-centred which made them very suitable to cut as a writing tool. Reed pens are still used by calligraphers today. Bamboo cane is often used as a substitute and is readily available. It is possible to cut reed pens with a thicker nib and they are used for larger writing.

Materials

- *Sharp knife*
- *Length of reed or bamboo*
- *Self-healing cutting mat*
- *Drinks can*

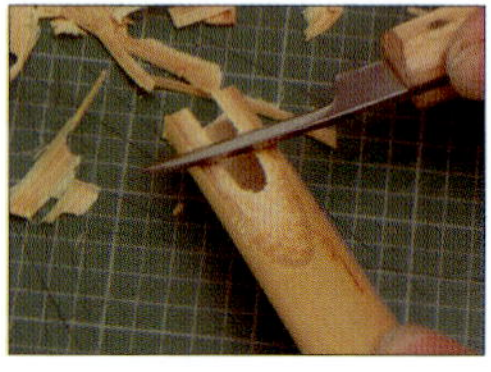

1 Using a sharp knife, cut the reed to about 20cm (8in). Cut a downward stroke, beginning 2.5cm (1in) from the end of the reed curving sharply to mid-way, and then bring the curve parallel with the reed shaft. Scrape away the soft pith.

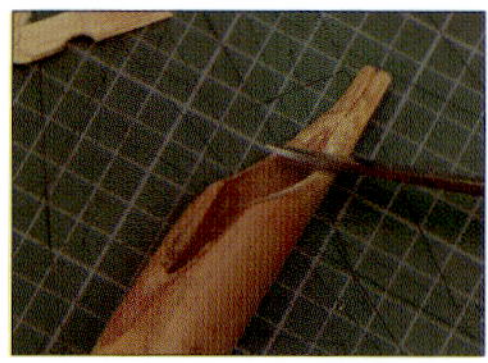

2 Cut the side sections to form the shoulders of the nib.

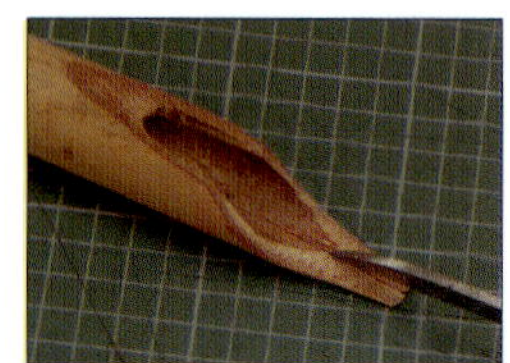

3 Make a vertical slit up the centre. Do not make this too long or the nib will separate when writing.

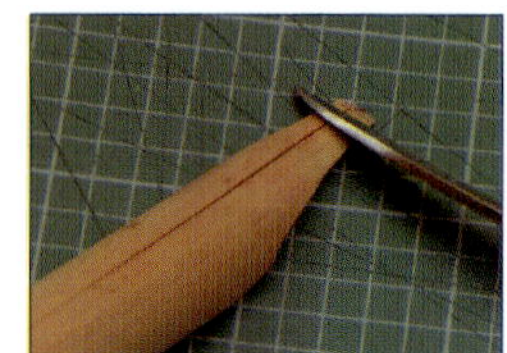

4 Cut across the top at an oblique angle of 30 degrees to shape the nib.

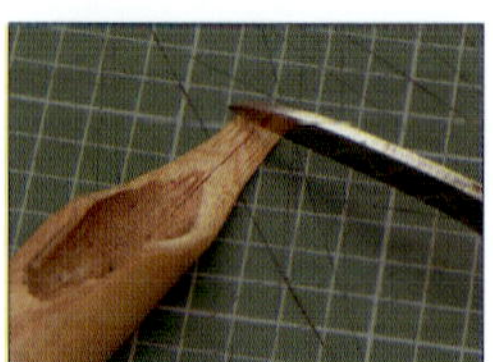

5 Cut the tip cleanly across to form a sharp writing edge at 90 degrees.

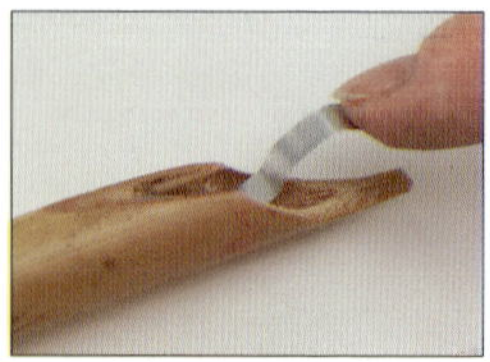

6 To make a reservoir, cut a strip of metal from a drinks can, bend it and insert it in the barrel. The ink sits behind the reservoir.

Curing and cutting a quill

Quills have been used for hundreds of years. Most calligraphers frequently use metal pens, but quills are still the preferred choice for writing on vellum because of their sensitivity and flexibility. Calligraphers mainly use goose, turkey and swan feathers, and crow for very fine writing. The best feathers for use with the right hand come from the first five flights of the left wing of the bird, and for a left-handed scribe, from the right wing of the bird. This is because the natural curve of the feather gives the correct balance in the hand.

Once prepared, the quill pen does not quite live up to its image of the beautiful plume – the quill is cut to a manageable length of about 20cm (8in) and stripped of its barbs, which makes it easier to handle.

Materials

- *Silver sand*
- *Cooker and pan*
- *Feather*
- *Sharp knife*
- *Self-healing cutting mat*

Tip: The drying process eliminates oils. Ideally, this should be carried out naturally, but this could take many months of drying. Instead an artificial heat source is used with a pan, but this needs to be kept gentle and very brief or the barrel becomes too brittle. The heating alters the quill from being soft textured and opaque to becoming harder.

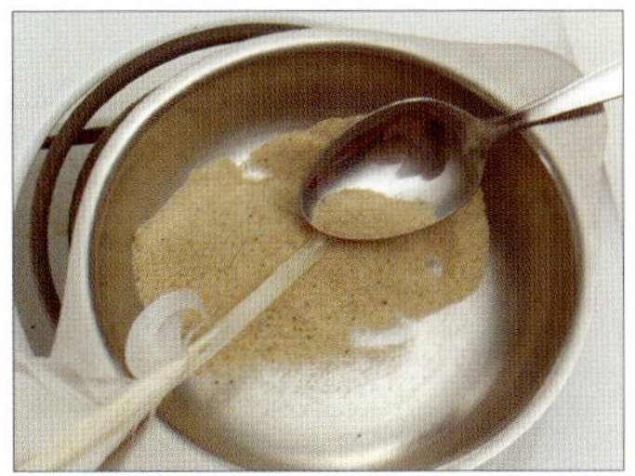

1 The quill needs to be cured so that the barrel is hardened. Before this is done, cut the sealed end of the barrel, then soak in water overnight. The next day heat the silver sand in a pan for about 15 minutes until really hot. Temper the quill by pouring hot sand down the upturned barrel. Insert the quill into the hot sand and leave for about 10–15 seconds (this is trial and error). If it is left too long, the nib will not crack cleanly and if under-cured, will be too rubbery. Cool the quill quickly by dipping it into cold water then shake it dry. The outer membrane is then scraped away using the back of a sharp knife.

2 Use a sharp knife to cut the quill. Cut the feathers to about 20cm (8in) in length and strip away the barbs.

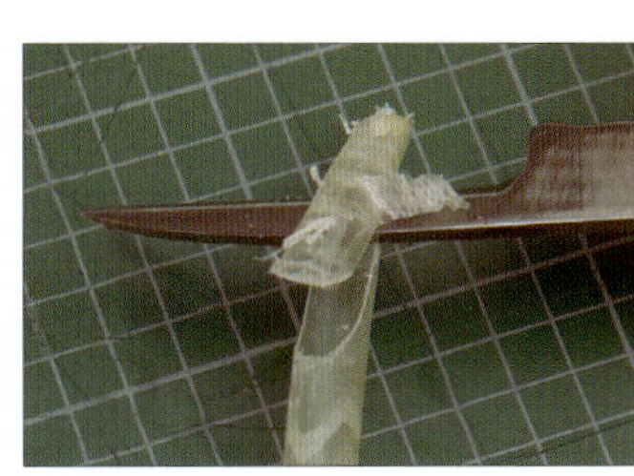

3 Make a long scoop on the underside of the barrel.

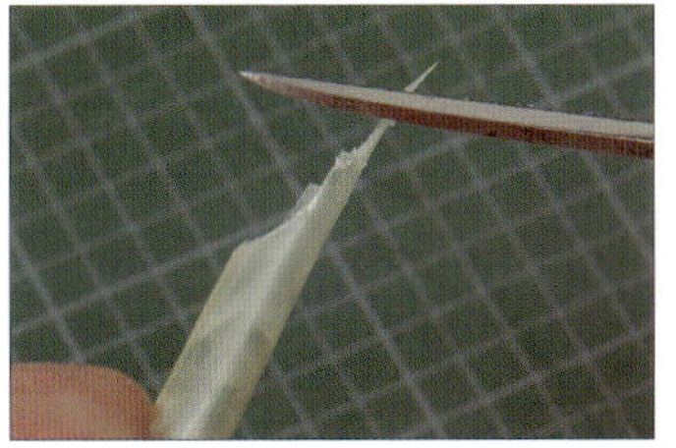

4 Scoop out the shoulders, matching both sides equally.

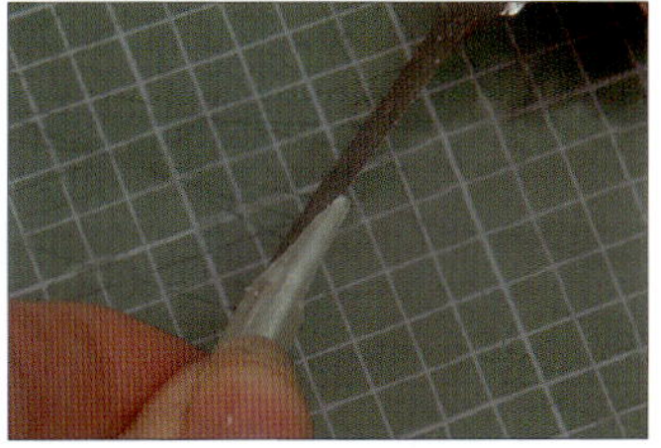

5 Place the top of the quill on a cutting mat. Place the knife blade in the centre of the nib and make a slit of one and a half times the nib width.

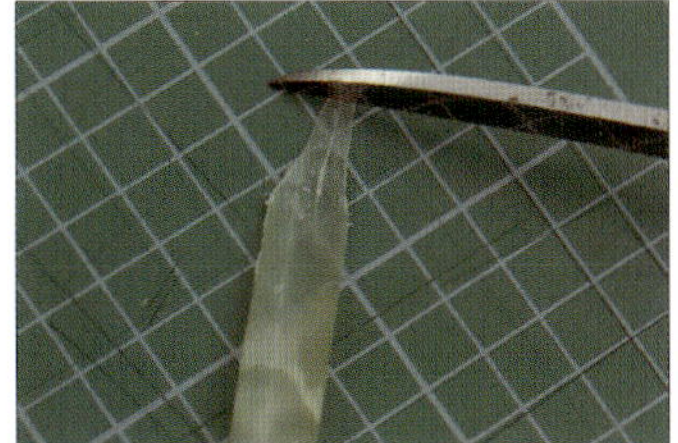

6 Trim the end of the quill with a small cut off the tip.

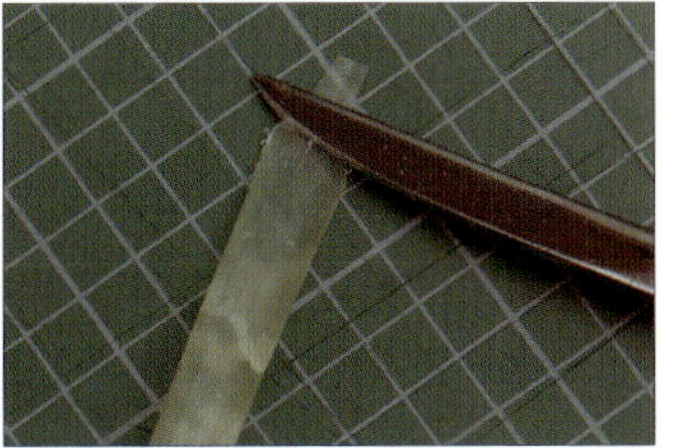

7 Scoop a thin sliver off the top of the nib.

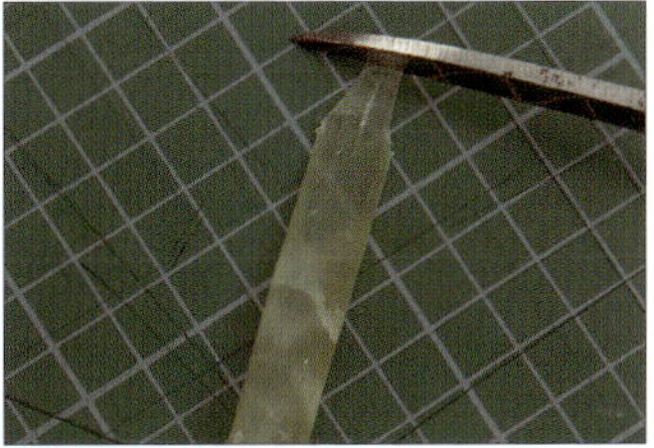

8 To square the nib, make a 90-degree clean cut.

Cut-paper lettering

Paper cutting has been a folk art ever since paper was invented in AD105 by Ts'ai Lun, an official in the court of Han Ho Ti, Emperor of China. It has not been widely recognized as an art form until recently, but artists and historians are becoming increasingly aware of its valuable folk heritage. Traditional techniques using cut paper include German *scherenschnitte*, Chinese *chien-chih*, Japanese *kirigami* or *mon-kiri*, Polish *wycinanki* and French *silhouettes*.

The craft of paper cutting is easily adapted to cut letters and may be used in conjunction with a piece of calligraphy or as a stand-alone design. The basic technique of cutting letters out of paper may be separated into two distinct categories – stencil and silhouette images. While similar, they each have their own 'rules'. These refer to whether it is the letter or the background that is cut out. For stencils, the letter is cut away, while for silhouettes it is the background that is lost.

Silhouette and stencil letters

On the left of this card is a silhouette, or positive letter, which is best thought of as a letter within a frame, ideally touching in at least three places. The letter stays while the background is cut away. On the right is a stencil or negative letter, which is removed from the paper leaving the letter-shaped hole, with the background firmly in place.

With practice it is possible to develop skills that allow elaborate lettering and designs to be cut out. It is important to remember when cutting around the curves of a shape or letter only to cut in small arcs, before stopping and moving the paper. Do not lift the knife, but keep it in the same position and continue cutting when the paper has been repositioned. This may seem a slow technique, but it will ensure a smoother shape to your cuts. Keep the blade upright – without slanting it to one side or the other – and make sure that the sharp edge is facing towards you. A sharp blade makes a great deal of difference to the quality of the cuts as well as the amount of effort that is needed to make them. A blade that is not sharp will produce uneven edges and poor curves so change the blade frequently. Choose the paper carefully because the thickness of the paper and the amount of detail in the letters also play a role in how successfully the letters are cut.

Tip: For crisp cutting, work in two directions – downwards and to the right. Turn the work to accommodate these directions. Left-handers should reverse the latter directions to work to the left and anticlockwise. At all times keep your free hand away from the cutting direction.

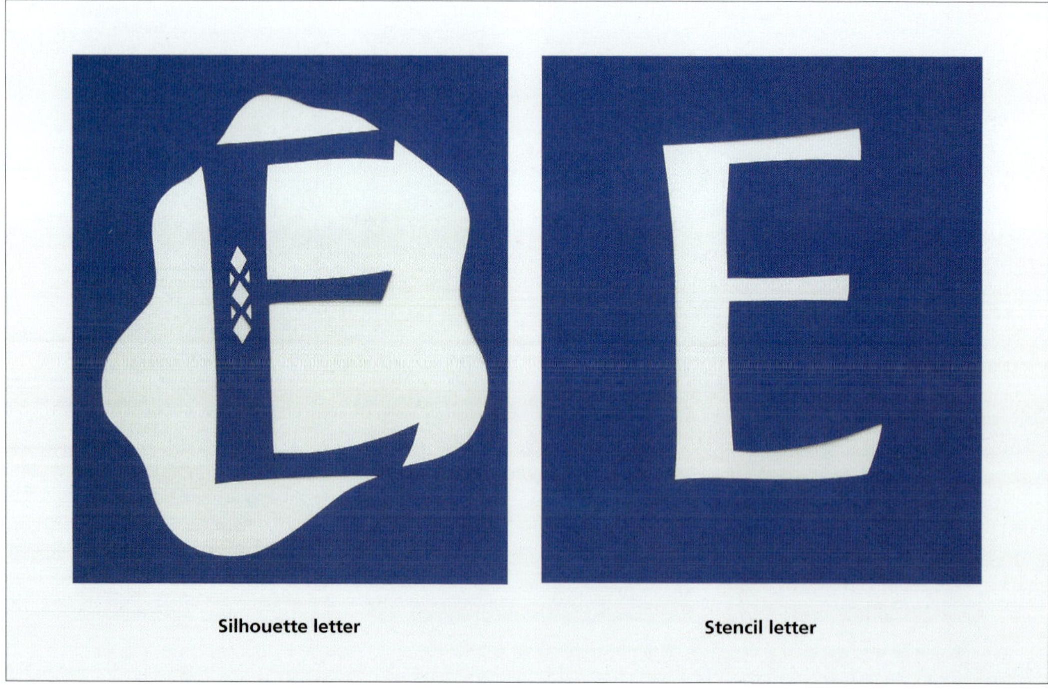

Silhouette letter **Stencil letter**

Making stencil letters

When cutting these stencils careful thought needs to be given to letters with enclosed areas that could simply fall out. If the stencil letter has a 'counter' or enclosed space, there needs to be a way to keep this 'island' in place as the letter is cut away. The letters with counters are: 'A', 'B', 'D', 'O', 'P', 'Q' and 'R' and 'a', 'b', 'd', 'e', 'g', 'o', 'p' and 'q'.

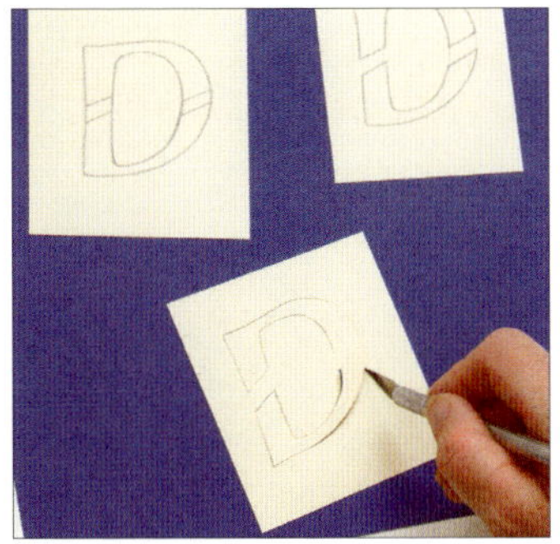

Cutting the counter ▲
Draw in pencil before you cut, to show where the letter will be cut. The addition of a 'pathway' such as a chevron can hold the middle of a letter, such as a 'D'.

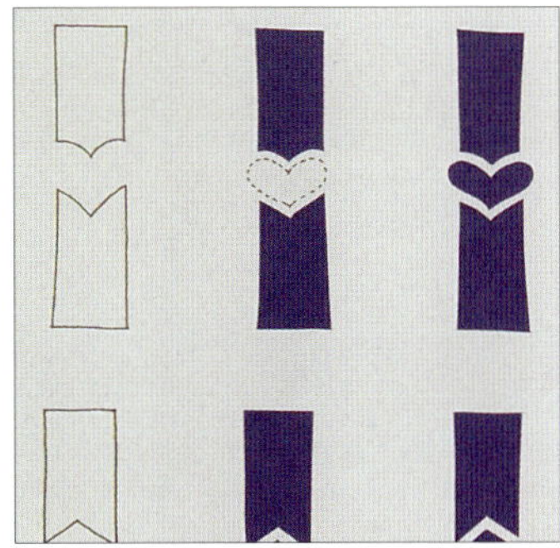

Using designs to create pathways ▲
Make use of designs to create 'pathways' of safety. Including shapes such as hearts or diamonds midway across the letter can create a pathway. Rub out any overlap points to avoid cutting and making mistakes.

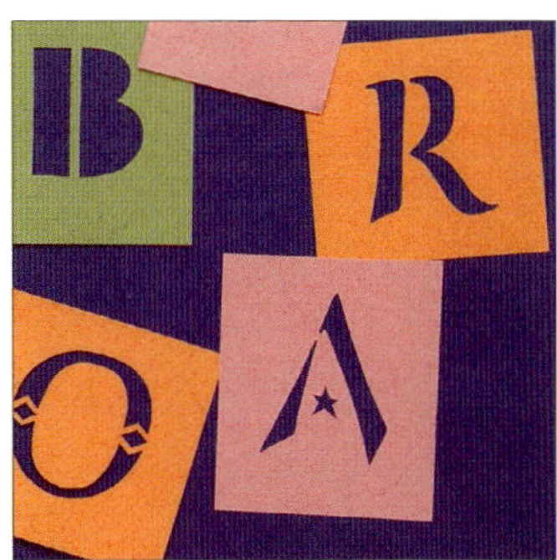

The finished letters ▲
These are some of the ways of making safe pathways on letters. When combining stencil letters within words, it is also important not to let them touch each other as the design will become physically unstable.

Practice exercise: **Making a stencil and silhouette letter**

When cutting silhouette letters, counter shapes and backgrounds are removed, but it is important that letters physically touch each other and their frame at overlap points, so that the design will be stable and hold together.

Materials
- *2H pencil*
- *Lightweight watercolour paper*
- *Craft (utility) knife or scalpel with a long, pointed blade*

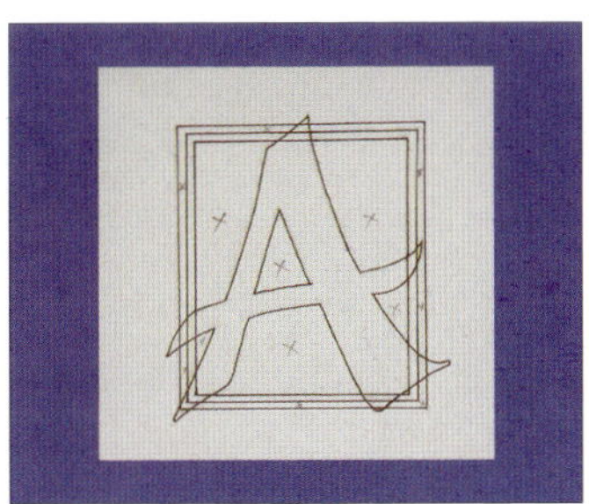

1 Draw the letter 'A' on to watercolour paper. Be very clear about where the cut is to be made, marking the spaces where the card can be cut away with an 'x'. To add a border around a silhouette letter, draw three lines in tandem, ensuring the letter protrudes beyond the outer line in at least three places and rubbing out the overlap areas.

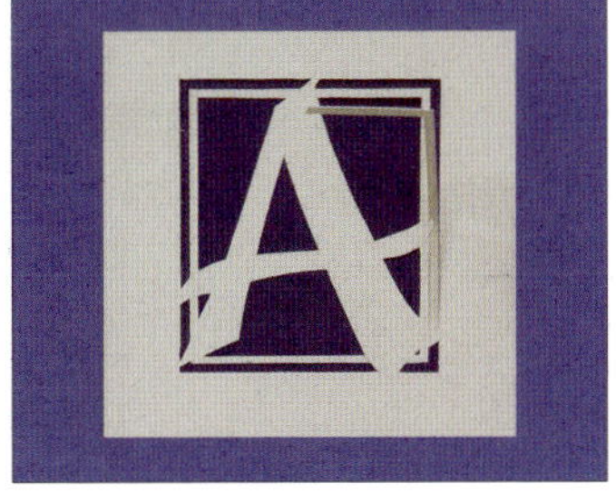

2 Cut a channel between the outer and middle lines and all other marked areas. Leave the border intact, because it keeps a pathway of safety.

Tip: Mark the areas to be cut and rub out overlap points. Do not just cut out the letter profile, or it will fall out.

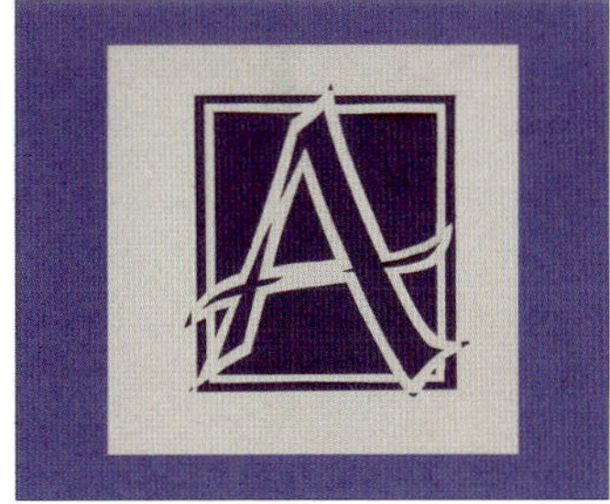

3 It is possible to combine both silhouette and stencil techniques, by further cutting into a silhouette letter. When doing so it must be remembered that stencil rules now apply, and care must again be taken to save the middles of letters.

Washes and backgrounds

There are many different effects that you can create with background washes. There is a wealth of possibilities if you consider using different media and tools. Dry brush techniques, clear film, spattering, spraying, rollers, sponge and textured cloth all produce different marks when used with paint or acrylic inks. With experimentation and practise, texture and visual excitement, mood and atmosphere can be achieved in the backgrounds to calligraphic work. There are lots of creative possibilities to be explored using washes, single or variegated, with dropped-in colour on the paper.

Before making washes and backgrounds it is wise to stretch the paper if it is under 300gsm (140lb) in weight. This means saturating the paper with water and then securing it on to a wooden board with brown paper tape. Overlap the tape at the corners, keep the board flat for drying and leave the paper attached until all the colour work is finished. When dry, the paper becomes taut and accepts any amount of watercolour without buckling or becoming wrinkled.

Tip: For best results use hot-pressed or cold-pressed papers for colour washes. Mix up enough paint to ensure you do not run short during an application. Thinly diluted watercolour paint will produce a more subtle wash effect, and applying the wash quickly will help avoid streaks and runs from forming.

Different effects

Try these washes and paint effects to create different backgrounds and patterns on paper.

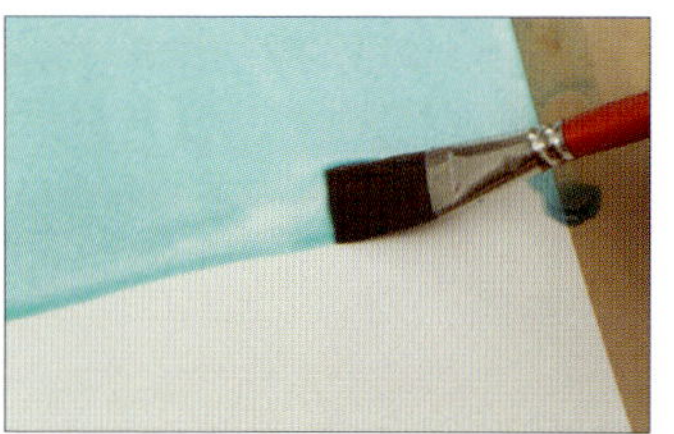

A single wash ▲
Raise the board at one end to apply the wash to the paper. Mix the watercolour paint or acrylic ink to a watery consistency. Dip a large brush in the paint and draw it across the paper to create a smooth wash.

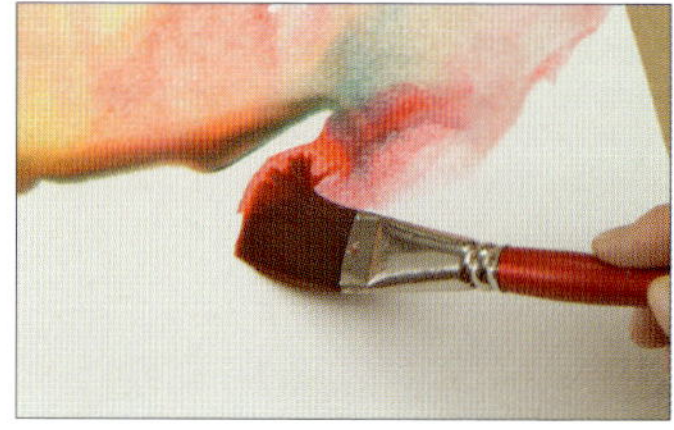

A variegated wash ▲
Mix up three separate colours. Dip the brush into the first colour and apply to the paper randomly. Rinse the brush and load with the second colour, adding it to the paper and blending into the spaces. Rinse the brush and add the final colour.

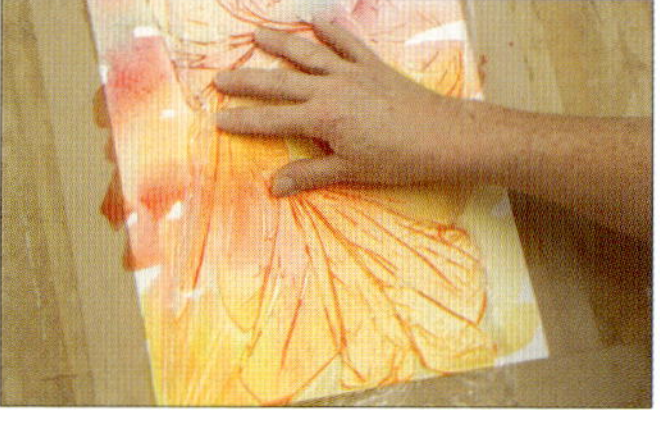

Using clear film or plastic wrap ▲
Paint a variegated wash on the paper, dropping in extra colour while it is still very wet. Drape a large piece of clear film on to the wet wash and drag it into different patterns. Leave to dry thoroughly before removing the film. This will create patterns in the colours.

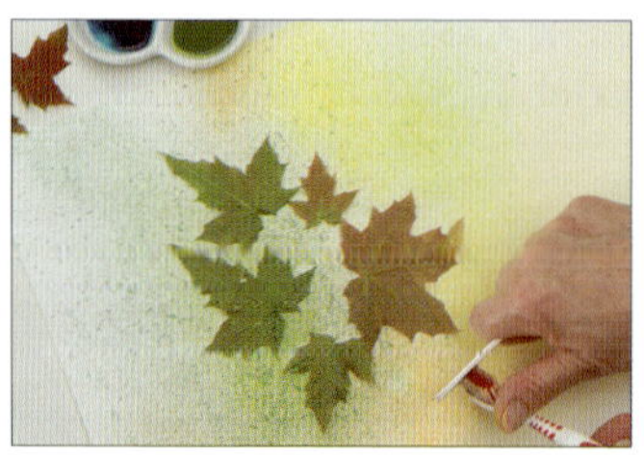

Spatter colour ▲
Use an old toothbrush loaded with paint. To spatter the paint drag a piece of card (stock) or a metal rule over the bristles towards yourself. Use a second brush for another colour. Alternatively, a spray bottle filled with paint can be used to create a similar effect.

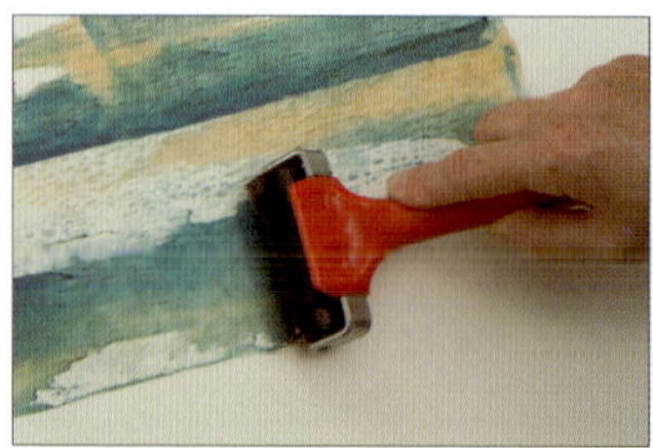

Using a roller ▲
A printmaking roller or commercial paint roller can be used. Each will create a different effect. Squeeze two different colours into a flat wide container and add water. Roller the colours together slightly before applying them in broad bands.

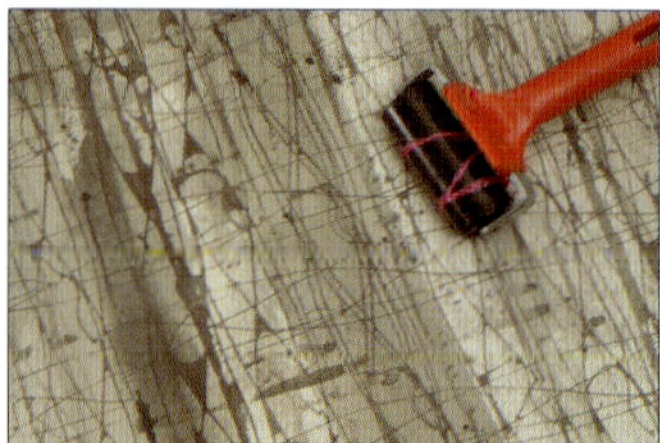

String around the roller ▲
The string creates interesting random patterns when it is used to roll ink or paint on to the paper. Thin string on a print roller has been used to create the effect shown here. For a different effect try strands of cotton around the roller.

Practice exercise: **A decorative card**

Practise background colours by blending washes and creating different effects on paper. Use a limited range of paint or ink colours to help you to remember the paint mixes. By using acrylic inks or casein paint in the background, your paper will have the added advantages of it being waterproof when dry, giving a soft pleasant surface on which to work and allowing easy removal of writing mistakes. If the paper is 300gsm (140lb) and small in size then it is not necessary to stretch it. The larger the piece of paper, the more water it will hold and the more buckled it will become if it is not taped to a board.

Materials

- *A selection of practice sheets*
- *Coloured card (stock)*
- *Decorative paper*
- *Craft glue*
- *White photocopy paper*
- *Ribbon*
- *A sequin or decorative motif or beads (optional)*

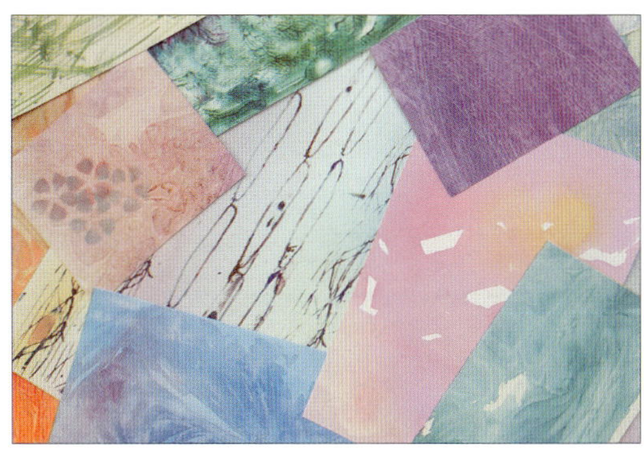

1 Create a variety of different textured and coloured paper, including different washes, patterns made with clear film (plastic wrap), spatter and coloured paper.

Tip: When using washes, varying the length of time that each colour is allowed to dry before adding another can create a more complex design with greater depth. Always wait until all the paint is completely dry before you start to write on the paper.

2 Cut a small sheet of coloured card in half, then fold each piece in half to create two separate cards. Cut some of the decorative pieces of paper into small rectangle or square shapes. Choose colour patterns that work harmoniously together and stick them to the cards with craft glue, piling different shapes on top of one another.

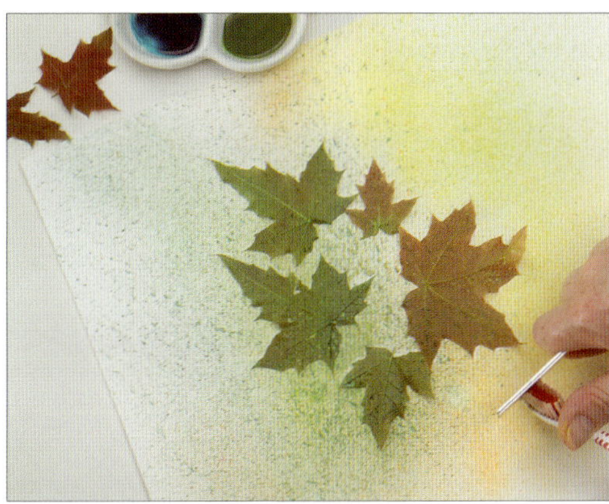

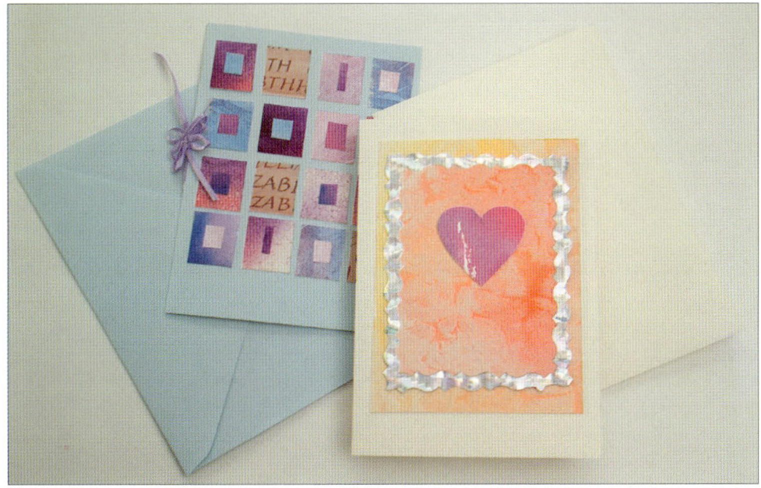

3 Finish the cards by adding a paper insert. For each card fold a small sheet of white photocopy paper in half and trim around the edges. Write your own message inside the folded paper and stick each one carefully into a card. Add a ribbon around the back spine making a neat bow on the outside. A sequin or decorative motif or beads can be added as a final decoration on the front of the cards.

Resists

Methods that are used to protect areas of work are called resists. This allows work to eventually appear through any processes that have covered them. The definition of 'resist' is 'to stop from reaching'. White gouache, a white candle and masking fluid can all be used to create a resist, and each will produce a different result. When using resist techniques, ensure each step has dried completely before going on to the next. If speed is important, work may be gently dried using a hairdryer. Make sure that your paper can withstand the resist soaking and sponging before you start your main work.

Experimenting with gouache

This resist is made by using dilute gouache on watercolour paper, covering it with colour and dissolving the gouache in hot water.

Materials

- *Bleed proof/permanent white gouache*
- *Watercolour paper*
- *Automatic pens*
- *Large brush or hake*
- *Waterproof ink or acrylic colour*
- *Bath of water*
- *Natural sponge*
- *Drawing board*
- *Brown paper gum strip*

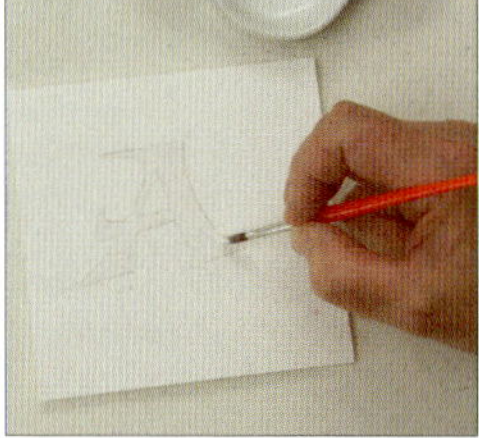

1 Using dilute white gouache (but not too dilute) on a piece of watercolour paper, write a large capital letter with the automatic pen. Allow to dry.

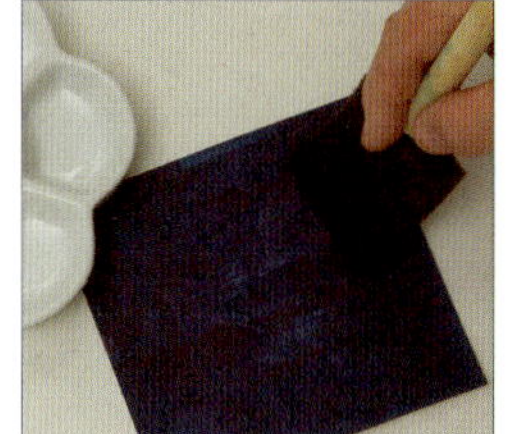

2 Fill a large wide brush with waterproof ink or acrylic colour and, with even strokes, cover the paper. Do not go back over a stroke as the gouache could dissolve. Allow to dry.

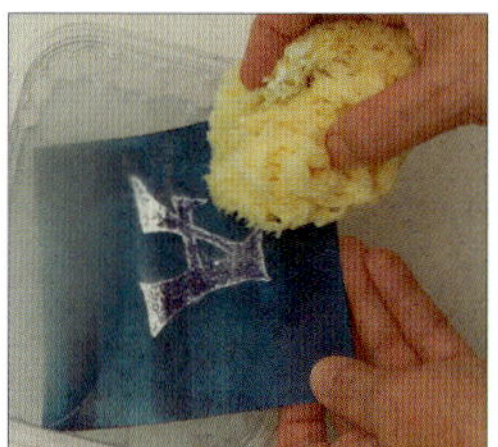

3 Soak the paper in water, either in a bath or under a tap. Gently rub the surface with a natural sponge. The gouache will dissolve and lift away taking the waterproof covering with it.

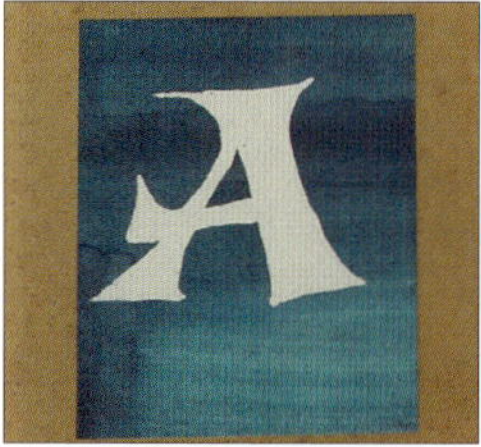

4 Place on a drawing board or similar and stretch with gum strip. Allow to dry before removing.

Experimenting with white candle wax

This method of resist uses the wax of a candle to form a resist against paint that is rolled over it.

Materials

- *Watercolour paper*
- *Waterproof ink*
- *Gouache paint in two colours diluted with water and washing-up liquid (liquid soap)*
- *Low-tack masking tape*
- *White candle*
- *Foam paint roller or equivalent*

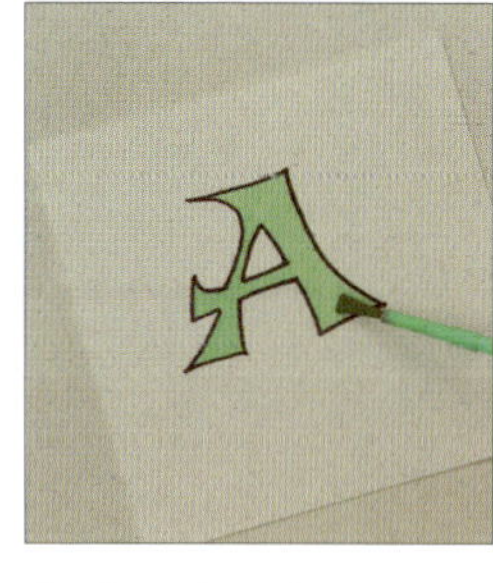

1 On a piece of watercolour paper draw the outline of a letter in waterproof ink. Fill in the shape with the darker of the gouache mixtures and leave to dry.

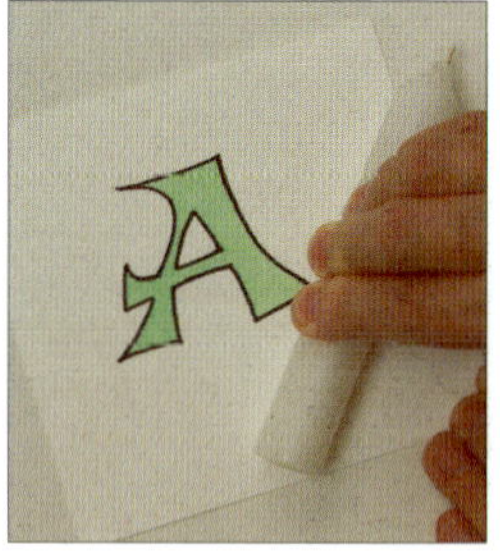

2 Outline the area of the design with low-tack masking tape, press down well to prevent seepage and vigorously rub the entire surface with the candle making sure that everything is well covered.

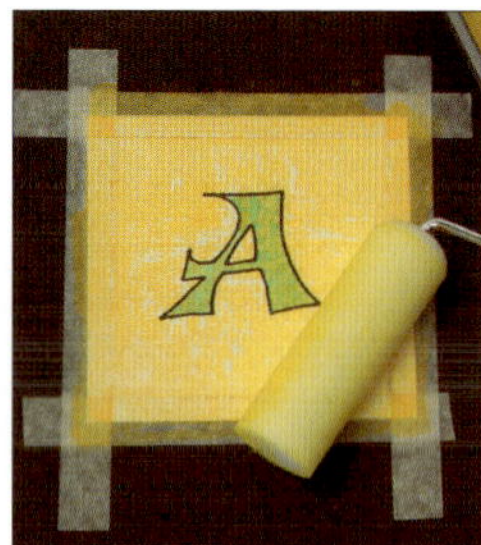

3 Using the foam paint roller, cover the surface with the paler gouache mixture; this should be very diluted. Leave to dry before carefully removing the masking tape.

Experimenting with masking fluid

This method of resist uses masking fluid to form a resist against watercolour that is brushed over it. This technique can be used to create quite intricate or delicate designs.

Materials

- *Watercolour paper*
- *Pencil*
- *Masking fluid*
- *Small and large paint brush*
- *Watercolour paint*

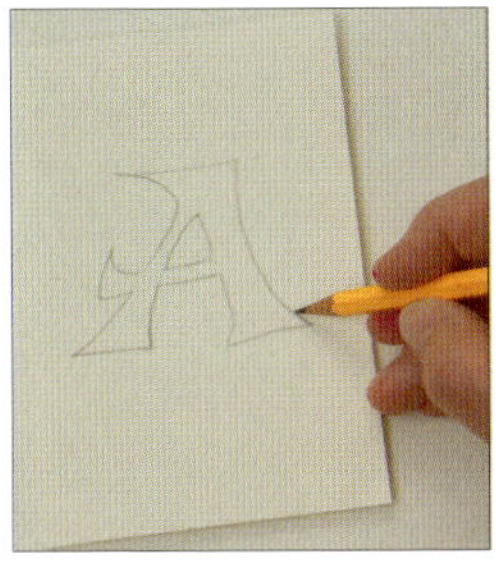

1 On a piece of watercolour paper draw an outline of the letter 'A'.

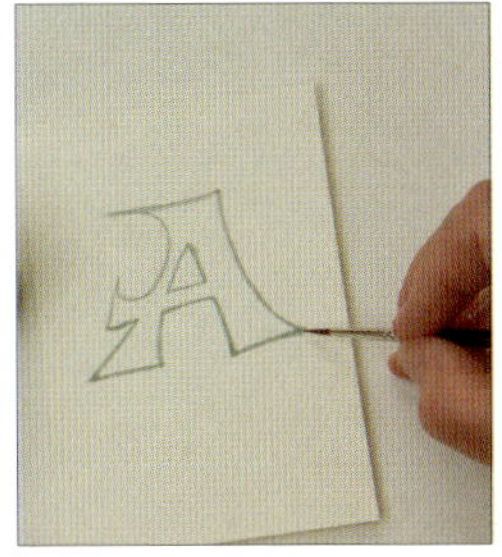

2 Paint over the outline of the letter with masking fluid. Allow to dry.

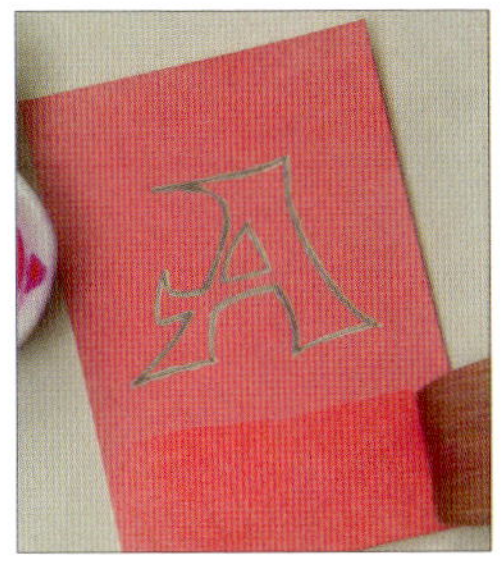

3 Using a large brush wash colour over the surface of the paper. Leave to dry.

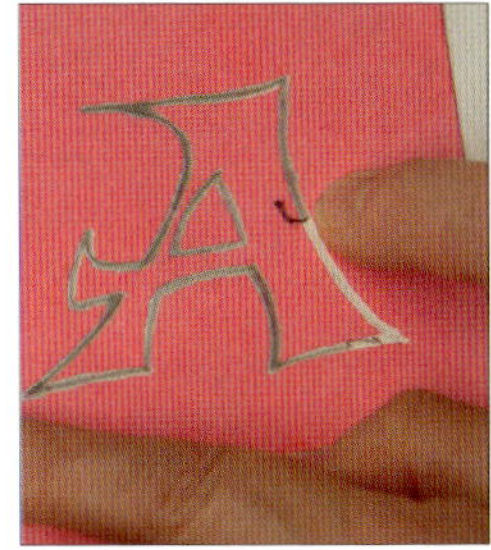

4 Gently remove the masking fluid by rubbing it with your finger.

Practice exercise: **AZ**

This exercise uses gouache to create an interesting layered resist. Two colours of paint are used, which mix to form a third, apart from in the places where the gouache resist has been applied. It is possible to use many different layers of colour.

Materials

- *White gouache*
- *Watercolour paper*
- *Small brush*
- *Large brush or hake*
- *Waterproof or acrylic paint (two colours – one darker than the other)*
- *Natural sponge*

Tip: If you do not want any white to appear on the page, paint a coloured wash on to the paper before adding the first resist. Leave this wash to dry thoroughly before adding the resist. The 'blank' area will then be the colour of the first wash.

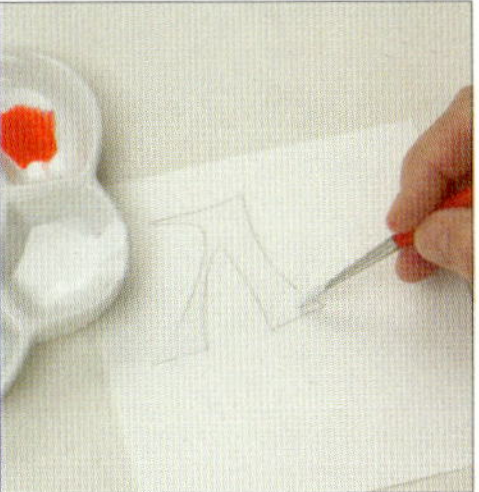

1 Using white gouache write a capital letter 'A' on to watercolour paper. Allow this to dry.

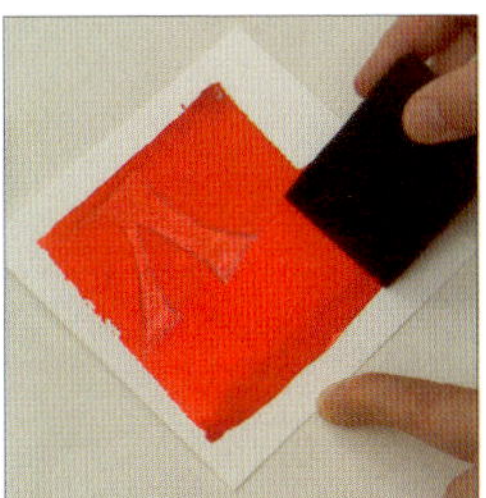

2 With a hake or similar wide brush, cover the surface of the paper with a wash of light coloured paint. Leave to dry.

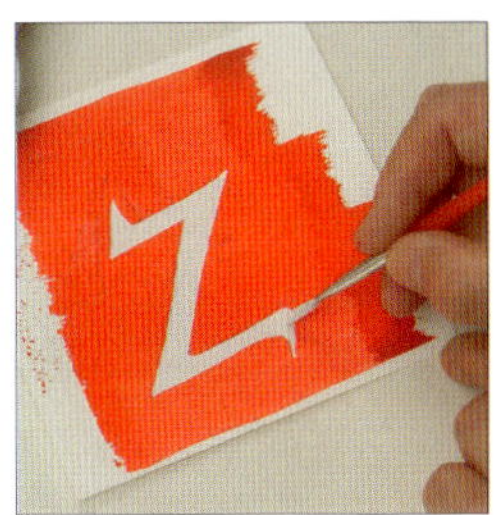

3 Using white gouache, write a capital letter 'Z' over the obliterated 'A' and once again leave to dry.

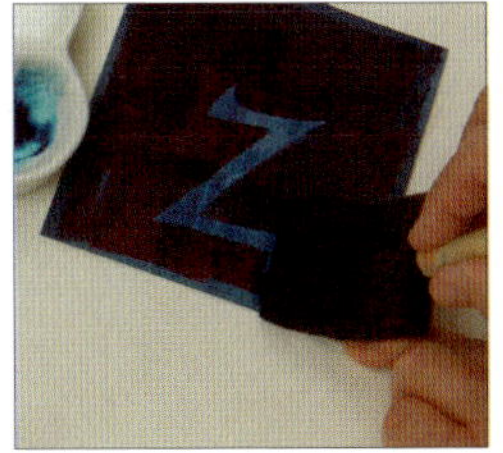

4 Cover the surface with a darker wash of waterproof or acrylic colour. Take more time over this than before, because the two colours need to dry.

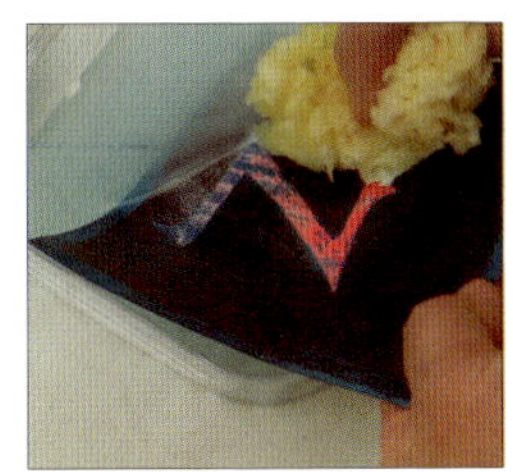

5 Allow the paint to dry before washing it off the area of resist and stretching.

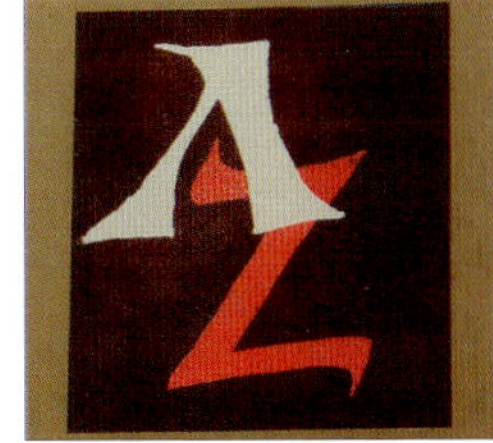

6 The finished resist before being removed from the board.

Gilding

Gold imparts a sense of richness and splendour to the page. It is a unique commodity and its specific qualities have been recognized by artists and artisans for thousands of years. It is pure, non-tarnishable and is one of the most malleable metals – which means it can be beaten into leaf by virtually the same methods as used in antiquity.

There are three methods of gilding: using powdered gold, applying gold leaf on to a gum base and burnishing gold leaf on a raised gesso base. Both flat and raised gold can be produced. Some techniques are easy and some are a little more technically demanding but most people will find a method which suits them and the piece they are working on.

Powdered gold

This type of gold is mixed with distilled water and gum arabic before being applied to the paper or other surface. It is often referred to as 'shell' gold (so called because the gold was originally sold in mussel shells), and is painted with a fine brush, or loaded into a pen. It dries flat and can be burnished, and patterns of lines and dots may be impressed into its surface with a pointed burnisher. The gold needs to be stirred from time to time to keep the particles well mixed. Powdered gold does not have the high brilliance of gold leaf, but using the two types of gold together can make a stunning contrast.

Gilding with gold leaf

This is quite a simple technique whereby wafer-thin sheets of gold are applied to a layer of gum. Traditionally only natural gums were used such as gum ammoniac, glair, parchment or vellum size. There are now synthetic adhesives which are equally suitable for gilding such as PVA (white) glue, acrylic gloss medium and gold water size. Gum ammoniac is easy to use. It can either be bought ready prepared or it can be made up and mixed with a little water and colour. Gesso, which is made mainly from plaster, can be made up or bought in cakes, and is the ideal base for gilding with loose leaf gold.

Practice exercise: **Using gum ammoniac to apply loose leaf gold**

This technique uses gum ammoniac, made from resin, as the base for laying loose leaf gold.

Materials
- *Gum ammoniac resin*
- *Plastic bag*
- *Rolling pin or hammer*
- *Small jars*
- *Distilled water*
- *Dish*
- *Muslin (cheesecloth)*
- *Liquid watercolour*
- *Brush*
- *Rolled paper*
- *Loose leaf gold*
- *Glassine paper*
- *Burnisher*
- *Clean cotton rag*
- *Paint and brush*

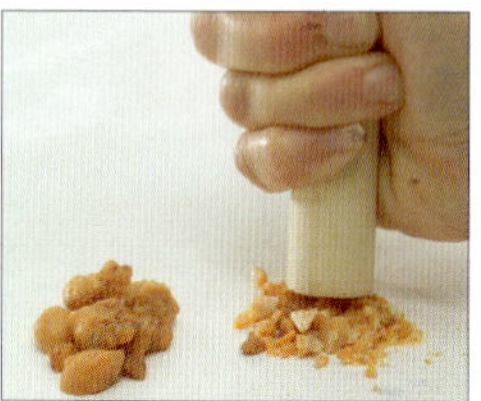

1 Put the gum ammoniac on a hard surface and crush the gum into fine pieces with a rolling pin or hammer.

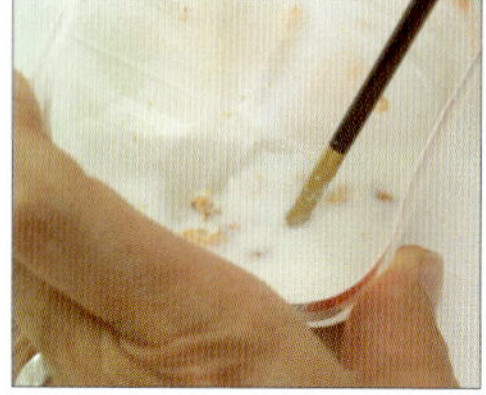

2 Transfer the pieces of crushed gum ammoniac to a small jar. Fill the jar with just enough distilled water to cover the gum, stir and leave overnight to dissolve.

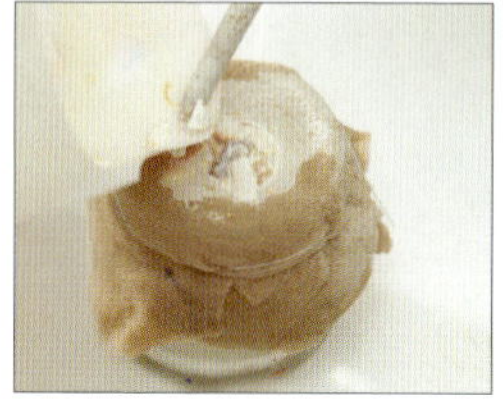

3 Strain the milky liquid through some muslin into another jar. Transfer to a dish. (Instead of using muslin you can use a piece of fabric cut from some old tights.)

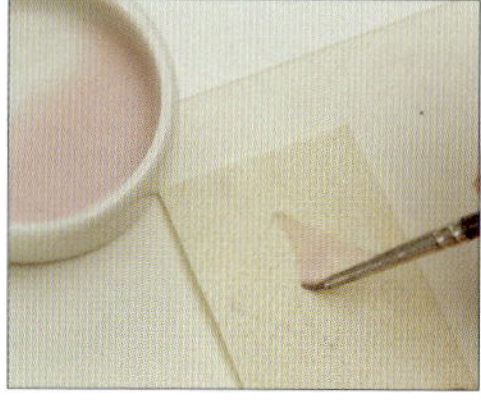

4 Add a couple of drops of liquid watercolour to the gum ammoniac and it is ready to use. Apply the gum to the surface using a paintbrush. Wash this brush.

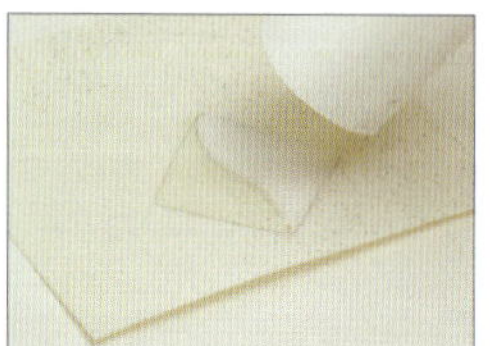

5 Using a piece of rolled-up paper, breathe on the letter to create a tacky surface.

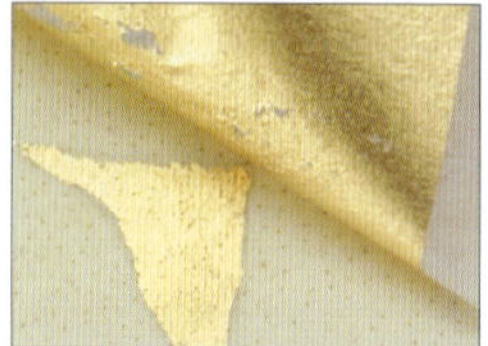

6 Apply a sheet of loose leaf gold and press down. Apply more gold on top if necessary.

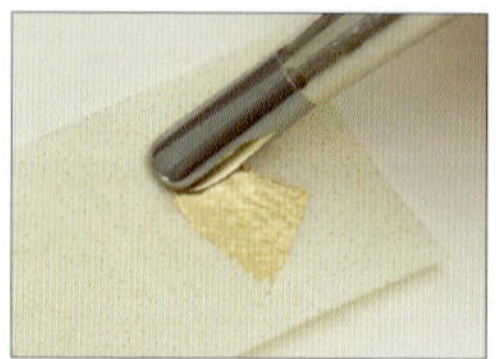

7 Brush away the excess gold and use the burnisher. Polish the gold with a clean cotton rag.

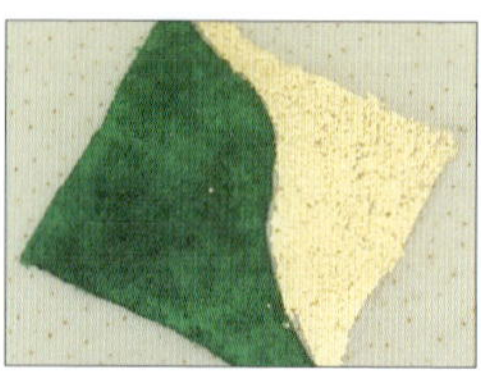

8 Complete the decoration. The gum ammoniac produces a flat layer of gold.

Practice exercise: **Using gesso to apply loose leaf gold**

This technique uses gesso to lay loose leaf gold. Gesso needs to be reconstituted before use, adding water to break up the pieces of gesso.

Materials

- *Distilled water*
- *Gesso*
- *Paintbrush*
- *Craft (utility) knife*
- *Burnisher*
- *Glassine paper*
- *Rolled paper*
- *Loose leaf gold*
- *Paint and brush*
- *Soft brush*
- *Clean cotton rag*

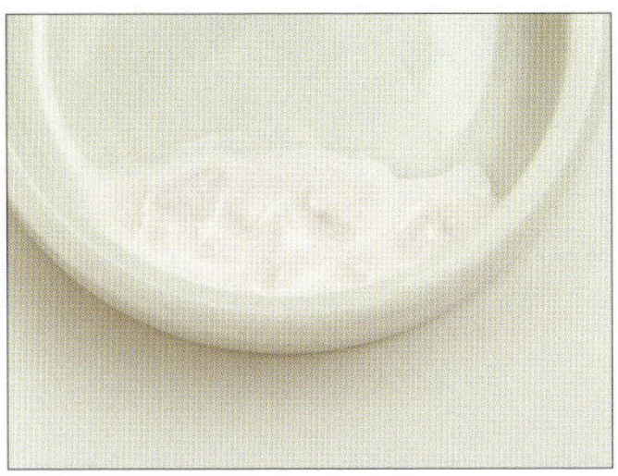

1 Add drops of distilled water to the gesso until it is the consistency of thin cream. Stir very gently to avoid air bubbles. If bubbles appear, blot them with a tissue.

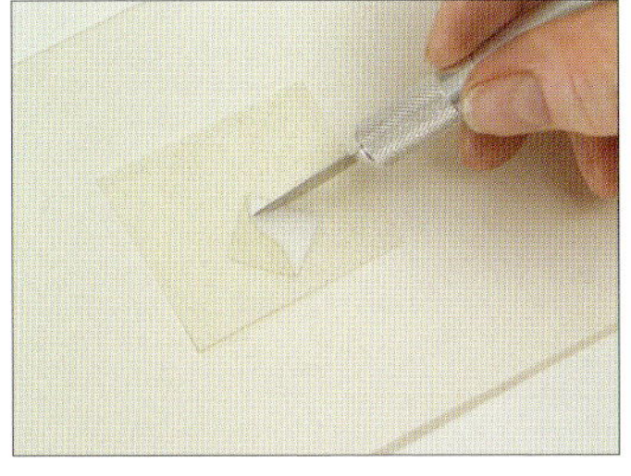

2 Load a paintbrush with this mixture and 'tease' the gesso into the shape. Leave to dry overnight. If it does not have an even surface, gently scrape it with a craft knife.

3 Burnish the gesso with a burnisher through glassine paper until the surface is completely smooth. This will encourage the gold leaf to adhere to the gesso.

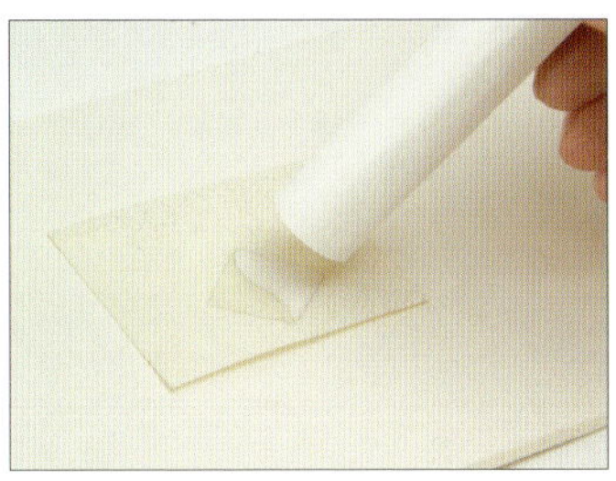

4 Breathe on to the gesso to create moisture, then quickly lay a sheet of loose leaf gold on it and apply pressure. If there are areas without gold, repeat this process.

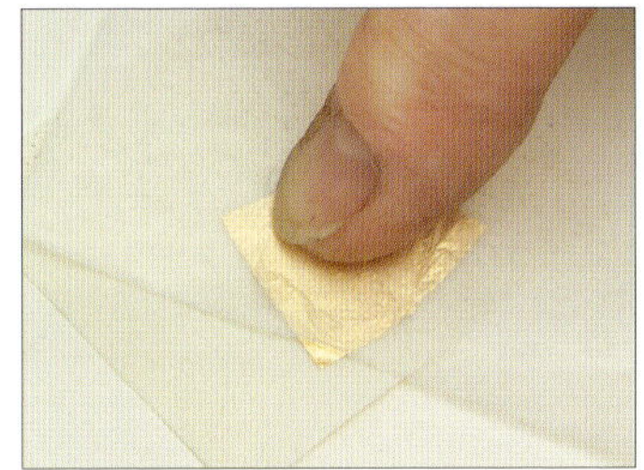

5 Leave for an hour or so before burnishing first with the burnisher through a piece of glassine paper and then directly with a finger through the glassine paper.

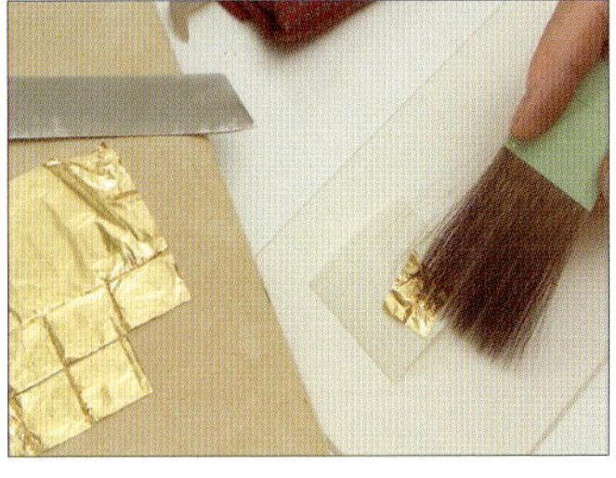

6 Applying additional layers of loose leaf gold will add even more brilliance. Brush away the excess gold with the soft brush, using short, light strokes to flick the gold away.

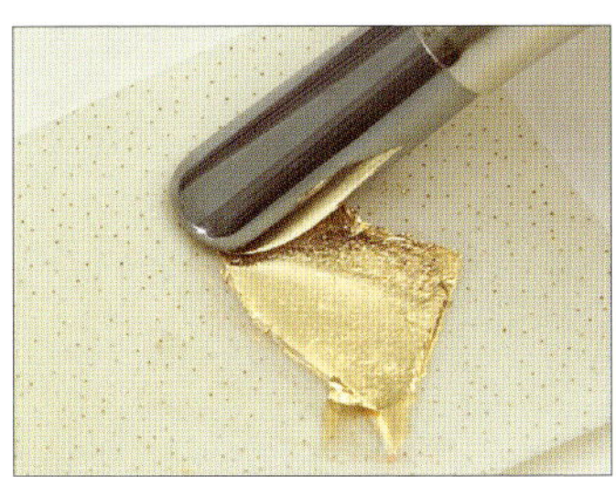

7 Burnish directly on to the gold, making sure that the gold has stuck at the edges.

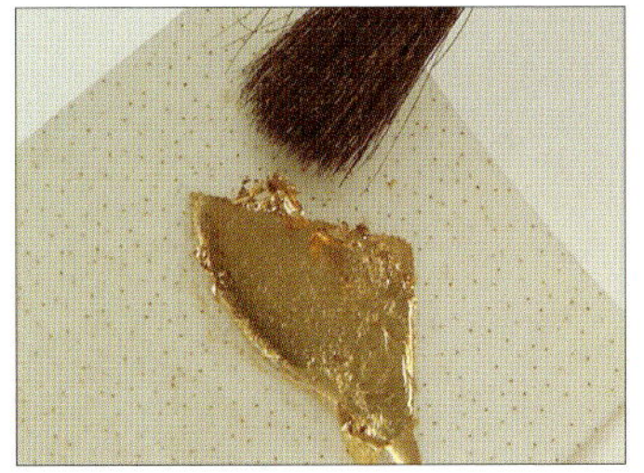

8 Brush away the loose gold at the edges. Continue brushing until all the surrounding gold leaf is removed. Burnish until smooth and polish with a clean cotton rag.

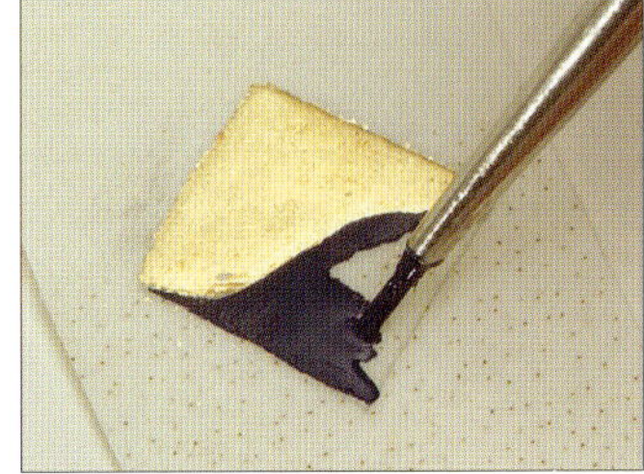

9 Complete the decoration. The gesso produces a raised gold finish to the piece.

Bookbinding

The art of physically assembling a book from a number of separate sheets of paper or other material is known as 'bookbinding'. Modern hand binding is not a difficult craft but it does require accuracy and patience. The papers that are held together within the case, or cover, are sometimes called the text block. The text blocks are usually sewn together with thread using methods such as stab sewing, in which the thread is sewn front to back through all the pages of the book. If the text block is to be illustrated using painted decoration, the paper used for the text block needs to be suited to ink or paint. The case for the book may be made of leather or cardboard, which may be covered by decorative paper. A half-bound book means that the spine and the corners of the cover are covered with leather or cloth, while the rest is covered with card or decorative paper. You can also use a lightweight board or a strong paper for the cover. There are so many book forms available that it is always possible to find the one that is most flattering for your calligraphy.

Tip: Never cut with the ruler or other straight edge held horizontally across the paper, always have the straight edge pointing away from you on the paper and draw the knife towards you. This will enable you to control the knife and to cut a clean and accurate line.

Creasing ▼
Check the grain of the paper before using a bone folder to crease sharply.

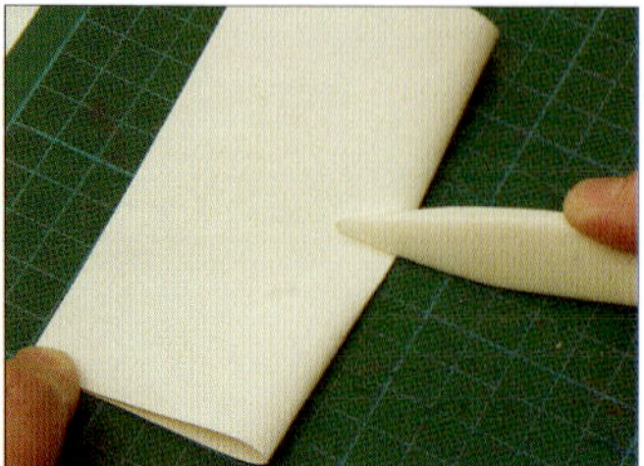

Bookbinding basics

Learning the bookbinding basics first will help you to work neatly and safely.

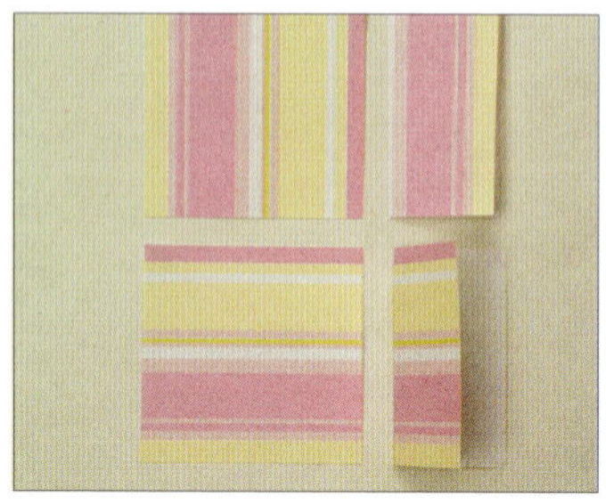

Finding the grain ▲
All machine-made paper, card (stock) or board has a grain. The grains should agree and run parallel to the spine of the book. Some paper is short grained, which means the grain runs parallel to the short side of the paper. The grain of long-grained paper runs parallel to the long side of the paper. Do not assume that the shape of a piece of paper, card or board or the pattern on a piece of paper indicates the direction of its grain.

To test for grain, use two identically sized squares of paper. Roll each square one side to the other horizontally and vertically. There will be a resistance to one of these moves. This happens when you are rolling against the grain. With a pencil, mark arrows showing the grain. Fold one square with the grain and one against the grain and observe that the first fold with the grain will be sharp and crisp. The second fold across the grain will be ragged and untidy. If you try to glue paper, card or board together when the grains do not agree, the work will bow.

Tip: The adhesives used in mainstream binding are PVA (white) glue, paste or a mixture of both. These are all very wet adhesives and are unsuitable for small bookbinding projects. A PH-neutral glue stick, however, is ideal.

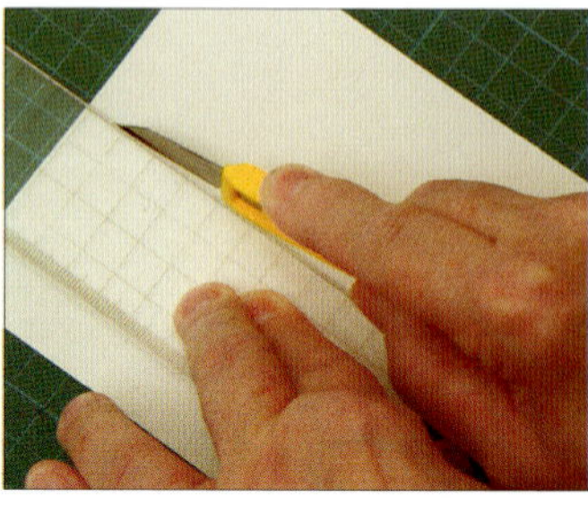

Cutting safely ▲
The best way of cutting paper in half is to measure the piece of paper and draw a line through the paper parallel to one of the edges. Place the paper on a self-healing cutting mat with the line at 90 degrees to yourself. Place the straight edge or ruler to this line and rest your non-dominant hand upon it. Press the knife to the cutting edge and draw it towards you. If it does not cut through the first time, repeat. Resist the temptation to press harder. Do not remove the straight edge until the paper has been cut through. For certainty, always measure twice and cut once.

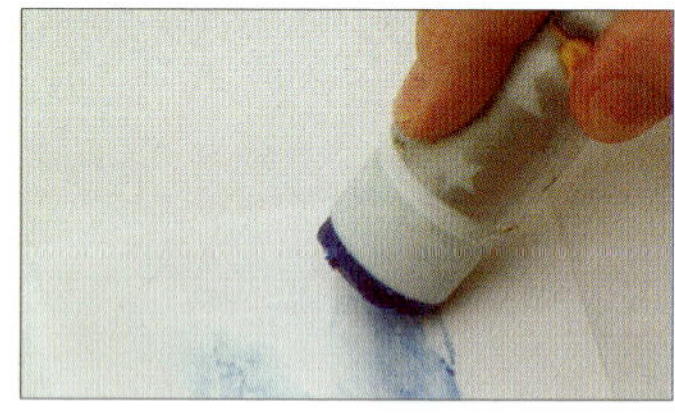

Gluing ▲
Get into the habit of gluing correctly. Place the piece of paper to be glued right side down on a piece of scrap paper. Apply the glue from the middle to the outside edges making sure that the surface of the paper is completely covered. The paper stays flat and does not crease. Do not glue from the sides to the middle of the paper because this can cause the paper to crease and buckle.

Mitring a corner

This is the process of neatening the corners of the book where the paper wraps and folds.

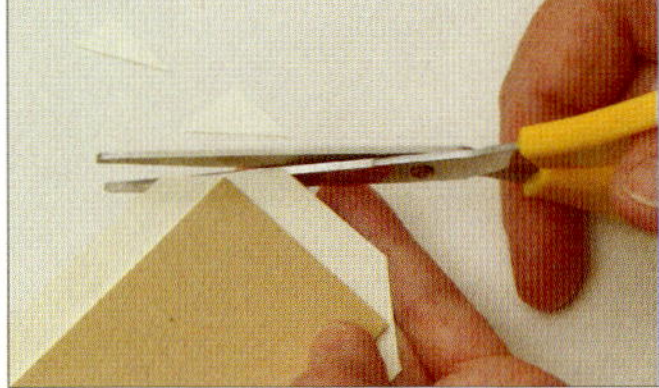

1 Take a small piece of board and a piece of cover paper 2.5cm (1in) larger all round. Glue the board and place on the middle of the reverse of the paper. Rub down well with a bone folder. With a pair of scissors trim away a triangle of paper at each corner leaving the depth of the board plus two thicknesses of paper. The base of each triangle should be at 45 degrees to the corner of the board.

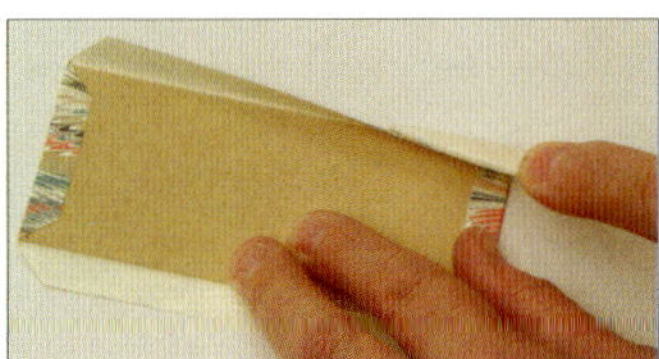

2 Place the board face down and fold down the projecting ends. Lift up the paper at the ends and glue them to the board, carefully tucking the ends around the two edges of the corners. Use the bone folder to press down the paper in place. Fold the adjacent edges.

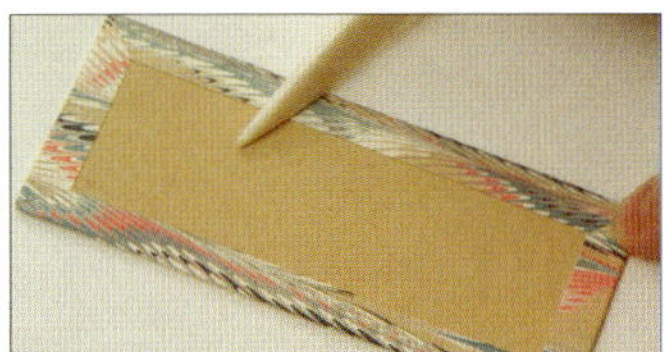

3 Lift and glue the sides and press in place using the bone folder. A nipping press (a small press used to apply pressure) can be applied, or the covered board can be left overnight under several heavy books.

Practice exercise: **Covering a mount**

This shows you how to cover a mount with a decorative paper, turning in the inside corners and edges so that it looks professionally finished.

Materials

- *Craft (utility) knife*
- *Decorative paper, e.g. marbled*
- *Purchased mount*
- *Straight edge or a ruler with a steel cutting edge*
- *Scrap paper (preferably shiny), for protection when gluing*
- *Glue stick*
- *Bone folder*
- *Self-healing cutting mat*

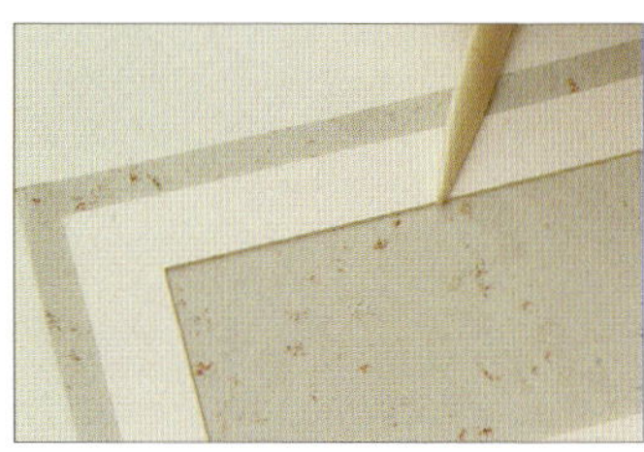

1 Cut a piece of decorative paper 2cm (3/4in) larger all round than the purchased mount. Glue the face of the mount and place centrally on the reverse side of the decorative paper. Use sharp strokes with the bone folder to ensure it adheres to the paper.

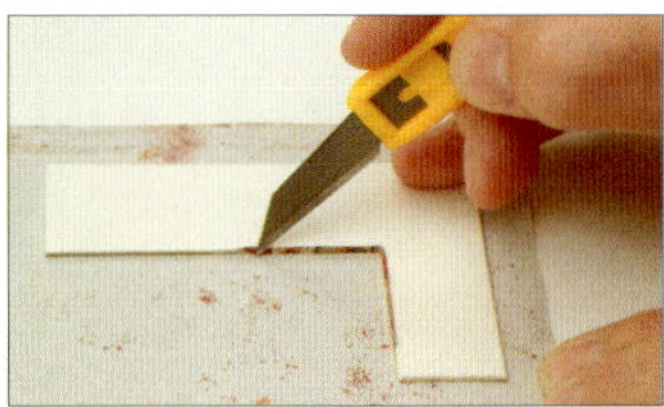

2 Cut four strips of the decorative paper the depth of the board by 5cm (2in). Glue these on the reverse sides and place one in each corner of the mount's aperture. These strips will serve to cover the slight gap that occurs when the cover paper is turned in around the aperture.

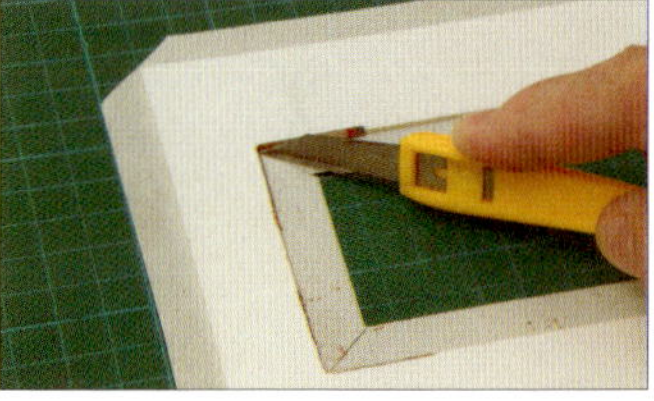

3 Trim away the paper at the corners and the centre of the mount's aperture leaving a margin of 1cm (1/2in). Cut the paper diagonally into the corners of the aperture.

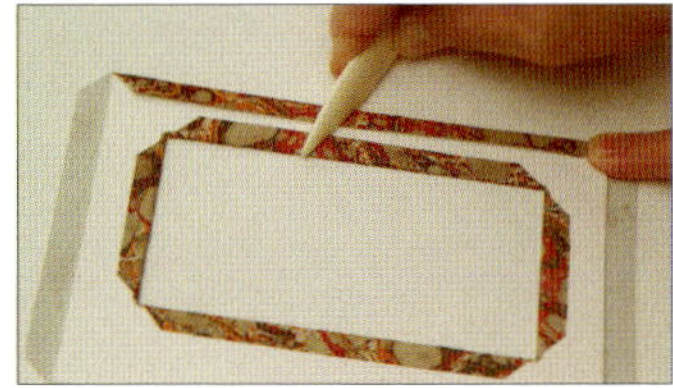

4 Glue the edges of the paper both around the frame and within the aperture. Turn these edges over the frame (this is termed 'turning in'), mitring the outside corners. Leave to dry under weights.

5 With an image or photograph added to the mount, it would make an ideal present for a friend or relative.

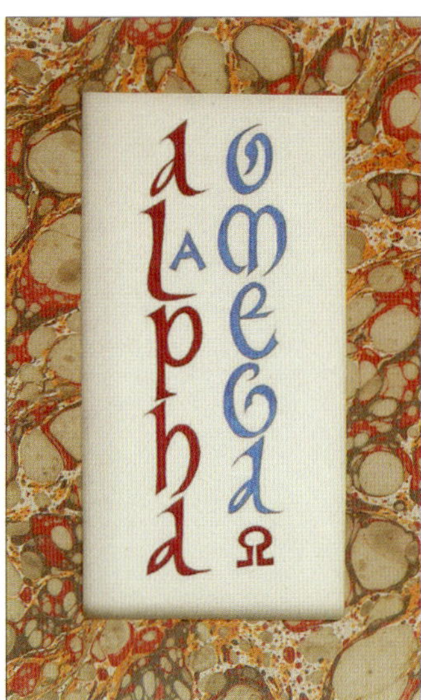

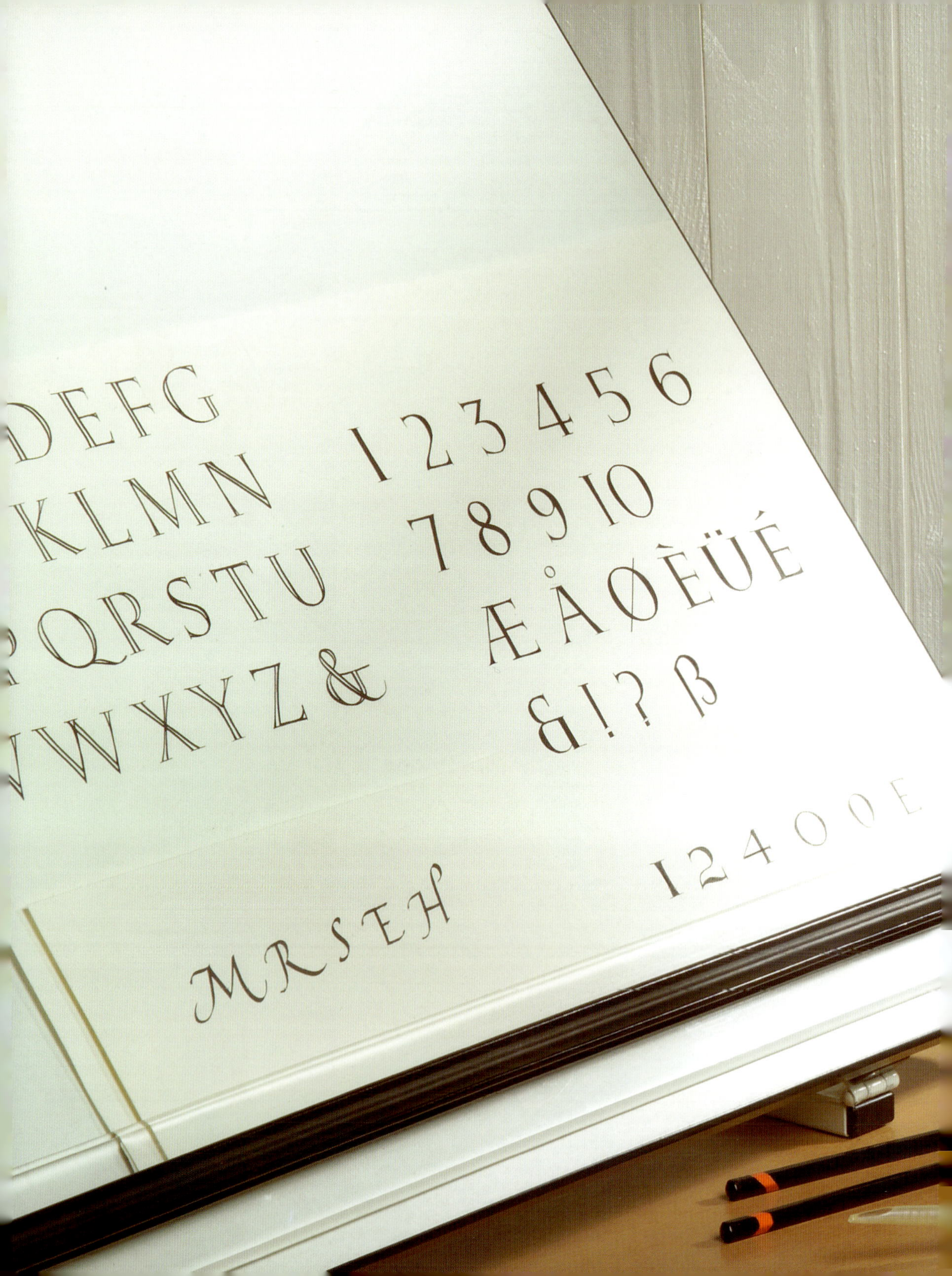

DEFG
KLMN
QRSTU
VWXYZ&

1 2 3 4 5 6
7 8 9 10
Æ Å Ø È Ü É
& ! ? ß

1 2 4 0 0 E

MRSEH

Alphabets

One of the joys of calligraphy is being able to choose a script that in some way expresses the meaning of the text. Hundreds of beautiful calligraphic alphabets have been developed over the centuries, and in this section 12 of the most popular are presented in detail. To enable you to accurately construct the individual letters, the alphabets are demonstrated in upper and lower case along with helpful markers to indicate the direction and order of the strokes used. Calligraphy, however, is not just a matter of mechanically following rules – it requires a feel for the style and flow of the scripts, and following the exercises that accompany each alphabet will help you to develop this. Practise the scripts, taking care to avoid the common mistakes, until you can write them fluently.

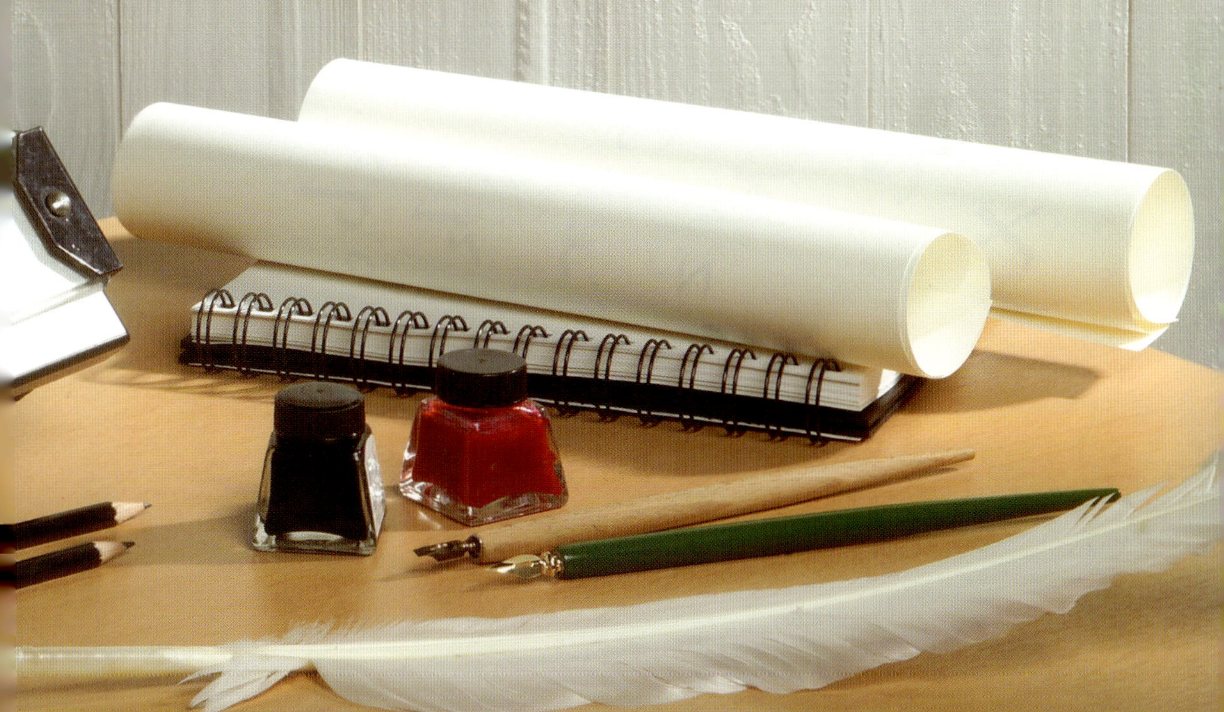

Foundational hand

The Foundational hand, also known as Round hand, was devised by Edward Johnston (1872–1944) following his studies of medieval manuscripts in the British Library. He based this hand on the writing of the Ramsey Psalter – an English Carolingian script with well-formed and consistent letterforms that was written around the end of the 10th century.

The Foundational hand is based on the circle made by two overlapping strokes of the pen. This cursive hand is written with a constant pen angle and few pen lifts. It is this constant angle that produces the characteristic 'thick' and 'thin' strokes of the letterforms.

In the 9th and 10th centuries either Uncial or Versal letters would have been used at the beginning of the Carolingian scripts on which Foundational hand is based. However, Roman Capitals are now used in conjunction with the Foundational hand. These capitals are based on the carved inscriptional letters used in Ancient Rome and their elegant proportions relate to the geometric proportions of a circle within a square. The Foundational alphabet can be divided into several groups, and the circle within a square construction is used as the guidelines for the proportions of the letters within each group. Circular letters follow the circle, rectangular letters are three-quarters the width of the square and narrow letters are half the width of the square. The only letters that do not fall into a group are the two wide capital letters 'M' and 'W'. The central part of the letter 'M' is constructed in the same way as 'V' and the legs extend right into the corners of the square. The letter 'W' is constructed as two 'V's side by side, making a very wide letter that extends beyond the boundaries of the square.

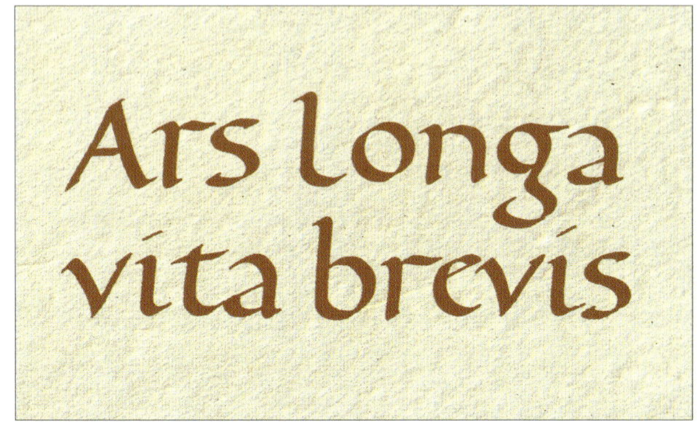

The basic rules

Foundational hand is a formal, upright script where each letter is made up of two or more strokes, which means that it has more pen lifts than a cursive script. The constant pen angle of 30 degrees controls the distribution of weight, creating thick and thin strokes. This pen angle must be maintained throughout in order to create good, rounded letterforms and strong arches. The letters should be evenly spaced for easy reading. An important characteristic of this hand is that the top curves of 'c' and 'r' are slightly flattened to help the eye travel along the line of writing.

LETTER HEIGHT
The Foundational letter height is four times the width of the nib. Turn the pen sideways to make squares with the nib, then rule the lines that far apart.

LETTER SLOPE
Foundational letters are upright and should not lean.

PEN ANGLES
Hold the nib at a constant angle of 30 degrees for all letters except for diagonals, where the first stroke is made with a pen angle of 45 degrees.

hp

h

p

45°

30°

Practice exercise: **Foundational hand**

Almost all the letterforms of this hand relate to the circle and arches, so practise by drawing controlled crescent moon shapes, beginning and ending on a thin point. Once this has been mastered, these semicircles can be attached to upright stems to create rounded letterforms or they can be extended into a downstroke to form arches. Begin high up and inside the stem to produce a strong rounded arch. Rounded serifs are used on entry and exit of strokes.

Group

Strokes (1st = red, 2nd = blue, 3rd = green)

Round or circular

cbpoedq

Note where the thin parts of the letters are. The first stroke of these letters should be a clean semicircular sweep, producing a shape like a crescent moon. Start at the top and move the pen downwards. The left and right edges of the pen form the circles.

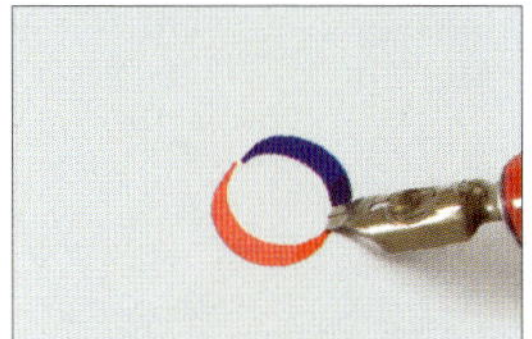

The letter 'o' is made by two overlapping semicircular strokes which produce the characteristic oval shape of the counter.

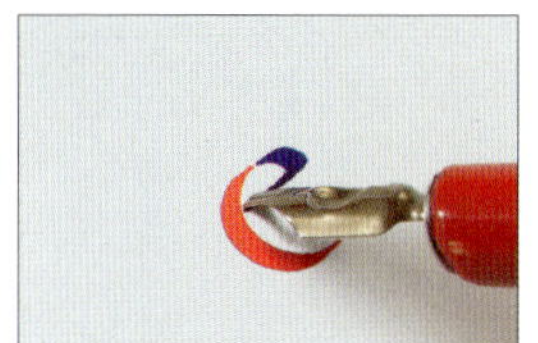

The back of the 'e' does not quite follow the circular 'o' but is flattened so it appears balanced. The top joins just above halfway.

Arched

lmnrhau

The arch joins the stem high up. Beginning with the pen in the stem, draw outwards in a wide curve, following the 'o' form. Start the letters with a strong, curved serif and end with a smaller curved serif. Keep the pen angle at 30 degrees throughout.

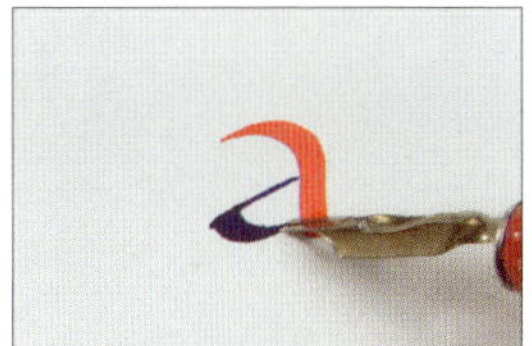

Draw an arch continuing into a straight stroke. The bowl of the letter begins halfway down the stem with the pen at 30 degrees.

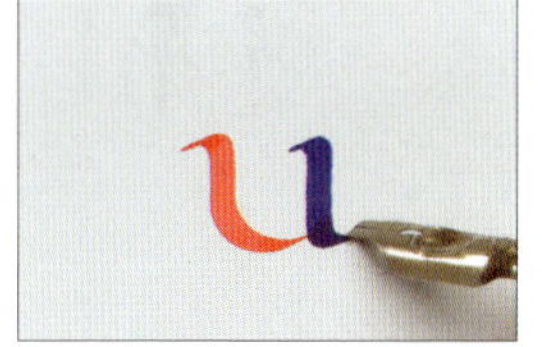

The 'u' follows the same line as an 'n' but upside down, producing a strong arch with no thin hairlines. Add the stem last.

Diagonal

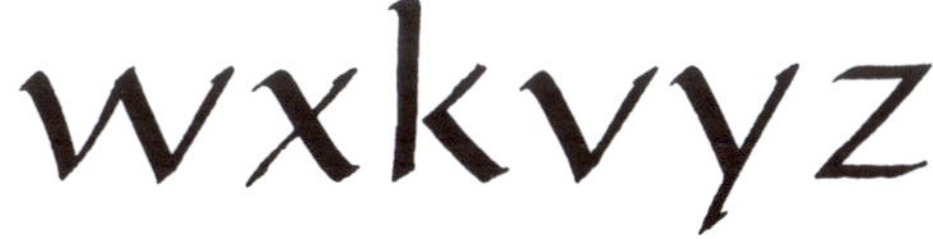

For the first stroke, hold the pen at the steeper angle of 45 degrees. This will prevent the stroke from being too thick. Take care not to make any curve on this stroke. Revert to a pen angle of 30 degrees for the second stroke.

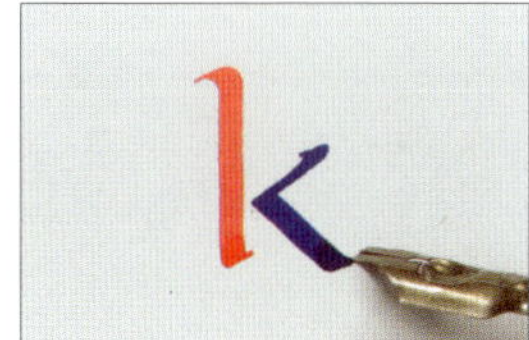

Start the ascender three nib widths above the body height. The second stroke is made in one continuous movement forming a right angle.

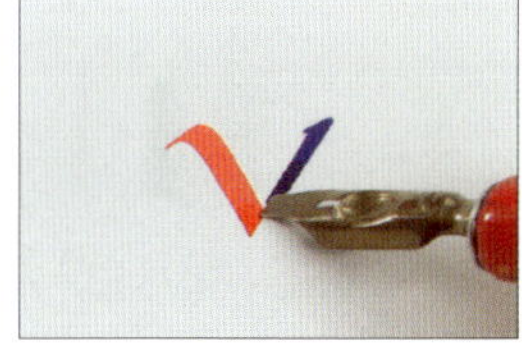

The pen angle is steepened for the thick stroke and the strokes should sit upright. The second stroke begins with a small, hooked serif.

Ungrouped

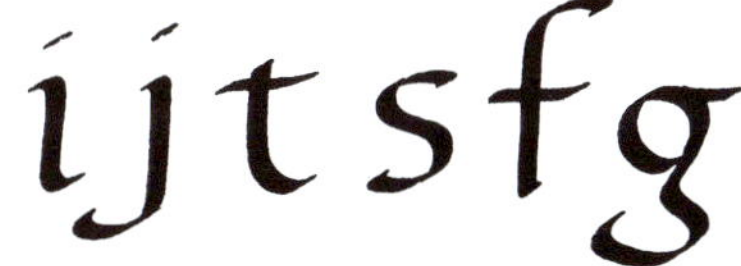

Keep the pen angle at 30 degrees for these letters. Remember to follow the smooth shape of the 'o' when drawing curves, rather than simply flicking the pen. Crossbars should sit just below the top line, and should protrude to nearly the width of the curve.

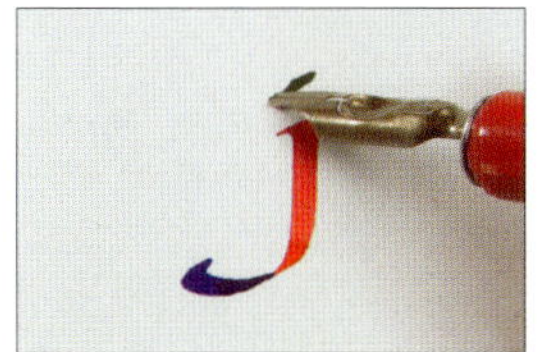

The base of the first stroke curves to relate to the 'i'. The second stroke begins with a small serif and neatly joins to this base.

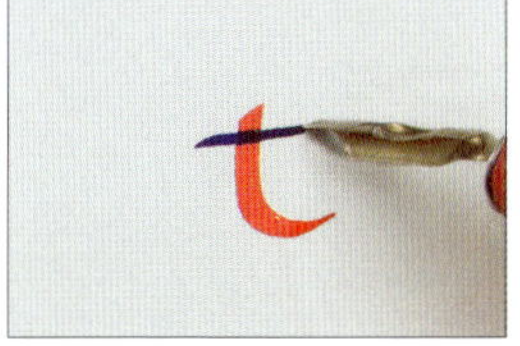

Start just above the top line. The crossbar forms the second stroke and is made by placing the nib at an angle just below the top line.

Foundational hand

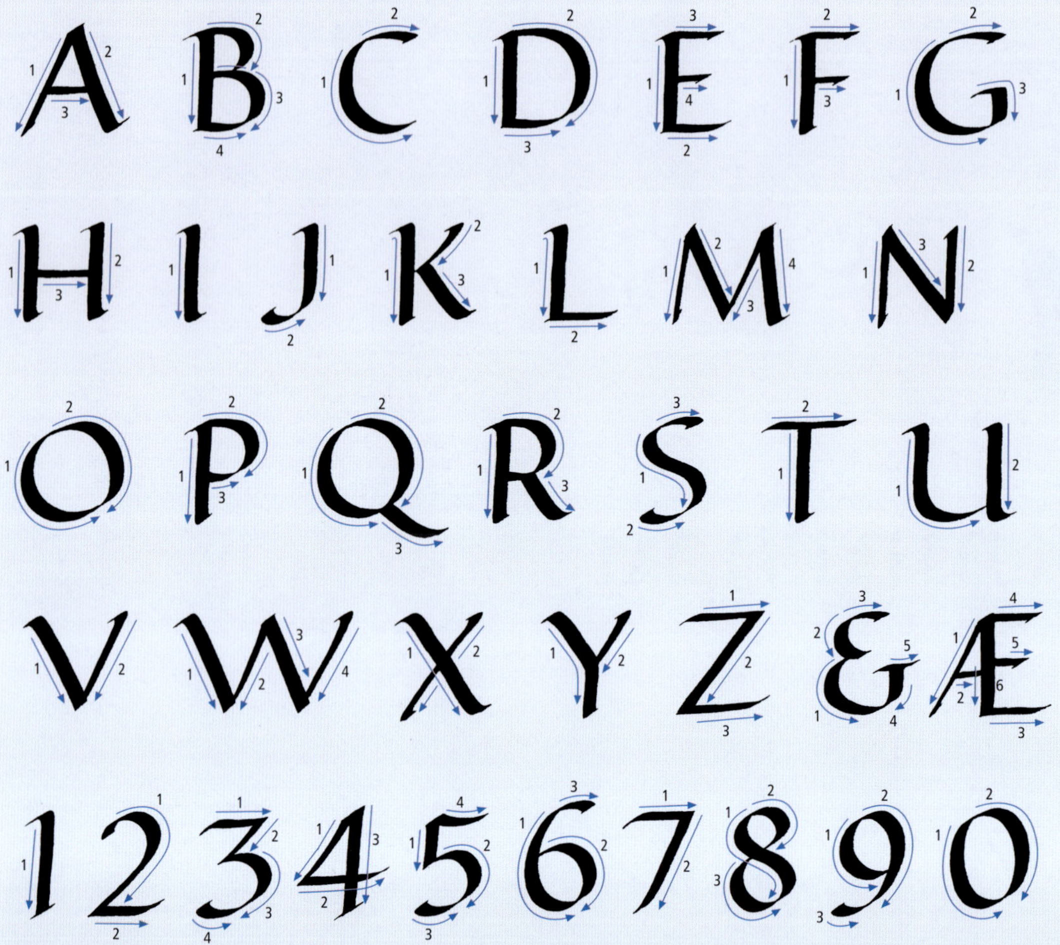

COMMON MISTAKES – CAPITALS

Often people start calligraphy with the Foundational hand and it is easy to establish incorrect letterforms. The most common place to go wrong with capitals is on the width of the letters and in keeping a correct pen angle. In addition to this, overlapping can cause unsightly dense areas.

The outer legs are too splayed and the 'v' is too narrow.

The top curve should be slightly flattened.

The bottom bowl should be slightly larger than the top with a smooth curve at the base.

Fatten the base of the bowl to avoid a dense join.

The diagonal stroke should be straight and not curved.

Strokes should cross slightly above half way up.

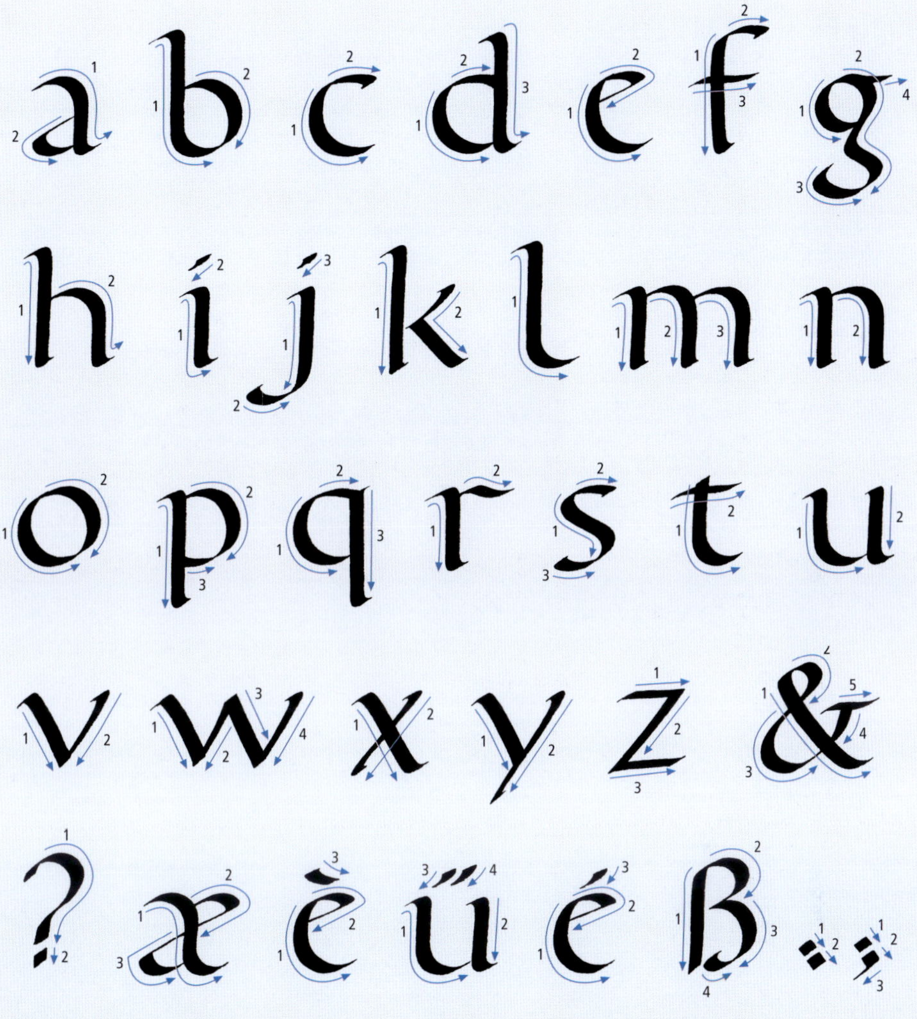

COMMON MISTAKES – LOWER CASE

A common mistake is to give letters the wrong shape. This is usually caused by not following the shape of the 'o'. As a result, the bowls of the letters will be too small, and arches will be weak and uneven.

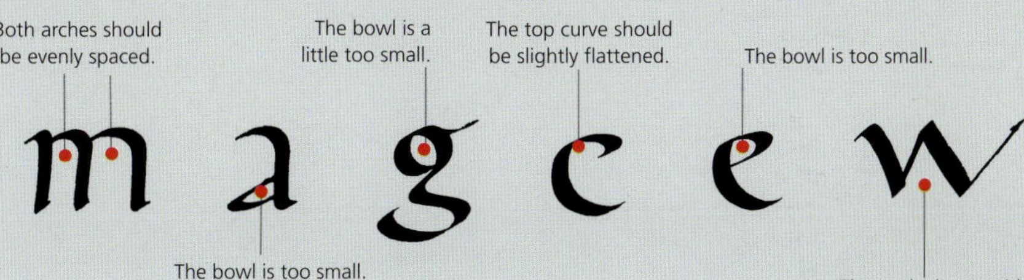

Roman Capitals

Roman Capitals are arguably the most important early ancestors of Western calligraphy. Two thousand years old, and originating from the beautiful letters inscribed in stone or marble in ancient Rome, they are now revered as classical models. Even today, the work of Roman craftsmen still exists throughout what used to be the Roman Empire for all to see.

The version of Roman Capitals shown here is lightweight, with small, elegant serifs. The letters maintain the classical Roman proportions, but are modelled on a more recent pen version developed in the medieval period by the famous Italian scribe Bartholomeo San Vito.

The Roman Capital letterforms are based in structure on the geometric proportions of the circle and the square. They can be divided into four groups: the circle within the square, three-quarter width, half width and the whole square or larger. It is helpful to try out these proportions first in pencil, making just skeleton monoline letters, perhaps on graph paper. Try them in width groups (as shown opposite) to familiarize yourself with the proportions before you begin to write using the edged pen. When you do write with the edged pen, ensure that you maintain the pen angle at 30 degrees. This angle can be flatter for the serifs if aiming for elegance. The serif endings may need to be finished off by using the corner of the nib. Diagonal strokes demand a 45-degree pen angle.

Close attention must be paid to the height and width of the letters if they are to be recreated with their true proportions. The letters need some space around them, so avoid crowding them too closely together.

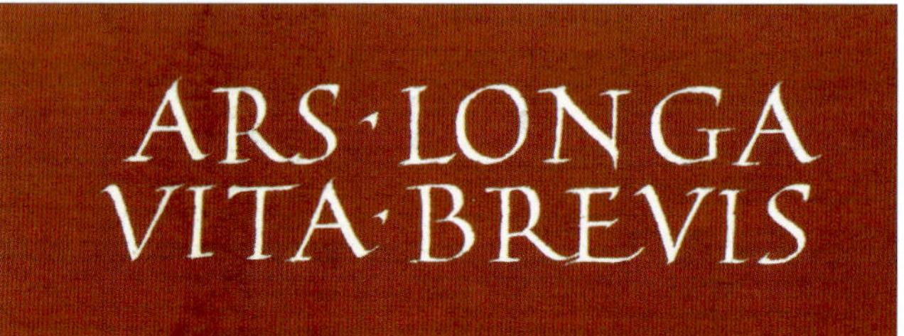

The basic rules

It is important to retain good pen control when writing Roman Capitals. In general, maintain a constant pen angle of 30 degrees. There are, however, a few exceptions to this rule that add elegance to the letterform. The upright strokes in 'N', and the first stroke in 'M', need a steeper pen angle of 60 degrees in order to make a thinner stroke. 'Z' needs a stronger diagonal stroke than 30 degrees will confer, so cheat and flatten the pen completely for a thicker stroke. You may find that in order to blend the serifs into the uprights, your pen needs to be well filled with ink; this helps the strokes flow together. In order to create serifs, a pen angle of 5 degrees may be adopted. Several different types of serif can be produced, requiring different levels of competence.

LETTER HEIGHT
The letters shown here are eight nib-widths, giving light elegance. You could try seven or even six nib widths, but take care not to allow the serifs to become too dominant.

LETTER SLOPE
The letters are upright, and should have no forward slope. Check that letters have not developed a lean by looking at the writing upside down.

PEN ANGLES
Thirty degrees is maintained overall, maybe a little flatter for elegance of serifs, a little steeper for the uprights of 'N' (to make them thinner) and flatter for the diagonal of 'Z' to make it thicker.

PH

P

H

30°

Practice exercise: **Roman Capitals**

Unlike all lower-case (minuscule) hands, Roman Capitals rely for their elegance on their geometry, and in particular on their widths relative to the circle and square. These widths are the basis upon which the groups of letters are formed. It is important to have a sound understanding of how Roman Capital letters are constructed before embarking upon reproducing the whole alphabet. An edged or broad pen may be used when writing this script.

Group

Strokes (1st = red, 2nd = blue, 3rd = green, 4th = mauve)

Circular

OCGDQ

All are formed as all or part of a circle. Make sure that your circle really is round and not oval, and that the letters that belong to this group have a round shape overall. 'D' is difficult to make rounded – you may find it helps if you pencil in the circle first.

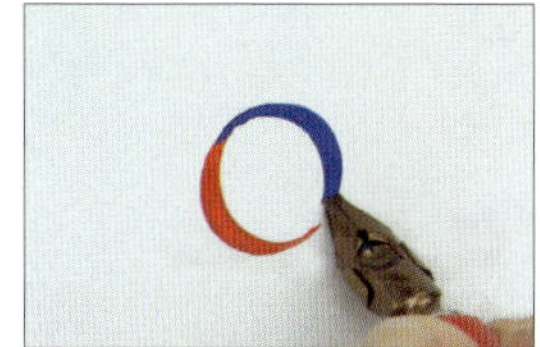

This letter is made in two 'half-moon' strokes pulled downwards and joined at the thin points.

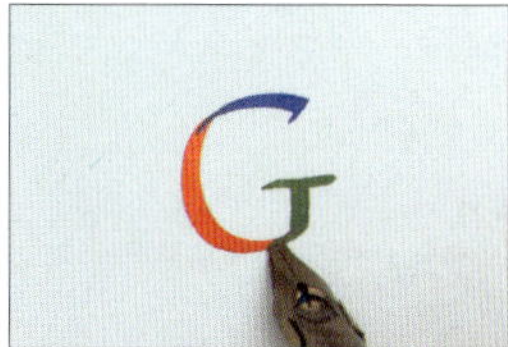

This letter has more parts; ensure it echoes the 'O' in shape, and blend the last stroke into the bottom without leaving a thin stroke.

Three-quarter width

HAVNTUXYZ

In geometric terms, these letters occupy the area where a circle in a square meets the two diagonal lines that cross it – equal to three-quarters of the width of the square. All the letters in this group occupy the same width – three-quarters of their height.

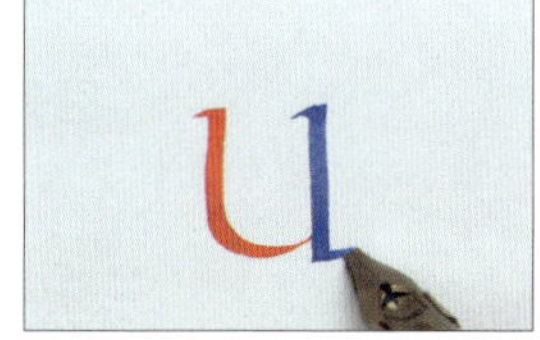

Make a confident curve finishing on a thin stroke, and bring the second stroke down to make an overlapped join.

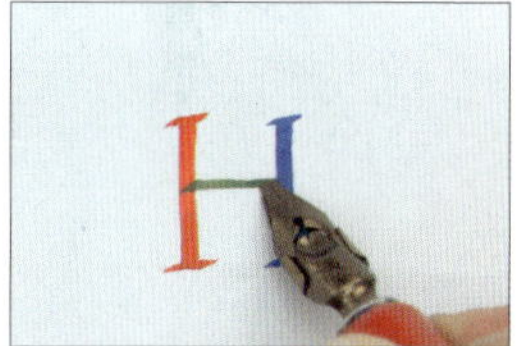

Judging the distance between the two uprights will need practice; ensure the crossbar is a little above the centre.

Half-width

BPRKSELFIJ

These letters are grouped together because, in geometric terms, the major part of the letter occupies just half of the square. In the case of 'R' and 'K', the tails of the letters will extend beyond the half of the square, and the letter 'I' is narrower than this.

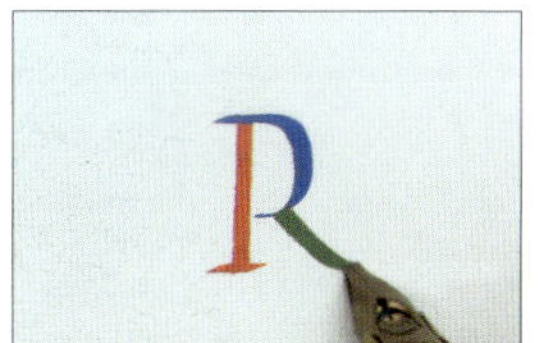

The top serif is made as part of the stroke that carries on to make the curve. The tail does not start from the stem, but from the curve.

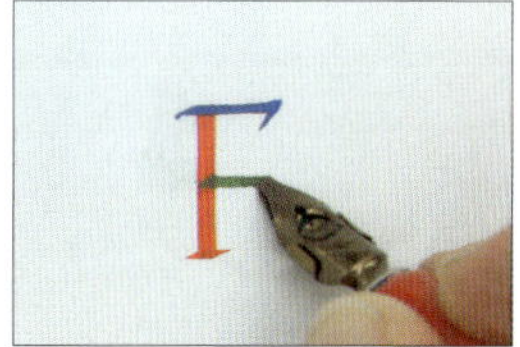

The top stroke starts as a serif to the left, and continues across with a slight twisting of the pen. Repeat for the central crossbar.

Broad-width

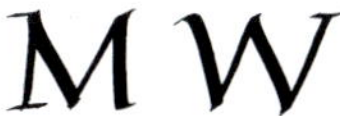

There are just two letters remaining: 'M' and 'W'. They are not upside-down versions of each other, so do not overdo the very slight splaying of 'M's legs. In geometric terms, 'M' mainly fits the shape of a square, whereas 'W' is two 'V's, making it very wide.

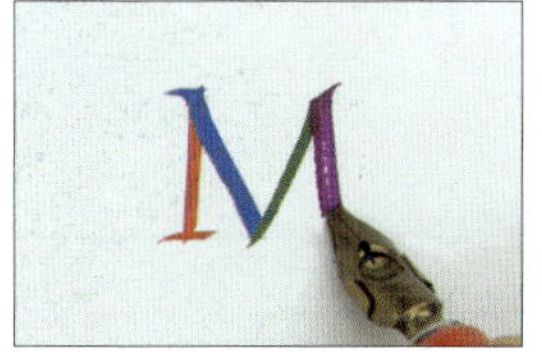

Make the first stroke with a steeper pen angle for a fine line; try not to allow the outer strokes to splay too much.

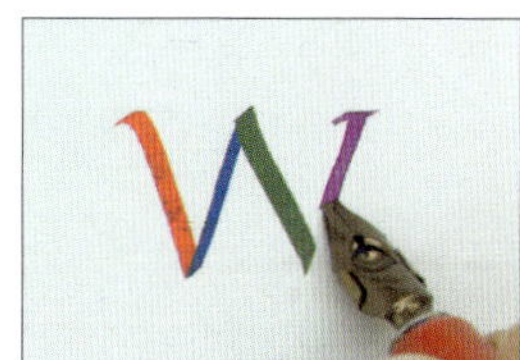

Put two 'V' shapes together, blending the joins by careful overlapping, especially at the bottom points.

Roman Capitals

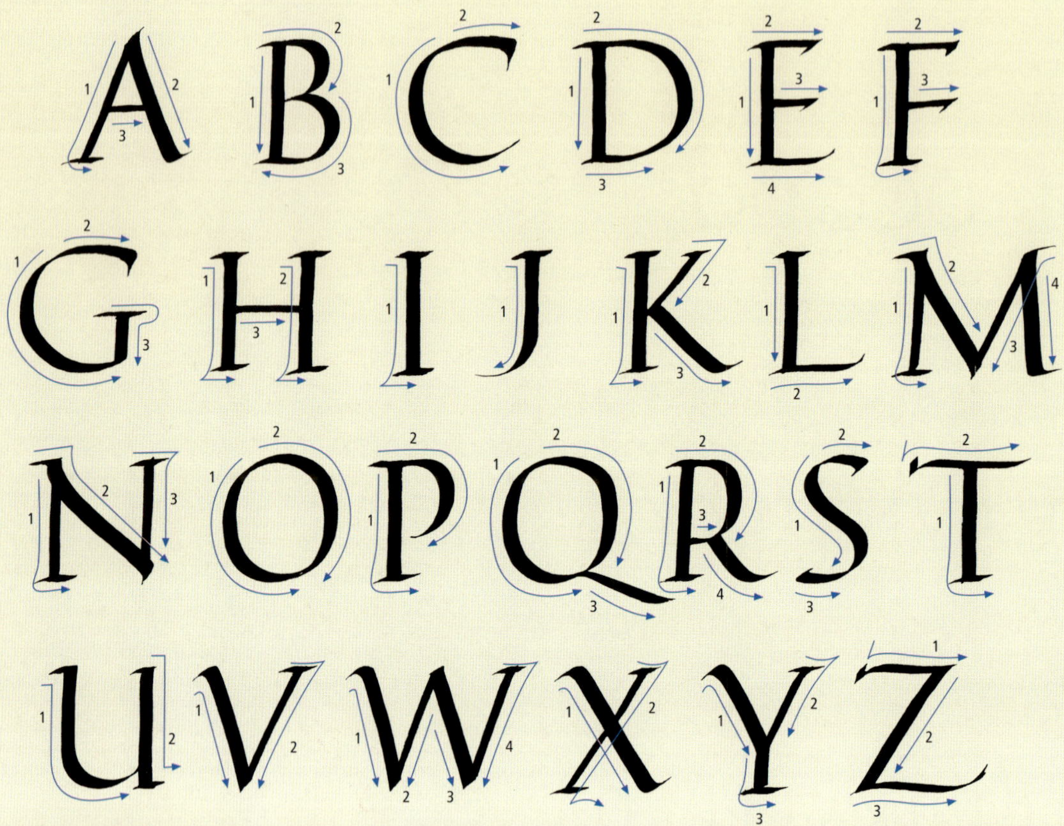

COMMON MISTAKES – CAPITALS

Mistakes of proportion are the most common problem with Roman Capitals, so you may prefer to trace the letters the first time, to help get the 'feel' of the balance of forms.

B R D M F G

Bottom bowl should be larger than top, for visual balance.

Too wide; this is a half-width letter.

Too narrow, this looks like half a circle – it should have a straight top to assist in gaining the width.

If the first stroke is sloping too much, the whole letter becomes an upside-down 'W'.

Too long; the horizontals should be a similar width.

Crossbar too low; throws the letter out of balance.

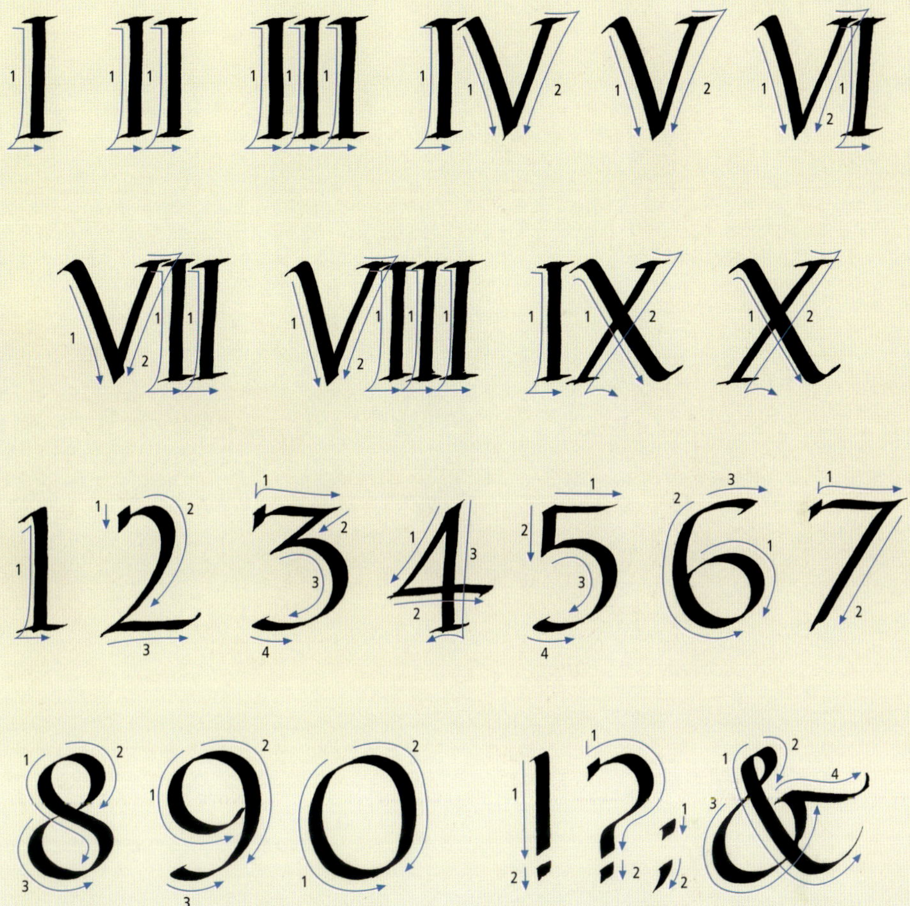

COMMON MISTAKES – NUMERALS AND SYMBOLS

Originally, of course, only Roman numerals would have been used with Roman Capitals. For speed, some writers join all the top and bottom serifs into horizontal bars. Arabic numerals were assimilated into the alphabet at a later date. They should generally be bottom-heavy so that they look balanced.

Divided too low, bottom bowl too small.

Top heavy; larger bowl should be at bottom for visual balance.

Top and bottom bowls too similar, make top bowl smaller.

Crossbar too high; makes it very small.

Small bowl, with lower stroke extending too far to bottom left.

Leaning backwards; start the first diagonal more upright.

Uncial hand

This script has a long history, developed around the 4th century AD or earlier. It is composed entirely of majuscules (capitals) which have no corresponding minuscules (lower-case letters) to accompany them. Minuscule forms had not yet evolved when Uncial was developed, but the few letters which extend above or below the body height ('D', 'H' and 'Q' for example) are the first signs of ascenders and descenders to come.

The precise origin of Uncials is uncertain, but they may have originated from north African scripts. They appear to combine Latin and Greek shapes – look at 'A', 'D' and 'E' (version with crossbar), 'H' and 'M', which seem to have Greek parentage. The early versions of Uncial appear to be quick to write, and this will have endeared them to scriptoria where dissemination of religious writings (including the bible) was the focus. They are known as 'book hands', or hands that were specifically evolved to suit writing at small scale.

Uncials became associated with Christianity, as they accompanied the spread of this 'religion of the book'. Luxury books of the time often incorporated very large writing (sometimes for practical purposes of being readable at a distance during a religious service). It is thought the term 'Uncial', which literally means 'inch-high', was an affectionate exaggeration of that size, and in the 19th century that name became the accepted name of the script.

Later versions of Uncial, used from the 7th to 9th centuries, became more complex, requiring twisting or 'manipulation' of the pen to obtain subtle wedged serifs, which would have slowed down the writing speed. Both forms are shown on the following pages, but follow the simple form before attempting the manipulated version, which requires more concentration.

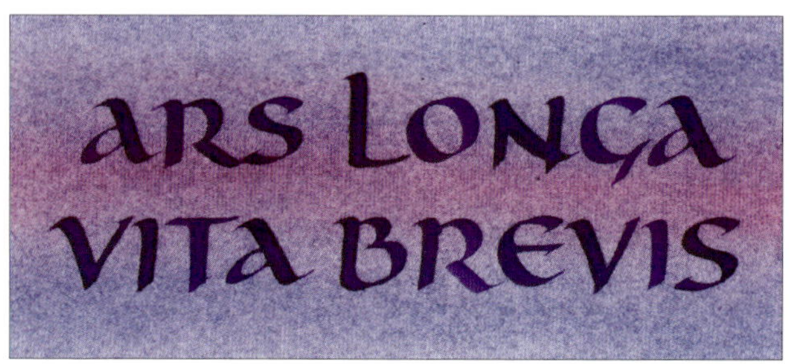

The basic rules

These letters are all very rounded, and may not come naturally to anyone who normally writes compressed forms. If this is the case, draw a row of circles lightly in pencil and write the letters on top, checking that each one maintains the rounded shape. All arches follow the round arches of 'O'. Even the diagonal letters correspond to the circle shape in width (except 'W', which incorporates two 'O's overlapped). Check that you have the pen at a flat pen angle, as steeper angles invite the pen to make narrower marks. Some letters have slight ascenders that are higher than the body height, or descenders that fall below the baseline, but these should be minimal in height, extending only between one and two nib widths. 'I' and 'J' are not dotted, because all Uncials are capital letters.

LETTER HEIGHT

The Uncials shown here are three and a half nib widths high, which provides the historically correct weight. However, they can also be written at four or more nib widths for lighter versions. The extensions are minimal, and must not exceed two nib widths.

LETTER SLOPE

These are upright letters and should not have a slope. Speed of writing occasionally creates a slight forward lean, but this is not good practice, so slow down if a slope creeps in.

PEN ANGLES

A comparatively flat angle is necessary for these letters, between 15 and 25 degrees. Check where your thinnest part in a curved letter comes – it should be very near the top, with the accompanying danger of weak arch joins.

Practice exercise: **Uncial hand**

For this script think 'fat and flat': very rounded, wide letters written with the pen at a very flat pen angle. They are fairly comfortable for left-handers; right-handers should tuck their elbow into their waist if having trouble with this pen angle. Keep checking that the thin strokes are near the top and bottom on curved letters, and that the horizontal strokes are much narrower than the upright strokes on straight letters.

Groups

Strokes (1st = red, 2nd = blue, 3rd = green)

Round or circular

ocdeegpqs

Most Uncial letters are rounded in shape. Try to see the secret 'O' in every letter, but remember that the Uncial 'O' is slightly wider than a circle. It may help to draw pencil circles to write over. There are two 'E's; the first 'E' in this group is Greek in origin.

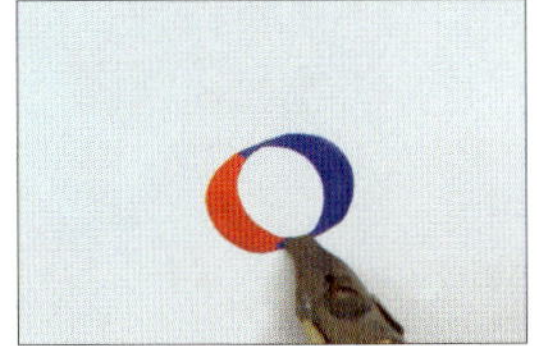

Make a half-moon curve from top to bottom, then blend in the second curve using a clockwise movement.

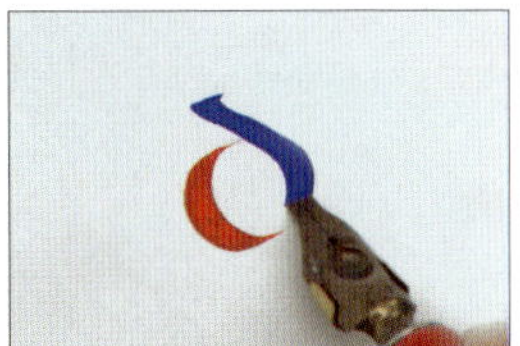

Start just like the 'O', then begin the second stroke above the line, completing the 'O' shape. Beware of flattening the right-hand side.

Diagonal

kvwxyzna

These letters still maintain the width of the 'O'. Watch your pen angle carefully so as not to make the diagonal strokes very much thicker than the upright strokes. The right-to-left diagonals should be thinner than their left-to-right counterparts.

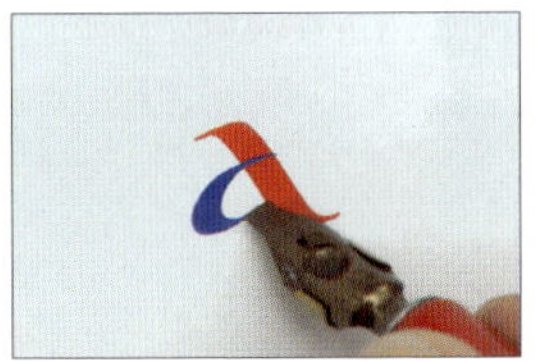

Make the first stroke a diagonal stroke, then, starting inside the diagonal, make a sweeping but tight curve.

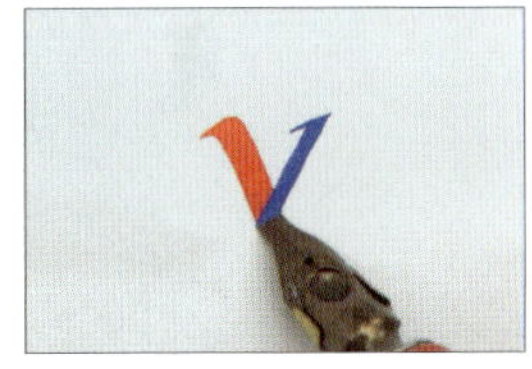

Pull the diagonal down at the shallow angle, and bring the second stroke down to overlap for a neat corner; check its thickness.

Arched

hmurb

A very flat pen angle puts the thinnest point of a curved letter near the top – just where it would join an upright for an arched letter. This can weaken the letter, so take care to start the curve inside the upright to make it look well attached.

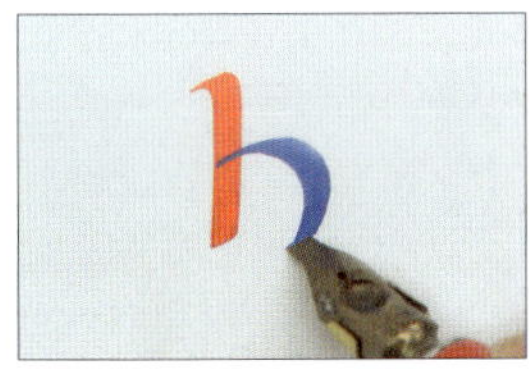

Start the upright stroke above the line, and firmly lock the curved stroke into it by starting within the stem. Note its roundness.

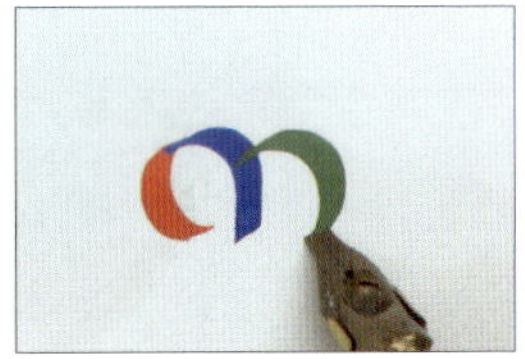

The first stroke is like 'O', the second forms an upright, and the last stroke repeats the curve with a firmly attached branching arch.

Straight

ijltf

These letters are the simplest, but they are useful for practising writing with the correct pen angle, as you can pay attention solely to attaining the desired difference in thickness between horizontals and verticals.

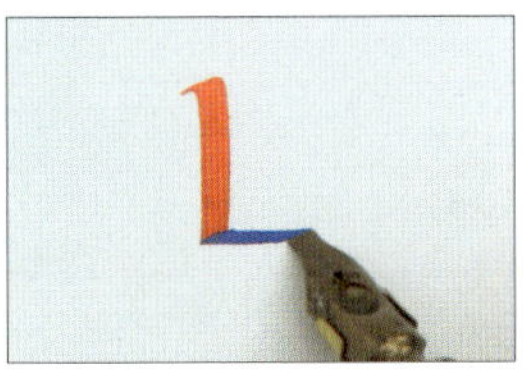

Start above the line with a minimal serif, and pull down for a strong vertical stroke, changing direction but not pen angle at the base.

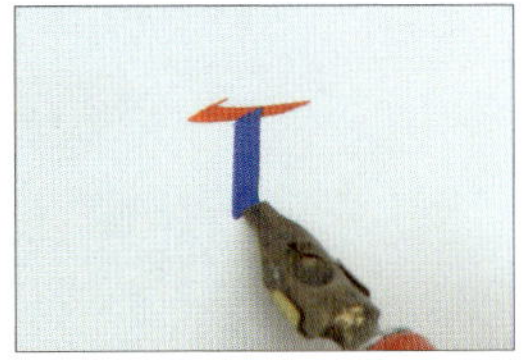

Start with the crossbar, as this will help when spacing text. Make a downstroke much thicker than the crossbar with the same pen angle.

Uncial hand

EARLY

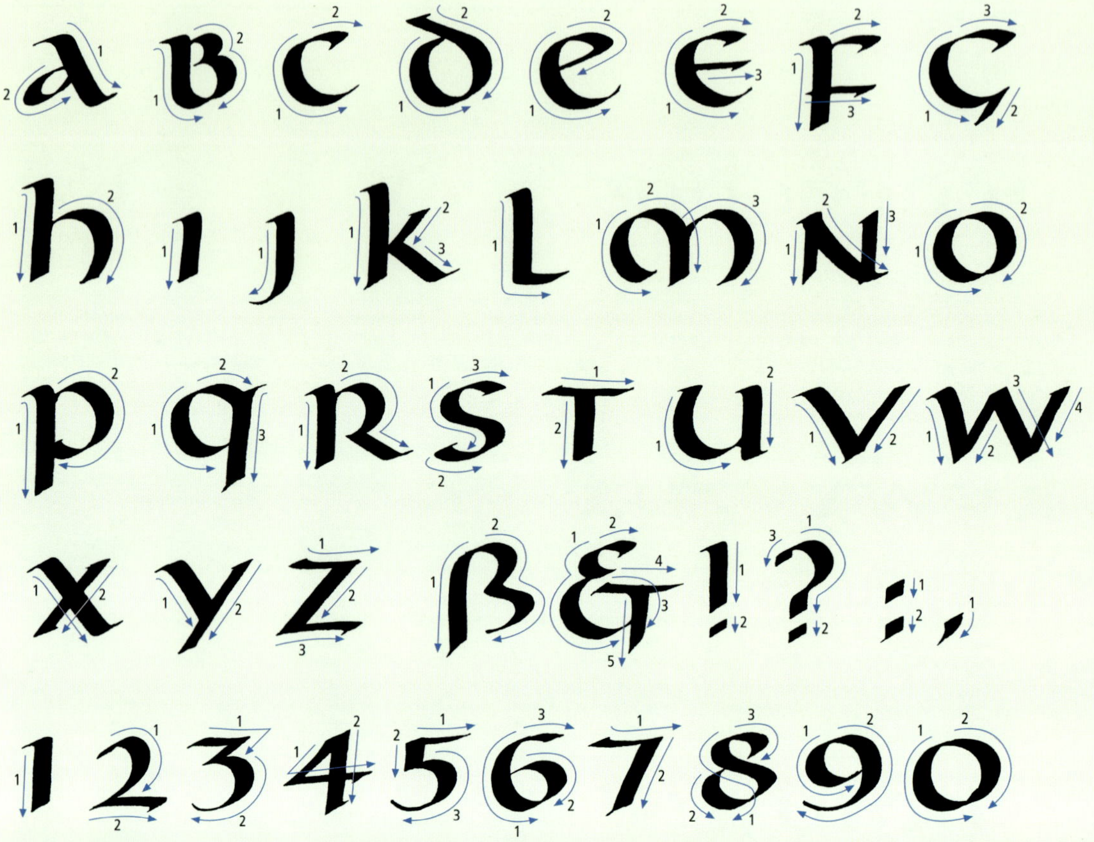

COMMON MISTAKES – EARLY UNCIALS

The main problem encountered with Uncials is not maintaining the roundness of every letter. It is this roundness that characterizes the overall texture in a block of Uncial writing – without it, the text loses its rhythm. Another mistake is to make ascenders too high and to place crossbars too high up the stem.

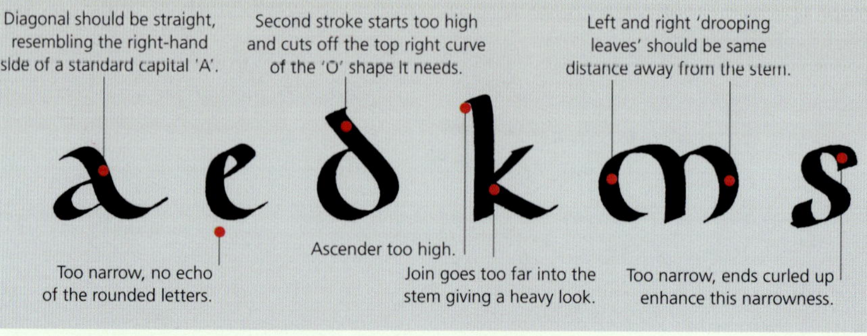

Diagonal should be straight, resembling the right-hand side of a standard capital 'A'.

Second stroke starts too high and cuts off the top right curve of the 'O' shape it needs.

Left and right 'drooping leaves' should be same distance away from the stem.

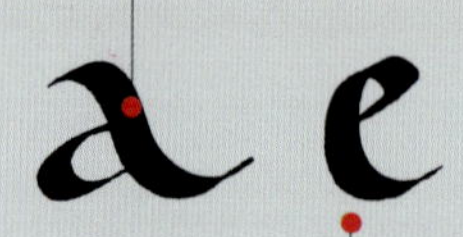

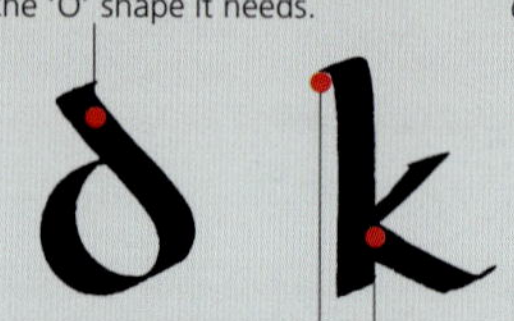

Too narrow, no echo of the rounded letters.

Ascender too high.

Join goes too far into the stem giving a heavy look.

Too narrow, ends curled up enhance this narrowness.

LATE

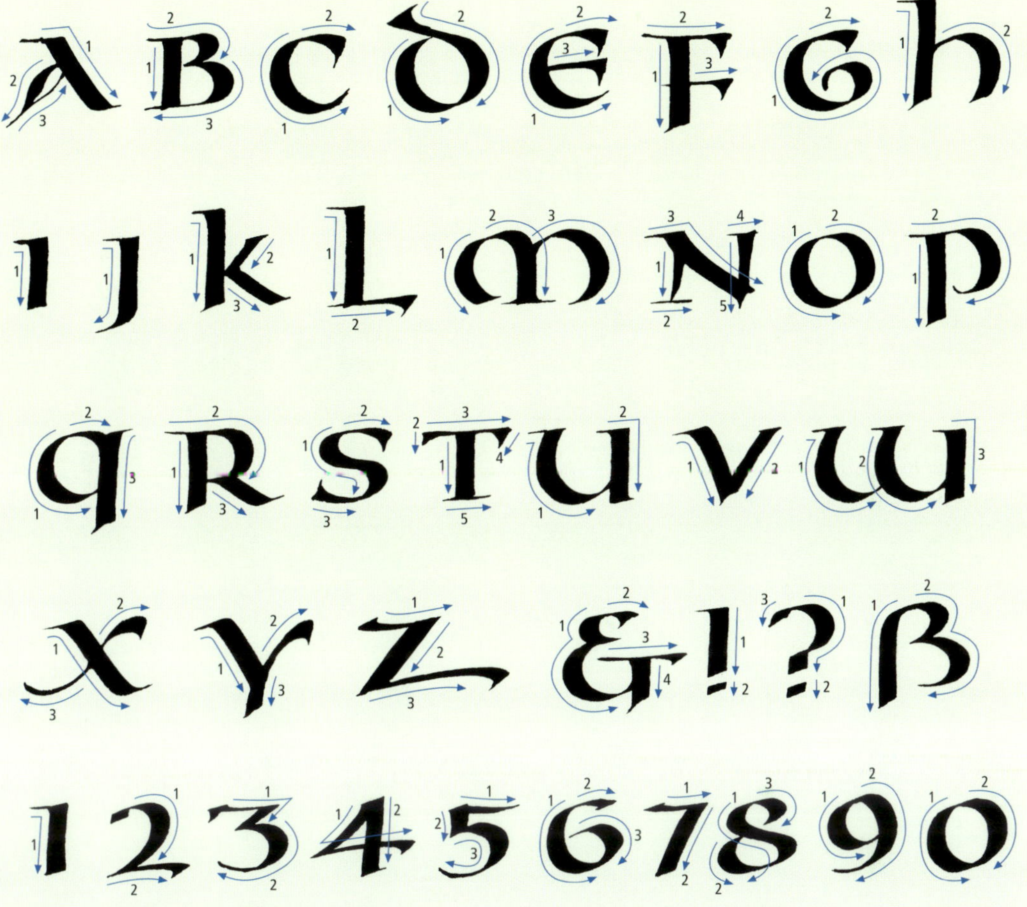

COMMON MISTAKES – LATE UNCIALS

The very flat pen angle is even more essential for these manipulated letters, as it creates contrasts of thickness, but take care with the twisted serifs which are its feature. These wedge shapes are made in a flowing movement twisting the pen from horizontal to near-vertical.

Top-heavy, give it a fatter body and a smaller head.

Too steep a pen angle, so both strokes are very similar in thickness – lacks contrast.

Horizontal stroke uncontrolled and wavy, manipulation required both ends.

Too narrow, not echoing the 'O' in width.

All strokes heavy, the uprights need manipulating for thinner strokes.

Extra serif on left unnecessary and in danger of looking like 'T'.

Gothic hand

Gothic was much despised by calligraphers in the early part of the 20th century, due no doubt in part to the previous generation's mistaken idea that it was first drawn and then 'filled-in'. Many bizarre versions of this writing appeared in the form of loyal addresses and freedoms of the city, which still emerge from time to time in manuscript sales. If influential calligrapher Edward Johnston had given as much attention to the Metz Pontifical as he gave to the Ramsey Psalter, the history of calligraphy might have been very different. Then instead of basing the introduction to calligraphy on the very circular shaped latter, with all the inherent problems of spacing, he could have inspired beginners to obtain the skill needed for control of the broad-edged pen with an easily spaced, simply constructed, straight-sided alphabet. Luckily Gothic, in all its various forms, is far too attractive and decorative a script for it to be consigned to obscurity for any length of time. The American calligrapher Ward Dunham was the champion of 'modern Gothic', a strong fierce hand that dominates all around it, or harmonizes beautifully with a more rhapsodic script, such as a delicate Italic – and where the attribute of script illegibility is shown to be a falsehood.

The defining characteristic of Gothic is the extreme density that has also earned it the name 'Blackletter'. Writing this hand is like beginning a war between the paper and the writing medium, one which the paper must lose. While the upper-case letters in Gothic are more decorative, the lower-case letters are almost geometric; the white spaces inside the letters should be kept the same width as the black strokes and the ascenders and descenders shallow. The sides of Gothic letters are very straight with many lines parallel to one another. Several Gothic letters are produced using identical strokes.

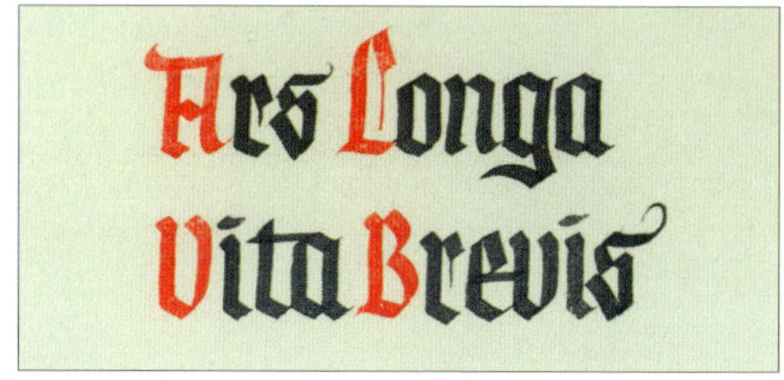

The basic rules

This is a modern version of a Gothic script and it is essential to bear in mind the importance of the writing's dominance over the area it covers, therefore a fairly flat pen angle of 30 degrees should be used. Medieval scribes had no 'official' majuscule letters for their Gothic scripts and so they borrowed heavily from the Roman Capitals and the Uncial forms. When these appeared too lightweight, they decorated them with diamonds, hairlines and small quill flicks to 'fill in' the white spaces. These letters seem over-elaborate for current use. However, the capitals chosen still maintain their link to the Roman and Uncial forms. If preferred, a simple weighted Roman capital is an effective alternative. Gothic majuscules should be used only sparingly. Keep them for the beginning of sentences and proper nouns – written in a block they become completely illegible.

LETTER HEIGHT

The x-height for this script is five nib widths. Height lines should be ruled before practising Gothic.

LETTER SLOPE

The Gothic hand is written without a slope. Gothic letters should remain upright and not be created with even the slightest of slants.

PEN ANGLES

This script is written with a pen angle of 30 degrees. The hairlines are drawn with the pen at an angle of 90 degrees or, for the letters 's' and 'x', with the left hand point of the nib.

90°

30°

Practice exercise: **Gothic hand**

Practise the dominant strokes of this hand: with an x-height of five nib widths and a pen angle of 30 degrees, draw the pen across and downwards to the right for one nib width. Without lifting the pen, draw it straight down the page for three nib widths and finally downwards to the right again for one nib width. Repeat this exercise several times; there should be only the space of one nib width between the vertical strokes. Do this before practising the letters described below.

Group — Strokes (1st = red, 2nd = blue, 3rd = green)

Oval

oabcdegq

A constant angle of 30 degrees is maintained while writing these letters except for when drawing the hairlines. Vertical lines are created close together.

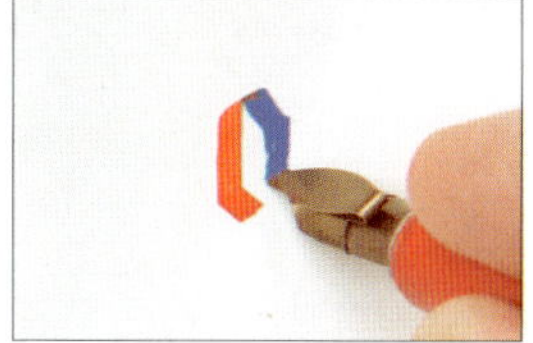

Both strokes are drawn with a pen angle of 30 degrees. The counter space needs to be the same width as the pen strokes.

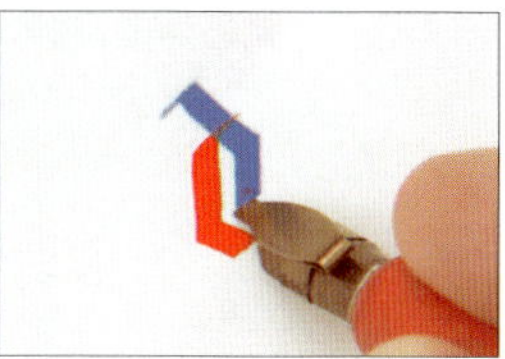

The second stroke (the ascender) starts above the x-height and to the left of the first stroke.

Arched

nmhkruvwy

Note that the last stroke of 'n' and 'm' has an upwards curved finish while the last stroke of 'h' curves below the line. The letter 'r' needs its base serif in order to limit the amount of white space around it.

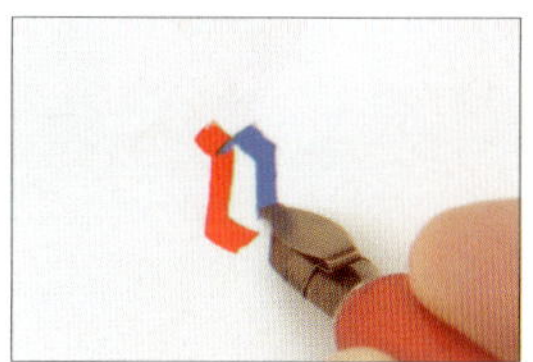

The letter 'n' is made from two strokes that are are almost identical. The second stroke ends with a curved serif.

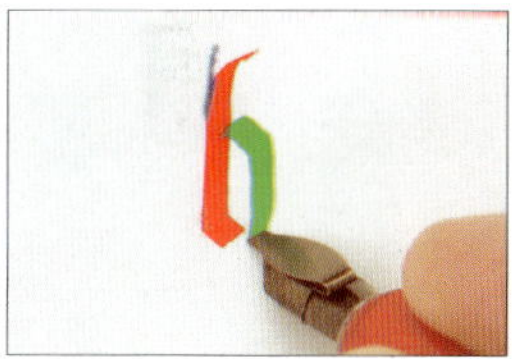

After the first stroke, draw a hairline at 90 degrees. The third stroke returns to 30 degrees finishing with a nib slide to the left.

Straight

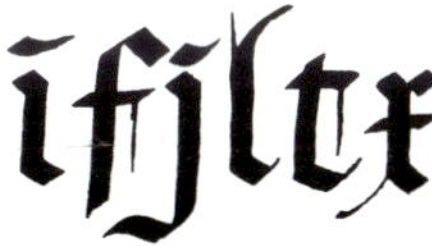

It was only with the introduction of Gothic writing that 'i' and 'j' acquired their dots, to aid legibility. To create the fine hairline for the letter 'x', place a spot of ink within the downstroke before attempting to draw out the line.

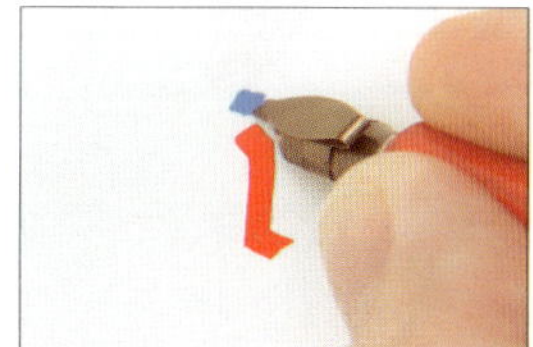

Draw the first stroke at 30 degrees, and keep the same angle of pen when drawing the dot.

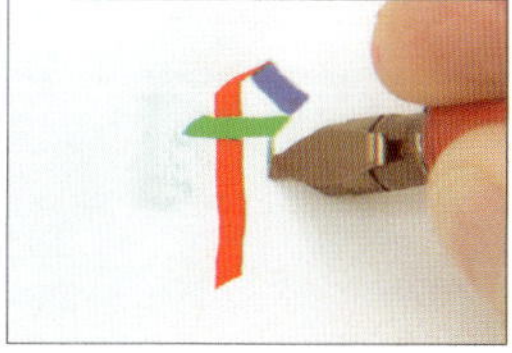

The first stroke starts as an ascender, finishing as a descender. The second stays above x-height, the crossbar hangs from x-height.

Ungrouped

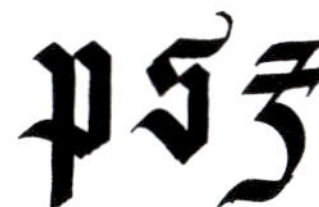

While these letters relate well to the rest of the alphabet, their complex construction keeps them in this separate category. None are difficult, although at first sight the 's' seems a little daunting.

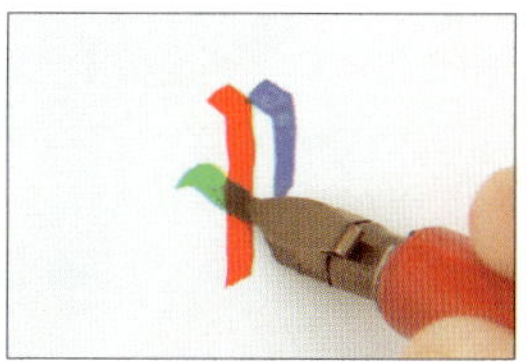

Make the descender, and repeat the style for the second stroke. The third stroke slides to the right and down to meet the second stroke.

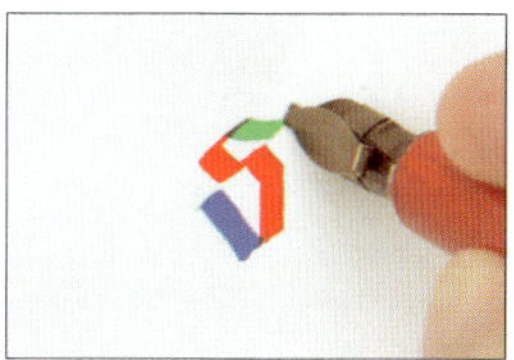

At x-height move one nib width following the path, then straight down. Touch with second stroke, and hang third stroke from x-height.

Gothic hand

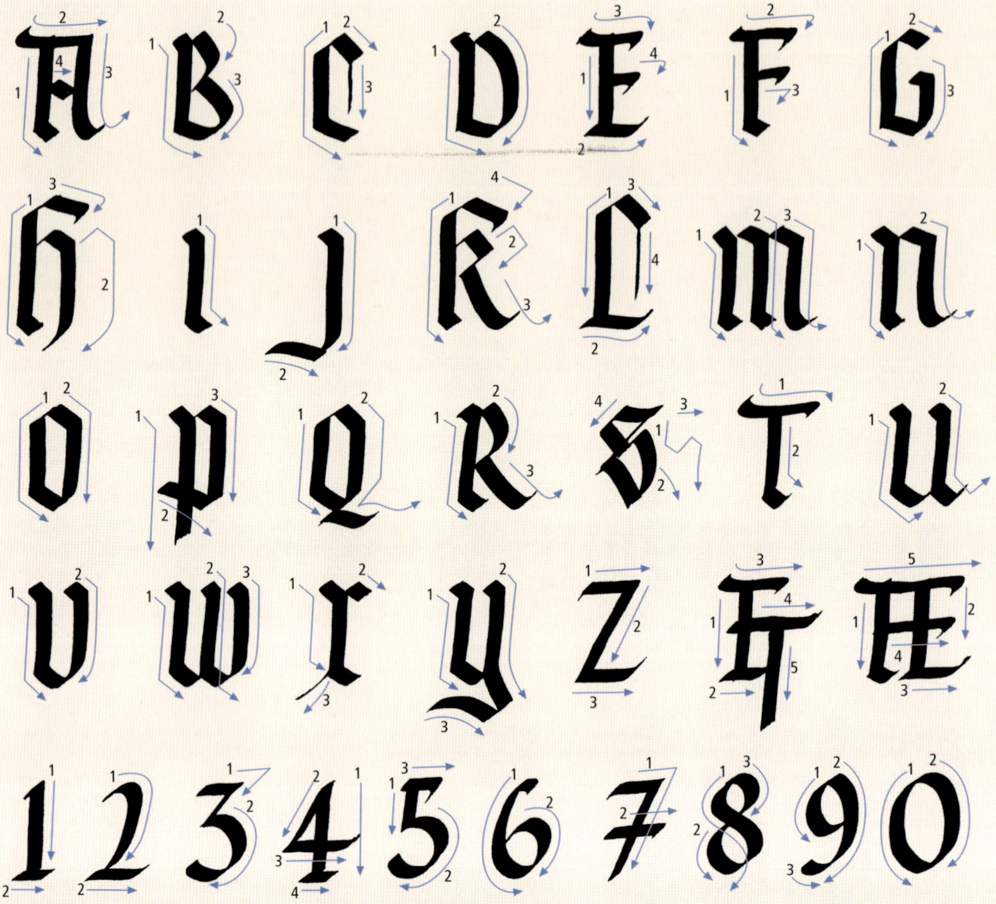

COMMON MISTAKES – CAPITALS

Having mastered the main structural elements of Gothic capital letters, they are not as difficult to recreate as they appear. Unlike, lower-case Gothic, capital letters are spacious and elegant. However, whole words should not be written in Gothic capitals as they are extremely hard to read. Common errors include groups of letters that do not appear consistent, and unbalanced letters.

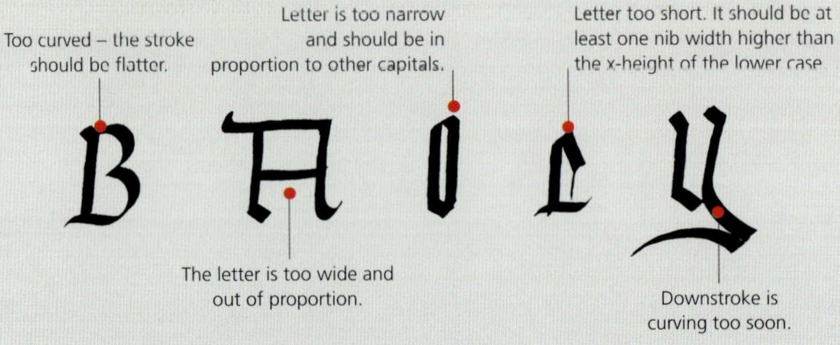

Too curved – the stroke should be flatter.

Letter is too narrow and should be in proportion to other capitals.

Letter too short. It should be at least one nib width higher than the x-height of the lower case

The letter is too wide and out of proportion.

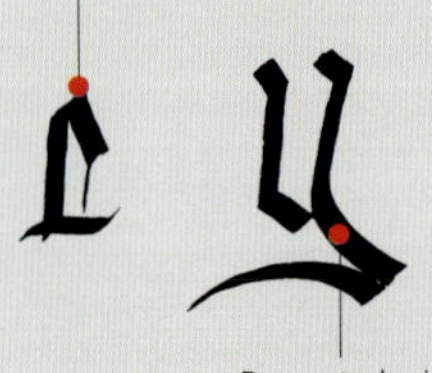

Downstroke is curving too soon.

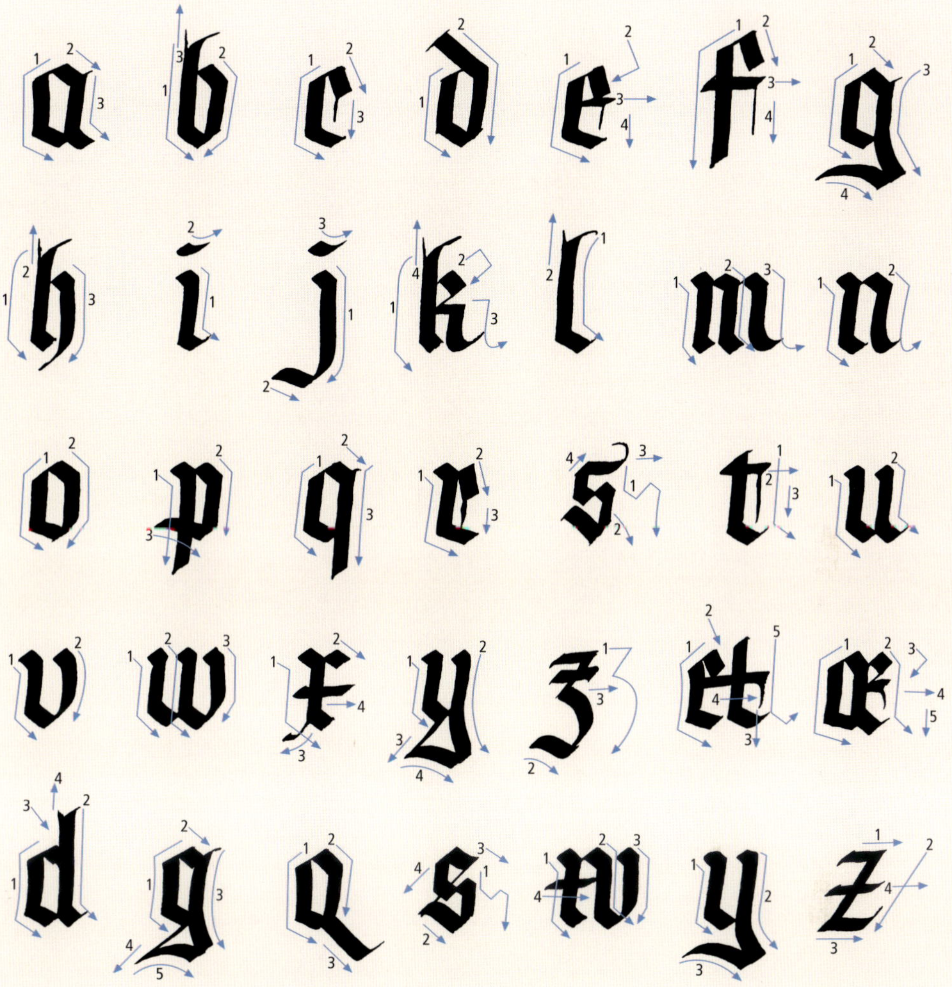

COMMON MISTAKES – LOWER CASE

With lower-case letters, spaces between words and lines should be as small as possible. A common mistake is the inclusion of a thin sideways stroke to make letters wider, or over-extension of ascenders and descenders. It may take time to adjust to such narrow letters without slim strokes and with few curves.

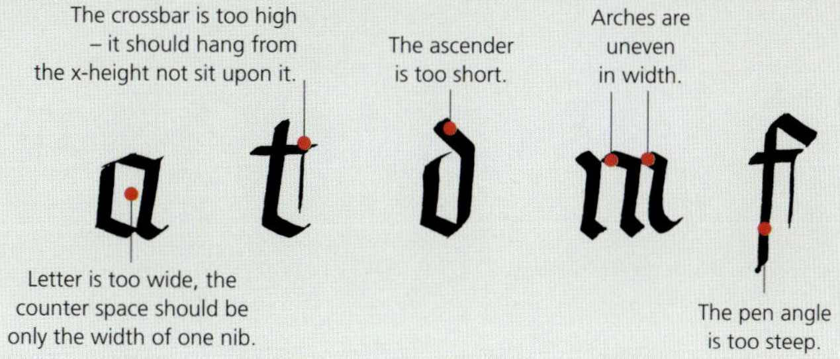

The crossbar is too high – it should hang from the x-height not sit upon it.

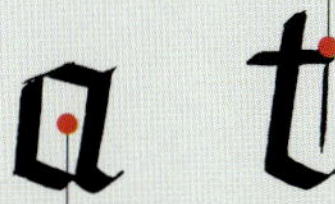

Letter is too wide, the counter space should be only the width of one nib.

The ascender is too short.

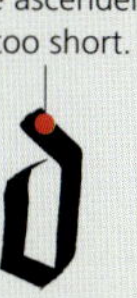

Arches are uneven in width.

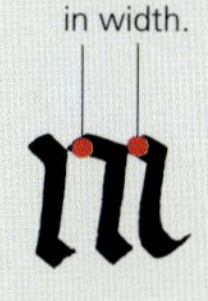

The pen angle is too steep.

Versal hand

The finest historical forms of Versal letters are to be found in 9th and 10th century manuscripts, in particular the Benedictional of Aethelwold, written in the late 10th century. A Versal was a single capital, usually larger than the main text, which marked the beginning of a paragraph or verse. Versals that were written at the beginning of the text to create a heading or to emphasize the importance of the words are called 'display capitals'. Often, freely drawn Uncial letters were used in the same way.

Versal letters in their simplest form are pen-drawn letters based on the proportions of the Roman Imperial Capital. The resulting form, however, is greatly influenced by the use of the pen. Both historical and modern Versals are made up of compound strokes of the pen.

Versal letters should be elegant and lightweight in character and should appear to have been executed effortlessly. Do not make the verticals too thick; remember they are only three nib widths at their widest point. Give the stem an elegant 'waist' but use minimal curving on the down strokes. Keep all serifs fine, with the pen held at either horizontal (0 degrees) or vertical (90 degrees).

Versals can be used for headings or as single initial letters, and they have been traditionally used as the underlying form for decorated and illuminated letters. Versal are extremely adaptable, and can be modernized, used with or without serifs, stretched, compressed, weighted at the top for added elegance or expanded to give heavy weighty letters. When sloped they work well with Italic minuscules.

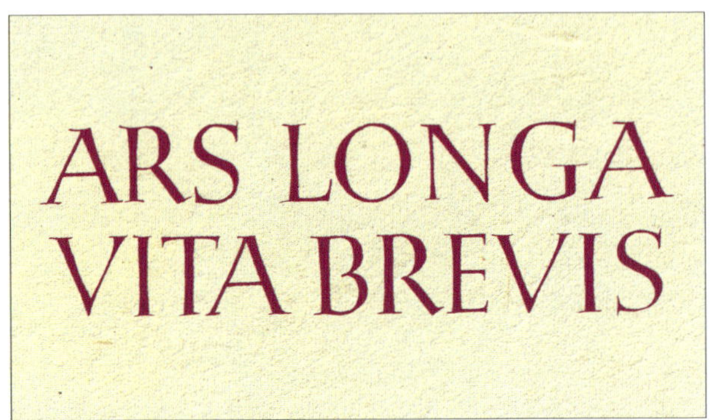

The basic rules

Each main or vertical stem is drawn with two outer strokes and is then filled or flooded with ink using the third stroke of the pen through the centre. The pen should be held so that it makes the widest line for horizontal, vertical and diagonal strokes and the thinnest lines for the serifs (the pen can be turned for the serifs). The letter is built up by drawing each vertical letter stem with the nib held horizontally (0 degrees). The crossbars and horizontal strokes of 'E', 'F' and 'L' use only one stroke with the pen held at 90 degrees to the line (with the pen nib at its fullest width). For the diagonal strokes, the curved strokes of 'O', 'C', 'G' and 'D' and 'Q' and other round strokes, as in 'R', 'P', 'S' and 'B', the pen nib is held at about 20 degrees to the writing line allowing the hand to move easily.

LETTER HEIGHT
Each letter is eight times the stem width. The stem is three nib widths at its widest point. The height of a letter is eight stem widths, which is therefore 8 x 3 = 24 nib-widths high.

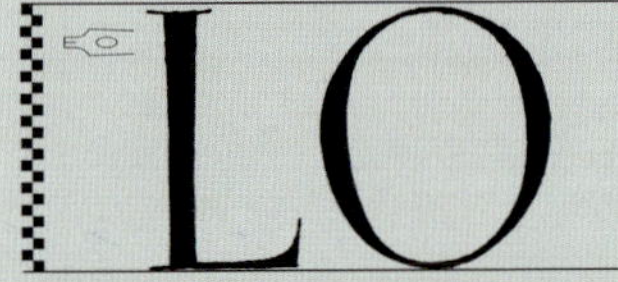

LETTER SLOPE
Versals are written upright unless they are being used with Italic, in which case they may be sloped.

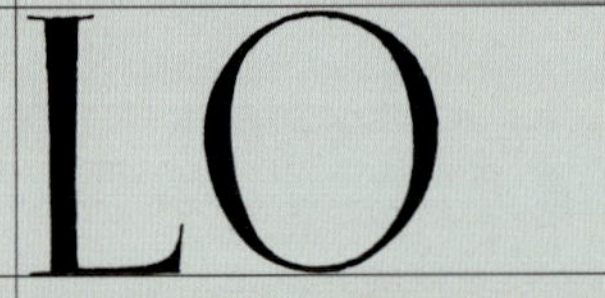

PEN ANGLES
Vertical strokes are written with the pen held horizontally to the line (0-degree angle). Horizontal strokes, i.e. crossbars are written with the pen nib held vertically to the line (90-degree angle), curved letters at 20 degrees. To enable you to draw the letter curves, the nib should be held at a slight angle (about 20 degrees).

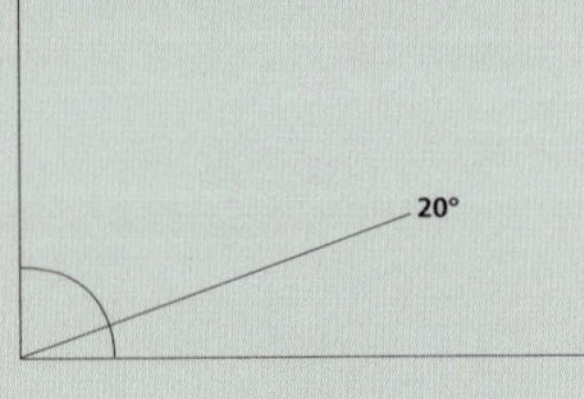

Practice exercise: **Versal hand**

With the pen held at 0 degrees, draw a series of vertical downstrokes. Practise drawing two of these strokes close together, slightly curving in at the centre, and fill in the gap between them. Keeping the pen at 90 degrees, draw the crossbars or horizontal lines. Finally, hold the pen at a 20-degree angle, and practise drawing semicircular curves and filling them. Skeleton Versal letters are shown to demonstrate the groups of strokes which will be filled in solidly to make the final Versal letter.

Group

Strokes (1st = red, 2nd = blue, 3rd = green)

Straight

EFHIJTL

Hold the pen nib at 0 degrees (horizontal) and draw the downward stem with two outer strokes, slightly waisted, with a third stroke filling the middle with ink or paint (not shown here). Each letter stem should be three nib widths at its widest point.

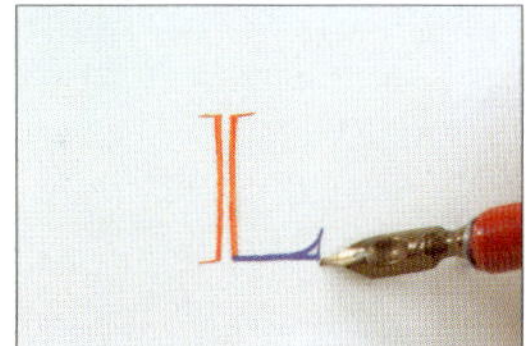

Draw the stem of the letter, waisting it halfway down. Hold the nib vertical to the line to draw a single stroke crossbar. Add serifs.

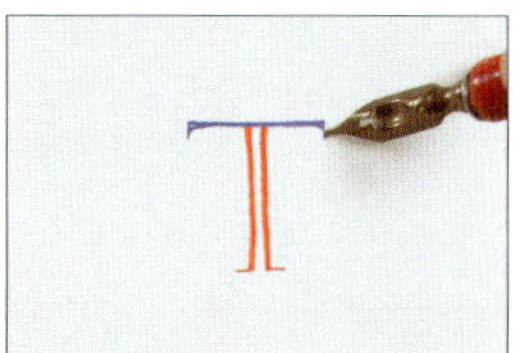

Draw the stem of the letter. With the nib held vertically (at 90 degrees) draw the crossbar on the top. Finish by drawing the serifs.

Diagonal

AMNV
WXZK

The vertical strokes are drawn in the same way as the letter stems. The thinner diagonal strokes should be drawn with the nib held at 0 degrees to create the line. The wide diagonals are formed by two strokes drawn with the nib at 20 degrees.

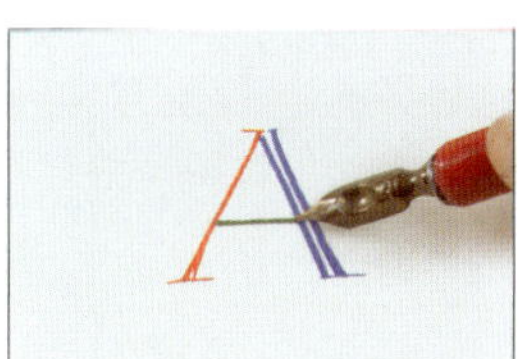

Draw the left and right diagonals with the nib at 0 and 20 degrees respectively. The crossbar is made with the nib held vertically.

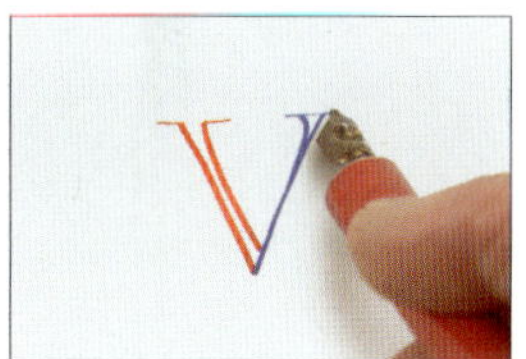

Draw two strokes with the nib at 20 degrees for the left diagonal, and one stroke at 0 degrees for the right diagonal. Add serifs.

Round or circular

OQCDG

To enable you to draw the curves of these letters the pen nib should be held at about 20 degrees. This angle allows for easy arm and hand movement. The angle can be altered slightly to build up the curved areas.

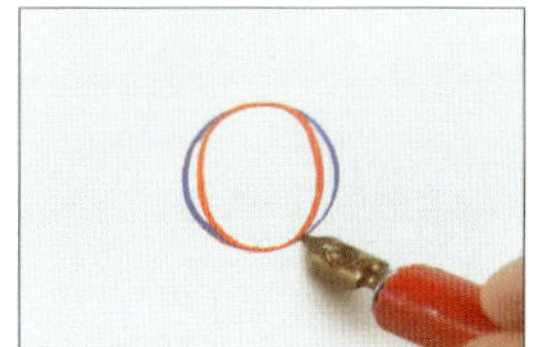

Draw the inside oval shape of the letter first with the nib at 20 degrees. Add the two outer shapes second.

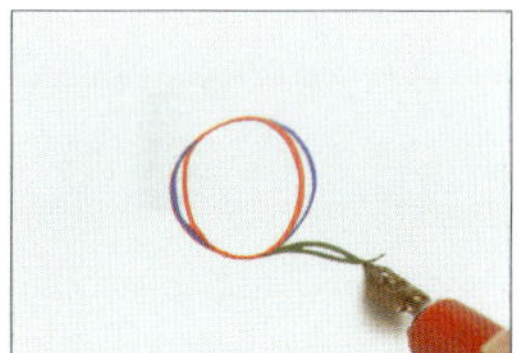

Draw the two inside oval strokes first and add the two outer round shapes at 20 degrees. Lastly add the tail using two strokes.

Combination

BRSUYP

These letters are written using a combination of two angles to produce the different shapes. The downward strokes are made with the pen nib at 0 degrees and the rounded shapes are created with the pen nib at 20 degrees.

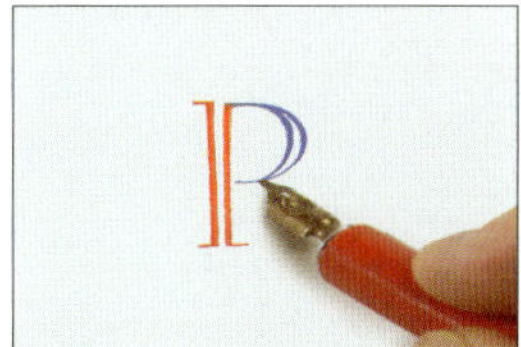

Draw the stem of the letter with the nib at 0 degrees. Change the nib to approximately 20 degrees to add the round shape.

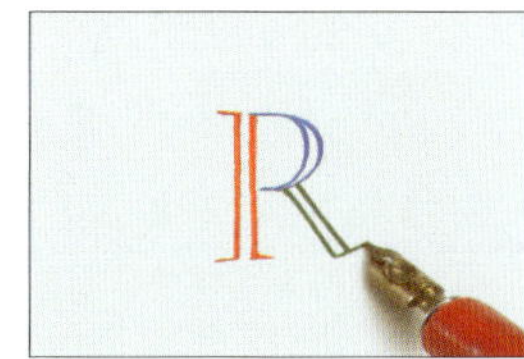

Draw the stem at 0 degrees, the rounded shape at 20 degrees and, finally, the diagonal foot also with the pen at 20 degrees.

Versal hand

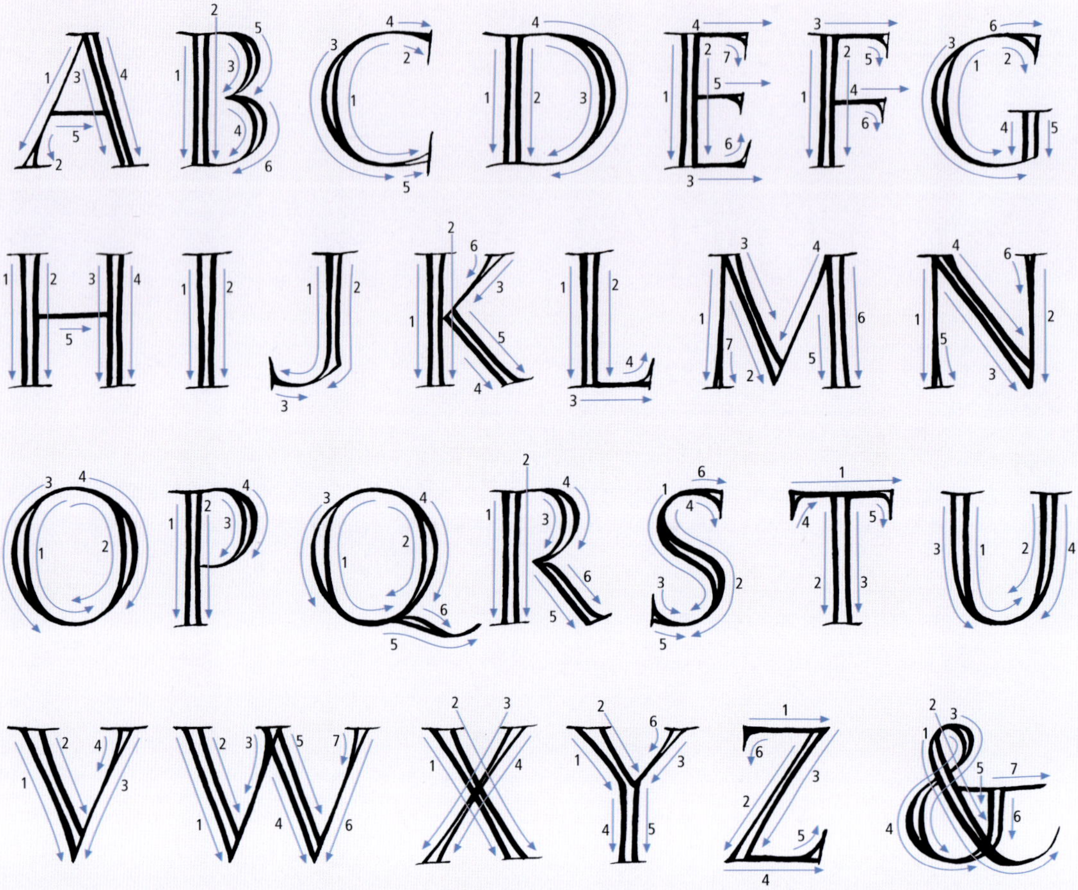

COMMON MISTAKES

The most common mistake made when using Versal hand is to give the letters excessive 'waists' either making the widest parts of the letter too wide, or the narrow parts too narrow. Waisting should be very elegant and subtle, and serifs on crossbars should not be too heavy.

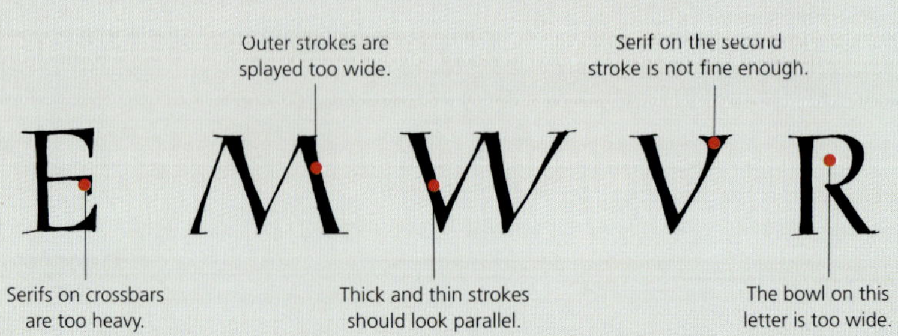

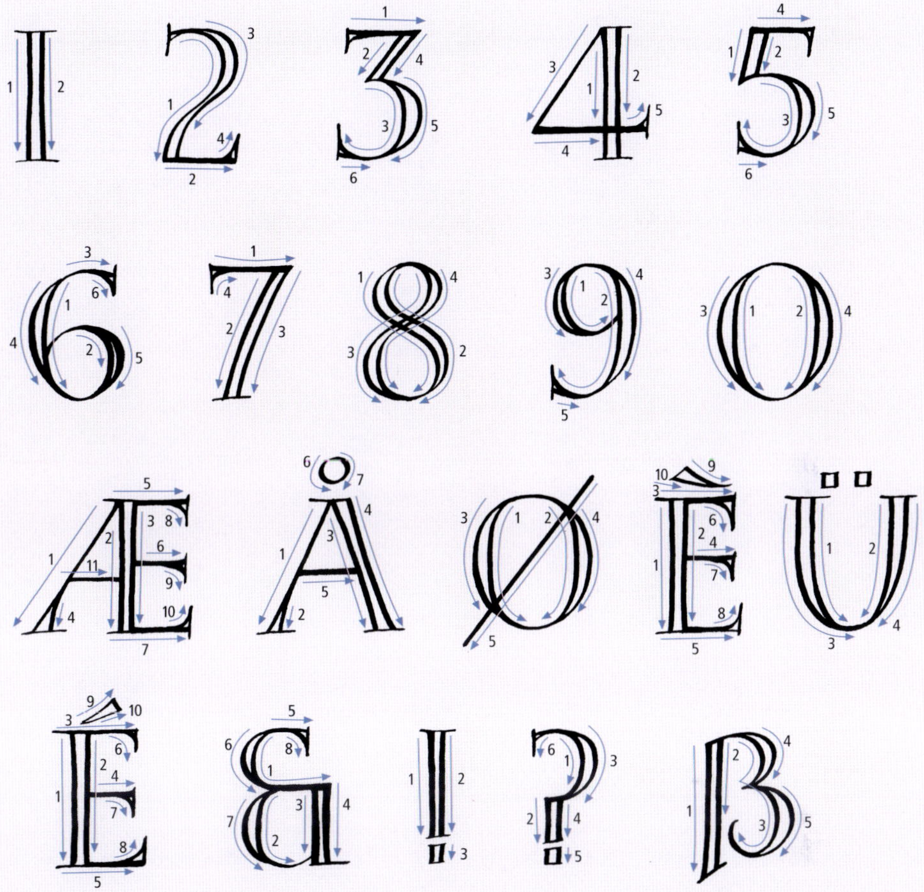

COMMON MISTAKES – NUMERALS AND SYMBOLS

Numbers should not appear too heavy or squat. As with the Versal letters, the lines and shapes should be elegant and rhythmic, and 'waisting' should not be too pronounced. Those numbers and figures that follow a circular shape should be slightly vertically elongated rather than completely round.

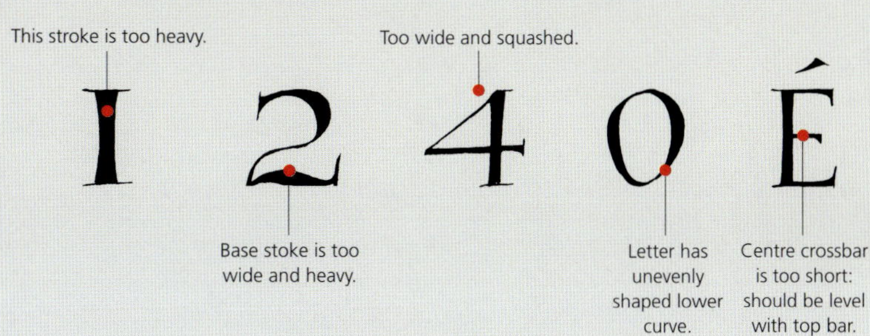

Italic hand

The name 'Italic' reveals this script's country of origin. It developed in Italy during the early Renaissance period of the 15th century. While the arts flourished, calligraphy manifested itself in painted and illuminated books of the period. The Italic hand was adopted by Pope Nicholas V for the papal chancery in the 15th century, and became known as Cancellaresca Corsiva, or Chancery Cursive.

Today, Italic is beloved of modern scribes. It is a flowing script that is created swiftly and demands few lifts of the pen. Italic differs from many other hands, being oval-shaped with a forward slope. It is written using a pen angle of between 35 and 45 degrees, which should remain constant.

This hand is a form of calligraphy that closely relates to handwriting, as the letters are formed with a rhythmic up-and-down movement, occasioned by one stroke developing from where the last stroke ended; this contrasts with Roman Capitals, for example, where each stroke is separate and often starts back at the top of the letter. The Italic script is very adaptable to variations, owing to its branching construction, and is ideal for flourishing (see Flourished Italics). Regular practice is recommended in order to develop a consistency in slope and width, and it is important to master the basic formal version before progressing to more complex Italic forms. In typography, any letterform that slopes is called italic, whereas in calligraphy a letter is only Italic if it conforms to the branching arch that is the defining feature of the Italic hand.

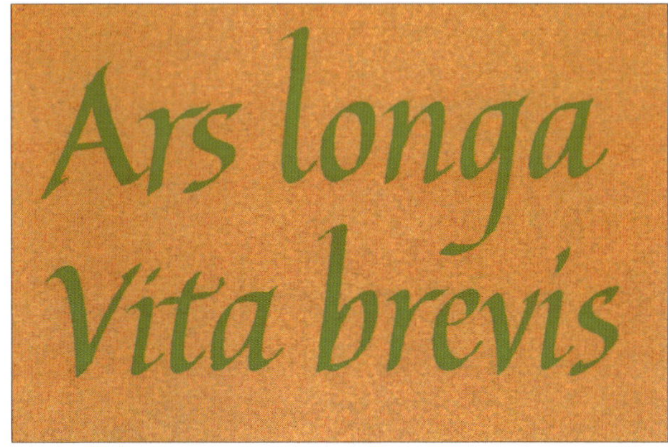

The basic rules

This is a slightly sloping, oval-shaped letterform with springing arches. The arch formation is the most important feature, and it distinguishes Italic from many other hands. You may wish to practise some pen patterns so that you become used to working with a pen angle of 30 to 45 degrees and a slope of 5 to 12 degrees. Practise with a pencil first, to develop the up-and-down rhythm used in 'm's and 'n's, and check where the arch emerges from the stem – it should be halfway. Look closely at 'u' – this needs to be identical in arch formation to 'n', branching halfway from the stem. All the arch shapes of the letters should be asymmetrical, and not too rounded.

LETTER HEIGHT
Five nib widths are the standard x-height for these letters, with ascenders and descenders extending up to five more nib widths above and below, although four is acceptable.

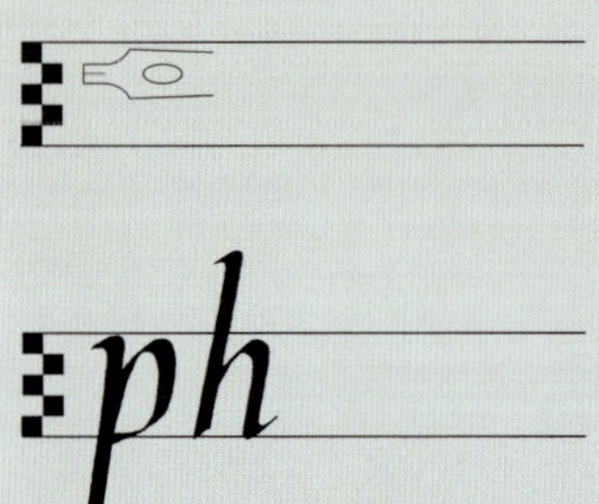

LETTER SLOPE
Between five and 12 degrees forward slope from the vertical is average for Italic, just ensure it is consistently the same throughout one piece of work.

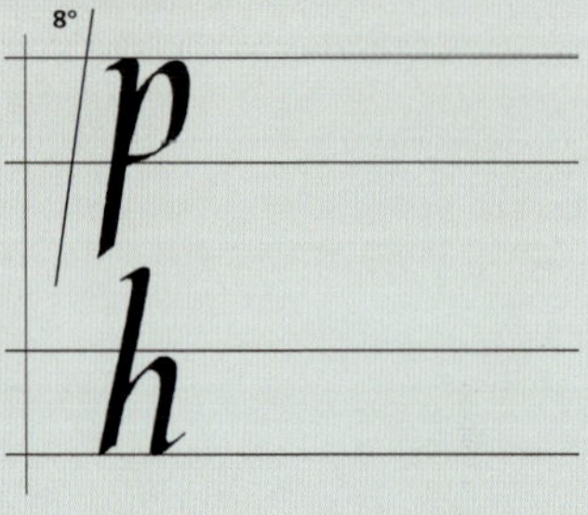

PEN ANGLES
Forty to forty-five degrees is the recommended angle for Italic lower case. However, it should be 30 degrees for the capitals, as 45 degrees will provide no difference in thickness of horizontals against vertical strokes.

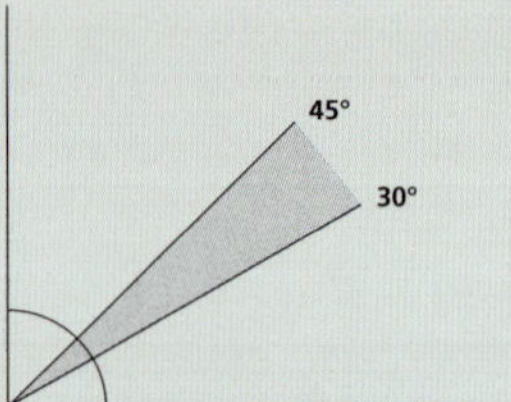

Practice exercise: **Italic hand**

If your pen resists the upward movement of the branching arches, lighten the pressure so that it does not dig into the paper – do not allow the pen to stop halfway. With 'n' and 'm' shapes, the pen moves from one stroke to the next without coming off the paper, and the arch emerges halfway up the stem. If your pen comes off, go back and try it again. When 'n' comes naturally, focus on the branching effect of 'u' and 'a' shapes which are the same format, upside down.

Group

Strokes (1st = red, 2nd = blue, 3rd = green)

Arched

nmrhpb

Practise with a pencil first if necessary, to make an 'n' shape without taking the tool off the paper. With 'p', where travelling all the way from a descender is too far, take the pen off the descender and start again on the baseline as if making an 'n'.

Start the ascender above the line, pause at baseline then move uphill, emerging halfway up the stem. Complete the downwards curve.

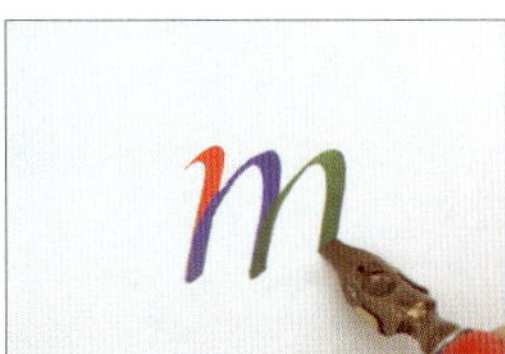

Make the first stem, pause at the baseline, rise and emerge halfway, make a tight corner down. Repeat stroke ending with an exit serif.

Base-arched

adgquy

These arches mimic the first group, but are upside down. The adding of a 'lid' can be left to the end. If it helps to maintain a rhythm of up-and-down, keep going without releasing the pen until the end.

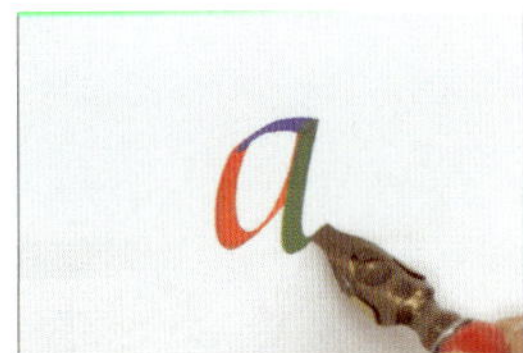

A tight stroke curves round and up to the topline. The lid is drawn next. The downstroke carries on where the upward curve finished.

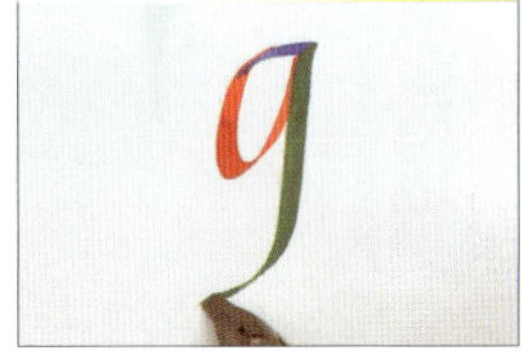

As in 'a', but with an extended downstroke that curves at the bottom. Finish with a horizontal, or add a stroke from the left.

Diagonals

vwxyzk

The angle in the top-left to bottom-right stroke needs to be adjusted to prevent it becoming thicker than any upright stroke. Use a steeper pen angle of about 50 degrees. The other diagonal must be thinner – try a 30-degree angle.

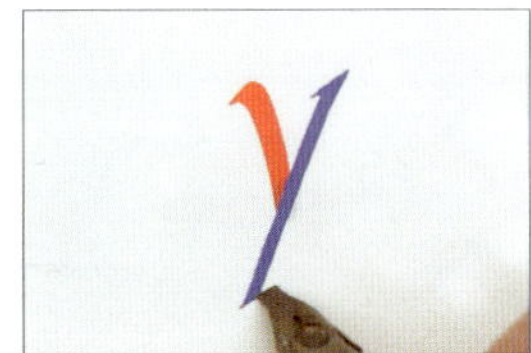

Steepen the pen angle to 50 degrees for the first stroke; flatten it to 30 degrees for the second. The descender should not bend.

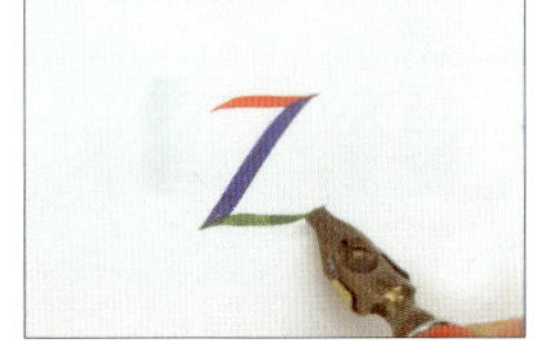

Make the horizontal stroke then completely flatten the pen angle for a thick diagonal. Complete the horizontal at the usual angle.

Ungrouped

ocesijfflt

'O' is frequently the governing letter of a hand, but in Italic it takes second place to 'n' and 'a'. However, it is essential to understand the smooth oval shape of the 'o', so that it can be matched to 'e' and 'c'. 'S' should also fit into a secret 'o' shape.

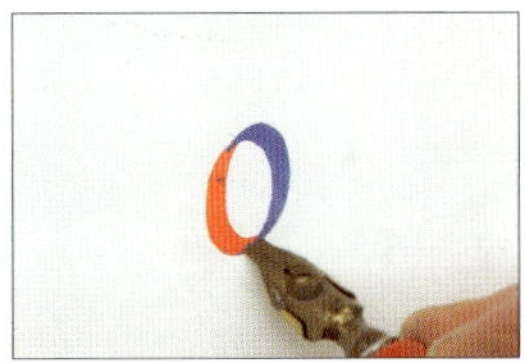

Start with a half-moon beginning and ending at the thinnest point. The second curve blends into the bottom curve.

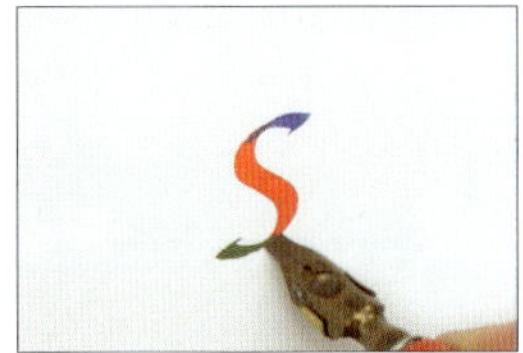

Start below the topline and flow left and right of two imaginary circles. Add end strokes with serifs that are straight rather than curved.

Italic hand

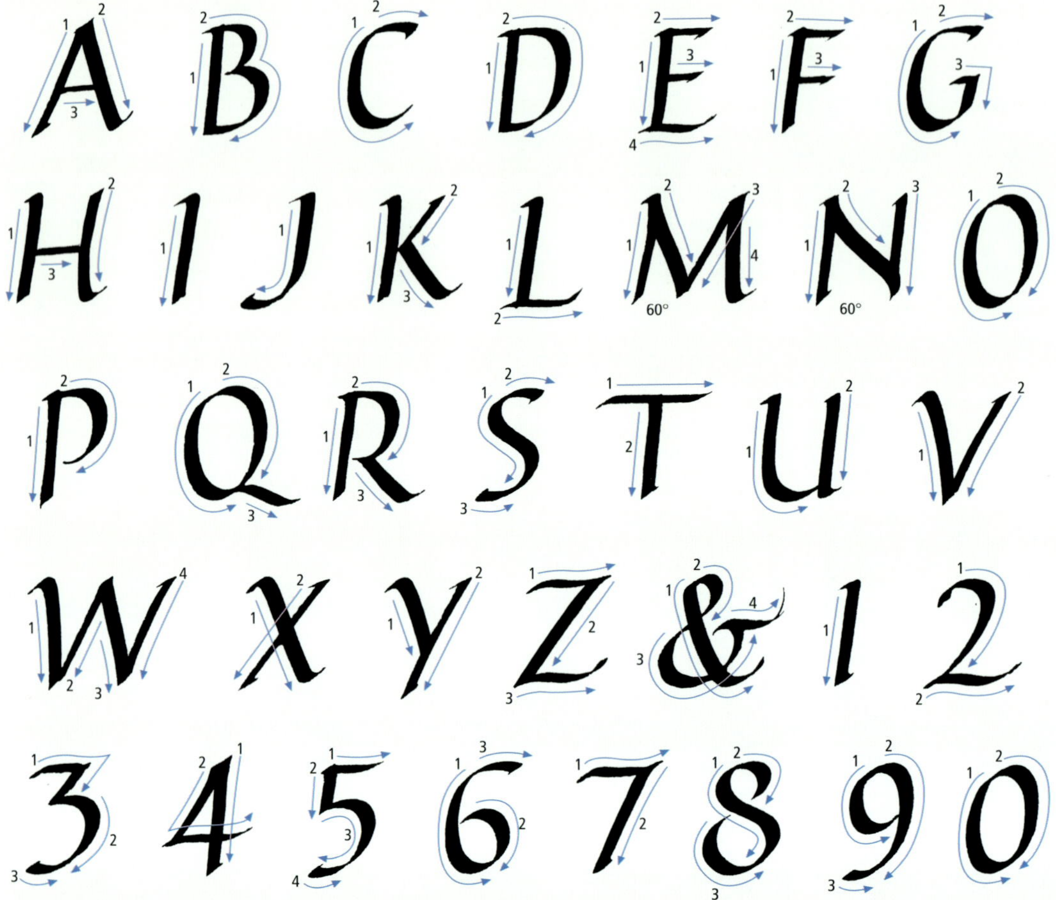

COMMON MISTAKES – CAPITALS

Italic letters are a compressed form of the Roman Capital but they should not be made either too wide or too narrow. Keep letters at a consistent forward slope and make firm joins by starting the next stroke inside the stem it joins.

Too narrow, with the top sloping forward too soon – uplift before curving round.

Uneven in widths, caused by the second stroke going too wide.

Three strokes all the same thickness – steepen pen angle to make the uprights thinner.

DOMZNS

Sloping backwards instead of forwards.

Diagonal too thin – need to flatten the pen to thicken this stroke.

Top heavy; better to be bottom-heavy for visual stability.

COMMON MISTAKES – LOWER CASE

Branching arches are a key part of this alphabet. They should not begin too high up the letter. The letters should be kept at a consistent forward slope (not more than 12 degrees from upright) throughout a piece of work. Do not make letters too rounded as they should be kept narrow.

Lacks essential upward branching arch – pen has come off at the bottom instead of going to the top.

Arch is not branching; should start from the baseline and emerge half way.

Not at the correct angle, and crossbar should sit higher.

Ascender is a little short, making it look squat.

Loop should be smaller and not pulled down which causes letter to fall backwards.

Uneven in shape, with corners.

Flourished Italic hand

The Italic hand was developed during the Italian Renaissance and was more elegant and rhythmically written than the Gothic hand of northern Europe at that time. Flourished Italic is a slightly more modern and exuberant version of formal Italic and one that is more adaptable for today's calligraphy. It is lightweight and elegant in its execution and has an energy that comes from being written with speed. The letters have a forward slope and springing arches. The basic letter shapes are that of Formal Italic but with fewer pen lifts. The proportions are the same: five nib widths for the body height of the minuscule letter and seven nib widths for the capitals. The actual stroke that forms the letter tends to be straight. The only strokes that curve into a flourish are the first and last strokes.

The Flourished Italic capitals, which are based on compressed sloped Roman Capitals, are also called swash capitals. The ascenders and descenders are the easiest to flourish and extend. The greater the decoration, the more space is required.

When executing more exuberant writing, extra consideration is needed for layout and design space. Be careful not to over-flourish the letters, as less is definitely better. Too many flourishes will make the words difficult to read. You may find it helps to decide on where to flourish by using a pencil.

The basic flourished letters shown on these pages are fairly restrained so that it is easy to see how they are constructed. As you gain more confidence and greater control over the pen, flourishing can become more adventurous, and innovative and exciting effects can be produced.

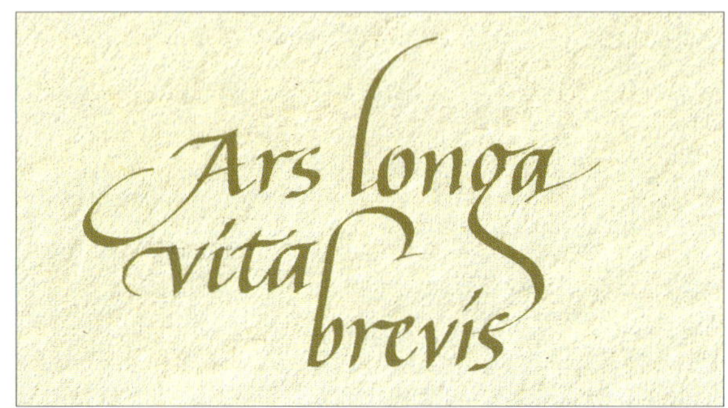

The basic rules

Attention needs to be given to the choice of paper. This should be easy to write on, with a surface that will not hinder the flow of the pen and ink. The pen nib should be smooth and easy to manipulate. For small writing the reservoir can be detached, giving the pen more flex. For the larger nib push the reservoir back from the edge allowing more of the nib to show. Load the pen before each flourish to ensure a good flow of ink. Ensure that the body height of the letter remains at five nib widths and continue to keep the Italic capitals at seven nib widths high or slightly less. The width of the letter forms are two-thirds body height to keep the proportions elegant. Modern Italic can sometimes be written in a more compressed and even pointed style to add interest to the writing.

LETTER HEIGHT

The x-height is five nib widths for the minuscules and seven nib widths for the capitals. The ascenders and descenders are normally three widths extra but can be more.

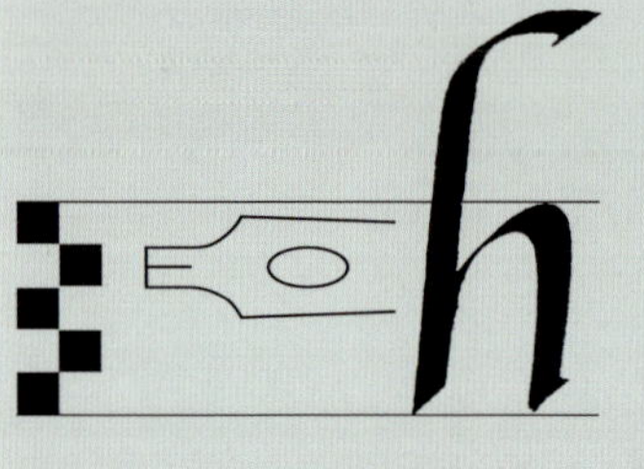

LETTER SLOPE

The letters are usually sloped between three and five degrees. They can slope 12 degrees or more but care will have to be taken over the angle of the pen nib to ensure that the letter weights are correct.

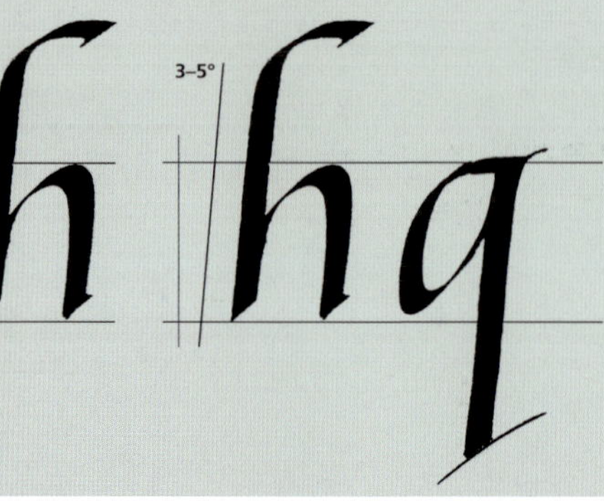

PEN ANGLES

The pen angles range between 30 and 45 degrees. There is some pen manipulation when flourishing to ensure easy movement on the paper. The average pen angle is about 40 degrees.

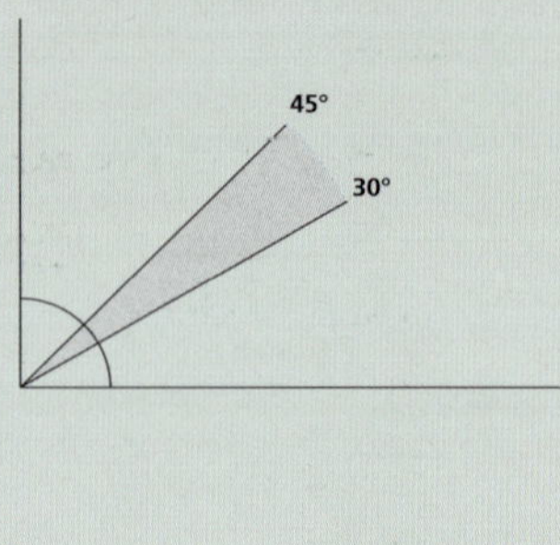

Practice exercise: **Flourished Italic hand**

Begin by writing in formal Italic. Lead into the chosen letters by extending the first serif before beginning the letter. Extend the exit stroke, for example with 'k' and 'z'. Try writing the ascenders taller and the descenders longer. Use a whole arm movement to create the letter, sweeping the pen off the paper at the end. Hold the pen lightly and write the shapes quite speedily. If you can do one or two letters well keep practising them to gain familiarity with the movements and confidence in what you are writing.

Group

Strokes (1st = red, 2nd = blue, 3rd = green)

Arched

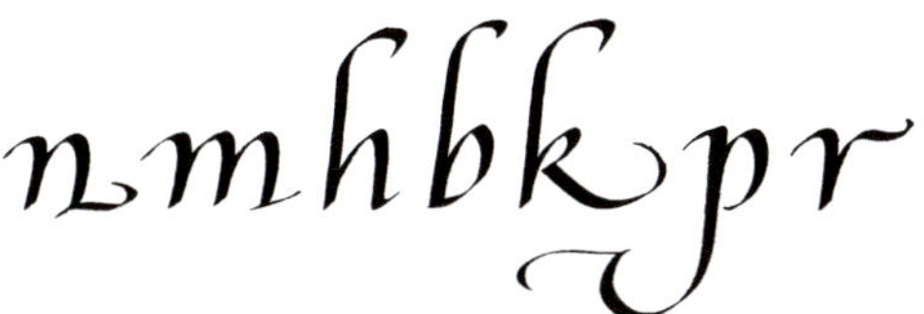

The letter 'n' is the key letter in this alphabet. The asymmetrical arch that springs from about two-thirds up the stem is the shape of all of the arched letters in Italic. Practise this stroke until you are confident writing it.

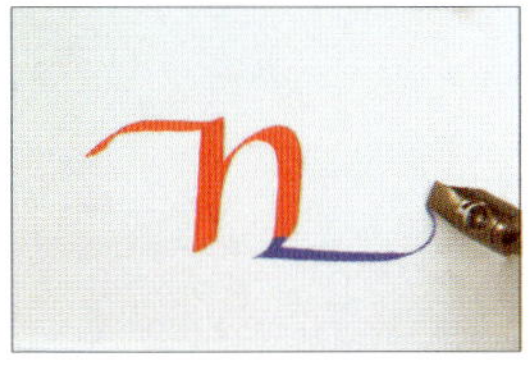

This letter is written in two strokes starting from the serif at the top, going down and springing up, round and down, with a flourish.

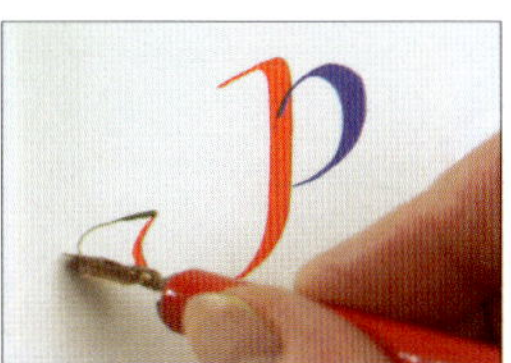

The downward stroke sweeps round to the left. Spring the second stroke from two thirds up the stem and round at the bottom. Flourish.

Base-arched

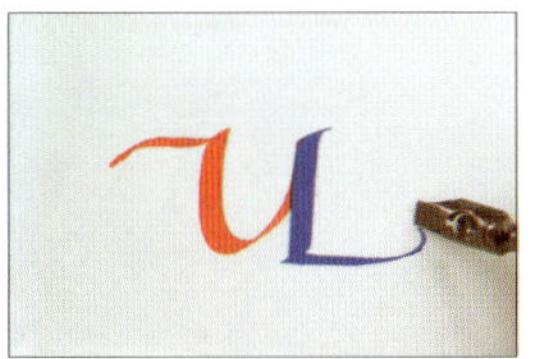

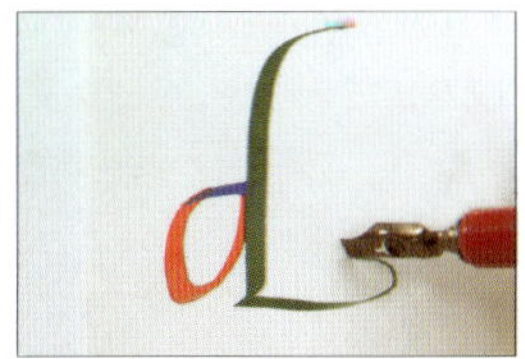

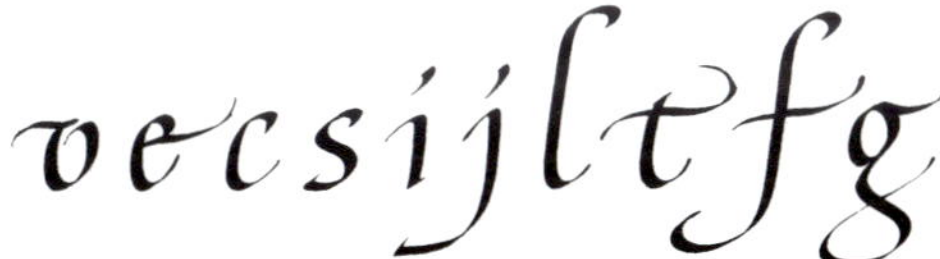

With arched letters, a variety of flourishes can be produced. Use a pen angle of 40 degrees and employ the whole hand to create the flourish on the first stroke.

The 'u' follows the shape of the 'n' but in reverse. Start with the arch, then draw the stem, finishing with the flourish at the baseline.

Create the bowl of 'd' with a lid. Curve in from the top right to start the ascender, down to the baseline and flourish outwards.

Round

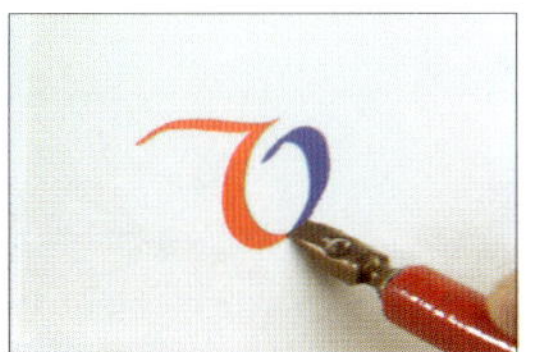

The round letters in this group begin with a downwards stroke. With 'e', the pen is moved downwards to create an oval shape with straight sides that curve when reaching the bottom.

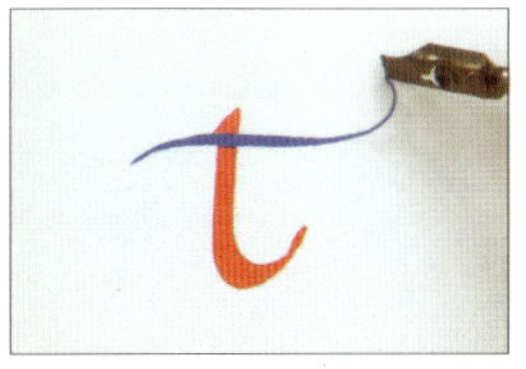

Lead in with a long serif to do the top of the letter and create the bowl. Add the second stroke from the top right.

Create the descender. The crossbar of the 't' can be flourished a long way depending on the space available either side.

Diagonal

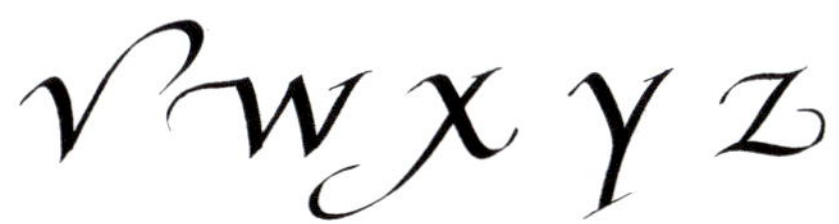

The nib may be flattened to 10 degrees in order to create the second diagonal in these letters. The flourishes can either be kept small or they can be extended to form quite elaborate designs.

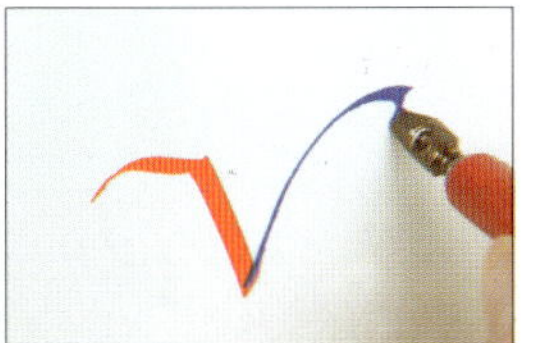

The first stroke can be extended from the front serif, and the second can be drawn up into a sweeping flourished curve.

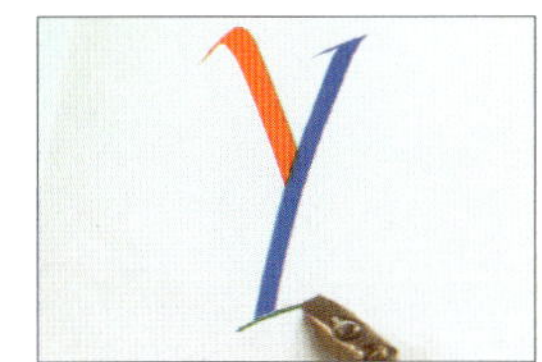

Pull down diagonally for the first stroke. Bring down the second stroke and flatten the pen angle. Add a third stroke to finish.

Flourished Italic hand

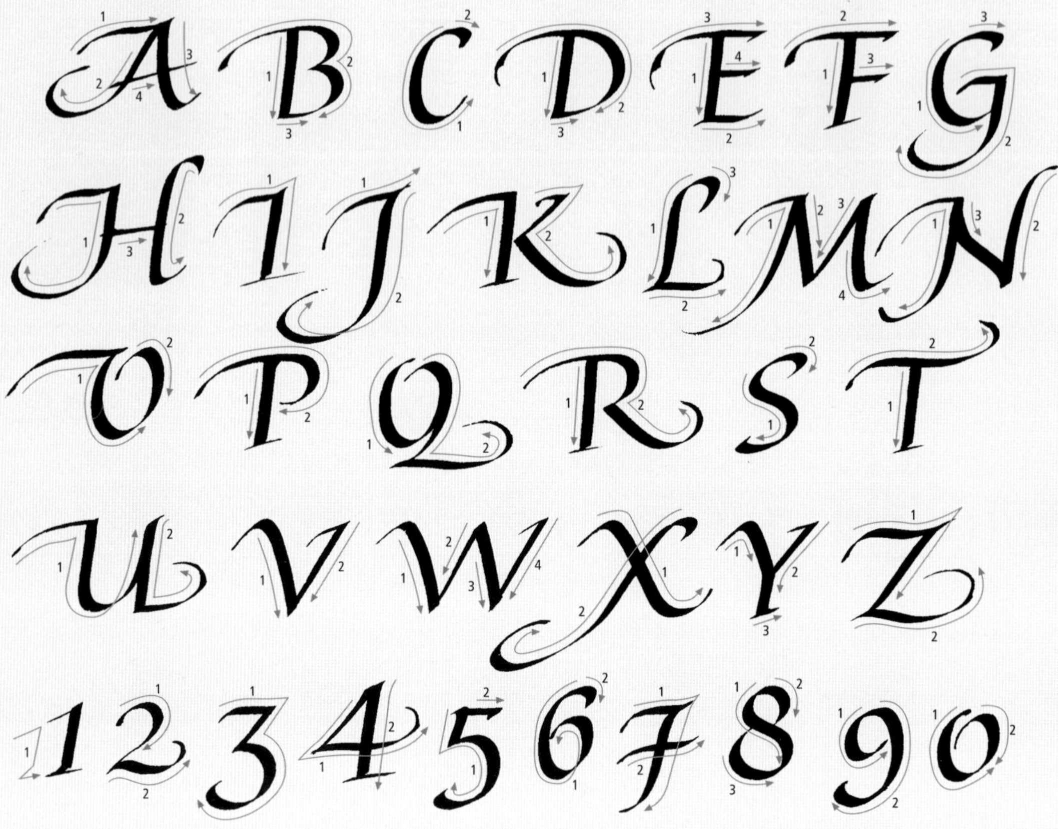

COMMON MISTAKES – CAPITALS

Flourished Italic capital letters should use the same spacing as the Italic script. Large flourishes will demand a greater distance between lines. Do not allow the letters to become too cramped. It may be a good idea to pencil in the path of any extending ascenders and descenders.

This letter is too ornate.

Bowl too tight.

Shape is too narrow.

Flourish too tight and curly.

Legs look splayed – keep under control.

Crossbar too short – should be level with top crossbar.

COMMON MISTAKES – LOWER CASE

The springing arches are the key to this alphabet. Do not start the arch too high on the stem because it will look like the round arch of Foundational hand. The arches in Flourished Italic spring from about two-thirds up the stem of the letter and are asymmetrical in shape.

The bowl is too round. Continue first stroke down, then lift stroke upwards to the top of the writing line.

The top part is too high.

The bottom stroke is too tightly curved, making it look contrived.

The second stroke is too short.

The letter shape is too mannered or curved.

The tail is too narrow.

Rustic hand

The Rustic script, which was widely used in the Roman Empire, was originally thought to have been a development of Roman Square Capitals. The discovery of early documents, however, has proved that it in fact pre-dates this script.

'Rustic' is perhaps something of a misnomer as it brings with it the whiff of country air and all things rural and casual. The Romans did have a script that relates to today's idea of 'bad handwriting', which they would use to 'scribble' on a wax tablet or write a quick note to a friend. However, this has nothing in common with the Rustic hand, which requires considerable calligraphic skill in order to obtain the changes of pen angle that are required on the majority of letters.

Rustic letters are both elongated and refined, with particularly slim stems. They were probably written with a reed or brush – certainly very large brushes must have been used to write the graffiti that can still be seen on the walls of Pompeii and Herculaneum. The script's rhythm is lively due to its weighty diagonals and serif strokes.

Although second only to Roman Capitals in its position of importance within a document, the Rustic script seems to have been relatively unpopular with medieval scribes and most examples appear to be poorly written. In manuscripts, Rustic was often written in a continuous stream, without spaces. By the 15th century it had ceased to be used, and it was only during the 20th century that an interest in this singular script fuelled a mini Rustic revival.

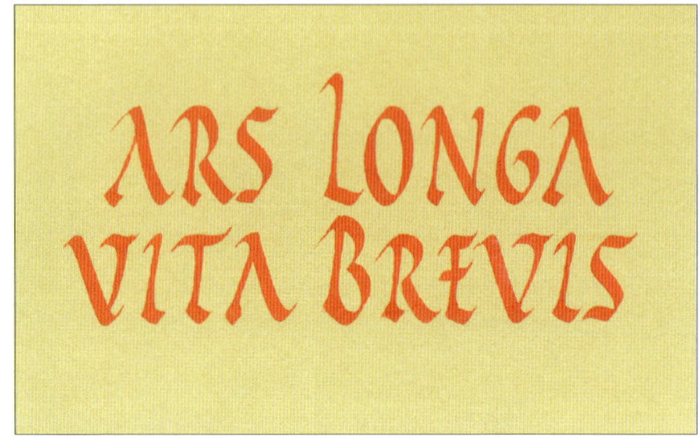

The basic rules

Rustic script is written at a relatively quick speed, and uses considerable variations in pen angle. In its original form the flexibility of the writing tool, probably a reed or a brush, would have allowed the change of pen angle and weight of stems to happen in one stroke. However, the modern metal nib is not as flexible and the effect is best achieved by using separate strokes. Many of the letterforms such as 'E' and 'T' are extremely narrow, and the difference in size between them and the wider letters such as 'M' and 'W' appears much greater than in classic Roman Capital letters. The interlinear space is minimal, probably no more than four nib widths.

LETTER HEIGHT
Seven nib widths for all letters except for 'B', 'F' and 'L'. These are written at eight nib widths.

LETTER SLOPE
This script should be written completely upright, without any slope.

PEN ANGLES
These vary from 80 degrees to 30 degrees. Right-handed calligraphers may find it easier to use a left-hand oblique nib.

80°

30°

Practice exercise: **Rustic hand**

It may take a little practice to retain the extremely steep pen angle used for this script. Before starting to write letters try making several hooked downstrokes to obtain the correct rhythm. The spacing between these strokes should be even and should reflect the normal letter spacing of this hand. Next, try holding the pen at 60 degrees and creating a series of oval shapes – drawing first the left side and then the right side. This will help to establish the hand movements needed for the rounded and oval parts of letters.

Group

Strokes (1st = red, 2nd = blue, 3rd = green)

Diagonal

A M N V
W X Y

While at first glance these letters may not appear to have much in common, practice will underline their family characteristics. Note that the third stroke of 'A' appears in all of these letters.

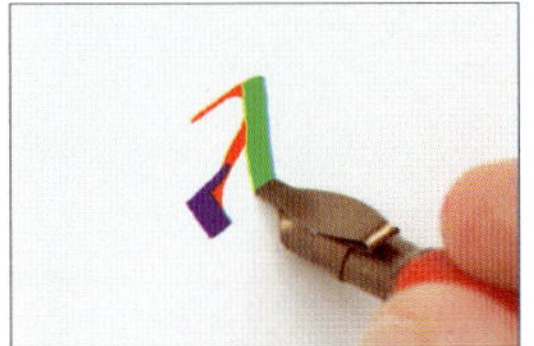

Swing the first diagonal stroke's base right. From the first stroke pull left, then right to produce the foot. Add the final diagonal stroke.

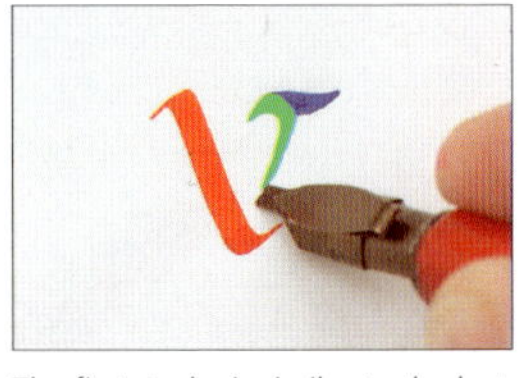

The first stroke is similar to the last stroke of 'A'. The right-hand serif is formed slightly flat.The final stroke should leave a finishing lift visible.

Straight

B D E F H I
K L P R T

The letter 'I' is the parent of this family. Note that the foot serif is elongated for the letters 'B', 'D', 'E' and 'L' and that the bowls of 'B', 'D', 'P' and 'R' continue the curve of the original serif in a downward movement.

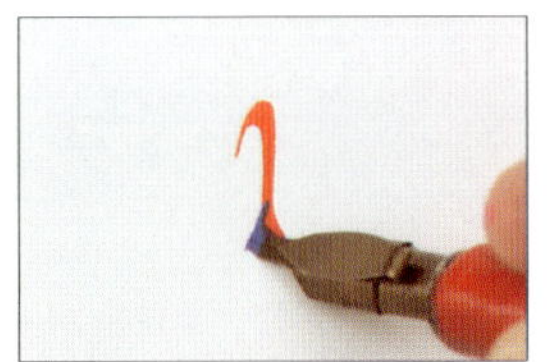

Emphasize the hooked serif and make a well-defined swing to the right at the end of the stroke. The second stroke starts within the first.

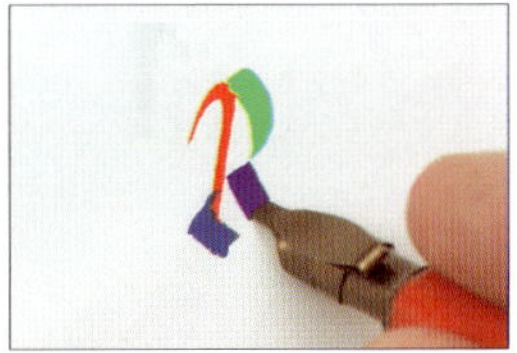

Construct a letter 'I', then with the pen within the curved serif, draw a bowl that meets the stem. Keep the angle to make the final stroke.

Oval

C G O Q

'O' is the parent of this family. Note how narrow it is. A pen angle of around 60 degrees is used to create these oval letters, and this angle needs to be maintained throughout the letter.

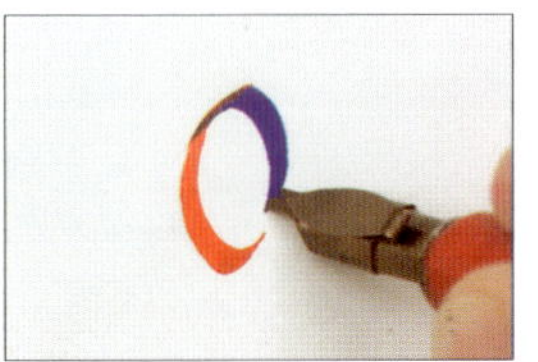

With a steep pen angle make the curved stroke. The second stroke reflects this shape and starts and finishes within the first stroke.

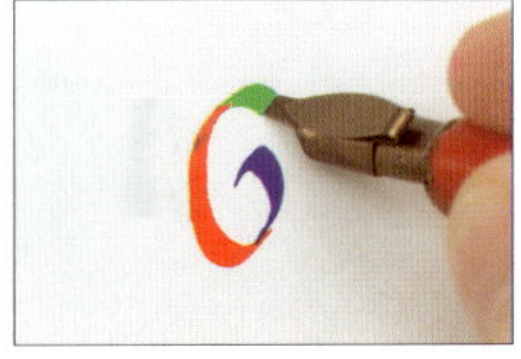

The first stroke is as for 'O'. The second starts just above the middle of the letter. For the top of the 'G' pull to the right, then lift slightly.

Ungrouped

J S U Z

Of these letters 'J' and 'U' have been designed to complement the rest of the alphabet as they did not exist in Roman times. Do ensure that the top and bottom strokes of 'S' are written with a concave curve, and that the letter appears upright.

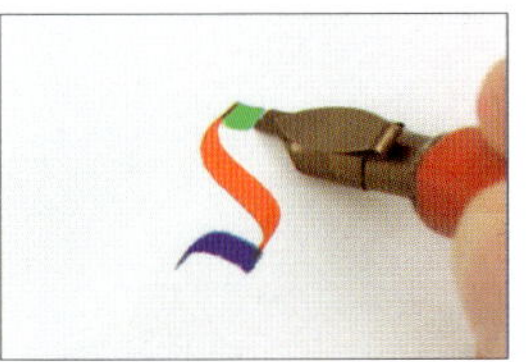

First draw the diagonal stroke with curved serifs to the right and left. The concave strokes at the head and tail should be kept short.

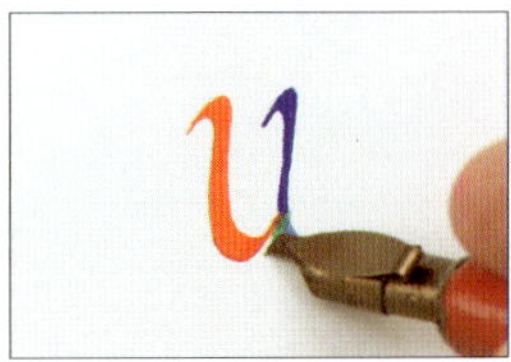

Begin the first stroke as for 'I' but finish with a curved bowl. The second and third strokes are the same as for a letter 'I'.

Rustic hand

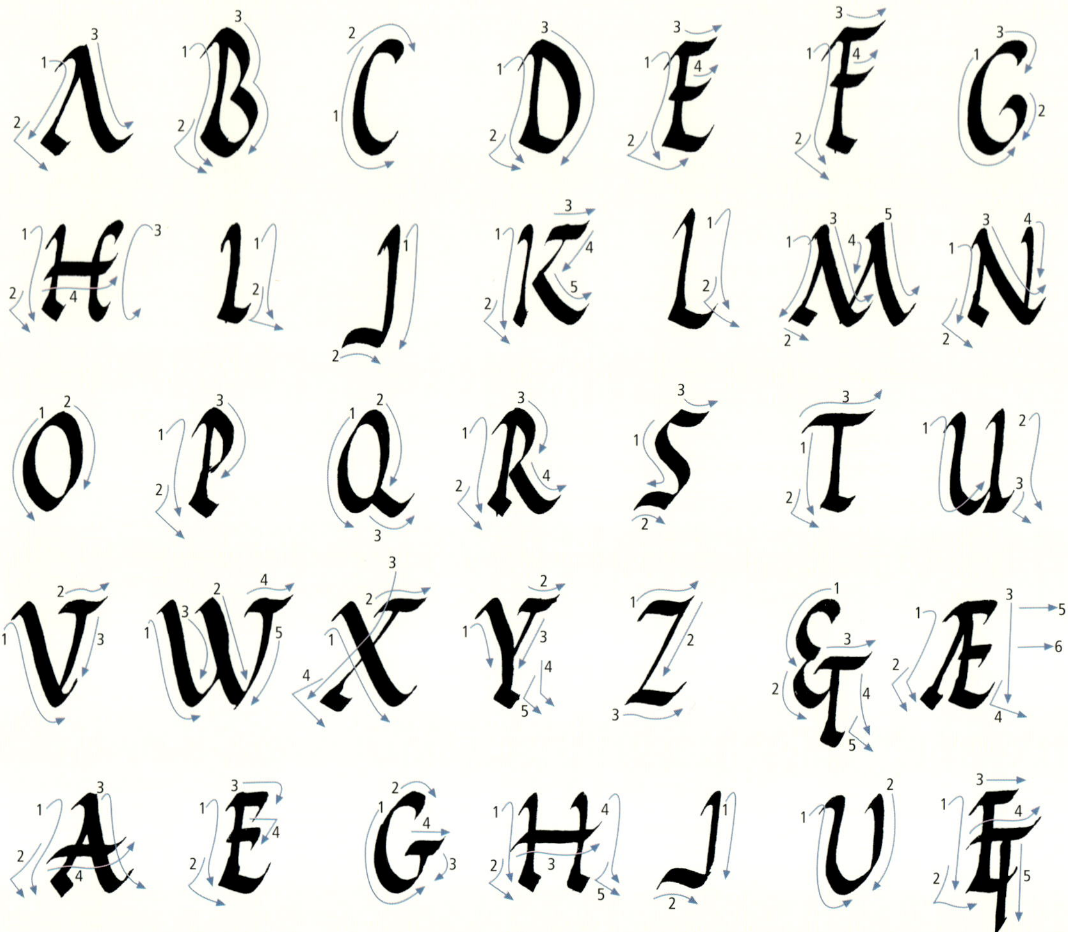

COMMON MISTAKES – CAPITALS

Some of the most common mistakes made with Rustic lettering occur when adding the serifs. Other mistakes include making the top and bottom strokes of 'S' concave. Keep the pen angle steep in order to produce thin vertical stems. Wide or round letters are always incorrect.

Lacking a hooked serif at the start.

Letter should be one nib width higher.

Bowl of letter is too rounded.

This letter is too wide.

Top and bottom strokes should not be concave curves.

Too conventional a shape. The hook serif on the second stroke is missing.

Incorrect foot serif – more akin to Gothic.

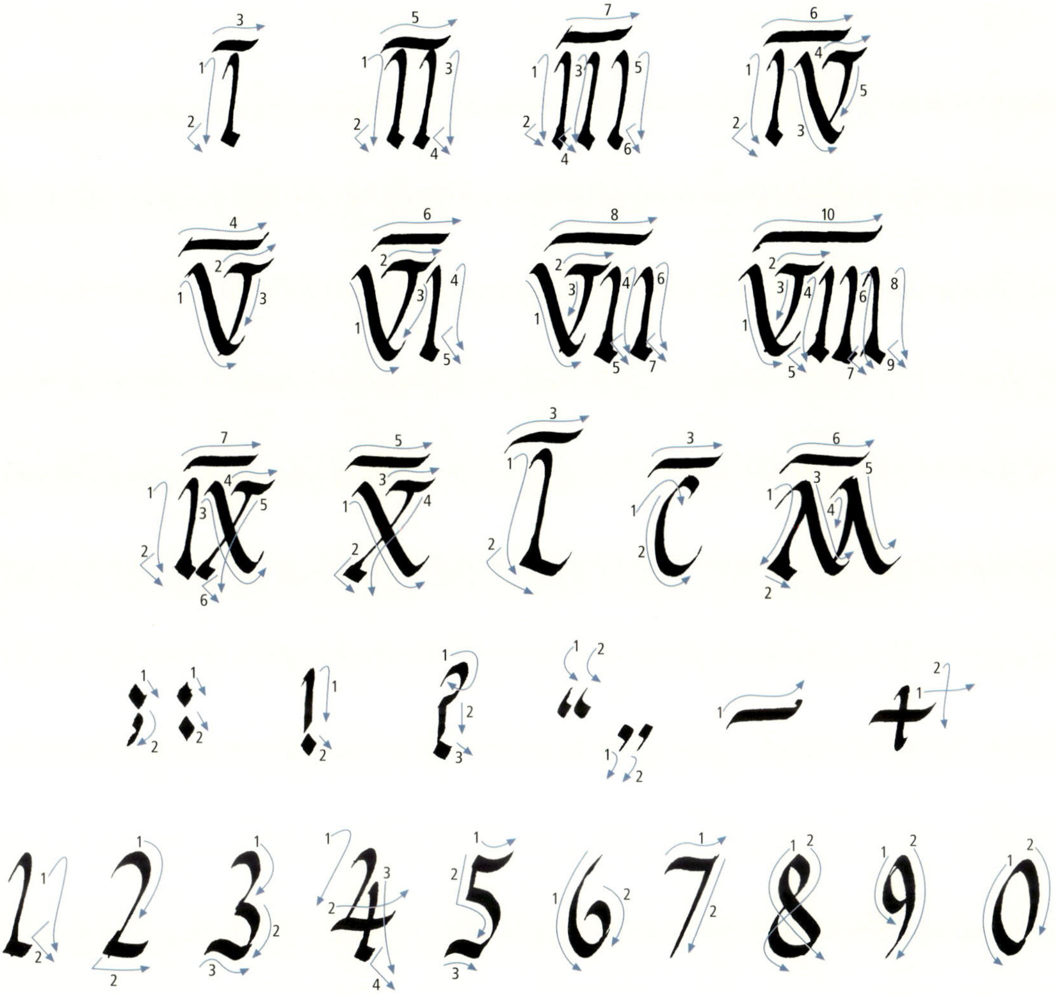

COMMON MISTAKES – NUMERALS AND SYMBOLS

Numbers and punctuation are just as important as letters in any finished piece of work and care should be taken so that unfamiliar shapes are not muddled giving a false impression. The overall effect should be one of harmony.

The 'L' should be one nib width higher to distinguish between the number 1 and 50.

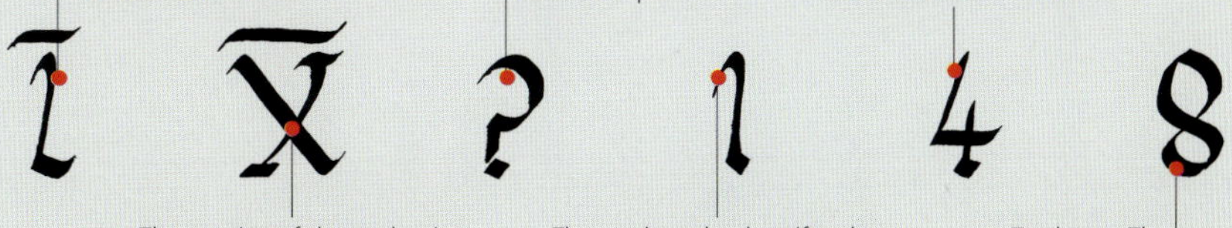

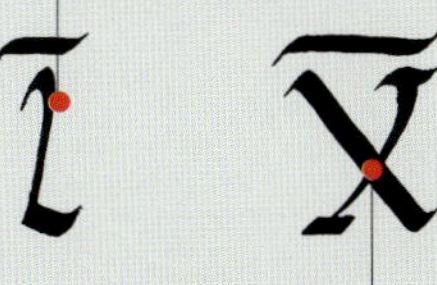

The crossing of the strokes is too low. It should be at or a little above the optical middle.

The bowl is too large for this narrow script.

The overlarge hook serif makes it difficult to distinguish this number 1 from a number 2.

Too conventional a shape as the hooked serif on the first stroke has been omitted.

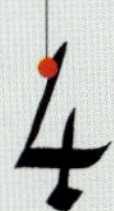

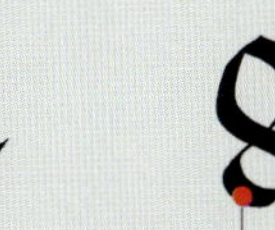

Top heavy. The bottom bowl should be the larger.

Carolingian hand

This beautiful hand is based on an extended 'o' shape, written at a constant angle of between 25 and 30 degrees. Carolingian evolved from Half-Uncial script in the court of King Charlemagne, who was king of the Franks from 768 to 814AD, Emperor of Rome and prime instigator of a widespread cultural revival. The script used here is based on the Moutier Grandval Bible written in St Martin's Abbey Scriptorium in Tours, France, in about 840AD.

Carolingian was used in the 9th and 10th centuries as a standard book hand. It has a gentle forward slope with tall, four nib width ascenders and descenders, and three nib widths for the main body of the letter. The cursive nature of the script makes it pleasant to execute and an elegant script to read. It also lends itself well to modern calligraphy. The space between the words is no more than the size of a lower-case 'o' but the space between lines is generous, at least three x-heights (or three body heights – equalling nine nib widths) to allow for tops and tails. The script should be written so that the upstrokes and overstrokes give the letters rhythm. Most letters are slightly wider than they are high. Avoid turning the pen to an angle other than 25 or 30 degrees when creating curved strokes as this produces lines that are thick in the wrong places. Because the hand is so rounded it requires practice when forming words from letters. Particularly long letters may leave a large space that affects the rhythm of the piece.

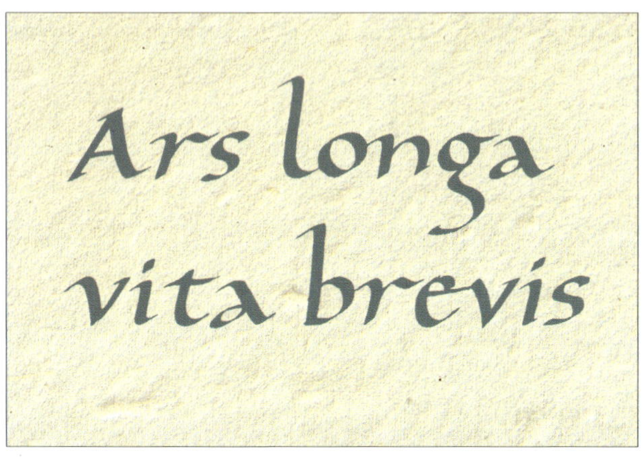

The basic rules

The alphabet is written with a shallow pen angle of between 25 and 30 degrees. The letters are very full and rounded. Both the round letters and the springing rounded arches of 'n', 'm', and 'h' are based on an extended 'o' shape. The main body of the letter is three nib widths high with an ascender and descender height of four nib widths. The letters have a very elegant and flowing look when written in quantity. The capitals that accompany this hand are based on Roman Capitals but are written at about five to six nib widths high. Edward Johnston chose the English Carolingian script used in the Ramsey Psalter as the model for his Foundational hand.

LETTER HEIGHT
The main body of the letter is three nib widths high with the ascenders and descenders at four nib widths.

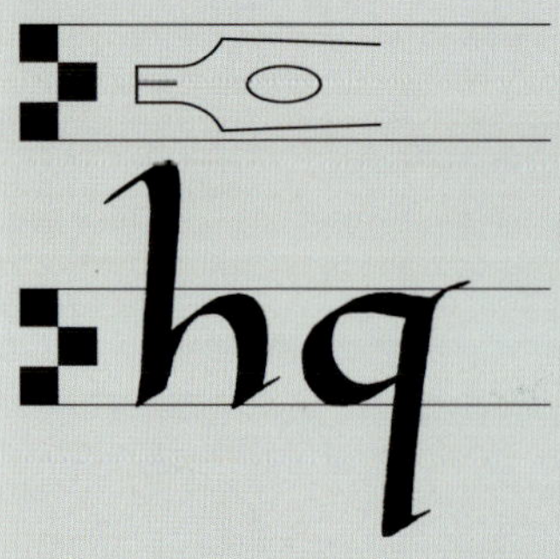

LETTER SLOPE
This alphabet is written at moderate speed and the letters slope forward at about five degrees from the vertical.

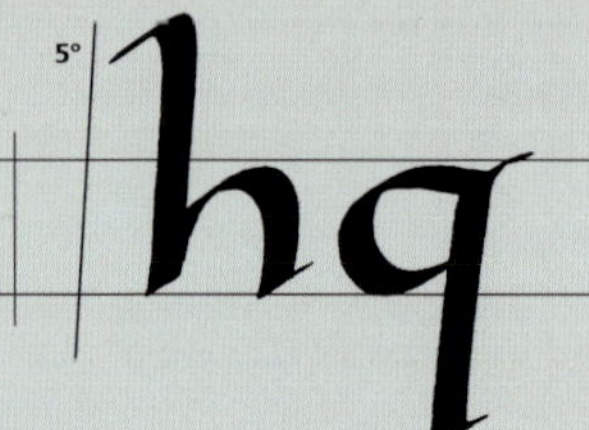

PEN ANGLES
The pen angle is about 25 to 30 degrees and is constant throughout the letters, giving a uniform rhythm to the script.

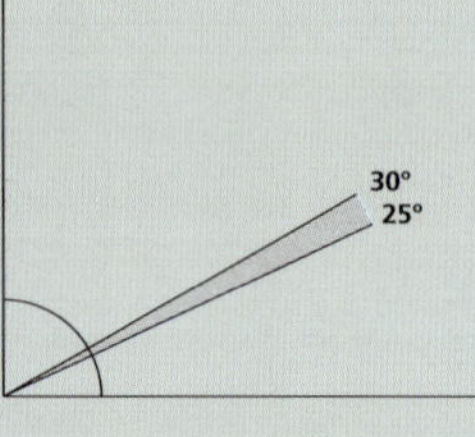

Practice exercise: **Carolingian hand**

The very rounded 'o' shape used in this script is slightly wider than a circle, with few lifts within the letters. Some letters do not have serifs on some of the strokes, most notably at the bottom of the first stroke of 'h', 'k', 'n', 'm' and 'r'. On historical models the finishing stroke on these letters often are pulled in to the left instead of displaying the usual serif ending. The written words have verve and a cursive quality about them which adds to the rhythm.

Group

Stroke (1st = red, 2nd = blue, 3rd = green)

Round or circular

cedqgo

The letters in this group are wider than they are high giving a fat, rounded appearance. Two overlapping strokes can be used to create the curved shape of the 'e' and 'o', beginning with a left-hand stroke.

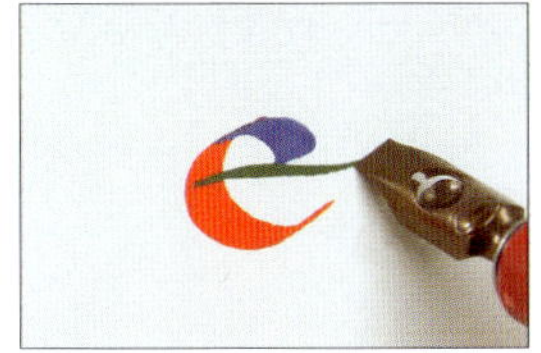

With the nib at 30 degrees write the left-hand curve first. Add the curved top and then add the crossbar with a flattened angle.

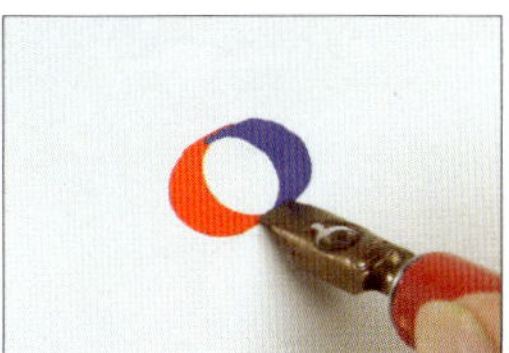

The first stroke keeps a nib angle of 30 degrees. Overlap the first stroke to make the second stroke, overlapping again at the bottom.

Arched

mhbprin

These letters contain the branching and springing round arches so typical of this hand. Attention should be given as to whether serifs are drawn at the top or bottom of the stroke.

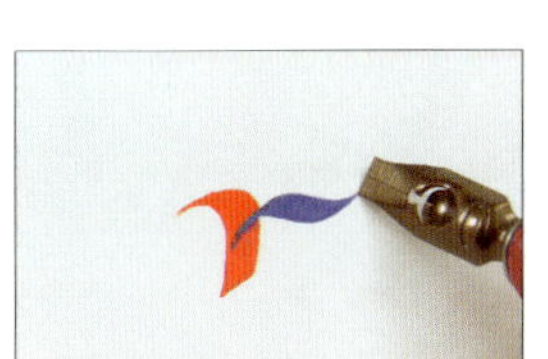

The first stroke has a small serif only at the top. Add the springing arch from about two thirds of the way up the stem.

The first stroke has a serif only at the top. Spring the second stroke in an arch to go to the baseline finishing with a small serif.

Combination

tyljfsu

Both straight and rounded features combine to create the shapes of the letters in this group. Take care to keep the distinction between the different elements.

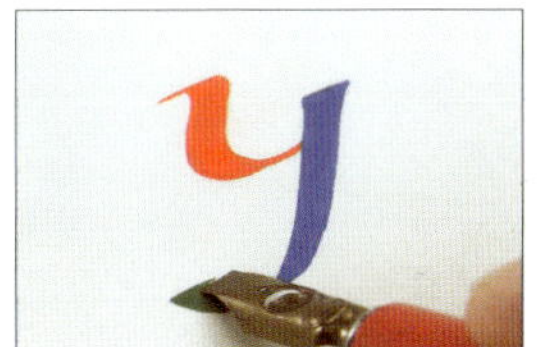

Keep the first stroke rounded. The second falls below the line until the pen line thins. Come back on to the existing line with a flat stroke.

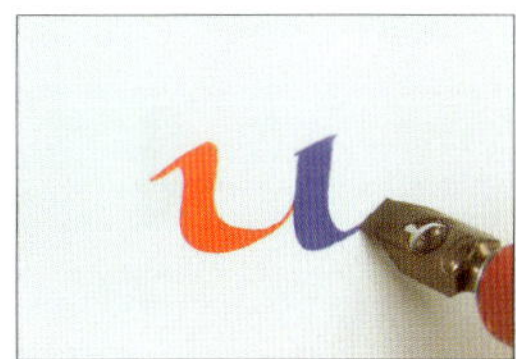

Make the first stroke and take it to the top of the letter space. Add the second stroke over the top of the first to go to the baseline.

Diagonal

kwxazv

Keep a constant angle of 30 degrees for these letters. You may wish to very slightly steepen the angle on the first stroke of 'v', 'w', 'x' and 'y', although this is not absolutely necessary.

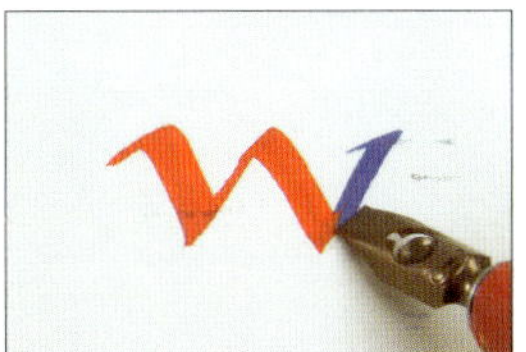

Start with a serif then write the first three stokes as one. Add the last stroke separately.

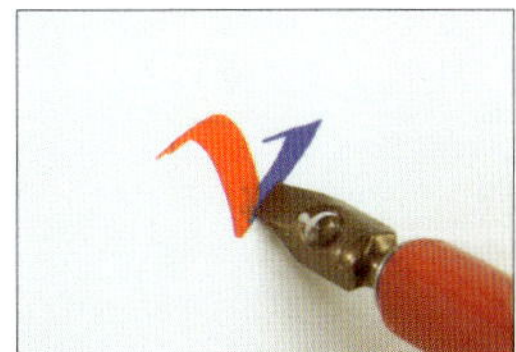

Write the first stroke with a serif. Flatten the angle to 25 degrees for the second stroke.

Carolingian hand

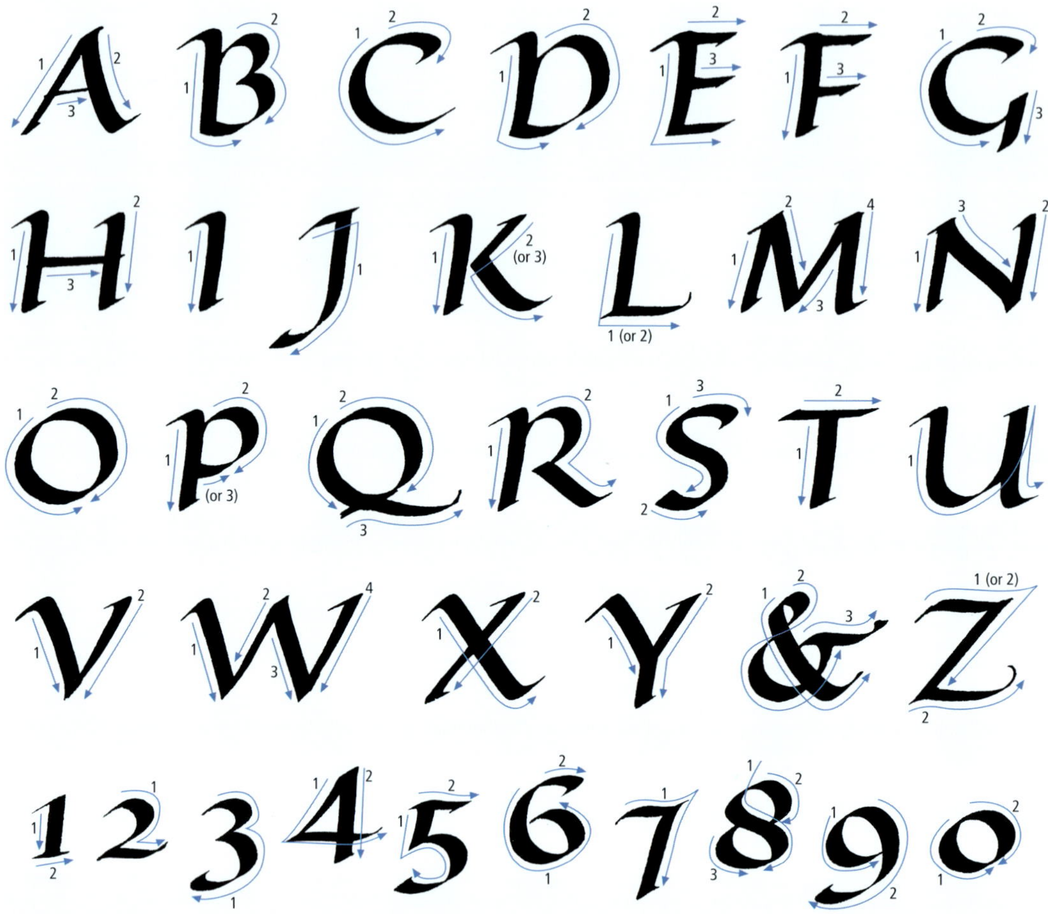

COMMON MISTAKES – CAPITALS

Carolingian hand's capital letters bear a strong resemblance to those of Foundational, but take on a slight lean. By keeping the pen at a 25 to 30-degree angle the letters can be kept generous; they should not, however, be splayed. Be careful not to produce letters that are too heavy.

Letter is too narrow.

Letter is too narrow and not rounded enough.

Centre diagonal is too curved.

Second stroke is too curved where it should be straight.

The foot is too curly.

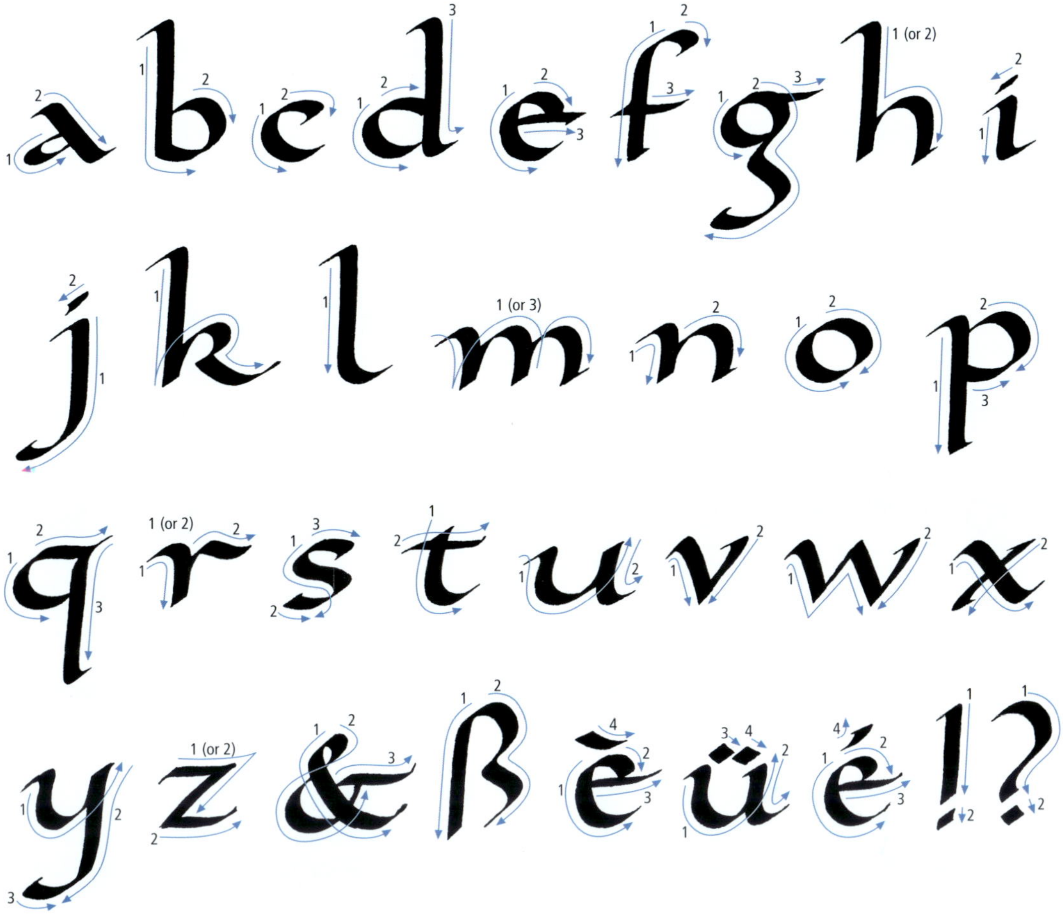

COMMON MISTAKES – LOWER CASE

Ensure that widths, arches, nib widths and ascender heights are correct to avoid producing letters that resemble a poor version of Foundational or Italic hand. Do not make the bowls of letters to tight, or descenders too curly.

Stroke is not sloped enough.

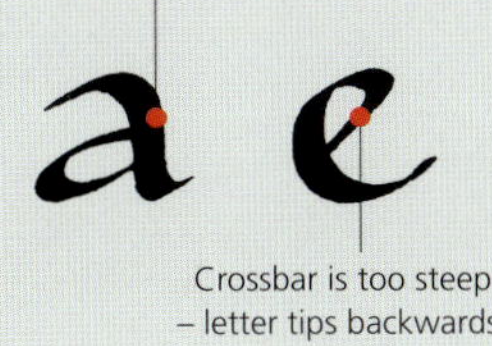

Crossbar is too steep – letter tips backwards.

Bowl is too large and descender too narrow.

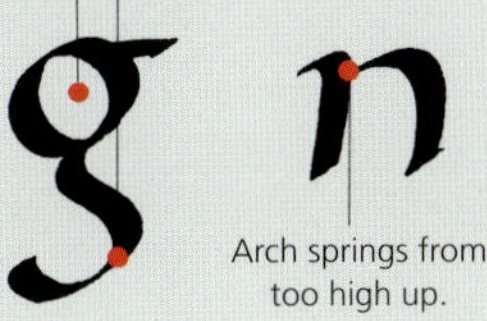

Arch springs from too high up.

Letter is too narrow. Strokes are too curly and should have flatter arches.

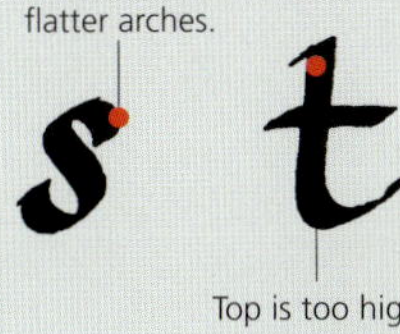

Top is too high and should have no top serif.

Copperplate hand

Developed in the 16th century from the Italic script, Copperplate is a flowing cursive hand that is the closest relation to modern handwriting of all the calligraphic scripts.

This hand was named Copperplate because it was based upon the writing used by engravers. In the late 16th century a new printing method developed whereby letters and designs were engraved in reverse on sheets or plates of copper using a pointed metal burin (engraving tool). The sharp point of the burin created a delicate line quite unlike that made by a square-edged pen. This spidery line soon became the vogue in Europe. The flexible pointed nib used for Copperplate writing on paper is designed to copy the effect of the burin. The nib produces a thick stroke when pressure is applied, which contrasts with the thin, wispy upward strokes of the hand. Many of the nibs used for Copperplate writing today were in production in the 19th century or before.

By the 19th century Copperplate had become the established hand of clerks and was taught in elementary schools to enhance the future prospects of pupils interested in advancing their career, since handwriting played an important role in many businesses. As well as being the main business hand, Copperplate was also the vernacular writing style of the period. It was taught by means of printed copybooks, such as George Bickham's *Universal Penman*, printed in 1741, and people developed their own variation of the hand using these exemplars.

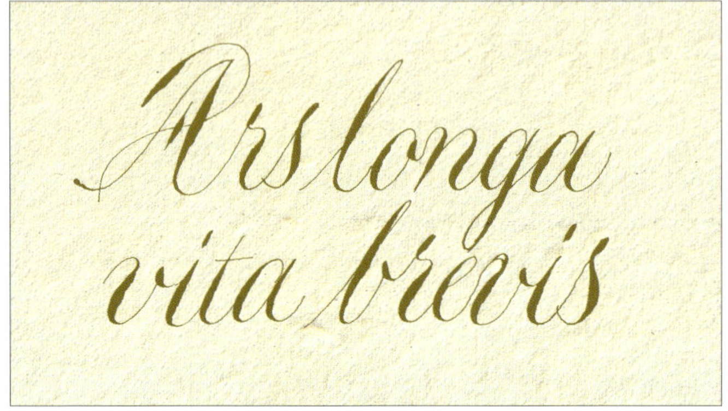

The basic rules

The characteristics of this hand are created by the basic form of an oval 'o' and a slope of 54 degrees. Unlike the edged pen, the pointed nib that is used for Copperplate writing can be used to write letters of any size and weight and so the x-height of the letters and the pen angle are not relevant. The pressure used to write Copperplate script is, however, very important in order to obtain the contrast of thick and thin strokes. Light pressure will reduce the flow of ink through the nib producing a delicate, thin stroke, whereas heavier pressure will open the nib slightly to let more ink through, thus producing a thicker line. Only apply pressure on the downstrokes.

LETTER HEIGHT
Letters written with a pointed nib cannot be measured in the same way as those written with a broad-edged nib. A variety of letter sizes and weights can be achieved by adjusting the body height (x-height) of the letters.

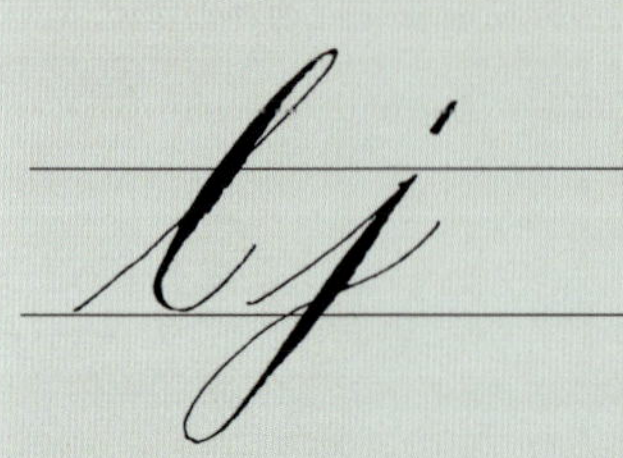

LETTER SLOPE
The slope of this hand is 54 degrees. Some faint guidelines will help to maintain this angle of writing.

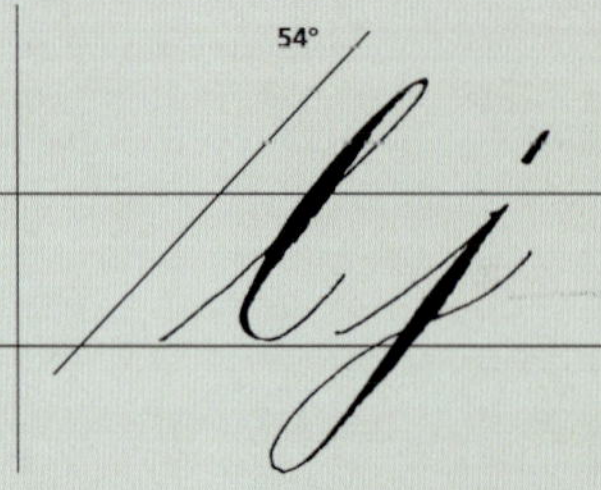

PEN ANGLES
There is no pen angle for Copperplate but the nib is pointed in the direction of the letter slope.

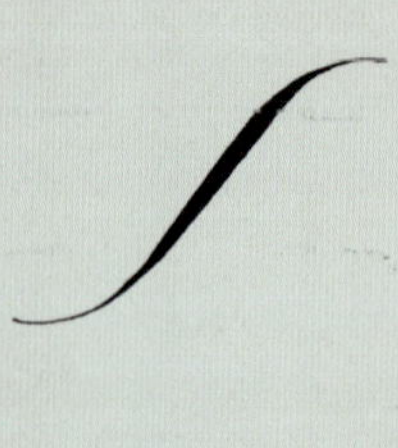

Practice exercise: **Copperplate hand**

Practise making the contrasting thick and thin strokes by increasing pressure on the nib on the downstrokes and applying only the lightest pressure on the upstrokes and ligatures. It helps to lay the paper flat and at an angle (anticlockwise) so that the slant of the letter slope is vertical to the body when writing. Try to leave even spaces between the thick strokes. Watch that the ascenders and descenders to not touch each other.

Group	Strokes (1st = red, 2nd = blue, 3rd = green)	

Oval

This group of letters follows the form of the elliptical or oval 'o'. Each letter is begun by drawing the elliptical shape in an anti-clockwise direction using increased pressure on the downward curve on the left side. The additional elements are then added.

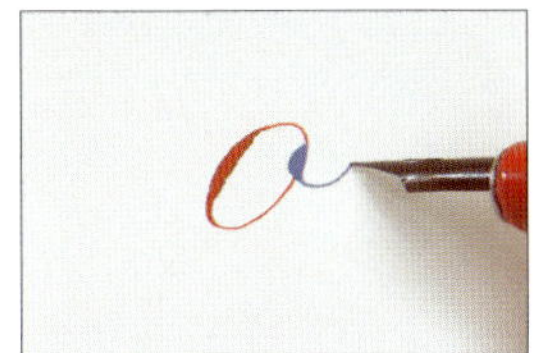

The elliptical bowl is drawn using more pressure on the left curve. The letter is finished with a small loop, which is flooded in with ink.

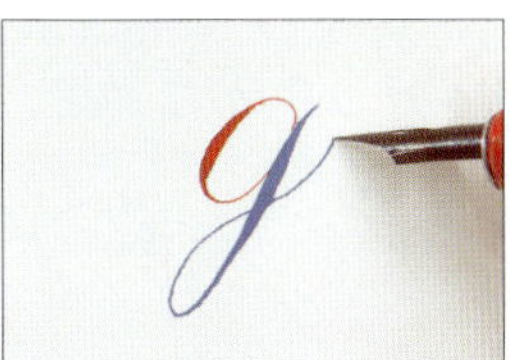

The bowl is drawn as for the 'o'. Next, a downward stroke is made with increased pressure in the middle, finishing in an upward loop.

Looped and straight

A light, curved, upward stroke is made as a ligature or lead-in stroke for letters in this group. Loops are made with light pressure on the pen, and this pressure is increased towards the centre of the downstroke to create a thicker line.

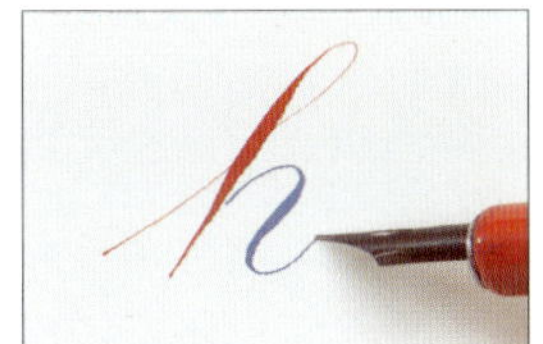

A curved upward stroke is drawn which makes a loop then the stem. The nib then continues up the stem and round to make an arch.

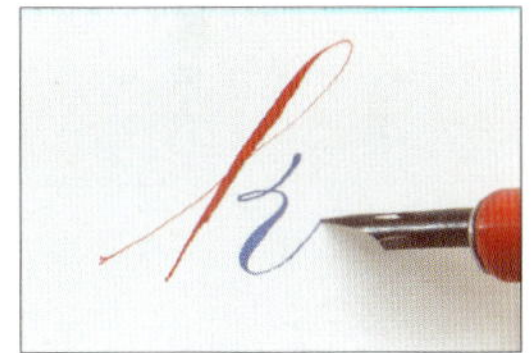

The first stroke is as for 'h'. Then, in a continuous movement, the nib is drawn down and round to form the bowl and leg of the letter.

Curved arches

Some arches are preceded by a straight downward stroke made with increased pressure. The arch springs from the base of the downstroke using a light upward movement leading into the curved arch and pressure is applied on the downward stroke.

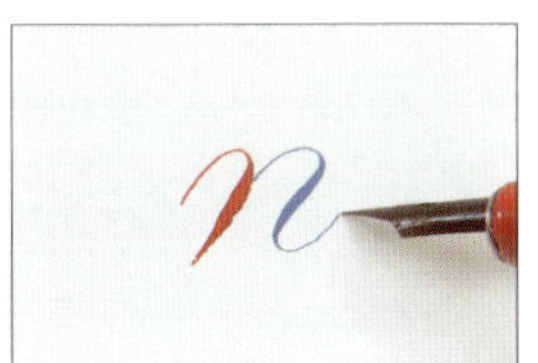

A small lead-in ligature begins the upward movement and increased pen pressure is applied to the downward stroke.

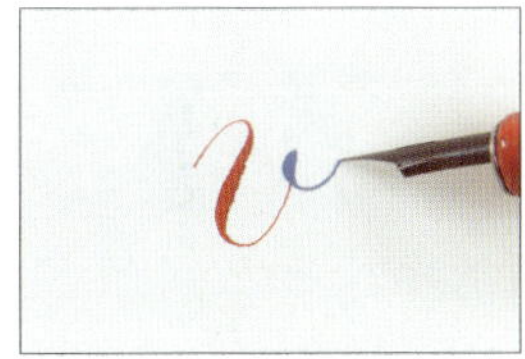

A thin arched stroke is made and pressure is applied to the down-ward curve. The stroke is finished with a small loop flooded with ink.

Ungrouped

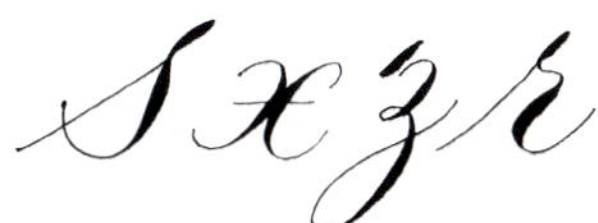

Although these letters do not fit into the other groups, the same basic rules are applied when writing them. Upwards strokes are made with light pressure and increased pressure is applied on the downstrokes. Aim to keep the letters looking balanced.

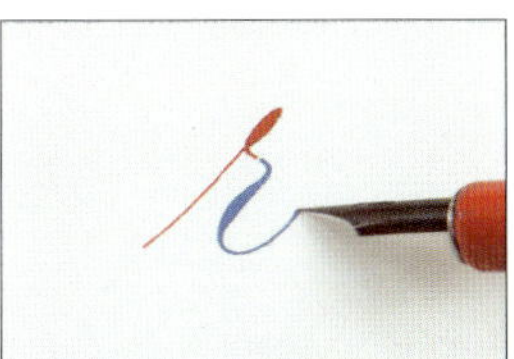

A ligature is made and a small elliptical shape is drawn and then flooded in with ink. The stroke continues with a small arch.

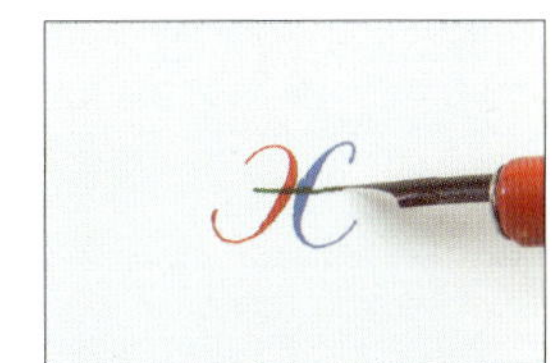

Pressure is applied to the centre of each curve and a thin crossbar is drawn through the centre using very light pressure.

Copperplate hand

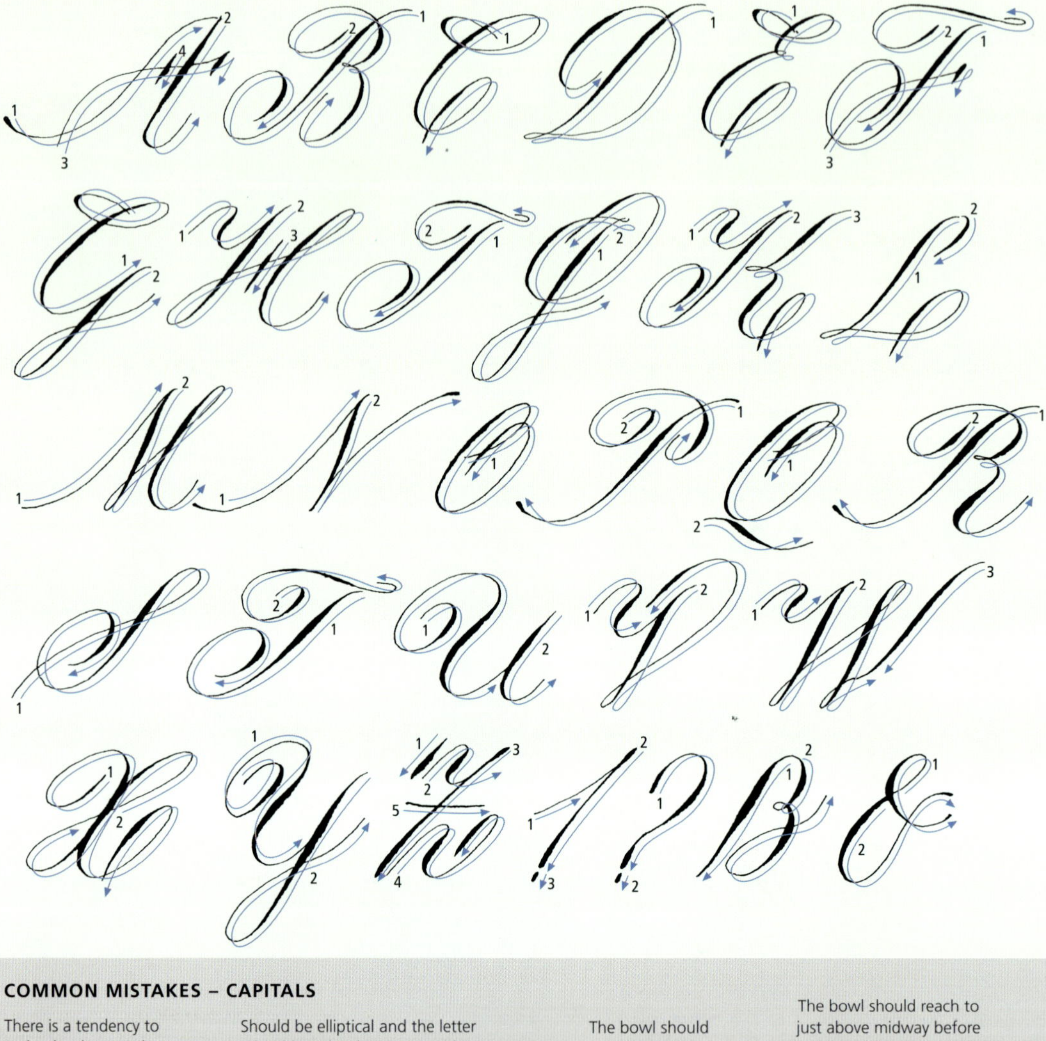

COMMON MISTAKES – CAPITALS

There is a tendency to make the downstroke too straight whereas this elegant line should begin with a curve and end with a curve. Letters are often written too wide with insufficient width of flourishing to the left of the downstroke.

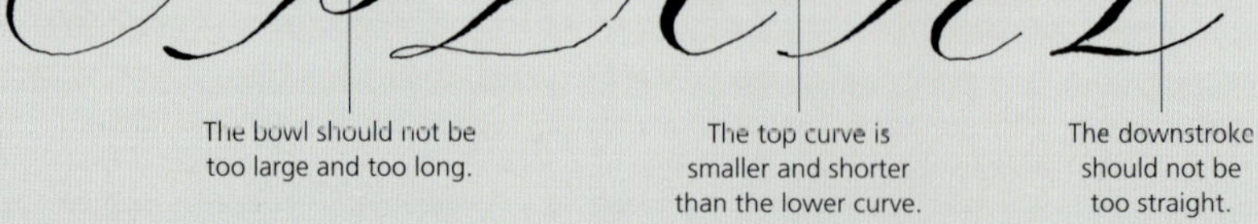

Should be elliptical and the letter should not be drawn too wide.

The bowl should be kept slim.

The bowl should reach to just above midway before the loop of the downstroke.

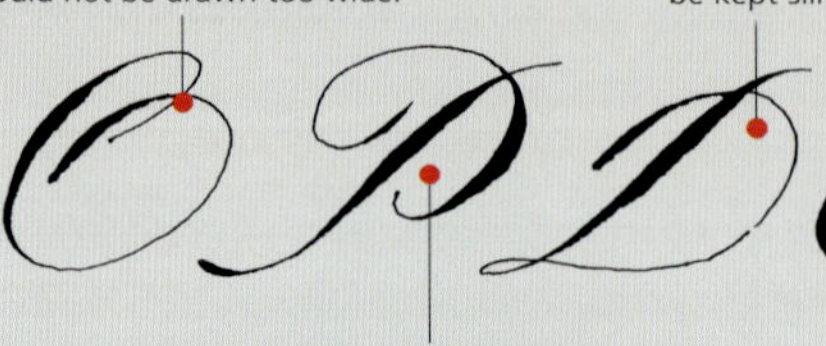

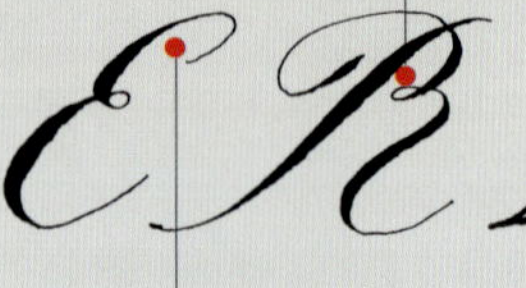

The bowl should not be too large and too long.

The top curve is smaller and shorter than the lower curve.

The downstroke should not be too straight.

COMMON MISTAKES – LOWER CASE

Letters are often constructed either too narrow or too wide. Aim for a visually even balance between letter-strokes and ligatures. If the change between thick and thin strokes is too sudden, the characteristic contrasts of the script are lost.

The two arches should be of equal width.

Do not apply pressure until after finishing the loop.

The small loop should be made above the line rather than extended too horizontally.

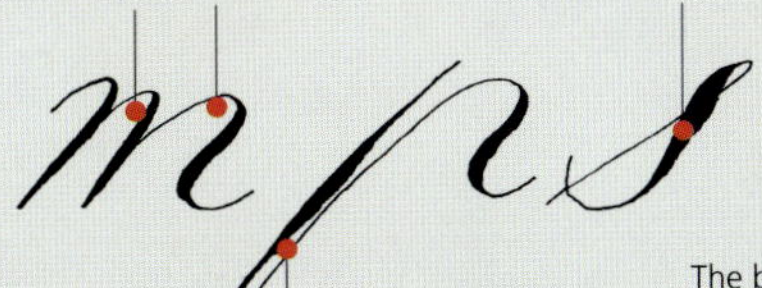

The thin upward ligature should be quite close to the downstroke and the bowl of the letter should not be too wide.

The bowl of the letter should be rounded and not too wide.

The base of the bowl should not be too wide but should follow the elliptical shape.

Batarde hand

The script known as Batarde is a cursive Gothic hand which is particularly decorative when well executed. Unlike its Gothic predecessors, Batarde is relatively informal and has a flowing style. When it is compared to Textura, the most widely recognized of the Gothic scripts, the real differences in rhythm and flow become very apparent. Although Batarde uses the pointed arches characteristic of Gothic scripts, its diagonal letters have a vigorous swing, which gives it much more movement than the very upright Textura. This hand appeared in French manuscripts between the 13th and 16th centuries.

Batarde is characterized by its short, bold body height and very long ascenders and descenders. This script has a characteristic 's' and 'f', which are made by twisting and drawing the nib to a greater angle for the long downstroke. A quill is the most suitable tool for this writing as the flexibility of the nib is ideal for such manipulation.

The elegant letters of Batarde hand were often illuminated, and many medieval manuscripts were complemented by lavish illustrations. This is particularly evident in the Books of Hours that were popular at the time. The upper case of the Batarde hand is very decorative with flamboyant hairlines and flourishes. Although they are certainly impressive, these letters are not always easily legible. They are therefore usually limited to the beginning of a paragraph or line, and are considered unsuitable for a long run of words.

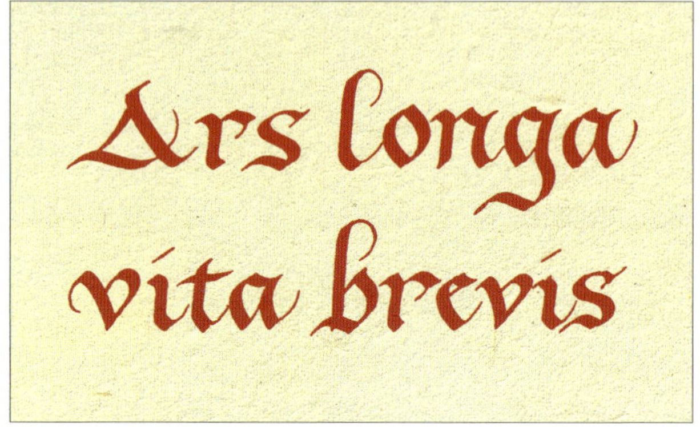

The basic rules

The key features of the lower case of Batarde are the pointed oval 'o' form and the sharp, pointed arches. The letters have a short body height with long ascenders and descenders. The slope of the letters is usually between 0 and 3 degrees although the long 's' and 'f' have a more exaggerated slant of around 10 degrees. The pen angle is usually between 35 and 45 degrees, but because some pen manipulation is involved in writing this script, a constant pen angle is not kept throughout. The flourishes and exaggerated ascenders and descenders use a number of up-and-over strokes, which you may need to practise before you can execute them in a controlled manner. It is also important to use a pen which will move smoothly over the paper for these upward strokes.

LETTER HEIGHT

The lower case of this hand is written with an x-height of three nib widths, with ascenders and descenders written at three nib widths. The upper case letters are written with an x-height of six nib widths.

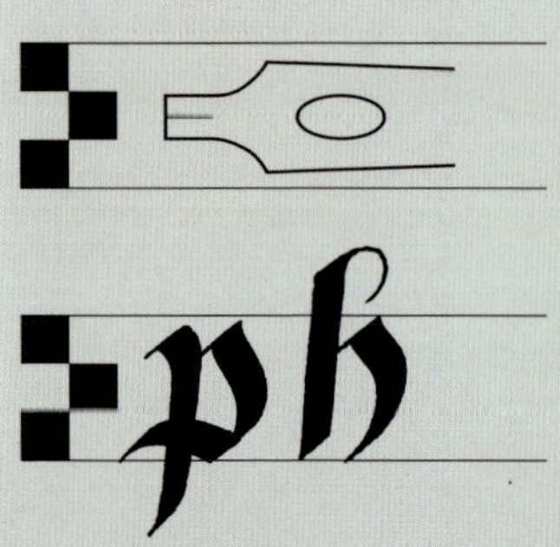

LETTER SLOPE

The slope of writing is usually between 0 and 3 degrees with the exception of letters 's' and 'f', which have an exaggerated slope of 10 degrees.

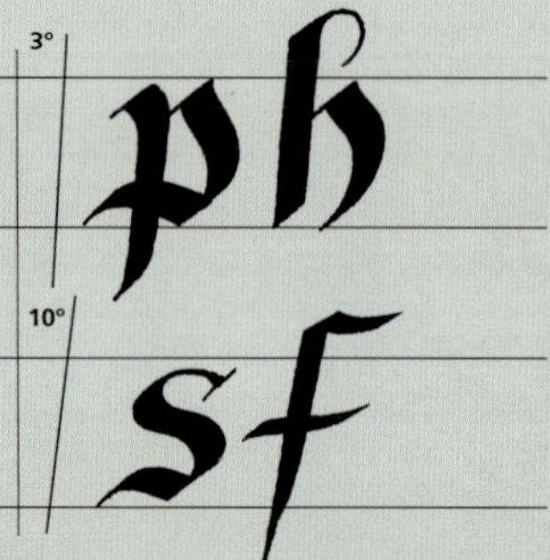

PEN ANGLES

The pen angle of this script is approximately 45 degrees although this does vary in some manuscripts between 35 and 45 degrees.

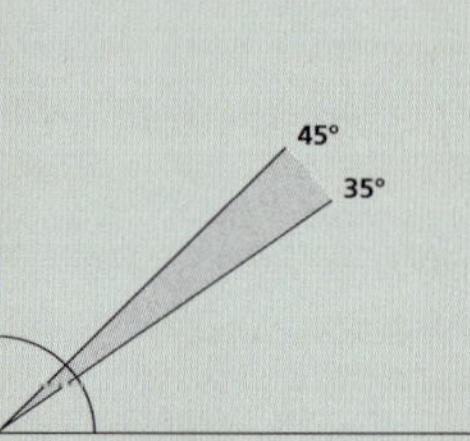

Practice exercise: **Batarde hand**

The strokes used in this hand are a little more difficult to create with a metal nib as it is not as flexible as a quill pen. This can be overcome as thin strokes may be created by dragging the ink along the corner of the nib for hairline strokes. Pressure is applied to the nib to create the fullness of the down stroke of 'f' and 's' and the nib is then twisted to form the long tapered point. Alternatively, the long stroke can be made with two pen strokes to create the width.

Group

Strokes (1st = red, 2nd = blue, 3rd = green, 4th = mauve)

Pointed oval

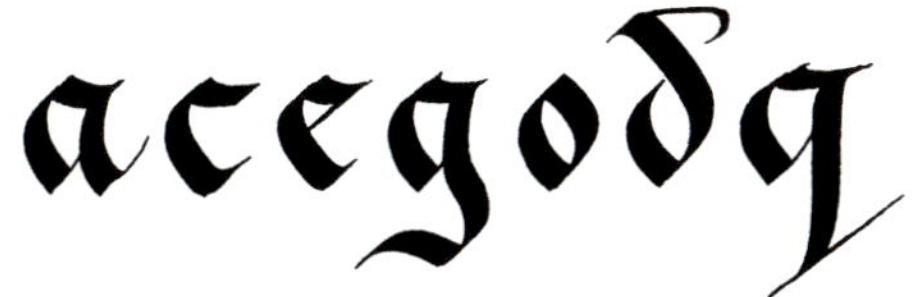

The letters in this group all begin in the same way, following the pointed elliptical curve of the 'o' form. The left-hand stroke is always drawn first.

Begin the letter 'o' with an anti-clockwise curve. Complete the letter with a clockwise curve, which links at the base.

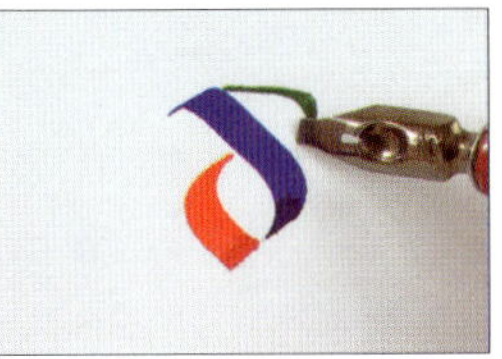

Begin the first stroke as an 'o'. The ascender projects beyond this stroke to the left. A hairline serif extends at the top of this.

Straight

These letters all begin with a straight stroke although the lead-in serif can vary from letter to letter. When this serif is delicate and looped, it should be made using the corner of the nib.

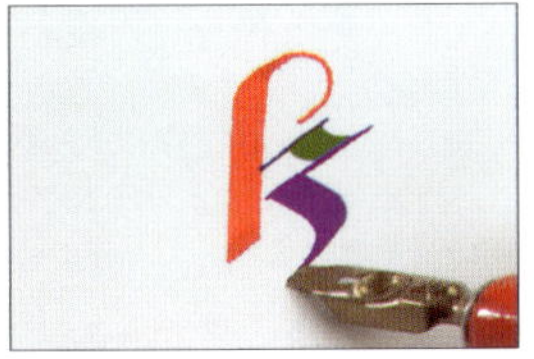

A hairline serif is looped at the top of the first stroke with the nib corner. Three strokes make up the rest of the letter.

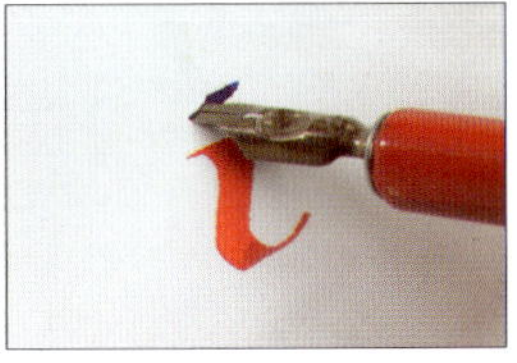

The 'i' is made by pulling diagonally from left to right then straight downwards and ending with a diagonal pull to the right and a dot.

Arched

The letters in this group all have asymmetric, pointed arches, which relate to the shape of the 'o'. The arch is started within the stem, and is formed by a thin upstroke drawn using the edge of the nib, followed by a thick downstroke.

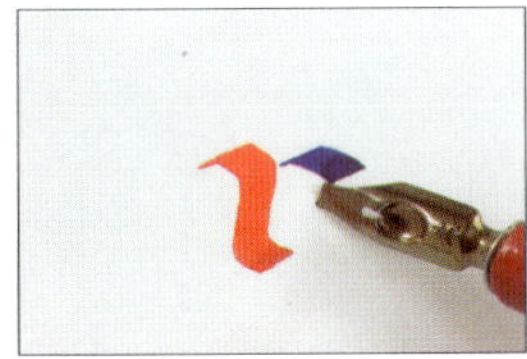

The first stroke of the letter 'r' is the same as for an 'i'. An upwards movement of the pen followed by a small curve forms the arch.

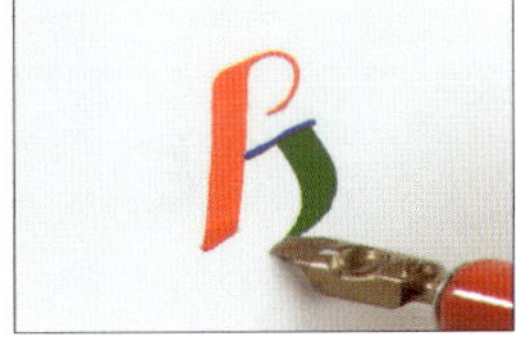

The first stroke is straight with a hairline serif. For the arch, the pen is drawn upwards, then continued downwards in one movement.

Ungrouped

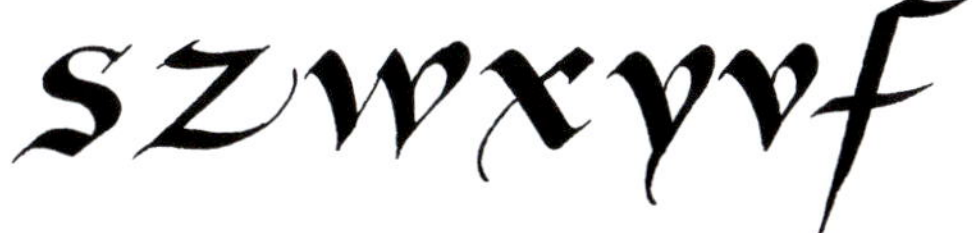

Make any hairline strokes using the edge of the pen. The letters 'x', 'w' and 'y' are looped on the right-hand side. This loop is formed using a single up-and-over stroke that begins halfway down the left-hand stroke and joins at its base.

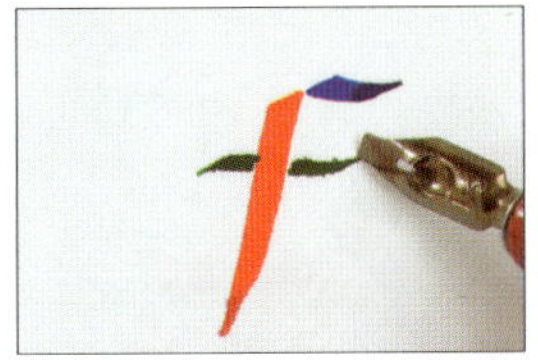

Firm pressure creates the thick downstroke. The nib is then twisted to a steep angle for the thin tail. The crossbar is added last.

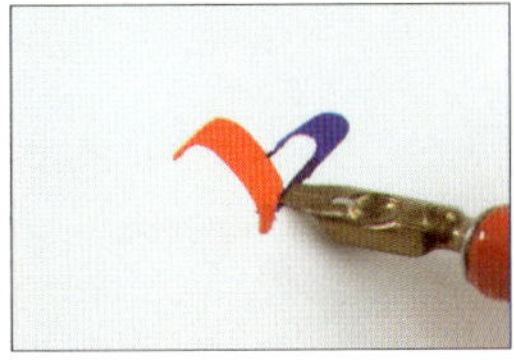

The first stroke is made with a diagonal movement. The second stroke is drawn up, over and down to the base of the first stroke.

Batarde hand

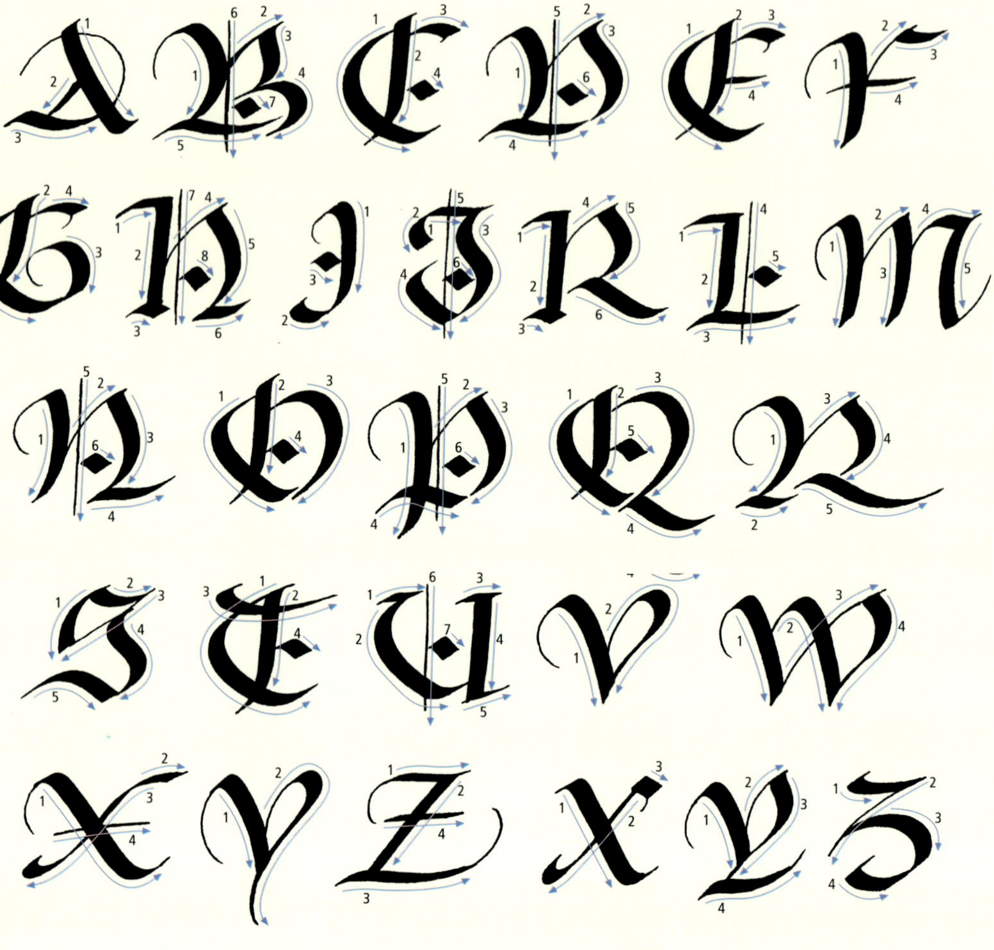

COMMON MISTAKES – CAPITALS

The capitals are bold and extravagant in width compared with the lower-case letters. One common mistake that is often made is that the letters are constructed too narrow – they should be very wide. Take care with ascenders, keep thick strokes wide and full, and check that the bowls are well rounded.

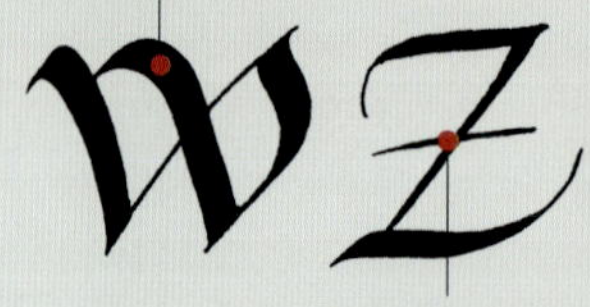

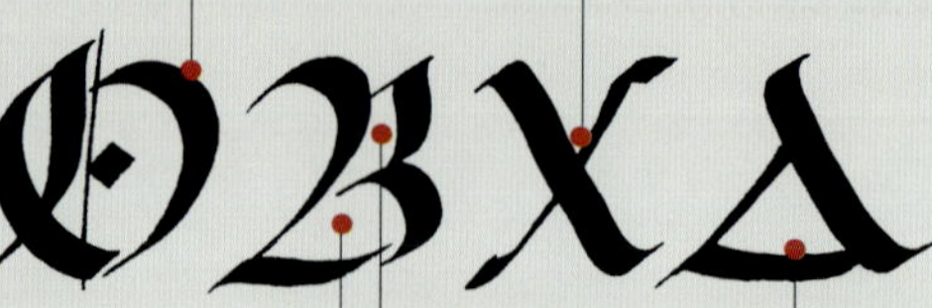

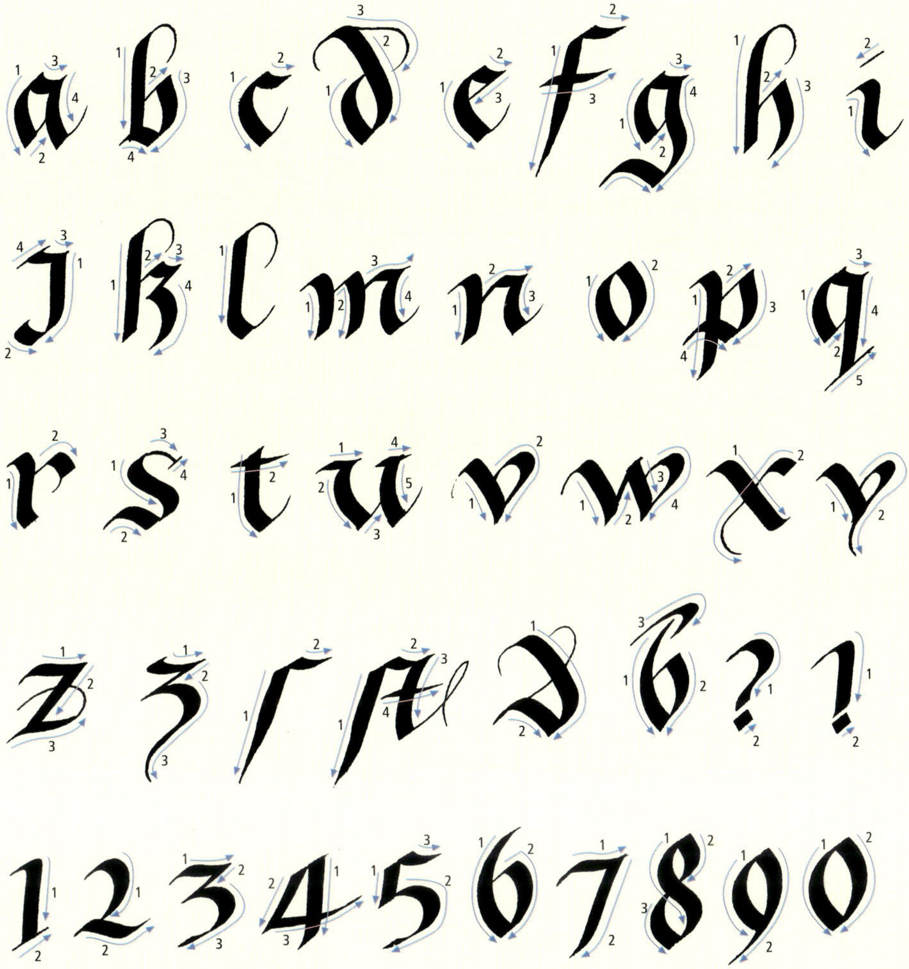

COMMON MISTAKES – LOWER CASE

There are many pen lifts with changes of nib angle, and much use of manipulation in this script which often interrupts the flow and rhythm. Keep the hand flowing without making the ascenders droopy or over-emphasizing the end strokes.

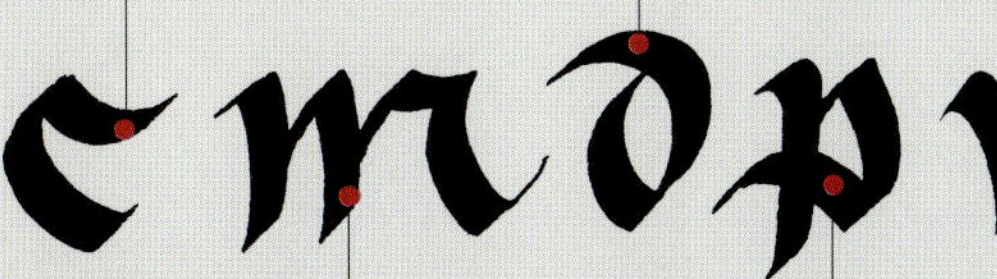

The curve is too accentuated and needs to be flatter.

The back of the ascender is longer and straighter before it curves.

Legs are unevenly spaced and the last stroke too close.

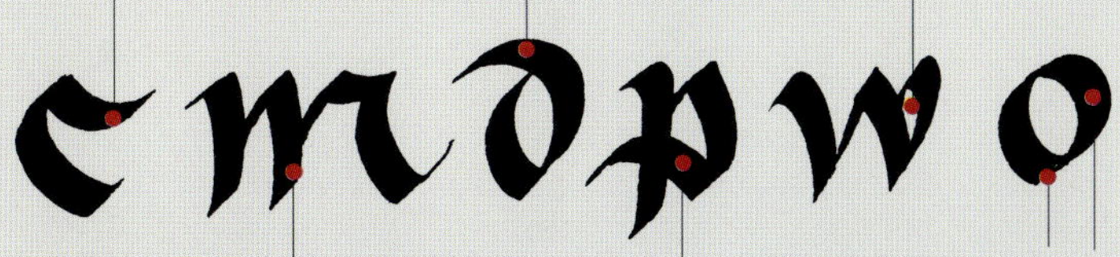

Legs are unevenly balanced and should be less cramped.

Stroke of the curve is too high and should be flattened to open up the bowl.

The shape is slightly too wide and the sharpened points not accentuated sufficiently.

Neuland hand

Most modern scripts used by calligraphers today are influenced by the writing of people who lived many centuries ago. This, however, is not true for Neuland, or 'New World' as it actually translates into English. Designed in 1923 by Rudolph Koch (1874–1934) as a typeface, the originality of its form, a sans serif with attitude, inspired its early use as a decorative script. Rudolph Koch cut the original punches freehand, which accounts for the irregularity in some of the sizing and gives Neuland its special feel. At first the written version was true to the typeface with very round counters. It takes a minimum of four strokes to write an original Neuland 'O'. However, during the course of time, tastes change, and even a script whose history is as well documented as that of Neuland is not immune to this. The 'O' and its associated letters are often, nowadays, written more simply, with counters that are pointed rather than round. This gives quite a different feel to the script, and makes it considerably quicker to write – a modern Neuland 'O' can be written in two strokes rather than four. The preferred style is a matter of choice but, for the sake of harmony, only one style should be used in any single piece of work.

Rudolph Koch often wrote this hand with a rule drawn between the lines and colour added to selected spaces producing a really fresh and striking visual effect. The eye-catching nature of Neuland has not diminished over the years, and it has been used by countless designers and advertisers from the 1920s up to the present day.

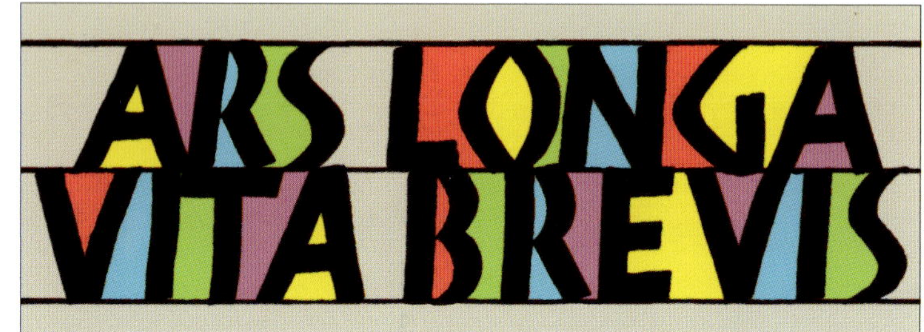

The basic rules

Because this script is based on a typeface, it does not have the inherent rhythm that a script that has developed over time from its writing instrument and usage has. The pen angle changes from stroke to stroke, and even within a stroke, but a guideline is to make vertical and diagonal strokes with a flat pen angle of 0 degrees, and horizontal strokes with the pen held at 90 degrees. The aim is always to achieve the maximum weight of line whatever the direction of the stroke. This gives the hand its characteristic boldness.

The original Neuland, with its round internal counters, has been joined by a variation with pointed internal counters. Both versions are fully illustrated here, but should not be intermixed. Take care to make joins of strokes clean and sharp, particularly in 'B' and 'R'.

LETTER HEIGHT

This should be no higher than four and a half nib widths and no lower than four nib widths. A height of four nib widths gives a heavier letter.

LETTER SLOPE

This script should be written without a slope.

PEN ANGLES

The majority of strokes are made with a pen angle of 0 degrees or 90 degrees. When writing round letters the angle varies to ensure that the width of the line remains constant.

90°

0°

Practice exercise: **Neuland hand**

Without forming letters, practise both vertical and horizontal strokes, making sure that the hand is turned to the correct position. Also practise drawing diagonal and curved lines, aiming to always hold the pen at an angle that gives the widest line possible. This is a constructed hand and therefore it lacks the fluency of a drawn script. Two types of Neuland are shown on the following pages – modern and traditional. The practice exercise follows the modern hand.

Group

Strokes (1st = red, 2nd = blue, 3rd = green)

Round or circular

O C G Q
B D P U R

It may be necessary to manipulate the pen angle to maintain the even thickness of the curved strokes. The curve ends with the line still at the same width. Note that the second stroke of 'O' and 'Q' begins and ends within the first stroke.

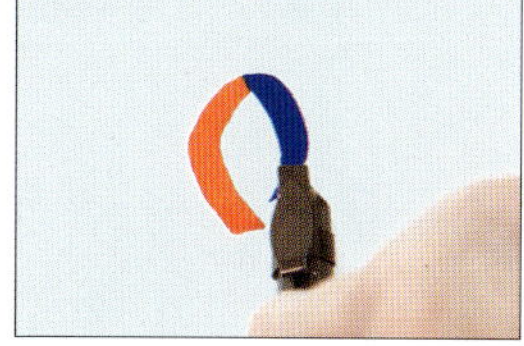

Both strokes are drawn with a flat pen angle of 0 degrees. The curve should not be angular nor should it be too pronounced.

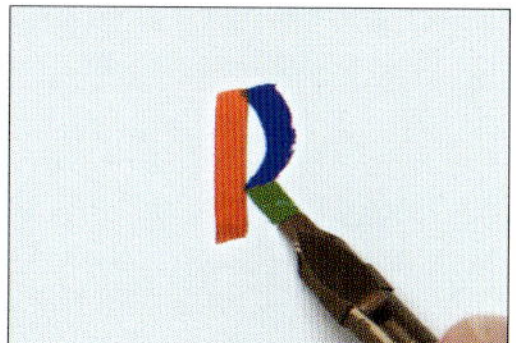

Both the first and second strokes are written with a flat pen angle of 0 degrees. The third stroke maintains a flat pen angle.

Straight

I E F H
J K L T

Probably the easiest group of letters. The pen angle should be 0 degrees for vertical strokes and 90 degrees for horizontal strokes. Where the strokes join, the second should start within the first. Note that the letter 'J' is the second stroke of the letter 'U'.

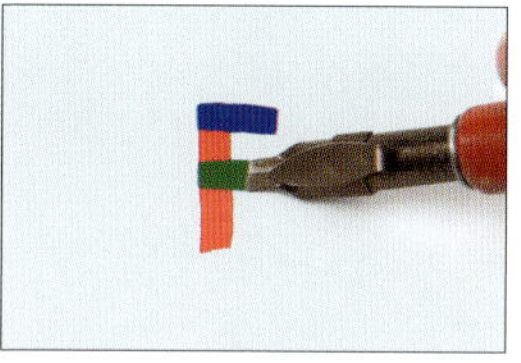

The second and third strokes start within the first. Keep the third stroke shorter than the second so that the letter is well balanced.

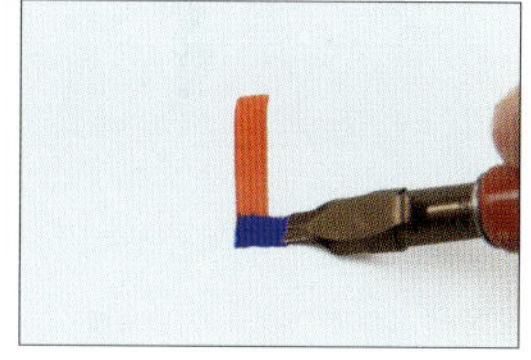

The first stroke is written with a flat pen angle of 0 degrees. The second stroke is written with a pen angle of 90 degrees.

Diagonal

A V M N
W X Y Z

A flat pen angle of 0 degrees must be maintained for all the diagonal strokes. Always start at the top of the letter and draw the pen downwards. The horizontal strokes are written with a pen angle of 90 degrees.

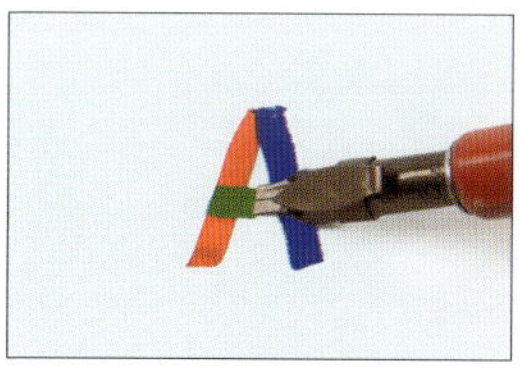

Make the diagonals using a flat pen angle. The third stroke starts within the first stroke and finishes well inside the second.

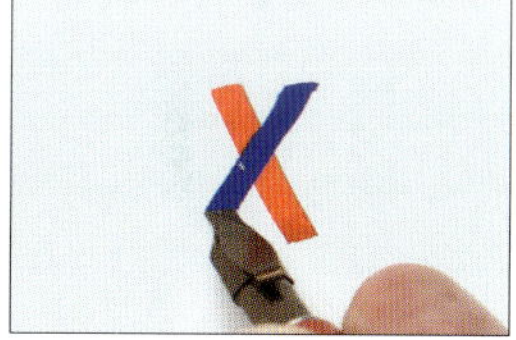

The second stroke starts at the top line a little bit in from where the bottom of the first stroke finishes. They cross at the optical middle.

Ungrouped

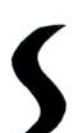

The 'S' does not fit in to any of the other groups. It is probably the most difficult of all the letters as it requires changes of direction and pen manipulation within the single stroke that forms the letter. Practice makes perfect!

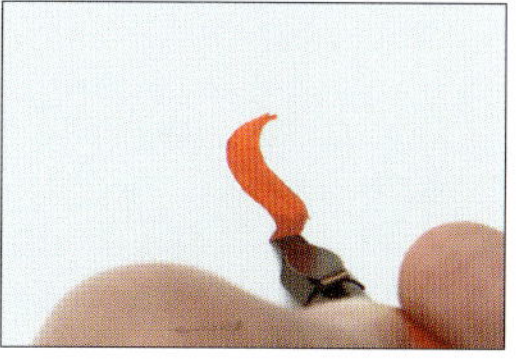

Start at the top of the letter and smoothly draw the pen downwards, manipulating the angle to keep an even thickness of line.

Tip: Neuland makes a big impact when used for posters and other similar projects. When written in black it really stands out and also photocopies well. Black gouache is often a better writing medium than black ink as it is easier to wash off nibs.

Neuland hand

MODERN

COMMON MISTAKES – MODERN

The characteristic of Neuland, whether the modern or the original version, is its extreme weight. While its letters are sans serif they have attitude and no weaknesses should be allowed to creep in.

Without the overlap of the first two strokes the letter appears weak.

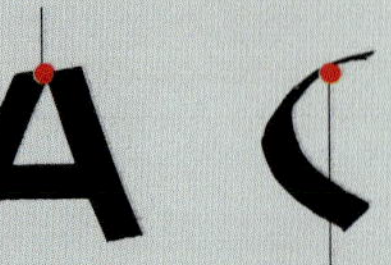

An incorrect pen angle has been used.

An incorrect pen angle has been used.

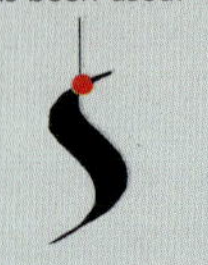

The curves are too exaggerated and the second stroke has not begun and finished within the first stroke.

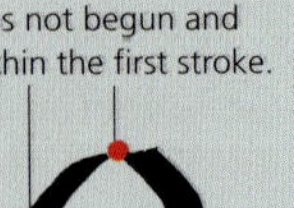

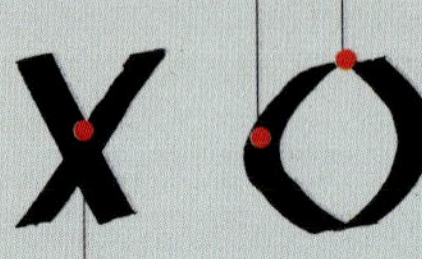

Letter is too wide and crosses too low.

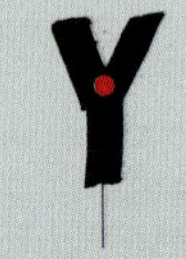

The 'V' shape of the 'Y' is too short.

TRADITIONAL

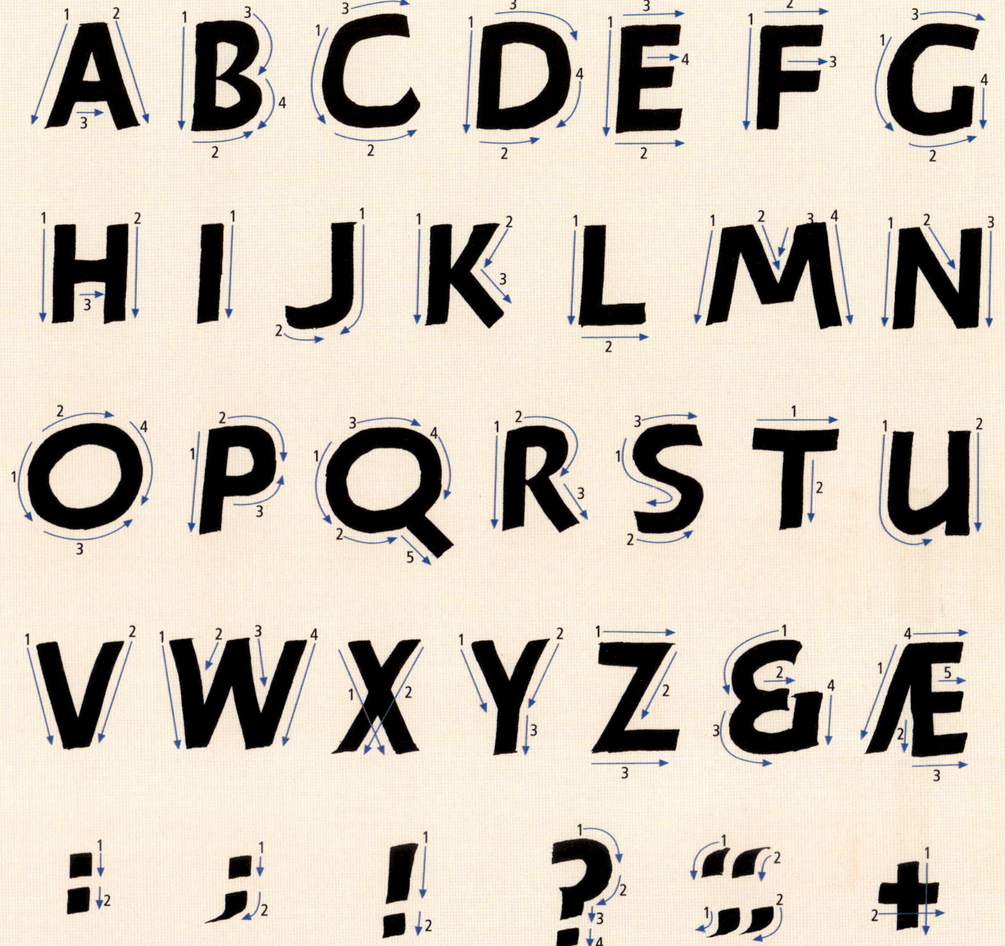

COMMON MISTAKES – TRADITIONAL

Take care to keep the letters even and balanced in appearance. Crossbars should be centrally positioned – neither too high nor too low. It is important to use the correct number of strokes to draw the circular shapes, otherwise the counters will look pointed.

Crossbar too high.

Letter too narrow.

Incorrect pen angle.

Pen angle not maintained on the curved stroke.

Crossbar too low.

Downstroke not in the middle of the crossbar.

Downstroke too high.

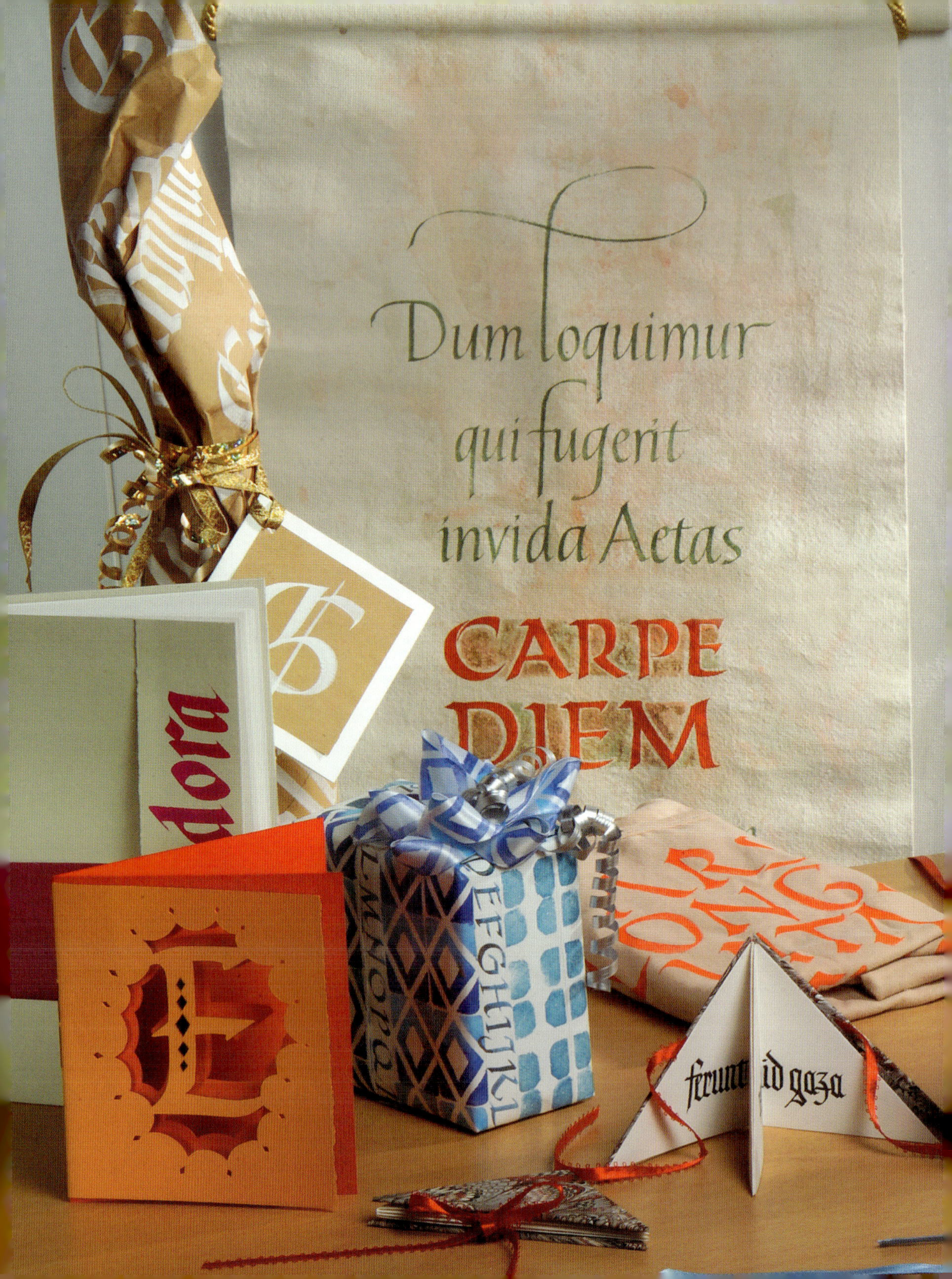
Dum loquimur
qui fugerit
invida Aetas
CARPE
DIEM

Calligraphic Projects

Having mastered the fundamental techniques of calligraphy, you can enjoy the rewarding process of putting calligraphic skills to creative use. This section contains 36 inspiring projects that enable you to practise calligraphy while creating a beautiful keepsake or gift. There is something for all occasions – from decorative boxes to handmade notebooks and scripted T-shirts – with each project allowing space for individual artistic expression and interpretation.

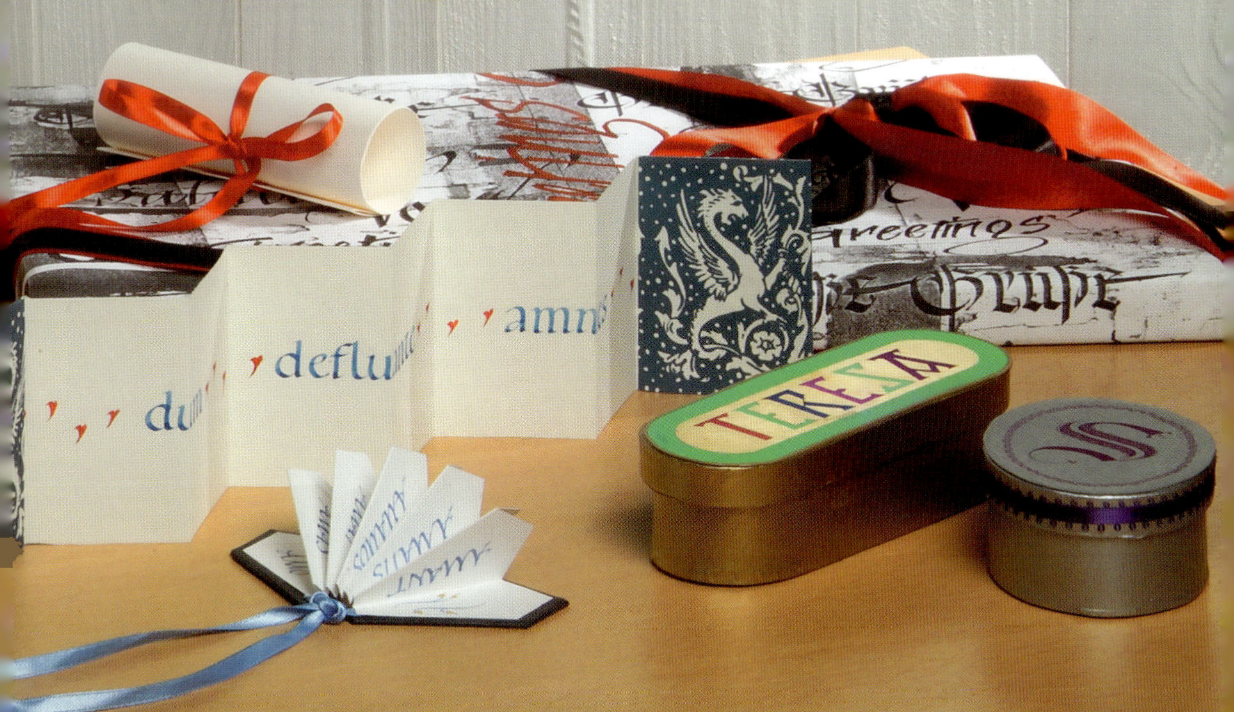

Quotation in graduated colour

Writing with coloured gouache paint or coloured ink is great fun, and will add extra interest to a piece of work. Creating a gradual change in the colour when writing the letters adds variation. All that is required is practice in loading the pen with different coloured paint from a brush, and in choosing colours that work well alongside each other. Learning to mix up each colour to achieve the best results is also important.

Gouache paint has been used for the writing as it has an opaque finish when dry, giving a good, even colour to the letters. Coloured inks are just as easy to use, but the calligraphy produced using inks is more transparent. Learning to blend colours together to create the best effect takes practice so it is worth having some trials first.

Begin by choosing only two colours from the three primary colours: red, blue and yellow. The two colours used in this project provide harmonious changes in colour – from red, through to orange and yellow.

Squeeze about 1cm (1/2in) primary red gouache into a mixing dish or palette and add water until the consistency resembles thin cream. Have your practice paper ready for writing. Load the brush with paint and feed the paint onto the dip pen by stroking it across the nib and reservoir. Practise the Foundational script in one colour first. Then try out the ideas on layout paper, before gradually mixing the colours as you write.

Materials

- *Mixing palette*
- *Gouache paints or coloured inks: primary red and cadmium yellow*
- *Two mixing brushes*
- *Two water pots*
- *Dip pen: William Mitchell 2 1/2 (medium nib)*
- *Layout or practice paper*
- *Kitchen paper*
- *Scalpel or craft (utility) knife*
- *Metal ruler*
- *Self-healing cutting mat*
- *Good quality white paper*
- *Card (stock) for mount, if required*

The design

This project combines primary red gouache and cadmium yellow. The quotation is written in Foundational script. The finished project is worked on good quality white paper but once you feel confident with the technique, you can start experimenting using coloured paper.

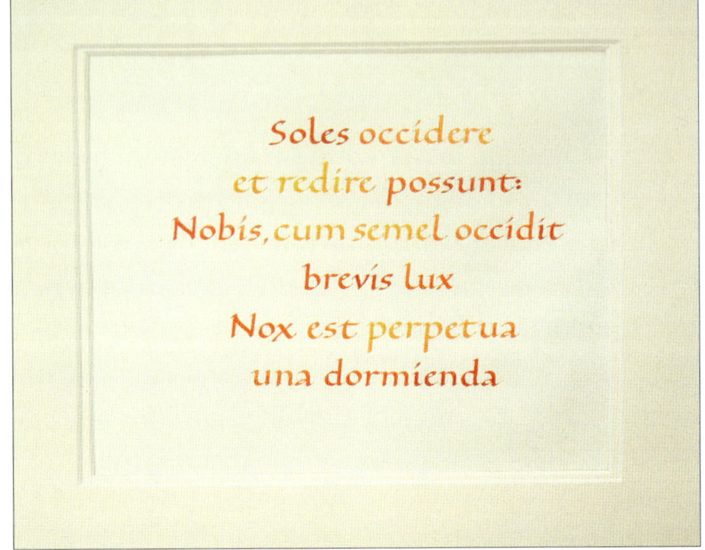

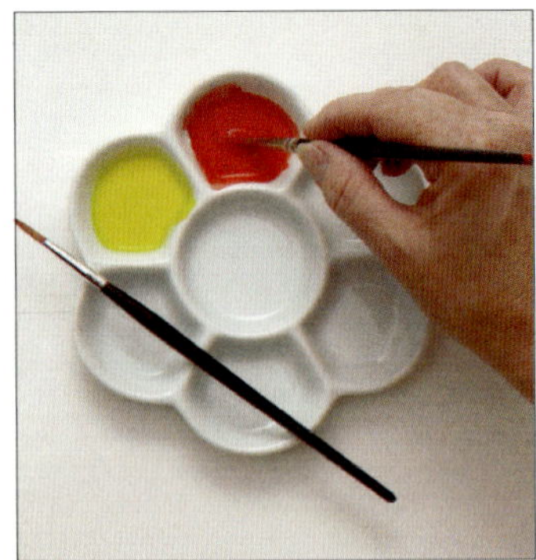

1 In separate sections of a palette or in separate mixing dishes combine primary red gouache and cadmium yellow gouache with water until each is of a thin, creamy consistency. Use a clean brush for each colour. Mix a generous amount of each so that you do not run out halfway through the writing.

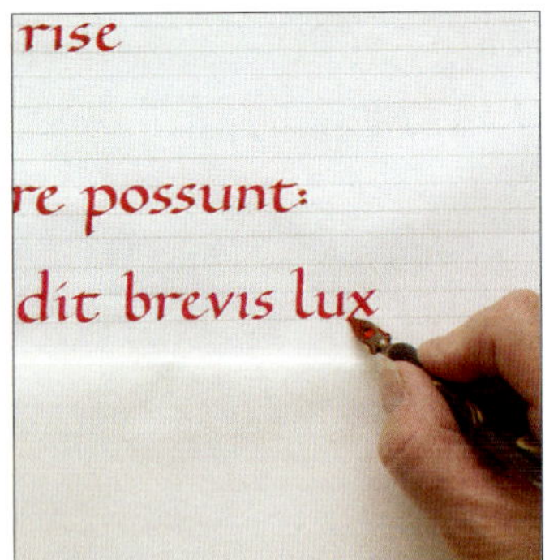

2 Use the dip pen to write out the quotation on a practice sheet of layout paper or similar, using one colour only. Load the brush with red gouache and feed the colour into the pen by stroking the brush across the reservoir and nib.

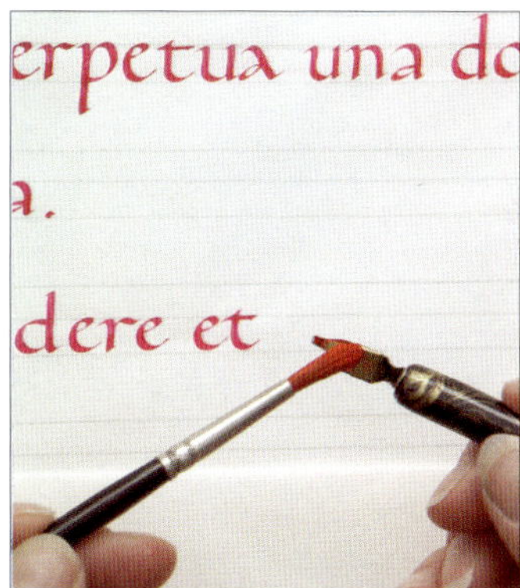

3 Write carefully and when required wipe the pen with the brush loaded with red paint, recharging to maintain the flow of colour.

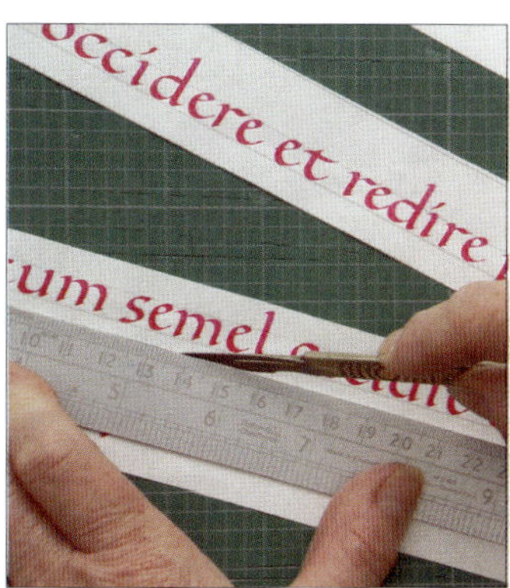

4 Cut the text into sections and arrange these on another piece of layout paper to create a good layout or design. Once you have decided on the layout to use, paste the text into position.

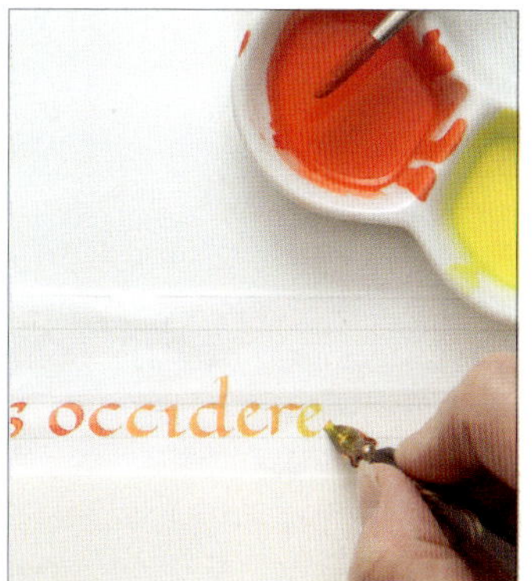

5 Practise writing using two colours. First, place another piece of layout paper over the top of the pasted design and begin to rewrite the quotation, using the original underneath as a guide. Use a different brush for each colour, wiping the nib with the different colours as you proceed. Blend the second colour into the first colour by carefully adding the second colour to the top of the pen nib with the second loaded brush. The colour will mix gradually in the pen as the paint travels through the nib on to the paper.

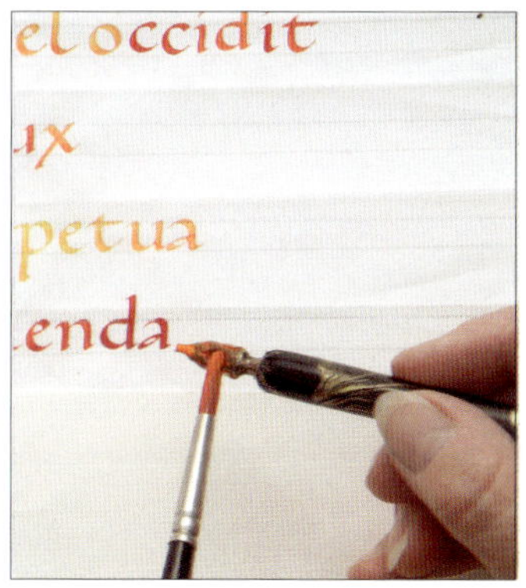

6 Change back to the first colour by loading the pen nib again from the top. The idea is to create gradual changes of colour throughout the writing. A subtle effect requires practice and your first attempts may not appear as gradual as you would like.

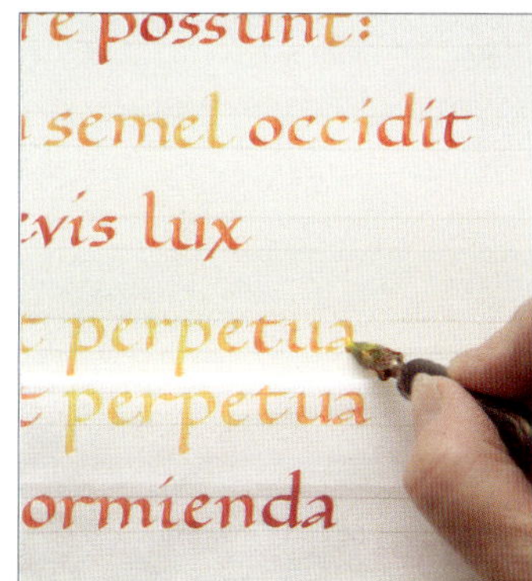

7 Change to good quality paper and prepare your guidelines for writing. Place a guard sheet underneath the section you are working on and, using the writing from your practice sheet as a guide, write out your quotation as the finished piece of work.

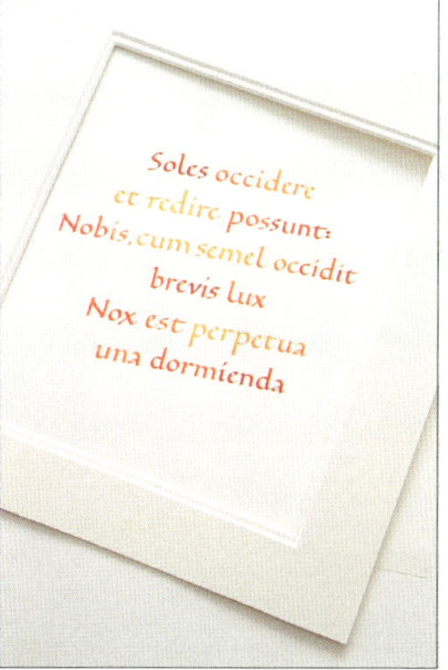

8 Cut or buy a small mount in a similar or contrasting colour to frame your quotation.

Tip: Sometimes it may be helpful to work with three colours especially if using a very dark colour such as dark blue and a very light colour such as a pale yellow. Mix the two colours that are being used to produce a mid-colour, in this case mid-green. You will then be working with three colours: dark blue, mid-green and pale yellow, using one pen but three brushes, one for each colour. This will give you a range of changes through your writing from yellow, yellow-green, mid-green, blue-green through to dark blue.

Flourished decorative letter

'Swash' or 'Flourished' Italic letters are based on Roman Capitals. The flourishes are the fluid extensions that make the letters appear decorative. Written at about seven nib widths with a slight forward slant, flourished Italics can be elegant and full of movement. They are also fun to do and can be used with added decoration on cards, at the beginning of a calligraphically written quotation, to spell out a child's name, or presented just as a single letter to be framed.

Every letter of the alphabet can be adapted in the same decorative way. You can use black ink, or write in colour and add detail within the shape of the letter itself, or you can decorate with gouache around the whole letter. If you are very ambitious, you can create a whole alphabet design using the same decorations for each letter, or instead create 26 individual patterns.

The main letter shape should be written with a large nib or an automatic pen. There are many different pens with large nibs you can use to create multiple strokes, including coit pens or even your own handmade reed and balsa wood pens. Try experimenting with different writing tools to expand your ideas and encourage creativity.

The more exuberant the writing the more thought needs to be given to the space allowed for layout and design; be careful not to over-flourish the letters. Flourishing can become even more adventurous, innovative and exciting with experience.

The design

In this project a flourished letter is created (and decorated with white gouache) by mixing up two colours. It could be used as an initial of a child's name and placed in a frame or on a card.

Materials

- *Gouache paints: ultramarine blue, primary red, lemon yellow, primary blue, zinc white and permanent white*
- *Brush for mixing paint*
- *Palette or mixing dishes*
- *Automatic pen or dip pen with a large nib*
- *Layout or practice paper*
- *Dip pen such as William Mitchell 5 (small nib)*
- *Hot-pressed watercolour paper*
- *Fine paintbrush No.000*
- *Two water pots*

Tip: Begin by writing in formal Italic. Lead into the chosen letters by extending the first serif – making it longer and more sweeping – before beginning the letter. Start with the letters you are most comfortable with.

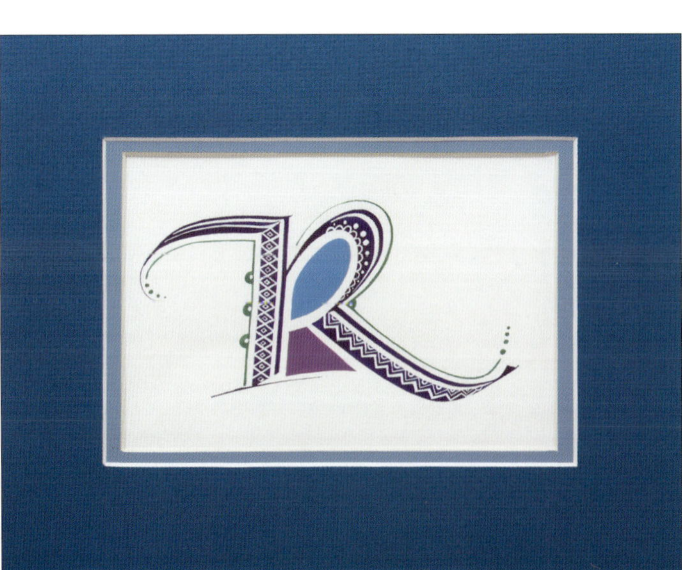

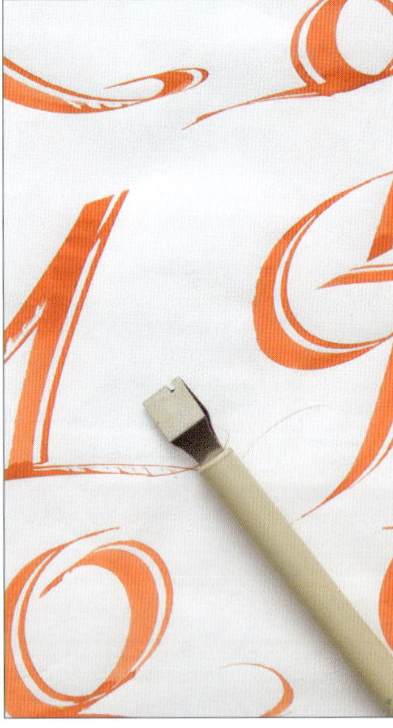

1 Mix some gouache paint in a palette or small container to the consistency of cream. Load your large pen with the paint and try creating some large, different flourished Italic capitals. Use layout paper to practise elongated serifs leading into and out of the letters. Do not be over ornate with your flourishes; try to keep them balanced and under control.

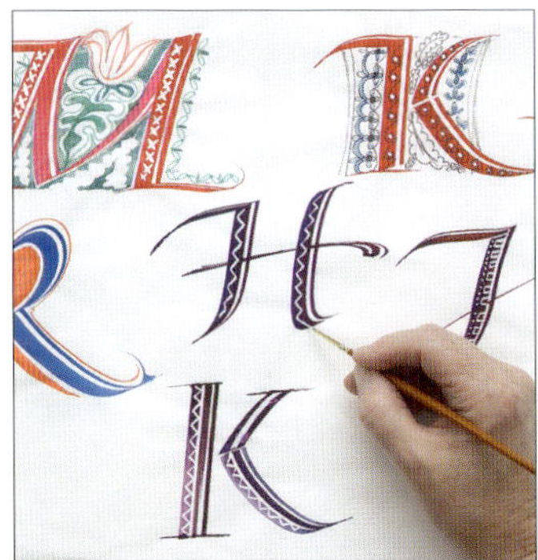

2 Try out some different decorative ideas, which you can add to the letter using the smaller nib and filigree lines and designs.

3 Choose a capital flourished Italic letter 'R' to develop and write it carefully on the watercolour paper with the large pen. Mix ultramarine blue and primary red gouache to make dark blue. Using a brush, load the nib with the colour. Do the stem first, twisting the pen to get the fine lines.

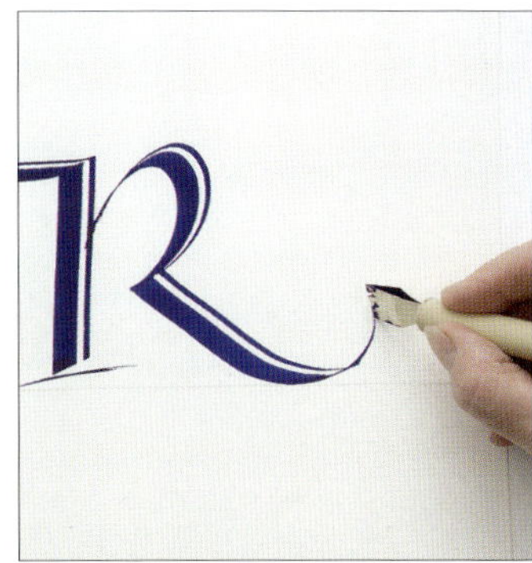

4 Add the fine lines to the flourishes with the edge of the pen nib for extra decoration.

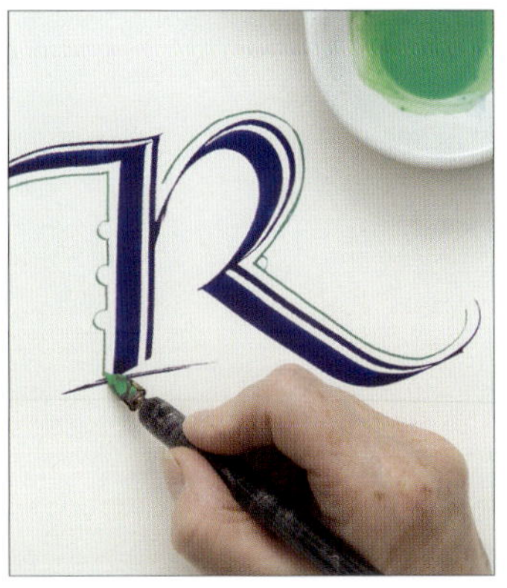

5 Add the fine lines around the letter in green – mix lemon yellow and primary blue gouache with a dip pen and a fine nib.

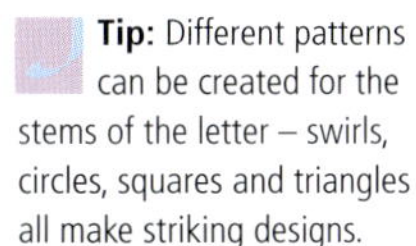

Tip: Different patterns can be created for the stems of the letter – swirls, circles, squares and triangles all make striking designs.

Tip: Various colour combinations can be used to write the letter and decorate the counters. Try out several ideas.

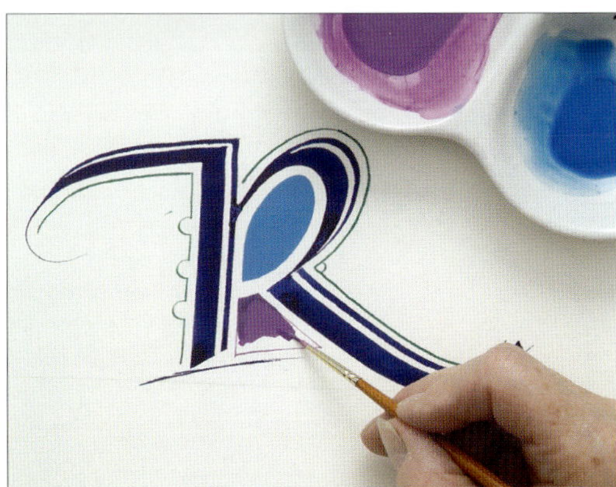

6 Add further embellishment to the letter by filling in the letter counter or centre with primary blue gouache and purple – a mix of primary blue and primary red.

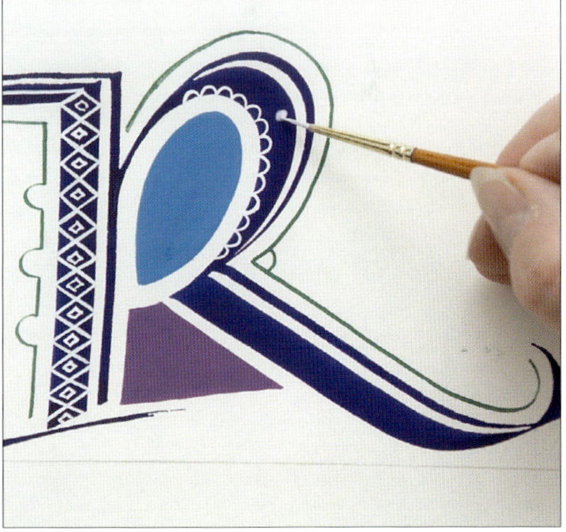

7 Paint filigree designs and dots on the letter with a fine brush and permanent white gouache to finish the letter. If you wish, frame your final letter with a matching colour.

One-word resist on a wash background

This is an excellent opportunity to work spontaneously with water and paint effects and to experiment with colour and texture. There are easy ways to produce exciting visual background effects by using a brush alone, as this project clearly demonstrates.

In this design a variegated wash is created with acrylic inks or watercolour paint and the colours are left to dry. A one-word resist is then added by writing over the background with a dip pen that has been dipped in art masking fluid. This forms an area of resist, which further paint cannot penetrate. The intensity and texture of the piece can be built up with colour using brush and paint effects. A toothbrush can be used to randomly spatter paint or ink over an area on the surface of the paper adding further texture and colour to the overall design of the piece.

To spatter colour on the surface of the paper, mix up paint to the consistency of thin cream. Dip the toothbrush into the paint or ink and, with the bristles uppermost, run a ruler or a narrow strip of stiff card over the top of the bristles towards you. This will create spatter away from you, over the paper's surface. Point the toothbrush to direct the spatter to the areas that you wish to cover. Different colours can be used. Rinse the toothbrush when you change colour, or use several toothbrushes – one for each colour. Different sized toothbrushes or other stiff brushes will create larger or smaller spatter. Experiment with the different effects you can produce – fine baby toothbrushes will produce fine dots of paint; nail brushes will produce larger dots of spatter.

Stencils can be used to make individual areas of interesting colour and texture. Gold and silver metallic powders add interest and sparkle to a project and will stick to wet paint. Think creatively about how you can make your project individual and exciting – the process of inventing different techniques when using paint introduces interesting and varied results that can be applied to all sorts of different projects.

The design

This project is centred around the word *Fantasia,* which is Italian for 'fantasy'. The word is written in Batarde script surrounded by random spatter and variegated washes. A star shape is stencilled in the background.

Materials

- *Layout or practice paper*
- *Dip pen: William Mitchell 0 or 1 (large nib)*
- *Watercolour paper*
- *A large brush*
- *Acrylic inks or watercolour paints*
- *Masking fluid*
- *Old newspapers and old toothbrushes*
- *Stencil or transparent sheet to cut a stencil*
- *Gold and silver metallic powders*
- *Water pots*
- *Mixing brushes*
- *Gum arabic (optional)*
- *Eraser*

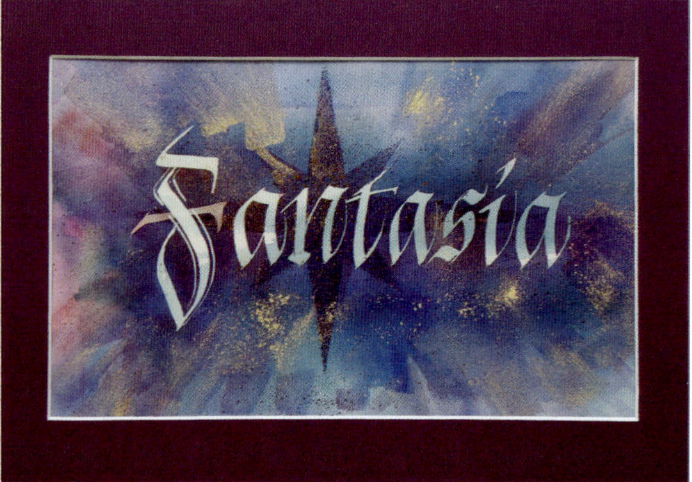

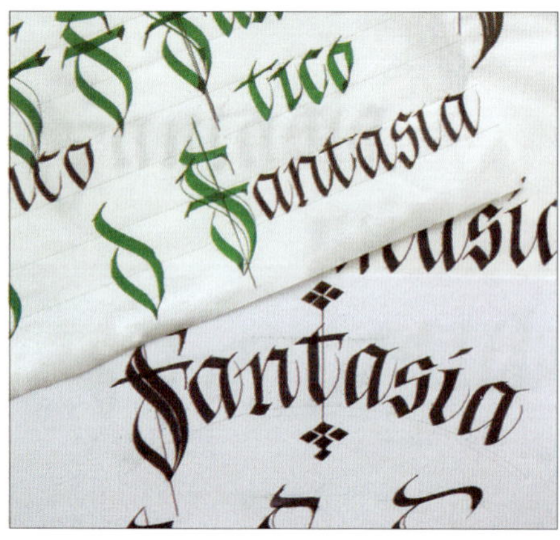

1 Practise writing the word *Fantasia* in Batarde script on your practice or layout paper. Decide on the size you wish your letters to be and the colours to be used in the design to convey the essence of the word you have chosen.

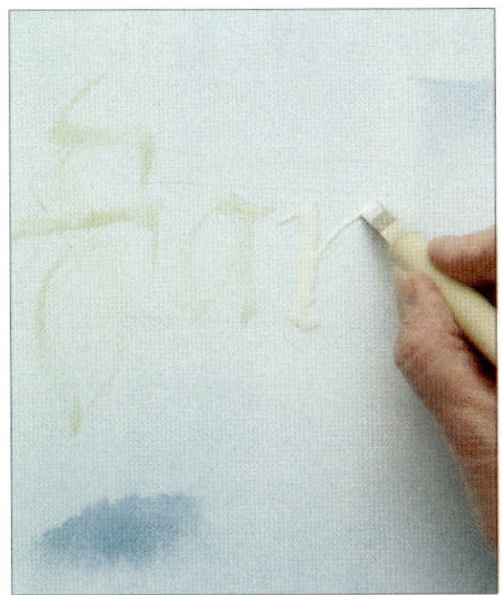

2 Using the watercolour paper, paint a variegated wash with acrylic inks. Leave to dry. Write in Batarde script the word *Fantasia* using a large pen, dipped in masking fluid. While the masking fluid is drying, prepare the area in which you are going to work by covering the surfaces with scrap paper or old sheets of newspaper.

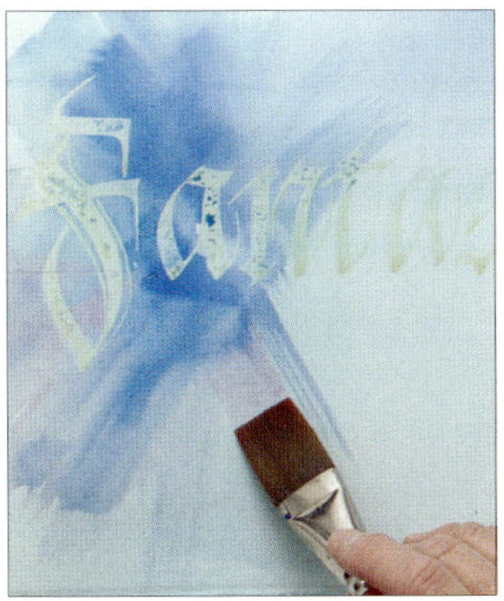

3 Paint small areas of the watercolour paper with random washes, using acrylic inks or watercolour paint, building up the colour. Leave to dry.

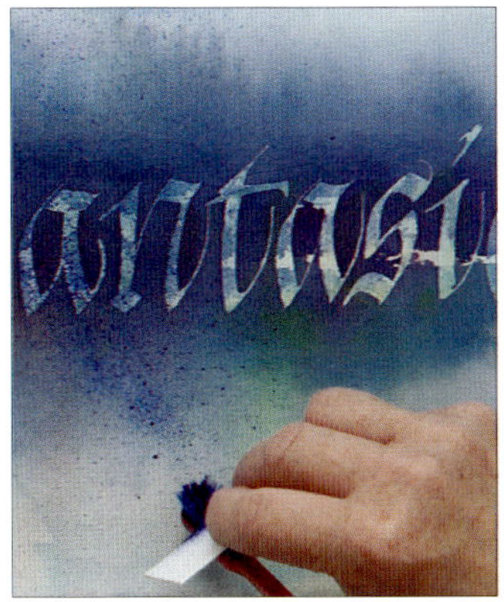

4 Use a toothbrush dipped in ink or paint to spatter different areas of the paper with fine sprays of colour to build up layers of different colours.

Tip: Test your spattering on newspaper first to perfect your technique. Also test on the newspaper just before spattering on to the piece of work. Sometimes it is easy to overload your brush with the ink or paint and then it blobs everywhere.

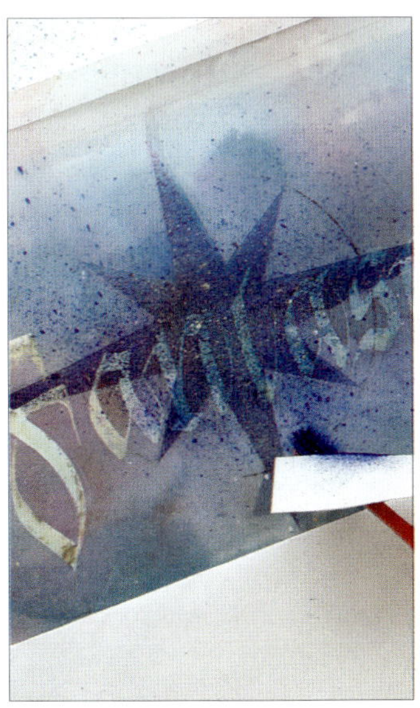

5 Choose a stencil shape, such as a star. Shield the rest of the work with paper. Spatter colour through the stencil to create a pattern.

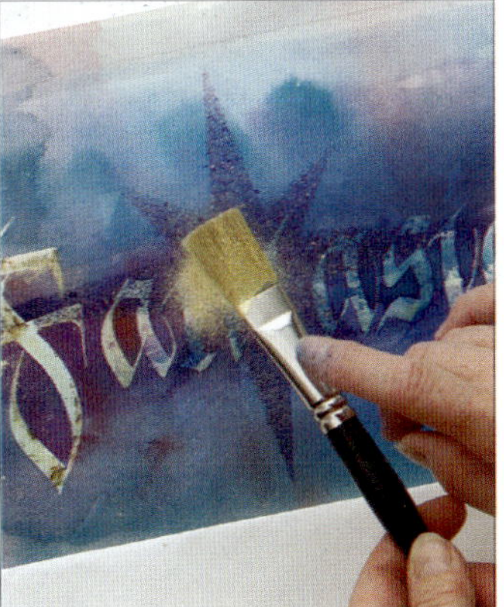

6 Before the stencil shape has fully dried, shake some gold or silver metallic powder over the design. It will stick to the wet paint and make it sparkle. Dust away the excess when dry. Alternatively, mix the metallic powder with water and two drops of gum arabic, which makes it stick to the paper and spatter the resulting gold or silver paint into your work. This paint can also be used in the pen to add decoration.

Tip: The spatter can be blended carefully with a large damp brush if it becomes too dotted. Carefully stroke the brush over the area to blend into the rest of the colour, and leave until dry.

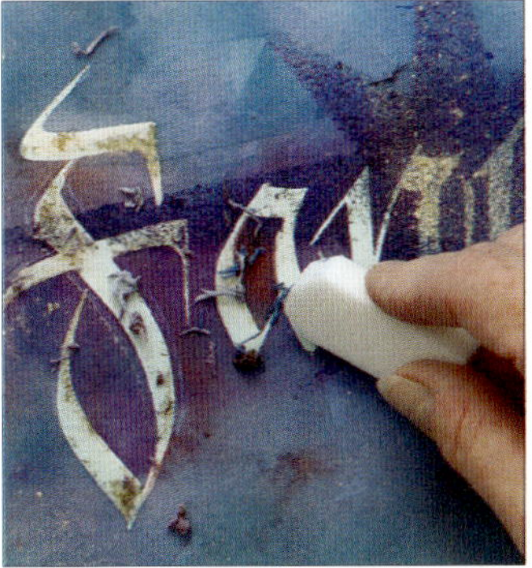

7 Finally, remove the masking fluid by carefully rubbing with an eraser, to reveal the hidden word underneath the layers of paint. If you wish, frame your artwork with a harmonious colour.

A poem and leaf print design

Printing can form the basis of interesting design and alleviates the need to draw or paint. This can be quite appealing for some calligraphers who are less confident about their artistic skills, or who would like to combine printing and calligraphy together in a simple and effective way.

In this project leaf printing is combined with calligraphy. Leaf prints are made by dropping leaves into gouache paint and then using an ink roller or brush to cover the leaves with paint. The leaf is pressed onto watercolour or coloured paper to create a design that combines with prose or poetry. This may relate to trees or flowers. Each subsequent print made with a painted leaf becomes a little paler than the previous imprint. For bold prints the paint will need to be replenished on each printing. Gouache paint will give dense, thick colour. Printing with acrylic inks produces a finer image.

Natural materials are ideal to use for design work. Leaves, ferns and grasses can all be used to create effective, quick results by dipping them in paint and printing them as a well arranged design. This project features a small mounted panel in green, which would make a delightful gift for a gardener.

Materials

- *Layout or practice paper*
- *Metal ruler*
- *Pencil*
- *Gouache paints: oxide of chromium and forest green, alizarin red and cadmium yellow, or acrylic inks*
- *Dip pens and various nibs, including William Mitchell 2 1/2 (medium nib)*
- *Scalpel or craft (utility) knife*
- *Self-healing cutting mat*
- *Glue*
- *Collection of small leaves*
- *Kitchen paper cut into squares*
- *Paintbrush*
- *Mixing palette or small tray*
- *Ink roller (optional)*
- *Tweezers (optional)*
- *Watercolour or coloured paper*
- *Card stock for mount*

The design

This is a design to complement a Latin poem about trees. Carolingian hand has been chosen to create a soft, natural feel, echoing a gently undulating landscape. The writing is in soft green oxide of chromium gouache colour with a small amount of forrest green. These colours were also used to print the leaves with the addition of alizarin red and cadmium yellow to add a more realistic feel.

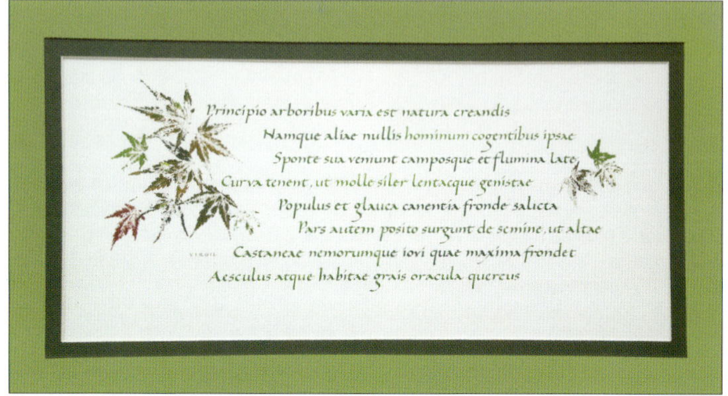

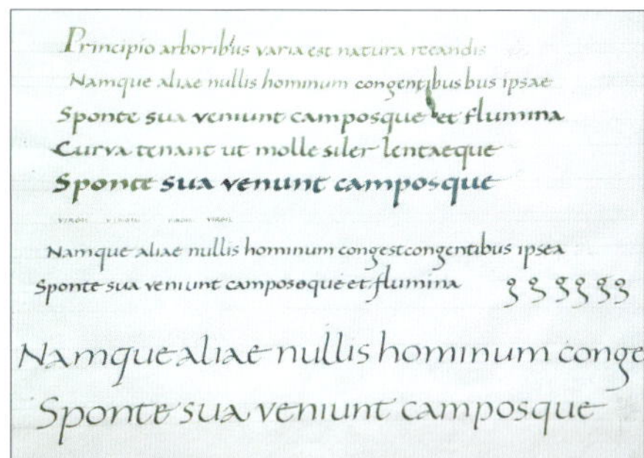

1 Rule up a piece of layout paper so you can practise the text. Write in colour using gouache paint or inks. Experiment with different letter weights and sizes of Carolingian script.

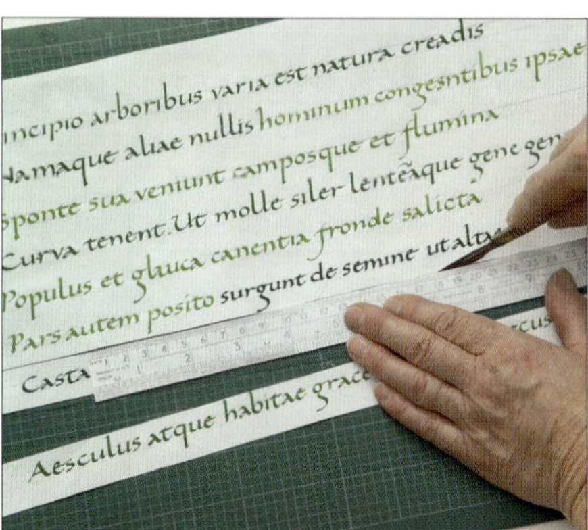

2 When the letterforms are correct and you have decided the size of the writing, write out the poem using the chosen nib. Try some different arrangements, remembering to include the leaves in each so that you can judge what your panel will look like when finished. Using a scalpel carefully cut out the writing in fine strips.

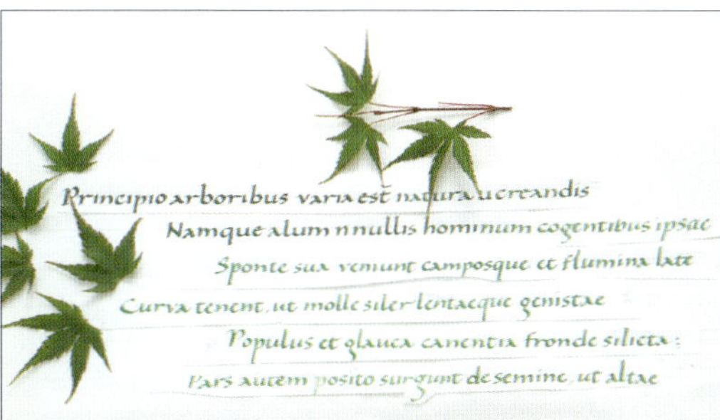

3 When you have decided on a design, paste the writing into position. Place the leaves on the paper, too, and quickly draw round each to give yourself a guide. You may wish to do some trial printings with the leaves.

> **Tip:** The small squares of kitchen paper used to press the leaf patterns help to prevent smudging with the paint. Small pieces of paper can be used instead, which will give you reversed leaf patterns. These can be used in card making.

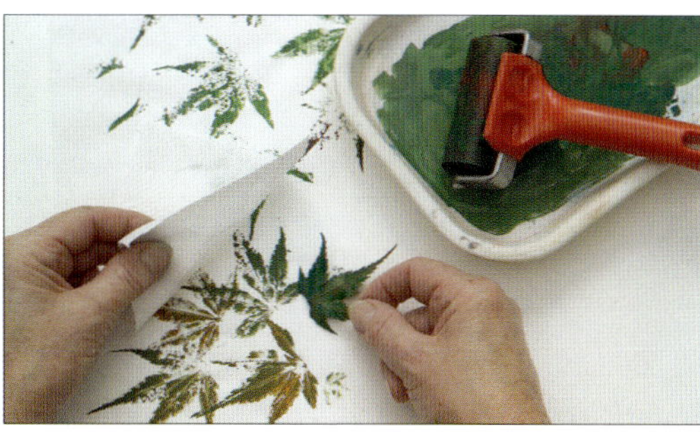

4 Squeeze the gouache colour, or acrylic ink, on to the small tray and mix them together with the ink roller or brush. Do not add water. Drop a leaf into the paint and press with the roller, or paint with the brush. The leaf will inevitably stick to the ink roller, but pick it off and lay it on to the paper in the position you have marked. Take a small piece of cut kitchen paper and press the leaf gently on to the paper. Remove it carefully with your fingers or tweezers. It may print a second time, though the impression will be much lighter. Discard the leaf when it becomes too wet.

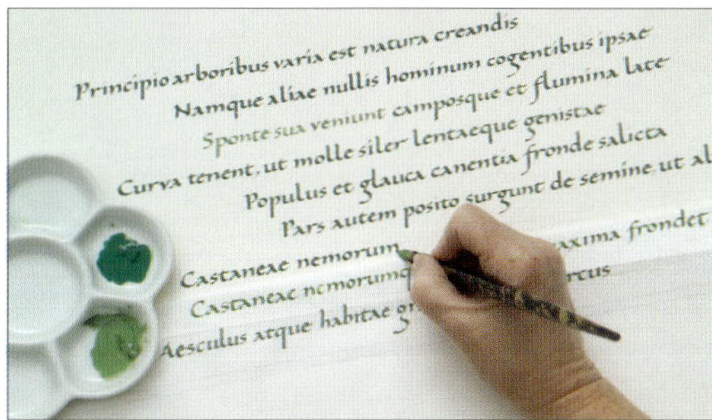

5 After practising leaf printing, rule up some good quality paper so you can begin on the project. Write the text first. When the text is dry, protect it against paint splashes by covering it with layout paper.

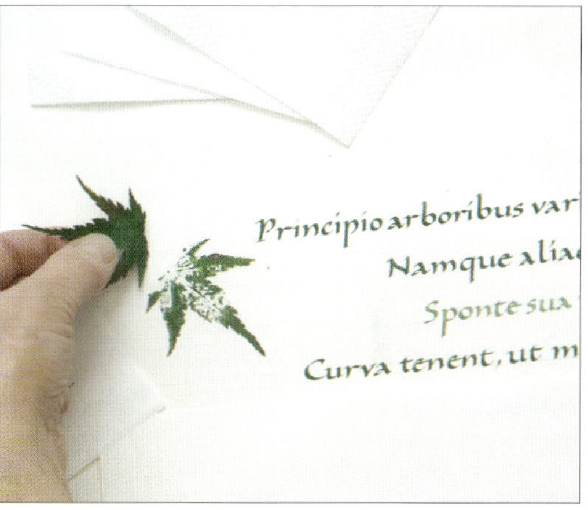

> **Tip:** If you choose leaves with strong textures the prints will appear more structured and interesting than without. If the leaves are very smooth, the resulting colour will be flat and solid.

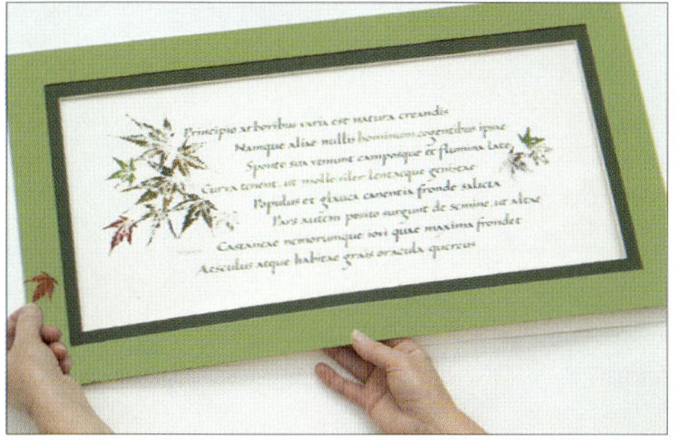

6 Print your leaf pattern, copying the design of your practice sheet. You may wish to enhance the leaf colours by adding small amounts of alizarin red and cadmium yellow to the colour in your palette, blending slightly with a roller or brush as before.

7 Mount your finished work in a suitable colour. You may find it effective to continue the leaf pattern on the mount.

Embellished gift box and tag

A hand-decorated box and tag gives a unique and personal touch to any gift. You can buy plain, undecorated cardboard boxes in a wide range of shapes and sizes from art and craft suppliers, or you may already have the perfect plain box at home, which you can use to decorate. If you wish, you can begin by painting a plain box with craft paint – and use this initial colour as the starting point of your design. A matching gift tag is easily created by reducing the tracing on a photocopier. This is then traced and transferred on to watercolour paper.

This project decorates the lid of a box with an initial letter to personalize it for a friend. The letter is outlined and then filled with gouache paint. Decorative detail is added and the letter finally embellished with silver paint. As a final touch, a ribbon is placed around the box and some ribbon attached to the matching gift tag.

There are many examples of initial letters in manuscripts from which you can take inspiration for your design. The letter in the project can be traced and then reduced or enlarged to fit your chosen box. You may prefer to transfer your chosen design directly on to the box lid, ready for decorating. However, if this is very small it will be quite difficult to work on. It is often easier to make a template by placing the lid of the box upside down on to some watercolour paper and drawing around the outside with a pencil. You will find it easier to work on a larger flat surface. When the design is completed, the template will be cut to shape and glued on to the lid of the box. Repeat the process for the gift tag by reducing the design on a photocopier by 30 per cent.

Tip: Consider making a box with a simple monogram by choosing two initial letters that work well together.

The design

An oval box has been selected for this project as the chosen letter 'S' fits very well into this shape. The box is painted silver with craft acrylic paint. The lid of the box is used as a template for the design and once finished will be cut out and glued on to the lid. A Versal letter 'S' is painted with purple gouache and embellished with silver. A simple decorative pen-made pattern encompasses the letter. A smaller version is made for the gift tag.

Materials

- *Small plain cardboard box with lid*
- *Layout or practice paper*
- *2B and 2H pencils*
- *Tracing paper*
- *Hot-pressed watercolour paper*
- *Photocopier*
- *Craft acrylic paint: silver*
- *Paint brushes, including size 0 brush*
- *Gouache paint: purple*
- *Pen with pointed nib: Gillott 303*
- *Scissors*
- *Hole punch*
- *PVA (white) or craft glue and brush*
- *Ribbon*

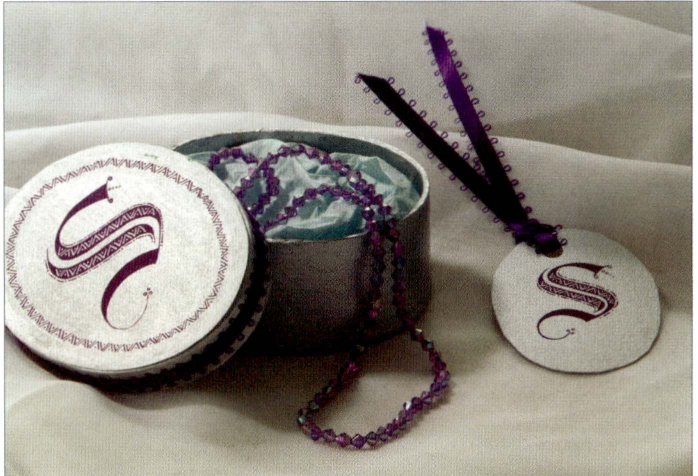

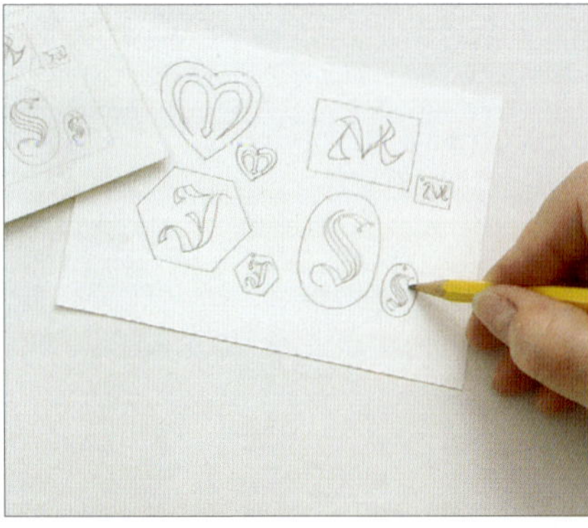

1 Consider the shape of your box and which kind of lettering would be most effective for it. A rounded letter is suitable for an oval box, while a small delicate letter might be suitable for a small heart-shaped box. For larger boxes a bolder letter would be more appropriate. Think whether the letter you have chosen may work well with a square, round or hexagonal box. Draw your design on to layout paper.

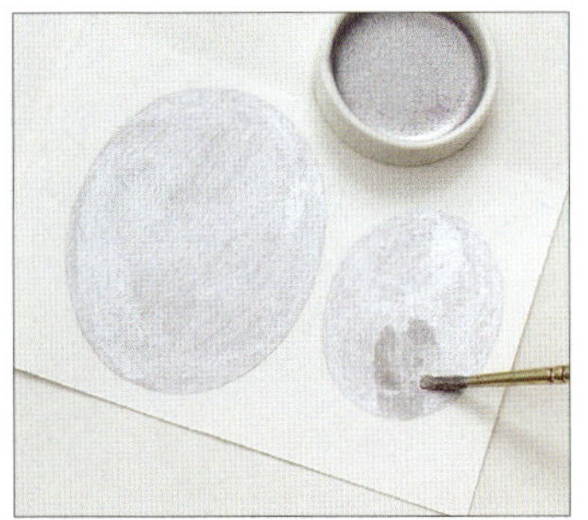

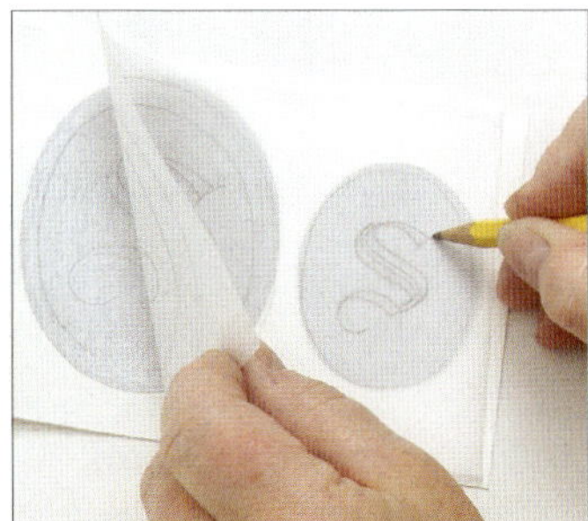

3 Trace down the Versal design on to the silver template and also trace the outline of the 80 per cent photocopy as a guideline for the decorative pattern. For the gift tag, trace and transfer the reduced design on to the smaller silver template.

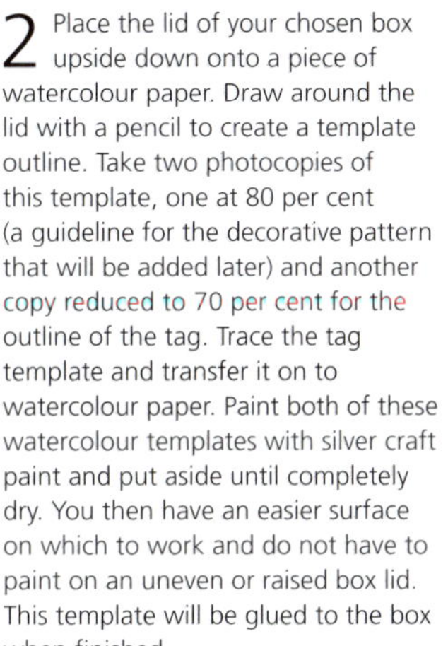

2 Place the lid of your chosen box upside down onto a piece of watercolour paper. Draw around the lid with a pencil to create a template outline. Take two photocopies of this template, one at 80 per cent (a guideline for the decorative pattern that will be added later) and another copy reduced to 70 per cent for the outline of the tag. Trace the tag template and transfer it on to watercolour paper. Paint both of these watercolour templates with silver craft paint and put aside until completely dry. You then have an easier surface on which to work and do not have to paint on an uneven or raised box lid. This template will be glued to the box when finished.

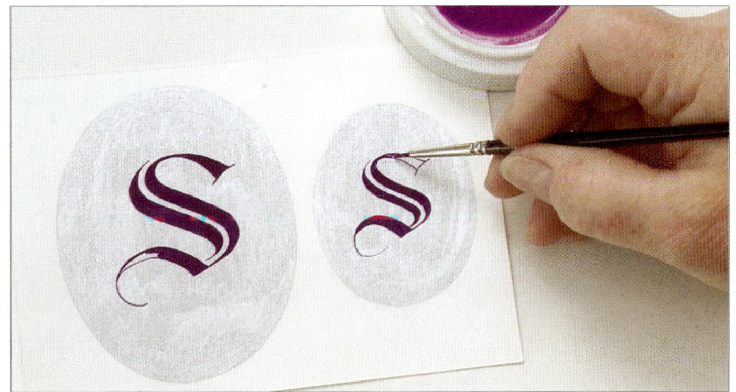

4 Outline the letter with some purple gouache paint using a pointed nib. Use a size 0 brush to paint the letter. Short, overlapping strokes will give you more control filling in the letter.

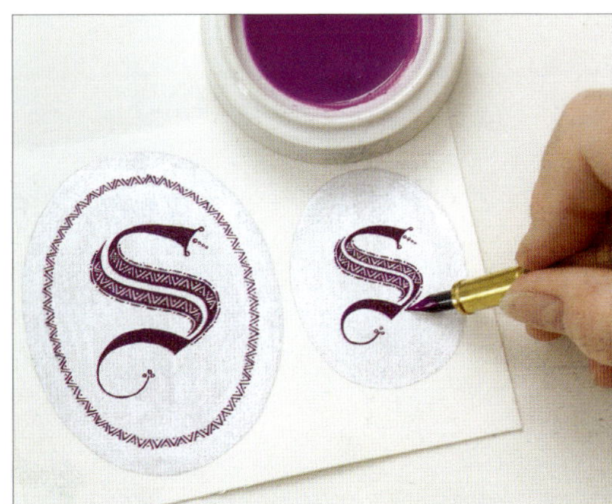

5 The lines and dots are now added using the pointed nib. The pen-made border is drawn and decorated with tiny dots. Once the paint has dried, slightly dilute some of the silver acrylic paint, or use silver gouache, and add the final embellishment to the letter. Then repeat the decorated initial to create the gift tag.

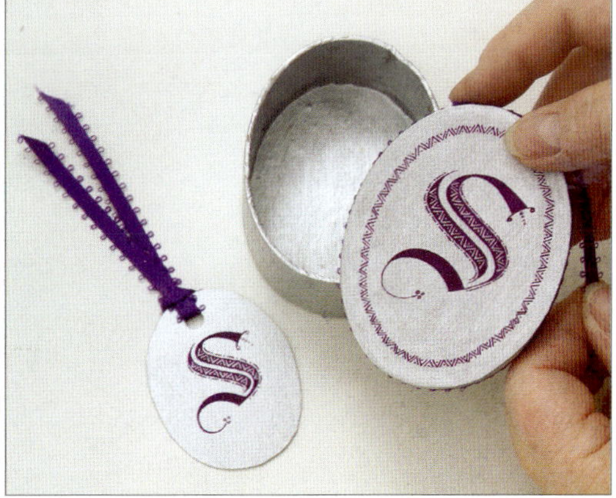

6 Carefully cut around each template. Make a hole in the top of the tag with a hole punch and thread some ribbon for a tie. Finally, glue your design on to the box lid with some craft glue or PVA glue, and place some ribbon around your completed box.

Decorated message on a pillow-box

This box is very easy to make and can be decorated in many different ways. You can use the template provided on this page to make a pillow-box of any size you like by reducing or enlarging it using a photocopier.

It is best to choose card that is 200gsm (90lb) or heavier. Generally, the larger the box, the thicker the card you need to use. The box in this project measures 10cm x 5cm (4in x 2in) at its narrowest point when folded. Use 250gsm (115lb) card if the size of the template is increased by 50 per cent or more.

A plain or textured card, in a colour of your choice, gives you an opportunity to create your own decoration. Adding a name or message will give the box a very personal touch.

Do not fold the card until you have finished your lettering, as it is far easier to work on a flat surface than on a curved area.

Experiment with ideas to decorate your box. A pleasing effect can be made by ruling chequered lines, painting every other square and writing an initial in the blank squares. For a special event such as a wedding, an appropriate decoration such as bells or horseshoes could be randomly placed with the name of the couple encircling each motif.

This project uses gouache paints and Gillot 404 pointed nib for ruling the lines and a William Mitchell 5 nib for the writing to create an interesting texture of lettering at angles using a variety of colours. Guidelines are ruled in pencil on the template measured 5mm (1/4in) apart with a 1cm (1/2in) gap between each set of lines. This will effectively repeat the pattern on both sides when the box is finally folded. The lines are then ruled over with alternate colours of red, green and purple gouache paint using the pointed nib. The ends have been left blank but this space could be used to add a name or personal message. Complete your box by tying ribbons around it in complementary colours and finishing with a bow.

The design

By using a slightly compressed Cursive Italic hand for this project, there is enough space to allow words to be repeated across the box. Choose your own colour scheme, whether striking or subtle. Alternating the use of a size 4 and size 6 nib for each letter of a word produces an interesting thick and thin design.

Materials

- *Tracing paper*
- *2H pencil*
- *Card (stock) in a weight to suit the size of box*
- *Photocopier*
- *Layout or practice paper*
- *Mixing brush*
- *Gouache paints: red, green, purple*
- *Dip pens: pointed nib Gillott 404 and William Mitchell 5 (small nib)*
- *Ruler with bevelled edge*
- *Scoring implement*
- *Scissors*
- *PVA (white) glue or craft glue and brush*
- *Ribbon*

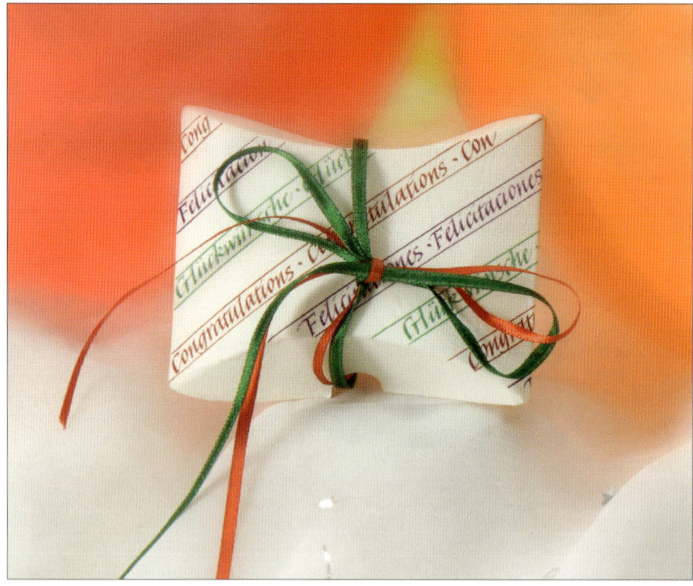

Template

enlarge by 200 per cent

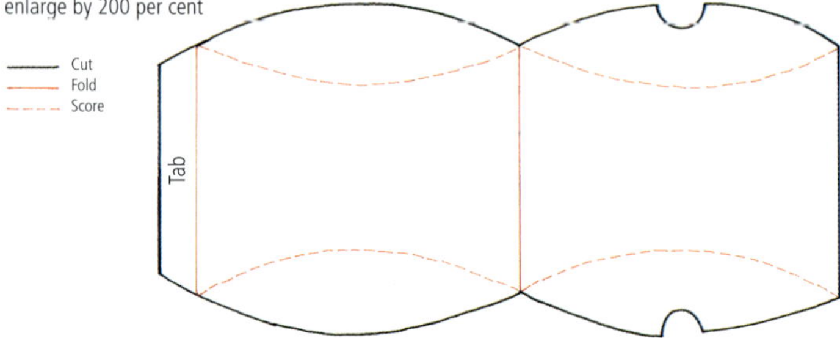

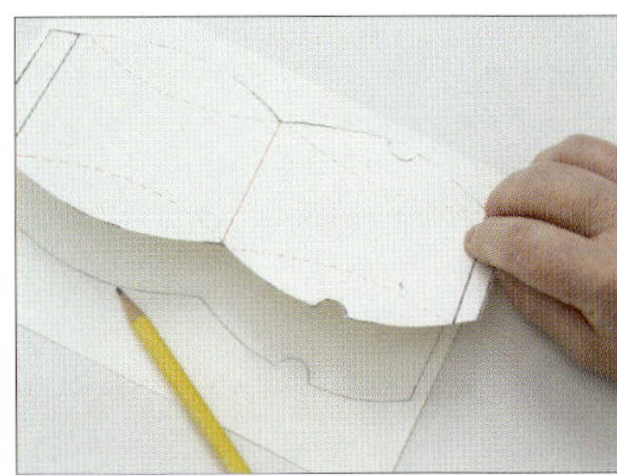

1 To make the box, first trace the template as shown here and transfer the design onto the card. Enlarge or reduce the template on a photocopier to a size that suits your purpose. Do not cut, score or fold the card at this stage.

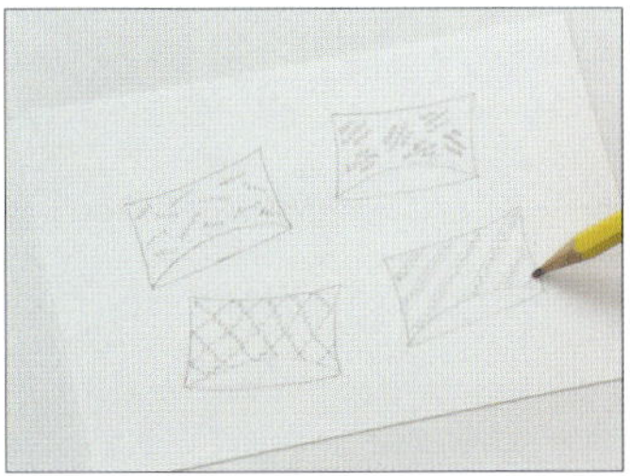

2 Try out some design ideas on layout paper. Experiment with random lettering, blocks or diagonal lines of text. Be bold and have fun with the colour scheme or else keep the colours subdued and elegant. Use a separate mixing brush for each colour and use a paint brush to fill the nib with gouache.

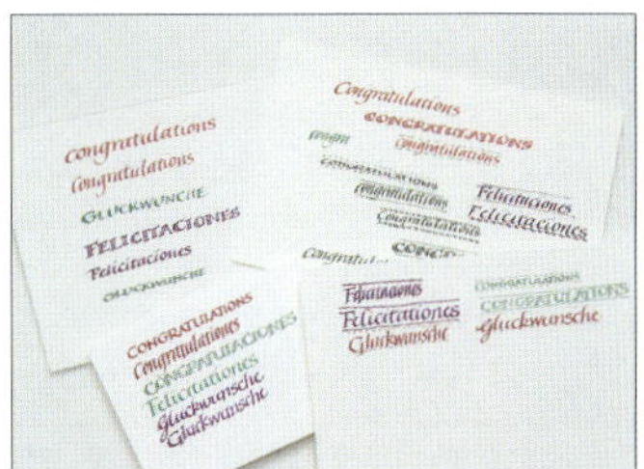

3 Write out the words in a range of sizes so that you can judge which will fit the box best. Try writing in different colours, too, to find the combination you prefer.

Tip: An old ball-point pen which has run out of ink is an ideal way of scoring along the tabs and fold lines.

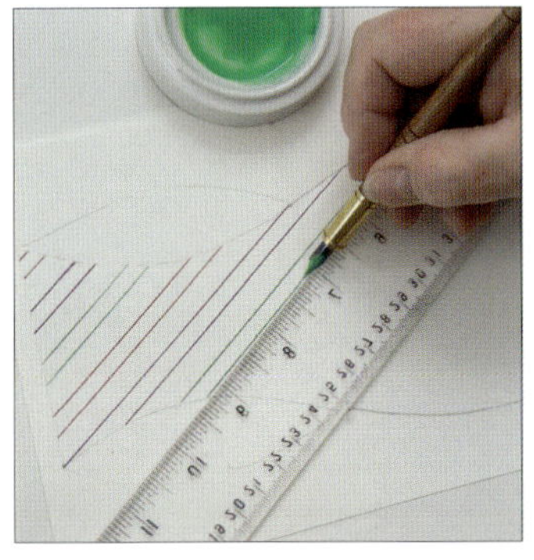

4 Use a pencil and ruler to draw some guidelines on to the card. The large dots indicate where to start. Now paint over the pencil lines by loading a pointed nib with a little gouache – too much will make a blob – and drawing the nib along the side of the ruler with the bevelled edge facing downwards. It will be easier to paint all the lines of one colour and wait until they have dried before proceeding with the next colour.

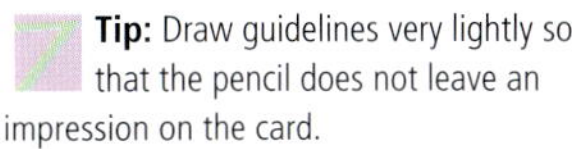

Tip: Draw guidelines very lightly so that the pencil does not leave an impression on the card.

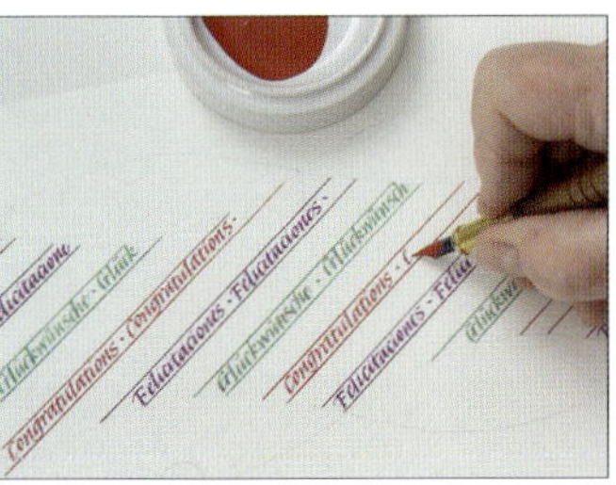

5 Write out the wording using a size 5 nib. Write out the lines with only one colour at a time and wait until the paint has dried before proceeding with the next colour. It helps to keep your work covered to avoid any smudges.

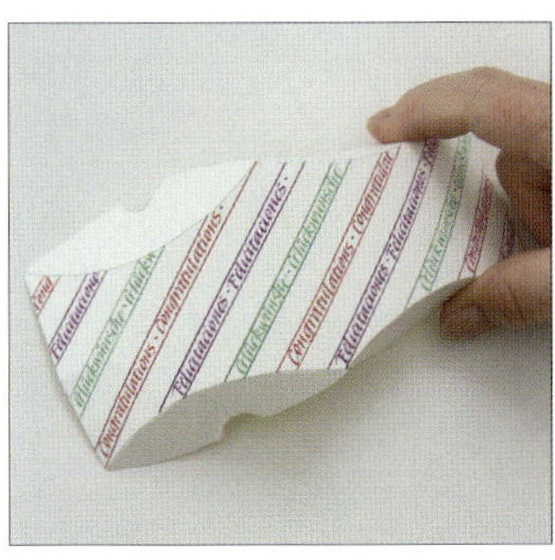

7 Carefully fold the card and press the box into shape. Glue the tab to seal the end of the box.

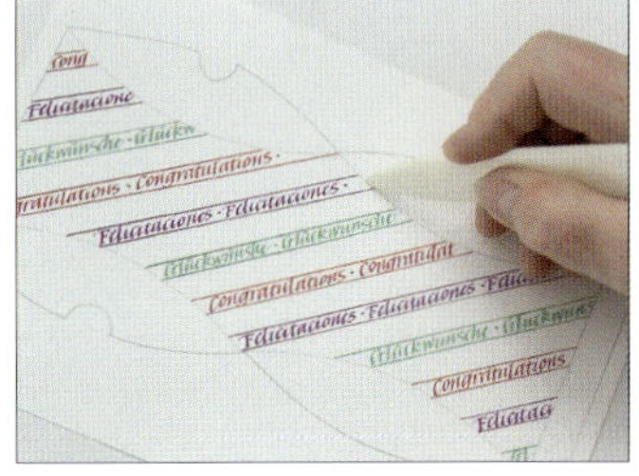

6 When the wording is dry, score along the lines indicated. Use a bone folder or other tool to score along the fold lines. Cut out the template.

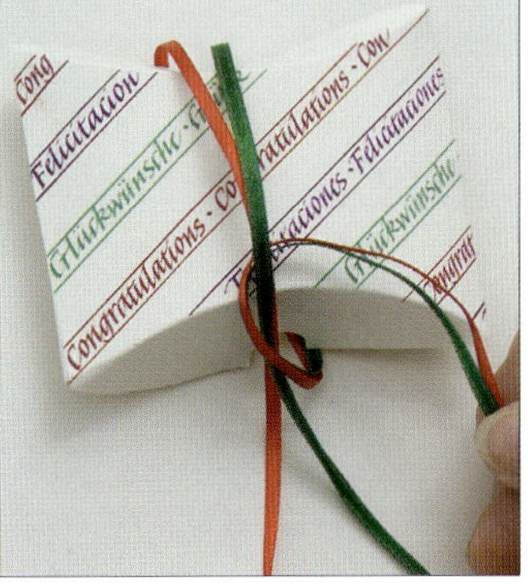

8 Add any final touches you may wish, such as ribbons in complementary colours.

Rubber-stamped wine label

This is a simple idea which can easily be adapted to all sorts of other labels for uses around the home. Making your own labels brings a warm and individual feel to any jar or bottle. This label is designed for use on a bottle of wine, but you can create all kinds of other labels for a variety of uses.

The label can be illustrated by using a variety of media. In this project a rubber stamp has been used to illustrate the label. You can create a rubber stamp from a craft block or plastic eraser by cutting out the shapes using a craft knife or a 'v'-groove linoleum tool to create the impression. The carving can be printed by using an ink pad or brushing on paint such as gouache or acrylic. While rubber stamping has been used as a simple and effective way of illustrating the wine label, other techniques could be used, such as watercolour painting or drawing with pen and ink or coloured pencils.

Adapt the label to suit your needs. It may be useful to create a generic design for your wine collection, or you may prefer to create individual labels. The description of the wine has been written clearly across the illustration using a bold colour as contrast.

Materials

- *Layout or practice paper*
- *HB and 2H pencils*
- *Coloured pencils*
- *Hot-pressed watercolour paper*
- *Ruler*
- *Pair of compasses*
- *Dip pens: William Mitchell 2, 3 and 4 (medium nibs)*
- *Scissors*
- *Glue stick*
- *Tracing paper*
- *Craft block or plastic square-edged eraser for the stamp*
- *Self-healing cutting mat*
- *Craft (utility) knife with curved blade or 'v'-groove linoleum-cut tool*
- *Ink pads (optional)*
- *Gouache paints: purple mixed with a little red, green and gold*
- *Paint brushes, including a size 0*
- *PVA (white) or craft glue and brush*

The design

This label for a bottle of wine features the 'house' name and the date of the wine written in Humanistic Cursive as a central feature, with a calligraphic border around the edge. The rubber stamp forms the decorative central motif.

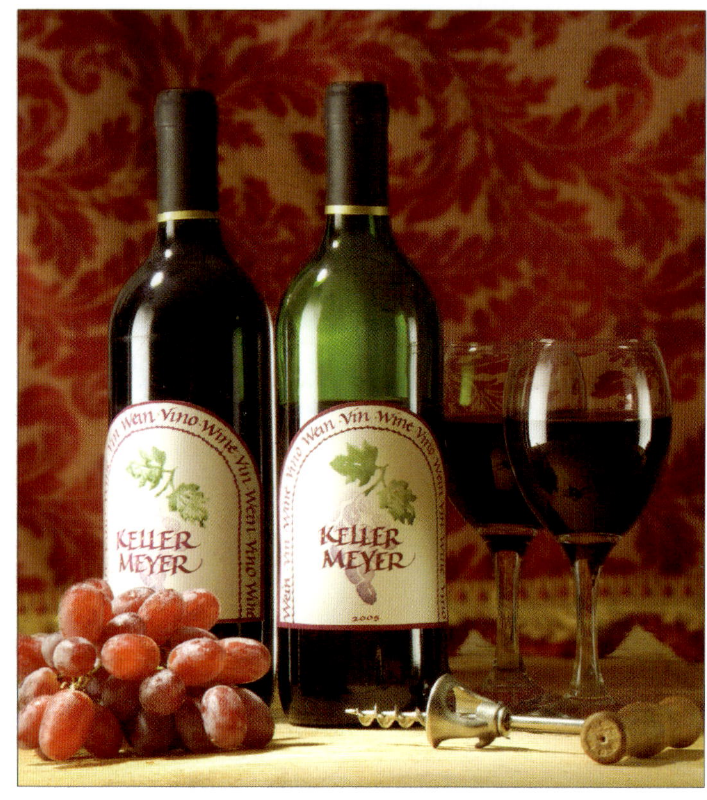

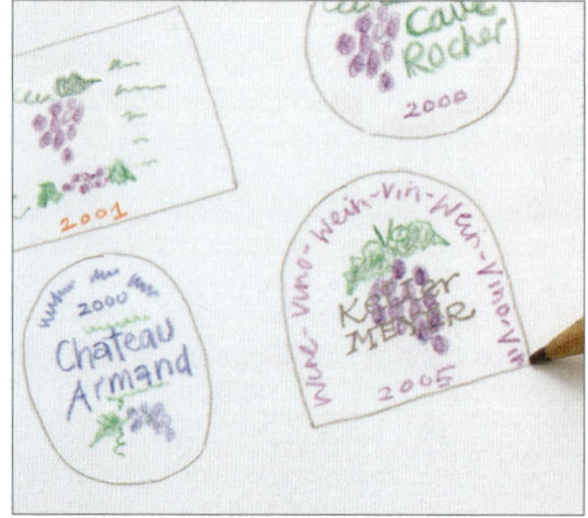

1 Begin by sketching out a few ideas on layout paper. Using coloured pencils will give you some idea of which colours work well together. Experiment with different shapes and sizes for labels.

Tip: Brush the glue from the centre outwards so that the glue does not seep underneath and spoil the label.

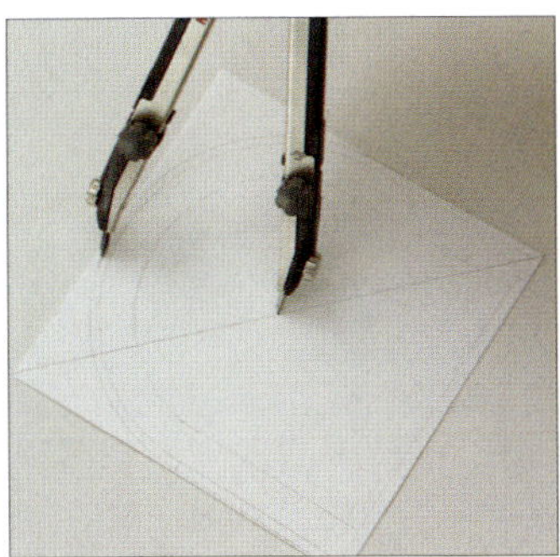

2 Once you have decided on the size of the label, you will have a clearer idea of how much space you have available for lettering and illustration. The label in this project is made by measuring 10cm x 10cm (4in x 4in) on to watercolour paper. Place a ruler diagonally from one corner to the other and mark the centre spot. Place the point of a ruling compass on this mark, open the compass to 5cm (2in) wide and draw an arc to form the top of the label. Repeat the arc 2mm (5/64in) smaller and again 1cm (1/2in) smaller for guidelines. Use a ruler to complete the side lines and base lines.

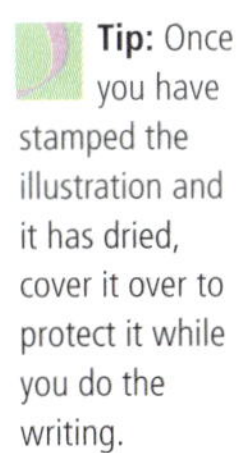

Tip: Once you have stamped the illustration and it has dried, cover it over to protect it while you do the writing.

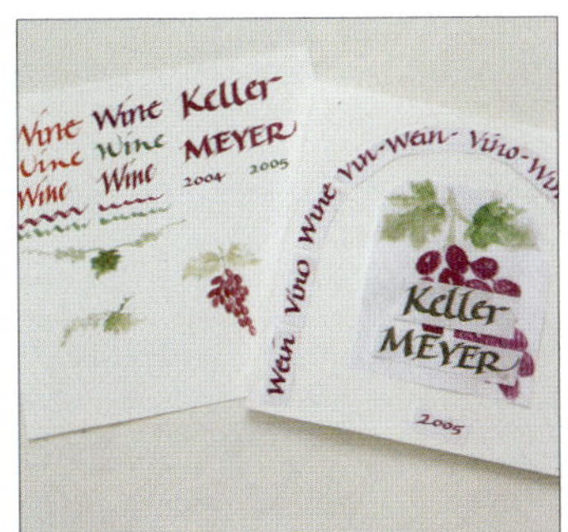

3 Try some writing trials, varying the styles, sizes and colours so as to emphasize the most important words on the label, and try out any ideas for illustration. Cut and paste the results to get the spacing right.

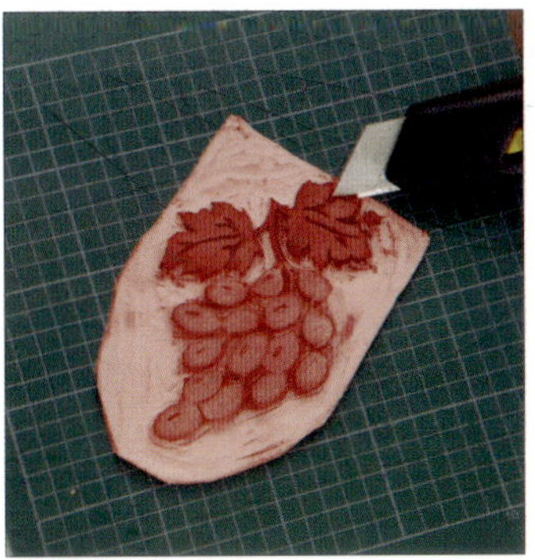

5 To carve the image, use a craft knife or 'v'-groove lino tool and cut away the parts of the image that you do not want printed, leaving the traced black lines. Carve unwanted areas away at an angle with short, shallow cuts.

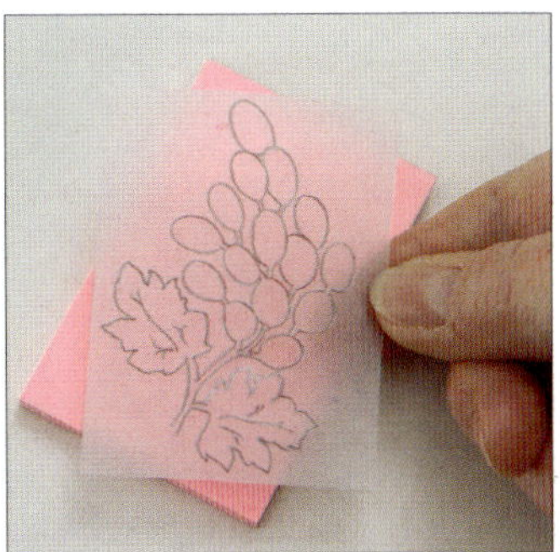

4 Trace your illustration onto tracing paper. Place the image face down on to the carving block or eraser and trace over the back of the tracing paper with a pencil to transfer the image.

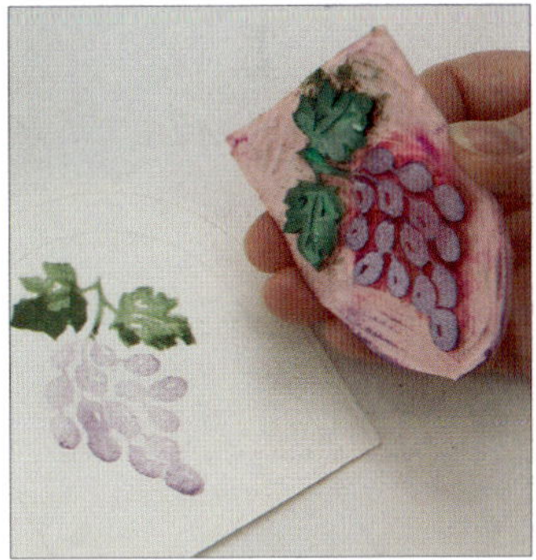

6 Mark some guidelines lightly with a pencil to show where the border will sit. Before using your stamp on the label, try practising on some spare paper until you are happy with the results. Cut out your label. Now stamp the illustration in the centre of the label.

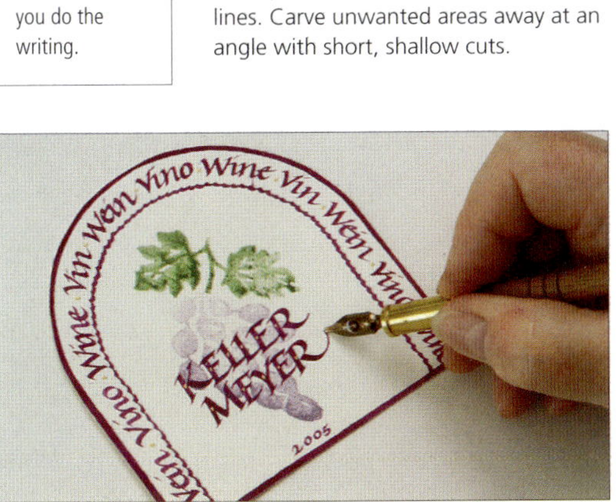

7 Using a size 0 brush, paint the 2mm (5/64in) border of the label. Write out the words *Wein, Vin, Wine, Vino* around the edge and add the pen-made border using a size 3 nib. Write the 'house' name with a size 2 nib and the year with a size 4 nib and add the little gold dots with a small brush. Finally, paste the label on to your bottle of wine.

Large-lettered notebook

This little notebook makes a wonderful holiday journal, baby or wedding book, or everyday 'book of memories'. It uses eight sheets of handwriting paper folded to make a book of 32 pages. The notebook is covered with a heavier dove-coloured jacket made of a print-making paper that feels like felt and is extremely soft and thick.

Conventional three-hole stitching holds the book together. The outside pockets are created by folding the outsize cover piece at the tail and the fore-edges, and inserting a contrasting pocket strip.

In this example the inserted strip picks up the colour (Bengal rose), of the lettering. These pockets provide useful spaces in which to tuck in memorabilia and the name on the flap – the only piece of calligraphy to feaure on the notebook – clearly identifies the owner or subject of the book.

Materials

- *Eight pieces of handwriting-weight paper for the signature*
- *Bone folder*
- *Ruler or metal cutting edge*
- *2H pencil*
- *Rives BFK print-making paper or similar paper for the cover*
- *Craft (utility) knife or scalpel*
- *Self-healing cutting mat*
- *Contrasting paper for the inner pocket*
- *Gouache paint in one colour*
- *Palette*
- *Automatic pen, size 4*
- *Glue stick*
- *Bradawl or awl*
- *Large-eyed tapestry needle*
- *Thick thread or string*
- *Scissors*
- *Beads (optional)*

Tip: Because the notebook is stitched with thick thread or string, it is possible to extend its life by replacing pages if required.

The design

Very little calligraphy is involved in this project – just one word. However, that single word defines the theme of the book. Here '*Theodora*' is strongly lettered using a large automatic pen and an Italic hand, with the reduced x-height of four nib widths. Also adding to the impact is the variation in stitching, which takes the thread through to the outside of the book – a variation on the conventional sewing, which starts from the centre of the book and sews the spine in a less conspicuous way.

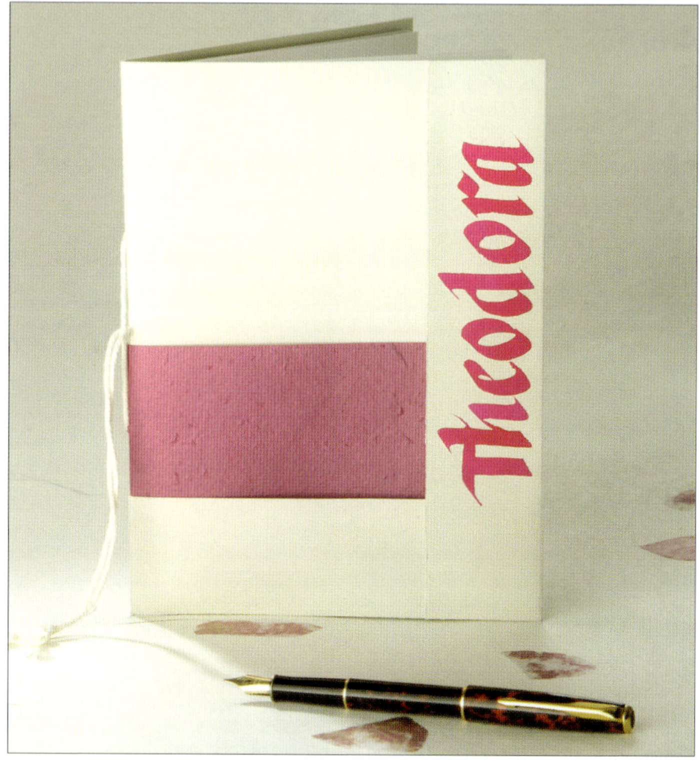

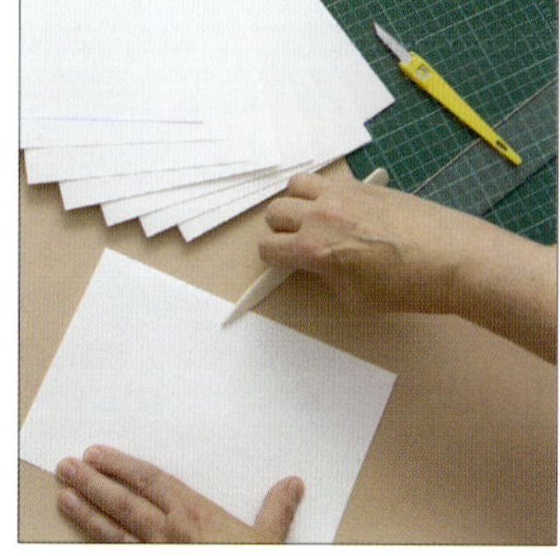

1 Check the grain of the eight sheets of paper. The grain should run parallel with the spine of the finished book. Use a bone folder to fold each sheet of paper in half, one at a time, then place the sheets neatly inside each other to form the signature. Note the measurements from head to tail (at the fore-edge and the spine) and from spine to fore-edge (at the head and the tail), then place your signature under a heavy book.

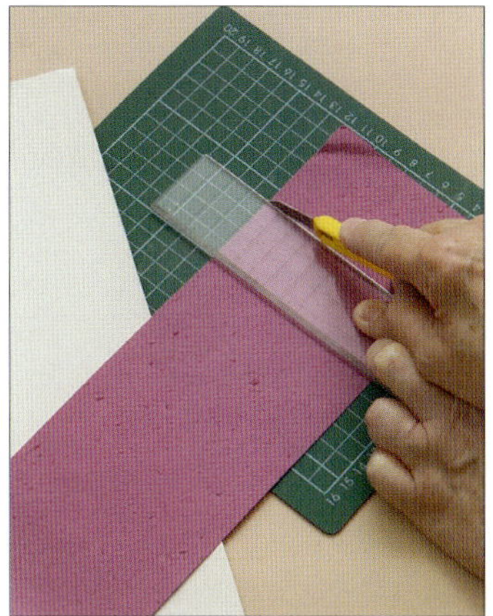

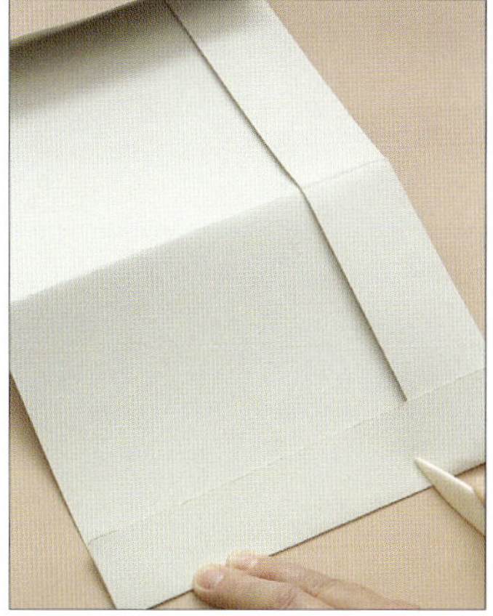

3 The cover and pocket strip should not be folded as crisply as the text block, so gently bring each piece together, short edge to short edge. Put the smaller piece – the pocket – to one side. Open out the larger piece – the cover – and, from the head, measure down the height of the signature plus 5mm (1/4in). Do this at both the fore-edges and the spine. Score and fold. Unfold and, from the spine to each fore-edge, measure the width of the book plus 5mm (1/4in). Score and fold. At the bottom corners of the cover will be overlapping creases. Trim these away.

2 Cut the cover paper one-and-a-quarter times the height of the book – the head to tail measurement – and two-and-a-half times the width of the book – the spine to fore-edge measurement. Now cut a strip of contrasting paper half the height and twice the width of the book. This will be used for the pocket strip.

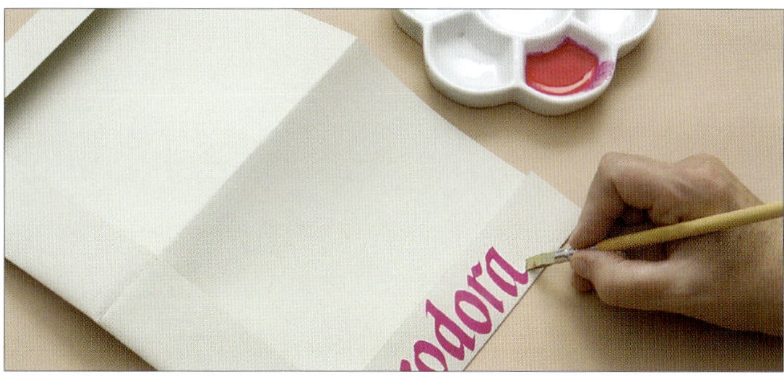

4 Use dilute gouache and a large pen such as an automatic size 4 to write your chosen word on the turn-back of the front flap.

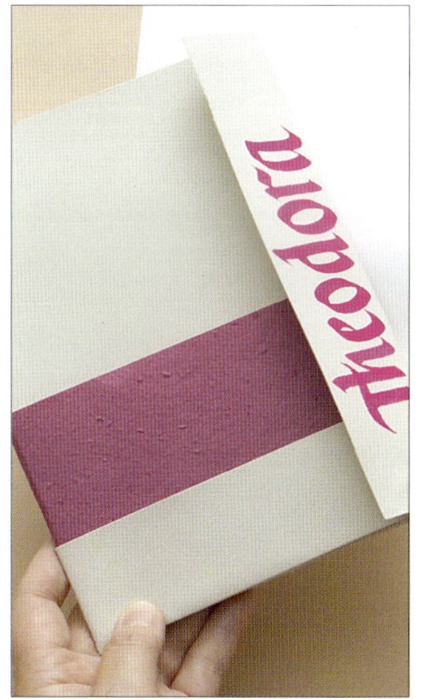

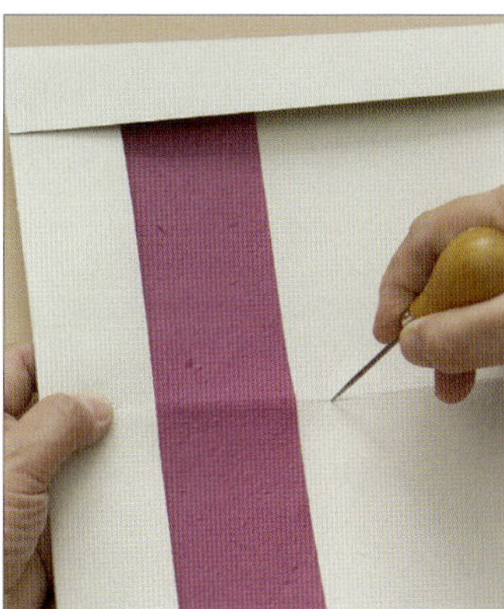

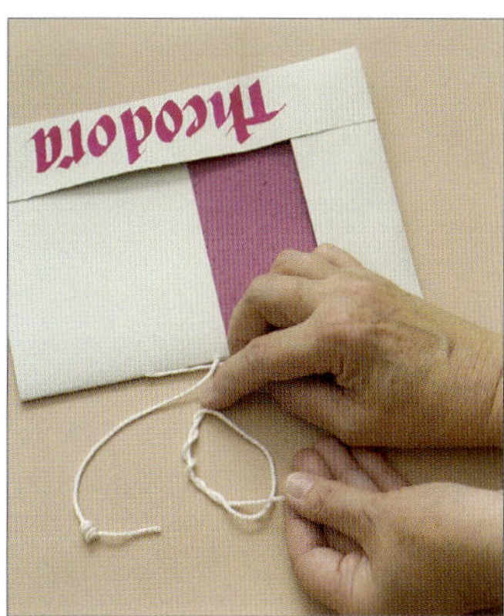

5 Fold up the flap at the tail of the cover and apply small dabs of glue to hold the fore-edge flaps back. Insert the pocket strip and wrap the cover evenly around the signature.

6 With the bradawl or awl, pierce three evenly spaced holes in the spine and, starting from the outside, sew the signature to the cover, finishing with a reef knot.

7 Tie a multi-wrapped overhand knot at each end of the thread, then trim and feather out the ends to make mock tassels. Alternatively, slip on some beads or charms.

Decorative concertina book

The concertina book was most likely to have been invented in China during the Heian period (794–1185). It was formed by folding a scroll backwards and forwards and adding covers to the front and back. It superseded the scroll which was difficult to store and awkward to use. Concertina books were often called *sempūyō*, or flutter books, because the concertina 'pages' were not attached to the spine so they could flutter out in the breeze. Books of this type were used traditionally for Buddhist *sutras* or for albums of painting or calligraphy.

This project creates a concertina book with eight identical sections. The text *dum defluante amnes* is Latin for 'until the rivers cease to flow'. The design has been used to make a Valentine's card, the theme being enforced by the decoration of pen-drawn hearts. After folding, the ends of the book are slipped into covers which, using origami techniques, complement the Chinese book construction. The outside covers are made from a piece of antique paper showing dragons. As dragons are a sign of good luck not only is the recipient assured of undying love but is also being sent good fortune.

The design

By using this folded form and the Foundational script, two simple but effective arts are united. The addition of small hearts, drawn with two easy pen strokes, turns this basic greetings card into a treasured keepsake.

Materials

- *Layout or practice paper*
- *Dip pens: such as William Mitchell $2\frac{1}{2}$ and $3\frac{1}{2}$ (medium nibs)*
- *Gouache paint in two diluted colours*
- *Hot-pressed watercolour paper*
- *Ruler with cutting edge*
- *2H pencil*
- *Eraser*
- *Self-healing cutting mat*
- *Craft (utility) knife*
- *Bone folder*
- *Card (stock)*
- *Decorative paper*

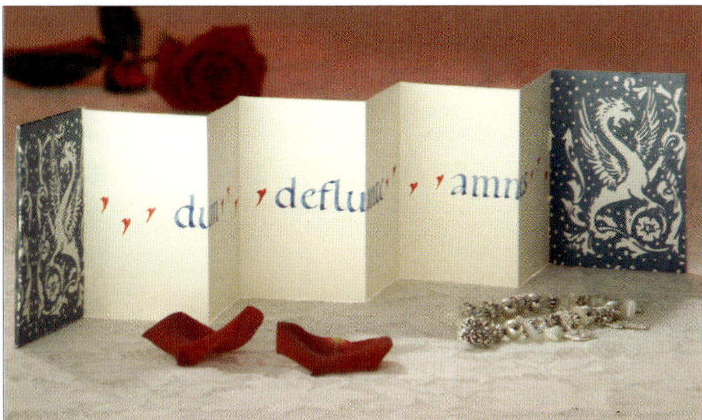

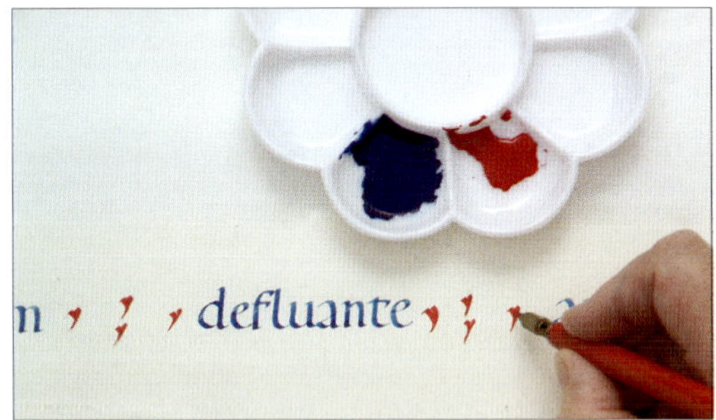

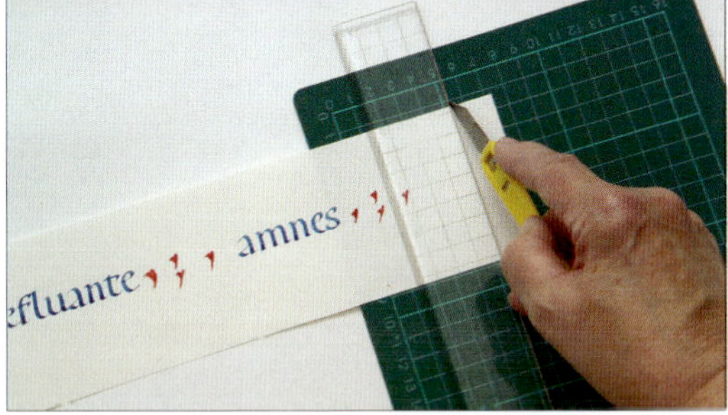

1 Practise the lettering and decoration on layout paper; this will help you choose what size nibs to use. When you are ready, start to work on the watercolour paper. It is best to write the final work on an oversize piece of paper. This means that you will be able to trim the paper and, if you have not quite centred the words, it will be possible to make allowances for this. Leaving a large space all around, rule up, write and decorate the text. The hearts look most effective if a nib two sizes smaller than the one you are using for the writing is used. When everything is thoroughly dry, erase your lines.

2 Measure the length of the line of writing. Divide this figure by 6 and multiply the answer by 8 to get measurement X. This is the length of paper needed for your concertina. To determine the width you need, divide X by 8 and multiply by 5 to get measurement Y. Cut the paper to measure X by Y, ensuring that the writing has an even amount of white space to the left and right, and lies slightly above the middle. This position is called the 'optical middle' and is more comfortably viewed by the human eye than the true middle.

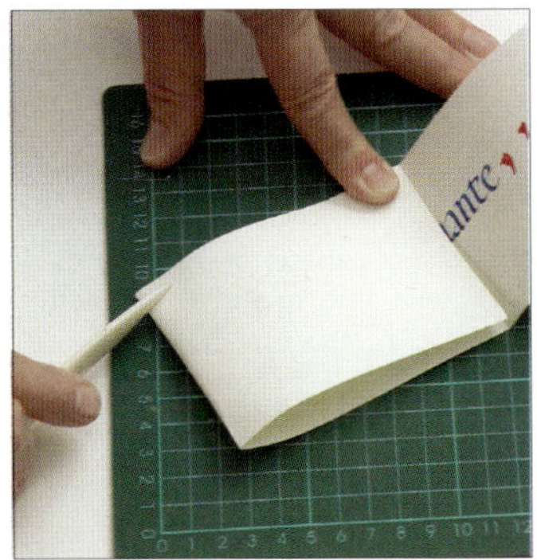

3 Using a bone folder to ensure a sharp crease, fold the paper in half, short edge to short edge and right side to right side. Using this fold as a 'gutter', fold one half in half again, written side to written side – so that the writing does not smudge or shine. Continue in this fashion until you have folded the strip into eight identical sections to form the concertina.

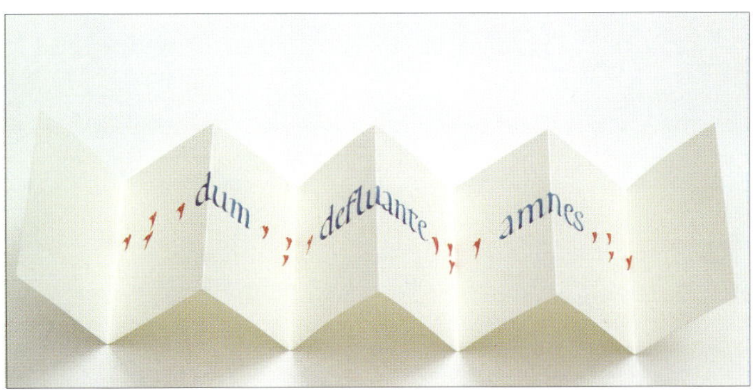

4 At this point the folds will not be in sequence. Change the directions of the folds to make sure you have a valley-mountain-valley-mountain sequence and that the concertina can be closed.

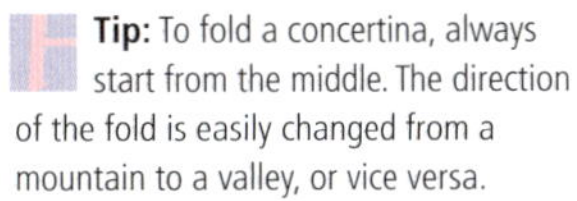

Tip: To fold a concertina, always start from the middle. The direction of the fold is easily changed from a mountain to a valley, or vice versa.

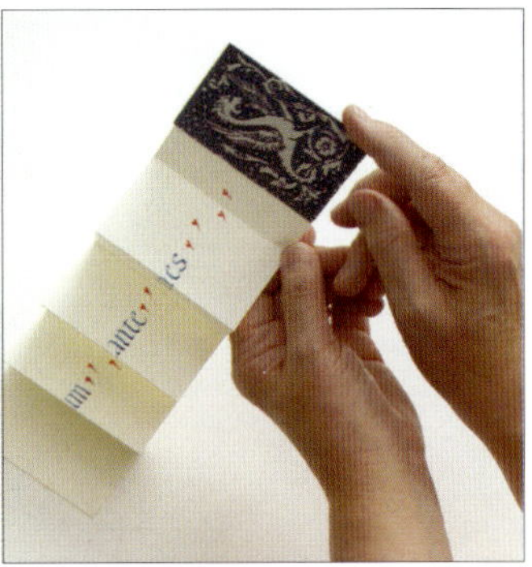

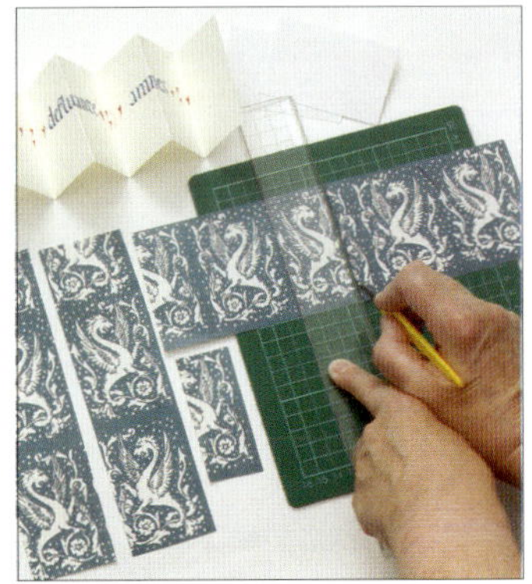

5 Measure the height and width of the folded concertina and cut two pieces of card to this exact measurement. Using decorative paper, cut two more pieces at twice the height of the concertina by the width of the concertina. Then cut two pieces twice the width of the concertina by the height. Finally, cut one piece three times the depth and once the height of the concertina.

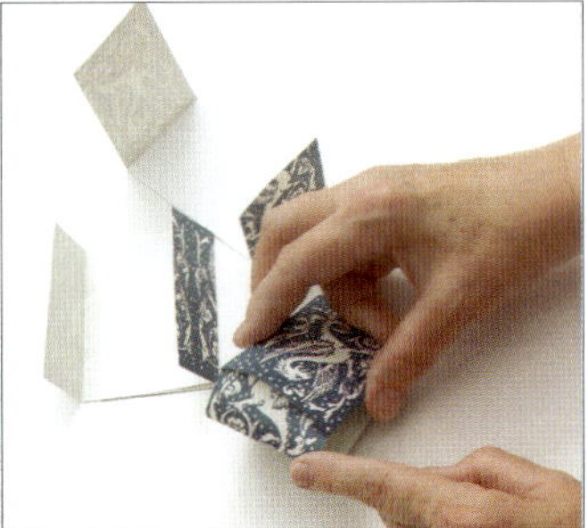

6 Fold one of the double-sized vertical pieces around a centrally placed piece of the card. Remove the card and repeat this exercise using the remaining vertical double-sized pieces of paper. Repeat with the double-sized horizontal pieces of paper. Place one of the 'horizontal' pieces of paper around a piece of the card and, with the open ends facing you, fold over and slide the ends of a vertical piece of paper over the card but inside the first piece of paper. This will lock together to form one cover. Repeat for the other cover.

7 Slide these covers on to the front and back sections of the concertina, if necessary cutting a sliver of paper from the outside sections to allow them to slide in easily. The amount that is trimmed should be as little as possible, or the covers will slip.

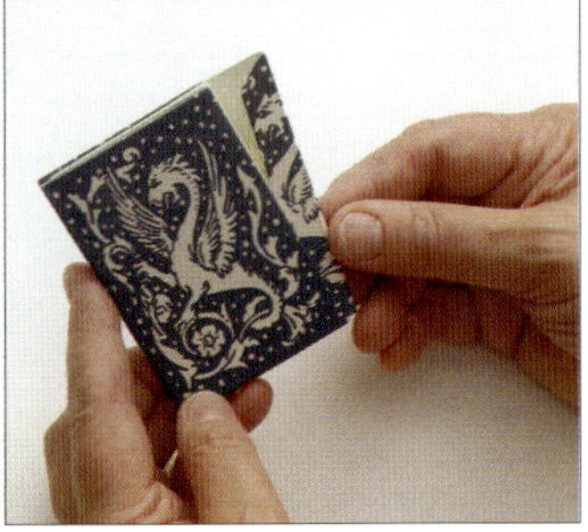

8 Measure the depth of the concertina and score the remaining strip of cover paper to provide a 'spine piece'. Crease firmly and slide into position to turn the concertina into a conventional book.

Triangular book with a centred script

The basic shape of this little book is formed by folding a square into eight equal triangles. The writing is centred on three sides of the square. It is an original and decorative vehicle for the Japanese verse form known as *haiku*, although of course it may be used to convey other messages.

Besides using the form as a *haiku* book, the triangular book makes a wonderful 'thank you', birthday, wedding or congratulations card, with a personalized message written inside. The attachment of the covered boards and ribbons turns a simple idea into a treasured object.

Materials

- *Hot-pressed watercolour paper*
- *2H pencil*
- *Ruler with cutting edge*
- *Eraser*
- *Gouache paint*
- *Dip pen (medium nib)*
- *Bone folder*
- *Self-healing cutting mat*
- *Craft (utility) knife or scalpel*
- *Card (stock) or small piece of mounting board*
- *Decorative paper for the cover*
- *Glue stick*
- *Ribbon*
- *Scrap paper, preferably shiny*
- *Weights*
- *Scissors*
- *Beads (optional)*

The design

Gothic, the script chosen for this project, is the easiest to space of all the calligraphic hands and its angularity, echoing the book's geometric design, ensures an overall harmony. Because it is so small only a scrap of decorative paper is needed for the cover, so any beautiful pieces you have hoarded because they 'might come in useful one day' are ideal for this project.

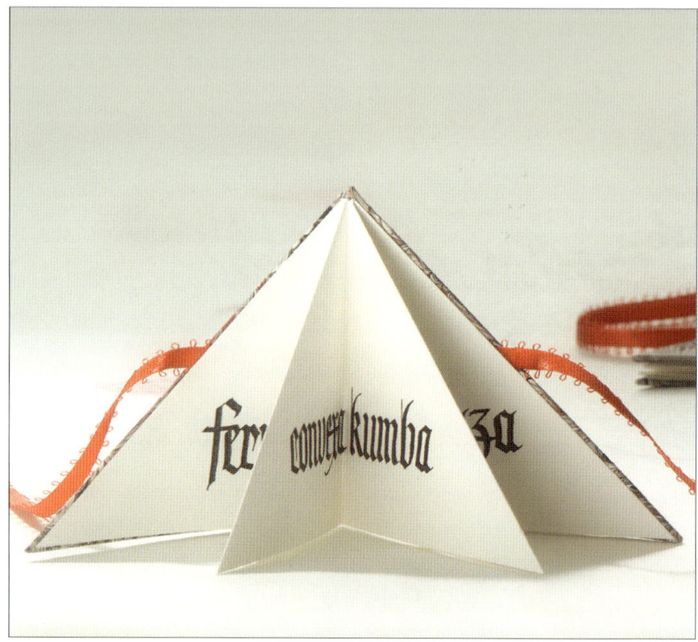

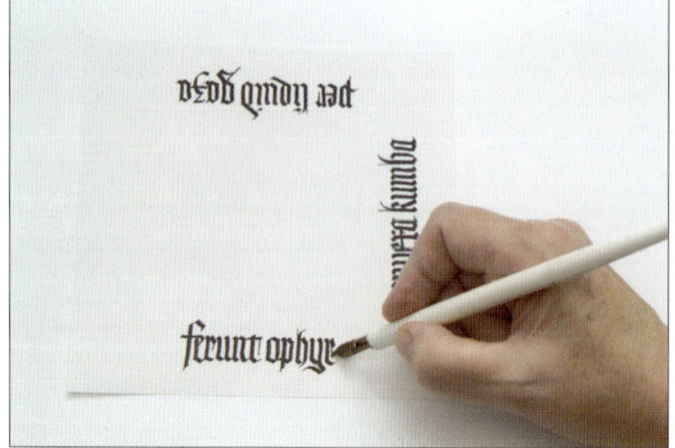

1 Rule up and write the *haiku*, or alternative text around three sides of the square cut to 20cm x 20cm (8in x 8in) making sure that each line of writing is centred within its own side. Erase any construction lines.

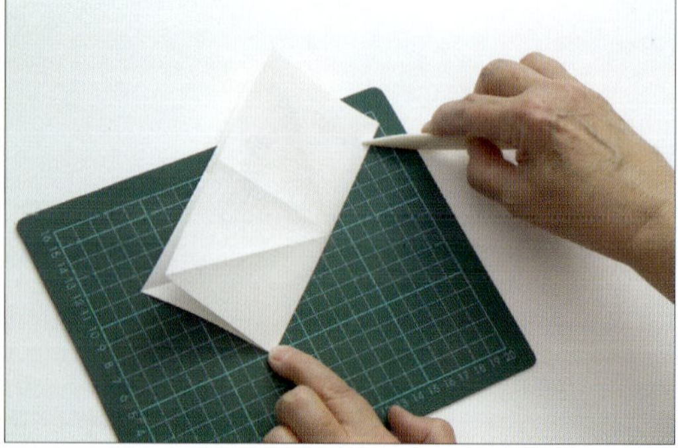

2 Using a bone folder to ensure crisp folds, fold the paper from side to side horizontally and vertically, then corner to corner bottom-left to top-right and top-left to bottom-right.

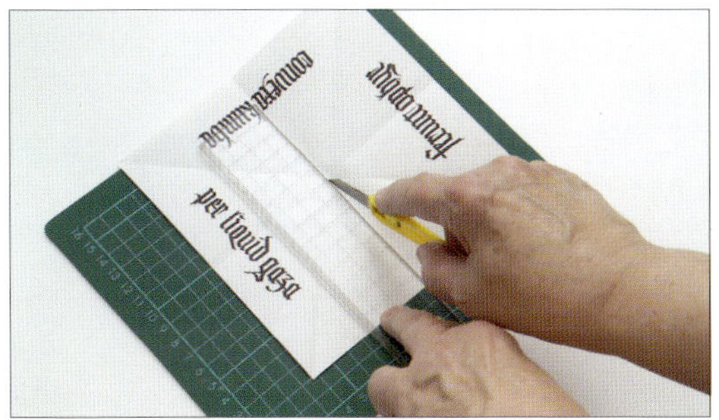

3 Cut through the paper along the fold from the centre to the middle of the unwritten section.

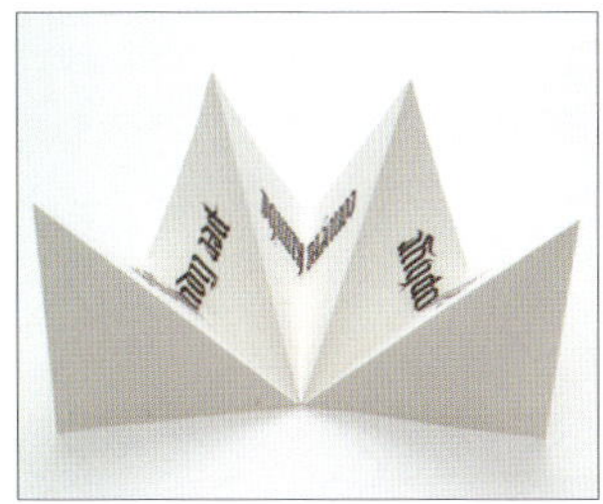

Tip: To centre work, write the words first on layout paper and place them above the writing line to help you space them correctly.

4 Change the direction of the folds, where necessary, so that they follow each other as a mountain or a valley to form a triangular concertina. Measure one of the resulting triangular sections.

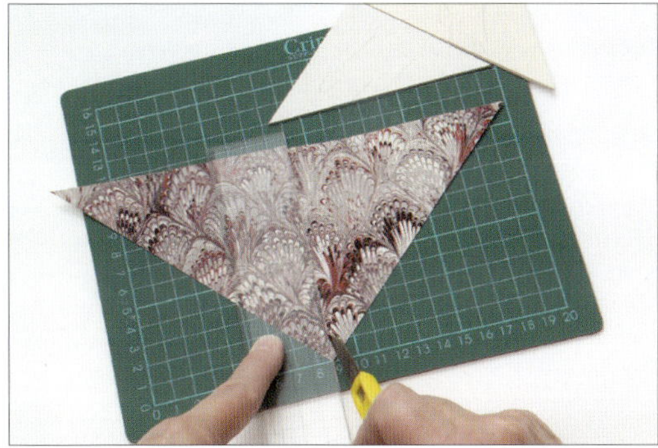

5 Referring to your measurements, cut two pieces of card (or board) to the size of a triangular section, and two pieces of cover paper, 1cm (1/2in) larger than the card all round, being careful to cut one piece of paper facing right and one piece facing left.

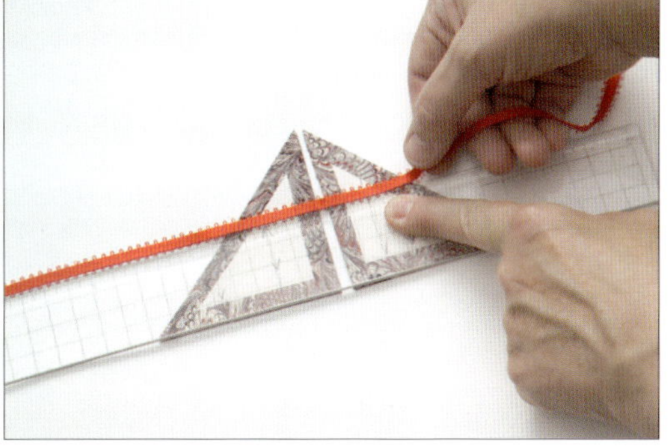

6 Carefully cover the card or board triangles with the decorative paper and glue. Lay the triangles face down, with the depth of the triangular concertina apart and the hypotenuses facing outwards. Place the ruler at the optical middle and draw a pencil line. Use this to help glue the ribbon to the cards. It need be only enough to make a hinge but can be longer if you prefer to use extravagant ties.

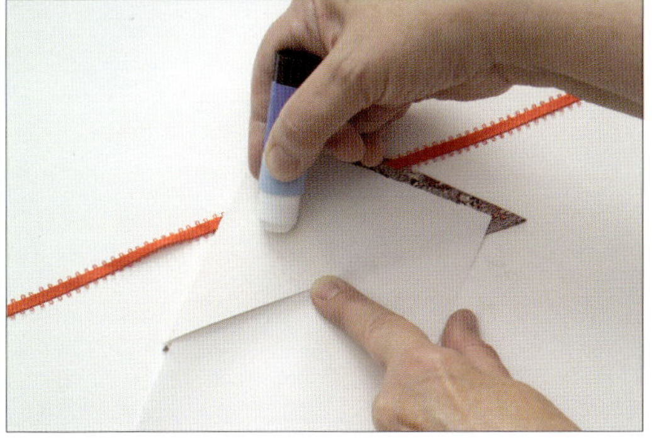

7 Slide scrap paper between the folds of the triangular concertina to protect it and glue the front section. Throw away the messy waste paper and attach the section to the reverse of the front board. Repeat these steps for the back section and board. Leave the book to dry under weights.

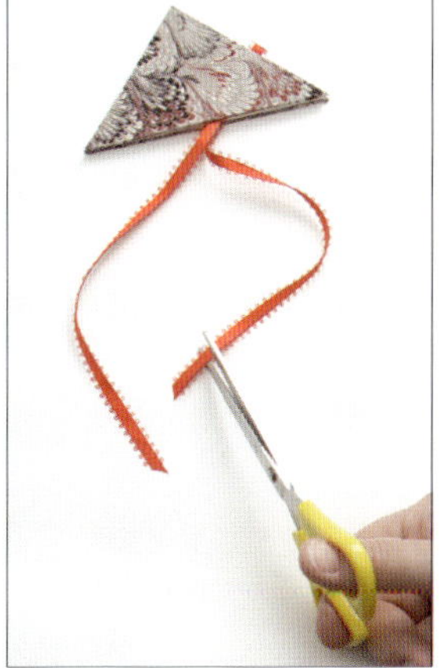

8 Finish the book by adding beads to the ribbon, or simply cut the ribbon ends diagonally, which will prevent fraying. Do not succumb to the temptation to cut 'fish tails' – they always fray.

Tip: To prevent 'show through' between the covers and the text, line the inside of the covers with decorative paper inserts.

Lotus book with a spiral script

The lotus fold is an ancient origami fold. In this book only one square of paper is folded and used to make the book. However, books may be made with several leaves, each created from individual squares of paper. It is thought that two leaves glued together resemble the flower of the lotus. A lotus may be folded using a circular piece of paper but, as that would emphasize the asymmetrical shape of the finished calligraphic spiral, the traditional square shape has been chosen. Writing around a spiral is much easier than you would think, and is very flattering to any standard of calligraphy. When closed, the square book gives no hint of the complex mysteries it encloses.

Make sure that there is plenty of ribbon available to make an extravagant tie in satin, velvet or silk as people often hang lotus books by their ribbons. If the paper or ribbon is very thick, or the text paper has 'show through', two smaller squares of decorative paper can be cut to line the inside of the cards. You can also cover the ribbon that is attached to each board with a small strip of masking tape.

The lotus fold takes a square and 'collapses' it into a square a quarter of its original size. In this project only one lotus is used, but you can join several of these folds together, openings outward, to make a more complex book. A lotus book is also an admirable vehicle to contain calligraphy that is written in straight lines. However, the shape of the lotus requires that the writing should run diagonally across the square of paper.

The design

Uncial is the ideal choice for this project – not only because it is a beautiful and round script, but also because its ascenders and descenders are relatively short and neat. By presenting the end result as a lotus book this exercise creates a charming gift, while enabling you to practise the art of producing calligraphy in the form of a spiral.

Materials

- *Layout or practice paper*
- *2H pencil*
- *Ruler with cutting edge*
- *Pair of compasses*
- *Hot-pressed watercolour paper*
- *Dip pen: William Mitchell $2\frac{1}{2}$ (medium nib)*
- *Gouache paint or ink in one colour*
- *Eraser*
- *Craft (utility) knife or scalpel*
- *Scissors*
- *Four strips of black paper*
- *Bone folder*
- *Card (stock)*
- *Decorative paper for cover*
- *Glue stick*
- *Scrap paper, preferably shiny*
- *Satin, velvet or silk ribbon, not florist's ribbon*

Tip: When writing in Uncials, it may be more comfortable to use a right-handed oblique nib.

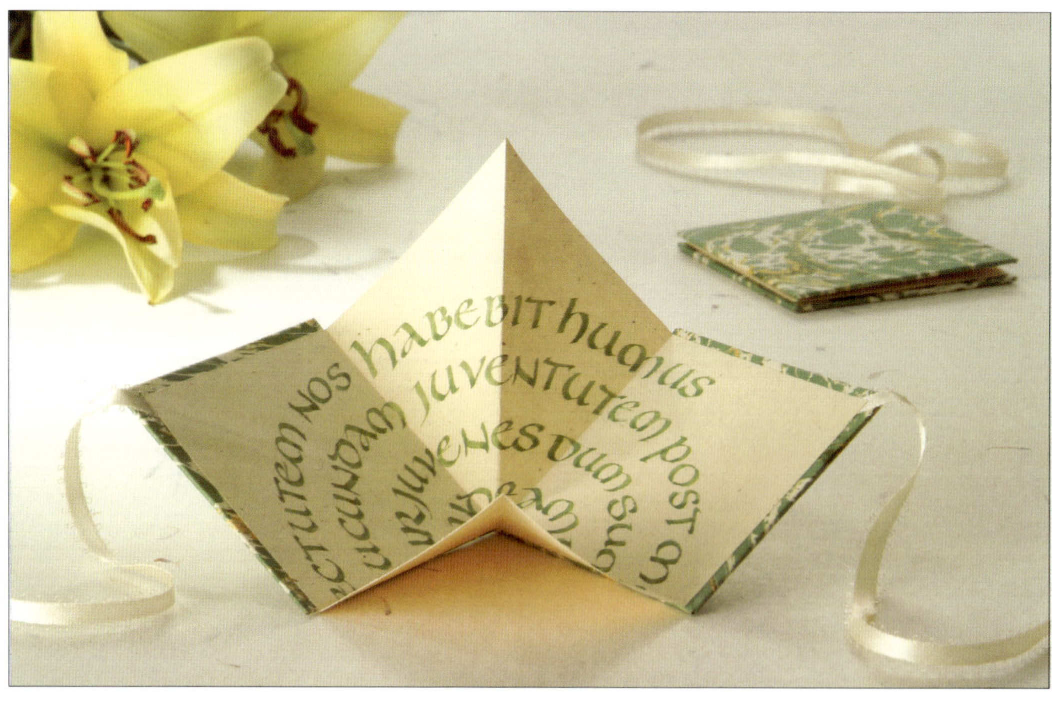

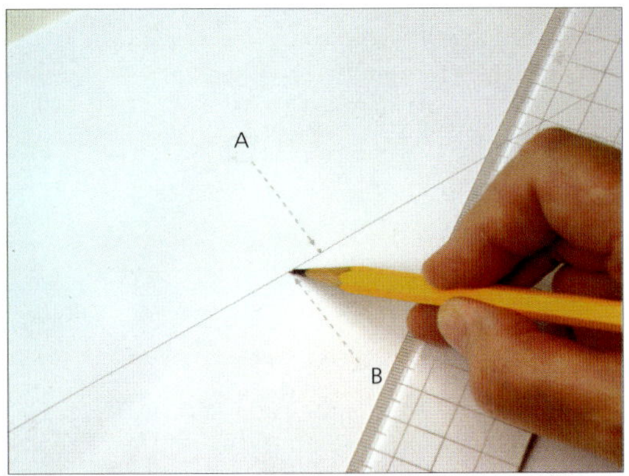

1 Using layout paper, practise drawing the spiral shape that will be the guide for your calligraphy. Draw a horizontal line and make two marks on it: 'A' and 'B'. Working from left to right, 'B' precedes 'A' and is on the underside of the line; 'A' is behind 'B' and sits on the top of the line. For the spiral to be compact, these two marks need to be close together.

Tip: If you are writing in a language that reads from right to left, your spiral needs to turn anti-clockwise. To ensure this, 'A' should precede 'B' on the horizontal line, sitting on the top. 'B' should follow 'A', on the underside of the line.

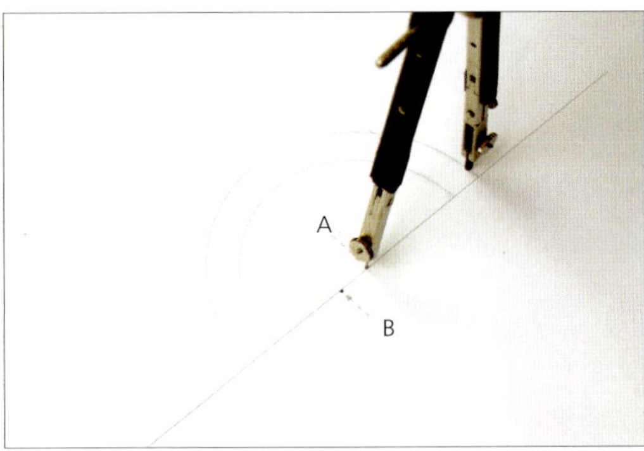

2 Using a pair of compasses, and point 'A' as the centre, draw two concentric semicircles. These need to be separated by the x-height of your chosen script.

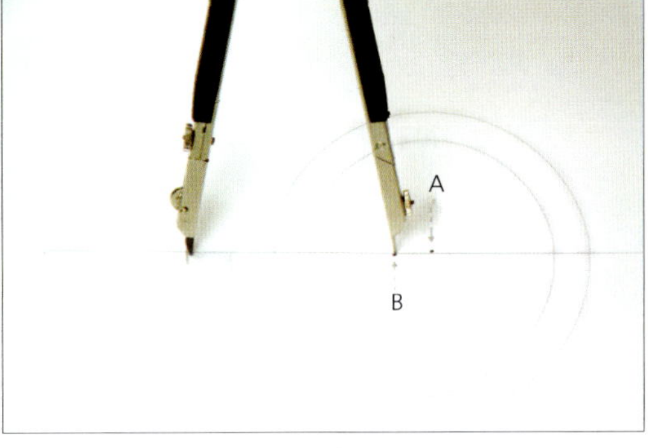

3 Using 'B' as the centre, draw another two concentric semicircles, adjusting the radii to touch the right-hand finishing points of the two semicircles you have already drawn.

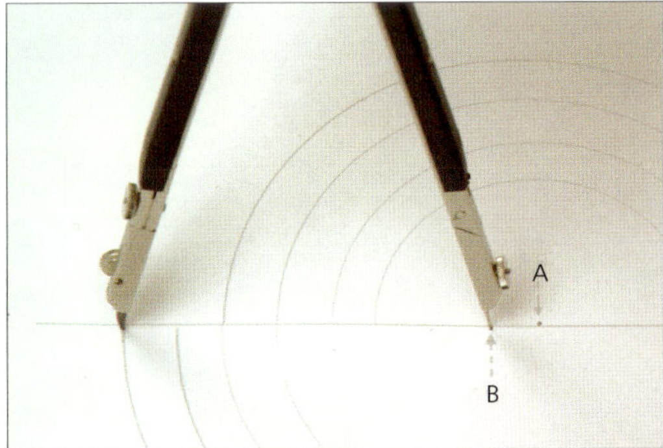

4 Return the compass to point 'A'. Draw another two concentric semicircles, touching the finishing points of the 'B'-centered semicircles. Continue moving between points 'A' and 'B' until the spiral is large enough to hold what you propose to write.

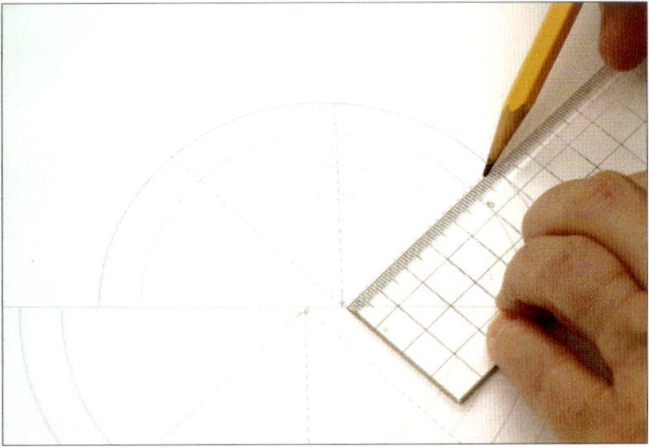

5 The axis of every letter needs to be parallel with its associated radius of the semicircle in which it is situated. To make this easier, pencil in radii for both semicircles. Note that these only share alignment along the original horizontal line. Having practised on layout paper, redraw the spiral on watercolour paper in exactly the same way.

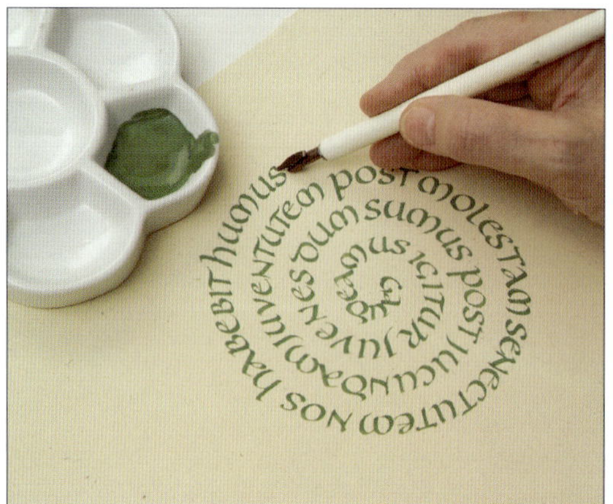

6 Write around the spiral using your chosen colour. Remember to keep turning your paper as you write. To prevent smudging, wait for the paint to dry at some points before continuing.

Tip: Black strips are used to work out the size and layout of the finished piece of calligraphy. If you have a large, unwanted picture mount, it is easier to cut this into two 'L' shapes and use these instead.

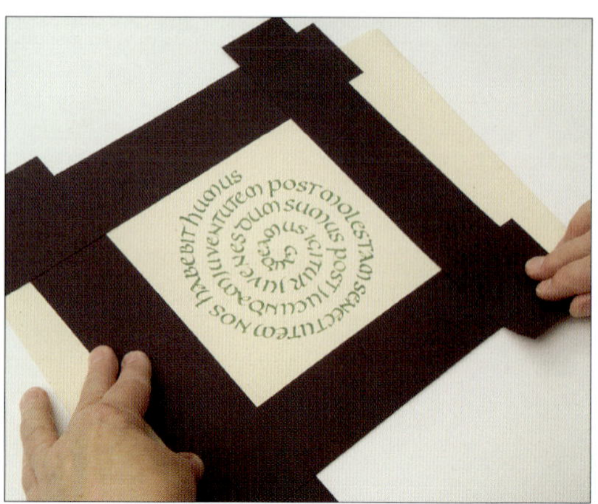

7 When the writing is complete, all the construction lines can be erased. At this stage, the spiral may look a little lopsided but this is easily put right. Take four strips of black paper or card and lay them around the work. Keep trying different orientations until you achieve one that you are happy with. Make careful pencil marks in the corners before removing the black strips and cutting the piece to the required shape. (Note: for this project the piece needs to be perfectly square. If you wanted to present your spiral as a finished broad sheet, you could choose a rectangular shape.)

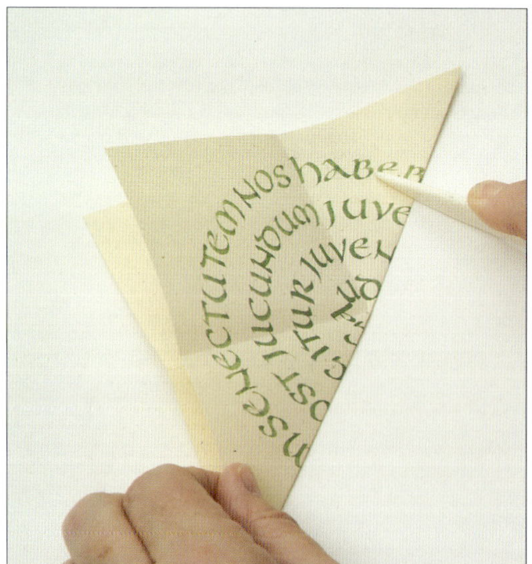

8 Fold the resulting square from side to side both horizontally and vertically. The calligraphy should be facing inwards. Turn the square over and fold once diagonally. Use a bone folder to ensure crisp folds.

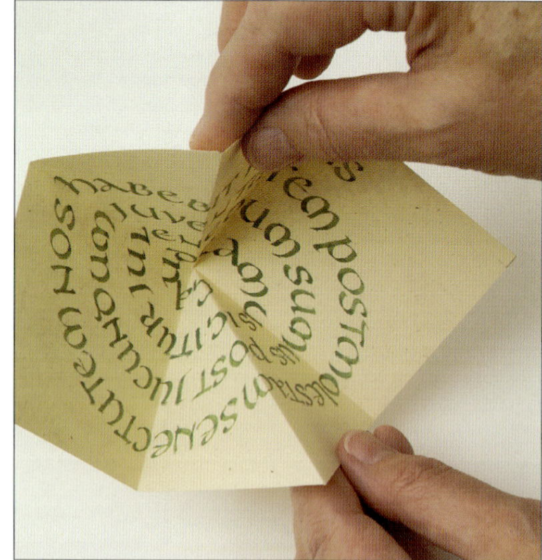

9 Pick up the square of paper and gently ease the diagonal crease together. The square will fold down into a square shape, which will be a quarter of its original size. This is the lotus fold.

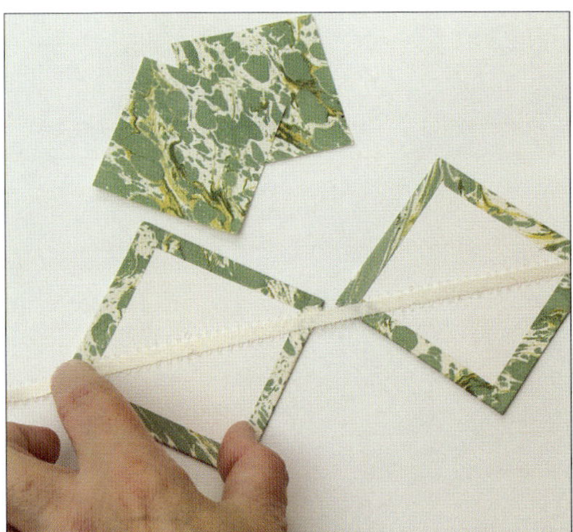

10 Measure this new, smaller square. You should be able to calculate its size from your original dimensions, but it is always safer to check. Cut two pieces of card to the same size, and two squares of decorative paper with an extra outside margin of 2.5cm (1in).

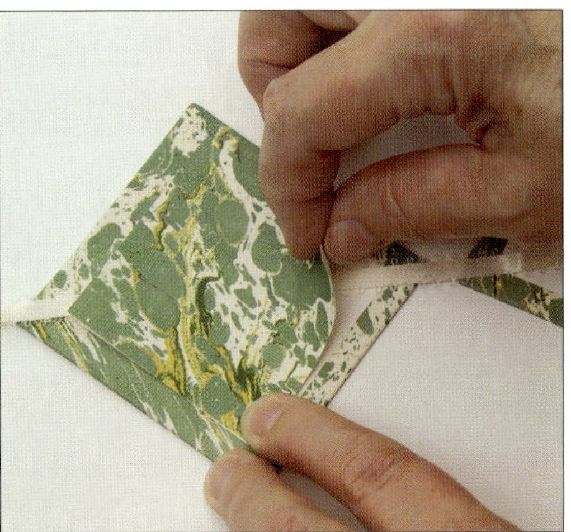

11 Lay the covered cards or boards face down, point to point and the depth of the lotus apart. If the space is too small the lotus will not open without damaging the covers. Glue straight across both cards horizontally. Fold the ribbon in half as a guide and lay it down on the glue. You may wish to line the insides of the covers to prevent 'show through'. Slide scrap paper between the folds of the lotus to protect it and glue the front section.

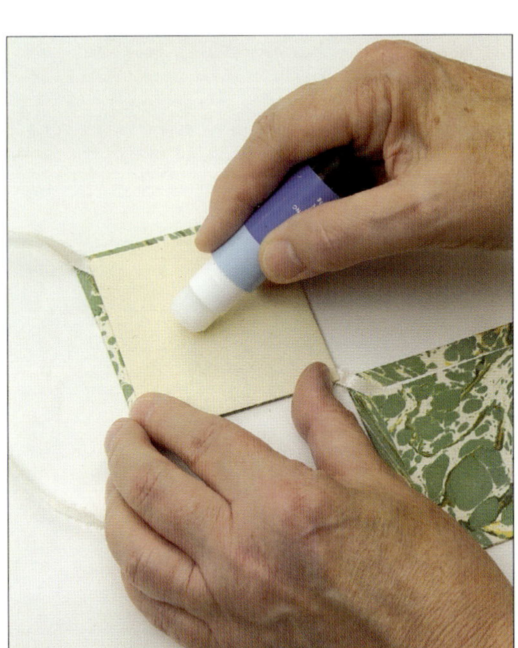

12 Throw away the messy waste paper and attach the front of the lotus to the reverse of the front board. Repeat these steps for the back of the lotus and board. Leave the book to dry under weights.

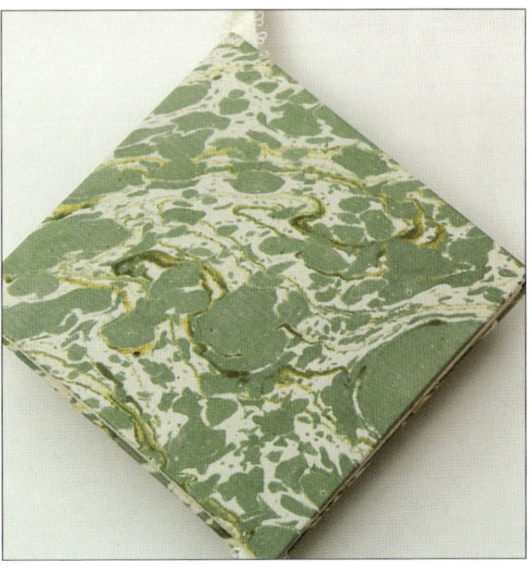

13 The finished book. These little books are so decorative that they can be displayed open or hanging up.

Rubber stamp patterns for place cards

This project is an excellent opportunity to bring something personal to a special occasion, such as a birthday dinner or wedding banquet. Once you have learnt the art of cutting your own designs for a rubber stamp this becomes an easy and effective way to create attractive single images, or repeat patterns for borders and larger areas.

A selection of place cards are created, which are then folded in order to stand up on a table. They have the individual name of each guest written on one side of the card, and are decorated around the edge by a rubber-stamped border. The guest's name can either be added to the card before you start stamping or can be written in afterwards – depending on the design you wish to create. You can attempt letters with the rubber stamp, but remember to cut them in reverse.

An infinite number of designs can be produced simply by overprinting with different colours or reversing the direction of a non-symmetrical stamp. Stamping can also be used to produce larger, more complex designs that combine several intricately cut stamps. The key to this project is to keep your stamping designs to basic geometric shapes as they are easy and quick to cut and make stunning patterns, especially if non-symmetrical. The designs can be turned through different angles for variety.

Tip: Have a damp cloth handy to clean stamps between colour changes, so stamping pads are not contaminated by different colours.

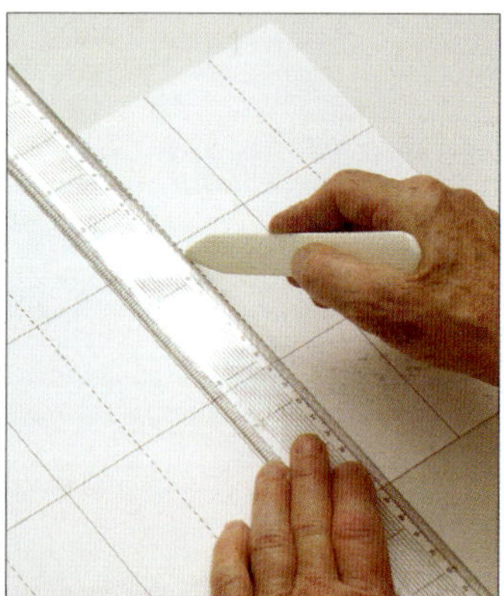

The design

The lettering in Italic is written before the 'v'-shaped cuts have been made in the stamps to produce an interesting border. Dots or tiny diamonds may be added once the cards have dried.

Materials

- *White card (stock)*
- *Bone folder*
- *Ruler and pencil*
- *Self-healing cutting mat*
- *Scalpel or craft (utility) knife*
- *Dip pen: various sizes*
- *Inks: various colours*
- *'Plastic' square-edged erasers*
- *Coloured stamping pads or foam*
- *Gouache paints and gel pens*

1 On a large sheet of card, rule up the place cards. A 7.5cm (3in) square is a recommended size to use. Divide this square in half lengthways to allow for the fold. Using a bone folder score all fold lines against a ruler to create a sharp indent in the card surface, ready for folding. Cut out the individual cards, but leave them unfolded.

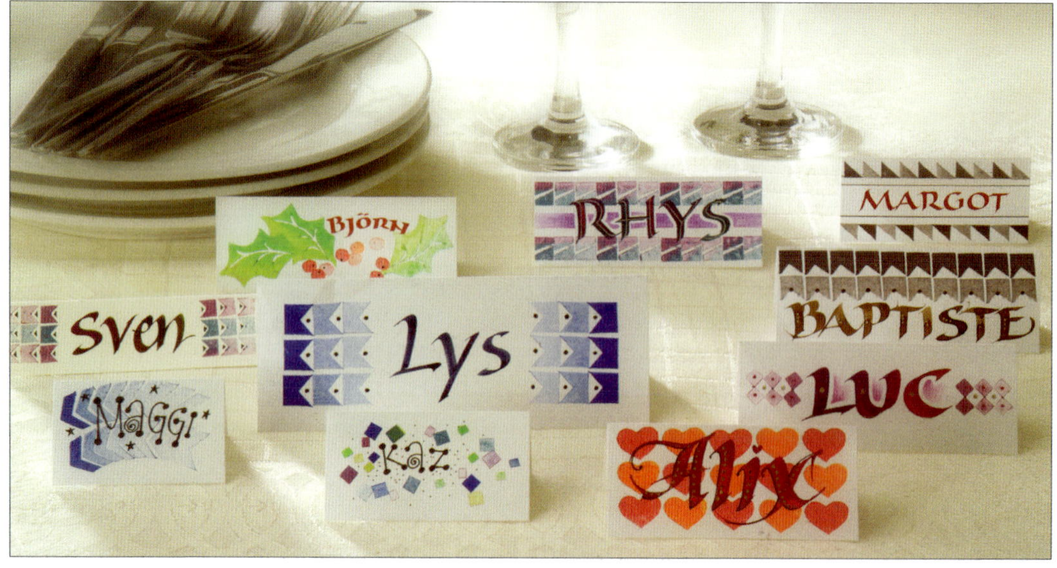

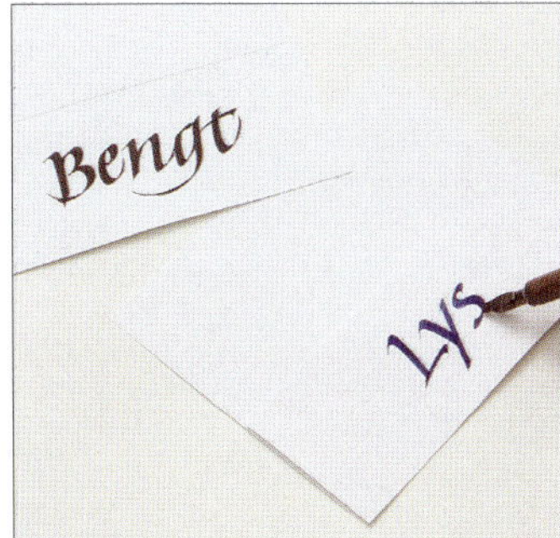

2 Write out the names of the guests in Italic lettering in your chosen colour on one side of the unfolded card. Allow to dry thoroughly. If you plan to stamp the whole surface of the card, you can write the name later, on top of the stamped design.

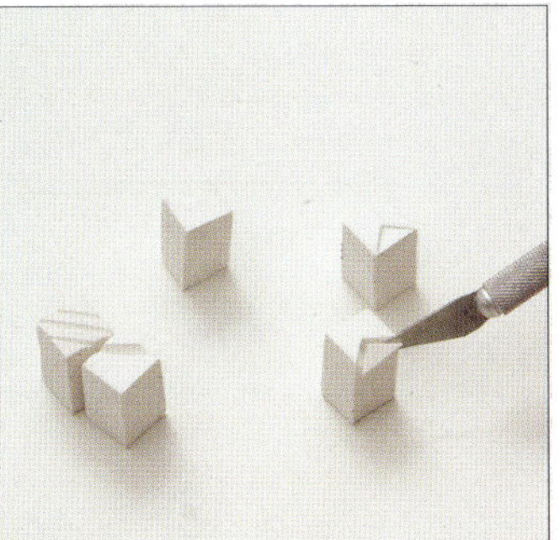

3 To prepare your rubber stamps, cut a small portion of an eraser, with the uncut edge at approximately 1cm (1/2in) square. This is the printing surface on which the design should be cut. If you attempt letters, they must be cut in reverse. Cut 'v'-shaped slivers from the printing surface of the stamp, with the blade entering at 45 degrees each time for clean cuts.

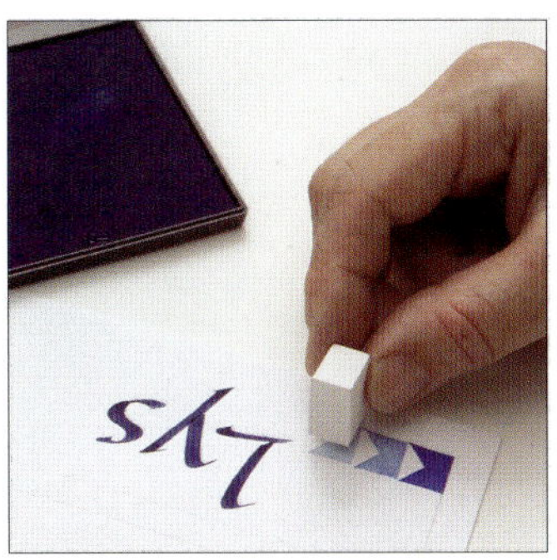

4 Whatever is cut away will show as a gap in the printing. Many varied designs may be achieved by simple cuts. A row of randomly placed 'v'-shaped cuts along the long edge of an eraser will create a terrific border pattern.

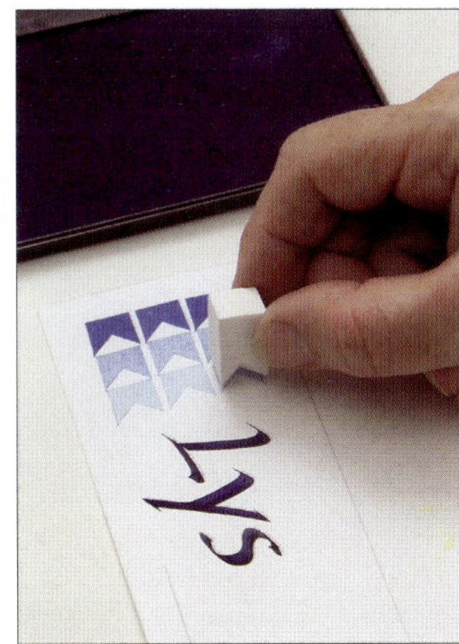

5 If this is your first attempt at printing, you will find it easier to use a purpose-made stamping pad, but you may also want to try making your own, with a little gouache spread on to a dampened foam pad. This adds texture to the prints. Practise stamping in rows, only re-inking every three or four prints. A pattern of repeated shapes, giving a graded tonal effect, makes a very attractive design, before and after the name.

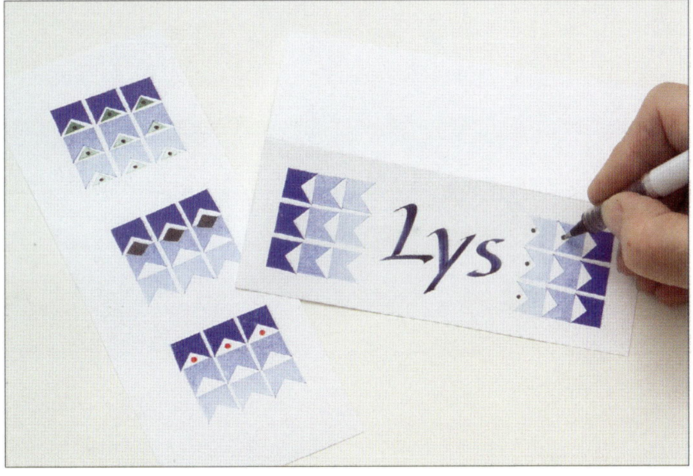

6 Once your cards are dry, you can fold them. You may want to add dots in black, gold or silver with gel pens. Alternatively the designs could be overstamped with further stamps of tiny diamonds or other shapes. Try out some ideas on a separate sheet. If you are writing over stamped designs, wait until the paint is fully dry before writing on top of it.

Tip: Stamp carefully and firmly, placing stamps in close proximity for the best results, in order to build up an effective pattern.

Tip: Keep the stamped designs simple, avoiding circular shapes as they are more difficult to cut. Keep your fingers away from the cutting direction.

Carolingian scroll

The scroll is an ancient invention, which predates the book by thousands of years. It usually consists of a parchment, papyrus, or paper roll adorned with writing and ornamentation. Some of the most beautiful scrolls are on display in museums, where they serve as a record in words and pictures of important historical events. The tradition continues today, as scrolls are used to commemorate important ceremonial occasions – such as the military tradition of granting 'Freedom of the City'. Scrolls are also often seen beautifully decorated with heraldry.

The scroll that is created in this project takes a more lighthearted approach, and could be made to celebrate a birthday or congratulate someone for passing an examination. The layout for this design is landscape rather than portrait, simply to minimize the number of lines you need to rule up. The name of the person being congratulated is written large in the centre, with smaller, flowing script arranged above and below to frame it, so you need to use two sizes of dip pens.

Traditionally, a ribbon was threaded through the top of a scroll in a complex arrangement to keep it closed, but the ribbon here is attached very simply to tie up the scroll and hold it in place. It is a good idea to select your ribbon first, if not choosing gold or silver, and mix your ink to match, as ribbon colours are limited.

The design

Use a sturdy paper such as cartridge or watercolour paper so that your scroll will roll up successfully and keep its shape. Carolingian script has been used for this scroll because it is wider than many hands but with elegant lengthy ascenders, giving a graceful effect even with few words.

Materials

- *Sheet of sturdy white cartridge or watercolour paper*
- *Pencil*
- *Ruler*
- *Layout or practice paper*
- *Pens in contrasting sizes: such as Speedball C-1 and C-3*
- *Gouache paints: orange, red and gold*
- *Mixing palettes and water pot*
- *Paintbrushes*
- *Craft (utility) knife*
- *Ribbon*

Tip: All machine-made papers have grain direction: the paper will feel stiff if it is rolled against the grain, but will roll more easily at right angles to it.

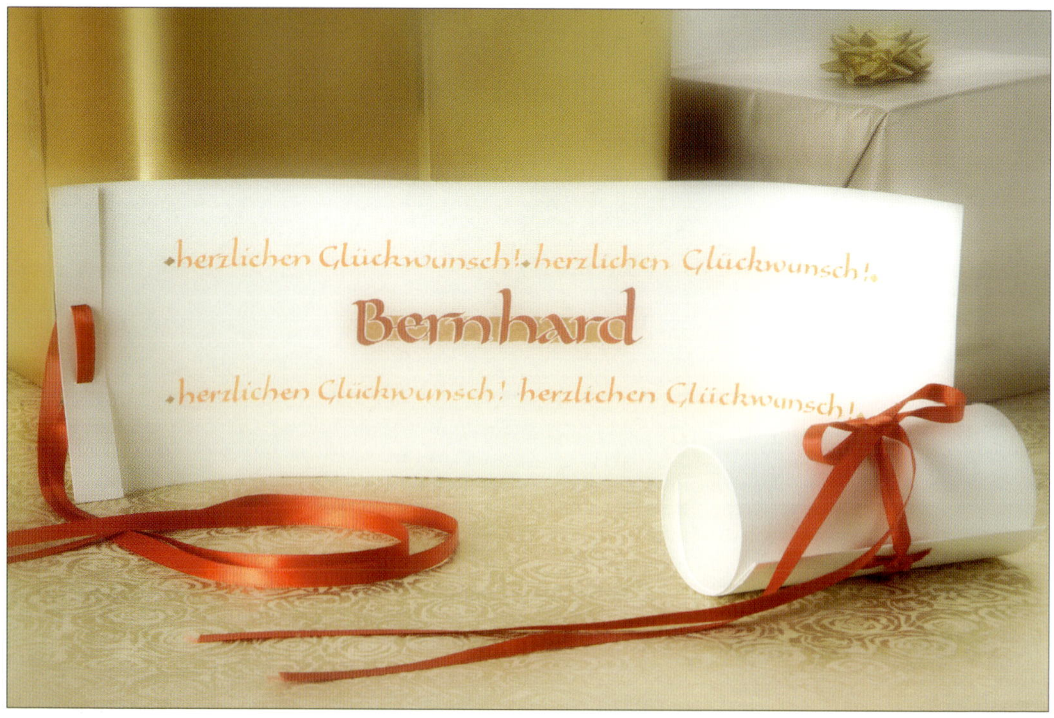

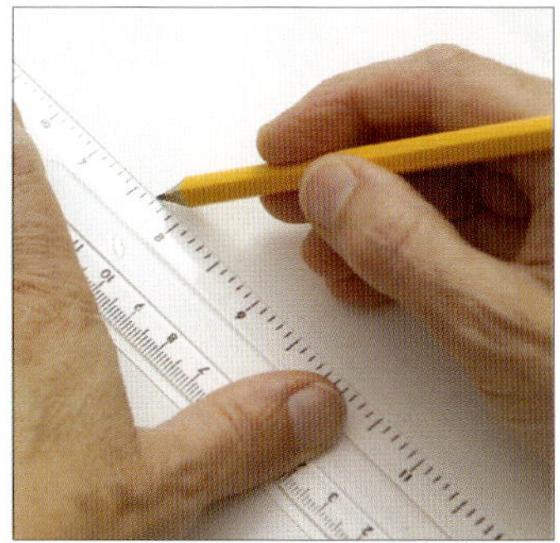

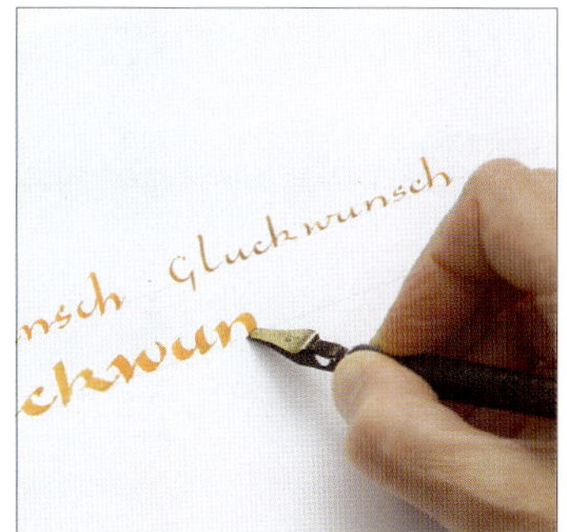

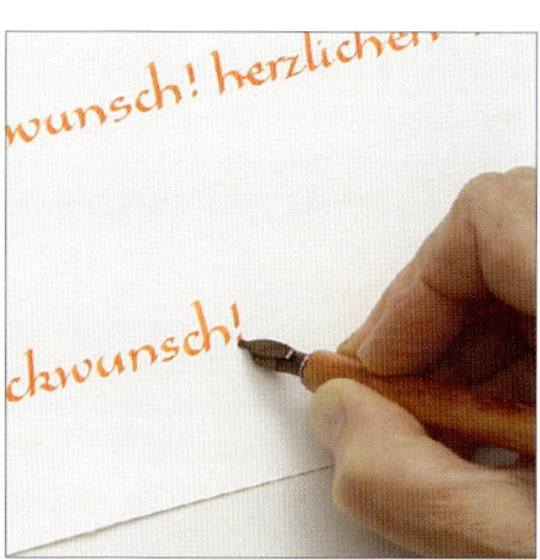

1 Select a sturdy paper, check the grain direction for ease of rolling, and trim to size – approximately 40cm (16in) long and 13cm (5in) wide. Rule lines working out from the centre, for the name, and a line of message above and below.

2 On a separate piece of layout paper, practise writing your chosen phrase in Carolingian; try it out in several sizes of pen. Create contrast by selecting a much larger pen to write the name.

3 Mix the gouache and write the top and bottom lines of small text on the scroll, taking care not to allow ascenders or descenders to intrude into the centre space.

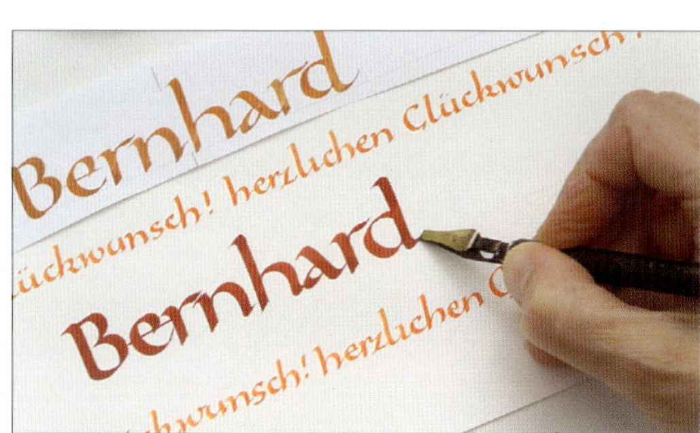

4 Wait until you are sure the first writing is dry, then carefully write the name in the central space in another colour, with the larger pen. Some pre-planning is necessary to ensure it sits in the middle; write it on another sheet first and lay this above your work as a guide.

Tip: When you fold over the left-hand edge of paper, score it lightly with the craft knife against a ruler to allow it to fold more sharply or use a bone folder.

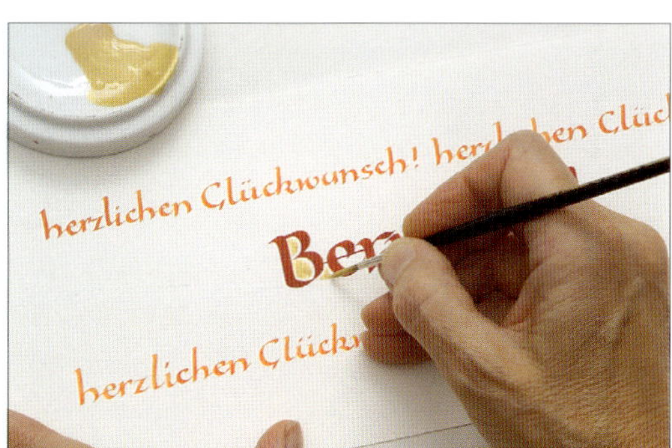

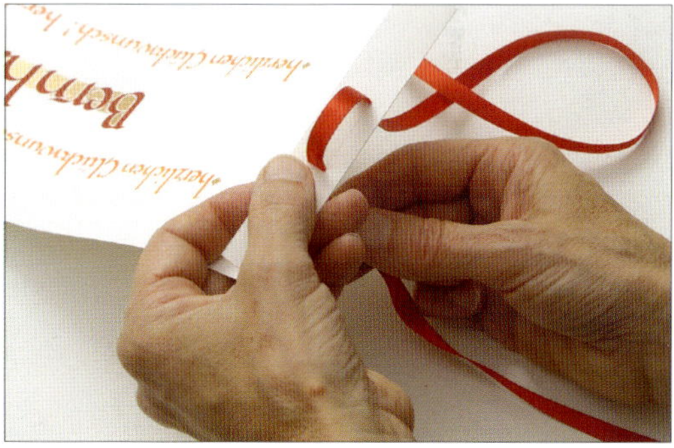

5 Mix the gold gouache to a fairly thick consistency, to fill in the counter spaces in some of the letters. Do not colour right up to the edge; leave a white line to separate the colours, to avoid runs and to allow the colours to stand out against each other.

6 Fold over 2cm (3/4in) of the left-hand edge, cut two slots with a craft knife through both layers, and thread through the ribbon. Roll up the scroll from the other end, so the ribbon's end is outermost. Tie up your finished scroll in a decorative bow. Scrolls are more commonly 'portrait' in layout; try this next time, with a more ambitious quantity of text, ruling more lines.

Calligraphic word with type

The advent of desktop publishing and the ease with which posters or leaflets can be produced on screen may appear to have made traditional calligraphy less important. In reality, a combination of methods whereby a single name or phrase in calligraphy is inserted into a sea of computer-generated type, can be very effective.

The degree of lettering perfection required will depend upon the use to which it will be put. If it is for a one-off occasion, perhaps saying 'Sale' or 'Exhibition', what is needed is legibility coupled with lively writing. If it is likely to be used many times, such as commercially in a business letterhead, or on packaging, then it will require much more refining, as small inconsistencies seen frequently will irritate and will spoil the effect. Graphic designers therefore have to spend a lot of time attending to fine details of shapes and spaces for company names or initials that are put together as logos, as these are intended to become immediately recognizable, and must be without any imperfections.

This project falls into the first category, but the refining process that is required for more ambitious logos, or artworks for business letterheads, is also touched upon. Logo design generally requires pages of trials, and the meticulous process of cutting and pasting the best letters together. However, this project concentrates on the fun of simply rendering a single calligraphic word, and incorporates colour using gouache paints for added vibrancy. Its destination is for scanning into a computer to be linked with a block of text, but if you lack the computer skills you can add the word freehand on to a previously typed page.

Tip: When using a brush for lettering, remember to twist your fingers and not your wrist.

The design

Here, a Latin version of the Lord's Prayer appears in capitals, with the focal point being the final calligraphic 'Amen' – which signals at a glance that this is a prayer. Uncials have particularly interesting forms for those four letters, and this script is historically appropriate as it was used to write bibles from the 4th century AD as Christianity spread in western Europe.

Materials

- *Felt-tipped pens*
- *Automatic pen or wide dip pen such as William Mitchell O*
- *Layout or practice paper*
- *Pencil*
- *Ruler*
- *Watercolour paper*
- *Gouache paints: ultramarine and magenta*
- *Mixing palette*
- *Paintbrushes*
- *Craft (utility) knife or scalpel*
- *Self-healing cutting mat*
- *Glue stick*

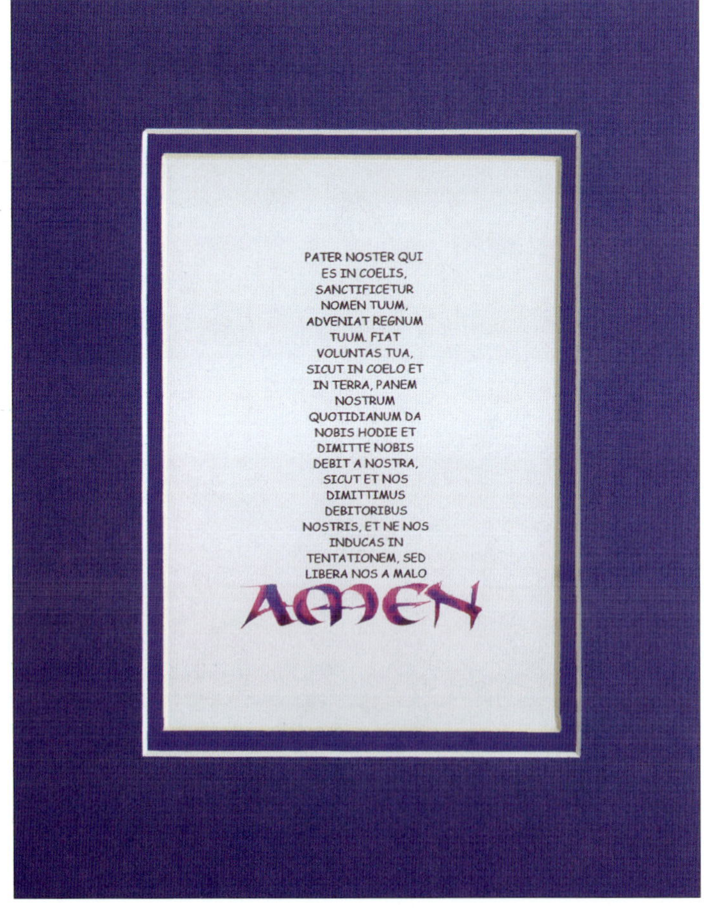

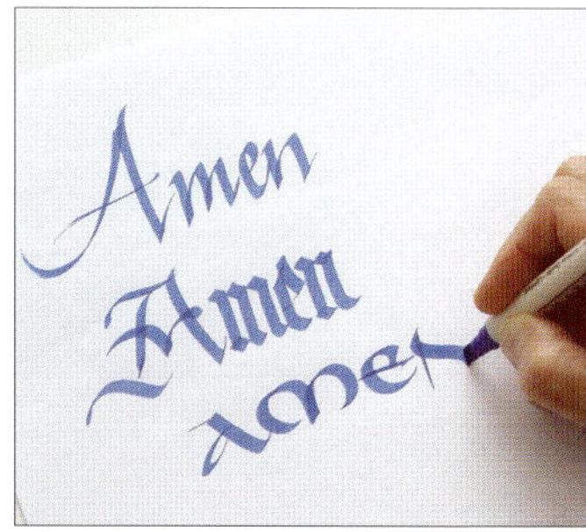

1 Explore your chosen word in various calligraphic formats to decide how to express the meaning. Gothic has a splendid 'A', but the narrowness of the complete word may not suit the layout. The letters have no ascenders or descenders and so will not easily lend themselves to flourishing, but the choice here of Uncial will allow plenty of lettering area in which to add colour.

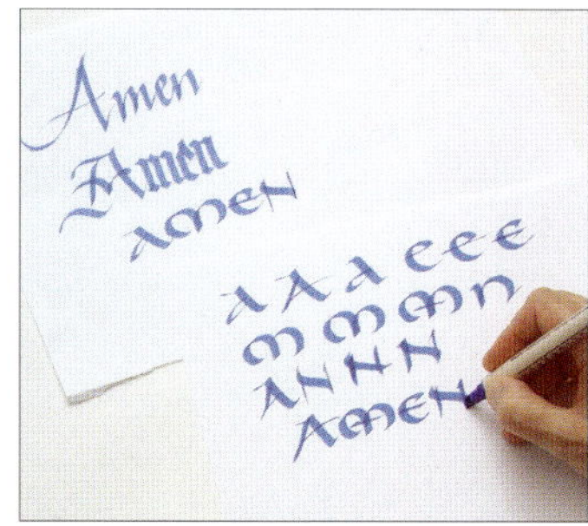

2 Once the script has been decided, the letters should be examined for any awkward combinations, and to check for inconsistencies of style. If this was a business logo, much more time would be spent at this stage in refining the details and making improvements in the design.

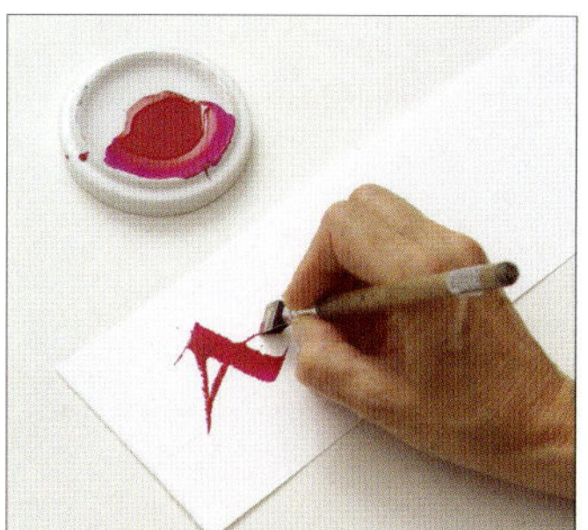

3 Mix two colours in the palette that will blend well together and check that they do not turn muddy when combined. Do not choose colours that oppose each other on the colour wheel, such as red and green. Write a letter in colour on the watercolour paper.

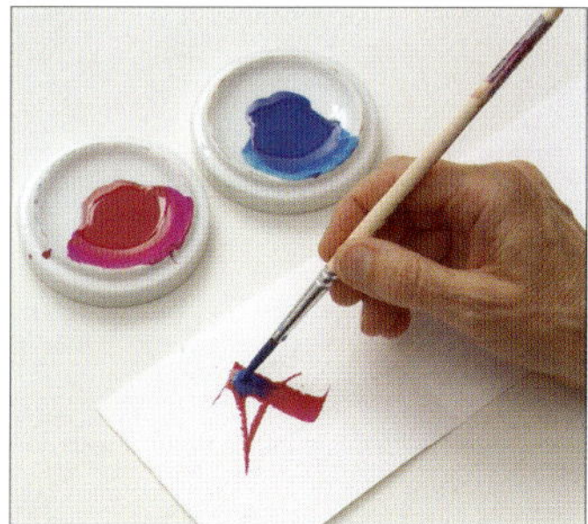

4 While the letter is still wet, charge a paintbrush with another colour and touch it on to the wet areas in the letter; watch the colour spread. Move the paper about to increase the spread if necessary. Continue this process for the rest of the word.

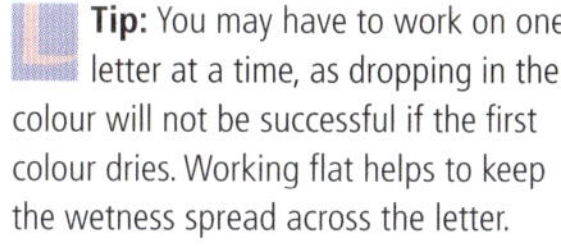

Tip: You may have to work on one letter at a time, as dropping in the colour will not be successful if the first colour dries. Working flat helps to keep the wetness spread across the letter.

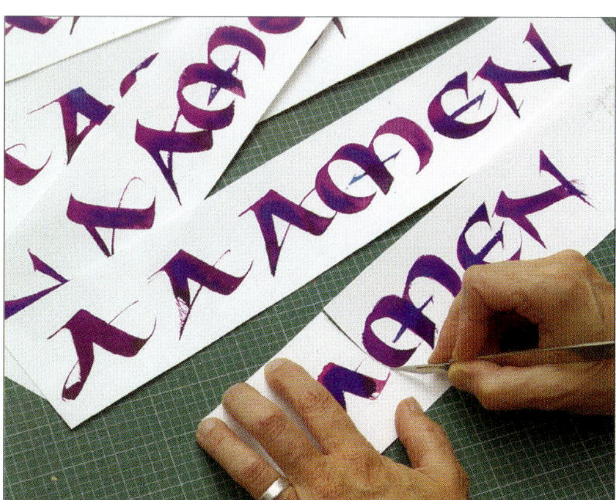

5 Select the best parts of the lettering. Often a word is successful except for one letter or the spacing needs adjusting. Make any changes by cutting and pasting the best letters or groups of letters to form the final word.

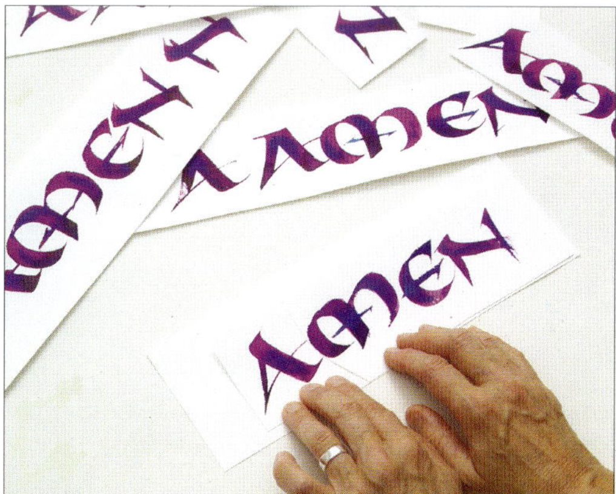

6 The completed title or logo has now been refined and is ready to be scanned into the computer. If you have the necessary skills, the paste-up exercise can be done on computer, but you may still find it quicker to physically cut and paste.

Brush lettering on cloth

It is possible to write on many more materials than paper, provided you are willing to experiment with the versatility of brushes. This project employs a fine pointed brush and uses a letterform that was traditionally drawn as decorative initials. In this project this initial design or monogram is used to decorate one corner of fine cloth.

It is advisable to keep the design simple if you plan to make a series of the same or a similar design. Initialled table napkins or handkerchiefs make excellent gifts. Choose a fabric that is thin enough to see through, as you need to be able to see the letters through the fabric in order to paint them accurately. If you cannot see the letters easily, use a lightbox or tape the fabric to a window. Fine cotton handkerchiefs are perfect, especially as they are already cut to size and finished. Alternatively, you could cut some fine lawn or muslin (cheesecloth) fabric. Fray the edges by pulling out several threads, then stitch along the solid edges to prevent further fraying.

In this project cotton handkerchiefs are painted with a single repeated letter 'R' in different colours, and are moved around to make a lettering square. You can choose your own initials, provided they combine and work well with each other; extra planning will be necessary if the letters are different widths.

Use fabric paints to work the lettering on to cloth, which can be bought from artists' suppliers. Do not use silk dyes, which are too watery and designed to spread – these letters need sharp edges. Add as little water as possible, while maintaining some flow of colour. Controlling the brush and the wetness of the paint will take some practice.

Materials

- *Alphabet exemplar*
- *Tracing paper*
- *Sharp pencil*
- *Squares of fine fabric*
- *Masking tape*
- *Mixing saucer or palette*
- *Water pot*
- *Fabric paints*
- *Narrow pointed brush*

The design

The Versal letterform, built up with several pen strokes, lends itself to fine pointed brush painting. Its geometric shapes also combine well when juxtaposed to make a pleasing pattern. Using two colours adds interest to the motif.

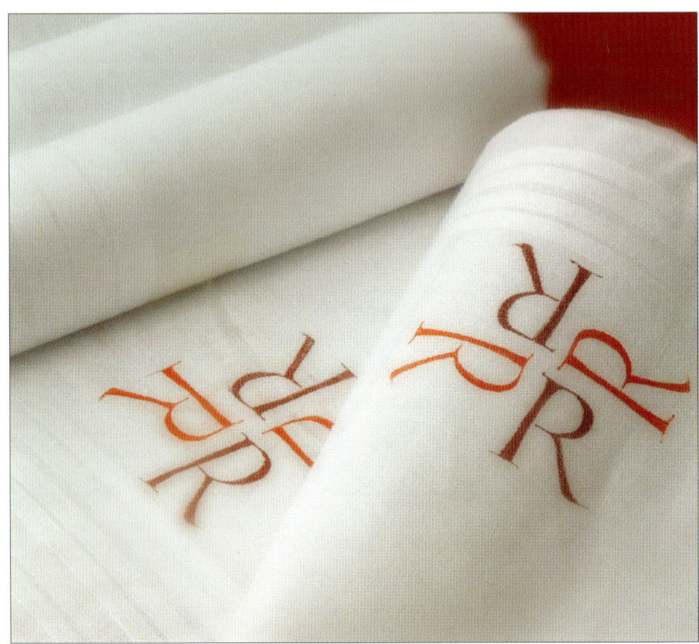

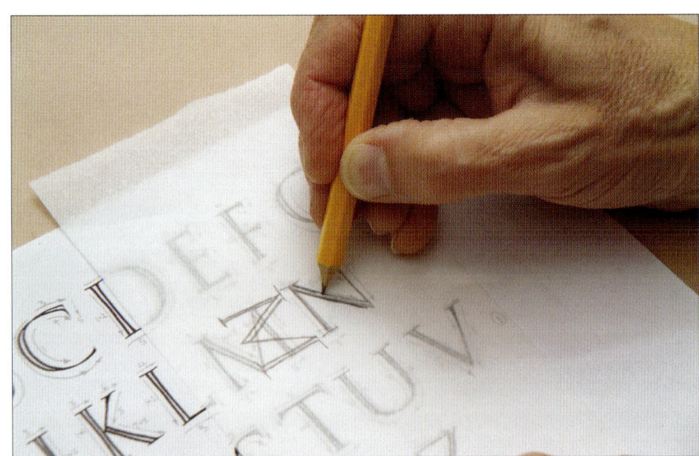

1 First select your letters and try out designs to see how they will combine by tracing one letter from the alphabet exemplar with a pencil then moving at right angles to fit another letter alongside.

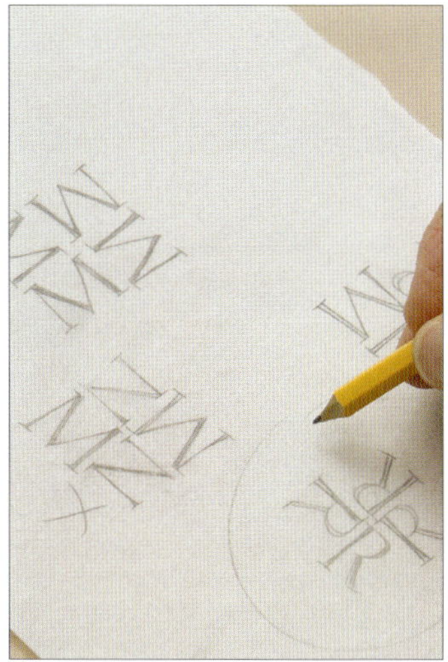

2 Here 'M' and 'N', and two 'M's together have been tried as combinations. If using two different letters, fit them together by keeping them closely spaced at the centre. The final choice here is a repeated 'R'.

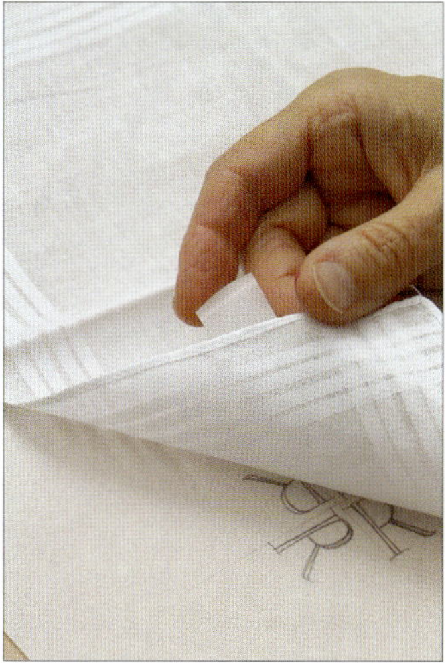

3 Attach thin fabric, or the corner of a handkerchief over the drawing with masking tape. Put some fabric paint in a saucer and add as little water as possible, so that the paint can flow without bleeding on the fabric.

Tip: Use a paintbrush with a fine point and reject any that have stray hairs. A springy nylon brush is ideal.

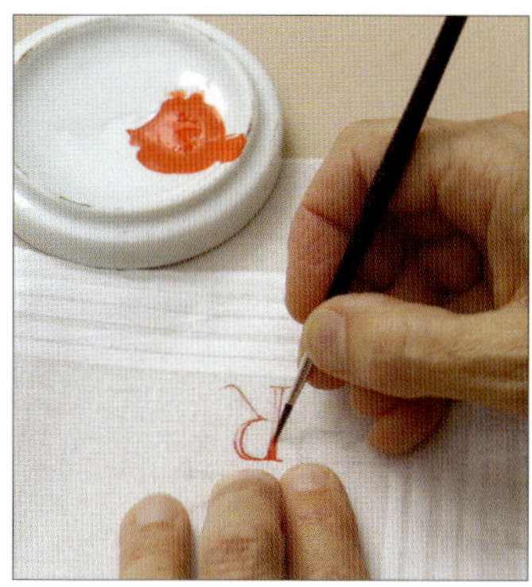

4 Carefully and accurately paint in your first letter, paying particular attention to the serifs; these must be rendered as fine lines and need a steady hand.

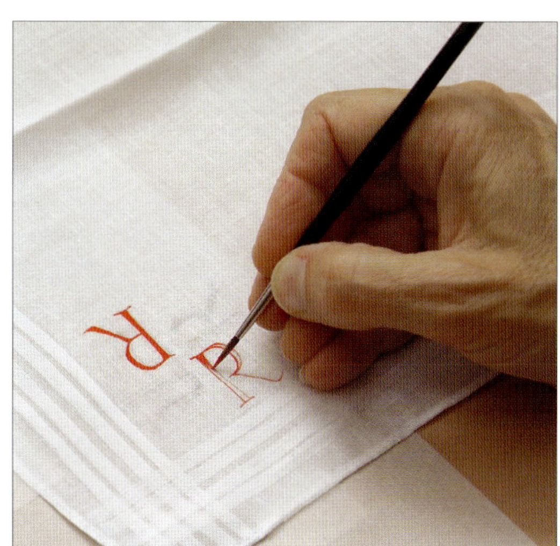

5 Repeat the opposite letter in the same colour. Try to ensure you see clearly your design underneath, for accuracy; outline a stem before filling it in.

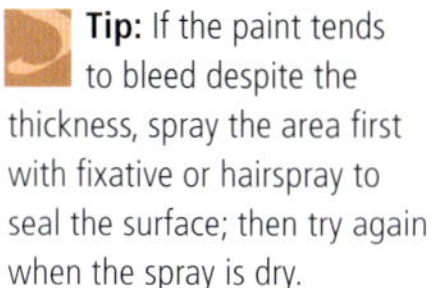

Tip: If the paint tends to bleed despite the thickness, spray the area first with fixative or hairspray to seal the surface; then try again when the spray is dry.

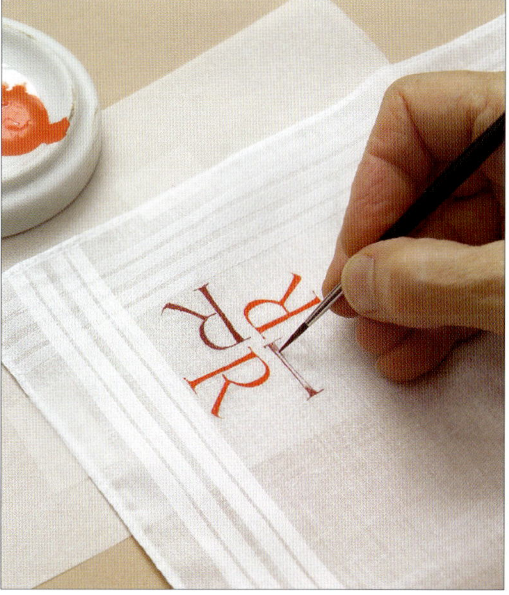

6 Use another colour for the second letter, here a darker red, again taking care to be accurate. Keep the fabric over or attached to the tracing at all times. Follow the paint label instructions for fixing the colour – usually by ironing.

Drawing up a perpetual calendar

A perpetual calendar is used to record significant dates that recur from year to year, such as birthdays or anniversaries, and is expected to last for some years. On a perpetual calendar the days of the week are not included as they vary from year to year. The calendar should be sturdy, to survive lengthy display, so it is worth spending some time selecting suitable paper, and refining the writing. Numerals rarely occur in large quantities, but in this project you can get a rhythm going as they need to be written in blocks. You do not need to leave as large a space for calendar entries as you would on a normal calendar.

The months of the year vary a great deal in length, which has implications when deciding layout. Repetition is one solution, and varied letter weights for decorative contrast. Here patterning is used to fill the areas decoratively. Simple squares of three different sizes are cut from erasers and used to make random overlapped patterns along the spaces left on the writing lines.

You will need a ruling pen, not as an expressive tool for writing, but for its original purpose – ruling lines in one of the colours used for the writing. However, if more convenient, a fine liner felt-tipped pen in a suitable colour could be substituted.

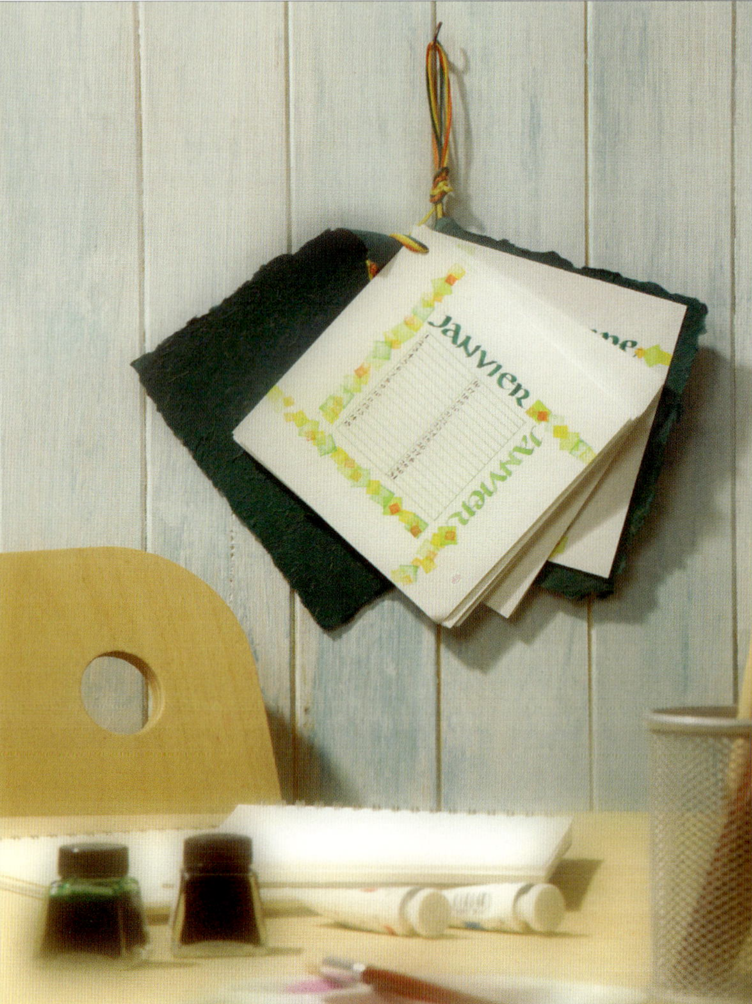

The design

This calendar is designed to hang on a wall, showing one month per page. Fitting the numbers on to a square, using two rows only, allows space for the user to make short entries. The months are written in Uncial. The pages are joined with a single hole punched in the corner, and threaded through with ribbon, providing creative opportunities if you enjoy using beads.

Materials

- *Layout or practice paper*
- *Dip pens, such as William Mitchell 1 (large nib) and 3½ (medium nib)*
- *Pencil and sharpener*
- *Ruler with a bevel edge*
- *Craft (utility) knife*
- *Self-healing cutting mat*
- *Glue stick*
- *Eraser*
- *Absorbent cloth*
- *Gouache paints: phthalo blue and lemon yellow*
- *Ruling pen or a fine liner felt-tipped pen*
- *Watercolour paper, cut to 17cm (6½in) square*
- *Coloured paper for cover*
- *Hole punch*
- *Ribbon and beads*

1 Numerals need time to get right. Practise them at a large size, then graduate through pen sizes to see how small you are prepared to go; aim for no bigger than a 1mm (3/64in) nib.

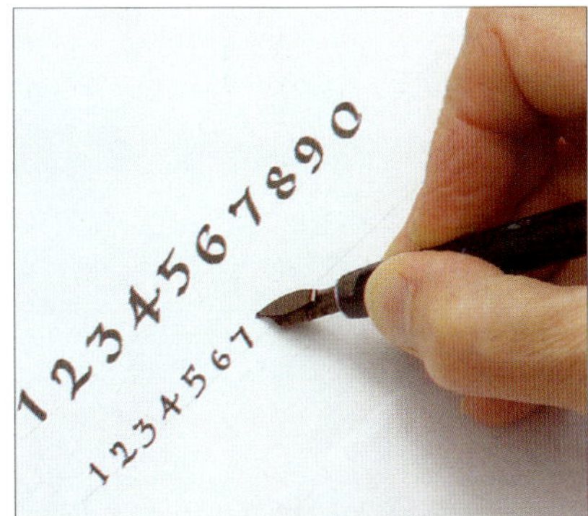

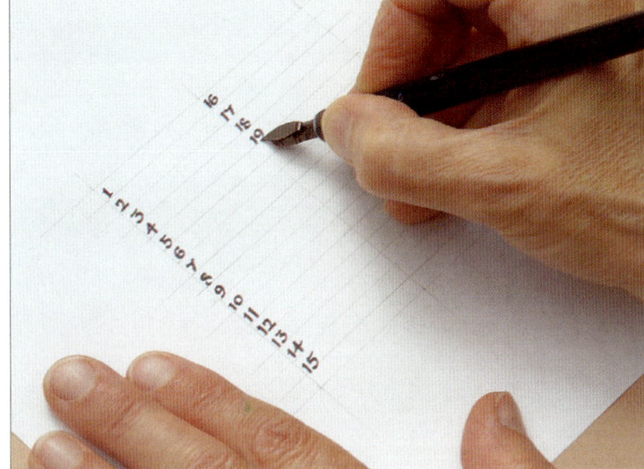

3 Practise writing the numbers downwards consecutively, 1-15 first row, and 16-31 – or less, for those shorter months – on the next, using a 1mm (3/64in) nib.

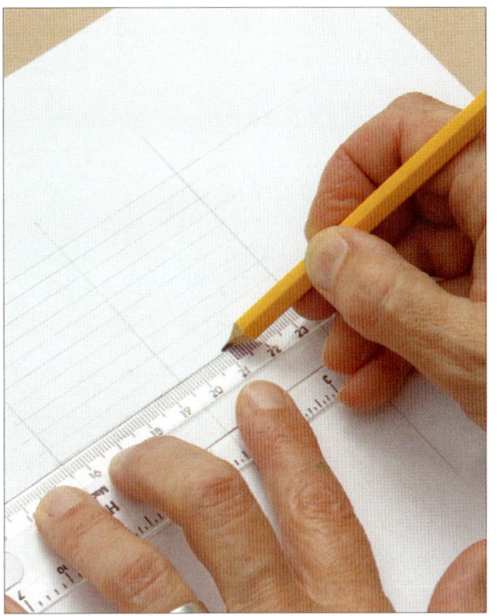

2 With a sharp pencil, rule lines to make a square 7.5cm x 7.5cm (3in x 3in) on practice paper, inside the overall 17cm (6 1/2in). Subdivide the square every 5mm (1/4in) all the way down, and just once across. The format will be the same for every month.

Tip: The ruling pen has a screw at the side to allow for cleaning, but also for adjusting the thickness of the ruled lines; screw it tight first, and make trials gradually unscrewing it until you are satisfied with the thickness; the paint needs to be thin or it will clog.

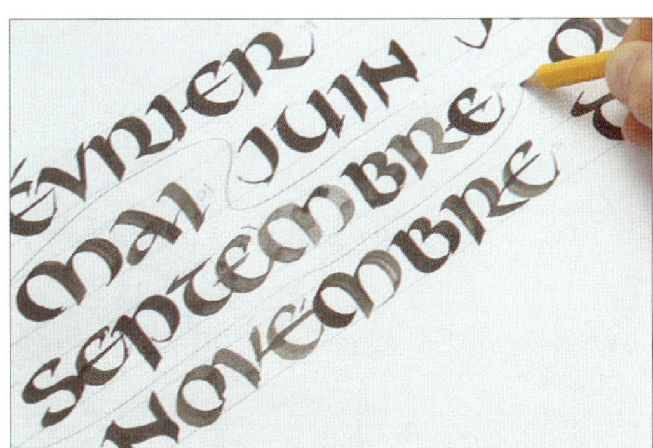

4 Now try out the months. These are written between lines at 1cm (1/2in). Compare your longest and shortest month to determine how they will fit in the same area.

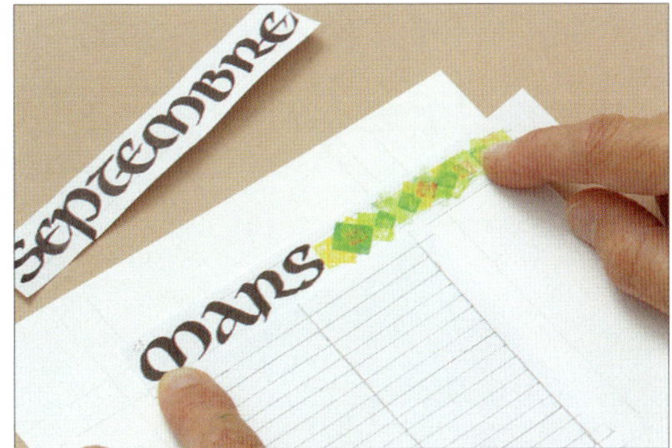

5 Prepare a paste-up to compare the look of a short month and a long one, placed against the square of numbers. Plan the final ruling-up at this stage; you will need to allow a space to separate the lettering from the numbers box.

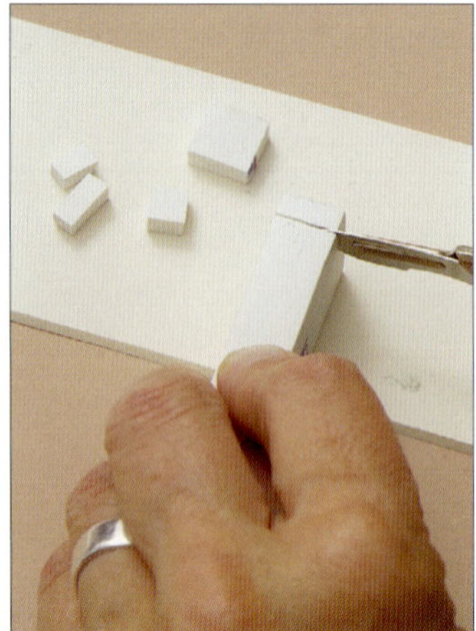

6 Cut simple rubber stamps for the pattern-making. Cut squares in three sizes from a plastic eraser, using a craft knife. More complex designs can also be cut, requiring more dexterity, or you could use ready-made stamps.

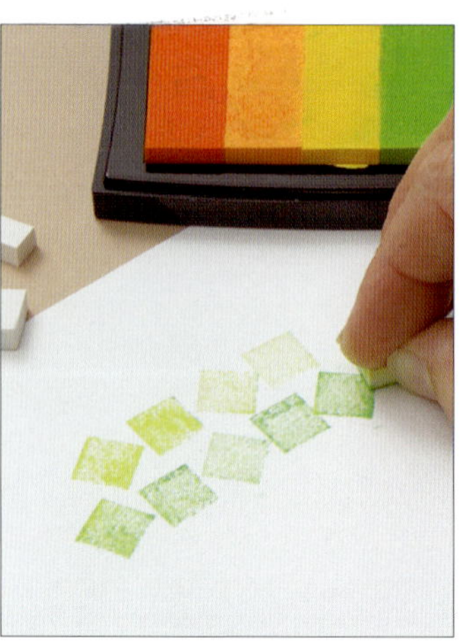

7 Use a small pad of absorbent soft cloth as a stamping pad, filled with paint mixed to an ink consistency, with a series of mixed colours that blend well together, or find a commercially produced multicoloured stamp pad.

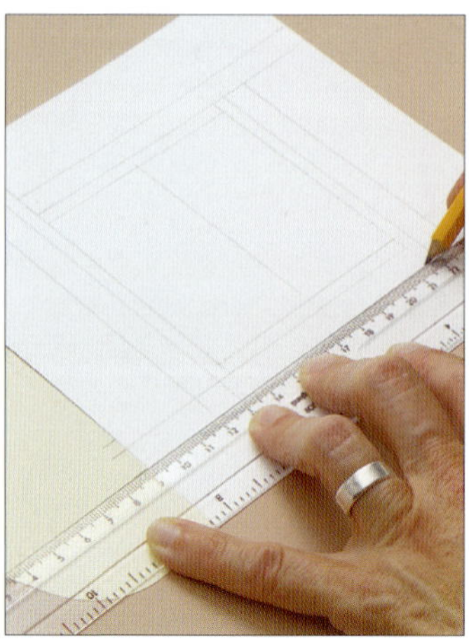

8 As there are 12 pages to rule up, it is worth preparing a template to save time. Mark all the measurements clearly on the edge of a strip of paper, and transfer them with a pencil on to the four edges of the square, then lightly rule across.

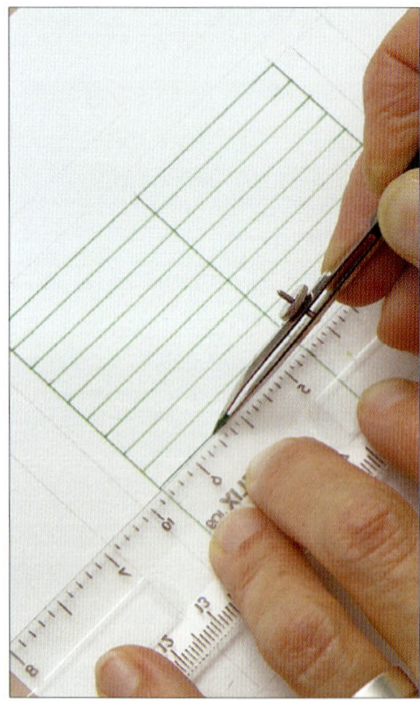

9 For the numerals box, rule all the lines in your chosen colour with the ruling pen. Make sure the ruler has its bevel edge up to prevent ink running underneath.

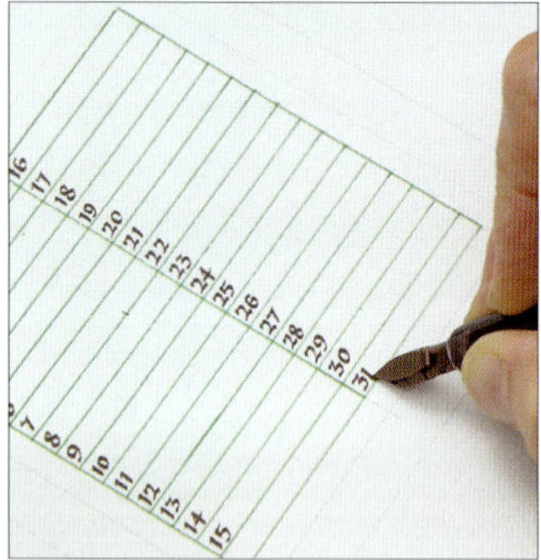

10 Write all the numerals first, noting which months have 31, 30 and 29, and reject any pages with mistakes.

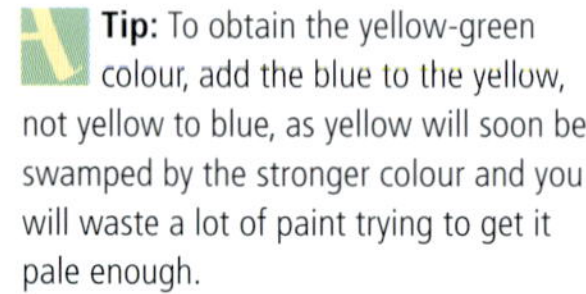

Tip: To obtain the yellow-green colour, add the blue to the yellow, not yellow to blue, as yellow will soon be swamped by the stronger colour and you will waste a lot of paint trying to get it pale enough.

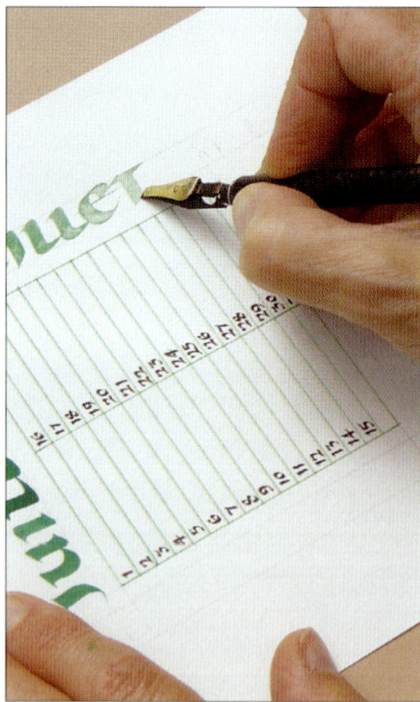

11 Then add the months, in a strong colour, here mixed with phthalo blue with a touch of lemon yellow. Write the second word in a more watery, yellower mix, so that it is less dominant than the first.

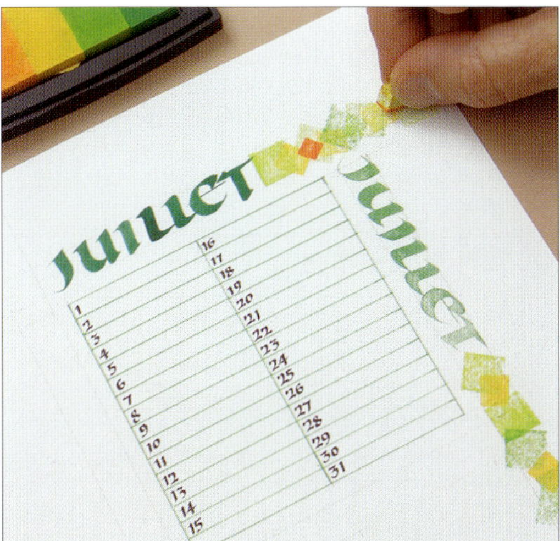

12 Do the stamping last, following the lines to bleed off the edges; experiment with colours and overlapping shapes and sizes. Make the stamping random, with lightest colours first.

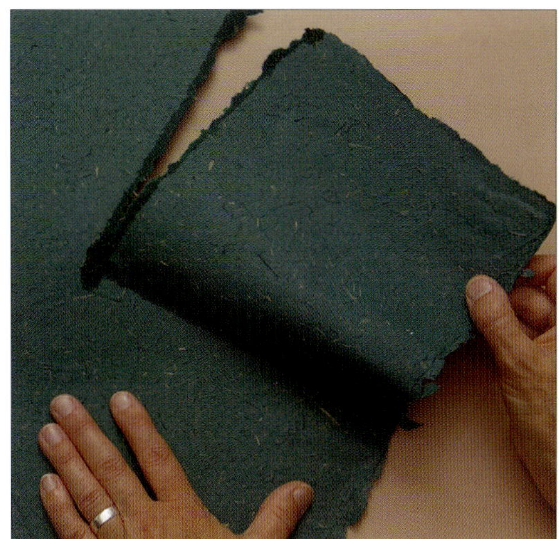

13 Assess the required size of a cover. Make it a little larger than the pages, to protect them. If using hand-made paper as here, you can trim the sides to mimic the deckle edge by running water from a paintbrush along a ruler, then pulling apart when the water has soaked in.

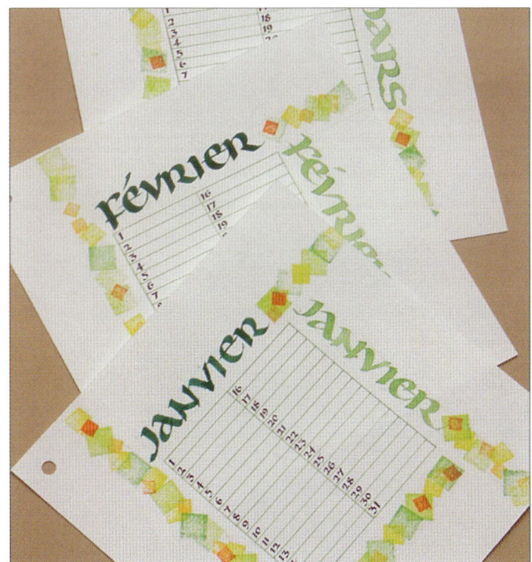

14 Assemble the pages in the right order, and use a hole puncher to make a hole in the corner. You will need to try this out on spare paper first, and when successfully positioned, mark how far in to push the paper by taping a piece of card to the machine.

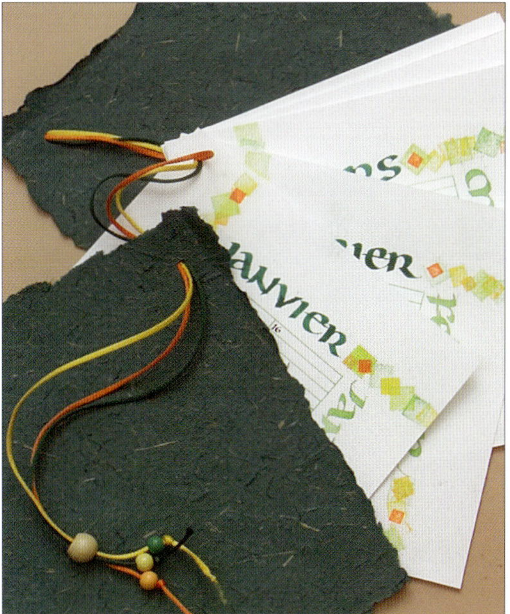

15 Fix all together with a ribbon and beads, choosing colours that repeat those used inside. Include a hanging thread to allow the calendar to be displayed on a wall for easy reference.

Curved lines on chalk pastels

Once you are confident in writing calligraphy along straight lines, you may want to try something more challenging. Many poems and quotations are expressive in nature and ask to be interpreted in a less rigid way than suggested by straight lines. Gentle, wavy lines may be the solution. However, they should not be overdone. Be aware that it is easy to overdo the curve of the waves. The curves should have gentle undulations, and parallel curves will help them blend into a design. Plan to vary the start and end point of each line of writing, in order to maintain the illusion of movement; wavy lines that all start ranged left are not usually so successful.

This project uses chalk pastels as a background. They can be purchased in many subtle colours and can usually be bought individually. The advantage of pastels is that you can choose to build up either a very subtle colour or a strong, powerful one, and they allow the beginner more control than watercolour paints. Chalk pastels are a dry medium, so will not make the paper cockle (wrinkle).

The design

The chosen text is a Celtic blessing about coming home safely. It is written in Uncial, and is arranged to fit offset on three lines, to give a feeling of movement. The background is laid first, using layers of pastel colours rubbed into the surface. The wavy lines are drawn in pastel so that they can be blended into the background after completing the writing in gouache.

Materials

- *Pencil*
- *Thin card (stock)*
- *Self-healing cutting mat*
- *Craft (utility) knife*
- *Chalk pastels: conte red, orange and ochre*
- *Cotton wool (balls)*
- *Smooth watercolour paper or cartridge paper*
- *Mixing palette*
- *Gouache paints: purple lake and ultramarine*
- *Dip pens, such as William Mitchell $1\frac{1}{2}$ and $2\frac{1}{2}$ (small nibs)*

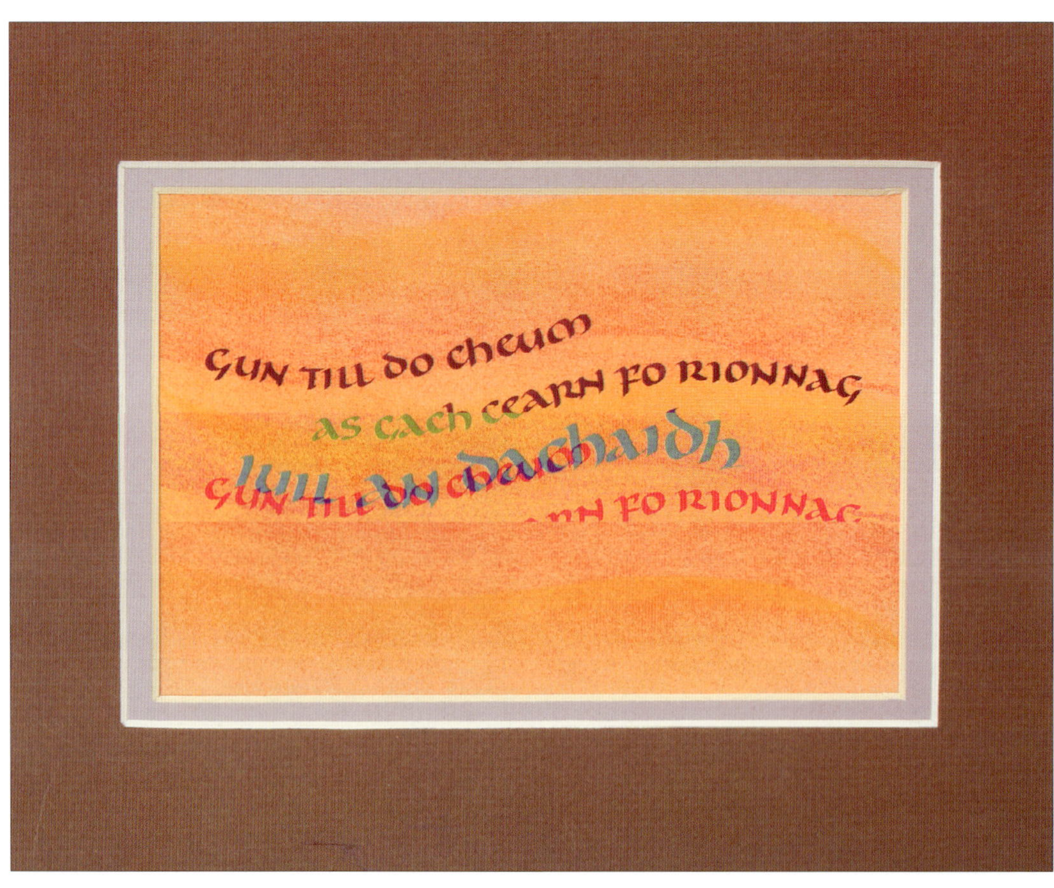

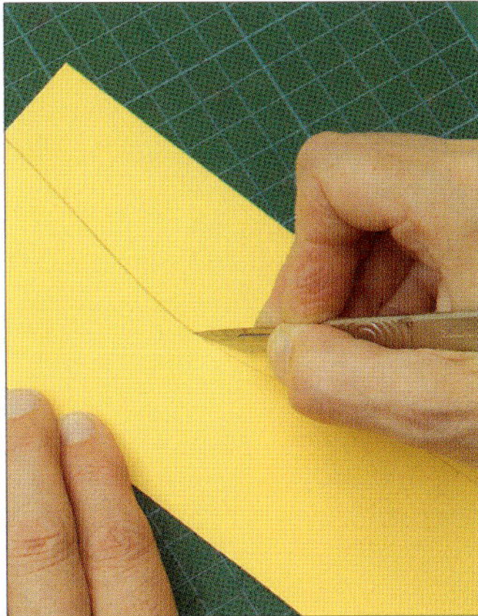

1 Pencil freehand a gentle curve on a piece of thin card. When you are satisfied with its profile, lay it on a cutting mat to protect your work surface and cut smoothly along the line with a craft knife to make a template.

Tip: You can spray with fixative or hairspray if you are concerned about the pastel smudging.

Tip: The harder you rub the pastel into the paper, the better the writing surface will be for sharp writing – loose chalk will clog the pen.

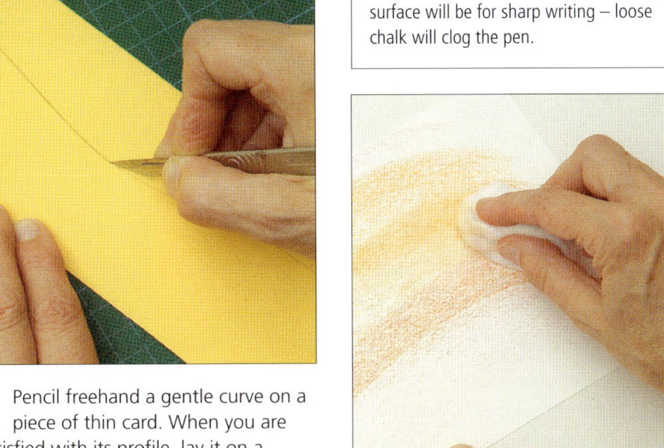

2 Select three pastel colours that work well together when mixed – red, orange and ochre are used here – rub them over the paper in wavy movements and press them firmly into the surface using a wad of cotton wool.

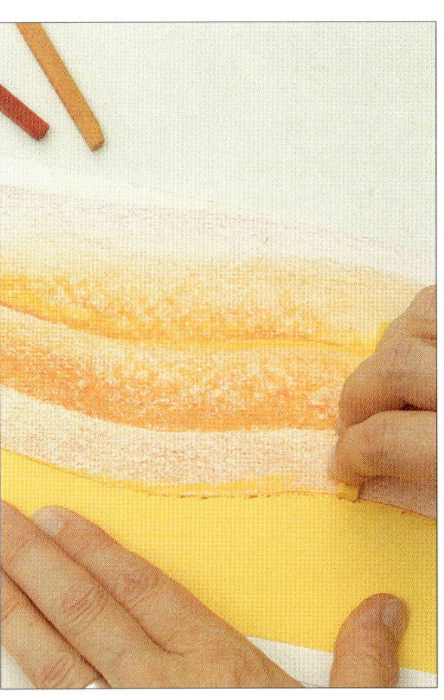

3 Lay the template over the colour background and use the pastel on its side to make a sweeping stroke along the curve of the template. Move the template down for the next line and repeat using another pastel colour, and so on for the third line. This should give sufficient mark for writing on – but you will have to manage without a top line.

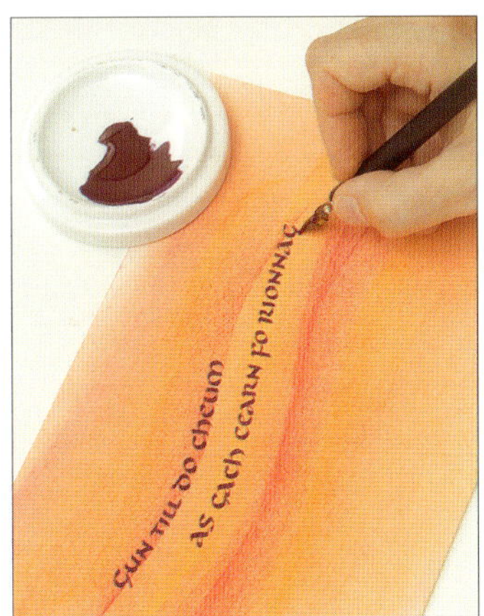

4 Mix the purple gouache paint to writing consistency and write the first line of text, moving the paper regularly so that the writing stays perpendicular to its line. You may have to press quite hard to make the paint stay on the pastel, but it will provide very sharp lettering.

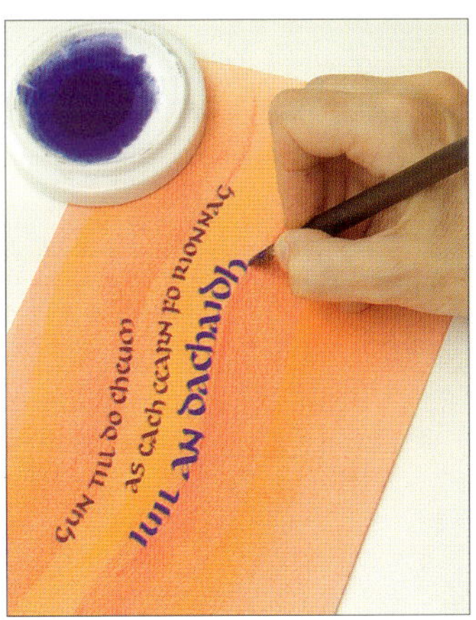

5 Use a bigger pen to write the last line, in ultramarine gouache, for emphasis. Leave it for some time to make sure it has dried before blending in the lines.

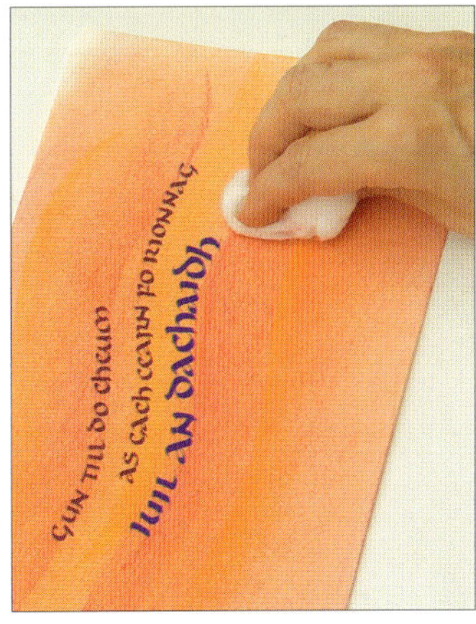

6 Erase the lines by rubbing in the pastel so that it blends into the background; this rubbing may slightly affect the paint in the writing, so take care not to write in too pale a colour. At this stage, you can touch up the background with extra depth of colour if needed.

Brush lettering on a T-shirt

Writing on T-shirt fabric can be very successful if you use a broad-edged brush rather than a pen. Choose a fabric paint if the T-shirt is likely to be washed frequently. Alternatively, if you are using a cheap T-shirt for a one-off occasion, use household emulsion paint which is available in sample pots – this dries as a waterproof paint but will eventually wear off in the wash. The positional area for the wording on an adult sized T-shirt is generally accepted to be a maximum 200mm (8in) wide, placed centrally. If the wording goes much wider, it will be lost in creases when the T-shirt is worn, although this will vary according to the size of the wearer. The choice of paint colour will be influenced by the colour of the T-shirt. If you find a bargain batch of navy blue T-shirts, choosing white paint will ensure your writing has dramatic impact. Pastel coloured T-shirts can cope with soft coloured paints, but when in doubt, choose black paint as it will always show up. A dramatic wording is a pleasing result.

Materials
- *Practice paper or brown Kraft paper*
- *Broad-edged brush, nylon, approx. 1cm (1/2in) wide*
- *Fabric paint or household emulsion (latex) paint: red*
- *Scissors*
- *Tape*
- *Ruler*
- *White chalk*
- *Plain cotton T-shirt*

The design

Rustic letterforms, with their tall, slender shape, lend themselves to a vertical arrangement, which suits the four short words of the quotation. To hold together as a design, the words need to be laid out close together with minimal space between the lines. One colour has been used here, but when you get more ambitious, you can consider including more colours. Keep the message brief. The Latin quotation chosen here translates as 'The art is long and life is short' (Hippocrates, c.460–375BC).

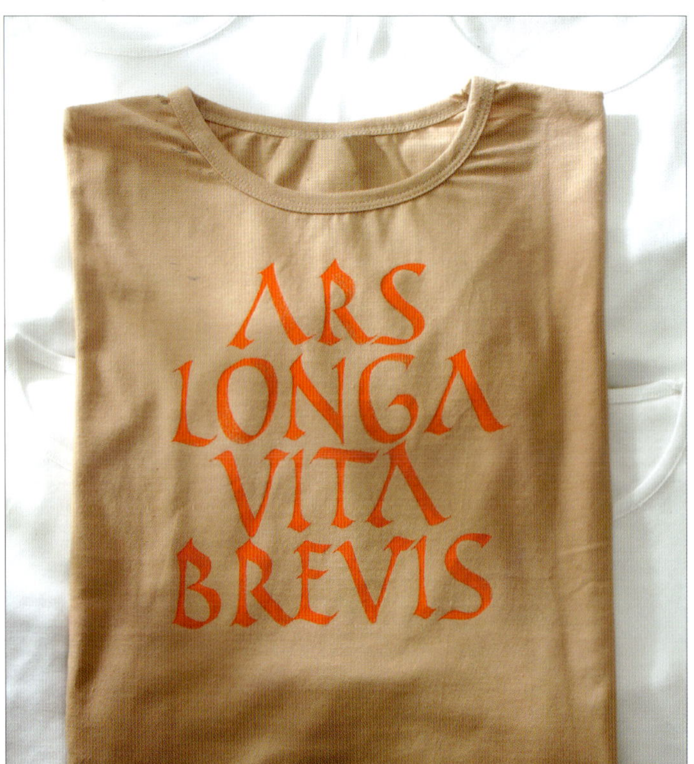

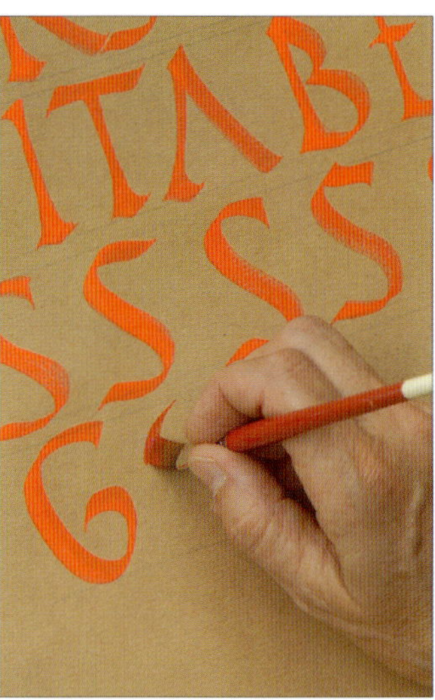

1 Practise the letterform, focusing on those letters needed for the quotation. If the broad-edged brush is a new tool for you, take time to adjust to its feel. If you can practise on the rough side of Kraft paper, this will give a resistance that is similar to the surface of fabric. For a 1cm (1/2in) brush, try letters that are 5cm (2in) high.

Tip: Light colours on dark T-shirts may need extra brushstrokes to obtain dense coverage of the paint and help it to read clearly.

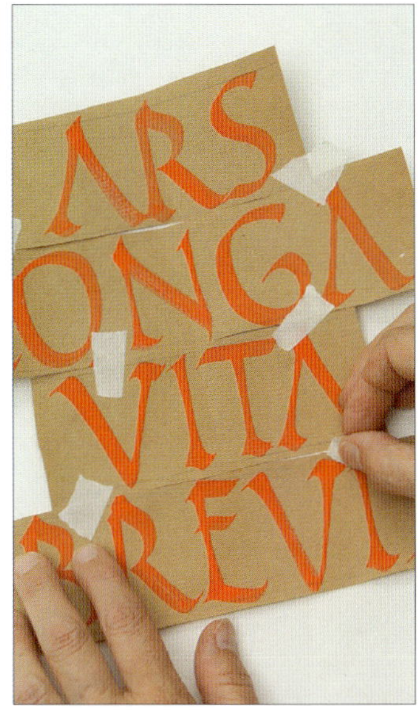

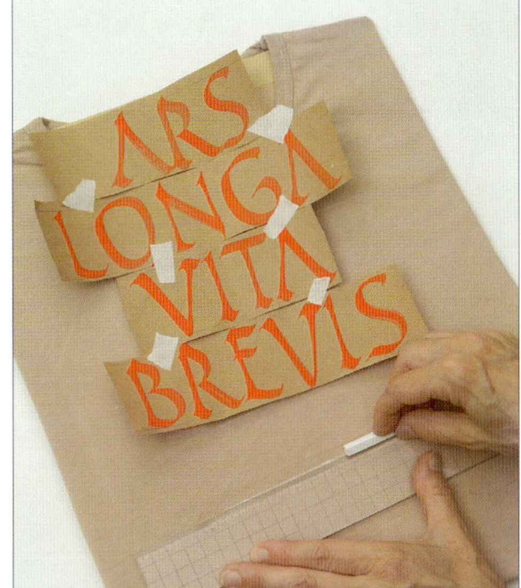

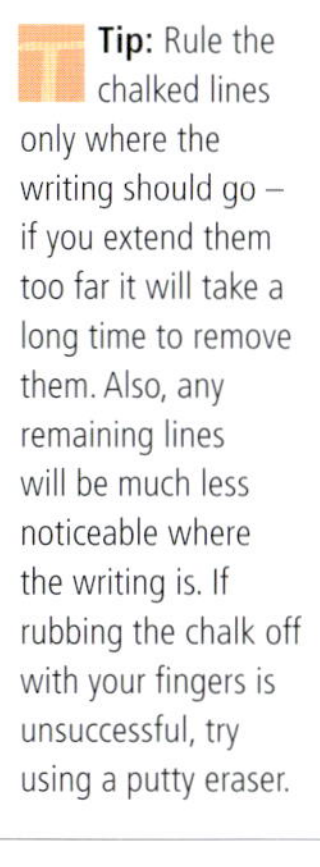

Tip: Rule the chalked lines only where the writing should go – if you extend them too far it will take a long time to remove them. Also, any remaining lines will be much less noticeable where the writing is. If rubbing the chalk off with your fingers is unsuccessful, try using a putty eraser.

2 Cut up the writing practice papers and arrange the words one above the other to check the fit of the final shape on your T-shirt. If it is for a child's T-shirt, you may need to rearrange the layout, or to redo it all smaller.

3 Wrap your T-shirt around something flat, such as a large piece of card (stock) and tape it steady, or simply tape it to a worksurface. Take measurements from your taped-up practice writing and lightly rule lines with chalk – trim the chalk to an edge if necessary.

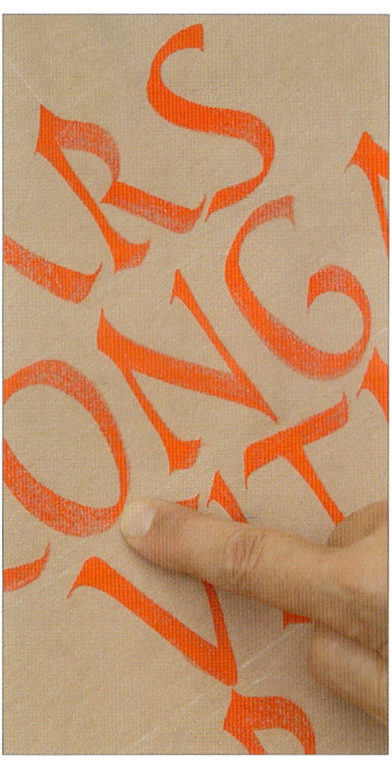

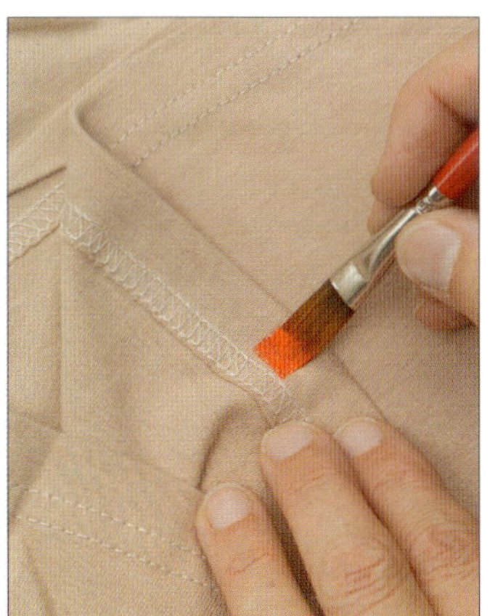

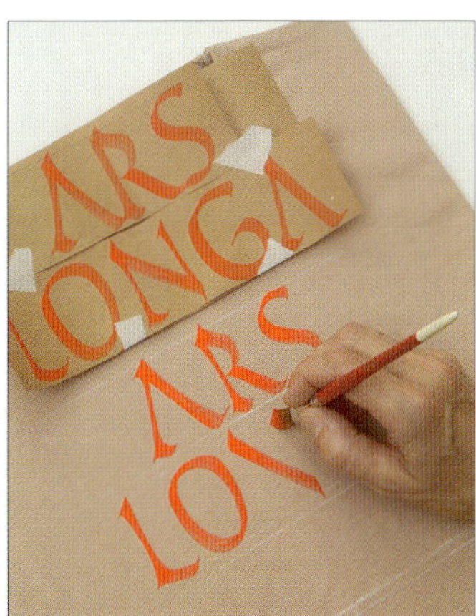

4 Test your paint on a non-visible area of the T-shirt first – an inside seam perhaps – to check it will show up and not bleed; add as little water as possible, and keep the brush wiped to a sharp chisel edge at all times.

5 Position the practice sheet directly above or below, for reference, and start painting. Recharge the brush frequently but wipe most of it off to maintain the chisel edge; too much paint on the brush will cause blobby marks.

6 When the writing is complete, leave it to dry then rub the chalk lines away with your finger. Remove the tape and iron it on the reverse to fix the paint or follow the directions on the fabric paint bottle.

Congratulations card with resist

Handmade cards are always a pleasure to receive, especially if the message is a joyous one. Decide on your greeting or message before you begin as this will help you choose the right colours for the finished card. If the message is bright and cheerful then the colour of the card can be bright and bold. A congratulatory card should be exuberant and vivid. Acrylic inks or luminous inks will give you this brilliance and are easy to write upon when dry as the paper surface becomes waterproof.

When making your card, plan your designs on layout paper first and practise your writing. This project uses a Carolingian script. Choose the colours and the media you wish to use. Pour some acrylic ink into the palette and mix with water. Paint the individual colours on to the paper allowing them to blend: this keeps them bright and fresh.

When the ink has dried write the message with a dip pen and art masking fluid. This forms an area of resist which paint cannot cover. The colour and texture of the card is created by brush and paint effects using a toothbrush spattered over the surface of the paper.

To spatter effectively, dip the brush into the ink and turn bristles uppermost. Draw a thin strip of card across the bristles toward you and the brush will spatter the design with ink. Make sure that you have shielded the area where you are working with old newspaper to stop the paint from sticking to everything.

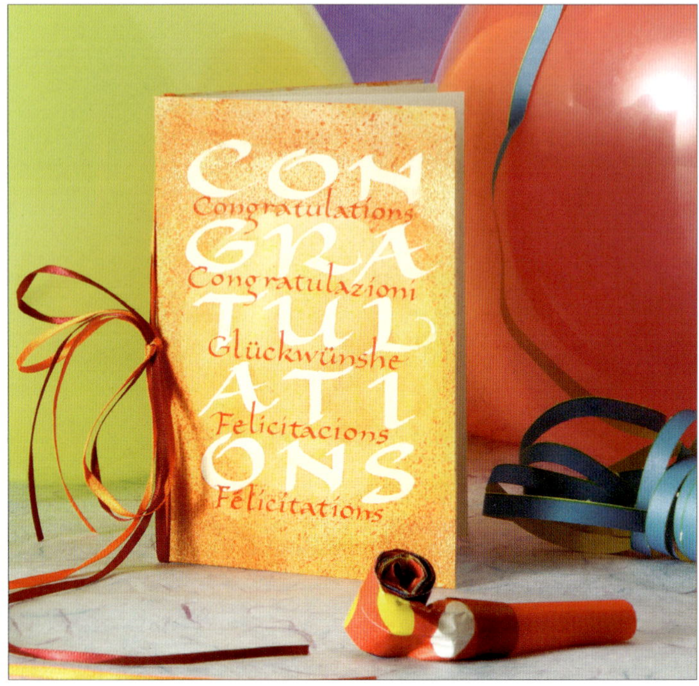

The design

The idea of the project is to produce a colourful card with a congratulations message in several languages that will fold well and fit a standard envelope. You can make an envelope for an individual card but if you wish to produce many of the same cards the cards will need to be folded to fit commercially-sized envelopes. You can design the card using standard-sized paper to ensure that when folded it fits into a standard envelope.

Materials

- *Photocopy paper or layout paper*
- *Dip pens: Speedball C-0 or William Mitchell 00 (large nib) and William Mitchell 3 (medium nib)*
- *Black ink*
- *Pencil*
- *Scissors*
- *Glue*
- *Hot-pressed watercolour paper*
- *Large paintbrush for ink washes*
- *Acrylic inks: red and yellow*
- *Gouache paints: scarlet lake and alizarin red*
- *Masking fluid*
- *Old toothbrush*
- *Stencil*
- *Eraser*
- *Matching envelope*
- *Ribbons*

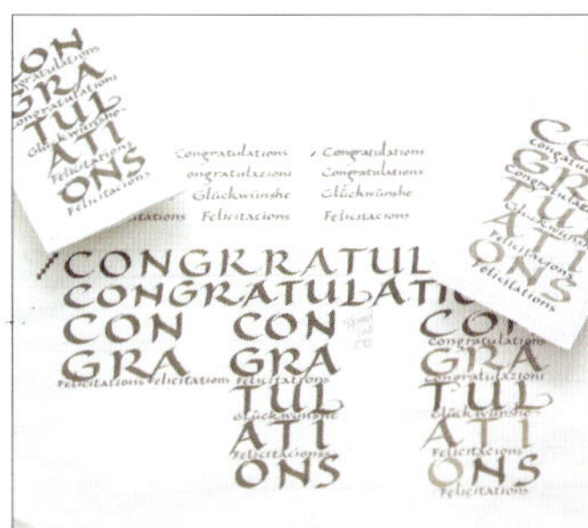

1 Practise your writing trying different sizes for the messages. Record the nib size used on the different trials. Create the design for your card and paste into a 'mock-up' of the card. This can be achieved by folding a sheet of photocopy paper in half then in half again and attaching the strips of your writing to the resulting card shape. Now you have an idea of what the finished card will look like.

2 Draw and cut the card size from the watercolour paper. Use the large brush and paint a bright background colour on your paper in the red and yellow acrylic ink. Mix the two colours to produce an orange, but also add both the red and yellow colours as you work allowing them to blend on the paper with the orange. This will keep the ink fresh and bright.

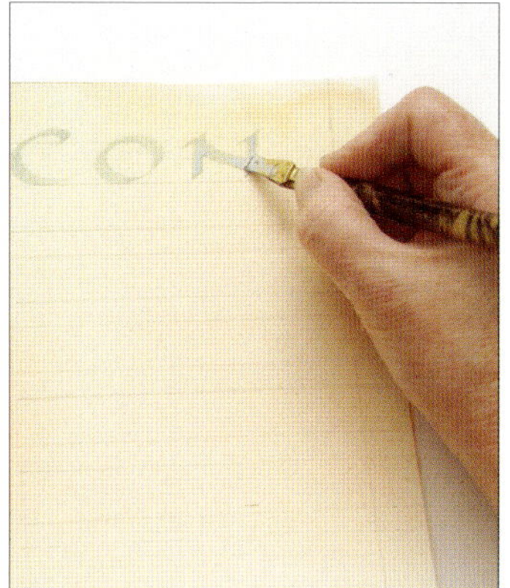

3 Wait until the paint dries then draw some faint writing lines on which to write using your mock up card as reference. Write your chosen word in masking fluid on the paper. Make the word look bright and happy.

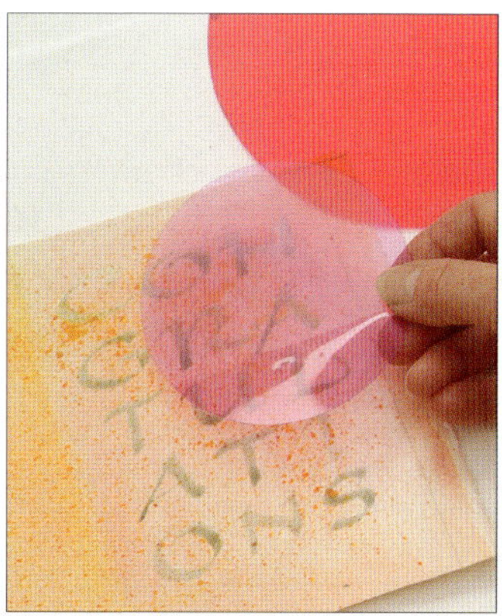

4 Once the masking fluid has dried, spatter the surface with acrylic ink using an old toothbrush. You could add further colour interest by spattering through a stencil shape.

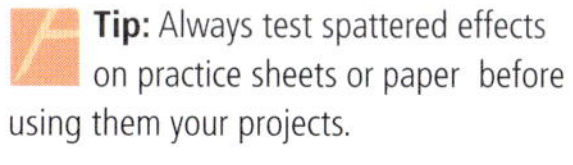

Tip: Always test spattered effects on practice sheets or paper before using them your projects.

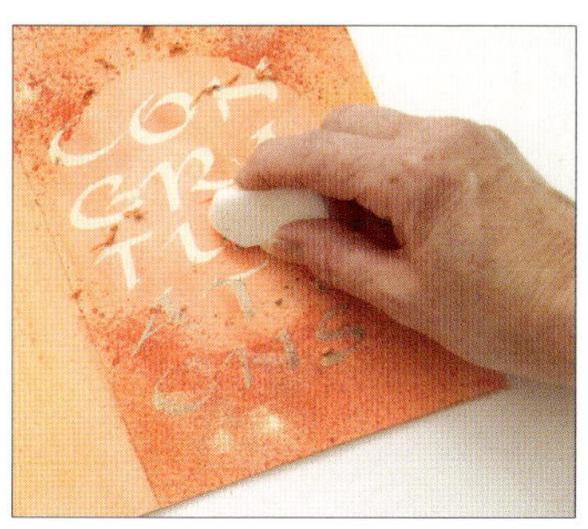

5 When all the colour has dried, remove the masking fluid from the paper by rubbing gently with your finger or using an eraser. The word will be revealed in the orange of the background colour.

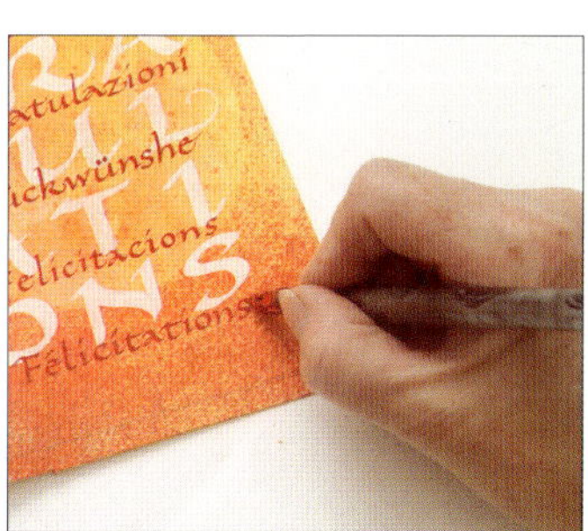

6 Mix up some scarlet lake and alizarin red gouache paint and, using a smaller pen nib size, write some smaller 'congratulations' messages on the card. Fold the card and trim it to the correct shape.

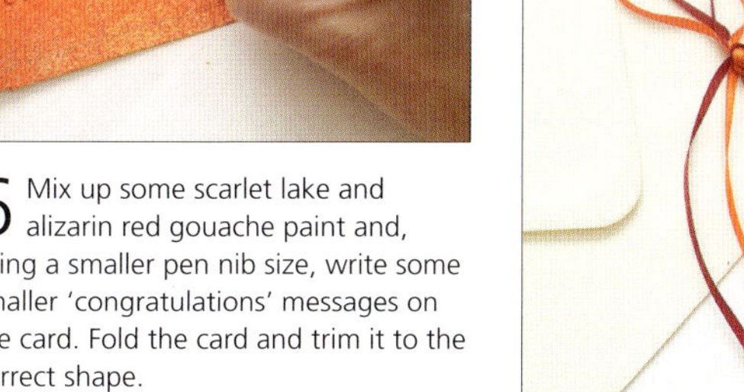

7 Fold a sheet of standard sized copy paper for the inside, to enable you to write your personal message. Put the white paper with your personal message inside the card and carefully stick with a thin line of glue.

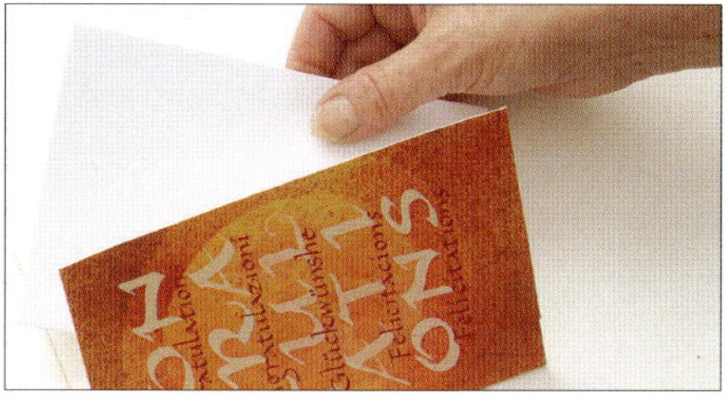

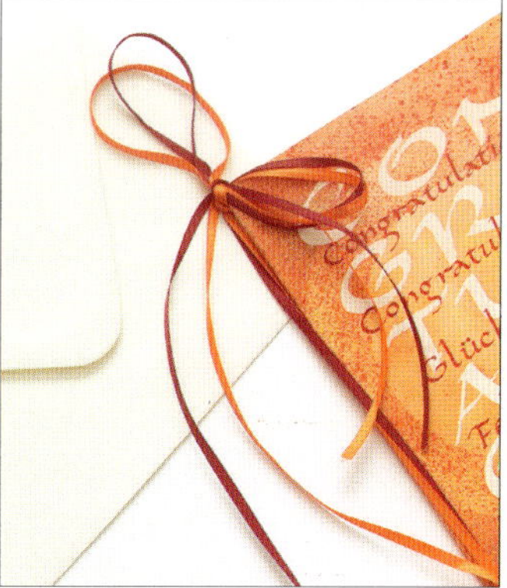

8 Finally, tie colourful ribbons round the spine of the card and match with an envelope.

Tip: Stencils can be bought ready made or you can cut your own designs with a craft knife or stencil cutter.

Gift wrap with painted background

This project involves rollering ink on to a quality lightweight paper to create a striking monochromatic background for gift wrap. Watery black ink is used which gives the paper an interesting textured effect. When the background is dry a message is written on the gift wrap using different sizes of pen nibs – which makes the same message appear different depending on the nib that has been chosen. Black ink or gouache is used for the first layer of writing. The paper is then given a quarter-turn before the message is written again, this time in a different, contrasting colour.

This project provides a good opportunity to use different types of pen. There are many to choose from besides the usual dip pen – coit pens, automatic pens, ruling pens, plus the pens that you can make yourself, such as quills, reed pens or cut balsawood pens. Each will produce a different mark.

To add to the fun of using a variety of writing tools, experiment with the interesting letter weights that can be produced by altering the letter nib width height. Using less than the standard x-height of a chosen script will make the letterform appear not only smaller but heavier and denser. Letters given a greater nib width height than the standard x-height of its letter style will appear lighter and more elegant.

The wrapped gift can be completed by the addition of a personalized tag.

Materials

- *Layout or practice paper*
- *Dip pens: in various sizes*
- *Ruling pen*
- *Automatic pen*
- *Scissors*
- *Glue*
- *One or two sheets of lightweight cartridge paper, white or coloured*
- *Transparent overlay or similar*
- *Old newspapers*
- *Printing ink roller or similar*
- *String*
- *Acrylic inks: black and red*
- *Gouache paints: black and red*
- *Ribbon*

The design

A complete alphabet script written in altered weights and sizes and with different pens can have great impact. This project features Flourished Italic and Gothic.

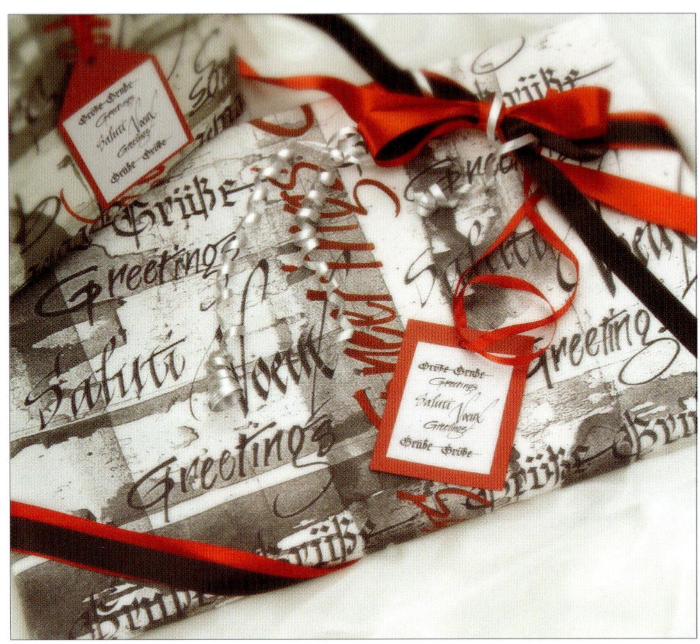

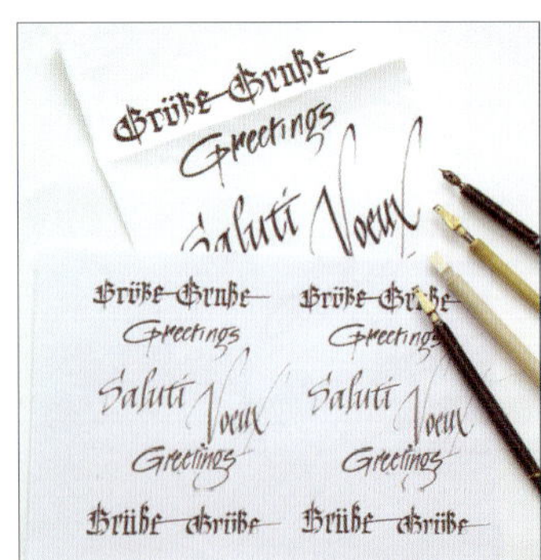

1 Using the layout paper, try writing some 'greetings' in Gothic and Flourished Italics. Try different sizes of pens and nibs; changing to an automatic pen or larger nib size will create heavier writing. Practise with further pen sizes within the same lines.

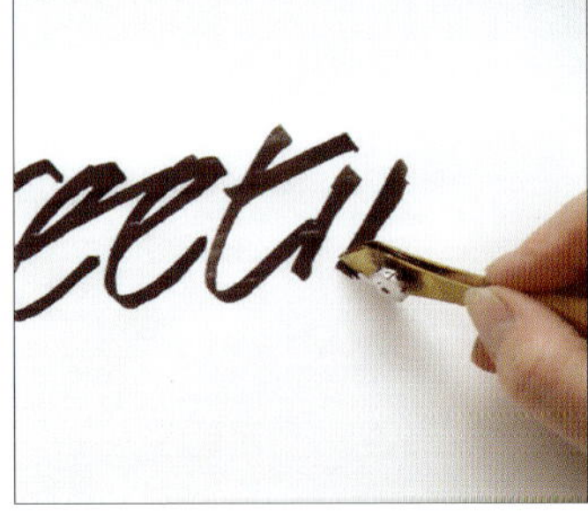

2 Try writing with the ruling pen, which will make the words appear particularly vibrant. Notice the differences in the weights of all your experimental writing examples. Remember to record the nib size used each time.

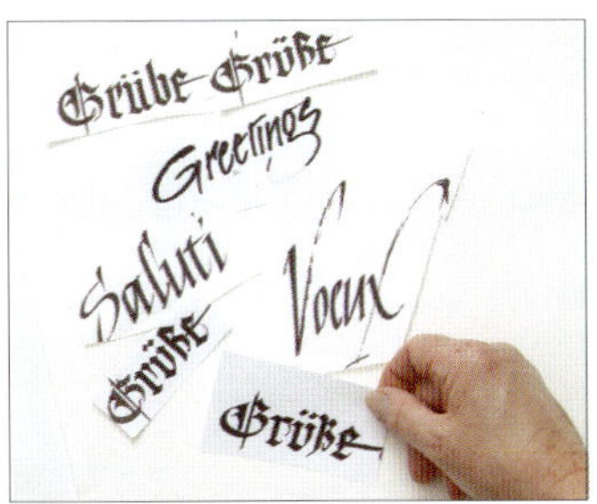

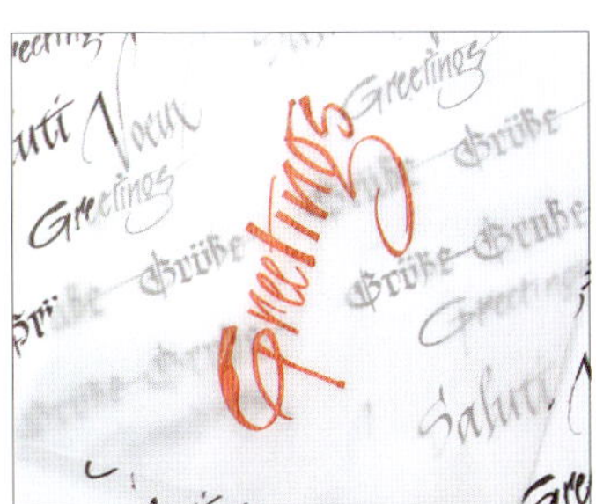

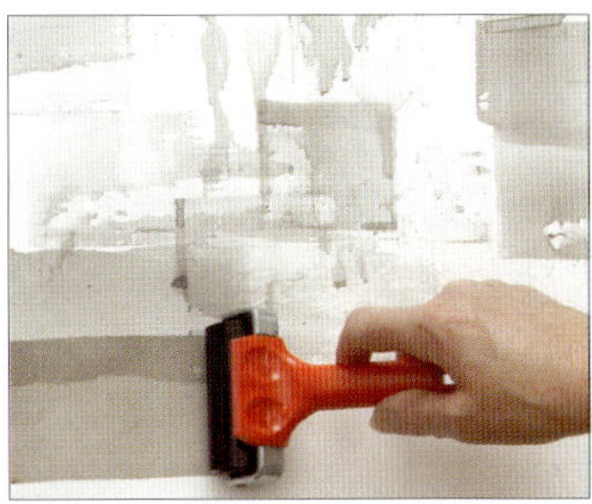

3 Cut and paste the various texts into different positions to create a design you like. The design will be repeated over the large sheet of cartridge paper so that the actual writing area will need to be no more than about 30cm x 20cm (12in x 8in). This will be repeated to cover all the paper.

4 Either photocopy some of the words on to a transparent overlay or write on a piece of drafting film or tracing paper and lay over your writing at different angles. This will make the design look busy, but exciting. Move the overlay around to view the effects.

5 Lay some old newspapers on the table to protect it from the roller carrying acrylic ink. Use a good quality piece of paper on which to lay a background colour. Pour some black acrylic ink into a tray and add water. Run the print roller through the ink and roll on to the paper, first one way, then the other, making random strokes of pattern.

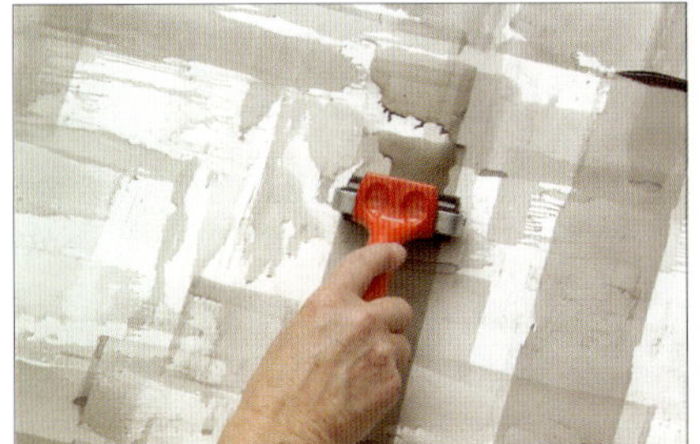

Tip: You can use coloured or textured paper instead of colouring your own. Black paper decorated with white and red writing always looks stunning.

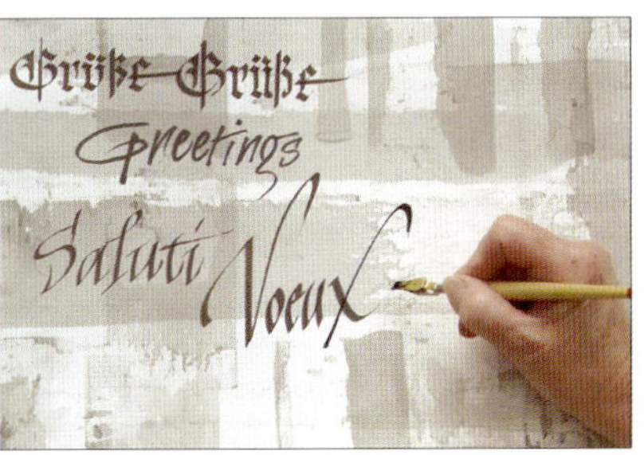

6 Create an all-over lightweight patterned background that will appear textured. The ink roller does not print the pattern the same all the time. By tying string around the roller other patterns can be produced. Do not use the ink too black, keep it watery and grey in colour. Let it dry thoroughly.

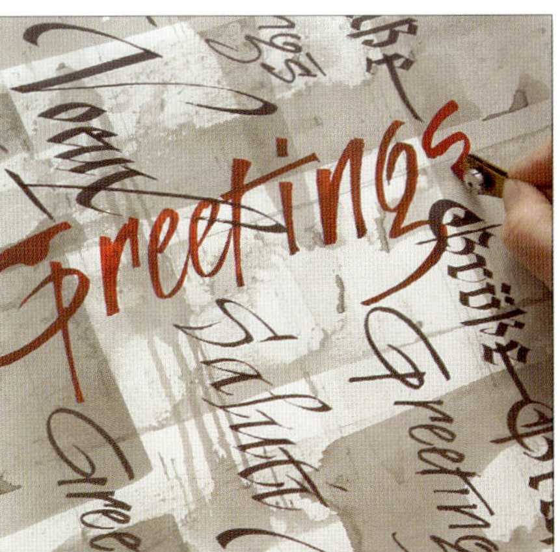

7 Write over the background with gouache paint or black ink. Draw in the guidelines using double pencils to help you place the writing correctly, then write your personal greetings.

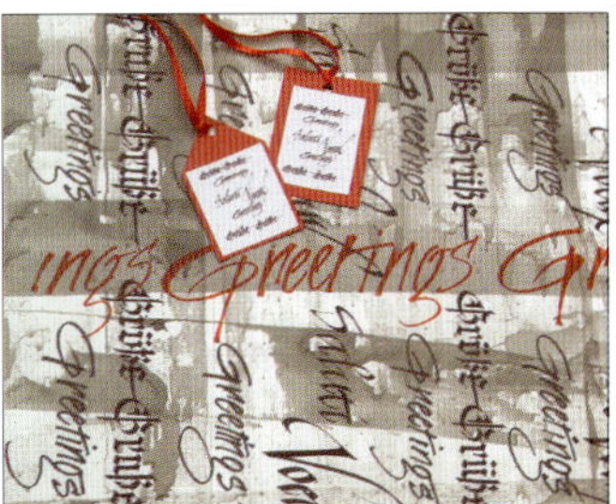

Tip: A completely different type of pattern can be produced by using a domestic roller that is used for house painting.

8 When your work is dry, turn the paper at 90 degrees. Mix up some gouache in the second, contrasting colour and write the greetings with a ruling pen according to your planned design.

9 The finished paper can be wrapped around a box and tied with ribbon. The gift tags can be made by repeating the pattern in smaller pens or by photocopying the original design.

Stamped gift wrap for a box

Very effective patterns can be created by repeating a design over a whole area with a rubber stamp. Create a stamp from erasers of various sizes or foam pads. If erasers are used, cut the shapes using a craft knife or linoleum cutting tools. Remember that the cut away areas on the eraser will not print.

Using a coloured ink pad or gouache paint, the cut motifs can be repeated many times. Stamping or printing is an ideal way to cover a large area such as gift wrap, and stamps are also ideal for producing repeat borders. Although it is possible to buy rubber or wooden stamps already made, it is very satisfying and inexpensive to make them yourself. Keeping the shapes of your initial designs uncomplicated makes the motifs easier to cut with the craft knife or linoleum cutting tool.

Leave a small narrow gap between the lines of patterns. Once printed into position on the gift wrap and dried, the gaps left can be filled with calligraphy using the dip pen and gold gouache or coloured ink. A calligraphic alphabet in an elegant script may work well here.

Materials

- *Layout or practice paper*
- *Coloured pencils or felt-tipped pens*
- *Pencils: 2B, 2H*
- *Two erasers*
- *Tracing paper*
- *Linoleum cutting tool or craft (utility) knife*
- *Coloured ink pad*
- *Kitchen paper or cloth for cleaning the stamps*
- *Thin cartridge paper or coloured paper*
- *Dip pen, such as William Mitchell 2 (large nib)*
- *Gouache: gold; or gold or black ink*
- *Ribbons*

Tip: The paper used for gift wrap should be quite lightweight – not more than around 100gsm (60lb). This will help ensure the decorated paper can easily be folded around the gift.

The design

The overall paper design is made by printing on thin paper with two cut erasers that have been pressed on to a variegated coloured stamp pad or into gouache paint. The lines of pattern can be alternated and the colours changed to create different patterns. The additional writing in the white spaces between the lines is Italic capitals written with gold or coloured gouache.

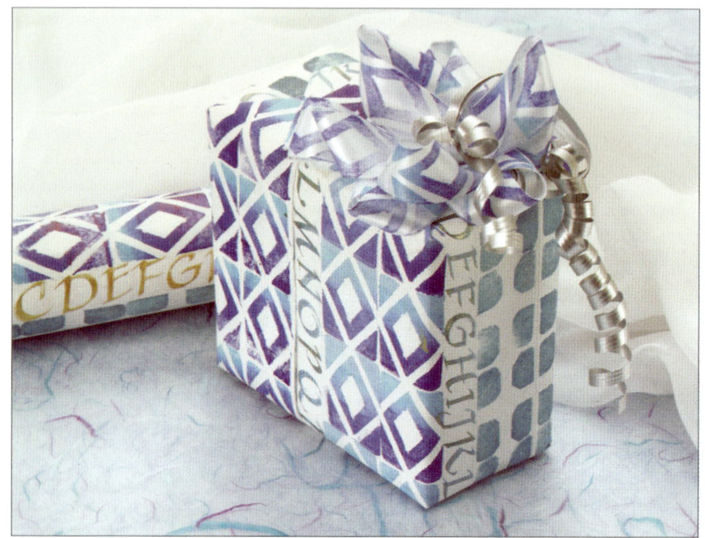

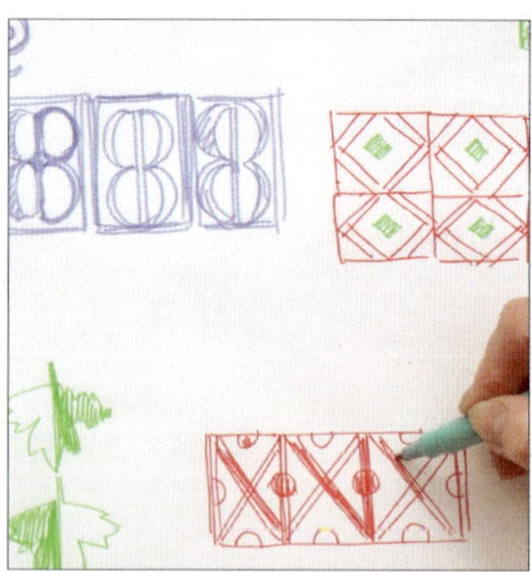

1 On the layout paper, using the coloured pencils or felt-tipped pens, create some interesting patterns that are likely to repeat well. Keep the patterns simple. Geometric designs are the most successful.

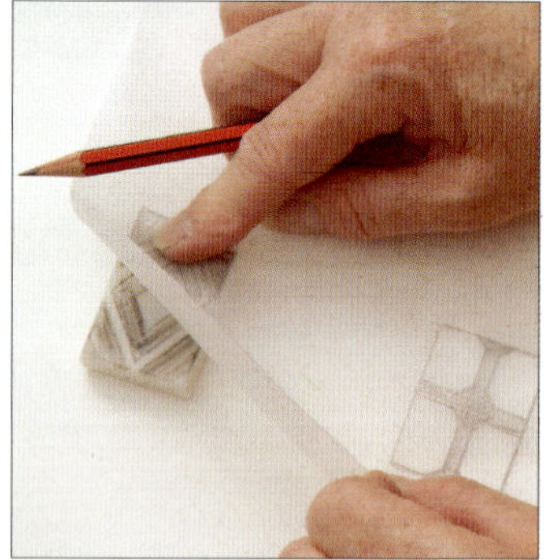

2 Trace two of the designs using a 2B pencil. Make sure that each of the designs will fit on to a separate eraser. Turn the tracing paper face down on to an eraser and scribble on the back of the design with a 2H pencil. This will transfer your first design on to the first eraser. Transfer the second design on to the second eraser in the same way.

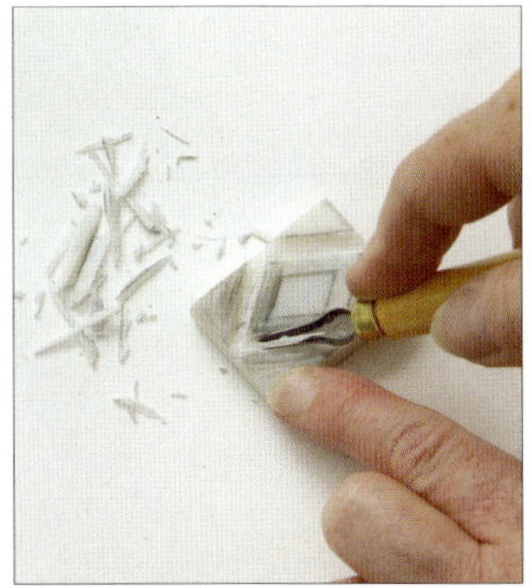

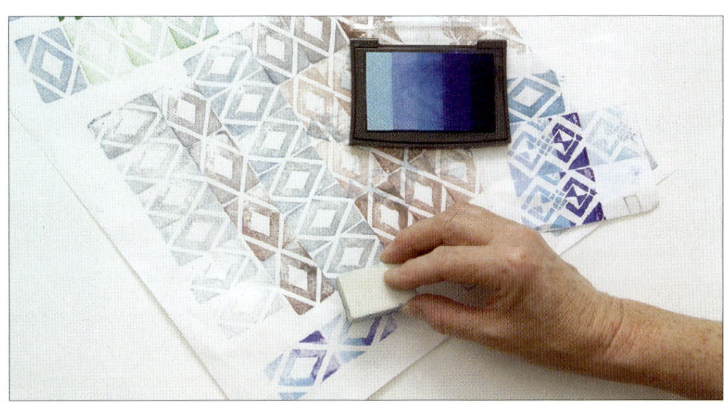

3 Take the first eraser, and using a cutting tool or craft knife, carefully cut away the areas of pattern that you do not wish to print. Take care not to cut towards your fingers. Remember that the parts of the eraser that remain will be the areas that will print colour. Test the pattern by placing the eraser on the ink pad and then printing on to waste paper. Check for jagged edges on the design and trim carefully.

4 Cut the second design in the same way, checking your progress on the inkpad and spare piece of paper. Test both patterns to see how well they work together. Make any adjustments. Try some different colour ideas, wiping the erasers on kitchen paper or an old cloth between colour changes.

Tip: Printing the stamp patterns on textured paper creates an interesting surface. You can also try rubber stamp printing on plain, coloured wrapping paper. Remember that the paper you use for this project should be thin enough to wrap around a gift.

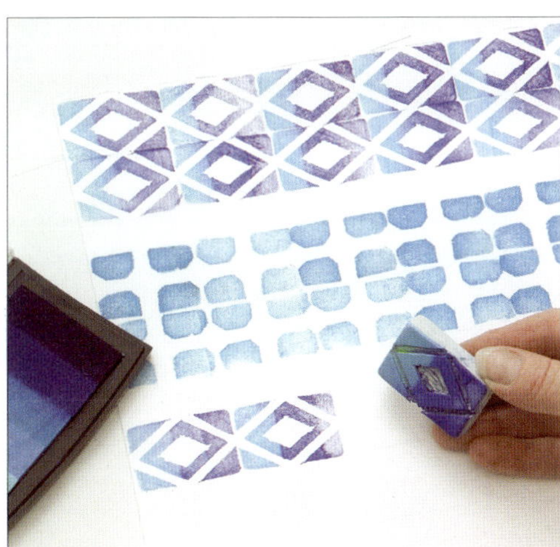

5 Now change to better quality paper, either white or coloured. Cover the whole of the paper with the stamped design, carefully replenishing the ink on the stamp from the ink pad when required. Carefully print the whole of your pattern on the paper, leaving about a 1cm (1/2in) gap between the rows of pattern. If you wish to change the colour of the design, wipe the eraser on a small piece of kitchen paper, press into the different colour and continue printing.

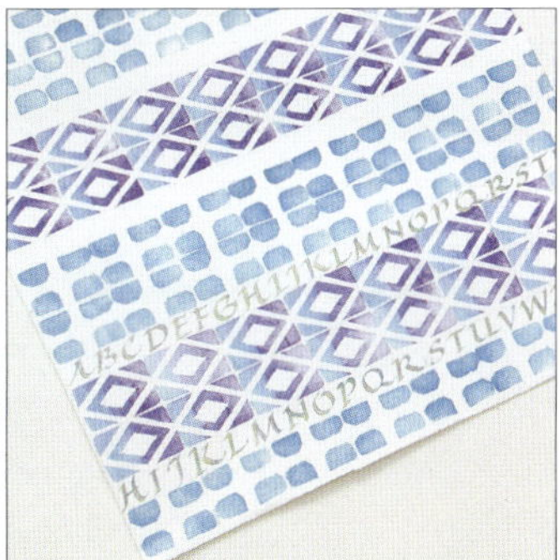

6 These long white gaps are filled with Italic capital letters for added decoration. Using a pen and gold gouache, or coloured or black ink, write the alphabet in these spaces.

7 Finally, wrap up the boxed gift and finish off with matching or contrasting ribbon. A pale-coloured ribbon can be decorated with one of the motifs to match the pattern on the paper. It can be printed with the cut eraser in the same way.

Copperplate address on an envelope

There is something very special about receiving a decorative, handwritten envelope and, in the age of computers, it makes it all the more individual. You could try this project for a one-off envelope, or make several for celebratory cards. You could even take it to a grander scale for that special occasion.

The hand chosen here is Copperplate, which is elegant and lends itself easily to flourishes and decoration, and will look good in several colours. If you do not have much experience in writing Copperplate, begin with fairly large writing. This will allow more space to cope with the thick and thin strokes of the script. To accommodate working at a larger size, a fairly large envelope should be used. You will be surprised how much space is needed for a handwritten address. With practice, you will know instinctively what size of envelope will suit your needs.

The design

This decorative envelope has been designed to incorporate various sizes of lettering and two colours. The large lettering is approximately 1cm (1/2in) high and the smaller approximately 7mm (3/8in) high. The Copperplate has been written with gouache using a pointed nib. If an envelope is to be posted it needs to be easily legible so it is good to bear this in mind when adding any decorative elements.

Materials

- *Dip pen with script nib, such as a Gillott 303 or 404, or Manuscript nib*
- *Black ink*
- *Layout or practice paper*
- *Envelopes*
- *Gouache paints: magenta and ultramarine; or coloured inks*
- *Pencil*
- *Ruler*
- *Protractor*
- *Mixing brushes*
- *Eraser*

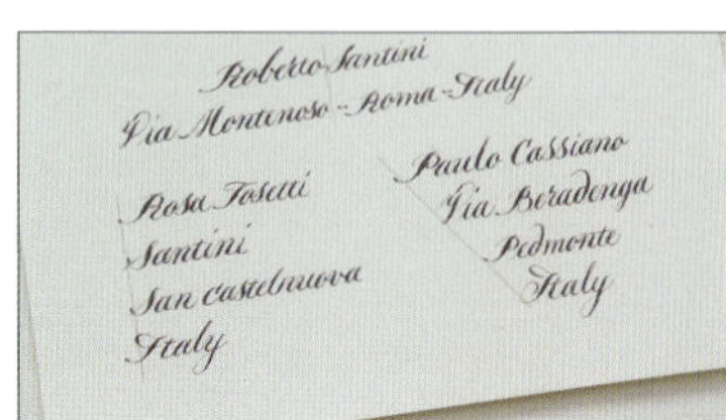

1 Jot down the name and address you are working with in a variety of ways – left aligned, offset or centred. The length of the lines in the address will have some bearing on which design you choose and also on the shape and size of envelope.

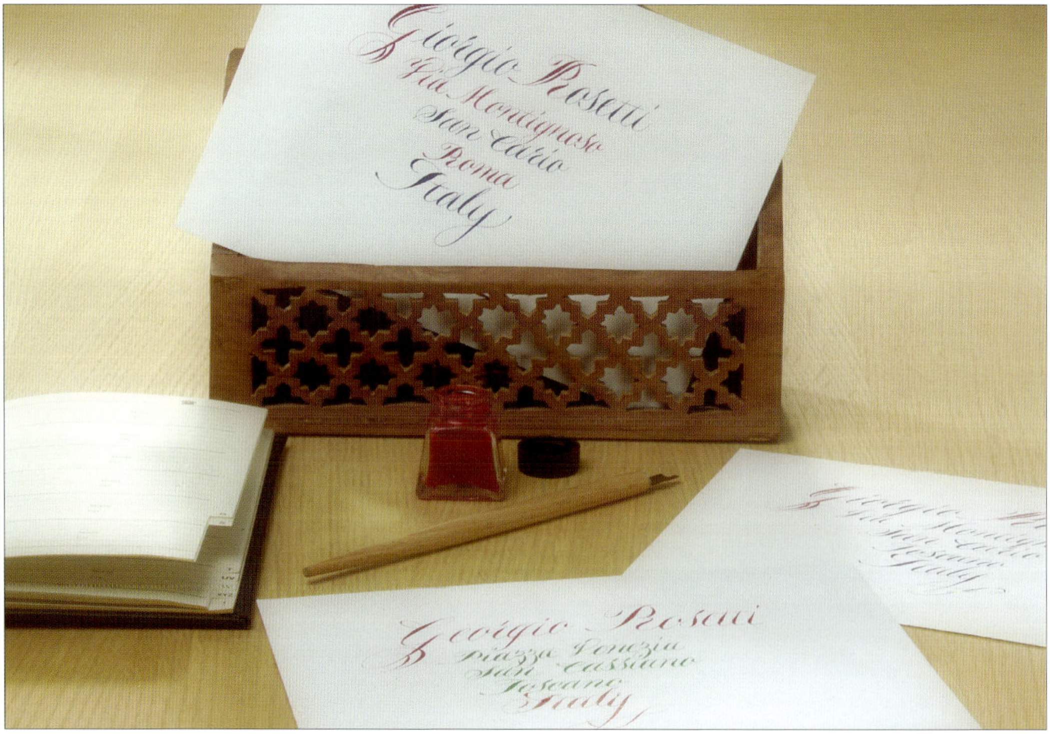

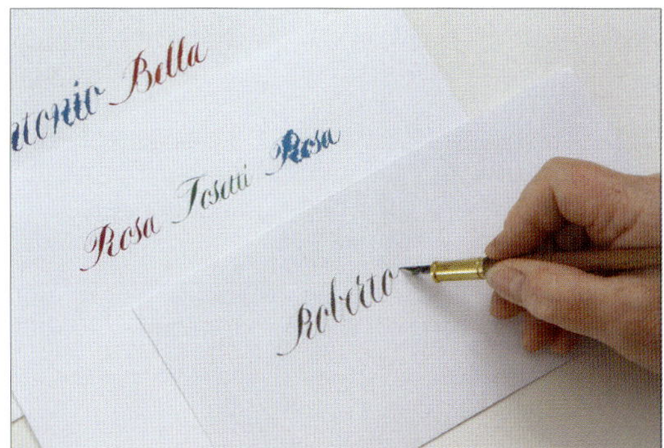

2 Do some writing trials on the type of envelope you intend to use. Sometimes the ink 'bleeds' on the envelope, spoiling the appearance of the lettering, so it is worthwhile doing some tests on a variety of envelopes to find a type that works well with the inks you are using.

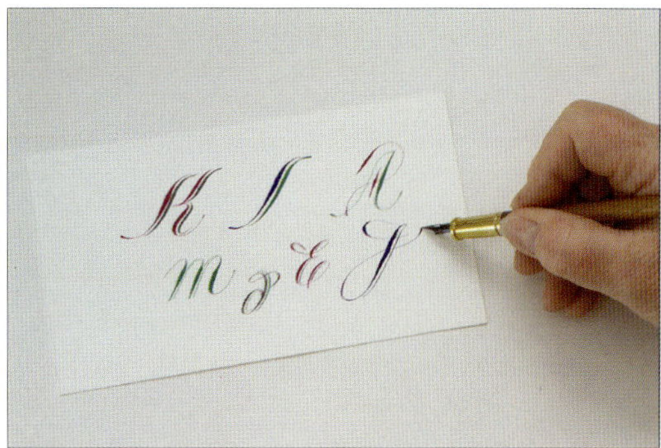

3 Try experimenting with colours. It is helpful to try out several colour combinations until you find one that is most suitable.

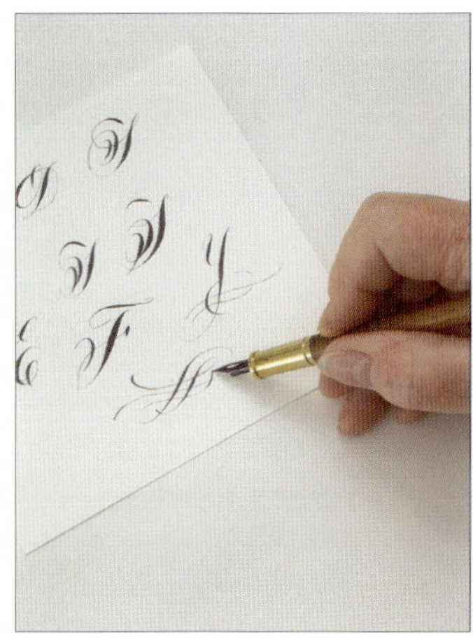

4 It can add interest to 'flourish' a letter. It is a good idea to practise on layout paper first. If necessary, the flourish can be drawn with a pencil to 'plan' the route.

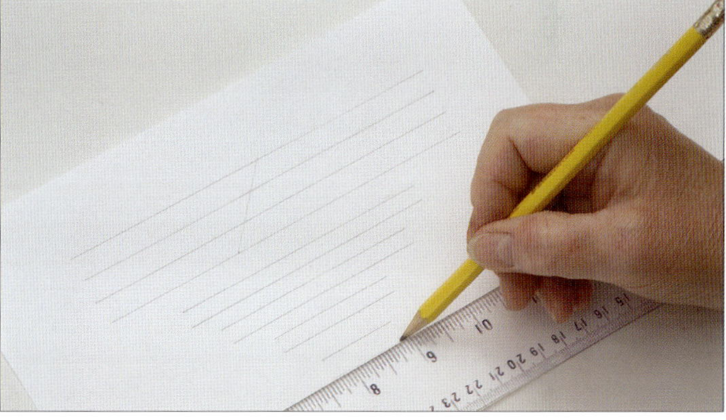

5 For this project use an envelope measuring 23cm x 15cm (9in x 6in) and lightly rule up and draw some guidelines. Measure three sets of guidelines for each line of writing (the top set for ascenders, the middle for the main body of writing and the bottom set for any descenders). The size of lettering is optional but as a guide measure 1cm (1/2in) for large lettering and 7mm (3/8in) for a smaller size. The slope of Copperplate writing is 54 degrees so if it helps, you could mark some guidelines using a protractor.

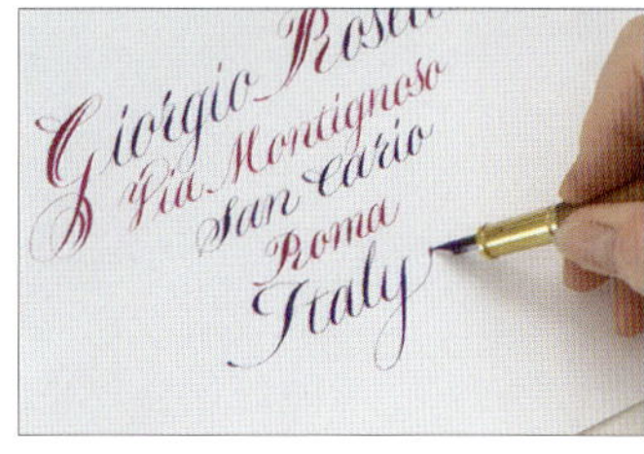

6 Mix up your chosen colours of gouache paints to the consistency of thin cream. If you are alternating colours it might be easier to use two different pens so that you do not need to keep rinsing the nib. Write out the envelope and when the writing has thoroughly dried carefully rub out the lines.

Tip: Keep your surface flat when writing Copperplate and dip the pen into the paint or inkpot until it completely covers the whole of the nib, which will ensure it is nicely loaded.

Dove calligram

The word 'calligram' was invented by poet and painter Guillaume Apollinaire at the beginning of the 20th century. A calligram is a word, phrase or poem in which the handwriting or script in the form of words is used to form part of the artwork. This calligram associates the word 'peace' with a symbol of peace – a dove – but a calligram can be created with many different words and associations. A calligram encourages an artist to manipulate the pen and break the rules. The results can look stunning on a card or as a design on a T-shirt. Interesting letter weights can be created by ignoring the nib-width rule or changing the nib-width ratio of the letterform. Try using an automatic pen in a small space. The result will be heavyweight writing. Conversely, a small pen in a large space will create tall, thin and lightweight calligraphy. Also try stretching and compressing letters and words to give a feeling of movement.

The design

Italic Capitals have been used for the small writing on this calligram of the dove. The word 'peace' is written in four other languages, using Italic minuscules and flourished Italic letters for some of the large lettering. Italic script is easy to manipulate into different shapes. Use the pen to make the writing very compressed, pointed, slanted, stretched, tall, small and so on.

Materials

- *Layout or practice paper*
- *Pencil*
- *Dip pens: in various sizes*
- *Tracing paper*
- *Lightweight watercolour paper*
- *Black ink or gouache paint*
- *Blotting paper*
- *Automatic pen*
- *Frame, if required*

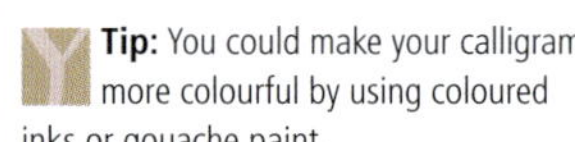

Tip: You could make your calligram more colourful by using coloured inks or gouache paint.

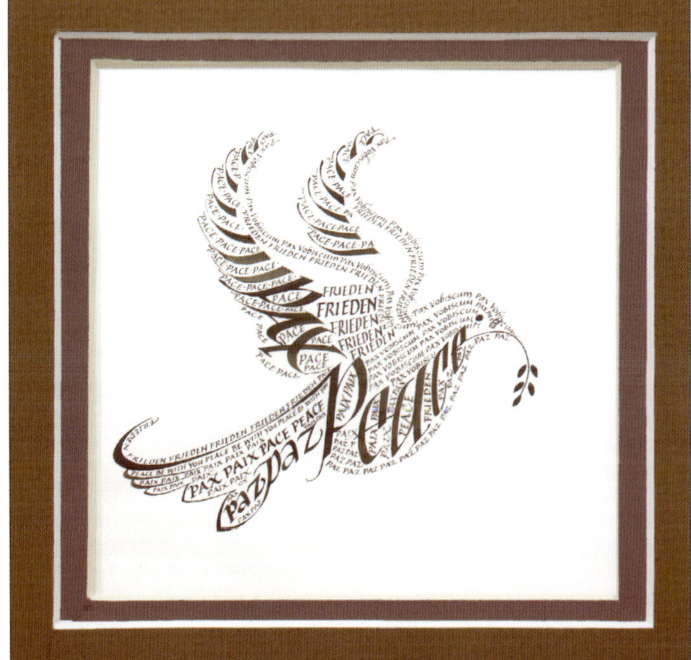

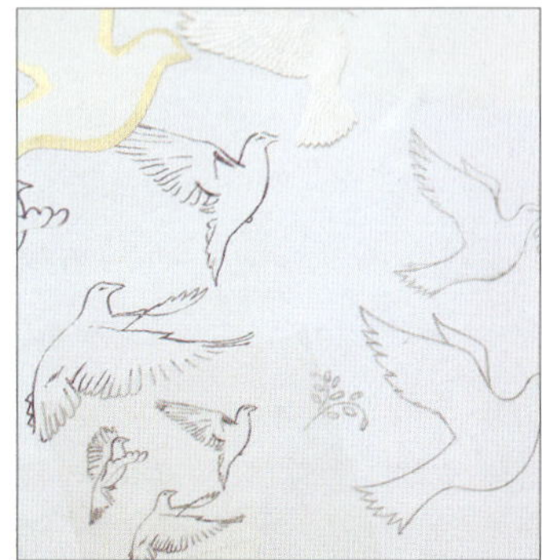

1 Using layout paper, draw some thumbnail sketches of the dove. If you prefer to find another idea, animals, flowers, butterflies, planes and cars are effective subjects to choose. You can trace your subject matter from a book or other sources, or try ideas that have been used before.

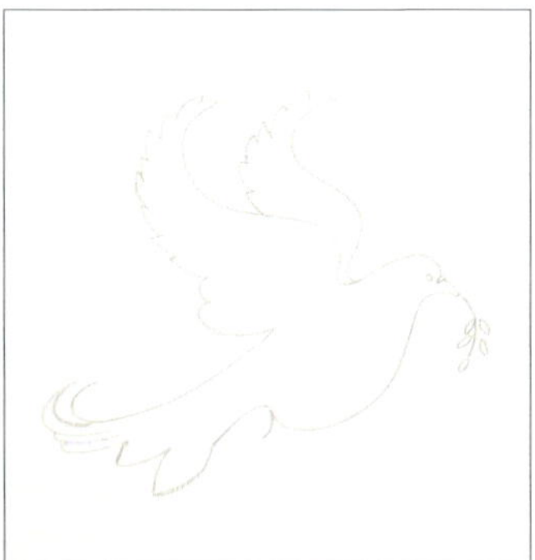

2 Draw the outline of the shape that works best. The dove has some long, curved lines that are easy to draw and which can be simplified into a flowing design. Remember to keep the design simple. Avoid complicated corners or lines.

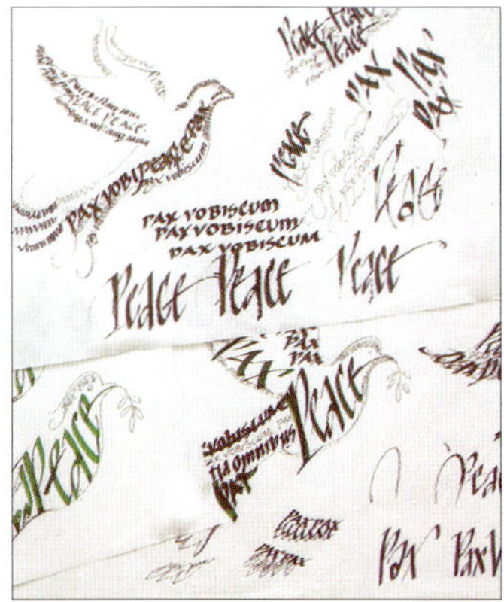

3 Using the pens, practise the writing for the calligram. Try different weights: make some words heavy and dense; some writing light and tall; some flourished and fine. Experiment with different pens and letter shapes.

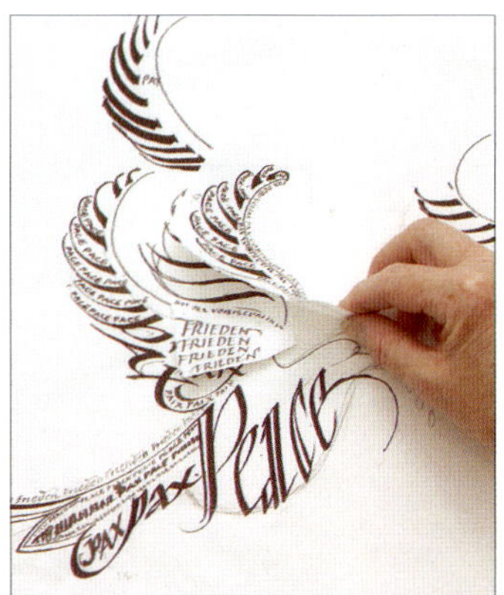

4 Take time to practise fitting the written words into the dove, so that you achieve a good balance of black on white when finished. It may take a while to get it right. Use overlays of layout paper or tracing paper to help it to all fit together. Then paste the words together on a sheet.

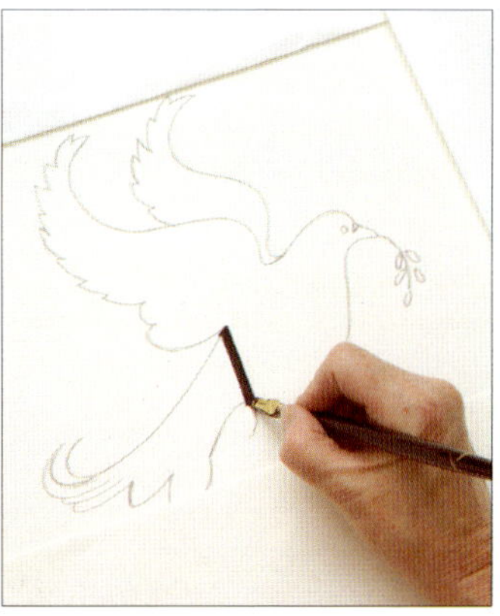

5 Transfer the outline on to good quality paper by tracing down the pencil shape. Use a cover guard sheet or blotting paper around the drawing as you write to prevent smudging the ink.

Tip: By using overlays written on tracing paper in the planning stage it is possible to fit the writing into the shape more easily. If you have the use of a lightbox, overlaying written areas and rearranging them over the light also helps to resolve the final design.

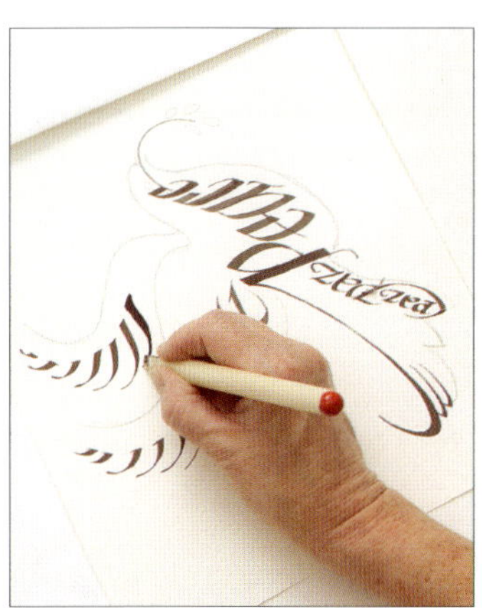

6 Using the automatic pen, do the larger penwork first: flourished Italic minuscules to create the form of the body and the flourish on the tail. Fill in with a slightly smaller pen-width size to create the feathers on the wings.

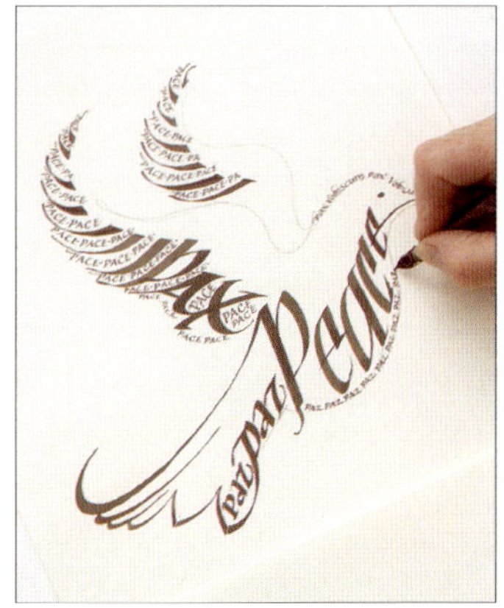

7 Carefully fill the rest of the dove shape with the small Italic capitals and flourished Italic minuscules, gradually filling the small spaces. Keep the writing following the form of the dove.

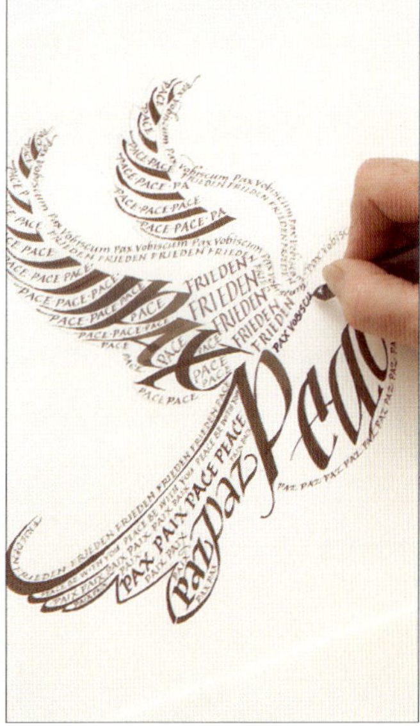

8 Finally, fill in the centre of the bird with rows of writing using a small nib. Frame the finished piece, if required.

Painted monogram

A monogram is a character or figure made up of two or more letters – often the two initials of a name. A monogram may vary from the simple and understated to a more elaborate or complex design. Some letters work well together but others are more difficult to arrange into a satisfactory design.

Whichever style of monogram you choose, there is the satisfaction of creating something truly exclusive. Try experimenting with colour. Coloured pencils are quick and easy to use for initial trials, then, when you have some idea of a design, try it with a pen. Simply changing the nib size or the height of the letters will alter the look of your monogram, so it is worth spending some time doing this. As a rough guide, the size of the monogram will probably need to be between 2.5cm and 4.5cm (1in to 1¾in).

A single colour scheme can look very elegant and a combination of two or even three colours can be exciting. Simple pen-drawn patterns and motifs can be used to embellish the initials. Letters can be adorned with flourishes but it is probably better to limit them to the first or last letter, depending on which lends itself most naturally.

The finished monogram can be applied to a range of uses. The design can be scanned and saved on a computer so that it can be printed when it is needed. The scale of the monogram can also be adjusted to complement the size of the item you are printing.

The design

In this project, the monogram is designed by using drawn and painted Versal letters on watercolour paper and painted in gouache. The initials are painted in two colours and a little decorative detail adorns the largest letter. The finished monogram will be used on stationery such as letterheads, invoices, notelets, labels and calling cards.

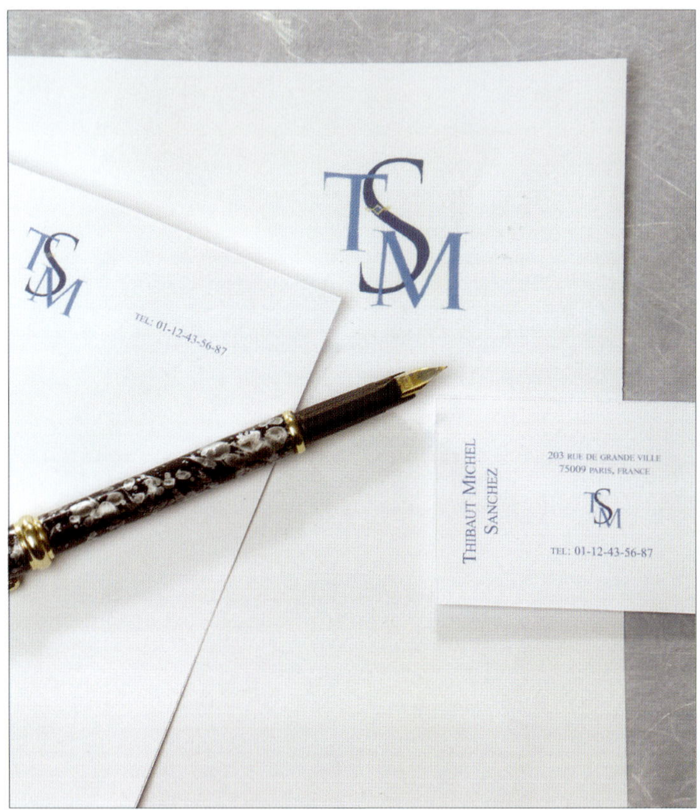

Materials

- *Layout or practice paper*
- *Pilot pens*
- *Dip pens in various sizes*
- *Watercolour ink or gouache*
- *Pencil*
- *Tracing paper*
- *Hot-pressed watercolour paper*
- *Tape*
- *Kitchen paper*
- *Scissors*
- *Paintbrush: size 00 or 1*
- *Gouache paint: cerulean, indigo, gold*
- *Writing paper, notelets etc. (optional)*

1 Spend some time drawing out different permutations of your chosen initials. It takes some letter juggling to find a design that is attractive and legible. First, try two letters that sit together but are separate.

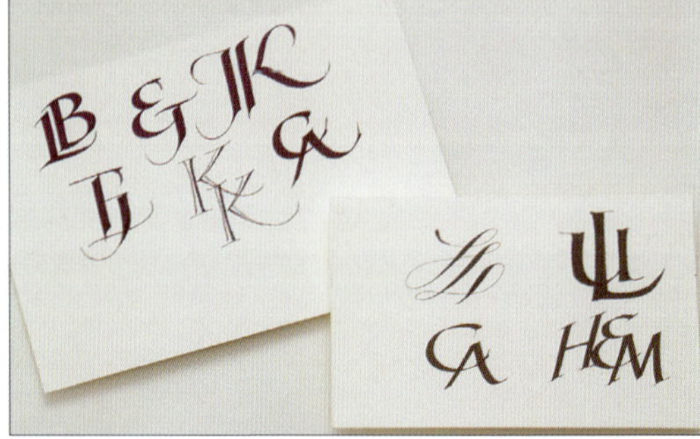

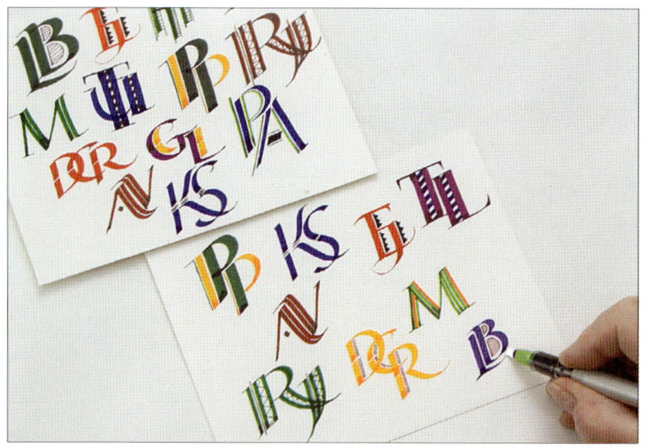

2 Now try some possible ways of linking two or three letters together. Letters could overlap, interlink or fit in to one another. There are many variations on styles of letterform, but remember that the design should not be over-complicated or too fussy as legibility is a main consideration. Introduce some colourways and add any decorative detail.

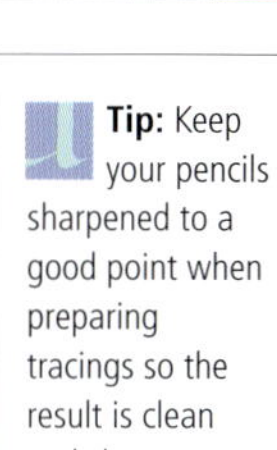

Tip: Keep your pencils sharpened to a good point when preparing tracings so the result is clean and clear.

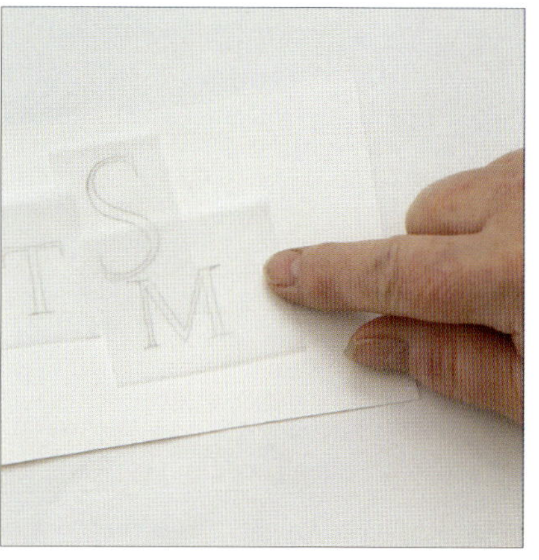

3 Once you have some idea of a design, pencil your letters separately on to some tracing paper and cut them into squares. Overlap the initials and try moving the tracing squares around until you are satisfied that the initials sit well together. Draw any additional ligatures, or joins that may be necessary to link the initials, or leave them separated if you prefer. If you wish to add any flourishes, draw them on to a separate piece of tracing paper, lay the tracing on the design and move it around until the position looks good.

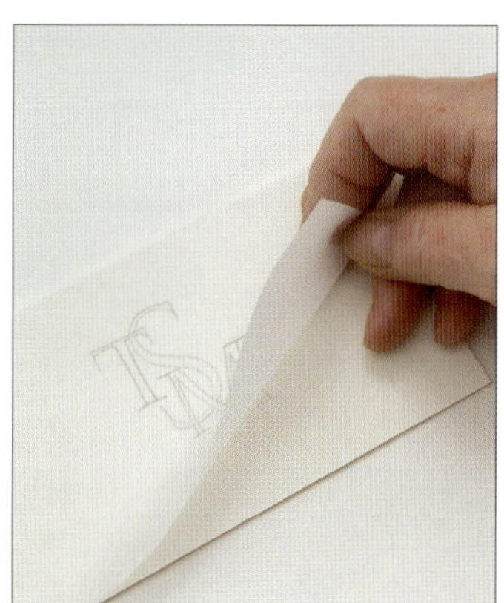

4 Trace down your design on to watercolour paper. Make your own carbon paper by scribbling over some tracing paper with an HB pencil until the piece is covered with graphite. Rub some kitchen paper over it to remove excessive graphite. Tape down the tracing into position and carefully slide the carbon paper underneath. Trace the design using a 2H pencil.

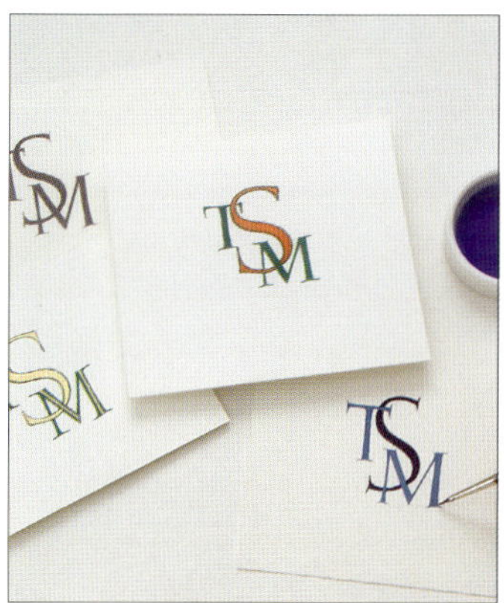

5 Mix up your gouache colours. Using a size 00 or 1 brush, paint one colour and leave to dry thoroughly before proceeding with the next colour. You can then try out some different colour combinations.

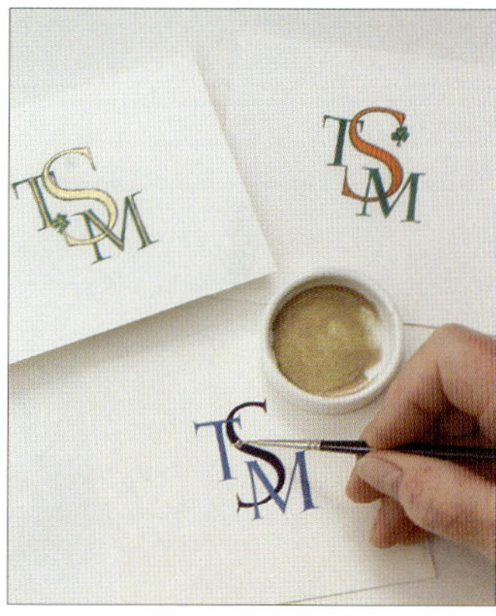

6 Add any decorative elements using either a pen or brush. If you have access to a computer, scan the monogram and save on file then print it on to your chosen article.

Bookmark with resist

There are many ways you can design a bookmark. It can have simple straight edges, be curved or pointed at the top or base, have a fringe-cut edge or be trimmed with some ribbon. The selection of paper alone has a bearing on the end result. You may want to try experimenting with some of the many textured papers available.

Borders can be very effective, whether simple pen-drawn patterns or more complicated designs, such as Celtic knotwork, an illuminated letter, a name, or a written quotation. There are many examples of illuminated or decorated letters from which you can seek inspiration, or you can create your own.

If you are making the bookmark to give with a book as a gift you could try reflecting the nature of the book, or the recipient's favourite hobby or pastime, in the design. This bookmark is created on watercolour paper or card with a quotation written in Classical Square Capitals from the Renaissance period. A striking effect is created with the use of masking fluid – a gum-based substance which resists liquids. A quotation is written using masking fluid brushed into the reservoir on the underside of the nib, and when the resist has thoroughly dried it is painted over with black ink. When the black ink has dried, the masking fluid is rubbed away with a soft eraser. The opposite side of the bookmark is written in black ink resulting in a bold contrast of black and white. The Latin quote written in this project *'verbatim & litteratim'* means 'word for word and letter for letter'. The bookmark is laminated to protect it. Finally a hole is punched in one end and an elegant black tassel is threaded through to complement the lettering.

Tip: Masking fluid is not the only form of resist. Candle wax will also create an area of resist against paint or inks, but is unsuitable for this project. Dilute gouache can be used but needs to be lifted away by immersing in water.

The design

In this project Classical Square Capitals have been chosen. These are closely related to the classic Roman inscriptional letters. Square Capitals are also known as San Vito Capitals, named after the 15th-century scribe Bartolomeo San Vito, who is known for his magnificent manuscripts.

Materials

- *Layout or practice paper*
- *Pencil*
- *Dip pens: William Mitchell 2 and 4 (medium and small nibs)*
- *Black Chinese ink or gouache*
- *Ruler*
- *Technical pen or pointed nib*
- *Card (stock) or heavy hot-pressed watercolour paper*
- *Masking fluid and old brush*
- *Paintbrush*
- *Eraser*
- *Craft (utility) knife*
- *Hole punch*
- *Black tassel*

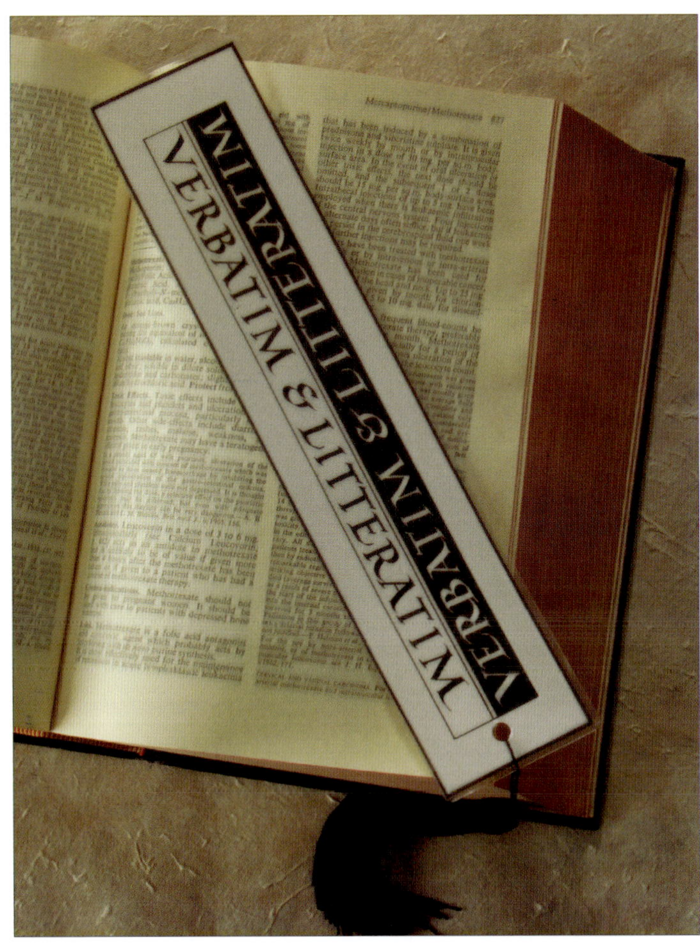

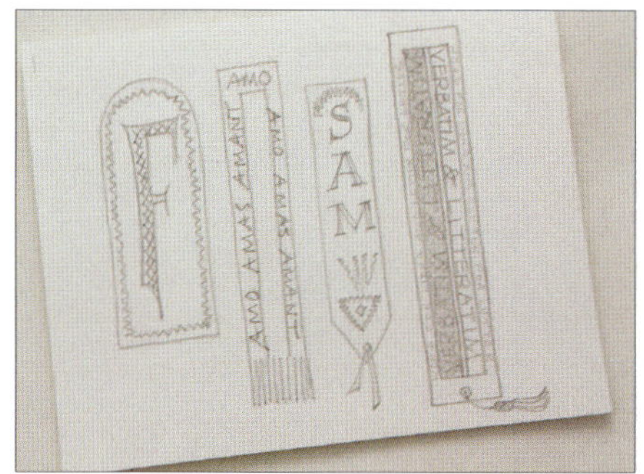

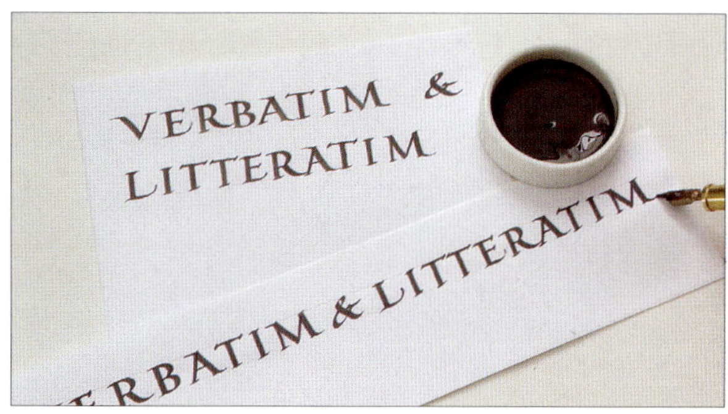

1 Draw thumbnail sketches on some layout paper to work out your ideas. Bear in mind the sizes of books for which you might use the bookmark. The scale of the bookmark needs to be relative to the size of the book: a small bookmark would be more suitable for a small book.

2 Write out the quotation on some layout paper so that you can gauge the dimensions needed for your bookmark.

Tip: Wash your brush and nib immediately after using masking fluid. It is difficult to remove once dry.

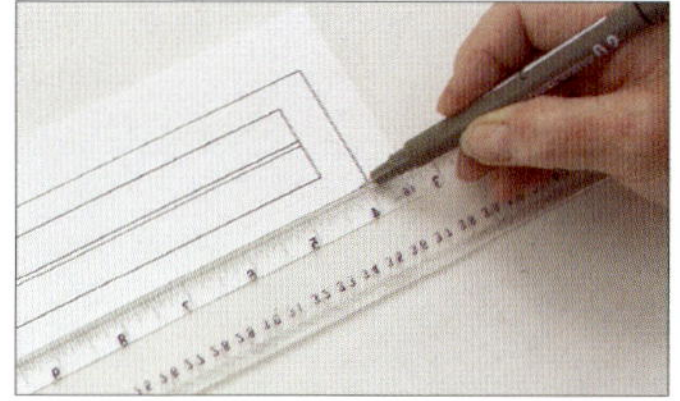

3 Measure and rule up lines for the overall dimensions of your chosen bookmark on to some watercolour paper. Rule lines with a ruling pen, a pointed nib or a technical pen using the bevel edge of a ruler. Write out the quotation around the outside border in small letters, using a size 4 nib, in black gouache or ink. Keep all the lettering facing outwards.

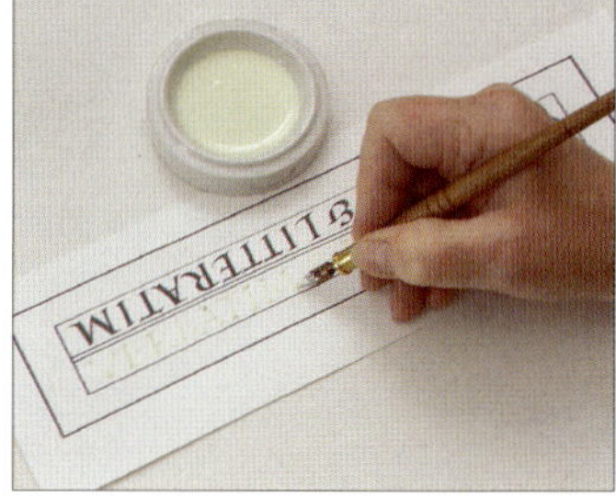

4 Write out the main quotation in large captials, with a size 2 nib, in the upper text box using black gouache or ink. Then write out the same words in the lower box using masking fluid. Mirror the writing so that the letters are back to back.

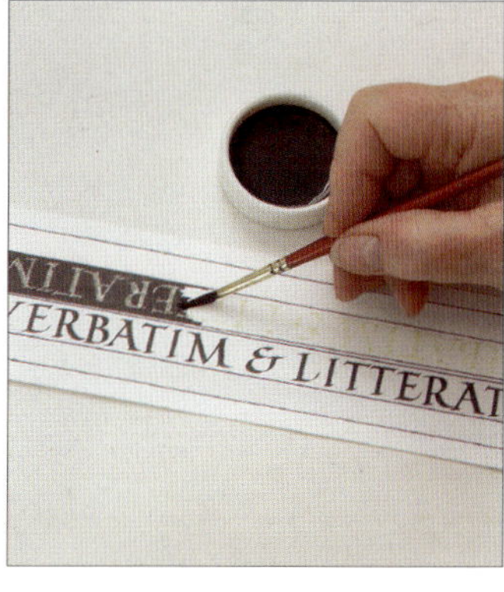

5 Paint over the masking fluid writing with black gouache or ink. Allow the paint to dry thoroughly.

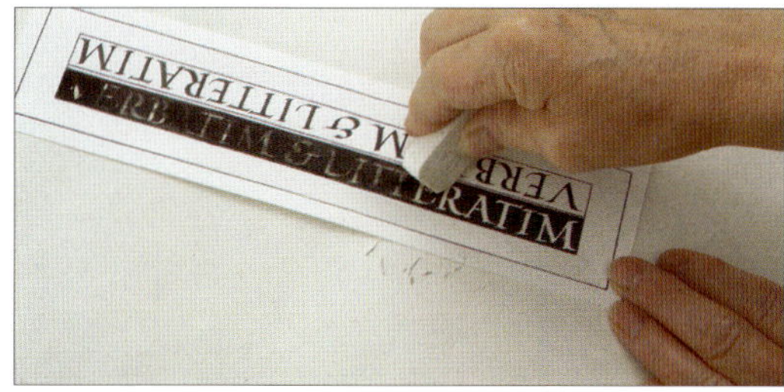

6 Rub off the masking fluid using an eraser. When the resist has been removed it will look as though the writing has been written in white on black.

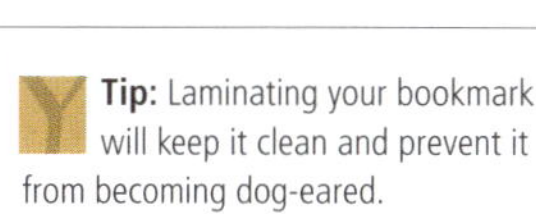

Tip: Laminating your bookmark will keep it clean and prevent it from becoming dog-eared.

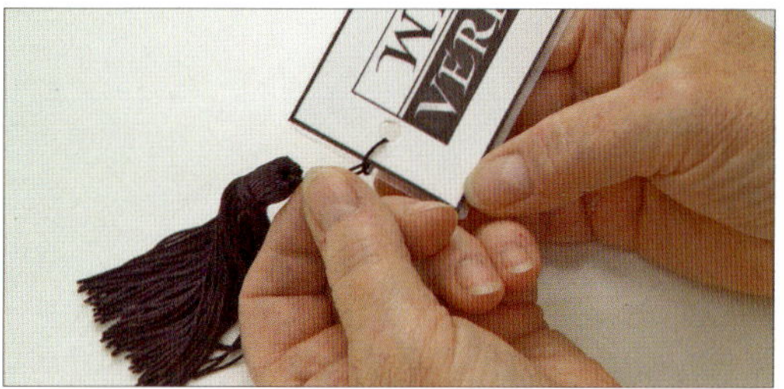

7 Remove any pencil lines with an eraser. Cut the bookmark to size with a craft knife and ruler. Laminate it, then use a hole punch to make a hole in one end. Finally, thread a black tassel through the hole and your bookmark is complete.

Greetings cards with diagonal writing

You can let your creativity flow when it comes to card design. Decide first on the shape. You can choose from a variety of styles such as 'tent' style, triangular, a tall thin card, or a square – your chosen word or text will play some role in your decision as it will dictate how much space you need. You also need to select card and paper, and you can be quite adventurous in this respect. Colour is an important consideration, too. Simply changing a colour scheme can alter the whole look of a card. It is worth mixing up a little colour and doing some trials on different papers to judge the various effects that can be created.

The greetings card has been made using a silver craft paper, which has a metallic look, in a single rectangular fold. A fold of red Chromatico paper (which looks like coloured tracing paper) is inserted inside the silver card. The bright colour works as a strong contrast to the metallic paper as well as a background for a message that could be written using a silver rollerball pen.

Materials

- *Silver metallic paper: Conqueror creative papers*
- *Red paper: Chromatico paper*
- *Layout paper*
- *Dip pens: in various sizes, including a William Mitchell 2 and a pointed nib*
- *Gouache paint: alizarin crimson*
- *Paintbrush for mixing*
- *Scissors*
- *Craft (utility) knife*
- *Glue stick*
- *Ruler*
- *Pencil*
- *Silver roller ball (ball point) pen, fine*
- *Thin red ribbon*

Tip: It is worth keeping your design simple for occasions when you want to send many cards, such as seasonal festivities.

The design

A lively script of capitals based on Uncials has been used for this card. A large pen size is used to produce bold letters and the small letters are written with a pointed nib in red gouache to reflect the colour of the insert.

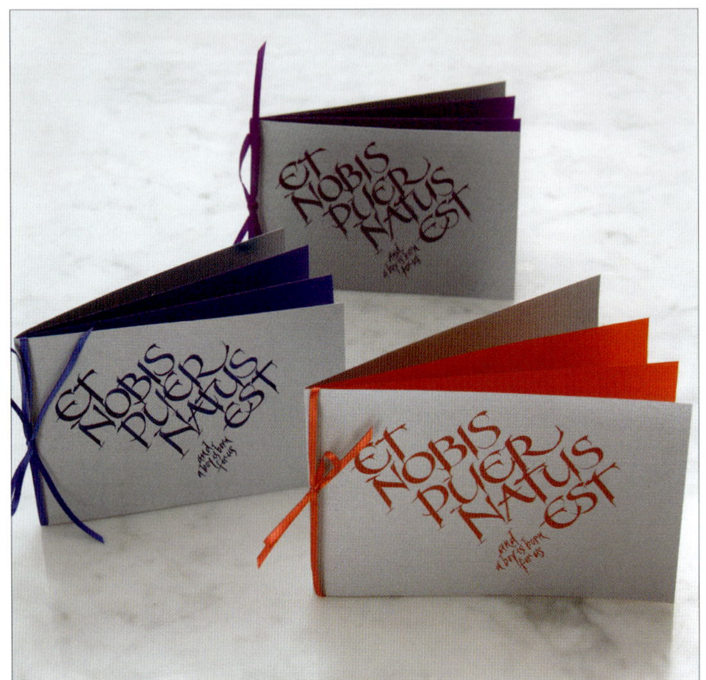

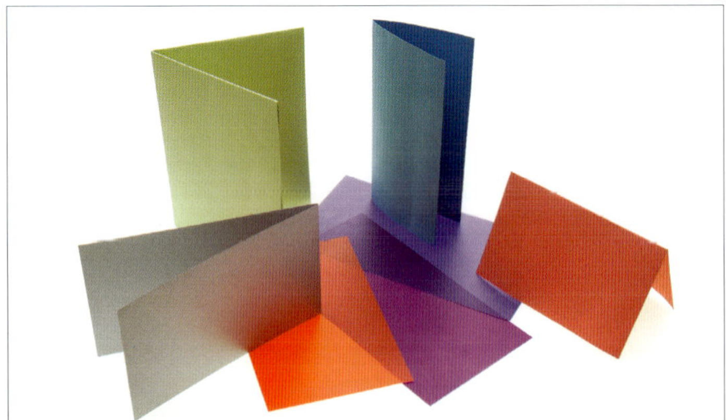

1 Make a selection of card folds with paper to see what works well for a finished card. This project uses silver metallic paper with an inserted fold of red Chromatico paper.

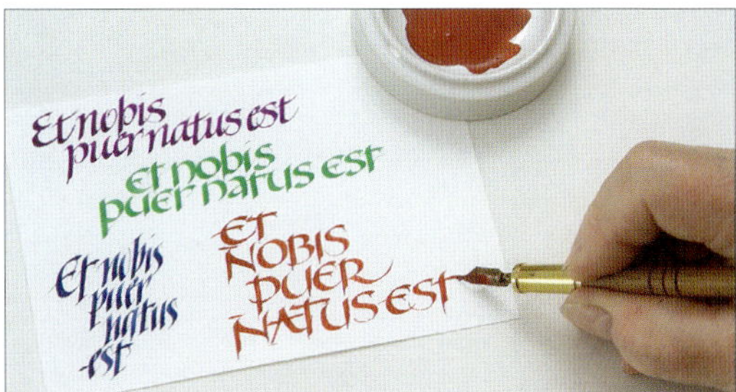

2 Practise various styles of writing and work out a layout for the design. On this card, the layout of lettering will be written diagonally across the card to create visual impact.

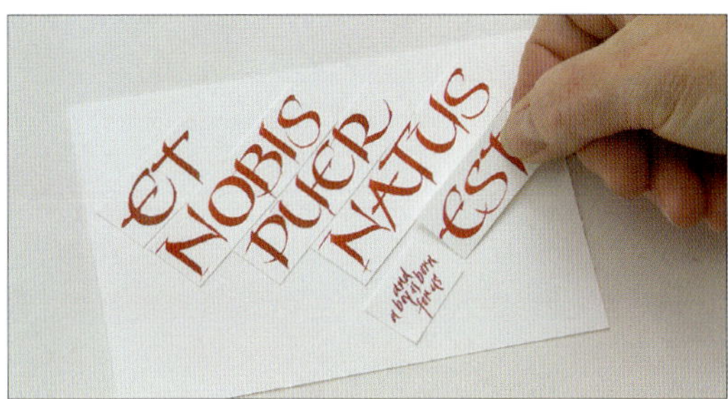

3 When you are satisfied with the writing, cut out the words and paste them on to some layout paper. Using repositionable glue will allow the words to be moved about on the paper until the layout is working well.

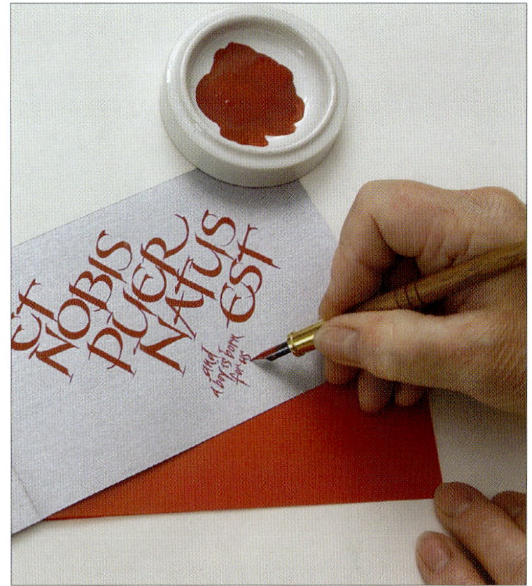

4 Using the silver metallic paper cut a piece measuring a width and height of 28cm x 10cm (11in x 4in). Carefully score the fold line, but do not fold it at this stage. Now cut a piece of red paper exactly the same size. If you need to rule up some guidelines for the writing on the silver paper, do this very lightly. Now mix up the paint and write out the words on the card using a size 2 nib for the large writing and a pointed nib for the small writing.

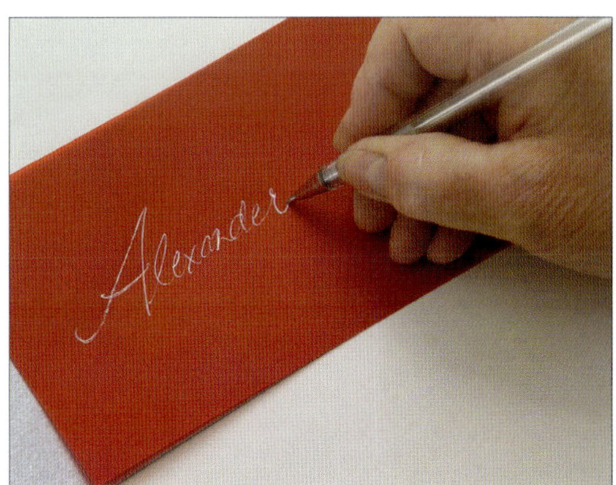

5 Once the writing has dried, the silver and red paper can be scored. Carefully make the folds and insert the red paper inside the silver card. Use a silver roller ball to write a name or personal message inside the card.

Tip: Do not forget that your card will need an envelope. A handmade card may not fit into a standard sized envelope, so it may be a good idea to make your own, using the same paper as the card.

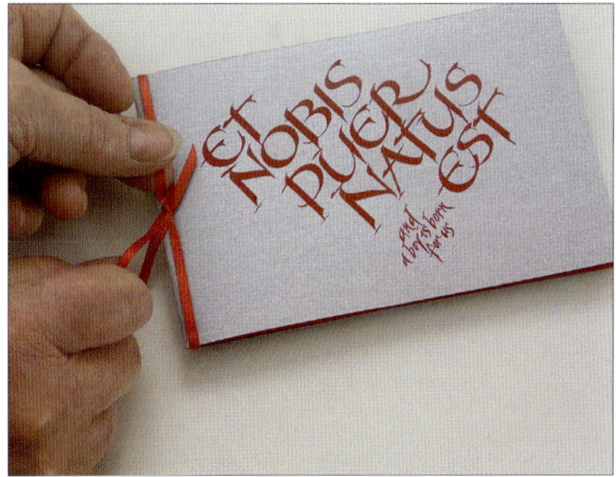

6 Tie some thin red ribbon around the card as a finishing touch to make the card look special.

Reversed-out bookplate

A bookplate is a label that indicates a book's ownership. Adorn a cherished volume with a bookplate and anyone you lend it to will have no chance of forgetting whose it is. The practice probably originated in Germany, where the earliest known example of a bookplate dates from the 15th century.

The bookplate created here has *Ex Libris,* Latin for 'from the books of', written across it, and you can personalize it with your own name. An elegant decorative effect is achieved by writing around the edges and by drawing simple pen patterns in the corners, made up of small oval loops forming butterflies.

You can easily create many bookplates to personalize a full collection of titles by using a photocopier to obtain multiple copies. Alternatively, you can scan the design into a computer using a scanner and the accompanying software. Choose a high number of pixels to ensure sharp definition. Take the resulting scan into a photo-manipulating package on your computer. By choosing 'invert' or 'negative' a black on white bookplate will show as white on black, which is much more eye-catching. By saving the bookplate design on the computer copies can be printed when needed.

The design

For this bookplate two weights of Modern Gothic script and pen patterns have been chosen as they will reproduce on a computer or photocopier very successfully. If you do not want any of the writing around the words *Ex Libris* in the centre to appear upside down, begin the writing at the bottom left-hand corner and continue to the top right across the top of the design. Then start at the bottom left-hand corner and once again travel to the top right, but this time traversing the bottom of the design.

Materials

- *Layout or practice paper*
- *Dip pens: in various sizes*
- *Gouache paint or ink: black*
- *Craft (utility) knife*
- *Self-healing cutting mat*
- *Ruler with cutting edge*
- *2H pencil*
- *Hot-pressed watercolour paper*
- *Deckle-edge scissors (optional)*

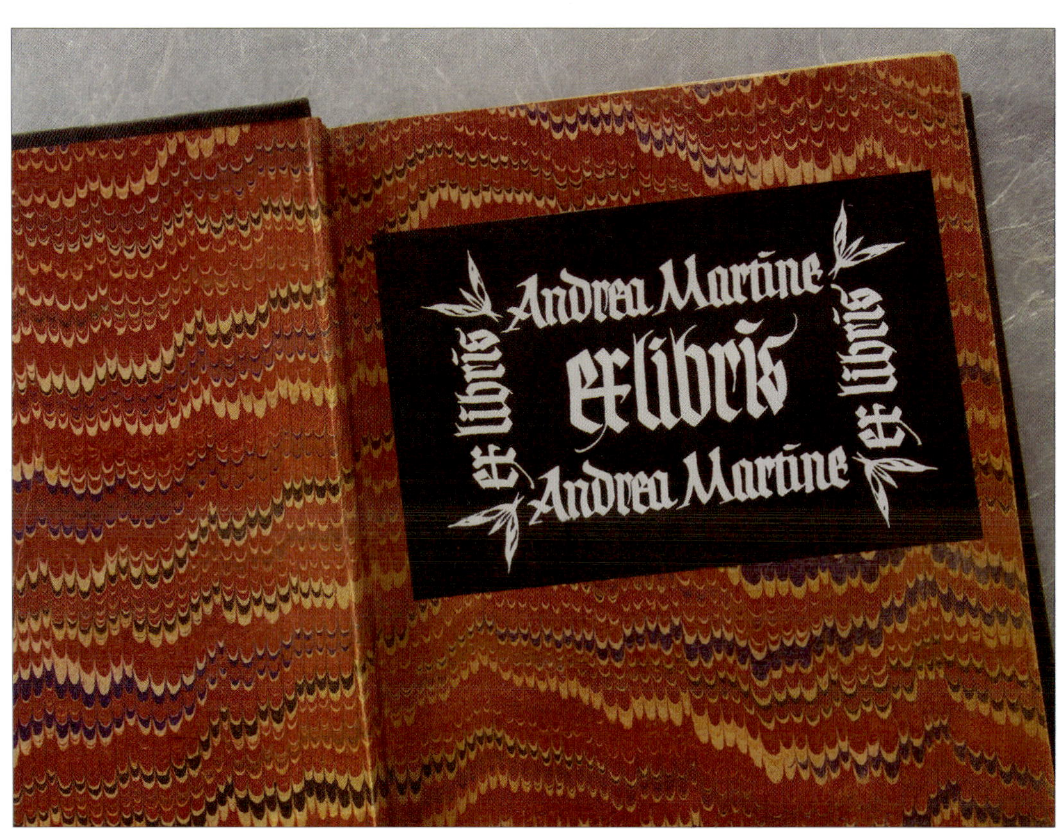

1 Experiment with various nib sizes. A strong contrast between *Ex Libris* and the name is desirable so a difference of at least two nib sizes is recommended. It may be useful to use large nibs and reduce the size on a photocopier.

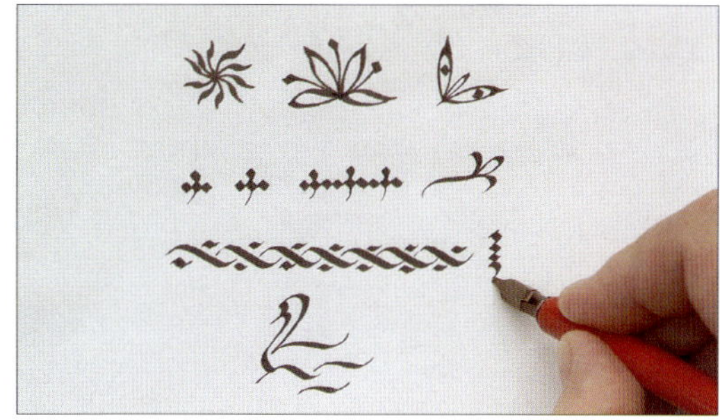

2 Practise making some simple pen patterns, again using different sized nibs. Your preferred pattern will be used to decorate the corners of your plate.

3 Once you have decided on the nibs, write the name several times on a strip of paper.

Tip: Use the nicest paper you can find for your bookplate, as this will reflect the quality of your personal library.

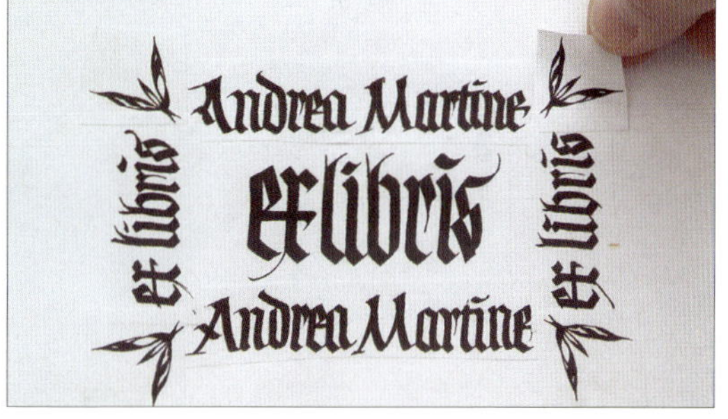

4 Try out various paste-ups. For this design the large lettered *Ex Libris* is being framed by smaller *Ex Libris* at the sides and the owner's name repeated top and bottom.

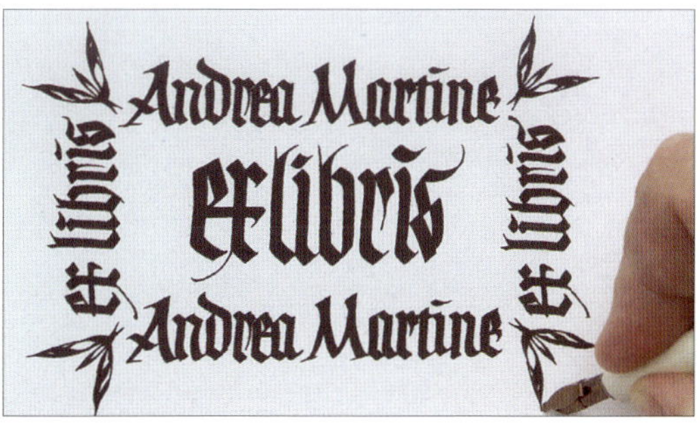

5 Once the layout has been decided, rule up and write on the watercolour paper. Any spaces in the corners can be filled with simple pen patterns. The pattern chosen here starts at the left-hand edge with a small oval loop, followed by a larger oval loop and a small oval loop to finish. Larger loops have been drawn around the outer ovals and, with the addition of antennae, the pattern has become a butterfly. This has been repeated in the other three corners.

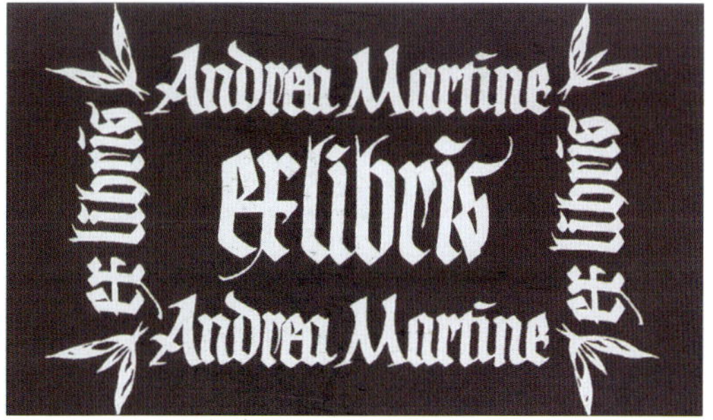

6 Scan and print out your bookplates – most photo-manipulating packages allow you to print multiple images on a single page and change or reverse the colours if you wish. You could choose a handmade paper, or one that appears handmade, to make the bookplate look as though it has history. Most photocopier machines and computer printers will accept lightweight hand-made paper though they may need to be hand-fed. You can cut out the bookplates using deckled-edge scissors to emphasize the effect.

Subtle colour lettering

This project is designed with a gardener in mind, since it uses the names of many plants that can be found in the garden. It is written in two colours, soft green and purple, to complement the theme. This form of subtle colour was introduced by well-known scribe Sam Somerville. While the colour distribution may appear random it is actually controlled by a mathematical progression starting with four letters written in green and four in purple, followed by three in green and five in purple, two in green and six in purple, one in green and seven in purple, two in green and six in purple, three in green and five in purple, and so it continues with the colours exchanging dominance and ebbing and flowing through the work. Individual words are separated by a small pink dash of colour.

Colour is a very personal choice. A cheerful and bright combination of colours that works well for one person may be a clash to someone else. In the 19th century, red and black was a very popular combination, but it is not recommended for this project, because the design requires more subtle colours. Complementary colours, such as red and green, which sit opposite each other on the colour wheel, are unlikely to be suitable because they contrast too strongly, whereas adjacent analogous colours such as blue and purple, orange and red, green and blue should look delightful. You do not even have to use different colours for this project: dark and light grey look wonderful together. Use two large calligraphy pens of the same size. In this example Brause 2mm (5/64in) nibs have been used.

Materials

- *Gouache: diluted in two colours*
- *Layout or practice paper*
- *Dip pen: Brause 2mm (5/64in)*
- *Ruler*
- *Pencil*
- *Black ink*
- *Coloured pencils*
- *Hot-pressed watercolour paper*
- *Eraser*
- *A coloured frame, if required*

The design

Neuland, the script chosen here, works well when written in a block. It is not a difficult script, which is all to the good as concentration is needed to ensure the designated colours are used in the correct places.

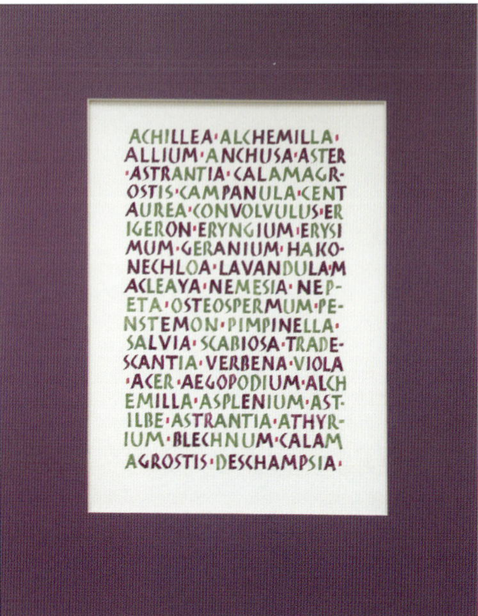

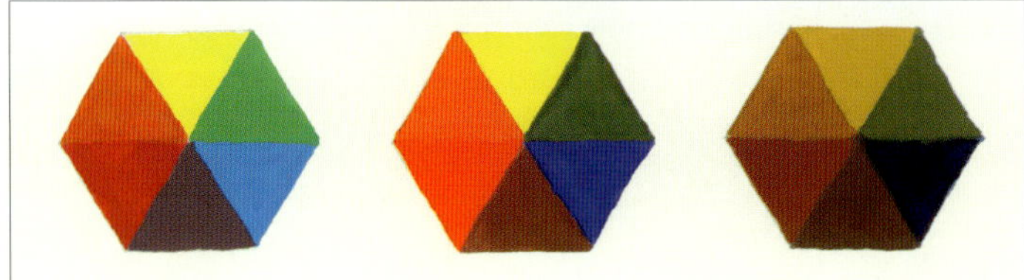

1 These three colour wheels are all based on the principle that the only three 'true' colours are red, blue and yellow, all the others are made by mixing. This would be true if it were possible to find these colours in an unadulterated form but this is not possible. Artists therefore choose to use two reds, two blues and two yellows: a warm and a cool version of each, for example cadmium red for warm, and magenta for cool. If you mix a warm colour with a cool colour the result is often disappointing. Therefore one wheel is dedicated to warm colours and the second to cool colours. However, there are also earth colours to choose from. Using yellow ochre for yellow, red ochre for red and indigo for blue, the third wheel shows subtler colours that can created by mixing. With these colour wheels in mind, experiment with colours from your collection. The colours below work well together.

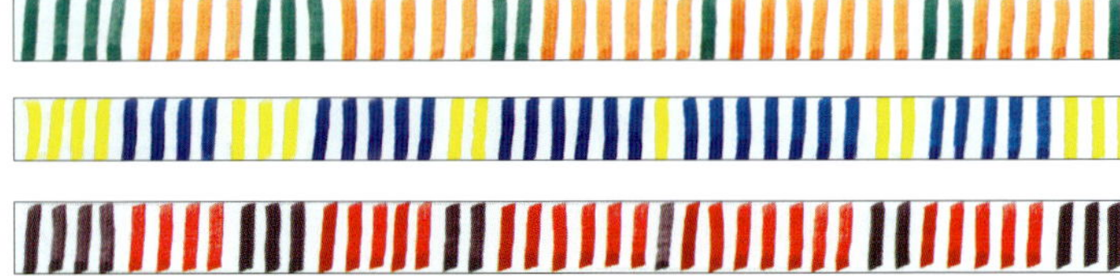

2 Once you have decided on the colours, rule up and write all of your text in black. This is a good opportunity to see how everything will sit on the page. If you are dissatisfied with your layout, now is the time to cut it all up and make a paste-up, to work out a final design.

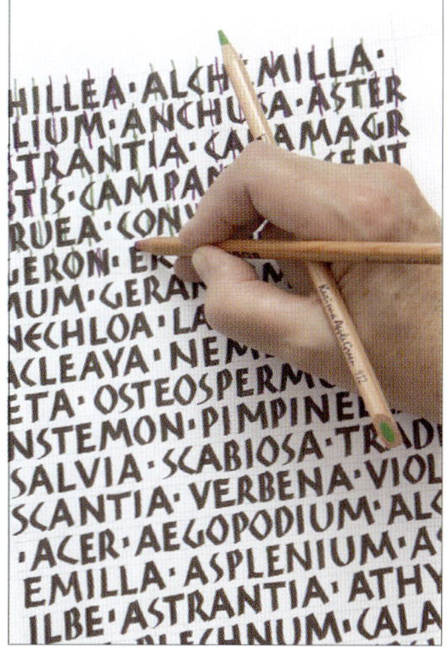

3 Select two pencils, as near in colour as possible to the gouaches you will be using, and go through the writing marking off each letter with the appropriate colour. Do not count spaces, full stops, paragraphs or anything else. Only the letters govern the progression 4/4, 3/5, 2/6, 1/7, 2/6, 3/5, 4/4, 5/3, 6/2, 7/1, and so on.

Tip: Though the main writing in this project uses two colours there is the addition of pink in the small dashes between the words. A good rule of thumb is to never use more than three colours in any piece of calligraphy.

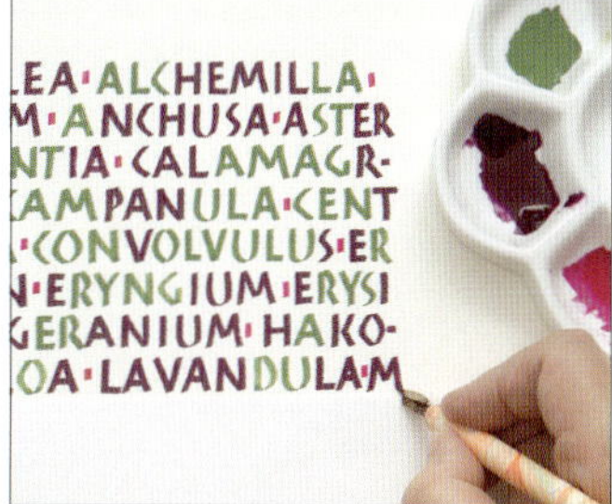

4 Rule up your good paper, mix up sufficient gouache and, using two pens, proceed to write. It is perfectly possible to complete this project with only one pen but this would mean repeatedly washing the nib before filling with a different colour.

Tip: If you make a mistake, do not worry – no one else is going to see it. Just continue with the correct sequence and try not to repeat the mistake.

5 When all the writing is completely dry, erase your guidelines and hold the piece of work up to a mirror. This way you will appreciate the wonderful flowing colours, without the words of the calligraphy getting in the way.

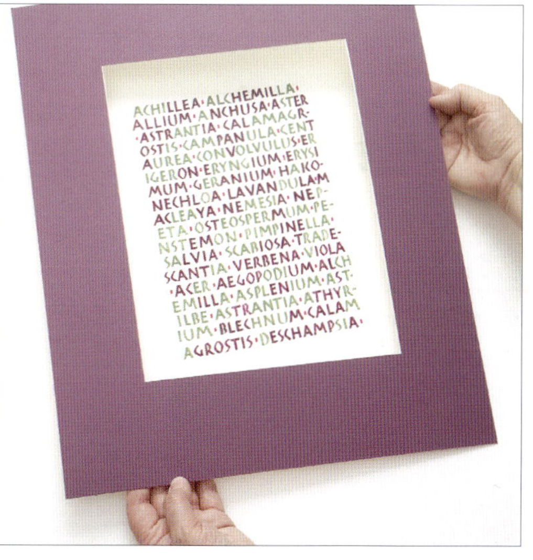

6 To finish off your work, choose a mount or frame that complements the colours of the lettering.

Cut letter cards

This project draws on techniques belonging to the delightful craft of paper pattern cutting, which has its roots in 4th–5th-century China. For centuries, Chinese children have learned paper cutting as part of their education and the paper cuts were used to decorate their homes. Thin paper was used and the subject matter was varied. Fierce dragons, flowers, birds and the gods are among the topics cut, always symbolizing good fortune and luck. Cut-paper patterns were used by all sections of Chinese society from royalty to peasantry, and in crafts as diverse as embroidery and pottery.

The techniques can be adapted to cut letters in paper, adding a new, exciting dimension to calligraphy, which can be used to create an attractive layered card, using two different colours of paper. The cut letter on the front of the card is shown off by the colour contrast of the insert. The card is embellished with tiny shapes such as cut-out diamonds, dots or stars, or drawn in gold fine line pen.

The design

Roman Capitals are used for silhouettes (positive letters) – the letter stays and the background is cut away. The letter within the 'frame' should ideally be attached in at least three places.

Tip: Almost any paper can be used for cut lettering, but a good weight for cards is around 160gsm (76lb), as this feels substantial but is not difficult to cut.

Materials

- *Automatic pen and ink, or two 2H pencils, taped together*
- *Layout or practice paper*
- *Tracing paper*
- *2H pencil*
- *Paper in two colours per card*
- *Scalpel or craft (utility) knife with long, pointed blade*
- *Self-healing cutting mat*
- *Masking tape*
- *Needle and thread, glue stick or padded sticky fixers*
- *Gold fine line pen*

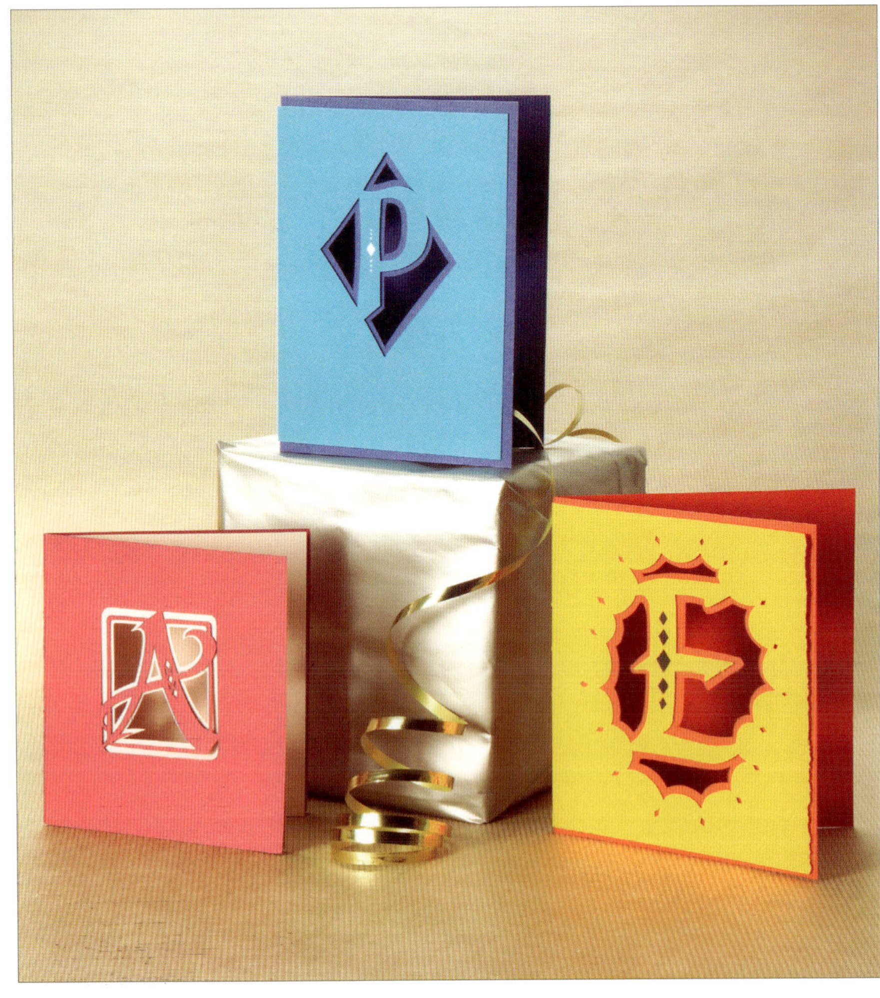

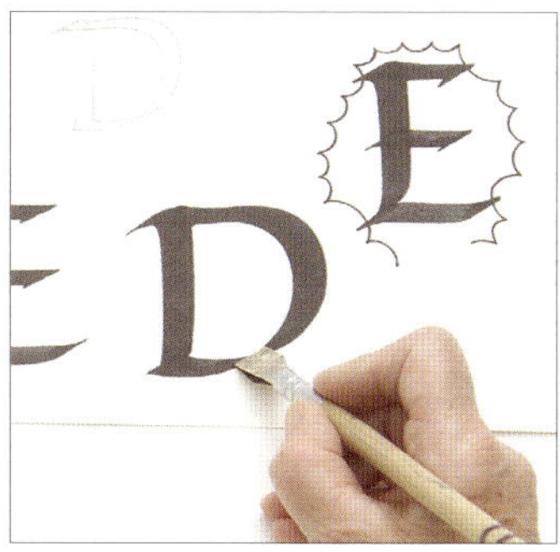

1 Using a large automatic pen and ink, or two pencils taped together, create some Roman Capitals approximately 6cm (2½in) high. Around your chosen letter, draw a shaped 'window' frame. It can be any shape – circular, diamond, cloud shaped, for example – but the drawn frame needs to overlap the letter in at least three places.

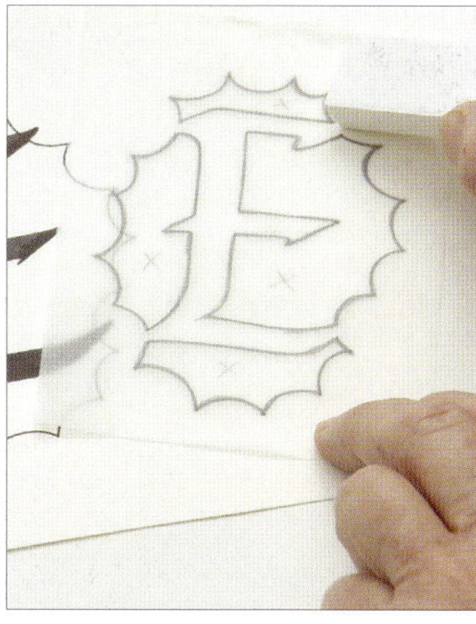

2 Trace the design, erasing the overlaps, to reduce the design to the four shaped background areas that will be cut away, leaving the letter firmly held in place. Mark each area to be cut out with a cross.

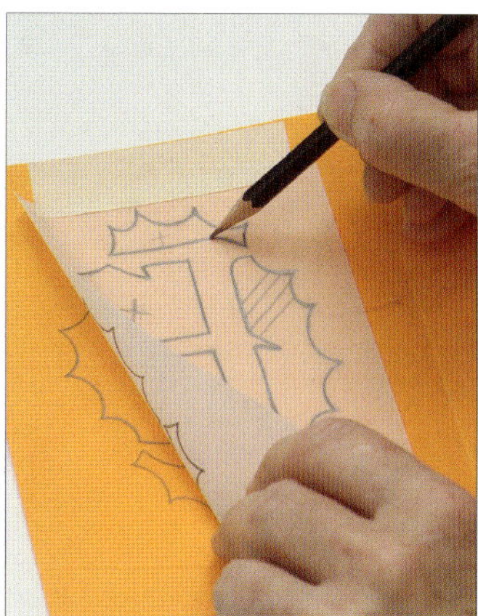

3 Transfer the design to the card by reversing the tracing paper and attaching it face down to the inside cover of a your prepared greetings card. Go over the lines with a sharp 2H pencil.

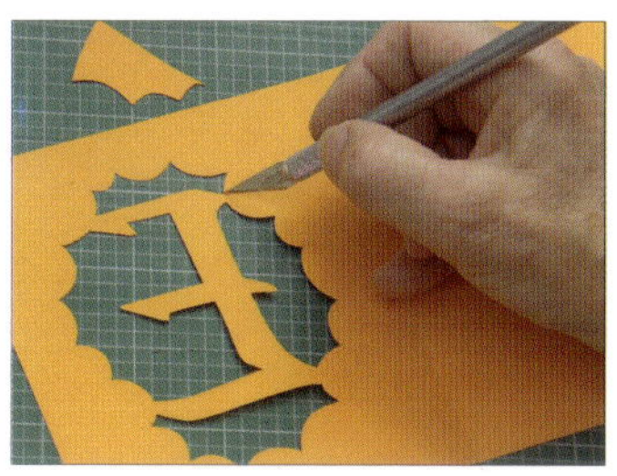

4 Holding the knife as if it were a pencil, keeping your fingers clear of cutting direction, cut out the background areas marked with a cross. Take care not to simply cut around the letter profile or the letter will become detached from its frame.

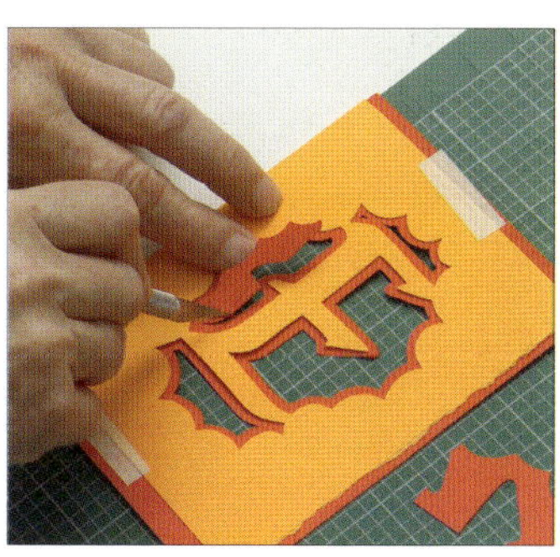

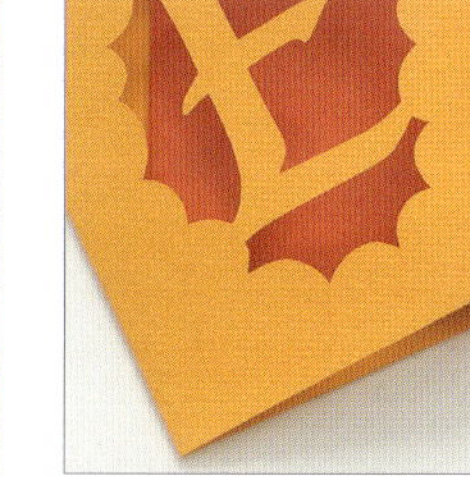

5 For the layered effect, prepare an inner card of a similar size and weight to the paper, then place this inside the completed outer section.

Tip: When cutting do not press too hard, as this will make the knife more difficult to control. You can always go over the cut line a second time to ensure the cut is complete.

6 Tape firmly together, with the cutting mat placed in between the back and front sections for protection. Working from the front of the card and through the cut letter design, mark a new cutting line on the inner surface, paralleling letter and frame, leaving a gap of 5mm (¼in).

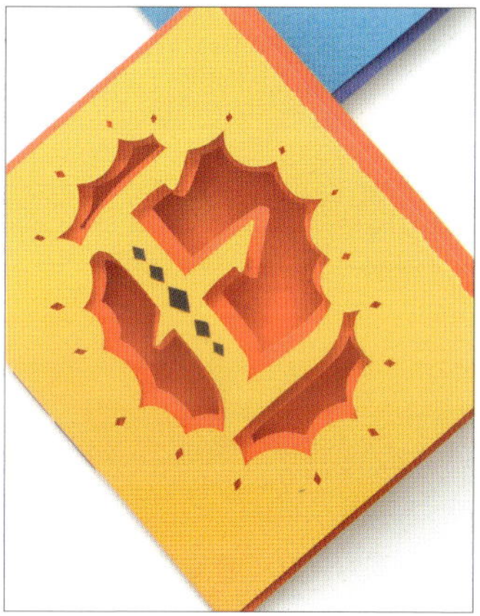

7 On completion, either sew the two sections together, or join them using a thin strip of glue on the back spine of the insert. Alternatively, instead of leaving the card insert freely hinged, try trimming the outer card in half, at the original fold line, and place small sticky fixer pads on the reverse of this outer section. Carefully mount this on to the inner section to create a 'decoupage' effect. Embellish with tiny cut paper diamonds and stars, or add dots of gold with a fine liner pen, if preferred.

Embossed designs for a letterhead

This project combines lettering skills for a letterhead with the art of embossing – shaping letters and patterns so that they are raised above the surface of the surrounding paper.

Embossing requires the use of a template and involves carefully and accurately cutting shapes out of a piece of thin card. Working from the reverse side, the surface of the paper is then gently pushed down into the cut shape. This creates a raised image on the front surface, casting shadows and giving an appearance of quality, which is suitable for both personal and business use.

Once you have cut your template it can be used many times, and the actual embossing is quick and easy to do. With practice you will acquire the necessary skills to be able to do crisp accurate cutting, making an infinite number of designs possible. Many papers emboss well and you might find it useful to keep a paper sample file of experiments and results. The best papers to use are those with a soft surface.

Materials

- *Dip pens: in various sizes*
- *Coloured inks*
- *Glue stick*
- *Layout or practice paper*
- *Watercolour paper or soft-surface paper such as BFK Rives*
- *2H pencils*
- *Craft (utility) knife*
- *Tracing paper*
- *Thin card (stock)*
- *Masking tape*
- *Embossing tool, or cable knitting needle*
- *Pastels*
- *Cotton bud (swab) or soft brush*
- *Crayon*

Tip: Always use a sharp blade for cutting stencils. For complex projects, you may have to replace the blades several times.

The design

This letterhead is made up of a personal name and address with an embossed initial letter, which can be subtly decorated with colour. The calligraphy is written using Foundational Hand and Roman Capitals in blue and black.

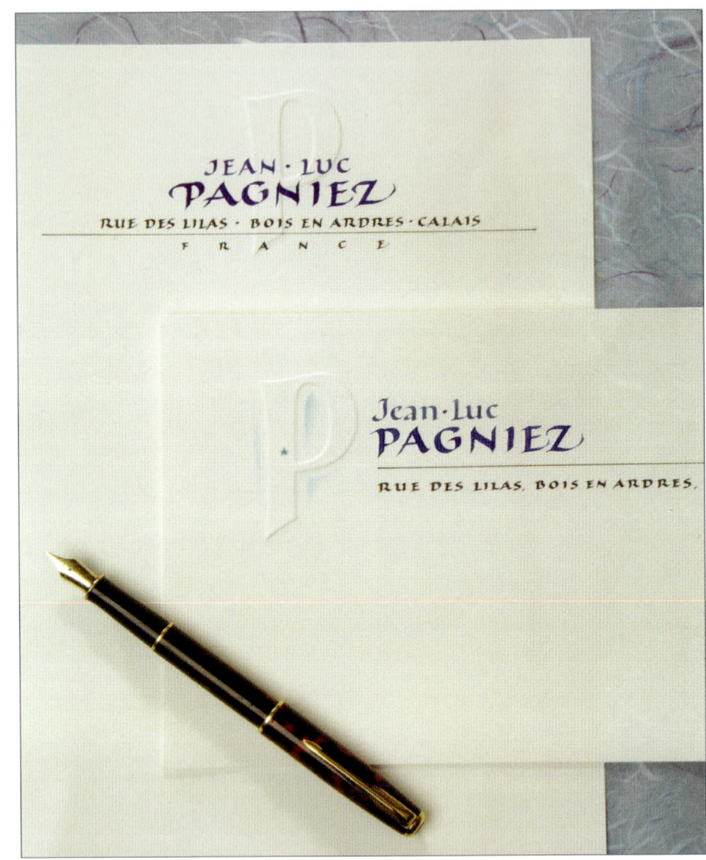

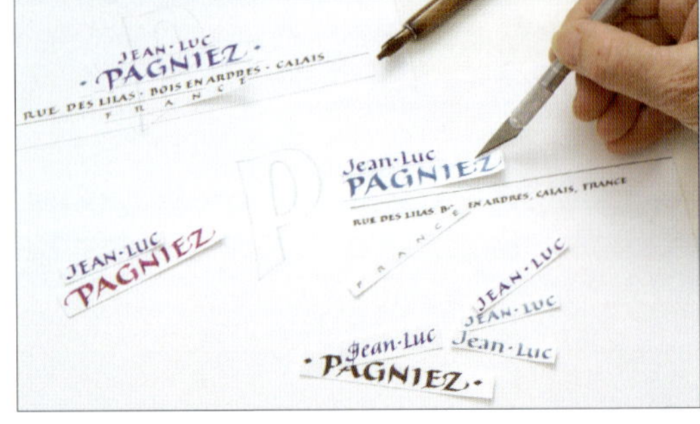

1 Design the lettering, using layout paper. Paste up your name and address strips leaving a space for the embossed image. Finalize the writing on the design and write out on a paper of your choice.

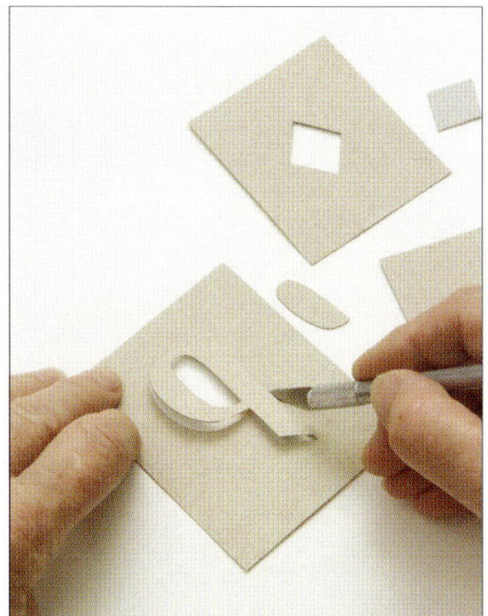

2 Draw or trace and transfer the image on to thin card. Cut out the shape, keeping your fingers clear of the cutting direction.

Tip: Keep your blade sharp, and overcut corners to ensure crisp cuts. If the blade is blunt you will leave tufts and they will show on the embossed surface.

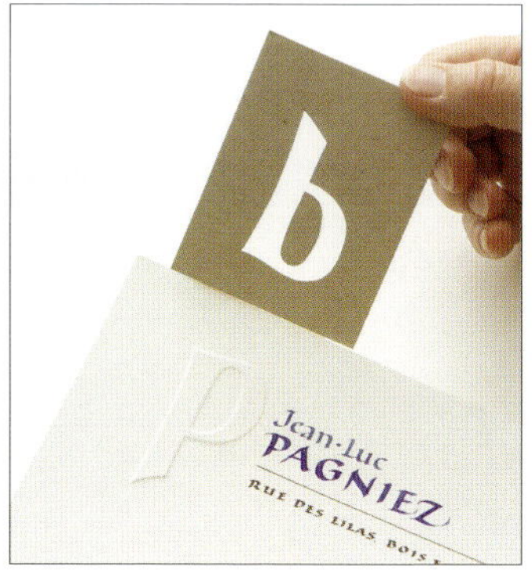

5 Use the hinge to check the quality of the embossing. If it is not crisp enough replace the hinged template, turn over and further emboss. Crisp edges and sharp points on corners are vital, so run the embossing tool firmly into the corners, to ensure good results.

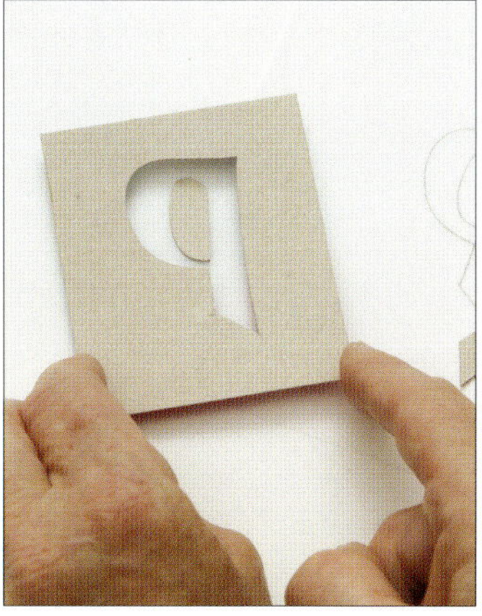

3 For letters with 'island' counters, stick the reverse image card template on to tracing paper. This backing allows you to stick the counter safely in place.

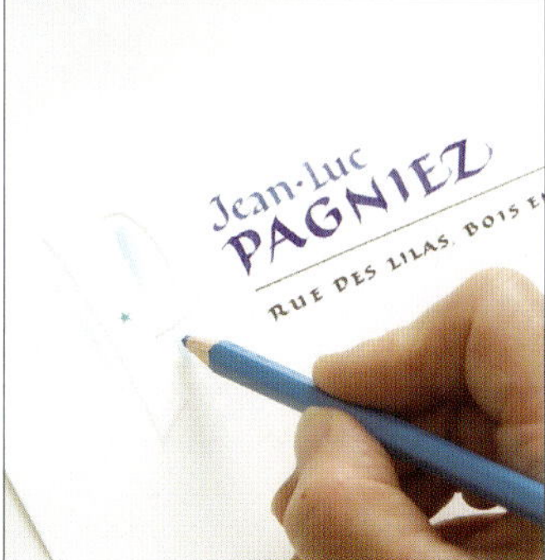

6 To add a blush of colour, scrape some dry pastel dust, using a cotton bud or soft brush, rubbing well in with a circular motion. Keep colour away from the embossed edge, or the subtle shadow effect will be lost. Use colour very sparingly. Alternatively, use a crayon to add final touches to the embossing.

Tip: When embossing, place the template down first, reverse face towards you if it is a letter, and position paper over, right side face down, and work from the reverse.

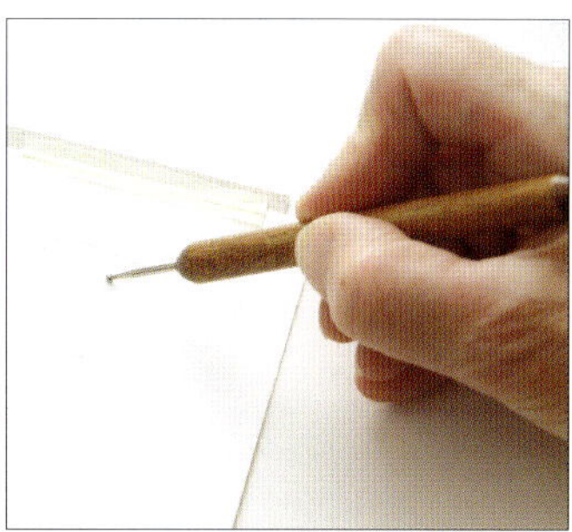

4 Once the lettering is complete, position the work face down on to the template and tape securely along one edge so that it acts as a hinge. To do this, place the template (reverse side up) against a window, to allow you to position it before taping it securely. Working on the reverse, gently run a fingernail into the depression, pushing the paper into the cut shape. Using the embossing tool, gently but firmly run it along the already depressed shape, working all around the perimeter, taking care to push well into the corners, to make crisp edges and points.

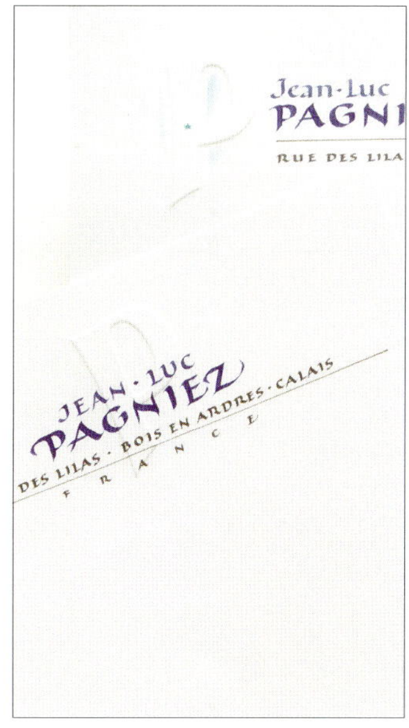

7 Prepare a variety of embossed images, some single and others with multiple embossings.

Alphabet on woven paper

Historically, the most important legal and other formal documents often had a wax seal affixed. Occasionally, when the cost of a vellum or parchment scroll was too high and paper was available, a paper design was woven and either applied to the document or woven directly into it.

This idea can be used to create an unusual textured effect for a design. Although the cutting and weaving in this project appears complex, the calligraphy itself is not. This means that you can spend some time and effort on the individual letters of the alphabet to make them as interesting or decorative as possible. Take the opportunity to try out variations on your usual calligraphic scripts or to develop new alphabets that you can use in other designs.

It is possible to create an even more intriguing piece of work by making several woven alphabets in different sizes and arranging them on a plain or coloured background. To do this mark up a much larger single sheet of paper with grids of different sizes and weave the strips into this, rather than making separate pieces of work and mounting them afterwards.

Another variation of this project is to cut the slits horizontally and weave the strips from top to bottom.

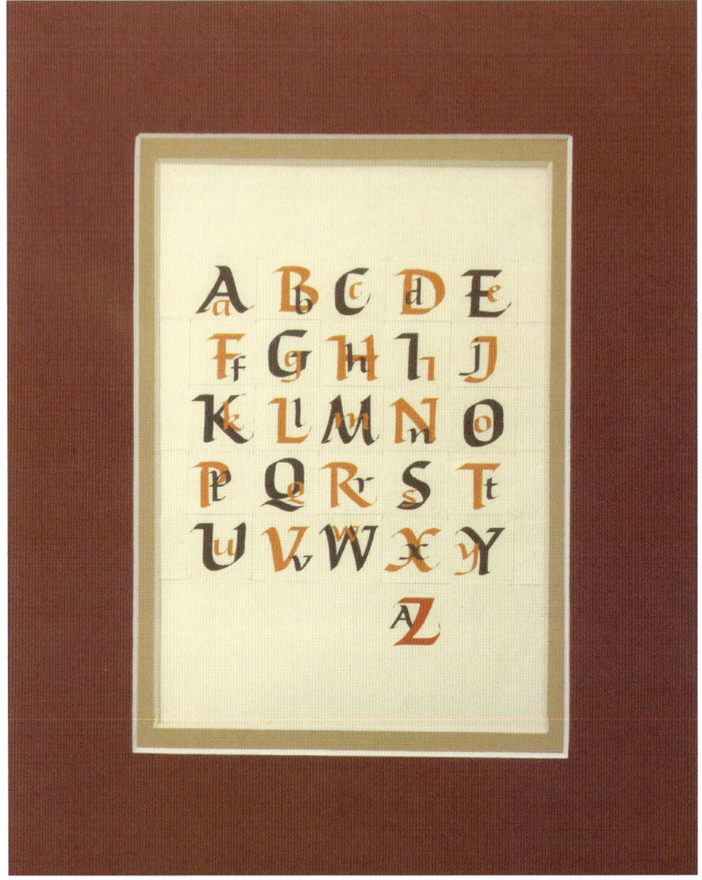

The design

Twelve of the letters are written in Italic on the grid and all the other letters, excluding 'Z', are written on the strips that are woven to form the alphabet.

Materials

- *Layout or practice paper*
- *Black and coloured writing ink*
- *Dip pens, such as William Mitchell 1 and 2*
- *Good quality paper*
- *Pencil*
- *Metal ruler, T-square or set square*
- *Scalpel or craft (utility) knife*
- *Eraser*
- *Tweezers (optional)*
- *Frame (optional)*

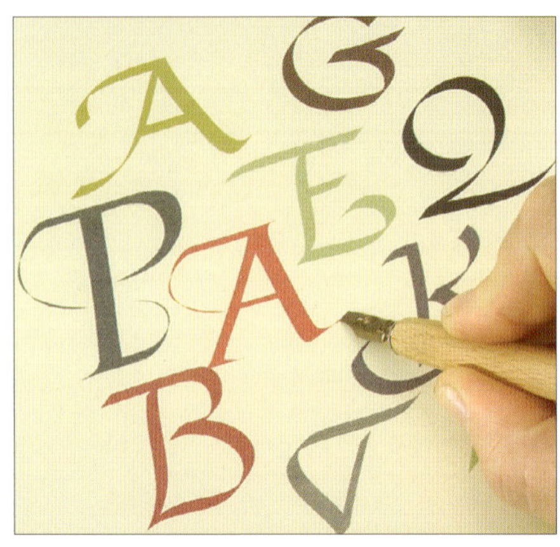

1 Write some letters of the alphabet in a range of styles on layout paper and choose one you want to use in the design. You can write capitals or lower case and mix them if you wish. Decide on a size for the final design without making it too large or too small. A basic module of 2cm (3/4in) square is a good size. Choose a good, strong paper. This can be white or coloured.

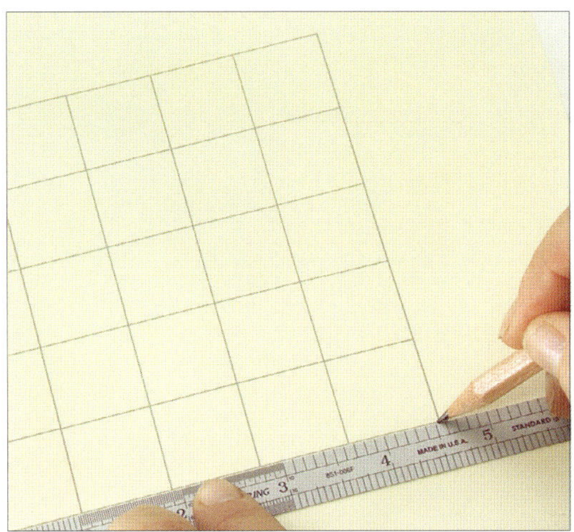

2 Mark up the paper lightly and accurately in pencil with a 5cm x 5cm (2in x 2in) square grid with a ruler. To be even more accurate use a T-square, set square or some other method that ensures that the grid lines are exactly at right angles to each other. Leave a margin of at least 10cm (4in) all around the grid. The surplus can be trimmed off afterwards.

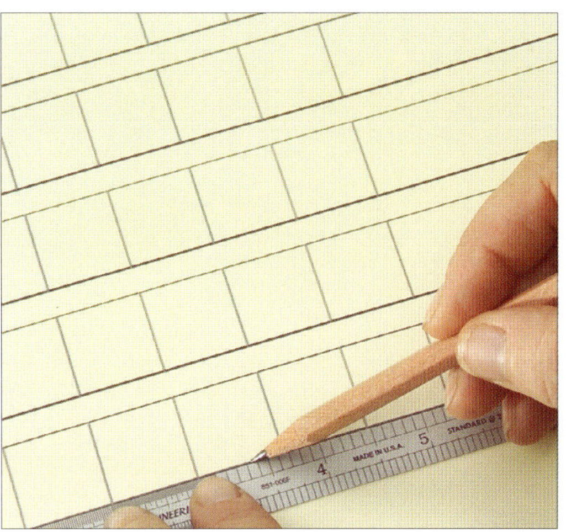

3 Measure and draw up paper strips to the width of the grid squares. Make them about 20cm (8in) longer than the width and height of your grid. These can be of the same or different paper from that on which you drew the initial grid. To make the weaving a little bit easier, make the width of the strips a tiny bit less than the grid squares.

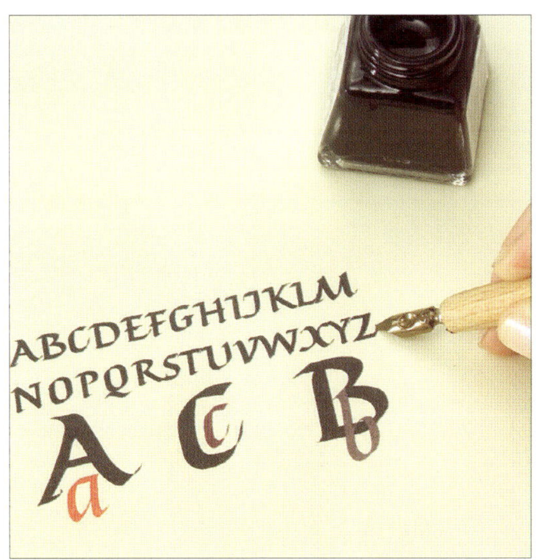

4 Plan out the letters for the whole alphabet. Experiment with variations on the letterform that has been selected. Try combining capitals and lower-case letters. Experiment with colour combinations. Remember that each letter or group of letters must fit with the squares of the grid.

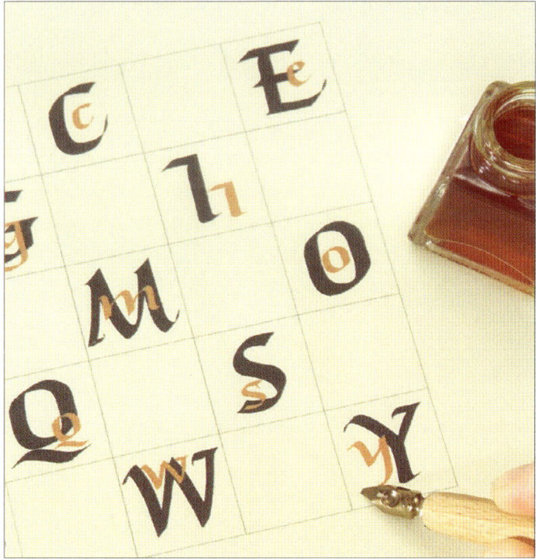

5 Write every second letter of the alphabet within the squares of the grid on the marked-up paper. This grid has capital letters in black and lower-case letters in orange. If two colours overlap, ensure that the first colour is dry before writing the second. Also, make sure that the medium of the second colour will not mix with that of the first letter.

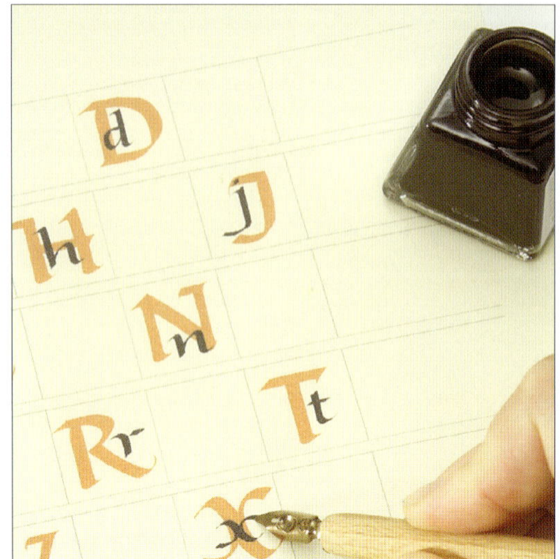

6 Write the remaining letters on every second square of the marked up sheet. The grid comprises 25 squares so this will leave the letter 'Z'. The colours of the capitals and lower-case letters have been reversed for the strips – the capitals are now orange and the lower-case letters black.

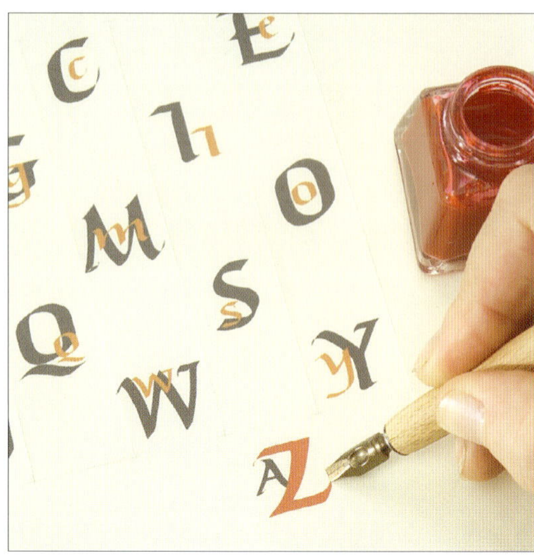

7 Decide on the position of the last letter 'Z' either on one of the strips or on the paper. This letter does not have to be the same as the others. In this example a small 'a' has been placed beside the 'Z' to suggest the whole alphabet. Red is used to contrast with the other letters.

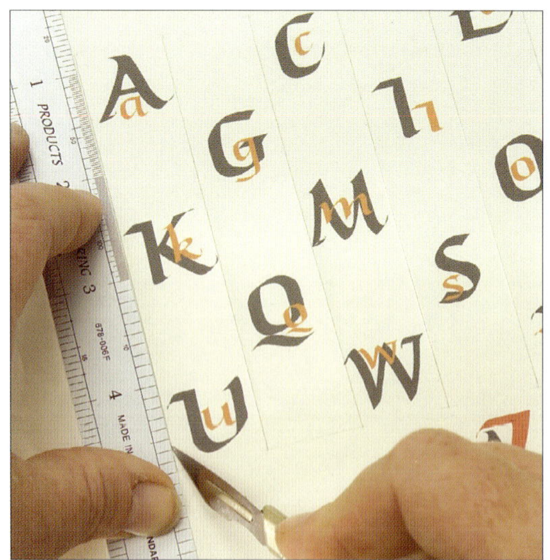

8 Cut six vertical slits on the paper within the grid to allow the strips of paper to be inserted and woven. Use a very sharp blade as any roughness will make weaving the strips of paper a little more difficult. Avoid extending cuts beyond the grid. If you cut the slits too long it will be hard to keep the paper strips in the correct position.

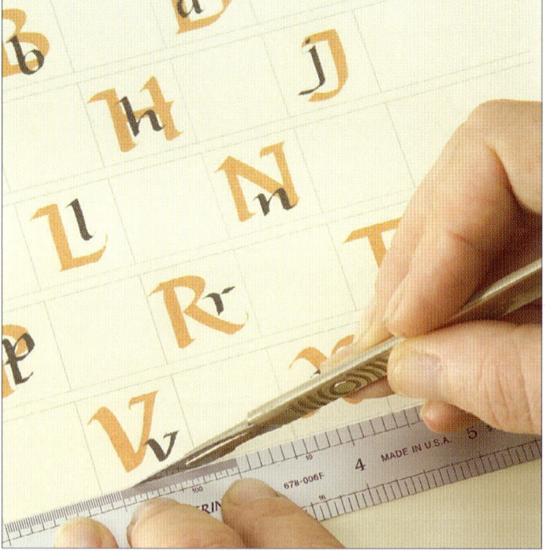

9 Cut the paper strips horizontally, using a scalpel and a metal ruler. When the lines have been cut, rub off the vertical lines that have been drawn between the letters using an eraser.

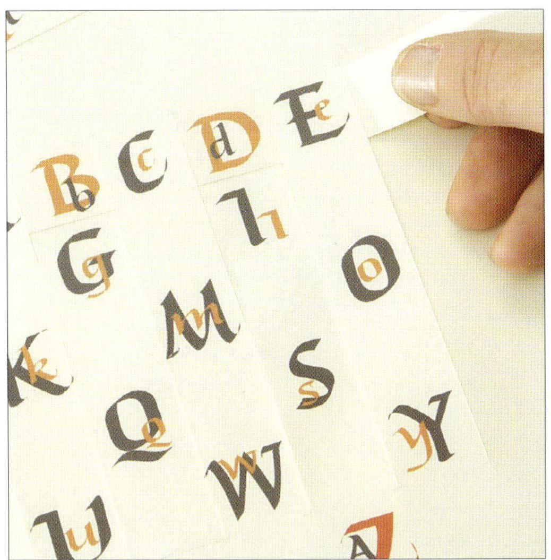

10 Feed the first paper strip (with the letters 'B' and 'D') through the slits, one at a time, from right to left. Feed it below the 'E', 'C' and 'A' and pull it through until the correct letters are positioned centrally with the squares. Push the strip upward until it butts up against the top of the slits.

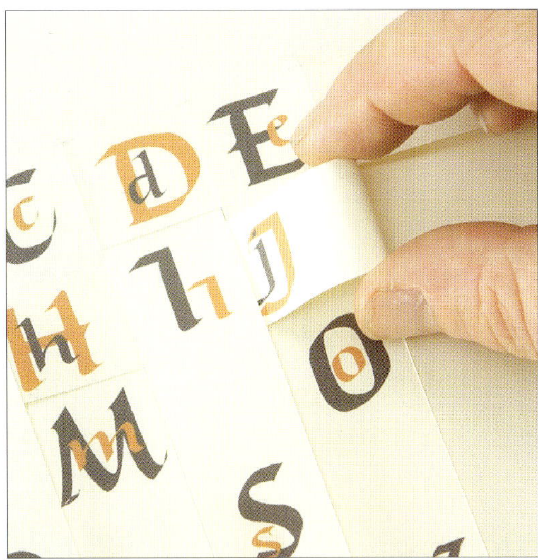

11 Similarly, feed the second strip (with the letters 'F', 'H' and 'J') through the slits from the right to the left. This time, feed it from below through the first slit under the 'I' and 'G' and downwards through the last (left) slit.

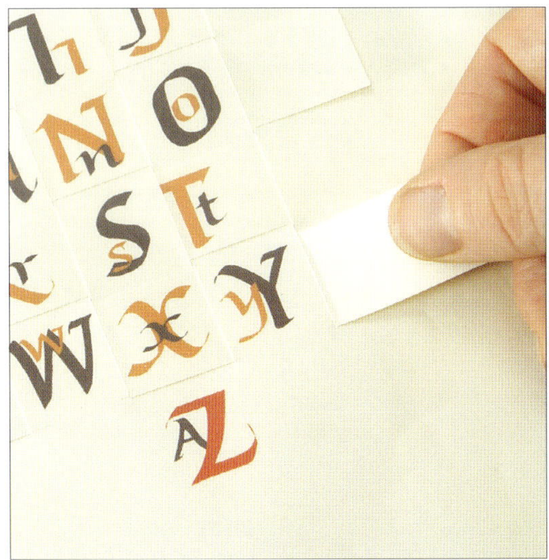

12 Continue feeding the other three strips alternately. The last strip will be the most difficult as the fit will be very tight. Make sure that the upper four strips are pushed hard up against each other. It may be helpful to use tweezers or some other method of gripping the leading edge of the strip. Cutting the leading edge to a point can also help.

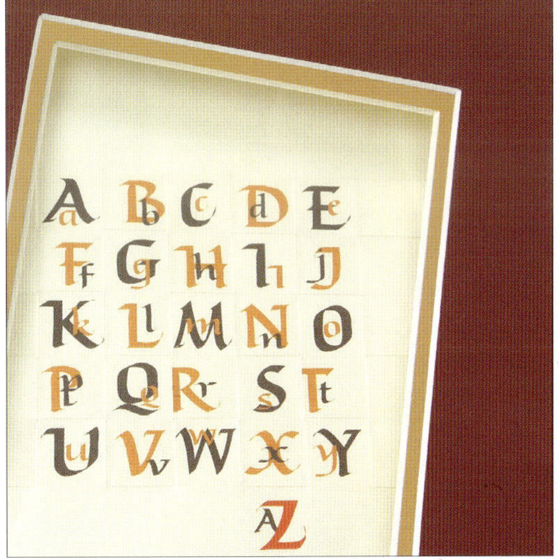

13 Trim the surplus paper from the strips leaving them the same length. Trim the calligraphy to its final size. Frame the calligraphy if desired with a matching frame.

Wall hanging using a broad-edged brush

This is an opportunity to exhibit your calligraphic skills on a grander scale by creating an elegant wall hanging. Getting the best results requires a skilful use of the broad-edged brush. To produce beautiful marks, the trick is to remember the edged brush is not a pen and so should not be used like one. Keep the paint as thick as possible, fill the brush and wipe most of it away, to preserve the chisel edge. Do this for every stroke, and the lettering will remain sharp. The calico will also accept large pens, providing it is prepared in the way shown here.

Unbleached calico can be bought from dressmaking or curtain-making stores. Writing on it directly is quite hard work as the surface of untreated calico is slightly water-resistant. For this project, household emulsion is first painted on to the calico, mixed with some glue to help flexibility and give a good writing surface. This also thickens the fabric and makes it sufficiently flat to work on without any need for stretching or extra preparation. If the paint has penetrated the surface, the edges will not fray when trimmed, so there is no need to neaten them by folding them over.

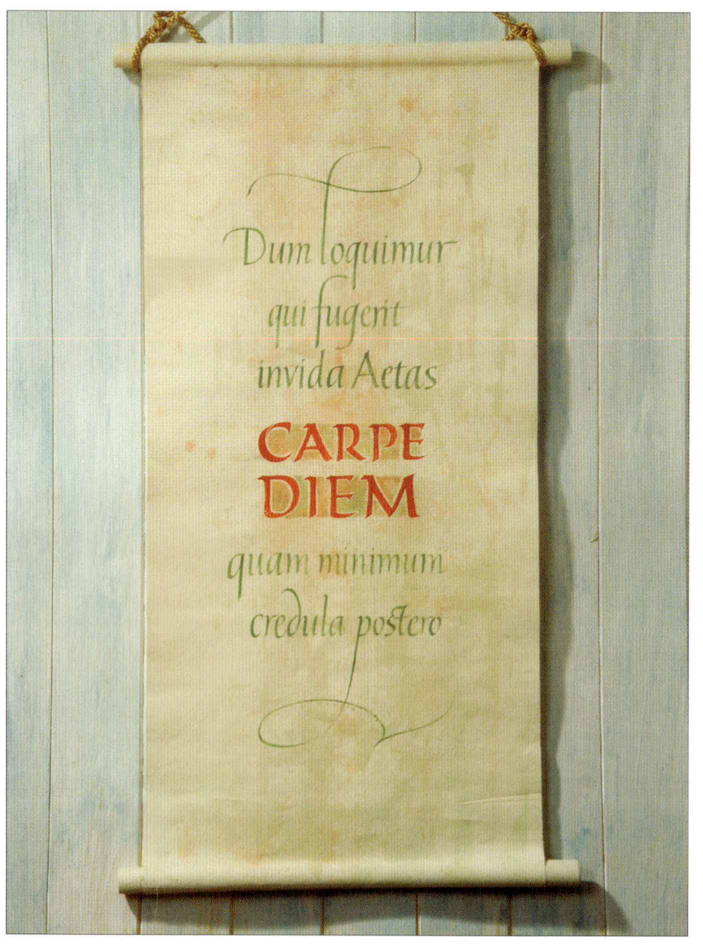

The design

This hanging is tall rather than wide, to give it more chance of fitting on a narrow wall. This practical shape does, however, mean there are more lines to rule, and quotations with long words can be awkward to accommodate. The Latin quotation, written using Roman Capitals and Flourished Italic, comes from Horace, and translates as 'While we talk, time is flying; seize the day, put no trust in the future'.

Materials

- *Dip pen, such as William Mitchell 3, (medium nib) and ink, or felt-tipped pen, for roughs*
- *Broad-edged brushes, 1cm (1/2in) wide and 5mm (1/4in) wide or automatic pens of approximately these sizes*
- *Layout paper or brown Kraft paper*
- *Craft (utility) knife, metal ruler, self-healing cutting mat*
- *Calico*
- *Household emulsion paint: white or cream, and PVA (white) glue*
- *Household paintbrush*
- *Old newspaper*
- *Fine abrasive paper*
- *Two equal lengths of dowel*
- *Mixing palette*
- *Gouache paints: oxide of chromium (green) and Chinese red*
- *Art roller and roller tray*
- *Water pot*
- *HB pencil*
- *Ruler*
- *Set square (optional)*
- *Sheet transfer gold leaf (optional)*
- *Oil pastels (optional)*
- *Coloured rope for hanging*

Tip: Practise all the writing on brown Kraft paper, or lining paper, obtainable from wallpaper stores; these have a slightly rough surface that will simulate the 'drag' of writing on calico, and give good sharp marks. Warming up first in this way can make all the difference to the finished result.

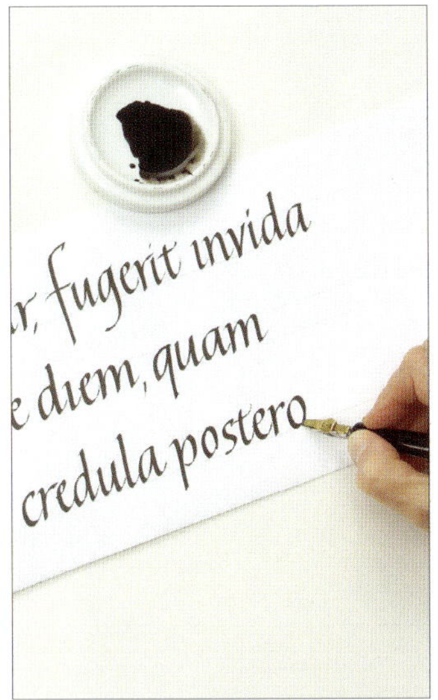

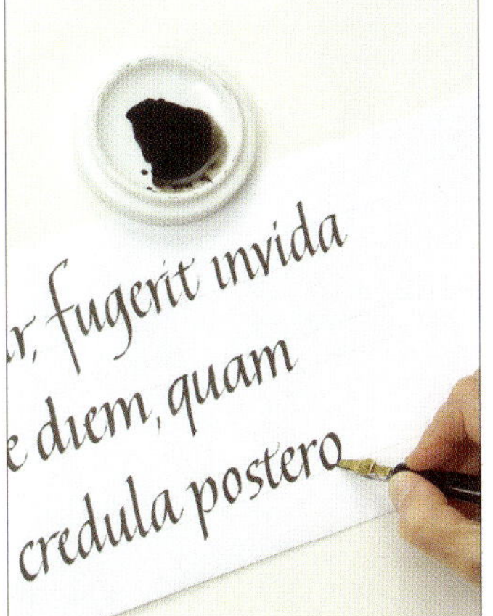

1 Try out the chosen quotation in Italic, with a dip pen or a felt-tipped pen. If you are using brushes, Kraft paper has a textured surface that will give the necessary 'drag' for good lettering. Use ordinary layout paper if pens are being used.

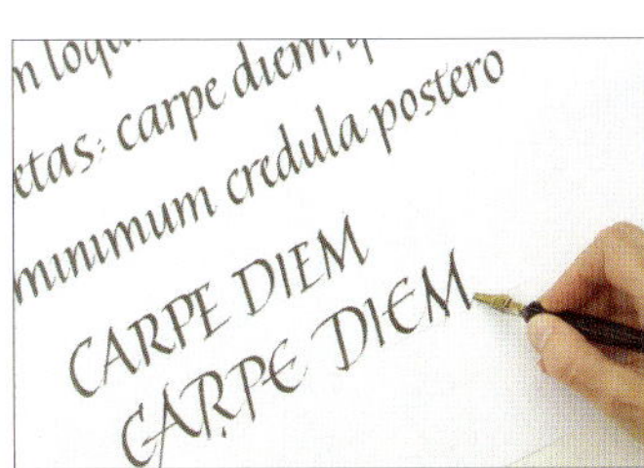

2 Pick a suitable phrase or word from your quotation to emphasize. This lettering can be written in a larger size, using Roman Capitals. *Carpe Diem* is a well-known phrase that will draw the reader's attention.

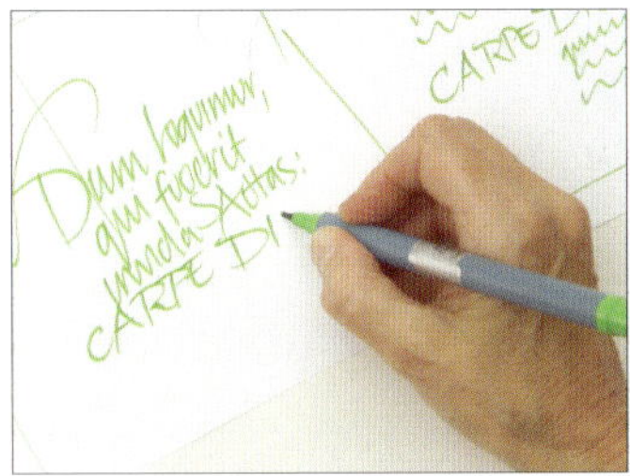

3 Do some trials so that you can practise the layout.

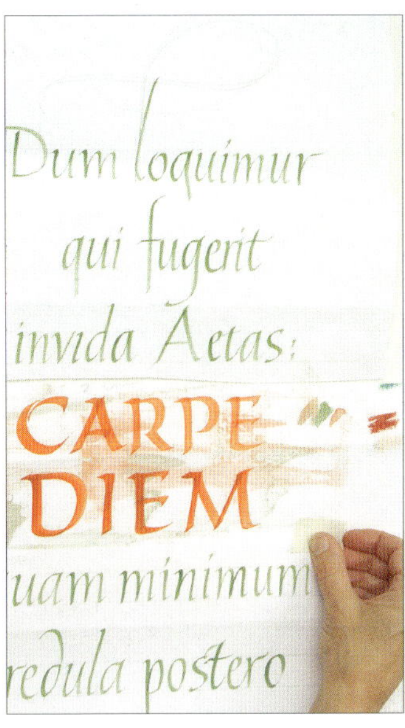

4 Write it all out in the sizes and tools you plan to use for the final work. Cut and paste it together into a design. If there is only one word per line, keep the interline spacing tight to bring the quotation together.

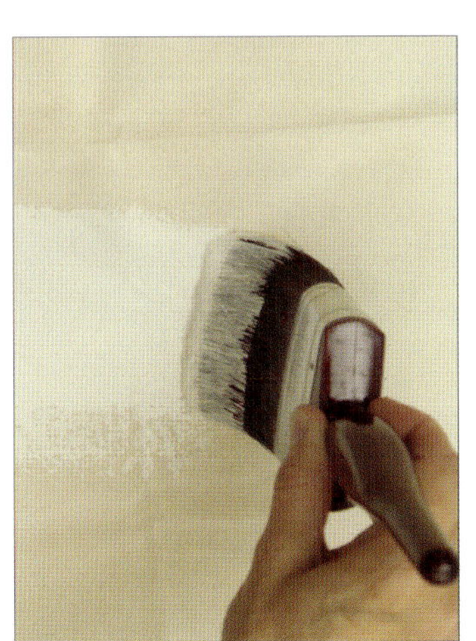

5 Prepare the calico by mixing household emulsion paint with PVA glue – approximately four parts paint to one part glue. Cover your work surface with old newspaper and then apply a layer of paint to the calico.

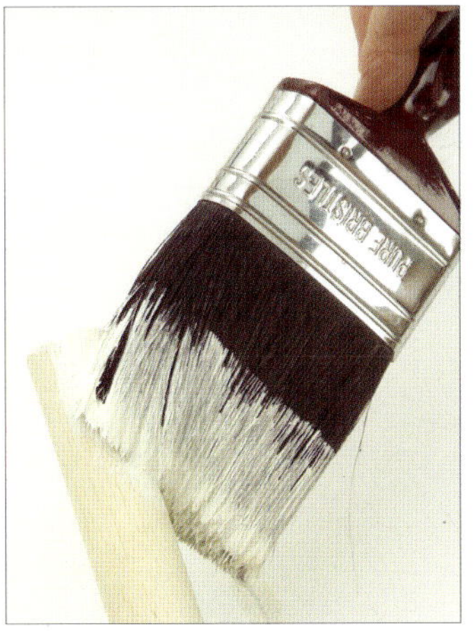

6 While the calico is drying, sand the ends of the lengths of dowel, and use emulsion to paint the parts that will show, unless you prefer to leave the wood bare.

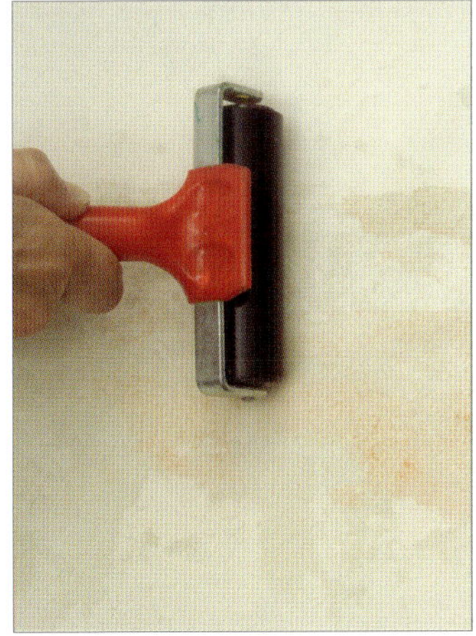

7 Mix up some of the red and green paint, but make it very watery, and apply it all over the surface in a vertical direction with the roller; apply one colour at a time but allow them to blend on the surface, providing a pale textured background. Leave to dry.

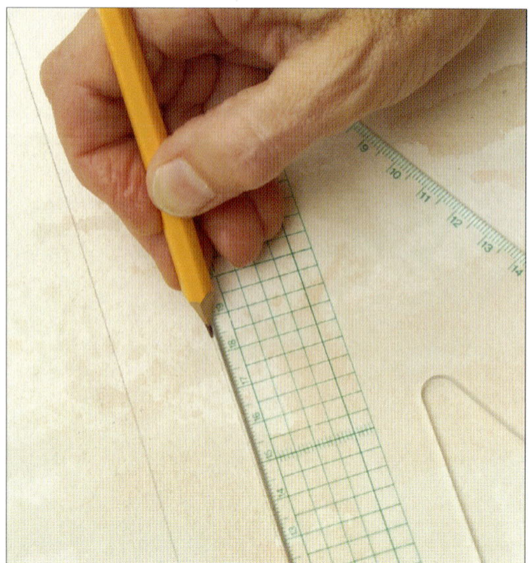

8 Allowing some space at the top and bottom of the calico length for rolling round the dowel, rule up the calico with fine lines using a pencil. Check first in a corner that the pencil can be erased without leaving a trace. To rule up, either measure down both sides of the calico and rule across, or if the calico edge is straight, use a set square as shown.

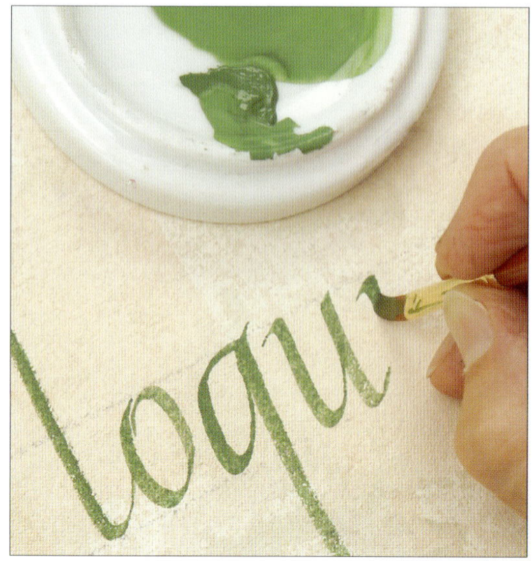

9 With the paste-up close at hand for reference, begin the lettering, using the oxide of chromium gouache. Keep the gouache as thick as will still come off the brush, to maintain drag. To preserve the chisel edge, fill the brush and wipe most of it away before every stroke.

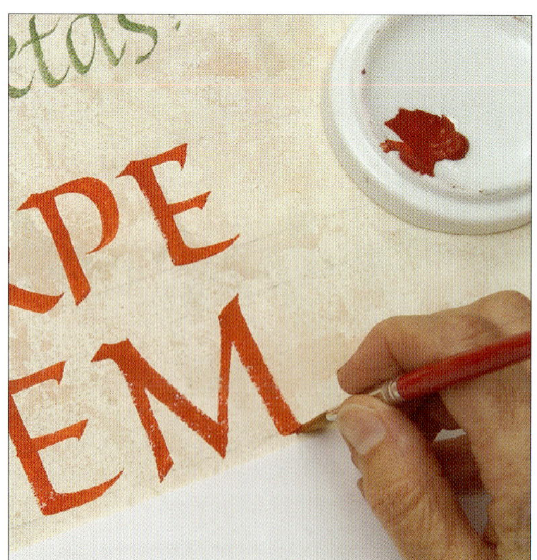

10 Write out *Carpe Diem* using a larger brush or pen, using the red gouache. These are heavyweight Roman Capitals, giving solid contrast to the wispier lower-case Italic.

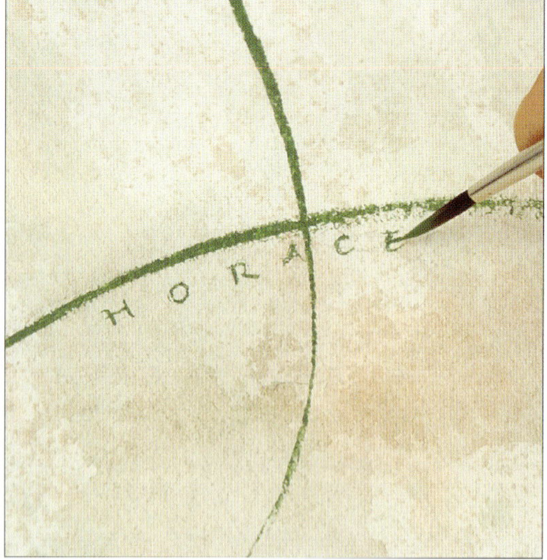

11 Complete the rest of the quotation in Italic, taking special care (by practising many times first) with the flourish. Use a very fine, pointed paintbrush to add the credit 'Horace' in small capitals, spread out along the curve of the flourish or alternatively in a line below.

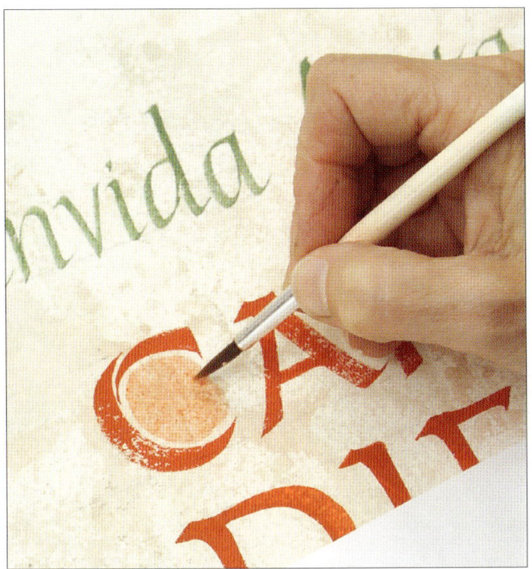

12 Add some delicate colour to the counters in the capitals by using very watery versions of the main colours, this time blending them into each other in each shape. Do not colour right up to the letter for fear of smudging. To make the chosen phrase really stand out, the colour can be applied in the spaces between the letters as well as in the counters.

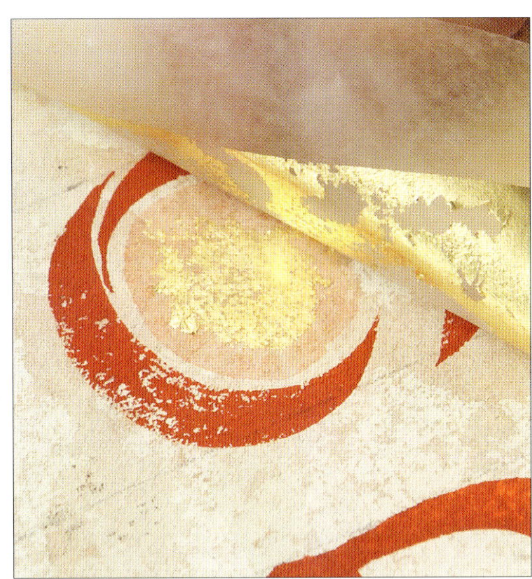

13 The final touch is to add some gold leaf. For a 'distressed' look with gold, rub an oil pastel over the area to be gilded and press the transfer gold lightly on to it. If more gold is required, press harder.

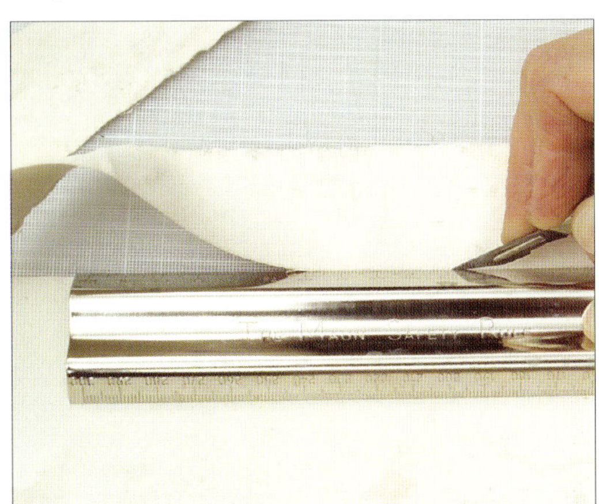

14 Working on a cutting mat or card, trim any uneven edges of the hanging with a craft knife, and attach the calico top and bottom to the prepared dowel. The simplest way to do this is to roll the calico round the dowel and fix it in place with PVA glue.

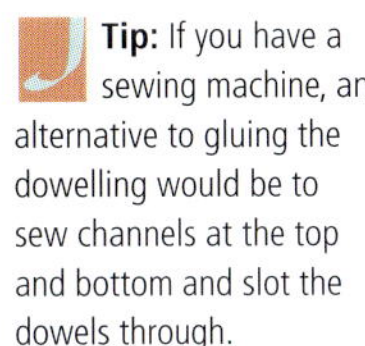

Tip: If you have a sewing machine, an alternative to gluing the dowelling would be to sew channels at the top and bottom and slot the dowels through.

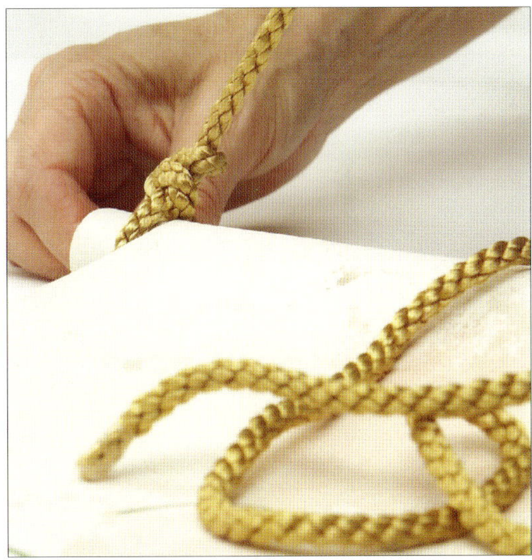

15 Attach the coloured rope along the top dowel and tie a decorative knot at each end, or loop the rope across the back to tie the ends together. Your wall hanging is now ready to display.

Gilded letter

The gilded lettering of medieval manuscripts is a rich visual treat. The gold appears so heavy and thick that it imbues the letters – usually stylized Versals or Lombardic letters – with an opulence that is truly remarkable. Even after hundreds of years hidden between heavy vellum pages the gleam remains, suggesting a text of importance.

The artists of today are no different from the artists of medieval times in their desire to design beautiful books and create precious artwork. The good news is that the materials are readily available and are not expensive. Decorating pages or panels of writing by adding real gold and other precious metals is immensely satisfying, and achieving stunning results need not be difficult.

A gilded calligraphic letter can be presented as a miniature work of art in its own right, as shown here, or placed as an initial to enhance a chosen word, or a paragraph of chosen text. Several letters grouped together will bring something extra special to a complete page of work. Further wonderful effects can be achieved with the addition of patterns and motifs within the design, painted with bright gouache paint.

Materials

- *Layout or practice paper*
- *Felt-tipped pens*
- *Tracing paper*
- *Hot-pressed watercolour paper*
- *HB and 2H pencils*
- *PVA (white) glue or craft glue*
- *Synthetic brushes, of various sizes*
- *Transfer gold leaf*
- *Glassine paper*
- *Agate burnisher or similar*
- *Square of silk*
- *Piece of glass*
- *Gesso (optional)*
- *Large brush*
- *Gouache paint: ultramarine, zinc white, scarlet lake, gold and permanent white*
- *Technical, fine dip or ruling pen*
- *Mount, if required*

The design

The letter that is used here is a modern Uncial 'H', which has been gilded and then decorated with gold and coloured diamonds. The letter has been painted in PVA as the medium on which to stick the gold. However, gesso can be used if you prefer. Once the gum has been laid the method of attaching the gold is the same. When the gold is polished both methods will produce a good bright shine but the gesso ground produces a slightly brighter, smoother brilliance on completion.

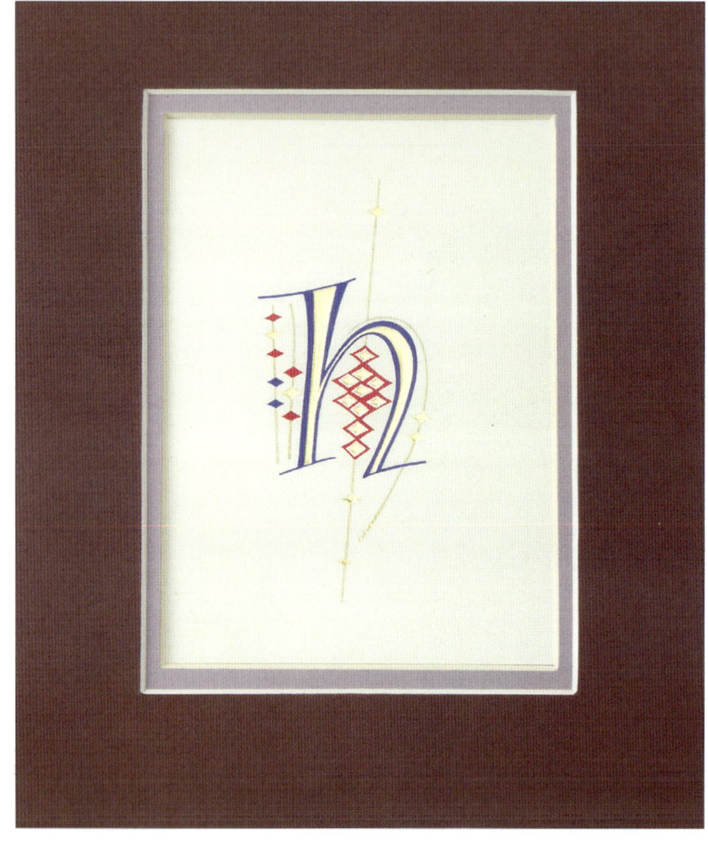

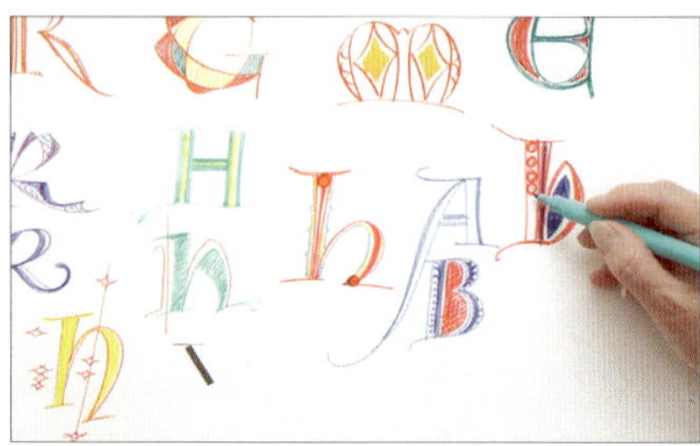

1 Design and sketch some letter shapes, adapted from Versals, Uncials or the Roman Capitals, with a felt-tipped pen or pencil. Add some simple decoration or change some of the shapes to enhance their effect. Add colour with felt-tipped pens as an aid to visualizing the finished project.

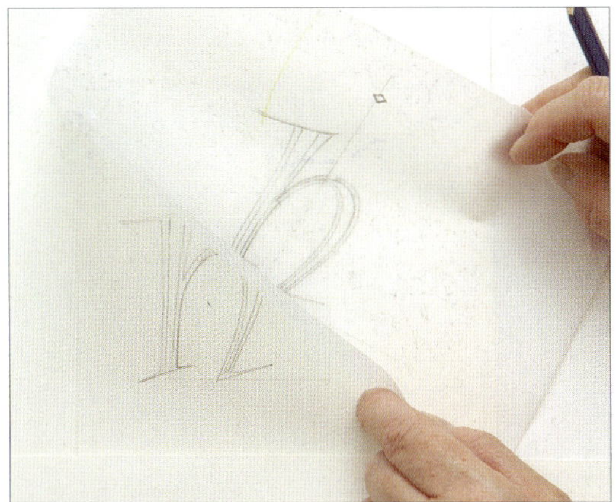

2 Choose a single letter and draw the shape on to tracing paper. Transfer the traced letter onto the watercolour paper and draw over the design with a sharp 2H pencil. The letter chosen for this project is a modern Uncial 'H'.

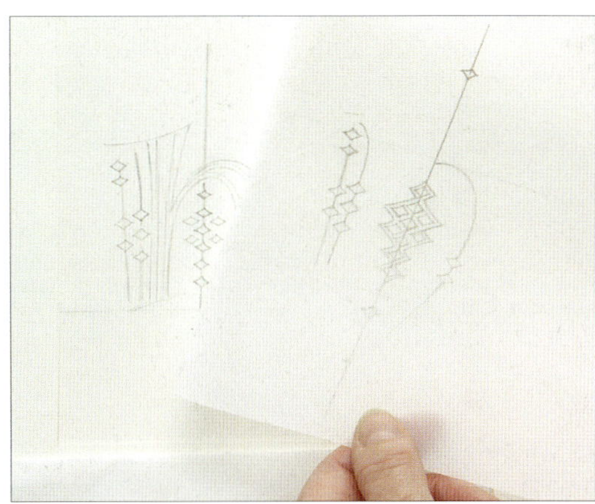

3 Draw some diamonds on to a separate piece of tracing paper and try the design over the letter. Add the diamond shapes around and inside the letter in a decorative way. Some of the diamonds will be painted in gold, and some in colour. Do not overdo the effect by drawing too many.

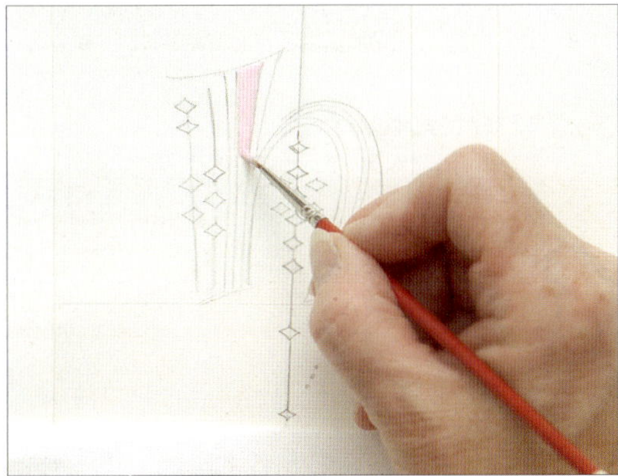

4 Paint the centre of the letter stem with PVA glue that has been coloured pink, using a synthetic 000 brush. Paint the diamonds that you plan to gild in glue, too. Leave the glue to dry, which will take 20–30 minutes, and arrange your gold leaf, glassine paper, burnisher, and a silk square close to hand. Protect your work with a paper shield, leaving only the design exposed.

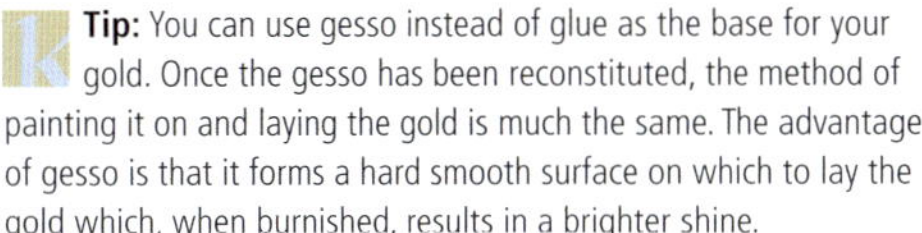

Tip: You can use gesso instead of glue as the base for your gold. Once the gesso has been reconstituted, the method of painting it on and laying the gold is much the same. The advantage of gesso is that it forms a hard smooth surface on which to lay the gold which, when burnished, results in a brighter shine.

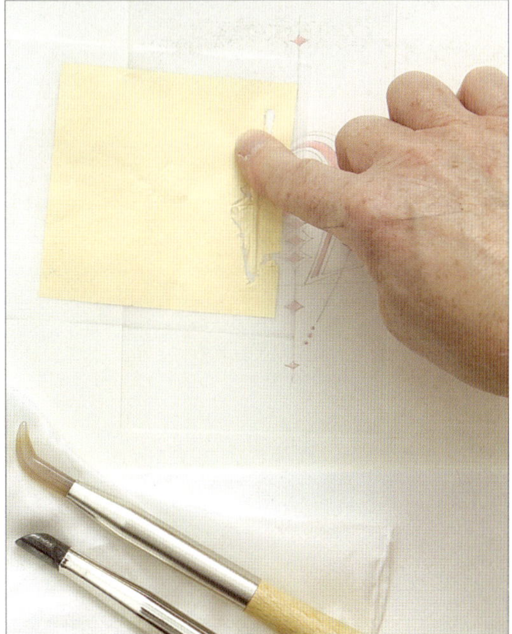

5 Place your work on a cold surface, ideally a piece of glass. Roll a small paper tube, about 7.5cm (3in) long. Place the tube against your mouth and breathe deeply on to the gum twice. Your warm breath will reactivate the glue and make it sticky. Quickly press the gold leaf, gold face down, on to the letter and rub it gently but firmly with your fingers.

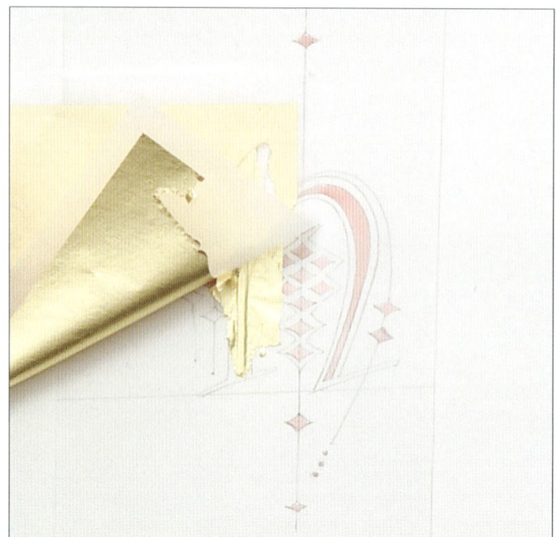

6 Lift the transfer and see how much gold has been deposited. To fill any gaps, breathe again through the tube and press the gold down firmly once more with your fingers. Repeat this process until the letter accepts the gold. When the letter is completely covered, still continue to press the transfer gold on to the letter. You no longer need to breathe on the letter beforehand, as the gold will now stick to itself.

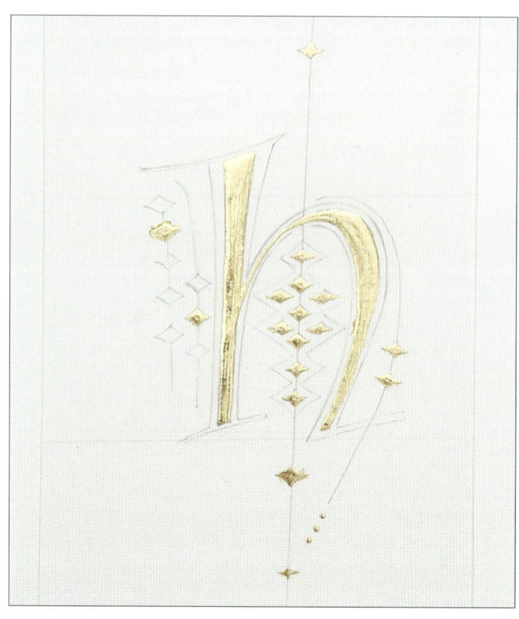

7 The more gold that is deposited the shinier the letter will appear when burnished. Once you are satisfied with the letter, gild the diamonds in the centre of the letter and most of the diamonds around the letter.

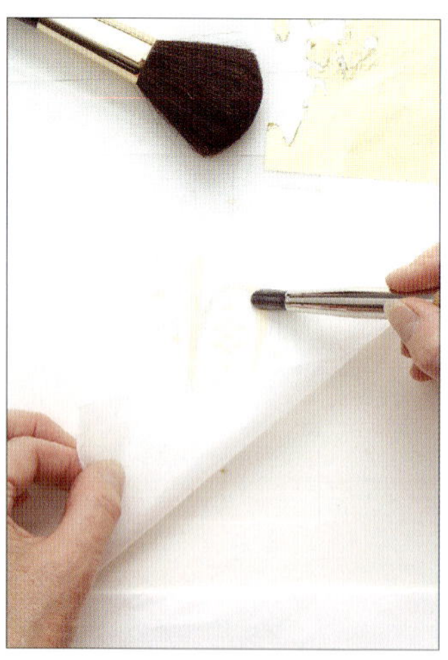

8 Brush away any excess gold with a large soft brush then use the burnisher to burnish the gold leaf through glassine paper. This will protect the gold surface. Try not to rub too hard as the gum may still be damp and the pressure will damage the gold surface.

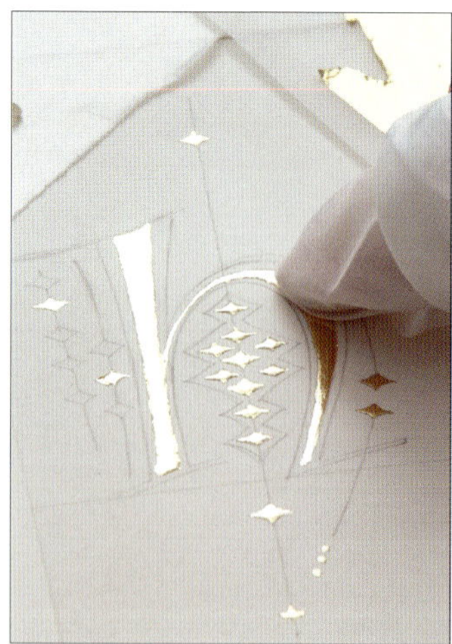

9 Finish by burnishing direct with the burnisher. Or it can be polished gently with a piece of silk.

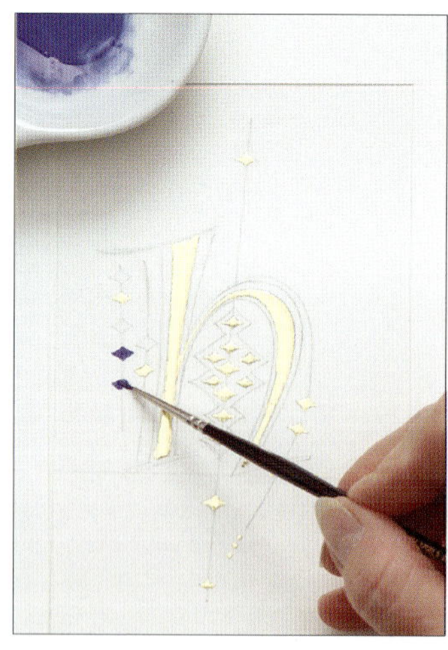

10 The letter is now ready to paint. Mix up some ultramarine plus a small amount of zinc white gouache paint, and paint two of the diamonds on the left of the letter in the blue.

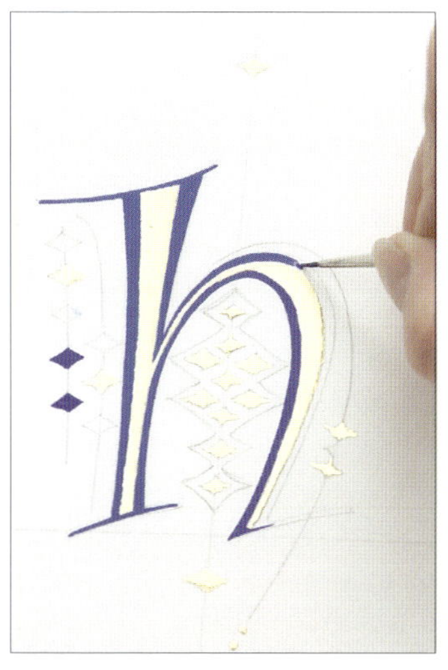

11 With the a fine brush, carefully paint a delicate blue line of colour around the letter stem.

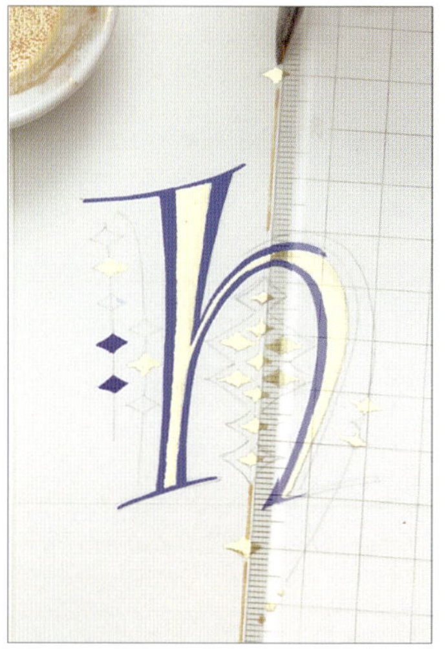

12 Add the fine lines to the design with a ruling pen, a coloured technical pen or a fine dip pen filled with gold gouache paint.

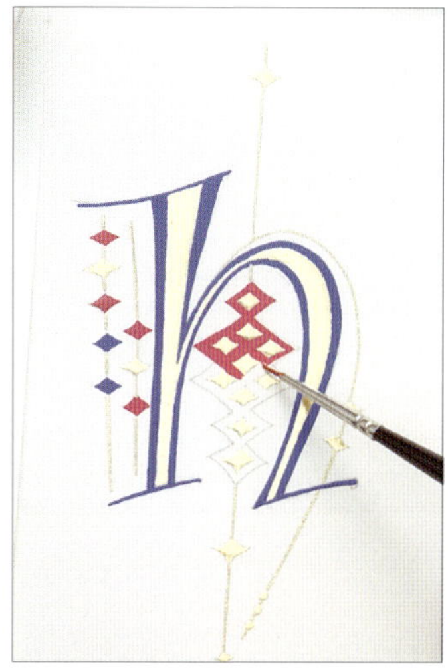

13 Mix scarlet lake red gouache with a touch of zinc white and paint diamonds on the side of the letter and around the gold diamonds in the centre of the letter.

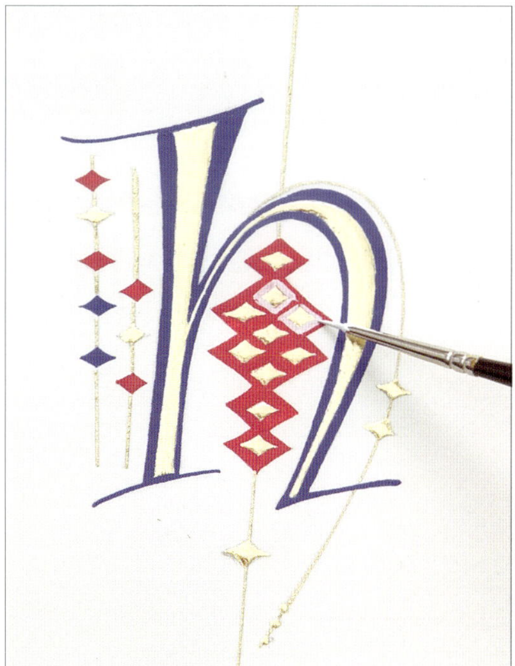

14 Finally, paint a border around the central gold diamonds in permanent white gouache.

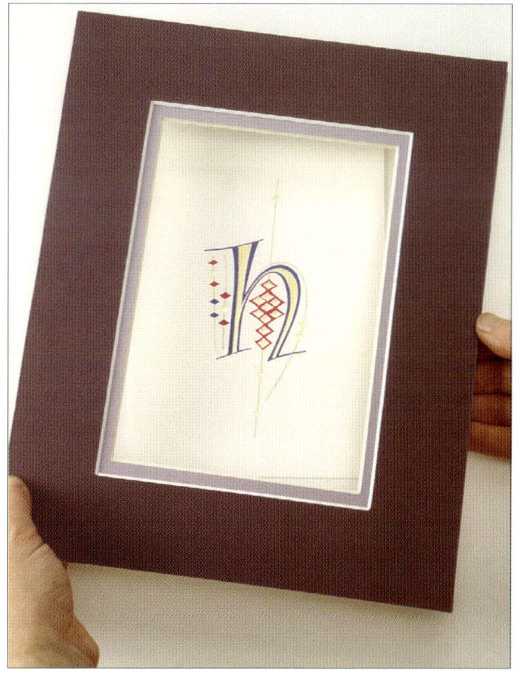

15 Mount the finished letter. Use a complementary colour for the mount so that the whole project is harmonious.

Illuminated letter

There is something magical about the richness of gold and most calligraphers will wish to try their hand at some form of gilding. The traditional method of laying gesso as a ground for gilding the letter 'Z' is used in this project. Furthermore diapering, a method often used in medieval manuscripts, is used to ornament the background of the illuminated letter. Diaper usually consists of geometric, floral or repeat motif patterns. These can range from very simple to quite complex patterns, producing very effective results.

To help locate the central point of each motif, a grid is drawn on tracing paper, and a square is then pencilled in. Dots are placed along each side of the box. Diagonal lines are used as a guide to join the dots and complete the grid.

Materials

- *Pencil*
- *Layout or practice paper*
- *Tracing paper*
- *Hot-pressed watercolour paper*
- *Ruler*
- *Gesso or PVA (white) glue*
- *Small vessel*
- *Distilled water and dropper*
- *Synthetic brushes*
- *Craft (utility) knife or scalpel*
- *Blotting paper*
- *Gold leaf (transfer, loose leaf optional)*
- *Glassine paper*
- *Burnisher*
- *Brush to remove loose gold*
- *Powdered gold or gold gouache*
- *Gouache paints: indigo blue mixed with a little ultramarine, gold*
- *Paintbrushes*
- *Pair of compasses*
- *Mount, if required*

Tip: If using PVA glue instead of gesso for the gilding technique, the glue can be applied in layers, allowing 30 minutes to dry between applications. The first application will be absorbed into the paper so one or two more layers will be needed to build up the ground.

The design

An elegant letter 'Z' adapted from Roman Capitals is used in this project. It is enclosed in a gold-edged painted border with a dark blue background. On this background the medieval method of diapering creates little motifs painted in gold.

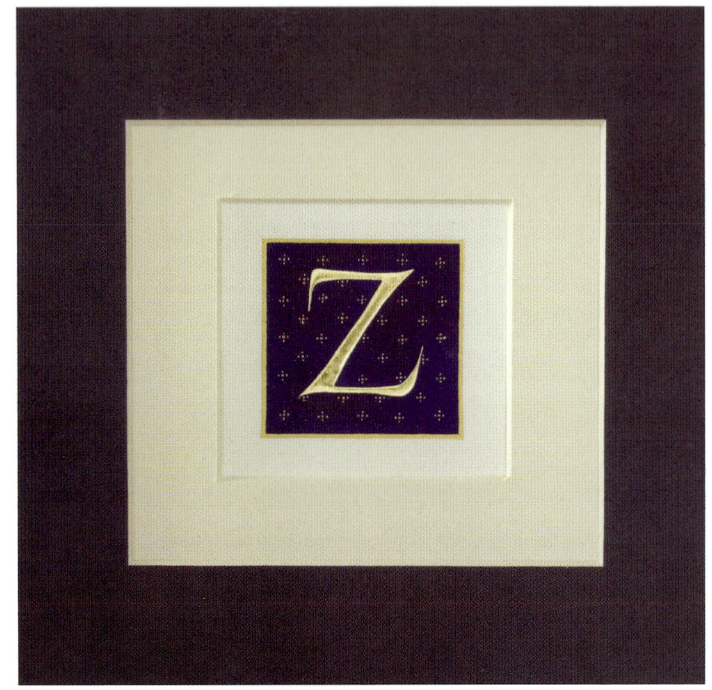

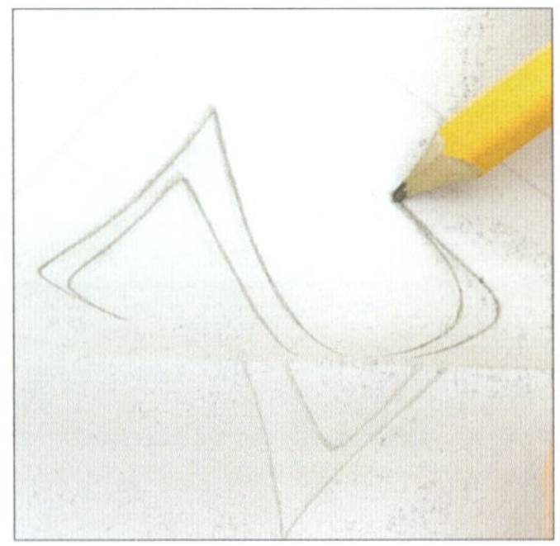

1 Sketch your letter on some layout paper. Versals or Roman Capitals are a good basis from which you can adapt your letter. Trace down the letter design on to watercolour paper.

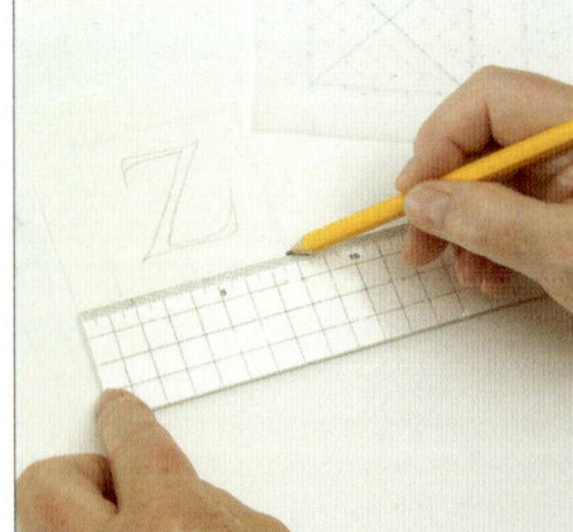

2 Draw a traced grid and mark up the dots that will create a decoration later. Draw an inner box 6cm x 6cm (2½in x 2½in) around the letter. Draw an outer box 1.5mm (1/16in) from the inner box to make a 'frame'.

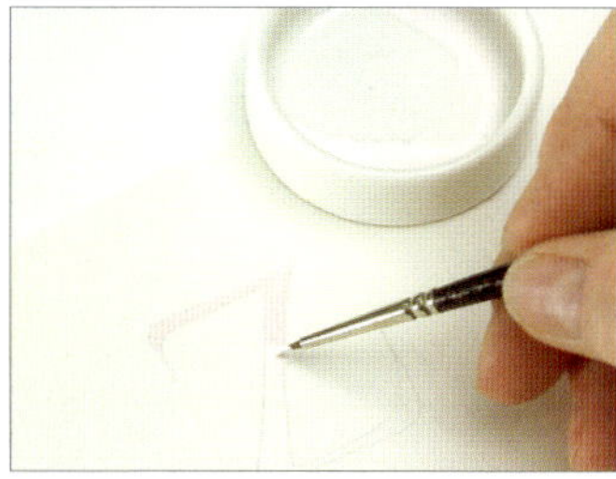

3 Reconstitute the gesso by breaking a cake of gesso into tiny pieces. Use a dropper and cover the gesso with two drops of distilled water and leave to soak for an hour. Stir very gently, avoiding creating any air bubbles, and if necessary add one or two more drops of distilled water until it is the consistency of thin cream. Apply the gesso by loading the brush and teasing the gesso into place with the tip of the brush, creating a nicely domed shape. Once the gesso has dried, any irregularities can be gently scraped away with a curved blade and burnished to a smooth surface.

4 Make a paper tube out of blotting paper and breathe on to the gesso to reactivate the glue and make the gesso sticky. Apply the transfer gold and press down firmly. Repeat the process until all the area is covered with gold. Leave the gesso to re-harden.

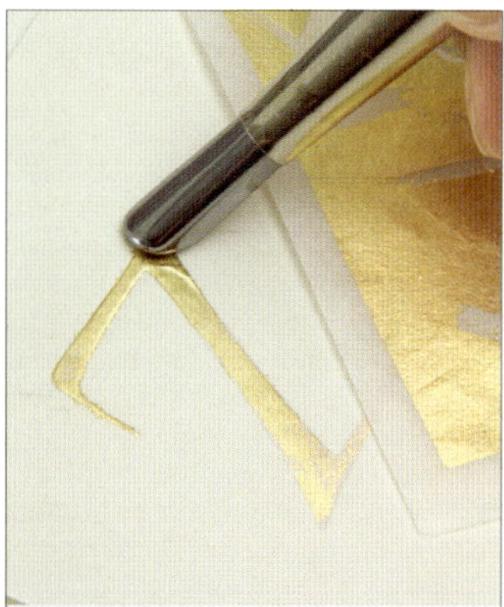

5 Burnish the gold leaf first through glassine paper and then directly on to the gold. For extra brilliance, a layer of loose-leaf gold can be applied and burnished.

Tip: To remove air bubbles from liquid gesso, add one drop of water but do not stir. The bubbles will disperse to the side of the vessel and can be gently removed with blotting paper.

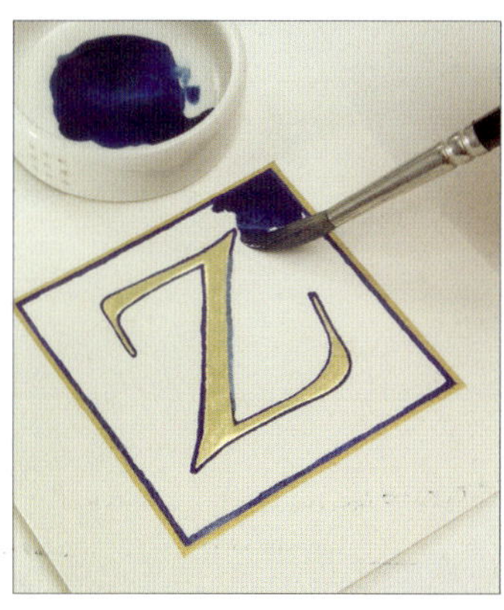

6 Paint the 'frame' with powdered gold or gold gouache. Mix up some indigo blue gouache and add a little ultramarine. Outline the letter, taking care not to get any paint over the gold, and also paint an outline inside the gold frame. Now load the brush with paint and fill in the background. Do not let any edges dry but keep adding more 'wet-into-wet' until the background is completed. The paint will then dry flat and even in colour.

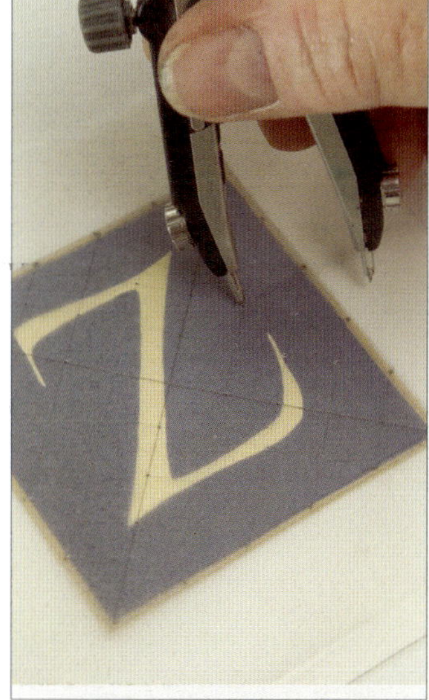

7 When the blue paint has completely dried, place the tracing grid over the work aligning the sides of the box. Use the point of a compass to mark each intersection.

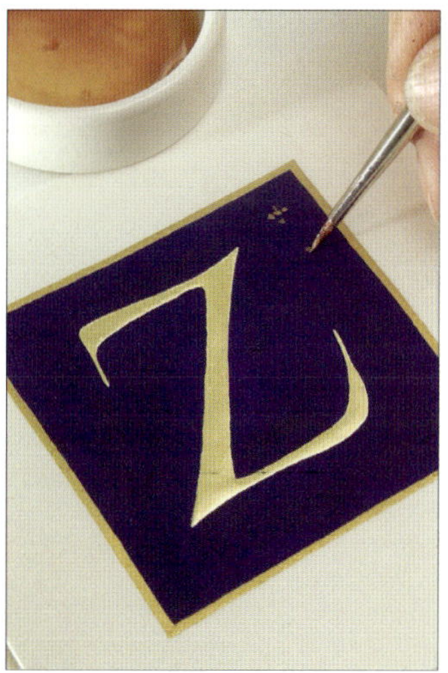

8 To diaper the background, place a little dot of gold on to each of the prick marks and encircle each dot with four little dots. If necessary, tidy up the gold frame with another layer of gold. The letter can be framed if required.

Fan book

Books can take many forms and in this example the shape of a fan has been chosen to send a message of love. During the 18th century, young people would convey messages to each other just by the way they held their fans so the shape seems a very suitable choice for this project and is stunning to look at. Making the fan requires accurate measuring, folding and cutting. The fan book was originally designed to stand next to a wedding cake but can, of course, be used to mark many other celebratory occasions. The ribbons flowing from its base should be velvet, satin, or silk, and form an integral part of this calligraphic *tour de force*.

This is a complicated book. Before attempting a finished fan, experiment first with layout paper until you are comfortable with the construction.

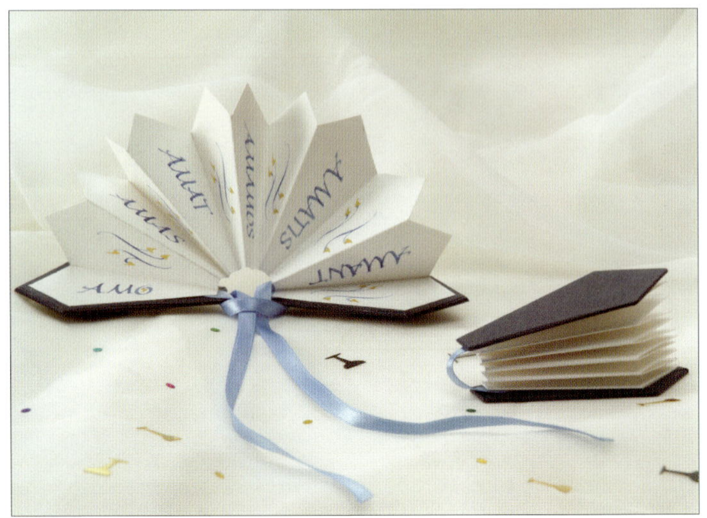

The design

The basic shape is a circle with lines of blue writing and flourishing radiating out like the spokes of a wheel. If used for a wedding the colour can echo that chosen for the wedding theme. The text – *amo, amas, amat, amamus, amatis, amant* – is the Latin verb 'to love', and is written in Italic based Free Capitals. The words are separated by flourishes embellished with gold.

Materials

- *Pair of compasses*
- *Hot-pressed watercolour paper*
- *Pencil*
- *Ruler with cutting edge*
- *Pens*
- *Gouache paints: ultramarine and gold*
- *Dip pen, such as William Mitchell 5 (fine nib)*
- *Eraser*
- *Bone folder*
- *Self-healing cutting mat*
- *Craft (utility) knife*
- *Scissors*
- *Card (stock) or mounting (mat) board*
- *Decorative paper*
- *Scrap paper (preferably shiny)*
- *Glue stick*
- *Ribbons: at least 1m (1yd)*

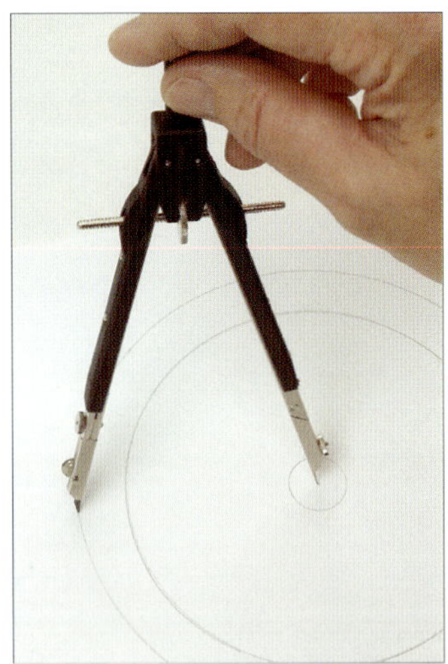

1 Using a pair of compasses, draw three concentric circles on the watercolour paper – the first one quite small, the second the diameter of the fan, and the third just a little larger, which will be cut away during the book's construction.

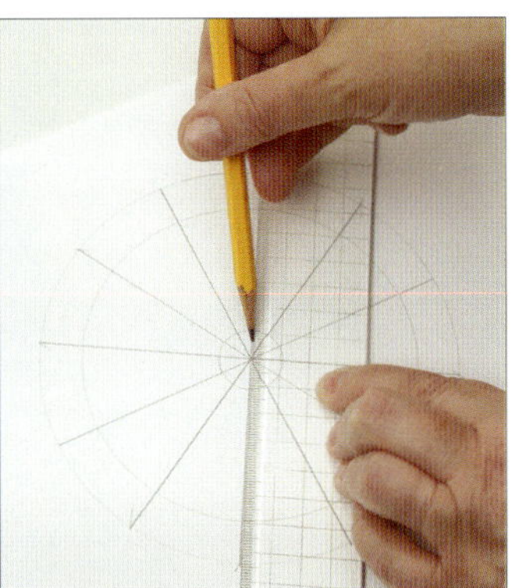

2 Divide the circles into 12. To do this, apply the rule that the radius of a circle can be stepped around its circumference six times. First draw two lines of diameter across the circles at right angles to each other. Open out the pair of compasses to the radius of the largest circle. Place the point at the end of one diameter, swing in a semi-circle, marking off where the pencil intersects the circumference. Do the same at the other end of this diameter and at the two ends of the other diameter. Draw radii from these marks to the centre of the circles. You should now have 12 segments.

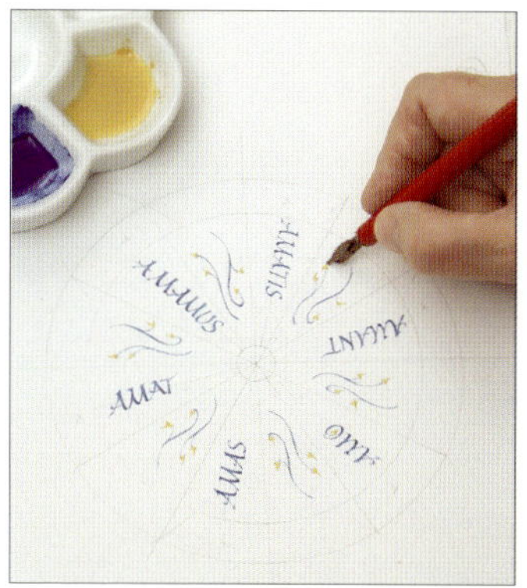

3 Rule up alternative segments and write out the Latin verb *amo*. With a finer pen, draw a flourish in the adjacent sections and decorate with pen-drawn hearts.

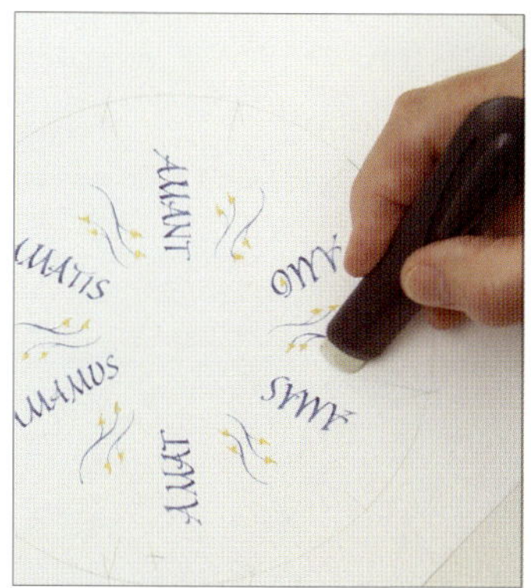

4 Erase the ruling up and the construction lines between the inner and outer circles. If these are erased later the fan may be damaged. Cut around the outer circle.

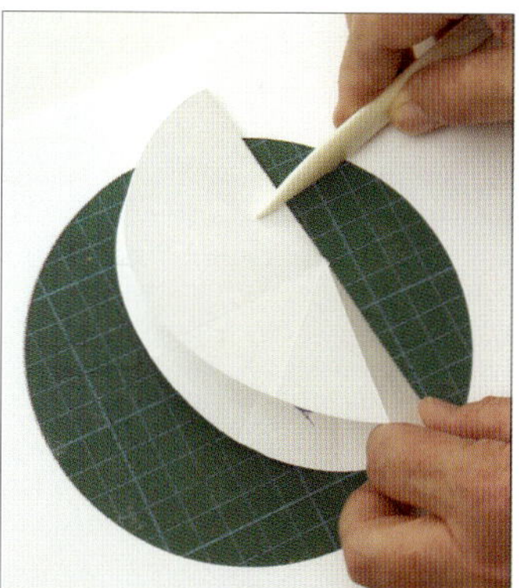

5 Using a bone folder, fold the circle into the 12 segments. Each time you fold the circle in half, the segments on the outer circles must meet.

Tip: Avoid erasing over metallic gouache. The mica filaments can easily be dislodged. Cut your eraser into small pieces so that you can get between the writing and design without going across the top.

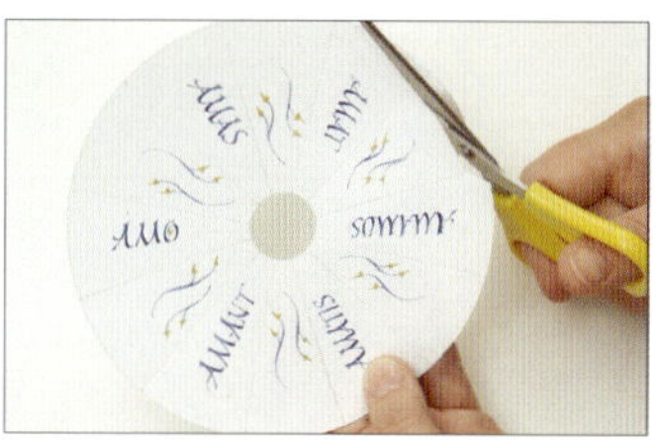

6 Cut away both the inner and outer circles (the latter was needed only to aid the folding process).

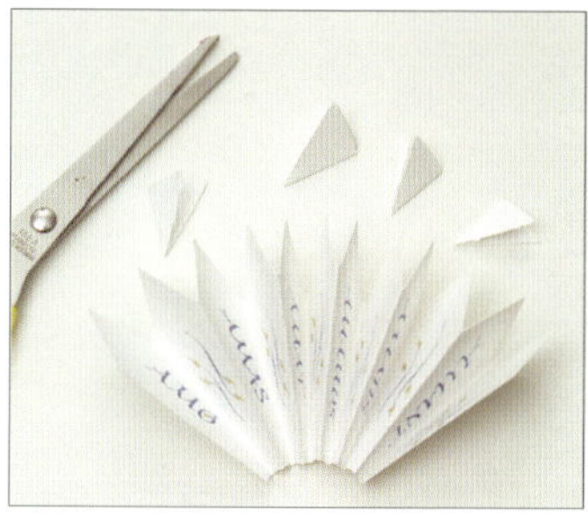

7 Cut the fold between the first and last segments and fold the fan accordian-style, in a valley–mountain–valley sequence. Use a sharp pair of scissors to cut off the pointed tops.

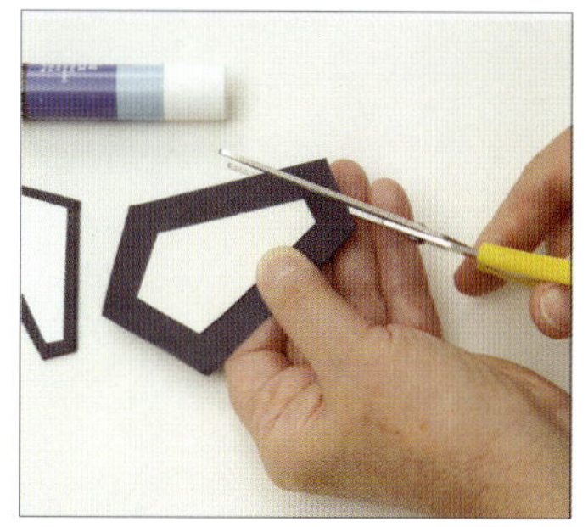

8 Measure an outside segment and cut two pieces of mounting board into the same shape but slightly larger all round. Then cut two pieces of the decorative paper the same shape but 1.5cm (3/4in) larger than the board all round. Cover the boards by gluing on the decorative paper.

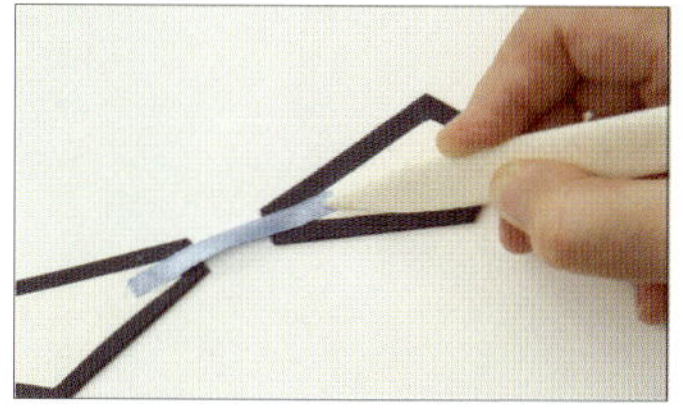

9 Cut a short length of ribbon and attach this to the 'wrong' side and lower ends of the board. Press down with the bone folder. If the decorative paper is very thick, or the fan paper very thin, line the inside of the board.

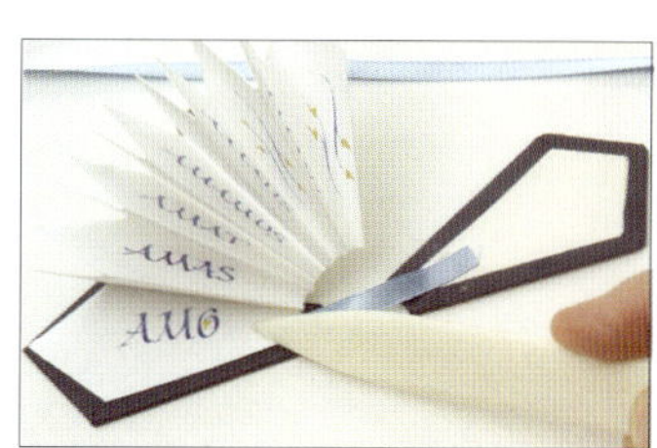

10 Apply glue to the reverse of the first section of the fan. Throw away the messy waste paper and attach the section to the reverse of the front board. Repeat these steps for the back section and board. Leave to dry under weights. Attach long ribbons to the ribbon loop – the longer and more extravagant the ribbons, the better.

Tip: Slide scrap paper between the folds of your text block to protect it and glue the front section.

Simple gallery book

Gallery books are a new type of book used by artists to display their work. By the action of folding and cutting the book appears to be a miniature art gallery with separate wings to display each illustration.

While gallery books are undoubtedly beautiful they involve making a 16-section accordian-style design and require an very long piece of paper. The variation shown here allows for fewer display panels but is simpler to construct, while retaining the impact of the original gallery book design.

This project involves an eight-section book. Cutting and gluing four specific sections together and cutting two other sections into horizontal thirds produces a simplified but still stunning gallery book that reflects a medieval diptych – the double-folding panels used as an altar or to carry a pair of religious pictures.

Even though this is meant to be a 'simple' gallery book, it is still complicated. Try a mock-up first using layout paper. Do not worry about the writing at this stage; just make pencil marks to show where the calligraphy or decoration will be.

Materials

- *Hot-pressed watercolour paper*
- *Pencil*
- *Gouache*
- *Ruler*
- *Two pens of contrasting sizes, such as Brause 2mm (5/64in) and Brause 1mm (3/64in)*
- *Scissors or craft (utility) knife*
- *Scrap paper (preferably shiny)*
- *Glue stick*
- *Weights*

Tip: A soapstone pencil is ideal for numbering and ruling up on dark backgrounds.

The design

Gallery books are intended to be eye-catching and this version is enhanced by the use of elegant small Roman Capitals for the body text, contrasting with large Uncial display letters. Two sizes of pen are needed to achieve the desired effect. In this project Brause 2mm (5/64in) and 1mm (3/64in) nibs are used.

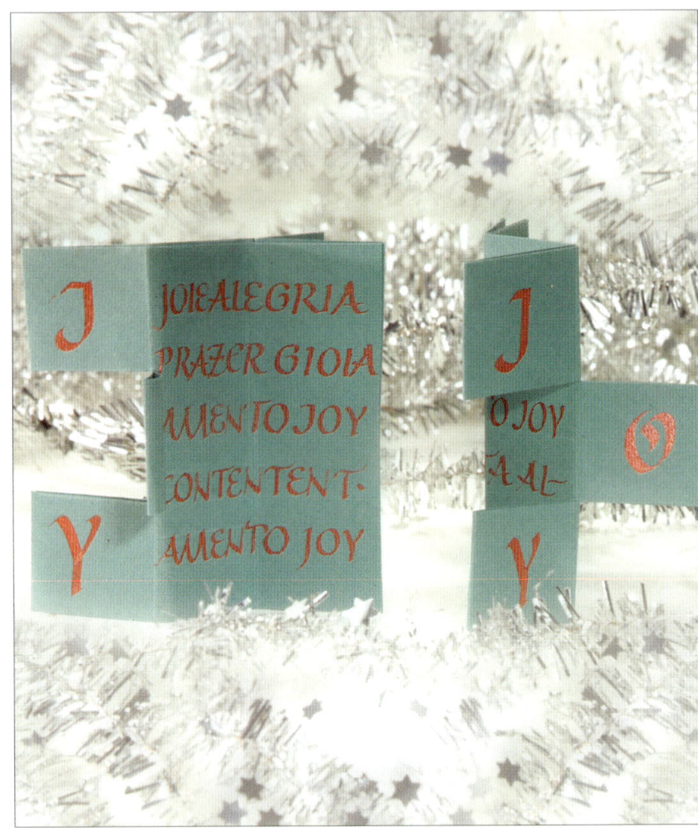

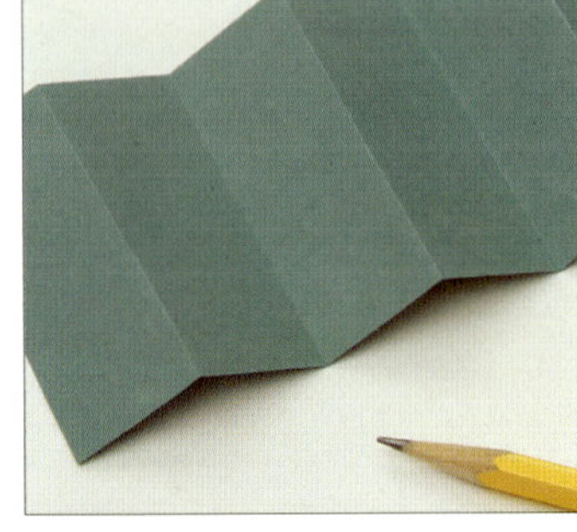

1 Using the watercolour paper prepare a long rectangular shape. Fold eight equally sized sections into an accordian-style concertina. Using a pencil, number the sections 1 to 8 on the front and 8 to 1 on the reverse.

Tip: This example uses three display panels, but the design works well with four panels or more.

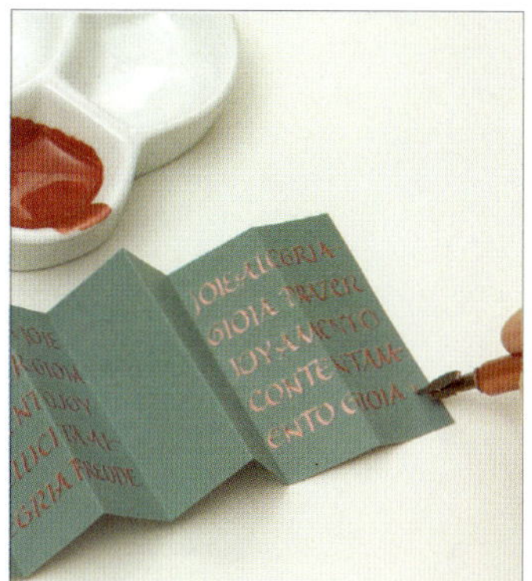

2 With the front facing you, rule up and write on sections 3 and 4 and 7 and 8 all the words you can find, in every language you can find, for 'Joy'. If you cannot find many, just keep repeating the ones you have, or use a quotation with the word 'joy' prominent within it. The writing can be vertical or horizontal. Leave it to dry before erasing your ruling lines.

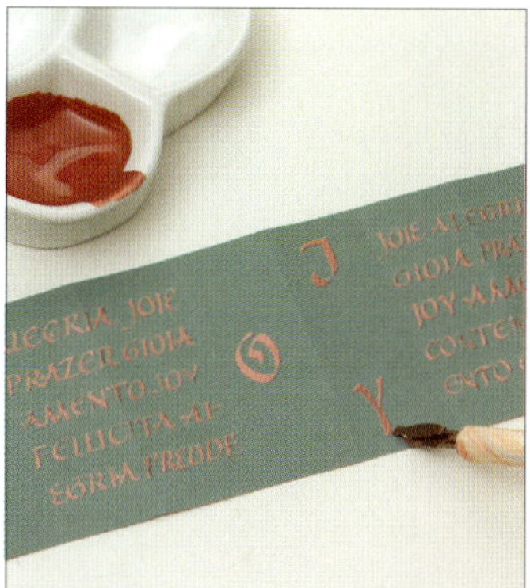

3 Measuring down from the head to the tail of the concertina, divide sections 5 and 6 into thirds and write the individual letters that form your words for 'joy' using the larger pen, on alternating panels. You will achieve a better contrast if your chosen script differs from the one used for the smaller writing.

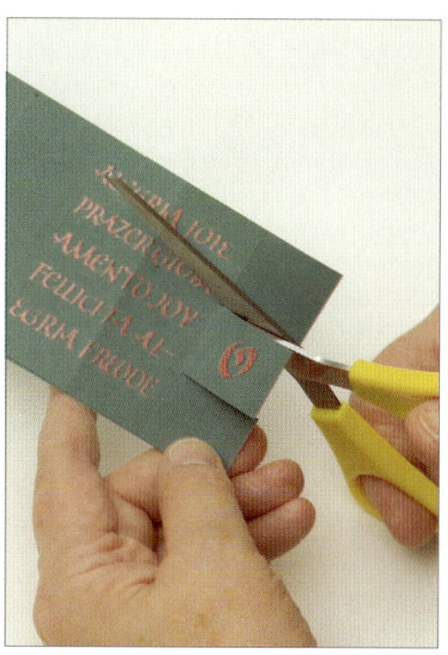

4 Carefully cut panels 5 and 6 into thirds horizontally using scissors or a craft knife.

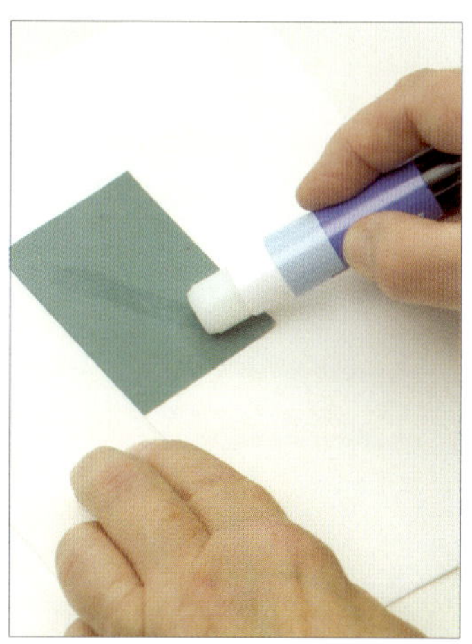

5 Turn the book over and lay it face down on to a piece of scrap paper. Carefully glue sections 1 and 2, having first covered the other sections with scrap paper for protection. Throw away the scrap paper.

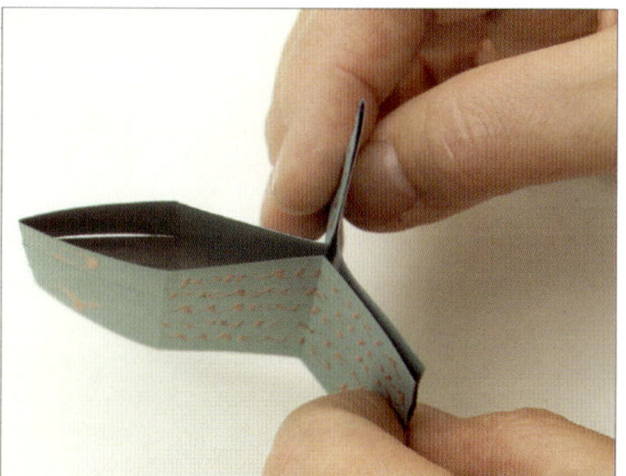

6 It is easier to complete the next step with the book held in your hands, rather than lying it flat. With the reverse side facing you, pinch together sections 2 and 3, gluing them together. Then bring the reverse of section 8 to the reverse of section 1 and glue these together. Sections 4 to 7 should now be touching back to back. Carefully bone down the two glued sections and leave to dry overnight. Put separate weights – books are ideal – on each of these sections, with the unglued 'tongue' standing up between them.

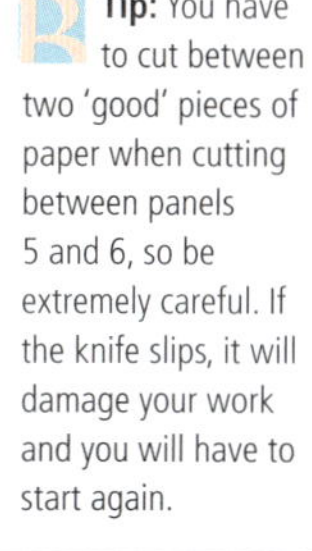

Tip: You have to cut between two 'good' pieces of paper when cutting between panels 5 and 6, so be extremely careful. If the knife slips, it will damage your work and you will have to start again.

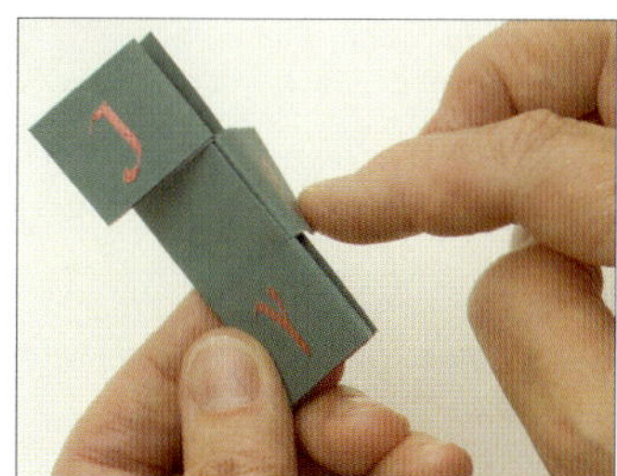

7 When the glue is completely dry, fold the resulting covers around the text, allowing the three display panels to enfold the whole book.

Glossary

Acrylic medium An adhesive that dries clear, used for sticking metal leaf.
Arch The curved part of a letter as it springs from the stem.
Ascender The rising stroke of the letter which extends above the x-height.
Automatic pens Poster pens ranging in size from 1 (smallest) to 6A (largest).
Baseline The bottom writing line on which the lettering sits.
Blending Merging adjacent colours or tones.
Body height This is also called the x-height and is the height of the letter not including the ascender and descender.
Book hand Any style of alphabet commonly used in book production before the development of printing. Also called a script.
Bowl The round or oval part of the letter formed by curved strokes, as in 'R', 'a', 'p' and 'q'.
Brause pen A German-made steep-nib dip pen. Nib size ranges from 1/2mm (1/64in) to 5mm (1/4 in).
Broad-edge pen A pen with a square-edged nib.
Burnish To rub a surface in order to make it shiny.
Charcoal Charred willow, beech or vine twigs, available as powder or sticks. It can also be mixed with a binder and pressed ('compressed' charcoal), creating sticks that are stronger than stick charcoal and do not break so easily. Charcoal pencils are also available.
Codex Book made up of folded and/or bound leaves forming successive pages.
Cold-pressed paper Paper with a medium-textured surface.
Colour mixing Optical colour mixing: applying one colour on top of another in such a way that both remain visible, although the appearance of each one is modified by the other. Also known as broken colour. Physical colour mixing: blending two or more colours together to create another colour.
Composition The way in which the elements of a drawing are arranged.
Conté crayon A drawing medium made from pigment and graphite bound with gum. Conté crayons are available as sticks and as pencils.
Cool colours Colours that contain blue and lie in the green-violet half of the colour wheel.
Counter The space that is contained within round parts of letters.
Cuneiform Early script with wedge-shaped signs, used by the Sumerians.
Cursive Linked or joined rapid writing creating a fluid effect.
Descender The tail of the letter which extends below the line, as in 'y' or 'p'.
Diaper patterns Designs created to ornament a surface with small patterns laid out on a grid.
Egg tempera Egg yolk added to ground pigment colour to make paint.
Emboss To indent on gold or to create a raised or indented surface on paper with a blunt tool through a stencil from the opposite side of the surface.
Eye level Where your eye level is in relation to the subject that you are drawing.
Fixative A substance sprayed on to drawings (especially charcoal and pastel) to prevent them from smudging.
Flourish An extended or exaggerated ascender or descender which is used to embellish the basic letterform.
Foreshortening The illusion that objects are compressed in length as they recede from your view.
Form See **Modelling.**
Format The shape of a drawing or painting. The most usual formats are landscape (a drawing that is wider than it is tall) and portrait (a drawing that is taller than it is wide).
Gesso A compound made from plaster of Paris, glue and white lead. Can be used to form a raised surface on to which layers of gold can be attached and polished.
Gild To apply gold to a surface using loose leaf, transfer or powdered gold.
Glassine paper A transparent paper with a non-stick or resistant surface used for protecting gold surfaces. Also called crystal parchment paper.
Gouache An opaque watercolour paint used when flat, dense colour is required (also called body colour).
Graphite Graphite is a natural form of crystallized carbon. To make a drawing

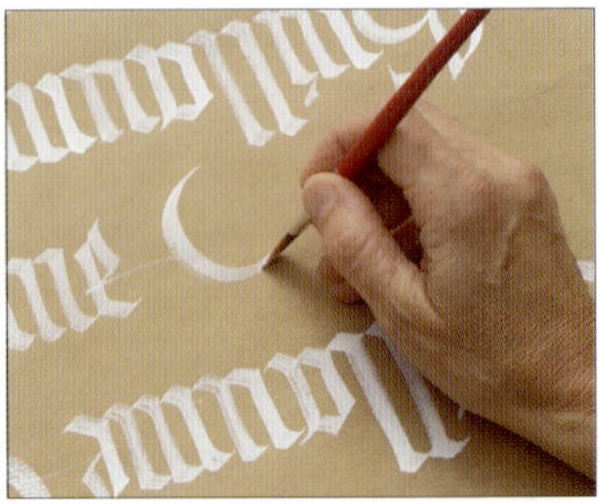

tool, it is mixed with ground clay and a binder and then moulded or extruded into strips for pencils or sticks. The more clay in the mix the harder the graphite stick or pencil is.
Ground A coating such as primer, which is applied to a drawing surface.
Gum ammoniac A resin in crystal form that can be activated with hot water to provide a sticky base for flat gilding.
Gum arabic Viscous substance from the acacia tree. Can be used as a glue, to aid paint adherence and as a resist.
Gum sandarac Lumps of gum which, when ground to a fine powder, can be dusted lightly on to paper or vellum to improve the surface.
Hatching Drawing a series of parallel lines, at any angle, to indicate shadow areas.
Highlight The point on an object where light strikes a reflective surface.
Hot-pressed paper Paper with a smooth surface.
Illumination The decoration of a manuscript, often using gold leaf burnished to a high shine.
Indent An additional space added to the usual margin at the beginning of a line of writing.
Interlinear spacing The spacing that occurs between lines allowing space for ascenders and descenders.
Layout The plan of a design showing spacing and organization of text.
Line and wash The technique of combining pen-and-ink work with a thin layer, or wash, of transparent paint (usually watercolour) or ink.
Logo A word or combination of letters designed to be used as a trademark, symbol or emblem.

Lower-case Small letters as distinct from capitals or upper case. Also called miniscule letters.
Majuscule A capital or upper-case letter.
Manikin A jointed wooden figure that can be moved into almost any pose, enabling the artist to study proportions and angles. Also known as a lay figure.
Manuscript A handwritten book or document.
Mask A material used to cover areas of a drawing, either to prevent marks from touching the paper underneath or to allow the artist to work right up to the mask to create a crisp edge.
Medium 1. The material in which an artist chooses to work ink, charcoal, pastel, etc. (The plural is 'media'.) 2. In painting, 'medium' is also a substance added to paint to alter the way in which it behaves – to make it thinner, for example. (The plural in this context is 'mediums'.)
Miniscule A lower-case letter
Modelling Emphasizing the light and shadow areas of a subject through the use of tone or colour, in order to create a three-dimensional impression.
Negative shapes The spaces between objects in a drawing, often (but not always) the background to the subject.
Nib width The width of the writing end (nib) of a broad-edged pen.
of a colour.
Palette Traditionally, the surface used for mixing paint.
Papyrus Paper-like substance made from the papyrus plant. Commonly used until the 3rd century ad.
Pen angle The angle that the writing tip of a broad-edged pen makes with a horizontal writing line.
Perspective A system whereby artists can create the illusion of three-dimensional space on the two-dimensional surface of the paper. Aerial perspective: the way the atmosphere, combined with distance, influences the appearance of things. Also known as atmospheric perspective. Linear perspective: this system exploits the fact that objects appear to be smaller the further away they are from the viewer. The system is based on the fact that all parallel lines, when extended from a receding surface, meet at a point in space known as the vanishing point. When such lines are plotted accurately on the paper, the relative sizes of objects will appear correct in the drawing. Single-point perspective: this occurs when objects are parallel to the picture plane. Lines parallel to the picture plane remain parallel, while parallel lines at 90° to the picture plane converge. Two-point perspective: this must be used when you can see two sides of an object. Each side is at a different angle to the viewer and therefore each side has its own vanishing point. Parallel lines will slant at different angles on each side.
Picture plane A imaginary vertical plane that defines the front of the picture area and corresponds with the surface of the drawing.
Pointed nib A nib with a sharply pointed end, such as those manufactured by Gillott. These are used for copperplate writing.
Positive shapes The tangible features (figures, trees, buildings, still-life objects etc.) that are being drawn.
PVA (polyvinyl acetate) glue A clear adhesive which dries clear and can be used to stick paper to paper and gold to paper. Also called white glue.
Recession The effect of making objects appear to recede into the distance by using aerial perspective and tone.
Resist A substance that prevents paint or ink from reaching the underlying material. When the resist is removed, a pattern or design is left.
Rough paper Paper with an extremely pronounced texture.
Sans serif A term denoting letters without serifs or finishing strokes.
Scriptorium A writing room, particularly in a medieval monastery.
Serif The beginning and the end part of the letterform. See also sans serif.
Sgraffito The technique of scratching off pigment to reveal an underlying colour or the white of the paper.
Skeleton letter The most basic form of a letter demonstrating its essential

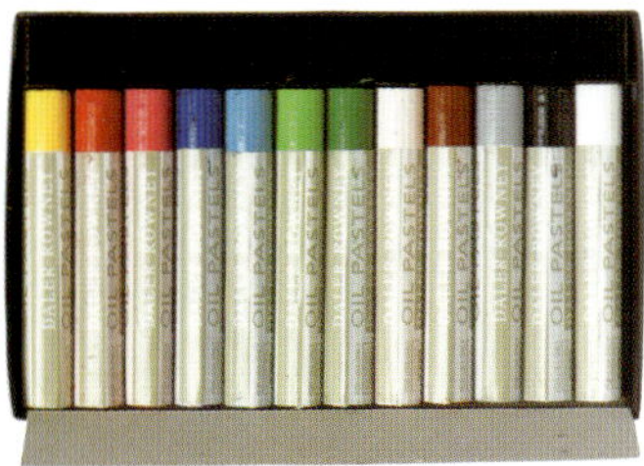

distinguishing characteristics.
Sketch A rough drawing or a preliminary attempt at working out a composition.
Speedball nibs American nibs ranging from C–0 (largest) to C–6 (smallest).
Stem Main vertical stroke of the letter.
Support The surface on which a drawing is made – usually paper, but board and surfaces prepared with acrylic gesso are also widely used.
Swash A simple flourish.
Tint A colour that has been lightened.
Tone The relative lightness or darkness
Tooth The texture of a support. Very smooth papers have little tooth.
Torchon A stump of tightly rolled paper with a pointed end, using for blending powdery mediums. Also known as paper stump or tortillon.
Uncials A very rounded hand that is composed entirely of capitals.
Upper-case Capital or large letters as distinct from lower-case. Also called majiscule letters.
Vanishing point In linear perspective, the point on the horizon at which parallel lines appear to converge.
Vector image In digital calligraphy, a graphics file that uses mathematical descriptions of lines, curves and angles.
Vellum Parchment made from calfskin which has been limed, scraped and prepared for either writing or painting.
Versals Elegant capital letters made by compound pen strokes.
Viewpoint The angle or position from which the artist draws his or her subject.
Warm colours Colours in which yellow or red are dominant.
William Mitchell pens Dip pens with nibs ranging in size from 0 (largest) to 6 (smallest).

Suppliers

Manufacturers

United Kingdom

Daler-Rowney UK Ltd
PO Box 10
Bracknell
Berkshire RG12 8ST
Tel: (01344) 461000
www.daler-rowney.com

Derwent Cumberland Pencil Co.
Greta Bridge
Keswick
Cumbria CA12 5NG
Tel: (017687) 73626
www.pencils.co.uk

Winsor & Newton
Whitefriars Avenue
Wealdstone
Middlesex HA3 5RH
Tel: (020) 8427 4343
www.winsornewton.com

W. Habberley Meadows Ltd (gold for illuminating and artists' materials)
5 Saxon Way
Chelmsley Wood
Birmingham B37 5AY
Tel: (0121) 770 0103
www.habberleymeadows.co.uk

William Cowley
Parchment and Vellum Works
97 Caldecote Street
Newport Pagnell
Buckinghamshire MK16 0DB
Tel: (01908) 610038

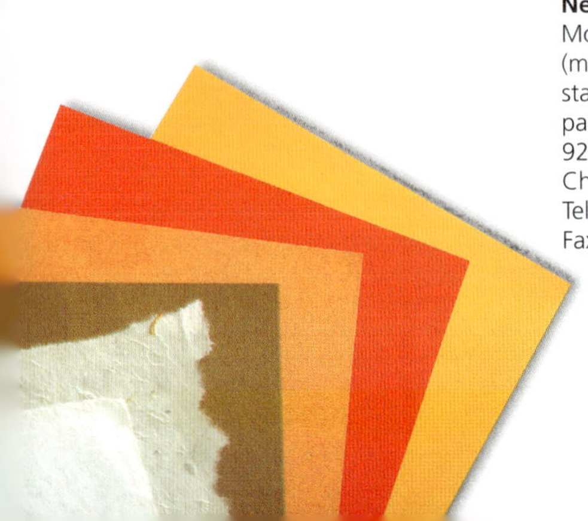

Germany

H Schmincke & Co.
Otto-Hahn-Strasse 2
D-40669 Erkath
Tel: (0211) 2509-0
Fax: (0211) 2509-461
www.schmincke.de

United States

Speedball Art Products Company (includes paints, inks, calligraphy pens and nibs)
2226 Speedball Road
Statesville
NC 28677
Tel: (800) 898-7224
Fax: (704) 838-1472
www.speedballart.com

Sanford North America (writing instruments and art materials)
Corporate Headquarters
Sanford
2707 Butterfield Road
Oak Brook, IL 60523
Tel: (800) 323-0749
www.sanfordcorp.com

Canada

Pentel of America (art materials and writing instruments)
2805 Columbia St
Torrance 90509
Canada
Tel: (310) 320-3831
Fax: (310) 533-0697

New Zealand

Montarga Art Stamps (manufacturers of rubber stamps, stamp pads, embossing powders, paper and cards)
922 Colombo St
Christchurch
Tel: (03) 366-9963
Fax: (03) 377-7963

Stockists

United Kingdom

Art Express
Sizers Court
Yeadon LS19 6DP
Tel: (0113) 250 0077
www.artexpress.co.uk

Atlantis Art Materials
7–9 Plumbers Row
London E1 1EQ
Tel: (020) 7377 8855
www.atlantisart.co.uk

Blots Pen and Ink Supplies (UK)
14 Lyndhurst Avenue
Prestwich
Manchester
M25 0GF
www.blotspens.co.uk

Ken Bromley Art Supplies
Curzon House, Curzon Road
Bolton BL1 4RW
Tel: (01204) 381900
www.artsupplies.co.uk

Calligraphity
(Specialist calligraphy/lettering books)
Gourock
Scotland PA19 1AF
1 Broderick Drive
Tel: (01475) 639668
www.calligraphity.com

Dominoes
66 High Street,
Leicester LE1 5YP
Tel: (0116) 2533363
Fax: (0116) 2628066
www.dominoestoys.co.uk

Hobbycraft
Specializes in arts and crafts materials. 20 stores in the UK.
Freephone 0800 027 2387
www.hobbycraft.co.uk

Jackson's Art Supplies Ltd
1 Farleigh Place
London N16 7SX
Tel: 0870 241 1849
www.jacksonsart.co.uk

Khadi Papers
Chilgrove
Chichester
PO18 9HU
Tel: (01243) 535314

Paintworks
99–101 Kingsland Road
London E2 8AG
Tel: (020) 7729 7451
www.paintworks.biz

Stuart R Stevenson
68 Clerkenwell Road
London EC1M 5QA
Tel: (020) 7253 1693
www.stuartstevenson.co.uk

The Studio Art Shop
13 Crawford Arcade
King Street
Stirling FK8 1AX
Tel: (01786) 446454
www.thestudioartshop.com

Turnham Arts & Crafts
2 Bedford Park Corner
Turnham Green Terrace
London W4 1LS
Tel: (020) 8995 2872

United States
Art Store
(15 stores nationwide)
www.artstore.com

The Art Supply Warehouse
5325 Departure Drive
Raleig, NC 27616-1835
Tel: (919) 878-5077
Fax: (919) 878-5075
www.aswexpress.com

Dick Blick Art Materials
PO Box 1267
Galesburg, IL 61402-1267
Tel: (800) 828-4548
www.dickblick.com
(More than 30 stores in 12 states)

Hobby Lobby
(More than 300 stores in 27 states)
www.hobbylobby.com

John Neal Bookseller
(books, calligraphy tools and
materials, gilding materials)
POB 9986
Greensboro
NC 27429
Tel: (336) 272 6139
Tel Toll Free: (800) 369 9598
www.JohnNealBooks.com

Michaels Stores
(More than 750 stores in 48 states)
8000 Bent Branch Drive
Irving, TX 75063
Tel: (800) 6432-4235
www.michaels.com

Rex Art
2263 SW 37 Avenue
Miami, FL 33145
Tel: (305) 445-1413
www.rexart.com

Canada
Colours Artist Suppliers
10660-105 Street
Edmonton
Alberta
Canada T5H 2W9
Tel: (800) 661-9945
www.artistsupplies.com

Curry's Art Store
490 Yonge Street
Toronto
Ontario
Tel: (416) 967-6666
www.currys.com

Island Blue Print
905 Fort Street
Victoria
British Columbia V8V 3K3
Tel: (250) 385-9786
www.islandblue.com

Kensington Art Supply
132 10th Street NW
Calgary
Alberta T2N 1V3
Tel: (403) 283-2288
Fax; (403) 26-7095
www.kensingtonartsupply.com

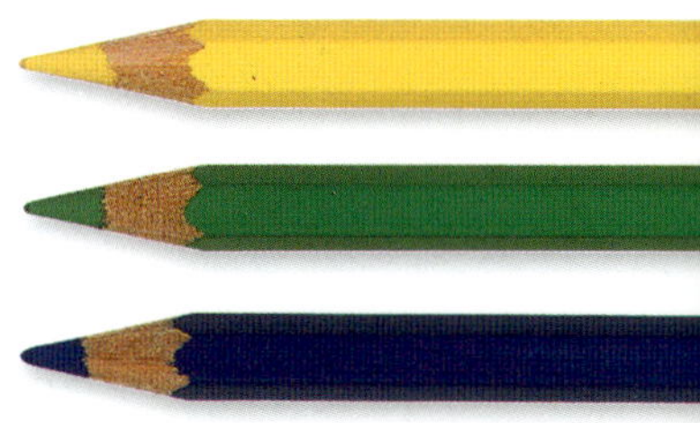

Australia
'Alphabetique'
Calligraphy Shop, Studio, Gallery
and Educational Centre (by
appointment)
225 Canterbury Village
Canterbury
Victoria 3126
Tel: (03) 9836-6616

The Artists Warehouse
65 Sheridan Street
Cairns
QLD 4870
Tel: (0740) 316-947
www.artistswarehouse.com.au

Oxford Art Supplies Pty Ltd
221–225 Oxford Street
Darlinghurst
NSW 2010
Tel: (02) 9360 4066
www.oxfordart.com.au

Premier Art Supplies
43 Gilles Street
Adelaide
SA 5000
Tel: (618) 8212 5922
www.premierart.com.au

New Zealand
Draw Art Supplies Ltd
PO Box 24022
5 Mahunga Drive
Mangere Bridge
Auckland
Tel: (09) 636-4989
www.draw-art.co.nz

Gordon Harris
170 Victoria Street
Wellington
Tel: (04) 385-2099
www.gordonharris.co.nz

Index

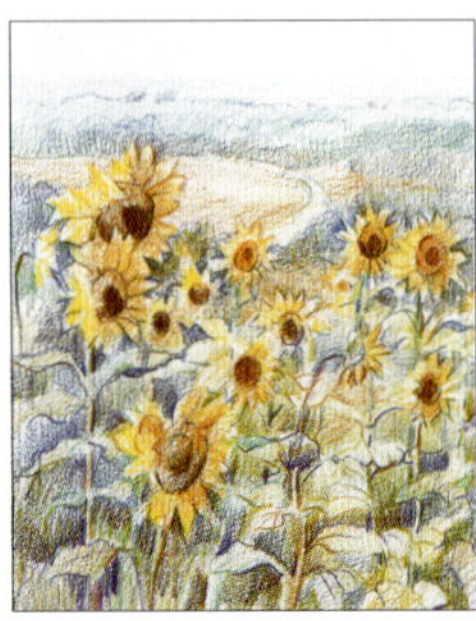

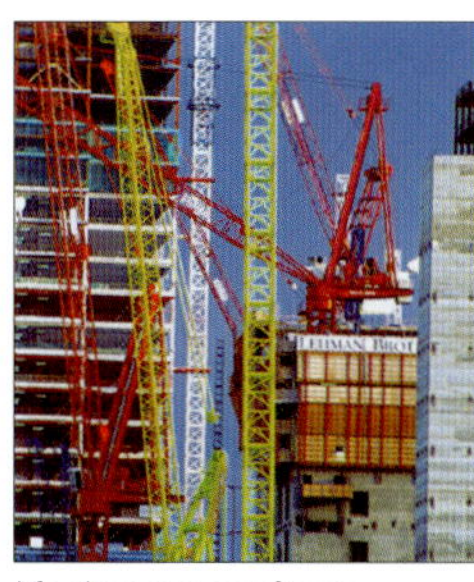

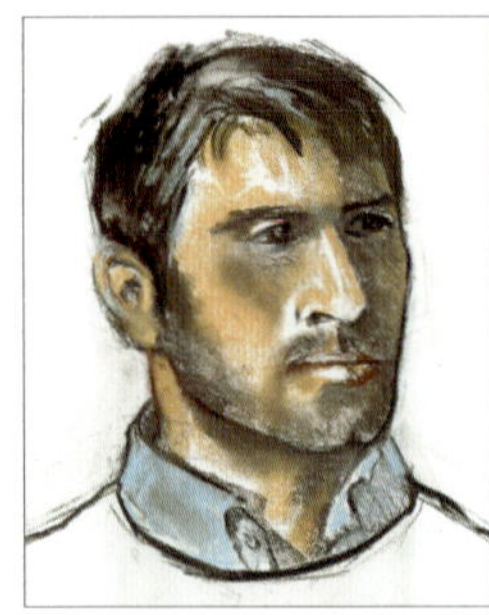

Acknowledgements

This edition is published by Southwater, an imprint of Anness Publishing Ltd, Hermes House, 88–89 Blackfriars Road, London SE1 8HA tel. 020 7401 2077; fax 020 7633 9499 www.southwaterbooks.com; www.annesspublishing.com

If you like the images in this book and would like to investigate using them for publishing, promotions or advertising, please visit our website www.practicalpictures.com for more information.

UK agent: The Manning Partnership Ltd; tel. 01225 478444; fax 01225 478440; sales@manning-partnership.co.uk
UK distributor: Book Trade Services; tel. 0116 2759086; fax 0116 2759090; uksales@booktradeservices.com; exportsales@booktradeservices.com
North American agent/distributor: National Book Network; tel. 301 459 3366; fax 301 429 5746; www.nbnbooks.com
Australian agent/distributor: Pan Macmillan Australia; tel. 1300 135 113; fax 1300 135 103; customer.service@macmillan.com.au
New Zealand agent/distributor: David Bateman Ltd; tel. (09) 415 7664; fax (09) 415 8892

Publisher: Joanna Lorenz
Editorial Director: Helen Sudell
Editors: Sarah Hoggett, Beverley Jollands
Designer: Nigel Partridge
Production Controller: Claire Rae

ETHICAL TRADING POLICY
Because of our ongoing ecological investment programme, you, as our customer, can have the pleasure and reassurance of knowing that a tree is being cultivated on your behalf to naturally replace the materials used to make the book you are holding. For further information about this scheme, go to www.annesspublishing.com/trees

Previously published in three separate volumes: *Mastering the Art of Drawing, Mastering the Art of Calligraphy* and *How to Paint and Draw.*

PUBLISHER'S NOTE
Although the advice and information in this book are believed to be accurate and true at the time of going to press, neither the authors nor the publisher can accept any legal responsibility or liability for any errors or omissions that may be made.

Contributing authors

Ian Sidaway trained as a graphic designer and has been working as an artist since 1970. He has authored almost 20 art technique and drawing books, including *The Practical Encyclopedia of Acrylics, Oils and Gouache*.

Janet Mehigan holds a degree in Education and is a Fellow of both the Society of Scribes and Illuminators (SSI) and of The Calligraphy and Lettering Arts Society (CLAS). She teaches calligraphy and art and runs workshops for students and calligraphic societies.

Mary Noble teaches, exhibits and takes commissions. She is a Fellow of both UK national societies, the SSI and the CLAS, and has written and co-authored several calligraphy books, many with Janet Mehigan.

Viva Lloyd has a Certificate in Calligraphy & Bookbinding and a Diploma in Calligraphy. She is a CLAS Accredited Tutor and travels widely teaching workshops. In 2000 she founded the Little Book Makers.

Maureen Sullivan studied Calligraphy, Illumination and Heraldry at Reigate School of Art & Design and has a degree in Calligraphy & Bookbinding. Maureen is a Fellow of the SSI, teaches workshops, takes commissions, has contributed to publications and is the author of *Craft in Motion.*

Dr George Thomson is a researcher/ practitioner in calligraphy and lettering and exhibits regularly in the UK, continental Europe, USA and Canada. He has lectured throughout Britain and North America.In addition to many academic papers on lettering, he has written a number of books on calligraphy.

Jan Pickett originally studied Graphics and she worked commercially as a children's illustrator before training for an art teaching career. Jan regularly teaches Adult Education classes, residential courses and day workshops. She is a Fellow of the CLAS and a Fellow of the SSI.

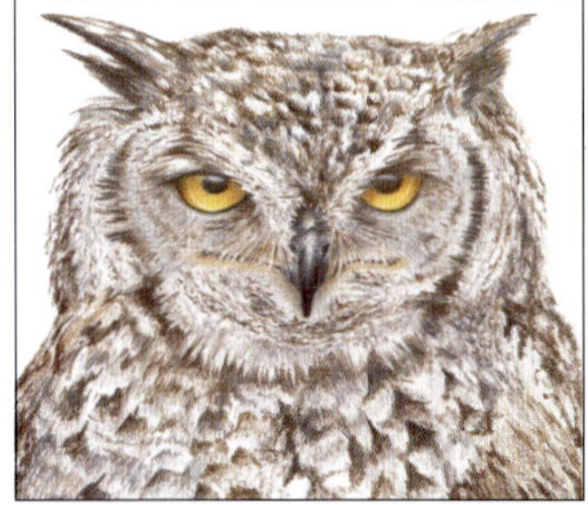

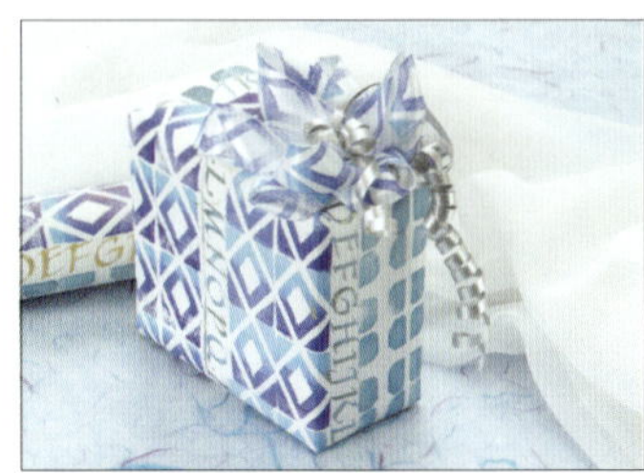

Janet Mehigan pp. 234–5, 350–1, 362–3, 388–391, 396–9, 404–7, 422–9, 462–7, 470–1, 494–7. **Mary Noble** pp. 334–347, 352–5, 376–383, 392–5, 448–461, 490–3. **Viva Lloyd** pp. 364–5, 368–9, 384–7, 400–3, 416–7, 436–445, 478–485, 500–1. **Maureen Sullivan** pp. 358–9, 366–7, 372–5, 408–411, 412–5, 430–5, 468–9, 472–7, 498–9. **Dr George Thomson** pp. 486–9. **Jan Pickett** pp. 360–1, 446–7, 482–3.

Special thanks to the following artists for step-by-step drawing demonstrations:
Diana Constance: pages 42–3, 62–3, 284–9, 310–4, 202–7, 208–211.
Douglas Druce: page 38–9.
Abigail Edgar: pages 31–1, 44–5, 48–9, 321–3, 92–5, 250–1, 112–3, 258–261, 124–5, 278–283, 440–1, 452–5, 1458–9, 462–5, 470–3, 172–5, 178–9, 198–9, 202–7, 304–9.
Suzy Herbert: pages 75–7, 146–9, 154–7, 186–9.
Wendy Jelbert: pages 79, 80–3, 108–9, 114–7, 118–121, 122–3, 132–5, 140–1, 162–3, 176–7, 192–5, 196–7, 236–9.
Melvyn Petterson: pages 110–1; 266–9, 126–7, 128–131, 136–9, 144–5, 150–3, 202–3, 232–5.
Paul Robinson: pages 84–7, 168–171.
Ian Sidaway: pages 28–9, 32–3, 34–5, 36–7, 40–1, 46–7, 48, 230, 78, 92, 96–7, 250 (top), 100–5, 252–5.
Effie Waverlin: 50–8.

Picture acknowledgements
Thanks to the following for permission to reproduce copyright photographs: Phil Dean: page 284 (left).Jon Hibberd: pages 266 (bottom left), 292 (top), 178 (top), 182 (top), 186 (bottom left), 192 (top), 202. Anthony Pickhaver: page 314 (right). Megan Fishpool: page 144 (top). Keith at Imageworks: page 304 (top) with thanks to Valerie and Ben Lorenz and Francesco Mangiacasale for modelling. 'Julian's Alphabet' p.328 by kind permission of Julian Barker.

Thanks to **Mike Hemsley** at wg photo for the digital studio photography (wgphoto.co.uk).